Studies in Pure Mathematics

To the Memory of Paul Turán

Birkhäuser Verlag
Basel · Boston · Stuttgart

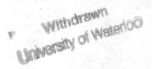

Library of Congress Cataloging in Publication Data

Main entry under title:
Studies in pure mathematics.
Includes index.
1. Mathematics—Addresses, essays, lectures.
2. Turán, P. (Paul) 1910—1976. I. Turán, P.
(Paul), 1910—1976. II. Erdős, Paul, 1913-
QA7.S845 510 81-17016
ISBN 3-7643-1288-2 AACR2

CIP-Kurztitelaufnahme der Deutschen Bibliothek

Studies in pure Mathematics: to the memory
of Paul Turán/Paul Erdős, ed. ... — Basel;
Boston; Stuttgart: Birkhäuser, 1983.
ISBN 3-7643-1288-2
NE: Erdős, Paul [Hrsg.]

Joint edition published by
Birkhäuser Verlag, Basel
and
Akadémiai Kiadó, Budapest
Printed in Hungary

ISBN 3-7643-1288-2

Contents

Editors' Preface

This volume, written by his friends, collaborators and students, is offered to the memory of Paul Turán.

Most of the papers they contributed discuss subjects related to his own fields of research. The wide range of topics reflects the versatility of his mathematical activity. His work has inspired many mathematicians in analytic number theory, theory of functions of a complex variable, interpolation and approximation theory, numerical algebra, differential equations, statistical group theory and theory of graphs.

Beyond the influence of his deep and important results he had the exceptional ability to communicate to others his enthusiasm for mathematics. One of the strengths of Turán was to ask unusual questions that became starting points of many further results, sometimes opening up new fields of research. We hope that this volume will illustrate this aspect of his work adequately.

Born in Budapest, on August 28, 1910, Paul Turán obtained his Ph. D. under L. Fejér in 1935. His love for mathematies enabled him to work even under inhuman circumstances during the darkest years of the Second World War. One of his major achievements, his power sum method originated in this period. After the war he was visiting professor in Denmark and in Princeton. In 1949 he became professor at the Eötvös Loránd University of Budapest, a member of the Hungarian Academy of Sciences and a leading figure of the Hungarian mathematical community. His untimely death on September 26, 1976 prevented him from working out a great many of the ideas he had so abundantly.

Even the relatively large extent of this volume did not permit to invite and include all desirable contributions.

We express our gratitude to the Akadémiai Kiadó for having made it possible for the many friends of Paul Turán to pay their tribute to a great mathematician.

The Editors

Preface

Personal reminiscences

I met Paul Turán first in September 1930 at the University of Budapest though we knew of each others existence since we both worked for the mathematical journal for high school students and our first joint paper appeared there, i.e. a solution of a problem which we obtained independently. At our first meeting I asked him if the sum of the reciprocals of the primes diverges or converges. He informed me that it diverges and he told me about the prime number theorem. (Seven or eight years earlier I learned from my father that the number of primes is infinite.)

We met and discussed mathematics nearly every day until I went to Manchester in October 1934, after that date until early September 1938 I spent half my time in England half in Hungary but when I was in England we corresponded a great deal. Our first joint paper dealt with elementary number theory, in which we deal with a problem of G. Grünwald and D. Lázár: Let $f(n)$ be the largest integer so that if $1 \leqq a_1 < \ldots < a_n$ are any set of n integers then $\prod_{1 \leqq i \leqq j \leqq n} (a_i + a_j)$ has at least $f(n)$ distinct prime factors.

We proved

$$c_1 \log n < f(n) < c_2 \frac{n}{\log n} \tag{1}$$

and we conjectured that $f(n)/\log n \to \infty$, which is still open.

Very soon we started our collaboration on interpolation which produced many more "serious" results.

From England I returned to Hungary for Christmas, Easter and summer vacations. In the spring of 1938 Hitler succeeded in disturbing my plans, but I could return to Hungary precariously in the summer of 1938. On September 3, 1938, I did not like the news and in the evening I was on my way to England and three and one-half weeks later to the USA. We corresponded until 1941, then there was an enforced gap of four years. As soon as possible we started our first postwar joint paper on the difference of consecutive primes which we wrote in correspondence. In this paper we stated a few problems which I find very interesting: Put $d_k = p_{k+1} - p_k$. Is it true that

$$d_k > d_{k+1} > d_{k+2} \quad \text{and} \quad d_k < d_{k+1} < d_{k+2}$$

both have infinitely many solutions? We also observed that we cannot prove that there is no k_0 for which

$$(-1)^j(d_{k_0+j}-d_{k_0+j-1}), \qquad j=1,2,\ldots$$

always has the same sign. I am of course sure that such a k_0 does not exist.

We met in the USA and Hungary in 1948–49 and wrote two papers on equidistribution, both of which I believe will outlive the authors. From that date we always corresponded but we could not meet until 1955. Our work on statistical group theory started around 1960 and in some sense is still continuing. We also worked with V. T. Sós (Mrs. Turán) and A. Meir (Meyer), a student of Turán, on applications of combinatorial analysis to geometry and various branches of analysis.

I knew that he was not long for this world but hoped to see him at Christmas. Our last mathematical discussion took place two weeks before his death — then I left for Canada and heard of his death there. — His last words which could be understood were O(1) — may his Theorems live forever.

I believe that Turán's most important and most original work was the discovery and development of the so-called power sum method. He applied this method to different branches of analysis and number theory. My contribution to this theory was minor and others are much more competent to write about it than I. Turán himself considered this as his most important work. One evening I found him working and asked him "what do you prove and conjecture". He was working on his book and answered "I am building my pyramid".

A particular strength of Turán was that he often found a question of a new type in a field which was far from his own. He generally solved a special case "just for orientation" as he was fond of saying and then he returned "home", i.e. to analytic number theory. This happened e.g. in the theory of extremal graphs now a flourishing subject (in this case though Turán occasionally returned and made some further important contributions) and in the theory of relations in set theory and also in probabilistic number theory. No doubt his important contributions in statistical group theory and in the theory of interpolation will live for the foreseeable future.

To end I can only quote from Hilbert's famous obituary of Minkowski, I have to be grateful to fate that it gave me such a friend and co-worker and that I could have him for such a long time.

Paul Erdős

Letter to Professor Paul Turán

Dear Professor Turán,

The letter form of these reminiscences is not merely a poetic device. A game with which ALFRÉD RÉNYI, one of the many students of yours whom you buried, saved a formal meeting some years ago, gave me the idea of writing humorous obituaries about living people, and although I did not do so, I could have sent you a version of this letter during your life. Almost since I first met you I delighted in turning against you your principles about mathematics, that you set forth with perseverence and courage. You always laughed heartily at this which emboldened me to write this letter in the same vein: contradicting whenever possible what you said about your own work and mathematics in general.

It is not because I was expecting you to die soon that I had chosen you as a subject for an obituary. For me you were always, up to the very end, youth personified. Not because you celebrated your fiftieth birthday by swimming across the Danube or things like that, but because your belief in mathematics never faltered no matter how hard life was for you. Although your love of mathematics went much deeper than loving one's own results, an important role in sustaining your interest was undoubtedly played by the many innovations which you presented to mathematics throughout your life. How did you do that?

While in a nazi labor camp, mounting poles and transporting bricks, you sought problems not requiring much computation, and it was there that you discovered your classical graph theorem that became the starting point of a flourishing theory on extremal graphs (giving the maximal number of edges in a graph with prescribed number of vertices containing no complete subgraph of prescribed size — the editor). You asserted, as in other cases too, that you had had luck in hitting upon the right problem.

The result that made you famous some years earlier was a simple proof of a theorem of Hardy and Ramanujan. This proof is now considered to mark the birth of probabilistic number theory. (The theorem states that the number of prime divisors of "almost all" numbers n is "approximately" loglog n, and his proof is based, in today's probabilistic language, on calculating the standard deviation and applying Tchebysheff's inequality — the editor.) Was it also good luck?

And what about your greatest discovery, the power sum method? In one of your several attempts at resolving the most outstanding problem of analytic number theory, RIEMANN's hypothesis on the zeros of the zeta function $\zeta(s)$, you observed that it is equivalent to $\zeta'/\zeta(s)$ having radius of regularity around s_0 at least $\operatorname{Re} s_0 - 1/2$ for $\operatorname{Re} s_0 > 1$, while by well-known approximations to $\zeta'/\zeta(s)$ this radius is

$$\left(\limsup_{\nu\to\infty} \sqrt[\nu]{\left|\sum_{\rho} 1/(s_0-\rho)^\nu\right|}\right)^{-1}$$

(ρ runs through the zeros of $\zeta(s)$) and this led you to replace the limit relation by inequalities

$$(*) \qquad \max_{m+1 \leqq \nu \leqq m+n} \left|\sum_{i=1}^{n} z_i^\nu\right| > \ldots$$

for sums of powers of general complex numbers. Though the most successful, this is only one of your several similar innovations. Rather than merely relying on good luck you went back to the very beginning, often building upon what seems a primitive observation like this one. Nevertheless, it must have required deep insight judging from the subsequent developments; you made your power sum inequalities into one of the basic methods of analysis with applications to different parts of mathematics ranging from analytic number theory (though you did not reach your final goal) through many branches of analysis to numerical methods. (The whole story is reminiscent of how your basic interest in number theory led you afterwards to many other fields.)

Your work is in fact applied mathematics in its true sense. In your case this means primarily applications in theoretical mathematics, but when you learned that your power-sum method is also related to numerical methods you studied numerical analysis and solved in theory one of its basic problems. This theory is likely to spawn new research towards practical solutions. (He constructed an algorithm furnishing with prescribed relative error a zero of a polynomial such that the length of the algorithm depends only on the degree of the polynomial and the error — the editor.) This is in rather sharp contrast with what you said about mathematics being only entertainment for you. Because of your birth you had no chance of getting a job as a mathematician before the war and you could only hope for doing it as a hobby. True, it was always great enjoyment for you but already then you were concentrating on important questions and never cared for *l'art pour l'art* problems (problems your power sum theory could have supplied in unlimited number).

You have been aware of the importance of your results and, though far from boasting, you carefully described their place in mathematics in your papers and lectures. Some felt you talked too much about them. However, what you said was always true and to the point. The only case in which I disagreed with you concerned your algebraic proof of your second main theorem (an inequality like (*) with an explicit constant on the right depending only on n and m under the normalization

$\max|z_i|=1$ — the editor). Your proof of the first main theorem (inequality under the normalization $\min|z_i|=1$ — the editor), uses algebraic identities only, whereas applications are mainly in analysis. You often called attention to this circumstance, and this was not idle talk either, for clarification of the true character, algebraic or analytic, of the first main theorem will undoubtedly lead to new developments. But when you presented such a proof for the deeper second main theorem by replacing the contour integration in the original one, I called it cheating, for it was essentially the same proof with the function theory disguised. You only laughed.

Once when I heard you lecturing on your results in potential theory (giving, among other things, estimates of potentials and capacity of sets in terms of the packing constants of geometry, an application of his graph theorem — the editor), I, too, felt that you were speaking too much. They are such beautiful results, they speak for themselves, but you took over the words from them.

The reason might be that, although you had a sense of beauty in mathematics, you did not attach too much importance to having beautiful results. As an example, here is a theorem from the comparative theory of primes, a theory which you in collaboration with another dear student you lost young, STANISLAW KNAPOWSKI, created out of some sporadic results with the aid of the power sum method.

For $(l, k)=1$, let $\pi(x, k, l)$ denote the number of primes $p \equiv l (\mathrm{mod}\ k)$ up to x. For $l \not\equiv 1 \pmod k$ and

$$T > \max(c, e_5(k), e_1(D^{-1}))$$

there exist then x_1 and x_2 in the interval $[\log_3 T, T]$ such that

$$\pi(x_1, k, 1) - \pi(x_1, k, l) > \sqrt{x_1}/\log x_1, \quad \pi(x_2, k, 1) - \pi(x_2, k, l) < -\sqrt{x_2}/\log x_2$$

provided that no Dirichlet L-function mod k vanishes for $0 < \mathrm{Re}\, s < 1$, $|\mathrm{Im}\, s| < D$ ($e_i($) and $\log_i$ stand for the i times iterated exponential and logarithm, respectively.)

No one would call this a beautiful theorem, yet every part of it concerns deep aspects of the problem such as sign changes by large positive and negative values, their localization, effectiveness in terms of only D, etc.

The proof of this and other results in the theory is extremely complicated, incorporating many auxiliary arguments and making use of your deepest "one-sided" power sum theorem, itself the combination of a great number of lemmas. This reminds me of your saying that it is not the theorem containing many lemmas that is important. I heard your saying quoted to justify "theorems" which are only insignificant variations on earlier results. You should have added that one ought to look at your work in approximation theory, partly joint work with among others PAUL ERDŐS, your life long friend with whom you fruitfully collaborated in many other areas as well to see what you meant by a theorem. Your 0–2 interpolation, a counterpart of Hermite interpolation prescribing the value and second derivative of polynomials or what you called rough theory of interpolation when Lebesgue constants can and fine theory when they cannot determine the rate of approximation or rational approximation to certain classes of functions, are all abounding in surprising new phenomena.

It was probably only to demonstrate your principle on the priority of theorem over proof that you once said that soon you would only be remembered by your characterization of the zeta function. (In the important problem of finding characteristic properties of the zeta function, he gave the monotonicity of coefficients and the existence of Euler product as such properties, both being relevant in existing methods concerning $\zeta(s)$ — the editor.) The proof is in fact a straightforward reduction to an earlier result by Paul Erdős, yet it shows the subject in a different light.

In the strong conviction that you will prove to be wrong and your work will long influence mathematics, the Hungarian Academy of Science, your friends, colleagues and pupils all over the world dedicate this volume with admiration, reverence and gratitude to your memory.

Budapest, 20th July, 1978

Gábor Halász

one of your many
mathematical children

Studies in Pure Mathematics
To the Memory of Paul Turán

An extremal problem in combinatorial number theory

by

H. L. ABBOTT and A. MEIR (Edmonton)

We consider in this paper an extremal problem in combinatorial number theory. Our work is related to the question of difference bases. For given positive integer n, a set of integers $0=a_1<a_2<\ldots<a_k=n$ is said to be a *difference set for n* if every integer v, $0<v<n$, can be written in the form $v=a_j-a_i$. Let $k(n)$ denote the minimum value of k over all difference bases for a given integer n. The problem of estimating $k(n)$ was first considered by A. Brauer [1] and subsequently by A. Rényi and L. Rédei [5], P. Erdős and I. S. Gál [3] and J. Leech [4]. The principal result is that $k(n)\sim\alpha n^{1/2}$, as $n\to\infty$, with a fixed positive constant α. Reasonably good estimates have been obtained for the value of α.

The question we wish to investigate here is as follows: A set of integers $0=a_0<a_1<\ldots<a_h=n$ is said to have *property* $P(n)$ if (i) $a_1=1$ and (ii) for every v, $0<v<n$, if $v=a_j-a_i$ then v has at least two such representations. Given n, we wish to estimate the minimum value $h(n)$ of h over all sets having property $P(n)$. A related but not identical problem was considered by Straus in [6]: For prime p, what is the greatest integer $f(p)$ so that in any set A of residues (mod p) with card $A\leqq f(p)$, one of the differences $x-y$, $x\in A$, $y\in A$ occurs (mod p) only once. Straus has shown that $1+\log_4(p-1)\leqq f(p)\leqq(2+o(1))\log_3 p$. Browkin, Divis and Schinzel, while considering a more general question, have improved the lower bound to $\log_2 p\leqq f(p)$. The above mentioned results do not imply our Theorems 1 and 2 below, since they refer to differences over finite fields. It is not difficult to see, however, that for p prime the inequality $f(p)\leqq h(p)-1$ holds. Our main results are:

Theorem 1.

$$h(n)>\frac{3}{2}\log_2 n+O(1).$$

Theorem 2. *For all n,*

$$h(n)\leqq 4\log_2 n.$$

It would be of interest to decide whether $\lim_{n\to\infty} h(n)/\log_2 n$ exists, and, if so, to determine its value. This we have not been able to do. It will follow from the proof of Theorem 2 that for infinitely many values of n, $h(n)<2\log_2 n+O(1)$. Hence if $\beta=\lim_{n\to\infty} h(n)/\log_2 n$ exists, we have $\frac{3}{2}\leqq\beta\leqq 2$.

Proof of Theorem 1. Let n be given and let $2^t\leqq n<2^{t+1}$. For $k\leqq t-2$ let J_k denote the set of integers contained in $(2^k, 2^{k+1}]\cup[n-2^{k+1}, n-2^k)$. Let S be a minimal subset of $\{0, 1, 2, \dots, n\}$ having property $P(n)$. Let a be the largest member of S not exceeding 2^k and b the least member of S not exceeding $n-2^k-1$. Then $v=b-a$ has to have a second representation, say $v=r-s$. Without loss of generality we may suppose that $r>b$ and $s>a$. Suppose that $J_k\cap S=\Phi$. This implies $s>2^{k+1}$ and hence $r-s<n-2^{k+1}$. However $b-a\geqq(n-2^k)-2^k=n-2^{k+1}$. This contradiction shows that $J_k\cap S\neq\Phi$ for each k, $0\leqq k\leqq t-2$. It follows immediately that

$$h(n)>\log_2 n+O(1).$$

We now show how the above argument may be refined. Suppose that for some $k\leqq t-3$, S has only two elements, say c and d, in common with $J_k\cup J_{k+1}$. We show that this leads to a contradiction. Let a and b have the same meaning as in the preceeding paragraph. We distinguish two cases; all others are essentially equivalent to one or other of these. Actually, we present a detailed argument in only one case.

Case 1: $2^k<c\leqq 2^{k+1}$, $n-2^{k+2}\leqq d<n-2^{k+1}$. We know that $v=b-a$ must have a second representation, say $v=r-s$. Now, $r\leqq d$ implies $r-s<n-2^{k+1}\leqq b-a$. Thus $r>b$ and $s>a$. From $s>c$ it follows that $s>2^{k+2}$ and this in turn yields $r-s<n-2^{k+2}<b-a$. Thus $s=c$ and we have

$$b-a=r-c. \tag{1}$$

$\mu=b-c$ has to have a second representation, say $\mu=u-v$. If $u>b$ then $v>c$ and hence $v>2^{k+2}$. Thus $u-v<n-2^{k+2}$, whereas $b-c\geqq(n-2^k)-2^{k+1}=n-3\cdot 2^k$. It follows that $u<b$. Also, $u<d$ implies $u-v<n-2^{k+2}$ and this again contradicts $b-c\geqq n-3\cdot 2^k$. Thus $u=d$ and we have

$$b-c=d-v, \quad \text{where} \quad v\leqq a\leqq 2^k. \tag{2}$$

From (2) we get

$$d=b-c+v\geqq b-c\geqq n-3\cdot 2^k. \tag{3}$$

$\lambda=d-a$ must have a second representation, say $\lambda=x-y$. $x<d$ implies $x-y<n-2^{k+2}$ while, by (3), $d-a\geqq(n-3\cdot 2^k)-2^k=n-2^{k+2}$. Thus $x>d$, and $y>a$. $y>c$ implies

$y > 2^{n+2}$ so that $x-y < n-2^{k+2}$ while $d-a < (n-2^{k+1})-2^k = n-3\cdot 2^k$. Thus $y=c$. Furthermore, $x > b$ implies $x-y > (n-2^k)-2^{k+1} = n-3\cdot 2^k > d-a$. Thus $x=b$ and we get

(4) $$d-a=b-c\,.$$

It is clear that $b-d > 2^k$. However, from (4) and (1) we get $b-d=c-a=r-b \leqq 2^k$. This is a contradiction. Thus, in this case, S must contain at least three members of $J_k \cup J_{k+1}$.

Case 2: $2^k < c \leqq 2^{k+1}$, $2^{k+1} \leqq d \leqq 2^{k+2}$. An argument, very similar to that used in Case 1, shows that $|S \cap (J_k \cup J_{k+1})| \geqq 3$ in this case as well.

Theorem 1 now follows easily.

Remark. Further improvement in the lower bound for $h(n)$ may perhaps be possible by considering three or more consecutive J_k's. A detailed analysis of this situation seems to be very laborious. Since we deemed it unlikely that it would lead to a best possible result, we have not pursued the matter further.

Proof of Theorem 2. Given n, we set $n=2(2^{t_1}+2^{t_2}+\ldots+2^{t_r})$ if n is even, and $n=2(2^{t_1}+2^{t_2}+\ldots+2^{t_r})$ if n is even, and $n=2(2^{t_1}+2^{t_2}+\ldots+2^{t_r})+1$ if n is odd, where $0 \leqq t_1 < t_2 < \ldots < t_r$. For $v=1, 2, \ldots, r-1$ we set $\sigma_v = \sum_{k=1}^{v} 2^{t_k}$ and define the sets of integers M_v by $M_v = \{\sigma_v + 2^{t_v}, \sigma_v + 2^{t_v+1}, \ldots, \sigma_v + 2^{t_{v+1}}\}$ for $v \geqq 1$ and $M_0 = \{0, 1, 2, 4, \ldots, 2^{t_1}\}$. Let $S_1 = \bigcup_{v=0}^{r-1} M_v$ and $S_2 = \{n-s : s \in S_1\}$. Then it is not difficult to check that the set $S = S_1 \cup S_2$ satisfies property $P(n)$. Hence $h(n) \leqq |S|$. Now,

$$|S_1| = t_1 + 2 + \sum_{k=1}^{r-1} (t_{k+1} - t_k + 1) = t_r + r + 1\,.$$

Hence

$$|S| = 2(t_r + r + 1)\,,$$

and since $r \leqq t_r + 1 \leqq \log_2 n$, we get $|S| \leqq 4 \log_2 n$.

This proves Theorem 2.

Remark. The proof shows that for all values of n for which $r = O(1)$, e.g. if n is a power of 2, we have the stronger result $h(n) \leqq 2 \log_2 n + O(1)$.

Added in proof. It follows from a presonal communication by E. G. STRAUS that the bound in Theorem 2 can be improved to $h(n) \leqq 2\lceil \log_2 n \rceil$

References

[1] A. BRAUER, A problem in additive number theory and its application in electrical engineering *J. Elisha Mitchell Sci. Soc.*, **61** (1945), 55–66.
[2] J. BROWKIN, B. DIVIS, A. SCHINZEL, Addition of sequences in general fields. *Monatsh. fr Math.*, **82** (1976), 261–268.
[3] P. ERDŐS and I. S. GÁL, On the representation of 1, 2, . . . , n by differences. *Indagationes Math.*, **10** (1948), 379–382.
[4] J. LEECH, On the representation of 1, 2, . . ., n by differences. *J. Lond. Math. Soc.*, **31** (1956), 160–169.
[5] L. RÉDEI and A. RÉNYI, On the representation of 1, 2, . . ., n by differences. *Mat. Sbornik*, **66** (NS 24) (1949), 385–389.
[6] E. G. STRAUS, Differences of residues (mod p). *J. Number Theory*, **8** (1976), 40–42.

THE UNIVERSITY OF ALBERTA
EDMONTON, CANADA

Studies in Pure Mathematics
To the Memory of Paul Turán

Every group admits a bad topology

by

M. AJTAI, I. HAVAS and J. KOMLÓS (Budapest)

Abstract

Every infinite Abelian group can be provided with a Hausdorff (group-) topology, in which the continuous characters (if there are any) do not separate the points.

Although formally this is a statement of (a counter-example in) harmonic analysis, the feature of the paper is essentially of a combinatorial construction involving number theory and probability.

Lemma 1 might be of independent interest for a number theorist.

§0. Introduction

A topological group is usually managable if it admits sufficiently many continuous characters (continuous multiplicative mappings to the complex unit circle), namely if any two points (elements of the group) can be separated by such a character ($\forall a, b \in G\ \exists \chi: \chi(a) \neq \chi(b)$).

It is important to find conditions implying this richness of H — the set of continuous characters; the most well-known is local compactness.

Now Imre Csiszár asked whether some conditions *only* on the group structure might do the same. In particular he asked whether or not *every* Hausdorff (group-) topology on the additive group Z of the integers automatically has sufficiently many continuous characters, for the sole reason that the group is nice and managable.

We are going to show that this is not so, and construct a topology on Z such that there will be *no* continuous characters except, of course, for the trivial $\chi_0 \equiv 1$, the principal character.

By giving two other constructions we also show that:

Theorem. *Every infinite Abelian group can be provided with a Hausdorff topology, in which the continuous characters do not separate the elements of the group.*

Of course, topology means group-topology, i.e. the group operation and the inverse should be continuous.

That the condition of commutativeness is essential (in fact, local finiteness would be sufficient), is shown by a construction of Shelah: a non-commutative infinite group admitting only the trivial topologies.

§1. Three particular groups

1A) The following lemma is well known, and it is an easy exercise:

Lemma 0. *Every infinite Abelian group contains one of the following groups as a subgroup*:

1) Z=*the additive group of the rational integers,*

2) $C(p_1, p_2, \ldots)$=*the (restricted) direct product of the cyclic groups* C_{p_i} *of order* p_i, *where* $p_1, p_2, \ldots$ *is a sequence of prime numbers, and either* $p=p_1=p_2=\ldots$, *or* $p_1<p_2<\ldots$,

3) C_{p^∞} *the multiplicative group of all p-power-th roots of unity (p is a prime), i.e.*

$$\{C_{p^\infty}\}=\{\exp(2\pi ik/p^r) \mid r=0,1,\ldots, k=0,,1,\ldots\}.$$

Recall that the (restricted) direct product of the groups $G_1, G_2, \ldots$ means the set of elements of the form $g_1^{r_1}g_2^{r_2}\ldots, r_i\geqq 0$, where all but a finite number of the exponents r_i are 0, i.e., we form finite products.

The operation is defined in the natural way.

Now the following proposition obviously implies the Theorem:

Theorem'. *Every one of the groups mentioned in Lemma* 0 *can be provided with a Hausdorff topology in which the only continuous character is* $\chi_0\equiv 1$.

Indeed, if G is an infinite Abelian group, then it contains one of the above groups G' say) as a subgroup, and then one can extend the crazy topology of G' to G in such a way that in G' the same sets remain open. Now, the restriction to G' of a continuous character is continuous on G', and thus it is identically equal to 1 on G'. Therefore, it cannot separate any two points of G'.

In §§2–4 we are going to construct the topologies mentioned in Theorem' separately for the three cases of Lemma 0 (more precisely, we prove existence only, since we use random construction). The most interesting case, however, is the first one, that of the group Z.

1B) The method of constructing a topology will be similar for all the above three cases.

We define a "norm" first — although we have a group G only, not a linear space, we will use the word norm for a function $\|\cdot\|: G\to[0,\infty)$, which has the following properties:

$$\|g_1g_2\|\leqq\|g_1\|+\|g_2\| \text{ (triangular inequality)}$$

$$\|g^{-1}\|=\|g\|$$

$$\|g\|=0 \quad \leftrightarrow g=e=\text{the unit of the group.}$$

If it satisfies the first two properties and $\|e\|=0$, *we will call it a semi-norm.*

In case $G=Z$ we will use additive notation, where the conditions read $\|x_1+x_2\|\leqq \leqq\|x_1\|+\|x_2\|$, $\|-x\|=\|x\|$, $\|x\|=0\leftrightarrow x=0$.

This norm will always be obtained through defining two sequences $a_1, a_2, \ldots$ ($a_i \in G$), and $\beta_1 > \beta_2 > \ldots$ (β_i are positive real numbers), $\lim \beta_n = 0$, then taking $\|g\| = \inf \sum \beta_i |\alpha_i|$, where the infimum is taken over all possible choices of finitely many integers α_i for which

$$g = \prod a_i^{\alpha_i},$$

(in case of Z this reads $g = \sum \alpha_i a_i$).

We will choose the sequence a_i in such a way that it generates the whole group, so that the set over which the infimum is extended, is non-empty. $\|\cdot\|$ is then a semi-norm, regardless of the choice of the sequences a_i, β_i. We will show then, that by choosing the elements a_i (and the numbers β_i) in an appropriate way, $\|\cdot\|$ becomes a norm. Thus the topology defined by calling a set a neighbourhood of e if it contains (an open) sphere $G_\varepsilon = \{g \in G \mid \|g\| < \varepsilon\}$, will be a Hausdorff group-topology. (The open sets can be described as ones which are neighbourhoods of every one of their points — where the neighbourhoods of g are the sets $gU_0 = \{gu \mid u \in U_0\}$, U_0 are neighbourhoods of e.)

We will thus choose our sequence a_i (and β_i) in such a way that the following three conditions be satisfied

G. the elements a_i generate the whole group,

N. $\|\cdot\|$ is a norm, i.e. $\|g\| = 0 \to g = e$,

C. for every character $\chi \neq \chi_0$ there is an $\varepsilon > 0$ such that no neighbourhood of e is contained in the set $\{g \in G \,\|\chi(g) - 1| < \varepsilon\}$.

This will be done by an explicit construction in case $G = C(p_1, p_2, \ldots)$, and by random constructions in the two other cases.

It would be the easy way to ensure N by assuming that given any $g \neq e$, we can delete sufficiently (but finitely) many elements from the sequence a_n, so that the subgroup generated by the tail does not contain g. But then a_n would be too rare to satisfy C. We will ensure instead that g cannot be expressed as a product of powers of elements in the tail of a_n with relatively small exponents, and that is what this norm is all about.

§2. The group Z

2A) We will need the following lemma, which is of independent interest:

Lemma 1. *Given any sequence $\varepsilon_n > 0$, $\varepsilon_n \to 0$, there is a sequence a_n of positive integers with*

$$\frac{a_{n+1}}{a_n} > 1 + \varepsilon_n$$

such that for any irrational α the sequence $a_n\alpha$ is uniformly distributed (mod 1), *and for any α rational, $\alpha = p/q$, $(p, q) = 1$, $a_n\alpha$ is u.d.* (mod 1) *on the set* $\{1/q, 2/q, \ldots, q/q\}$.

Remark. It is an easy exercise to show that if a_n is a sequence of positive integers and $a_{n+1}/a_n \geqq 2$, then there are irrational numbers α for which $a_n\alpha$ is *not* uniformly distributed mod 1. P. Erdős and S. J. Taylor [1] showed that the number 2 above can be replaced by any $q > 1$, and the Hausdorff measure of those α-s is 1.

BERNARD DE MATHAN [2] proved that this remains true even if we replace the words "uniformly distributed" by "everywhere dense".

Thus, our lemma says that these statements are best possible — the exponential growth cannot be weakened.

Proof. We give a random construction. Let $I_n=[u_n, v_n]$ be an arbitrary sequence of intervals with the following properties

(i) $$v_n=\exp\{o(n)\}$$

(ii) $$\frac{1}{N}\sum_{n=1}^{N} 1/|I_n|\to 0 \quad (\text{e.g. } |I_n|\to\infty).$$

Let us choose the number a_n at random uniformly distributed on the integers of I_n, and independently for different values of n. We show that with probability 1

(+) $$\lim_{N\to\infty}\frac{1}{N}\sum_{n=1}^{N}\exp\{2\pi i m\alpha a_n\}=0$$

holds for *all* α irrational and integer $m>0$, and also for $\alpha=p/q$, $(p,q)=1$, and $m=1, 2, \ldots, q-1$.

We are going to use the following estimation:

Lemma 2. *Let $X_1, X_2, \ldots, X_N$ be independent complex-valued random variables.*

$$|X_n|\leqq 1, \quad n=1,\ldots,N; \quad S_N=X_1+\ldots+X_N,$$

$0<\varepsilon<1$ *arbitrary. Then the condition* $|ES_N|\leqq\frac{\varepsilon}{4}N$ *implies*

$$P(|S_N|>\varepsilon N)<4\exp\left\{-\frac{\varepsilon^2}{100}N\right\}.$$

The proof of Lemma 2 is a routine application of Markov's inequality: $P(Y>x)\leqq\frac{EY}{x}$ for non-negative random variables Y, and $x>0$.

Since $|S_N|\leqq|\mathrm{Re}\,S_N|+|\mathrm{Im}\,S_N|$

$$P(|S_N|>\varepsilon N)\leqq P\left(|\mathrm{Re}\,S_N|>\frac{\varepsilon}{2}N\right)+P\left(|\mathrm{Im}\,S_N|>\frac{\varepsilon}{2}N\right).$$

Thus, it is enough to show that for real- valued X_n the conditions $|X_n|\leqq 1$, $|ES_N|\leqq \frac{\varepsilon}{2}N$ imply

$$P(|S_N|>\varepsilon N)<2\exp\left\{-\frac{4\varepsilon^2}{100}N\right\}.$$

Now for any $0<t<1$

$$P(S_N>\varepsilon N)=P(\exp tS_N>\exp t\varepsilon N)\leqq\exp\{-t\varepsilon N\}E\exp tS_N=$$

$$=\exp\{-t\varepsilon N\}\sum_{n=1}^{N}E\exp tX_n<\exp\{-t\varepsilon N\}\sum_{n=1}^{N}E(1+tX_n+t^2)<$$

$$<\exp\{-t\varepsilon N\}\exp\{tES_N+Nt^2\}.<\exp\left\{-t\frac{\varepsilon}{2}N+Nt^2\right\}.$$

Taking $t=\frac{\varepsilon}{4}$, we get the bound $\exp\left\{-\frac{\varepsilon^2}{16}N\right\}<\exp\left\{-\frac{4\varepsilon^2}{100}N\right\}$. The same argument works for $P(S_N<-\varepsilon N\}$ using $(-S_N)$ in the above estimation.

Now fix m and apply Lemma 2 for the random variables

$$X_n=\exp\{2\pi im\alpha a_n\},\qquad n=1,\ldots,N.$$

$$|EX_n|=\left|\frac{1-\exp\{2\pi im\alpha|I_n|\}}{1-\exp\{2\pi im\alpha\}}\right|\cdot\frac{1}{|I_n|}\leqq\frac{2}{|I_n|}\,\frac{1}{|1-\exp\{2\pi im\alpha\}|}\leqq\frac{1}{2\gamma|I_n|}$$

if only the distance of α from the nearest rational number of the form $\frac{j}{m}$ (denote this distance by $d_m(\alpha)$), is at least γ.

Thus for given $\delta>0$ we have

$$|ES_N|<\frac{1}{2d_m(\alpha)}\sum_{n=1}^{N}\frac{1}{|I_n|}<\frac{\delta}{4}N,$$

if only
$$d_m(\alpha)>\frac{2}{\delta}\frac{1}{N}\sum_{n=1}^{N}1/|I_n|=q_N.$$

Hence for such α

$$P\left(\left|\sum_{n=1}^{N}\exp\{2\pi im\alpha a_n\}\right|>\delta N\right)<4\exp\left\{-\frac{\delta^2}{100}N\right\}.$$

Thus

$$P\left(\left|\sum_{n=1}^{N}\exp\{2\pi im\alpha a_n\}\right|>\delta N \text{ for some } \alpha \text{ of the form } j\exp\left\{-\frac{\delta^2}{200}N\right\},\ j \text{ integer},\right.$$
$$\left.0<\alpha<1,\ d_m(\alpha)>q_N\}\right)<4\exp\left\{-\frac{\delta^2}{200}N\right\}.$$

Now for any $0<\alpha'<1$, $d_m(\alpha')>q_N$, one can find an α of the form $j\exp\left\{-\frac{\delta^2}{200}N\right\}$, j integer, $0<\alpha<1$, $d_m(\alpha)>q_N$, such that $|\alpha'-\alpha|<\exp\left\{-\frac{\delta^2}{200}N\right\}$ (assuming N is so large that $\exp\left\{-\frac{\delta^2}{200}N\right\}<\frac{1}{m}-2q_N$).

We have

$$\left|\sum_{n=1}^{N}\exp\{2\pi i m\alpha' a_n\}\right| \leqq \left|\sum_{n=1}^{N}\exp\{2\pi i m\alpha a_n\}\right| + \sum_{n=1}^{N}|\exp\{2\pi i m\alpha' a_n\}-\exp\{2\pi i m\alpha a_n\}|$$

and the latter term is at most

$$2\pi m|\alpha'-\alpha|\sum_{n=1}^{N}a_n<2\pi m\exp\left\{-\frac{\delta^2}{200}N\right\}Na_N<\delta N$$

if only $a_N<\frac{\delta}{2\pi m}\exp\left\{\frac{\delta^2}{200}N\right\}$, which holds if

$$(*) \qquad v_N<\frac{\delta}{2\pi m}\exp\left\{\frac{\delta^2}{200}N\right\}.$$

Thus, under the condition (*), for the event

$$A_N(\delta,m)=\left\{\left|\sum_{n=1}^{N}\exp\{2\pi i m\alpha a_n\}\right|<2\delta N \textit{ for all } \alpha,\ 0<\alpha<1,\ d_m(\alpha)>q_N\right\}$$

we have $\sum_{N=1} P(\bar{A}_N)<\sum_{N=1}4\exp\left\{-\frac{\delta^2}{200}N\right\}<\infty$, and applying the Borel–Cantelli lemma we get that, with probability 1, $A_N(\delta,m)$ holds for all N from some $N_0=N_0(\omega)$ on. I.e. with probability 1 for any α, $0<\alpha<1$, $\alpha\neq\frac{j}{m}$

$\limsup_{N\to\infty}\left|\frac{1}{N}\sum_{n=1}^{N}\exp\{2\pi i m\alpha a_n\}\right|\leqq 2\delta$. Since δ was arbitrary, we get

$$\lim_{N\to\infty}\frac{1}{N}\sum_{n=1}^{N}\exp\{2\pi i m\alpha a_n\}=0 \text{ for all } \alpha,\ 0<\alpha<1,\ \alpha\neq\frac{j}{m}.$$

Thus (+) holds if only $q_N\to 0$ and (*) is satisfied for any given δ and m, and $N>N_0(\delta,m)$; but this is assumed by (i) and (ii).

This proves Lemma 1, since (ii) is compatible with the extra condition $u_{n+1} > (1+\varepsilon_n)v_n$

ERDŐS suggested the following

Remark to Lemma 1:

We have actually shown that if $a_n = \exp\{o(n)\}$, and d_n is an arbitrary sequence tending to infinity, then there is a b_n such that $a_n \leqq b_n < a_n + d_n$, and the sequence $b_n\alpha$ is uniformly distributed mod 1 for every α.

2B) In Lemma 1 we have proved not only that there is a sequence with the required properties, but our random sequence has these properties with probability 1, if we select the sequence in the random way described at the beginning of the proof, and (i) and (ii) hold. That allows us to impose further conditions on the sequence, as we do in the next section.

2C) Now we turn to the random construction of the topology on Z.

As mentioned in §1, we metrize Z as follows:

Let us be given two sequences $1 = a_1 < a_2 < \dots$ (positive integers), and $\beta_1 > \beta_2 > \dots$ (real numbers), $\beta_n \to 0$. We define a semi-norm on Z:

For $x \in Z$ write x, in every possible way, as a finite sum $x = \sum \alpha_i a_i$, with integer coefficients α_i. Then the semi-norm of x is

$$\|x\| = \inf \sum_i \beta_i |\alpha_i| .$$

where the infimum is taken over all possible finite sums $\sum \alpha_i a_i = x$, α_i integer.

$\|x\|$ is only a semi-norm, since $\|x\| = 0$ might happen for $x \neq 0$. As will be seen, $\|\cdot\|$ becomes a norm for almost all choices of a_n.

(This definition of $\|\cdot\|$ is more natural than it looks, for if we choose some elements a_n from smaller and smaller neighbourhoods of 0, then many elements of the form $\sum \alpha_i a_i$ occur automatically in slightly larger neighbourhoods.

After months of looking at the terribly complicated sets of the neighbourhood-system, we realized that we had, in fact, a simple metric structure.)

2D) We want to choose the sequence a_n (and β_n) in such a way that the following two conditions hold ($a_1 = 1$ generates the group):

N. $\|\cdot\|$ is a norm.

C. For every non-trivial character $\chi \neq \chi_0$ there is an $\varepsilon > 0$ such that no neighbourhood of 0 is contained in the set $\{x \in Z \mid |\chi(x) - 1| < \varepsilon\}$.

C expresses that there are no continuous characters other than χ_0.

While *N* requires that a_n be rather a rare sequence, *C* holds only if a_n consists of sufficiently many integers. Fortunately, there is a compromise, for Lemma 1 implies that we can choose almost exponantially rare sequences a_n such that *C* still holds, and this is rare enough for *N* (actually $a_n = n^{\omega(n)}$, $\omega(n) \to \infty$, would be sufficient).

We choose the sequence a_n according to the random construction described in the proof of Lemma 1:

Let $I_n=[u_n, v_n]$ be a sequence of intervals, where

$$u_n=2^{[n^{1/2}]}$$

$$v_n=u_n+2^{[n^{1/3}]}.$$

Choose the numbers a_n at random uniformly distributed on the integers of I_n, and independently for different values of n.

According to (*) after Lemma 1, the sequence a_n has the following property with probability 1: given any non-integer real number α, for infinitely many n we have

$$1/3\leqq\{\alpha a_n\}\leqq 2/3,$$

where $\{x\}$ stands for the fraction part of x. And since the only characters on Z are $\chi_\alpha(a)=e^{2\pi i\alpha a}$, C holds with probability 1 (with $\varepsilon=\sqrt{3}$ for any $\chi\in H$, $\chi\neq\chi_0$), since $\|a_n\|\leqq\beta_n\to 0$ if $n\to\infty$.

2E) We show now that N holds (with probability 1), i.e. $\|\cdot\|$ is a norm.

Given $x\neq 0$ and $\alpha_1,\ldots,\alpha_N$, $\alpha_N\neq 0$, for the probability that $\sum\alpha_i a_i=x$ we have $P\left(\sum_{i=1}^N \alpha_i a_i=x\right)\leqq\dfrac{1}{d_N}$, where d_N is the number of integers on the interval I_n, i.e. $d_N=2^{[n^{1/3}]}+1$. Indeed, this is obviously true if the values $a_1,\ldots,a_{N-1}$ have already been given, and therefore it is also true for their average $(P(\cdot)=EP(\cdot\,|a_1,\ldots,a_{N-1}))$.

We claim now that there are not too many choices for the integers α_i such that

$$\sum_{i=1}^N \beta_i|\alpha_i|<1 \qquad \text{(say)}.$$

Indeed, since β_n is decreasing, we have

$$\sum_{i=1}^N |\alpha_i| < \frac{1}{\beta_N} < \left[\frac{1}{\beta_N}\right]+1=M,$$

and thus we have at most

$$\binom{N+M-1}{N-1}=\binom{N+M-1}{M}<N^M$$

choices for the numbers $|\alpha_i|$. And since at most M of the α-s are non-zero, we have at most $2^M N^M$ choices for the numbers α_i in order to satisfy $\sum_{i=1}^N \beta_i|\alpha_i|<1$.

Thus, for a fixed non-zero integer x we get

$$P_N(x)=P\text{ (there are integers }\alpha_1,\ldots,\alpha_N,\ \alpha_N\neq 0,$$

$$\sum_{i=1}^{N} \beta_i|\alpha_i|<1 \text{ (such that } \sum_{i=1}^{N} \alpha_i a_i = x) < (2N)^{1+1/\beta_N} \cdot \frac{1}{d_N}.$$

Choosing the sequence β_N slow enough, say $\beta_N = \dfrac{1}{\log(N+1)}$, we get

$$P_N(x) = O(2^{-n^{1/4}}).$$

Whence $\sum_{N=1}^{\infty} P_N(x) < \infty$, and according to the Borel–Cantelli lemma, with a probability 1 only finitely many of the events $P_N(x)$, $N=1, 2, \ldots$ occur.

Thus — with probability 1 — a non-zero x cannot be written as $x = \sum_{i=1}^{N} \alpha_i a_i$, $\alpha_N \neq 0$, $\sum_{i=1}^{N} \beta_i|\alpha_i|<1$ if $N > N_0 = N_0(\omega, x)$. For $N \leqq N_0$ we have, on the other hand,

$$\sum_{i=1}^{N} \beta_i|\alpha_i| \geqq \beta_N \geqq \beta_{N_0} > 0.$$

This is true for every $x \neq 0$, thus $\|\cdot\|$ is a norm with probability 1, i.e. for almost all choices of the sequence a_n.

This proves Theorem′ for the group Z.

§3. The group $C(p_1, p_2, \ldots)$

3A) For this group we give a proper (non-random) construction. The elements g of the group $G = C(p_1, p_2, \ldots)$ can be represented as follows:

$g = c_1^{r_1} \ldots c_n^{r_n}, n \geqq 1, c_j^{p_j} = e =$ unit of G, where for $g \neq e$ one can assume that $0 < r_n < p_n$. Thus they are represented as finite vectors

$$(r_1, \ldots, r_n),\ n \geqq 1,\quad 0 \leqq r_j < p_j,\quad r_n \neq 0 \qquad \text{(except for } e).$$

A character χ is given by an infinite vector $(h_1, h_2, \ldots)$, $0 \leqq h_j < p_j$, where χ acts on g as follows:

$$\chi(g_1^{r_1} \ldots g_n^{r_n}) = \varepsilon_1^{h_1 r_1} \ldots \varepsilon_n^{h_n r_n}, \qquad \text{where} \qquad \varepsilon_j = e^{2\pi i/p_j}.$$

Order the elements g by the lexicographical order, and let $g_0 = e, g_1, g_2, \ldots$ be the list of the elements of G in this order. Thus an element g_j with $j \leqq 2^n \left(\leqq \prod_{i=1}^{n} p_i \right)$ contains only the base elements $c_1, \ldots, c_n$ in its representation.

Now our semi-norm will be defined as

$$\|g\| = \inf \sum \beta_i |\alpha_i|,$$

where $\beta_1 > \beta_2 > \ldots, \beta_n \to 0$, and the infimum is extended over all choices of finitely many integers α_i, such that $g = \prod_i a_i^{\alpha_i}$, where the definition of a_i will follow in a minute. Obviously, we can restrict the exponents α_i in the range of the infimum by the condition $|\alpha_i| <$ order of a_i, and we do so.

The sequence a_n consists of all elements of the form

$$c_j^{r_j}, \quad 0 \leqq r_j < p_j,$$

(the generators), and also the elements

$$b_j = b_j(g_j) = g_j \cdot \prod_{k=2^j+1}^{2^{j+1}} c_k .$$

Order these elements into one sequence a_n by listing after b_j all the elements $c_j^{r_j}$, $0 \leqq r_j < p_j$.

We show now that N and C are satisfied. The latter is easy, for it says that there are sufficiently many elements in a_n — and thus in the neighbourhoods of e. N is harder, for it needs that a_n is not too dense.

3B) Let $\chi \neq \chi_0$ be a character, and let $\delta > 0$ be arbitrarily small. We show that there is an element g such that

$$\|g\| < \delta \text{ and yet } |\chi(g) - 1| \geqq \sqrt{3} .$$

If $\chi = (h_1, h_2, \ldots)$ is such that for some s $h_s \neq 0$ but $h_t = 0$ for all $t > s$, then let r_s be defined by

$$r_s h_s \equiv [p_s/2] \pmod{p_s}, \quad 0 < r_s < p_s .$$

Choose an integer $t > s$, and let $g_j = c_s^{r_s} c_t$, $b_j = b_j(g_j)$.

Now $\chi(b_j) = \chi(c_s^{r_s})\chi(c_t) \prod \chi(c_k) = \chi(c_s^{r_s}) = e^{2\pi i [p_s/2]/p_s}$, and thus $|\chi(b_j) - 1| \geqq \sqrt{3}$.

On the other hand, the element b_j belongs to the sequence a_n. Thus, if t was large enough, we have $\|b_j\| < \delta$, since $\|a_n\| \leqq \beta_n \to 0$, if $n \to \infty$.

Assume now that χ is such that infinitely many of the numbers h_i are non-zero. Let s be one of those, and set $g_j = c_s^{r_s}$, where r_s is defined above. The value of $\chi(g_j)$ is the same as above. On the other hand, g_j is in a_n, and thus if s was chosen large enough, we have $\|g_j\| < \delta$.

Thus c holds with $\varepsilon = \sqrt{3}$ for any $\chi \neq \chi_0$.

3C) Let us show now that if g is any element different from e, then $\|g\| > 0$.

Assume that g is written in the form $\prod a_i^{\alpha_i}$, $|\alpha_i| <$ order of a_i. Let us estimate the number $\sum \beta_i |\alpha_i|$ from below. There are only finitely many generating elements c_i occurring in g, say $g = c_1^{\gamma_1} \ldots c_n^{\gamma_n}$. If none of the elements a_i contains other generators, then there is no problem, since there are only finitely many such representations, giving a positive infimum.

Consider now a representation, where some a_i contain other generators than $c_1, \ldots, c_n$. There must be some b_j-s among them, consider the one with the largest j, say $b_J = a_N$. Since it contains the generators c_k for all $2^J < k \leqq 2^{J+1}$, and obviously no other b_j does any of them, we *either* have the elements $c_k^{r_k}$ (as a_i-s) in the representation $g = \prod a_i^{\alpha_i}$ for *all* $2^J < k \leqq 2^{J+1}$, (the r_k-s are some integers $0 < r_k < p_k$) — call this case 1, *or* b_j is raised to such a power α that some of the c_k-s disappeared — case 2.

If $p_1 = p_2 = \ldots$, then case 2 cannot happen, while if $p_1 < p_2 < \ldots$, then case 2 implies that $\sum \beta_i |\alpha_i| \geqq \beta_N p_{2^J}$, and since $N < J + \prod_{i=1}^{J} p_i = N(J)$, we get

$$\sum \beta_i |\alpha_i| > \beta_{N(J)} p_{2^J}.$$

In case 1 let $c_k^{r_k} = a_{l(k)}$, and then $\sum \beta_i |\alpha_i| \geqq \sum_{k=2^J}^{2^{J+1}} \beta_{l(k)}$. Now $l(k) < N(k)$, and hence we get the lower bound $2^J \cdot \beta_{N(2^J)}$.

Choosing the sequence β_n so slow that both $\beta_{N(J)} p_{2^J}$ and $\beta_{N(2^J)} \cdot 2^J$ be larger than 1/2 for any $J \geqq 1$ $\left(\text{say } \beta_n = \dfrac{K}{\log\log(n+2)}\right)$, we get that

$$\inf \sum \beta_i |\alpha_i| > 0, \qquad \text{if only } g \neq e.$$

$$\prod a_i^{\alpha_i} = g$$

§4. The group C_{p^∞}

4A) The elements of $G = C_{p^\infty}$ are of the form $e^{2\pi i k/p^n}$, and thus we can identify them by the fractions k/p^n, where $0 < k < p^n$, and $(k, p) = 1$ — except for the element 0 (corresponding to 1 of the original numbers).

Now a character χ can be identified by an infinite vector $(h_1, h_2, \ldots)$ of integer entries, where

$$0 \leqq h_n < p^n,$$

and

$$h_{n+1} \equiv h_n (\text{mod } p^n), \qquad n = 1, 2, \ldots,$$

i.e. $h_{n+1} = h_n + i \cdot p^n$, $0 \leqq i < p$. χ acts on $g = \dfrac{k}{p^n}$ as follows:

$$\chi(k/p^n) = e^{2\pi i h_n k/p^n}.$$

It is clear that for $\chi \neq \chi_0$ there are only finitely many zeros among the integers h_n. Just as in §§2–3, we choose some sequence $a_n \in G$ and also a sequence of real numbers $\beta_1 > \beta_2 > \ldots$, $\beta_n \to 0$, and define a semi-norm on G: for $x \in G$

$$\|x\| = \inf \sum \beta_i |\alpha_i|,$$

where the infimum is extended over all finite sets of integers α_i for which

$$x=\sum \alpha_i a_i \pmod 1 .$$

(Since any infinite sequence $a_n \in G$ generates G, the set of the infimum is non-empty.)

We have to choose a_n (and β_n) in such a way that

N. $\|\cdot\|$ is a norm,

C. For every $\chi \neq \chi_0$ there is an $\varepsilon > 0$ such that no neighbourhood of 0 is a subset of the set $\{x \in G \mid |\chi(x)-1| < \varepsilon\}$.

4B) Let us put all the elements $1/p^n$, $n=1, 2, \ldots$ to the sequence a_n, to start with. Now either the sequence h_n is constant from some n on, or $p^n - h_n$ is constant, or the interval $\left[\frac{1}{p+1}, \frac{p}{p+1}\right]$ is visited by infinitely many of the numbers h_n/p^n.

In the last case C is satisfied, since $\chi(1/p^n)=e^{2\pi i h_n/p^n}$ is at least as far from 1 for these n-s as $\left|e^{\frac{2\pi i}{p+1}}-1\right| = 2\left(1-\cos\frac{2\pi}{p+1}\right) > 0$; and $1/p^n$ is an a_i, and $\|a_i\| \leqq \beta_i \to 0$.

We still have to put a lot more elements into a_n in order to satisfy C in the first two cases, i.e. when

$$\chi_h(x)=e^{2\pi i h x},$$

where h is a non-zero integer. (It is amazing that the nicest characters, which map the unit circle into itself by simply raising the elements to an integer power h, cause the most problems.)

This can be done, obviously, by requesting that the sequence a_n be everywhere dense on (0, 1). (That is why we called this topology crazy in the beginning of the paper, for the neighbourhoods of any point are everywhere dense on the unit circle.)

4C) Thus our last task is to ensure N, i.e. to construct a sequence a_n of diadic rationals (and a sequence $\beta_1 > \beta_2 > \ldots, \beta_n \to 0$) such that $0 < a_n < 1$, a_n is everywhere dense in (0, 1), all the numbers $1/p^m$ belong to a_n, and

$$\bigcap_{M=1} B_M = \{0\},$$

where B_M is defined as $B_M = \left\{ \sum_{i=M} \alpha_i a_i \mid \alpha_i \text{ are integers, all but finitely many are zeros, and } \sum_{i=M} \beta_i |\alpha_i| < 1 \right\}$.

It seems likely that this last problem can be solved by an explicit construction, but we were unable to do it, that is why we give a random construction again. (We doubt, however, that an explicit construction could easily be made in case of the group Z.)

Let

$$\beta_n = 1/\log(n+1), \quad a_{2n-1} = 1/p^n, \quad n=1, 2, \ldots,$$

and define $a_{2n}=k/p^n$, where the number k is chosen from among the possible p^n values $0, 1, \ldots, p^n-1$ at random, and uniformly. Perform these random choices independently for different values of n.

To show that a_n is everywhere dense in (0, 1) with probability 1, fix a rational interval (r, s), $0<r<s<1$. For the probability that infinitely many a_{2n} fall into (r, s), we have the lower bound

$$P\,(\text{infinitely many } a_{2n}\in(r,s))\geqq\limsup_{n=\infty}(a_{2n}\in(r,s))=s-r>0\,.$$

And since a_{2n} are independent, according to the KOLMOGOROV 0–1 law, our probability must be equal to 1 (since it cannot be 0). In order to show that the tail $\bigcap_{M=1} B_M$ is trivial (contains 0 only), we proceed a similar way as in §2.

Let us fix an x, $0<x<1$. We want to show that

$$\lim_{M=\infty} P(x\in B_M)=0\,.$$

Given the integers α_{2i}, $2i\geqq M$, $\alpha_{2N}\neq 0$, $\alpha_{2i}=0$ for $2i>2N$, and also the integers α_{2i-1}, $M\leqq 2i-1\leqq 4N$, we let vary only the numbers α_{2i-1}, $2i-1>4N$. Since under the condition $\sum\beta_j|\alpha_j|<1$ we have

$$\left|\sum_{2i-1>4N}\alpha_{2i-1}a_{2i-1}\right|=\left|\sum_{2i-1>4N}\frac{\alpha_{2i-1}}{p^i}\right|<\frac{2\log(2N)}{p^{2N}}\,,$$

which is smaller than $\frac{1}{2}\cdot\frac{1}{p^N}$, the numbers $\sum_{2i-1>4N}\alpha_{2i-1}a_{2i-1}$ vary on an interval smaller than $1/p^N$.

Thus P (x can be written as a finite sum $x=\sum_{j\geqq M}\alpha_j a_j$ with the prescribed α_j-s and arbitrary α_{2i-1} for $2i-1>4N$, $\sum_{j\geqq M}\beta_j|\alpha_j|<1$)

$$\sup_y P(\alpha_{2N}a_{2N}=y)=\frac{(|\alpha_{2N}|,p^N)}{p^N}\leqq\frac{|\alpha_{2N}|}{p^N}<\frac{1/\beta_{2N}}{p^N}=\frac{\log(2N+1)}{p^N}\,.$$

Now we proved in §2 that the number of choices for integers α_i, $i\leqq 4N$ for which

$$\sum_{i\leqq 4N}\beta_i|\alpha_i|<1$$

is less than $(8N)^{1/\beta_{4N}}<e^{2\log^2 N}$.

Whence the probability

$$P(x\in B_M)\leqq\sum_{N\geqq M}e^{2\log^2 N}\cdot\frac{\log(2N+1)}{p^N}<\frac{1}{M}\to 0$$

as $M\to\infty$. Thus x belongs to all B_M only with probability zero.

References

[1] P. ERDŐS–S. J. TAYLOR, On the set of points of convergence of a lacunary trigonometric series and the equidistribution properties of related sequences. *Proc. London Math. Soc.* (3) **7** (1957), 598–615.

[2] BERNARD DE MATHAN, Sur un problème de densité mod 1. *Comptes Rendus*, Tome 287 — Séries A et B No. 5 (18 Sept. 1978)

MATHEMATICAL INSTITUTE
OF THE HUNGARIAN ACADEMY
OF SCIENCES
H-1053 BUDAPEST,
REÁLTANODA U. 13–15, HUNGARY

EÖTVÖS LORÁND UNIVERSITY
H-1088 BUDAPEST, MÚZEUM KRT. 6–8
HUNGARY

Studies in Pure Mathematics
à la mémoire de Paul Turán

Sur certains changements de variable des séries de puissances

par

L. ALPÁR (Budapest)

1. — Dans la note [6] TURÁN a démontré le théorème suivant souvant cité:

Théorème A. — *Étant donné le paramètre complexe* ζ, $0<|\zeta|<1$, *il existe une fonction*

$$f_1(z)=\sum_{\nu=0}^{\infty} a_\nu z^\nu$$

analytique dans le cercle $|z|<1$ *et telle qu'en un point* z_1, $|z_1|=1$, *la série* $\sum a_\nu z_1^\nu$ *converge, donc* $f_1(z)$ *est définie, et si l'on pose*

$$f_1\left(\frac{z-\zeta}{1-\bar{\zeta}z}\right)=f_2(z)=\sum_{n=0}^{\infty} b_n z^n \quad (b_n=b_n(\zeta)),$$

la fonction $f_2(z)$ *est aussi analytique pour* $|z|<1$, *pourtant au point* z_2, $|z_2|=1$, *donné par l'équation* $z_1=(z_2-\zeta)/(1-\bar{\zeta}z_2)$, *la série* $\sum b_n z_2^n$ *diverge, malgré que* $f_2(z_2)=f_1(z_1)$ *a une valeur bien déterminée.*

En d'autres termes: *La convergence locale des séries de puissances sur leur circonférence de convergence n'est pas un invariant conforme.*

Nous allons établir une preuve nouvelle du Théorème A montrant de plus qu'il existe f_1 telle que $\sum a_\nu z_1^\nu$ converge, mais que $\sum b_n z_2^n$ ne soit pas sommable (C, δ) pour un $\delta \in [0, 1/2)$ donné. On comprendra mieux le sense de cette assertion en évoquant notre résultat suivant ([1] Théorème 2, p. 100). Si l'on fixe d'avance les paramètres ζ, $k \geqq 0$ et $\delta \in [0, 1/2)$, il existe $f_1=f_1(z; \zeta, k, \delta)$ telle que $\sum a_\nu z_1^\nu$ soit sommable (C, k), et que $\sum b_n z_2^n$ ne soit pas sommable $(C, k+\delta)$ avec le δ donné.

Néanmoins la démonstration que nous allons exposer n'est pas seulement différente de celle de TURAN ou de celle que nous avons publiée antérieurement, mais elle met aussi en relief le fond du phénomène en question.

Théorème. — *Étant donnés les paramètres* $\zeta(0<|\zeta|<1)$ *et* $\delta \in [0, 1/2)$, *il existe une fonction*

$$f_1(z) = \sum_{\nu=0}^{\infty} a_\nu z^\nu \tag{1.1}$$

analytique dans le cercle $|z|<1$ *et telle qu'en un point* z_1, $|z_1|=1$, *la série* $\sum a_\nu z_1^\nu$ *converge, donc* $f_1(z_1)$ *est définie, et si l'on pose*

$$f_1\left(\frac{z-\zeta}{1-\bar{\zeta}z}\right) = f_2(z) = \sum_{n=0}^{\infty} b_n z^n \quad (b_n = b_n(\zeta)) \tag{1.2}$$

la fonction $f_2(z)$ *est aussi analytique pour* $|z|<1$, *pourtant au point* z_2, $|z_2|=1$, *solution de l'équation* $z_1 = (z_2-\zeta)/(1-\bar{\zeta}z_2)$, *la série* $\sum b_n z_2^n$ *n'est pas sommable* (C, δ), *malgré que* $f_1(z_1) = f_2(z_2)$ *a une valeur bien déterminée.*

2. — La démonstration du Théorème s'appuie sur trois lemmes.

Lemme 1. — *Soient* $[c_{n\nu}]$ $(n=0, 1, 2, \ldots; \nu=0, 1, 2, \ldots)$ *une matrice infinie,* $\{x_\nu\}_{\nu=0}^{\infty}$ *et* $\{y_n\}_{n=0}^{\infty}$ *deux suites infinies liées par la relation*

$$y_n = \sum_{\nu=0}^{\infty} c_{n\nu} x_\nu \quad (n=0, 1, 2, \ldots). \tag{2.1}$$

Pour que la série $\sum y_n$ *soit sommable* (C, δ) $(\delta \geqq 0)$ *chaque fois que la série* $\sum x_\nu$ *converge, il est nécessaire:*

(I) *que chaque colonne de la matrice* $[c_{n\nu}]$ *soit sommable* (C, δ), *c'est-à-dire que les quantités*

$$(C, \delta)\text{-}\sum_{n=0}^{\infty} c_{n\nu} \quad (\nu=0, 1, 2, \ldots) \tag{2.2}$$

soient finies;

(II) *qu'il existe une constante* $K>0$ *telle que*

$$\sum_{\nu=0}^{\infty} |c_{n\nu} - c_{n,\nu+1}| < K(n^\delta + 1) \quad (n=0, 1, 2, \ldots). \tag{2.3}$$

Démonstration du Lemme 1. — Comme il s'agit de prouver la nécessité des conditions indiquées, il faut admettre que $\sum y_n$ est sommable (C, δ) chaque fois que $\sum x_\nu$ est convergente et, en premier lieu, que dans ce cas les séries (2.1) convergent. C'est qui arrive, si

$$\sum_{\nu=0}^{\infty} |c_{n\nu} - c_{n,\nu+1}| < \infty \quad (n=0, 1, 2, \ldots) \tag{2.4}$$

(voir p.e. [3] Theorem 7, p. 51). Or, (2.3) contient (2.4) qui, de cette raison, ne figure pas comme condition distincte dans l'énoncé du Lemme 1. Toutefois seule la convergence des séries (2.1) ne permet de conclure davantage que (2.4).

Pour voir que les quantités (2.2) doivent être finies choisissons comme $\{x_\nu\}$ la suite dans laquelle $x_\nu=0$, si $\nu\neq\mu$ et $x_\mu=1$. Alors $\sum x_\nu=1$ est convergente, $y_n=c_{n\mu}$ et (2.2) doit représenter une quantité finie pour que la série particulière $\sum y_n=\sum c_{n\mu}$ soit sommable (C,δ).

Il en résulte de plus que $c_{n\nu}=o(n^\delta)$ $(n\to\infty)$ pour tout ν.

Pour montrer la nécessité de (2.3) observons tout d'abord que $\sum y_n$ étant sommable (C,δ), on a aussi $y_n=o(n^\delta)$ $(n\to\infty)$.

La relation (2.4) rend légitime une transformation d'Abel des séries (2.1). Posons donc $\xi_\nu=\sum_{\mu=0}^{\nu} x_\mu$, nous obtenons ainsi, après une division par $(n^\delta+1)$,

$$\eta_n=\frac{y_n}{n^\delta+1}=\sum_{\nu=0}^{\infty}\frac{c_{n\nu}-c_{n,\nu+1}}{n^\delta+1}\xi_\nu \quad (n=0,1,2,\ldots).$$

$\{\xi_\nu\}_{\nu=0}^{\infty}$ est une suite convergente arbitraire, tandis que $\eta_n\to 0$, $n\to\infty$. La matrice

$$\left[\frac{c_{n\nu}-c_{n,\nu+1}}{n^{\delta+1}}\right]=[d_{n\nu}] \quad (n=0,1,2,\ldots;\nu=0,1,2,\ldots)$$

transforme donc chaque suite convergente en une suite convergente vers zéro. Par conséquent, en vertu du théorème de Kojima–Schur, la matrice $[d_{n\nu}]$ satisfait aux conditions ci-après: il y a une constante $K>0$ indépendante de n telle que

$$\sum_{\nu=0}^{\infty}|d_{n\nu}|<K; \tag{2.5}$$

ils existent les limites finies

$$\lim_{n\to\infty} d_{n\nu}=d_\nu \quad (\nu=0,1,2,\ldots); \quad \lim_{n\to\infty}\sum_{\nu=0}^{\infty} d_{n\nu}=d$$

et, si $\xi_\nu\to\xi$ est une suite convergente quelconque, on a

$$\eta_n\to d\xi+\sum_{\nu=0}^{\infty} d_\nu(\xi_\nu-\xi)=0.$$

Il s'ensuit que chaque $d_\nu=0$ et $d=0$. En effet, $d_\nu=0$ puisque $c_{n\nu}=o(n^\delta)$ pour tout ν fixé et $d=0$, car

$$\sum_{\nu=0}^{\infty} d_{n\nu}=\sum_{\nu=0}^{\infty}(c_{n\nu}-c_{n,\nu+1})/(n^\delta+1)=c_{no}/(n^\delta+1)\to 0.$$

Enfin (2.3) est une conséquence immédiate de (2.5).

3. — Les fonctions qui figurent dans les Lemmes 2 et 3 sont à variable et à valeurs réelles.

Lemme 2. — *Si* $p(u) \in C^2$, $|p''(u)| > \kappa > 0$ $(\kappa = \text{const.})$, $q(u)$ *est monotone dans l'intervalle* $[a, b]$ *et*

$$A = \int_a^b e^{ip(u)} q(u)\, du\,,$$

alors

$$|A| \leqq \frac{8}{\pi} (|q(a)| + |q(b)|) \kappa^{-1/2}\,. \tag{3.1}$$

Démonstration du Lemme 2. — On écrit A sous la forme

$$A = \int_a^b \cos p(u) \cdot q(u)\, du + i \int_a^b \sin p(u) \cdot q(u)\, du = A_1 + iA_2$$

et on applique le second théorème de la moyenne pour évaluer A_1 et A_2. Nous aurons

$$A_1 = q(a) \int_a^\tau \cos p(u) \cdot du + q(b) \int_\tau^b \cos p(u) \cdot du \quad (a \leqq \tau \leqq b)\,.$$

Ces intégrales peuvent être majorées à l'aide du lemme de Van der Corput ([7] I, p. 197), ce qui donne

$$|A_1| \leqq \frac{4}{\pi} (|q(a)| + |q(b)|) \kappa^{-1/2}\,.$$

$|A_2|$ étant majorée par la même quantité, on obtient (3.1).

Lemme 3. — *On suppose que la fonction* $h(t)$ *jouit des propriétés suivantes:*
(i) $h(t) = t + h_0(t)$, $h_0(t) = h_0(t + 2\pi)$, $h_0(0) = 0$;
(ii) $h_0 \in C^2$; $h'(t) \neq 0$ *resp.* $h_0(t) \neq -1$;
(iii) $h''(t) = h_0''(t)$ *a un nombre fini de zéros dans* $[0, 2\pi]$.

Soit de plus

$$e^{i\nu h(t)} = \sum_{n=-\infty}^{\infty} a_{n\nu} e^{int} \quad (\nu = 0, \pm 1, \pm 2, \ldots). \tag{3.2}$$

Il existe alors une constante $\lambda > 0$ *telle que*

$$\lambda |n|^{1/2} < \sum_{\nu=-\infty}^{\infty} |a_{n\nu} - a_{n,\nu+1}| \quad (n = 0, \pm 1, \pm 2, \ldots)\,. \tag{3.3}$$

Démonstration du Lemme 3. — Comme $h'(t) \neq 0$, la fonction $h(t) = u$ a un inverse, soit $t = g(u)$, ayant manifestement la même structure que $h(t)$; c'est que $g(u) = u + g_0(u)$, $g_0(u) = g_0(u + 2\pi)$, $g_0(0) = 0$, $g'(u) = 1/h'(t) \neq 0$, $g''(u) = -h''(t)[h'(t)]^{-3}$ est continue et $g(u)$ remplit la condition (iii).

On a d'autre part, en vertu (3.2) et avec le changement de variable signalé,

$$(3.4) \qquad \begin{aligned} a_{n\nu} - a_{n,\nu+1} &= \frac{1}{2\pi} \int_0^{2\pi} e^{i\nu h(t) - int}(1 - e^{ih(t)})\, dt = \\ &= \frac{1}{2\pi} \int_0^{2\pi} e^{i\nu u - ing(u)}(1 - e^{iu})\, g'(u)\, du \end{aligned}$$

d'où il vient

$$(3.5) \qquad \sum_{\nu=-\infty}^{\infty} |a_{n\nu} - a_{n,\nu+1}|^2 = \frac{1}{2\pi} \int_0^{2\pi} |1 - e^{iu}|^2 g'^2(u)\, du = \alpha^2 > 0 .$$

Il en découle que (3.3) est vérifié pour $n = 0$. On admettra donc pour ce qui suit que $n \neq 0$.

Posons ensuite $(a_{n\nu} - a_{n,\nu+1})/\alpha = \alpha_{n\nu}$, nous avons alors, selon (3.4) et (3.5),

$$(3.6) \qquad \alpha_{n\nu} = \frac{-i}{\alpha\pi} \int_0^{2\pi} e^{i(\nu+1/2)u - ing(u)} \sin\frac{u}{2} \cdot g'(u)\, du; \qquad \sum_{\nu=-\infty}^{\infty} |\alpha_{n\nu}|^2 = 1 .$$

Au sense des propriétés de $g(u)$ il y a apparement un intervalle $I \subset [0, 2\pi]$ dans lequel $|g''(u)| \geqq \kappa > 0$ et $\sin\frac{u}{2} \cdot g'(u)$ est monotone. De cette manière on prend dans I comme p et q du Lemme 2 les fonctions $p(u) = (\nu + 1/2)u - ng(u)$ et $q(u) = \sin\frac{u}{2} \cdot g'(u)$ et l'on considère l'intégrale

$$\beta_{n\nu} = \frac{-i}{\alpha\pi} \int_I e^{i(\nu+1/2)u - ing(u)} \sin\frac{u}{2} \cdot g'(u)\, du .$$

Nous en tirons au moyen du Lemme 2

$$(3.7) \qquad |\beta_{n\nu}| \leqq c_0(\kappa|n|)^{-1/2} = \varepsilon \quad (n \neq 0)$$

pour tout ν, c_0 étant une constante convenablement choisie.

Soit de plus $\alpha_{n\nu}=\beta_{n\nu}+\gamma_{n\nu}$ et $J=[0, 2\pi]\backslash I$. Il est simple de voir que

$$\sum_{\nu=-\infty}^{\infty} |\alpha_{n\nu}|^2 = \sum_{\nu=-\infty}^{\infty} |\beta_{n\nu}|^2 + \sum_{\nu=-\infty}^{\infty} |\gamma_{n\nu}|^2 = 1 \tag{3.8}$$

avec

$$\sum_{\nu=-\infty}^{\infty} |\gamma_{n\nu}|^2 = \frac{2}{\alpha^2\pi} \int_J \sin^2 \frac{u}{2} \cdot g'^2(u)\, du = c_1 < 1$$

où c_1 est indépendante de n.

Lorsque $|\alpha_{n\nu}| > H\varepsilon$, $H>1$ étant une constante, il résulte de (3.7) que $\frac{H}{H-1}|\gamma_{n\nu}| > |\alpha_{n\nu}|$ et, par suite,

$$\sum_{|\alpha_{n\nu}|>H\varepsilon} |\alpha_{n\nu}|^2 < \left(\frac{H}{H-1}\right)^2 \sum_{\nu=-\infty}^{\infty} |\gamma_{n\nu}|^2 = \left(\frac{H}{H-1}\right)^2 c_1 = 1-\vartheta$$

quel que soit n. Choisissons H pour avoir $0<\vartheta<1$. On en conclut, vu (3.6) ou (3.8),

$$\sum_{\nu=-\infty}^{\infty} |\alpha_{n\nu}| \geqq \sum_{|\alpha_{n\nu}|\leqq H\varepsilon} |\alpha_{n\nu}| > \frac{1}{H\varepsilon} \sum_{|\alpha_{n\nu}|\leqq H\varepsilon} |\alpha_{n\nu}|^2 > \frac{\vartheta}{H\varepsilon},$$

d'où l'inégalité (3.3).

Remarque. — La preuve du Lemme 3 utilise une idée de LEIBENZON [5]. — Le Lemme 3 montre certaine analogie avec deux propositions de KAHANE ([4] Théorème IV, p. 253; Théorème V, p. 254) et avec trois de nos résultats ([2] Théorème 1, p. 280; Théorème 3, p. 282; Remarque, p. 283). Toutefois dans ces notes on envisage de sommes du type $\sum_{n=-\infty}^{\infty} |a_{n\nu}|^{2-\sigma}$ où n est l'indice variable et non ν ($\alpha=1$ dans [4] et $0<\sigma<2$ dans [2]).

4. — Démonstration du Théorème. — Revenons maintenant sur les expressions (1.1) et (1.2). Supposons, pour simplifier le calcul, que $\zeta=r$ est réel et positif ($0<r<1$) et que $z_1=1$. Alors on a aussi $z_2=1$. Dans ces circonstances il faut prouver que la convergence de la série $\sum a_\nu$ n'entraîne pas nécessairement la sommabilité (C, δ) de la série $\sum b_n$, si $0\leqq\delta<1/2$.

Ceci posé, on aura

$$f_1\left(\frac{z-r}{1-rz}\right) = \sum_{\nu=0}^{\infty} a_\nu \left(\frac{z-r}{1-rz}\right)^\nu = f_2(z) = \sum_{n=0}^{\infty} b_n z^n \tag{4.1}$$

où les séries en question sont uniformément convergentes pour $|z|=\rho<1$. Par conséquent on déduit de (4.1)

$$b_n = \sum_{\nu=0}^{\infty} a_\nu \frac{1}{2\pi i} \cdot \int\limits_{|z|=\rho} \left(\frac{z-r}{1-rz}\right)^\nu \frac{dz}{z^{n+1}} = \sum_{\nu=0}^{\infty} \omega_{n\nu} a_\nu .$$

Les coefficients b_n sont donc les transformés de la suite $\{a_\nu\}_{\nu=0}^{\infty}$ par la matrice $[\omega_{n\nu}]$. On voit que $\omega_{n\nu}$ est le n-ième coefficient dans la série de Maclaurin de $\left(\frac{z-r}{1-rz}\right)^\nu$. Cette fonction étant analytique pour $|z|<r^{-1}$, l'expression de $\omega_{n\nu}$ s'écrit aussi sous la forme

(4.2) $$\omega_{n\nu} = \frac{1}{2\pi i} \int\limits_{|z|=1} \left(\frac{z-r}{1-rz}\right)^\nu \frac{dz}{z^{n+1}} \quad (n=0, 1, 2, \ldots, \nu=0, 1, 2, \ldots).$$

Écrivons en conséquence $z=e^{it}$, nous aurons

$$\frac{e^{it}-r}{1-re^{it}} = e^{ih(t)}; \quad h(t) = t - i \log \frac{1-re^{-it}}{1-re^{it}} = t + h_0(t).$$

On vérific facilement que $h(t)$ jouit des propriétés des fonctions définies dans le Lemme 3. En effet, $h_0(t)$ est **2π-périodique,**

$$h'(t) = \frac{1-r^2}{1-2r\cos t + r^2} > 0, \quad h''(t) = \frac{-2r(1-r^2)\sin t}{(1-2r\cos t + r^2)^2},$$

$h''(t)$ est continue et n'a que trois zéros dans $[0, 2\pi]$. $h(t)$ est même analytique le longue de l'axe des t, $h(-t) = -h(t)$ et, vu (4.2),

(4.3) $$e^{i\nu h(t)} = \sum_{n=0}^{\infty} \omega_{n\nu} e^{int} \quad (\nu=0, 1, 2, \ldots).$$

Pour appliquer la formule (3.3), il faut tenir compte également des valeurs négatives des n et des ν. Or, d'après (4.3), $\omega_{n\nu}=0$ quand $n<0$, $\nu>0$; puis $h(t)$ étant impaire, $\omega_{n\nu} = \omega_{-n,-\nu}$ et $\omega_{n,-\nu}=0$, si $n>0$, $\nu>0$, enfin $\omega_{00}=1$ et $\omega_{n0}=0$, $n\neq 0$. Nous obtenons ainsi, grâce à (3.3),

$$\sum_{\nu=0}^{\infty} |\omega_{n\nu} - \omega_{n,\nu+1}| > \lambda n^{1/2} \quad (n=0, 1, 2, \ldots).$$

La matrice $[\omega_{n\nu}]$ ne réalise donc pas la condition (2.3) du Lemme 1, si $0 \leqq \delta < 1/2$. Par conséquent il existe une série convergente $\sum a_\nu$ dont la transformée, la série $\sum b_n$ n'est pas sommable (C, δ).

Références

[1] ALPÁR, L., Remarque sur la sommabilité des séries de Taylor sur leurs cercles de convergence, III. *Publ. Math. Inst. Hungarian Acad. Sci.* **5** (1960), 97–152.

[2] ALPÁR, L., Sur une classe particulière de séries de Fourier à certaines puissances absolument convergentes. *Studia Sci. Math. Hung.* **3** (1968), 279–286.

[3] HARDY, G. H., *Divergent Series.* Clarendon Press, Oxford, 1956.

[4] KAHANE, J.-P., Sur certaines classes de séries de Fourier absolument convergentes. *J. de Math. Pures et Appl.* **35** (1956), 249–259.

[5] ЛЕЙБЕНЗОН, З. Л.: О кольце функций с абсолютно сходящимисн рядами фуръе, *Успехи математических наук*, **9** (1954), No. *3.* 157–162.

[6] TURÁN, P., A remark concerning the behaviour of a power series on the periphery of its convergence circle. *Acad. Serbe Sci. Publ. Inst. Math.* **12** (1958), 19–26.

[7] ZYGMUND, A., *Trigonometric Series.* University Press, Cambridge, 1959.

INSTITUT MATHÉMATIQUE
DE L'ACADÉMIE HONGROISE DES SCIENCES
H-1053 BUDAPEST, REÁLTANODA U. 13–15.
HONGRIE

Studies in Pure Mathematics
To the Memory of Paul Turán

The spherical derivative of meromorphic functions with relatively few poles

by

J. M. ANDERSON and J. CLUNIE (London)

1. Introduction

Suppose that $f(z)$ is a function meromorphic in the plane **C** and let

$$\rho(f(z)) = \frac{|f'(z)|}{1+|f(z)|^2}$$

denote the spherical derivative of $f(z)$. For $r>0$ we set

$$\mu(r, f) = \max\{\rho(f(z)) : |z| = r\}.$$

We shall assume acquaintance with the standard terminology of the NEVANLINNA theory (see e.g. [3]) and shall use the notations

$$T(r, f), \delta(a, f), \log M(r, f), N(r, a)\ldots$$

etc. without further specification.

In [2] the relationship of the growth of $\mu(r, f)$ to that of $T(r, f)$ or $\log M(r, f)$ when $f(z)$ is entire is dealt with fairly comprehensively. The results for entire functions differ significantly from those for meromorphic functions.

We cite two theorems

Theorem A. ([4] Theorem 1). *If* $f(z)$ *is meromorphic in* **C**, *then*

(1) $$\limsup_{r\to\infty} r\mu(r, f) \geq \frac{1}{2}.$$

Theorem B. ([2] Theorem 2). *If* $f(z)$ *is entire and transcendental then*

(2) $$\limsup_{r\to\infty} \frac{r\mu(r, f)}{\log r} = \infty.$$

Both of these results are sharp. However, in [1] we observed that if $f(z)$ is meromorphic and transcendental, and if $\delta(\infty, f)>0$ then, in place of (1) we have

$$\limsup_{r\to\infty} r\mu(r, f)=\infty. \tag{3}$$

We also remarked in [1], p. 271 that if

$$\rho(f(z))=O\left(\frac{1}{|z|}\right) \quad (z\to\infty) \tag{4}$$

then it is an "open question" whether $f(z)$ can possess a VALIRON deficient value. However over 40 years earlier OSTROWSKI had proved ([5] pp. 245–246) a much stronger result, namely that if $f(z)$ satisfies (4) then

$$n(r, a)-n(r, b)=O(1) \quad (r\to\infty)$$

for all $a, b\in \mathbf{C}\cup\{\infty\}$. We regret that we were unaware of this result of OSTROWSKI at that time.

This result of OSTROWSKI, together with Theorem B, suggests that (3) might not be the best possible. This is indeed the case and in the present paper we show that if $f(z)$ is meromorphic (and transcendental) and of order zero with $\delta(\infty, f)>0$ then the maximal behaviour of $\mu(r, f)$ resembles that of entire functions and, in particular, it will follow that (2) holds for any transcendental meromorphic function $f(z)$ with $\delta(\infty, f)>0$.

2. Statement of results

The three theorems following are analogous to results for entire functions in [2]. This latter paper also contains results for entire functions of any positive finite order. It seems quite probable that the analogous results for meromorphic functions with $\delta(\infty, f)>0$ are also true, though perhaps with some restrictions on the actual size of $\delta(\infty, f)$. We discuss this question in §7.

Theorem 1. *Let $f(z)$ be a transcendental meromorphic function of order zero with $\delta(\infty, f)>0$. Then*

$$\limsup_{r\to\infty} \frac{r\mu(r, f)}{T(r, f)}>0.$$

Corollary. *If $f(z)$ is a transcendental meromorphic function with $\delta(\infty, f)>0$ then* (2) *holds.*

Theorem 2. *Let $f(z)$ be a meromorphic function with $\delta(\infty, f)>0$. Suppose that $\Phi(r)\uparrow\infty$ as $r\uparrow\infty$ and that*

$$\limsup_{r\to\infty} T(r,f)/\Phi(r)(\log r)^{\alpha} \quad >0,\ T(r,f)=O(\log r)^{\alpha+1} \quad (r\to\infty),$$

where $2<\alpha<\infty$. Then

$$\limsup_{r\to\infty} \frac{r\mu(r,f)}{\Phi(r)(\log r)^{\alpha-1}}>0.$$

Theorem 3. *Suppose that $\Phi(r)\uparrow$ as $r\uparrow\infty$ and let $f(z)$ be a transcendental meromorphic function with $\delta(\infty, f)>0$ and such that*

$$T(r,f)=O\left(\frac{(\log r)^2}{\Phi(r)}\right) \quad (r\to\infty).$$

Then

$$\limsup_{r\to\infty} \frac{r\mu(r,f)}{\Phi(r)\log r}=\infty.$$

Theorem 1 and its Corollary are the best possible — the necessary examples, in the form of entire functions, are contained in [2], Theorems 6 and 7. Theorems 2 and 3 exhibit the slightly curious phenomenon, already apparent in [2], that (2) is best possible only for functions whose growth is essentially like $(\log r)^2$.

3. Preliminary lemmas

Lemma 1. *Suppose that $h(z)$ is meromorphic in $|z|\leqq R$ and that $|h(z)|\geqq 1$ there. Let $\zeta_1, \zeta_2, \ldots, \zeta_n$ denote the poles of $h(z)$ in $|z|<R$, and let*

$$B(z)=\prod_{k=1}^{n} \frac{R(z-\zeta_k)}{R^2-\bar{\zeta}_k z}.$$

Then, for $|z|=r<R$,

$$\frac{R-r}{R+r}\log|h(0)\,B(0)|\leqq \log|h(z)\,B(z)|\leqq \frac{R+r}{R-r}\log|h(0)\,B(0)|.$$

Proof. We assume, without loss of generality, that $h(z)$ has no poles on $|z|=R$. Consider $H(z)=h(z)B(z)$. Then $H(z)$ is analytic and non-zero for $|z|<R$ and on $|z|=R$, $|H(z)|=|h(z)|>1$. Hence by the maximum principle $|H(z)|>1$ for $|z|\leqq R$. In particular $\log|H(0)|>0$. If we represent $\log|H(z)|$ as a Poisson integral of its boundary values on $|z|=R$ and use an obvious estimate we obtain

$$\frac{R-r}{R+r}\log|H(0)|\leqq\log|H(z)|\leqq\frac{R+r}{R-r}\log|H(0)|,$$

which is the result of the lemma.

Lemma 2. *Suppose that $h(z)$ satisfies the hypothesis of Lemma* 1, *that* $|h(z_0)|=1$ for *some* z_0 *with* $|z_0|=R$ *and that* $|h(0)|\geqq 2$. *Then for some* ζ *with* $|\zeta|<R$

$$\rho(h(\zeta))\geqq\frac{1}{(10\log 2)R}\log\left(|h(0)|\cdot\frac{\prod_{k=1}^{n}|\zeta_k|}{R^n}\right).$$

Proof. Let τ be the point of largest modulus on the segment $[0, z_0]$ such that $|h(\tau)|=2$. Then

$$1\leqq\left|\int_{\tau}^{z_0}h'(w)\,dw\right|\leqq(R-|\tau|)|h'(\zeta)|$$

for some ζ in $[\tau, z_0]$. Since $|h(\zeta)|\leqq 2$

$$\rho(h(\zeta))\geqq\frac{1}{5}|h'(\zeta)|\geqq\frac{1}{5}\frac{1}{R-|\tau|}. \tag{5}$$

But, by Lemma 1,

$$\frac{R-|\tau|}{R+|\tau|}\log|h(0)\,B(0)|\leqq\log 2\,|B(\tau)|\leqq\log 2$$

and so

$$\frac{1}{R-|\tau|}\geqq\frac{1}{(R+|\tau|)\log 2}\log|h(0)B(0)|\geqq\frac{1}{2R\log 2}\log|h(0)B(0)|.$$

This estimate, together with (5) gives the desired result.

If $f(z)$ is an entire function of genus zero we introduce the notation

$$Q(r)=r\int_{r}^{\infty}\frac{N(t,0,f)}{t^2}\,dt,$$

noting that the integral converges. We require the following lemma, which is in [6], pp. 55–65.

Lemma 3. *Let $f(z)$ be an entire function of genus zero with $f(0)=1$ and zeros $\{z_k\}_{k=1}^{\infty}$. Then*

$$N(r,0,f)\leqq \log M(r,f)\leqq \log \prod_{1}^{\infty}\left(1+\frac{r}{|z_k|}\right)=r\int_{0}^{\infty}\frac{n(t)dt}{(t+r)t}\leqq$$

$$\leqq N(r,0,f)+r\int_{r}^{\infty}\frac{n(t)dt}{t^2}=Q(r).$$

If $f(z)$ is of order zero then

$$N(r,0,f)\sim Q(r)$$

or, equivalently,

$$r\int_{r}^{\infty}\frac{n(t)dt}{t^2}=o(N(r,0,f))$$

as $r\to\infty$ through some unbounded set of values of r.

4. Proof of Theorem 1

In the proof of Theorem 1 we make extensive use of Lemma 3 without specific reference. We make a number of inessential assumptions for the sake of simplification: 1) we suppose $f(z)=f_1(z)/f_2(z)$, where $f_1(z)$, $f_2(z)$ are entire functions without common zeros, and $f_1(0)=f_2(0)=1$; 2) $T(r,f)\sim N(r,0,f)\ (r\to\infty)$; 3) given $r>0$ and $\Phi_0\in(-\pi,\pi)$ there is a Φ with $\Phi-\Phi_0\leqq\frac{\pi}{6}$ and $f_1(re^{i\Phi})=M(r,f_1)$. We can always achieve 3) by considering $f(z^6)$ in place of $f(z)$ if necessary.

Consider now an unbounded set of values of ρ such that, as $\rho\to\infty$

$$\rho\int_{\rho}^{\infty}\frac{n(t,0,f)}{t^2}dt=o(N(\rho,0,f)).$$

For large ρ we have

$$\log M(\rho,f_1)>(1-o(1))\rho\int_{\rho}^{\infty}\frac{N(t,0,f)dt}{t^2}>\left(1-\frac{\delta}{4}\right)T(\rho,f)\quad(\rho\to\infty). \tag{6}$$

Also, if $\{z_k\}_1^{\infty}$ are the poles of $f(z)$, then

$$\log \prod_1^\infty \left(1+\frac{r}{|z_k|}\right) \leqq r \int_r^\infty \frac{N(t,\infty,f)}{t^2}\,dt\,.$$

For all large t we have

$$N(t,\infty,f) < \left(1-\frac{\delta}{2}\right) N(t,0,f)\,,$$

where $\delta = \delta(\infty, f)$. Hence, for sufficiently large ρ as above we have, for $|z| = \rho$ and $|f_1(z)| = M(\rho, f_1)$

$$\text{(7)} \qquad \log|f(z)| \geqq \log\left[\frac{M(\rho,f_1)}{\prod_1^\infty \left(1+\frac{\rho}{|z_k|}\right)}\right] \geqq \frac{\delta}{4}\rho \int_\rho^\infty \frac{N(t,0,f)}{t^2}\,dt > \frac{\delta}{4} T(\rho,f)\,.$$

Let ρ' be the largest number not exceeding ρ such that $|f(z)| \leqq 1$ at some point on $|z| = \rho'$. Note that ρ' takes arbitrarily large values. We set $\Delta = \exp(-5\delta^{-1})$ and consider two cases

a) $\rho' \geqq \rho\Delta$ b) $\rho' < \rho\Delta$.

Case a) $\rho' \geqq \rho\Delta$.

Suppose that $|f(\rho' e^{i\Phi_0})| \leqq 1$. Then if $|f_1(\rho e^{i\Phi})| = M(\rho, f_1)$ and $|\Phi - \Phi_0| \leqq \frac{\pi}{6}$, i.e. assumption 3) above is fulfilled, then it is an obvious geometrical fact that $|\rho' e^{i\Phi_0} - \rho e^{i\Phi}| < \eta\rho$ where $\eta = \eta(\Delta) < 1$. We let $z_0 = \rho e^{i\Phi}$ and apply Lemma 2 to $h(z) = f(z_0 + z)$. If R is the radius of the largest disc in which $|h(z)| > 1$ then $R \leqq |\rho' e^{i\Phi_0} - \rho e^{i\Phi}| < \eta\rho$. From Lemma 2 we obtain

$$\text{(8)} \qquad \rho(f(\zeta)) > \frac{1}{10(\log 2)R}\left[\log|f(z_0)| R^{-n} \prod_{k=1}^n |z_0 - \zeta_k|\right],$$

for some ζ satisfying $|\zeta - z_0| < R$. Here $\zeta_1, \ldots, \zeta_n$ denote the poles of $f(z)$ in $|z - z_0| < R$. If, now $\prod'$ denotes the product over the remaining poles $\{z_k\}$ of $f(z)$ we obtain, using (7)

$$\log\left[|f(z_0)| R^{-n} \prod_{k=1}^n |z_0 - \zeta_k|\right] = \log\left[\frac{M(\rho,f_1)}{\prod_k' \left|1-\frac{z_0}{z_k}\right|} \cdot \frac{\prod_{k=1}^n |\zeta_k|}{R^n}\right] \geqq$$

$$\geqq \log\left[\frac{M(\rho,f_1)}{\prod_k' \left(1+\frac{\rho}{|z_k|}\right)} \cdot \prod_{k=1}^n \left(\frac{|\zeta_k|}{\rho + |\zeta_k|}\right)\right] = \log\left[\frac{M(\rho,f_1)}{\prod\left(1+\frac{\rho}{|z_k|}\right)}\right] > \frac{\delta}{4} T(\rho,f)\,.$$

Noting that $(1-\eta)\rho<|\zeta|\leqq 2\rho$ we obtain from (8) that

$$\mu(t, f)>k_1\frac{T(\rho, f)}{t}, \tag{9}$$

where k_1 is a constant >0 and t is some number satisfying $(1-\eta)\rho\leqq t\leqq 2\rho$.

We now use k to denote a generic constant not necessarily the same at each occurrence. It follows from our choice of ρ that

$$\rho\int_{2\rho}^{\infty}\frac{n(t, 0, f)}{t^2}\,dt<kN(\rho, 0, f)\quad(\rho\to\infty) \tag{10}$$

and so

$$n(2\rho, 0, f)<kN(\rho, 0, f).$$

Hence

$$N(2\rho, 0, f)\leqq N(\rho, 0, f)+n(2\rho, 0, f)\log 2<kN(\rho, 0, f).$$

Thus for $(1-\eta)\rho<t\leqq 2\rho$

$$T(t, f)\leqq T(2\rho, f)\sim N(2\rho, 0, f)<kT(\rho, f).$$

This estimate together with (9) gives the desired result in case a).

Case b) $\rho'<\rho\Delta$

In this case we define $r_0=\rho'\exp\left(\frac{5}{\delta}\right)<\rho$ and show that (6) and (10) hold with ρ replaced by r_0. Since $\rho'=r_0\Delta$ this reduces case b) to case a) and so completes the proof of Theorem 1. Since $f(z)$ has no zeros in $\rho'\leqq|z|\leqq\rho$ we have $n(t, 0, f)=n(\rho', 0, f)$ for $\rho'\leqq t\leqq\rho$. If r satisfies $\rho'\leqq r\leqq\rho$ we write $r=\sigma\rho'$ so that $1\leqq\sigma\leqq\frac{\rho}{\rho'}$. Then .

$$\frac{r\displaystyle\int_r^{\infty}\frac{n(t, 0, f)}{t^2}\,dt}{N(r, 0, f)}=\frac{rn(\rho', 0, f)\displaystyle\int_r^{\rho}\frac{dt}{t^2}+r\int_{\rho}^{\infty}\frac{n(t, 0, f)}{t^2}\,dt}{N(\rho', 0, f)+n(\rho', 0, f)\log\dfrac{r}{\rho'}}\leqq\frac{1}{\log\sigma}+\frac{\gamma\sigma}{\alpha+\beta\log\sigma},$$

where $\alpha=N(\rho', 0, f)$, $\beta=n(\rho', 0, f)$ and $\nu=\rho'\int\limits_{\rho}^{\infty}\frac{n(t, 0, f)}{t^2}\,dt$. If we set $F(\sigma)=\frac{\sigma}{\alpha+\beta\log\sigma}$ then $F(\sigma)$ is increasing for $\sigma>e$ since then

$$F'(\sigma)=\frac{\alpha+\beta\log\frac{\sigma}{e}}{(\alpha+\beta\log\sigma)^2}\geqq 0.$$

Hence, choosing $r=r_0$, for which $\sigma=\exp\left(\frac{5}{\delta}\right)$ we obtain

$$\frac{r_0\int\limits_{r_0}^{\infty}\frac{n(t, 0, f)}{t^2}\,dt}{N(r_0, 0, f)}\leqq\frac{\delta}{5}+\gamma F(\sigma/\sigma')=\frac{\delta}{5}+\frac{\rho\int\limits_{\rho}^{\infty}\frac{n(t, 0, f)}{t^2}\,dt}{N\left(\rho, \frac{1}{f}\right)}=\frac{\delta}{5}+o(1)\quad\text{as}\quad\rho\to\infty,$$

since the last term tends to zero as ρ approaches infinity. Thus (10) holds with ρ replaced by r_0. On integrating by parts we obtain

$$r_0\int\limits_{r_0}^{\infty}\frac{N(t, 0, f)}{t^2}\,dt\leqq\left(\frac{\delta}{5}+o(1)\right)N(r_0, 0, f)$$

for r_0 sufficiently large, and it is easily verified that this implies (6), with ρ replaced by r_0. Theorem 1 is now proved.

To prove the corollary we use the Ahlfors–Shimizu characteristic $T_0(r, f)$ of a meromorphic function $f(z)$, given by

$$T_0(r, f)=\int\limits_0^r\frac{S(t, f)}{t}\,dt,$$

where

$$S(r, f)=\frac{1}{\pi}\int\limits_0^r\int\limits_0^{2\pi}\rho^2(f(te^{i\Theta}))\,t\,dt\,d\Theta.$$

If, for a meromorphic function $f(z)$, $\mu(t, f)=O(t^{-1}\log t)\,(t\to\infty)$ then $T_0(r, f)=O((\log r)^4)\,(r\to\infty)$. Hence the result of the corollary is only significant for functions of very small growth, and these are dealt with by Theorem 1 since $\log r=o(T(r, f))\,(r\to\infty)$.

5. Proof of Theorem 2

As before, we denote a generic constant by k. It is easy to verify that, under the hypotheses of Theorem 2,

$$n(r,0,f)=O((\log r)^{\alpha}) \quad (r\to\infty),$$

$$r\int_r^{\infty}\frac{n(t,0,f)}{t^2}\,dt=O((\log r)^{\alpha}) \quad (r\to\infty).$$

We assume as before that $N(r,0,f)\sim T(r,f)$. Hence for a set of values r

$$N(r,0,f)>k\Phi(r)(\log r)^{\alpha}.$$

and so

$$N\left(\frac{r}{2},0,f\right)\geqq N(r,0,f)-n(r,0,f)\log 2>k\Phi(r)(\log r)^{\alpha}.$$

For such a set of values of r we set $\rho=\frac{r}{2}$ and argue as in the proof of Theorem 1.

In Case a) we find that

$$\limsup_{r\to\infty}\frac{r\mu(r,f)}{\Phi(r)(\log r)^{\alpha}}>0,$$

which is a stronger result than that stated.

In Case b) we obtain as in the proof of Theorem 1, that, for some arbitrarily large t

$$t\mu(t,f)\geqq kT(r_0,f), \tag{11}$$

where $(1-\eta)r_0\ t\leqq 2r_0\leqq 2\rho$ (using the notation of Theorem 1). But

$$n\left(\frac{\rho}{2},0,f\right)\log\frac{\rho}{2}\geqq k\int_0^{\rho/2}\frac{n(t,0,f)}{t}\,dt\geqq k\left\{N(\rho,0,f)-\int_{\rho/2}^{\rho}\frac{n(t,0,f)}{t}\,dt\right\}\geqq$$

$$\geqq k\Phi(2\rho)(\log\rho)^{\alpha}$$

Since $n(t,0,f)=n(\rho',0,f)=n\left(\frac{\rho}{2},0,f\right)$ $(\rho'\leqq t\leqq\rho)$ we see that

$$T(r_0,f)\sim N(r_0,f)\geqq\int_{\rho'}^{r_0}\frac{n(t,0,f)}{t}\,dt\geqq k\Phi(2\rho)(\log\rho)^{\alpha-1}\geqq k\Phi(t)(\log t)^{\alpha-1}.$$

This estimate, combined with (11) proves Theorem 2.

6. Proof of Theorem 3

We only sketch the proof in this case. We assume, as in the proof of Theorem 1, that the simplifying assumptions 1), 2) and 3) are fulfilled. It is easy to check, in the present case that $n(r, 0, f) = O\left(\frac{\log r}{\Phi(r)}\right)$ $(r \to \infty)$ and that

$$N(r, 0, f) \sim Q(r)$$

as $r \to \infty$ unrestrictedly. We use this observation freely in the proof.

Consider now a large r such that $f(z) = 0$ at some point of the circle $|z| = r$. It is known ([6], p. 64) that if $\beta(r) = \left(\frac{\log r}{\Phi(r) \log M(r, f_1)}\right)^{1/2}$ then, for some ρ satisfying $r - kr\beta^2(r) < \rho < r$, we have

$$\log |f_1(z)| = (1 + o(1)) \log M(\rho, f)$$

on $|z| = \rho$. Hence by Lemma 3 and the argument used in the proof of Theorem 1 we find that for all large r there is a ρ with $r - kr\beta^2(r) < \rho < r$ such that, on $|z| = \rho$,

$$\log \left[\frac{|f_1(z)|}{\prod_1^\infty \left(1 + \frac{\rho}{|z_k|}\right)} \right] \geqq kT(\rho, f)$$

where $z_1, z_2, \ldots$ are the poles of $f(z)$.

If $f_1(re^{i\Phi_0}) = 0$ we apply Lemma 2 to $h(z) = f(\rho e^{i\Phi_0} + z)$ in the largest disc in which $|h(z)| \geqq 1$ and argue as in the proof of Theorem 1 to obtain

$$\rho(f(\zeta)) \geqq \frac{kT(\rho, f)}{r\beta^2(r)}$$

for some ζ satisfying $r - kr\beta^2(r) \leqq |\zeta| \leqq r$. It follows that, for some large r, there exist t and ρ satisfying $\frac{r}{2} \leqq t, \rho \leqq r$ such that

$$\mu(t, f) \geqq k \frac{T(\rho, f)}{r} \cdot \frac{\Phi(r) \log M(r, f_1)}{\log r} \geqq k \frac{\Phi(t) \log t}{t} \cdot \frac{T(\rho, f)}{\log \rho} \cdot \frac{\log M(r, f_1)}{\log r}.$$

Since the last two quotients on the right-hand side above tend to ∞ as $r \to \infty$, the result follows.

7. Concluding remarks

We are unable to decide the extent to which Theorem 1 remains valid for meromorphic functions of positive order. Indeed, there seems no reason a priori why Theorem 1 should not remain valid for any meromorphic function. Our methods of proof would require the use of some results like Teichmüller's theorem ([3], Theorem 4.11) and so would be valid only for order $\rho < \frac{1}{2}$ and $\delta > 1 - \cos \pi\rho$. Even in that case it is not clear that the method would be successful — the difficulties arise in discussing Case b) in Theorem 1. Since our results in any case would be at best fragmentary, we do not choose to pursue the matter further here.

References

[1] J. M. ANDERSON and J. CLUNIE, Slowly growing meromorphic functions. *Comment. Math. Helv.*, **40** (1966), 267–280.
[2] J. CLUNIE and W. K. HAYMAN, The spherical derivative of integral and meromorphic functions. *Comment. Math. Helv.*, **40** (1966), 117–148.
[3] W. K. HAYMAN, *Meromorphic Functions*, Oxford 1964.
[4] O. LEHTO, The spherical derivative of a meromorphic function in the neighbourhood of an isolated singularity. *Comment. Math. Helv.*, **33** (1959), 196–205.
[5] O. OSTROWSKI, Über Folgen analytischer Funktionen und einige Verschärfungen des Picardschen Satzes. *Math. Zeitschr.*, **24** (1926), 215–258.
[6] G. VALIRON, *Fonctions entières d'ordre fini et fonctions méromorphes.* (Genève 1960).

MATHEMATICS DEPARTMENT
UNIVERSITY COLLEGE,
LONDON W. C. 1.

MATHEMATICS DEPARTMENT
IMPERIAL COLLEGE,
LONDON S. W. 7.

Studies in Pure Mathematics
To the Memory of Paul Turán

A generalization of ultraspherical polynomials*

by

R. ASKEY and MOURAD E.-H. ISMAIL (Madison)

Abstract

Some old polynomials of L. J. ROGERS are orthogonal. Their weight function is given. The connection coefficient problem, which ROGERS solved by guessing the formula and proving it by induction, is derived in a natural way and some other formulas are obtained. These polynomials generalize zonal spherical harmonics on spheres and include as special cases polynomials that are spherical functions on rank one spaces over reductive p-adic groups. A limiting case contains some Jacobi polynomials studied by HYLLERAAS that arose in work on the Yukawa potential.

1. Introduction

FEJÉR [21] introduced the following class of polynomials. Let

(1.1) $$f(z)=\sum_{n=0}^{\infty} a_n z^n$$

be a function analytic in a neighbourhood of the origin with a_n real. Form

(1.2) $$|f(re^{i\Theta})|^2=\sum_{n=0}^{\infty} P_n(\cos\Theta)r^n,$$

so that

(1.3) $$P_n(\cos\Theta)=\sum_{k=0}^{n} a_k a_{n-k}\cos(n-2k)\Theta.$$

* Sponsored in part by:
The United States Army under Contract No. DAAG29-75-C-0024;
The National Science Foundation under Grant No. MPS75-06687-IV;
The National Research Council of Canada under Grant A4522; and
The McMaster University Research Board under Grant 7593.

$P_n(x)$ is a polynomial of degree n, and is called a generalized Legendre polynomial since $f(z)=(1-z)^{-1/2}$ gives the Legendre polynomials. More generally, $f(z)=(1-z)^{-\lambda}$ gives the ultraspherical polynomials $C_n^\lambda(x)$. The orthogonality relation for the ultraspherical polynomials when $\lambda>-\frac{1}{2}$ is

(1.4)
$$\int_{-1}^{1} C_n^\lambda(x)C_m^\lambda(x)(1-x^2)^{\lambda-1/2}dx=0, \quad m\neq n,$$
$$dx=\frac{(2\lambda)_n\Gamma\left(\frac{1}{2}\right)\Gamma\left(\lambda+\frac{1}{2}\right)}{n!(n+\lambda)\Gamma(\lambda)}, \quad m=n.$$

FEJÉR and SZEGŐ obtained a number of interesting facts about these generalized Legendre polynomials, some of which are summarized in [40, Chapter VI]. FELDHEIM [23] and LANCEVICKI [32] determined when the generalized Legendre polynomials are orthogonal by showing that the polynomials must satisfy a specific recurrence relation. However they did not obtain an explicit representation for the polynomials and they were unable to find the weight function. We will find both the polynomials and the weight function. These polynomials are not new. They were studied extensively by ROGERS in the third of an important series of papers [36]. The only results from this series of papers that are well known are two identities that RAMANUJAN rediscovered and are now known as the Rogers–Ramanujan identities. However there are many other interesting identities (some are reproved in [6]), and the polynomials in the third paper are probably more interesting and important than any other results in Rogers' papers, including the Rogers–Ramanujan identities. We will summarize some of the results of ROGERS obtained for these polynomials and add a few new ones.

The key to obtaining explicit formulas is to use the q-binomial theorem and basic hypergeometric series. The binomial theorem can be written as

(1.5)
$$(1-x)^{-a}=\sum_{n=0}^{\infty}\frac{(a)_n}{n!}x^n$$

where

(1.6)
$$(a)_n=\Gamma(n+a)/\Gamma(a)=a(a+1)\dots(a+n-1).$$

The q-binomial theorem [5, Th. 2.1] is

(1.7)
$$\sum_{n=0}^{\infty}\frac{(a;q)_n}{(q;q)_n}x^n=\frac{(ax;q)_\infty}{(x;q)_\infty}, \quad |x|<1, \quad |q|<1,$$

where

(1.8)
$$(a;q)_\infty=\prod_{n=0}^{\infty}(1-aq^n), \quad |q|<1,$$

and

$$(1.9) \qquad (a;q)_n = \frac{(a;q)_\infty}{(aq^n;q)_\infty} = (1-a)(1-aq)\dots(1-aq^{n-1}).$$

More general hypergeometric and basic hypergeometric series are given by

$$(1.10) \qquad {}_rF_s\left(\begin{matrix} a_1, \dots, a_r \\ b_1, \dots, b_s \end{matrix}; x\right) = \sum_{n=0}^{\infty} \frac{(a_1)_n \dots (a_r)_n}{(b_1)_n \dots (b_s)_n} \frac{x^n}{n!}$$

and

$$(1.11) \qquad {}_{r+1}\varphi_r\left(\begin{matrix} a_1, \dots, a_{r+1} \\ b_1, \dots, b_r \end{matrix}; q, x\right) = \sum_{n=0}^{\infty} \frac{(a_1;q)_n \dots (a_{r+1};q)_n}{(b_1;q)_n \dots (b_r;q)_n} \frac{x^n}{(q;q)_n}.$$

To motivate the study of the polynomials implicitly found by Feldheim and Lancevicki we remark that their generating function will turn out to be

$$(1.12) \qquad \frac{(\beta re^{i\Theta};q)_\infty(\beta re^{-i\Theta};q)_\infty}{(\alpha re^{i\Theta};q)_\infty(\alpha re^{-i\Theta};q)_\infty} = \sum_{n=0}^{\infty} P_n(\cos\Theta)r^n,$$

which is a very natural analogue of the classical generating function

$$(1.13) \qquad (1-2r\cos\Theta+r^2)^{-\lambda} = \sum_{n=0}^{\infty} C_n^\lambda(\cos\Theta)r^n.$$

For $1-2r\cos\Theta+r^2=(1-re^{i\Theta})(1-re^{-i\Theta})$, and the analogy between the binomial theorem as given in (1.5) and the q-binomial theorem in (1.7) shows that the function $(\beta re^{i\Theta};q)_\infty/(\alpha re^{i\Theta};q)_\infty$ is a natural substitute for $(1-re^{i\Theta})^{-\lambda}$.

2. The orthogonal generalized Legendre polynomials

If a set of polynomials is orthogonal and satisfies $P_n(-x)=(-1)^n P_n(x)$, then it must satisfy the three term recurrence relation

$$(2.1) \qquad 2b_n x P_n(x) = P_{n+1}(x) + \lambda_n P_{n-1}(x), \quad n=0, 1, \dots,$$
$$P_0(x)=1, \quad P_{-1}(x)=0.$$

Feldheim [23] determined b_n and λ_n for the generalized Legendre polynomials that are orthogonal. His result is

$$b_n = b_1 + (b_1 - b_0)\frac{\sinh(n-1)\xi}{\sinh(n+1)\xi}, \quad n = 0, 1, \ldots,$$

$$\lambda_n = b_1^2 + 2b_1(b_1 - b_0)\frac{\sinh(n-1)\xi}{\sinh(n+1)\xi} + (b_1 - b_0)^2\frac{\sinh(n-3)\xi}{\sinh(n+1)\xi}.$$

The coefficients in the original power series for $f(z)$ satisfy

(2.2) $$b_n = a_n/a_{n-1}.$$

Setting $q = \exp(-2\xi)$, we rewrite these as .

(2.3) $$b_n = b_1 + (b_1 - b_0)q\frac{(1-q^{n-1})}{(1-q^{n+1})},$$

(2.4) $$\lambda_n = b_1^2 + 2b_1(b_1 - b_0)q\frac{(1-q^{n-1})}{(1-q^{n+1})} + (b_1 - b_0)^2 q^2\frac{(1-q^{n-3})}{(1-q^{n+1})}.$$

With these choices of b_n and λ_n, formula (2.1) can be written as

$$2x[b_1(1+q) - b_0 q - (b_1 q + b_1 - b_0)q^n]P_n(x) =$$
$$= (1-q^{n+1})P_{n+1}(x) + [(b_1 + b_1 q - b_0 q)^2 - q^{n-1}(b_1 + b_1 q - b_0)^2]P_{n-1}(x).$$

Set $b_1 + b_1 q - b_0 q = \alpha$ and $b_1 q + b_1 - b_0 = \beta$. This gives

(2.5) $$2x[\alpha - \beta q^n]P_n(x) = (1-q^{n+1})P_{n+1}(x) + [\alpha^2 - \beta^2 q^{n-1}]P_{n-1}(x).$$

To find the polynomials $P_n(x)$, multiply (2.5) by r^{n+1} and sum, recalling that $P_{-1}(x) = 0$, and $P_0(x) = 1$. If

$$f(r, x) = \sum_{n=0}^{\infty} P_n(x) r^n,$$

the resulting equation is

$$2x\alpha r f(r, x) - 2x\beta r f(qr, x) =$$
$$= f(r, x) - 1 - [f(qr, x) - 1] + \alpha^2 r^2 f(r, x) - \beta^2 r^2 f(qr, x)$$

or

(2.6) $$(1 - 2x\alpha r + \alpha^2 r^2) f(r, x) = (1 - 2x\beta r + \beta^2 r^2) f(qr, x).$$

Set $x = \cos\Theta$ and rewrite (2.6) as

(2.7) $$f(r, \cos\Theta) = \frac{(1-\beta r e^{i\Theta})(1-\beta r e^{-i\Theta})}{(1-\alpha r e^{i\Theta})(1-\alpha r e^{-i\Theta})} f(qr, \cos\Theta).$$

Iterate (2.7) to obtain

$$f(r,\cos\Theta)=\frac{(\beta re^{i\Theta};q)_n(\beta re^{-i\Theta};q)_n}{(\alpha re^{i\Theta};q)_n(\alpha re^{-i\Theta};q)_n}f(q^n r,\cos\Theta). \tag{2.8}$$

Then let $n\to\infty$. The result is

$$f(r,\cos\Theta)=\frac{(\beta re^{i\Theta};q)_\infty(\beta re^{-i\Theta};q)_\infty}{(\alpha re^{i\Theta};q)_\infty(\alpha re^{-i\Theta};q)_\infty}=\sum_{n=0}^{\infty}P_n(\cos\Theta)r^n. \tag{2.9}$$

This is the generating function stated in (1.12).

The above derivation was formal, but it is easy to justify it, since the function $f(z,\cos\Theta)$ is analytic for $|z|<|\alpha|^{-1}$. There is no loss in generality in taking $\alpha=1$, for it can be removed by scaling. With this simplification define $C_n(x;\beta|q)$ by

$$\sum_{n=0}^{\infty}C_n(x;\beta|q)r^n=\frac{(\beta e^{i\Theta}r;q)_\infty(\beta e^{-i\Theta}r;q)_\infty}{(e^{i\Theta}r;q)_\infty(e^{-i\Theta}r;q)_\infty}. \tag{2.10}$$

We will use x and $\cos\Theta$ interchangeably. When $\beta=q^\lambda$ it is easy to see that

$$\lim_{q\to1^-}C_n(x;q^\lambda|q)=C_n^\lambda(x). \tag{2.11}$$

This follows from either the generating function (2.10), using

$$\lim_{q\to1^-}\frac{(q^\lambda x;q)_\infty}{(x;q)_\infty}=\lim_{q\to1^-}\sum_{n=0}^{\infty}\frac{(q^\lambda;q)_n}{(q;q)_n}x^n=\sum_{n=0}^{\infty}\frac{(\lambda)_n}{n!}x^n=(1-x)^{-\lambda}, \tag{2.12}$$

or from the recurrence relation

$$2x[1-\beta q^n]C_n(x;\beta|q)=(1-q^{n+1})C_{n+1}(x;\beta|q)+(1-\beta^2q^{n-1})C_{n-1}(x;\beta|q) \tag{2.13}$$

which becomes

$$2x(n+\lambda)C_n^\lambda(x)=(n+1)C_{n+1}^\lambda(x)+(n+2\lambda-1)C_{n-1}^\lambda(x) \tag{2.14}$$

when $\beta=q^\lambda$, every term is divided by $1-q$ and $q\to1^-$.

If $C_n(x;\beta|q)=k_nr_n(x;\beta|q)$ with $k_n=(\beta;q)_n/(q;q)_n$, then (2.13) becomes

$$2xr_n(x)=r_{n+1}(x)+\frac{(1-\beta^2q^{n-1})(1-q^n)}{(1-\beta q^{n-1})(1-\beta q^n)}r_{n-1}(x). \tag{2.15}$$

Now we see that the case $|q|>1$ can be reduced to the case $|q|<1$ when β is replaced by β^{-1}. Thus there was no loss in generality in assuming $|q|\leqq1$. We use β rather than q^λ since β could be negative, and the case $\beta=0$ is very important. The conditions for orthogonality can be obtained from (2.15). See [20], [27, Ch. II, Th. 1.5]. It is necessary and sufficient that

$$\frac{(1-\beta^2 q^{n-1})(1-q^n)}{(1-\beta q^{n-1})(1-\beta q^n)}>0, \quad n=1,2,\ldots.$$

When $0<q<1$, the cases $n=1$ and $n=2$ imply $-1<\beta<q^{-1/2}$, and these conditions are easily seen to be sufficient. When $-1<q<0$ the cases $n=1$, $n=2$, and $n=3$ imply $-1<\beta<-q^{-1}$ and these conditions are sufficient. The trivial case $q=0$ holds when $\beta>-1$. The only way this inequality can hold when $q\to 1$ is to have $\beta=q^\lambda$, in which case the condition is $\lambda>-\frac{1}{2}$. Finally the case $q\to -1$ can only hold when $\beta=|q|^\lambda$ and $\lambda>-1$ or $\beta=-|q|^\lambda$ and $\lambda>0$.

3. Explicit representations for the continuous q-ultraspherical polynomials

There is another set of orthogonal polynomials that are basic hypergeometric series and have the ultraspherical polynomials as limits when $q\to 1$. These will be called the discrete q-ultraspherical polynomials, because their distribution function is a discrete measure. See [7]. The weight functions for the polynomials under consideration in this paper are absolutely continuous when $|\beta|<1$, so these polynomials will be called the continuous q-ultraspherical polynomials. The adjective will be used in both cases, since it is not clear which will be more important.

To find an explicit representation use the q-binomial theorem (1.7) in the generating function (2.10). The result is ($x=\cos\Theta$)

(3.1)
$$\begin{aligned} C_n(x;\beta|q) &= \sum_{k=0}^{n} \frac{(\beta;q)_k(\beta;q)_{n-k}}{(q;q)_k(q;q)_{n-k}} e^{i(n-2k)\Theta} \\ &= \sum_{k=0}^{n} \frac{(\beta;q)_k(\beta;q)_{n-k}}{(q;q)_k(q;q)_{n-k}} \cos(n-2k)\Theta \\ &= \frac{(\beta;q)_n}{(q;q)_n} e^{in\Theta} \sum_{k=0}^{n} \frac{(q^{-n};q)_k(\beta;q)_k}{(q^{1-n}\beta^{-1};q)_k(q;q)_k} (q\beta^{-1}e^{-2i\Theta})^k \end{aligned}$$

since $(a;q)_{n-k}=\dfrac{(a;q)_n q^{k(k+1)/2}}{(-aq^n)^k(q^{1-n}a^{-1};q)_k}$. This gives

(3.2)
$$C_n(\cos\Theta;\beta|q)=\frac{(\beta;q)_n}{(q;q)_n} e^{in\Theta}\,{}_2\varphi_1\left(\begin{matrix} q^{-n},\beta \\ q^{1-n}\beta^{-1}\end{matrix};q,q\beta^{-1}e^{-2i\Theta}\right).$$

Another representation can be obtained as a special case of a more general set of orthogonal polynomials considered in [12]. The polynomials are

$$(3.3)\qquad P_n(x)={}_4\varphi_3\left(\begin{matrix}q^{-n}, q^{n-1}abcd, ae^{i\Theta}, ae^{-i\Theta}\\ ab, ac, ad\end{matrix};q,q\right)$$

$x=\cos\Theta$. Their recurrence relation is

$$(3.4)\qquad 2xP_n(x)=a_nP_{n+1}(x)-(a_n+c_n-a-a^{-1})P_n(x)+c_nP_{n-1}(x),$$

where

$$(3.5)\qquad a_n=\frac{(1-abq^n)(1-acq^n)(1-adq^n)(1-abcdq^{n-1})}{a(1-abcdq^{2n-1})(1-abcdq^{2n})},$$

$$(3.6)\qquad c_n=\frac{a(1-q^n)(1-bcq^{n-1})(1-bdq^{n-1})(1-cdq^{n-1})}{(1-abcdq^{2n-2})(1-abcdq^{2n-1})}.$$

First set $c=-a$, $d=-b$. In this case the weight function is even and $a_n+c_n=a+a^{-1}$. Then set $b=aq^{1/2}$. With these specializations, the coefficients a_n and c_n are

$$(3.7)\qquad a_n=\frac{(1-a^4q^n)}{a(1-a^2q^n)},$$

$$(3.8)\qquad c_n=\frac{a(1-q^n)}{(1-a^2q^n)}.$$

Set $P_n(x)=k_ns_n(x)$ with $k_n=a^n(a^2;q)_n/(a^4;q)_n$. The recurrence relation (3.4) becomes

$$(3.9)\qquad 2xs_n(x)=s_{n+1}(x)+\frac{(1-a^4q^{n-1})(1-q^n)}{(1-a^2q^{n-1})(1-a^2q^n)}s_{n-1}(x).$$

This gives $r_n(x)=s_n(x)$ with $\beta=a^2$, where $r_n(x)$ satisfies (2.15). Combining the above formulas we see that

$$(3.10)\qquad C_n(\cos\Theta;\beta|q)=\frac{(\beta^2;q)_n}{\beta^{n/2}(q;q)_n}\,{}_4\varphi_3\left(\begin{matrix}q^{-n}, q^n\beta^2, \beta^{1/2}e^{i\Theta}, \beta^{1/2}e^{-i\Theta}\\ \beta q^{1/2}, -\beta q^{1/2}, -\beta\end{matrix};q,q\right).$$

Another way of writing (3.10) is

$$(3.11)\qquad C_n(x;\beta|q)=\frac{(\beta^2;q)_n}{\beta^{n/2}(q;q)_n}\sum_{k=0}^{n}\frac{(q^{-n};q)_k(q^n\beta^2;q)_k\prod_{j=0}^{k-1}(1-2\beta^{1/2}xq^j+\beta q^{2j})}{(\beta q^{1/2};q)_k(-\beta q^{1/2};q)_k(-\beta;q)_k(q;q)_k}q^k.$$

This is probably as close as one can get to a single sum that gives these polynomials as a series in the polynomial variable x. Another formula which shows the polynomial character of $C_n(x;\beta|q)$ is

(3.12) $$C_n(x;\beta|q)=\sum_{k=0}^{n}\frac{(\beta;q)_k(\beta;q)_{n-k}}{(q;q)_k(q;q)_{n-k}}T_{n-2k}(x),$$

where $T_n(x)$ is the Chebychev polynomial of the first kind defined by $T_n(\cos\Theta)=\cos n\Theta$. Two interesting formulas follow from (3.12). One is the special case $\beta=q$.

(3.13) $$C_n(\cos\Theta;q|q)=\sum_{k=0}^{n}\cos(n-2k)\Theta=\frac{\sin(n+1)\Theta}{\sin\Theta}.$$

The second is

(3.14) $$\lim_{\beta\to 1}(1-q^n)\frac{C_n(\cos\Theta;\beta|q)}{2(1-\beta)}=\cos n\Theta,\quad n=1,2,\ldots.$$

Observe that in both cases the polynomials are independent of q.

In the case of ultraspherical polynomials the zeros of the polynomials $C_n^\lambda(x)$ have absolute values that decrease as λ increases. This suggests that the zeros of $C_n(\cos\Theta;q^\lambda|q)$ lie between the zeros of $\cos n\Theta$ and $\sin(n+1)\Theta$ when $0<\lambda<1$ and $0<q<1$. FELDHEIM [23] has shown this, but his notation is so much at variance with ours that we give a new proof. By a theorem of FEJÉR [22], [40, Theorem 6.5.2] it is sufficient to show that the coefficients are a moment sequence on [0, 1], i.e.

$$a_n=\int_0^1 t^n d\mu(t),\quad d\mu(t)\geqq 0.$$

Thus we need

(3.15) $$\frac{(q^\lambda;q)_n}{(q;q)_n}=\int_0^1 t^n d\mu(t).$$

Let $d\mu$ have a point mass equal to

$$\frac{(q^\lambda;q)_\infty(q^{1-\lambda};q)_\infty}{(q;q)_\infty^2}\,\frac{t^\lambda(tq;q)_\infty}{(tq^{1-\lambda};q)_\infty}\quad\text{at}\quad t=q^i,\quad i=0,1,\ldots.$$

When $0<\lambda<1$ this mass is positive, and the q-binomial theorem (1.7) shows that (3.15) holds. The inequalities for the zeros are

(3.16)
$$\frac{\pi\left(k-\frac{1}{2}\right)}{n}\leqq\Theta_{k,n}^\lambda\leqq\frac{k\pi}{n+1},\quad 0<\lambda<1,\quad 0<q<1,\quad k=1,\ldots,\left[\frac{n}{2}\right],$$
$$\frac{k\pi}{n+1}\leqq\Theta_{k,n}^\lambda\leqq\frac{\pi\left(k-\frac{1}{2}\right)}{n},\quad 0<\lambda<1,\quad 0<q<1,\quad k=\left[\frac{n}{2}\right],\ldots,n$$

where $\Theta_{k,n}^{\lambda}$ are the zeros of $C_n(\cos\Theta; q^{\lambda}|q)$ ordered by $\Theta_{k,n}^{\lambda} < \Theta_{k+1,n}^{\lambda}$. There is equality in (3.16) only when n is odd and $k=(n+1)/2$.

An unlikely looking formula follows on equating the basic hypergeometric series in (3.2) and (3.10). It can be written as

$$(3.17)\qquad {}_2\varphi_1\left(\begin{matrix} q^{-n}, a^2 \\ q^{1-n}a^{-2} \end{matrix}; q, \frac{qx^2}{a^2}\right) = \frac{x^n(a^4;q)_n}{a^n(a^2;q)_n}\, {}_4\varphi_3\left(\begin{matrix} q^{-n}, q^n a^4, ax, ax^{-1} \\ a^2q^{1/2}, -a^2q^{1/2}, -a^2 \end{matrix}; q, q\right).$$

When $a=q^{\alpha/2}$ and the limit $q\to 1^-$ is taken the resulting identity is

$$(3.18)\qquad {}_2F_1\left(\begin{matrix} -n, \alpha \\ 1-n-\alpha \end{matrix}; x^2\right) = \frac{x^n(2\alpha)_n}{(\alpha)_n}\, {}_2F_1\left[\begin{matrix} -n, n+2\alpha \\ \alpha+\frac{1}{2} \end{matrix}; -\frac{(1-x)^2}{4x}\right].$$

This is one of the iterated quadratic transformations. The first quadratic type transformation for basic hypergeometric series seems to be that of Carlitz [17]. Another is given in [7], where the discrete q-ultraspherical polynomials are related to some discrete q-Jacobi polynomials. Another will be given in [12].

An interesting inequality follows from (3.1),

$$(3.19)\qquad |C_n(x;\beta|q)| \leqq C_n(1;\beta|q), \quad -1<\beta<1, \quad -1<q<1.$$

For $|\cos(n-2k)\Theta| \leqq 1$ and $(\beta;q)_k>0$, $(q;q)_k>0$ when $-1<\beta<1$, $-1<q<1$.

Unlike the classical case of $C_n^{\lambda}(x)$, when

$$(3.20)\qquad C_n^{\lambda}(1) = \frac{(2\lambda)_n}{n!},$$

it is impossible to find the value $C_n(1;\beta|q)$ as a simple product. There are two interesting points where the value can be given as a product. From (2.10)

$$\sum_{n=0}^{\infty} C_n(0;\beta|q)r^n = \frac{(\beta ir;q)_\infty(-\beta ir;q)_\infty}{(ir;q)_\infty(-ir;q)_\infty} = \frac{(-\beta^2r^2;q^2)_\infty}{(-r^2;q^2)_\infty} =$$

$$= \sum_{n=0}^{\infty} \frac{(\beta^2;q^2)_n}{(q^2;q^2)_n}(-1)^n r^{2n}$$

so

$$(3.21)\qquad C_{2n}(0;\beta|q) = (-1)^n \frac{(\beta^2;q^2)_n}{(q^2;q^2)_n}$$

$$C_{2n+1}(0;\beta|q) = 0.$$

Heine [28], see also [5, Cor. 2.4] found an analogue of Gauss' sum of ${}_2F_1\left(\begin{matrix} a, b \\ c \end{matrix}; 1\right)$. It is

(3.22)
$$ {}_2\varphi_1\left(\begin{matrix} a, b \\ c \end{matrix}; q, \frac{c}{ab}\right) = \frac{\left(\frac{c}{a}; q\right)_\infty \cdot \left(\frac{c}{b}; q\right)_\infty}{\left(\frac{c}{ab}; q\right)_\infty (c; q)_\infty}, \quad \left|\frac{c}{ab}\right| < 1, \quad |q| < 1 . $$

If the series terminates this is the correct value without the condition $\left|\frac{c}{ab}\right| < 1$.

Set $e^{2i\theta} = \beta$ in (3.2). This gives

(3.23)
$$ C_n\left(\frac{\beta^{1/2} + \beta^{-1/2}}{2}; \beta|q\right) = \frac{(\beta^2; q)_n}{(q; q)_n} \beta^{-n/2}, \quad 0 < \beta < q^{-1/2} . $$

When $1 < \beta < q^{-1/2}$ this is interesting, for then

$$ \lim_{n\to\infty} C_n\left(\frac{\beta^{1/2} + \beta^{-1/2}}{2}; \beta|q\right) = 0 . $$

This goes to zero fast enough so the distribution function has a point mass at $x = (\beta^{1/2} + \beta^{-1/2})/2$ when $1 < \beta < q^{-1/2}$, see [33]. By symmetry there is also one at $x = -(\beta^{1/2} + \beta^{-1/2})/2$. These are the only point masses when $1 < \beta < q^{-1/2}$.

For convenience the first four of these polynomials are given next.

(3.24)
$$ \begin{aligned} C_0(x; \beta|q) &= 1 \\ C_1(x; \beta|q) &= \frac{2(1-\beta)}{(1-q)} x \\ C_2(x; \beta|q) &= \frac{4(1-\beta)(1-\beta q)}{(1-q)(1-q^2)} x^2 - \frac{(1-\beta^2)}{(1-q^2)} \\ C_3(x; \beta|q) &= \frac{8(1-\beta)(1-\beta q)(1-\beta q^2)}{(1-q)(1-q^2)(1-q^3)} x^3 - \\ &\quad - \frac{2x(1-\beta)[2+q+\beta(1-q^2)-\beta^2 q(1+2q)]}{(1-q^2)(1-q^3)} . \end{aligned} $$

From this point on the formulas become more complicated.

Another useful expression for $C_n(\cos\Theta; \beta|q)$ can be obtained by applying the q-analogue of the Pfaff–Kummer transformation to (3.2). This transformation is

(3.25)
$$ {}_2\varphi_1\left(\begin{matrix} a, b \\ c \end{matrix}; q, x\right) = \frac{(ax; q)_\infty}{(x; q)_\infty} \sum_{n=0}^{\infty} \frac{\left(\frac{c}{b}; q\right)_n (a; q)_n (-xb)^n q^{\binom{n}{2}}}{(c; q)_n (q; q)_n (ax; q)_n} . $$

See ANDREWS [4] for a proof of this formula. The resulting formula is

(3.26)
$$C_n(\cos\Theta;\beta|q)=\frac{(\beta;q)_n}{(q;q)_n}e^{in\Theta}(\beta^{-1}e^{-2i\Theta}q^{1-n};q)_n\times$$
$$\times\sum_{k=0}^{\infty}\frac{(q^{-n};q)_k(q^{1-n}\beta^{-2};q)_k q^{\binom{k}{2}}(-qe^{-2i\Theta})^k}{(q^{1-n}\beta^{-1};q)_k(q^{1-n}\beta^{-1}e^{-2i\Theta};q)_k(q;q)_k}.$$

Now sum this series in the opposite direction, i.e. replace k by $n-k$, and simplify to obtain

(3.27)
$$C_n(\cos\Theta;\beta|q)=\frac{(\beta^2;q)_n e^{-in\Theta}}{(q;q)_n\beta^n}\,{}_3\varphi_2\left(\begin{matrix}q^{-n},\beta,\beta e^{2i\Theta}\\ \beta^2,0\end{matrix};q,q\right).$$

From this it is easy to obtain the generating function

(3.28)
$$\sum_{n=0}^{\infty}\frac{C_n(\cos\Theta;\beta|q)}{(\beta^2;q)_n}q^{\binom{n}{2}}(\beta r)^n=(-re^{-i\Theta};q)_\infty\,{}_2\varphi_1\left(\begin{matrix}\beta,\beta e^{2i\Theta}\\ \beta^2\end{matrix};q,-re^{-i\Theta}\right).$$

4. The orthogonality relation

The orthogonality relation for the q-Wilson polynomials defined in (3.3) is

(4.1)
$$\int_{-1}^{1}\frac{P_n(x)P_m(x)\prod_{k=0}^{\infty}(1-2(2x^2-1)q^k+q^{2k})}{h(x,a)h(x,b)h(x,c)h(x,d)}\frac{dx}{\sqrt{1-x^2}}=$$
$$=\begin{cases}0 & m\neq n\\ \dfrac{2\pi a^{2n}(bc;q)_n(bd;q)_n(cd;q)_n(q;q)_n(1-abcdq^{n-1})}{(ab;q)_n(ac;q)_n(ad;q)_n(abcd;q)_n(1-abcdq^{2n-1})}\times & \\ \quad\times\dfrac{(abcd;q)_\infty}{(ab;q)_\infty(ac;q)_\infty(ad;q)_\infty(bc;q)_\infty(bd;q)_\infty(cd;q)_\infty(q;q)_\infty} & m=n\end{cases}$$

when $|a|$, $|b|$, $|c|$, $|d|<1$, where

(4.2)
$$h(x,a)=\prod_{n=0}^{\infty}(1-2axq^n+a^2q^{2n}).$$

In general there will be finitely many mass points outside $(-1,1)$. See [12] for details.

For the continuous q-ultraspherical polynomials when $|\beta|<1$, the specializations of the last section lead to

(4.3)
$$\int_{-1}^{1} C_n(x;\beta|q)C_m(x;\beta|q)w_\beta(x)(1-x^2)^{-1/2}dx = 2\pi\frac{(1-\beta)}{(1-\beta q^n)}\frac{(\beta^2;q)_n}{(q;q)_n}\frac{(\beta;q)_\infty(\beta q;q)_\infty}{(\beta^2;q)_\infty(q;q)_\infty}\delta_{m,n}$$

where

(4.4)
$$w_\beta(x) = \prod_{k=0}^{\infty}\frac{(1-2(2x^2-1)q^k+q^{2k})}{(1-2(2x^2-1)q^k\beta+q^{2k}\beta^2)}.$$

This can also be written as

(4.5)
$$w_\beta(\cos\Theta) = \frac{(e^{2i\Theta};q)_\infty(e^{-2i\Theta};q)_\infty}{(\beta e^{2i\Theta};q)_\infty(\beta e^{-2i\Theta};q)_\infty}.$$

To get a better idea of this weight function observe that

$$w_{q^2}(x)(1-x^2)^{-1/2} = (4-4x^2)((1+q)^2-4qx^2)(1-x^2)^{-1/2}.$$

When $q=1$ this becomes $4^2(1-x^2)^{2-1/2}$.

Before considering other special cases we will give a direct proof of the orthogonality relation (4.3). There are two reasons for this. One is that no other proof has appeared yet, and the three other proofs that we know use results that are not needed in the present proof. Also this proof will give a direct proof of an important identity of ROGERS [36].

As a first step we compute a trigonometric moment that is of independent interest,

$$\int_0^\pi e^{2ik\Theta}w_\beta(\cos\Theta)d\Theta = \int_0^\pi e^{2ik\Theta}\prod_{n=0}^{\infty}\frac{(1-e^{2i\Theta}q^n)(1-e^{-2i\Theta}q^n)}{(1-e^{2i\Theta}\beta q^n)(1-e^{-2i\Theta}\beta q^n)}d\Theta.$$

Use the q-binomial theorem,

$$\frac{(e^{2i\Theta};q)_\infty}{(\beta e^{2i\Theta};q)_\infty} = \sum_{n=0}^{\infty}\frac{(\beta^{-1};q)_n}{(q;q)_n}\beta^n e^{2in\Theta},$$

to get

$$\int_0^\pi e^{2ik\Theta}w_\beta(\cos\Theta)d\Theta = \sum_{n=0}^{\infty}\frac{(\beta^{-1};q)_n}{(q;q)_n}\beta^n\sum_{m=0}^{\infty}\frac{(\beta^{-1};q)_m}{(q;q)_m}\beta^m\int_0^\pi e^{2i(k+n-m)\Theta}d\Theta$$

$$= \pi\sum_{n=0}^{\infty}\frac{(\beta^{-1};q)_n(\beta^{-1};q)_{k+n}}{(q;q)_n(q;q)_{k+n}}\beta^{k+2n}$$

$$= \pi\beta^k\frac{(\beta^{-1};q)_k}{(q;q)_k}\,{}_2\varphi_1\left(\begin{matrix}\beta^{-1}, q^k\beta^{-1}\\ q^{k+1}\end{matrix};q,\beta^2\right).$$

HEINE [28], [29, p. 106], see also [5, Cor. 2.2], gave an important transformation of the general ${}_2\varphi_1$,

$$(4.6)\qquad {}_2\varphi_1\left(\begin{matrix}a, b\\ c\end{matrix}; q, x\right)=\frac{(ax;q)_\infty(b;q)_\infty}{(x;q)_\infty(c;q)_\infty}\,{}_2\varphi_1\left[\begin{matrix}\frac{c}{b}, x\\ ax\end{matrix}; q, b\right].$$

The iterate of this is

$$(4.7)\qquad {}_2\varphi_1\left(\begin{matrix}a, b\\ c\end{matrix}; q, x\right)=\frac{(bx;q)_\infty\left(\frac{c}{b};q\right)_\infty}{(x;q)_\infty(c;q)_\infty}\,{}_2\varphi_1\left[\begin{matrix}\frac{abx}{c}, b\\ bx\end{matrix}; q, \frac{c}{b}\right].$$

Use (4.7) on the ${}_2\varphi_1$ above to get

$$\int_0^\pi e^{2ik\Theta}w_\beta(\cos\Theta)\,d\Theta=\frac{\pi\beta^k(\beta^{-1};q)_k(\beta;q)_\infty(\beta q^{k+1};q)_\infty}{(q;q)_k(\beta^2;q)_\infty(q^{k+1};q)_\infty}\,{}_2\varphi_1\left(\begin{matrix}q^{-1}, \beta^{-1}\\ \beta\end{matrix}; q, \beta q^{k+1}\right).$$

Summing this ${}_2\varphi_1$ (there are only two non-zero terms) gives

$$(4.8)\qquad \int_0^\pi e^{2ik\Theta}w_\beta(\cos\Theta)\,d\Theta=\frac{\pi\beta^k(\beta^{-1};q)_k(1+q^k)}{(\beta q;q)_k}\,\frac{(\beta;q)_\infty(\beta q;q)_\infty}{(q;q)_\infty(\beta^2,q)_\infty},$$

$|\beta|<1$. The condition $|\beta|<1$ was used to expand $w_\beta(\cos\Theta)$ by the q-binomial theorem, and the series that was used does not converge when $\beta^2\geqq 1$. The case $\beta=1$ is trivial, since $w_1(\cos\Theta)=1$. In this case

$$\int_0^\pi e^{2ik\Theta}w_1(\cos\Theta)\,d\Theta=\begin{cases}0, & k=\pm 1, \pm 2, \ldots,\\ \pi, & k=0.\end{cases}$$

To continue the proof of the orthogonality relation consider

$$\int_0^\pi C_n(\cos\Theta;\beta|q)\,T_{n-2k}(\cos\Theta)\,w_\beta(\cos\Theta)\,d\Theta$$

where

$$T_n(\cos\Theta)=\cos n\Theta.$$

This integral is

$$\sum_{j=0}^{n}\frac{(\beta;q)_j(\beta;q)_{n-j}}{(q;q)_j(q;q)_{n-j}}\int_0^\pi e^{i(n-2j)\Theta}\left[\frac{e^{i(n-2k)\Theta}+e^{-i(n-2k)\Theta}}{2}\right]w_\beta(\cos\Theta)d\Theta=$$

$$=\frac{1}{2}\sum_{j=0}^{n}\frac{(\beta;q)_j(\beta;q)_{n-j}}{(q;q)_j(q;q)_{n-j}}\int_0^\pi[e^{2i(n-j-k)\Theta}+e^{2i(k-j)\Theta}]w_\beta(\cos\Theta)\,d\Theta=$$

$$=\frac{\pi}{2}\frac{(\beta;q)_\infty(\beta q;q)_\infty}{(\beta^2;q)_\infty(q;q)_\infty}[I_{n-k}+I_k]$$

where

$$I_k=\sum_{j=0}^{n}\frac{(\beta;q)_j(\beta;q)_{n-j}}{(q;q)_j(q;q)_{n-j}}\frac{\beta^{k-j}(\beta^{-1};q)_{k-j}}{(\beta q;q)_{k-j}}(1+q^{k-j}).$$

Use

$$\frac{(a;q)_{n-j}}{(b;q)_{n-j}}=\frac{(a;q)_n}{(b;q)_n}\frac{(q^{1-n}b^{-1};q)_j}{(q^{1-n}a^{-1};q)_j}\left(\frac{b}{a}\right)^j$$

to rewrite this as

$$(4.9)\quad I_k=\frac{(\beta;q)_n(\beta^{-1};q)_k}{(q;q)_n(\beta q;q)_k}\beta^k(1+q^k)\sum_{j=0}^{n}\frac{(q^{-n};q)_j(q^{-k}\beta^{-1};q)_j(\beta;q)_j(-q^{1-k};q)_j}{(q;q)_j(q^{1-n}\beta^{-1};q)_j(q^{1-k}\beta;q)_j(-q^{-k};q)_j}q^j.$$

This sum is a balanced ${}_4\varphi_3$ (i.e. the product of the numerator parameters times q is the product of the denominator parameters that are listed in the ${}_4\varphi_3$) and so may be transformed by

$$(4.10)\quad {}_4\varphi_3\left(\begin{matrix}q^{-n},a,b,c\\ d,e,f\end{matrix};q,q\right)=\left(\frac{bc}{d}\right)^n\frac{\left(\frac{de}{bc};q\right)_n\left(\frac{df}{bc};q\right)_n}{(e;q)_n(f;q)_n}{}_4\varphi_3\left[\begin{matrix}q^{-n},a,\frac{d}{c},\frac{d}{b}\\ d,\frac{de}{bc},\frac{df}{bc}\end{matrix};q,q\right]$$

where $q^{1-n}abc=def$. See [7] or [12] for this transformation. Let $d=-q^{-k}$, $a=\beta$. This gives

$$I_k=\frac{(\beta;q)_n(\beta^{-1};q)_k\beta^{k-n}(1+q^k)q^{(1-k)n}(q^{k-n};q)_n(\beta^2;q)_n}{(q;q)_n(\beta q;q)_k(q^{1-n}\beta^{-1};q)_n(q^{1-k}\beta;q)_n}\times$$

$$(4.11)\qquad \times\,{}_4\varphi_3\left(\begin{matrix}q^{-n},\beta,q^{-1},-\beta\\ -q^{-k},q^{k-n},\beta^2\end{matrix};q,q\right)=$$

$$=(\beta q)^k\frac{(1-q^{n-2k})(\beta^{-1};q)_k(\beta^2;q)_n(q^{1-k};q)_{n-1}}{(1-q^{1-k}\beta)(\beta q;q)_k(q;q)_n(q^{2-k}\beta;q)_{n-1}}.$$

Thus $I_k=0$, $k=1, 2, \ldots, n-1$, and $I_0=I_n=(\beta^2;q)_n/(\beta q;q)_n$. Since

$$T_n(x)=2^{n-1}x^n+\ldots,\quad n=1,2,\ldots,\quad T_0(x)=1,$$

and

$$C_n(x;\beta|q)=2^n\frac{(\beta;q)_n}{(q;q)_n}x^n+\ldots,\quad n=0,1,\ldots,$$

it is easy to check that (4.3) holds.

The argument above is easy when $|\beta|<1$, it would be more complicated for the values of β with $|\beta|>1$ when the polynomials are orthogonal with respect to a positive measure. Rather than try to carry out this argument (we have not tried) or introduce the methods that we know will lead to this orthogonality we will now use the orthogonality to find some important identities. The complete orthogonality relations will be given in [11] and [12]. Different methods are used in these two papers.

The argument above did not need $k=0, 1, \ldots, n$. Let k be successively $-k$ and $n+k$ in (4.11). A calculation gives

$$\int_0^\pi C_n(\cos\Theta;\beta|q)T_{n+2k}(\cos\Theta)w_\beta(\cos\Theta)d\Theta = \tag{4.12}$$
$$=\frac{\pi\beta^k(\beta^{-1};q)_k(q;q)_{n+k}}{(q;q)_k(q;q)_n}\frac{(1-q^{n+2k})}{(1-q^{n+k})}\frac{(\beta;q)_\infty(\beta q^{n+k+1};q)_\infty}{(q;q)_\infty(\beta^2q^n;q)_\infty},\quad k=1,2,\ldots.$$

Using the orthogonality relation (4.3) and (4.12) gives

$$T_n(x)=\sum_{k=0}^{[\frac{n}{2}]}\beta^k\frac{(\beta^{-1};q)_k(q;q)_{n-k}(1-q^n)(1-\beta q^{n-2k})}{(q;q)_k(\beta q;q)_{n-k}(1-q^{n-k})2(1-\beta)}C_{n-2k}(x;\beta|q). \tag{4.13}$$

Then if (4.13) is used on the right-hand side of (3.12), the result is

$$C_n(x;\gamma|q)=\sum_{k=0}^{[\frac{n}{2}]}\frac{(\gamma;q)_k(\gamma;q)_{n-k}(q;q)_{n-2k}}{(q;q)_k(q;q)_{n-k}(\beta q;q)_{n-2k}}(1-\beta q^{n-2k})\times \tag{4.14}$$
$$\times{}_6\varphi_5\left(\begin{matrix}q^{n-2k}, q^{n/2-k+1}, -q^{n/2-k+1}, \gamma q^{n-k}, \beta^{-1}, q^{-k}\\ q^{n/2-k}, -q^{n/2-k}, \gamma^{-1}q^{1-k}, \beta q^{n+1-2k}, q^{n+1-k}\end{matrix};q,\frac{\beta q}{\gamma}\right)\frac{C_{n-2k}(x;\beta|q)}{(1-\beta)}.$$

The ${}_6\varphi_5$ is very well poised and so can be summed by a theorem of JACKSON [37, p. 96]. The resulting series is

$$C_n(x;\gamma|q)=\sum_{k=0}^{[\frac{n}{2}]}\beta^k\frac{(\gamma\beta^{-1};q)_k(\gamma;q)_{n-k}}{(q;q)_k(\beta q;q)_{n-k}}\frac{(1-\beta q^{n-2k})}{(1-\beta)}C_{n-2k}(x;\beta|q). \tag{4.15}$$

This very important formula was found by Rogers [36]. He obtained it by finding the coefficients for small values of n, guessing the answer, and then proving it by induction. The special case when $\gamma=0$ and $\beta=1$ was used in his second paper [35] to obtain the identities

(4.16)
$$\sum_{n=0}^{\infty} \frac{q^{n^2}}{(q;q)_n} = \frac{1}{(q;q^5)_\infty (q^4;q^5)_\infty}$$

and

(4.17)
$$\sum_{n=0}^{\infty} \frac{q^{n^2+n}}{(q;q)_n} = \frac{1}{(q^2;q^5)_\infty (q^3;q^5)_\infty}.$$

While it is not particularly easy to read and understand these papers of Rogers, we have found it easier to read them after understanding the polynomials of Rogers. It is also easier to read them in the order [36], [35], [34] rather than the order in which they were written. These papers are very interesting and contain many other important results. Probably the most interesting is

(4.18)
$$C_m(x;\beta|q)C_n(x;\beta|q) = \sum_{k=0}^{\min(m,n)} a(k,m,n) C_{m+n-2k}(x;\beta|q),$$
$$a(k,m,n) = \frac{(q;q)_{m+n-2k}(\beta;q)_{n-k}(\beta;q)_{m-k}(\beta;q)_k(\beta^2;q)_{m+n-k}(1-\beta q^{m+n-2k})}{(\beta^2;q)_{m+n-2k}(q;q)_{n-k}(q;q)_{m-k}(q;q)_k(\beta q;q)_{m+n-k}(1-\beta)}.$$

Rogers found this result in the same way he found (4.15), by working out the coefficients for small m, guessing the answer, and proving it by induction. We do not have a better proof of (4.18) at this time.

Rogers [36] pointed out that the special case $q=1$, $\beta=q^\lambda$ is an important result for spherical harmonics. However no one picked up this result from [36] and the special case $\beta=q^\lambda$, $q=1$ of (4.18) was next stated by Dougall [19] almost twenty-five years later. The only special cases that were known before Rogers found the general result were the trivial cases $\beta=1$, which is equivalent to

$$\cos n\Theta \cos m\Theta = \frac{1}{2}[\cos(n+m)\Theta + \cos(n-m)\Theta],$$

$\beta=q$, which is

$$\frac{\sin(n+1)\Theta}{\sin\Theta}\,\frac{\sin(m+1)\Theta}{\sin\Theta} = \sum_{k=0}^{\min(m,n)} \frac{\sin(m+n+1-2k)\Theta}{\sin\Theta},$$

and one nontrivial case, $\beta=q^{1/2}$, $q=1$,

$$P_n(x)P_m(x) = \sum_{k=0}^{\min(m,n)} \frac{m+n+\frac{1}{2}-2k}{m+n+\frac{1}{2}-k}\,\frac{\left(\frac{1}{2}\right)_k\left(\frac{1}{2}\right)_{m-k}\left(\frac{1}{2}\right)_{n-k}\cdot(m+n-k)!}{k!(m-k)!(n-k)!\left(\frac{1}{2}\right)_{m+n-k}} P_{m+n-2k}(x).$$

a result of FERRERS [24, Example 10, p. 156] and ADAMS [1]. See Chapter 5 of [9] for a summary of some of the known results on the linearization problem.

Formulas (4.15) and (4.18) can be inverted. The inverse of (4.18) is

$$\frac{(\beta;q)_m(\beta;q)_n}{(q;q)_m(q;q)_n} C_{m+n}(x;\beta|q) =$$

$$= \frac{(\beta;q)_{m+n}}{(q;q)_{m+n}} \sum_{k=0}^{\min(m,n)} b(k,m,n) C_{m-k}(x;\beta|q) C_{n-k}(x;\beta|q), \tag{4.19}$$

$$b(k,m,n) = \frac{(q^{-m-n}\beta^{-2};q)_k (1-q^{2k-m-n}\beta^{-2})(\beta^{-1};q)_k}{(q;q)_k (1-q^{-m-n}\beta^{-2})(q^{1-m-n}\beta^{-1};q)_k} \left(\frac{\beta^2}{q}\right)^k.$$

The limiting case $\beta = q^\lambda$, $q=1$ of (4.19) was found by AL-SALAM [3]. A proof of (4.19) can be given following his proof; use (4.18) to replace $C_{m-k}(x;\beta|q)C_{n-k}(x;\beta|q)$ and invert the order of summation. The resulting series is a very well poised ${}_6\varphi_5$, which is summed by JACKSON's result. Details are left to the reader.

The other inverse is

$$w_\beta(x) C_n(x;\beta|q) = \sum_{k=0}^{\infty} a(k,n) C_{n+2k}(x;\gamma|q) w_\gamma(x),$$

(4.20)

$$a(k,n) = \frac{\beta^k (\gamma/\beta;q)_k (q^{n+1};q)_{2k} (\gamma^2 q^{n+2k};q)_\infty (\beta q^{n+k+1};q)_\infty (\beta;q)_\infty (1-\gamma q^{n+2k})}{(q;q)_k (\gamma q^{n+k};q)_\infty (\beta^2 q^n;q)_\infty (\gamma;q)_\infty}.$$

This follows from (4.15) by the general argument given by ASKEY in [8]. The series (4.20) converges when $|\beta|<1$, $|q|<1$. For $|a(k,n)| = O(\beta^k)$ and

$$|C_{n+2k}(x;\gamma|q)| \leqq (n+1) \max_k \left|\frac{(\gamma;q)_k}{(q;q)_k}\right| = A(\gamma,q)(n+1)$$

for γ, q fixed, $|q|<1$.

ROGERS [36] found a number of other formulas. The reader is referred to [36] for these results.

5. Special cases

It is not surprising that interesting results are found when $q \to 1$. However it is surprising that an interesting result could be found by letting $q \to 0$. To see this consider the generating function (2.10) when $q=0$. It is

$$\frac{1-2\beta r\cos\Theta+\beta^2 r^2}{1-2r\cos\Theta+r^2} = \frac{(1-\beta r e^{i\Theta})(1-\beta r e^{-i\Theta})}{(1-re^{i\Theta})(1-re^{-i\Theta})} = \sum_{n=0}^{\infty} C_n(\cos\Theta;\beta,0) r^n. \tag{5.1}$$

A partial fraction decomposition gives

(5.2)
$$C_n(\cos\Theta;\beta|0)=2\beta(1-\beta)\cos n\Theta+(1-\beta)^2\frac{\sin(n+1)\Theta}{\sin\Theta},\quad n=1,2,\dots,$$
$$C_0(\cos\Theta;\beta|0)=1$$

or

$$C_n(x;\beta|0)=2\beta(1-\beta)T_n(x)+(1-\beta)^2U_n(x),\quad n=1,2,\dots,$$
$$C_0(x;\beta|0)=1\,.$$

These can also be written as

$$C_n(\cos\Theta;\beta|0)=(1-\beta)\frac{\sin(n+1)\Theta}{\sin\Theta}-\beta(1-\beta)\frac{\sin(n-1)\Theta}{\sin\Theta},\quad n=1,2,\dots,$$
$$C_0(\cos\Theta;\beta|0)=1$$

or

$$C_n(x;\beta|0)=(1-\beta)U_n(x)-\beta(1-\beta)U_{n-2}(x),\quad n=1,2,3,\dots,$$
$$C_0(x;\beta|0)=1\,.$$

The orthogonality relation is

(5.3)
$$\int_{-1}^{1}C_n(x;\beta|0)C_m(x;\beta|0)\frac{(1-x^2)^{1/2}}{(1+\beta)^2-4\beta x^2}\,dx=\frac{\pi}{2}(1-\beta)^2\delta_{m,n},\quad (m,n)\neq(0,0)$$
$$\int_{-1}^{1}[C_0(x;\beta|0)]^2\frac{(1-x^2)^{1/2}}{(1+\beta)^2-4\beta x^2}\,dx=\frac{\pi}{2(1+\beta)}$$

when $|\beta|<1$.

This is a known result. It follows easily from the SZEGŐ–BERNSTEIN theory [14], [40, §2.6]; it was also given by KARLIN and MCGREGOR [31]. When $\beta>1$ there are two point masses that need to be added outside $[-1,1]$. See KARLIN and MCGREGOR [31]. Some of these functions are spherical functions on rank one spaces over reductive p-adic groups. See CARTIER [18].

The case $q\to1$ gives the classical ultraspherical polynomials. The main point of interest here is the way the weight functions converge as $q\to1$. Recall that

(5.4)
$$\int_{-1}^{1}\prod_{n=0}^{\infty}\frac{(1-2(2x^2-1)q^n+q^{2n})}{(1-2(2x^2-1)\beta q^n+\beta^2q^{2n})}\frac{dx}{\sqrt{1-x^2}}=2\pi\frac{(\beta;q)_\infty(\beta q;q)_\infty}{(q;q)_\infty(\beta^2;q)_\infty}\,.$$

Let $\beta=q^\lambda$ and $x=e^{i\Theta}$. Then (5.4) becomes

(5.5) $$\int_0^\pi \prod_{n=0}^{\infty}\frac{(1-e^{2i\Theta}q^n)}{(1-e^{2i\Theta}q^{n+\lambda})}\prod_{n=0}^{\infty}\frac{(1-e^{-2i\Theta}q^n)}{(1-e^{-2i\Theta}q^{n+\lambda})}\,d\Theta=2\pi\frac{(q^\lambda;q)_\infty(q^{\lambda+1};q)_\infty}{(q^{2\lambda};q)_\infty(q;q)_\infty}.$$

The q-gamma function $\Gamma_q(x)$ is defined by

(5.6) $$\Gamma_q(x)=\frac{(q;q)_\infty}{(q^x;q)_\infty}(1-q)^{1-x},\quad 0<q<1.$$

In [10] it was shown that $\lim\limits_{q\to 1-}\Gamma_q(x)=\Gamma(x)$. The limit on the right-hand side of (5.5) can be written as

(5.7) $$\frac{2\pi\Gamma_q(2\lambda)}{\Gamma_q(\lambda)\Gamma_q(\lambda+1)}\to\frac{2\pi\Gamma(2\lambda)}{\Gamma(\lambda)\Gamma(\lambda+1)}\quad\text{as}\quad q\to 1.$$

The left-hand side of (5.5) is

$$\int_0^\pi {}_1\varphi_0(q^{-\lambda};q,q^\lambda e^{2i\Theta})\,{}_1\varphi_0(q^{-\lambda};q,q^\lambda e^{-2i\Theta})\,d\Theta,$$

and formally this converges to

$$\int_0^\pi(1-e^{2i\Theta})^\lambda(1-e^{-2i\Theta})^\lambda d\Theta=\int_0^\pi(2-2\cos\Theta)^\lambda d\Theta=2^{2\lambda}\int_0^\pi\left(\sin\frac{\Theta}{2}\right)^{2\lambda}d\Theta.$$

The formal argument can be justified since

$${}_1\varphi_0(\mathbf{a};q,x)=\frac{(ax;q)_\infty}{(x;q)_\infty}$$

and

$${}_1F_0(\mathbf{a};x)=(1-x)^{-a}$$

are functions which are analytic for $|x|<1$ and have extensions to the complex plane cut along $(-\infty,-1)$ and

$$\lim_{q\to 1}{}_1\varphi_0(\mathbf{q}^a;q,x)={}_1F_0(\mathbf{a};x).$$

Another interesting case is $q\to -1$. Consider the case $\beta = -|q|^\lambda$. Set $q=-p$. Then

$$W_{-|q|^\lambda,q}(\cos\Theta) = \left|\frac{(e^{2i\Theta};q)_\infty}{(-|q|^\lambda e^{2i\Theta};q)_\infty}\right|^2 = \left|\frac{(e^{2i\Theta};q^2)_\infty(qe^{2i\Theta};q^2)_\infty}{(-|q|^\lambda e^{2i\Theta};q^2)_\infty(-q|q|^\lambda e^{2i\Theta};q^2)_\infty}\right|^2$$

$$= \left|\frac{(e^{2i\Theta};p^2)_\infty(-pe^{2i\Theta};p^2)_\infty}{(p^{\lambda+1}e^{2i\Theta};p^2)_\infty(-p^\lambda e^{2i\Theta};p^2)_\infty}\right|^2$$

$$= |{}_1\varphi_0(p^{-(\lambda+1)};p^2,p^{\lambda+1}e^{2i\Theta})\,{}_1\varphi_0(p^{-(\lambda-1)};p^2,-p^\lambda e^{2i\Theta})|^2 .$$

As $p\to 1$ this converges to

$$\left|{}_1F_0\left(\begin{matrix}-(\lambda+1)/2\\ -\end{matrix};e^{2i\Theta}\right){}_1F_0\left(\begin{matrix}(1-\lambda)/2\\ -\end{matrix};-e^{2i\Theta}\right)\right|^2 =$$

$$= |(1-e^{2i\Theta})^{(\lambda+1)/2}(1+e^{2i\Theta})^{(\lambda-1)/2}|^2 = (2-2\cos 2\Theta)^{(\lambda+1)/2}(2+2\cos 2\Theta)^{(\lambda-1)/2} =$$

$$= 2^{\lambda+1}(\sin^2\Theta)^{(\lambda+1)/2}2^{\lambda-1}(\cos^2\Theta)^{(\lambda-1)/2} = 2^{2\lambda}(1-x^2)^{(\lambda+1)/2}|x|^{\lambda-1} .$$

Set

(5.8) $$N_n^\lambda(\cos\Theta) = \lim_{q\to -1} C_n(\cos\Theta; -|q|^\lambda|q) .$$

Then

(5.9) $$\int_{-1}^{1} N_m^\lambda(x)N_n^\lambda(n)\,(1-x^2)^{\lambda/2}|x|^{\lambda-1}\,dx = 0, \quad m\neq n .$$

A change of variables gives

(5.10) $$N_{2m}^\lambda(x) = a_m P_m^{(\frac{\lambda}{2},\frac{\lambda}{2}-1)}(2x^2-1),$$

(5.11) $$N_{2m+1}^\lambda(x) = b_m x P_m^{(\frac{\lambda}{2},\frac{\lambda}{2})}(2x^2-1),$$

where the Jacobi polynomial $P_n^{(\alpha,\beta)}(x)$ is defined by

(5.12) $$P_n^{(\alpha,\beta)}(x) = \frac{(\alpha+1)_n}{n!}\,{}_2F_1\left(\begin{matrix}-n,\,n+\alpha+\beta+1\\ \alpha+1\end{matrix};\frac{1-x}{2}\right).$$

They are orthogonal on $(-1, 1)$ with respect to $(1-x)^\alpha(1+x)^\beta$. The constants a_m and b_m in (5.10) and (5.11) can be determined by keeping track of the constants that occur in the various orthogonality relations, they can be determined from the recurrence relations or the coefficient of x^n in one of the explicit formulas for $C_n(x;\beta|q)$ can be computed under the specialization $\beta=-|q|^\lambda$ and $q\to -1$, and can be compared with the coefficient of x^n in (5.12). The last is the easiest method. The results are

(5.13) $$N_{2m}^{\lambda}(x)=\frac{(\lambda)_m}{\left(\frac{\lambda}{2}\right)_m}P_m^{\left(\frac{\lambda}{2},\frac{\lambda}{2}-1\right)}(2x^2-1)$$

and

(5.14) $$N_{2m+1}^{\lambda}(x)=2x\frac{(\lambda+1)_m}{\left(\frac{\lambda+1}{2}\right)_m}P_m^{\left(\frac{\lambda}{2},\frac{\lambda}{2}\right)}(2x^2-1).$$

Now we can see the real reason for the existence of a surprising result of HYLLERAAS [30]. The coefficients in the expansion

(5.15) $$P_n^{(\alpha,\beta)}(x)P_m^{(\alpha,\beta)}(x)=\sum_{k=|n-m|}^{n+m}a(k,m,n)P_k^{(\alpha,\beta)}(x)$$

are of interest. The case $\alpha=\beta$ is the special case $\beta=q^{\alpha+1/2}$, $q\to 1$ of (4.18). The coefficients in (5.15) are not usually given as a single term, which they are when $\alpha=\beta$. They are usually a sum of products, rather than just a product. HYLLERAAS found one other case when the coefficients are given by a product, the case $\alpha=\beta+1$. This follows from (4.18) when n and m are even, $\beta=-|q|^{\lambda}$ and $q\to -1$.

The case $\beta=|q|^{\lambda}$, $q\to -1$ leads to similar results, but nothing new, so it will not be considered here.

6. The continuous q-Hermite polynomials

The last special case that will be mentioned is the case $\beta=0$. With a different normalization they will be called the continuous q-Hermite polynomials,

(6.1) $$H_n(x|q)=(q,q)_nC_n(x;0|q).$$

The recurrence relation becomes

(6.2) $$2xH_n(x|q)=H_{n+1}(x|q)+(1-q^n)H_{n-1}(x|q).$$

The generating function (2.10) becomes

(6.3) $$\frac{1}{|(re^{i\Theta};q)_\infty|^2}=\sum_{n=0}^{\infty}\frac{H_n(\cos\Theta|q)r^n}{(q;q)_n}$$

or

(6.4) $$\frac{1}{\prod_{n=0}^{\infty}(1-2xrq^n+r^2q^{2n})}=\sum_{n=0}^{\infty}\frac{H_n(x|q)r^n}{(q;q)_n}.$$

ROGERS [35] and later SZEGŐ [39] and CARLITZ [15], [16] studied these polynomials extensively. CARLITZ used a different variable and normalization, so his results need a slight translation to correspond to those of ROGERS and special cases of formulas in this paper. He uses a variable and normalization that make it clear that the functions are polynomials in this variable. However the price he has to pay of losing the nice orthogonality relation is so high that we will use the notation above.

The q-extension of Mehler's bilateral sum for Hermite polynomials is

$$\text{(6.5)} \qquad \frac{(r^2;q)_\infty}{|(re^{i(\Theta+\varphi)};q)_\infty (re^{i(\Theta-\varphi)};q)_\infty|^2} = \sum_{n=0}^{\infty} \frac{H_n(\cos\Theta|q)H_n(\cos\varphi|q)r^n}{(q;q)_n}.$$

See [40, Problem 23] for MEHLER's formula. A beautiful combinatorial proof of MEHLER's formula has been given by FOATA [25]. Formula (6.5) is one of the few results that have been found for q-Hermite polynomials that has not been extended to q-ultraspherical polynomials.

The orthogonality relation (4.3) becomes

$$\text{(6.6)} \qquad \int_{-1}^{1} H_n(x|q)H_m(x|q) \prod_{k=0}^{\infty} (1-2(2x^2-1)q^k+q^{2k})(1-x^2)^{-1/2}\,dx = \frac{2\pi(q;q)_n}{(q;q)_\infty}\delta_{m,n},$$

so (6.5) is the analogue of MEHLER's formula. For they both have the form

$$\sum_{n=0}^{\infty} \frac{p_n(x)p_n(y)r^n}{h_n}$$

with

$$h_n = \int_a^b [p_n(x)]^2 w(x)\,dx.$$

The orthogonality relation (6.6) was given by ALLAWAY [2].

The reader should now read the papers of ROGERS [34], [35], and [36] to see how he used the q-Hermite polynomials to obtain the Rogers–Ramanujan identities and many other results.

There are many open problems. The most important is to find spaces on which these polynomials live, presumably as spherical functions. Then groups acting on these spaces need to be used to derive addition formulas. It would be interesting to find a combinatorial interpretation of the q-Hermite polynomials, and then use it to give a combinatorial proof of (6.5). SLEPIAN [38] has a very important multisum extension of MEHLER's formula and FOATA and GARSIA [26] have found a combinatorial proof of this formula. A similar formula for the continuous q-Hermite polynomials should be obtained.

References

[1] J. C. ADAMS, On the expression of the product of any two Legendre's coefficients by means of a series of Legendre's coefficients, *Proc. Royal Soc. London*, **27** (1878), 63–71.

[2] W. ALLAWAY, *The identification of a class of orthogonal polynomial sets*. Ph. D. thesis, U. of Alberta, Edmonton, Alberta, Canada, 1972.

[3] W. A. AL-SALAM, On the product of two Legendre polynomials, *Math. Scand.*, **4** (1956), 239–242.

[4] G. ANDREWS, On the q-analog of Kummer's theorem and applications, *Duke Math. J.*, **40** (1973), 525–528.

[5] G. ANDREWS, The Theory of Partitions, *Encyclopedia of Mathematics and Its Applications*, Vol. **2**, Addison–Wesley, Reading, MA., 1977.

[6] G. ANDREWS and R. ASKEY, Enumeration of partitions: The role of Eulerian series and q-orthogonal polynomials, *Higher Combinatorics*, ed. M. Aigner, D. Reidel, Dordrecht, Boston, 1977, 3–26.

[7] G. ANDREWS and R. ASKEY, q-analogues of the classical orthogonal polynomials and applications, to appear.

[8] R. ASKEY, Orthogonal expansions with positive coefficients, *Proc. Amer. Math. Soc.*, **16** (1965), 1191–1194.

[9] R. ASKEY, Orthogonal Polynomials and Special Functions, *Regional Conference Series in Applied Mathematics*, **21,** SIAM, Philadelphia, 1975.

[10] R. ASKEY, The q-gamma and q-beta functions, *Applicable Analysis*, **8** (1978), 125–141.

[11] R. ASKEY and M. ISMAIL, Recurrence relations, continued fractions and orthogonal polynomials, to appear.

[12] R. ASKEY and J. WILSON, Some basic hypergeometric orthogonals polynomials that generalize Jacobi polynomials, to appear as *Memoir of Amer. Math. Soc.*

[13] W. N. BAILEY, *Generalized Hypergeometric Series*, Cambridge Univ. Press, Cambridge, 1935.

[14] S. BERNSTEIN, Sur les polynômes orthogonaux relatifs à un segment fini, *J. de Math.*, (9) Vol. **9** (1930), 127–177; Vol. **10** (1931), 219–286.

[15] L. CARLITZ, Some polynomials related to theta functions, *Ann. Math. Pura Appl.*, Ser. 4, **41** (1955), 359–373.

[16] L. CARLITZ, Some polynomials related to theta functions, *Duke Math. J.*, **24** (1957), 521–527.

[17] L. CARLITZ, Some formulas of F. H. JACKSON, *Monatshefte für Math.*, **73** (1969), 193–198.

[18] P. CARTIER, Harmonic analysis on trees, Harmonic Analysis on Homogeneous Spaces, ed. C. C. Moore, *Proc. Symp. Pure Math.*, **26** (1973), Amer. Math. Soc. Providence, R. I., 419–424.

[19] J. DOUGALL, A theorem of SONINE in Bessel functions, with two extensions to spherical harmonics, *Proc. Edinburgh Math. Soc.*, **37** (1919), 33–47.

[20] J. FAVARD, Sur les polynômes de Tchebycheff, *C. R. Acad. Sci. Paris*, **200** (1935), 2052–2055.

[21] L. FEJÉR, Abschätzungen für die Legendreschen und verwandte Polynome, *Math. Zeit.*, **24** (1925), 285–294, *Gesammelte Arbeiten II*, 161–175.

[22] L. FEJÉR, Potenzreihen mit mehrfach monotoner Koeffizientenfolge und ihre Legendre Polynome, *Proc. Camb. Phil. Soc.*, **31** (1935), 307–316, *Gesammelte Arbeiten II*, 621–631.

[23] E. FELDHEIM, Sur les polynomes généralisés de Legendre, *Izv. Akad. Nauk. SSSR Ser. Math.*, **5** (1941), 241–248, Russian Transl. ibid, 248–254.

[24] N. M. FERRERS, *An Elementary Treatise on Spherical Harmonics and Subjects Connected with Them*, Macmillan, London, 1877.

[25] D. FOATA, A combinatorial proof of the MEHLER formula, *J. Comb. Th. (A)*, **24** (1978), 367–376.

[26] D. FOATA and A. M. GARSIA, A combinatorial approach to MEHLER formulas for Hermite polynomials, Relations between Combinatitories and Other Parts of Mathematics, ed. D. K. Ray-Chandhuri, *Proc. Symp. Pure Math.*, **34** (1979), Amer Math. Soc., Providence, R. I. 169–179.

[27] G. FREUD, *Orthogonale Polynome*, Birkhäuser-Verlag, Basel and Stuttgart, 1969.

[28] E. HEINE, Untersuchungen über die Reihe ..., *J. Reine Angew. Math.*, **34** (1847), 285–328.

[29] E. HEINE, *Theorie der Kugelfunctionen*, Berlin, 1878.

[30] E. HYLLERAAS, Linearization of products of Jacobi polynomials, *Math. Scand.*, **10** (1962), 189–200.

[31] S. KARLIN and J. MCGREGOR, Random walks, *Illinois J. Math.*, **3** (1959), 66–81.

[32] I. L. LANZEWIZKY, Über die Orthogonalität der Fejér-Szegöschen Polynome, *C. R. (Dokl.) Acad. Sci. URSS*, **31** (1941), 199–200.
[33] P. NÉVAI, *Orthogonal Polynomials*, Memoirs of the Amer. Math. Soc., No 213, Providence R. I. 1979.
[34] L. J. ROGERS, On the expansion of some infinite products, *Proc. London Math. Soc.*, **24** (1893), 337–352.
[35] L. J. ROGERS, Second memoir on the expansion of certain infinite products, *Proc. London Math. Soc.*, **25** (1894), 318–343.
[36] L. J. ROGERS, Third memoir on the expansion of certain infinite products, *Proc. London Math. Soc.*, **26** (1895), 15–32.
[37] L. J. SLATER, *Generalized Hypergeometric Functions*, Cambridge Univ. Press, Cambridge, 1966.
[38] D. SLEPIAN, On thè symmetrized Kronecker power of a matrix and extensions of Mehler's formula for Hermite polynomials, *SIAM J. Math. Anal.*, **3** (1972), 606–616.
[39] G. SZEGŐ, Ein Beitrag zur Theorie der Thetafunktionen, *Sitz. Preuss. Akad. Wiss. Phys. Math. Kl.*, **19** (1926), 242–252. Collected Worls, Birkhäuser-Boston, Vol. **I,** 795–805.
[40] G. SZEGŐ, *Orthogonal Polynomials*, Amer. Math. Soc. Coll. Publ. XXIII, fourth edition, Providence, R. I., 1975.

UNIVERSITY OF WISCONSIN, MADISON
MATHEMATICS RESEARCH CENTER
U.S.A.

ARIZONA STATE UNIVERSITY
U.S.A.

Studies in Pure Mathematics
To the Memory of Paul Turán

A Blaschke product with a level-set of infinite length

by

C. BELNA and G. PIRANIAN* (University Park and Ann Arbor)

A recent paper by PIRANIAN and A. WEITSMAN [1] describes an outer function f in the unit disk D such that, for uncountably many values R, the R-level-set $\{z : |f(z)| = R\}$ has infinite length. We shall now show that an inner function can also have a level-set of infinite length.

Let $A(z) = \exp[(z+1)/(z-1)]$ $(|z|<1)$, and for each a in $D - \{0\}$ let $T = T_a$ denote the function defined by the formula

$$T(\zeta) = \frac{\zeta - a}{1 - \bar{a}\zeta} \quad (|\zeta| < 1).$$

Corresponding to each positive number R and each nonconstant holomorphic function f in D, let $\mathbf{L}(R, f)$ denote the length of the R-level-set $\{z : |f(z)| = R\}$.

Theorem. *With the notation of the preceding paragraph, the function* $f = T \circ A$ *has the property that*

$$\mathbf{L}(|a|, f) = \infty$$

and

$$\mathbf{L}(R, f) = O(|R - |a||^{-1/2})$$

if $0 < R < 1$ *and* $R \neq |a|$.

Remark. The function $T \circ A$ is a Blaschke product, because it is an inner function whose radial limit is nowhere 0. Our estimate shows that the length $\mathbf{L}(R, f)$ is a well-behaved function of R in two senses: it is an integrable function of R, and it is finite except for one value of R, which happens to be the modulus of the omitted value of the Blaschke product.

* The authors gratefully acknowledge support from the National Science Foundation.

In the proof of the theorem, we shall use the notation

$$X+iY=Z(z)=\frac{z+1}{z-1}, \quad \zeta(z)=\exp Z(z), \quad w(z)=T(\zeta).$$

We denote by γ the circle $|w|=|a|$ and by γ^* its image under T^{-1}. Since T maps the points 0 and $c=2a/(1+|a|^2)$ onto the points $-a$ and a, respectively, the maximum modulus of ζ on γ^* is $|c|$.

The inverse image of $\gamma^*-\{0\}$ under the mapping $Z\to\zeta=\exp Z$ consists of infinitely many curves Δ_n $(n=0,\pm 1,\pm 2,\ldots)$ with the following properties:

(i) Δ_0 lies in a horizontal strip that contains the real axis and has width 2π;

(ii) Δ_0 lies in the half-plane $X\leqq \log|c|$, and it has exactly one point on the line $X=\log|c|$ (we shall denote this point by $\operatorname{Log} c$);

(iii) the closure of Δ_0 is a simple closed curve through the point at infinity (recall that γ^* passes through the origin);

(iv) the curve Δ_n is obtained from Δ_0 by the translation $Z\to Z+2n\pi i$.

Let δ_n denote the inverse image of Δ_n under the mapping $z\to Z=(z+1)/(z-1)$. Then the closure of δ_n is a Jordan curve that passes through the point $z=1$. Because the mapping $z\to(z+1)/(z-1)$ is an involution, the inverse image of the point $Z_n=\operatorname{Log} c+2n\pi i$ is $z_n=(Z_n+1)/(Z_n-1)$; clearly,

$$z_n-1=2/(Z_n-1)\sim 1/n\pi i.$$

The length of δ_n is greater than $2|z_n-1|$, and for all large values of $|n|$ it is therefore greater than $1/2|n|$. Consequently, the $|a|$-level-set of f has infinite length.

It remains to investigate the length $\mathbf{L}(R,f)$ for values R in (0, 1) other than $|a|$. Let $\gamma_R=\{w:|w|=R\}$, and let $\gamma_R^*=T^{-1}(\gamma_R)$. If $0<R<|a|$, the point $\zeta=0$ lies outside the circle γ_R^*, and under the mapping $\zeta=\exp Z$ the inverse image of γ_R^* consists of a loop $\Delta_{R,0}$ and all loops $\Delta_{R,n}$ that can be obtained from it by a translation $Z\to Z+2n\pi i$ $(|n|=1,2,\ldots)$. If $|a|<R<1$, the point $\zeta=0$ lies inside the circle γ_R^*, and the inverse image of γ_R^* consists of a wavy arc $\Delta_{R,0}$ in the strip $-\pi\leqq Y\leqq\pi$ and all copies $\Delta_{R,n}$ that can be obtained from it by a translation $Z\to Z+2n\pi i$ $(|n|=1,2,\ldots)$.

In both cases, the minimum and maximum moduli of ζ on γ_R are

$$c_R=\frac{|R-|a||}{1-|a|R} \quad\text{and}\quad c_R'=\frac{R+|a|}{1+|a|R},$$

and the loops or waves of the set $\cup_n\Delta_{R,n}$ lie in the vertical strip $X_1\leqq X\leqq X_2$, where

$$X_1=\log c_R \quad\text{and}\quad X_2=\log c_R'.$$

To estimate the length of the inverse image in the z-plane of the set $\cup_n\Delta_{R,n}$ we use the derivative of the locally defined function $z=f^{-1}(w)$. Clearly,

$$\frac{dw}{dz} = T'(\zeta)A'(z) = -2T'(\zeta)\frac{1}{(z-1)^2}\exp\frac{z+1}{z-1} = -2T'(\zeta)\frac{\zeta}{(z-1)^2},$$

and since

$$|T'(\zeta)| = \frac{1-|a|^2}{|1-\bar{a}\zeta|^2} > \frac{1-|a|^2}{(1+|a|)^2} = \frac{1-|a|}{1+|a|},$$

it follows that

$$\left|\frac{dz}{dw}\right| < \frac{1+|a|}{1-|a|} \cdot \frac{|z-1|^2}{2|\zeta|} = K_1|z-1|^2/|\zeta|.$$

To obtain an upper bound on the integral of $|dz/dw|$ on the universal covering curve of γ_R, we divide γ_R into two portions γ'_R and γ''_R on the basis of the inequalities

$$|\zeta| \leqq |R-|a||^{1/2} \quad \text{and} \quad |\zeta| \geqq |R-|a||^{1/2}.$$

Now γ'_R has length less than $K_2|R-|a||^{1/2}$, since $|T'(\zeta)| < (1+|a|)/(1-|a|)$ in the unit disk, and $|\zeta| \geqq c_R > |R-|a||$ if $T(\zeta)$ lies on γ_R; therefore we can assert that for $|n| = 1, 2, \ldots$ the inverse image of $\Delta_{R,n}$ has length less than

$$K_3|R-|a||^{-1/2}|z_n^*-1|^2,$$

where z_n^* is the point on the inverse image farthest from 1. Because the point $Z_n^* = Z(z_n^*)$ lies on $\Delta_{R,n}$ and $z_n^* = (Z_n^*+1)/(Z_n^*-1)$, we see that

$$|z_n^*-1| = 2/|Z_n^*-1| < K_4/|n|$$

if $|n| = 1, 2, \ldots$. The length of the inverse image of $\Delta_{R,0}$ has a bound K_5 independent of R, and consequently $\mathsf{L}(R, f) < K_6|R-|a||^{-1/2}$. This completes the proof.

In a private communication, PETER JONES informs us that he has independently constructed a Blaschke product possessing a level-set of infinite length. JONES begins with the bounded harmonic function (in the upper half-plane) whose boundary-value on the segment $(n, n+1)$ of the real axis is $(1+(-1)^n)/2$. He feels that his method is so similar to ours that publication would not be justified.

Reference

[1] G. PIRANIAN and A. WEITSMAN, Level sets of infinite length, *Comment. Math. Helv.*, 53 (1978), 161–164.

PENNSYLVANIA STATE UNIVERSITY

UNIVERSITY OF MICHIGAN

Studies in Pure Mathematics
To the Memory of Paul Turán

On complete bipartite subgraphs contained in spanning tree complements

by

B. BOLLOBÁS (Cambridge), F. R. K. CHUNG (Murray Hill)
and R. L. GRAHAM (Murray Hill)

Abstract

The celebrated theorem of TURÁN answers the following question exactly:

How many edges can a graph with n vertices have without containing the complete graph K_r as a subgraph?

In a recent paper, ERDŐS, FAUDREE, ROUSSEAU and SCHELP investigate the analogous question for the complete bipartite graph $K_{a,b}$. In particular, they study the following problem: What is the largest number $f(n, k)$ such that no matter how $f(n, k)$ edges are deleted from K_n, the resulting graph always contains $K_{a,b}$ as a subgraph for all a and b satisfying $a+b \leqq n-k$. ERDŐS et al. show that for $\varepsilon < e^{-4}$, it is always possible to remove slightly more than $n/2$ edges from K_n and thereby prevent the occurrence of some $K_{a,b}$ in the remaining graph for $a+b \leqq n-[\varepsilon n]$.

The same authors also raise the question of estimating $f(n, k)$ when the removed edges form a *spanning subtree* of K_n. In this note we show that it is possible to obtain surprisingly sharp estimates for this problem.

Introduction

The celebrated theorem of TURÁN [3] answers the following question exactly:

How many edges can a graph with n vertices have without containing the complete graph K_r as a subgraph?

In a recent paper [2], ERDŐS, FAUDREE, ROUSSEAU and SCHELP investigate the analogous question for the complete bipartite graph $K_{a,b}$. In particular, they study the following problem: What is the largest number $f(n, k)$ such that no matter how $f(n, k)$ edges are deleted from K_n, the resulting graph always contains $K_{a,b}$ as a subgraph for all a and b satisfying $a+b \leqq n-k$.

They find that a rather abrupt change occurs as k increases from 1 to 2 by proving:

(i) $f(n, 0) = \lceil n/2 \rceil - 1$, $n \geqq 2$;

(ii) $f(n, 1) = \left\lceil \dfrac{n+1}{2} \right\rceil$, $n \geqq 3$;

(iii) For fixed $k \geqq 2$ there exist positive constants A and B (depending on k) such that for n sufficiently large

$$n/2 + A\sqrt{n} < f(n, k) < n/2 + B\sqrt{n}.$$

(iv) For $0 < \varepsilon < e^{-4}$, there is a $\delta = \delta(\varepsilon) > 0$ so that for n sufficiently large

$$f(n, [\varepsilon n]) < \left(\frac{1}{2} + \delta\right)n .$$

The last result shows that it is always possible to remove slightly more than $n/2$ edges and thereby prevent the occurrence of some $K_{a,b}$ in the remaining graph for $a+b \leqq n-[\varepsilon n]$.

In [2] ERDŐS et al. raise the question of estimating $f(n, k)$ when the removed edges form a *spanning subtree* of K_n. In this case, a relatively large number $(n-1)$ of edges are removed, but they are required to be rather well-behaved. In this note we show that it is possible to obtain remarkably sharp estimates for this problem.

The main result

Let $f(n)$ denote the least integer with the property that for any spanning tree T of K_n and any $a+b \leqq n-f(n)$, $K_{a,b} \subseteq K_n - T$.

Theorem.

$$f(n) = (1+o(1))\frac{\log n}{\log 3}.$$

Proof. Let $\varepsilon > 0$ be fixed. We first show that

$$f(n) > (1-\varepsilon)\frac{\log n}{\log 3} \qquad (1)$$

for infinitely many n. Suppose (1) fails to hold for all sufficiently large n. Take n to be of the form

$$n = (1+3+\ldots+3^{2r-1}) = \frac{1}{2}(3^{2r}-1)$$

for a large r to be specified later. For the spanning tree T of K_n we choose T_{2r}, the complete *ternary* tree with $2r$ levels (see Fig. 1)

Finally, we take a to be $\frac{1}{4}(3^{2r}-1)$.

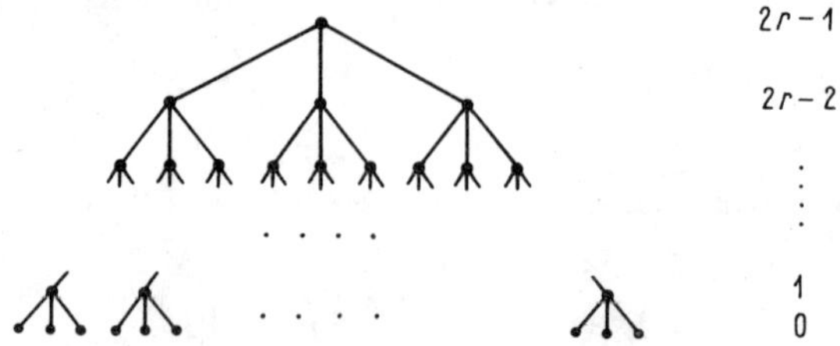

Fig.1. T_{2r}, the Complete Ternary Tree with $2r$ Levels

Assume now that for a fixed $\varepsilon>0$ there is a number b with

$$a+b>n-(1-\varepsilon)\frac{\log n}{\log 3}$$

such that $K_{a,b}\subseteq K_n-T_{2r}$. Note that expressed to the base 3,

$$n=\overbrace{11\ldots11}^{2r},\quad a=\overbrace{202\ldots02}^{r\,2\text{'s}}.$$

Also,

$$\frac{\log n}{\log 3}<2r-\frac{\log 2}{\log 3}<2r\,.$$

Thus,

$$b>n-a-(1-\varepsilon)\frac{\log n}{\log 3}>n-a-2(1-\varepsilon)r\,. \tag{2}$$

The number of vertices of K_n which do not belong to $K_{a,b}$ is just $n-(a+b)$ which is at most

$$(1-\varepsilon)\frac{\log n}{\log 3}<2(1-\varepsilon)r\,.$$

Their removal splits T_{2r} up into components C_i. The two vertex sets A and B of $K_{a,b}$ (where $|A|=a$, $|B|=b$) must each be contained in disjoint unions of these C_i. The plan is to show that any union of C_i's which contains at least a vertices must in fact contain more than $a+2(1-\varepsilon)r$ vertices, leaving fewer than $n-(a+2(1-\varepsilon)r)<b$ vertices from which to form B, which of course is a contradiction.

Let the number $n-(a+b)$ of vertices which do not belong to $K_{a,b}$ be denoted by αr. Thus

$$\alpha<2(1-\varepsilon)\,.$$

We must make a careful analysis of the sizes and relationships of the components C_i into which T_{2r} is partitioned by the removal of the αr unused vertices.

To begin with, we will always remove lower level vertices before higher level vertices, i.e., vertices closer to the bottom are removed first. Thus, if vertex v in level m is removed then the top (parent) tree loses $\frac{1}{2}(3^{m+1}-1)$ vertices and three new complete ternary trees T_m are formed, each with $\frac{1}{2}(3^m-1)$ vertices (see Fig. 2). We say that the resulting four quantities

$$-\frac{1}{2}(3^{m+1}-1)\,,\quad \frac{1}{2}(3^m-1)\,,\quad \frac{1}{2}(3^m-1)\,,\quad \frac{1}{2}(3^m-1)$$

form a *family*.

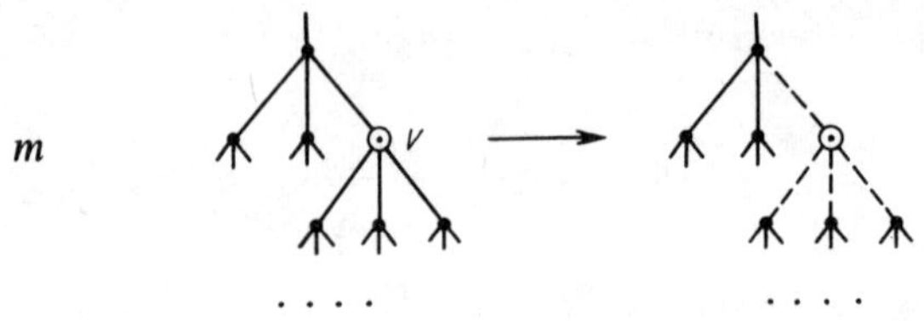

Fig. 2

After all αr points have been deleted, $\alpha r+1$ families will be formed. Let us examine what happens if some of the C_i are combined to form a set C containing A. The cardinality $|C|$ of C is a sum of $|C_i|$. For each family of the form $-\frac{1}{2}(3^{m+1}-1), \frac{1}{2}(3^m-1), \frac{1}{2}(3^m-1), \frac{1}{2}(3^m-1)$ there are just 8 possible sums it can contribute to $|C|$, depending on which members of the family occur in C. These sums are:

$$-\frac{1}{2}(3\cdot 3^m-1),\ -\frac{1}{2}(2\cdot 3^m),\ -\frac{1}{2}(3^m+1),\ -1,$$

$$\frac{1}{2}(3^m-1), \frac{1}{2}(2\cdot 3^m-2), \frac{1}{2}(3\cdot 3^m-3) \quad \text{and} \quad 0.$$

Hence, each family contributes an amount of the form $\frac{1}{2}(\delta\cdot 3^m+\gamma)$ to $|C|$ where $\delta=\pm 3, \pm 2, \pm 1$ or 0 and $|\gamma|\leqq 3$.

Since $A\subseteq C$ then

$$\frac{1}{4}(3^{2r}-1)=a=|A|\leqq|C|=\sum_{i=0}^{\alpha r}\frac{1}{2}(\delta_i\cdot 3^{m_i}+\gamma_i) \tag{3}$$

Thus, we have

$$\frac{1}{2}(3^{2r}-1)\leqq\sum_{i=0}^{\alpha r}\delta_i 3^{m_i}+\sum_{i=0}^{\alpha r}\gamma_i\leqq\sum_{i=0}^{\alpha r}\delta_i 3^{m_i}+3(\alpha r+1). \tag{4}$$

Since $3(\alpha r+1)$ has at most

$$\left\lceil\frac{\log 3(\alpha r+1)}{\log 3}\right\rceil\leqq\frac{2\log r}{\log 3}$$

nonzero digits base 3 (for large r) then $\frac{1}{2}(3^{2r}-1)-\sum_{i=0}^{\alpha r}\gamma_i$ has the form

$$\overbrace{111\ldots 11}^{2r-v}x_1\ldots x_v \quad \text{(base 3)}$$

where $v<\dfrac{2\log r}{\log 3}$.

So, by (4) we have

(5) $$\sum_{i=0}^{\alpha r} \delta_i 3^{m_i} \geqq \overbrace{111\ldots11}^{2r-v} x_1 \ldots x_v \geqq \sum_{j=1}^{2r-v} 3^{v+j-1}$$

where $v < \frac{2\log r}{\log 3}$, $\alpha < 2(1-\varepsilon)$ and $\delta_i = \pm 3, \pm 2, \pm 1$ or 0.

We now proceed to normalize the sum $\sum_{i=0}^{\alpha r} \delta_i 3^{m_i}$. To begin with, we may assume that $|\delta_i| \leqq 2$ since otherwise, we simply increase m_i by one. Next, observe that if $m_i = m_j$ for some $i \neq j$ then by writing

$$\delta_i + \delta_j = 3\delta_{i'} + \delta_{j'}$$

with $|\delta_{i'}| \leqq 1$, $|\delta_{j'}| \leqq 2$, we have

$$\delta_i 3^{m_i} + \delta_j 3^{m_j} = \delta_{i'} 3^{m_i+1} + \delta_{j'} 3^{m_i}$$

where either at least one more δ is 0 or $\sum_i |\delta_i|$ has decreased. Hence, we can continue this process until all the m_i in (5) are distinct. We can therefore rewrite

$$\sum_{i=0}^{\alpha r} \delta_i 3^{m_i} \quad \text{as} \quad \sum_{i=0}^{2r} \beta_i 3^i$$

where $\beta_i = \pm 2, \pm 1$ or 0 and *at most* $\alpha r + 1$ β's *are nonzero.* Equation (5) becomes

(5′) $$\sum_{i=0}^{2r} \beta_i 3^i \geqq \sum_{j=1}^{2r-v} 3^{v+j-1}.$$

Next, suppose for some i we have

$$\beta_{i+1} = 2, \quad \beta_i = -2.$$

Since

$$2 \cdot 3^{i+1} - 2 \cdot 3^i = 1 \cdot 3^{i+1} + 1 \cdot 3^i$$

we can replace these β's by the new values $\beta_{i+1} = 1$, $\beta_i = 1$, thereby decreasing $\sum_i |\beta_i|$. In the same way $(\beta_{i+1}, \beta_i) = (1, -2), (2, -1)$ and $(1, -1)$ can be replaced by $(\beta_{i+1}, \beta_i) = (0, 1), (1, 2)$ and $(0, 2)$, respectively, thereby either decreasing $\sum_i |\beta_i|$ or keeping $\sum_i |\beta_i|$ constant and decreasing the number of negative β's. Hence, we may assume that in the sequence $\bar{\beta} = (\beta_{2r}, \beta_{2r-1}, \ldots, \beta_0)$, no positive β_{i+1} is followed by a negative β_i.

Let i_0 be the largest index such that $\beta_{i_0} \neq 1$, $i_0 < 2r$. We know that $i_0 \geqq (2-\alpha)r$ since at most $\alpha r + 1$ β's are nonzero. There are several possibilities:

(a) Suppose $\beta_{2r} \neq 0$. Then by the construction of the C_i, β_{2r} is positive and by the normalization process, $\beta_{2r-1} \geqq 0$ so that

(6) $$\sum_{i=0}^{2r} \beta_i 3^i \geqq 3^{2r} - 2 \sum_{i=0}^{2r-2} 3^i > 3^{2r} - 3^{2r-1} = 2 \cdot 3^{2r-1}.$$

(b) Suppose $\beta_{2r}=0$ and $\beta_{i_0}=0$. Thus, $\bar{\beta}$ looks like

$$\bar{\beta}=(0, 1, 1, \ldots, 1, 0, \beta_{i_0-1}, \ldots, \beta_0)$$

and

$$\sum_{i=0}^{2r} \beta_i 3^i \leqq \sum_{i=i_0+1}^{2r-1} 3^i + 2 \cdot \sum_{i=0}^{i_0-1} 3^i < \sum_{i=i_0}^{2r-1} 3^i$$

which contradicts (5′) for large r since

$$v < \frac{2 \log r}{\log 3} \quad \text{and} \quad i_0 \geqq (2-\alpha) r > 2\varepsilon r.$$

(c) Suppose $\beta_{2r}=0$ and $\beta_{i_0}=2$. Thus, $\bar{\beta}$ looks like

$$\bar{\beta}=(0, 1, 1, \ldots, 1, 2, \beta_{i_0-1}, \ldots, \beta_0)$$

where $\beta_{i_0-1} \geqq 0$ by the normalization process. Hence

(7) $$\sum_{i=0}^{2r} \beta_i 3^i \geqq \sum_{i=i_0+1}^{2r-1} 3^i + 2 \cdot 3^{i_0} - 2 \cdot \sum_{i=0}^{i_0-2} 3^i > \sum_{i=i_0}^{2r-1} 3^i + 2 \cdot 3^{i_0-1}.$$

Note that the preceding arguments apply even if $i_0 = 2r-1$. Therefore, if (5′) holds then by (6) and (7)

(8) $$\begin{aligned} |C| = \frac{1}{2} \sum_{i=0}^{\alpha r} (\delta_i 3^{m_i} + \gamma_i) \geqq \frac{1}{2} \sum_{i=0}^{2r} \beta_i 3^i - \frac{3}{2}(\alpha r + 1) > \\ > \frac{1}{2} \sum_{i=i_0}^{2r-1} 3^i + 3^{i_0-1} - \frac{3}{2}(\alpha r + 1). \end{aligned}$$

Consequently, the number of vertices of K_n which can be used for B is at most

(9) $$\begin{aligned} n - \alpha r - |C| < n - \frac{1}{2} \sum_{i=i_0}^{2r-1} 3^i - 3^{i_0-1} + \frac{3}{2}(\alpha r + 1) - \alpha r < \\ < \frac{1}{2} \sum_{i=i_0}^{2r-1} 3^i + \sum_{i=0}^{i_0-2} 3^i + \alpha r < \frac{1}{2} \sum_{i=i_0}^{2r-1} 3^i + \frac{1}{6} \cdot 3^{i_0} + \alpha r. \end{aligned}$$

On the other hand, by (2)

$$|B| = b > n - a - 2(1-\varepsilon) r$$

(10)
$$>\frac{1}{2}\sum_{i=0}^{2r-1}3^i-2(1-\varepsilon)r=\frac{1}{2}\sum_{i=i_0}^{2r-1}3^i+\frac{1}{2}\sum_{i=0}^{i_0-1}3^i-2(1-\varepsilon)r>$$
$$>\frac{1}{2}\sum_{i=i_0}^{2r-1}3^i+\frac{1}{4}\cdot 3^{i_0}-2r\,.$$

Since $\alpha<2$ and $i_0>2\varepsilon r$ then (9) and (10) are contradictory for large r. This shows that (1) must hold for infinitely many n.

To show that in fact (1) holds for all sufficiently large n, a very similar but somewhat more detailed calculation must be made. In place of a complete ternary tree we now use for T a "balanced" ternary tree $T(n)$ on n points. These trees are structurally very similar to complete ternary trees. However, they have the property that when a vertex at level m is removed from $T(n)$, the three new trees formed from vertices at levels below m are all balanced ternary trees on sets of vertices which now can differ by at most one in cardinality. It is not hard to show that such trees exist on any number of vertices. By keeping careful track of the perturbations produced by these trees in the preceding argument, a similar contradiction results. In fact, this argument shows that

$$f(n)>\frac{\log n}{\log 3}-\frac{(1+\varepsilon)\log n}{\log\log n}$$

for any fixed $\varepsilon>0$ and all sufficiently large n.

We next must show that

(11)
$$f(n)<(1+\varepsilon)\frac{\log n}{\log 3}$$

for all sufficiently large n. The basic fact we need for the proof of (11) is the following result.

Lemma. (F. R. K. Chung and R. L. Graham [1]). *Let T be a tree with at least α vertices. Then for some vertex p of T, the components $T_1, \ldots, T_d$ of T formed by the removal of p (and all incident edges) contain a subset $T_{i_1}, \ldots, T_{i_k}$ such that*

$$\alpha\leqq\sum_{j=1}^{k}|T_{i_j}|\leqq 2\alpha\,.$$

It follows from repeated application of the lemma that any number $x<|T|-\left\lceil\frac{\log|T|}{\log 3}\right\rceil$ can be written as a sum of component sizes formed by the deletion of at most $\left\lceil\frac{\log|T|}{\log 3}\right\rceil$ vertices from T. For, each time we delete a vertex, we can guarantee that with the new components formed, the distance from the target value a to a sum of component sizes we can achieve decreases by a factor of at most 1/3, since if a correction term Δ is needed at stage j, the by generating a component sum in $\left(\frac{2}{3}\Delta, \frac{4}{3}\Delta\right)$ the new correction term is at most $\frac{1}{3}\Delta$. (The reader should have no difficulty filling in the details.) This proves (11) and the theorem is proved.

It would be interesting to know to what extent results like this hold for almost all a, b with $a+b$ small enough, and, more generally, for almost all spanning trees of K_n.

References

[1] F. R. K. Chung and R. L. Graham, On Graphs Which Contain all Small Trees. *J. Combinatorial Theory (B)*, **24** (1978), 14–23.

[2] P. Erdos, R. J. Faudree, C. C. Rousseau and R. H. Schelp, *On the Extremal Problem for Complete Bipartite Graphs*, to appear

[3] P. Turán, On an Extremal Problem in Graph Theory (Hungarian), *Mat. Fiz. Lapok*, **48** (1941) 436–452.

CAMBRIDGE UNIVERSITY
UNITED KINGDOM

BELL LABORATORIES
MURRAY HILL, NJ 07974
U.S.A.

Studies in Pure Mathematics
To the Memory of Paul Turán

On an open problem of Paul Turán concerning 3-graphs

by

W. G. BROWN (Montréal)*

1. The third of PAUL TURÁN's 1961 list of *Research Problems* [4] reads:

"If $2 \leqq l < k < n$, then what is the minimal number μ of combinations $C_1, C_2, \ldots, C_\mu$ taken l at a time out of 1, 2, . . ., n with the property that each combination taken k at a time out of 1, 2, . . ., n contains at least one C_j? (For $l=2$ the question is settled with exhibiting the only minimal C-system in my paper "Egy gráfelméleti szélsőérték-feladatról", *Mat. és Fiz. Lapok* (1941) 436–451, in Hungarian with German abstract.)"

The values of the numbers μ are still unknown for $l > 2$. We shall be concerned in this paper with the simplest open case, viz. $l=3$, in a complementary form.

Terminology and notation will conform with those of, for example, the author's paper [3] with V. T. Sós and P. ERDŐS. Denoting by $K^{(3)}(k)$ the complete 3-graph on k vertices — that having all $k(k-1)(k-2)/6$ possible triples — we would seek to determine numbers $\text{ex}(n, k) = \text{ex}(n, K^{(3)}(k))$, the maximum number m of triples for which there exists a 3-graph $G^{(3)}(n, m)$ containing no $K^{(3)}(k)$; the set of 3-graphs which contain no $K^{(3)}(k)$ for which the extremum is realized (the *extremal graphs*) will be denoted by $\text{EX}(n, k)$.

A plausible conjecture for the values of $\text{ex}(n, k)$ has been available in the literature for some time. RINGEL [1] and others have observed that, in the case $k=5$, this conjectured number of triples is attained for two quite distinct families of 3-graphs.

It is the purpose of this note to describe a similar phenomenon for the case $k=4$: namely, that if the conjectured value for $\text{ex}(n, 4)$ is correct, then $\text{EX}(n, 4)$ contains more than one extremal 3-graph (for $n > 6$).

* This research was supported in part by the Natural Sciences and Engineering Research Council of Canada, under Operating Grant No. A2984.

2. The conjecture

The conjectured value of $\mathrm{ex}(n, 4)$ is the number of triples in the following 3-graph: the n vertices are partitioned into classes A_1, A_2, A_3 containing respectively $[n/3]$, $[(n+1)/3]$, $[(n+2)/3]$ vertices; the following triples are selected:

(i) all triples formed by two distinct vertices in some A_i and one vertex in A_{i+1} (subscripts modulo 3); and

(ii) all triples formed from one vertex in each of A_1, A_2, A_3 (cf. [1], [2]).

The number of triples can be shown to be

$$\begin{cases} m^2(5m-3)/2 & n=3m \\ m(5m^2+2m-1)/2 & n=3m+1 \\ m(m+1)(5m+2)/2 & n=3m+2 \end{cases}$$

all of magnitude $5n^3/54+O(n^2)$ as $n\to\infty$.

3. The class of possible extremal 3-graphs

We shall describe a 3-parameter class of 3-graphs on n vertices which contain no complete $K^{(3)}(4)$. All members of a 1-parameter family of these will be seen to have the number of triples of the example discussed in the preceding section. This family will include the example which gave rise to the conjecture.

The n vertices are again to be partitioned into three classes A_1, A_2, A_3, having, as before, respectively $[n/3]$, $[(n+1)/3]$, $[(n+2)/3]$ members. Let three non-negative integers b_1, b_2, b_3 be given, respectively not exceeding the cardinalities of A_1, A_2, A_3. Now let each A_i be partitioned into parts B_i and C_i, where B_i contains exactly b_i vertices.

The triples to be selected are as follows (subscripts modulo 3):

(i-a) all triples having two vertices in some A_i and the third vertex in A_{i+1}, except those having all vertices in $B_i\cup B_{i+1}$;

(i-b) all triples having two vertices in some A_i and a third vertex in B_{i-1}, except those having no vertex in B_i; and

(iii) all triples having one vertex in each of A_1, A_2, A_3 except those having exactly one vertex in $C_1\cup C_2\cup C_3$.

The 3-graphs considered in Section 2 above are obtained by taking $b_1=b_2=b_3=0$. More generally, however, it can be shown that all such 3-graphs with equal values of the three parameters b_1, b_2, b_3 yield the conjectured extremal number. (We do not claim that these are the only values of the parameters with this property, however.)

To show that this construction yields several distinct 3-graphs, we consider the numbers of triples which contain pairs of vertices. (Our discussion will be confined to the case where n is divisible by 3, but can easily be adapted to the other two cases.) In general there are seven different types of pairs of vertices, namely,

I. both vertices in the same A_i: one in B_i and one in C_i;
II. both vertices in the same B_i;
III. both vertices in the same C_i;
IV. one vertex in B_i and one in B_{i+1};
V. one vertex in B_i and one in C_{i+1};
VI. one vertex in C_i and one in B_{i+1};
VII. one vertex in C_i and one in C_{i+1}.

When $n=3m$, the numbers of triples containing these pairs are respectively (taking b as the common value of $b_1, b_2, b_3/m+b, m, m, 2m-1, 2m-1, 2m-b-1, 2m-1$. While we do not claim that there are m distinct sets of values possible, we assert that at least cn distinct 3-graphs can be constructed in this fashion. For example, when $n=9$, the value $b=0$ yields the familiar example, in which there are only two distinct numbers in this sequence: 3, and 5; the 3-graphs corresponding to $b=1$ and $b=2$ are isomorphic, and give rise to the set of "valencies" $\{4, 5\}$ for pairs of vertices.

4. Conclusion

Lest the reader conjecture that our construction — even where the parameters b_1, b_2, b_3 are unconstrained — yield all extremal 3-graphs in $\mathrm{EX}(n, 4)$, we hasten to remark that this is not the case. A counter-example exists with $n=7$ vertices.

References

[1] G. Ringel, Extremal Problems in the Theory of Graphs, Theory of Graphs and its Applications (Proc. Sympos. Smolenice, 1963), pp. 85–90. Publ. House Czechoslovak Acad. Sci., Prague, 1964.
[2] M. Simonovits, Extremal graph problems with conditions, Combinatorial Theory and its Applications III, *Colloquia Math. Soc. J. Bolyai*, 4, North-Holland Publishing Co., Amsterdam–London, 1970, 999–1012.
[3] V. T. Sós, P. Erdős and W. G. Brown, On the existence of triangulated spheres in 3-graphs, and related problems, *Period. Math. Hung.*, 3 (1973), 221–228.
[4] P. Turán, Research Problems, *Magy. Tud. Akad. Mat. Kut. Int. Közl.*, 6 (1961), 417–423.

MCGILL UNIVERSITY
MONTRÉAL, CANADA

Studies in Pure Mathematics
To the Memory of Paul Turán

On the decomposition of graphs into complete bipartite subgraphs

by

F. R. K. CHUNG (Murray Hill), P. ERDŐS (Budapest)
and J. SPENCER* (Stony Brook)

Abstract

For a given graph G, we consider a **B**-decomposition of G, i.e., a decomposition of G into complete bipartite subgraphs $G_1, \dots, G_t$, such that any edge of G is in exactly one of the G_i's. Let $\alpha(G; \mathbf{B})$ denote the minimum value of $\sum_i |V(G_i)|$ over all **B**-decompositions of G. Let $\alpha(n; \mathbf{B})$ denote the maximum value of $\alpha(G; \mathbf{B})$ over all graphs on n vertices.

A **B**-covering of G is a collection of complete bipartite subgraphs $G_1', G_2', \dots, G_t'$, such that any edge of G is in at least one of the G_i'. Let $\beta(G; \mathbf{B})$ denote the minimum value of $\sum_i |V(G_i')|$ over all **B**-coverings of G and let $\beta(n; \mathbf{B})$ denote the maximum value of $\beta(G; \mathbf{B})$ over all graphs on n vertices.

In this paper, we show that for any positive ε, we have

$$(1-\varepsilon)\frac{n^2}{2e\log n} < \beta(n; \mathbf{B}) \leqq \alpha(n; \mathbf{B}) < (1+\varepsilon)\frac{n^2}{2\log n}$$

where $e = 2.718\dots$ is the base of natural logarithms, provided n is sufficiently large.

Introduction

For a finite graph G, a *decomposition* P of G is a family of subgraphs $G_1, G_2, \dots, G_t$, such that any edge in G is an edge of exactly one of the G_i' s. If all G_i' s belong to a specified class of graphs **H**, such a decomposition will be called an **H**-decomposition of G (see [2]).

Let f denote a *cost function* for graphs which assigns certain non-negative real values to all graphs. Sometimes it is desirable to decompose a given graph into subgraphs in **H** such that the total "cost" (the sum of the cost function values of all subgraphs) is minimized. In other words, for a given graph G, we consider the following:

* Work done while a consultant at Bell Laboratories.

$$\alpha_f(G;\mathbf{H})=\min_P \sum_i f(G_i)$$

where $P=\{G_1, G_2, \ldots, G_t\}$ ranges over all $\mathbf{H}$-decompositions of G.

Also of interest to us will be the quantity

$$\alpha_f(n;\mathbf{H})=\max_G \alpha_f(G;\mathbf{H})$$

where G ranges over all graphs on n vertices.

If we take f_0 to be the counting function, which assigns value 1 to any graph, and $\mathbf{P}$ is the family of all planar graphs, then $\alpha_{f_0}(G; \mathbf{P})$ is simply the thickness of G. If $\mathbf{F}$ denotes the family of forests, then $\alpha_{f_0}(G; \mathbf{F})$ is called the arboricity of G (see [6]). Many results along these lines are available. The reader is referred to [2] for a brief survey.

In this paper, we will deal almost exclusively with the case in which $\mathbf{H}$ is $\mathbf{B}$, the family of complete bipartite graphs. By a theorem in [5], the value of $\alpha_{f_0}(n; \mathbf{B})$ is given by:

$$\alpha_{f_0}(n;\mathbf{B})=n-1\,.$$

We consider the cost function f_1 where the value $f_1(G)$ is just the number of vertices in G. In the remaining part of the paper, we abbreviate $\alpha(n)=\alpha_{f_1}(n; \mathbf{B})$ and $\alpha(G)= =\alpha_{f_1}(G; \mathbf{B})$. In particular, we show for any given ε and sufficiently large n,

$$(1)\qquad (1-\varepsilon)\frac{n^2}{2e\log n}<\alpha(n)<(1+\varepsilon)\frac{n^2}{2\log n}$$

where e satisfies $\ln e=1$.

An $\mathbf{H}$-covering of G is a collection of subgraphs of G, say $G'_1, \ldots, G'_{t'}$, such that any edge of G is in at least one of the G'_i, and all G'_i are in $\mathbf{H}$. For a given cost function f, we can define

$$\beta_f(G;\mathbf{H})=\min_P \sum_i f(G'_i)$$

where $P=\{G'_1, \ldots, G'_{t'}\}$ ranges over all $\mathbf{H}$-coverings of G.

It is easily seen that

$$\beta_f(G;\mathbf{H})\leqq\alpha_f(G;\mathbf{H})$$

and

$$\beta_f(n;\mathbf{H})\leqq\alpha_f(n;\mathbf{H})\,.$$

We will show that the asymptotic growth of $\beta_{f_1}(n; \mathbf{B})$ is quite similar to $\alpha_{f_1}(n; \mathbf{B})$. In fact, we will obtain the same upper and lower bounds for $\beta_{f_1}(n; \mathbf{B})$ as those for $\alpha_{f_1}(n; \mathbf{B})$ in (1).

A lower bound

We derive these bounds mainly by probabilistic methods, which have been extensively described in the book by two of the authors [4].

Theorem 1. $\alpha(n) \geqq (1-\varepsilon)\dfrac{n^2}{2e \log n}$ *for any given positive* ε *and sufficiently large n.*

Proof. Let us consider a random graph G with n vertices and $\lfloor n^2/2e \rfloor$ edges. The probability of G containing a complete bipartite subgraph $K_{a,b}$ is bounded above by

$$\binom{n}{a}\binom{n}{b} e^{-ab} < e^{(a+b)\log n - ab}$$

(where $\lfloor x \rfloor$ and $\lceil x \rceil$ denote the greatest integer less than x and the least integer greater than x, respectively.)

Let S denote the set of all unordered pairs $\{a, b\}$ satisfying

$$1 \leqq a, b \leqq n, \frac{a+b}{ab} < \frac{1-\varepsilon}{\log n}.$$

The probability of G containing one of the complete bipartite subgraphs $K_{a,b}$ with $\dfrac{a+b}{ab} < \dfrac{1-\varepsilon}{\log n}$ is bounded above by

$$\sum_{\{a,b\} \in S} \binom{n}{a}\binom{n}{b} e^{-ab} < \sum_{\{a,b\} \in S} e^{-\varepsilon ab} < \sum_{\{a,b\} \in S} e^{-\varepsilon(\log n)^2} < n^2 e^{-\varepsilon(\log n)^2} < 1$$

for large n.

Therefore, there exists a graph G with n vertices and $\lfloor n^2/2e \rfloor$ edges such that G does not contain any $K_{a,b}$ as a subgraph. Let $P = \{G_1, G_2, \ldots, G_t\}$ denote a **B**-decomposition of G such that $\alpha(G)$ is the sum of the sizes of vertex set $V(G_i)$ of G_i, i.e.,

$$\alpha(G) = \sum_{i=1}^{t} |V(G_i)|.$$

For any edge (u, v) in G, we define

$$f(u, v) = \frac{|V G_i)|}{|E(G_i)|}$$

where $\{u, v\}$ is in $E(G_i)$, the edge set of G_i.

It is easily seen that

$$\alpha(G) = \sum_{\{u,v\}} f(u, v).$$

Since G does not contain $K_{a,b}$ as a subgraph, any $G_i = K_{c,d}$, $1 \leqq i \leqq t$, satisfies that $\frac{c+d}{cd} \geqq \frac{1-\varepsilon}{\log n}$. Thus we have

$$f(u, v) \geqq \frac{1-\varepsilon}{\log n} \quad \text{for any } \{u, v\} \text{ in } E(G).$$

and

$$\alpha(n) > \alpha(G) > \frac{(1-\varepsilon)n^2}{2e \log n}$$

for sufficiently large n. This proves the theorem.

An upper bound

First, we shall prove a preliminary result.

Lemma. *For any $\varepsilon > 0$ any graph on n vertices and $\rho \binom{n}{2}$ edges contains a complete bipartite graph $K_{s,t}$ as a subgraph where $t = \lfloor 1(1-\varepsilon)n\rho^s \rfloor$ and $s < \varepsilon \rho n$ for n sufficiently large.*

Proof. Suppose G has n vertices and $\rho \binom{n}{2}$ edges and G does not contain $K_{s,t}$ as a subgraph. From the proof in [3], the following holds:

$$n(\rho n - s)^s \leqq (t-1) \cdot n^s. \tag{2}$$

However, on the other hand, we have

$$(t-1)n^s < tn^s \leqq (1-\varepsilon)n^{1+s}\rho^s < n(\rho n - s)^s$$

since $s < \varepsilon \rho n$.

This contradicts (2). Thus G must contain $K_{s,t}$.

Theorem 2. *For any given ε, we have*

$$\alpha(n) < (1+\varepsilon) \frac{n^2}{2 \log n} \tag{3}$$

if n is large enough.

Proof. From Lemma 1, one can easily verify that a graph G on $\rho \binom{n}{2}$ edges and n vertices contains a subgraph H isomorphic to $K_{s,t}$, where $s = \lfloor (1-\varepsilon_1) \log n \log (1/\rho) \rfloor$ and $t = \lfloor s^2 \log (1/\rho) \rfloor$ and $\varepsilon_1 > \frac{(\log n)^2}{\rho n}$. We will decompose G into complete bipartite subgraphs by a "greedy algorithm". Given G we find a subgraph H isomorphic to $K_{s,t}$ and let G_1 to be the subgraph of G containing all edges of G except those in H. Now, we find a subgraph H_1 isomorphic to K_{s_1,t_1} and let G_2 to be a subgraph of G_1 containing all edges of G_1 except those in H_1 and continue in this fashion until only $\varepsilon_2 \frac{n^2}{\log n}$ edges are left. Thus G is decomposed into $H, H_1, \ldots,$ together with $\varepsilon_2 \frac{n^2}{\log n}$ edges and we have the following recursive relation

(4) $$\alpha(G) \leqq s + t + \alpha(G_1).$$

We will prove by induction that for a give $\varepsilon < \varepsilon_2 < \varepsilon_1$, $\varepsilon_3 > 0$ and sufficiently large n the following holds,

(5) $$\alpha(G) \leqq (1+\varepsilon_2) \frac{n^2}{2 \log n} \int_0^{\rho} \log(1/x)\,dx + 2\varepsilon_2 \frac{n^2}{\log n}.$$

Suppose (5) holds for any graph H with $|E(H)| < \rho \binom{n}{2}$. From (4), we have

$$\alpha(G) \leqq (1-\varepsilon_2)(\log n)^2/(\log(1/\rho))^3 + (1+\varepsilon_2) \frac{n^2}{2 \log n} \int_0^{\rho'} \log(1/x) dx + 2\varepsilon_2 \frac{n^2}{\log n}$$

where $\rho' = (|E(G)| - st) \Big/ \binom{n}{2}$ for n sufficiently large. It suffices to show that

$$(1-\varepsilon_2)\ (\log n)^2/\log(1/\rho))^3 + (1+\varepsilon_2) \frac{n^2}{2 \log n} \int_0^{\rho'} \log(1/x)\,dx \leqq$$

$$\leqq (1+\varepsilon_2) \frac{n^2}{2 \log n} \int_0^{\rho'} \log(1/x)\,dx$$

This can be verified by straightforward calculation. Thus (5) is proved and we have

$$\alpha(n) \leqq (1+\varepsilon_2) \frac{n^2}{2 \log n} \int_0^{1} \log(1/x) dx + 2\varepsilon_2 \frac{n^2}{\log n} \leqq (1+\varepsilon) \frac{n^2}{2 \log n}$$

for given $\varepsilon > 0$. Theorem 2 is proved.

By slightly modifying the proofs of Theorem 1, we can easily prove the following.

Theorem 3.

$$\beta_{f_1}(n; \mathbf{B}) \geqq (1-\varepsilon) \frac{n^2}{2e \log n}$$

for any positive ε and sufficiently large n.

Therefore we have

$$(1-\varepsilon)\frac{n^2}{2e\log n} < \beta_{f_1}(n;\mathbf{B}) \leqq \alpha_{f_1}(n;\mathbf{B}) < (1+\varepsilon)\frac{n^2}{2\log n}$$

for any given positive ε and sufficiently large n, which summarizes the main results of the paper.

Some related question

As we noted earlier, the lower bound is obtained by a probabilistic method which is nonconstructive. It would be of great interest to find an explicit construction of a graph G on n vertices, $c_1n^2/\log n$ edges (or c_2n^2 edges) which does not contain an $K_{c_3\log n, c_3\log n}$ as a subgraph for some constants c_1, c_2 and c_3.

Another interesting problem which has long been conjectured [4] concerns the Turán number $T(K_{t,t};n)$, the maximum number of edges a graph on n vertices can have which does not contain $K_{t,t}$ as a subgraph. Is it true that

$$T(K_{t,t};n) = O(n^{2-1/t})?$$

For the case $t=3$, the above equality has been verified in [1].

In this paper, we have shown that $\alpha_{f_1}(n;\mathbf{B}) = O(n^2/\log n)$. However, we do not know the existence of

$$\lim_{n\to\infty}\frac{\alpha_{f_1}(n;\mathbf{B})}{n^2/\log n} \quad \text{or} \quad \lim_{n\to\infty}\frac{\beta_{f_1}(n;\mathbf{B})}{n^2/\log n},$$

obviously.

Let $\mathbf{G}_n$ be the set of all the $2^{\binom{n}{2}}$ labelled graphs on n vertices. It would be of interest to evaluate $\sum_{G\in\mathbf{G}_n}\alpha_{f_1}(G;\mathbf{B})$. It is not unreasonable to conjecture that

$$\lim_{n\to\infty}\frac{\sum_{G\in\mathbf{G}_n}\alpha_{f_1}(G;\mathbf{B})}{2^{\binom{n}{2}}\,n^2/\log n} = c$$

exists and c is probably equal to $\lim_{n\to\infty}\frac{\alpha_{f_1}(n;\mathbf{B})}{n^2/\log n}$. We can also ask the analogous question for $\beta_{f_1}(G;\mathbf{B})$.

Let $\mathbf{G}_{n,m}$ be the set of all graphs on n vertices and m edges. We can define $\alpha_f(n,m;\mathbf{H})$ to be the maximum value of $\alpha_f(G;\mathbf{H})$ where G ranges over all graphs in $\mathbf{G}_{n,m}$. In this paper we investigate $\alpha_{f_1}(n,m;\mathbf{B})$ where m is about $n^2/2e$. One could also investigate $\alpha_{f_1}(n,m;\mathbf{B})$ or $\beta_{f_1}(n,m;\mathbf{B})$. In particular, we can ask the problem of determining m so that $\alpha(n,m;\mathbf{B})$ is maximized or to find the range for m for which we have $\alpha(n,m;\mathbf{B}) = o(n^2)$.

References

[1] W. G. Brown, On Graph That do not Contain a Thomson Graph, *Canad. Math. Bull.* **9** (1966), 281–285.

[2] F. R. K. Chung, On the Decomposition of Graphs, *SIAM J. on Algebraic and Discrete Methods*, **2** (1981), 1–12.

[3] F. R. K. Chung and R. L. Graham, On Multicolor Ramsey Numbers for Complete Bipartite Graphs, J. C. T. **18**, (1975), 164–169.

[4] P. Erdős and J. Spencer, Probabilistic Methods in Combinatorics, Academic Press, New York, 1974.

[5] R. L. Graham and H. O. Pollak, On the Addressing Problem for Loop Switching, *Bell Sys. Tech. Jour.*, **50** (1971), 2495–2519.

[6] F. Harary, *Graph Theory*, Addison-Wesley, New York, 1969.

BELL LABORATORIES
MURRAY HILL, NJ 07974
U.S.A.

MATHEMATICAL INSTITUTE OF THE HUNGARIAN ACADEMY
OF SCIENCES
H 1053 BUDAPEST
REÁLTANODA U. 13–15
HUNGARY

SUNY STONY BROOK
STONY BROOK, NY
U.S.A.

Studies in Pure Mathematics
To the Memory of Paul Turán

Syntopogenous spaces and zero-set spaces

by

Á. CSÁSZÁR (Budapest)

0. Introduction

Syntopogenous spaces were studied in details in the monograph [1] in order to give a common generalization of topological spaces, proximity spaces, quasi-uniform spaces and uniform spaces. Zero-set spaces have been introduced in [5] as a generalization of the structure composed of a set equipped with a topology and of the system of all zero-sets of real-valued functions continuous with respect to this topology.

The purpose of this paper is to show that zero-set spaces are essentially special syntopogenous spaces and to investigate their relation to general syntopogenous spaces. Many of the results are contained (without proofs), with emphasis on categorical aspects, in the paper [2]. Some of them generalize or restate results of [5] and show that the tools of the theory of syntopogenous spaces are useful in studying zero-set spaces.

In connection with syntopogenous spaces we use the terminology and notation of [1]. In particular, a *semi-topogenous order* on a set X is a binary relation on 2^X (i.e. a subset of $2^X \times 2^X$), denoted by $<$, such that

(0.1) $$\emptyset < \emptyset, \quad X < X,$$

(0.2) $$A < B \text{ implies } A \subset B,$$

(0.3) $$A' \subset A < B \subset B' \subset X \text{ implies } A' < B'.$$

A *topogenous order* on X is a semi-topogenous order satisfying

(0.4) $$A_i < B_i \quad (i = 1, \ldots, n) \text{ implies } \bigcup_1^n A_i < \bigcup_1^n B_i, \quad \bigcap_1^n A_i < \bigcap_1^n B_i.$$

A *syntopogenous structure* on X is a set $\mathcal{S}$ of topogenous orders that is *directed*, i.e. $<_1, <_2 \in \mathcal{S}$ implies the existence of $<_3 \in \mathcal{S}$ such that $<_1 \cup <_2 \subset <_3$, and *idempotent*, i.e. $< \in \mathcal{S}$ implies the existence of $<' \in \mathcal{S}$ such that $< \subset <'^2 = <'<'$. Here $\cup$, $\subset$ are used for (semi-)topogenous orders as subsets of $2^X \times 2^X$ and $<_1 <_2$ denotes the composition in $2^X \times 2^X$. A *syntopogenous space* is a pair $[X, \mathscr{S}]$ composed of a set X and a syntopogenous structure $\mathscr{S}$ on X. We refer to [1] for further information.

A *zero-set structure* on X is a system $\mathfrak{Z}$ of subsets of X such that

(0.5) $$\emptyset, X \in \mathfrak{Z},$$

(0.6) $$Z_i \in \mathfrak{Z} \quad (i=1, \ldots, n) \text{ implies } \bigcup_1^n Z_i \in \mathfrak{Z},$$

(0.7) $$Z_i \in \mathfrak{Z} \quad (i \in \mathbf{N}) \text{ implies } \bigcap_1^\infty Z_i \in \mathfrak{Z},$$

(0.8) $$Z \in \mathfrak{Z} \text{ implies the existence of } Z_i \in \mathfrak{Z} \text{ such that } X - Z = \bigcup_1^\infty Z_i,$$

(0.9) $Z_1, Z_2 \in \mathfrak{Z}$, $Z_1 \cap Z_2 = \emptyset$ implies the existence of C_1, C_2 such that $X - C_i \in \mathfrak{Z}$, $Z_i \subset C_i$ and $C_1 \cap C_2 = \emptyset$.

(0.5), (0.6) and (0.7) may be summarized by saying that $\mathfrak{Z}$ is a *δ-lattice* in X. A system $\mathfrak{Z}$ of subsets of X satisfying (0.8) can be said to be *perfect*, and a system satisfying (0.9) to be *normal*. For a system $\mathfrak{Z}$ of subsets of X, we shall denote by $\mathfrak{Z}^c$ the system of all complements $X - Z$ ($Z \in \mathfrak{Z}$).

A *zero-set space* is a pair $(X, \mathfrak{Z})$ of a set X and a zero-set structure $\mathfrak{Z}$ on X. If $(X, \mathfrak{Z})$ and $(X', \mathfrak{Z}')$ are zero-set spaces, then a map $f: X \to X'$ is said to be a *zero-set map* iff $Z' \in \mathfrak{Z}'$ implies $f^{-1}(Z') \in \mathfrak{Z}$.

1. *z*-spaces

We can associate a syntopogenous space with an arbitrary zero-set space $(X, \mathfrak{Z})$:

(1.1) ([2], Theorem 1). *If $(X, \mathfrak{Z})$ is a zero-set space, denote by $<(\mathfrak{Z})$ the topogenous order generated by the system of sets $\mathfrak{Z}^c$. Then $\mathscr{L}(\mathfrak{Z}) = \{<(\mathfrak{Z})\}$ is a simple syntopogenous structure on X. The correspondence of $\mathfrak{Z}$ and $<(\mathfrak{Z})$ is one-to-one because*

(1.2) $$A <(\mathfrak{Z}) B \textit{ iff there is a } C \in \mathfrak{Z}^c \textit{ such that } A \subset C \subset B,$$

(1.3) $$Z \in \mathfrak{Z} \textit{ iff } X - Z <(\mathfrak{Z}) X - Z.$$

Proof. According to the definition of a semi-topogenous order generated by a system of sets ([1], (2.1)), (1.2) and (1.3) are immediate. $<(\mathfrak{Z})$ is a topogenous order since $\mathfrak{Z}$ and $\mathfrak{Z}^c$ are lattices ([1], (3.3)). Clearly $<(\mathfrak{Z})^2 = <(\mathfrak{Z})$ so that $\mathscr{L}(\mathfrak{Z})$ is idempotent and a simple ([1], (7.7)) syntopogenous structure. ■

(1.4) ([2], Theorem 2). *Let $(X, \mathfrak{Z})$ and $(X', \mathfrak{Z}')$ be zero-set spaces. A map $f: X \to X'$ is a zero-set map iff it is $(\mathscr{L}(\mathfrak{Z}), \mathscr{L}(\mathfrak{Z}'))$-continuous.*

Proof. If f is a zero-set map and $A' <(\mathfrak{Z}') B'$ then $A' \subset C' \subset B'$ for a suitable $C' \in \mathfrak{Z}'^c$, hence

$$f^{-1}(A')\subset f^{-1}(C')\subset f^{-1}(B'),$$
$$f^{-1}(C')\in \mathfrak{Z}^c \quad\text{and}\quad f^{-1}(A')<(\mathfrak{Z})f^{-1}(B').$$

Thus f is $(\mathscr{Z}(\mathfrak{Z}), \mathscr{Z}(\mathfrak{Z}'))$-continuous by [1], (10.2). Conversely, if f is $(\mathscr{Z}(\mathfrak{Z}), \mathscr{Z}(\mathfrak{Z}'))$-continuous and $Z'\in\mathfrak{Z}'$, then $X'-Z'<(\mathfrak{Z}')X-Z'$ by (1.3), hence

$$f^{-1}(X-Z')<(\mathfrak{Z})f^{-1}(X-Z')$$

and

$$X-f^{-1}(Z')<(\mathfrak{Z})X-f^{-1}(Z')$$

so that $f^{-1}(Z')\in\mathfrak{Z}$ by (1.3). ■

We say that $\mathscr{Z}(\mathfrak{Z})$ is the syntopogenous structure *associated* with the zero-set structure $\mathfrak{Z}$, or that $\mathfrak{Z}$ is associated with $\mathscr{Z}(\mathfrak{Z})$. Similarly, the syntopogenous space $[X, \mathscr{Z}(\mathfrak{Z})]$ and the zero-set space $(X, \mathfrak{Z})$ are said to be associated with each other.

We look for a characterization of those syntopogenous spaces that are associated with zero-set spaces. For this purpose, we need some definitions.

A semi-topogenous order $<$ is said to be *strongly idempotent* iff $A<B$ implies the existence of a set C such that $A\subset C<C\subset B$. A syntopogenous structure $\mathscr{S}$ and a syntopogenous space $[X, \mathscr{S}]$ are said to be strongly idempotent iff each $<\in\mathscr{S}$ is a strongly idempotent topogenous order.

(1.5) *A semi-topogenous order $<$ on X is strongly idempotent iff there exists a system $\mathfrak{S}$ of subsets of X such that $<$ is generated by $\mathfrak{S}$.*

Proof. The semi-topogenous order generated by a system $\mathfrak{S}$ is strongly idempotent by [1], (2.1). Conversely, if $<$ is strongly idempotent and $\mathfrak{S}$ denotes the system of all subsets S of X satisfying $S<S$, then $\emptyset, X\in\mathfrak{S}$ and, by definition, $A<B$ iff there is an $S\in\mathfrak{S}$ such that $A\subset S\subset B$, i.e. $<$ is generated by $\mathfrak{S}$. ■

We recall ([3], (2.2)) that a topogenous order $<$ is said to be *normal* iff $<^c<\subset<<^c$ (for the definition of $<^c$, see [1], (2.6)). A topogenous structure ([1], (7.7)) $\mathscr{T}=\{<\}$ or a topogenous space $[X,\mathscr{T}]$ are said to be normal ([3], (2.3)) iff $<$ is a normal topogenous order.

A semi-topogenous order $<$ on X will said to be *countably perfect* iff

(1.6) $$A_i<B_i \quad (i\in\mathbf{N}) \quad\text{implies}\quad \bigcup_{i\in\mathbf{N}} A_i<\bigcup_{i\in\mathbf{N}} B_i.$$

A perfect semi-topogenous order (that satisfies (1.6) for an arbitrary index set I instead of $\mathbf{N}$, cf. [1], p. 24) is countably perfect. A syntopogenous structure $\mathscr{S}$ and a syntopogenous space $[X, \mathscr{S}]$ are said to be countably perfect iff each $<\in\mathscr{S}$ is a countably perfect topogenous order.

If $<$ is a semi-topogenous order on X, let us denote by $<^\pi$ the following subset of $2^X\times 2^X$:

(1.7) $A<^\pi B$ iff there exist A_i, B_i $(i\in\mathbf{N})$ such that $A=\bigcup_1^\infty A_i$, $B=\bigcup_1^\infty B_i$, and $A_i<B_i$ for each $i\in\mathbf{N}$.

(1.8) *For an arbitrary semi-topogenous order* $<$, *the relation* $<^{\pi}$ *is the coarsest countably perfect semi-topogenous order finer than* $<$.

Proof. $\emptyset < \emptyset$ and $X < X$ imply $\emptyset <^{\pi} \emptyset$ and $X <^{\pi} X$ respectively. Similarly, the validity of (0.2) for $<$ implies its validity for $<^{\pi}$. If $A' \subset A <^{\pi} B \subset B'$, $A = \bigcup_1^{\infty} A_i$, $B = \bigcup_1^{\infty} B_i$, $A_i < B_i$, *then*

$$A' = \bigcup_1^{\infty} (A' \cap A_i), \quad B' = \bigcup_1^{\infty} B_i'$$

where $B_i' = B'$ for each i, and by (0.3)

$$A' \cap A_i \subset A_i < B_i \subset B_i' \quad (i \in \mathbf{N}),$$

hence $A' <^{\pi} B'$. Thus $<^{\pi}$ is a semi-topogenous order.

If $A_k <^{\pi} B_k$ for $k \in \mathbf{N}$, and

$$A_k = \bigcup_{i=1}^{\infty} A_{ki}, \quad B_k = \bigcup_{i=1}^{\infty} B_{ki}, \quad A_{ki} < B_{ki} \quad (k, i \in \mathbf{N}),$$

then

$$A = \bigcup_{k=1}^{\infty} A_k = \bigcup_{k=1}^{\infty} \bigcup_{i=1}^{\infty} A_{ki}, \quad B = \bigcup_{k=1}^{\infty} B_k = \bigcup_{k=1}^{\infty} \bigcup_{i=1}^{\infty} B_{ki},$$

hence $A <^{\pi} B$. Thus $<^{\pi}$ is countably perfect.

Clearly $A < B$ implies $A <^{\pi} B$. Finally if $<'$ is a countably perfect semi-topogenous order finer than $<$, then $A <^{\pi} B$ implies $A <' B$ since $A_i <' B_i$ in (1.7). ■

A semi-topogenous order $<$ will be said to be *semi-symmetric* iff $< \subset <^{c\pi}$. If $<$ is symmetric (i.e. if $<^c = <$, see [1], p. 9) then it is semi-symmetric by (1.8). A syntopogenous structure $\mathscr{S}$ (or a syntopogenous space $[X, \mathscr{S}]$) is semi-symmetric iff each $< \in \mathscr{S}$ is semi-symmetric.

It is now easy to prove:

(1.9) ([2], Theorem 4). *For a syntopogenous space* $[X, \mathscr{S}]$, *there exists a zero-set structure* $\mathfrak{Z}$ *on* X *such that* $\mathscr{S} = \mathscr{Z}(\mathfrak{Z})$ *iff* $\mathscr{S}$ *is simple, strongly idempotent, normal, countably perfect and semi-symmetric.*

Proof. Assume $\mathscr{S} = \mathscr{Z}(\mathfrak{Z})$ for a zero-set structure $\mathfrak{Z}$. Then $\mathscr{S} = \{<(\mathfrak{Z})\}$ so that $\mathscr{S}$ is simple and strongly idempotent by (1.2) and (1.5). If $A <(\mathfrak{Z})^c <(\mathfrak{Z}) B$ then there is a set C satisfying $A <(\mathfrak{Z})^c C <(\mathfrak{Z}) B$, hence there are sets $Z_1, Z_2 \in \mathfrak{Z}$ such that

$$X - C \subset X - Z_1 \subset X - A, \quad C \subset X - Z_2 \subset B,$$

i.e.

$$A \subset Z_1 \subset C \subset X - Z_2 \subset B.$$

Therefore the normality of $\mathfrak{Z}$ implies the existence of C_1, C_2 such that $Z_i \subset C_i$, $X - C_i \in \mathfrak{Z}$, $C_1 \cap C_2 = \emptyset$. Then

$$A \subset Z_1 \subset C_1 \subset X - C_2 \subset X - Z_2 \subset B$$

and

$$A < (\mathfrak{Z}) C_1 < (\mathfrak{Z})^c B\,;$$

the latter relation follows from $X - B \subset C_2 \subset X - C_1$. Thus $<(\mathfrak{Z})$ is normal.

Suppose now $A_i < (\mathfrak{Z}) B_i$ for $i \in \mathbf{N}$, i.e.

$$A_i \subset X - Z_i \subset B_i\,, \quad Z_i \in \mathfrak{Z}\,.$$

Then

$$\bigcup_1^\infty A_i \subset X - \bigcap_1^\infty Z_i \subset \bigcup_1^\infty B_i$$

and $\bigcap_1^\infty Z_i \in \mathfrak{Z}$ by (0.7). Hence $<(\mathfrak{Z})$ is countably perfect.

Finally assume $A < (\mathfrak{Z}) B$, i.e. $A \subset X - Z \subset B$, $Z \in \mathfrak{Z}$. By (0.8) we have $X - Z = \bigcup_1^\infty Z_i$, $Z_i \in \mathfrak{Z}$. Hence

$$A = \bigcup_1^\infty (A \cap Z_i)\,, \quad B = \bigcup_1^\infty B_i \quad (B_i = B)\,,$$

$$X - B_i = X - B \subset X - Z_i \subset X - (A \cap Z_i)\,,$$

i.e.

$$A \cap Z_i < (\mathfrak{Z})^c B_i \quad \text{and} \quad A < (\mathfrak{Z})^{c\pi} B\,.$$

Thus $<(\mathfrak{Z})$ is semi-symmetric.

Suppose now conversely that $\mathcal{S}$ is simple, strongly idempotent, normal, countably perfect and semi-symmetric. Set $\mathcal{S} = \{<\}$. By (1.5) $<$ is generated by a system $\mathfrak{C}$ of subsets of X. Since $<$ is a topogenous order, $\mathfrak{C}$ is a lattice by [1], (3.3). Let $\mathfrak{Z}$ be the system $\mathfrak{C}^c$, then $\mathfrak{Z}$ is a lattice as well.

If $Z_i \in \mathfrak{Z}$ for $i \in \mathbf{N}$, then $X - Z_i < X - Z_i$ by [1], (2.1), and, since $<$ is countably perfect,

$$\bigcup_1^\infty (X - Z_i) = X - \bigcap_1^\infty Z_i < X - \bigcap_1^\infty Z_i$$

so that $\bigcap_1^\infty Z_i \in \mathfrak{Z}$ and $\mathfrak{Z}$ is a δ-lattice.

For $Z \in \mathfrak{Z}$, i.e. $X - Z < X - Z$, we have

$$X - Z <^{c\pi} X - Z$$

because $<$ is semi-symmetric. Hence

$$X - Z = \bigcup_1^\infty A_i\,, \quad X - Z = \bigcup_1^\infty B_i\,, \quad A_i <^c B_i$$

and a fortiori $A_i <^c X - Z$. Therefore

$$Z \subset X - Z_i \subset X - A_i, \quad A_i \subset Z_i \subset X - Z$$

for suitable sets $Z_i \in \mathfrak{Z}$. Thus

$$X - Z = \bigcup_1^\infty Z_i\,,$$

and (0.8) is fulfilled.

Finally let $Z_i \in \mathfrak{Z}$ $(i=1, 2)$, $Z_1 \cap Z_2 = \emptyset$. Then

$$Z_1 <^c Z_1 \subset X - Z_2 < X - Z_2\,,$$

and by the normality of $<$ there is a set C satisfying $Z_1 < C <^c X - Z_2$, i.e.

$$Z_1 \subset C_1 \subset C \subset X - C_2 \subset X - Z_2$$

for suitable sets C_i such that $X - C_i \in \mathfrak{Z}$. Hence (0.9) is fulfilled, $\mathfrak{Z}$ is a zero-set structure and $< = <(\mathfrak{Z})$. ■

A simple, strongly idempotent, normal, countably perfect and semi-symmetric syntopogenous structure is said to be a *z-structure*, and a syntopogenous space $[X, \mathscr{S}]$ such that $\mathscr{S}$ is a z-structure will be called a *z-space*. Thus z-spaces are in a one-to-one relation to zero-set spaces in the sense of (1.1).

2. The operation π

We investigate the properties of the operation π that assigns $<^\pi$ to an arbitrary semi-topogenous order $<$. Its most essential properties are summarized in the following statement:

(2.1) ([2], Theorem 3). *The operation π is an elementary operation* (in the sense of [1], p. 69).

Proof. By (1.8), $< \subset <^\pi = <^{\pi\pi}$ for every semi-topogenous order $<$. By (1.7), $<_1 \subset <_2$ obviously implies $<_1^\pi \subset <_2^\pi$.

If $A <^{2\pi} B$ then

$$A = \bigcup_1^\infty A_i, \quad B = \bigcup_1^\infty B_i, \quad A_i < C_i < B_i \quad (i \in \mathbf{N}),$$

hence

$$A <^\pi \bigcup_1^\infty C_i <^\pi B\,, \quad A <^{\pi 2} B\,.$$

If $A <^{\pi q} B$ then by [1], (3.6)

$$A = \bigcup_{i=1}^{m} A_i, \quad B = \bigcap_{j=1}^{n} B_j, \quad A_i <^{\pi} B_j$$

for each i and j. Hence by (1.7)

$$A_i = \bigcup_{k=1}^{\infty} A_{ijk}, \quad A_{ijk} < B_j \quad (i=1, \ldots, m; \quad j=1, \ldots, n; \quad k \in \mathbf{N}).$$

Let (C_{ih}) $(h \in \mathbf{N})$ be a sequence composed of all sets of the form

$$A_{i1k_1} \cap A_{i2k_2} \cap \ldots \cap A_{ink_n}.$$

Then

$$A = \bigcup_{h=1}^{\infty} C_{ih}, \quad C_{ih} <^{q} \bigcap_{j=1}^{n} B_j = B, \quad D_h = \bigcup_{i=1}^{m} C_{ih} <^{q} B \quad (h \in \mathbf{N})$$

and

$$A = \bigcup_{i=1}^{m} \bigcup_{h=1}^{\infty} C_{ih} = \bigcup_{h=1}^{\infty} D_h <^{q\pi} B$$

so that $<^{\pi q} \subset <^{q\pi}$.

If $f: X' \to X$ is a map and $<$ is a semi-topogenous order on X then $A f^{-1}(<^{\pi})B$ implies by [1], (6.1)

$$f(A) <^{\pi} X - f(X' - B),$$

i.e.

$$f(A) = \bigcup_{1}^{\infty} A_i, \quad A_i < X - f(X' - B) \quad (i \in \mathbf{N})$$

so that

$$A = \bigcup_{1}^{\infty} (A \cap f^{-1}(A_i)),$$

$$f(A \cap f^{-1}(A_i)) \subset A_i < X - f(X' - B),$$

$$A \cap f^{-1}(A_i) f^{-1}(<) B$$

and $A f^{-1}(<)^{\pi} B$. Conversely, the latter formula implies

$$A = \bigcup_{1}^{\infty} C_i, \quad f(C_i) < X - f(X' - B) \quad (i \in \mathbf{N}),$$

hence

$$f(A) = \bigcup_{1}^{\infty} f(C_i), \quad f(A) <^{\pi} X - f(X' - B)$$

and

$$A f^{-1}(<^{\pi}) B. \blacksquare$$

Hence, by [1], (8.8), together with $<$ also $<^{\pi}$ is a topogenous order. By [1], (8.23) and (8.33), if $\mathscr{S}$ is a syntopogenous structure then $\mathscr{S}^{\pi}=\{<^{\pi}: <\in\mathscr{S}\}$ is a similar structure. In particular, if $\mathscr{S}$ is simple, then the same holds for $\mathscr{S}^{\pi}$. If $f:X\to X'$ is $(\mathscr{S}, \mathscr{S}')$-continuous then it is $(\mathscr{S}^{\pi}, \mathscr{S}'^{\pi})$-continuous by [1], (10.12). All this proves [2], Theorem 3.

(2.2) *For every semi-topogenous order* $<$, *we have*

$$<^{\pi p}=<^{p}.$$

Proof. By (1.7) and [1], (4.4) clearly $<^{\pi}\subset<^{p}$, hence $<^{\pi p}\subset<^{pp}=<^{p}$. On the other hand $<\subset<^{\pi}$ implies $<^{p}\subset<^{\pi p}$. ■

3. $C(\mathscr{S})$ and $C^*(\mathscr{S})$

We shall define an operation that assigns a z-structure to every syntopogenous structure $\mathscr{S}$. For this purpose, we need first some results concerning the system of all continuous (or bounded and continuous) real-valued functions defined on a syntopogenous space $[X, \mathscr{S}]$. In order to do this, we have to equip the real line **R** with a standard syntopogenous structure with respect to which the continuity is understood.

Let us consider on **R** the syntopogenous structure $\mathscr{H}$ composed of all symmetric (and biperfect) topogenous orders $<_{\varepsilon}$ $(\varepsilon>0)$ where

$$A<_{\varepsilon}B \quad \text{iff} \quad x\in A, \quad |y-x|<\varepsilon \text{ implies } y\in B \quad (A, B\subset\mathbf{R}).$$

(Cf. [1], p. 87, where the present order $<_{\varepsilon}$ is denoted by $<_{\varepsilon}^{sb}$.) For an arbitrary syntopogenous space $[X, \mathscr{S}]$, we denote by $C(\mathscr{S})$ the system of all $(\mathscr{S}, \mathscr{H})$-continuous functions $f:X\to\mathbf{R}$ and by $C^*(\mathscr{S})$ the system of all bounded functions $f\in C(\mathscr{S})$.

If $\mathscr{S}$ is symmetric and biperfect and $\mathscr{U}$ denotes the uniform structure associated with $\mathscr{S}$, then by [1], (10.26) $C(\mathscr{S})$ consists of all real-valued functions uniformly continuous with respect to $\mathscr{U}$. Similarly, if $\mathscr{T}$ is a topogenous structure or a topology, then, by [1], (10.12) and (10.10), $C(\mathscr{T})$ consists of all $(\mathscr{T}, \mathscr{H}^{t})$ or all $(\mathscr{T}, \mathscr{H}^{tp})$-continuous functions respectively; therefore, in the case of a topology, [1], (10.28) implies that $C(\mathscr{T})$ consists of all continuous real-valued functions (with respect to the euclidean topology of **R**).

(3.1) *If* $f\in C(\mathscr{S})$, $c\in\mathbf{R}$ *then*

$$f+c, \quad cf, \quad |f|, \quad \max(f, c,), \quad \min(f, c)\in C(\mathscr{S}).$$

Proof. By [1], (10.7) it suffices to observe that each of the functions g_i is $(\mathscr{H}, \mathscr{H})$-continuous where

$$g_1(t)=t+c, \quad g_2(t)=ct, \quad g_3(t)=|t|,$$

$$g_4(t)=\max(t, c), \quad g_5(t)=\min(t, c).$$

This in turn is an easy consequence of [1], (10.26). ■

(3.2) $C(\mathscr{S})$ *is complete* (i.e. $f_n \in C(\mathscr{S})$ implies $f \in C(\mathscr{S})$ if $f_n \to f$ uniformly).

Proof. For $\varepsilon > 0$, select n_0 such that $n \geqq n_0$ implies $|f_n - f| < \varepsilon/3$. Assume A, $B \subset \mathbf{R}$, $A <_\varepsilon B$, and set

$C = S(A, \varepsilon/3) = \{y \in \mathbf{R}$: there is $x \in A$ such that $|y - x| < \varepsilon/3\}$,

$$D = S(C, \varepsilon/3).$$

Then $f^{-1}(A) \subset f_n^{-1}(C)$ for $n \geqq n_0$, and for the same n $f_n^{-1}(D) \subset f^{-1}(B)$ because $S(D, \varepsilon/3) \subset S(A, \varepsilon) \subset B$. By the $(\mathscr{S}, \mathscr{H})$-continuity of f_{n_0}, there is a $< \in \mathscr{S}$ (depending only on ε) such that $M <_{\varepsilon/3} N$ implies $f_{n_0}^{-1}(M) < f_{n_0}^{-1}(N)$. Since $C <_{\varepsilon/3} D$, we have

$$f^{-1}(A) \subset f_{n_0}^{-1}(C) < f_{n_0}^{-1}(D) \subset f^{-1}(B). \blacksquare$$

(3.3) $C^*(\mathscr{S})$ *is a complete vector lattice containing all constants.*

Proof. (3.2) clearly implies that $C^*(\mathscr{S})$ is complete. On the other hand, $f, g \in C^*(\mathscr{S})$, $c \in \mathbf{R}$ implies

$$f + g,\ \max(f, g),\ \min(f, g),\ cf,\ c \in C^*(\mathscr{S})$$

by [1], (11.84) and (3.1). ■

Let us now denote by $\mathfrak{Z}(\mathscr{S})$ the system of all zero-sets

$$Z(f) = \{x \in X : f(x) = 0\}$$

belonging to all functions $f \in C(\mathscr{S})$. By (3.1) $\mathfrak{Z}(\mathscr{S})$ is also the system of all $Z(f)$ for $f \in C^*(\mathscr{S})$. Moreover, we can say:

(3.4) $\mathfrak{Z}(\mathscr{S})$ *coincides with the system of all sets*

$$X(f \geqq 0) = \{x \in X : f(x) \geqq 0) \quad (f \in C(\mathscr{S}))$$

and also with the system of all sets

$$X(f \geqq c) = \{x \in X : f(x) \geqq c\} \quad (f \in C(\mathscr{S}), c \in \mathbf{R})$$

or with that of all sets

$$X(f \leqq c) = \{x \in X : f(x) \leqq c\} \quad (f \in C(\mathscr{S}), c \in \mathbf{R}).$$

The same remains true if we replace $C(\mathscr{S})$ *by* $C^*(\mathscr{S})$.

Proof. By (3.1) everything follows from the identities

$$X(f \geqq 0) = Z(\min(f, 0)), \quad X(f \geqq c) = X(f - c \geqq 0),$$

$$X(f \leqq c) = X(-f + c \geqq 0), \quad Z(f) = X(-|f| \geqq 0) = X(|f| \leqq 0). \blacksquare$$

(3.5) *If Φ is a complete vector lattice containing all constants, composed of real-valued functions defined on X, then the system $\{Z(f): f \in \Phi\} = \mathfrak{Z}$ is a zero-set structure. In particular, $\mathfrak{Z}(\mathscr{S})$ is a zero-set structure for every syntopogenous structure $\mathscr{S}$.*

Proof. By [4], Proposition (3.1), $\mathfrak{Z}$ coincides with the system of all sets $X(f \geqq c)$ $(f \in \Phi, c \in \mathbf{R})$. Hence by [4], Proposition (3.2), $\mathfrak{Z}$ is a δ-lattice and satisfies (0.8).

Assume $Z_1, Z_2 \in \mathfrak{Z}$, $Z_1 \cap Z_2 = \emptyset$. Then there is f_i such that $Z_i = Z(f_i)$. We can suppose $f_i \geqq 0$ because $Z(f_i) = Z(|f_i|)$. Now $f_2 - f_1, f_1 - f_2 \in \Phi$ and the sets

$$C_1 = X(f_2 - f_1 > 0), \quad C_2 = X(f_1 - f_2 > 0)$$

satisfy $Z_i \subset C_i$, $X - C_i \in \mathfrak{Z}$ and $C_1 \cap C_2 = \emptyset$. Thus $\mathfrak{Z}$ fulfils (0.9).

For the case of $\mathfrak{Z}(\mathscr{S})$ we can apply (3.3). ■

(3.6) *If $\mathscr{S}_1 < \mathscr{S}_2$ then $C(\mathscr{S}_1) \subset C(\mathscr{S}_2)$, $C^*(\mathscr{S}_1) \subset C^*(\mathscr{S}_2)$, $\mathfrak{Z}(\mathscr{S}_1) \subset \mathfrak{Z}(\mathscr{S}_2)$.*

Proof. [1], (10.10). ■

An important result in the opposite direction is the following one:

(3.7) $C^*(\mathscr{S}) = C^*(\mathscr{S}^t)$ *for every syntopogenous structure $\mathscr{S}$. Consequently $\mathfrak{Z}(\mathscr{S}) = \mathfrak{Z}(\mathscr{S}^t)$.*

Proof. By (3.6) $C^*(\mathscr{S}) \subset C^*(\mathscr{S}^t)$. Conversely if $f \in C^*(\mathscr{S}^t)$ then $f(X) \subset I$ where I is a bounded interval of $\mathbf{R}$, and f is $(\mathscr{S}^t, \mathscr{H})$-continuous. For a given $\varepsilon > 0$, set

$$I = \bigcup_1^n I_k$$

where each I_k is an interval of length less than $\varepsilon/2$, and $I'_k = S(I_k, \varepsilon/2)$. Since $I_k <_{\varepsilon/2} I'_k$, we have $f^{-1}(I_k) < f^{-1}(I'_k)$ for the topogenous order $<$ satisfying $\mathscr{S}^t = \{<\}$. Hence there are, by [1], (8.38), topogenous orders $<_k \in \mathscr{S}$ such that $f^{-1}(I_k) <_k f^{-1}(I'_k)$ $(k = 1, \ldots, n)$; select $<' \in \mathscr{S}$ satisfying $<_k \subset <'$ for each k.

Now if $A, B \subset \mathbf{R}$, $A <_\varepsilon B$, then $A \cap I_k \neq \emptyset$ implies $I'_k \subset B$; denote by K the set of those k for which this is true. Then

$$f^{-1}(A) \subset \bigcup_{k \in K} f^{-1}(I_k) <' \bigcup_{k \in K} f^{-1}(I'_k) \subset f^{-1}(B).$$

Thus $<' \in \mathscr{S}$ corresponds to $<_\varepsilon$ in the sense of the $(\mathscr{S}, \mathscr{H})$-continuity of f so that $f \in C^*(\mathscr{S})$. ■

4. The operation σ

Let $\mathscr{T}$ be a topogenous structure on X, $\mathscr{T} = \{<\}$. Let us define a relation $<^\sigma$ on $2^X \times 2^X$ by

(4.1) $A <^\sigma B$ iff there exists an $f \in C(\mathscr{T})$ such that $0 \leqq f \leqq 1$, $f(x) = 0$ for $x \in A$, $f(x) = 1$ for $x \in X - B$.

(4.2) ([2], Theorem 7). *$<^\sigma$ is a symmetric topogenous order on X, and $\mathscr{T}^\sigma=\{<^\sigma\}$ is the finest symmetric topogenous structure coarser than $\mathscr{T}$. $\mathscr{T}^{\sigma\sigma}=\mathscr{T}^\sigma$, and $\mathscr{T}$ is symmetric iff $\mathscr{T}=\mathscr{T}^\sigma$.*

Proof. $\emptyset<^\sigma\emptyset$ is shown by $f=1$, $X<^\sigma X$ by $f=0$. (0.2) and (0.3) are obvious. If $A_i<^\sigma B_i$ is shown by f_i (i$=1, \ldots, n$) then

$$\bigcup_1^n A_i<^\sigma\bigcup_1^n B_i$$

is shown by $\min(f_1, \ldots, f_n)$ and

$$\bigcap_1^n A_i<^\sigma\bigcap_1^n B_i$$

by $\max(f_1, \ldots, f_n)$. If f shows $A<^\sigma B$, then $1-f$ shows $X-B<^\sigma X-A$. Of course, (3.3) is needed for proving that all these functions belong to $C(\mathscr{T})$.

If $0\leqq f\leqq 1$, $f(x)=0$ for $x\in A$, $f(x)=1$ for $x\in X-B$, then set $C = X(f<1/2)$. Now $\min(2f, 1)$ shows $A<^\sigma C$ and $\max(2f-1, 0)$ shows $C<^\sigma B$, according to (3.3).

Therefore $\mathscr{T}^\sigma$ is a symmetric topogenous structure. Since $\{0\}<_1(-\infty, 1)$ on the real line, $A<^\sigma B$ implies $A<B$ so that $\mathscr{T}^\sigma<\mathscr{T}$. On the other hand, if $\mathscr{T}'$ is a symmetric topogenous structure and $\mathscr{T}'<\mathscr{T}$, then $\mathscr{T}'=\{<'\}$ and $A<'B$ imply by [1], (12.41) that there exists a $(\mathscr{T}', \mathscr{I})$-continuous f satisfying $0\leqq f\leqq 1$, $f(x)=0$ for $x\in A$, $f(x)=1$ for $x\in X-B$. This f is $(\mathscr{T}', \mathscr{H})$-continuous by [1], (10.34) and $(\mathscr{T}, \mathscr{H})$-continuous by [1], (10.10). Hence $A<^\sigma B$ and $\mathscr{T}'<\mathscr{T}^\sigma$. The remaining statements are now obvious. ∎

(4.3) ([2], Theorem 8) *Let $[X, \mathscr{T}]$ and $[X', \mathscr{T}']$ be two topogenous spaces. If g is $(\mathscr{T}, \mathscr{T}')$-continuous then it is $(\mathscr{T}^\sigma, \mathscr{T}'^\sigma)$-continuous. In particular, $\mathscr{T}_1<\mathscr{T}_2$ implies $\mathscr{T}_1^\sigma<\mathscr{T}_2^\sigma$.*

Proof. Set $\mathscr{T}=\{<\}$, $\mathscr{T}'=\{<'\}$. If $A<'^\sigma B$ then there is a $(\mathscr{T}', \mathscr{H})$-continuous f such that $0\leqq f\leqq 1$, $f(x)=0$ for $x\in A$, $f(x)=1$ for $x\in X'-B$. Then $f\circ g$ is $(\mathscr{T}, \mathscr{H})$-continuous by [1], (10.7) and shows that

$$g^{-1}(A)<^\sigma g^{-1}(B).$$

The last statement follows from [1], (10.6). ∎

(4.4) ([2], Theorem 9). *If $\mathscr{T}=\{<\}$ is a normal topogenous structure then $<^\sigma=<^c<$*

Proof. [3], (2.20). ∎

The following statement is somewhat similar to (3.7):

(4.5) *If $\mathscr{T}$ is an arbitrary topogenous structure then $C(\mathscr{T}^\sigma)=C(\mathscr{T})$, $C^*(\mathscr{T}^\sigma)=C^*(\mathscr{T})$, $\mathfrak{Z}(\mathscr{T}^\sigma)=\mathfrak{Z}(\mathscr{T})$.*

Proof. By (4.2) and (3.6) $C(\mathscr{T}^\sigma) \subset C(\mathscr{T})$. On the other hand, if f is $(\mathscr{T}, \mathscr{H})$-continuous, then it is $(\mathscr{T}, \mathscr{H}^t)$-continuous by [1], (10.12), hence $(\mathscr{T}^\sigma, \mathscr{H}^t)$-continuous by (4.3) and (4.2), and $(\mathscr{T}^\sigma, \mathscr{H})$-continuous by [1], (10.10). ∎

(4.6) *If* $\mathscr{Z}$ *is a z-structure then* $\mathscr{Z} = \mathscr{Z}^{\sigma\pi}$.

Proof. Set $\mathscr{Z} = \{<\}$. By (4.2) $<^\sigma \subset <$, hence $<^{\sigma\pi} \subset <^\pi = <$ by (2.1) and (1.8). On the other hand, $< = <(\mathfrak{Z})$ by (1.9) for some zero-set structure $\mathfrak{Z}$. Hence $A < B$ implies $A \subset C \subset B$ for a suitable $C \in \mathfrak{Z}^c$, then $C = \bigcup_1^\infty Z_i$ for some sets $Z_i \in \mathfrak{Z}$ so that $Z_i <^c Z_i \subset$ $\subset C < C$ for each i. Therefore $Z_i <^\sigma C$ by (4.4), then $C <^{\sigma\pi} C$, whence $A <^{\sigma\pi} B$. ∎

(4.7) *If* $\mathscr{T}$ *is a topology, then* $\mathscr{T}^{\sigma p}$ *is the finest uniformizable topology coarser than* $\mathscr{T}$, *and* $\mathscr{T}^\sigma = \mathscr{T}^{\sigma p \sigma}$ *is associated with the finest proximity compatible with* $\mathscr{T}^{\sigma p}$.

Proof. $\mathscr{T}^\sigma < \mathscr{T}$ by (4.2), hence $\mathscr{T}^{\sigma p} < \mathscr{T}^p = \mathscr{T}$. $\mathscr{T}^\sigma$ is symmetric, hence $\mathscr{T}^{\sigma p}$ is a uniformizable topology by [1] (12.61). If $\mathscr{T}' < \mathscr{T}$ is a uniformizable topology, then $\mathscr{T}' = \mathscr{T}''^p$ for some symmetric topogenous structure $\mathscr{T}''$, and $\mathscr{T}'' < \mathscr{T}' < \mathscr{T}$ implies $\mathscr{T}'' < \mathscr{T}^\sigma$, $\mathscr{T}' = \mathscr{T}''^p < \mathscr{T}^{\sigma p}$.

$\mathscr{T}^\sigma < \mathscr{T}^{\sigma p} < \mathscr{T}$ implies $\mathscr{T}^{\sigma\sigma} < \mathscr{T}^{\sigma p \sigma} < \mathscr{T}^\sigma$ by (4.3) so that $\mathscr{T}^\sigma = \mathscr{T}^{\sigma p \sigma}$ by (4.2), and this is the finest symmetric topogenous structure $\mathscr{T}'$ satisfying $\mathscr{T}'^p = \mathscr{T}^{\sigma p}$. ∎

5. The operation z

We know from (3.5) that $\mathfrak{Z}(\mathscr{S})$ is a zero-set structure for every syntopogenous structure $\mathscr{S}$. Hence $\mathscr{Z}(\mathfrak{Z}(\mathscr{S}))$ is a z-structure, let us denote it by $\mathscr{S}$.

(5.1) ([2], Theorem 5). *For an arbitrary syntopogenous structure* $\mathscr{S}$, $\mathscr{S}^z$ *is a z-structure.* $\mathscr{S}^z = \mathscr{S}$ *holds iff* $\mathscr{S}$ *is a z-structure, hence* $\mathscr{S}^{zz} = \mathscr{S}^z$ *for every* $\mathscr{S}$. *If g is* $(\mathscr{S}, \mathscr{S}')$*-continuous, then it is* $(\mathscr{S}^z, \mathscr{S}'^z)$*-continuous as well. In particular,* $\mathscr{S}_1 < \mathscr{S}_2$ *implies* $\mathscr{S}_1^z < \mathscr{S}_2^z$.

Proof. $\mathscr{S}^z$ is a z-structure by definition, hence $\mathscr{S}^z = \mathscr{S}$ implies that $\mathscr{S}$ is a z-structure. Conversely, suppose that $\mathscr{S} = \{<\}$ is a z-structure. Then $\mathscr{S} = \mathscr{Z}(\mathfrak{Z})$, $< = <(\mathfrak{Z})$ for some zero-set structure $\mathfrak{Z}$ (cf. (1.9)). Hence $Z \in \mathfrak{Z}$ implies $C < C$ for $C = X - Z$, thus $C = \bigcup_1^\infty A_i$, $A_i <^\sigma C$ by (4.6). Consequently there exist functions $f_i \in C(\mathscr{S})$ satisfying $0 \leq f_i \leq 1$, $f_i(x) = 0$ for $x \in A_i$, $f_i(x) = 1$ for $x \in X - C$; then $A_i \subset C_i \subset C$ for $C_i = X(f_i < 1/2)$ and $C_i \in \mathfrak{Z}(\mathscr{S})^c$ by (3.4), hence

$$Z = \bigcap_1^\infty (X - C_i) \in \mathfrak{Z}(\mathscr{S})$$

by (3.5). Thus $\mathfrak{Z} \subset \mathfrak{Z}(\mathscr{S})$.

On the other hand, assume $Z \in \mathfrak{Z}(\mathscr{S})$, $Z = Z(f)$, $f \in C(\mathscr{S})$. Then $Z = \bigcap_1^\infty C_i$ for $C_i = X(|f| < 1/n)$ and the function $1 - \min(n|f|, 1) \in C(\mathscr{S})$ (cf. (3.1)) shows that $X - C_i <^\sigma X - Z$, hence $X - Z <^{\sigma\pi} X - Z$ or $X - Z < X - Z$ by (4.4). Therefore $Z \in \mathfrak{Z}$, $\mathfrak{Z}(\mathscr{S}) \subset \mathfrak{Z}$, and $\mathscr{Z}(\mathfrak{Z}) = \mathscr{Z}(\mathfrak{Z}(\mathscr{S})) = \mathscr{S}^z$.

If $g: X \to X'$ is $(\mathscr{S}, \mathscr{S}')$-continuous for given syntopogenous spaces $[X, \mathscr{S}]$ and $[X', \mathscr{S}']$, then $f \in C(\mathscr{S}')$ implies $f \circ g \in C(\mathscr{S})$, hence $Z' \in \mathfrak{Z}(\mathscr{S}')$, $Z' = Z(f)$, $f \in C(\mathscr{S}')$ implies $g^{-1}(Z') = Z(f \circ g) \in \mathfrak{Z}(\mathscr{S})$ and g is $(\mathscr{S}^z, \mathscr{S}'^z)$-continuous by (1.4). ■

(5.2) ([2], Theorem 12). *For every syntopogenous structure $\mathscr{S}$, we have*

$$\mathscr{S}^z = \mathscr{S}^{tz} = \mathscr{S}^{t\sigma z}.$$

Proof. By (3.7) and (4.5) $\mathfrak{Z}(\mathscr{S}) = \mathfrak{Z}(\mathscr{S}^t) = \mathfrak{Z}(\mathscr{S}^{t\sigma})$. ■

(5.3) *If $\mathscr{S}$ is a symmetric syntopogenous structure, then $\mathscr{S} < \mathscr{S}^z$.*

Proof. Since $\mathscr{S} < \mathscr{S}^t$, $\mathscr{S}^t$ is symmetric by [1], (8.56) and $\mathscr{S}^z = \mathscr{S}^{tz}$ by (5.2), it suffices to consider a symmetric topogenous structure $\mathscr{T} = \{<\}$. Now $\mathscr{T} = \mathscr{T}^\sigma$ by (4.2), hence $A < B$ implies the existence of $f \in C(\mathscr{T})$ such that $0 \leqq f \leqq 1$, $f(x) = 0$ for $x \in A$, $f(x) = 1$ for $x \in X - B$. Then $A \subset C \subset B$ for $C = X(f < 1/2)$ and $C \in \mathfrak{Z}(\mathscr{T})^c$ by (3.4), so that $A <' B$ for $\{<'\} = \mathscr{T}^z$. ■

(5.4) *If $\mathscr{Z}$ is a z-structure then $\mathscr{Z}^{\sigma z} = \mathscr{Z}$.*

Proof. By (5.1) and (5.2)

$$\mathscr{Z} = \mathscr{Z}^z = \mathscr{Z}^{t\sigma z} = \mathscr{Z}^{\sigma z}$$

because $\mathscr{Z}$ is simple, hence $\mathscr{Z} = \mathscr{Z}^t$. ■

(5.5) *If $\mathscr{T}$ is a symmetric topogenous structure, $\mathscr{Z}$ is a z-structure, and $\mathscr{T}^z < \mathscr{Z}$, then $\mathscr{T} < \mathscr{Z}^\sigma$.*

Proof. By (5.3) $\mathscr{T} < \mathscr{T}^z < \mathscr{Z}$, and (4.2) can be applied. ■

(5.6) *If $\mathscr{T}$ is a symmetric topogenous structure then $\mathscr{T}^z = \mathscr{T}^\pi$. Consequently $\mathscr{T}^z = \mathscr{T}^{\sigma\pi}$ for an arbitrary topogenous structure, and $\mathscr{T}^{zp} = \mathscr{T}^{\sigma p} < \mathscr{T}^p$. Further $\mathscr{S}^z = \mathscr{S}^{t\sigma\pi}$ for every syntopogenous structure. A syntopogenous structure is a z-structure iff it is of the form $\mathscr{T}^\pi$ for a symmetric topogenous structure $\mathscr{T}$.*

Proof. Set $\mathscr{T} = \{<\}$, $\mathscr{T}^z = \{<'\}$. If $\mathscr{T}$ is symmetric and $A <' B$, then there is a $Z \in \mathfrak{Z}(\mathscr{T})$ such that $A \subset X - Z \subset B$. Hence $Z = Z(f), f \in C(\mathscr{T})$, and $Z = \bigcap_1^\infty C_n$ for the sets $C_n = X(|f| < 1/n)$. Since $\{0\} <_{1/n} (-1/n, 1/n)$, we have $Z < C_n$, $X - C_n < X - Z$, and

$X-Z=\bigcup_1^\infty (X-C_n)$ implies $X-Z<^\pi X-Z$ so that $A<^\pi_* B$. On the other hand, $<\subset<'$ by (5.3) and $<'^\pi=<^\pi$ by (1.8) and (1.9), hence $<^\pi\subset<$.

If $\mathscr{T}$ is an arbitrary topogenous structure, we have $\mathscr{T}^z=\mathscr{T}^{\sigma z}$ by (5.2) and $\mathscr{T}^\sigma$ is symmetric by (4.2), whence $\mathscr{T}^z=\mathscr{T}^{\sigma\pi}$, $\mathscr{T}^{zp}=\mathscr{T}^{\sigma\pi p}=\mathscr{T}^{\sigma p}$ by (2.2). Hence $\mathscr{T}^\sigma<\mathscr{T}$ implies $\mathscr{T}^{\sigma p}<\mathscr{T}^p$.

If $\mathscr{S}$ is a syntopogenous structure, then $\mathscr{S}^z=\mathscr{S}^{tz}$ by (5.2), whence $\mathscr{S}^z=\mathscr{S}^{t\sigma\pi}$. The last statement is obtained from (5.4) and (5.1). ■

By (5.5) $\mathscr{T}<\mathscr{T}^{z\sigma}$ for every symmetric topogenous structure $\mathscr{T}$, and $\mathscr{T}^{zp}=\mathscr{T}^p$ by (5.6), $\mathscr{T}^{z\sigma z}=\mathscr{T}^z$ by (5.4). Hence

$$\mathscr{T}^p=\mathscr{T}^{zp}=\mathscr{T}^{z\sigma zp}=\mathscr{T}^{z\sigma p} \tag{5.7}$$

again by (5.6). Thus $\mathscr{T}\neq\mathscr{T}^{z\sigma}$ whenever $\mathscr{T}$ is not associated with the finest proximity compatible with $\mathscr{T}^p$.

(5.8) ([2], Theorem 6). *A z-structure $\mathscr{Z}$ is perfect iff it is a perfectly normal topology, $\mathscr{Z}$ is symmetric iff $\mathscr{Z}=\mathscr{Z}(\mathfrak{Z})$ for a σ-algebra $\mathfrak{Z}$.*

Proof. Suppose $\mathscr{Z}$ is perfect. Then $\mathscr{Z}$, as a perfect topogenous space, is a topology, and if $\mathscr{Z}=\mathscr{Z}(\mathfrak{Z})$, then $\mathfrak{Z}$ coincides with the family of all sets closed with respect to $\mathscr{Z}$ (cf. [1], (7.20)). By (0.8) and (0.9) $\mathscr{Z}$ is perfectly normal.

Conversely if $\mathscr{T}$ is a perfectly normal topology, then $\mathscr{T}$ is generated by the family of all open sets, and that of all closed sets, denoted by $\mathfrak{Z}$, satisfies (0.5)–(0.9). Hence $\mathscr{T}$ is a perfect z-structure.

If $\mathscr{Z}$ is a symmetric z-structure, $\mathscr{Z}=\mathscr{Z}(\mathfrak{Z})=\{<\}$, then $Z\in\mathfrak{Z}$ implies $X-Z<X-Z$, hence $Z<Z$ and $X-Z\in\mathfrak{Z}$. From (0.5) and (0.7) we get that $\mathfrak{Z}$ is a σ-algebra. Conversely if $\mathfrak{Z}$ is a σ-algebra then it clearly satisfies (0.5)–(0.9) so that $\mathscr{Z}(\mathfrak{Z})$ is a z-structure. If $\mathscr{Z}(\mathfrak{Z})=\{<\}$ and $A<B$, then $A\subset X-Z\subset B$ for some $Z\in\mathfrak{Z}$, hence $X-B\subset Z\subset X-A$ and $X-Z\in\mathfrak{Z}$ so that $X-B<X-A$ and $\mathscr{Z}(\mathfrak{Z})$ is symmetric. ■

(5.9) *If $\mathscr{T}$ is a topology, then $\mathscr{T}^{zp}<\mathscr{T}$, $\mathscr{T}^{zpz}=\mathscr{T}^z$. $\mathscr{T}^{zp}=\mathscr{T}$ holds iff $\mathscr{T}$ is a uniformizable topology.*

Proof. By (5.6) $\mathscr{T}^{zp}=\mathscr{T}^{\sigma p}$. From (4.2) $\mathscr{T}^\sigma<\mathscr{T}$, hence if $\mathscr{T}^p=\mathscr{T}$ then $\mathscr{T}^{zp}=\mathscr{T}^{\sigma p}<$ $<\mathscr{T}^p=\mathscr{T}$. Thus by (5.1)

$$\mathscr{T}^{zpz}<\mathscr{T}^z=\mathscr{T}^{zz}<\mathscr{T}^{zpz}.$$

$\mathscr{T}^{zp}=\mathscr{T}$ iff $\mathscr{T}^{\sigma p}=\mathscr{T}$ iff $\mathscr{T}$ is a uniformizable topology by (4.7). ■

We shall describe the elements of $C(\mathscr{Z})$ for a z-structure $\mathscr{Z}$.

(5.10) *$\mathfrak{Z}(\mathscr{H})$ consists of all sets closed with respect to the topology $\mathscr{H}^{tp}$* (i.e. the euclidean topology of **R**).

Proof. If f is $(\mathscr{H}, \mathscr{H})$-continuous, then it is $(\mathscr{H}^{tp}, \mathscr{H}^{tp})$-continuous by [1], (10.12), hence $Z(f)$ is $\mathscr{H}^{tp}$-closed. Conversely if $F \subset \mathbf{R}$ is $\mathscr{H}^{tp}$-closed, then

$$f(x) = \inf\{|y-x| : y \in F\}$$

is clearly $(\mathscr{H}, \mathscr{H})$-continuous and $Z(f) = F$. ■

(5.11) *If* $\mathfrak{Z}$ *is a zero-set structure on* X, $\mathscr{Z} = \mathscr{Z}(\mathfrak{Z})$, *then* $C(\mathscr{Z})$ *consists of all functions* f *such that* $X(f \geqq c) \in \mathfrak{Z}$ *and* $X(f \leqq c) \in \mathfrak{Z}$ *for every* $c \in \mathbf{R}$.

Proof. If $f \in C(\mathscr{Z})$, then f is $(\mathscr{Z}, \mathscr{H})$-continuous, hence $(\mathscr{Z}, \mathscr{H}^z)$-continuous by (5.1) so that $f^{-1}(Z) \in \mathfrak{Z}$ for every $Z \in \mathfrak{Z}(\mathscr{H})$ (cf. (1.4)); in particular $X(f \geqq c) \in \mathfrak{Z}$ and $X(f \leqq c) \in \mathfrak{Z}$ by (5.10).

Conversely if all sets $X(f \geqq c)$ and $X(f \leqq c)$ belong to $\mathfrak{Z}$, then f is $(\mathscr{Z}, \mathscr{H}^z)$-continuous by (1.4) and (5.10), because each $\mathscr{H}^{tp}$-closed set is the countable intersection of finite unions of sets of the form $(-\infty, c]$ and $[c, +\infty)$. Thus f is $(\mathscr{Z}, \mathscr{H})$-continuous by [1], (10.10). ■

(5.12) *If* $\mathfrak{Z}$ *is a zero-set structure on* X, $\mathscr{Z} = \mathscr{Z}(\mathfrak{Z})$, *then* $\mathfrak{Z} = \mathfrak{Z}(\mathscr{Z})$.

Proof. By (5.11) $Z(f) \in \mathfrak{Z}$ for each $f \in C(\mathscr{Z})$. Conversely if $Z \in \mathfrak{Z}$, then $\mathscr{Z}^z = \mathscr{Z}$ implies that $Z = Z(f)$ for some $f \in C(\mathscr{Z})$. ■

6. Initial structures of z-structures

We begin with a simple remark concerning semi-topogenous orders generated by systems of sets:

(6.1) *Let* $<$ *be a semi-topogenous order on* X, *generated by a system* $\mathfrak{S}$ *of sets, and* $g: Y \to X$. *Then* $g^{-1}(<)$ *is generated by the system*

$$g^{-1}(\mathfrak{S}) = \{g^{-1}(S) : S \in \mathfrak{S}\}.$$

Proof. By [1], (6.2),

$$A g^{-1}(<) B \quad \text{iff} \quad g(A) < X - g(Y - B).$$

Hence $A g^{-1}(<) B$ iff $g(A) \subset S \subset X - g(Y-B)$ for some $S \in \mathfrak{S}$, i.e. iff $A \subset g^{-1}(S) \subset B$ for the same S. ■

Now we can prove that the inverse image of a z-structure is a z-structure:

(6.2) *Let* $\mathfrak{Z}$ *be a zero-set structure on* X, $\mathscr{Z} = \mathscr{Z}(\mathfrak{Z})$, $g: Y \to X$. *Then* $g^{-1}(\mathfrak{Z})$ *is a zero-set structure and*

$$g^{-1}(\mathscr{Z}) = \mathscr{Z}(g^{-1}(\mathfrak{Z})).$$

Proof. By (1.1) and (6.1) it suffices to prove that $g^{-1}(\mathfrak{Z})$ is a zero-set structure on Y.

Now we know from (5.1) that $\mathfrak{Z}=\mathfrak{Z}(\mathscr{Z})$, i.e. $\mathfrak{Z}$ coincides with all sets $Z(f)$ for $f \in C^*(\mathscr{Z})$. By (3.3) $C^*(\mathscr{Z})$ is a complete vector lattice containing all constants. We show that

$$\Phi = C^*(\mathscr{Z}) \circ g = \{f \circ g : f \in C^*(\mathscr{Z})\}$$

is a complete vector lattice as well, containing all constants. This is obvious except the completeness.

Suppose $f_n \in C^*(\mathscr{Z})$ and $f_n \circ g \to h$ uniformly. By passing over to a subsequence we can assume

$$|f_n \circ g - h| \leqq 2^{-n-1}$$

for $n \in \mathbf{N}$. By denoting $h_1 = f_1$, $h_{n+1} = f_{n+1} - f_n$, we have

$$h = \sum_1^\infty h_n \circ g\,, \quad |h_n \circ g| \leqq 2^{-n} \quad (n>1)\,.$$

Define $k_1 = h_1$,

$$k_n = \max(-2^{-n}, \min(h_n, 2^{-n})) \quad (n>1)\,.$$

Then clearly $h_n, k_n \in C^*(\mathscr{Z})$, and $h_n \circ g = k_n \circ g \quad (n \in \mathbf{N})$. Moreover,

$$\sum_1^\infty k_n = k \in C^*(\mathscr{Z})$$

because the series converges uniformly. Hence $h = k \circ g$, $h \in \Phi$.

This being established, the system

$$\mathfrak{Z}' = \{Z(h) : h \in \Phi\}$$

is a zero-set structure by (3.5). Since $Z(f \circ g) = g^{-1}(Z(f))$, we obtain $\mathfrak{Z}' = g^{-1}(\mathfrak{Z})$. ■

Observe that the validity of each of the conditions (0.5)–(0.8) obviously implies its validity for $g^{-1}(\mathfrak{Z})$ instead of $\mathfrak{Z}$. However, this is not true for (0.9), as is shown by an injective map and the system of all closed sets of a normal but not hereditarily normal topology.

(6.3) *Let* $[X, \mathscr{S}]$ *be a syntopogenous space and* $g: Y \to X$. *Then*

(6.4) $$g^{-1}(\mathscr{S}^z) < g^{-1}(\mathscr{S})^z\,.$$

Proof. Obviously $C(\mathscr{S}) \circ g \subset C(g^{-1}(\mathscr{S}))$ by [1], (10.7) and (10.16), hence $Z \in \mathfrak{Z}(\mathscr{S})$ implies $g^{-1}(Z) \in \mathfrak{Z}(g^{-1}(\mathscr{S}))$. By (6.2) $g^{-1}(\mathscr{S}^z)$ consists of $<(g^{-1}(\mathfrak{Z}(\mathscr{S}))$, and this in turn is coarser than $<(\mathfrak{Z}(g^{-1}(\mathscr{S}))$, the only element of $g^{-1}(\mathscr{S})^z$. ■

In general, the symbol $<$ cannot be replaced by equality in (6.4). In fact, let $[Y, \mathscr{T}']$ be a discrete topological space, Y uncountable, and $[X, \mathscr{T}]$ the one-point compactification of $[Y, \mathscr{T}']$, $X = Y \cup \{p\}$. Then $\mathfrak{Z}(\mathscr{T}')$ consists of all subsets of Y, while the elements of $\mathfrak{Z}(\mathscr{T})$ are closed G_δ-s, hence either finite subsets of Y or sets containing p and having a countable complement (observe that an open neighbourhood of p has finite complement). Hence $g^{-1}(\mathscr{T}) = \mathscr{T}'$, $g^{-1}(\mathfrak{Z}(\mathscr{T})) \neq \mathfrak{Z}(\mathscr{T}')$, $g^{-1}(\mathscr{T}^z) \neq \mathscr{T}'^5$ for the canonical injection $g: Y \to X$.

There are, however, two important cases when equality is valid in (6.4):

(6.5) *If* $[X, \mathscr{S}]$ *is a syntopogenous space,* $\mathscr{S} < \mathscr{S}^z$, $g: Y \to X$, *then*

$$g^{-1}(\mathscr{S}^z) = g^{-1}(\mathscr{S})^z .$$

Proof. The assumption $\mathscr{S} < \mathscr{S}^z$ implies $g^{-1}(\mathscr{S}) < g^{-1}(\mathscr{S}^z)$ by [1], (9.3), hence

$$g^{-1}(\mathscr{S})^z < g^{-1}(\mathscr{S}^z)^z = g^{-1}(\mathscr{S}^z)$$

by (5.1) and (6.2). Then (6.3) can be applied. ■

By (5.3), the hypothesis of (6.5) is fulfilled in particular if $\mathscr{S}$ is symmetric.

For the other statement, similar to (6.5), let us first prove the following lemma:

(6.6) *Let* $[X, \mathscr{S}]$ *and* $[Z, \mathscr{S}']$ *be syntopogenous spaces,* $\mathscr{S}'$ *separated, and* $g: Y \to X$ *surjective. Then each* $(g^{-1}(\mathscr{S}), \mathscr{S}')$*-continuous map* h *can be factorized in the form* $h = f \circ g$ *with an* $(\mathscr{S}, \mathscr{S}')$*-continuous* f.

Proof. If $x, y \in Y$, $h(x) \neq h(y)$, then there is a $<' \in \mathscr{S}'$ such that, say, $h(x) <' Z - \{h(y)\}$, and then a $< \in \mathscr{S}$ such that

$$h^{-1}(h(x)) g^{-1}(<) Y - h^{-1}(h(y))$$

and a fortiori

$$x g^{-1}(<) Y - \{y\}, \quad g(x) < X - \{g(y)\}, \quad g(x) \neq g(y) .$$

In other words, $g(x) = g(y)$ implies $h(x) = h(y)$. Therefore there exists a map $f: X \to Z$ satisfying $h = f \circ g$. Now select, for a given $<' \in \mathscr{S}'$, an order $< \in \mathscr{S}$ satisfying $h^{-1}(<') \subset g^{-1}(<)$. Then $A <' B$ implies

$$h^{-1}(A) g^{-1}(<) h^{-1}(B) ,$$

i.e.

$$g(h^{-1}(A)) < X - g(Y - h^{-1}(B)) .$$

Since g is surjective,

$$g(h^{-1}(A)) = g(g^{-1}(f^{-1}(A)) = f^{-1}(A) ,$$

$$g(Y - h^{-1}(B)) = g(g^{-1}(f^{-1}(Z - B))) = f^{-1}(Z - B) ,$$

so that $f^{-1}(A) < f^{-1}(B)$. This shows the $(\mathscr{S}, \mathscr{S}')$-continuity of f. ■

(6.7) *If* $[X, \mathcal{S}]$ *is a syntopogenous space and* $g: Y \to X$ *is a surjective map, then*

$$C(g^{-1}(\mathcal{S})) = C(\mathcal{S}) \circ g, \quad C^*(g^{-1}(\mathcal{S})) = C^*(\mathcal{S}) \circ g.$$

$$\mathfrak{Z}(g^{-1}(\mathcal{S})) = g^{-1}(\mathfrak{Z}(\mathcal{S})),$$

consequently

$$g^{-1}(\mathcal{S}^z) = g^{-1}(\mathcal{S})^z.$$

Proof. The first three equalities are obtained from (6.6) for $[Z, \mathcal{S}'] = [\mathbf{R}, \mathcal{H}]$ because $C(\mathcal{S}) \circ g \subset C(g^{-1}(\mathcal{S}))$ is obvious. ■

Now we turn to the study of suprema of z-structures.

(6.8) *Let* $\mathcal{S}_i$ $(i \in I \neq \emptyset)$ *be syntopogenous structures on* X. *Then*

$$(\bigvee_{i \in I} \mathcal{S}_i^z)^z < (\bigvee_{i \in I} \mathcal{S}_i)^z.$$

If $\mathcal{S}_i < \mathcal{S}_i^z$ *for each* $i \in I$, *then*

$$(\bigvee_{i \in I} \mathcal{S}_i^z)^z = (\bigvee_{i \in I} \mathcal{S}_i)^z.$$

In particular, for z-structures $\mathcal{Z}_i$ *on* X, $(\bigvee_{i \in I} \mathcal{Z}_i)^z$ *is the coarsest z-structure on X finer than each* $\mathcal{Z}_i$.

Proof. Denote $\bigvee_{i \in I} \mathcal{S}_i = \mathcal{S}$. Then $\mathcal{S}_i < \mathcal{S}$ for every i, hence $\mathcal{S}_i^z < \mathcal{S}^z$ by (5.1), further $\bigvee_{i \in I} \mathcal{S}_i^z < \mathcal{S}^z$ by [1], (8.89), so that by (5.1)

$$(\bigvee_{i \in I} \mathcal{S}_i^z)^z < \mathcal{S}^{zz} = \mathcal{S}^z.$$

If $\mathcal{S}_i < \mathcal{S}_i^z$ for each i, then

$$\mathcal{S} = \bigvee_{i \in I} \mathcal{S}_i < \bigvee_{i \in I} \mathcal{S}_i^z$$

and

$$\mathcal{S}^z < (\bigvee_{i \in I} \mathcal{S}_i^z)^z.$$

For z-structures $\mathcal{Z}_i$, we have $\mathcal{Z}_i < \bigvee_{i \in I} \mathcal{Z}_i$ for each i, hence

$$\mathcal{Z}_i = \mathcal{Z}_i^z < (\bigvee_{i \in I} \mathcal{Z}_i)^z = \mathcal{Z}$$

so that $\mathscr{Z}$ is a z-structure finer than each $\mathscr{Z}_i$. Conversely if $\mathscr{Z}'$ is a z-structure finer than each $\mathscr{Z}_i$, then

$$\bigvee_{i\in I} \mathscr{Z}_i < \mathscr{Z}', \quad \mathscr{Z} = (\bigvee_{i\in I} \mathscr{Z}_i)^z < \mathscr{Z}'^z = \mathscr{Z}'. \blacksquare$$

We can add the following construction to the last statement:

(6.9) *Let* $\mathfrak{Z}_i$ $(i\in I\neq\emptyset)$ *be zero-set structures on* X, $\mathscr{Z}_i = \mathscr{Z}(\mathfrak{Z}_i)$, $\mathscr{Z} = (\bigvee_{i\in I} \mathscr{Z}_i)^z$, $\mathscr{Z} = \mathscr{Z}(\mathfrak{Z})$. *Then* $\mathfrak{Z}$ *consists of all countable intersections of finite unions of elements of the system* $\mathfrak{S} = \bigcup_{i\in I} \mathfrak{Z}_i$.

Proof. By (6.8) $\mathscr{Z}_i < \mathscr{Z}$ for each i, hence clearly $\mathfrak{Z}_i \subset \mathfrak{Z}$. Of course, the finite unions of elements of $\mathfrak{S}$ and all countable intersections of these unions belong to $\mathfrak{Z}$.

Conversely if $Z\in\mathfrak{Z}$, then $Z = Z(f)$ for some $f\in C(\mathscr{S})$ where $\mathscr{S} = \bigvee_{i\in I} \mathscr{Z}_i$. Consider the sets $C_n = X(|f| < 1/n)$. Since $(-\infty, -1/n]\cup[1/n, +\infty) <_{1/n} \mathbf{R} - \{0\}$ on the real line, there exists, for a given n, an order $<_n \in \mathscr{S}$ satisfying $X - C_n <_n X - Z$, and by [1], (8.89)

$$<_n = (\bigcup_{j=1}^{k_n} <_{nj})^q$$

for suitable orders $\{<_{nj}\} = \mathscr{Z}_{i_{nj}}$. Therefore by [1], (3.6), we have

$$X - C_n = \bigcup_{s=1}^{p_n} A_{ns}, \quad X - Z = \bigcap_{t=1}^{q_n} B_{nt}, \quad A_{ns} <_{nj(n,s,t)} B_{nt}$$

for suitable p_n, q_n, A_{ns}, B_{nt} and $j(n, s, t)$. Thus

$$A_{ns} \subset X - Z_{nst} \subset B_{nt} \quad (Z_{nst} \in \mathfrak{Z}_{i_{nj(n,s,t)}}),$$

and

$$A_{ns} \subset \bigcap_{t=1}^{q_n} (X - Z_{nst}) = X - \bigcup_{t=1}^{q_n} Z_{nst} \subset \bigcap_{t=1}^{q_n} B_{nt} = X - Z,$$

$$X - C_n \subset \bigcup_{s=1}^{p_n} (X - \bigcup_{t=1}^{q_n} Z_{nst}) = X - \bigcap_{s=1}^{p_n} \bigcup_{t=1}^{q_n} Z_{nst} \subset X - Z;$$

since $Z = \bigcap_1^\infty C_n$, we have

$$X - Z = X - \bigcap_{n=1}^{\infty} \bigcap_{s=1}^{p_n} \bigcup_{t=1}^{q_n} Z_{nst}, \quad Z_{nst} \in \mathfrak{S}. \blacksquare$$

(6.10) *Let* $[X_i, \mathscr{Z}_i]$ *be z-spaces for* $i \in I \neq \emptyset$, *and* $g_i: X \to X_i$ *be given maps. Then*

$$\mathscr{Z} = (\bigvee_{i \in I} g_i^{-1}(\mathscr{Z}_i))^z$$

is the coarsest z-structure $\mathscr{Z}'$ *on* X *such that every* g_i *is* $(\mathscr{Z}', \mathscr{Z}_i)$*-continuous.*

Proof. The map g_i is $(g_i^{-1}(\mathscr{Z}_i), \mathscr{Z}_i)$-continuous by [1], (10.16), hence $(\mathscr{Z}, \mathscr{Z}_i)$-continuous by [1], (10.10) and (5.1). Conversely if each g_i is $(\mathscr{Z}', \mathscr{Z}_i)$-continuous for a z-structure $\mathscr{Z}'$, then $g_i^{-1}(\mathscr{Z}_i) < \mathscr{Z}'$ for $i \in I$ and $\mathscr{Z} < \mathscr{Z}'$ by (6.8). ■

In particular, we get from [1], (11.4):

(6.11) *Let* $[X_i, \mathscr{Z}_i]$ *be z-spaces for* $i \in I \neq \emptyset$, $X = \mathsf{X}_{i \in I} X_i$. *Then*

$$\mathscr{Z} = (\mathsf{X}_{i \in I} \mathscr{Z}_i)^z$$

is the coarsest z-structure $\mathscr{Z}'$ *on* X *such that each projection* $p_i: X \to X_i$ *is* $(\mathscr{Z}', \mathscr{Z}_i)$*-continuous.* ■

(6.12) *If* $[X_i, \mathscr{S}_i]$ *are syntopogenous spaces for* $i \in I \neq \emptyset$, *and* $\mathscr{S}_i < \mathscr{S}_i^z$ *for each i, then*

$$(\mathsf{X}_{i \in I} \mathscr{S}_i)^z = (\mathsf{X}_{i \in I} \mathscr{S}_i^z)^z .$$

Proof. [1], (11.4) shows that

$$\mathsf{X}_{i \in I} \mathscr{S}_i = \bigvee_{i \in I} p_i^{-1}(\mathscr{S}_i), \quad \mathsf{X}_{i \in I} \mathscr{S}_i^z = \bigvee_{i \in I} p_i^{-1}(\mathscr{S}_i^z)$$

for the projections p_i. Now

$$p_i^{-1}(\mathscr{S}_i^z) = p_i^{-1}(\mathscr{S}_i)^z$$

by (6.5) or (6.7), further $\mathscr{S}_i < \mathscr{S}_i^z$ implies

$$p_i^{-1}(\mathscr{S}_i) < p_i^{-1}(\mathscr{S}_i^z) = p_i^{-1}(\mathscr{S}_i)^z$$

by [1], (9.3), hence (6.8) furnishes the statement. ■

7. z-refined syntopogenous structures

We saw several times that syntopogenous structures $\mathscr{S}$ satisfying $\mathscr{S} < \mathscr{S}^z$ possess special advantageous properties. Let us call *z-refined* a structure of this kind. By (5.1) each z-structure, (5.3) each symmetric syntopogenous structure is z-refined. According to (5.8) and (5.9), if $\mathscr{T}$ is a topology but not perfectly normal, then $\mathscr{T}$ is not z-refined.

(7.1) ([2], Theorem 10). *If $\mathscr{S}$ is a z-refined syntopogenous structure, then $\mathscr{S}^z$ is the coarsest z-structure finer than $\mathscr{S}$.*

Proof. If $\mathscr{S} < \mathscr{Z}$ for a z-structure $\mathscr{Z}$ then $\mathscr{S}^z < \mathscr{Z}^z = \mathscr{Z}$ by (5.1). ■

(7.2) *$\mathscr{S}$ is z-refined iff $\mathscr{S}^t$ is z-refined.*

Proof. $\mathscr{S} < \mathscr{S}^z$ implies $\mathscr{S}^t < \mathscr{S}^{zt} = \mathscr{S}^z = \mathscr{S}^{tz}$ by (5.2). Conversely $\mathscr{S}^t < \mathscr{S}^{tz}$ implies

$$\mathscr{S} < \mathscr{S}^t < \mathscr{S}^{tz} = \mathscr{S}^z. \ ■$$

(7.3) *If $\mathscr{S}$ is z-refined on X and $g: Y \to X$, then $g^{-1}(\mathscr{S})$ is z-refined.*

Proof. $g^{-1}(\mathscr{S}) < g^{-1}(\mathscr{S}^z) = g^{-1}(\mathscr{S})^z$ by (6.5). ■

(7.4) *If $\mathscr{S}_i$ are z-refined on X for $i \in I \neq \emptyset$, then $\mathscr{S} = \bigvee_{i \in I} \mathscr{S}_i$ is z-refined.*

Proof. By hypothesis

$$\bigvee_{i \in I} \mathscr{S}_i < \bigvee_{i \in I} \mathscr{S}_i^z,$$

and $\mathscr{S}_i^z < \bigvee_{i \in I} \mathscr{S}_i^z$ implies by (6.8)

$$\mathscr{S}_i^z = \mathscr{S}_i^{zz} < \bigvee_{i \in I} \mathscr{S}_i^z)^z = (\bigvee_{i \in I} \mathscr{S}_i)^z.$$

Finally

$$\bigvee_{i \in I} \mathscr{S}_i^z < \bigvee_{i \in I} \mathscr{S}_i)^z. \ ■$$

(7.5) *If $[X_i, \mathscr{S}_i]$ are syntopogenous spaces for $i \in I \neq \emptyset$ and each $\mathscr{S}_i$ is z-refined, then $\mathsf{X}_{i \in I} \mathscr{S}_i$ is z-refined.*

Proof. [1], (11.4), (7.3) and (7.4). ■

Conversely, we can prove:

(7.6) *If $\mathsf{X}_{i \in I} \mathscr{S}_i$ is z-refined, then so is each $\mathscr{S}_i$.*

Proof. By [1], (11.29), $[X_i, \mathscr{S}_i]$ is isomorphic to a subspace of $[\mathsf{X}_{i \in I} X_i, \mathsf{X}_{i \in I} \mathscr{S}_i]$, and (7.3) can be applied. ■

The following example shows that there exist topogenous structures $\mathscr{T}$ such that neither $\mathscr{T} < \mathscr{T}^z$ nor $\mathscr{T}^z < \mathscr{T}$ is true. Let $X = \mathbf{R}$ and $<_\varepsilon^+$ denote the (biperfect) topogenous order on $\mathbf{R}$ defined by

$$A <_\varepsilon^+ B \quad \text{iff} \quad S^+(A, \varepsilon) = \bigcup_{x \in A} [x, x+\varepsilon) \subset B\,.$$

For $\mathscr{T} = \mathscr{S}^t$ we have $C^*(\mathscr{T}) = C^*(\mathscr{S})$ by (3.7) where $\mathscr{S}$ denotes the syntopogenous structure composed of all orders $<_\varepsilon^+$. On the other hand $C(\mathscr{S}) = C(\mathscr{H})$ since $S^+(A, \varepsilon) \subset S(A, \varepsilon)$ for every $A \subset \mathbf{R}$, hence $<_\varepsilon \subset <_\varepsilon^+$, $\mathscr{H} < \mathscr{S}$ and $C(\mathscr{H}) \subset C(\mathscr{S})$, while an $(\mathscr{S}, \mathscr{H})$-continuous f is $(\mathscr{H}, \mathscr{H})$-continuous because if $x \leqq y < x + \delta$ implies $|f(y) - f(x)| < \varepsilon$ for some $\varepsilon > 0$, $\delta > 0$ and every $x, y \in \mathbf{R}$, then $|y - x| < \delta$ implies $|f(y) - f(x)| < \varepsilon$ as well. Therefore $\mathfrak{Z}(\mathscr{T}) = \mathfrak{Z}(\mathscr{S}) = \mathfrak{Z}(\mathscr{H})$, which coincides with the system of all closed sets in $\mathbf{R}$ with respect to the euclidean topology $\mathscr{T}_0$ (cf. (5.10)). Hence $\mathscr{T}^z$ is the euclidean topology itself by (1.1). Now $\{0\} <_1^+ [0, 1)$, hence $\{0\} < [0, 1)$ for $\{<\} = \mathscr{T}$, but there is no $\mathscr{T}_0$-open set G satisfying $0 \in G \subset [0, 1)$. On the other hand $(0, 1)$ is $\mathscr{T}_0$-open but $(0, 1)$ $<_\varepsilon^+$ $(0, 1)$ does not hold for any $\varepsilon > 0$.

The same example shows that $\mathscr{T}^{zp} \neq \mathscr{T}^p$ in general (cf. (5.6)) for a topogenous structure $\mathscr{T}$. In fact, $\mathscr{T}^{zp}$ is the euclidean topology of the real line while $\mathscr{T}^p$ clearly coincides with the topology of the Sorgenfrey line (for which the intervals $[a, b)$ constitute a base).

However, the above equality is valid for z-refined topogenous structures:

(7.7) *If $\mathscr{T}$ is a z-refined topogenous structure then $\mathscr{T}^{zp} = \mathscr{T}^p$.*

Proof. By (5.6) $\mathscr{T}^{zp} < \mathscr{T}^p$. On the other hand if $\mathscr{T} < \mathscr{T}^z$ then obviously $\mathscr{T}^p < \mathscr{T}^{zp}$. ■

The following propositions contribute to the characterization of z-refined structures; according to (7.2) it is enough to consider topogenous structures.

(7.8) *A z-refined topogenous structure is semi-symmetric.*

Proof. By (5.6) $\mathscr{T} < \mathscr{T}^z$ implies $\mathscr{T} < \mathscr{T}^{\sigma\pi}$. Now $\mathscr{T}^\sigma < \mathscr{T}$ and $\mathscr{T}^\sigma$ is symmetric by (4.2), hence $\mathscr{T}^{\sigma c} = \mathscr{T}^\sigma < \mathscr{T}^c$ by [1], (2.11), and $\mathscr{T}^{\sigma\pi} < \mathscr{T}^{c\pi}$ by (2.1) so that $\mathscr{T} < \mathscr{T}^{c\pi}$. ■

Conversely we can prove:.

(7.9) ([2], Theorem 11). *A semi-symmetric and normal topogenous structure is z-refined.*

Proof. Let $\mathscr{T} = \{<\}$ be semi-symmetric and normal. If $A < B$ then there is a C such that $A < C < B$, then, by $< \subset <^{c\pi}$, $A = \bigcup_1^\infty A_n$ and $A_n <^c C$ for every $n \in \mathbf{N}$. Now by (4.4) $A_n <^c < B$ implies $A_n <' B$ where $\{<'\} = \mathscr{T}^\sigma$. Hence $A <'^\pi B$, i.e. $\mathscr{T} < \mathscr{T}^{\sigma\pi} = \mathscr{T}^z$ by (5.6). ■

It would be interesting to know whether there exist non-normal z-refined topogenous structures.

8. The operation y

Let us consider, for an arbitrary syntopogenous structure $\mathscr{S}$, the operation

$$\mathscr{S}^y = \mathscr{S}^{z\sigma}. \tag{8.1}$$

(8.2) ([2], Theorem 13). *$\mathscr{S}^y$ is the finest symmetric topogenous structure $\mathscr{T}$ satisfying $\mathscr{T}^z = \mathscr{S}^z$.*

Proof. By (4.2) $\mathscr{S}^y$ is a symmetric topogenous structure and $\mathscr{S}^{yz} = \mathscr{S}^{z\sigma z} = \mathscr{S}^z$ by (5.4). If $\mathscr{T}$ is a symmetric topogenous structure such that $\mathscr{T}^z = \mathscr{S}^z$ then $\mathscr{T} < \mathscr{S}^{z\sigma} = \mathscr{S}^y$ by (5.5). ■

(8.3) ([2], Theorem 14). *If $\mathscr{S}$ is a syntopogenous structure, then*

$$\mathscr{S}^{yy} = \mathscr{S}^y, \quad \mathscr{S}^{yp} = \mathscr{S}^{zp}.$$

If $[X, \mathscr{S}]$ and $[X', \mathscr{S}']$ are syntopogenous spaces and $f: X \to X'$ is $(\mathscr{S}, \mathscr{S}')$-continuous then it is $(\mathscr{S}^y, \mathscr{S}'^y)$-continuous; in particular, $\mathscr{S}_1 < \mathscr{S}_2$ implies $\mathscr{S}_1^y < \mathscr{S}_2^y$.

Proof. $\mathscr{S}^{yy} = \mathscr{S}^{yz\sigma} = \mathscr{S}^{z\sigma} = \mathscr{S}^y$ by (8.2). $\mathscr{S}^{yp} = \mathscr{S}^{y\sigma p} = \mathscr{S}^{yzp}$ by (5.6) since $\mathscr{S}^y$ is a symmetric topogenous structure. The remaining part follows from (5.1) and (4.3). ■

(8.4) ([2], Theorem 16) *For a topogenous structure $\mathscr{T}$, the equality $\mathscr{T}^{yp} = \mathscr{T}$ holds iff $\mathscr{T}$ is a uniformizable topology.*

Proof. (8.3) and (5.9). ■

Let us call a topogenous structure $\mathscr{T}$ a *y-structure* iff it fulfils $\mathscr{T}^y = \mathscr{T}$. A syntopogenous structure $\mathscr{S}$ will be said to be *y-refined* iff $\mathscr{S} < \mathscr{S}^y$.

(8.5) ([2], Theorem 15). *If $\mathscr{S}$ is a y-refined syntopogenous structure, then $\mathscr{S}^y$ is the coarsest y-structure finer than $\mathscr{S}$. Every symmetric syntopogenous structure is y-refined and every y-refined structure is z-refined.*

Proof. If $\mathscr{S} < \mathscr{S}^y$ then $\mathscr{S}^y$ is, by (8.3), a y-structure finer than $\mathscr{S}$. If $\mathscr{T}$ is a y-structure finer than $\mathscr{S}$ then $\mathscr{S} < \mathscr{T}$ implies $\mathscr{S}^y < \mathscr{T}^y = \mathscr{T}$. If $\mathscr{S}$ is symmetric then $\mathscr{S}^y = \mathscr{S}^{z\sigma} = \mathscr{S}^{tz\sigma}$ and $\mathscr{S} < \mathscr{S}^t < \mathscr{S}^{tz\sigma}$ by (5.5). Finally by (4.2) $\mathscr{S} < \mathscr{S}^y = \mathscr{S}^{z\sigma}$ implies $\mathscr{S} < \mathscr{S}^z$. ■

It would be interesting to know whether there exist non-symmetric y-refined structures.

References

[1] Á. Császár, *Foundations of general topology*, Budapest—Oxford—London—New York—Paris, 1963.
[2] Á. Császár, Topogenous spaces and zero-set spaces, *Abh. Akad. Wiss. DDR*, 1979, Nr. 4N, 19–24.
[3] Á. Császár, Normality is productive, *Colloquia Soc. J. Bolyai*, **23** (1978), 323–341.
[4] Á. Császár and M. Laczkovich, Some remarks on discrete Baire classes, *Acta Math. Acad. Sci. Hung.*, **33** (1979), 51–70.
[5] H. Gordon, Rings of functions determined by zero-sets, *Pacific J. Math.*, **36** (1971), 133–157.

EÖTVÖS LORÁND UNIVERSITY
H-1088 BUDAPEST MÚZEUM KRT. 6–8.
HUNGARY

Studies in Pure Mathematics
To the Memory of Paul Turán

Automata on one symbol

by

J. DÉNES, (Budapest), K. H. KIM* and F. W. ROUSH* (Montgomery)

Abstract

We obtain bounds on the number of states of a one symbol deterministic automaton needed for the automaton to be equivalent to an arbitrary nondeterministic automaton on n states. We conjecture that they are best possible.

1. Introduction

In this paper we use the concepts of Boolean matrix and binary relation interchangeably. Let B_n denote the set of $n\times n$ Boolean matrices and $\mathbf{n}$ the set $\{1, 2, \ldots, n\}$.

Definition 1. An *n-state, one symbol, nondeterministic automation* $\bar{A}$ is a triple $(\mathbf{A}, \mathbf{I}, \mathbf{F})$ where $\mathbf{A}\in B_n$ and I, $F\subset\mathbf{n}$. An integer $j\geqq 0$ is said to be *good* for $\bar{A}$ if and only if $\mathbf{I}\mathbf{A}^j\cap\mathbf{F}\neq\emptyset$. An *n-state, one symbol, deterministic automaton* D is a triple $(\Theta, \mathbf{i}, \mathbf{F})$ where Θ is a transformation on $\mathbf{n}$, $\mathbf{i}\in\mathbf{n}$ and $F\subset\mathbf{n}$. An integer $j\geqq 0$ is a said to be *good* for D if and only if $\Theta^j(\mathbf{i})\in\mathbf{F}$. Two n-state, one symbol automata are said to be equivalent if an integer $j\geqq 0$ is good for one if and only if it is good for the other.

These definitions can conveniently be recast into a form which involves only Boolean vectors and matrices. By a Boolean matrix we mean a matrix whose elements belong to two element Boolean algebra $\beta=\{0, 1\}$. For example, $0+0=0\cdot 0=$ $=1\cdot 0=0\cdot 1=0$, $1+1=0+1=1+0=1$.

If

$$\mathbf{A}=\begin{bmatrix}1 & 0 & 1\\ 0 & 0 & 1\\ 1 & 1 & 0\end{bmatrix},\qquad \mathbf{B}=\begin{bmatrix}0 & 0 & 1\\ 1 & 0 & 1\\ 0 & 1 & 1\end{bmatrix},$$

then

$$\mathbf{A}+\mathbf{B}=\begin{bmatrix}1 & 0 & 1\\ 1 & 0 & 1\\ 1 & 1 & 1\end{bmatrix},\qquad \mathbf{AB}=\begin{bmatrix}0 & 1 & 1\\ 0 & 1 & 1\\ 1 & 0 & 1\end{bmatrix},$$

* This research was supported in part by Alabama State University Faculty Research Grant R-18-6.

An n-state, one symbol, nondeterministic automaton is a triple $(\mathbf{v}, \mathbf{A}, \mathbf{w})$ where $\mathbf{A} \in B_n$, $\mathbf{v}$ is a row vector and $\mathbf{w}$ is a column vector. An n-state, one symbol, deterministic automaton is a triple $(\mathbf{v}, \mathbf{A}, \mathbf{w})$ such that $\mathbf{A}$ is the matrix of a transformation, i.e. has exactly one 1 entry per row, and $\mathbf{v}$ has exactly one 1 entry. Two automata are equivalent if and only if the series of numbers $\mathbf{v}\mathbf{A}^j\mathbf{w}$ coincide.

Definition 2. The *index* of a Boolean matrix $\mathbf{A}$ is the least positive integer k such that $\mathbf{A}^{k+d} = \mathbf{A}^k$ for some positive integer d. The *period* of $\mathbf{A}$ is the least positive integer d such that $\mathbf{A}^{k+d} = \mathbf{A}^k$ for some positive integer k. The period of an automaton $\bar{A}$ is the least positive integer d such that $\mathbf{v}\mathbf{A}^{j+d}\mathbf{w} = \mathbf{v}\mathbf{A}^j\mathbf{w}$ for all sufficiently large j. The index of an automaton $\bar{A}$ is the least integer $k \geqq 0$ such that $\mathbf{v}\mathbf{A}^{j+d}\mathbf{w} = \mathbf{v}\mathbf{A}^j\mathbf{w}$ for all $j \geqq k$, where d is the period of $\bar{A}$. The index of an automaton, but not a matrix, may be zero. The index and period of $\bar{A}$ cannot exceed the index and period of $\mathbf{A}$.

Example 1. The automaton

$$(0 \quad 0 \quad 1), \quad \begin{bmatrix} 0 & 1 & 0 \\ 1 & 0 & 0 \\ 1 & 0 & 1 \end{bmatrix}, \quad \begin{bmatrix} 0 \\ 1 \\ 0 \end{bmatrix}$$

has index 2 and period 1. The matrix $\mathbf{A}$ has index 2 and period 2.

It can be observed that the minimum number of states required by a deterministic automaton equivalent to $\bar{A}$ is

$$\text{index } \bar{A} + \text{period } \bar{A} .$$

For background on automata, see MANDL [1] and MARKOWSKY [2]. The interested reader can find further details on Boolean matrices considered as adjacency matrices of graphs in [6].

2. Preliminary results

Definition 3. A Boolean matrix $\mathbf{A}$ is *indecomposable* if and only if there does not exist a permutation matrix $\mathbf{P}$ such that $\mathbf{P}\mathbf{A}\mathbf{P}^T$ has the form

$$\begin{bmatrix} * & 0 \\ * & * \end{bmatrix}$$

where the diagonal blocks are square.

It is known that for any Boolean matrix $\mathbf{A}$ there exists a permutation matrix $\mathbf{P}$ such that $\mathbf{P}\mathbf{A}\mathbf{P}^T$ has the form

$$\begin{bmatrix} \mathbf{A}_{11} & 0 & \cdots & 0 \\ * & \mathbf{A}_{22} & \cdots & 0 \\ & \cdots & \cdots & \\ * & * & \cdots & \mathbf{A}_{mm} \end{bmatrix}$$

where each $\mathbf{A}_{ii}$ is indecomposable or is zero (see SCHWARZ [5], ROSENBLATT [4]). Here $\mathbf{P}^T$ denotes the transpose of $\mathbf{P}$.

For any indecomposable matrix $\mathbf{A}$ there exists a permutation matrix $\mathbf{Q}$ such that $\mathbf{QAQ}^T$ has the form

$$\begin{bmatrix} 0 & \mathbf{A}_{12} & 0 & \dots & 0 \\ 0 & 0 & \mathbf{A}_{23} & \dots & 0 \\ 0 & 0 & 0 & \dots & 0 \\ & \dots & \dots & \dots & \\ \mathbf{A}_{d1} & 0 & 0 & \dots & 0 \end{bmatrix}$$

where d is the period of $\mathbf{A}$. So the period of an indecomposable matrix cannot exceed its dimension (see MINC [3]).

Lemma 1. *Let* $\mathbf{A}$ *be a matrix in block triangular form whose main diagonal blocks are indecomposable matrices or zero. Suppose that the* $\mathbf{A}_{ii}$ *and* $\mathbf{A}_{jj}$ *blocks are nonzero and have relatively prime periods. Then the block* $\mathbf{A}_{ij}^{(e)}$ *is either zero for all e or is completely filled with ones for all sufficiently large k.*

Proof. The blocks $\mathbf{A}_{ii}$ and $\mathbf{A}_{jj}$, being indecomposable, must have at least one 1 in each row and column. Therefore the blocks $\mathbf{A}_{ii}^{(e)}$ and $\mathbf{A}_{jj}^{(e)}$ must have at least one 1 in each row and column. And

$$\mathbf{A}_{ij}^{(e)} \geqq \mathbf{A}_{ij}^{(e-i)} \mathbf{A}_{ij}^{(m)}$$

will then be nonzero for all $e \geqq m$, if $\mathbf{A}_{ij}^{(m)}$ is nonzero for any m. Let $G(\mathbf{A}_{ii})$ denote the cyclic group consisting of all $\mathbf{A}_{ii}^{(e)}$ for $e >$ index $\mathbf{A}_{ii}$ and let $G(\mathbf{A}_{jj})$ be the corresponding group. Let d_1, d_2 be the orders of $G(\mathbf{A}_{ii})$ and $G(\mathbf{A}_{jj})$ and let g_1, g_2 be the generators of the respective groups.

Suppose that $\mathbf{A}_{ij}^{(m)}$ is nonzero. Then

$$\mathbf{A}_{ij}^{(e)} \geqq \sum (\mathbf{A}_{ii})^{e-m-t} \mathbf{A}_{ij}^{(m)} (\mathbf{A}_{jj})^t .$$

This implies that for large e, (since $(d_1, d_2) = 1$)

$$\mathbf{A}_{ij}^{(e)} \geqq \sum_{f=1}^{d_1} \sum_{h=1}^{d_2} g_1^f \mathbf{A}_{ij}^{(m)} g_2^h = \left(\sum_{f=1}^{\delta_1} g_1^f \right) \mathbf{A}_{ij}^{(m)} \left(\sum_{f=1}^{d_2} g_2^h \right)$$

holds.

The first and last factors will be indecomposable and idempotent so they must be matrices consisting entirely of ones. So the total product will consist entirely of ones. So for all sufficiently large e, $\mathbf{A}_{ij}^{(e)}$ will consist entirely of 1 entries. This proves the lemma.

Lemma 2. *There exists for any even integer* $y > 3$ *indecomposable* $y \times y$ *matrix of period* 2 *and index*

$$2\left(\frac{y}{2} - 1\right)^2 + 2 .$$

For any odd integer $y>3$ there exists $y\times y$ matrix of period 2 and index

$$2\left(\frac{y-1}{2}-1\right)^2+3.$$

Proof. For **y** even we take a matrix of the form

$$\begin{bmatrix} 0 & \mathbf{I} \\ \mathbf{B} & 0 \end{bmatrix}$$

where **B** has index

$$\left(\frac{y}{2}-1\right)^2+1.$$

For any integer n there exists a column rank $n-1$ matrix of index $(n-1)^2+2$ namely

$$\begin{bmatrix} \mathbf{A} & 0 \\ \mathbf{v} & 0 \end{bmatrix}$$

where **A** is an $(n-1)\times(n-1)$ matrix of index $(n-1)^2+1$ and **v** is a vector containing only one 1 such that

$$\mathbf{v}\mathbf{A}^{(n-1)^2}<(1, 1, \dots, 1).$$

In fact we will assume **A** has the standard form

$$\begin{bmatrix} 0 & 1 & 0 & \dots & 0 \\ 0 & 0 & 1 & \dots & 0 \\ 0 & 0 & 0 & \dots & 0 \\ \dots & \dots & \dots & \dots & \dots \\ 1 & 0 & 0 & \dots & 1 \\ 1 & 0 & 0 & \dots & 0 \end{bmatrix}.$$

The matrix

$$\begin{bmatrix} \mathbf{A} & 0 \\ \mathbf{v} & 0 \end{bmatrix}$$

can be factored as $\mathbf{H}_1\mathbf{H}_2$ where $\mathbf{H}_1$ is an $n\times(n-1)$ matrix and $\mathbf{H}_2$ is an $(n-1)\times n$ matrix. In fact we can choose $\mathbf{H}_2$ to be the $(n-1)\times(n-1)$ identity matrix with its last row repeated. Then the matrix

$$\begin{bmatrix} 0 & \mathbf{H}_1 \\ \mathbf{H}_2 & 0 \end{bmatrix}$$

if raised to the

$$2\left(\frac{y-1}{2}-1\right)^2+2$$

power will not equal to same matrix to the

$$2\left(\frac{y-1}{2}-1\right)^2+4$$

power. Therefore it will satisfy the conditions of the lemma for n odd.

Example 2. For $n=4, 5$ we have the matrices

$$\begin{bmatrix} 0 & 0 & 1 & 0 \\ 0 & 0 & 0 & 1 \\ 1 & 1 & 0 & 0 \\ 1 & 0 & 0 & 0 \end{bmatrix}, \quad \begin{bmatrix} 0 & 0 & 0 & 1 & 1 \\ 0 & 0 & 0 & 1 & 0 \\ 0 & 0 & 0 & 0 & 1 \\ 1 & 0 & 0 & 0 & 0 \\ 0 & 1 & 0 & 0 & 0 \end{bmatrix},$$

of indexes 4 and 5 respectively.

3. Main results

Definition 4. The number c_n is the largest possible size of a cyclic subgroup of the symmetric group on n symbols. (For bounds on c_n see [7].)

Theorem 3. *Let* (**A**, **I**, **F**) *be an n-state, one symbol, nondeterministic automaton, of period d and index k. Assume* $n>2$.

(1) *If* $d>c_{n-2}$ *then* $k\leqq 1$. *If* $d>c_{n-1}$ *then* $k=0$.

(2) *If* $c_n=c_{n-y}$ *there exists an* (**A**, **I**, **F**) *with* $d=c_n$ *and* $k=y$, *for* $y>0$.

(3) *If* $c_n=c_{n-y}$ *and* $c_n>c_{n-y-1}$ *and* $4|c_n$ *or* $2\nmid c_n$ *and* $y>3$ *then there exists an* (**A**, **I**, **F**) *with* $d=c_n$ *and*

$$k=2\left(\frac{y}{2}-1\right)^2+2 \quad or \quad k=2\left(\frac{y-1}{2}-1\right)^2+3$$

according as y is even or odd.

(4) *If* $c_n=c_{n-y}$ *and* $c_n>c_{n-y-1}$ *and* $y>1$ *and* $4\nmid c_n$ *and* $2|c_n$, *then there exists an* (**A**, **I**, **F**) *with* $d=c_n$ *and*

$$k=2\left(\frac{y}{2}\right)^2+2 \quad or \quad k=2\left(\frac{y-1}{2}\right)^2+3$$

according as y is even or odd.

Proof. Suppose $d > c_{n-2}$. We first show that no two indecomposable blocks of **A** can have periods with greatest common divisor larger than one. Suppose $p > 1$ divides the periods of two cycles c, d. Assume $c \leqq d$. If $c = p$, replace the blocks of periods c, d by a d cycle and at least two 1-cycles. If $c > p$ replace the blocks of period c, d by a d cycle and a $\frac{c}{p}$ cycle and at least two 1 cycles. Therefore there exists a permutation of order d with at least two 1 cycles. Therefore there exists a permutation of order $d > c_{n-2}$ and degree $n-2$. This is a contradiction. Therefore no two indecomposable blocks can have periods with greatest common divisor greater than one.

The same argument shows that no indecomposable block of **A** can have size more than one larger than its period, and if some block does have size larger than its period, no main diagonal blocks are zero.

Case 1. No main diagonal blocks are zero. We first prove that the main diagonal blocks must be periodic. Let **B** be such a block. Then **B** must be indecomposable. If its period were 1, again we would have $d \leqq c_{n-2}$. For some permutation matrix **P**,

$$\mathbf{PBP}^T = \begin{bmatrix} 0 & B_{12} & 0 & \dots & 0 \\ 0 & 0 & B_{23} & \dots & 0 \\ 0 & 0 & 0 & \dots & 0 \\ \dots & \dots & \dots & \dots & \dots \\ B_{m1} & 0 & 0 & \dots & 0 \end{bmatrix}.$$

At most one diagonal block of $\mathbf{PBP}^T$ can have size > 1. Therefore each block of $\mathbf{PBP}^T$ off the diagonal is either $1 \times r$ or $r \times 1$ for some r. The fact that **B** is indecomposable implies it has at least one 1 in each row and column. Therefore all blocks $\mathbf{B}_{i,i+1}$ and $\mathbf{B}_{m1}$ consist entirely of ones. This implies **B** is periodic.

Now which blocks of **A** could possibly be nonperiodic? The only possibilities are blocks below the diagonal in which a 1 entry exists in some power of **A**. But Lemma 1 implies such blocks must fill completely with ones. Then if $\mathbf{I} \times \mathbf{F}$ contains a pair in such a block, every number is eventually good and $d = 1$. Therefore $\mathbf{I} \times \mathbf{F}$ can contain entries only in periodic blocks. So the set of good numbers is periodic, and $k = 1$.

If $d > c_{n-1}$ then no zero diagonal blocks can occur, every diagonal block must be a cycle and any two cycles must have greatest common divisor 1. Any off diagonal entry of **A** containing an element of $\mathbf{I} \times \mathbf{F}$ must always be zero. Therefore as far as $\mathbf{I} \times \mathbf{F}$ is concerned, **A** may as well be a permutation matrix. Therefore $k = 0$

Case 2 is proved by taking **A** to be the direct sum of a permutation matrix of degree $n - y$ *and order* c_n, and a nilpotent $y \times y$ matrix of index y. The set $\mathbf{I} \times \mathbf{F}$ is to include one entry from each cycle of the permutation, and the last nonzero entry of the nilpotent matrix. The entries of the permutation are chosen so that they are zero on the $y-1$ power of **A**. Then $y-1$ will be a good number whereas $y - 1 + c_n$ will not. So the index is y. Also the period will be c_n.

Case 3 is proved by taking **A** to be the direct sum of a permutation matrix of degree $n-y$ and order c_n and a $y \times y$ matrix as in Lemma 2. In the following we let **E** be the identity matrix. The set $\mathbf{I} \times \mathbf{F}$ is to include one entry from each cycle of the permutation and an entry of

$$\begin{bmatrix} 0 & \mathbf{H}_1 \\ \mathbf{H}_2 & 0 \end{bmatrix} \quad \text{or} \quad \begin{bmatrix} 0 & \mathbf{E} \\ \mathbf{B} & 0 \end{bmatrix}$$

to the $2\left(\frac{y-1}{2}-1\right)^2+2$ power (respectively $2\left(\frac{y}{2}-1\right)^2+1$ power) to the power which is zero but becomes 1 in higher even power. In addition we require that the entries from the permutation cycles be zero on the $2\left(\frac{y-1}{2}-1\right)^2+2$ respectively $2\left(\frac{y}{2}-1\right)^2+1$ power of **A**. By assumption, $4|c_n$ or $2\not| c_n$. We require in addition that the entry from any permutation cycle of **A** which is divisible by 4 be one only for odd powers. Therefore it will not be hidden by the 1 appearing every even power in the bottom summand. Then the period of the automaton will be c_n and the index will be as stated.

Case 4. Here $4\not| c_n$. Since $c_n = c_{n-2}$, $2|c_n$. Let **A** be the direct sum of a $(n-y-2) \times \times (n-y-2)$ permutation matrix of period $\frac{c_n}{2}$ and a $(y+2) \times (y+2)$ matrix as in Lemma 2. Choose $\mathbf{I} \times \mathbf{F}$ to include one entry of each cycle of the permutation and an entry of

$$\begin{bmatrix} 0 & \mathbf{H}_1 \\ \mathbf{H}_2 & 0 \end{bmatrix} \quad \begin{bmatrix} 0 & \mathbf{E} \\ \mathbf{B} & 0 \end{bmatrix}$$

to the $\left(\frac{y-1}{2}-1\right)^2+2$ (respectively $2\left(\frac{y}{2}-1\right)^2+1$) power which is zero but becomes 1 in higher even powers. Require that the entries in the permutation matrices be zero in A to the $2\left(\frac{y-1}{2}-1\right)^2+2$ (respectively $2\left(\frac{y-1}{2}+1\right)$ power. Then the index of the automaton will be $2\left(\frac{y-1}{2}-1\right)^2+3$, respectively $2\left(\frac{y}{2}-1\right)^2+2$. And the period will be c_n. This completes the proof.

Conjecture. *Any nondeterministic automaton on one symbol, with n-state is equivalent to a one symbol deterministic automaton with the following numbers of states.*

(i) *For* $n<19$, $(n-1)^2+2$.

(ii) *For* $n \geqq 19$, *if* $c_n > c_{n-1}$, c_n *states. If* $c_n = c_{n-1} > c_{n-2}$, c_n+1 *states.*

(iii) *For* $n>19$, *if* $c_n = c_{n-y} > c_{n-y-1}$ *and* $y>3$, $c_n+2\left(\frac{y}{2}-1\right)^2+2$ *states for y even and* $c_n+2\left(\frac{y-1}{2}-1\right)^2+3$ *states for y odd.*

(*iv*) *If* $n > 19$, $c_n = c_{n-y} > c_{n-y-1}$ *and* $y = 2$ *or* 3 *and* $4|c_n$ *or* $2\nmid c_n$, $c_n + y$ *states.*
(*v*) *If* $n > 19$, $c_n = c_{n-y} > c_{n-y-1}$, *and* $y = 2$ *or* 3 *and* $2|c_n$ *and* $4\nmid c_n$, $c_n + y + 2$ *states.*

It follows from our theorem that if this conjecture is true, it gives the best possible bound on the number of states. The last case follows from part (4) of the theorem. For further problems in this respect see [8].

References

[1] R. MANDL, Precise bounds associated with the subset construction on various classes of nondeterministic finite automata, *Proc. 7th Annual Princeton Conf. on Information Sciences and Systems*, 1973, 263–267.
[2] G. MARKOWSKY, Bounds on the index and period of a binary relation on a finite set, *Semigroup Forum*, **13** (1977), 253–259.
[3] H. MINC, *Nonnegative matrices*, Lecture Note, Technion-Israel Institute of Technology, Haifa, Israel, 1974.
[4] D. ROSENBLATT, On the graphs and asymptotic forms of finite Boolean relation matrices, *Naval Research Logistics Quartely*, **4** (1957), 151–167.
[5] S. SCHWARZ, On the semigroup of binary relations on a finite set, *Czech. Math. Jour.*, **20–95** (1970), 632–679.
[6] SEDLACEK, Uvod do teorie grafu, Academia, Praha, 1977.
[7] M. SZALAY, On the maximal order in S_n and S_n^*, Acta Arith., **37** (1980), 321–331.
[8] J. DÉNES, Research Problems, Europ. J. Comb., **1** (1980), 207–209.

INSTITUTE FOR CO-ORDINATION
OF COMPUTER TECHNIQUES
BUDAPEST, HUNGARY

MATHEMATICS RESEARCH GROUP
ALABAMA STATE UNIVERSITY
MONTGOMERY, ALABAMA 36101
U.S.A.

Studies in Pure Mathematics
To the Memory of Paul Turán

On a problem of Lehmer

by

E. DOBROWOLSKI (Wroclaw), W. LAWTON (Pasadena) and
A. SCHINZEL (Warszawa)

D. H. LEHMER [6] asked whether for every $\varepsilon>0$ there exists a monic polynomial $g \in \mathbf{Z}[z]$ such that

$$1<\prod_{g(\alpha)=0} \max(1,|\alpha|)<1+\varepsilon .$$

(Here and in the sequel every zero α is counted with its multiplicity.)

P. E. BLANKSBY and H. L. MONTGOMERY [1] and more recently the first named author [2] have given lower bounds for

$$M(g)=\prod_{g(\alpha)=0} \max(1,|\alpha|)$$

in terms of the degree of g. The second named author [5] announced the existence of a bound depending only on the number of non-zero coefficients of g. The aim of this paper is to exhibit such a bound. We shall prove

Theorem. *If $g(z) \in \mathbf{Z}[z]$ is a monic polynomial with $g(0)\neq 0$ that is not a product of cyclotomic polynomials then*

$$M(g) \geqq 1+\frac{1}{\exp_{k+1} 2k^2}$$

where k is the number of non-zero coefficients of g.

In the proof we shall use the vector notation and denote by $h(\mathbf{r})$ or $l(\mathbf{r})$ the maximum of the absolute values of the entries of a vector $\mathbf{r}$ or their sum respectively. The same notation is used for matrices.

Lemma 1. *Let $F(z)=\sum_{j\in\mathcal{J}} a_j z^j \in \mathbf{C}[z]$ and suppose that F has a zero $c\neq 0$ of multiplicity $\geqq J=|\mathcal{J}|$. Then $F\equiv 0$.*

Proof. This is Lemma 1 in [7]. It has been however proved earlier by G. HAJÓS [4] as was kindly pointed out to us by MR. A. MĄKOWSKI.

To formulate the next lemma we need some notation. Let

$$F(\mathbf{z})=F(z_1,\ldots,z_N)=\sum_{\mathbf{j}\in\mathscr{J}} a(\mathbf{j})z_1^{j_1}\ldots z_N^{j_N}, \tag{1}$$

where $\mathbf{j}=(j_1,\ldots,j_N)$, the j_n are integers and $\mathscr{J}$ is a finite set such that $a(\mathbf{j})\neq 0$ for $\mathbf{j}\in\mathscr{J}$. We set

$$\mathscr{J}-\mathscr{J}=\{\mathbf{j}_1-\mathbf{j}_2:\mathbf{j}_i\in\mathscr{J}\},\quad J=|\mathscr{J}|,\quad D=\max_{\mathbf{j}\in\mathscr{J}}\max_{1\leqq n\leqq N}|j_n|;\quad \min_{\mathbf{j}\in\mathscr{J}} j_n=d_n;$$

$$IF(z)=F(z)\prod_{n=1}^{N} z_n^{-d_n},\quad h(F)=\max_{\mathbf{j}\in\mathscr{J}}|a(\mathbf{j})|,\quad l(F)=\sum_{\mathbf{j}\in\mathscr{J}}|a(\mathbf{j})|.$$

We let Φ_m denote the mth cyclotomic polynomial and we say that Φ is an extended cyclotomic polynomial if

$$\psi(z)=I\Phi_m(z_1^{v_1}\ldots z_N^{v_N})$$

for some set of coprime integers v_n.

Lemma 2. *Let $F(z)$ be a polynomial of the form* (1), $\mathbf{r}=(r_1,\ldots,r_N)\in\mathbf{Z}^N$ *and suppose that F is not divisible by any extended cyclotomic polynomial but*

$$\Phi_m(z)|IF(z^{r_1},\ldots,z^{r_N}).$$

Then there are linearly independent vectors $\mathbf{v}^{(i)}\in\mathscr{J}-\mathscr{J}$, $i=1,2$ for which

$$m|(\mathbf{v}^{(1)}\cdot\mathbf{r},\mathbf{v}^{(2)}\cdot\mathbf{r})P,\quad \textit{where}\quad P=\prod_{p\leqq J}p.$$

Proof is the same as proof of Lemma 3 in [7] up to formula (9) on p. 200. The subsequent argument is unnecessary since in the notation of the above paper (8) and (9) imply

$$I\Phi_l(z_1^{v_1}\ldots z_N^{v_N})|F(\mathbf{z})$$

and since $\Phi_{ld}(z)|\Phi_l(z^d)$ the left-hand side is divisible by an extended cyclotomic polynomial.

Lemma 3. *Let $F(\mathbf{z})$ be a polynomial of the form* (1), $\mathbf{r}\in\mathbf{Z}^N$. *If F is not divisible by any extended cyclotomic polynomial but the sum of degrees of all cyclotomic factors of $IF(z^{r_1},\ldots,z^{r_N})$ counted with multiplicities exceeds $\frac{1}{2}$ the degree of $IF(z^{r_1},\ldots,z^{r_N})$ then $\mathbf{v}\cdot\mathbf{r}=0$ for some vector $\mathbf{v}\in\mathbf{z}^N$ such that*

$$0<h(\mathbf{v})<2PJ^5D.$$

Proof. If $IF(z^{r_1}, \ldots, z^{r_N})$ has fewer than J terms then $\mathbf{j}^{(1)} \cdot \mathbf{r} = \mathbf{j}^{(2)} \cdot \mathbf{r}$ for some $\mathbf{j}^{(i)} \in \mathcal{J}$ and it suffices to take $\mathbf{v} = \mathbf{j}^{(1)} - \mathbf{j}^{(2)}$.

If $IF(z^{r_1}, \ldots, z^{r_N})$ has J distinct terms then its degree is given by

$$\Delta = \max_{\mathbf{j} \in \mathcal{J}} \mathbf{j} \cdot \mathbf{r} - \min_{\mathbf{j} \in \mathcal{J}} \mathbf{j} \cdot \mathbf{r} .$$

On the other hand from the condition of the lemma and from Lemma 1 we have

$$\frac{1}{2} \Delta < \sum_{m \in M} \gamma(m)\, \varphi(m) < J \sum_{m \in M} \varphi(m)$$

where $m \in M$ if $\Phi_m(z)$ divides $IF(z^{r_1}, \ldots, z^{r_N})$ with multiplicity $\gamma(m) > 0$.

Let $V = \{(\mathbf{u}, \mathbf{v}) \colon \mathbf{u}, \mathbf{v} \in \mathcal{J} - \mathcal{J}, \text{ rank } (\mathbf{u}, \mathbf{v}) = 2\}$. Then by Lemma 2

$$\frac{1}{2} \Delta < J \sum_{(\mathbf{u}, \mathbf{v}) \in V} \; \sum_{m | (\mathbf{u} \cdot \mathbf{r}, \mathbf{w} \cdot \mathbf{r}) P} \varphi(m) = PJ \sum_{(\mathbf{u}, \mathbf{v}) \in V} (\mathbf{u} \cdot \mathbf{r}, \mathbf{v} \cdot \mathbf{r}) .$$

But V contains less than $\frac{1}{2} J^4$ elements*, so there is a pair $(\mathbf{u}, \mathbf{w}) \in V$ for which $d = (\mathbf{u} \cdot \mathbf{r}, \mathbf{w} \cdot \mathbf{r}) > \Delta P^{-1} J^{-5}$. Put $u = \mathbf{u} \cdot \mathbf{r}/d$, $w = \mathbf{w} \cdot \mathbf{r}/d$.

Then

$$|u| \leqq PJ^5 |\mathbf{u} \cdot \mathbf{r}| / \Delta \leqq PJ^5$$

and similarly $|w| \leqq PJ^5$. Put $\mathbf{v} = w\mathbf{u} - u\mathbf{w}$. Then $\mathbf{v} \cdot \mathbf{r} = 0$, $\mathbf{v} \neq \mathbf{0}$ and

$$h(\mathbf{v}) < 2PJ^5 D .$$

Lemma 4. *For any non-zero vector* $\mathbf{n} \in \mathbf{Z}^K$ *there exists an integral matrix* $\mathbf{M} = [m_{ij}]_{\substack{i \leqq N \\ j \leqq K}}$ *and a vector* $\mathbf{r} \in \mathbf{Z}^N$ *such that* $N \leqq K$,

(2) $$\mathbf{n} = \mathbf{r}\mathbf{M} ,$$

(3) $$h(\mathbf{M}) \leqq \exp_{K-N+1} 2(K^2 - N^2) ,$$

(4) $$\mathbf{v} \cdot \mathbf{r} = 0, \quad \mathbf{v} \in \mathbf{Z}^N \quad \textit{implies}$$

$$\mathbf{v} = \mathbf{0} \quad \textit{or} \quad h(\mathbf{v}) > \exp 3(2h(\mathbf{M}) + 1)^N .$$

Proof. The identity matrix $\mathbf{M}$ and $\mathbf{r} = \mathbf{n}$ satisfy the conditions (2) and (3) with $N = K$. Take a matrix $\mathbf{M}_0$ and a vector $\mathbf{r}_0$ that satisfy these conditions and correspond to the least possible N. We shall show that they also satisfy the conditions (4). Suppose to the contrary that there exists a $\mathbf{v} \in \mathbf{Z}^N$ such that

* In the proof of Theorem 1 in [7] it is stated incorrectly that V contains less than J^2 elements, but the error is reparable.

(5) $$\mathbf{v}\cdot\mathbf{r}_0=0 \quad\text{and}\quad 0<h(\mathbf{v})\leqq\exp 3(2h(\mathbf{M}_0)+1)^N .$$

The set of all integral vectors $\mathbf{r}$ satisfying (5) forms a lattice L. If say, $v_1\neq 0$ this lattice contains $N-1$ linearly independent vectors

$$[-v_2, v_1, 0, \dots, 0], [-v_3, 0, v_1, 0, \dots, 0], \dots, [-v_N, 0, \dots, 0, v_1].$$

Hence L has a basis $\mathbf{r}_1, \dots, \mathbf{r}_{N-1}$ satisfying

(6) $$h(\mathbf{r}_i)\leqq(N-1)\,h(\mathbf{v})$$

and we have

$$\mathbf{r}_0=\sum_{i=1}^{N-1} s_i\mathbf{r}_i, \quad \mathbf{s}=[s_1, \dots, s_{N-1}]\in\mathbf{Z}^{N-1}$$

$$\mathbf{n}=\sum_{i=1}^{N-1} s_i\mathbf{r}_i\mathbf{M}_0=\mathbf{s}\mathbf{R}\mathbf{M}_0 ,$$

where

$$R=\begin{bmatrix}\mathbf{r}_1\\ \vdots\\ \mathbf{r}_{N-1}\end{bmatrix}.$$

It follows from (3), (5) and (6) that

$$h(\mathbf{RM}_0)\leqq Nh(\mathbf{R})h(\mathbf{M}_0)\leqq N(N-1)\,h(\mathbf{v})\exp_{K-N+1}2(K^2-N^2)\leqq$$
$$\leqq\exp 3\,(2\exp_{K-N+1}2(K^2-N^2)+1)^N$$

and by a tedious computation we find that (for $K>1$) the right-hand side does not exceed

$$\exp_{K-N+2}2(K^2-(N-1)^2)$$

which contradicts the choice of N. For $K=1$ (4) holds trivially.

Lemma 5. *Any polynomial $g(z)\in\mathbf{Z}[z]$ with $K+1$ terms and $g(0)\neq 0$ that is not a constant multiple of the product of cyclotomic polynomials has a divisor $f(z)\in\mathbf{Z}[z]$ such that $f(z)$ has at most $\exp_K 2\,K^2$ non zero coefficients and that the sum of the degrees of all cyclotomic factors of f counted with multiplicities does not exceed $\frac{1}{2}$ degree of $f=\frac{1}{2}|f|$.*

Proof. Let

$$g(z)=b_0+\sum_{j=1}^{K} b_jx^{n_j}, \quad n_j \text{ distinct}.$$

By Lemma 4 there exists an integral matrix $\mathbf{M}=[m_{ij}]$ and a vector $\mathbf{r}\in\mathbf{Z}^N$ such that $N\leqq K$

$$[n_1,\dots,n_K]=\mathbf{rM}$$

(7)

$$h(\mathbf{M})\leqq\exp_K(2K^2-2)$$

and

(8) $$\mathbf{v}\cdot\mathbf{r}=0,\quad \mathbf{v}\in\mathbf{Z}^N \text{ implies } \mathbf{v}=\mathbf{0} \text{ or } h(\mathbf{v})>\exp 3(2h(\mathbf{M})+1)^N .$$

Let us put

$$G(z_1,\dots,z_N)=I\left(b_0+\sum_{j=1}^{K} b_j\sum_{i=1}^{N} z_i^{m_{ij}}\right).$$

The degree of G in z_i does not exceed $2h(\mathbf{M})$ for any $i\leqq N$. We have

(9) $$g(z)=IG(z^{r_1},\dots,z^{r_N})$$

and the assumption about g implies that G is not a constant multiple of the product of extended cyclotomic polynomials. Let

$$G(z_1,\dots,z_N)=E(z_1,\dots,z_N)\,F(z_1,\dots,z_N),$$

where $E, F\in\mathbf{Z}[z_1,\dots,z_N]$ and $F\neq$const is not divisible by any extended cyclotomic polynomial. Let us represent F in the form (1). We have

(10) $$D\leqq 2h(\mathbf{M}),$$

(11) $$1<J\leqq(2h(\mathbf{M})+1)^N .$$

Now, set

$$f(z)=IF(z^{r_1},\dots,z^{r_N}).$$

By (9) $f(z)|g(z)$. Moreover in virtue of (8) and (10) the number of terms in $f(z)$ is $J>1$, thus f is non-constant and by (7) and (11)

$$J\leqq(2\exp_K(2K^2-2)+1)^K\leqq\exp_K 2K^2 .$$

If the sum of the degrees of all cyclotomic factors of $f(z)$ counted with multiplicities would exceed $\frac{1}{2}|f|$ we should have by Lemma 4 a relation

$$\mathbf{v}\cdot\mathbf{r}=0,\quad\text{where}\quad 0<h(\mathbf{v})<2J^5PD .$$

However by (10) and (11)

$$2J^3PD<4h(\mathbf{M})\,(2h(\mathbf{M})+1)^{3N}\prod_{P\leqq(2h(\mathbf{M})+1)^N} p\leqq\exp 3(2h(\mathbf{M})+1)^N$$

which contradicts (8).

Lemma 6. *If α is a non-zero algebraic integer of degree n, α is not a root of unity, and p is a prime number then*

$$\left| \prod_{i,j=1}^{n} (\alpha_i^p - \alpha_j) \right| \geqq p^n ,$$

where α_i are the conjugates of α.

Proof. This is Lemma 2 of [2].

Lemma 7. *If α is a non-zero algebraic integer of degree n, α is not a root of unity and $f(\alpha)=0$, $f \in \mathbf{Z}[z]$ of degree $|f|$ then*

$$M(\alpha) = \prod_{i=1}^{n} \max(1, |\alpha_i|) \geqq 1 + \frac{n}{|f| \exp 2l(f)} .$$

Proof. Let

$$f(x) = a_0 + \sum_{j=1}^{J-1} a_j z^{n_j}, \quad a_j \neq 0, \quad n_j \text{ distinct};$$

$$Q = \prod_{p \leqq l(f)} p .$$

Suppose that $f(\alpha^{1+iQ})=0$ for $i=0, \ldots, J-1$. Considering this as a system of linear equations for $a_j\alpha^{n_j}$ we get that

$$\det |\alpha^{iQn_j}|_{0 \leqq i,j < J} = 0 ,$$

thus

$$\prod_{0 \leqq i < j < J} (\alpha^{Qn_i} - \alpha^{Qn_j}) = 0 \quad (n_0 = 0)$$

and α is a root of unity, a contradiction. Thus there exists an integer $i<J$ such that

$$f(\alpha^{1+iQ}) \neq 0 .$$

Let d be the least divisor of $1+iQ$ such that

$$f(\alpha^d) \neq 0 .$$

Clearly $1<d<JQ$. Moreover taking for p any prime factor of d we have

$$f(\alpha^{d/p}) = 0, \quad f(\alpha_j^{d/p}) = 0 .$$

Taking norms from $\mathbf{Q}(\alpha)$ to $\mathbf{Q}$ we get

$$\prod_{i,j=1}^{n} (\alpha_i^d - \alpha_j^{d/p}) | Nf(\alpha^d) ,$$

the product is to be taken over $\alpha_j^{d/f}$ distinct and since $f(\alpha^d)\neq 0$ we infer from Lemma 7 that

$$|Nf(\alpha^d)|\geqq p^n .$$

However

$$|Nf(\alpha^d)|\leqq l(f)^n\left(\prod_{i=1}^{n}\max(1,|\alpha_i|)\right)^{d|f|}.$$

Hence

$$\prod_{i=1}^{n}\max(1,|\alpha_i|)\geqq\left(\frac{p}{l(f)}\right)^{n/d|f|}.$$

On the other hand $p|d$ implies $p\nmid Q$, $p>l(f)$. Thus

$$\prod_{i=1}^{n}\max(1,|\alpha_i|)\geqq\exp\left(\frac{n}{d|f|(l(f)+1)}\right)\geqq$$

$$\geqq 1+\frac{n}{|f|(l(f)+1)JQ}\geqq 1+\frac{n}{|f|\exp 2l(f)}.$$

Lemma 8. *If f_1, $c\in\mathbf{Z}[z]$, f_1 is monic, non-divisible by z or by any cyclotomic polynomial and all its zeros are zeros of c then*

$$M(f_1)\geqq 1+\frac{|f_1|}{|c|\exp 2l(c)}.$$

Proof. Let α_i $(1\leqq i\leqq r)$ form a maximal system of pairwise non-conjugate zeros of f_1, let n_i be the degree and e_i the multiplicity of α_i as a zero of f_1. We have

$$M(f_1)=\prod_{i=1}^{r}M(\alpha_i)^{e_i}$$

hence by Lemma 7

$$M(f_1)\geqq\prod_{i=1}^{r}\left(1+\frac{n_i}{|c|\exp 2l(c)}\right)^{e_i}\geqq 1+\frac{\sum_{i=1}^{r}n_ie_i}{|c|\exp 2l(c)}=1+\frac{|f_1|}{|c|\exp 2l(c)}.$$

Lemma 9. *Let $\mathbf{a}\in\mathbf{Z}^J$ be a vector and $B>1$ a real number. Then there exist vectors $\mathbf{c}\in\mathbf{Z}^J$ and $\mathbf{r}\in\mathbf{Q}^J$ and a rational number q such that*

$$\mathbf{a}=\mathbf{r}+q\mathbf{c}, \tag{12}$$

$$0<l(\mathbf{c})\leqq(JB)^J+B^{-1}, \tag{13}$$

$$q\geqq Bl(\mathbf{r}). \tag{14}$$

Proof. Let $A>1$ be a real number. By Dirichlet's theorem there exists a rational integer t, $1\leqq t\leqq A^J$ such that

$$\left\| t\frac{a_i}{l(\mathbf{a})} \right\| \leqq A^{-1} \quad \text{for} \quad i=1,2,\dots,J$$

where $[a_1, a_2, \dots, a_J]=\mathbf{a}$.

Take $A=JB$ and $q=\dfrac{l(\mathbf{a})}{t}$.

Define the vector $\mathbf{c}=[c_1, c_2, \dots, c_J]$ by the conditions

$$\left\| t\frac{a_i}{l(\mathbf{a})} \right\| = \left| t\frac{a_i}{l(\mathbf{a})} - c_i \right|, \quad c_i \in \mathbf{Z} \quad \text{for} \quad i=1,2,\dots,J$$

and the vector $\mathbf{r}=[r_1, r_2, \dots, r_J]$ by $\mathbf{r}=\mathbf{a}-q\mathbf{c}$. The above conditions do not determine c_i uniquely, but assure that $\operatorname{sgn} c_i=\operatorname{sgn} a_i$.

Then (12) holds trivially. As to (13) note the inequality

$$\left| t-\sum_{i=1}^{J} |c_i| \right| = \left| \sum_{i=1}^{J} \left(t\frac{|a_i|}{l(\mathbf{a})} - |c_i| \right) \right| \leqq \sum_{i=1}^{J} \left| t\frac{a_i}{l(\mathbf{a})} - c_i \right| \leqq JA^{-1} < 1.$$

Thus $t\geqq 1$ implies $l(\mathbf{c})>0$.

On the other hand

$$l(\mathbf{c})=\sum_{i=1}^{J} |c_i| \leqq \sum_{i=1}^{J} \left(\left| t\frac{c_i}{l(\mathbf{c})} \right| + A^{-1} \right) = t + JA^{-1} \leqq (JB)^J + B^{-1}.$$

Finally

$$l(\mathbf{r})=\sum_{i=1}^{J} |a_i - qc_i| = q\sum_{i=1}^{J} \left| t\frac{|a_i|}{l(\mathbf{a})} - c_i \right| \leqq qB^{-1}.$$

which proves (14).

Proof of the theorem. By Lemma 5 $g(z)$ has a divisor $f(z)$ such that the number J of non-zero coefficients of f satisfies

(15) $$J \leqq \exp_{k-1} 2(k-1)^2$$

and if P is the product of all cyclotomic factors of f counted with multiplicities then

$$|P| \leqq \frac{1}{2}|f|.$$

Let $f(z)=\sum_{j=1}^{J} a_j z^{n_j}$, $0=n_1<n_2<\ldots<n_J$. Take in Lemma 9, $\mathbf{a}=[a_1, \ldots, a_J]$, $B=1+\frac{1}{\exp 2J^J}$. By that Lemma there exist vectors $\mathbf{c}\in\mathbf{Z}^J$ and $\mathbf{r}\in\mathbf{Q}^J$ and a rational number q satisfying (12), (13) and (14). Put

$$c(z)=\sum_{j=1}^{J} c_j z^{n_j}, \quad r(z)=\sum_{j=1}^{J} r_j z^{n_j}$$

and let

$$f(z)=P(z)f_1(z)f_2(z),$$

where $f_1, f_2\in\mathbf{Z}[z]$, all zeros of f_1 are zeros of c and $(f_2, c)=1$, moreover f_1, f_2 are monic. By (13) $c(z)\neq 0$. If $|f_1|\geqq|f_2|$ we apply Lemma 8 and get

$$M(f_1)\geqq 1+\frac{|f_1|}{|c|\exp 2l(c)}.$$

However

$$|f_1|\geqq\frac{1}{2}(|f|-|P|)\geqq\frac{1}{4}|f|\geqq\frac{1}{2}|c|$$

and by (13)

$$l(c)=l(\mathbf{c})\leqq(JB)^J+B^{-1}\leqq J^J+\frac{3}{2}\quad(J\geqq 2).$$

Hence

$$M(f_1)\geqq 1+\frac{1}{4\exp(2J^J+3)}.$$

If $|f_1|\leqq|f_2|$ we apply Lemma 9 and get from (12)

$$f(z)=r(z)+qc(z)$$

where $r(z)\neq 0$ (otherwise $f_2(z)=1$). Let $\alpha_1, \alpha_2, \ldots, \alpha_{|f_2|}$ be all the zero of f_2 listed with multiplicities. We have $f(\alpha_i)=0$, $c(\alpha_i)\neq 0$, hence

$$-r(\alpha_i)=qc(\alpha_i),\quad \prod_{i=1}^{|f_2|}|r(\alpha_i)|=q^{|f_2|}\prod_{i=1}^{|f_2|}|c(\alpha_i)|$$

and by (14)

$$l(\mathbf{r})^{|f_2|}M(f_2)^{|r|}\geqq q^{|f_2|}\geqq(Bl(\mathbf{r}))^{|f_2|}.$$

Since $l(\mathbf{r})>0$ and $|r|\leqq|f|$ it follows that

$$M(f_2)\geqq B^{|f_2|/|f|}\geqq B^{\frac{1}{4}}\geqq 1+\frac{1}{4(\exp 2J^J+1)}.$$

Therefore in both cases

$$M(g) \geqq \max\{M(f_1), M(f_2)\} \geqq 1 + \frac{1}{4\exp(2J^J+3)}.$$

However by (15) and a tedious computation

$$4\exp(2J^J+3) \leqq \exp(2J^J+5) \leqq \exp_2 J^2 \leqq \exp_{k+1} 2k^2.$$

References

[1] P. E. BLANKSBY and H. L. MONTGOMERY, Algebraic integers near the unit circle, *Acta Arith.*, **18** (1971), 355–369.

[2] E. DOBROWOLSKI, On a question of Lehmer and the number of irreducible factors of a polynomial, *Acta Arith.*, **34** (1979), 391–401.

[3] A. O. GELFOND, *Transcendental and algebraic numbers*. New York 1960.

[4] G. HAJÓS, Solution of problem 41 (in Hungarian), *Mat. Lapok*, **4** (1953), 40–41.

[5] W. LAWTON, Asymptotic properties of roots of polynomials, preliminary report, *Proceedings of the Seventh Iranian National Mathematical Conference*, Azarabadegan University, Tabris, Iran, March 1976.

[6] D. H. LEHMER, Factorization of certain cyclotomic functions, *Ann. Math.*, (2), **34** (1933), 461–479.

[7] H. L. MONTGOMERY and A. SCHINZEL, Some arithmetic properties of polynomials in several variables, pp. 195–203 in *Transcendence Theory; Advances and Applications*, London–New York–San Francisco 1977.

WROCLAW UNIVERSITY,
INSTITUTE OF MATHEMATICS,
WROCLAW, POLAND

JET PROPULSION LABORATORY
CALIFORNIA INSTITUTTE OF TECHNOLOGY
PASADENA, CALIFORNIA, U.S.A.

INSTITUTE OF MATHEMATICS
POLISH ACADEMY OF SCIENCES, WARSZAWA, POLAND AND
INSTITUT MITTAG-LEFFLER
DJURSHOLM, SWEDEN

Studies in Pure Mathematics
To the Memory of Paul Turán

On extrermal polynomials

by

Á. ELBERT (Budapest)

Let $\mathscr{P}$ be the set of polynomials of the form

(1) $$p(x)=(x+1)^{n_1}(x-1)^{n_2}\sum_{i=0}^{n_3} a_i x^i ,$$

where n_1, n_2, n_3 are nonnegative integers, and the coefficients a_i $(i=0, 1, \ldots, n_3)$ are real (the complex case will be commented later). For the sake of convenience we set

$$n=n_1+n_2+n_3 , \quad n_1=n\alpha , \quad n_2=n\beta .$$

Let us suppose that

(2) $$|p(x)|\leqq 1 \quad \text{for} \quad -1\leqq x\leqq 1 .$$

Then we are interested in finding an estimate on $|p(x)|$ for all real $x\in(-\infty, \infty)$ (and also in the complex plane **C**). Even on the interval $[-1, 1]$ it is possible to sharpen the estimate (2) exploiting the special form of $p(x)$ by (1). The problem was posed by G. G. Lorentz [1] in special case ($n_2=0$) and recently was solved completely by E. B. Saff, R. S. Varga and coworkers (see [2] and the references therein). They made use of some asymptotic properties of Jacobi polynomials and of a lemma (see Corollary 2.2 in [2]) which will be recapitulated here.

Lemma. *Let a, b be real numbers with* $-1<a<b<1$, *and let*

(3) $$\Phi(z)=\frac{\sqrt{z-a}+\sqrt{z-b}}{\sqrt{z-a}-\sqrt{z-b}}, \quad z\in \mathbf{C}^*\backslash[a, b]$$

(where $\mathbf{C}^*$ *denotes the extended complex plane) for some suitable branch of the square root function so that* $w=\Phi(z)$ *maps* $\mathbf{C}^*\backslash[a, b]$ *into* $|w|>1$. *Then for* $p(x)\in\mathscr{P}$ *and for all*

$z \in \mathbf{C}^* \setminus [a, b]$

(4) $$|p(z)| \leq \max_{a \leq x \leq b} |p(x)| \cdot |\Phi(z)|^n \left| \frac{\Phi(z) - \Phi(-1)}{\Phi(-1)\,\Phi(z) - 1} \right|^{n_1} \left| \frac{\Phi(z) - \Phi(1)}{\Phi(1)\Phi(z) - 1} \right|^{n_2}.$$

The Jacobi polynomials come into play when the values a and b are to be chosen so that the estimate in (4) be optimal.

It was found that this is the case when

(5) $$\left.\begin{matrix} b \\ a \end{matrix}\right\} = \alpha^2 - \beta^2 \pm \sqrt{(1+\alpha+\beta)(1+\alpha-\beta)(1-\alpha+\beta)(1-\alpha-\beta)}\,.$$

This formula shows that $a<b$ except when $\alpha+\beta=1$. Since the case $\alpha+\beta=1$ is uninteresting we may assume that $\alpha+\beta<1$ or equivalently $a<b$.

Our aim here is to give another proof for the inequality (4) together with (5) in the *real* case (i.e. when the coefficients a_i and the independent variable x are real) using properties of some extremal polynomials in $\mathscr{P}$ and asymptotic results of [3]. In the complex case we can not say more then what Lemma states.

Let $\mathscr{P}^*$ be the subset of $\mathscr{P}$ whose elements are of the form

(6) $$p(x) = (x+1)^{n_1}(x-1)^{n_2}(x^{n_3} + a_{n_3-1}x^{n_3-1} + \ldots + a_1 x + a_0)\,,$$

and let $\mu_n = \mu_n(n_1, n_2, n_3)$ be defined by

(7) $$\mu_n = \min_{p \in \mathscr{P}^*} \max_{-1 \leq x \leq 1} |p(x)|\,.$$

It is clear that there is exactly one polynomial $p_n^*(x) \in \mathscr{P}^*$ satisfying the relation

(8) $$\max_{-1 \leq x \leq 1} |p_n^*(x)| = \mu_n\,.$$

These polynomials $p_n^*(x)$ (for different values of n_1, n_2, n_3) are the extremal polynomials in question and they have the following properties:

Property 1: they can be written as

$$p_n^*(x) = (x+1)^{n_1}(x-1)^{n_2} \prod_{i=1}^{n_3} (x - x_i)\,,$$

where $x_i = x_i(n_1, n_2, n_3)$, $-1 < x_1 < x_2 < \ldots < x_{n_3} < 1$.

Property 2: for each extremal polynomial $p_n^*(x)$ there is a sequence of extremal points $\{\xi_j\}_{j=0}^{n_3}$ depending on n_1, n_2, n_3 such that

(9) $$-1 \leq \xi_0 < x_1 < \xi_1 < \ldots < x_{n_3} < \xi_{n_3} \leq 1\,,$$

(10) $$p_n^*(\xi_j) = (-1)^{n_2+n_3-j}\mu_n, \quad j = 0, 1, \ldots, n_3\,.$$

(This is the so-called Chebycheff alternation property of extremal polynomials).

Let $\rho_n(x)$ be introduced by

$$(11)\qquad \rho_n(x)=\begin{cases} \dfrac{1}{n(x_{i+1}-x_i)}, & x_i\leqq x\leqq x_{i+1} \quad \text{for} \quad i=1,2,\ldots,n_3-1,\\ 0 & \text{elsewhere.}\end{cases}$$

Let $\{p^*_{n^{(\nu)}}(x)\}_{\nu=1}^{\infty}$ be a sequence of extremal polynomials such that

$$(12)\qquad \lim_{\nu\to\infty}\frac{n_1^{(\nu)}}{n^{(\nu)}}=\alpha,\quad \lim_{\nu\to\infty}\frac{n_2^{(\nu)}}{n^{(\nu)}}=\beta,$$

where α, β are fixed nonnegative numbers, $\alpha+\beta\leqq 1$. Then according to the main result of [3] we have

$$(13)\qquad \frac{1}{n^{(\nu)}}\log|p^*_{n^{(\nu)}}(x)|\Rightarrow\varphi(x)=\alpha\log|x+1|+\beta\log|x-1|+\int_a^b\log|x-t|\gamma(t)dt$$

as $\nu\to\infty$, where $\Rightarrow$means the convergence in measure, the values a and b are the *same* as in (5), and

$$(14)\qquad \lim_{\nu\to\infty}\rho_{n^{(\nu)}}(x)=\gamma(x) \text{ for almost everywhere in } [-1,1],$$

and

$$\gamma(x)=\begin{cases}\dfrac{1}{\pi}\dfrac{\sqrt{(b-x)(x-a)}}{1-x^2} & \text{for} \quad a\leqq x\leqq b,\\ 0 & \text{elsewhere.}\end{cases}$$

On the interval $[a,b]$ we have in (13) that

$$(15)\qquad \varphi(x)=\lim_{\nu\to\infty}\frac{1}{n^{(\nu)}}\log\mu_{n^{(\nu)}}=\log\frac{\sqrt{\mu(\alpha,\beta)}}{2},$$

where

$$\mu(\alpha,\beta)=(1+\alpha+\beta)^{1+\alpha+\beta}(1+\alpha-\beta)^{1+\alpha-\beta}(1-\alpha+\beta)^{1-\alpha+\beta}(1-\alpha-\beta)^{1-\alpha-\beta}.$$

We remark here that in [3] the sequences $\{n_1^{(\nu)}/n^{(\nu)}\}_{\nu=1}^{\infty}$ and $\{n_2^{(\nu)}/n^{(\nu)}\}_{\nu=1}^{\infty}$ were nondecreasing, but looking over the proof we can see that this circumstance makes no difficulties in modifying the proof to be valid for the cases when we know only the fact of convergence in (12).

A somewhat tedious computation yields for $\varphi(x)$ by (13)

$$(16)\qquad \varphi'(x)=\frac{S(x;a,b)}{\sqrt{1-x^2}},\quad x\neq\pm 1,$$

where

$$S(x;a,b)=\begin{cases}\sqrt{(a-x)(b-x)} & \text{for } x\leqq a\\ 0 & \text{for } a\leqq x\leqq b\\ -\sqrt{(a-x)(b-x)} & \text{for } x\geqq b.\end{cases}$$

Let us introduce the quantities $\bar{a}$ and $\bar{b}$ for the sequence of polynomials $\{p^*_{n^{(\nu)}}(x)\}_{\nu=1}^{\infty}$ with (12) by

$$\text{(17)}\qquad \begin{aligned}\bar{a}&=\liminf_{\nu\to\infty}\xi_0(n_1^{(\nu)},n_2^{(\nu)},n_3^{(\nu)})\\ \bar{b}&=\limsup_{\nu\to\infty}\xi_{n_3}(n_1^{(\nu)},n_2^{(\nu)},n_3^{(\nu)}).\end{aligned}$$

By (9) it is clear that $\bar{a}\leqq a$ and $b\leqq\bar{b}$. Since the relations (13), (14) give rather global description of the individual zeros and extremal points of $p^*_{n^{(\nu)}}(x)$, therefore the next theorem will not be a trivial one.

Theorem 1. *Let $\{p^*_{n^{(\nu)}}(x)\}_{\nu=1}^{\infty}$ be a sequence of extremal polynomials satisfying* (12) *with the restriction $\alpha+\beta<1$. Then the quantities $\bar{a}$ and $\bar{b}$ introduced in* (17) *fulfil the relations $\bar{a}=a$ and $\bar{b}=b$, where a and b are given in* (5).

Proof. The cases $a=-1$ and $b=1$ are trivial since by (17) $-1\leqq\bar{a}\leqq a$ and $b\leqq\bar{b}\leqq 1$ and only the equality can be true.

Let us show first the validity of $a=\bar{a}$ for $a>-1$. Since (5) gives

$$\alpha=\frac{\sqrt{(1+a)(1+b)}}{2},\quad \beta=\frac{\sqrt{(1-a)(1-b)}}{2}$$

(see also [3], p. 260) thus $\alpha>0$ in this case. By (12) we have that $\alpha^{(\nu)}=n_1^{(\nu)}/n^{(\nu)}>0$ for $\nu\geqq\nu_0$, where ν_0 is sufficiently large. For $\alpha+\beta<1$, there is some $\nu_1\geqq\nu_0$ such that $\alpha^{(\nu)}<1$ for $\nu\geqq\nu_1$.

Let $d^{(\nu)}$ be the solution of the equation

$$\text{(18)}\qquad (1+x)^{\alpha^{(\nu)}}(1-x)^{1-\alpha^{(\nu)}}=\frac{1}{2}\qquad -1\leqq x\leqq 0,\quad \nu\geqq\nu_1.$$

This equation has exactly one solution since the function on the left hand side strictly increases on $[-1,1-2\alpha^{(\nu)}]$ from 0 to its maximum and it strictly decreases on $[1-2\alpha^{(\nu)},1]$ from this maximum to 0 and at $x=0$ it takes on the value 1.

The solution $d^{(\nu)}$ depends continuously on $\alpha^{(\nu)}$ for $0<\alpha^{(\nu)}<1$ hence there exists the limit defined by

$$\text{(18')}\qquad d=\lim_{\nu\to\infty}d^{(\nu)},$$

and d is the solution of (18) if we replace α instead of $\alpha^{(\nu)}$. Hence $d > -1$.

We are going to show that $\bar{a} \geqq d$. For $|x-y| < 1-x$ if $-1 \leqq x < 0$ and $-1 < y < 1$, therefore by Property 1 we have

$$|p^*_{n^{(\nu)}}(x)| = (x+1)^{n_1^{(\nu)}}(1-x)^{n_2^{(\nu)}} \prod_{i=1}^{n_3^{(\nu)}} |x - x_i^{(\nu)}| <$$

$$< (x+1)^{n_1^{(\nu)}}(1-x)^{n_2^{(\nu)}+n_3^{(\nu)}} \quad \text{for} \quad -1 < x < 0 ,$$

hence by the definition of $d^{(\nu)}$

$$|p^*_{n^{(\nu)}}(x)| < \frac{1}{2^{n^{(\nu)}}} \quad \text{for} \quad -1 < x < d^{(\nu)}, \quad \nu \geqq \nu_1 . \tag{19}$$

On the other hand Theorem 1 in [3] states that

$$\max_{-1 \leqq x \leqq 1} |p^*_{n^{(\nu)}}(x)| = \mu_{n^{(\nu)}} > 2^{-n^{(\nu)}} [\mu(\alpha^{(\nu)}, \beta^{(\nu)})]^{n^{(\nu)}/2} , \tag{20}$$

where $\beta^{(\nu)} = n_2^{(\nu)}/n^{(\nu)}$. The function $\mu(\alpha, \beta)$ in (15) is strictly increasing in its both variables hence for $0 < \alpha^{(\nu)} < 1$

$$\mu(\alpha^{(\nu)}, \beta^{(\nu)}) \geqq \mu(\alpha^{(\nu)}, 0) > \mu(0, 0) = 1 ,$$

therefore by (20) $\mu_{n^{(\nu)}} > 2^{-n^{(\nu)}}$ and by (10) we have for $\xi_0^{(\nu)} = \xi_0(n_1^{(\nu)}, n_2^{(\nu)}, n_3^{(\nu)})$

$$|p^*_{n^{(\nu)}}(\xi_0^{(\nu)})| = \mu_{n^{(\nu)}} > 2^{-n^{(\nu)}} .$$

Thus by (19) $\xi_0^{(\nu)}$ cannot be in the interval $[-1, d^{(\nu)}]$, i.e. $\xi_0^{(\nu)} > d^{(\nu)}$ if $\nu > \nu_1$. Let ν tend to ∞ here then (18′) implies $\bar{a} \geqq d > -1$ as we stated.

Before going further we make an observation. If x_i and x_{i+1} are consecutive zeros of $p_n^*(x)$ in $(-1, 1)$ then it follows from (11) that

$$\int_{x_i}^{x_{i+1}} \rho_n(x)\,dx = \frac{1}{n} .$$

Hence if we know about any interval $[c, d] \subset (-1, 1)$ that

$$n \int_c^d \rho_n(x)\,dx \geqq 2 ,$$

then there are at least two zeros of $p_n^*(x)$ on it.

Taking into consideration that

$$\int_{-1}^{1} \rho_n(x)\,dx = \frac{n_3 - 1}{n} ,$$

we have by (12), (14)

$$\lim_{\nu\to\infty}\int_{-1}^{1}\rho_{n^{(\nu)}}(x)dx=\int_a^b\gamma(x)dx=1-\alpha-\beta$$

and

$$\lim_{\nu\to\infty}\int_a^b\rho_{n^{(\nu)}}(x)dx=1-\alpha-\beta>0\,.$$

Thus for some sufficiently large $\nu_2\geqq\nu_1$ the inequality

$$n^{(\nu)}\int_a^b\rho_{n^{(\nu)}}(x)dx>2\quad\text{for}\quad \nu\geqq\nu_2 \tag{21}$$

holds hence every polynomial $p^*_{n^{(\nu)}}(x)$ with $\nu\geqq\nu_2$ has at least two zeros on $[a, b]$ and consequently it has at least one extremal point between them. Let $\xi_k^{(\nu)}$ $(k=k^{(\nu)})$ denote the smallest extremal point of $p^*_{n^{(\nu)}}(x)$ which is still in $[a, b]$ for $\nu\geqq\nu_2$. We state that

$$\lim_{\nu\to\infty}\xi_k^{(\nu)}=a\,. \tag{22}$$

Suppose that (22) is not true. Then there would be a subsequence of $\{n^{(\nu)}\}_{\nu=\nu_2}^{\infty}$, denoted by $\{n^{(\nu_l)}\}_{l=1}^{\infty}$ for which the corresponding extremal points $\xi_k^{(\nu_l)}$ satisfy

$$\lim_{l\to\infty}\xi_k^{(\nu_l)}=a'>a\,. \tag{23}$$

Owing to the definition of $\xi_k^{(\nu)}$'s there is at most one zero of $p^*_{n^{(\nu)}}(x)$ on $[a, \xi_k^{(\nu)}]$, hence our observation gives

$$n^{(\nu)}\int_a^{\xi_k^{(\nu)}}\rho_{n^{(\nu)}}(x)dx<2\,. \tag{24}$$

But (14) and (23) imply

$$\lim_{l\to\infty}\int_a^{\xi_k^{(\nu_l)}}\rho_{n^{(\nu_l)}}(x)dx=\int_a^{a'}\gamma(x)dx\,,$$

which contradicts to (24), thus (22) is true.

Now we shall prove the equality $\bar{a}=a$ for $a>-1$. Suppose the contrary which is $\bar{a}<a$.

By (17) there is a subsequence of $\{n^{(\nu)}\}_{\nu=1}^{\infty}$ such that the sequence of the corresponding ξ_0's is convergent to $\bar{a}$. For the sake of simplicity we shall denote this subsequence again by $\{n^{(\nu)}\}_{\nu=1}^{\infty}$ and then

$$\lim\xi_0^{(\nu)}=\bar{a}\,. \tag{17'}$$

In [3] it was introduced the set $I_\nu(\varepsilon, c)$ for $0<\varepsilon, c<1$ by

$$I_\nu(\varepsilon, c)=[-1, -1+\varepsilon]\cup[1-\varepsilon, 1]\cup\bigcup_{i=1}^{n_3^{(\nu)}}\left[x_i^{(\nu)}-\frac{c}{n^{(\nu)}}, x_i^{(\nu)}+\frac{c}{n^{(\nu)}}\right],$$

and it was shown (see formula (32) in [3]) with our notations that for $x\in[-1, 1]\setminus I_\nu(\varepsilon, c)$

$$\frac{1}{n^{(\nu)}}\log|p^*_{n^{(\nu)}}(x)|=\alpha^{(\nu)}\log|x+1|+\beta^{(\nu)}\log|x-1|+\Psi_\nu(x)+ \tag{25}$$
$$+\Theta\left[\frac{1}{n^{(\nu)}}\log\frac{1}{\sqrt{\varepsilon(2-\varepsilon)}}+\frac{3}{2n^{(\nu)}}\log\frac{n_3^{(\nu)}}{c}\right],$$

where $|\Theta|<1$ and

$$\Psi_\nu(x)=\int_{-1}^{1}\log|x-t|\rho_{n^{(\nu)}}(t)dt\,.$$

The sequence $\{\Psi_\nu(x)\}_{\nu=1}^{\infty}$ is equicontinuous, because there is a strictly increasing continuous function $\eta(h)$ defined on $[0, h_0]$, $h_0=(3-\sqrt{5})/2$ such that $\eta(0)=0$ and for every real x the relation

$$|\Psi_\nu(x+h)-\Psi_\nu(x)|<\eta(h)\quad\text{for}\quad 0<h<h_0,\quad \nu=1, 2, \ldots \tag{26}$$

is valid (see (29) in [3]).

We want to apply (25) for $x=\xi_0^{(\nu)}$ and for $x=\xi_k^{(\nu)}$, therefore we must ensure that these points belong not to $I_\nu(\varepsilon, c)$ for sufficiently large ν's if ε and c are sufficiently small. By (22) and (17′) we have that if $\varepsilon<\min\{1-a, \bar{a}+1\}=\varepsilon_0$ then $\xi_0^{(\nu)}, \xi_k^{(\nu)}\notin$ $\notin[-1, -1+\varepsilon]\cup[1-\varepsilon, 1]$ if ν is sufficiently large. Here we must know that $a<1$ and $\bar{a}>-1$. Both are true since by one of our assumptions $a<b$ and $b\leqq 1$. On the other hand we have shown above that $\bar{a}\geqq d>-1$.

Our indirect assumption is $\bar{a}<a$ hence (17′) and (22) imply that $k=k^{(\nu)}>0$. By (21) there are at least two zeros of $p^*_{n^{(\nu)}}(x)$ for $\nu\geqq\nu_2$ on $[a, b]$ hence $k^{(\nu)}<n_3^{(\nu)}$. Thus we should consider the differences

$$x_1^{(\nu)}-\xi_0^{(\nu)},\ \xi_k^{(\nu)}-x_k^{(\nu)},\ x_{k+1}^{(\nu)}-\xi_k^{(\nu)}\,.$$

Applying a theorem due to S. Bernstein [4] we have for $p^*_{n^{(\nu)}}(x)$

$$|p^{*\prime}_{n^{(\nu)}}(x)|\leqq\frac{n^{(\nu)}\mu_{n^{(\nu)}}}{\sqrt{1-x^2}},\quad -1<x<1\,,$$

hence by (10)

$$\mu_{n^{(\nu)}}=|p^*_{n^{(\nu)}}(\xi_0^{(\nu)})|=\left|\int_{\xi_0^{(\nu)}}^{x_1^{(\nu)}}p^{*\prime}_{n^{(\nu)}}(x)dx\right|\leqq n^{(\nu)}\mu_{n^{(\nu)}}\int_{\xi_0^{(\nu)}}^{x_1^{(\nu)}}\frac{dx}{\sqrt{1-x^2}},$$

consequently

$$x_1^{(\nu)} > \xi_0^{(\nu)} \cos \frac{1}{n^{(\nu)}} + \sqrt{1-\xi_0^{(\nu)^2}} \sin \frac{1}{n^{(\nu)}} .$$

Then it follows from (17′)

$$\liminf_{\nu\to\infty} n^{(\nu)}(x_1^{(\nu)} - \xi_0^{(\nu)}) \geqq \sqrt{1-\bar{a}^2} .$$

Taking into consideration (22) we have similarly for $\xi_k^{(\nu)}$

$$\liminf_{\nu\to\infty} n^{(\nu)}(\xi_k^{(\nu)} - x_k^{(\nu)}) \geqq \sqrt{1-a^2} ,$$

$$\liminf_{\nu\to\infty} n^{(\nu)}(x_{k+1}^{(\nu)} - \xi_k^{(\nu)}) \geqq \sqrt{1-a^2} .$$

Let $c_0 = \min\{\sqrt{1-\bar{a}^2}, \sqrt{1-a^2}\}$. If we choose and fix the values c, ε so that $0<\varepsilon<\varepsilon_0$, $0<c<c_0$, then $\xi_0^{(\nu)}, \xi_k^{(\nu)} \notin I_\nu(\varepsilon, c)$ for all $\nu \geqq \nu_3$ where $\nu_3 \geqq \nu_2$ and ν_3 is sufficiently large. Hence by (17′) and (26) we have

$$\lim_{\nu\to\infty} (\Psi_\nu(\xi_0^{(\nu)}) - \psi_\nu(\bar{a})) = 0,$$

by (14)

$$\lim_{\nu\to\infty} \psi_\nu(\bar{a}) = \int_a^b \log|\bar{a}-t|\gamma(t)\,dt ,$$

and so by (25)

$$\lim_{\nu\to\infty} \frac{1}{n^{(\nu)}} \log|p^*_{n^{(\nu)}}(\xi_0^{(\nu)})| = \alpha \log|\bar{a}+1| + \beta \log|\bar{a}-1| + \int_a^b \log|\bar{a}-t|\gamma(t)\,dt = \varphi(\bar{a})$$

and similarly by (22)

$$\lim_{\nu\to\infty} \frac{1}{n^{(\nu)}} \log|p^*_{n^{(\nu)}}(\xi_k^{(\nu)})| = \varphi(a) .$$

On the other hand by (10) it is $|p^*_{n^{(\nu)}}(\xi_0^{(\nu)})| = |p^*_{n^{(\nu)}}(\xi_k^{(\nu)})|$ therefore $\varphi(a) = \varphi(\bar{a})$, i.e.

$$0 = \varphi(a) - \varphi(\bar{a}) = \int_{\bar{a}}^{a} \varphi'(x)\,dx ,$$

which contradicts to the assumption $\bar{a} < a$ since by (16) the integrand $\varphi'(x) > 0$ and continuous on $(-1, a)$.

The proof of the equality $b = \bar{b}$ goes in similar manner and the proof of Theorem 1 is complete.

Let us introduce the Chebycheff like polynomials by

$$p_n(x) = \frac{1}{\mu_n} p_n^*(x) . \tag{27}$$

It is clear that $p_n(x) \in \mathscr{P}$ and $p_n(x)$ fulfils the relation (2). In the case $n_1 = n_2 = 0$ we have $p_n(x) = T_n(x)$, i.e. the well-known Chebycheff polynomials of nth order. That is the reason why we call the polynomials $p_n(x)$ here Chebycheff like polynomials.

Theorem 2. *Let $p(x)$ be a polynomial in $\mathscr{P}$ satisfying the relation (2). Let the polynomial $p_n(x)$ be the corresponding Chebycheff like polynomial (i.e. with same n_1, n_2, n_3 as in $p(x)$) and let $n_3 > 0$. Then*

$$|p(x)| \leqq |p_n(x)| \quad \textit{for all real} \quad x \notin [\xi_0, \xi_{n_3}] \cup \{-1\} \cup \{1\}. \tag{28}$$

Concerning the extremal point ξ_0 the following possibilities can take place. If $n_1 = 0$ then $\xi_0 = -1$ and either $|p(-1)| < 1$ or $|p(-1)| = 1$ and $|p'(-1)| \leqq |p_n'(-1)|$. If $n_1 > 0$ then $\xi_0 > -1$ and $|p(\xi_0)| \leqq 1$.

In the relations where $\leqq$ stands, the equality holds if and only if $p(x) = \pm p_n(x)$. Similar statement is true for ξ_{n_3}.

(Concerning this theorem see also Theorem 3.3 in [2]).

Proof. Let us consider the case $x > \xi_{n_3}$. Suppose that there is a polynomial $p(x) \in \mathscr{P}$ different from $p_n(x)$ and $-p_n(x)$ and suppose that there is a value $\bar{x} > \xi_{n_3'}$ $\bar{x} \neq 1$ satisfying $|p(\bar{x})| \geqq p_n(\bar{x})|$ then we should led to a contradiction.

Let ε be defined by $\varepsilon = \operatorname{sign}(p(\bar{x})/p_n(\bar{x}))$ and consider the polynomial

$$r(x) = (x+1)^{-n_1}(x-1)^{-n_2}[p_n(x) - \varepsilon p(x)].$$

Since $p, p_n \in \mathscr{P}$ therefore $r(x)$ is a polynomial of the order not greater than n_3. By (2) and (10), (27) we have

$$(-1)^{n_3 - j} r(\xi_j) \geqq 0 \quad j = 0, 1, \ldots, n_3,$$

and the indirect assumption implies that $r(\bar{x}) \leqq 0$. Hence the polynomial $r(x)$ would have at least $n_3 + 1$ zeros, i.e. $r(x) \equiv 0$, and so $p(x) = \varepsilon p_n(x)$, which contradicts to our assumption $p(x) \neq \pm p_n(x)$.

Let us consider the extremal point ξ_{n_3}. If $n_2 = 0$ then $\xi_{n_3} = 1$ since otherwise it would be for $\xi_{n_3} < 1$ by Property 1 that $p_n(1) > p_n(\xi_{n_3}) = 1$ in contradiction to (2). Hence $p_n(1) = 1$. When $|p(1)| < 1$ then there is nothing to prove. When $|p(1)| = 1$ then $p(1) = \pm 1$ and let $q(x) = p(1)p(x)$. So we have $q(1) = 1$, $q(x) \in \mathscr{P}$. From the inequality $q(x) \leqq 1$ for $-1 \leqq x \leqq 1$ it follows that $q'(1) \geqq 0$. On the other hand the just proved inquality (28) gives $q(x) \leqq p_n(x)$ for $x > 1$ and so $|p'(1)| = q'(1) \leqq p_n'(1)$. If $q'(1) = p_n'(1)$ here then the polynomial $r(x)$, defined by

$$r(x) = (x+1)^{-n_1}[p_n(x) - q(x)]$$

has a double zero at $x = 1$ and $(-1)^{n_3 - j} r(\xi_j) \geqq 0$ for $j = 0, 1, \ldots, n_3 - 1$, therefore $r(x)$ has at least $2 + (n_3 - 1) = n_3 + 1$ zeros, i.e. $r(x) \equiv 0$ and the equalities $|p(1)| = p_n(1)$, $|p'(1)| = p_n'(1)$ are possible only for $p(x) = \pm p_n(x)$.

In the case $n_2>0$ it is clear that $-1<\xi_{n_3}<1$. By (2) $|p(\xi_{n_3})|\leqq 1$ hence we should examine the case of equality. If $|p(\xi_{n_3})|=1$ then $p'(\xi_{n_3})=0$, hence the polynomial

$$r(x)=(x+1)^{-n_1}(x-1)^{-n_2}[p_n(x)-p(\xi_{n_3})p(x)]$$

has double zero at $x=\xi_{n_3}$ and thus we arrive to $r(x)\equiv 0$, i.e. $p(x)=\pm p_n(x)$.

The case $x<\xi_0$ can be treated in similar manner which completes the proof.

Now we can pass over to establish an inequality similar to (4).

Theorem 3. *Let $p(x)$ be a polynomial in $\mathcal{P}(n_1, n_2, n_3)$ satisfying relation* (2) *and let $n_3>0$. Then*

$$|p(x)|<2^n e^{n\varphi(x)}\{\mu(\alpha, \beta)\}^{-n/2} \quad \textit{for} \quad x\notin(a, b)\cup\{-1\}\cup\{1\}, \tag{29}$$

where $n=n_1+n_2+n_3$, $\alpha=n_1/n$, $\beta=n_2/n$ and a, b are defined by (5) *and the functions $\varphi(x)$, $\mu(\alpha, \beta)$* by (13), (14), *resp.*

Proof. Let us consider the set of polynomials $\mathcal{P}_\nu=\mathcal{P}(2^\nu n_1,\ 2^\nu n_2,\ 2^\nu n_3)$ for $\nu=0, 1, \ldots$. Let $n^{(\nu)}=2^\nu n$, $n_i^{(\nu)}=2^\nu n_i$ for $i=1, 2, 3$ and let $p_{n^{(\nu)}}(x)$ be the Chebycheff like polynomial in $\mathcal{P}_\nu$. By Theorem 2 we have

$$|p(x)|\leqq|p_{n^{(\nu)}}(x)| \quad \text{for} \quad x\notin[\xi_0^{(\nu)}, \xi_{n_3}^{(\nu)}]\cup\{-1\}\cup\{1\}. \tag{30}$$

Let us consider the polynomial $q(x)=[p_{n^{(\nu)}}(x)]^2$ $(\nu=0, 1, \ldots)$. It is clear that $q(x)\in\mathcal{P}_{\nu+1}$. Since $q(x)\geqq 0$ for all x's, $q(x)$ has not the Chebycheff alternation property therefore $q(x)\neq\pm p_{n^{(\nu+1)}}(x)$. Applying again Theorem 2 for $q(x)$ we have

$$p^2_{n^{(\nu)}}(x)<|p_{n^{(\nu+1)}}(x)| \quad \text{for} \quad x\notin[\xi_0^{(\nu+1)}, \xi_{n_3}^{(\nu+1)}]\cup\{-1\}\cup\{1\}. \tag{31}$$

Moreover Theorem 2 gives in the case $n_1=0$ that $n_1^{(\nu)}=0$, $\xi_0^{(\nu)}=-1$ for $\nu=0, 1, \ldots$ and in the case $n_1>0$ that $n_1^{(\nu)}>0$, $\xi_0^{(\nu)}>-1$ and

$$p^2_{n^{(\nu)}}(\xi_0^{(\nu+1)})<|p_{n^{(\nu+1)}}(\xi_0^{(\nu+1)})|=1.$$

This inquality together with (31) implies

$$\xi_0^{(\nu)}>\xi_0^{(\nu+1)} \quad \nu=0, 1, 2, \ldots \quad \text{if} \quad n_1>0, \tag{32}$$

and similarly

$$\xi_{n_3}^{(\nu)}<\xi_{n_3}^{(\nu+1)} \quad \nu=0, 1, 2, \ldots \quad \text{if} \quad n_2>0.$$

By (27) the sequence of polynomials $\{\mu_{n^{(\nu)}}p_{n^{(\nu)}}(x)\}_{\nu=0}^{\infty}$ mets all the requirements of Theorem 1 thus

$$\lim_{\nu\to\infty}\xi_0^{(\nu)}=a, \qquad \lim_{\nu\to\infty}\xi_{n_3}^{(\nu)}=b. \tag{33}$$

It is clear that $\bigcup_{\nu=0}^{\infty}[\xi_0^{(\nu)}\xi_{n_3}^{(\nu)}]\cup\{-1\}\cup\{1\}=(a,b)\cup\{-1\}\cup\{1\}=U$ hence by (30), (31) we have simultaneously

$$|p(x)|^{\frac{1}{n}} \leqq |p_{n^{(0)}}(x)|^{\frac{1}{n}} < |p_{n^{(1)}}(x)|^{\frac{1}{n^{(1)}}} < \dots < |p_{n^{(\nu)}}(x)|^{\frac{1}{n^{(\nu)}}} < \dots \quad \text{for} \quad x \notin U. \tag{34}$$

Letting $\nu\to\infty$ here and making use of relations (13), (15) we have from (34)

$$|p(x)| < e^{n\varphi(x)}\left(\frac{\sqrt{\mu(\alpha,\beta)}}{2}\right)^{-n} \quad \text{for} \quad x \notin U.$$

It is not difficult to show making use of (25) that the convergence in (13) is common, pointwise for $x \notin U$. Hence Theorem 3 is proved.

As an interesting byproduct of the proof of Theorem 3 we can establish the next theorem.

Theorem 4. *Let $p_n^*(x)$ be the extremal polynomial in $\mathscr{P}^*(n_1, n_2, n_3)$ with $n_3>0$. Let ξ_0, ξ_{n_3} be the smallest and the largest extremal points of it. Let $\alpha=n_1/n$, $\beta=n_2/n$ and let a, b be defined by* (5). *Then*

$$\xi_0 \underset{(=)}{>} a \underset{(=)}{>} -1 \quad \textit{when} \quad n_1 \underset{(=)}{>} 0,$$

$$\xi_{n_3} \underset{(=)}{<} b \underset{(=)}{<} 1 \quad \textit{when} \quad n_2 \underset{(=)}{<} 0.$$

Proof. Based on the relations (32), (33) and on Theorem 2.

In order to compare (4) and Theorem 3 we need to evaluate the function $\varphi(x)$. After a cumbersome calculation of the finite integral in (13) we have by (14), (15)

$$\begin{aligned} &\frac{2}{\sqrt{\mu(\alpha,\beta)}}e^{\varphi(x)} = \\ &= \frac{|x+1|^{\alpha}|x-1|^{\beta}(\sqrt{|x-a|}+\sqrt{|x-b|})^2(b-a)^{\alpha+\beta-1}}{(\sqrt{1+b}\sqrt{|x-a|}+\sqrt{1+a}\sqrt{|x-b|})^{2\alpha}(\sqrt{1-b}\sqrt{|x-a|}+\sqrt{1-a}\sqrt{|x-b|})^{2\beta}} \\ &\qquad \text{for} \quad x \notin (a,b) \end{aligned} \tag{35}$$

which agrees with (4) in real case. Moreover we can see that in Theorem 3 the "less" relation holds while in (4) only "less or equal". Finally we remark that our limiting procedure using Chebycheff like polynomials ensures that the base of power in (29) of Theorem 3 given explicitly in (35) can not be smaller for $x \notin (a,b)\cup\{-1\}\cup\{1\}$ i.e. the result is sharp in this sense.

Acknowledgement

It is my sad duty to acknowledge that this paper would not have been written without the standing encouragement of the late Professor PAUL TURÁN.

References

[1] LORENTZ, G. G., *Approximation by incomplete polynomials (problems and results), Padé and rational approximation: theory and applications*, (eds.: E. B. Saff and R. S. Varga), pp. 289–302, Acad. Press Inc., N. Y., 1977.

[2] LACHANCE, M.; SAFF, E. B.; VARGA, R. S.; Bounds for incomplete polynomials vanishing at both endpoints of an interval, *Constructive approaches to mathematical models* (Proc. Conf. in honor of R. J. Duffin. Pittsburgh, Pa., 1978), pp. 421–437, Acad. Press, N. Y., 1979.

[3] ELBERT, Á., Some inequalities concerning polynomials having only real zeros, *Stud. Sci. Math. Hung.*, **6** (1971), 251–261.

[4] BERNSTEIN, S., Sur quelques propriétés asymptotiques des polynomes, *Comptes Rendus Acad. Sci. Paris*, **157** (1913), 1055–1057.

MATHEMATICAL INSTITUTE OF THE
HUNGARIAN ACADEMY OF SCIENCES
H-1053 BUDAPEST, REÁLTANODA U. 13–15.
HUNGARY

Studies in Pure Mathematics
To the Memory of Paul Turán

Subsequences of primes in residue classes to prime moduli

by

P. D. T. A. ELLIOTT* (Boulder)

In a recent paper [1] the author proved that in order for a strongly-additive arithmetic function $f(n)$ to satisfy

$$\sum_{n \leqq x} |f(n+1) - f(n)|^2 \leqq c_1 x$$

for some constant c_1 and all $x \geqq 1$, it is both necessary and sufficient that there be a further constant A so that the series

$$\sum p^{-1} |f(p) - A \log p|^2, \quad p \text{ prime},$$

be convergent. An important part in the proof was played by an inequality of the type

$$(1) \qquad \sum_{q \leqq Q} (q-1) \sum_{l=1}^{q-1} \Bigg| \sum_{\substack{p \leqq x \\ p \equiv l (\mathrm{mod}\, q)}} a_p - \frac{1}{q-1} \sum_{p \leqq x} a_p \Bigg|^2 \leqq \Delta(x, Q) \sum_{p \leqq x} |a_p|^2,$$

with

$$(2) \qquad \Delta(x, Q) = c_2 x (\log x)^{-1} + D(Q).$$

Here c_2 is an absolute constant, $D(Q)$ a non-explicit function of Q alone, and the inequality is valid for all $x \geqq 2$, $Q \geqq 2$, and complex numbers a_p. As is usual p q are generic symbols for prime numbers. The presence of the factor $(\log x)^{-1}$ in the expression for $\Delta(x, Q)$ was essential.

The inequality (1) might be compared with a result of Wolke [12].

In order to obtain a quantitative formulation of the theorem concerning additive functions it appears desirable to have an explicit and "not-too-large" estimate for $D(Q)$ in (2). We indicate here how to obtain the following result.

* Partially supported by NSF Contract No. MCS 75–08233

Theorem. *The inequality*

$$\sum_{q\leqq Q}(q-1)\sum_{l=1}^{q-1}\left|\sum_{\substack{p\leqq x\\ p\equiv l(\mathrm{mod}\ q)}} a_p-\frac{1}{q-1}\sum_{p\leqq x} a_p\right|^2\leqq c_3\left(\frac{x}{\log x}+Q^5\right)\sum_{p\leqq x}|a_p|^2$$

holds with some constant c_3, uniformly for all complex numbers a_p, $2\leqq p\leqq x$, and real numbers $x\geqq 2$, $Q\geqq 2$.

Remarks. As we shall presently indicate, the term Q^5 may be slightly improved.

Let $\chi(\ )$ be a non-principal cubic character (mod q), $q\equiv 1$ (mod 3). Let $\rho\neq 1$ be a cube root of unity and let $w(q)$ be the least *prime* p such that $\chi(p)=\rho$. Since $\chi(p)=\rho$ if and only if p belongs to one of a certain $(q-1)/3$ reduced residue classes (mod q), we see that whenever $w(q)>x(\geqq 2)$ then

$$(q-1)\sum_{l=1}^{q-1}\left|\sum_{\substack{p\leqq x\\ p\equiv l(\mathrm{mod}\ q)}} -\frac{1}{q-1}\sum_{p\leqq x} 1\right|^2\geqq \pi(x)^2/3.$$

Hence the number N of primes q, not exceeding Q, for which $w(q)>x$ satisfies

$$N\pi(x)^2/3\leqq c_3(x(\log x)^{-1}+Q^5)\pi(x).$$

In particular, there are positive constants b and c, effectively computable, so that for all primes $q\leqq Q$, $q\equiv 1$ (mod 3), with the possible exception of at most b, the bound $w(q)<cQ^5$ is satisfied. This ends the remarks.

For a Dirichlet character χ let

$$\mathbf{L}(s,\chi)=\sum_{n=1}^{\infty}\chi(n)n^{-s},\quad s=\sigma+it,$$

denote the corresponding **L**-series. For real numbers α and T, $1/2\leqq\alpha\leqq 1$, $T\geqq 2$, let $N(\alpha, T,\chi)$ denote the number of zeros of $\mathbf{L}(s,\chi)$ which lie in the rectangle $\alpha\leqq\sigma\leqq 1$, $|t|\leqq T$. For the duration of this paper we shall assume that

$$\sum_{D\leqq Q}\ \sum_{\chi(\mathrm{mod}\ D)}^{*} N(\alpha, T,\chi_1\chi)\leqq c_4Q^{A(1-\alpha)}T^B \tag{3}$$

holds uniformly for $1/2\leqq\alpha\leqq 1$, $T\geqq 2$, primitive characters χ_1 to moduli not exceeding Q, with absolute constants c_4, A and B. Here * denotes, as usual, that summation is restricted to primitive characters. Note that there are no terms on the right-hand side of this inequality which involve $\log Q$. This will be important. It is advantageous that A be small, but B need not be. This is convenient, for on occasion in problems of this type a larger value of B permits a smaller value for A (see, for example, HUXLEY [4]).

If $A>3$ is fixed then an argument of JUTILA [6] guarantees the validity of an inequality of the type (3) over some interval $1-\delta\leqq\sigma\leqq 1$, where δ depends only upon A.

Over the range $1/2 \leqq \sigma \leqq 1-\delta$ the argument of MONTGOMERY [9] Chapter 12 may be simply modified to give (3) with A having any fixed value greater than 5. The extra character χ_1 may be adopted into the HALÁSZ method at no further expense. A fourth-moment result which is appropriate to our circumstances may be obtained by means of some kind of approximate functional equation such as in [8]; see also RAMACHANDRA [11].

More complicated arguments lead to smaller permissible values for A. Thus, HUXLEY's argument [5] §8, pp. 168–169 allows any fixed $A > 54/11$. For a survey of related results see JUTILA [7].

Let $k(\geqq 2)$ be a positive integer and define

$$W(x, \chi) = -\sum_{n \leqq x} \left(1 - \frac{n}{x}\right)^k \chi(n)\Lambda(n)$$

where χ is a non-principal character (mod D), $D \geqq 2$, and $\Lambda(n)$ is von Mangoldt's function. We obtain a representation for $W(x, \chi)$ in terms of the zeros of the associated **L**-series.

Define the function

$$f(s) = f_k(s) = \frac{k!}{s(s+1)\dots(s+k)}.$$

Contour integration shows that if $\lambda > 0$ then

$$\frac{1}{2\pi i} \int_{\lambda - i\infty}^{\lambda + i\infty} f_k(s) y^s \, ds = \begin{cases} 0 & \text{if } 0 < y \leqq 1, \\ \left(1 - \dfrac{1}{y}\right)^k & \text{if } y \geqq 1. \end{cases}$$

Hence, if $b = 1 + (\log x)^{-1}$ and $T \geqq 2$,

$$W(x, \chi) = \frac{1}{2\pi i} \int_{b - i\infty}^{b + i\infty} f(s) \frac{\mathbf{L}'}{\mathbf{L}}(s, \chi) x^s \, ds =$$

$$= \frac{1}{2\pi i} \int_{b - iT}^{b + iT} f(s) \frac{\mathbf{L}'}{\mathbf{L}}(s, \chi) x^s \, ds + O(T^{-k+1} x \log x).$$

In the standard manner of obtaining so-called "explicit formulae" (see, for example, PRÁCHAR [10], Kap. VII) we deform the line-segment $\sigma = b$, $|t| \leqq T$ into the union of the line-segments $b - iT \to -\frac{1}{2} - iT$, $-\frac{1}{2} - iT \to -\frac{1}{2} + iT$, $-\frac{1}{2} + iT \to b + iT$; it being perhaps necessary to change the value of T by an amount less than one in absolute value. In this way we introduce integrals which are

$$O\left(\frac{x}{T^{k-1}}\log^2 DT + x^{-1/2}\log^2 D\right).$$

Here we have made use of Sätze 4.2, 4.3 of PRACHAR [10], Kap. VII. The deformation encloses poles corresponding to the zeros of $\mathbf{L}(s, \chi)$ and (whether or not $\mathbf{L}(0, \chi)=0$) a pole at $s=0$ owing to the presence of the kernel $f(s)$. The zeros $\rho=\beta+i\gamma\neq 0$ of $\mathbf{L}(s, \chi)$ lie in the rectangle $0<\beta<1$, $|\gamma|\leqq T$ and have corresponding residue $f(\rho)x^{\rho}$ counted with multiplicity.

Suppose that in the neighborhood of $s=0$ we have

$$\frac{\mathbf{L}'}{\mathbf{L}}(s, \chi)=\frac{1}{s}(u+vs+\ldots),$$

then the residue at $s=0$ will be

$$v+u(\log x+e_k)$$

where e_k is a constant depending only upon k. Since χ is primitive it has a functional equation which shows that $\mathbf{L}(s, \chi)$ can have at most a simple zero at $s=0$; thus $u=0$ or 1. The value of v may of course depend upon the character χ.

We have so far that

$$W(x, \chi)=\sum_{\substack{0<\beta\leqq 1\\ |\gamma|\leqq T}} f(\rho)x^{\rho}+v+O\left(\log x+\frac{x}{T^{k-1}}\log^2 DT+x^{-1/2}\log^2 D\right).$$

Moreover, $W(2, \chi)=O(1)$; subtracting it (and its representation) gives

$$(4)\quad W(x, \chi)=\sum_{\substack{0<\beta\leqq 1\\ |\gamma|\leqq T}} f(\rho)(x^{\rho}-2^{\rho})+O\left(\log x+\frac{x}{T^{k-1}}\log^2 DT+x^{-1/2}\log^2 D\right).$$

We now 'remove' the zeros with $\beta\leqq 1/2$.

According to a long-established result (see PRACHAR [10] Kap. IV) there can be at most one zero, and that a simple one, which lies in the rectangle

$$1-\frac{c_5}{\log D}\leqq\sigma<1, \quad |t|\leqq 2$$

for a certain positive absolute constant c_5. Let us call this ("Siegel") zero ρ_0. From its functional equation $\mathbf{L}(s, \chi)$ will have the zero $1-\rho_0$ in the rectangle $0\leqq\sigma\leqq c_5(\log D)^{-1}$, $|t|\leqq 2$, and no others save possibly for the zero at $s=0$ already mentioned. If $1-\rho_0$ occurs then

$$(1-\rho_0)^{-1}\{x^{1-\rho_0}-2^{1-\rho_0}\}=\int_2^x y^{-\rho_0}dy=O\left(\int_2^x y^{-1/2}du\right)=O(x^{1/2}).$$

Moreover, we shall then have $(1-\rho_0)f(1-\rho_0)=O(1)$.

For any integer j

$$|\rho+j|^2=\beta^2+(\gamma+j)^2\geqq\beta^2+\gamma^2=|\rho|^2$$

so that $|f(\rho)|\leqq|\rho|^{-k}$. Hence for any $m>1$

$$\sum_{\substack{0<\beta\leqq 1/2\\ m<|\gamma|\leqq 2m}} |f(\rho)||x^\rho-2^\rho|=O(x^{1/2}m^{-k+1}\log 2\,mD)$$

Since each **L**-series has $O(2m\log 2mD)$ zeros in the rectangle $0\leqq\beta\leqq 1$, $|\gamma|\leqq 2m$, (PRACHAR [10], Kap. VII, Satz 3.4). Summing over $m=2,4,\ldots$, and not exceeding T we see that the zeros with $\beta\leqq 1/2$ and $|\gamma|>2$ contribute towards $W(x,\chi)$ an amount which is $O(x^{1/2}\log D)$. Similarly the zeros with $|\gamma|\leqq 2$ contribute $O(x^{1/2}\log D+(\log D)^2)$.

Since $k\geqq 2$ we choose an unbounded sequence of T-values and readily obtain the estimate

$$W(x,\chi)=\sum_{1/2<\beta<1} f(\rho)(x^\rho-2^\rho)+O(x^{1/2}\log D+(\log D)^2)\,.$$

The following result is now clear.

Lemma 1. *For* $x>2$

$$|W(x,\chi)|\leqq 2\sum_{1/2<\beta<1} x^\beta|\rho|^{-k}+O(x^{1/2}\log D+(\log D)^2)\,.$$

In what follows we choose a value $k>B$.

Lemma 2. *Let* χ_1 *be a primitive character to a modulus not exceeding* Q. *Assume that* (3) *is valid. Let* $\varepsilon>0$ *be fixed. Then the inequality*

$$\sum_{D\leqq Q}\ \sideset{}{^*}\sum_{\chi(\mathrm{mod}\,D)} |W(x,\chi_1\chi)|\leqq c_6x+O(x^{1/2}Q^2\log Q+Q^{A+\varepsilon})$$

where the constants depend at most upon ε, k *and* B, *holds uniformly for all* $x\geqq 2$, $Q\geqq 2$ *and permissible characters* χ_1.

Proof. If $m>1$ then

(5) $$\sum_{\substack{1/2<\beta<1\\ m<|\gamma|\leqq 2m}} x^\beta|\rho|^{-k}\leqq m^{-k}\sum_{\substack{1/2<\beta<1\\ |\gamma|\leqq 2m}} x^\beta=-m^{-k}\int_{1/2}^{1} x^\sigma dN(\sigma,2m)$$

where

$$N(\sigma,T)=\sum_{D\leqq Q}\ \sideset{}{^*}\sum_{\chi(\mathrm{mod}\,D)} N(\sigma,T,\chi_1\chi)\,.$$

Integrating by parts and appealing to the upper-bound (3), the integral in (5) is

$$-m^{-k}\{xN(1,2m)-x^{1/2}N(1/2,2m)\}+m^{-k}\log x\int_{1/2}^{1}x^{\sigma}N(\sigma,2m)d\sigma=$$

$$=O(m^{-k+B}x^{1/2}Q^{A/2})+O(m^{-k+B}\log x\int_{1/2}^{1}Q^{A}(xQ^{-A})^{\sigma}d\sigma).$$

If $Q^{A+\varepsilon}<x$ the final integral is $O(x(\log x)^{-1})$. If $Q^{A+\varepsilon}\geqq x$ but $Q^{A}\leqq 2x$ then this same integral is at most

$$O\left(\int_{1/2}^{1}x^{\sigma}(Q^{A})^{1-\sigma}d\sigma\right)=O(x)=O(Q^{A+2\varepsilon}(\log x)^{-1}).$$

If $Q^{A}>2x$ then $(xQ^{-A})^{\sigma}\leqq(xQ^{-A})^{1/2}$ uniformly for $1/2\leqq\sigma\leqq 1$, and the integral is again $O(Q^{A+2\varepsilon}(\log x)^{-1})$.

Summing over $m=2,4,\ldots$, taking into account those zeros for which $|\gamma|\leqq 2$, and then lemma 1, we obtain the inequality of lemma 2 with 2ε in place of ε.

Lemma 3. *If the condition* (3) *holds, then for any fixed* $\varepsilon>0$ *the inequality*

$$\sum_{D\leqq Q}\ \sum_{\chi(\mathrm{mod}\,D)}^{*}\left|\sum_{p\leqq x}a_p\chi(p)\right|^2\leqq c_7\left(\frac{x}{\log x}+\frac{x^{1/2}Q^2\log Q}{\log x}+Q^{A+\varepsilon}\right)\sum_{p\leqq x}|a_p|^2$$

holds uniformly for all complex numbers a_p, *and real numbers* $x\geqq 2$, $Q\geqq 2$.

Remark. From this result we shall readily deduce the theorem.

Proof. Let $\chi_j(n)$, $j=1,\ldots,J$, denote the various primitive characters to moduli not exceeding Q. Consider the sum

$$\sum_{n\leqq x}\left(1-\frac{n}{x}\right)^{k}\Lambda(n)\left|\sum_{j=1}^{J}d_j\chi_j(n)\right|^2. \tag{6}$$

Expanding the inner square and interchanging the order of summation we obtain

$$\sum_{j,k=1}^{J}d_j\bar{d}_k\sum_{n\leqq x}\left(1-\frac{n}{x}\right)^{k}\Lambda(n)\chi_j\bar{\chi}_k(n). \tag{7}$$

Whenever $j=k$ the inner sum is not more than

$$\sum_{n\leqq x}\left(1-\frac{n}{x}\right)^{k}\Lambda(n)=O(x).$$

If $j \neq k$ then it is $W(x, \chi\bar{\chi}_k)$ where χ_j and $\bar{\chi}_k$ are primitive characters. Since $|d_j \ \bar{d}_h| \leqq |(|d_j|^2 + |d_k|^2)/2$, the terms in (7) with $j \neq k$ altogether contribute not more than

$$\sum_{r=1}^{J} |d_r|^2 \cdot \max_k \sum_{j=1}^{J} |W(x, \chi_j\bar{\chi}_k)|.$$

Applying Lemma 2 we see that the sum at (6) does not exceed

$$c_8(x + x^{1/2}Q^2 \log Q + Q^{A+\varepsilon}) \sum_{j=1}^{J} |d_j|^2 .$$

Over the range $(x/2)^{1/2} < n \leqq x/2$ the inequalities

$$\left(1 - \frac{n}{x}\right)^k \geqq 2^{-k}, \quad \Lambda(n) \geqq \frac{1}{4} \log x$$

hold whenever n is a prime. Hence (replacing x by $2x$)

$$\sum_{x^{1/2} < p \leqq x} \left| \sum_{j=1}^{J} d_j\chi_j(p) \right|^2 \leqq c_9 \left(\frac{x}{\log x} + \frac{x^{1/2}Q^2 \log Q}{\log x} + \frac{Q^{A+\varepsilon}}{\log x} \right) \sum_{j=1}^{J} |d_j|^2 .$$

Replacing x by $x^{1/2}$, $x^{1/4}$, ..., and summing we obtain the inequality

$$\sum_{p \leqq x} \left| \sum_{j=1}^{J} d_j\chi_j(p) \right|^2 \leqq c_7 \left(\frac{x}{\log x} + x^{1/2}Q^2 \frac{\log Q}{\log x} + Q^{A+\varepsilon} \right) \sum_{j=1}^{J} |d_j|^2 .$$

This inequality holds for all complex numbers d_j, and is dual to that in the statement of Lemma 3 (see Elliott [2], [3]).

This completes the proof of Lemma 3.

Remark. If the L-series to Dirichlet characters have no zeros in the half-plane $\sigma > 1/2$ then the term $Q^{A+\varepsilon}$ in the result of Lemma 3 may be omitted.

Proof of theorem. We first note the identity

$$(q-1) \sum_{l=1}^{q-1} \left| \sum_{\substack{p \leqq x \\ p \equiv l (\mathrm{mod}\ q)}} a_p - \frac{1}{q-1} \sum_{\substack{p \leqq x \\ p \neq q}} a_p \right|^2 = \sum_{\chi (\mathrm{mod}\ q)} \left| \sum_{p \leqq x} a_p\chi(p) \right|^2 ,$$

χ running over the non-principal (primitive) characters (mod q). This together with Lemma 3 shows that an inequality of type (1) holds with

$$\Delta(x, Q) = c_7 \left(\frac{x}{\log x} + \frac{x^{1/2}Q^2 \log Q}{\log x} + Q^{A+\varepsilon} \right).$$

For any fixed value of $A>4$ the second of the three terms in the brackets is dominated by either the first or the third term, in particular

$$\Delta(x, Q)<c_{10}\left(\frac{x}{\log x}+Q^{A+\varepsilon}\right).$$

Since, as we indicated earlier, the inequality (3) holds with a value of A less than 5, the theorem is proved.

Remarks. If a weak form of the 'density hypothesis' holds then any fixed $A>4$ is to be expected, which could lead to a result of the type (1) and (2) with $D(Q)<D^{4+\varepsilon}$.

On the appropriate Riemann hypothesis the above argument gives a permissible

$$\Delta(x, Q)<c_{11}\left(\frac{x}{\log x}+\frac{x^{1/2}Q^2\log Q}{\log x}+Q^2(\log Q)^2\right),$$

and so $D(Q)<c_{12}Q^4\log Q$. Perhaps, on analogy with the large sieve, $D(Q)<Q^2(\log Q)^{c_{13}}$ holds for some constant c_{13}.

An argument of a type given in the author's paper [2] shows that any function $D(Q)$ in (2) must satisfy $D(Q)\geqq c_{14}Q^2(\log Q)^{-1}$ for some positive absolute constant c_{12} and all $Q\geqq 2$.

References

[1] P. D. T. A. ELLIOTT, On the differences of additive arithmetic functions, *Mathematika*, **24** (1977), 153–165.

[2] P. D. T. A. ELLIOTT, On inequalities of Large Sieve type, *Acta Arithmetica*, **18** (1971), 405–422.

[3] P. D. T. A. ELLIOTT, *Probabilistic Number Theory, Springer New York*, 1979/1980.

[4] M. N. HUXLEY, An imperfect hybrid zero-density theorem, *J. London Math. Soc.*, (2) **13** (1976), 53–56.

[5] M. N. HUXLEY, Large values of Dirichlet polynomials *II*, *Acta Arith.* **27** (1975), 159–169.

[6] M. JUTILA, On Linnik's constant, *Math. Scand.*, **41** (1977), 45–62.

[7] M. JUTILA, Progress in the theory of **L**-functions, *Paris, Séminaire Delange-Pisot-Poitou*, 1975/76.

[8] A. F. LAVRIK, A functional equation for Dirichlet **L**-series and the problem of divisors in arithmetic progressions, *Izv. Akad. Nauk. SSSR. Ser. Mat.*, **30** (1966), 433–448.

[9] H. MONTGOMERY, *Topics in Multiplicative Number Theory*, Lecture Notes in Math. **227**, Springer, Berlin, 1971.

[10] K. PRACHAR, *Primzahlverteilung*, Springer, Berlin, 1957.

[11] K. RAMACHANDRA, A simple proof of the Mean Fourth Power Estimate of $\zeta\left(\frac{1}{2}+it\right)$ and $\mathbf{L}\left(\frac{1}{2}+it\right)$, *Ann. Scuola Norm. Sup. Pisa Sci. Fis. Mat.* **1974** (1), 81–97.

[12] D. WOLKE, Farey-Brüche mit primen Nenner und das grosse Sieb, *Math. Zeit.*, **114** (1970), 145–158.

BOULDER, COLORADO
U.S.A.

Studies in Pure Mathematics
To the Memory of Paul Turán

Some asymptotic formulas on generalized divisor functions I

by

P. ERDŐS and A. SÁRKÖZY (Budapest)

1. Throughout this paper, we use the following notations:

$c, c_1, c_2, \ldots, X_0, X_1, \ldots$ denote positive absolute constants. We denote the number of the elements of the finite set S by $|S|$. We write $e^x = \exp(x)$. $v(n)$ denotes the number of the distinct prime factors of n. We denote the least prime factor of n by $p(n)$, while the greatest prime factor of n is denoted by $P(n)$.

Let A be a finite or infinite sequence of positive integers $a_1 < a_2 < \ldots$. Then we write

$$N_A(x) = \sum_{\substack{a \in A \\ a \leqq x}} 1,$$

$$f_A(x) = \sum_{\substack{a \in A \\ a \leqq x}} \frac{1}{a},$$

$$d_A(n) = \sum_{\substack{a \in A \\ a/n}} 1$$

(in other words, $d_A(n)$ denotes the number of divisors amongst the a_i's) and

$$D_A(x) = \max_{1 \leqq n \leqq x} d_A(x).$$

The aim of this paper is to investigate the function $D_A(x)$. Clearly

(1) $$\sum_{1 \leqq n \leqq x} d_A(n) = x f_A(x) + O(x).$$

One would expect that if $N_A(x) \to +\infty$ then also

(2) $$\lim_{x \to +\infty} \frac{D_A(x)}{f_A(x)} = +\infty.$$

(2) is trivial if $f_A(x) < C$ thus we can assume

$$f_A(x) \to +\infty. \tag{3}$$

The special case when

$$(a_i, a_j) = 1 \quad \text{for all} \quad 1 \leqq i < j \tag{4}$$

was posed as a problem in [2]. Furthermore, we guessed there that condition (4) can be dropped, in other words, (2) holds for all infinite sequences. To our great surprise, we disproved (2); Section 2 will be devoted to the counter-example. On the other hand, we prove in Section 3 that $\liminf_{x\to+\infty} N_A(x)\left(\frac{x \log\log x}{\log x}\right)^{-1} > c_1$ implies (2). We believe that also the weaker condition $f_A(x)(\log\log x)^{-1} \to +\infty$ implies (2). We hope to return to this question in a subsequent paper.

Furthermore, we prove in Section 3 that (3) implies that

$$\limsup_{x\to+\infty} \frac{D_A(x)}{f_A(x)} = +\infty. \tag{5}$$

Perhaps

$$\limsup_{x\to+\infty} D_A(x)/f_A(x)^{(1-\varepsilon)\log f_A(x)} = +\infty$$

also holds; we will return to this problem in Part II of this paper. In Section 3, we prove several other theorems concerning various sharpenings of (2) and (5).

Theorem 1. *There exist positive constants c_2, c_3 and an infinite sequence A of positive integers such that for an infinite sequence $x_1 < x_2 < \ldots < x_k < \ldots$ of positive integers we have*

$$f_A(x_k) > c_2 \log\log x_k \tag{6}$$

and

$$\frac{D_A(x_k)}{f_A(x_k)} < c_3. \tag{7}$$

Proof. We are going to construct finite sequences satisfying inequalities corresponding to (6) and (7) at first.

By a theorem of HARDY and RAMANUJAN [5], there exist positive constants δ and X_1 such that if $x > X_1$ then uniformly for all $\sqrt{x} \leqq y \leqq x$, the conditions $b \leqq y$ and $\nu(b) < 2 \log\log x$ hold for all but $\frac{y}{(\log x)^\delta}$ integers b. (See also [1].)

For any positive integer $x \geqq 10$ and for $1 \leqq j \leqq (\log x)^{\delta/2}$, let $B_j(x)$ denote the set of those integers b for which

(i) $\frac{x}{2^j} < b \leqq \frac{x}{2^{j-1}}$,

(ii) $p(b) > 2^j$,

(iii) $\mu(b) \neq 0$

and

(iv) $\nu(b) < 2 \log\log x$

hold and let

$$B(x) = \bigcup_{1 \leqq j \leqq (\log x)^{\delta/2}} B_j(x).$$

We will show that there exist constants X_2 and c_4 such that for $x \geqq X_2$, we have

$$\sum_{b \in B(x)} \frac{1}{b} > c_4 \log\log x \tag{8}$$

and

$$D_{B(x)}(x) < 2 \log\log x. \tag{9}$$

By using standard methods of the prime number theory (see e.g. [3] or [4]), it can be shown easily that there exist constants c_5 and X_3 such that if $x > X_3$ then uniformly for all y and z for which $\sqrt{x} < y$ and $z \leqq 2^{(\log x)^{\delta/2}}$, the number of the integers b satisfying the conditions $y \leqq b \leqq 2y$, $p(b) > z$ and $\mu(b) \neq 0$ is greater than

$$c_5 y \prod_{p \leqq z}\left(1 - \frac{1}{p}\right) \prod_{p > z}\left(1 - \frac{1}{p^2}\right) > c_6 \frac{y}{\log z}.$$

Thus for $x > X_3$, the number of the integers b satisfying (i), (ii) and (iii) (for fixed j) is greater than

$$c_6 \frac{x/2^j}{\log 2^j} = c_7 \frac{x}{j 2^j}$$

uniformly for $1 \leqq j \leqq (\log x)^{\delta/2}$.

On the other hand, by

$$\frac{x}{2^j} \geqq \frac{x}{2^{(\log x)^{\delta/2}}} > \frac{x}{\sqrt{x}} = \sqrt{x},$$

the definition of δ yields that for $x > X_1$, (iv) holds for all but

$$\frac{x/2^{j-1}}{(\log x)^\delta} = \frac{x}{2^{j-1}(\log x)^\delta}$$

of the integers b satisfying (i).

Thus for $x \geqq X_4$, we have

$$|B_j(x)| > c_7 \frac{x}{j2^j} - \frac{x}{2^{j-1}(\log x)^\delta} = c_7 \frac{x}{j2^j}\left(1 - \frac{2}{c_7}\frac{j}{(\log x)^\delta}\right) > c_8 \frac{x}{j2^j}$$

for all $1 \leqq j \leqq (\log x)^{\delta/2}$, hence

$$\sum_{b \in B(x)} \frac{1}{b} = \sum_{1 \leqq j \leqq (\log x)^{\delta/2}} \sum_{b \in B_j(x)} \frac{1}{b} \geqq \sum_{1 \leqq j \leqq (\log x)^{\delta/2}} \sum_{b \in B_j(x)} \frac{1}{x/2^{j-1}} =$$

$$= \sum_{1 \leqq j \leqq (\log x)^{\delta/2}} |B_j(x)| \frac{2^{j-1}}{x} > \sum_{1 \leqq j \leqq (\log x)^{\delta/2}} c_8 \frac{1}{2j} > c_9 \log (\log x)^{\delta/2} > c_{10} \log \log x$$

for $x > X_5$ which proves (8).

In order to prove (9), note that if

$$b_1 u = b_2 v \leqq x$$

for some positive integers $b_1 \in B(x)$, $b_2 \in B(x)$, u, v, and $b_1 < b_2$ then by the construction of the set $B(x)$, we have

$$p(b_1) > \frac{x}{b_1} \geqq u = \frac{b_2}{b_1} v > v$$

thus $(b_1, v) = 1$ and $b_1 = \dfrac{b_2 v}{u} \Big/ b_2 v$, hence b_1 / b_2. Thus if $n \leqq x$, and $b_1 < b_2 < \ldots < b_r$ denote all the positive integers b_i such that $b_i \in B(x)$ and b_i / n then

$$b_1 / b_2 / \ldots / b_r \tag{10}$$

must hold. By the construction of the set $B(x)$, we have

$$\mu(b_r) \neq 0 \tag{11}$$

and

$$\nu(b_r) < 2 \log \log x . \tag{12}$$

(10) and (11) imply that

$$\nu(b_1) < \nu(b_2) < \ldots < \nu(b_r)$$

thus with respect to (12),

$$d_{B(x)}(n)=r\leqq \nu(b_r)<2\log\log x$$

for all $n\leqq x$ which proves (9).

Finally, let $x_1=\max\{10,\ [X_2]+1\}$ and $x_k=[\exp\{\exp(\exp x_{k-1})\}]+1$ for $k=2, 3, \dots$, and let

$$A=\bigcup_{k=1}^{+\infty} B(x_k)\,.$$

Then by (8), we have

$$f_A(x_k)=\sum_{\substack{a\in A\\ a\leqq x_k}}\frac{1}{a}\geqq\sum_{a\in B(x_k)}\frac{1}{a}>c_4\log\log x_k \tag{13}$$

for $k=1, 2, \dots$ which proves (6).

Furthermore, (9) yields that for $k=2, 3, \dots$ and $n\leqq x_k$, we have

$$d_A(n)\leqq\sum_{i=1}^{k}d_{B(x_i)}(n)=\sum_{i=1}^{k-1}d_{B(x_i)}(n)+d_{B(x_k)}(n)\leqq$$

$$\leqq\sum_{i=1}^{k-1}\sum_{b\in B(x_i)}1+D_{B(x_k)}(x_k)<\sum_{b\leqq x_{k-1}}1+2\log\log x_k=$$

$$=x_{k-1}+2\log\log x_k<\log\log\log x_k+2\log\log x_k<3\log\log x_k$$

hence

$$D_A(x_k)<3\log\log x_k\,. \tag{14}$$

(13) and (14) yield (7) and the proof of Theorem 1 is completed.

We note that we could sharpen Theorem 1 in the following way:

Theorem 1′. *There exists an infinite sequence A of positive integers such that for an infinite sequence $x_1<x_2<\dots<x_k<\dots$ of positive integers we have*

$$\liminf_{k\to+\infty}\frac{f_A(x_k)}{e^{-\gamma}\log\log x_k}=1 \tag{6′}$$

and

$$\limsup_{k\to+\infty}\frac{D_A(x_k)}{f_A(x_k)}=1 \tag{7′}$$

where γ denotes the Euler-constant.

Note that (7′) is best possible as (1) shows.

In fact, Theorem 1’ could be proved by the following construction:

Let x_1 be a large number, and for $k=2, 3, \ldots$, let x_k be sufficiently large in terms of k and x_{k-1}. For $k=1, 2, \ldots$, let $B(x_k)$ denote the set of those integers b for which

(i) $x_k^{1/2} < b < x_k$,

(ii) $p(b) > \frac{x_k}{b}$,

(iii) $\mu(b) \neq 0$,

(iv) $\nu(b) < \left(1+\frac{1}{k}\right) \log\log x_k$,

(v) if the prime factors of b are $p_1 < p_2 < \ldots < p_{\nu(b)}$ then $p_{i+1} > p_1 p_2 \ldots p_i$ holds for less than $\left(1+\frac{2}{k}\right) e^{-\gamma} \log\log x_k$ of the integers $1 \leqq i \leqq \nu(b)$.

Finally, let

$$A = \bigcup_{k=1}^{+\infty} B(x_k).$$

It can be shown easily that for this sequence A, we have

$$\limsup_{k\to+\infty} \frac{D_A(x_k)}{e^{-\gamma} \log\log x_k} \leqq 1. \tag{15}$$

Combining the methods of probability theory with Brun's sieve (see e.g. [3] or [4]) it can be proved that also (6′) holds. However, this proof would be very complicated; this is the reason of that that we have worked out the weaker version discussed in Theorem 1. (1), (6′) and (15) yield also (7′).

Theorem 2. *If*

$$\lim_{x\to+\infty} f_A(x) = +\infty \tag{16}$$

then we have

$$\limsup_{x\to+\infty} D_A(x) \left(\frac{\log x}{\log\log x}\right)^{-1} \geqq 1. \tag{17}$$

Note that this theorem is best possible as the sequence A consisting of all the prime number shows.

Proof. We are going to show at first that (16) implies that for all $\varepsilon > 0$, there exist infinitely many integers y such that

$$N_A(y) > \frac{y}{(\log y)^{1+\varepsilon}}. \tag{18}$$

In fact, let us assume indirectly that for some $\varepsilon>0$ and $y>y_0(\varepsilon)$ we have

$$N_A(y)\leqq \frac{y}{(\log y)^{1+\varepsilon}}.$$

Then partial summation yields that for $x\to+\infty$ we have

$$f_A(x)=\sum_{a\leqq x}\frac{1}{a}=\sum_{y=1}^{x}\frac{N_A(y)-N_A(y-1)}{y}=\sum_{y=1}^{x}N_A(y)\left(\frac{1}{y}-\frac{1}{y+1}\right)+\frac{N_A(x)}{x+1}=$$

$$=\sum_{y=1}^{x}\frac{N_A(y)}{y(y+1)}+\frac{N_A(x)}{x+1}=O\left(\sum_{y=1}^{x}\frac{y/(\log y)^{1+\varepsilon}}{y^2}\right)+O\left(\frac{x/(\log x)^{1+\varepsilon}}{x}\right)=$$

$$=O\left(\sum_{y=1}^{x}\frac{1}{y(\log y)^{1+\varepsilon}}\right)+O\left(\frac{1}{(\log x)^{1+\varepsilon}}\right)=O(1)$$

in contradiction with (16) and this contradiction proves the existence of infinitely many integers y satisfying (18) (for all $\varepsilon>0$).

Let us fix some $\varepsilon>0$ and let y be a large integer satisfying (18). Put

$$X=\prod_{\substack{a\in A\\ a\leqq y}}a.$$

Then

$$X\leqq\prod_{\substack{a\in A\\ a\leqq y}}y=y^{N_A(y)}$$

hence

$$\log X\leqq N_A(y)\log y, \tag{19}$$

and for large y, we have

$$\log X=\sum_{\substack{a\in A\\ a\leqq y}}\log a\geqq\sum_{\substack{a\in A\\ 3\leqq a\leqq y}}\log a>$$

$$>\sum_{\substack{a\in A\\ 3\leqq a\leqq y}}\log 3=(N_A(y)-N_A(2))\log 3\geqq(N_A(y)-2)\log 3>N_A(y)$$

thus by (18),

$$\log\log X>\log N_A(y)>\log\frac{y}{(\log y)^{1+\varepsilon}}>(1-\varepsilon)\log y \tag{20}$$

for sufficiently large y.

(19) and (20) yield that

$$N_A(y) \geqq \frac{\log X}{\log y} > \frac{\log X}{\frac{1}{1-\varepsilon} \log\log X} = (1-\varepsilon)\frac{\log X}{\log\log X}. \tag{21}$$

Furthermore, we have

$$D_A(X) \geqq d_A(X) = \sum_{\substack{a \in A \\ a/X}} 1 \geqq N_A(y) \tag{22}$$

since $X = \prod_{\substack{a \in A \\ a \leqq y}} a$ is divisible by all the $N_A(y)$ integers a satisfying $a \in A$, $a \leqq y$.

(21) and (22) yield that

$$D_A(X) > (1-\varepsilon)\frac{\log X}{\log\log X}.$$

For all $\varepsilon > 0$, this holds for infinitely many integers X and this proves (17).

Theorem 3. *If* $x > X_0$ *and*

$$N_A(x) > 5\frac{x \log\log x}{\log x} \tag{23}$$

then there exists a positive integer X *such that*

$$\frac{x}{\log x} < X < \exp(x) \tag{24}$$

and

$$\frac{d_A(X)}{\log X} > \exp\left(\frac{1}{20}\frac{\log x}{x} N_A(x)\right). \tag{25}$$

Note that by (23) and (24), the right-hand side of (25) is

$$\exp\left(\frac{1}{5}\frac{\log x}{x} N_A(x)\right) > \exp(\log\log x) = \log x > \log\log X \to +\infty$$

as $x \to +\infty$.

Theorem 4. *If* A *is an infinite sequence such that*

$$\liminf_{x \to +\infty} N_A(x)\left(\frac{x \log\log x}{\log x}\right)^{-1} > 5 \tag{26}$$

then we have

$$\lim_{x\to+\infty}\frac{D_A(x)}{\log x}=+\infty. \tag{27}$$

Note that for large x, we have

$$f_A(x)=\sum_{\substack{a\in A\\ a\leqq x}}\frac{1}{a}\leqq\sum_{a\leqq x}\frac{1}{a}<2\log x \tag{28}$$

thus (25) implies that also

$$\lim_{x\to+\infty}\frac{D_A(x)}{f_A(x)}=+\infty$$

holds.

We are going to prove Theorems 3 and 4 simultaneously.

Proof of Theorems 3 and 4. Assume that $x>X_0$ and for a finite or infinite sequence A, we have

$$N_A(x)>5\frac{x\log\log x}{\log x}. \tag{29}$$

Let t be a real number such that

$$\frac{5}{4}\log\log x\leqq\log t\leqq\frac{1}{4}\frac{\log x}{x}N_A(x). \tag{30}$$

Then obviously, we have

$$\log t\leqq\frac{1}{4}\frac{\log x}{x}x=\frac{1}{4}\log x$$

hence

$$t\leqq x^{1/4}. \tag{31}$$

Let A^* denote the set of those integers a for which $a\in A$, $a\leqq x$ and $P(a)>\frac{x}{t}$ hold. It is well known that

$$\sum_{p\leqq y}\frac{1}{p}=\log\log y+c_{11}+O\left(\frac{1}{\log y}\right). \tag{32}$$

(30), (31) and (32) yield that

$$\sum_{\substack{1\leqq n\leqq x\\ P(n)>x/t}}1\leqq\sum_{x/t<p\leqq x}\ \sum_{\substack{1\leqq n\leqq x\\ p/n}}1=$$

$$=\sum_{x/t<p\leqq x}\left[\frac{x}{p}\right]\leqq\sum_{x/t<p\leqq x}\frac{x}{p}=x\left(\sum_{p\leqq x}\frac{1}{p}-\sum_{p\leqq x/t}\frac{1}{p}\right)=$$

(33)

$$= x\left\{\left(\log\log x + c_{11} + O\left(\frac{1}{\log x}\right)\right) - \left(\log\log x/t + c_{11} + O\left(\frac{1}{\log x/t}\right)\right)\right\} =$$

$$= -x\log\left(1 - \frac{\log t}{\log x}\right) + O\left(\frac{x}{\log x}\right) < 2x\frac{\log t}{\log x} + O\left(\frac{x}{\log x}\right) < 3x\frac{\log t}{\log x}$$

since

$$-\log(1-y) = \sum_{k=1}^{+\infty}\frac{y^k}{k} < \sum_{k=1}^{+\infty} y^k = \frac{y}{1-y} < 2y \quad \text{for} \quad 0 < y < \frac{1}{2},$$

and

$$0 < \frac{\log t}{\log x} < \frac{1}{4}$$

by (30) and (31).

(30) and (33) yield that

$$|A^*| \geqq N_A(x) - \sum_{\substack{1 \leqq n \leqq x \\ P(n) > x/t}} 1 = N_A(x)\left(1 - \frac{1}{N_A(x)}\sum_{\substack{1 \leqq n \leqq x \\ P(n) > x/t}} 1\right) =$$

(34)

$$= N_A(x)\left(1 - \frac{\log x}{4x\log t}\sum_{\substack{1 \leqq n \leqq x \\ P(n) > x/t}} 1\right) > N_A(x)\left(1 - \frac{\log x}{4x\log t}\cdot 3x\frac{\log t}{\log x}\right) = \frac{1}{4}N_A(x).$$

Let us denote the least common multiple of the elements of A^* by X. Then with respect to (34), we have

$$d_A(X) \geqq d_{A^*}(X) = |A^*| > \frac{1}{4}N_A(x). \tag{35}$$

Furthermore, if $a \in A^*$ then $a \leqq x$ and $P(a) \leqq x/t$ thus we have

$$a \Big| \prod_{p \leqq x/t} p^{[\log x/\log p]}$$

hence

$$X \Big| \prod_{p \leqq x/t} p^{[\log x/\log p]}$$

which implies that

$$X \leqq \prod_{p \leqq x/t} p^{[\log x/\log p]} \leqq p \prod_{p \leqq x/t} x = x^{\pi(x/t)}. \tag{36}$$

Using the prime number theorem or a more elementary theorem, we obtain from (36) with respect to (31) that

$$\log X \leqq \pi(x/t)\log x < 2\frac{x/t}{\log x/t}\log x \leqq \tag{37}$$

$$\leqq 2\frac{x}{t\log(x/x^{1/4})}\log x = \frac{8}{3}\frac{x}{t}.$$

In order to deduce Theorem 3 from the construction above, assume that A satisfies the conditions in Theorem 3, and put

$$\log t = \frac{1}{4}\frac{\log x}{x}N_A(x). \tag{38}$$

Then by (23), we have

$$\log t > \frac{1}{4}\frac{\log x}{x}\cdot 5\frac{x\log\log x}{\log x} = \frac{5}{4}\log\log x, \tag{39}$$

while the second inequality in (30) holds by the definition of t. Thus by (23), (35), (37) and (38), the construction above yields the existence of an integer X such that

$$\frac{d_A(X)}{\log X} > \frac{N_A(x)/4}{8x/3t} = \frac{3}{32}\cdot\frac{N_A(x)t}{x} = \frac{3}{32}\cdot\frac{N_A(x)}{x}\exp\left(\frac{1}{4}\cdot\frac{\log x}{x}N_A(x)\right) =$$

$$= \exp\left(\frac{1}{4}\cdot\frac{\log x}{x}N_A(x) + \log\frac{3}{32}\cdot\frac{N_A(x)}{x}\right) >$$

$$> \exp\left(\frac{1}{4}\cdot\frac{\log x}{x}N_A(x) + \log\frac{3}{32}\cdot\frac{5\log\log x}{\log x}\right) >$$

$$> \exp\left(\frac{1}{4}\cdot\frac{\log x}{x}N_A(x) - \log\log x\right) >$$

$$> \exp\left\{\frac{1}{4}\cdot\frac{\log x}{x}N_A(x)\left(1 - 4\cdot\frac{1}{N_A(x)}\cdot\frac{x\log\log x}{\log x}\right)\right\} >$$

$$> \exp\left\{\frac{1}{4}\cdot\frac{\log x}{x}N_A(x)\left(1-\frac{4}{5}\right)\right\} = \exp\left(\frac{1}{20}\cdot\frac{\log x}{x}N_A(x)\right).$$

Finally, by the definition of X and with respect to (23) and (34), we have

$$X \geqq \max_{a\in A^*} a \geqq |A^*| > \frac{1}{4}N_A(x) > \frac{1}{4}\cdot 5\frac{x\log\log x}{\log x} > \frac{x}{\log x},$$

while (36) and (39) yield that

$$X < \exp\left(\frac{8}{3}\cdot\frac{x}{t}\right) < \exp\left(\frac{8}{3}\cdot\frac{x}{(\log x)^{5/4}}\right) < \exp(x)$$

and this completes the proof of Theorem 3.

In order to prove Theorem 4, assume that an infinite sequence A satisfies (26) and let y be a large number; we are going to show by using the construction above that $\frac{D_A(y)}{\log y}$ is large. Define x by

$$x = \frac{1}{3}\log y(\log\log y)^{5/4}$$

and put $t = (\log x)^{5/4}$. Then for sufficiently large y, (29) holds by (26). Furthermore,

$$\frac{1}{4}\frac{\log x}{x}N_A(x) > \frac{1}{4}\frac{\log x}{x}\cdot 5\frac{x\log\log x}{\log x} = \frac{5}{4}\log\log x = \log t$$

thus also (30) holds. The construction above yields the existence of an integer X such that (35) and (37) hold. We obtain from (37) that

$$X < \exp\left(\frac{3}{8}\frac{x}{t}\right) = \exp\left\{\frac{8}{3}\cdot\frac{1}{3}\frac{\log y(\log\log y)^{5/4}}{\left(\log\left(\frac{1}{3}\log y(\log\log y)^{5/4}\right)\right)^{5/4}}\right\} <$$

$$< \exp\left(\frac{8}{9}\frac{\log y\,(\log\log y)^{5/4}}{(\log\log y)^{5/4}}\right) = y^{8/9} < y,$$

thus with respect to (29) and (35), we have

$$\frac{D_A(y)}{\log y} \geqq \frac{d_A(X)}{\log y} > \frac{N_A(x)/4}{\log y} > \frac{4}{5}\frac{x\log\log x}{\log x\log y} =$$

$$= \frac{4}{5}\frac{\frac{1}{3}\log y\,(\log\log y)^{5/4}\log\log\left(\frac{1}{3}\log y\,(\log\log y)^{5/4}\right)}{\log\left(\frac{1}{3}\log y\,(\log\log y)^{5/4}\right)\log y} > \tag{40}$$

$$> \frac{4}{15}\frac{(\log\log y)^{5/4}\log\log\log y}{2\log\log y} > \frac{2}{15}(\log\log y)^{1/4}\log\log\log y$$

which completes the proof of Theorem 4.

Theorems 3 and 4 are best possible (except the values of the constants on the right hand sides of (23) and (26), respectively) as the following theorem shows:

Theorem 5. *There exists an infinite sequence A of positive integers such that*

(41)
$$\lim_{x\to+\infty} \inf N_A(x)\left(\frac{x\log\log x}{\log x}\right)^{-1} \geqq 1$$

and

(42)
$$d_A(x) \leqq \log x$$

for all x.

Proof. Let A consist of all the integers a of the form $a=pk$ where p is a prime number and $1\leqq k\leqq \log p$. Then by the prime number theorem (or a more elementary theorem) and (32) we have

$$\sum_{\substack{a\in A\\ a\leqq x}} 1 = \sum_{p\leqq x}\ \sum_{1\leqq k\leqq \min\{\log p,\, x/p\}} 1 \geqq \sum_{\frac{x}{\log x-2\log\log x}<p\leqq x}\ \sum_{1\leqq k\leqq \frac{x}{p}} 1 \geqq$$

$$\geqq \sum_{\frac{x}{\log x-2\log\log x}<p\leqq x}\left(\frac{x}{p}-1\right) = x\left(\sum_{p\leqq x}\frac{1}{p} - \sum_{p\leqq \frac{x}{\log x-2\log\log x}}\frac{1}{p}\right) + O\left(\frac{x}{\log x}\right) =$$

$$= x\left(\log\log x - \log\log\frac{x}{\log x-2\log\log x} + O\left(\frac{1}{\log x}\right)\right) + O\left(\frac{x}{\log x}\right) =$$

$$= -x\log\left(1-\frac{\log(\log x-2\log\log x}{\log x}\right) + O\left(\frac{x}{\log x}\right) =$$

$$= (1+o(1))\frac{x\log(\log x-2\log\log x)}{\log x} + O\left(\frac{x}{\log x}\right) = (1+o(1))\frac{x\log\log x}{\log x}$$

which proves (41).

Let $x\geqq 2$ be an integer and let $x=p_1^{\alpha_1}p_2^{\alpha_2}\dots p_r^{\alpha_r}$ where $p_1<p_2<\dots<p_r$ are prime numbers and $\alpha_1,\alpha_2,\dots,\alpha_r$ are positive integers. For $i=1,2,\dots,r$, let S_i denote the set of the integers a for which $a\in A$, a/x and $P(a)=p_i$ hold.

By the definition of the set A, $a\in S_i$ implies that a can be written in the form $a=p_ik$ where $1\leqq k\leqq \log p_i$. Thus obviously, we have

$$|S_i| \leqq \sum_{1\leqq k\leqq \log p_i} 1 \leqq \log p_i$$

hence

$$d_A(x)=\sum_{\substack{a\in A\\ a/x}} 1=\sum_{i=1}^{r}\sum_{\substack{a\in A\\ a/x\\ P(a)=p_i}} 1=\sum_{i=1}^{r}|S_i|\leqq\sum_{i=1}^{r}\log p_i=$$

$$=\log\left(\prod_{i=1}^{r}p_i\right)\leqq\log\left(\prod_{i=1}^{r}p_i^{\alpha_i}\right)\leqq\log x$$

and this completes the proof of Theorem 5.

Theorems 2 and 3 imply that

Theorem 6. *If*

$$\lim_{x\to+\infty} f_A(x)=+\infty$$

then we have

$$\limsup_{x\to+\infty}\frac{D_A(x)}{f_A(x)}=+\infty. \tag{43}$$

Proof. Assume at first that

$$f_A(x)=o\left(\frac{\log x}{\log\log x}\right). \tag{44}$$

We have

$$\frac{D_A(x)}{f_A(x)}=\frac{D_A(x)}{\frac{\log x}{\log\log x}}\cdot\frac{\frac{\log x}{\log\log x}}{f_A(x)}.$$

Here the first factor is $\geqq\frac{1}{2}$ for infinitely many integers x by Theorem 2, while the second factor tends to $+\infty$ by (44) which implies (43).

Assume now that

$$\limsup_{x\to+\infty}\frac{f_A(x)}{\frac{\log x}{\log\log x}}>0. \tag{45}$$

We are going to show that this implies that there exist infinitely many integers x satisfying

$$N_A(x)>5\frac{x\log\log x}{\log x}. \tag{46}$$

Assume indirectly that for $x>X_0$ we have

$$N_A(x)\leqq 5\frac{x\log\log x}{\log x}.$$

Then partial summation yields that

$$f_A(x)=\sum_{\substack{a\in A\\ a\leqq x}}\frac{1}{a}=\sum_{y\leqq x}\frac{N_A(y)-N_A(y-1)}{y}=\sum_{y\leqq x}N_A(y)\left(\frac{1}{y}-\frac{1}{y+1}\right)+\frac{N_A(x)}{x+1}=$$

$$=\sum_{y\leqq x}\frac{N_A(y)}{y(y+1)}+\frac{N_A(x)}{x+1}\leqq\sum_{y\leqq x}\frac{N_A(y)}{y^2}+\frac{N_A(x)}{x}=$$

$$=O\left(\sum_{y\leqq x}\frac{\log\log y}{y\log y}\right)+O\left(\frac{\log\log x}{\log x}\right)=O((\log\log x)^2)$$

in contradiction with (45) which proves the existence of infinitely many integers satisfying (46). By Theorem 3, this implies that

(47) $$\limsup_{x\to+\infty}\frac{D_A(x)}{\log x}=+\infty.$$

Obviously, we have

$$f_A(x)=\sum_{\substack{a\in A\\ a\leqq x}}\frac{1}{a}\leqq\sum_{a\leqq x}\frac{1}{a}\sim\log x$$

thus

(48) $$\liminf_{x\to+\infty}\frac{\log x}{f_A(x)}\geqq 1.$$

(47) and (48) yield that

$$\limsup_{x\to+\infty}\frac{D_A(x)}{f_A(x)}=\limsup_{x\to+\infty}\frac{D_A(x)}{\log x}\cdot\frac{\log x}{f_A(x)}=+\infty$$

and this completes the proof of Theorem 6.

References

[1] P. Erdős, An asymptotic inequality in the theory of numbers (in Russian), *Vestnik Leningrad. Univ.*, **15** (1960), no. *13*, 41–49.

[2] Problem 483, *Nieuw Archief voor Wiskunde*, **25** (1977), 424–425.

[3] H. Halberstam and H. E. Richert, *Sieve methods*, Academic Press, London–New York–San Francisco, 1974.

[4] H. Halberstam and K. F. Roth, *Sequences*, vol. I, Oxford at the Clarendon Press, Oxford, 1966.

[5] G. H. Hardy and S. Ramanujan, The normal number of prime factors of a number *n*, *Quarterly Journal of Mathematics*, **48** (1920), 76–92.

MATHEMATICAL INSTITUTE
OF THE HUNGARIAN ACADEMY OF SCIENCES
H-1053 BUDAPEST, REÁLTANODA U. 13–15.
HUNGARY

Studies in Pure Mathematics
To the Memory of Paul Turán

On a generalization of Turán's graph-theorem

by

P. ERDŐS and V. T. SÓS (Budapest)

The so-called extremal graph theory started with the well-known theorem of TURÁN [12], [13]. He determined the smallest integer $f(n; k)$ so that every graph $G(n; e)$ of n vertices and $e > f(n; k)$ edges contains a complete graph of k vertices. A general problem in extremal graph theory can be formulated as follows: Let L be a fixed graph and $f(n; L)$ the smallest integer so that every graph of n vertices having more than $f(n; L)$ edges contains a graph isomorphic to L as a subgraph. One of the general theorems in this theory is the ERDŐS–SIMONOVITS [5], see also ERDŐS–STONE [7] theorem which states as follows:

Let the chromatic number of L be $\chi(L)$ and $\chi(L) = r \geqq 3$. Then

$$f(n; L) = (1 + o(1))\left(1 - \frac{1}{r-1}\right)\frac{n^2}{2}.$$

For the case $r = 2$ the theorem only states $f(n; L) = o(n^2)$ but some sharper theorems are also known [1], [4], [8], [9]. The exact value of $f(n; L)$ is known only for very few graphs [2], [3], [10], [11] and if $\chi(L) = 2$ even asymptotic formulas are rarely known.

Now we state Turán's theorem in the exact form:

We use—as above—the notation $f(n; k)$ instead of $f(n; K_k)$.

Theorem (TURÁN). *Let $n = (k-1)t + r$; $0 \leqq r < k-1$. Then*

$$f(n; k) = \frac{1}{2}\frac{k-2}{k-2}n^2 - \frac{1}{2}r\left(1 - \frac{r}{k-1}\right).$$

The only graph (up to isomorphism) of n vertices and $f(n; k)$ edges which does not contain a K_k is the complete $(k-1)$-chromatic graph $K_{k-1}(n_1, \ldots, n_{k-1})$ with n_i vertices in its i'th class where

$$n = n_1 + \ldots + n_k \quad \text{and} \quad |n_i - n_j| \leqq 1 \quad \text{for} \quad 1 \leqq i < j \leqq n.$$

In this note we first of all prove a generalization of this theorem.

We need the following definition and notations:

Let $G=\langle V;E\rangle$ be a graph with vertex set $V=\{v_1,\ldots,v_n\}$ an edge-set E. The star $S_G^i=\langle V_i;E_i\rangle$ of a vertex $v_i\in V$ is the graph spanned by those vertices of G which are joined by an edge to v_i. (*I.e.* $E_i=\{(v_\nu,v_\mu):(v_\nu,v_\mu)\in E,\ v_\nu,v_\mu\in V_i\}$.) Let $d_i=|V_i|$, $e_i=|E_i|$ for $i=1,\ldots,n$.

The above described $K_{k-1}(n_1,\ldots,n_{k-1})$ will be denoted by $T_{k-1,n}$.

Theorem. *Let $G=\langle V;E\rangle$ be a graph with $|V|=n$ and $e=|E|>f(n;k)$. Then for at least one vertex $v_i\in V$ we have*

$$e_i>f(d_i;k-1).$$

The only graph G with $|V|=n$, $|E|=f(n;k)$ and $e_i\leqq f(d_i;k-1)$ for $i=1,\ldots,n$ is the "Turán-graph" $T_{k-1,n}$.

This theorem clearly implies Turán's theorem. At first sight it seems to be deeper but it turns out that the proof is very simple.

Proof. Let

$$d_i\equiv r_i \bmod (k-2)\,;\quad 0\leqq r_i<k-2\,.$$

Supposing

$$e_i\leqq f(d_i;k-1)\quad\text{for}\quad 1\leqq i\leqq n \tag{1}$$

we shall show

$$e\leqq f(n;k)\,. \tag{2}$$

Since $\sum_1^n e_i=3T$ where T is the number of triangles in G and

$$3T\geqq \sum_{(v_i,v_j)\in E}((d_i+d_j)-n)=\sum_1^n d_i^2-en\,, \tag{3}$$

we have

$$\sum_{i=1}^n d_i^2-en\leqq \sum_{i=1}^n e_i\leqq \sum_{i=1}^n f(d_i;k-1)$$

(4)

$$\sum_{i=1}^n d_i^2-\sum_{i=1}^n f(d_i;k-1)\leqq en$$

Using $\sum_{i=1}^n d_i=2e$ as the first simple result we get

$$\sum_{i=1}^n d_i^2-\sum_{i=1}^n f(d_i;k-1)=\frac{1}{2}\frac{k-1}{k-2}\sum_{i=1}^n d_i^2+\sum_{i=1}^n\frac{r_i}{2}\left(1-\frac{r_i}{k-2}\right)\geqq\frac{1}{2}\frac{k-1}{k-2}\left(\frac{2e}{n}\right)^2 n\,. \tag{5}$$

From (4) and (5) we get

$$e \leqq \frac{1}{2}\frac{k-2}{k-1}n^2 . \tag{6}$$

This gives the desired result in the case $k-1/n$. To get (2) for the general case write

$$e = \frac{1}{2}\frac{k-2}{k-1}n^2 - \frac{r}{2}\left(1 - \frac{r}{k-1}\right) + \Delta . \tag{7}$$

From (6) we know already that

$$\Delta \leqq \frac{r}{2}\left(1 - \frac{r}{k-1}\right)$$

and we may suppose $\Delta > 0$.

As one can see easily, under the condition

$$\sum_{i=1}^{n} d_i = 2e$$

the minimal value of $\sum_{i=1}^{n} d_i^2 - \sum_{i=1}^{n} f(d_i; k-2)$ is taken for the system (d_i^*) where

$$|d_i^* - d_j^*| \leqq 1 ; \quad 1 \leqq i < j \leqq n .$$

For this (d_i^*) system we get easily—for a suitable choice of the indices—

$$d_i^* = \begin{cases} n-(t+1) = (k-2)t+r & \text{if } 1 \leqq i \leqq rt - 2\Delta \\ n-t = (k-2)t+r-1 & \text{if } rt-2\Delta < i \leqq n = (k-1)t+r \end{cases} \tag{9}$$

(from $\Delta \leqq \frac{r}{2}\left(1 - \frac{r}{k-2}\right)$ we have $2\Delta \leqq r$), and consequently

$$r_i^* = \begin{cases} r, & \text{if } 1 \leqq i \leqq rt - 2 \\ r-1, & \text{if } \mathrm{rt} - 2\Delta < r \leqq (k-1)t + r . \end{cases} \tag{10}$$

Hence, as an easy computation shows

$$\text{(11)} \sum d_i^2 - \sum f(d_i, k-2) \geqq f(n; k) + \frac{k-1}{k-2}\Delta(2(n-t-1)+(k-2)-2r+1) .$$

From (4) and this

$$\frac{k-1}{k-2}\Delta(2(n-t-1)+k-2-2r+1) \leqq \Delta n$$

follows which contradicts to $\Delta > 0$.

From the above reasoning it also follows easily that

$$(12)\qquad \begin{aligned} &e = f(n;k) \quad \text{and} \\ &e_i \leqq f(d_i; k-2) \quad \text{for} \quad i = 1, \dots, n \end{aligned}$$

holds if and only if G is the "Turán-graph" $T_{k-1,n}$.

Namely (12) holds only if we have equality in (11), our system (d_i) is the system (d_i^*) and we have equality in (3).

Problems and remarks

One can try to find other extremal problems for which an analogous method applies.

(a) Consider the case of a pyramid. A pyramid P is a graph where $V = \{x, y_1, \dots, y_k\}$ and $E = \{(x, y_i), (y_i, y_{i+1}); 1 \leqq i \leqq k\}$ with $y_{k+1} = y_k$. It is known [6] that any $G(V; E)$ with $|V| = n$ and $|E| \geqq \frac{n^2}{4} + \frac{n}{2}$ contains a pyramid. By a similar method we used one can show that a graph with $e \geqq \frac{n^2}{4} + \frac{n}{2}$ contains a vertex where S_G^i contains more than d_i edges.

This phenomenon does not remain valid if we fix the size of the pyramid.

In the above examples the L graphs under consideration were such that they had a vertex which is joined to all other vertices and in this case we had to consider only the S_G^i star graphs; the existence of a proper subgraph in S_G^i assured the existence of a subgraph in G isomorphic to L. Now an analogous phenomenon may occur for complete bipartite graphs.

(b) Let us consider the case of a $K_{2,2,2}$. In Erdős and Simonovits [6] proved that

$$f(n; K_{2,2,2}) = \frac{n^2}{4} + cn^{3/2} + O(n^{3/2})$$

for a certain c which value can be determined. A relatively simple computation proves that every G with $|V| = n$, $|E| = \frac{n^2}{4} + c^* n^{3/2}$ contains two vertices for whose the intersection of their stars contains enough edges to ensure a c_4. But we have not proved that $c^* = c$.

Added in proof. The same result was also proved by Bollobás and Eldridge and recently a very simple proof was found by Bondy which will appear soon.

References

[1] W. J. Brown, On graphs that do not contain a Thomson graph, *Canad. Math. Bull.*, **9** (1966), 281–285.
[2] P. Erdős, Extremal problems in Graph Theory, *Theory of graphs and its applications*, 29–36, Publ. House Czechoslovak Acad. Sci., Prague, 1964.
[3] P. Erdős and T. Gallai, On maximal paths and circuits of graphs, *Acta Math. Acad. Sci. Hung.*, **10** (1959), 337–356.
[4] P. Erdős, A. Rényi and V. T. Sós, On a problem of graph theory, *Studia Sci. Math. Hung.*, **1** (1966), 215–235.
[5] P. Erdős and M. Simonovits, A limit theorem in graph theory, *Studia Sci. Math. Hung.*, **1** (1966), 51–57.
[6] P. Erdős and M. Simonovits, On extremal graph-problem, *Acta Math. Acad. Sci. Hung.*, **22** (1971), 275–282.
[7] P. Erdős and A. H. Stone, On the structure of linear graphs, *Bull. Amer. Math. Soc.*, **52** (1946), 1087–1091.
[8] C. Hylten and Cavallius, On a combinatorial problem, *Coll. Math.*, **6** (1958), 59–65.
[9] T. Kővári, V. T. Sós and P. Turán, On a problem of K. Zarankiewicz, *Coll. Math.*, **3** (1954), 50–57.
[10] M. Simonovits, Extremal graph problems with simmetrical extremal graphs, *Discrete Math.*, **7** (1974), 349–376.
[11] M. Simonovits, A method for solving extremal problems in graph theory; stability problems, *Theory of Graphs, Proc. Coll. Tihany*, Hungary (1966), 279–319.
[12] P. Turán, On an extremal problem in graph theory, (in Hungarian), *Mat. Fiz. Lapok*, **48** (1941), 436–452.
[13] P. Turán, On the theory of graphs, *Coll. Math.*, **3** (1954), 19–30.

MATHEMATICAL INSTITUTE
OF THE HUNGARIAN ACADEMY OF SCIENCES
H-1053 BUDAPEST, REÁLTANODA U. 13—15.
HUNGARY

EÖTVÖS LORÁND UNIVERSITY
H-1088 BUDAPEST, MÚZEUM KRT. 6—8.
HUNGARY

Studies in Pure Mathematics
To the Memory of Paul Turán

On some problems of J. Dénes and P. Turán

by

P. ERDŐS and M. SZALAY (Budapest)

1. In what follows we are dealing with some statistical properties of partitions resp. unequal partitions of positive integers. We introduce the notation

$$\Pi = \begin{Bmatrix} \lambda_1 + \lambda_2 + \ldots + \lambda_m = n \\ \lambda_1 \geqq \lambda_2 \geqq \ldots \geqq \lambda_m \geqq 1 \end{Bmatrix} \tag{1.1}$$

for a generic partition Π of n where

$$m = m(\Pi) \quad \text{and the} \quad \lambda_\mu\text{'s are integers.} \tag{1.2}$$

Let $p(n)$ denote the number of partitions of n. According to the classical result of G. H. Hardy and S. Ramanujan (see [1]),

$$p(n) = (1 + o(1)) \frac{1}{4n\sqrt{3}} \exp\left(\frac{2\pi}{\sqrt{6}}\sqrt{n}\right). \tag{1.3}$$

(The o-sign and later the O-sign refer to $n \to \infty$.)

2. J. Dénes raised the following interesting problem. What is the number of pairs (Π_1, Π_2) of partitions of n which do not have equal *subsums*? This problem has not been solved yet but its investigation led P. Turán to some unexpected phenomena. The pairs with the Dénes property* are obviously contained in the set of pairs of partitions not having common *summands*. P. Turán proved (see [6]) that the number of pairs of partitions (of n) having no common summands is

$$\exp\left((1 + o(1))\pi\sqrt{2n}\right) \tag{2.1}$$

* Apart from the common complete subsums of course, we exclude the pair $(\lambda_1 = n, \lambda_1 = n)$ here.

at most. This estimation shows that the number of pairs with the Dénes property is "small" (in comparison with the total number $p(n)^2$ of the pairs). This smallness suggested that "almost all" pairs (i.e., with the exception of $o(p(n)^2)$ pairs at most) have "many" common summands. Indeed, P. TURÁN proved (see [6]) that almost all pairs of partitions of n contain

$$\left(\frac{\sqrt{6}}{4\pi} - o(1)\right)\sqrt{n}\log n \tag{2.2}$$

common summands at least (*with multiplicity*). Afterwards P. TURÁN proved an analogue of the above result for k-tuples of partitions with fixed integer $k \geqq 2$ (see [7]). This result was generalized for $k = o(\sqrt{n})$ by C. POMERANCE [2].

Thinking of the fact (which is easy to prove) that "almost all" partitions of n (i.e., with the exception of $o(p(n))$ partitions at most) contain 1 as summand $[\sqrt{n}(\omega(n))^{-1}]$-times at least ($\omega(n) \nearrow \infty$ arbitrarily slowly) one can imagine that the phenomenon (2.2) is perhaps caused by certain summands of *great multiplicity*. That this is *not* the "real" reason turned out in [8]. Namely, in his paper [8] P. TURÁN proved the existence of

$$(1 - o(1))\frac{\sqrt{3}}{\pi k 2^{k-1}}\sqrt{n} \tag{2.3}$$

common summands in "almost all" k-tuples of *unequal partitions* of the form

$$\Pi^* = \left\{\begin{matrix} \alpha_1 + \alpha_2 + \ldots + \alpha_m = n \\ \alpha_1 > \alpha_2 > \ldots > \alpha_m \geqq 1 \end{matrix}\right\} \tag{2.4}$$

where

$$m = m(\Pi^*) \quad \text{and the} \quad \alpha_\mu\text{'s are integers.} \tag{2.5}$$

We remind the reader that G. H. HARDY and S. RAMANUJAN's formula (see [1]) asserts the relation

$$q(n) = \frac{1+o(1)}{4n^{3/4}3^{1/4}}\exp\left(\frac{\pi}{\sqrt{3}}\sqrt{n}\right) \tag{2.6}$$

for the number $q(n)$ of *unequal partitions* (2.4)–(2.5) of n.

3. Another approach to the original problem would be, as P. TURÁN proposed, the investigation of the integers which can be represented by subsums. This investigation led us to other surprising phenomena we are dealing with in this paper. Our Theorem I yields that (not in the strongest form) *almost all* partitions of n represent *all* integers k of $[1, n]$ as subsums, i.e., in the form

$$k = \sum_{j=1}^{S_k} \lambda_{i_j} \qquad (i_j \neq i_l \quad \text{for} \quad j \neq l). \tag{3.1}$$

The analogue of this assertion does not hold for *unequal partitions* (e.g., it is easy to see that $k=1$ cannot be represented in a positive percentage of the unequal partitions of n) but our Theorem II yields a weaker result of similar type.

4. Let $M(n)$ denote the number of such partitions Π of n for which it is *not* true that every integer k of the interval $[1, n]$ is representable by a subsum of Π. Then we assert

Theorem I.

$$M(n) = \left(1 + O\left(\frac{\log^{30} n}{\sqrt{n}}\right)\right)\frac{\pi}{\sqrt{6n}}\, p(n)\,. \tag{4.1}$$

Corollary. *The number of partitions of n which represent all integers k of the interval* $[1, n]$ *as subsums is*

$$\left(1 - \frac{\pi}{\sqrt{6n}} + O\left(\frac{\log^{30} n}{n}\right)\right)p(n)\,, \tag{4.2}$$

consequently, almost all partitions of n represent all integers k of $[1, n]$ *as subsums.*

For the proof of Theorem I, we need a number of lemmata. We use the results of P. Turán and M. Szalay on the distribution of summands in the partitions of n (see [3], [4], [5]).

5. Using the notation (1.1), we define

$$S_1(n, \Pi, \Lambda) = \sum_{\substack{\lambda_\mu \geqq \Lambda \\ \lambda_\mu \in \Pi \text{ (with multiplicity)}}} 1. \tag{5.1}$$

Lemma 1 (M. Szalay–P. Turán [3], Corollary of Theorem II). *If* Λ *is restricted by*

$$11 \log n \leqq \Lambda \leqq \frac{\sqrt{6}}{2\pi}\sqrt{n}\log n - 3\sqrt{n}\log\log n \tag{5.2}$$

then the relation

$$S_1(n, \Pi, \Lambda) = \left(1 + O\left(\frac{1}{\log n}\right)\right)\frac{\sqrt{6}}{\pi}\sqrt{n}\log\frac{1}{1-\exp\left(-\frac{\pi\Lambda}{\sqrt{6n}}\right)} \tag{5.3}$$

holds uniformly in (5.2) *apart from*

$$c p(n)\, n^{-5/4}\log n \tag{5.4}$$

exceptional Π*'s at most.*

Throughout this paper c's stand for explicitly calculable positive constants not necessarily the same in different occurrences.

Lemma 2 (M. SZALAY–P. TURÁN [5], Corollary 1). *With the restriction*

$$\log^6 n \leqq \mu \leqq \frac{\sqrt{6}}{2\pi}\sqrt{n}\log n - 5\sqrt{n}\log\log n \tag{5.5}$$

the relation

$$\lambda_\mu = \left(1 + O\left(\frac{1}{\log n}\right)\right)\frac{\sqrt{6}}{\pi}\sqrt{n}\log\frac{1}{1-\exp\left(-\frac{\pi\mu}{\sqrt{6n}}\right)} \tag{5.6}$$

holds uniformly with the exception of $cp(n)\,n^{-5/4}\log n$ partitions of n at most.

Lemma 3 (M. SZALAY–P. TURÁN [5], Lemma 4). *The inequalities*

$$\lambda_1 \leqq 5\frac{\sqrt{6}}{2\pi}\sqrt{n}\log n \tag{5.7}$$

and

$$m \leqq 5\frac{\sqrt{6}}{2\pi}\sqrt{n}\log n \tag{5.8}$$

hold with the exception of $cp(n)\,n^{-2}$ Π's at most.

Lemma 4. *Using the abbreviation*

$$U(k) = \log\frac{1}{1-\exp\left(-\frac{\pi k}{\sqrt{6n}}\right)}, \tag{5.9}$$

we have, for

$$\log^7 n \leqq k \leqq \frac{\sqrt{6}}{2\pi}\sqrt{n}\log n - 9\frac{\sqrt{6}}{\pi}\sqrt{n}\log\log n, \tag{5.10}$$

the uniform estimation

$$\sum_{\mu=k}^{m}\lambda_\mu = \left(1 + O\left(\frac{1}{\log n}\right)\right)\frac{6}{\pi^2}n\int_0^{U(k)}\frac{x}{\exp(x)-1}\,dx \tag{5.11}$$

apart from $cp(n)\,n^{-5/4}\log n$ Π's at most.

Proof. Owing to Lemma 2 and Lemma 3, we have

$$\sum_{\mu=k}^{m}\lambda_\mu = \sum_{\mu\in I}\lambda_\mu + O(m)\,O(\log^7 n)$$

where

$$I = \left[k, \frac{\sqrt{6}}{2\pi}\sqrt{n}\log n - 7\frac{\sqrt{6}}{\pi}\sqrt{n}\log\log n\right],$$

i.e.,

$$\sum_{\mu=k}^{m} \lambda_\mu = \sum_{\mu\in I} \lambda_\mu + O(\sqrt{n}\log^8 n) =$$

$$= \sum_{\substack{\mu\in I\\ \mu\,\text{integer}}} \left(1+O\left(\frac{1}{\log n}\right)\right)\frac{\sqrt{6}}{\pi}\sqrt{n}\log\frac{1}{1-\exp\left(-\frac{\pi\mu}{\sqrt{6n}}\right)} + O(\sqrt{n}\log^8 n) =$$

$$= \left(1+O\left(\frac{1}{\log n}\right)\right)\left\{\int_I \frac{\sqrt{6}}{\pi}\sqrt{n}\log\frac{1}{1-\exp\left(-\frac{\pi x}{\sqrt{6n}}\right)}\,dx + O(\sqrt{n}\log n)\right\} +$$

$$+ O(\sqrt{n}\log^8 n) =$$

$$= \left(1+O\left(\frac{1}{\log n}\right)\right)\cdot$$

$$\cdot\left\{\int_k^\infty \frac{\sqrt{6}}{\pi}\sqrt{n}\log\frac{1}{1-\exp\left(-\frac{\pi x}{\sqrt{6n}}\right)}\,dx + O(\sqrt{n}\log^7 n)\right\} + O(\sqrt{n}\log^8 n).$$

Here, the last integral is

$$\geqq \frac{6}{\pi^2}\sqrt{n}\log^9 n,$$

thus,

$$\sum_{\mu=k}^{m} \lambda_\mu = \left(1+O\left(\frac{1}{\log n}\right)\right)\int_k^\infty \frac{\sqrt{6}}{\pi}\sqrt{n}\log\frac{1}{1-\exp\left(-\frac{\pi x}{\sqrt{6n}}\right)}\,dx =$$

$$= \left(1+O\left(\frac{1}{\log n}\right)\right)\frac{6}{\pi^2}n\int_0^{U(k)} \frac{y}{\exp(y)-1}\,dy$$

$$\left(\text{with } y = \log\frac{1}{1-\exp\left(-\frac{\pi x}{\sqrt{6n}}\right)}\right).$$

Lemma 5. *There exists a positive constant c such that dropping* $cp(n)n^{-5/4}\log n$ *suitable partitions of n at most, the remaining ones have the property that*

$$\lambda_\mu \geqq \log^{10} n > 0 \tag{5.12}$$

implies

$$\lambda_\mu \leqq \lambda_{\mu+1} + \lambda_{\mu+2} + \ldots + \lambda_m . \tag{5.13}$$

Proof. After dropping $cp(n)\,n^{-5/4}\log n$ Π's at most all the previous lemmata will be applicable. Owing to Lemma 2,

$$\lambda_{\left[\frac{\sqrt{6}}{2\pi}\sqrt{n}\log n - 9\frac{\sqrt{6}}{\pi}\sqrt{n}\log\log n\right]} < c\log^{9.1} n < \log^{10} n$$

for $n > n_0$. Therefore, for sufficiently large n,

$$\lambda_\mu \geqq \log^{10} n$$

implies

$$1 \leqq \mu \leqq \frac{\sqrt{6}}{2\pi}\sqrt{n}\log n - 9\frac{\sqrt{6}}{\pi}\sqrt{n}\log\log n - 1 . \tag{5.14}$$

For

$$n > n_1 \quad \text{and} \quad 1 \leqq \mu \leqq \left[\frac{\sqrt{6}}{\pi}\sqrt{n}\right] - 1 , \tag{5.15}$$

Lemma 4 and Lemma 3 yield that

$$\lambda_{\mu+1} + \lambda_{\mu+2} + \ldots + \lambda_m \geqq \lambda_{\left[\frac{\sqrt{6}}{\pi}\sqrt{n}\right]} + \ldots + \lambda_m \geqq$$

$$\geqq \frac{3}{\pi^2} n \int_0^{\log\frac{1}{1-\exp(-1)}} \frac{x}{\exp(x)-1}\,dx > 5\frac{\sqrt{6}}{2\pi}\sqrt{n}\log n \geqq \lambda_1 \geqq \lambda_\mu ,$$

thus the inequality (5.13) holds in the case (5.15). Next let

$$n > n_2 , \quad \left[\frac{\sqrt{6}}{\pi}\sqrt{n}\right] \leqq \mu \leqq \frac{\sqrt{6}}{2\pi}\sqrt{n}\log n - 9\frac{\sqrt{6}}{\pi}\sqrt{n}\log\log n - 1 . \tag{5.16}$$

Then, owing to Lemma 4 resp. Lemma 2, we get

$$\lambda_{\mu+1} + \lambda_{\mu+2} + \ldots + \lambda_m \geqq \frac{3}{\pi^2} n \int_0^{\exp\left(-\frac{\pi(\mu+1)}{\sqrt{6n}}\right)} \frac{x}{\exp(x)-1}\,dx \geqq$$

$$\geqq \frac{3}{\pi^2} n \int\limits_0^{\exp\left(-\frac{\pi(\mu+1)}{\sqrt{6n}}\right)} \frac{1}{e-1} dx > \frac{3}{2\pi^2} n \exp\left(-\frac{\pi(\mu+1)}{\sqrt{6n}}\right) > \frac{1}{100} n \exp\left(-\frac{\pi\mu}{\sqrt{6n}}\right),$$

resp.

$$\lambda_\mu \leqq c\sqrt{n} \exp\left(-\frac{\pi\mu}{\sqrt{6n}}\right) < \frac{1}{100} n \exp\left(-\frac{\pi\mu}{\sqrt{6n}}\right).$$

These estimations imply (5.13) in the case (5.16). Thus, Lemma 5 is proved for sufficiently large n and the increase of the constant c completes the proof for all n.

6. We shall use HARDY–RAMANUJAN's stronger formula (see [1]) in the form

$$(6.1)\quad p(n) = \frac{\exp\left(\frac{2\pi}{\sqrt{6}}\sqrt{n-\frac{1}{24}}\right)}{4\left(n-\frac{1}{24}\right)\sqrt{3}} \left\{1 - \frac{\sqrt{6}}{2\pi\sqrt{n-\frac{1}{24}}}\right\} + O\left(\exp\left(0.51 \cdot \frac{2\pi}{\sqrt{6}}\sqrt{n}\right)\right).$$

One can get easily from (6.1) that

$$(6.2)\qquad p(n) = \frac{1}{4n\sqrt{3}}\left\{1 - \left(\frac{\sqrt{6}}{2\pi} + \frac{\pi}{24\sqrt{6}}\right)\frac{1}{\sqrt{n}} + O\left(\frac{1}{n}\right)\right\} \exp\left(\frac{2\pi}{\sqrt{6}}\sqrt{n}\right).$$

Let $p_1(n)$ denote the number of partitions of n not containing 1 as summand. We have obviously

$$(6.3)\qquad p_1(n) = p(n) - p(n-1) \quad \text{for} \quad n > 1$$

and using (6.2) we get

$$p_1(n) = p(n)\left(1 - \frac{p(n-1)}{p(n)}\right) = p(n)\left(1 - \left(1 + O\left(\frac{1}{n}\right)\right)\exp\left(-\frac{2\pi}{\sqrt{6}}\frac{1}{\sqrt{n}+\sqrt{n-1}}\right)\right) =$$

$$= p(n)\left(\frac{\pi}{\sqrt{6n}} + O\left(\frac{1}{n}\right)\right).$$

Thus we have proved

Lemma 6.

$$(6.4)\qquad p_1(n) = p(n) - p(n-1) = \left(1 + O\left(\frac{1}{\sqrt{n}}\right)\right)\frac{\pi}{\sqrt{6n}}\, p(n)$$

for $n > 1$.

To the representations of the "small" integers we shall need the number $p(n, i, j)$ of partitions of n containing neither the summand i nor the summand j where i, j are integers and

$$1 \leqq i < j . \tag{6.5}$$

Now we assert

Lemma 7. *Under the restrictions*

$$1 \leqq i < j \leqq \log^{10} n, \quad n > c , \tag{6.6}$$

the relations

$$\begin{aligned} p(n, i, j) &= p(n) - p(n-i) - p(n-j) + p(n-i-j) = \\ &= O\left(\frac{\log^{20} n}{n} p(n)\right) = O\left(\frac{\log^{20} n}{\sqrt{n}} p_1(n)\right) \end{aligned} \tag{6.7}$$

hold.

Proof. The relation

$$1 + \sum_{n=1}^{\infty} p(n, i, j) y^n = \prod_{\substack{\nu=1 \\ \nu \neq i, j}}^{\infty}{}' \frac{1}{1 - y^\nu}$$

holds obviously for $0 < y < 1$. From this we get

$$1 + \sum_{n=1}^{\infty} p(n, i, j) y^n = (1 - y^i)(1 - y^j)\left(1 + \sum_{n=1}^{\infty} p(n) y^n\right),$$

i.e.,

$$p(n, i, j) = p(n) - p(n-i) - p(n-j) + p(n-i-j) \tag{6.8}$$

for $n > i + j$.

Using (6.8), (6.6) and (6.2) we get

$$p(n, i, j) = p(n)\left\{1 - \frac{p(n-i)}{p(n)} - \frac{p(n-j)}{p(n)}\left(1 - \frac{p(n-i-j)}{p(n-j)}\right)\right\} =$$

$$= p(n)\left\{1 - \left(1 + O\left(\frac{i}{n}\right)\right)\exp\left(-\frac{2\pi}{\sqrt{6}} \frac{i}{\sqrt{n} + \sqrt{n-i}}\right) - \right.$$

$$- \left(1 + O\left(\frac{j}{n}\right)\right)\exp\left(-\frac{2\pi}{\sqrt{6}} \frac{j}{\sqrt{n} + \sqrt{n-j}}\right) \times$$

$$\times\left(1-\left(1+O\left(\frac{i}{n}\right)\right)\exp\left(-\frac{2\pi}{\sqrt{6}}\frac{i}{\sqrt{n-j}+\sqrt{n-i-j}}\right)\right)\Bigg\}=$$

$$=p(n)\left\{1-\left(1-\frac{\pi}{\sqrt{6n}}i+O\left(\frac{\log^{20}n}{n}\right)\right)-\right.$$

$$\left.-\left(1-\frac{\pi}{\sqrt{6n}}j+O\left(\frac{\log^{20}n}{n}\right)\right)\left(\frac{\pi}{\sqrt{6n}}i+O\left(\frac{\log^{20}n}{n}\right)\right)\right\}=$$

$$=p(n)O\left(\frac{\log^{20}n}{n}\right)=O\left(\frac{\log^{20}n}{\sqrt{n}}p_1(n)\right).$$

7. Now we turn to the proof of Theorem I. Owing to Lemma 6, we have obviously

$$M(n)\geqq p_1(n)=p(n)-p(n-1)=\left(1+O\left(\frac{1}{\sqrt{n}}\right)\right)\frac{\pi}{\sqrt{6n}}p(n) \tag{7.1}$$

for $n>c$ and we have to prove only the estimation

$$M(n)-p_1(n)\leqq c\frac{\log^{30}n}{\sqrt{n}}p_1(n) \tag{7.2}$$

for $n>c$, i.e., we have to prove that the $p(n-1)$ partitions of n $(>c)$ containing 1 as summand represent all integers k of the interval $[1, n]$ by subsums apart from

$$c\frac{\log^{30}n}{\sqrt{n}}p_1(n) \tag{7.3}$$

partitions in question at most.

The partitions of n containing 1 as summand represent 1 and we investigate the representations of 2, 3 and 4 for $n>c$.

The number of partitions of n $(>c)$ containing 1 as summand but not representing 2 is obviously

$$=p(n-1,1,2)\leqq c\frac{\log^{20}n}{\sqrt{n}}p_1(n) \tag{7.4}$$

owing to Lemma 7.

The number of partitions of n $(>c)$ containing 1 as summand but not representing 3 resp. 4 is obviously

$$\leqq p(n,2,3)\leqq c\frac{\log^{20}n}{\sqrt{n}}p_1(n) \tag{7.5}$$

resp.

$$\leqq p(n, 3, 4) \leqq c \frac{\log^{20} n}{\sqrt{n}} p_1(n) \tag{7.6}$$

owing to Lemma 7.

(7.4), (7.5) and (7.6) yield that the partitions of n ($>c$) containing 1 as summand represent 1, 2, 3 and 4 by subsums apart from

$$c \frac{\log^{20} n}{\sqrt{n}} p_1(n) \tag{7.7}$$

partitions in question at most.

Next let

$$n > c, \quad 5 \leqq k \leqq \log^{10} n . \tag{7.8}$$

Taking into consideration Lemma 7 and (7.7) too,

$$k=(k-1)+1 \quad \text{or} \quad k=(k-2)+2 \quad \text{or} \quad k=(k-2)+1+1$$

is a representation of k by a subsum apart from

$$c \frac{\log^{20} n}{\sqrt{n}} p_1(n) + p(n, k-2, k-1) \leqq c \frac{\log^{20} n}{\sqrt{n}} p_1(n) \tag{7.9}$$

partitions in question at most.

These estimations show that the partitions of n ($>c$) *containing* 1 *as summand* represent *all* integers k of $[1, \log^{10} n]$ by subsums apart from

$$(\log^{10} n)\, c \frac{\log^{20} n}{\sqrt{n}} p_1(n) \tag{7.10}$$

partitions in question at most. Increasing the constant c we can apply also Lemma 5 for the remaining partitions owing to

$$cp(n)\, n^{-5/4} \log n < c \frac{\log^{30} n}{\sqrt{n}} p_1(n) .$$

After dropping

$$c \frac{\log^{30} n}{\sqrt{n}} p_1(n)$$

exceptional partitions in question at most let Π be an arbitrary partition of n ($>c$) from the remaining ones and k an integer with

$$1 \leqq k \leqq n . \tag{7.11}$$

We prove by induction that k is representable by a subsum of Π. This assertion has been proved for $1 \leqq k \leqq \log^{10} n$ (and is trivial for $k=n$). We assume that

$$\log^{10} n < k < n \tag{7.12}$$

and that

$$\begin{cases} \text{all the positive integers less than } k \text{ are representable} \\ \text{by subsums of } \Pi. \end{cases} \tag{7.13}$$

Let

$$\lambda_0 \overset{\text{def}}{=} n \tag{7.14}$$

and define the index $\mu \geqq 0$ by

$$\lambda_\mu > k \geqq \lambda_{\mu+1} \tag{7.15}$$

which makes sense owing to $\lambda_0 > k$ and $1 = \lambda_m < k$. Now, $\lambda_\mu > k > \log^{10} n$ and Lemma 5 preclude the possibility of

$$(n>)k \geqq \lambda_{\mu+1} + \lambda_{\mu+2} + \ldots + \lambda_m \tag{7.16}$$

because (7.16) would imply $\mu \neq 0$ and

$$\lambda_\mu > \lambda_{\mu+1} + \lambda_{\mu+2} + \ldots + \lambda_m$$

in contradiction with (5.13). Therefore, we can define an index v by

$$\lambda_{\mu+1} + \lambda_{\mu+2} + \ldots + \lambda_v + \lambda_{v+1} > k \geqq \lambda_{\mu+1} + \lambda_{\mu+2} + \ldots + \lambda_v . \tag{7.17}$$

This gives that

$$O \leqq k - \lambda_{\mu+1} - \lambda_{\mu+2} - \ldots - \lambda_v < \lambda_{v+1} \leqq \lambda_{\mu+1} \leqq k . \tag{7.18}$$

If $k \neq \lambda_{\mu+1} + \lambda_{\mu+2} + \ldots + \lambda_v$ then (7.13) and (7.18) make it sure that

$$k - \lambda_{\mu+1} - \ldots - \lambda_v = \sum_{j=1}^{s} \lambda_{i_j} < \lambda_{v+1}$$

where

$$v+1 < i_1 < i_2 < \ldots < i_s . \tag{7.19}$$

Then,

$$k = \lambda_{\mu+1} + \ldots + \lambda_v + \lambda_{i_1} + \ldots + \lambda_{i_s}$$

is a representation of k by a subsum owing to (7.19) and Theorem I is completely proved.

8. For the proof of Theorem II we shall use, for

$$\text{(8.1)} \qquad \operatorname{Re} z > 0,$$

the function

$$\text{(8.2)} \qquad f(z) \overset{\text{def}}{=} \prod_{\nu=1}^{\infty} \frac{1}{1-\exp(-\nu z)} = 1 + \sum_{n=1}^{\infty} p(n) \exp(-nz)$$

and the well-known formula

$$\text{(8.3)} \qquad f(z) = \exp\left(\frac{\pi^2}{6z} + \frac{1}{2}\log\frac{z}{2\pi} + o(1)\right) \quad \text{for} \quad z \to 0$$

in all angles

$$\text{(8.4)} \qquad |\arc z| \leqq \kappa < \frac{\pi}{2}$$

(log means the principal logarithm).

These give that

$$\text{(8.5)} \qquad \prod_{\nu=1}^{\infty} (1+\exp(-\nu z)) = \frac{f(z)}{f(2z)} = \exp\left(\frac{\pi^2}{12z} - \frac{1}{2}\log 2 + o(1)\right) \quad \text{for} \quad z \to 0$$

under the restriction (8.4).

9. We use the notation

$$\text{(9.1)} \qquad \Pi^* = \begin{Bmatrix} \alpha_1 + \alpha_2 + \dots + \alpha_m = n \\ \alpha_1 > \alpha_2 > \dots > \alpha_m \geqq 1 \end{Bmatrix}$$

for a generic *unequal partition* Π^* of n where

$$\text{(9.2)} \qquad m = m(\Pi^*) \quad \text{and the } \alpha_\mu\text{'s are integers.}$$

According to HARDY–RAMANUJAN'S formula (see [1]), the relation

$$\text{(9.3)} \qquad q(n) = \frac{1+o(1)}{4n^{3/4}\, 3^{1/4}} \exp\left(\frac{\pi}{\sqrt{3}}\sqrt{n}\right)$$

holds for the number $q(n)$ of *unequal partitions* of n.

Then, as it was indicated in **3**, we assert

Theorem II. *Let k_0 be an integer with*

$$\text{(9.4)} \qquad 1 \leqq k_0 \leqq \frac{n}{2}.$$

Then, the unequal partitions of n represent all integers k of the interval $[k_0, n-k_0]$ *as subsums apart from*

(9.5) $$(20\,(2/\sqrt{3})^{-k_0}+cn^{-1/10})q(n)$$

unequal partitions of n at most.

10. The proof of Theorem II requires some lemmata.

Lemma 8. *Let* k_0 *be an integer with*

(10.1) $$1 \leqq k_0 \leqq n^{1/5}.$$

Then, for $n>c$, *the unequal partitions of n represent all integers k of the interval* $[k_0, n^{1/5}]$ *as subsums of two terms apart from*

(10.2) $$20\,(2/\sqrt{3})^{-k_0}q(n)$$

unequal partitions of n at most.

Proof. For arbitrary positive integers n and k with $k \geqq 3$, let $q(n, k)$ denote the number of *unequal partitions* of n containing only one of s and $k-s$ *at most* (as summand) for every integer s of the interval $[1, t]$ where $t=[(k-1)/2]$ (i.e., *not* having subsums of the form $(k-s)+s$ with $k-s>s\geqq 1$). We are going to prove that the inequality

(10.3) $$q(n, k) < 2\,(2/\sqrt{3})^{-k}q(n)$$

holds for

(10.4) $$n>c, \quad 3 \leqq k \leqq n^{1/5}.$$

Let us observe that the relation

(10.5) $$1+\sum_{n=1}^{\infty} q(n, k)\, w^n = \left\{\prod_{s=1}^{t} \frac{1+w^s+w^{k-s}}{(1+w^s)(1+w^{k-s})}\right\} \prod_{v=1}^{\infty} (1+w^v)$$

holds for $|w|<1$. Cauchy's formula gives the representation

(10.6) $$q(n, k) = \frac{1}{2\pi i} \int\limits_{|w|=\rho} w^{-n-1} \left\{\prod_{s=1}^{t}\left(1-\frac{w^k}{(1+w^s)(1+w^{k-s})}\right)\right\} \prod_{v=1}^{\infty} (1+w^v)\, dw$$

for $0<\rho<1$. Let us define $g_k(z)$ by

(10.7) $$g_k(z) = \left\{\prod_{s=1}^{t}\left(1-\frac{\exp(-kz)}{(1+\exp(-sz))(1+\exp(-(k-s)z))}\right)\right\} \prod_{v=1}^{\infty} (1+\exp(-vz))$$

for

(10.8) $$x=\operatorname{Re} z>0.$$

Then we have

(10.9) $$q(n,k)=\frac{1}{2\pi}\int_{-\pi}^{\pi} g_k(x+iy)\exp(n(x+iy))\,dy$$

for $x>0$.

Let C_0 be a sufficiently large constant and ε fixed with $0<\varepsilon<10^{-2}$. We choose

(10.10) $$x=x_0=\frac{\pi}{2\sqrt{3}}n^{-1/2},\quad y_1=n^{-3/4+\varepsilon/3},\quad y_2=C_0x_0$$

and investigate (10.9) as

$$q(n,k)=\frac{1}{2\pi}\int_{-\pi}^{\pi} g_k(x_0+iy)\exp(nx_0+iny)\,dy=\frac{1}{2\pi}\left\{\int_{-\pi}^{-y_2}+\int_{-y_2}^{-y_1}+\int_{-y_1}^{y_1}+\int_{y_1}^{y_2}+\int_{y_2}^{\pi}\right\}.$$

(We use some ideas of G. A. Freiman's $p(n)$-estimation.)

For

(10.11) $$n>c,\quad 3\leqq k\leqq n^{1/5}\quad\text{and}\quad |y|\leqq y_2,$$

we can apply (8.4)–(8.5) and get

$$\prod_{\nu=1}^{\infty}(1+\exp(-\nu(x_0+iy)))=\exp\left(\frac{\pi^2}{12(x_0+iy)}-\frac{1}{2}\log 2+o(1)\right)\quad(\text{for } n\to\infty),$$

further,

$$\exp\left(\sum_{s=1}^{t}\log\left(1-\frac{\exp(-k(x_0+iy))}{(1+\exp(-s(x_0+iy)))(1+\exp(-(k-s)(x_0+iy)))}\right)\right)=$$

$$=\exp\left(\sum_{s=1}^{t}\log\left(1-\frac{1}{4}+O(kn^{-1/2})\right)\right)=$$

$$=\exp\left(t\log\frac{3}{4}+O(tkn^{-1/2})\right)=\exp\left(t\log\frac{3}{4}+O(n^{-1/10})\right)$$

under the restriction (10.11). Consequently, the relation

(10.12) $$g_k(x_0+iy)=\exp\left(t\log\frac{3}{4}+\frac{\pi^2}{12(x_0+iy)}-\frac{1}{2}\log 2+o(1)\right)$$

holds under the restriction (10.11).

First,

$$\frac{1}{2\pi}\int_{-y_1}^{y_1} g_k(x_0+iy)\exp(nx_0+iny)\,dy=$$

$$=\frac{1}{2\pi}\int_{-y_1}^{y_1}\exp\left\{t\log\frac{3}{4}+\frac{\pi^2}{12x_0}\left(1-i\frac{y}{x_0}-\left(\frac{y}{x_0}\right)^2+O\left(\left(\frac{y_1}{x_0}\right)^3\right)\right)+\right.$$

$$\left.+nx_0+iny-\frac{1}{2}\log 2+o(1)\right\}dy=$$

$$=\frac{1}{2\pi}\int_{-y_1}^{y_1}\exp\left(t\log\frac{3}{4}+\frac{\pi}{\sqrt{3}}\sqrt{n}-\frac{2\sqrt{3}}{\pi}n^{3/2}y^2+O(n^{-1/4+\varepsilon})-\frac{1}{2}\log 2+o(1)\right)dy=$$

$$=\frac{1+o(1)}{2\pi\sqrt{2}}\left(\frac{3}{4}\right)^t\exp\left(\frac{\pi}{\sqrt{3}}\sqrt{n}\right)\int_{-y_1}^{y_1}\exp\left(-\frac{2\sqrt{3}}{\pi}n^{3/2}y^2\right)dy=$$

$$=\frac{1+o(1)}{2\pi\sqrt{2}}\left(\frac{3}{4}\right)^t\exp\left(\frac{\pi}{\sqrt{3}}\sqrt{n}\right)\sqrt{\frac{\pi}{2}}\,3^{-1/4}n^{-3/4}\left\{\int_{-\infty}^{+\infty}\exp(-u^2)\,du+o(1)\right\}=$$

$$=\frac{1+o(1)}{4n^{3/4}3^{1/4}}\left(\frac{3}{4}\right)^t\exp\left(\frac{\pi}{\sqrt{3}}\sqrt{n}\right)=(1+o(1))\left(\frac{3}{4}\right)^t q(n)\,.$$

Next,

$$\frac{1}{2\pi}\left|\int_{-y_2}^{-y_1}+\int_{y_1}^{y_2}\right|\leqq\frac{1}{\pi}\int_{y_1}^{y_2}\exp\left(t\log\frac{3}{4}+\frac{\pi^2x_0}{12(x_0^2+y^2)}+nx_0+O(1)\right)dy\leqq$$

$$\leqq c\left(\frac{3}{4}\right)^t\exp\left(\frac{\pi^2x_0}{12(x_0^2+y_1^2)}+nx_0\right)=$$

$$=c\left(\frac{3}{4}\right)^t\exp\left(\frac{\pi^2}{12x_0}\left(1-\frac{y_1^2}{x_0^2}+O\left(\frac{y_1^4}{x_0^4}\right)\right)+nx_0\right)\leqq$$

$$\leqq c\left(\frac{3}{4}\right)^t\exp\left(\frac{\pi}{\sqrt{3}}\sqrt{n}-\frac{2\sqrt{3}}{\pi}n^{2\varepsilon/3}\right)=o(1)\left(\frac{3}{4}\right)^t q(n)\,.$$

Finally, we have to estimate the expression

$$\frac{1}{2\pi}\left|\int_{-\pi}^{-y_2} + \int_{y_2}^{\pi}\right|.$$

For

$$n>c, \quad 3\leqq k\leqq n^{1/5} \quad \text{and } y_2\leqq |y|\leqq \pi, \tag{10.13}$$

we get (with $z=x_0+iy$)

$$\exp\left(\operatorname{Re}\sum_{\nu=1}^{\infty}\log(1+\exp(-\nu z))\right)=\exp\left(\operatorname{Re}\sum_{\nu=1}^{\infty}\sum_{\mu=1}^{\infty}\frac{(-1)^{\mu-1}}{\mu}\exp(-\nu\mu z)\right)=$$

$$=\exp\left(\operatorname{Re}\sum_{\mu=1}^{\infty}\frac{(-1)^{\mu-1}}{\mu(\exp(\mu z)-1)}\right)\leqq\exp\left(\sum_{\mu=1}^{\infty}\frac{1}{\mu}|\exp(\mu z)-1|^{-1}\right)=$$

$$=\exp\left(\sum_{\mu=1}^{\infty}\frac{1}{\mu}\left((\exp(\mu x_0)-1)^2+4\exp(\mu x_0)\sin^2\frac{\mu y}{2}\right)^{-1/2}\right)\leqq$$

$$\leqq\exp\left(\left(2\sin\frac{|y|}{2}\right)^{-1}+\sum_{\mu=2}^{\infty}\frac{1}{\mu^2 x_0}\right)\leqq\exp\left(\frac{1}{x_0}\left(\frac{\pi^2}{6}-1+\frac{\pi}{2C_0}\right)\right)$$

and

$$\prod_{s=1}^{t}\left|1-\frac{\exp(-kz)}{(1+\exp(-sz))(1+\exp(-(k-s)z))}\right|\leqq$$

$$\leqq\prod_{s=1}^{t}\left(1+\frac{1}{(1-\exp(-sx_0))(1-\exp(-(k-s)x_0))}\right)\leqq\left(1+\frac{1}{(1-\exp(-x_0))^2}\right)^t\leqq$$

$$\leqq(cn)^t\leqq\exp(k\log(cn))\leqq\exp(n^{1/4})=\exp\left(\frac{o(1)}{x_0}\right).$$

Therefore,

$$\frac{1}{2\pi}\left|\int_{-\pi}^{-y_2}+\int_{y_2}^{\pi}\right|\leqq\frac{1}{\pi}\int_{y_2}^{\pi}\exp\left(\frac{1}{x_0}\left(\frac{\pi^2}{6}-1+\frac{\pi}{2C_0}+o(1)\right)+nx_0\right)dy\leqq$$

$$\leqq\exp\left(\frac{\pi}{\sqrt{3}}\sqrt{n}-\frac{2\sqrt{3}}{\pi}\sqrt{n}\left(1-\frac{\pi^2}{12}-\frac{\pi}{2C_0}-o(1)\right)\right)=o(1)\left(\frac{3}{4}\right)^t q(n)$$

owing to (10.10) and (10.13).

Thus we have proved the estimation

(10.14) $$q(n,k)=(1+o(1))\left(\frac{3}{4}\right)^t q(n)<2\left(\frac{2}{\sqrt{3}}\right)^{-k} q(n)$$

for

(10.15) $$n>c, \quad 3\leqq k\leqq n^{1/5}.$$

The assertion of Lemma 8 is trivial for $k_0=1$, 2 owing to $20(2/\sqrt{3})^{-2}>1$. For $3\leqq k_0\leqq n^{1/5}$, the total number of the exceptional unequal partitions is

$$\leqq \sum_{k=k_0}^{[n^{1/5}]} q(n,k)\leqq 2q(n)\sum_{k=k_0}^{\infty}\left(\frac{2}{\sqrt{3}}\right)^{-k}<20\left(\frac{2}{\sqrt{3}}\right)^{-k_0} q(n)$$

and Lemma 8 is completely proved.

11. Now we assert

Lemma 9. *The unequal partitions of $n(>c)$ represent all integers k of the interval*

(11.1) $$\left[n^{1/5}, \left(1+\frac{1}{5}\right)\frac{\sqrt{3}}{\pi}\sqrt{n}\log n\right]$$

as subsums of four terms at most apart from

(11.2) $$cq(n)n^{-4}$$

unequal partitions of n at most.

Proof. For arbitrary positive integers n and k with $k\geqq 10$ and the notations

(11.3) $$t_1=\left[\frac{k}{4}\right]+1, \quad t_2=\left[\frac{k-1}{2}\right], \quad t=t_2-t_1+1,$$

let $q_1(n,k)$ denote the number of unequal partitions of n containing only one of s and $k-s$ *at most* (as summand) for every integer s of the interval $[t_1, t_2]$ (i.e., *not* having subsums of the form $(k-s)+s$ with $k-s>s>k/4$).

Let us observe that the relation

(11.4) $$1+\sum_{n=1}^{\infty} q_1(n,k)\exp(-nx)=$$
$$=\left\{\prod_{s=t_1}^{t_2}\frac{1+\exp(-sx)+\exp(-(k-s)x)}{(1+\exp(-sx))(1+\exp(-(k-s)x))}\right\}\prod_{v=1}^{\infty}(1+\exp(-vx))$$

holds for $x>0$. (11.4) yields that

$$q_1(n,k)\exp(-nx)\leqq$$

$$\leqq\left\{\prod_{s=t_1}^{t_2}\left(1-\frac{\exp(-kx)}{(1+\exp(-sx))(1+\exp(-(k-s)x))}\right)\right\}\prod_{v=1}^{\infty}(1+\exp(-vx))\leqq$$

$$\leqq\left\{\prod_{s=t_1}^{t_2}\left(1-\frac{1}{4}\exp(-kx)\right)\right\}\prod_{v=1}^{\infty}(1+\exp(-vx)),$$

i.e.,

$$q_1(n,k)\leqq\left\{\prod_{v=1}^{\infty}(1+\exp(-vx))\right\}\exp\left(nx+t\log\left(1-\frac{1}{4}\exp(-kx)\right)\right)$$

for $x>0$.

Choosing

(11.5) $$x=x_0=\frac{\pi}{2\sqrt{3}}n^{-1/2}$$

and using (8.4)–(8.5), we get

$$q_1(n,k)\leqq\left\{\prod_{v=1}^{\infty}(1+\exp(-vx_0))\right\}\exp\left(nx_0-\frac{t}{4}\exp(-kx_0)\right)\leqq$$

$$\leqq c\exp\left(\frac{\pi^2}{12x_0}+nx_0-\frac{k}{16}\exp(-kx_0)\right)=$$

$$=c\exp\left(\frac{\pi}{\sqrt{3}}\sqrt{n}-\frac{k}{16}\exp(-kx_0)\right)$$

i.e.,

(11.6) $$q_1(n,k)\leqq cq(n)\exp\left(\frac{3}{4}\log n-\frac{k}{16}\exp\left(-\frac{\pi k}{2\sqrt{3n}}\right)\right).$$

For

(11.7) $$n>c,\quad n^{1/5}\leqq k\leqq\frac{2\sqrt{3}}{\pi}\sqrt{n},$$

we get

(11.8) $$q_1(n,k)\leqq cq(n)\exp\left(\frac{3}{4}\log n-\frac{1}{16e}n^{1/5}\right)<cq(n)n^{-5}.$$

For

(11.9) $$n>c,\quad\frac{2\sqrt{3}}{\pi}\sqrt{n}\leqq k\leqq\left(1-\frac{1}{100}\right)\frac{\sqrt{3}}{\pi}\sqrt{n}\log n,$$

(11.6) gives the estimation

(11.10)
$$q_1(n, k) \leqq cq(n) \exp\left(\frac{3}{4}\log n - \frac{2\sqrt{3n}}{16\pi}\exp\left(-\left(\frac{1}{2}-\frac{1}{200}\right)\log n\right)\right) =$$
$$= cq(n) \exp\left(\frac{3}{4}\log n - \frac{2\sqrt{3}}{16\pi} n^{1/200}\right) < cq(n) n^{-5}.$$

(11.7)–(11.10) show that the unequal partitions of $n(>c)$ represent all integers k of the interval

(11.11)
$$I_1 = \left[n^{1/5}, \left(1-\frac{1}{100}\right)\frac{\sqrt{3}}{\pi}\sqrt{n}\log n\right]$$

as subsums of the form

(11.12)
$$k = (k-s)+s \quad \text{with} \quad k-s>s>k/4$$

apart from

$$\sum_{\substack{k \in I_1 \\ k \text{ integer}}} q_1(n, k) < cq(n) n^{-4}$$

unequal partitions of n at most. After dropping these exceptional unequal partitions let

$$\Pi^* = \begin{cases} \alpha_1+\alpha_2+\ldots+\alpha_m = n \\ \alpha_1>\alpha_2>\ldots>\alpha_m \geqq 1 \end{cases}$$

be an arbitrary unequal partition of $n(>c)$ from the remaining ones and k an arbitrary integer with

(11.13)
$$\left(1-\frac{1}{100}\right)\frac{\sqrt{3}}{\pi}\sqrt{n}\log n \leqq k \leqq \left(1+\frac{1}{5}\right)\frac{\sqrt{3}}{\pi}\sqrt{n}\log n .$$

Let

$$k_1 = \left[\left(1-\frac{1}{100}\right)\frac{\sqrt{3}}{\pi}\sqrt{n}\log n - n^{1/5}\right], \quad k_2 = k-k_1 .$$

Then we can use the property (11.11)–(11.12) of Π^* owing to $k_1, k_2 \in I_1$. Thus,

$$k_1 = \alpha_{u_1}+\alpha_{v_1}, \quad \alpha_{u_1} > \alpha_{v_1} > \frac{k_1}{4},$$

$$k_2 = \alpha_{u_2}+\alpha_{v_2}, \quad \alpha_{u_2} > \alpha_{v_2} > \frac{k_2}{4},$$

and

$$k_2 < \left(\frac{1}{5} + \frac{2}{100}\right)\frac{\sqrt{3}}{\pi}\sqrt{n}\log n < \frac{k_1}{4}.$$

Therefore,

(11.14)
$$k = \alpha_{u_1} + \alpha_{v_1} + \alpha_{u_2} + \alpha_{v_2}$$

is a representation of k by a subsum of Π^* owing to

$$\alpha_{u_1} > \alpha_{v_1} > \frac{k_1}{4} > k_2 > \alpha_{u_2} > \alpha_{v_2}.$$

(11.11)–(11.14) prove Lemma 9.

In order to show that the upper value in (11.1) "usually" exceeds the maximal summand, using the notation (9.1) we assert

Lemma 10. *If $\beta = \beta(n)$ is restricted by*

(11.15)
$$0 < \beta < \frac{\pi}{4\sqrt{3}} \cdot \frac{\sqrt{n}}{\log n} - \frac{1}{2}$$

then the inequality

(11.16)
$$\alpha_1 \leqq (1+2\beta)\frac{\sqrt{3}}{\pi}\sqrt{n}\log n$$

holds with the exception of $cq(n)n^{-\beta}$ Π^*'s at most. In particular, the inequality

(11.17)
$$\alpha_1 \leqq \left(1 + \frac{1}{5}\right)\frac{\sqrt{3}}{\pi}\sqrt{n}\log n$$

holds for all but

(11.18)
$$cq(n)n^{-1/10}$$

Π^*'s at most.

Proof. In order to estimate the number of the exceptional Π^*'s, let

$$F \overset{\text{def}}{=} \left[(1+2\beta)\frac{\sqrt{3}}{\pi}\sqrt{n}\log n\right] + 1.$$

The number of Π^*'s with $\alpha_1 = j$, $F \leqq j \leqq n-1$ is $\leqq q(n-j)$. Hence, the number of the exceptional Π^*'s is

$$\leqq \sum_{j=F}^{n-1} q(n-j) + 1 = 1 + \sum_{l=1}^{n-F} q(l).$$

Using (9.3) we get

$$1+\sum_{l=1}^{n-F} q(l)\leqq c+c\sum_{l=1}^{n-F} l^{-3/4}\exp\left(\frac{\pi}{\sqrt{3}}\sqrt{l}\right)\leqq$$

$$\leqq c+c\int_{1}^{n-F+1} x^{-3/4}\exp\left(\frac{\pi}{\sqrt{3}}\sqrt{x}\right)dx\leqq c+c(n-F+1)^{-1/4}\exp\left(\frac{\pi}{\sqrt{3}}\sqrt{n-F+1}\right).$$

Owing to (11.15), we have

$$n-F+1\geqq\frac{n}{2}.$$

Consequently,

$$c+c(n-F+1)^{-1/4}\exp\left(\frac{\pi}{\sqrt{3}}\sqrt{n-F+1}\right)\leqq cq(n)n^{1/2}\exp\left\{-\frac{\pi}{\sqrt{3}}(\sqrt{n}-\sqrt{n-F+1})\right\}=$$

$$=cq(n)n^{1/2}\exp\left\{-\frac{\pi}{\sqrt{3}}\cdot\frac{\left[(1+2\beta)\frac{\sqrt{3}}{\pi}\sqrt{n}\log n\right]}{\sqrt{n}+\sqrt{n-F+1}}\right\}\leqq cq(n)n^{-\beta}.$$

Q.e.d.

12. Continuing the representation by induction, we can see that Lemma 9 and (11.17)–(11.18) preclude the possibility of an inequality analogous to (7.16) (since now $\mu+1$ would be 1). Another difficulty is, however, caused by the lack of the "small" integers representable. In order to avoid this difficulty we assert

Lemma 11. *Dropping*

$$cq(n)\exp(-10^{-3}n^{1/12}) \tag{12.1}$$

exceptional unequal partitions of n at most, each Π^* of $n(>c)$ from the remaining ones has a summand in the interval

$$\left(\frac{\tau}{2},\frac{2\tau}{3}\right] \tag{12.2}$$

for every integer τ restricted by

$$10^{-2}\sqrt{n}\leqq\tau\leqq\left(1+\frac{1}{4}\right)\frac{\sqrt{3}}{\pi}\sqrt{n}\log n. \tag{12.3}$$

Proof. For arbitrary positive integers n and τ with $\tau\geqq 6$, let $q_2(n,\tau)$ denote the number of unequal partitions of n *not* having summands from the interval $(\tau/2, 2\tau/3]$.

Then, the relation

$$(12.4)\qquad 1+\sum_{n=1}^{\infty} q_2(n,\tau)\exp(-nx)= \\ =\left\{\prod_{\nu=1}^{[\tau/2]}(1+\exp(-\nu x))\right\}\prod_{\mu=[2\tau/3]+1}^{\infty}(1+\exp(-\mu x))$$

holds for $x>0$. (12.4) yields that

$$q_2(n,\tau)\exp(-nx)\leqq\left\{\prod_{\nu=1}^{\infty}(1+\exp(-\nu x))\right\}\prod_{\mu=[\tau/2]+1}^{[2\tau/3]}(1+\exp(-\mu x))^{-1}\leqq$$

$$\leqq\left\{\prod_{\nu=1}^{\infty}(1+\exp(-\nu x))\right\}\left(1+\exp\left(-\frac{2\tau}{3}x\right)\right)^{-[2\tau/3]+[\tau/2]},$$

i.e.,

$$q_2(n,\tau)\leqq\left\{\prod_{\nu=1}^{\infty}(1+\exp(-\nu x))\right\}\exp\left(nx-\left(\left[\frac{2\tau}{3}\right]-\left[\frac{\tau}{2}\right]\right)\log\left(1+\exp\left(-\frac{2\tau}{3}x\right)\right)\right)$$

for $x>0$.

Choosing

$$(12.5)\qquad x=x_0=\frac{\pi}{2\sqrt{3}}n^{-1/2}$$

and using (8.4)–(8.5), we get

$$(12.6)\qquad q_2(n,\tau)\leqq c\exp\left(\frac{\pi^2}{12x_0}+nx_0-\frac{\tau}{6}\log\left(1+\exp\left(-\frac{2\tau}{3}x_0\right)\right)\right).$$

Taking into consideration (12.3), the estimation (12.6) gives that, for $n>c$,

$$q_2(n,\tau)\leqq c\exp\left(\frac{\pi}{\sqrt{3}}\sqrt{n}-\frac{1}{600}\sqrt{n}\log\left(1+\exp\left(-\frac{5}{12}\log n\right)\right)\right)\leqq$$

$$\leqq c\exp\left(\frac{\pi}{\sqrt{3}}\sqrt{n}-\frac{1}{700}n^{1/12}\right)\leqq cq(n)\exp\left(-\frac{1}{800}n^{1/12}\right).$$

This yields that the number of the exceptional Π^*'s is

$$\leqq\sum_{\substack{10^{-2}\sqrt{n}\leqq\tau\leqq\left(1+\frac{1}{4}\right)\frac{\sqrt{3}}{\pi}\sqrt{n}\log n\\ \tau\ \text{integer}}} q_2(n,\tau)<cq(n)\exp(-10^{-3}n^{1/12}).$$

Q.e.d.

13. Finally, we assert

Lemma 12. *The unequal partitions of $n(>c)$ represent all integers k of the interval*

$$\left[n^{1/5}, \frac{1}{2}n\right] \tag{13.1}$$

as subsums apart from

$$cq(n)\, n^{-1/10} \tag{13.2}$$

unequal partitions of n at most.

Proof. After dropping

$$cq(n)\, n^{-1/10}$$

exceptional unequal partitions of $n(>c)$ at most Lemma 9, Lemma 11 and (11.17) from Lemma 10 will be applicable. Let

$$\Pi^* = \begin{Bmatrix} \alpha_1 + \alpha_2 + \ldots + \alpha_m = n \\ \alpha_1 > \alpha_2 > \ldots > \alpha_m \geqq 1 \end{Bmatrix}$$

be an arbitrary unequal partition of n from the remaining ones and k an integer with

$$n^{1/5} \leqq k \leqq \frac{1}{2}n\,. \tag{13.3}$$

We prove by induction that k is representable by a subsum of Π^*. This assertion has been proved for

$$n^{1/5} \leqq k \leqq \left(1 + \frac{1}{5}\right)\frac{\sqrt{3}}{\pi}\sqrt{n}\log n$$

by Lemma 9. We assume that

$$\left(1 + \frac{1}{5}\right)\frac{\sqrt{3}}{\pi}\sqrt{n}\log n < k \leqq \frac{1}{2}n \tag{13.4}$$

and that

$$\begin{cases} \text{all integers of } [n^{1/5}, k-1] \text{ are representable} \\ \text{by subsums of } \Pi^*. \end{cases} \tag{13.5}$$

Owing to (11.17) and (13.4), we have

$$\alpha_1 < k \leqq \frac{1}{2}n < \alpha_1 + \alpha_2 + \ldots + \alpha_m = n\,. \tag{13.6}$$

Therefore, we can define an index ν by

(13.7) $$\alpha_1+\alpha_2+\ldots+\alpha_\nu \leqq k < \alpha_1+\alpha_2+\ldots+\alpha_\nu+\alpha_{\nu+1}\,.$$

This gives that

(13.8) $$0 \leqq \Delta \overset{\text{def}}{=} k-\alpha_1-\alpha_2-\ldots-\alpha_\nu < \alpha_{\nu+1} < \alpha_1 < k\,.$$

For

$$n^{1/5} \leqq \Delta (<k),$$

(13.5) and (13.8) make it sure that

$$k-\alpha_1-\ldots-\alpha_\nu = \sum_{j=1}^{s} \alpha_{i_j} < \alpha_{\nu+1}$$

where

(13.9) $$\nu+1 < i_1 < i_2 < \ldots < i_s\,.$$

Then,

$$k=\alpha_1+\alpha_2+\ldots+\alpha_\nu+\alpha_{i_1}+\ldots+\alpha_{i_s}$$

is a representation of k by a subsum owing to (13.9). The case $\Delta=0$ is trivial. The only problematic case we have to investigate is

(13.10) $$1 \leqq \Delta < n^{1/5}\,.$$

We have obviously

(13.11) $$m < \sqrt{2n}$$

$\left(\text{from } n=\alpha_1+\ldots+\alpha_m \geqq m+\ldots+1 > \frac{1}{2}m^2\right)$. (13.4) and (13.7) give that

$$\alpha_{\nu+1}+\ldots+\alpha_m = n-(\alpha_1+\ldots+\alpha_\nu) \geqq n-k \geqq \frac{n}{2},$$

consequently,

$$\frac{n}{2} \leqq \alpha_{\nu+1}+\ldots+\alpha_m \leqq (m-\nu)\alpha_{\nu+1} < \sqrt{2n}\,\alpha_{\nu+1}$$

owing to (13.11). Thus we have

(13.12) $$\alpha_\nu > \alpha_{\nu+1} > \frac{1}{2\sqrt{2}}\sqrt{n} > 10^{-2}\sqrt{n}\,.$$

Choosing

(13.13) $$\tau = \alpha_\nu + \Delta$$

we get

$$10^{-2}\sqrt{n}<\alpha_\nu<\tau<\alpha_1+n^{1/5}<\left(1+\frac{1}{4}\right)\frac{\sqrt{3}}{\pi}\sqrt{n}\log n \tag{13.14}$$

for $n>c$ from (13.12), (13.10) and (11.17). (13.14) shows that (12.3) is satisfied with the choice (13.13). Applying Lemma 11, we get an index μ with

$$\frac{\alpha_\nu}{2}+\frac{\Delta}{2}=\frac{\tau}{2}<\alpha_\mu\leqq\frac{2\tau}{3}=\frac{2\alpha_\nu}{3}+\frac{2\Delta}{3}. \tag{13.15}$$

Then,

$$\alpha_\mu<\frac{2\alpha_\nu}{3}+n^{1/5}=\alpha_\nu-\left(\frac{1}{3}\alpha_\nu-n^{1/5}\right)<\alpha_\nu-\left(\frac{1}{6\sqrt{2}}\sqrt{n}-n^{1/5}\right)<\alpha_\nu$$

for $n>c$ owing to (13.15), (13.10) and (13.12). Consequently,

$$\nu<\mu. \tag{13.16}$$

Let

$$\Delta_1=\tau-\alpha_\mu. \tag{13.17}$$

Then we get

$$k=\alpha_1+\alpha_2+\ldots+\alpha_{\nu-1}+\alpha_\mu+\Delta_1 \tag{13.18}$$

from (13.8), (13.13) and (13.17). Further,

$$\Delta_1=\tau-\alpha_\mu<2\alpha_\mu-\alpha_\mu=\alpha_\mu<\alpha_1\leqq\left(1+\frac{1}{5}\right)\frac{\sqrt{3}}{\pi}\sqrt{n}\log n \tag{13.19}$$

and

$$\Delta_1=\tau-\alpha_\mu\geqq\frac{1}{3}\tau>\frac{1}{300}\sqrt{n}>n^{1/5}$$

for $n>c$ from (13.17), (13.15), (11.17) and (13.14). Now, we can apply Lemma 9 for Δ_1. This yields that

$$\Delta_1=\sum_{j=1}^{u}\alpha_{r_j} \tag{13.20}$$

with

$$\mu<r_1<r_2<\ldots<r_u \tag{13.21}$$

owing to (13.19). Consequently,

$$k=\alpha_1+\alpha_2+\ldots+\alpha_{\nu-1}+\alpha_\mu+\alpha_{r_1}+\ldots+\alpha_{r_u}$$

is a representation of k by a subsum owing to (13.18), (13.20), (13.16) and (13.21). This settles the case (13.10) and Lemma 12 is completely proved.

Now, Lemma 8 and Lemma 12 prove Theorem II for $k_0 \leqq k \leqq \frac{1}{2}n$ and for $\frac{1}{2}n < k \leqq n - k_0$ too by means of the complementary subsums.

References

[1] G. H. HARDY and S. RAMANUJAN, Asymptotic formulae in combinatory analysis, *Proc. London Math. Soc.* (2), **17** (1918), 75–115, esp. formula (1.55).

[2] C. POMERANCE, oral communication.

[3] M. SZALAY and P. TURÁN, On some problems of the statistical theory of partitions with application to characters of the symmetric group, I. *Acta Math. Acad. Sci. Hungar.*, **29** (1977), 361–379.

[4] M. SZALAY and P. TURÁN, On some problems of the statistical theory of partitions with application to characters of the symmetric group, II, *Acta Math. Acad. Sci. Hungar.*, **29** (1977), 381–392.

[5] M. SZALAY and P. TURÁN, On some problems of the statistical theory of partitions with application to characters of the symmetric group, III, *Acta Math. Acad. Sci. Hungar.*, **32** (1978), 129–155.

[6] P. TURÁN, On some connections between combinatorics and group theory. In: *Colloquia Math. Soc. J. Bolyai* **4**. *Combinatorial Theory and Its Applications* (Balatonfüred, 1969), 1055–1082.

[7] P. TURÁN, Combinatorics, partitions, group theory. In: *Colloquio Int. s. Teorie Combinatorie* (Roma, 3–15 settembre 1973), Roma, Accademia Nazionale dei Lincei, 1976, Tomo II, 181–200.

[8] P. TURÁN, On a property of partitions, *J. of Number Theory*, **6** (1974), 405–411.

MATHEMATICAL INSTITUTE
OF THE HUNGARIAN ACADEMY OF SCIENCES
REÁLTANODA U. 13–15.
H-1053 BUDAPEST,
HUNGARY

DEPARTMENT OF ALGEBRA AND NUMBER THEORY
EÖTVÖS LORÁND UNIVERSITY
MÚZEUM KÖRÚT 6–8
H-1088 BUDAPEST,
HUNGARY

Studies in Pure Mathematics
To the Memory of Paul Turán

On sums and products of integers

by

P. ERDŐS and E. SZEMERÉDI (Budapest)

Let $1 \leqq a_1 < \ldots < a_n$ be a sequence of integers Consider the integers of the form

$$a_i + a_j, \quad a_i a_j, \quad 1 \leqq i \leqq j \leqq n. \tag{1}$$

It is tempting to conjecture that for every $\varepsilon > 0$ there is an n_0 so that for every $n > n_0$ there are more than $n^{2-\varepsilon}$ distinct integers of the form (1). We are very far from being able to prove this, but we prove the following weaker

Theorem 1. *Denote by $f(n)$ the largest integer so that for every $\{a_1, a_2, \ldots, a_n\}$ there are at least $f(n)$ distinct integers of the form* (1). *Then*

$$n^{1+c_1} < f(n) < n^2 \exp(-c_2 \log n / \log \log n). \tag{2}$$

We expect that the upper bound in (2) may be close to the "truth".

More generally we conjecture that for every k and $n > n_0(k)$ there are more than $n^{k-\varepsilon}$ distinct integers of the form

$$a_{i_1} + \ldots + a_{i_k}, \quad \prod_{j=1}^{k} a_{i_j}$$

At the moment we do not see how to attack this plausible conjecture.

Denote now by $g(n)$ the largest integer so that for every $\{a_1, \ldots, a_n\}$ there are at least $g(n)$ distinct integers of the form

$$\sum_{i=1}^{n} \varepsilon_i a_i, \quad \prod_{i=1}^{n} a_i^{\varepsilon_i} \quad (\varepsilon_i = 0 \text{ or } 1) \tag{3}$$

We conjecture that for $n > n_0(k)$, $g(n) > n^k$. Unfortunately we have not been able to prove this and perhaps we overlook a simple idea. We prove

Theorem 2.

$$g(n) < \exp(c_3 \log^2 n/\log\log n).$$

Again we believe (without too much evidence) that Theorem 2 may be close to the final truth. Perhaps our conjectures remain true if the a's are real or complex numbers.

Some more conjectures: Let $\mathcal{G}(n, k)$ be a graph of n vertices $x_1, x_2, \ldots, x_n$ and k edges. Make correspond a_i to x_i. Consider the set of $2k$ integers.

$$\{a_i + a_j, \quad a_i a_j\} \tag{4}$$

where x_i is joined to x_j. We conjecture that for every $\varepsilon > 0$ and $0 < \alpha \leqq 1$ if $k > n^{1+\alpha}$ then there are more than $n^{1+\alpha-\varepsilon}$ distinct integers of the form (4). Our proof of Theorem 1 does not seem to apply here. The conjecture very likely remains true if the a's can be real numbers. P. ERDŐS once thought that the conjecture may hold even if we only assume $k > cn$, but A. RUBIN showed that this is not true if the a's can be real numbers and it perhaps fails even if the a's are restricted to be positive integers.

Finally we state a few related problems. Let $a_i b_i = T$ $i = 1, 2, \ldots, n$. Consider the sums

$$a_{i_1} + a_{i_2}, \quad b_{i_1} + b_{i_2}, \quad a_{i_1} + b_{i_2} \quad 1 \leqq i_1 \leqq i_2 \leqq n.$$

Is it true that all but one of three sets have more than n^{1+c} distinct elements?

Consider the sets $\{k(n-k), 1 \leqq k < n\}$ and $\{l(m-l), 1 \leqq l < m\}$. Can one estimate the number of integers which are common to both sets?

Let $a_1, \ldots, a_n$ be such that there are only cn distinct sums of the form $a_i + a_j$, $1 \leqq i \leqq j \leqq n$. Then there certainly must be more than $n^{2-\varepsilon}$ distinct products of the form $a_i a_j$, $1 \leqq i \leqq j \leqq n$. Perhaps there are more than $n^2/(\log n)^\varepsilon$ products of the form $a_i a_j$, $1 \leqq i \leqq j \leqq n$. The deep results of FREIMAN can possibly be used here [1].

Finally a problem of different kind. Let $2n - 1 \leqq t \leqq \frac{n^2+n}{2}$. It is easy to see that one can find a sequence of integers $a_1 < \ldots < a_n$ so that there should be exactly t distinct integers in the sequence $a_i + a_j$, $1 \leqq i \leqq j \leqq n$. We do not know for which t is it possible to find a sequence $a_1 < \ldots < a_n$ so that there should be exactly t distinct integers of the form

$$\sum_{i=1}^{n} \varepsilon_i a_i, \quad \varepsilon_i = 0 \text{ or } 1.$$

It is probably even more difficult to find out for which $t > f(n)$ is there a sequence $a_1 \ldots < a_n$ so that there are exactly t distinct integers of the form (1).

First we prove Theorem 2 which will not be difficult. Let x be large. The a's are the integers of the form

$$\Pi p_i^{\alpha_i}, \quad p_i < (\log x)^{2/3}, \quad 0 \leqq \alpha_i \leqq (\log x)^{1/3}.$$

Put

$$[(\log x)^{1/3}] = t, \quad \pi([(\log x)^{2/3}]) = (1 + o(1)) \frac{3(\log x)^{2/3}}{2 \log\log x} = l. \tag{5}$$

The number of a's is

$$(6)\qquad n=(t+1)^l = \exp\left(\frac{1}{2}(\log x)^{2/3}\right).$$

All the a's are less than x, thus the number of the distinct sums is less than x^2.

Next we have to estimate the number of the distinct product of the form $\prod_{i=1}^{n} a_i^{\varepsilon_i}$, $\varepsilon_i=0$ or 1. These integers are all composed of the first l primes. The highest exponent of a prime p which can occur in $\prod_{i=1}^{n} a_i^{\varepsilon_i}$ is at most $tn<(t+1)^{l-1}=(t+1)n$. Thus the number of the integers of the form $\prod_{i=1}^{n} a_i^{\varepsilon_i}$ $\varepsilon_i=0$ or 1, is less than

$$(7)\qquad ((t+1)n)^l=(t+1)^{l^2+l}.$$

To complete the proof of Theorem 2 we only have to show by (5) and (6) that

$$(8)\qquad n^{c\log n/\log\log n}>(t+1)^{l^2+l}+x^2.$$

(8) immediately follows from (5) and (6), which completes the proof of Theorem 2.

Now we prove Theorem 1. First we prove the right side of (2). This will be a standard and comparatively simple estimation. We do not try to obtain the largest possible value of c_2 since we are not at all sure that the term $n^2\exp\left(-\frac{c_2\log n}{\log\log n}\right)$ is the final truth.

To prove the right side of (2) let $2j$ be the largest even integer not exceeding $\frac{\log x}{3\log\log x}$, $s=\pi((\log x)^3)$. The a_i are the integers of the form

$$(9)\qquad \prod_{i=1}^{2j} p_i^{\varepsilon_i},\quad p_i<(\log x)^3,\qquad \varepsilon_i=0 \text{ or } 1.$$

These integers are clearly all less than x. Their number clearly equals

$$(10)\qquad t_x=\binom{s}{2j}=x^{2/3+o(1)}.$$

The number of distinct integers of the form a_i+a_j is by (10) and $a_i<x$ less than $2x<t_x^{3/2+o(1)}$ and thus can be neglected. Next we have to estimate the number of distinct integers of the form a_ia_k. We split these integers into two classes. In the first class are the a_ia_k for which ($v(n)$ denotes the number of distinct prime factors of n)

$$v((a_i,a_k))>j.$$

The number of these integers is by a simple computation less than

$$t_x \log x \binom{2j}{j}\binom{s}{j} < t_x \log x\, 2^{2j}(\log x)^{(2+o(1))j} < t_x x^{1/3+o(1)}.$$

Thus the numbers of the first class can be also neglected.

Now if $a_i a_k$ is in the second class we can write

$$a_i a_k = Q^2 L$$

where $Q=(a_i, a_k)$ is squarefree and L is the product of two relatively prime squarefree integers having $2j - v(Q)$ prime factors, where $v(Q) < j = \dfrac{\log x}{6 \log\log x}$. But then clearly Q^2L can be written in at least $\binom{2j}{j}$ ways as the product of two numbers a_i, a_k, $v(a_i, a_k) = Q$. Thus the number of integers in the second class is less than

$$t_x^2\, 2^{-\frac{\log x}{3 \log\log x}}.$$

which proves the right side of (2).

To complete the proof of Theorem 1 we now have to prove the left side of (2), and this in fact is the main novelty and difficulty of our paper. We make no attempt to get a large value for c_1 as stated in the introduction $c_1 > 1-\varepsilon$ for every $\varepsilon > 0$ and our method cannot even give $c_1 = \dfrac{1}{2}$.

First a few remarks. If $a_n < n^k$ our Theorem follows trivially with $c_1 > 1-\varepsilon$, thus the only difficulty is if some of the a's are very large. First we prove that we can assume without loss of generality that all the a_i are in some interval $u \leqq a_j \leqq 2u$.

Denote by S_i the set of a_j's satisfying $2^i < a_j \leqq 2^{i+1}$. First observe that we can assume without loss of generality that

$$(11) \qquad |S_i| = 0 \quad \text{or} \quad |S_i| \geqq n^{1/4}.$$

Assume that (11) does not hold. Let $S_{i_1}, \ldots, S_{i_k}$ satisfy

$$(12) \qquad 0 < |S_{i_j}| < n^{1/4}, \quad 1 \leqq j \leqq k.$$

If $\bigcup_{j=1}^{k} |S_{i_j}| < \dfrac{n}{2}$ we simply omit all the a's satisfying (12) and we only work with the remaining a's and since their number is greater than $\dfrac{n}{2}$ this clearly can be done. If $\bigcup_{j=1}^{k} |S_{i_j}| \geqq \dfrac{n}{2}$ then by (12) clearly $k \geqq n^{3/4}/2$. Let a_{i_j} be an arbitrary element of

S_{i_j}, $j=1, 2, \ldots k$, $k \geqq n^{3/4}/2$. Clearly $a_{i_{2j+2}} > 2a_{i_{2j}}$ and thus the sums

$$a_{i_{2j_1}} + a_{i_{2j_2}}, \quad 2 \leqq j_1 < j_2 \leqq k$$

are all distinct, so there are at least $\frac{n^{\frac{3}{2}}}{\delta}$ distinct sums of the form $a_u + a_v$, $1 \leqq u < v \leqq n$, which proves Theorem 1 if (11) does not hold.

Thus we can now assume that (11) holds.

Now we state the crucial

Lemma. *Let $m < b_1 < \ldots < b_t \leqq 2m$. Then the number of distinct integers of the form*

$$b_i + b_j, \quad b_i b_j, \quad 1 \leqq i < j \leqq t$$

is greater than $\varepsilon t^{1+\alpha}$ for some $\alpha > 0$ and $\varepsilon > 0$.

Suppose that our Lemma has already been proved. Then by (11) and our Lemma the number of distinct integers of the form $a_i + a_j$, $a_i a_j$ is at least

$$\sum{}' \varepsilon |S_i|^{1+\alpha} > c n^{1+\alpha/4} \tag{13}$$

(where the dash indicates that the summation is extended over the i satisfying $|S_i| \geqq n^{1/4}$) (13) of course gives the left side of (2) and hence proves Theorem 1.

Thus we only have to prove our Lemma. Put $[t^{1/8}] = s$. Denote by B_i the set of b's $\{b_{(i-1)s+1}, \ldots, b_{is}\}$. In other words we divided the index set of the b's into $[t^{7/8}]$ sets of size $[t^{1/8}]$. Denote by $B = B_r$ the B_j of smallest diameter (i.e. $b_{(j-1)s+1} - b_{js}$ is minimal). Observe now that if $u - v \geqq 10$ and $(u \neq r,\ v \neq r)$ $b_1 \in B$, $b_2 \in B$, $b_3 \in B_u$, $b_4 \in B_v$ then $b_1 + b_3 \neq b_2 + b_4$ and $b_1 b_3 \neq b_2 b_4$. This is obvious for the sum and nearly obvious for the product. Put $b_2 = b_1 + x$, $b_4 = b_3 - y$. Then if $b_1 b_3 = b_2 b_4$ we would have $b_1 b_3 = (b_1 + x)(b_3 - y)$ or $xy = b_3 x - b_1 y$ and this easily leads to a contradiction since $y > 10x$ by the minimality property of $B = B_r$ and $u - v \geqq 10$. Further $1/2 < b_3/b_1 < 2$. Thus $b_3 x - b_1 y < 0 < xy$ which is impossible.

Consider now the $s^7/10$ B_j's, $j \equiv 1 \pmod{10}$. We divide the indices j into two classes. In the first class are the indices j for which the number of distinct integers of the form

$$b_i + b_l, \quad b_i b_l, \quad b_i \in B, \quad b_l \in B_j$$

is greater than $s^{1+8\alpha}$. If at least half of the indices belong to the first class then our Lemma immediately follows since the number of distinct integers of the form $b_i + b_j$, $b_i b_j$ is greater than $\frac{1}{10} \cdot \frac{1}{2} \cdot s^7 s^{1+8\alpha} = \frac{1}{20} t^{1+\alpha}$ which proves the Lemma in this case.

Let now j be an index of the second class. We remind the reader that in this case the number of distinct integers of the form $b_u + b_v$, $b_u b_v$, $b_u \in B$, $b_v \in B_j$ is less than $s^{1+8\alpha}$.

We want to find six integers $b_1, b_2, b_3, b_4, b_5, b_6$, $b_i \in B_j$ $(i=1, 2)$, $b_i \in B$ $(3 \leqq i \leqq 6)$, satisfying

$$b_1+b_3=b_2+b_4 \quad \text{and} \quad b_1 b_5=b_2 b_6 . \tag{14}$$

Consider the s^2 products $b_u b_v$, $b_u \in B$, $b_v \in B_j$. Since B_j is in the second class there are fewer than $s^{1+8\alpha}$ distinct integers of this form. Therefore there is a T so that $T=b_u b_v$ has at least $s^{1-8\alpha}$ solutions. Put

$$T=b_{u_r} b_{v_r}, \quad b_{u_r} \in B \qquad b_{v_r} \in B_j, \quad 1 \leqq r \leqq s^{1-8\alpha} \quad .$$

Consider now the $s^{2-16\alpha}$ sums of the form $b_{u_w}+b_{v_j}$. For sufficiently small α these sums clearly cannot all be different.

Thus there are indices u_w, v_l, u_p, v_q so that $b_{u_w}+b_{v_l}=b_{u_p}+b_{v_q}$. But $b_{u_l} b_{v_l}=b_{u_q} b_{v_q}$. Thus b_{u_w}, b_{u_p}, b_{u_l}, $b_{u_q} \in B$, b_{v_l}, $b_{v_q} \in B_j$ are our required six integers. Observe that if b_3, b_4, b_5, b_6 are fixed there is at most one b_1, b_2 pair which solves (14).

We have at least $\frac{1}{2} \cdot \frac{1}{10} \cdot s^7$ B_j's in the second class and the number of different b_3, b_4, b_5, b_6 quadrouples is at most s^4. This contradicts our observation, and this contradiction completes the proof of Theorem 1.

Reference

[1] FREIMAN, G. A., *Foundations of a structural theory of set addition.* Translations of Math. Monographs, Amer. Math. Soc., Vol. 37. Providence R.I. 1973.

MATHEMATICAL INSTITUTE OF THE
HUNGARIAN ACADEMY OF SCIENCES
H-1053 BUDAPEST, REÁLTANODA U. 13—15.
HUNGARY

Studies in Pure Mathematics
To the Memory of Paul Turán

On the growth of meromorphic functions on rays

by

W. H. J. FUCHS* (Cornell Univ.)

In this paper I investigate the behaviour of

$$(1) \qquad L = \liminf_{r\to\infty} |\log|f(re^{i\delta})| + \log|f(re^{-i\delta})||/N(r)$$

where f is a meromorphic function of non-integral order λ,

$$N(r) = N(r, f) + N(r, 1/f)$$

and

$$0 \leqq \delta < \pi .$$

(Since $N(r)$ can be $\equiv 0$ for functions of integer order, the restriction to non-integral λ is necessary.) The method of attack is based on an idea of A. A. Goldberg [3] who used it in the study of lim inf $\log|f(r)|/T(r)$. I shall prove

Theorem 1. *Let* $f(z)$ *be a meromorphic function of nonintegral order* λ. *Then* L, *defined by* (1), *satisfies*

$$L \leqq C(\lambda, \delta) \quad (0 \leqq \delta < \pi)$$

where

$$(2) \qquad C(\lambda, \delta) = \frac{2\lambda\pi \max\{|\cos\lambda\delta|, |\cos\lambda(\pi-\delta)|\}}{|\sin\pi\lambda|}.$$

For entire functions and for δ restricted to a much smaller range this result is proved in [2]. However, under these more restrictive assumptions the proof in [2] gives the

* Research carried out with support by NSF grant MCS 76-0654.

stronger result that there is a sequence $r_n \to \infty$ $(n \to \infty)$ such that

$$\log|f(r_n e^{i\vartheta + i\delta}) f(r_n e^{i\vartheta - i\delta})| > (C(\lambda, \delta - \varepsilon_n) N(r) \quad (0 \leqq \vartheta < 2\pi, \varepsilon_n \to 0).$$

By considering canonical products of order λ with negative zeros and $N(r) = N(r, 1/f) \sim r^\lambda/\lambda$ it can be seen that (2) is best possible.

We shall use the standard notations of Nevanlinna theory. The letter K denotes a positive number depending, at most, on λ, the value of K many be different at different occurrences. Fixed constants are denoted by $K_1, K_2 \dots$.

In §1 a few general results about meromorphic functions of non-integral order are collected. §2 contains the proof of Theorem 1 except for the construction of an auxiliary function which is deferred to §3.

We shall assume, without loss of generality that $f(0) \neq 0, \infty$.

§1. It is well known [5, p. 103] that

$$N(r) = N(r, f) + N(r, 1/f)$$

has Pólya peaks of order λ. This means that one can find $\tau_1, \tau_2, \dots, \tau_n \to \infty$ and positive ε_n, $\varepsilon_n \to 0$, such that

(1.1) $$N(r) \leqq N(\tau_n)(r/\tau_n)^{\lambda - \varepsilon_n} \quad (0 \leqq r \leqq \tau_n)$$

$$N(r) \leqq N(\tau_n)(r/\tau_n)^{\lambda + \varepsilon_n} \quad (\tau_n \leqq r).$$

Further, since λ is not an integer,

(1.2) $$T(\tau_n) < K_1 N(\tau_n) \quad (\tau_n > r_0).$$

By (1.1) for a fixed value of r and the First Fundamental Theorem of Nevanlinna Theory.

(1.3) $$\lim_{n \to \infty} \frac{\log N(\tau_n)}{\log \tau_n} = \lambda.$$

Let $\lambda(r)$ be a proximate order, i.e. a piece-wise differentiable, positive function satisfying

(1.4) $$\lambda(r) \to \lambda \quad (r \to \infty)$$

(1.5) $$\lambda'(r) r \log r \to 0 \quad (r \to \infty).$$

Note that (1.5) implies

(1.6) $$r^{\lambda(r) - \lambda(t)} = 1 + o(1) \quad \left(r \to \infty; \frac{1}{4} r \leqq t \leqq 4r\right)$$

Lemma 1. *If $\tau=\tau_m$ and $\sigma=\tau_n>\tau$ are Pólya peaks of $N(r)$, and if*

$$\frac{1}{4}\tau<t<\frac{1}{2}\tau \quad \frac{1}{4}\sigma<s<\frac{1}{2}\sigma,$$

then, for $\tau>\tau_0$, $T(r)=T(r,f)$,

$$\int_t^s T(r)r^{-\lambda(r)-1}\,dr<K\int_t^s N(r)r^{-\lambda(r)-1}\,dr+K(N(\tau)\tau^{-\lambda(\tau)}+N(\sigma)\sigma^{-\lambda(\sigma)}). \tag{1.7}$$

Proof. Let $p=[\lambda]<\lambda<p+1$. For meromorphic functions of order λ [5, p. 102]

$$T(r)<Kr^p\int_0^r N(u)u^{-p-1}du+Kr^{p+1}\int_r^\infty N(u)u^{-p-2}\,du \quad (r>r_0).$$

Therefore

$$\int_t^s T(r)r^{-\lambda(r)-1}\,dr<\int_t^\sigma T(r)r^{-\lambda(r)-1}\,dr<$$

$$<K\int_t^\sigma r^{p-\lambda(r)-1}\,dr\int_0^t N(u)u^{-p-1}\,du+K\int_t^\sigma r^{p-\lambda(r)-1}\,dr\int_t^r N(u)u^{-p-1}\,du+$$

$$+K\int_t^\sigma r^{p-\lambda(r)}\,dr\int_\sigma^\infty N(u)u^{-p-2}\,du+K\int_t^\sigma r^{p-\lambda(r)}\,dr\int_r^\sigma N(u)u^{-p-2}\,du=I_1+I_2+I_3+I_4.$$

From the properties of proximate orders it follows easily that [4, p. 73]

$$\begin{aligned}&\int_t^\infty r^{p-\lambda(r)-1}\,dr<Kt^{p-\lambda(t)}\\ &\int_0^t r^{p-\lambda(r)}\,dr<Kt^{p+1-\lambda(t)}.\end{aligned} \tag{1.8}$$

By (1.8), (1.6), (1.1) and the inequality

$$t<\tau<4t$$

$$I_1<K\int_t^\infty r^{p-\lambda(r)-1}\,dr\int_0^\tau N(u)u^{-p-1}\,du<$$

$$<Kt^{p-\lambda(t)}N(\tau)\tau^{\varepsilon-\lambda}\int_0^\tau u^{\lambda-\varepsilon-p-1}\,du<Kt^{p-\lambda(\tau)}N(\tau)\tau^{-p}<KN(\tau)\tau^{-\lambda(\tau)}.$$

Similarly

$$I_3<KN(\sigma)\sigma^{-\lambda(\sigma)}.$$

By an interchange of the order of integration and (1.8)

$$I_2 < K \int_t^\sigma N(u)u^{-p-1}\,du \int_u^\sigma r^{p-\lambda(r)-1}\,dr < K \int_t^\sigma N(u)u^{-\lambda(u)-1}\,du$$

and by the same method

$$I_4 < K \int_t^\sigma N(u)u^{-\lambda(u)-1}\,du\,.$$

We have proved

$$\int_t^s T(r)r^{-\lambda(r)-1}\,dr < K \int_t^\sigma N(r)r^{-\lambda(r)-1}\,dr + KN(\tau)\tau^{-\lambda(\tau)}\,.$$

But, by (1.6)

$$+KN(\sigma)\sigma^{-\lambda(\sigma)}\,.$$

$$\int_s^\sigma N(r)r^{-\lambda(r)-1}\,dr < KN(\sigma) \int_{1/4\sigma}^\sigma r^{-\lambda(\sigma)-1}\,dr < KN(\sigma)\sigma^{-\lambda(\sigma)}\,.$$

This completes the proof of the Lemma.

§2. In §3 we shall construct a function $\lambda(r)$ which in addition to the properties of a proximate order satisfies the conditions

(a) $\lambda'(r)$ is continuous and $\lambda(r)$ has a piecewise continuous second derivative such that

$$\lambda''(r)r^2 \log r \to 0 \quad (r \to \infty) \tag{2.1}$$

(b) For a sub-sequence of Pólya peaks (which we shall denote by $t_1 < t_2 < t_3 \ldots$)

$$N(t_n) = t_n^{\lambda(t_n)}\,. \tag{2.2}$$

Note that (2.2) implies

$$\int^\infty N(r)r^{-\lambda(r)-1}\,dr = \infty\,. \tag{2.3}$$

For, at a Pólya-peak t_n, by (2.2) and (1.6)

$$\int_{t_n}^{2t_n} N(r)r^{-\lambda(r)-1}\,dr \geqq N(t_n)t_n^{-\lambda(t_n)} \int_{t_n}^{2t_n} t_n^{\lambda(t_n)} r^{-\lambda(r)-1}\,dr \geqq$$

$$\geqq \int_{t_n}^{2t_n} \left(\frac{1}{2}r\right)^{\lambda(t_n)} r^{-\lambda(r)-1}\,dr \geqq K \int_{t_n}^{2t_n} r^{-1}\,dr = K_0\,.$$

Proof of Theorem 1. We shall apply Green's formula

$$(2.4)\qquad (1/2\pi)\int_B (u\Delta v - v\Delta u)\,dS = (1/2\pi)\int_{\partial B}\left(u\frac{\partial v}{\partial n} - v\frac{\partial u}{\partial n}\right)ds$$

to

$$u(z)=u(re^{i\vartheta})=\log|f(z)|,\ v(re^{i\vartheta})=r^{-\lambda(r)}\cos\lambda(\vartheta-\pi)$$

in the region B obtained from

$$t<r<s,\quad 0<\vartheta<2\pi$$

by removing small disks centered at the poles b_μ and the zeros a_ν of $f(z)$.

By straightforward calculation

$$\Delta v = \frac{1}{r}\frac{\partial}{\partial r}\left(r\frac{\partial v}{\partial r}\right) + \frac{1}{r^2}\frac{\partial^2 v}{\partial\vartheta^2} = o(r^{-\lambda(r)-2}),$$

uniformly in ϑ. Therefore

$$\left|\int_B (u\Delta v - v\Delta u)\,dS\right| = \left|\int u\Delta v\,ds\right| < \int_t^s r\,dr\int_0^{2\pi} |\log|f(re^{i\vartheta})||\,|\Delta v|\,d\vartheta =$$

$$= o\left(\int_t^s T(r)r^{-\lambda(r)-1}\,dr\right)\quad (t\to\infty),$$

because

$$(2.5)\qquad \int_0^{2\pi} |\log|f(re^{i\vartheta})||\,d\vartheta < 2\pi(m(r,f)+m(r,1/f)) < KT(r).$$

We must now consider the right-hand side of (2.4). For simplicity assume that there are no zeros or poles on $r=s$ and on $r=t$.

As the radii of the excluded disks around the poles $b_\mu = |b_\mu|e^{i\beta_\mu}$ and the zeros $a_\nu = |a_\nu|e^{i\alpha_\nu}$ tend to 0, the contribution of the boundaries of the disks to the right-hand side of (2.4) becomes

$$\sum |a_\nu|^{-\lambda(|a_\nu|)}\cos\lambda(\alpha_\nu-\pi) - \sum |b_\mu|^{-\lambda(|b_\mu|)}\cos\lambda(\beta_\mu-\pi).$$

Here the summation is over all zeros and poles in $t<r<s$ and the arguments must be chosen in $0\leqq\alpha_\nu,\ \beta_\mu<2\pi$.

On the straight line boundary of B we have

$$\left.\frac{\partial u}{\partial n}\right|_{\arg\vartheta=0} = -\left.\frac{\partial u}{\partial n}\right|_{\arg\vartheta=2\pi}$$

$$\left.\frac{\partial v}{\partial n}\right|_{\arg\vartheta=0} = \left.\frac{\partial v}{\partial n}\right|_{\arg\vartheta=2\pi} = -\frac{1}{r}\frac{\partial v}{\partial\vartheta} = -\lambda r^{-\lambda(r)}\sin\lambda\pi.$$

Therefore the contribution of this boundary to the right-hand side of (2.4) is

$$-\pi^{-1}\lambda \sin \pi\lambda \int_t^s r^{-\lambda(r)} \log|f(r)|dr .$$

On the circle $r=t$

$$|v| \leqq t^{-\lambda(t)}, \quad \left|\frac{\partial v}{\partial n}\right| < Kt^{-\lambda(t)-1} ,$$

$$\left|\frac{\partial u}{\partial n}\right| = \left| -\frac{\partial}{\partial r} \log|f(re^{i\vartheta})|\right|_{r=t} \leqq \left| -\frac{\partial}{\partial r} \log f(re^{i\vartheta})\right|_{r=t} = \left|\frac{f'}{f}(te^{i\vartheta})\right| .$$

The contribution of $r=t$ to (2.4) is in absolute value less than

$$K \int_0^{2\pi} |\log|f(te^{i\vartheta})||t^{-\lambda(t)-1} t d\vartheta + K \int_0^{2\pi} \left|\frac{f'}{f}(te^{i\vartheta})\right| t^{-\lambda(t)} dt . \tag{2.6}$$

By (2.5) the first integral in (2.6) is less than $KT(t)t^{-\lambda(t)}$. For the second integral in (2.6) we have the estimate

$$\int_0^{2\pi} \left|\frac{f'}{f}(te^{i\vartheta})\right| dt < KT(2t) ,$$

provided t is suitably chosen; every interval $(R, 2R)$ contains a suitable t [1]. Therefore

$$\left| \int_{r=t} \left(u \frac{\partial v}{\partial n} - v \frac{\partial u}{\partial n} \right) ds \right| < KT(2t) t^{-\lambda(t)} , \tag{2.7}$$

provided t is chosen suitably. Similarly, for suitable s

$$\left| \int_{r=s} \left(u \frac{\partial v}{\partial n} - v \frac{\partial u}{\partial n} \right) ds \right| < KT(2s) s^{-\lambda(s)} . \tag{2.8}$$

Collecting all the information (2.4) becomes

$$\begin{aligned} &(\lambda \sin \lambda\pi/\pi) \int_t^s r^{-\lambda(r)-1} \log|f(r)|dr = \\ &= \sum |a_\nu|^{-\lambda(|a_\nu|)} \cos \lambda(\alpha_\nu - \pi) - \sum |b_\mu|^{-\lambda(|b_\mu|)} \cos \lambda(\beta_\mu - \pi) + E . \end{aligned} \tag{2.9}$$

Here the summations are over all zeros $|a_\nu|e^{i\alpha_\nu}$ and all poles $|b_\mu|e^{i\beta_\mu}$ in $t<r<s$ and

$$0 < \alpha_\nu, \beta_\mu < 2\pi .$$

The letter E from now on denotes a function of t and s satisfying

$$(2.10)\qquad |E|<K(T(2t)t^{-\lambda(t)}+T(2s)s^{-\lambda(s)})+o\left(\int_t^s T(r)r^{-\lambda(r)-1}dr\right)\quad (t<s,\ t\to\infty).$$

If $f(z)$ is changed into $f(ze^{i\delta})$ $(0<\delta<\pi)$, the sums on the right-hand side of (2.9) become

$$(2.11)\qquad \begin{aligned}&\sum_{\delta\leqq\alpha_\nu<2\pi}|a_\nu|^{-\lambda(|a_\nu|)}\cos\lambda(\alpha_\nu-\delta-\pi)+\sum_{0\leqq\alpha_\nu<\delta}|a_\nu|^{-\lambda(|a_\nu|)}\cos\lambda(\alpha_\nu-\delta+\pi)-\\ &-\sum_{\delta\leqq\beta_\mu<2\pi}|b_\mu|^{-\lambda(|b_\mu|)}\cos\lambda(\beta_\mu-\delta-\pi)-\sum_{0\leqq\beta_\mu<\delta}|b_\mu|^{-\lambda(|b_\mu|)}\cos\lambda(\beta_\mu-\delta+\pi),\end{aligned}$$

because of the convention that the arguments of zeros and poles lie in $[0, 2\pi)$.

If we change this convention by demanding that $-\delta<\alpha_\nu,\ \beta_\mu<2\pi-\delta$, then (2.11) becomes

$$(2.12)\qquad \begin{aligned}&\sum_{|\alpha_\nu|<\delta}|a_\nu|^{-\lambda(|a_\nu|)}\cos\lambda(\alpha_\nu-\delta+\pi)+\sum_{\delta\leqq\alpha_\nu<2\pi-\delta}|a_\nu|^{-\lambda(|a_\nu|)}\cos\lambda(\alpha_\nu-\delta-\pi)-\\ &-\sum_{|\beta_\mu|<\delta}|b_\mu|^{-\lambda(|b_\mu|)}\cos\lambda(\beta_\mu-\delta+\pi)-\sum_{\delta\leqq\beta_\mu<2\pi-\delta}|b_\mu|^{-\lambda(|b_\mu|)}\cos\lambda(\beta_\mu-\delta-\pi).\end{aligned}$$

Similarly, if $f(z)$ is replaced by $f(ze^{-i\delta})$ the sums on the right-hand side of (2.9) have to be replaced by

$$(2.13)\qquad \begin{aligned}&\sum_{|\alpha_\nu|<\delta}|a_\nu|^{-\lambda(|a_\nu|)}\cos\lambda(\alpha_\nu+\delta-\pi)+\sum_{\delta\leqq\alpha_\nu<2\pi-\delta}|a_\nu|^{-\lambda(|a_\nu|)}\cos\lambda(\alpha_\nu+\delta-\pi)-\\ &-\sum_{|b_\mu|<\delta}|b_\mu|^{-\lambda(|b_\mu|)}\cos\lambda(\beta_\mu+\delta-\pi)-\sum_{\delta\leqq\beta_\mu<2\pi-\delta}|b_\mu|^{-\lambda(|b_\mu|)}\cos\lambda(\beta_\mu+\delta-\pi).\end{aligned}$$

It now follows from (2.9), (2.12) and (2.13) that

$$(\lambda\sin\lambda\pi/\pi)\int^s r^{-\lambda(r)-1}\log|f(re^{i\delta})f(re^{i\delta})|dr=$$

$$\begin{aligned}&=2\sum_{|\alpha_\nu|<\delta}|a_\nu|^{-\lambda(|a_\nu|)}\cos\lambda\alpha_\nu\cos\lambda(\pi-\delta)+2\sum_{\delta\leqq\alpha_\nu\leqq2\pi-\delta}|a_\nu|^{-\lambda(|a_\nu|)}\cos\lambda(\alpha_\nu-\pi)\cos\lambda\delta-\\ &-2\sum_{|\beta_\mu|<\delta}|b_\mu|^{-\lambda(|b_\mu|)}\cos\lambda\beta_\mu\cos\lambda(\pi-\delta)-2\sum_{\delta\leqq\beta_\mu\leqq2\pi-\delta}|b_\mu|^{-\lambda(|b_\mu|)}\cos\lambda(\beta_\mu-\pi)\cos\lambda\delta+E.\end{aligned}$$

Letting the α_ν and β_μ vary while keeping $|a_\nu|$, $|b_\mu|$ fixed we see that

$$|\lambda\sin\lambda\pi/2\pi|\int_t^s r^{-\lambda(r)-1}\log|f(re^{i\delta})f(re^{-i\delta})|dr\leqq$$

(2.14)

$$\leqq \max\{|\cos\lambda\delta|, |\cos\lambda(\pi-\delta)|\}\sum\{|a_\nu|^{-\lambda(|a_\nu|)}+|b_\mu|^{-\lambda(|b_\mu|)}\}+E\,.$$

With

$$n(r)=n(r,f)+n(r,1/f)\,,$$

$$\Sigma=\sum(|a_\nu|^{-\lambda(|a_\nu|)}+|b_\mu|^{-\lambda(|b_\mu|)})=\int_t^s r^{-\lambda(r)}dn(r)=$$

$$=n(s)s^{-\lambda(s)}-n(t)t^{-\lambda(t)}-\int_t^s n(r)\frac{d}{dr}(r^{-\lambda(r)})dr\,,$$

$$\Sigma=n(s)s^{-\lambda(s)}-n(t)t^{-\lambda(t)}+\lambda\int_t^s r^{-\lambda(r)-1}n(r)dr+F\,.$$

By (1.4) and (1.5)

$$F=\int_t^s r^{-\lambda(r)-1}n(r)\{\lambda(r)-\lambda+\lambda'(r)r\log r\}dr=o(\int_t^s r^{-\lambda(r)-1}n(r)dr)\quad(t\to\infty)\,.$$

The inequality $n(u)\log 2<N(2u)$ and one further integration by part show that

$$\Sigma=\lambda^2\int_t^s r^{-\lambda(r)-1}N(r)dr+o(\int_t^s r^{-\lambda(r)-1}N(r)dr)+KN(2s)s^{-\lambda(s)}+$$

(2.15)

$$+KN(2t)t^{-\lambda(t)}=\lambda^2\int_t^s r^{-\lambda(r)-1}N(r)dr+E\,.$$

Hence (2.14) can be rewritten

$$|\sin\lambda\pi/2\lambda\pi|\int_t^s r^{-\lambda(r)-1}\log|f(re^{i\delta})f(re^{-i\delta})|dr\leqq$$

(2.16)

$$\leqq\max\{|\cos\lambda\delta|, |\cos\lambda(\pi-\delta)|\}\int_t^s r^{-\lambda(r)-1}N(r)dr+E\,.$$

Next we show that given $R>0$ and $\varepsilon>0$ there are t and s, $R<t<s$ such that in (2.16)

(2.17)

$$|E|<K\varepsilon\int_t^s r^{-\lambda(r-1)}N(r)dr\,.$$

From the sequence of Pólya peaks satisfying (2.2) choose $\tau=t_k>4R$. Select t, $\frac{1}{4}\tau<t<\frac{1}{2}\tau$, such that (2.7) holds. Then, by (1.2), (1.6) and (2.2)

(2.18) $$T(2t)t^{-\lambda(t)} < T(\tau)\left(\frac{1}{4}\tau\right)^{-\lambda(t)} < KN(\tau)\tau^{-\lambda(\tau)}\,\tau^{\lambda(\tau)-\lambda(t)} < K\,.$$

It follows from (2.3) that, given $M>0$, it is possible to find a Pólya peak $t_l=\sigma$ satisfying (2.2) such that

(2.19) $$\int_t^{\sigma/4} N(r)r^{-\lambda(r)-1}dr > M\,.$$

Choose s, $\frac{1}{4}\sigma < s < \frac{1}{2}\sigma$ such that (2.8) holds. By the reasoning of (2.18)

(2.20) $$T(2s)s^{-\lambda(s)} < K\,.$$

By (2.10), (2.18), (2.20), Lemma 1 and (2.2) the E-term in (2.16) satisfies for $t > t_0(\varepsilon)$

$$|E| < K_1 + K_2\varepsilon \int_t^s N(r)r^{-\lambda(r)-1}dr\,.$$

If M in (2.19) is chosen so that

$$K_1 < MK_2\varepsilon\,,$$

then (2.17) holds with $K=2K_2$. By (2.16) and (2.17)

$$\int_t^s r^{-\lambda(r)-1}\{\log|f(re^{i\delta})f(re^{-i\delta})| - [C(\lambda,\delta)+2K_2\varepsilon]N(r)\}dr \leqq 0$$

for some arbitrarily large t and s. Hence

$$\liminf \log|f(re^{i\delta})f(re^{-i\delta})|/N(r) \leqq C(\lambda,\delta) + 2K_2\varepsilon\,.$$

Similarly, by considering $1/f(z)$

$$\liminf(-\log|f(re^{i\delta})f(re^{-i\delta})|/N(r)) \leqq C(\lambda,\delta) + 2K_2\varepsilon\,.$$

Theorem 1 follows on letting $\varepsilon\to 0$.

§3. It remains to construct the proximate order $\lambda(r)$ satisfying (1.4), (1.5), (2.1) and (2.2).

We begin by defining, for given $t>e$, an auxiliary function

$$\varphi_t(r) = \varphi(r) \quad (r \geqq t)\,.$$

Let

$$\varphi(r) = -\log\log r + \log\log t + \frac{r-t}{t\log t} \quad (t \leqq r \leqq 2t)\,.$$

Then

$$\varphi(t) = \varphi'(t) = 0\,,$$

$$0 < \varphi'(r) < \frac{1}{t \log t} < \frac{4}{r \log r} \quad (t \leqq r \leqq 2t) \tag{3.1}$$

and

$$\frac{1}{2t \log t} < \varphi'(2t) < \frac{1}{t \log t}\,. \tag{3.2}$$

Beyond $r = 2t$ let

$$\varphi(r) = 2t \log 2t \varphi'(2t)\,(\log \log r - \log \log t) + \varphi(2t) \quad (2t \leqq r \leqq u)\,. \tag{3.3}$$

The end point u of this interval is determined by the condition

$$\varphi(u) = 1\,. \tag{3.4}$$

By (3.1), (3.2) and (3.3) $\varphi(r) \in C^1[t, u]$ and

$$0 < \varphi'(r) < \frac{4}{r \log r} \quad (t \leqq r \leqq u)\,. \tag{3.5}$$

For $u \leqq r \leqq v$ let

$$\varphi(r) = 2u \log u \varphi'(u)\,\{\log \log r - \log \log t\} - (r - t)\varphi'(u) \quad (u \leqq r \leqq v)\,.$$

The point v is determined by

$$\varphi'(v) = \frac{2u \log u \varphi'(u)}{v \log v} - \varphi'(u) = 0\,.$$

Obviously $v < 2u$ and

$$0 < \varphi'(r) < \varphi'(u) < \frac{4}{u \log u} < \frac{16}{r \log r} \quad (u \leqq r < v)\,. \tag{3.6}$$

For $r > v$ let

$$\varphi(r) = \varphi(v) \quad (r \geqq v)\,. \tag{3.7}$$

Note that $v = v(t)$ depends on t.

By (3.5), (3.6) and (3.7)

$$0 \leqq \varphi'(r) < \frac{16}{r \log r} \quad (r \geqq t)\,.$$

Also, by the formulae for $\varphi(r)$,

$$\varphi''(r) = O\left(\left|\frac{d^2}{dr^2} \log \log r\right|\right) = O\left(\frac{1}{r^2 \log r}\right)$$

where the constant implied by the O-notation is independent of t.

We can now define simultaneously $\lambda(r)$ and the sequence $\{t_k\}$ of Pólya-peaks for which (2.2) holds.

Let $\tau_1, \tau_2, \ldots$ be a sequence of Pólya peaks of $N(r)$. Choose $t_1 > e$ among the τ's. Let t_2 be the least τ_k such that $t_2 \geqq v(t_1)$. Choose

$$\lambda(r) = \frac{\log N(t_1)}{\log t_1} + \alpha_1 \varphi_{t_1}(r) \quad (t_1 \leqq r \leqq t_2)$$

where α_1 is adjusted so that

$$\lambda(t_2) = \frac{\log N(t_2)}{\log t_2}.$$

Now repeat the same process with t_2 in place of t_1: If $\lambda(r)$ has been defined up to $r = t_j$, let t_{j+1} be the least Pólya peak τ satisfying $t_{j+1} \geqq v(t_j)$. Put

$$\lambda(r) = \frac{\log N(t_j)}{\log t_j} + \alpha_j \varphi_{t_j}(r) \quad (t_j \leqq r \leqq t_{j+1})$$

where α_j is chosen so that

$$\lambda(t_{j+1}) = \frac{\log N(t_{j+1})}{\log t_{j+1}}.$$

Since, by (3.4) and (3.6),

$$\varphi_{t_j}(t_{j+1}) = \varphi(v(t_j)) > \varphi(u) = 1,$$

$$|\alpha_j| < \left| \frac{\log N(t_j)}{\log t_j} - \frac{\log N(t_{j+1})}{\log t_{j+1}} \right|.$$

Therefore, by (1.3), $\alpha_j \to 0$ as $j \to \infty$. It is now easy to check that $\lambda(r)$ satisfies the conditions (1.4), (1.5), (2.1) and (2.2).

Bibliography

[1] W. H. J. Fuchs, A theorem on the Nevanlinna deficiencies of meromorphic functions of finite order, *Ann. of Math.*, **68** (1958), 203–209.

[2] W. H. J. Fuchs, An inequality involving the absolute value of an entire function and the counting function of its zeros, *Comm. Mat. Helvetici*, **53** (1978), 135–141.

[3] A. A. Goldberg, On the growth of an entire function on a line, *Dokl. Ak. Nauk. USSR*, **152** (1963), 1049–1050.

[4] A. A. Goldberg and I. V. Ostrovskii, *Distribution of Values of Meromorphic Functions*, (In Russian) Nauka, Moscow 1970.

[5] W. K. Hayman, *Meromorphic Functions*, Oxford University Press, 1964.

DEPARTMENT OF MATHEMATICS
CORNELL UNIVERSITY,
ITHACA, N. Y. 14853
U.S.A.

Studies in Pure Mathematics
To the Memory of Paul Turán

Entire functions and their derivative on an asymptotic arc

by

D. GAIER (Giessen) and B. KJELLBERG (Stockholm)

1. Introduction and result

In this note we take up a problem that we have studied already in two previous papers [2], [4]. Let f be an entire function of order ρ, finite type, and assume that there exists an arc Γ extending from 0 to ∞ on which f is bounded. What can we say about the behavior of f' on Γ?

If $\rho = \frac{1}{2}$, f' is also bounded on Γ (see [2], p. 136) while this becomes false for $\rho > 1/2$ and even for functions of order 1/2, maximum type (see [4]). However, we can show that f' will be at most of polynomial growth on Γ.

Theorem. *Let f be an entire function with*

$$|f(z)| = O(1)e^{A|z|^\rho} \quad (z \in \mathbf{C}, \rho > 0),$$

and assume that $|f(z)| = O(1)$ for z on an arc *Γ extending from* 0 *to* ∞. *Then we have*

$$|f'(z)| = O(1)|z|^{2\rho-1} \quad (z \in \Gamma). \tag{1}$$

The exponent $2\rho - 1$ cannot be replaced by a smaller number.

Remarks. 1. Notice that for $0 < \rho < 1/2$ the theorem becomes empty since in this case there is no arc Γ on which f is bounded.

2. If we replace $|f(z)| = O(1)$ by other growth conditions on Γ, we may obtain results similar to (1). For example $|f(z)| = O(|z|^\gamma)$ $(\gamma > 0)$ implies $|f'(z)| = O(|z|^{2\rho-1+\gamma})$ for $z \to \infty$ on Γ, and $|f(z)| = O(e^{B|z|^\alpha})$ $(0 < \alpha < \rho)$ implies $|f'(z)| = O(e^{B'|z|^\alpha})$ for each $B' > B$.

2. Proof of the estimate (1)

As in [2] we use the following

Lemma. *Let F be regular in* $\{z: |z| < R\}$ *and* $|F(z)| \leqq e^K$ $(K > 0)$ *there, and assume that* $|F(z)| \leqq 1$ *for z on an* arc *connecting* $z=0$ *to* $z=R$. *Then*

$$|F(z)| \leqq \exp\left\{\frac{4}{\pi} K \left(\frac{r}{R}\right)^{1/2}\right\} \quad \text{for} \quad |z| = r < R. \tag{2}$$

In order to prove (1) we take $z_0 \in \Gamma$ and have

$$|f(z)| \leqq M \exp\{A(|z_0| + R)^\rho\} \quad \text{in} \quad \{z: |z - z_0| \leqq R\}$$

and

$$|f(z)| \leqq M \quad \text{on} \quad \{z: |z - z_0| \leqq R\} \cap \Gamma$$

which certainly contains an arc connecting z_0 to a point on $\{z: |z - z_0| = R\}$. The Lemma yields

$$|f(z)| \leqq M \exp\left\{\frac{4}{\pi} A(|z_0| + R)^\rho \left(\frac{r}{R}\right)^{1/2}\right\} \quad \text{on} \quad \{z: |z - z_0| = r < R\}.$$

Cauchy's formula for $f'(z_0)$ gives

$$|f'(z_0)| \leqq M \frac{e^{c\sqrt{r}}}{r} \quad \text{with} \quad c = \frac{4}{\pi} A(|z_0| + R)^\rho R^{-1/2},$$

and choosing $r = A^2/c^2 < R$ we obtain

$$|f'(z_0)| \leqq M e^A \left(\frac{4}{\pi}\right)^2 \frac{(|z_0| + R)^{2\rho}}{R}.$$

This holds for all $R > 0$. Now choose $R = \frac{1}{2}|z_0|$ to obtain

$$|f'(z_0)| \leqq N |z_0|^{2\rho - 1}$$

with a certain constant N which is our desired result.

3. Functions with large values of f' in the case $\frac{1}{2} \leqq \rho < 1$

We are going to use an entire function f of order ρ, constructed in [4] for the purpose of obtaining an example where $f(z) \to 0$ for $z \to \infty$ along an arc Γ' but not $f'(z)$. The only case of interest in [4] was $1/2 < \rho < 1$, but the construction remains valid for $\rho = 1/2$.

Let us mention here briefly that the construction of f begins by forming a function u, being harmonic and positive to the left of Γ (see Fig. 1), zero on Γ and in the rest of the plane. The choice of a Γ symmetric to $\mathbf{R}$ simplifies the following arguments somewhat. Observe that Γ contains a sequence of segments $P_n Q_n P_n$; in [4] the length l_n of $P_n Q_n$ was $l_n = \dfrac{R_n}{(\log R_n)^2}$, where R_n denotes the distance from P_n to the origin.

Since u is subharmonic in the whole plane and of order $\rho < 1$ it has the representation (choosing $u(0) = 1$)

$$u(z) = 1 + \int_{\Gamma} \log \left| 1 - \frac{z}{t} \right| d\mu(t) \tag{3}$$

where $\mu(t)$ is an increasing function as t traverses Γ in the direction indicated in Fig. 1. The construction continues by taking $d[\mu(t)]$ instead of $d\mu(t)$ which gives an

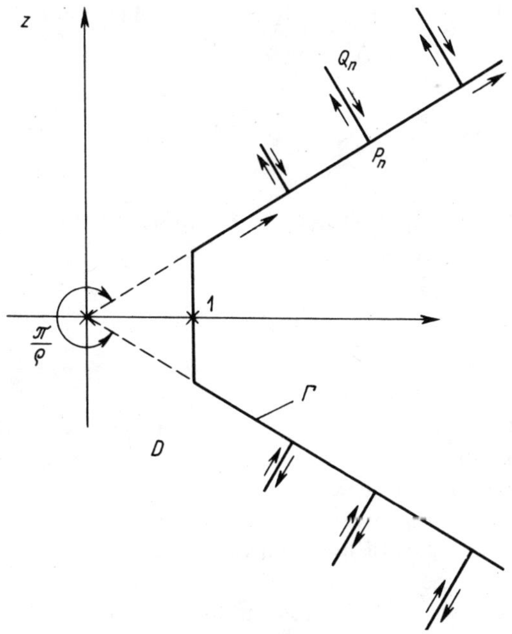

Fig. 1

infinite series $h(z)$ instead of $u(z)$. Removing a few terms from h we obtain $\log|f|$ where f is an entire function in the form of a simple Weierstrass product; see (7.5) in [4] where Σ has to be replaced by a product.

Our construction ensures that $f(z)\to 0$ as $z\to\infty$ along Γ, in fact $|f(z)|\leqq\frac{1}{|z|}$ there. Near the peaks Q_n the modulus $|f(z)|$ has a rapid growth: If z is a point on the prolongation of P_nQ_n, at a distance δ from Q_n, with $\frac{1}{R_n}<\delta<\frac{l_n}{4}$, we have according to (8.2) in [4]

$$\log|f(z)|>\frac{\sqrt{\delta}\,R_n^{\rho-\frac{1}{2}}}{150\log R_n}-53\log R_n. \tag{4}$$

Let us now use this to conclude the proof of the theorem. Let $z=Q_n'$ be the point on the prolongation of P_nQ_n nearest to Q_n where $|f(Q_n')|=1$. It follows from (4) that the distance δ' from Q_n to Q_n' is less than the number δ which makes the right hand member of (4) zero:

$$\delta'<(150\cdot 53)^2\cdot\frac{(\log R_n)^4}{R_n^{2\rho-1}}.$$

If we denote by M_n the maximum of $|f'(z)|$ on Q_nQ_n' we get

$$1-\frac{1}{R_n}\leqq|f(Q_n')-f(Q_n)|=\left|\int_{Q_n}^{Q_n'}f'(z)\,dz\right|\leqq M_n\cdot\delta'$$

and hence

$$M_n\geqq K\cdot\frac{R_n^{2\rho-1}}{(\log R_n)^4}$$

for some constant $K>0$.

Let us then adjoin the pieces $Q_nQ_n'Q_n$ to Γ and we obtain an arc Γ' on which f is bounded but on which there are points $z\to\infty$ with

$$|f'(z)|\geqq L\cdot\frac{|z|^{2\rho-1}}{(\log|z|)^4}. \tag{5}$$

Thus the exponent in (1) is the right one. By choosing $l_n=R_n(\log R_n)^{-1-\varepsilon}$ $(\varepsilon>0)$, we could have obtained $2+2\varepsilon$ instead of 4 in (5); for further improvements probably some other construction is needed.

One thing still remains to be done. In [4] it is only shown that u and therefore f is of order ρ, but it might be of maximal type. We now show that u, and therefore f, is actually of mean type of order ρ.

In order to see this, we give a representation of u in D by a conformal mapping. Let D_ζ be the image of D under the mapping $\zeta=(1-z)^\rho$, and let h be the conformal mapping of D_ζ onto $\{w\colon \operatorname{Re} w>0\}$ with $h(1)=1$. Then we have

$$u(z)=\operatorname{Re} h(\zeta) \quad \text{where} \quad \zeta=(1-z)^\rho, \quad \text{for} \qquad z\in D\,.$$

To estimate the growth of u, we make use of an old result of Ahlfors ([1], p. 38) concerning the angular derivative of h at ∞; for this topic see for example Gattegno–Ostrowski ([3], pp. 17 ff.). First, an elementary calculation shows that the boundary of D_ζ lies between the imaginary axis of the ζ-plane and a curve γ symmetric with respect to $\mathbf{R}$ and described as

$$\gamma=\left\{re^{i\varphi}\colon |\varphi|=\frac{\pi}{2}-\delta(r) \quad \text{with} \qquad \delta(r)\leqq\frac{\text{Const}}{(\log(2+\text{r}))^2}\right\}$$

so that

$$\int_1^\infty \frac{\delta(r)}{r}\,dr<\infty.$$

From this follows that the angular derivative of h at ∞ exists and is $\neq 0$ and $\neq\infty$; in particular

$$\frac{h(t)}{t}\to A \quad \text{for} \qquad t\to+\infty \qquad \text{with} \qquad A\in\mathbf{R},\ A\neq 0\,.$$

Observing $u(-R)=h[(1+R)^\rho]$ we therefore have

$$\frac{u(-R)}{R^\rho}\to A \quad \text{for} \qquad R\to\infty. \tag{6}$$

Now notice that because of the symmetry of Γ, we have $u(z)=u(\bar{z})$ and so $d\mu(t)=d\mu(\bar{t})$ in the representation (3). This formula gives therefore

$$\max\{u(z)\colon |z|=R\}=u(-R)\,,$$

and (6) shows then that u is of exact order ρ, mean type.

4. The case $\rho\geqq 1$

For each ρ in $1/2\leqq\rho<1$, we have produced an entire function f_ρ of order ρ, mean type, and an arc Γ_ρ such that f_ρ was bounded on Γ_ρ but f_ρ' satisfied (5) at some points $z\to\infty$ on Γ_ρ.

Now put

$$F(z)=f_\rho(z^k) \quad (k=2,3,\ldots,\text{fixed})$$

which is of order $k\rho$, mean type, and let γ be the arc extending from 1 to ∞ such that $z \in \gamma$ gives $z^k \in \Gamma_\rho$. Again, F is bounded on γ, and its derivative satisfies

$$|F'(z)| = |f_\rho'(z^k)| \cdot |kz^{k-1}| \geqq kL \frac{|z^k|^{2\rho-1}|z|^{k-1}}{(\log |z^k|)^4},$$

at some points $z \to \infty$ on γ. The numerator is $|z|^{2(k\rho)-1}$, and this shows that the exponent in (1) cannot be reduced for functions of order $k\rho$ where $k=2, 3, \ldots$ and $1/2 \leqq \rho < 1$. All orders $\geqq 1/2$ are thus covered, and the proof of our theorem is complete.

References

[1] AHLFORS, L. V., Untersuchungen zur Theorie der konformen Abbildung und der ganzen Funktionen. *Acta Soc. Sci. Fennicae Nova Ser.* **A1**, No. 9, 40 pp. (1930).

[2] DELANGE, H. and GAIER, D., Über asymptotische Wege analytischer Funktionen und ihrer Ableitungen. Archiv Math. **7** (1956), 135–142.

[3] GATTEGNO, C. and OSTROWSKI, A., Représentation conforme à la frontière; domaines particuliers. Paris, 1949.

[4] KJELLBERG, B. and SANDSTRÖM, B., Asymptotic values of an entire function and its derivative. *Ann. Acad. Sci. Fennicae Ser. A. I. Mathematica* **2** (1976), 257–267.

MATHEMATISCHES INSTITUT
DER UNIVERSITÄT GIESSEN
ARNDTSTRASSE 2
D 63 GIESSEN

ROYAL INSTITUTE OF TECHNOLOGY
DIVISION OF MATHEMATICS
S 10044 STOCKHOLM 70

Studies in Pure Mathematics
To the Memory of Paul Turán

Orthogonal polynomials and rational approximation of holomorphic functions

by

T. GANELIUS (Göteborg)

1. Introduction

In this note some known results for orthogonal polynomials and interpolation will be applied to certain problems on rational approximation of holomorphic functions. A typical application is the rational approximation of x^s on an interval I of the positive real axis. In this case the best rational approximation $r_n(x^s, I)$ satisfies

$$0 < K_1 \leqq r_n(x^s, I) \exp(2n/C(I)) \leqq K_2 .$$

The positive constants K_1 and K_2 depend on the interval and s, but are independent of n. The capacity of the condenser formed by I and the negative real axis is called $C(I)$, i.e. $C(I)$ is the Green capacity of I with respect to the plane cut along the negative axis.

This kind of approximation, where the degree of approximation is the square of the corresponding degree of approximation for functions in general, holomorphic in the same domain, has been studied by GONČAR [4] (cf. also GANELIUS [2,3]). Our discussion is based on GONČAR's approach.

The main idea is to show that the well-known methods from the theory of orthogonal polynomials can be applied to this kind of approximation problems. In this way we are able to make some of GONČAR's results more precise and we also give some slight extensions.

Theorem. *Let μ be a positive measure on $E=[-1, 1]$ and define $f \in H(S^2 \backslash E)$ by*

$$f(z) = \int \frac{d\mu(x)}{x-z}. \tag{1.1}$$

Let G be a compact set, disjoint from E, symmetric with respect to the real axis and with a boundary that is a Jordan curve of bounded rotation. For the best rational approximation $r_n(f, G)$ to f on G we then have

$$r_n(f, G) \leqq K_2 \exp(-2n/C(G, E)), \tag{1.2}$$

where the capacity of the condenser formed by E and G is denoted C(G, E). If $\int \log \mu'(x)dx/\sqrt{1-x^2} > -\infty$ *and G is an interval on the positive real axis, then*

$$r_n(f, G) \geqq K_1 \exp(-2n/C(G, E)). \tag{1.3}$$

The positive constants K_1 *and* K_2 *depend on* μ *and the geometry, but are independent of n.*

Another way to phrase this result is to say that $r_n(f, G)$ is of the order ρ^{-2n}, where ρ is the ratio of the radii in an annulus conformally equivalent to the complement of $G \cup E$. The most important case with G equal to a real interval is treated by GONČAR in [4], where he determines $\lim r_n^{1/n}$.

2. The approximation method

There is a standard method (see e.g. WALSH [6, ch. VIII]) to obtain rational approximations on a set G to a function f, holomorphic in a neighborhood of G. We consider the integral

$$\rho_n(z) = \frac{R_n(z)}{2\pi i} \int_C \frac{f(\zeta)}{R_n(\zeta)} \frac{d\zeta}{\zeta - z}, \tag{2.1}$$

where C is a rectifiable contour surrounding G and $R_n = S_n/T_n$ is a rational function of order n with zeros in G. If the zeros of the polynomial S_n are called $\{a_k\}_1^n$, simple calculation of residues gives

$$\rho_n(z) = f(z) - U_n(z),$$

the rational function U_n being given by

$$U_n(z) = \frac{S_n(z)}{T_n(z)} \sum \frac{T_n(a_k)}{z - a_k} \cdot \frac{f(a_k)}{S_n'(a_k)}.$$

From this representation we infer that any upper bound for $|\rho_n(z)|$ on G also is an upper bound for the best rational approximation $r_n(f, G)$. If f is holomorphic on the complement of E, we move the contour C towards the boundary of E, and it is readily seen that

$$\overline{\lim}\ r_n^{1/n} \leqq \exp(-1/C(G, E)),$$

since R_n can be chosen so that (cf. (2.7) and (2.8) below)

$$(\max_G |R_n| / \min_E |R_n|)^{1/n} \to \exp(-1/C(G, E)).$$

(For a general result of this type, see WIDOM [7].)

To obtain a better degree of approximation it is natural (cf. GONČAR [4] for the following) to try

(2.2) $$\sigma_n(z)=\frac{1}{2\pi i}\frac{\omega_{2n}(z)}{V_n(z)T_n(z)}\int_C \frac{T_n(\zeta)f(\zeta)-P_{n-1}(\zeta)}{\omega_{2n}(\zeta)}\frac{V_n(\zeta)}{\zeta-z}d\zeta=f(z)-\frac{P_{n-1}(z)}{T_n(z)},$$

where $\omega_{2n}(z)=\prod_1^{2n}(z-a_i)$ with $a_i\in G$, and P_{n-1}/T_n interpolates f at the points $\{a_i\}$. The polynomial V_n is arbitrary.

If $z\in G$ our assumptions imply that

$$\int_C \frac{P_{n-1}(\zeta)V_n(\zeta)}{\omega_{2n}(\zeta)(\zeta-z)}d\zeta=0,$$

since there are no poles outside C. Specializing by taking $V_n=T_n$ and $\omega_{2n}=S_n^2$ we can rewrite (2.2) as

(2.3) $$\sigma_n(z)=\frac{1}{2\pi i}\left(\frac{S_n(z)}{T_n(z)}\right)^2\int_C \frac{T_n(\zeta)^2}{S_n(\zeta)^2}\frac{f(\zeta)}{\zeta-z}d\zeta.$$

We have thus obtained squares of the rationals, but we are not free to choose T_n. As soon as S_n is fixed, T_n is determined (except for a constant). The polynomial T_n is characterized by the fact that

(2.4) $$\int_C \frac{\zeta^m T_n(\zeta)f(\zeta)}{S_n(\zeta)^2}d\zeta=0, \quad \text{for} \qquad m=0,1,\dots,n-1.$$

This is immediate since

$$\int_C \frac{\zeta^m(T_n(\zeta)f(\zeta)-P_{n-1}(\zeta))}{S_n(\zeta)^2}d\zeta=0,$$

and the integral of the last term vanishes.

We next introduce the special form of f assumed in our theorem. Putting $f=\int(x-z)^{-1}d\mu(x)$ we get after a change of the order of integration, that (2.3) can be written

(2.5) $$\sigma_n(z)=\left(\frac{S_n(z)}{T_n(z)}\right)^2\int\left(\frac{T_n(x)}{S_n(x)}\right)^2\frac{d\mu(x)}{x-z}$$

and the conditions (2.4) on T_n become

$$\int x^m T_n(x) \frac{d\mu(x)}{S_n(x)^2} = 0. \tag{2.6}$$

From now on we assume that the points of interpolation are taken symmetrically on G, so that $S_n(x)^2 > 0$ for $x \in E$.

The following facts for rational functions will be useful. It is well known that for all rationals R_n of order n it holds

$$\max_G |R_n| / \min_E |R_n| \geqq \exp(-n/C(G, E)). \tag{2.7}$$

In the other direction (see [3]) we have

If G is of bounded rotation, there is a rational R_n with zeros on G and poles on E, such that,

$$\max_G |R_n| / \min_E |R_n| \leqq M \exp(-n/C(G, E)). \tag{2.8}$$

Here as in the sequel M denotes a positive constant depending on the configuration but independent of n.

3. Inequalities for orthogonal polynomials

The following lemma (cf. FREUD [1, p. 121]) will be useful.

Lemma. *Let $\{Q_n\}$ be the orthonormal set of polynomials belonging to the weight $d\alpha$ on $E = [-1, 1]$. If Π_{n-1} is an arbitrary polynomial of degree $(n-1)$, then*

$$|\Pi_{n-1}(z)| \leqq 2(\operatorname{dist}(z, E))^{-1} \|\Pi_{n-1}\|_{2,\alpha} |Q_n(z)|, \tag{3.1}$$

where $\|\Pi_{n-1}\|_{2,\alpha}^2 = \int |\Pi_{n-1}(x)|^2 d\alpha(x)$.

For the proof we express Π_{n-1} by Lagrange interpolation in the zeros $(x_i)_1^n$ of Q_n and get

$$\Pi_{n-1}(z) = \frac{k_{n-1}}{k_n} \sum_{i=1}^{n} \lambda_i \frac{Q_{n-1}(x_i)\,\Pi_{n-1}(x_i)}{z - x_i} Q_n(z).$$

Here $\{\lambda_i\}$ are the Christoffel numbers and k_n is the leading coefficient in Q_n. It is known (see e.g. [1, p. 45]) that $0 < k_{n-1}/k_n \leqq 2$.

Hence

$$|\Pi_{n-1}(z)\,\mathrm{dist}\,(z,E)|^2 \leqq 4|Q_n(z)|^2\left(\sum\lambda_i Q_{n-1}(x_i)^2\right)\left(\sum\lambda_i \Pi_{n-1}(x_i)^2\right)=$$

$$=4|Q_n(z)|^2 \int Q_{n-1}(x)^2\,d\alpha(x)\int|\Pi_{n-1}(x)|^2 d\alpha(x),$$

and (3.1) follows.

The other facts about orthogonal polynomials we shall refer to are the following (see e.g. SZEGŐ [5, p. 294] or FREUD [1, p. 194]).

Let $\{Q_i\}_0^\infty$ be the orthonormal set of polynomials belonging to the weight $d\mu$ and let $\{\Phi_i\}_0^\infty$ with $\Phi_i(w)=\kappa_i w^i+\ldots+\gamma_i$, be the associated ortho-normal set on the unit circle with the weight $d\alpha(\vartheta)=|d\mu(\cos\vartheta)|$. Then

$$\sqrt{2\pi}(1+\kappa_{2n}^{-1}\gamma_{2n})^{1/2}Q_n(z)=w^{-n}\Phi_{2n}(w)+w^n\Phi_{2n}(w^{-1}),$$

where $z=\frac{1}{2}(w+w^{-1})$. Since all zeros of Φ_{2n} are inside the unit circle and the coefficients are real

$$|Q_n(z)|\leqq M|w|^{-n}|\Phi_{2n}(w)|,\quad |w|>1\,. \tag{3.2}$$

The condition imposed on μ' for the second part of the theorem can be written $\int\log\alpha'(\vartheta)\,d\vartheta>-\infty$. Hence (see [5, p. 276]) there is a function $D\in H^2(U)$ with boundary values $D(e^{i\vartheta})$ such that $\alpha'(\vartheta)=|D(e^{i\vartheta})|^2$. We also recall that, since $S_n(x)$ is positive on E, it can be written

$$S_n(z)=h(w)h(w^{-1}),\quad z=\frac{1}{2}(w+w^{-1}), \tag{3.3}$$

where h is of degree n and has all zeros outside the unit circle.

4. Proof of the theorem

The upper bound of the theorem now follows easily. Taking T_n in (2.5) as the nth orthogonal polynomial belonging to the weight $(S_n(x))^{-2}d\mu(x)$, we get

$$|\sigma_n(z)|\leqq M\left|\frac{S_n(z)}{T_n(z)}\right|^2.$$

Application of the lemma gives

$$|\sigma_n(z)|\leqq M\left|\frac{S_n(z)}{\Pi_{n-1}(z)}\right|^2\int\left|\frac{\Pi_{n-1}(x)}{S_n(x)}\right|^2 d\mu(x), \tag{4.1}$$

where both the polynomials are at our disposal. Choosing $S_n(z)/\Pi_{n-1}(z) = (z-a_0)\,R_{n-1}(z)$, where R_{n-1} is given by (2.8) and $a_0 \in G$ we get

$$r_n(f, G) \leqq \max_G |\sigma_n(z)| \leqq \|\mu\| \exp(-2n/C(G, E)).$$

Hence the first part of the theorem is proved.

The obtain lower bounds for r_n we specialize G to be an interval I, so that the Tchebycheff theorem can be applied, telling us that the best rational approximand is an interpolating rational. It is suitable to consider approximation by rationals of the form $M_{n-1}(x)/T_n(x)$, interpolating at $2n$ points (the orthogonality condition implies that the rational function of best approximation among these in fact has numerator and denominator of degree exactly $(n-1)$ and n). Then there is a rational with the double deviation from f, that interpolates at n poles of double multiplicity. As remarked above the Tchebycheff theorem implies that

$$2r_{n-1}(f, I) \geqq \max_{z \in I} |\sigma_n(z)|. \tag{4.2}$$

To estimate $|\sigma_n(z)|$ we apply (2.5) and find that

$$r_{n-1}(f, I) \geqq M \left| \frac{S_n(z)}{T_n(z)} \right|^2, \tag{4.3}$$

choosing T_n as the nth orthogonal polynomial belonging to the weight $d\mu(x)/S_n(x)^2$ so the orthogonality conditions (2.6) are satisfied. We recall (3.3) and if we can show that (see below; cf. [5, Theorem 12.1.1])

$$|T_n(z) \leqq M |w|^n |h(w^{-1})|^2, \quad |w| > 1, \quad x \in I, \tag{4.4}$$

combination of (4.4) and (4.3) gives

$$r_{n-1}(f, I) \geqq M \left| \frac{h(w)}{w^n h(w^{-1})} \right|^2. \tag{4.5}$$

Since $\min_{z \in E} |w^{-n} h(w)/h(w^{-1})| = 1$, it follows from (2.7) and (4.5) that

$$r_{n-1}(f, I) \geqq M \exp(-2n/C(I, E)),$$

where we have used the conformal invariance of the capacity.

The inequality (4.4) can be obtained in the following way by a residue calculation. Let $|w| > 1$ and Φ_m an orthogonal polynomial belonging to $\alpha'(\vartheta) S_n(\cos\vartheta)^{-2}$. In the notation of section 3 we have

$$\left|\frac{\Phi_m(w)D(w^{-1})(w^2-1)}{w^{m+2}h(w^{-1})^2}\right|^2 = \left|\frac{1}{2\pi i}\int\limits_{|\zeta|=1}\frac{\Phi_m(\zeta)D(\zeta^{-1})(w\zeta-1)}{\zeta^{m+2}h(\zeta^{-1})^2(\zeta-w)}\,d\zeta\right|^2 \leqq$$

$$\leqq\frac{1}{2\pi}\int\left|\frac{\Phi_m(e^{i\vartheta})}{S_n(\cos\vartheta)}\right|^2 d\alpha(\vartheta),$$

and (4.4) follows by (3.2).

References

[1] G. FREUD, *Orthogonale Polynome*, Akadémiai Kiadó, Budapest 1969.
[2] T. GANELIUS, Rational approximation in the complex plane and on the line, *Ann. Acad. Sci. Fenn. Ser. A. I.*, **2** (1976), 129–145.
[3] T. GANELIUS, Some extremal functions and approximation, *Colloquia. Math. Soc. J. Bolyai* **19**, Fourier Analysis and Approximation Theory, Budapest 1976, 371–381.
[4] A. A. GONČAR, On the degree of rational approximation to certain analytic functions, (in Russian) *Mat. Sb.*, **105** (1978), 147–163.
[5] G. SZEGŐ, *Orthogonal polynomials*. Fourth edition. Amer. Math. Soc., New York 1975.
[6] J. L. WALSH, *Interpolation and approximation*. Fifth edition. Amer. Math. Soc., New York 1969.
[7] H. WIDOM, Rational approximation and *n*-dimensional diameter, *J. Approximation Theory*, **5** (1972), 343–361.

UNIVERSITY OF GÖTEBORG
SWEDEN

Studies in Pure Mathematics
To the Memory of Paul Turán

Norm form equations and explicit lower bounds for linear forms with algebraic coefficients

by

K. GYŐRY (Debrecen) and Z. Z. PAPP (Budapest)

1. Explicit bounds for the solutions of norm form equations

Let $L \subset K$ be algebraic number fields with degrees $[L:\mathbf{Q}]=l$ and $[K:L]=n \geqq 3$. Let R_K, h_K and D_K denote the regulator, the class number and the absolute value of the discriminant of K, and let r be the number of fundamental units in K. Suppose $\alpha_2, \ldots, \alpha_k$ are elements in K with heights[1] $\leqq H$ and with respective degrees $n_i \geqq 3$ $(2 \leqq i \leqq k)$ over L such that $K = L(\alpha_2, \ldots, \alpha_k)$ and $n_2 \ldots n_k = n$. Let $0 \neq \mu \in L$ with $H(\mu) \leqq m$. As a consequence of a more general result we proved in [11] that all solutions $(x_1, \ldots, x_k) \in \mathbf{Z}_L^k$ of the norm form equation

$$\mathrm{Norm}_{K/L}(x_1 + \alpha_2 x_2 + \ldots + \alpha_k x_k) = \mu \tag{1}$$

satisfy

$$\max_{1 \leqq i \leqq k} \overline{|x_i|} < \exp\{(8\, l\, n^*)^{32(l\, n^*+1)} D_K^{3n^*/n} (\log D_K)^{3\, l\, n^* - 1} (D_K^{3n^*/2n} + \log (mH))\}, \tag{2}$$

where $n^* = n(n-1)(n-2)$. In the case $k=2$ this implies Baker's famous theorem on the Thue equation [4]. When $L=\mathbf{Q}$, for $\mathbf{Z}$-modules $\{1, \alpha_2, \ldots, \alpha_k\}$ of the above type our result makes effective Schmidt's well-known theorem on norm form equations [21].

Our estimate (2) enables us to derive nontrivial explicit lower bounds for linear forms $x_1 + \alpha_2 x_2 + \ldots + \alpha_k x_k$ at integer points in $\mathbf{Z}_L^k$. The purpose of the present paper is to improve (2) and to derive from this improvement the best known lower bounds for some linear forms.

If $k=2$ and $L=\mathbf{Q}$, (1) is essentially the Thue equation. In this case the estimates of Sprindzuk [25] and Stark [26] provide better upper bounds in D_K than (2). Following a more direct deduction than what we needed in [11], from the recent estimates of Baker [5] or van der Poorten and Loxton [18] for linear forms in the logarithms of algebraic

[1] Throughout the paper we use standard notation. By the height $H(\alpha)$ of an algebraic number α we mean the usual height. As usual, $\overline{|\alpha|}$ denotes the maximum absolute value of the conjugates of α and $\overline{|F|}$ denotes the maximum absolute value of the conjugates of the coefficients of a polynomial $F(x)$ with algebraic coefficients. $\mathbf{Z}_L$ signifies the ring of integers of an algebraic number field L.

numbers we are able to derive bounds for the solutions of (1) which are the best known for $k=2$ too. We shall prove the following improvement of (2).

Theorem 1. *Let $L, K, \alpha_2, \ldots, \alpha_k$ and μ be as above. Then all solutions $(x_1, \ldots, x_k) \in \mathbf{Z}_L^k$ of (1) satisfy*

$$\max_{1 \leq i \leq k} \overline{|x_i|} < \exp\{C R_K (\log R_K^*)^2 (R_K + \log(mH))\} \tag{3}$$

and

$$\max_{1 \leq i \leq k} \overline{|x_i|} < \exp\{C h_K^{-1} D_K^{1/2} (\log D_K)^{2N} (h_K^{-1} D_K^{1/2} + \log(mH))\} \tag{4}$$

where $N = l\,n$, $C = (25(r+3)N)^{15(r+3)}$ and $R_K^* = \max(R_K, e)$.

As a consequence of Theorem 1 we get the best known bounds for the solutions of the generalized Thue equation.

Corollary. *Let L be as above with discriminant D_L and let $F(x, y) \in \mathbf{Z}_L[x, y]$ be an irreducible binary form of degree $n \geq 3$ with $\overline{|F|} \leq \mathscr{H}$. Let α be a root of $F(x, 1) = 0$ and D_K and R_K be the absolute value of the discriminant and regulator respectively of $K = L(\alpha)$. Suppose μ is a non-zero algebraic integer in L with $\overline{|\mu|} \leq m$. Then all solutions $(x, y) \in \mathbf{Z}_L^2$ of the generalized Thue equation*

$$F(x, y) = \mu \tag{5}$$

satisfy

$$\max(\overline{|x|}, \overline{|y|}) < \exp\{C N^2 R_K (\log R_K^*)^2 (R_K + \log(2m\mathscr{H}))\} \tag{6}$$

$$\max(\overline{|x|}, \overline{|y|}) < \exp\{C N^2 h_K^{-1} D_K^{1/2} (\log D_K)^{2N} (h_K^{-1} D_K^{1/2} + \log(2m\mathscr{H}))\} \tag{7}$$

and

$$\max(\overline{|x|}, \overline{|y|}) < \exp\{C N^{2(N+1)} n^{7n} (\mathscr{H}^{l(n-1)} |D_L|)^{n/2} (\log(2\mathscr{H}|D_L|))^{2N} [(\mathscr{H}^{l(n-1)}|D_L|)^{n/2} + \log m]\} \tag{8}$$

with the N, C, R_K^* defined in Theorem 1.

If $|N_{L/\mathbf{Q}}(\mu)|$ is not small relative to m, (6), (7) and (8) improve our previous estimate obtained in [11] for the solutions of (5).

$\mathfrak{p}$-adic generalizations to the Thue–Mahler equation have been obtained by KOTOV and SPRINDŽUK [13], [14] and KOTOV [12]. We remark that by specializing the results of [13], [14] and [12] to the equation (5) one gets slightly weaker estimates in certain parameters than (6), (7), (8) and the bounds in [13], [14] and [12] are not expressed explicitly in terms of l and n.

2. Explicit lower bounds for some linear forms with algebraic coefficients

Suppose $\alpha_1, \ldots, \alpha_k$ are algebraic numbers such that $1, \alpha_1, \ldots, \alpha_k$ are linearly independent over the rationals and denote by n the degree of the number field $\mathbf{Q}(\alpha_1, \ldots, \alpha_k)=K$. By a generalization of a well-known theorem of LIOUVILLE [15] there exists an effectively computable positive constant $c_1=c_1(\alpha_1, \ldots, \alpha_k)$ such that for any k-tuples of rational integers $x_1, \ldots, x_k$ with $|\mathbf{x}|=\max(|x_1|, \ldots, |x_k|)>0$

$$\|x_1\alpha_1+\ldots+x_k\alpha_k\|>c_1|\mathbf{x}|^{-\frac{n-\sigma}{\sigma}} \tag{9}$$

holds[2] where $\sigma=1$ or $\sigma=2$ according as K is real or not. As a generalization of ROTH's famous theorem [19] SCHMIDT [20] proved that for any $\kappa>\dfrac{k+1-\sigma}{\sigma}$ there exists a constant $c_2=c_2(\kappa, \alpha_1, \ldots, \alpha_k)$ such that

$$\|x_1\alpha_1+\ldots+x_k\alpha_k\|>c_2|\mathbf{x}|^{-\kappa} \tag{10}$$

for any k-tuples of rational integers $x_1, \ldots, x_k$ with $|\mathbf{x}|>0$. (In fact, SCHMIDT has obtained a series of results both stronger and more general than this; see e.g. SCHMIDT's survey paper [22].) In contrast with LIOUVILLE's inequality, it is not possible to evaluate the constant c_2 by the THUE–SIEGEL–ROTH–SCHMIDT method.

For certain algebraic numbers $\alpha_1, \ldots, \alpha_k$, given essentially by fractional powers of rationals, considerable effective refinements of the exponent in (9) have been established by BAKER [1], [2], [3], FELDMAN [7], [8] and OSGOOD [16], [17]. When applicable, the methods applied in these works give surprisingly strong estimates.

For $k=1$, the first effective improvement of (9) in the general case was obtained by BAKER [4]. Later FELDMAN proved [9] that

$$\|x\alpha_1\|>c_3|x|^{-\kappa}$$

for all integers $x\neq 0$, where c_3, κ are positive numbers, effectively computable in terms of α, with $\kappa<n-1$. Recently KOTOV and SPRINDŽUK [14] have obtained a $\mathfrak{p}$-adic generalization of FELDMAN's theorem.

Theorem 1 enables us to establish an effective improvement of (9) for every $k\geq 1$ and for a wide class of algebraic numbers $\alpha_1, \ldots, \alpha_k$. To these numbers the above mentioned methods of BAKER, FELDMAN and OSGOOD are not applicable in general.

To state our theorems we need some notations and assumptions. Let again $L\subset K$ be algebraic number fields with the parameters given above. Denote by R_L the regulator of L and suppose $\alpha_1, \ldots, \alpha_k$ are elements in K with heights $\leq H$ and with respective degrees $n_i\geq 3$ $(1\leq i\leq k)$ over L such that $K=L(\alpha_1, \ldots, \alpha_k)$ and $n_1 \ldots n_k=n$. We suppose that there are s real and $2t$ complex conjugates to K over $\mathbf{Q}$. Denote by Ω the set of Archimedean valuations $|\ldots|_v$ of K, where v is one of the natural numbers 1, 2,

[2] $\|\xi\|$ denotes the distance from ξ to the nearest integer.

$\ldots, s+t$. For $\beta \in K$ put $\|\beta\|_v = |\beta|_v^{m_v}$ where $m_v = [K_v:\mathbf{Q}_v]$. Under the above conditions we have the following

Theorem 2. *Let Γ be a subset of Ω and denote by s' and t' respectively the number of real and complex valuations in Γ. Let $x_0, x_1, \ldots, x_k$ be algebraic integers in L, not all zero. Then there exists a unit ε in L such that*

$$\prod_{v \in \Gamma} \|(\varepsilon x_0) + (\varepsilon x_1)\alpha_1 + \ldots + (\varepsilon x_k)\alpha_k\|_v > c_4 X^{-N+s'+2t'+\tau_4}, \quad X = \max_{0 \le i \le k} \overline{|\varepsilon x_i|} \tag{11}$$

where $c_4 = (2kH)^{-N+s'+2t'-kn-1} \exp\{-R_K - 6nl^3 R_L\}$ and $\tau_4 = (CR_K(\log R_K^*)^2)^{-1}$, C being the constant defined in Theorem 1.

Of particular interest is the special case $L = \mathbf{Q}$.

Corollary. *Let $\alpha_1, \ldots, \alpha_k$ be algebraic numbers with heights $\le H$ and with degrees at least 3 such that the degree n of $K = \mathbf{Q}(\alpha_1, \ldots, \alpha_k)$ is $\deg \alpha_1 \ldots \deg \alpha_k$. Then we have for any rational integer k-tuples $x_1, \ldots, x_k$ with $|\mathbf{x}| = \max(|x_1|, \ldots, |x_k|) > 0$*

$$\|x_1\alpha_1 + \ldots + x_k\alpha_k\| > c_5 |\mathbf{x}|^{-\frac{n-\sigma-\tau_5}{\sigma}} \tag{12}$$

where $c_5 = (2kH)^{\frac{-2n+2\sigma-kn-1+\tau_5}{\sigma}} \exp\{-R_K - 6n\}$, $\tau_5 = (C^* R_K(\log R_K^*)^2)^{-1}$, $C^* = (25(r+3)n)^{15(r+3)}$ and $\sigma = 1$ or $\sigma = 2$ according as K is real or not.

When $k=1$, our Corollary provides, with explicitly computed constants c_3, κ, FELDMAN's theorem quoted above [9]. Namely, if α is a real algebraic number with height $\le H$ and degree $n \ge 3$ and $K = \mathbf{Q}(\alpha)$, then we have, with the above τ_5,

$$\left|\alpha - \frac{y}{x}\right| > \frac{(2H)^{-3n+1+\tau_5} \exp\{-R_K - 6n\}}{x^{n-\tau_5}} \tag{13}$$

for every rational $\frac{y}{x}$ with $x > 0$.

We return now to the general case. Let L be as above, and let ϑ be an algebraic number with height $\le H$ and with degree $n \ge 3$ over L. Write $K = L(\vartheta)$ and define s, $2t$ and Ω as above. As another consequence of Theorem 1 we have the following

Theorem 3. *Let Γ be a subset of Ω and denote by s' and t' respectively the number of real and complex valuations in Γ. Suppose $\alpha \in L$. If α is an algebraic integer, we have*

$$\prod_{v \in \Gamma} \|\vartheta - \alpha\|_v > c_6 (H(\alpha))^{-nl+s'+2t'+\tau_6} \tag{14}$$

where $c_6=(4H)^{-nl+s'+2t'-n-1}\exp\{-R_K-6nl^3R_L\}$ *and* $\tau_6=(2lCR_K(\log R_K^*)^2)^{-1}$ *with the constant C defined in Theorem 1. If* α *is not integral, then*

$$\prod_{v\in\Gamma}\|\vartheta-\alpha\|_v>c_6(H(\alpha))^{-nl+\tau_6}. \tag{15}$$

This theorem is in fact a special case of Theorem 3 of Kotov and Sprindžuk [14]. In [14] the authors proved (14) and (15) with Γ containing a finite number of Archimedean and non-Archimedean valuations. However, in [14] it is assumed that $n\geqq 5$ and the constants corresponding to our c_6 and τ_6 are not expressed explicitly.

We remark that the exponents in our estimates (11), (12), (13), (14), (15) depend only on K and Γ. Since R_K can be estimated from above by k, H, l, D_L and $[K:\mathbf{Q}]$, we can easily get explicit estimates in the exponents of which these latter parameters occur.

3. Proofs

Proof of Theorem 1. In proving our theorem we shall use some ideas of Baker [4] and Stark [26] applied earlier to the Thue equation.

Suppose that (1) is solvable in algebraic integers of L and let $x_1, \ldots, x_k$ be any fixed solution of (1). Put $X=\max\limits_{2\leqq i\leqq k}\overline{|x_i|}$. If $X=0$, (3) obviously holds. We may suppose without loss of generality that $X=\overline{|x_k|}>0$. Further, we suppose that

$$X>\exp\{rc_7R_K+2l\log(2m)+6N^3\log(4kH)\} \tag{16}$$

where $c_7=\left(\dfrac{6rN^2}{\log N}\right)^r$.

Consider an arbitrary isomorphism $K\to K'$ into the complex numbers and denote by $x_1', \ldots, x_k', \mu', \alpha_2', \ldots, \alpha_k', L'$ the conjugates of $x_1, \ldots, x_k, \mu, \alpha_2, \ldots, \alpha_k, L$ respectively under this isomorphism. $x_1', \ldots, x_k'$ satisfy the equation

$$\mathrm{Norm}_{K'/L'}(x_1'+\alpha_2'x_2'+\ldots+\alpha_k'x_k')=\mu'. \tag{17}$$

Suppose that $X'=\max\limits_{2\leqq i\leqq k}|x_i'|=|x_f'|$.

Denote by $\alpha_i'=\alpha_{i,1}', \ldots, \alpha_{i,n_i}'$ the roots of the minimal defining polynomial of α_i' over L'. Putting

$$\beta'_{j_2\ldots j_k}=x_1'+\alpha'_{2,j_2}x_2'+\ldots+\alpha'_{k,j_k}x_k' \quad (j_i=1, \ldots, n_i;\, i=2, \ldots, k), \tag{18}$$

in view of $K'=L'(\alpha_2', \ldots, \alpha_k')$ and $[K':L']=n_2\ldots n_k$ (17) can be written in the form

$$\prod_{j_2=1}^{n_2}\cdots\prod_{j_k=1}^{n_k}\beta'_{j_2\ldots j_k}=\mu'. \tag{19}$$

Consider the products $\prod_{j_f=1}^{n_f} |\beta'_{j_2\ldots j_k}|$ for fixed $j_2, \ldots, j_{f-1}, j_{f+1}, \ldots, j_k$ and suppose that they take their minimum for $j'_2, \ldots, j'_{f-1}, j'_{f+1}, \ldots, j'_k$. We may now, for simplicity, omit the indices $j'_2, \ldots, j'_{f-1}, j'_{f+1}, \ldots, j'_k$ and assume that $\beta'_{j'_2\ldots j'_{f-1}j_fj'_{f+1}\ldots j'_k} = \beta'_{j_j}$. Then (17) implies

$$\prod_{j_f=1}^{n_f} |\beta'_{j_f}| \leqq |\mu'|^{n_f/n} \leqq (2m)^{n_f/n}. \tag{20}$$

Let $a_f > 0$ denote the leading coefficient of the minimal defining polynomial of α'_f over $\mathbf{Z}$. Then $a_f(\alpha'_{f,i} - \alpha'_{f,j})$ is a non-zero algebraic integer for any $i \neq j$ with $1 \leqq i, j \leqq n_f$ and we have

$$a_f|\alpha'_{f,i} - \alpha'_{f,j}| \leqq 2\overline{|a_f\alpha'_f|} \leqq 4H, \tag{21}$$

whence

$$|\alpha'_{f,i} - \alpha'_{f,j}| \geqq (4H)^{-ln_f(ln_f-1)}. \tag{22}$$

Suppose now that $|\beta'_q| \leqq |\beta'_j|$ for some q and for any j with $1 \leqq j$, $q \leqq n_f$ and $j \neq q$. We have for each of these β'_j

$$|\beta'_j| \geqq |\beta'_q - \beta'_j| - |\beta'_q|$$

and this together with (18) and (22) implies

$$|\beta'_j| \geqq \frac{1}{2}|\beta'_q - \beta'_j| = \frac{1}{2}X'|\alpha'_{f,q} - \alpha'_{f,j}| \geqq \frac{1}{2}X'(4H)^{-ln_f(ln_f-1)}. \tag{23}$$

It follows from (20) and (23) that

$$|\beta'_q| < 2^{n_f-1}(2m)^{n_f/n}(4H)^{ln_f(ln_f-1)(n_f-1)}X'^{-n_f+1}. \tag{24}$$

If $X' > 2(2m)^{1/n}(4H)^{l(ln_f-1)^2}$, then by (24) we get for any $\beta'_{j_2\ldots j_k}$

$$|\beta'_{j_2\ldots j_k}| \leqq |\beta'_{j_2\ldots j_k} - \beta'_q| + |\beta'_q| \leqq 4kHX' \leqq 4kHX.$$

Otherwise, if $X' \leqq 2(2m)^{1/n}(4H)^{l(ln_f-1)^2}$, from (17) it follows that

$$|x'_1| \leqq n(2nkHX^*)^n + 2m$$

where $X^* = \max(X', 1)$ and by (16) we obtain again

$$|\beta'_{j_2\ldots j_k}| \leqq 4kHX \tag{25}$$

for each $\beta'_{j_2 \dots j_k}$. Further, since $\mu' a^n$ is an algebraic integer in L with $a = a_2 \dots a_k$, if $|\beta'_{j_2 \dots j_k}| < 1$ then

$$1 < \frac{1}{|\beta'_{j_2 \dots j_k}|} \leqq \frac{(4kHX)^{n-1}}{|\mu'|} \leqq (4kHX)^{n-1} H^{(k-1)N} (2m)^{l-1}. \tag{26}$$

We suppose that there are s real conjugate fields to K and $2t$ complex conjugates to K over $\mathbf{Q}$ and that they are chosen in the usual manner: if α is in K then $\alpha^{(j)}$ is real for $j = 1, \dots, s$ and $\alpha^{(j+t)} = \overline{\alpha^{(j)}}$ for $j = s+1, \dots, s+t$. Let $e_j = 1$ if $1 \leqq j \leqq s$ and $e_j = 2$ if $s+1 \leqq j \leqq s+t$. It follows from the work of Siegel [24] (combining it with a recent result of Dobrowolski [6]; cf. [10], Lemma 2) that there exist independent units $\eta_1, \dots, \eta_r$ in K such that

$$\prod_{i=1}^{r} \max(\log \overline{|\eta_i|}, 1) < c_7 R_K \tag{27}$$

and the absolute values of the elements of the inverse matrix of $(e_j \log |\eta_i^{(j)}|)_{1 \leqq i,j \leqq r}$ do not exceed $c_8 = \dfrac{6r!N^2}{\log N}$.

Write $\beta_{1,\dots,1} = \beta$ and $|N_{K/\mathbf{Q}}(\beta)| = M$. As is well known (see e.g. [10], Lemma 3), there exist rational integers $b_1, \dots, b_r$ such that

$$\gamma = \beta \eta_1^{b_1} \dots \eta_r^{b_r} \tag{28}$$

and

$$|\log| M^{-1/N} \gamma^{(j)}|| \leqq \frac{c_7 r}{2} R_K, \quad j = 1, \dots, N. \tag{29}$$

We may get bounds for the integers $b_1, \dots, b_r$ from the equations

$$\begin{aligned} & b_1 e_j \log |\eta_1^{(j)}| + \dots + b_r e_j \log |\eta_r^{(j)}| = e_j \log |\gamma^{(j)}/\beta^{(j)}| = \\ & = e_j \log | M^{-1/N} \gamma^{(j)}| + \frac{e_j}{N} \log M - e_j \log |\beta^{(j)}|, \quad j = 1, \dots, r. \end{aligned} \tag{30}$$

Since $M = |N_{L/\mathbf{Q}}(\mu)|$, we get

$$|\log M| \leqq l \log(2m) + kN \log H.$$

This together with (25) and (29) implies that the right side of (30) in absolute value is less than

$$c_7 r R_K + 4l \log(2m) + 4kN \log H + 2n \log(4kHX).$$

In view of (16) we get from (30)

$$\max_{1\le i\le r} |b_i| \leqq 3rnc_8 \log X\,. \tag{31}$$

Consider now an isomorphism $K\to K'$ into $\mathbf{C}$ for which $x_k\to x'_k$ and $|x'_k|=\overline{|x_k|}$. For the β'_q defined above we have now

$$|\beta'_q|<2^{n_k-1}(2m)^{n_k/n}(4H)^{ln_k(ln_k-1)(n_k-1)}X^{-n_k+1}\,. \tag{32}$$

Further, consider two β'_g, β'_h with $1\leqq g, h\leqq n_k$, $g\neq h$, $g, h\neq q$ and use the identity

$$(\alpha'_{k,g}-\alpha'_{k,q})\beta'_h-(\alpha'_{k,h}-\alpha'_{k,q})\beta'_g=(\alpha'_{k,g}-\alpha'_{k,h})\beta'_q. \tag{33}$$

We have by (28)

$$\alpha_1^{b_1}\dots\alpha_r^{b_r}\alpha_{r+1}-1=\frac{\alpha'_{k,g}-\alpha'_{k,h}}{\alpha'_{k,h}-\alpha'_{k,q}}\cdot\frac{\beta'_q}{\beta'_g} \tag{34}$$

where

$$\alpha_i=\begin{cases}\eta'_{i,g}/\eta'_{i,h}, & i=1,\dots,r\\ \dfrac{\alpha'_{k,g}-\alpha'_{k,q}}{\alpha'_{k,h}-\alpha'_{k,q}}\cdot\dfrac{\gamma'_h}{\gamma'_g}, & i=r+1\end{cases}$$

and $\eta'_{i,g}$, γ'_g (resp. $\eta'_{i,h}$, γ'_h) denote the conjugates of η_i, γ corresponding to β'_g (resp. to β'_h). By (34), (21), (22), (23), (32) and (16)

$$0<|\alpha_1^{b_1}\dots\alpha_r^{b_r}\alpha_{r+1}-1|<(2m)^{n_k/n}(4H)^{l^3n_k^3}X^{-n_k}<\frac{1}{2}X^{-2}\,. \tag{35}$$

Let $\alpha_0=-1$. We get from (35) with $B=3r^2nc_8\log X$, $\delta=(3r^2nc_8)^{-1}$

$$0<|b_0\log\alpha_0+b_1\log\alpha_1+\dots+b_r\log\alpha_r-\log\alpha_{r+1}^{-1}|<e^{-2\log X}<e^{-\delta B} \tag{36}$$

where b_0 is a rational integer and log denotes the principal value. So

$$|b_0|\leqq|b_1|+\dots+|b_r|$$

and by (31)

$$\max_{0\le i\le r}|b_i|\leqq B\,. \tag{37}$$

We shall now apply Theorem 3 of VAN DER POORTEN and LOXTON [18] to (36). For this we need some estimates. Put $A_i=\max(H(\alpha_i), e^e)$ for $i=0,\dots,r$. Since

$$H(\alpha_i)\leqq(2\overline{|\eta'_{i,g}/\eta'_{i,h}|})^{N(n-1)}\leqq(2\overline{|\eta_i|}^N)^{N(n-1)},$$

by (27) we have

$$\log A_i<2(n-1)N^2\max(\log\overline{|\eta_i|},1)\,. \tag{38}$$

From (38) and (27) it follows that

(39) $$\Omega' = \log A_0 \log A_1 \ldots \log A_r < c_7 c_9 R_K$$

where $c_9 = e[2(n-1)N^2]^r$. Put $T = c_{10}\Omega' \log \Omega'$ with $c_{10} = (25(r+3)N)^{10(r+3)}$ and set $A = [8H^k(2m)^{l/n} e^{8c_7 r R_K}]^{N^2(n-2)}$. We have $A_i < A$ for any i. Since $a\gamma$ is an algebraic integer, by (21) and (29) we obtain

$$H(\alpha_{r+1}) \leqq (\overline{|a_k(\alpha'_{k,g} - \alpha'_{k,q}) a\gamma'_h|} + \overline{|a_k(\alpha'_{k,h} - \alpha'_{k,q})\, a\gamma'_g|})^{N(n-1)(n-2)} \leqq A.$$

Obviously $\delta \leqq c_{10}^{-1/2}\, T$. Applying now VAN DER POORTEN and LOXTON's theorem [18], we get from (36)

$$B < \delta^{-1}\, T \log(\delta^{-1}\, T) \log A\,.$$

By virtue of (39) this implies

$$\log X < c_{11} R_K (\log R_K^*)^2 \,(R_K + \log(mH))$$

where $c_{11} = 48 c_{10} c_7^2 c_9 (\log c_7)(\log c_{10})(rN^2(n-2))$. If x'_1 is any of the conjugates of x_1, for $\beta'_{j_2 \ldots j_k} = x'_1 + \ldots + \alpha'_{k,j_k} x'_k$ (25) holds. Consequently

$$|x'_1| = |\beta'_{j_2 \ldots j_k} - (\alpha'_{2,j_2} x'_2 + \ldots + \alpha'_{k,j_k} x'_k)| \leqq 6kHX$$

and

(40) $$\max_{1 \leqq i \leqq k} \overline{|x_i|} < \exp\{2c_{11} R_K (\log R_K^*)^2\, (R_K + \log(mH))\}\,.$$

Since $2c_{11} < (25(r+3)N)^{15(r+3)}$ we get (3).

It follows from a theorem of SIEGEL [24] that

$$R_K h_K < c_{12} D_K^{1/2} \,(\log D_K)^{N-1}$$

with $c_{12} = 8N^2$ and so from (40) we obtain

$$\max_{1 \leqq i \leqq k} \overline{|x_i|} < \exp\{2c_{11} c_{12}^2 N^2 h_K^{-1} D_K^{1/2} (\log D_K)^{2N} (h_K^{-1} D_K^{1/2} + \log(mH))\}\,.$$

In view of $2 \cdot c_{11} \cdot c_{12}^2 N < (25(r+3)N)^{15(r+3)}$ this implies (4).

Proof of the Corollary of Theorem 1. Let a_0 be the leading coefficient of $F(x, 1)$. (5) can be written in the form

$$\mathrm{Norm}_{K/L}(x - \alpha y) = \mu / a_0\,.$$

We have

$$H(\mu/a_0) \leqq (\overline{|\mu|} + \overline{|a_0|})^l \leqq (2m + 2\mathscr{H})^l\,.$$

Denote by $F^{(1)}(x,y)=F(x,y),\ldots,F^{(l)}(x,y)$ the polynomials whose coefficients are conjugates of the corresponding coefficients of $F(x,y)$ over L. Then $\mathcal{F}(x,y)=$ $=\prod_{i=1}^{l} F^{(i)}(x,y)\in\mathbf{Z}[x,y]$ and the maximum absolute value of the coefficients of $\mathcal{F}$ is less than $(n+1)^{l-1}\mathcal{H}^l$. Since $\mathcal{F}(x,1)$ is divisible by the minimal defining polynomial of α over $\mathbf{Z}$, we get (cf. SIEGEL [23], Hilfssatz III)

$$H(\alpha)\leqq N!(n+1)^{l-1}\mathcal{H}^l .$$

Now (6) and (7) follow immediately from (3) and (4).

Using BAKER's [4] and STARK's [26] arguments, we get $n^{5n}(\mathcal{H}/|a_0|)^{2n-2}$ as an upper bound for the absolute value of the discriminant of $a_0^{-1}F(x,1)$. Since the relative discriminant $D_{K/L}(a_0\alpha)$ is $a_0^{n(n-1)}$ times this, we get

$$|D_{K/L}(a_0\alpha)|\leqq n^{5n}\mathcal{H}^{2n-2}|a_0|^{n^3-3n+2}.$$

Repeating this argument for each conjugate of $F(x,1)$ over L, we obtain

$$\overline{|D_{K/L}(a_0\alpha)|}\leqq n^{5n}\mathcal{H}^{n(n-1)}.$$

So we have

$$D_K\leqq|N_{L/\mathbf{Q}}(D_{K/L}(a_0\alpha))||D_L|^n\leqq(n^{5n}\mathcal{H}^{n-1})^N|D_L|^n$$

and (8) follows from (7).

Proof of Theorem 2. By the assumption made on $\alpha_1,\ldots,\alpha_k$ $l(\mathbf{x})=x_0+x_1\alpha_1+$ $+\ldots+x_k\alpha_k\neq 0$. Put

$$N_{K/L}(l(\mathbf{x}))=\mu . \tag{41}$$

Let a denote the product of the leading coefficients of the minimal defining polynomials of $\alpha_1,\ldots,\alpha_k$. Then $a^n\mu$ is an algebraic integer in L. There exists a unit ε in L such that for $\mu'=\mu\varepsilon^n$

$$\overline{|\mu'|}\leqq|N_{L/\mathbf{Q}}(\mu)|^{1/l}\exp\{6nl^{3l-1}R_L\}$$

holds (cf. [10], Lemma 3). So

$$H(\mu')\leqq a^n(2\overline{|\mu'|})^l\leqq H^{kn}|N_{L/\mathbf{Q}}(\mu')|\exp\{6nl^{3l}R_L\}. \tag{42}$$

From (41) we get

$$N_{K/L}(\varepsilon x_0+\varepsilon x_1\alpha_1+\ldots+\varepsilon x_k\alpha_k)=\mu'. \tag{43}$$

By Theorem 1 we have

$$X = \max_{0 \leq i \leq k} \overline{|x_i \varepsilon|} < \exp\{CR_K(\log R_K^*)^2 (R_K + \log H + \log H(\mu'))\},$$

whence, by (42),

$$|N_{L/\mathbf{Q}}(\mu')| > \rho X^{\tau_4} \tag{44}$$

where $\rho = H^{-kn-1} \exp\{-R_K - 6nl^{31}R_L\}$.

From (43) it follows that

$$\prod_{v \in \Omega} \|\varepsilon x_0 + \varepsilon x_1 \alpha_1 + \ldots + \varepsilon x_k \alpha_k\|_v = |N_{L/\mathbf{Q}}(\mu')|. \tag{45}$$

Since

$$\|\varepsilon x_0 + \varepsilon x_1 \alpha_1 + \ldots + \varepsilon x_k \alpha_k\|_v \leq (1 + k + kH)^{m_v} X^{m_v}$$

for each $v \in \Omega$, we obtain from (45)

$$\prod_{v \in \Gamma} \|\varepsilon x_0 + \ldots + \varepsilon x_k \alpha_k\|_v \geq \frac{|N_{L/\mathbf{Q}}(\mu')|}{((1 + k + kH)X)^{N - s' - 2t'}}.$$

This together with (44) implies (11).

Proof of the Corollary of Theorem 2. Let $-y$ be the nearest integer to $x_1\alpha_1 + \ldots + x_k\alpha_k$. Then we have

$$\|x_1\alpha_1 + \ldots + x_k\alpha_k\| = |y + x_1\alpha_1 + \ldots + x_k\alpha_k| > 0.$$

In case $\|x_1\alpha_1 + \ldots + x_k\alpha_k\| \geq 1$ (12) obviously holds. If $\|x_1\alpha_1 + \ldots + x_k\alpha_k\| < 1$, we obtain $|y| \leq 1 + k(1 + H)|\mathbf{x}|$. Applying now Theorem 2 to the linear form $y + x_1\alpha_1 + \ldots + x_k\alpha_k$, (12) follows at once.

Proof of Theorem 3. We shall follow the proof of Theorem 2. Denote by a the leading coefficient in the minimal defining polynomial of α over $\mathbf{Z}$. There exists a unit ε in L such that

$$N_{K/L}(\varepsilon a \vartheta - \varepsilon a \alpha) = \mu \tag{46}$$

and

$$H(\mu') \leq |N_{L/\mathbf{Q}}(\mu')| \cdot H^n \exp\{6nl^{31}R_L\}.$$

By Theorem 1 we have

$$\begin{aligned} \max(\overline{|\varepsilon a|}, \overline{|\varepsilon a \alpha|}) &< \exp\{CR_K(\log R_K^*)^2 (R_K + \log H + \log H(\mu'))\} < \\ &< \exp\{CR_K(\log R_K^*)^2 (R_K + (n+1)\log H + 6nl^{31}R_L + \log |N_{L/\mathbf{Q}}(\mu')|)\}. \end{aligned} \tag{47}$$

Since

$$H(\alpha)=H\left(\frac{\varepsilon a\alpha}{\varepsilon a}\right)\leqq(\lceil\overline{\varepsilon a}\rceil+\lceil\overline{\varepsilon a\alpha}\rceil)^l,$$

it follows from (47) that

(48) $$|N_{L/\mathbf{Q}}(\mu')|>\rho' H(\alpha)^{\tau_6}$$

where $\rho'=H^{-(n+1)}\exp\{-R_K-6nl^{3l}R_L\}$.

From (46) we get

(49) $$\prod_{v\in\Omega}\|a\vartheta-a\alpha\|_v=|N_{L/\mathbf{Q}}(\mu')|.$$

In view of the estimate

$$\|a\vartheta-a\alpha\|_v\leqq(4H)^{m_v}H(\alpha)^{m_v}$$

(49) and (48) imply

$$\prod_{v\in\Gamma}\|\vartheta-\alpha\|_v>\rho'(4H)^{-nl+s'+2t'}H(\alpha)^{-nl+s'+2t'+\tau_6}a^{-s'-2t'}$$

and this proves (14).

If α is not integral, by $a\leqq H(\alpha)$ we get (15).

References

[1] A. Baker, Rational approximations to certain algebraic numbers, *Proc. London Math. Soc.* (*3*) **14** (1964), 385–98.

[2] A. Baker, Rational approximations to $\sqrt[3]{2}$ and other algebraic numbers, *Quart. J. Math. Oxford*, **15** (1964), 375–83.

[3] A. Baker, Simultaneous rational approximations to certain algebraic numbers, *Proc. Camb. Phil. Soc.*, **63** (1967), 693–702.

[4] A. Baker, Contributions to the theory of Diophantine equations, *Philos. Trans. Roy. Soc. London, Ser. A*, **263** (1968), 173–208.

[5] A. Baker, *The theory of linear forms in logarithms, Transcendence theory: advances and applications*, pp. 1–27 (Ed. by A. Baker and D. Masser). Academic Press, London–New York–San Francisco, 1977.

[6] E. Dobrowolski, On the maximal modulus of conjugates of an algebraic integer, *Bull. Acad. Polon. Sci.*, to appear.

[7] N. I. Feldman, Estimation of an incomplete linear form in certain algebraic numbers (Russian), *Mat. Zametki*, **7** (1970), 569–80.

[8] N. I. Feldman, Diophantine equations with a finite number of solutions (Russian), *Vestnik Moskov. Univ. Ser. I*, **26** (1971), 52–58.

[9] N. I. Feldman, An effective refinement of the exponent in Liouville's theorem (in Russian), *Izv. Akad. Nauk SSSR*, **35** (1971), 973–90.

[10] K. Győry, On the solutions of linear diophantine equations in algebraic integers of bounded norm, *Annales Univ. Sci. Budapest*, to appear.

[11] K. GYŐRY and Z. Z. PAPP, Effective estimates for the integer solutions of norm form and discriminant form equations, *Publ. Math.*, to appear.

[12] S. V. KOTOV, The Thue–Mahler equation in relative fields (Russian), *Acta Arith.*, **27** (1975), 293–315.

[13] S. V. KOTOV and V. G. SPRINDŽUK, An effective analysis of the Thue–Mahler equation in relative fields (Russian), *Dokl. Akad. Nauk BSSR*, **17** (1973), 393–95.

[14] S. V. KOTOV and V. G. SPRINDŽUK, The Thue–Mahler equation in relative fields and approximation of algebraic numbers by algebraic numbers (in Russian), *Izv. Akad. Nauk SSSR*, **41** (1977), 723–51.

[15] J. LIOUVILLE, Sur des classes très étendues de quantités dont la valeur n'est ni algébrique, ni même réductible à des irrationelles algébriques, *C. R. Acad. Sci. Paris*, **18** (1844), 883–85 and 910–11.

[16] CHARLES F. OSGOOD, The simultane diophantine approximation of certain k-th roots, *Proc. Camb. Phil. Soc.*, **67** (1970), 75–86.

[17] CHARLES F. OSGOOD, On the simultaneous diophantine approximation of values of certain algebraic functions, *Acta Arith.*, **19** (1971), 343–86.

[18] A. J. VAN DER POORTEN and J. H. LOXTON, Multiplicative relations in number fields, *Bull. Austral. Math. Soc.*, **16** (1977), 83–98. *Corregindum and addendum*, ibid. **17** (1977), 151–55.

[19] K. F. ROTH, Rational approximations to algebraic numbers, *Mathematika*, **2** (1955), 1–20.

[20] W. M. SCHMIDT, Simultaneous approximation to algebraic numbers by rationals, *Acta Math.*, **125** (1970), 189–201.

[21] W. M. SCHMIDT, Linearformen mit algebraischen Koeffizienten, II., *Math. Ann.*, **191** (1971), 1–20.

[22] W. M. SCHMIDT, Approximations to algebraic numbers, *Enseignement Math.*, **17** (1971), 187–253.

[23] C. L. SIEGEL, Approximation algebraischer Zahlen, *Math. Z.*, **10** (1921), 173–213.

[24] C. L. SIEGEL, Abschätzung von Einheiten, *Nachr. Akad. Wiss. Göttingen, Math.-Phys. Kl. II* (1969), 71–86.

[25] V. G. SPRINDŽUK, On an estimate for solutions of Thue's equation (Russian), *Izv. Akad. Nauk SSSR*, **36** (1972), 712–41.

[26] H. M. STARK, Effective estimates of solutions of some diophantine equations, *Acta Arith.*, **24** (1973), 251–59.

Added in proof. The results of the present paper have recently been generalized (with other estimates) by the first author (*see e.g. Archiv der Math.*, **35** (1980), 438–446, and *Publ. Math.* (*Debrecen*), **28** (1981), 89–98).

KOSSUTH LAJOS UNIVERSITY
DEBRECEN
HUNGARY

EXPERIMENTAL INSTITUTE
OF THE HUNGARIAN POST-OFFICE ADMINISTRATION
BUDAPEST, HUNGARY

Studies in Pure Mathematics
To the Memory of Paul Turán

On the first and second main theorem in Turán's theory of power sums

by

G. HALÁSZ (Budapest)

A basic inequality of TURÁN [1] states

$$|f(0)| \leqq (2e(a+1))^n \max_{a \leqq x \leqq a+1} |f(x)| \quad (a>0) \tag{1}$$

for

$$f(x) = \sum_{j=1}^{n} b_j e^{\lambda_j x}$$

with arbitrary complex numbers b_j, λ_j subject only to $\operatorname{Re} \lambda_j \geqq 0$. It has a number of applications in various problems of analysis (see [1] or a forthcoming more complete English edition [2]). For some of these applications it would be important to have the accurate constant factor up to $\exp(o(n))$ in this and related results.

We shall only be concerned with asymptotic behaviour. By taking limits in an obvious way, the inequality remains valid for any polynomial of degree n as $f(x)$ and Tchebycheff's polynomials belonging to the interval $[a, a+1]$ show that Turán's constant is rather sharp as $a \to +\infty$. This is not the case for $a \to +0$ when $2e(a+1) \to 2e$ whereas one would expect 1 as limit here. This is the content of our

Theorem 1.

$$|f(0)| \leqq 30 n^2 e^{6n\sqrt{a}} \max_{a \leqq x \leqq a+1} |f(x)|$$

for $\operatorname{Re} \lambda_j \geqq 0$, $0 < a \leqq 1$.

The dependence on a is sharp as the above Tchebycheff polynomials show. It would be interesting to see whether they also furnish the best possible constant in place of our 6. No attempt is made here and in the sequel to fully exploit our method as far as constants like this or less important powers of n as factors are concerned.

A significant special case $f(t)=g(e^{it})$ of (1) where

$$g(z)=\sum_{j=1}^{n} b_j z^{n_j}$$

is a polynomial of n terms (though of arbitrary degree) estimates max $|g(z)|$ on $|z|=1$ by the maximum on a subarc. $f(t)$ being periodic then, this leads to estimating $|f(0)|$ by values on both sides, e.g. by

$$\max_{a\leqq|x|\leqq a+1} |f(x)|.$$

For small a nothing better than Theorem 1 is known whereas $\sqrt{a}$ can probably be replaced by a in this case which, if true, would be sharp.[1]

Now, Turán derives his inequality (1) from the following discrete version, his first main theorem

$$(2)\qquad |s_0|<\left(\frac{2e(m+n)}{n}\right)^n \max_{m+1\leqq\nu\leqq m+n} |s_\nu| \quad (m\geqq 0 \text{ integer})$$

where

$$s_\nu=\sum_{j=1}^{n} b_j z_j^\nu$$

with $|z_j|\geqq 1$ (by choosing $m=[an]$, $z_j=\exp\left(\frac{a}{m+1}\lambda_j\right)$ where

$$(3)\qquad |s_\nu|=\left|f\left(\frac{a}{m+1}\nu\right)\right|\leqq \max_{a\leqq x\leqq a+1} |f(x)| \quad (m+1\leqq\nu\leqq m+n).$$

For this, independently by de Bruijn and Makai (see [2]), the sharp factor was also determined:

$$\sum_{l=0}^{n-1}\binom{m+l}{l}2^l$$

which even for $m=0$ grows exponentially. In the application to the continuous case there is, however, no reason for using only n (= the number of terms) values of ν and Theorem 1 will in fact be a corollary of the following inequality for longer intervals.

[1] For this case of two intervals it was only shown by the author that Turán type inequalities hold without any condition on λ_j. This will appear in [2].

Theorem 1′.

$$|s_0| \leqq \left(\frac{\sqrt{m}\,N}{n} + \sqrt{N}\right) e^{n\left(\frac{4n}{N}+6\sqrt{\frac{m}{N}}\right)} \max_{m+1 \leqq v \leqq m+N} |s_v|$$

for $|z_j| \geqq 1$, $N \geqq n$.

It is interesting to note that already for $N = [cmn^2/\log n]$ the factor will become a power of n and m.

TURÁN's second main theorem concerns the deeper case when only one of the z_j is known to be large:

$$\min_{l=1,\ldots,n} \left|\sum_{j=1}^{l} b_j\right| \leqq \left(\frac{8e(m+n)}{n}\right)^n \max_{m+1 \leqq v \leqq m+n} |s_v|$$

if $1 = |z_1| \geqq |z_2| \geqq \ldots \geqq |z_n|$ (see [1] or [2]).

This has numerous applications first of all in analytic number theory and that is obviously the reason why he in [2] raised the problem of generalizing this similarly to Theorem 1' for longer intervals.

Theorem 2.

$$\min_{l=1,\ldots,n} \left|\sum_{j=1}^{l} b_j\right| \leqq \frac{4N^{3/2}}{n} \exp\left[30n\left(\frac{1}{\log(N/n)} + \frac{1}{\log(N/m)}\right)\right] \cdot \max_{m+1 \leqq v \leqq m+N} |s_v|$$

for $m, n \leqq N$, $1 = |z_1| \geqq |z_2| \geqq \ldots \geqq |z_n|$.

Because of only a logarithmic improvement for N large compared to m and n this, however, is not likely to be useful in applications.

Proof of Theorem 1'. We start off with Turán's method in a form suitable for both his main theorems.

With coefficients c_v $(m+1 \leqq v \leqq m+N)$ to be determined later we have

$$\sum_{v=m+1}^{m+N} c_v s_v = \sum_{j=1}^{n} b_j \sum_{v=m+1}^{m+N} c_v z_j^v = \sum_{j=1}^{n} b_j = s_0$$

provided that

$$\sum_{v=m+1}^{m+N} c_v z_j^v = 1 \quad (j = 1, \ldots, n)$$

implying

(4) $$|s_0| \leqq \max_{m+1 \leqq v \leqq m+N} |s_v| \sum_{v=m+1}^{m+N} |c_v| \,.$$

We thus have to construct a polynomial

$$P(z)=1-\sum_{\nu=m+1}^{m+N} c_\nu z^\nu \tag{5}$$

vanishing at all the z_j and having a gap from $\nu=2$ to $\nu=m$. We seek it in the form

$$P(z)=R(z)\,Q(z)$$

where $R(z)$, a polynomial of degree $\leqq N$ is to take care of the first condition:

$$R(z_j)=0 \quad (j=1, \ldots, n)$$

and $Q(z)$ of the second: assuming that $R(z)$ does not vanish for $|z|<1$ we define

$$\frac{1}{R(z)}=\sum_{l=0}^{\infty} a_l z^l \quad (|z|<1)$$

and

$$Q(z)=\sum_{l=0}^{m} a_l z^l .$$

$P(z)$ will then in fact have the desired form and in order to estimate its coefficients we represent it on $|z|=1$ as

$$\begin{aligned} P(z)&=R(z)\frac{1}{2\pi i}\int\limits_{|\xi|=r}\frac{d\xi}{R(\xi z)(1-\xi)\xi^{m+1}}= \\ &=\frac{R(z)z^{m+1}}{2\pi i}\int\limits_{|\xi|=r}\frac{d\xi}{R(\xi)(z-\xi)\xi^{m+1}}. \end{aligned} \tag{6} \qquad (r<1,\,|z|=1)$$

In Turán's case $N=n$ the unique choice up to a constant factor of $R(z)$ is

$$\prod_{j=1}^{n}\left(1-\frac{z}{z_j}\right).$$

(In fact, as is easy to see, $P(z)$ itself is also uniquely determined by the requirements.) Here we have, however, more liberty in choosing it and in order to make it neither small nor large as the above integral formula requires we put

$$R(z)=\prod_{j=1}^{n} h\left(\frac{z}{z_j}\right)$$

where $h(z)$ is a polynomial of degree $k=[N/n]$ as defined in Lemma below. The qualitative requirements are obviously satisfied and by $|z_j|\geqq 1$ and (iii) of Lemma we also have

$$|R(z)|\leqq(\max_{|z|=1}|h(z)|)^n\leqq\left(1+\frac{2}{k}\right)^n<e^{\frac{2n}{k}}\quad(|z|=1)$$

and by (iv) of Lemma

$$|R(\xi)|\geqq(\min_{|\xi|\leqq r}|h(\xi)|)^n\geqq e^{-\frac{4n}{k}\frac{r}{1-r}}\quad(|\xi|=r).$$

(6) then gives, using also $k\geqq\frac{N}{2n}$,

$$|P(z)|\leqq\frac{1}{1-r}e^{\frac{2n}{k}+\frac{4n}{k}\frac{r}{1-r}}r^{-m}\leqq\frac{1}{1-r}e^{\frac{4n^2}{N}+\frac{8n^2}{N}\frac{r}{1-r}+m\frac{1-r}{r}}.\quad(|z|=1).$$

Optimizing the exponential part by taking

$$\frac{1-r}{r}=\sqrt{\frac{8n^2}{mN}},\quad r=\frac{1}{1+\sqrt{\frac{8n^2}{mN}}}$$

we get

$$|P(z)|<\left(\frac{\sqrt{mN}}{n}+1\right)e^{\frac{4n^2}{N}+6n\sqrt{\frac{m}{N}}}\quad(|z|=1).$$

For the coefficients in (5) of $P(z)$ this implies by the Cauchy–Schwartz inequality and Parseval's formula

$$\sum_{\nu=m+1}^{m+N}|c_\nu|\leqq\sqrt{N\sum_{\nu=m+1}^{m+N}|c_\nu|^2}<\sqrt{N}\left(\frac{\sqrt{mN}}{n}+1\right)e^{\frac{4n^2}{N}+6n\sqrt{\frac{m}{N}}}$$

and recalling (4) Theorem 1′ follows.

Proof of Theorem 1. We define as in (3) $z_j=\exp\left(\frac{a}{m+1}\lambda_j\right)$ with $m=[aN]$ in which case

$$|s_\nu|=\left|f\left(\frac{a}{m+1}\nu\right)\right|\max_{a\leqq x\leqq a+1}|f(x)|.\quad(m+1\leqq\nu\leqq m+N)$$

The factor in Theorem 1′ then becomes

$$\left(\frac{N\sqrt{m}}{n}+\sqrt{N}\right)e^{\frac{4n^2}{N}+6n\sqrt{\frac{m}{N}}}<30n^2e^{6n\sqrt{a}}$$

e.g. for $N=4n^2$ and the proof is completed.

Lemma. *For every integer k there exists a polynomial h(z) of degree k such that*

$$\text{(i)}\quad h(0)=1,\quad \text{(ii)}\quad h(1)=0,\quad \text{(iii)}\quad |h(z)|\leqq 1+\frac{2}{k},$$

$$\text{(iv)}\quad |h(z)|\geqq e^{-\frac{4|z|}{k(1-|z|)}}. \qquad (|z|\leqq 1).$$

The order of magnitude in (iii) is sharp. For the problem mentioned concerning the constant 6 in Theorem 1 it would be interesting to find the best value in place of our 2.[2]

Proof of Lemma. The function

$$\frac{z}{c-z}=\sum_{l=1}^{\infty}\left(\frac{z}{c}\right)^{l} \quad (|z|<1, c>1)$$

maps the unit disc onto the disc with $\left[-\frac{1}{c+1},\frac{1}{c-1}\right]$ as diameter. This being convex,

$$h^*(z)=\sum_{l=1}^{k}\left(1-\frac{l}{k+1}\right)\left(\frac{z}{c}\right)^{l} \quad (|z|<1),$$

according to a classical result of Fejér, also takes values in this disc. Hence, if

$$h^*(1)\geqq\frac{1}{2(c-1)},$$

then

$$|h^*(z)-h^*(1)|\leqq h^*(1)+\frac{1}{c+1} \quad (|z|<1).$$

In fact we have

$$h^*(1)=\sum_{l=1}^{k}\left(1-\frac{l}{k+1}\right)\frac{1}{c^l}\geqq\sum_{l=1}^{\infty}\frac{1}{c^l}-\frac{1}{k+1}\sum_{l=1}^{\infty}\frac{l}{c^l}=$$

$$=\frac{1}{c-1}-\frac{c}{(k+1)(c-1)^2}=\frac{1}{2(c-1)}$$

where we have chosen $c=\frac{k+1}{k-1}$ for $k>1$ (the lemma is trivial for $k=1$). Let

$$h^{**}(z)=\frac{h^*(1)-h^*(z)}{h^*(1)}$$

[2] Theorems 1, 1′ and Lemma are earlier results of the author (see [3]). Another proof has been later given for Lemma by RAHMAN and STENGER [4]. (The origin of the problem due to misunderstanding incorrectly stated there.)

Then $h^{**}(0)=1$, $h^{**}(1)=0$ and

$$|h^{**}(z)| \leqq \frac{h^{*}(1)+\dfrac{1}{c+1}}{h^{*}(1)} \leqq 1+\frac{2(c-1)}{c+1}=1+\frac{2}{k}.$$

As for (iv), it might have zeros ρ_i in $|z|<1$. But then

$$h(z)=\frac{h^{**}(z)\prod \rho_i}{\prod \dfrac{\rho_i-z}{1-z\bar{\rho}_i}},$$

also a polynomial of degree k, is different from zero for $|z|<1$, $h(0)=1$, $h(1)=0$, and

$$|h(z)|=|h^{**}(z)|\prod|\rho_i| \leqq |h^{**}(z)| \leqq 1+\frac{2}{k}(|z|=1).$$

(iv) can now be deduced by general function theoretic means.

$$u(z)=\log h(z)=\sum_{l=1}^{\infty} d_l z^l$$

is regular for $|z|<1$ having real part at most $\log(1+2/k)<2/k$.

$$\frac{2}{k}-u(z)=\frac{2}{k}-\sum_{l=1}^{\infty} d_l z^l$$

is then of positive real part and so

$$|d_l r^l|=\frac{2}{2\pi}\left|\int_0^{2\pi} e^{-il\varphi}\,\mathrm{Re}\left(\frac{2}{k}-u(re^{i\varphi})\right)d\varphi\right| \leqq$$

$$\leqq \frac{2}{2\pi}\int_0^{2\pi} \mathrm{Re}\left(\frac{2}{k}-u(re^{i\varphi})\right)d\varphi=\frac{4}{k} \quad (r<1)$$

and $r \to 1-0$ gives

$$|d_l| \leqq \frac{4}{k},$$

$$|u(z)| \leqq \frac{4}{k}\sum_{l=1}^{\infty}|z|^l=\frac{4|z|}{k(1-|z|)},$$

$$\log|h(z)|=\mathrm{Re}\,u(z) \geqq -\frac{4|z|}{k(1-|z|)}.$$

Q.e.d.

Proof of Theorem 2. Keeping the condition $R(z_j)=0$ $(j=1, \ldots, n)$ on the polynomial $R(z)$ of degree $\leqq N$, the integral formula (6) defines a $P(z)$ with the same properties as in the proof of Theorem 1′ if $R(z)\neq 0$ for $|z|\leqq r$. We have, however, no information on $\min|z_j|$ and let us, therefore, see what (6) gives for arbitrary $r<1$.

We can replace integration on $|\xi|=r$ by $|\xi|=R\to\infty$, the contribution of the latter tending to 0. Collecting residues we get for the right-hand side of (6) the value

$$R(z)z^{m+1}\left(\frac{1}{R(z)z^{m+1}}-\sum_{|\rho|>r}\frac{1}{R'(\rho)(z-\rho)\rho^{m+1}}\right)=$$

$$=1-\sum_{|\rho|>r}\frac{R(z)z^{m+1}}{R'(\rho)(z-\rho)\rho^{m+1}}\qquad(|z|=1, r<1)$$

where ρ runs through zeros of $R(z)$. This is again a polynomial of the form

$$P(z)=1-\sum_{\nu=m+1}^{m+N}c_\nu z^\nu \tag{7}$$

having the value 0 for all ρ with $|\rho|>r$ and 1 for $|\rho|<r$. (We have tacitly assumed that the zeros avoid $|\xi|=r$ and that they are all simple but the latter assumption, by taking limits, can obviously be dropped.) This leads to the formula

$$\sum_{\nu=m+1}^{m+N}c_\nu s_\nu=\sum_{j=1}^{n}b_j\sum_{\nu=m+1}^{m+N}c_\nu z_j^\nu=\sum_{|z_j|>r}b_j\,.$$

Owing to the ordering of the z_j, the last sum is a partial sum of the b_j, non-empty because of $|z_1|=1>r$ and so

$$\max_{m+1\leqq\nu\leqq m+N}|s_\nu|\sum_{\nu=m+1}^{m+N}|c_\nu|\geqq\min_{l=1,\ldots,n}\left|\sum_{j=1}^{l}b_j\right|. \tag{8}$$

Thus it again suffices to estimate (6) for any $r<1$.

We again use Lemma with $k=[N/n]$ but consider, in order to remain in the unit disc ($|z_j|\leqq 1$!),

$$\prod_{j=1}^{n}h(z\bar{z}_j)\,.$$

This has zeros for $1/\bar{z}_j$ and we reflect them into z_j by defining

$$R(z)=\prod_{j=1}^{n}h(z\bar{z}_j)\frac{z-z_j}{1-z\bar{z}_j}\,.$$

Lemma yields

$$|R(z)| \leqq \left(1+\frac{2}{k}\right)^n < e^{\frac{2n}{k}} \quad (|z|=1),$$

$$|R(\xi)| \geqq e^{-\frac{4nr}{k(1-r)}} \prod_{j=1}^{n} \left|\frac{\xi - z_j}{1-\xi \bar{z}_j}\right| \geqq$$

$$\geqq e^{-\frac{4nr}{k(1-r)} - \sum_{j=1}^{n} \log \frac{1-r|z_j|}{|r-|z_j||}}. \quad (|\xi|=r)$$

These give in (6)

(9) $$|P(z)| \leqq \frac{1}{1-r} e^{\frac{2n}{k} + \frac{4nr}{k(1-r)} + \sum_{j=1}^{n} \log \frac{1-r|z_j|}{|r-|z_j||} + m\frac{1-r}{r}}. \quad (|z|=1).$$

To eliminate the dependence on z_j we observe that for $0 \leqq s \leqq 1$

$$\int_{-1}^{1} \frac{1}{1-u^2} \log \frac{1-us}{|u-s|} du,$$

(applying the transformation $u = \frac{v+s}{1+vs}$ that leaves the hyperbolic length element $dv/(1-v^2)$ invariant), has, independently of s, the value

$$\int_{-1}^{1} \frac{1}{1-v^2} \log \frac{1}{|v|} dv = \frac{\pi^2}{4}$$

(by expanding $1/(1-v^2)$ and integrating term by term by parts). Hence

$$\int_{-1}^{1} \frac{1}{1-u^2} \sum_{j=1}^{n} \log \frac{1-u|z_j|}{|u-|z_j||} du \leqq \frac{\pi^2}{4} n.$$

For $1/2 \leqq \alpha < \beta < 1$ to be chosen later this implies the existence of an r in $[\alpha, \beta]$ fulfilling

$$\sum_{j=1}^{n} \log \frac{1-r|z_j|}{|r-|z_j||} \leqq \frac{\frac{\pi^2}{4} n}{\int_{\alpha}^{\beta} \frac{du}{1-u^2}} < \frac{5n}{\log \frac{1-\alpha}{1-\beta}}.$$

With this r, using also $k \geqq N/2n$, (9) becomes

$$(10) \qquad |P(z)| < \frac{1}{1-\beta} e^{\frac{4n^2}{N} + \frac{8n^2}{N(1-\beta)} + \frac{5n}{\log(1-\alpha)/(1-\beta)} + 2m(1-\alpha)} . \quad (|z|=1).$$

We balance the last three terms by setting, with the abbreviation $K=(1-\alpha)/(1-\beta)>1$,

$$\frac{n^2}{N(1-\beta)} = \frac{n}{\log K} = m(1-\alpha),$$

i.e.

$$(11) \qquad 1-\beta = \frac{n \log K}{N}, \quad 1-\alpha = \frac{n}{m \log K},$$

$$K = \frac{1-\alpha}{1-\beta} = \frac{N}{m \log^2 K}, \quad K \log^2 K = \frac{N}{m} \quad (K>1).$$

From the latter it follows

$$(12) \qquad K \geqq \max\sqrt{N/m};\ 1, 7)$$

and our estimation (10) becomes

$$(13) \qquad |P(z)| \leqq \frac{N}{n \log K} e^{\frac{4n^2}{N} + \frac{15n}{\log K}} \leqq \frac{2N}{n} e^{\frac{4n^2}{N} + \frac{30n}{\log(N/m)}}$$

provided that the condition $\alpha \geqq 1/2$ is satisfied. If not, then by (11) and (12)

$$\frac{n}{m \log\sqrt{(N/m)}} \geqq \frac{1}{2},$$

and putting $\alpha = 1/2$ the last term in (10) becomes

$$2m(1-\alpha) = m \leqq \frac{4n}{\log(N/m)}$$

and in order to balance the two others we set

$$\frac{n^2}{N(1-\beta)} = \frac{n}{\log K},$$

i.e.

$$1-\beta = \frac{n \log K}{N}, \quad K = \frac{1/2}{1-\beta},$$

$$K \log K = \frac{N}{2n}$$

implying

$$K \geqq \max\left(\sqrt{(N/m)}; 1, 3\right)$$

in which case we have for (10)

$$|P(z)| \leqq \frac{N}{n \log K} e^{\frac{4n^2}{N} + \frac{13n}{\log K} + m} \leqq 4 \frac{N}{n} e^{\frac{4n^2}{016x} + \frac{26n}{\log(N/n)} + \frac{4n}{\log(N/m)}}.$$

Comparing with (13) we get in any case

$$|P(z)| \leqq 4 \frac{N}{n} e^{30n\left(\frac{1}{\log(N/n)} + \frac{1}{\log(N/m)}\right)}$$

and recalling (7) and (8) the proof is completed the same way as that of Theorem 1′.

References

[1] TURÁN, P., *Über eine neue Methode der Analysis und ihre Anwendungen*, Akadémiai Kiadó, Budapest, 1953.

[2] TURÁN, P., *On a new method in the analysis and its applications*, to appear in the Wiley Interscience Tracts series.

[3] HALÁSZ, G., Über die Turánsche Ungleichung für Lückenpolynome, *Tagungsbericht*. 7/1972, *Math. Forschungsinstitut Oberwolfach, Funktionentheorie.*

[4] RAHMAN, Q. I. and STENGER, F., An extremal problem for polynomials with a prescribed zero, *Proc. Amer.. Math. Soc.*, **43** (1974), 84–90.

MATHEMATICAL INSTITUTE
OF THE HUNGARIAN ACADEMY OF SCIENCES
H-1053 BUDAPEST, REÁLTANODA U. 13–15.
HUNGARY

Studies in Pure Mathematics
To the Memory of Paul Turán

Generalized ramsey theory VIII.
The size ramsey number of small graphs

by

FRANK HARARY and ZEVI MILLER (Ann Arbor)

Abstract

The ramsey number $r(F)$ of a graph F with no isolates has been much studied. We now investigate its size Ramsey number $\zeta(F)$ defined as the minimum q such that there exists a graph G with q edges for which every 2-coloring of $E(G)$ has a monochromatic F. The size ramsey number of a graph has also been studied by CHVÁTAL, ERDŐS, FAUDREE, ROUSSEAU and SCHELP. We obtain the exact values of $\zeta(F)$ for stars, stripes and several small graphs. We conclude with a list of unsolved problems.

1. Introduction

The generalized ramsey number $r(F)$ of a graph F has been defined [1] as the smallest integer p such that every 2-coloring of the edges of K_p yields a monochromatic F. This number and variants of it have been the subject of numerous investigations, including the first seven papers [1–7] in this series. We now consider the *size ramsey number* $\zeta(F)$ defined as the minimum number of edges that a graph must have in order that any 2-coloring of its edges yield a monochromatic F. Independently, ERDŐS, FAUDREE, SCHELP and ROUSSEAU [18] discovered and studied the same invariant, denoting it by $\hat{r}(F)$.

Some relationships between $\zeta(F)$ and $r(F)$ are immediately apparent. The fact that $\zeta(F)$ is finite follows from the obvious inequality $\zeta(F) \leq \binom{r(F)}{2}$. For some F, for example $F = P_3$, we have the equality $\zeta(F) = \binom{r(F)}{2}$. This is not always the case, however, as shown by the numbers $\zeta(2K_2) = 3$, $r(2K_2) = 5$, and several others.

Our object is to find the numbers $\zeta(F)$ for the "small graphs" F having at most four points and no isolates (other than $K_4 - x$ for which we obtain an upper bound).

All terminology not explicitly defined in this paper will follow the book [8]. In particular, all graphs are finite with no loops or multiple edges. The number of points in G is $p(G)$ and the number of lines is $q(G)$. If $v \in V(G)$, then its neighborhood $N(v)$ is the set of points adjacent to v. If S and T are disjoint subsets of $V(G)$, we define $X(S, T)$ as the set of edges in G having one point in S and the other in T. Also if $S \subset V(G)$, let $\langle S \rangle$ be the subgraph of G induced by the points of S. The degree of a point v will be denoted by $d(v)$.

If there is a 2-coloring of $E(G)$ with no monochromatic F, it is called an *F-free coloring* of G, and G is said to be *F-free colorable*. The notation $G \to F$ will mean that in any 2-coloring of $E(G)$, a monochromatic F occurs. If $G \to F$, and $G-x$ is F-free colorable for every edge x, then G is called *edge minimal with respect to* $G \to F$. Thus if F is connected, then G must be connected. When we say a *coloring of G* or a *2-coloring of G*, we will mean a 2-coloring of $E(G)$.

In the figures which illustrate 2-colorings of various graphs, we will use the colors red and green with a solid line indicating red, and a dashed line green. A wavy line will indicate a missing edge.

There are graphs F for which the size ramsey numbers are easily calculated, and examples of these are given in Theorem 1. In general we have found that the exact determination of ζ requires rather involved arguments, even for some of the small graphs. We give such arguments in Theorem 2, and we derive the upper bound $\zeta(K_4-x) \leqq 44$ in Theorem 3, the corresponding lower bound still being open. Our experience shows that the exact determination of $\zeta(F)$ for graphs F which are not "small" or complete is extremely difficult, and in most cases intractable when the number of points exceeds five.

2. Size ramsey numbers for stars and stripes

The numbers $\zeta(F)$ for stars and stripes are given in Theorem 1. We begin by stating as a lemma some well known basic observations.

Lemma 1a. *The size ramsey number ζ of any graph G with q lines and ramsey number r satisfies the inequalities*

$$2q-1 \leqq \zeta \leqq \binom{r}{2}.$$

Proof. The upper bound follows immediately from the definitions. For the lower bound, observe that every graph H with at most $2q-2$ edges can be 2-colored so that each color appears on at most $q-1$ edges. Such a graph can therefore never satisfy $H \to G$. The lower bound follows. ■

The ramsey numbers for stars given by $2r(K_{1,n}) = 4n-1+(-1)^n$ was already mentioned in [2]. The name *stripes* was given to the graphs nK_2 by COCKAYNE and LORIMER [12] who noted that $r(nK_2) = 3n-1$.

Theorem 1. *The size ramsey numbers of the stars $K_{1,n}$ and the stripes nK_2 are given by* $\zeta(K_{1,n}) = \zeta(nK_2) = 2n-1$.

Proof. In both cases the lower bound for the size ramsey number follows from Lemma 1. To prove the upper bound, it only remains to find graphs G, H satisfying $G \to K_{1,n}$, $H \to nK_2$, and $q(G) = q(H) = 2n-1$. These graphs are $G = K_{1,2n-1}$ and $H = (2n-1)K_2$.

3. The size ramsey number for small graphs

In Theorem 2 we present the numbers $\zeta(F)$ for all but one small graph and the upper bound $\zeta(K_4 - x) \leqq 44$ which we believe is exact. The results are summarized in Table 1. The number $\zeta(K_4) = 153$ follows from a theorem of Chvátal whose proof appears in [18] and will be included in the next section for completeness.

In the proofs below we employ a method which consists of two main stages. In the first stage we get a prospective value for $\zeta(F)$ by finding the maximum number n of edges whose removal from $K_{r(F)}$ results in a graph G such that $G \to F$. The prospective value is then $\binom{r(F)}{2} - n$, and it follows immediately that $\zeta(F) \leqq \binom{r(F)}{2} - n$. To prove the other inequality, we must show that if $G \to F$, then $q(G) \geqq \binom{r(F)}{2} - n$. The second stage consists in verifying this inequality by showing that if G is edge minimal with respect to $G \to F$, then $q(G) \geqq \binom{r(F)}{2} - n$. Since every graph H satisfying $H \to F$ contains such a G, we would be done.

We state a useful Lemma.

Lemma 2a. *Let G be K_3-free colorable. If F and some $v \in V(F)$ satisfy*
(1) $F - v \cong G$,
(2) $d(v) \leqq 3$, *or* $d(v) = 4$ *and* $q(F) \leqq 18$,
then F is K_3-free colorable.

Proof. Let f be a K_3-free coloring of $F - v$. In addition to the colors red and green in f, give a third color, say yellow, to all the edges of $\overline{F - v}$. Now in $\langle N(v)\rangle \cup \langle \overline{N(v)}\rangle$, the complete graph on the neighborhood of v, either all edges are yellow or there is a pair of edges of different colors. In the former case, a K_3-free coloring of F is gotten by combining f with a green coloring of $X(v, N(v))$. We may therefore assume that there are two edges with different colors in $\langle N(v)\rangle$.

Suppose first that $d(v) \leqq 3$ since any subgraph of a K_3-free colorable graph is K_3-free colorable. Let $N(v) = \{t_1, t_2, t_3\}$ with t_1t_2 and t_2t_3 having different colors. As one of t_1t_2, t_2t_3 is red or green we can say t_1t_2 is green. Now let vt_1, vt_2 be red while vt_3 is green. This coloring of $X(v, N(v))$ combined with f yields a K_3-free coloring of F.

Now suppose that $d(v) = 4$ and $q(F) \leqq 18$. A simple verification shows that if $\langle N(v)\rangle \neq K_4$ there exists a 2-coloring of $X(v, N(v))$ which combined with f yields a K_3-free coloring of F. We may therefore suppose that $\langle N(v)\rangle \cong K_4$, and we let $V(N(v)) = \{s, t, z, w\}$.

Suppose to the contrary that $F \to K_3$. Our first reduction will be to show that the coloring of $\langle N(v)\rangle$ induced by f is one of the two shown in Fig. 1. To see this, note that any K_3-free coloring of K_4 other than the two in Fig. 1 has the property that there exists a pair of independent edges of opposite color, say st green and zw red. Now let vs and vt be red while vz and vw are green. This coloring of $X(v, N(v))$ combined with f yields a K_3-free coloring of F, a contradiction.

Fig. 1. The possible colorings of $\langle N(v)\rangle$ induced by f

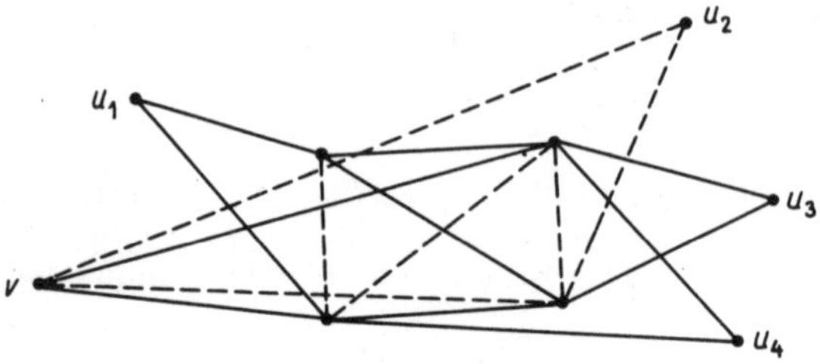

Fig. 2. A K_3-free coloring of F

We may therefore assume without loss of generality that $\langle N(v)\rangle$ is colored as in Fig. 1a. We will show that for each green edge e in $\langle N(v)\rangle$, there exists a point $u\in V(F-N(v)-v)$ such that u is attached by a red edge to each point of e. For suppose st is green in $\langle N(v)\rangle$. Then color $\{vz, vw\}$ red, $\{vs, vt\}$ green, and change st to red. If no point u exists with us and ut red, then the coloring just described combined with f on $F-v-st$ yields a K_3-free coloring of F. Hence to each green line in $\langle N(v)\rangle$ we find a point u as described above, thus getting the 4 points $\{u_1, u_2, u_3, u_4\}$. Note that no two of the u_i coincide since then by their definition it would follow that there is a red K_3 in the coloring of $F-v$ by f.

The above remarks imply that the subgraph $T=\langle v, N(v), u_1, u_2, u_3, u_4\rangle$ of F has at least 18 edges. Since $g(F)\leqq 18$ and $T\subset F$, it follows that $T=F$ and that the structure of T derived above determines T (and hence F) uniquely. The graph F is shown in Fig. 2 with a K_3-free coloring, and the lemma is proved. ■

Theorem 2. *The size ramsey numbers of the small graphs are given in*:

Table 1

F	K_2	P_3	K_3	P_4	$2K_2$	$K_{1,3}$	$K_{1,3}+x$	C_4	K_4-x	K_4
$\zeta(F)$	1	3	15	7	3	5	19	15	$\leqq 44$	153

Remark. As the proofs are long and sometimes tedious, we include the details only for $K_{1,3}+x$ as well as the verification of the upper bound in Table 1 for K_4-x.

Proof that $\zeta(C_4)=15$. It is well known that $r(C_4)=6$, so that by Lemma 1a we have $\zeta(C_4)\leqq 15$. The converse argument is much longer. A proof has just been announced by ROUSSEAU and SHEEHAN [19] who studied the size ramsey number of bipartite graphs. An outline of our proof proceeds as follows.

To prove that $\zeta(C_4)\geqq 15$, we must show that every graph G satisfying $q(G)\leqq 14$ can be C_4-free colored. It is easily verified that K_6-x can be so colored. Since every graph G satisfying $q(G)\leqq 14$ and $p(G)\leqq 6$ is a subgraph of K_6-x, it can be C_4-free colored too. We therefore suppose that a graph G satisfying $G\rightarrow C_4$, $p(G)\geqq 7$, and $q(G)\leqq 14$ exists, and then derive a contradiction.

This is accomplished by considering edge minimal graphs. That is, the supposed graph G must contain an edge minimal subgraph H with respect to $H\rightarrow C_4$. We then derive a contradiction by showing that a C_4-free coloring of H can always be found. The idea is to force the degrees of the points of H to be high. This is shown by inferring from the assumption that the degrees are low that a C_4-free coloring of H can be constructed which can be extended to a C_4-free coloring of G. The rest of the proof consists of developing the details of an algorithm for finding such a C_4-free coloring of H.

It is amusing to note that this proof utilized (at some stage in the algorithm) the well known theorem of PÓSA [15] giving sufficient conditions for a graph to be hamiltonian in terms of its degree sequence.

As in [8, p. 12], $K_{1,3}+x$ is drawn by adding one new edge to $K_{1,3}$, and K_4-x by removing one edge from K_4.

Proof that $\zeta(K_{1,3}+x)=19$. We begin by proving the inequality $\zeta(K_{1,3}+x)\leqq 19$. For this we will define the following graph H having 7 points and 19 edges, and we will show $H\rightarrow K_{1,3}+x$. To form H, take a subgraph H' isomorphic to K_6, and join the seventh point r to any four of the points in H'.

Consider any 2-coloring of H. It is well known that at least two monochromatic triangles, T_1 and T_2, occur in the coloring of H' induced by the coloring of H. It is also known [13] that if a 2-coloring of K_6 contains *exactly* two monochromatic triangles T_1 and T_2, then the number of points in $T_1\cap T_2$ may be 0, 1, or 2. It is convenient to call these cases (a), (b), (c). It was found that T_1 and T_2 have different colors if and only if (b) holds.

First we will reduce our proof to the case where H' contains two monochromatic triangles that are related in one of the three ways (a), (b), or (c) given above. For suppose such a pair T_1 and T_2 does not exist. Then there are two monochromatic triangles Q_1 and Q_2 which are either disjoint and have different colors, or have just one common point and have the same color. By the result of [13], there are at least three monochromatic triangles in H'.

Let Q_3 be a third such triangle and suppose without loss of generality that Q_1 and Q_3 have the same color. If Q_1 and Q_2 are disjoint, then Q_3 and Q_1 share either an edge or a point so that a monochromatic $K_{1,3}+x$ occurs with edges in $Q_3\cup Q_1$. If Q_1 and Q_2 have one common point, then a monochromatic $K_{1,3}+x$ exists having its edges in $Q_1\cup Q_2$.

Let us then consider separately each of the cases (a), (b) and (c).

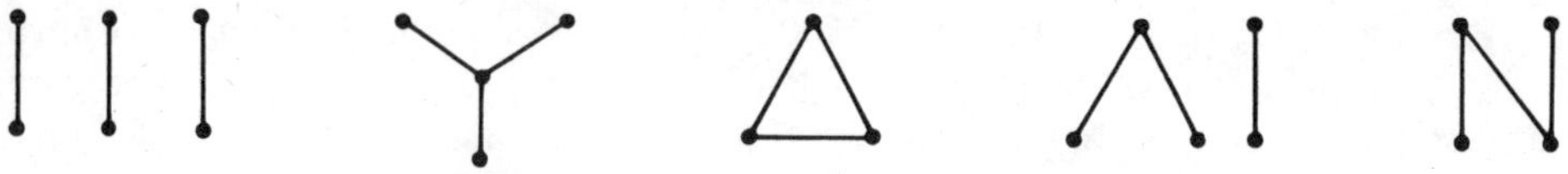

Fig. 3. The five graphs induced by three edges

Suppose first that (a) holds, and that both T_1 and T_2 are green with point sets $\{u_1, u_2, u_3\}$ and $\{v_1, v_2, v_3\}$. To avoid a green $K_{1,3}+x$, all edges u_iv_j are red. For the same reason, the edges ru_i, rv_i are red. Since r is on 4 such edges, there are 3 points in $N(r)$ with the property that not all of them are in the same monochromatic triangle. It follows that the graph induced by these 3 points and r contains a red $K_{1,3}+x$.

If (b) holds, we show that H' already contains a monochromatic $K_{1,3}+x$. The triangles T_1 and T_2 have different colors. Hence any edge in $X(T_1, T_2)$ must play the role of the edge x in either a red or green $K_{1,3}+x$.

Finally, if (c) holds, then the monochromatic $K_{1,3}+x$ occurs among the edges of T_1 and T_2.

We now begin the proof that $\zeta(K_{1,3}+x) \geqq 19$. This verification is rather involved and quite long. As usual, the proof is split into the two cases $p \leqq r(K_{1,3}+x)=7$ and $p \geqq r(K_{1,3}+x)+1=8$. That is, we will first show that if $H \to K_{1,3}$ and $p(H) \leqq 7$, then $q(H) \geqq 19$, and then do the same when $p(H) \geqq 8$.

For the case $p(H) \leqq 7$, it obviously suffices to find $(K_{1,3}+x)$-free colorings of all graphs obtained by removing 3 edges from K_7. Each possible graph J induced by 3 edges is displayed in Fig. 3. In Fig. 4, a $(K_{1,3}+x)$-free coloring of the graph $K_7 - E(J)$ for each J is given. In each diagram of Fig. 4, the area enclosed by the Jordan curve represents a subgraph H' of H having 6 points.

The coloring of H' is denoted by either "2Δ" or "Δ-free". To explain these names, we begin with a coloring of K_6 given by taking 2 disjoint green triangles T_1 and T_2 and coloring the remaining edges of K_6 red. The name 2Δ refers to a coloring of H' obtained by taking the above coloring of K_6 and possibly removing one or two edges from the two green triangles. The triangles T_1 and T_2 in H' are drawn, and the appropriate drawing of each edge on T_1 and T_2 is given according to whether the edge is present (dashed) or absent (wavy). Examples of 2Δ-colorings are shown in Figs 4a, 4b, and 4c. A *Δ-free coloring* is a 2-coloring of $H' = K_6 - x$ which has no monochromatic triangle. Examples of this coloring are in Figs 4d and 4c. It is easily checked that the colorings displayed in Fig. 4 are all $(K_{1,3}+x)$-free. Thus we have settled the case $p(H) \leqq 7$.

We now pass to the case $p \geqq 8$. Now let H be an edge minimal graph with respect to $H \to K_{1,3}$ and satisfying $p(H) \geqq 8$. We must show that $q(H) \geqq 19$, so assume to the contrary that $q(H) \leqq 18$.

We now make certain reductions concerning possible degree sets of pairs of adjacent points. First we prove that if v and w are adjacent in H, then not both v and w have degree at most 2. For suppose this were false, and an adjacent pair v, w satisfy $d(v) \leqq 2$ and $d(w) \leqq 2$. By edge minimality, $H - vw$ has a $(K_{1,3}+x)$-free 2-coloring. If either v or w

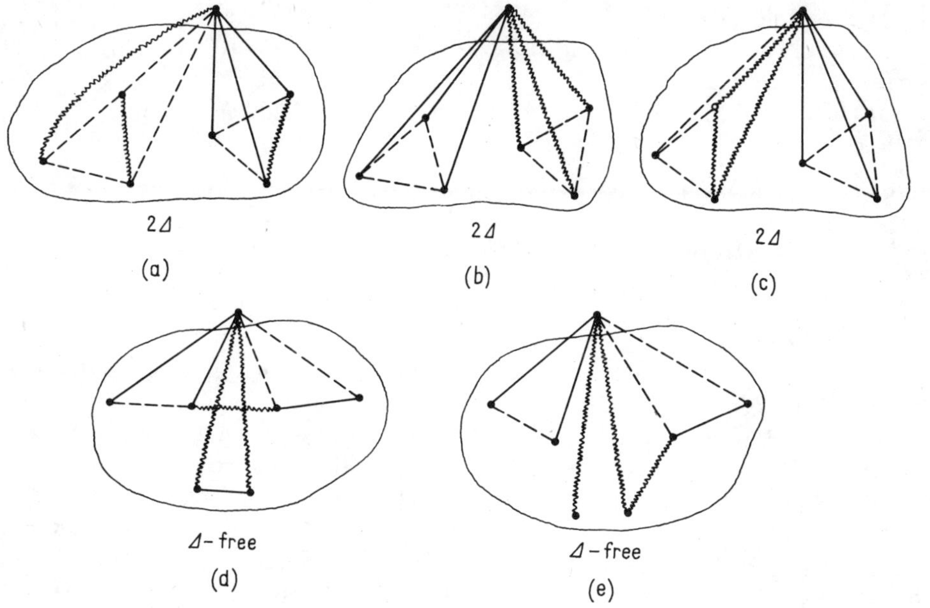

Fig. 4. The $(K_{1,3}+x)$-free colorings of the (7, 18) graphs.

has degree 1, then any coloring of vw combined with the $(K_{1,3}+x)$-free coloring of $H-vw$ yields a $(K_{1,3}+x)$-free coloring of H. Suppose then that $d(v)=2$ and $d(w)=2$. Let y (or z) be the edge other than vw incident with v (or w). If y and z have the same color, say red, in the coloring of $H-vw$, color vw green. Otherwise, give vw either color. Now combining the $(K_{1,3}+x)$-free coloring of $H-vw$ with this coloring of vw gives a $(K_{1,3}+x)$-free coloring of H, a contradiction.

Arguments similar to the one just given also show that there does not exist a pair of adjacent points having degrees 1 and 3, or 2 and 3.

Observe now that H contains no point of degree 4. For if v were such a point, then $q(H-v)\leqq 14$. Since $\zeta(K_3)=15$, there exists a K_3-free coloring of H. Then by Lemma 2a, there is a K_3-free (and hence a $(K_{1,3}+x)$-free) coloring of H, a contradiction.

We now show that the remarks above imply that there exists no set $S\subset V(H)$ satisfying $\sum_{v\in S} d(v)=4$. The connectedness of H implies that the set S consists of either four points of degree 1, or two points of degree 2, or one point of degree 1 and one point of degree 3. The discussion above shows that no two points of S are adjacent. Hence we have $|X(S, H-S)|=4$, so that $q(H-X(S, H-S))\leqq 14$. Since $\zeta(K_3)\leqq 15$, a K_3-free coloring of $H-X(S, H-S)$ exists. It follows from Lemma 2a that H can also be given a K_3-free (hence a $(K_{1,3}+x)$-free) coloring in each of the three possible cases. Hence no such set S exists.

We now use the assertions proved above to show that H contains no point v with $d(v)=1$. For if such a point v exists, then the discussion above implies that one of the following holds:

(1) $d(s) \geqq 5$ for all $s \in H - v$.

(2) There exists w such that $d(w) = 2$, w is not adjacent to v, and $d(s) \geqq 5$ for all $s \in H - \{v, w\}$.

(3) There are at most 2 other points u, t having degree 1 and $d(s) \geqq 5$ for all $s \in H - \{u, v, w\}$.

Suppose (1) holds. By Euler's equation, we have $q(H) \geqq \frac{1}{2}(1 + (p(H) - 1) \cdot 5)$. Since $p(H) \geqq 8$ and $q(H) \leqq 18$, it follows that $p(H) = 8$ and that the degree sequence of H is 15555555. Hence there is a point $r \in H - v$ whose degree in $H - v$, $d(r, H - v)$, is 4. Thus $q(H - v - r) \leqq 13$, so that $\zeta(K_3) = 15$ and Lemma 2a imply that $H - v$ is K_3-free colorable. Hence H is $(K_{1,3} + x)$-free colorable, a contradiction.

Suppose (2) holds. Combining Euler's equation with $q(H) \leqq 18$, we get $p(H) = 8$. If $q(H) \leqq 17$, then $q(H - v - w) \leqq 14$ holds. Now $\zeta(K_3) = 15$ and Lemma 2a give a K_3-free (hence a $(K_{1,3} + x)$-free) coloring of H. We may therefore assume that $H - v - w$ is K_6. A $(K_{1,3} + x)$-free coloring of H is then gotten by taking the 2Δ-coloring of K_6 described previously, say with 2 green triangles, and coloring the edges incident with v and w red.

Suppose finally that (3) holds. Let R be the set of points of degree 1 in H. If $|R| = 1$, then we are in case (1) which has been resolved. If $|R| = 2$, then Euler's equation and $q(H) \leqq 18$ combine to show that $p(H) = 8$. Thus $H - r \subseteq K_6$, and it would suffice to find a $(K_{1,3} + x)$-free coloring of H under the assumption $H - R = K_6$. But this is easily done by using the 2Δ-coloring of $H - R$ with green triangles and coloring $X(R, H - R)$ red. If $|R| = 3$, then we have $p(H) = 9$ or 8 so that $|H - R| = 6$ or 5. If $|H - R| = 6$, the argument just given provides a $(K_{1,3} + x)$-free coloring of H. If $|H - R| = 5$, then we can even find a K_3-free coloring of H by taking such a coloring of $H - R$ and combining it with any coloring of $X(R, H - R)$. This final contradiction shows that H contains no points of degree 1.

We now show that H contains no points of degree 2 or 3. Let W be the set of such points, and suppose first $|W| = 1$. If $v \in W$ and $d(v) = 3$, then since H contains no points of degree 4 or 1 we get $q(H) \geqq \frac{1}{2}(3 + 5(p(H) - 1) \geqq 19$, contradicting $q(H) \leqq 18$. We thus have $d(v) = 2$. Since $q(H) \leqq 18$, for $t \in H - v$ we have $d(t) \geqq 5$. As the number of points of odd degree is even, we get $q(H) = 18$ and 255555556 for the degree sequence of H. Hence $H - v$ contains a point w of degree 4. Thus $q(H - v - w) = 13$, and on applying $\zeta(K_3) = 15$ and Lemma 2a twice, we get a K_3-free (hence a $(K_{1,3} + x)$-free) coloring for H. We may therefore assume that $|W| \geqq 2$. If $v, w \in W$ satisfy $d(v) = d(w) = 2$ or $d(v) = 2$ and $d(w) = 3$, then v and w are not adjacent by previous arguments. Hence $q(H - v - w) \leqq 14$ so we get a K_3-free coloring of H as above. We may therefore assume that there exist $v, w \in W$ with $d(v) = d(w) = 3$. Then regardless of whether v and w are adjacent, we have $q(H - v - w) \leqq 14$ and a K_3-free coloring of H as above follows. We have thus shown that $\delta(H) \geqq 5$.

The final contradiction to $q(H) \leqq 18$ now comes by combining $\delta(H) \geqq 5$, $p(H) = 8$, and Euler's equation to get $q(H) \geqq 20$. It follows that $q(H) \geqq 19$, as desired. ■

We now establish that $\zeta(K_4 - x) \leqq 44$ but this upper bound is reduced to 39 in [21].

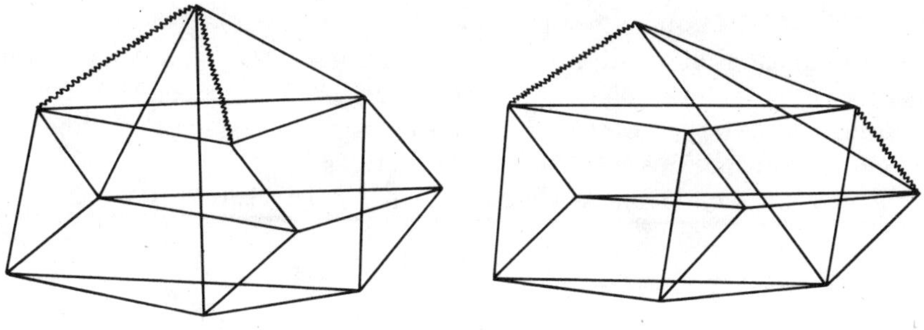

(a) (b)

Fig. 5. (K_4+x)-free colorings of $K_{10}-E(P_3)$ and $K_{10}-E(2K_2)$

Proof. $\zeta(K_4-x)\leqq 44$. We prove in fact that if there exists a graph $H\to K_4-x$ with $q(H)\leqq 43$, then $11\leqq p(H)\leqq 17$.

To prove the first assertion, we will show that any 2-coloring of $K_{10}-x$ yields a monochromatic K_4-x. Let v be a point of degree 9 in $K_{10}-x$. Then without loss of generality v is greenly joined to 5 points u_i, $1\leqq i\leqq 5$. Consider the graph F on 5 points induced by the u_i. If F contains a green P_3, then v and this P_3 induce a green K_4-x. Hence F contains no green P_3, so that at most 2 edges of F are green. Thus at least 7 edges of F are red. But it is easily seen that any red graph on 5 points and 7 edges contains a red K_4-x. Thus any 2-coloring of $K_{10}-x$ yields a monochromatic K_4-x, so that $\zeta(K_4-x)\leqq 44$.

Now let $H\to K_4-x$ and $q(H)\leqq 43$. First we will show that $p(H)\geqq 11$ by displaying (K_4-x)-free 2-colorings of the graphs obtained by removing 2 edges from K_{10}. Then using a degree argument, we will show that $p(H)\leqq 17$.

If $p(H)\leqq 10$, then H is either $K_{10}-E(2K_2)$ or $K_{10}-E(P_3)$. A (K_4-x)-free coloring of H for the first case is given in Fig. 5a, and for the second case in Fig. 5b. We give only the red graph since the green graph is obtained by complementation in K_{10}. Note that we have made use of a (K_4-x)-free coloring of K_9 having $K_3\times K_3$ as its red subgraph. The missing edges are wavy lines.

We will now show that $p(H)\leqq 17$. Observe that to do this it would suffice to show that $\delta(H)\geqq 5$. For then Euler's equation combined with $q(H)\leqq 43$ immediately implies that $p(H)\leqq 17$. Note also that to show $\delta(H)\geqq 5$, we need only prove that H contains no points of degree 4 since any subgraph of a (K_4-x)-free colorable graph is also (K_4-x)-free colorable. Suppose then to the contrary that H contains a point v of degree 4. We will derive a contradiction using an argument that is similar to one already given.

We may of course assume that H is edge minimal with respect to $H\to K_4-x$. Then there is a (K_4-x)-free 2-coloring f of $\langle N(v)\rangle$. Our object is to find a coloring of $X(v, N(v))$ which combined with f yields a $K_4-x)$-free coloring of H. Let us consider the 3-coloring of the edges of $N=\langle N(v)\rangle\cup\overline{\langle N(v)\rangle}$ obtained by combining f with a yellow coloring of the edges of $\overline{\langle N(v)\rangle}$. If all edges of N are yellow, then any coloring of $X(v, N(v))$ will do. If any edge of N is yellow, then it is easy to find the desired red-green coloring of $X(v, N(v))$. Assume then that $N=\langle N(v)\rangle=K_4$, and let $N(v)=\{t, u, w, z\}$. If there is a pair of independent edges of opposite color in $E(\langle N(v)\rangle)$, say tu green and wz red, then the desired coloring of $X(v, N(v))$ is vt, vu red and vw, vz green. If no such pair of edges exists, then $\langle N(v)\rangle$ is colored in one of the two ways given in Fig. 3 above. The desired coloring of H is possible, and we are done. ■

The number $\zeta(K_4)=153$ follows as a consequence of the theorem in the next section.

3. Complete graphs

Of course one can also define the off-diagonal size ramsey number $\zeta(F, H)$ for two graphs F and H as the minimum number of lines in a graph G such that for every 2-coloring of $E(G)$ there is a green F or a red H. We will say that a graph G is (F, H)-free colored if there is a 2-coloring of G in which neither a green F or a red H occur. Also, we write $G\rightarrow(F, H)$ if every 2-coloring of G yields either a green F or a red H. Aside from the calculation of $\zeta(F, H)$ for various F and H, a natural problem is to determine which pairs of graphs $\{F, H\}$ satisfy $\zeta(F, H)=\binom{r(F, H)}{2}$. For the special case of complete graphs this problem has been settled by V. CHVÁTAL, as noted in [18]. We include his elegant proof for completeness. Clearly this result yields the numbers $\zeta(K_3)$ and $\zeta(K_4)$. Let $r(m, n)$ stand for $r(K_m, K_n)$.

Theorem C (Chvátal). *If G is connected, $G\rightarrow(K_m, K_n)$, and $q(G)\leqq\binom{r(m, n)}{2}$, then G is $K_{r(m,n)}$. In particular, we have $\zeta(K_m, K_n)=\binom{r(m, n)}{2}$.*

Proof. Let G be connected of order p with $q(G)\leqq\binom{r(m, n)}{2}$ and $G\neq K_{r(m,n)}$. We will show that $G\not\rightarrow(K_m, K_n)$. This is certainly true if $p<r(m, n)$ since $K_{r(m,n)-1}$ can be given a (K_m, K_n)-free coloring. So let us take $p\geqq r(m, n)$ and assume by induction that the result holds for every graph other than $K_{r(m,n)}$ of order less than p with at most $\binom{r(m, n)}{2}$ edges.

We now proceed to find a (K_m, K_n)-free coloring of G. Note that since $p\geqq r(m, n)$, $q\leqq\binom{r(m, n)}{2}$ and $G\neq K_{r(m,n)}$, we know that G is not complete. Let u and v be non-adjacent points of G, and we write for later convenience $G_u=G-v$, $G_v=G-u$, and $H=G-\{u, v\}$. Observe that in order to find a (K_m, K_n)-free coloring of G, it would suffice to find colorings of G_u and G_v agreeing on H in which neither a red K_m nor a green K_n occurs. For if this could be done, then the coloring of G obtained by combining the colorings of G_u and G_v compatibly is (K_m, K_n)-free since any monochromatic complete graph must be wholly contained in the coloring of G_u or of G_v.

We now construct the required colorings of G_u and G_v. Let $Z=N(u)\cup N(v)$, and let H_u be the graph obtained from G_u by adding all edges of the form uz, $z\in Z-N(u)$, and let H_v be similarly defined. Note that H_u and H_v are isomorphic graphs of order $p-1$ having at most $\binom{r(m,n)}{2}$ edges. If we knew that $H_u, H_v \neq K_{r(m,n)}$, then induction yields a (K_m, K_n)-free coloring of both H_u and H_v. Since $H_u \simeq H_v$ and $H_u \supset G_u$, $H_v \supset G_v$, it follows that there exist (K_m, K_n)-free colorings of G_u and G_v which agree on H.

It therefore remains to show that H_u, $H_v \neq K_{r(m,n)}$. Hence we assume that the isomorphic graphs H_u and H_v are both $K_{r(m,n)}$. Then $H \simeq K_{r(m,n)-1}$ while the condition $q(G) \leqq \binom{r(m,n)}{2}$ implies that $(N(u), N(v))$ is a partition of $V(H)$. But then there exists a point $w\in H$ such that u and w are nonadjacent and $N(u)\cap N(w)\neq\emptyset$, a contradiction. Hence $H_u=H_v\neq K_{r(m,n)}$ and so we can simply let w play the role of v, and the proof goes through as above. The theorem is thus proved. ■

Corollary. $\zeta(K_4)=\binom{18}{2}=153.$

In [18], asymptotic relations between ζ and the classical ramsey number are explored, and bounds are given for the values $\zeta(G)$ for certain classes of graphs G. As an example, the problem of which infinite sequences $\{G_n\}$ of graphs satisfy $\lim_{n\to\infty} \frac{\zeta(G_n)}{r(G_n)}=0$ is explored. The bounds for ζ are derived using probabilistic methods.

4. Unsolved problems

All of the questions which have been asked in [14] concerning the ramsey number $r(F)$ of a graph F can be posed as well for the size ramsey number $\zeta(F)$. Surveys of generalized ramsey theory and of edge colorings of noncomplete graphs are given in Burr [10, 11]. Six additional problems follow.

A. Analogously with Beineke and Schwenk [9], we can define the bipartite edge ramsey number for which all three graphs F, H, and G are bipartite, see also Problem 6 of [14]. We conjecture that for the complete bipartite graphs $K_{m,n}$, a result analogous to Chvátal's Theorem C will hold.

B. Sumner [16] studied the connected ramsey number $r_c(F, H)$ defined as follows. A graph T is *coconnected* if both T and its complement $\bar{T}$ are connected. For two graphs F and H, he defined $r_c(F, H)$ to be the smallest integer $n\geqq 4$ such that if T is a connected graph on at least n vertices, then $F\subset T$ or $H\subset \bar{T}$. The edge analogue of $r_c(F, H)$ would be the smallest n such that there exists a coconnected graph on n edges, and if R is a coconnected graph on at least n edges, then $F\subset R$ or $H\subset \bar{R}$. What are connected ramsey numbers and the size analogues for small graphs F and H?

C. In [4], the ramsey multiplicity of F was defined as the minimum number of monochromatic occurrences of F among all 2-colorings of the edges of the complete graph of order $r(F)$. One can immediately define the *size ramsey multiplicity* as the minimum number of monochromatic occurrences of F among all 2-colorings of all graphs H satisfying $H \to F$ and $q(H) = \zeta(F)$. What are the size-ramsey multiplicities for the small graphs?

D. Ramsey numbers for digraphs were introduced in [5] where it was observed that $r(D_1, D_2)$ exists if and only if at least one of the two digraphs is acyclic. For an acyclic digraph D we may thus define the obvious arc analogue of $r(D_1, D_2)$. It remains to calculate the arc ramsey numbers for the small digraphs considered in [5].

E. In [6], ramsey numbers for plexes were introduced. These are pure 2-dimensional simplicial complexes, also known as 3-uniform hypergraphs. In [17] DUKE studied precisely the size ramsey number for plexes. In fact, his work was the original stimulus for this article. Duke determined this number for a few families of plexes.

F. We conjecture that $\zeta(K_4 - x) = 44$. The crude lower bound $\zeta(K_4 - x) \geqq 28$ is easily obtained by noting that if a graph H satisfies $H \to K_4 - x$ and $q(H) \leqq 43$, then the proof of $\zeta(K_4 - x) \leqq 44$ given in Theorem 2 shows that $11 \leqq p(H) \leqq 17$ and $\delta(H) \geqq 5$. Euler's equation then yields $q(H) \geqq 28$.

G. A very nice exact result concerning the size ramsey number of multiple copies of stars was derived by BURR, ERDŐS, FAUDREE, ROUSSEAU and SCHELP in [20]. They proved that

$$\zeta(mK_{1,r}, nK_{1,s}) = (m+n-1)(r+s-1),$$

which of course generalizes the obvious result of our Theorem 1. It would seem natural to conjecture the still more general equation

$$\zeta(n_1 K(1, r_1), \ldots, n_c K(1, r_c)) = (\Sigma n_i - 1)(\Sigma r_i - 1)$$

for c colors.

H. In addition to these questions, one can ask for the exact values of the off-diagonal edge ramsey numbers of the small graphs.

References

[1] V. CHVÁTAL and F. HARARY, Generalized ramsey theory for graphs I: Diagonal numbers. *Periodica Math. Hungar.*, **3** (1973), 113–122.

[2] V. CHVÁTAL and F. HARARY, Generalized ramsey theory for graphs II: Small diagonal numbers. *Proc. Amer. Math. Soc.*, **41** (1972), 389–394.

[3] V. CHVÁTAL and F. HARARY, Generalized ramsey theory for graphs III: Small off-diagonal numbers. *Pacific J. Math.*, **41** (1972), 335–345.

[4] F. HARARY and G. PRINS, Generalized ramsey theory for graphs IV: The Ramsey multiplicity of a graph. *Networks*, **4** (1974), 163–173.

[5] F. HARARY and P. HELL, Generalized ramsey theory for graphs V: The ramsey number of a digraph. *Bull. London Math. Soc.*, **6** (1974), 175–182; **7** (1975), 87–88.

[6] R. A. DUKE and F. HARARY, Generalized ramsey theory VI: Ramsey numbers for small plexes. *J. Australian Math. Soc.*, (Series A) **22** (1976), 400–409.

[7] F. HARARY and A. J. SCHWENK, Generalized ramsey theory VII: Multigraphs and networks. *Networks*, to appear.

[8] F. HARARY, *Graph Theory*, Addison-Wesley, Reading (1969).

[9] L. W. Beineke and A. J. Schwenk, On a bipartite form of the Ramsey problem. *Proceedings of the Fifth British Combinatorial Conference* (C. St. J. A. Nash-Williams and J. Sheehan, eds.), Utilitas, Winnipeg (1976), 17–22.

[10] S. A. Burr, Generalized ramsey theory for graphs — a survey. *Graphs and Combinatorics* (R. Bari and F. Harary, eds.), Springer, Berlin (1974), 52–75.

[11] S. A. Burr, On noncomplete ramsey constructions. *Topics in Graph Theory* (F. Harary, ed.), New York Acad. Sci., (1979), 148–159.

[12] E. J. Cockayne and P. J. Lorimer, The ramsey number for stripes. *J. Australian Math. Soc.*, **19** (1975), 252–256.

[13] F. Harary, The two-triangle case of the acquaintance graph. *Math. Mag.*, **45** (1972), 130 135.

[14] F. Harary, The foremost open problems in generalized Ramsey theory, *Proceedings of the Fifth British Combinatorial Conference* (C. St. J. A. Nash-Williams and J. Sheehan, eds.), Utilitas, Winnipeg (1976), 269–282.

[15] L. Pósa, A theorem concerning hamiltonian lines. *Magyar Tud. Akad. Mat. Kutató Int. Közl.*, **7** (1962), 225–226.

[16] D. P. Sumner, The connected ramsey number. *Discrete Math.* **14** (1976), 91–97.

[17] R. A. Duke, Some extremal problems for simple two-complexes. *Springer Lecture Notes Math.*, **642** (1978), 148–159.

[18] P. Erdős, R. J. Faudree, C. C. Rousseau, R. H. Schelp, The size ramsey number. *Periodica Math. Hungar.*, **9** (1978), 145–161.

[19] C. C. Rousseau and J. Sheehan, Size ramsey numbers for bipartite graphs (Abstract). *Notices Amer. Math. Soc.*, (Jan. 1978) A36.

[20] S. A. Burr, P. Erdős, R. J. Faudree, C. C. Rousseau, R. H. Schelp, Ramsey-minimal graphs for multiple copies. *Indag. Math.*, **40** (1978), 187–195.

[21] R. J. Faudree and J. Sheehan, Size Ramsey numbers for small order graphs. *J. Graph Theory*, to appear.

UNIVERSITY OF MICHIGAN
ANN ARBOR, U.S.A.

Studies in Pure Mathematics
To the Memory of Paul Turán

The asymptotic distribution of the order of elements in alternating semigroups and in partial transformation semigroups

by

B. HARRIS (Madison)*

Abstract

The asymptotic distributions of the order of elements in alternating semigroups and in partial transformation semigroups are obtained and shown to coincide with that for the symmetric semigroup.

1. Introduction

In the papers by P. Erdős and P. Turán [9–12], various questions concerning statistical characteristics of the symmetric group on n letters, S_n, for large n, are studied. In particular let P denote a generic element of S_n and let $O(P)$ be the order of P. Then if $K(n, x)$ is the number of elements of S_n satisfying

(1) $$\log O(P) \leqq \frac{1}{2}\log^2 n + \frac{x}{\sqrt{3}}\log^{3/2} n,$$

we have

(2) $$\lim_{n\to\infty} \frac{K(n,x)}{n!} = \frac{1}{\sqrt{2\pi}} \int_{-\infty}^{x} e^{-t^2/2}dt.$$

Equivalently, if P is "chosen at random" from S_n, define

$$Z = \left(\log O(P) - \frac{1}{2}\log^2 n\right)\Big/\frac{1}{\sqrt{3}}\log^{3/2} n;$$

then the distribution of Z converges to the standard normal distribution as $n\to\infty$. In J. Dénes, P. Erdős and P. Turán [8], this result was extended to the alternating group on

* Sponsored by the United States Army under Contract No. DAAG29–75–C–0024.

n letters A_n. Letting $L(n, x)$ be the number of elements of A_n satisfying (1), they showed that

$$\lim_{n\to\infty} \frac{L(n, x)}{n!/2} = \frac{1}{\sqrt{2\pi}} \int_{-\infty}^{x} e^{-t^2/2} dt . \tag{3}$$

In [11], the analogous result to (1) and (2) for the symmetric semigroup T_n was obtained. Specifically T_n is the set of all mappings of $X_n = \{x_1, x_2, \ldots, x_n\}$ into X_n. With no loss of generality, we can take $X_n = \{1, 2, \ldots, n\}$. If $\alpha, \beta \in T_n$, then the product $\alpha\beta \in T_n$ is defined by $(\alpha\beta)x = \alpha(\beta(x))$ for all $x \in X_n$. There is a one-to-one correspondence between the elements of T_n and the class of labeled directed graphs on n vertices, with each vertex having exactly one edge leaving it. Such a graph may be constructed by the following procedure: if $\alpha(x) = x_1$, draw the directed edge from x to x_1 (if $x = x_1$; draw a loop at x_1). For each $\alpha \in T_n$, we divide X_n into two classes, cyclical and non-cyclical elements. An $x \in X_n$ is said to be cyclical under α if there is an $m > 0$ with $\alpha^m(x) = x$. The set of cyclical elements under α will be denoted by C_α. The restriction of α to C_α will be denoted by α^*. α^* is a one-to-one mapping of C_α onto C_α and thus permutes the elements of C_α. DÉNES [3, 4, 5, 7] has called α^* the main permutation of α. Further for each $x \in X_n$, there is a least integer $r = r_\alpha(x) \geqq 0$ such that $\alpha^r(x) \in C_\alpha$. We call r the α-height of x, defining the height of α by $h(\alpha) = \max_{x \in X_n} r_\alpha(x)$.

Then for any $\alpha \in T_n$, the order of α, $O(\alpha)$, is defined as the number of distinct elements of T_n in the set $\{\alpha, \alpha^2, \ldots\}$. It is easily seen that if α is a permutation, this definition reduces to the usual definition. DÉNES [3, 4, 5] has shown that this is equivalent to

$$O(\alpha) = O(\alpha^*) + \max(0, h(\alpha) - 1)$$

and also equivalent to defining $O(\alpha)$ as the least m such that for $0 < q \leqq m$, $\alpha^q = \alpha^{m+1}$.

Then, in HARRIS [13], it was shown that for $M(n, x)$, the number of elements of T_n satisfying

$$\log O(\alpha) \leqq \frac{1}{8} \log^2 n + \frac{x}{\sqrt{24}} \log^{3/2} n, \tag{4}$$

we have

$$\lim_{n\to\infty} \frac{M(n, x)}{n^n} = \frac{1}{\sqrt{2\pi}} \int_{-\infty}^{x} e^{-t^2/2} dt . \tag{5}$$

In the present paper, the result is extended to the alternating semigroup K_n and to the partial transformation semigroup P_n. The alternating semigroup on n letters is defined by

$$K_n = (T_n - S_n) \cup A_n . \tag{6}$$

The partial transformation semigroup is the semigroup of all transformations whose domain and range are subsets of X_n. The significance of the alternating semigroup and various results concerning it may be found in J. M. Howie [15], J. Dénes [6], K. H. Kim and J. Dénes [17], Chapter IV, N. Ito [16] and O. Ore [18]. Some results for the partial transformation semigroup may be found in J. Baillieul [1] and C. D. Bass and K. H. Kim [2].

In Section 2 the asymptotic distribution of the order of elements in alternating semigroups is obtained and in Section 3 the corresponding result for the partial transformation semigroup is given.

2. The asymptotic distribution of $O(\alpha)$, $\alpha \in K_n$

We now show that the asymptotic distribution of the order of elements in the alternating semigroup is identical with that for the symmetric semigroup.

Clearly

$$|T_n| = n^n, \quad |K_n| = n^n - n!/2. \tag{7}$$

Let $K_n(B) = \{\alpha \in K_n : O(\alpha) \in B\}$ and let $T_n(B) = \{\alpha \in T_n : O(\alpha) \in B\}$, where B is any set of positive integers. Then, clearly

$$|T_n(B)| - n!/2 \leqq |K_n(B)| \leqq |T_n(B)|. \tag{8}$$

It is convenient to proceed using language and notation equivalent to assuming that the elements of K_n are equally likely and selected at random. Then $\alpha \in K_n$ is a random variable taking values in K_n. Using such notation, we have

$$P\{\alpha \in K_n(B)\} = |K_n(B)|/(n^n - n!/2). \tag{9}$$

Hence, from (8), we have

$$P\{\alpha \in K_n(B)\} \leqq |T_n(B)|/(n^n - n!/2) = \frac{|T_n(B)|}{n^n} \frac{n^n}{n^n - n!/2};$$

thus,

$$P\{\alpha \in K_n(B)\} \leqq P(\alpha \in T_n(B)\}(1 - \delta(n))^{-1}, \tag{10}$$

where $\delta(n) \to 0$ as $n \to \infty$. Also, from (8) and (9),

$$P\{\alpha \in K_n(B)\} \geqq \frac{|T_n(B)| - n!/2}{n^n - n!/2} \geqq \frac{|T_n(B)| - n!/2}{n^n}$$

yields

$$P\{\alpha \in T_n(B)\} \geqq P\{\alpha \in T_n(B)\} - \delta(n). \tag{11}$$

Thus combining (10) and (11), we get

$$\lim_{n \to \infty} P\{\alpha \in K_n(B)\} = P\{\alpha \in T_n(B)\}$$

and hence if $N(n, x)$ is the number of elements of K_n with

$$\log O(\alpha) \leq \frac{1}{8}\log^2 n + \frac{x}{\sqrt{24}}\log^{3/2} n,$$

then

$$\lim_{n\to\infty} \frac{N(n, x)}{n^n - n!/2} = \frac{1}{\sqrt{2\pi}} \int_{-\infty}^{x} e^{-t^2/2} dt \,. \tag{12}$$

Remarks. This problem was suggested by Dr. J. Dénes and appears in a list of research problems in combinatorics that he has circulated, where it is identified as problem 4.4. There he conjectured that the asymptotic distribution for the alternating semigroup would be the same as that for the alternating group. There is however an interesting parallel of a different kind. If P belongs either to the alternating group or symmetric group on n letters,

$$\sqrt{3}\log^{-3/2}\left(\log O(P) - \frac{1}{2}\log^2 n\right)$$

has the standard normal distribution. Further if α belongs either to the symmetric semigroup or alternating semigroup on n letters, then

$$\sqrt{24}\log^{-3/2} n\left(\log O(\alpha) - \frac{1}{8}\log^2 n\right)$$

has the standard normal distribution.

3. The asymptotic distribution of the order of elements in partial transformation semigroups

In order to represent $\beta \in P_n$ as a labeled directed graph as described in section one, we replace X_n by $X_n^* = \{0, 1, \ldots, n\}$ and represent $\beta \in P_n$ by the mapping α of X_n^* into X_n^* such that if x is in the domain of β, $\alpha(x) = \beta(x)$ and if x is not in the domain of β, $\alpha(x) = 0$. Note that this implies $\alpha(0) = 0$. It is obvious that there is a one-to-one correspondence between the elements of P_n and the mappings obtained in this manner. Furthermore this correspondence preserves the order of the mapping. Thus we can regard P_n as a particular subset of T_{n+1}. The above argument also makes it obvious that

$$|P_n| = (n+1)^n \,. \tag{13}$$

We will proceed by regarding the mappings α defined above as the elements of P_n and assume that they are selected at random with equal probabilities.

In the directed graph representation of α, since $\alpha(0)=0$, 0 is the vertex of a loop. Thus $O(\alpha^*)=O(\hat{\alpha})$, where $\hat{\alpha}$ is the permutation determined by restricting α to $C_\alpha\backslash\{0\}=C_{\hat{\alpha}}$. Thus

$$O(\alpha)=O(\hat{\alpha})+\max(0, h(\alpha)-1). \tag{14}$$

If $C_\alpha\backslash\{0\}=\Phi$, we set $O(\hat{\alpha})=1$.

For $\alpha\in T_n$, $L(\alpha)=|C_\alpha|$ is a random variable taking values in $\{1, 2, \ldots, n\}$. In B. HARRIS [13], it was shown that

$$P\{L(\alpha)=l\}=p(l, n)=\frac{(n-1)!l}{(n-l)!n^l}, \quad l=1, 2, \ldots, n. \tag{15}$$

For $\alpha\in P_n$, let $L_1(\alpha)=|C_{\hat{\alpha}}|$. $L_1(\alpha)$ is a random variable with values in $\{0, 1, \ldots, n\}$ and

$$P\{L_1(l)=l\}=r(l, n)=\frac{n!(l+1)}{(n-l)!(n+1)^{l+1}}, \quad l=0, 1, \ldots, n. \tag{16}$$

We present (16) without proof at this time. This result is contained in a paper under preparation and can easily be established by extending Corollary 2 to Theorem 1 in B. HARRIS and L. SCHOENFELD [14] to the partial transformation semigroup.

Comparing (15) and (16), we see that

$$p(l+1, n+1)=r(l, n), \quad l=0, 1, \ldots, n. \tag{17}$$

This observation permits us to apply the methods of B. HARRIS [13] with no essential changes. It is readily observed that the hypotheses of all lemmas are satisfied. In particular, if $C_{\hat{\alpha}}=\{x_{i1}, x_{i2}, \ldots, x_{il}\}$, where the x_{ij}'s are any l distinct elements of X_n. Then

$$P\{\hat{\alpha}=\hat{\alpha}_0|C_{\hat{\alpha}f}=\{x_{r1}, x_{r2}, \ldots, x_{rl}\}=1/l!,$$

where $\hat{\alpha}_0$ is any specified permutation of the elements of $C_{\hat{\alpha}}$. This symmetry condition is essential to the use of the results in [13} and is the technical reason for using $C_{\hat{\alpha}}$ instead of C_α.

Thus, from (17), we immediately obtain the following:

Theorem. *If $R(n, x)$ is the number of elements of P_n with $\log O(\alpha)\leq\frac{1}{8}\log^2 n+$ $+\frac{x}{\sqrt{24}}\log^{3/2} n$, then*

$$\lim_{n\to\infty}\frac{P(n, x)}{(n+1)^n}=\frac{1}{\sqrt{2\pi}}\int_{\infty}^{x} e^{-t^2/2}dt.$$

*

I deem it a singular honor to participate in this volume commemorating the death of Professor Paul Turán, who was a dear friend and who inspired much of my scientific efforts. His death is a great loss to mathematics and to each of us personally.

References

[1] J. Baillieul, Green's relations in finite function semigroups, *Aequationes Mathematicae*, **1** (1972), 22–27.
[2] C. D. Bass and K. H. Kim, Combinatorial properties of partial transformation semigroups, 1971, unpublished.
[3] J. Dénes, Connections between transformation semigroups and graphs; in *Theory of Graphs* (Internat. Sympos., Rome, 1966), 93–101. Gordon and Beach, N. Y., 1967.
[4] J. Dénes, On transformations, transformation-semigroups and groups; in *Theory of Graphs, Proceedings of the Colloquium held at Tihany*, Hungary, September 1966, 65–75. Academic Press, New York, 1968.
[5] J. Dénes, Some combinatorial properties of transformations and their connection with the theory of graphs, *J. Combinatorial Theory*, **9** (1969), 108–116.
[6] J. Dénes, Leképezések és leképezés félcsoportok, I, *Magyar Tudományos Akadémia Matematikai Fizikai Osztályának Közleményei*, **19** (1969), 247–269.
[7] J. Dénes, On graph representation of semigroups, *Proceedings of the Calgary International Conference on Combinatorial Structures and their Applications*, 55–57. Edited by Richard Guy et al., Gordon and Beach, N. Y., 1970.
[8] J. Dénes, P. Erdős and P. Turán, On some statistical properties of the alternating group of degree *n*, *Enseignement Math.*, 2, **15** (1969), 89–99.
[9] P. Erdős and P. Turán, On some problems of a statistical group theory. I., *Z. Wahrscheinlichkeitstheorie und Verw. Gebiete*, **4** (1965), 175–186.
[10] P. Erdős and P. Turán, On some problems of a statistical group theory, II, *Acta Math. Acad. Sci. Hungar.*, **18** (1967), 151–163.
[11] P. Erdős and P. Turán, On some problems of a statistical group theory. III, *Acta Math. Acad. Sci. Hungar.*, **18** (1967), 309—320.
[12] P. Erdős and P. Turán, On some problems of a statistical group theory. IV., *Acta Math. Acad. Sci. Hungar.*, **19** (1968), 413–435.
[13] B. Harris, The asymptotic distribution of the order of elements in symmetric semigroups, *J. Combinatorial Theory Ser. A*, **15** (1973), 66–74.
[14] B. Harris and L. Schoenfeld, A composition theorem for the enumeration of certain subsets of the symmetric semigroup, in "*Graph Theory and its Applications*", B. Harris, Ed., Academic Press, New York, 1970.
[15] J. M. Howie, The subsemigroup generated by the idempotents of a full transformation semigroup, *J. London Math. Soc.*, **41** (1966), 707–716.
[16] N. Ito, A theorem on the alternating group, *Math. Japonica*, **2** (1951), 59–60.
[17] K. H. Kim and J. Dénes, *Boolean Matrix Theory and Applications*, Unpublished Book Manuscript.
[18] O. Ore, Some remarks on commutators, *Proc. Amer. Math. Soc.*, **2** (1951), 307–314.

UNIVERSITY OF WISCONSIN–MADISON
MATHEMATICS RESEARCH CENTER
U.S.A.

Studies in Pure Mathematics
To the Memory of Paul Turán

On the minimum of a subharmonic function on a connected set

by

W. K. HAYMAN (London) and B. KJELLBERG (Stockholm)

1. Introduction and statement of earlier results

Suppose that $u(z)$ is subharmonic (s. h.) and not constant in the open plane. An interesting special case occurs when

$$u(z)=\log|f(z)|, \tag{1.1}$$

where $f(z)$ is entire, but all our theorems remain true and will be stated for general s. h. functions. We write

$$u^+(z)=\max(u(z), 0)$$

$$B(r)=\max_{|z|=r} u^+(z).$$

The order λ and lower order μ are defined by

$$\lambda=\overline{\lim_{r\to\infty}}\frac{\log B(r)}{\log r}, \quad \mu=\underline{\lim_{r\to\infty}}\frac{\log B(r)}{\log r}$$

Thus $0\leqq\mu\leqq\lambda\leqq\infty$. If $\lambda=\mu$ we say that $u(z)$ has regular growth. If $0<\lambda<\infty$, we also define the type,

$$\alpha=\overline{\lim_{r\to\infty}}\frac{B(r)}{r^\lambda},$$

and say that $u(z)$ has minimal, mean or maximal type, according as $\alpha=0$, $0<\alpha<\infty$ or $\alpha=\infty$.

The function $B(r)$ is an increasing convex function of $\log r$. We write for any complex z

$$B(z)=B(|z|) \tag{1.2}$$

and observe that $B(z)$ is a s. h. function of z.

The aim of this paper is to show that $u(z)$ cannot in general be much smaller than $-B(z)$ in a suitable sense. In this direction we quote some classical results.

We write

$$A(r) = \inf_{|z|=r} u(z) \quad .$$

WIMAN [12] proved

Theorem A. *If $u(z)$ is harmonic then*

$$\overline{\lim_{r\to 1}} \frac{A(r)}{B(r)} \geqq -1 .$$

This led Wiman to conjecture that Theorem A extends to functions of the form (1.1). In this direction BEURLING [1] proved

Theorem B. *If $u(z)$ is s. h. and not constant in the plane and ϑ is fixed and real then*

$$\overline{\lim_{r\to\infty}} \frac{u(re^{i\vartheta})}{B(r)} \geqq -1 .$$

In fact BEURLING proved rather more than this and for future reference we quote the following more precise

Theorem B′. *If $K > 1$, and $u(z)$ is s. h. in $|z| < R$ and satisfies for some fixed real ϑ*

$$u(re^{i\vartheta}) < -KB(r), \quad 0 < r < R .$$

then

$$u(z) \leqq 0 , \quad \text{for} \quad |z| < CR ,$$

where the constant C depends only on K.

For functions of lower order $\mu < 1$ the following result is due to the second author [8] sharpening earlier theorems of LITTLEWOOD [9], WIMAN [11], VALIRON [10] and HEINS [6].

Theorem C. *If $0 < \mu < 1$, and*

$$A(r) < \cos(\pi\mu) B(r) + O(1) \quad \text{as} \quad r \to \infty$$

then

$$\frac{B(r)}{r^{\mu}} \to \alpha ,$$

where $0 < \alpha \leqq \infty$.

The case $\mu = 1$ was treated by the first author [5].

Theorem D. *If*

$$A(r) < -B(r) + O(1), \quad \text{as} \quad r \to \infty$$

then either $u(x+iy)$ *is linear in* (x, y) *or*

$$\frac{B(r)}{r} \to +\infty .$$

For functions of order or lower order greater than one no such precise results are known. We quote the following Theorem which is due to LITTLEWOOD [9] at least in the case (1.1) and with order instead of lower order. The full result follows immediately if we apply Littlewood's technique to Theorem C.

Theorem E. *If* $\mu < \infty$, *then*

$$\overline{\lim_{r \to \infty}} \frac{A(r)}{B(r)} \geqq -C(\mu)$$

where the constant $C(\mu)$ *depends only on* μ.

Wiman's conjecture is equivalent to $C(\mu) = 1$. Unfortunately this result is false and the correct order of magnitude of $C(\mu)$ is $\log \mu$ as $\mu \to +\infty$ [3]. For functions of positive lower order we have [ibid.]

Theorem F. *If* $\mu > 0$ *and* $\varepsilon > 0$, *then we have*

$$A(r) > -\left(\frac{e^2}{\pi} + \varepsilon\right) B(r) \log \log B(r)$$

for a set E of values of r, having positive lower density, i.e. such that

$$\underline{\lim_{r \to \infty}} \frac{m(r)}{r} \geqq C_1(\varepsilon),$$

where $m(r)$ *is the measure of the part of E in* $[O, r]$ *and the constant* $C_1(\varepsilon)$ *depends only on* ε.

The order of magnitude in Theorem F (though not the constant) is also best possible.

2. Statement of our results

Since Wiman's original conjecture is false and the theory of $A(r)$ is somewhat unsatisfactory it is natural to see whether we can obtain an analogue of Theorem B if we replace the ray $\arg z = \vartheta$ by an unbounded connected set. Counter examples to Theorems E and F show that it is not enough to consider a set which meets every circle $|z| = r$ for large r. We shall prove the following results.

Theorem 1. *Suppose that $u(z)$ is s. h. and not constant in the plane and that $K>1$. Then the set where*

$$u(z)+KB(z)<0 \tag{2.1}$$

has no unbounded components.

Corollary. *If Γ is a path from z_0 to ∞ then* (2.1) *cannot hold at every point of Γ.*

Clearly the above result fails for $K=1$, as the function $u(x+iy)=x-1$ shows. The following theorems show nevertheless that even the case $K=1$ of (2.1) implies considerable restrictions on the curve and on the function.

Theorem 2. *Suppose that with the hypothesis of Theorem 1 the set where*

$$u(z)+B(z)<0 \tag{2.2}$$

has an unbounded component. Then $u(z)$ has infinite lower order or else regular growth and mean or minimal type of order λ where $1<\lambda<\infty$, or u is linear.

To state our final result we need some notions of density for a set E on the positive real axis. If $E(a, b)$ is the part of E in the interval (a, b) we say that E has finite logarithmic measure if

$$\int_{E(1,\infty)} \frac{dt}{t} < \infty . \tag{2.3}$$

We say that E has logarithmic density δ if

$$\lim_{r\to\infty} \frac{1}{\log r} \int_{E(1,r)} \frac{dt}{t} = \delta . \tag{2.4}$$

We have

Theorem 3. *If with the hypothesis of Theorem 2 there is a path Γ from a finite point to ∞ on which* (2.2) *holds, then Γ has a limiting direction ϑ in the sense that*

$$\arg z\to\vartheta \quad \text{as} \quad z\to\infty \quad \text{on} \quad \Gamma, \tag{2.5}$$

without restriction if $\mu=\infty$, and for all z on Γ with the exception of a set Γ_0 such that the set $\{|z| \mid z\in\Gamma_0\}$ has logarithmic density zero, if $\mu<\infty$.

Before proving these results we wish to make the following remarks. The first author proved Theorem 1 for a large absolute constant $K=A_0$ and conjectured the result as stated [3]. Soon afterwards Professor BEURLING showed the second author in a conversation a simple argument for proving Theorem 1 for any $K>3$. Recalling this earlier conversation with BEURLING we have now been able to prove the results stated above. Our argument proceeds as follows. We start with a generalisation of the reflection principle suggested by BEURLING. Next we need a harmonic measure estimate. This leads, under the hypothesis that (2.1) holds on an unbounded connected set, to a sector in which $u(z)$ is bounded above by a negative multiple of $B(z)$. Finally we obtain from this a contradiction which proves Theorem 1. Here some rather delicate growth estimates as well as Poisson's formula for a sector are required for the case $\lambda=\infty$.

Theorems 2 and 3 then follow fairly simply by similar methods.

3. Reflection principles and proof of Theorem 1 for $K>3$

We now suppose that $u(z)$ is s. h. and not constant in the open plane and that

$$u(z)+KB(z)<0, \quad z\in G \tag{3.1}$$

where G is an unbounded connected set and $K\geqq 1$. We also suppose without loss of generality that G contains the origin. For if z_0 is a point of G, γ is the line segment joining 0 to z_0, and if $u(z)<M$ on $|z|\leqq|z_0|$, then the function $v(z)=u(z)-M$ satisfies the analogue of (3.1) on $G\cup\gamma$.

Since u is s. h. and so upper semi-continuous, the set G is open. Thus there exists a polygonal line Γ joining the origin to an arbitrary point z_1 of G, such that (3.1) holds on Γ and $B(z)$ is given by (1.2). It is in this form that we use (3.1). We start with the following reflection principle, whose use in this connection was suggested to us by Professor BEURLING.

Lemma 1. *Suppose that $z_0=r_0e^{i\vartheta_0}$ is a point of G. Then*

$$u(re^{i\vartheta_0})<\left(\frac{1-K}{2}\right)B(r), \quad 0\leqq r\leqq r_0. \tag{3.2}$$

Before proving Lemma 1 we note, following BEURLING, that Theorem 1 for $K>3$ follows at once from Lemma 1 and Theorem B′. In fact if $K>3$, then $K'=\frac{1}{2}(K-1)>1$ and (3.2) shows, since G is unbounded, that we have

$$u(re^{i\vartheta_0})<-K'B(r), \quad 0<r<r_0$$

for some arbitrarily large r_0 and ϑ_0 depending on r_0. Thus in view of Theorem B′ we have $u(z)\leqq 0$ for $|z|<Cr_0$ and so for all complex z. Thus $u(z)$ is constant, contrary to hypothesis.

We proceed to prove Lemma 1.

Suppose that Γ is a polygonal Jordan arc with endpoints 0, z_0 on which (3.1) holds. We assume that Γ has only a finite number of points of intersection with the segment

$0, z_0$. Suppose that z_1, z_2 are two successive such points of intersection on this segment, so that z_1, z_2 bound an arc γ_1 of Γ, which does not meet the segment $\gamma_0 : z_1 z_2$ except at the end points.

Let D_1 be the Jordan domain bounded by γ_0 and γ_1. Let D_1^* be the reflection of D_1 in γ_0 and set

$$D = D_1 \cup \gamma_0 \cup D_1^* .$$

In D we consider

$$v(z) = u(z) + u(z^*) + (K-1)B(z)$$

where z^* is the reflection of z in γ_0. Clearly $v(z)$ is s. h. in D and, if z is any boundary point of D, either z or z^* belongs to Γ. Thus

$$v(z) < 0$$

on the boundary of D and so at every point of D since v is s. h. In particular we have on γ_0

$$2u(z) < (1-K)B(z) .$$

Thus (3.2) holds at every point of the segment $z_1 z_2$ and this proves Lemma 1.

We need an extension of Lemma 1 to the case when z_0 lies near Γ. To do this we define a harmonic function $\omega(z)$ as follows. Suppose that $z_0 = re^{i\vartheta_0}$ is not on Γ and let $z_1 = re^{i\vartheta_1}$ be a point on Γ, such that the arc γ_1 given by

$$z = re^{i\vartheta}, \quad \vartheta_0 < \vartheta < \vartheta_1$$

does not meet Γ. Next let $z_2 = r_2 e^{i\vartheta_0}$ be a point on Γ, such that the segment $\gamma_2 : z_2 z_0$ does not meet Γ. Let γ be the arc $z_1 z_2$ of Γ. Then the Jordan curve $\gamma\gamma_2\gamma_1$ bounds a domain D_0. We define a harmonic measure $\omega(z)$ as follows. The function $\omega(z)$ vanishes on γ, $\omega(z) = 1$ on γ_1 and the normal derivative of $\omega(z)$ is zero on γ_2. If D_0^* is the reflection of D_0 in γ_2, we obtain a simply connected domain $D = D_0 \cup \gamma_2 \cup D_0^*$ on a Riemann surface by joining D_0 to D_0^* along γ_2, but regarding points of D_0 and D_0^* as different. Then $\omega(z)$ is harmonic and bounded in D

$$\omega(z) = 1 \quad \text{on} \quad \gamma_1 \cup \gamma_1^* ,$$

$$\omega(z) = 0 \quad \text{on} \quad \gamma \cup \gamma^* .$$

We now prove

Lemma 2. *If $\omega(z)$ is defined as above then for z in D*

$$v(z) = u(z) + u(z^*) - (K+1)B(r)\omega(z) + (K-1)B(z) \leqq 0 . \tag{3.3}$$

We consider $u(z)$ in the Riemann domain D. Clearly at points of γ we have $u(z) + KB(z) < 0$, $u(z^*) - B(z) \leqq 0$ and $\omega(z) = 0$. Thus (3.3) is valid on γ. Similarly (3.3) is valid on γ^*.

Finally on γ_1 we have

$$u(z)+u(z^*)+(K-1)B(z)\leqq(K+1)B(r)=(K+1)B(r)\omega(z),$$

so that (3.3) holds on γ_1. Thus (3.3) holds at each point of the boundary of D and since $u(z)$ is s. h. in D the inequality holds also at points inside D.

We now have to assume $K>1$, and set

$$K=1+4\eta. \tag{3.4}$$

We can then prove

Lemma 3. *Suppose that $\omega(z)$ is defined as above and that $r_2<r_1<r$. If we have for all points on that* arc *γ_3 of $D\cap(|z|=r_1)$, which is bisected by γ_2*

$$\omega(z)\leqq\frac{\eta}{1+2\eta}\frac{B(r_1)}{B(r)}, \tag{3.5}$$

then we have for $z=\rho e^{i\vartheta_0}$, $0<\rho<r_1$

$$u(z)\leqq-\eta B(z). \tag{3.6}$$

It is sufficient to prove Lemma 3 if $r_2<\rho<r_1$, since for $\rho<r_2$ the result follows from Lemma 1. We consider $u(z)$ on the arc γ_3, and deduce from (3.3) and (3.5)

$$u(z)+u(z^*)\leqq(2+4\eta)B(r)\omega(z)-4\eta B(z)\leqq-2\eta B(z). \tag{3.7}$$

Also γ_3 divides D into two domains, one of which, D' say, contains the points $z=\rho e^{i\vartheta_0}$, $r_2<\rho<r_1$. We now consider on the boundary of D' the s. h. function

$$v_1(z)=u(z)+u(z^*)+2\eta B(z).$$

At points of γ_3 we have by (3.7)

$$v_1(z)\leqq 0. \tag{3.8}$$

If ζ is another boundary point of D' either ζ or ζ^* belongs to Γ and at such points ζ we have

$$v_1(z)\leqq(-1-4\eta+1)B(z)+2\eta B(z)\leqq 0.$$

Thus (3.8) holds on the boundary of D' and so throughout D'. Setting $z=z^*$, we deduce Lemma 3.

4. An estimate for harmonic measure

In order to make effective use of Lemma 3 we need an estimate for $\omega(z)$. A number of such estimates exist in the literature. A convenient starting point is the following result, [2, Theorem 4 and Theorem 5, (3. 8)]

Lemma 4. *Let Ω be an open set in the s plane ($s=\sigma+i\tau$) given by*

$$\vartheta_1(\sigma)<\tau<\vartheta_2(\sigma), \quad \sigma\in E. \tag{4.1}$$

We denote the segment (4.1) *by ϑ_σ, the length of ϑ_σ by*

$$\vartheta(\sigma)=\vartheta_2(\sigma)-\vartheta_1(\sigma),$$

and write

$$I=\int_E \frac{d\sigma}{\vartheta(\sigma)}.$$

Suppose that Ω is mapped (1, 1) *conformally onto a subset of the unit disk $|w|<1$, in such a way that the images g_σ of ϑ_σ for σ in E form crosscuts in $|w|<1$ which separate the points $w=0$, ρ. Then*

$$\frac{1}{2}\log\frac{1+\rho}{1-\rho}\geqq d_0(I)>\frac{\pi I}{2}-\log 2.$$

We deduce

Lemma 5. *With the hypothesis of Lemma 3, let $2t\,\vartheta(t)$ be the length of that* arc *γ_t of the intersection of D with $|z|=t$, which contains the point $te^{i\vartheta_0}$. Then we have on γ_3*

$$\omega(z)<\frac{16}{\pi}\exp\left\{-\frac{\pi}{2}\int_{r_1}^{r}\frac{dt}{t\vartheta(t)}\right\}. \tag{4.2}$$

We map the domain D of the previous section onto the domain G consisting of the disk $|w|<1$ cut along the real axis from -1 to 0, in such a way that the arc $\gamma_1\cup\gamma_1^*$ maps onto the segment $[-1, 0]$ and a fixed point z_3 on γ_3 maps onto $w=\rho$. Since D is a Jordan domain on a Riemann surface such a map is possible. Further harmonic measure is unaltered by this conformal map. Thus $\omega(z_3)$ is equal to the harmonic measure at $w=\rho$ of the segment $[-1, 0]$ with respect to G, i.e.

$$\omega(z_3)=1-\frac{4}{\pi}\tan^{-1}\sqrt{\rho}=\frac{4}{\pi}\tan^{-1}\left(\frac{1-\sqrt{\rho}}{1+\sqrt{\rho}}\right). \tag{4.3}$$

Thus to prove Lemma 5 we need to obtain a suitable lower bound for ρ. To do this we use Lemma 4. We make a transformation

$$s=\log z=\sigma+i\tau.$$

Under this map D corresponds to a simply-connected domain Δ over the s plane. The arc γ_t corresponds to a segment ϑ_σ

$$\vartheta_1(e^\sigma)<\tau<\vartheta_2(e^\sigma)$$

in the s-plane, where $\sigma=\log t$, $\vartheta_1+\vartheta_2=2\vartheta_0$, and

$$\vartheta_2(e^\sigma)-\vartheta_1(e^\sigma)=2\vartheta(e^\sigma).$$

If we denote the image of ϑ_σ in the w-plane by g_σ then it is clear that the arcs g_σ form crosscuts in $|w|<1$, which separate $w=0$, ρ.

Thus we apply Lemma 4, and writing $\sigma_1=\log r_1$, $\sigma_2=\log r$, we deduce

$$\frac{1}{2}\log\frac{1+\rho}{1-\rho}\geqq\frac{\pi}{2}\int_{\sigma_1}^{\sigma_2}\frac{d\sigma}{2\vartheta(e^\sigma)}-\log 2=\frac{\pi}{4}\int_{r_1}^{r}\frac{dt}{t\vartheta(t)}-\log 2. \tag{4.4}$$

Again

$$\tan^{-1}\frac{1-\sqrt{\rho}}{1+\sqrt{\rho}}<\frac{1-\sqrt{\rho}}{1+\sqrt{\rho}}=\frac{1-\rho}{1+\rho+2\sqrt{\rho}}<\frac{1-\rho}{1+\rho}. \tag{4.5}$$

Thus, using (4.3) to (4.5), we deduce that

$$\omega(z_3)<\frac{4}{\pi}\frac{1-\rho}{1+\rho}<\frac{16}{\pi}\exp\left\{-\frac{\pi}{2}\int_{r_1}^{r}\frac{dt}{\vartheta(t)}\right\}.$$

This proves Lemma 5.

5. A sector in which u is bounded above

We continue to assume that $K>1$ and define for any positive r

$$k(r)=\inf\frac{\log B(r_2)-\log B(r_1)+A_1(K)}{\log r_2-\log r_1} \tag{5.1}$$

where

$$A_1(K)=\log\left\{\frac{32}{\pi}\frac{K+1}{K-1}\right\} \tag{5.2}$$

and the infimum is taken over all pairs r_1, r_2, such that $r<r_1<r_2$. The quantity $k(r)$ plays the role of the lower order μ in our subsequent argument. It is evident that $k(r)$ is finite and increases with r and further that

$$0 \leqq k(r) \leqq \mu, \quad 0<r<\infty. \tag{5.3}$$

We now prove

Lemma 6. *Suppose that $u(z)$ satisfies* (3.1) *with $K=1+4\eta>1$. Then, if $r>0$, there exist ϑ_1, ϑ_2 depending on r such that*

$$u(z) \leqq -\eta B(z), \quad |z| \leqq r, \quad \vartheta_1 \leqq \arg z \leqq \vartheta_2 . \tag{5.4}$$

Here

$$\vartheta_2 - \vartheta_1 \geqq \frac{\pi}{k(r)}, \tag{5.5}$$

where $k(r)$ is given by (5.1).

Given $k'>k(r)$ we choose r_1, r_2, such that

$$r<r_1<r_2$$

and

$$\log B(r_2) < \log B(r_1) + k' \log (r_2/r_1) - A_1(K) . \tag{5.6}$$

We proceed to prove Lemma 6 with k' instead of $k(r)$.

By hypothesis G contains an arc Γ_1 joining $|z|=r_1$ and $|z|=r_2$ in $r_1<|z|<r_2$. Let Φ_1, Φ_2 be the lower and upper bounds of $\arg z$ on Γ_1. If $\Phi_2-\Phi_1 \geqq \pi/k'$ our result follows from Lemma 1. Thus we may assume that

$$\Phi_2 - \Phi_1 < \frac{\pi}{k'} . \tag{5.7}$$

We now define ϑ_1, ϑ_2 as follows. For any ρ with $r_1<\rho<r_2$ let $\vartheta_1(\rho)$ be the smallest number such that $\Phi_1 \leqq \vartheta_1(\rho) \leqq \Phi_2$ and $\rho \exp\{i\vartheta_1(\rho)\}$ lies on Γ_1. Similarly we define $\vartheta_2(\rho)$ to be the largest number such that $\Phi_1 \leqq \vartheta_2(\rho) \leqq \Phi_2$ and $\rho \exp\{i\vartheta_2(\rho)\}$ lies on Γ_1. Now we define ϑ_1 to be the least number, such that $\vartheta_1<\Phi_1$ and

$$\int_{r_1}^{r_2} \frac{d\rho}{\rho\{\vartheta_1(\rho)-\vartheta_1\}} \geqq \frac{2k'}{\pi} \log\left(\frac{r_2}{r_1}\right). \tag{5.8}$$

If no such numbers exist we define $\vartheta_1 = \Phi_1$. Similarly ϑ_2 is defined to be the greatest number such that $\vartheta_2 > \Phi_2$ and

$$\int_{r_1}^{r_2} \frac{d\rho}{\rho\{\vartheta_2 - \vartheta_2(\rho)\}} \geqq \frac{2k'}{\pi} \log\left(\frac{r_2}{r_1}\right). \tag{5.9}$$

If no such number exists we define $\vartheta_2 = \Phi_2$. We proceed to prove that

$$\vartheta_2 - \vartheta_1 \geqq \frac{\pi}{k'}. \tag{5.10}$$

To see this take $\vartheta_1', \vartheta_2'$, so that $\vartheta_1' < \vartheta_1 < \vartheta_2 < \vartheta_2'$. Then

$$\int_{r_1}^{r_2} \frac{d\rho}{\rho(\vartheta_2' - \vartheta_2(\rho))} < \frac{2k'}{\pi} \log\left(\frac{r_2}{r_1}\right),$$

$$\int_{r_1}^{r_2} \frac{d\rho}{\rho(\vartheta_2(\rho) - \vartheta_1')} \leqq \int_{r_1}^{r_2} \frac{d\rho}{\rho(\vartheta_1(\rho) - \vartheta_1')} < \frac{2k'}{\pi} \log\left(\frac{r_2}{r_1}\right).$$

Thus in view of Schwarz's inequality we have

$$\int_{r_1}^{r_2} (\vartheta_2' - \vartheta_2(\rho)) \frac{d\rho}{\rho} \geqq \left(\log\left(\frac{r_2}{r_1}\right)\right)^2 \Big/ \int_{r_1}^{r_2} \frac{d\rho}{\rho(\vartheta_2' - \vartheta_2(\rho))} > \frac{\pi}{2k'} \log\left(\frac{r_2}{r_1}\right).$$

Similarly

$$\int_{r_1}^{r_2} (\vartheta_2(\rho) - \vartheta_1') \frac{d\rho}{\rho} \geqq \int_{r_1}^{r_2} (\vartheta_1(\rho) - \vartheta_1') \frac{d\rho}{\rho} > \frac{\pi}{2k'} \log\left(\frac{r_2}{r_1}\right).$$

On adding these inequalities we obtain (5.10) with $\vartheta_1', \vartheta_2'$ instead of ϑ_1, ϑ_2. Since we may choose $\vartheta_1', \vartheta_2'$ as near to ϑ_1, ϑ_2 as we please we deduce (5.10).

We now suppose that $\vartheta_1 < \vartheta < \vartheta_2$ and proceed to prove that

$$u(\rho e^{i\vartheta}) \leq -\eta B(\rho), \quad 0 < \rho < r_1. \tag{5.11}$$

It is enough to consider the cases when $\vartheta_1 < \vartheta < \Phi_1$ or $\Phi_2 < \vartheta < \vartheta_2$, since otherwise (5.11) follows from Lemma 1. Suppose then that

$$\vartheta_1 < \vartheta < \Phi_1.$$

We deduce from (5.8) and (5.6) that

$$\int_{r_1}^{r_2} \frac{d\rho}{\rho\{\vartheta_1(\rho)-\vartheta\}} > \frac{2k'}{\pi} \log\left(\frac{r_2}{r_1}\right) > \frac{2}{\pi}(\log B(r_2) - \log B(r_1) + A_1(K)).$$

It now follows from Lemma 5 that if D is constructed as in Lemma 3 with ϑ, r_1, r_2 instead of ϑ_0, r_1, r then we have on $|z|=r_1$

$$\omega(z) < \frac{16}{\pi} \exp\left\{-\frac{\pi}{2}\int_{r_1}^{r_2} \frac{d\rho}{\rho\{\vartheta_1(\rho)-\vartheta\}}\right\} < \frac{16}{\pi}\exp\{\log B(r_1) - \log B(r_2) - A_1(K)\} =$$

$$= \frac{16}{\pi}\frac{B(r_1)}{B(r_2)} \exp\{-A_1(K)\} = \frac{\eta}{1+2\eta}\frac{B(r_1)}{B(r_2)}.$$

Now Lemma 3 yields (5.11). The inequality (5.11) thus holds for $\vartheta_1 < \vartheta < \Phi_1$ and similarly for $\Phi_2 < \vartheta < \vartheta_2$, and so for $\vartheta_1 < \vartheta < \vartheta_2$. Also ϑ_1, ϑ_2 satisfy (5.10) for a fixed $k' > k(r)$. Thus Lemma 6 holds with k' instead of $k(r)$.

We now set $k' = k(r) + \varepsilon_n$ for a positive integer n, where $\varepsilon_n \to 0$, and construct the corresponding numbers $\vartheta_1^{(n)}, \vartheta_2^{(n)}$. Clearly at least one line $\arg z = \vartheta_0$ belongs to infinitely many intervals $(\vartheta_1^{(n)}, \vartheta_2^{(n)})$.

By taking subsequences if necessary, we obtain sequences $\vartheta_1^{(n)}$, $\vartheta_2^{(n)}$, such that $\vartheta_1^{(n)} < \vartheta_0 < \vartheta_2^{(n)}$ and (5.4) holds for $\vartheta_1^{(n)} < \vartheta < \vartheta_2^{(n)}$ and each n. Thus if

$$\vartheta_1 = \underline{\lim}\, \vartheta_1(n), \quad \vartheta_2 = \overline{\lim}\, \vartheta_2(n),$$

we deduce that (5.4) holds for $\vartheta_1 < \vartheta < \vartheta_2$ and clearly $\vartheta_2 - \vartheta_1 \geqq \pi/k(r)$.

It remains to consider the cases $\vartheta = \vartheta_1$ or $\vartheta = \vartheta_2$. If for instance $z_0 = \rho e^{i\vartheta_1}$, where $0 \leqq \rho \leqq r$, we set

$$v(z) = u(z) + \eta B(z).$$

Thus we have for all sufficiently small ε

$$\inf_{|z-z_0|=\varepsilon} v(z) \leqq 0. \tag{5.12}$$

Since $v(z)$ is s. h. at z_0 (5.12) implies that $v(z_0) \leqq 0$, in view of the Milloux–Schmidt inequality (see e.g. [7, p. 109]). This completes the proof of Lemma 6.

6. Poisson's formula in a sector

We shall be able to deduce from Lemma 6 and (5.1) that $u(z)$ has for many values of r an extremely small minimum on $|z|=r$, compared with $B(r)$, thus obtaining a contradiction. For this purpose we prove

Lemma 7. *Suppose that $u(z)$ satisfies the conclusion of Lemma 6, and set $\vartheta_0=\frac{1}{2}(\vartheta_1+\vartheta_2)$. Then for $\rho<r$, we have*

$$\frac{u(\rho e^{i\vartheta_0})}{B(\rho)}<-A_2\frac{k}{k-k_1}\left(1-\left(\frac{\rho}{r}\right)^{k-k_1}\right) \tag{6.1}$$

where $k=k(r)$, $k_1=k(\rho)$, $A_2=(K-1)^2/\{128(K+1)\}$, and we assume $k>k_1$. If $k=k_1$, we replace the right hand side in (6.1) by $-kA_2\log(r/\rho)$.

Suppose first that $k=k(r)=1$, $\vartheta_2=-\vartheta_1=\frac{\pi}{2}$, and $\vartheta_0=0$. We deduce from (5.4) that we have for $\arg z=\mp\frac{\pi}{2}$

$$u(z)\leqq-\eta B(z).$$

Thus the function $u(z)$ is dominated in $|z|<r$, $|\arg z|<\frac{\pi}{2}$ by the bounded harmonic function $v(z)$ in the right half plane with boundary values

$$v(\mp iy)=-\eta B(y),\quad 0<y<r$$
$$v(iy)=0,\quad |y|>r.$$

For clearly $v(z)\geqq-\eta B(r)$ on $|z|=r$, $|\arg z|<\frac{\pi}{2}$, since $B(\rho)$ increases with ρ. Now Poisson's formula for the half-plane yields

$$u(\rho)\leqq v(\rho)=\frac{1}{\pi}\int_{-r}^{r}\frac{\rho v(iy)\,dy}{\rho^2+y^2}\leqq\frac{-\eta\rho}{\pi}\int_{\rho}^{r}\frac{B(t)\,dt}{t^2}. \tag{6.2}$$

If $k\neq1$, but $\vartheta_2=-\vartheta_1=\pi/(2k)$, we apply the inequality (6.2) to

$$U(z)=u(z^{1/k}).$$

This yields

$$u(\rho^{1/k})\leqq\frac{-\eta\rho}{\pi}\int_{\rho}^{r}\frac{B(t^{1/k})\,dt}{t^2},$$

where

$$B(R)=\max_{|z|=R^k} U^+(z)=\max_{|z|=R} u^+(z).$$

Setting $\rho^{1/k}=\rho_1$, $r^{1/k}=r_1$, $t^{1/k}=t_1$, we deduce

$$u(\rho_1)\leqq\frac{-\eta}{\pi}\rho_1^k\int_{\rho_1}^{r_1}\frac{B(t_1)kt_1^{k-1}dt_1}{t_1^{2k}}=-\frac{k\eta\rho_1^k}{\pi}\int_{\rho_1}^{r_1}\frac{B(t_1)dt_1}{t_1^{1+k}}. \tag{6.3}$$

We now recall the definition (5.1) of $k(r)$ and deduce that

$$\frac{B(t_1)}{B(\rho_1)}\geqq A_3\left(\frac{t_1}{\rho_1}\right)^{k_1},$$

where $k_1=k(\rho_1)$ and $A_3=\exp(-A_1)$. Thus (6.3) yields

$$u(\rho_1)\leqq\frac{-kA_3\eta\rho_1^{k-k_1}B(\rho_1)}{\pi}\int_{\rho_1}^{r_1}t_1^{k_1-k-1}dt_1=$$

$$=\frac{-A_3\eta B(\rho_1)}{\pi}\frac{k}{k-k_1}\left\{1-\left(\frac{\rho_1}{r_1}\right)^{k-k_1}\right\}. \tag{6.4}$$

This yields (6.1) when we replace ρ_1, r_1 by ρ, r and set

$$A_2=\frac{A_3}{\pi}\eta=\frac{1}{\pi}\frac{K-1}{4}\cdot\frac{\pi}{32}\frac{K-1}{K+1}=\frac{(K-1)^2}{128(K+1)}.$$

If $k=k_1$ we must replace (6.4) by

$$u(\rho_1)\leqq -kA_2B(\rho_1)\log(r_1/\rho_1).$$

If $\vartheta_0\neq 0$ we obtain the desired conclusion, by considering $u(ze^{i\vartheta_0})$ instead of $u(z)$. Thus Lemma 7 is proved in all cases.

We need a further inequality relating $B(r)$ and $k(r)$. This is

Lemma 8. *With the hypothesis of Lemma 6 we have*

$$\overline{\lim_{r\to\infty}}\frac{B(r)}{r^{k(r)}}<\infty.$$

We choose r_0 so that $1<r_0<2$ and

$$\inf_{|z|=r_0} u(z)=m>-\infty.$$

Let $S(r)$ be the sector

$$\vartheta_1<\arg z<\vartheta_2, \quad 0<|z|<r,$$

and let $\omega(z)$ be the harmonic measure of the circle $|z|=r$ with respect to $S(r)$. Since $u(z)\leqq 0$ in $S(r)$ and $u(z)$ satisfies (5.4) we deduce that

$$u(z)\leqq -\eta B(r)\,\omega(z).$$

Set $\vartheta_0=\dfrac{1}{2}(\vartheta_1+\vartheta_2)$. Then it is easy to show that

$$\omega(r_0e^{i\vartheta_0})=\frac{4}{\pi}\tan^{-1}\left\{\left(\frac{r_0}{r}\right)^{k(r)}\right\}>\left(\frac{r_0}{r}\right)^{k(r)}.$$

Thus

$$m\leqq u(z_0)\leqq -\eta B(r)\left(\frac{r_0}{r}\right)^{k(r)}<-\frac{\eta B(r)}{r^{k(r)}},$$

i.e.

$$\frac{B(r)}{r^{k(r)}}<\frac{-m}{\eta}, \quad r_0<r<\infty$$

and this proves Lemma 8.

7. Proof of Theorem 1 when $k(r)$ grows slowly

We shall prove Theorem 1 by deducing a contradiction from Theorem F and Lemma 7. We deduce from Lemma 8 that

$$\log B(r)<k(r)\log r+O(1), \quad \text{as} \quad r\to\infty. \tag{7.1}$$

Our proof is divided into two cases according to whether $k(r)$ or $\log r$ is the dominant term on the right-hand side of (7.1). In this section we suppose that

$$\lim_{r\to\infty}\frac{k(r)}{(\log r)^{1/4}}=0. \tag{7.2}$$

We write

$$k_n=k(2^{n^2}),$$

and deduce

Lemma 9. *If* (7.2) *holds there exist arbitrarily large positive integers n, such that*

$$k_n < n^{\frac{1}{2}}$$

and

$$k_n - k_{n-1} < n^{-\frac{1}{2}}.$$

If $k_n = 0$ for all n, Lemma 9 is trivial. Otherwise k_n is nondecreasing and so strictly positive for $n \geqq n_0$ say. Given a positive integer $N > n_0$, we choose ε less than one and so small that

$$k_n > \varepsilon n^{\frac{1}{2}}, \quad n_0 \leqq n \leqq N.$$

We then choose n to be the smallest integer such that $n > N$ and

$$k_n < \varepsilon n^{\frac{1}{2}}. \tag{7.3}$$

If no such integer exists we obtain a contradiction from (7.2). For in this case suppose that $r > 2^{N^2}$ and let n be the integer such that

$$2^{n^2} < r \leqq 2^{(n+1)^2}.$$

Then

$$k(r) \geqq k_n \geqq \varepsilon n^{\frac{1}{2}} > \frac{1}{2} \varepsilon (n+1)^{\frac{1}{2}} > \frac{1}{2} \varepsilon \left(\frac{\log r}{\log 2} \right)^{\frac{1}{4}}.$$

This inequality holds for all large r, contrary to (7.2). Thus we may choose n to be the first integer greater than N to satisfy (7.3) and so

$$k_{n-1} \geqq \varepsilon (n-1)^{\frac{1}{2}}$$

and

$$k_n - k_{n-1} < \varepsilon \{ n^{\frac{1}{2}} - (n-1)^{\frac{1}{2}} \} < \varepsilon n^{-\frac{1}{2}} < n^{-\frac{1}{2}},$$

since $\varepsilon < 1$. Since $n > N$ and N may be chosen as large as we please, we have proved Lemma 9.

We now choose n as in Lemma 9, with $n \geqq 4$ and apply Lemma 7 with

$$2^{(n-1)^2} \leqq \rho < 2^{n^2 - n + 1}, \quad r = 2^{n^2}, \tag{7.4}$$

We write $k - k_1 = \tau$, $\log (r/\rho) = h$, so that (6.1) yields

$$\frac{u(\rho e^{i\vartheta_0})}{B(\rho)} < -A_2 k \frac{1}{\tau} (1 - e^{-\tau h}) < -\frac{C}{\tau} (1 - e^{-\tau h}),$$

where C is a positive constant independent of h. For if $k<\frac{1}{2}$ for large r, we obtain a contradiction from Lemma 6. We deduce from Lemma 9 that $\tau<n^{-1/2}$. Thus if $\tau h>1$, we obtain

$$\frac{u(\rho e^{i\vartheta_0})}{B(\rho)}<-\frac{C}{2\tau}<-\frac{1}{2}Cn^{\frac{1}{2}}, \tag{7.5}$$

and if $\tau h\leqq 1$ we obtain

$$\frac{u(\rho e^{i\vartheta_0})}{B(\rho)}<-\frac{C}{e\tau}\tau h\leqq-\frac{C}{e}(n-1)\log 2.$$

Thus (7.5) holds for ρ in the range (7.4) and some arbitrarily large n.

Again we deduce from (7.1) and Lemma 9 that for ρ in the range (7.4), we have

$$\log B(\rho)<k(\rho)\log\rho+O(1)=O(n^{5/2}).$$

Thus (7.5) yields

$$A(\rho)=\inf_{|z|=\rho}u(z)\leqq u(\rho e^{i\vartheta_0})<-C'B(\rho)\{\log B(\rho)\}^{\frac{1}{5}}, \tag{7.6}$$

where C' is another positive constant.

This inequality holds for $\rho_n\leqq\rho\leqq\rho'_n$, where

$$\rho_n=2^{n^2-2n+1},\quad \rho'_n=2^{n^2-n+1},$$

so that

$$\frac{\rho'_n}{\rho_n}\to\infty.$$

However it follows from Theorem F, that if ρ_n, ρ'_n/ρ_n exceed a fixed constant there exists ρ in the range $\rho_n\leqq\rho\leqq\rho'_n$, such that

$$A(\rho)>-3B(\rho)\log\log B(\rho).$$

This contradicts (7.6) and the contradiction establishes Theorem 1, with the hypothesis (7.2).

8. Proof of Theorem 1, when $k(r)$ grows rapidly

We now suppose that (7.2) is false. This implies that

$$\log \rho = O\{k(\rho)\}^4,$$

and so, using (7.1) we deduce that

$$\log B(\rho) = O\{k(\rho)\}^5, \quad \text{as} \quad \rho \to \infty .$$

Using Theorem F, we deduce that

$$A(\rho) > -15B(\rho)\log k(\rho) \tag{8.1}$$

on a set E having positive lower density.

In order to obtain our contradiction from this and (6.1) we need a final lemma concerning the growth of positive increasing functions. This is

Lemma 10. *If $\Phi(x)$ is a positive, nondecreasing function for $x \geqq x_0$, then if α, β are constants such that $0 < \beta < 1$, $\alpha > 1 - \beta$, we have*

$$\Phi\{x + \Phi(x)^{-\alpha}\} < \Phi(x) + \Phi(x)^{\beta} \tag{8.2}$$

for all $x > x_0$ outside a set e of finite measure.

We define sequences x_n, y_n as follows. If x_{n-1} has already been defined we set

$$y_{n-1} = \Phi(x_{n-1}) .$$

If (8.2) holds for all sufficiently large x there is nothing to prove. Thus we may assume that (8.2) is false for an unbounded set of x and define x_n' to be the lower bound of all x for which (8.2) is false and

$$x \geqq x_{n-1} + y_{n-1}^{-\alpha} .$$

We then define x_n to be a number such that

$$x_n' \leqq x_n < x_n' + 2^{-n}$$

and such that (8.2) is false for $x = x_n$, i.e.

$$\Phi\{x_n + \Phi(x_n)^{-\alpha}\} \geqq \Phi(x_n) + \Phi(x_n)^{\beta} .$$

Thus x_n, y_n are defined for all n.

Since $\Phi(x)$ increases with x we deduce that for $n \geqq 1$

$$y_n = \Phi(x_n) \geqq \Phi(x_{n-1} + y_{n-1}^{-\alpha}) \geqq y_{n-1} + y_{n-1}^{\beta} . \tag{8.3}$$

The sequences x_n, y_n increase with n. If y_n tends to a finite limit l, we deduce that

$$l \geqq l + l^{\beta} .$$

Thus $y_n \to \infty$ with n and hence so does x_n.

We next write $p = 1/(1-\beta)$ and show that

$$y_n \geqq C n^p , \quad n \geqq 1 \tag{8.4}$$

where C is a positive constant. To do this we note that for $n \geqq 1$

$$(n+1)^p - n^p \leqq p(n+1)^{p-1} \leqq A n^{p-1} ,$$

where $A = p 2^{p-1}$.

Suppose now that (8.4) holds for n. Then (8.3) shows that

$$y_{n+1} \geqq y_n + y_n^{\beta} \geqq C n^p + C^{\beta} n^{p\beta} = C n^p + C^{\beta} n^{p-1} \geqq C(n+1)^p$$

if

$$C^{\beta} \geqq CA , \quad \text{i.e.} \quad C^{1-\beta} \leqq A^{-1} .$$

Thus (8.4) holds, provided that

$$C = \min \{ y_1 , A^{-1/(1-\beta)} \} .$$

We deduce that

$$\sum_{1}^{\infty} y_n^{-\alpha} \leqq \sum_{1}^{\infty} (C n^p)^{-\alpha} < \infty , \tag{8.5}$$

since $p\alpha > 1$ by hypothesis.

Also it follows from our construction that if $\boldsymbol{e}$ is the union of the intervals $[x_n, x_n + y_n^{-\alpha}]$ and $[x_n', x_n' + 2^{-n}]$ then (8.2) holds outside $\boldsymbol{e}$. Further $\boldsymbol{e}$ has finite measure in view of (8.5). Thus Lemma 10 is proved.

We note that Lemma 10 fails if $\alpha = 1 - \beta$ and $\Phi(x) = e^x$, since then we have for $h = \Phi(x)^{-\alpha} = e^{-\alpha x}$ and all real x

$$\Phi(x+h) > e^x + h e^x = e^x + e^{\beta x} = \Phi(x) + \Phi(x)^{\beta} .$$

To complete the proof of Theorem 1 we apply Lemma 9 with $\alpha = \beta = \frac{2}{3}$ to

$$\Phi(x) = k(e^x) ,$$

where $k(\rho)$ is the function of Lemma 6. Thus unless $\log\rho$ belongs to a set e of finite measure, i.e. unless ρ belongs to a set E_1 of finite logarithmic measure, we may in Lemma 7 set

$$h=\log\frac{r}{\rho}=k(\rho)^{-\frac{2}{3}}=k_1^{-\frac{2}{3}},$$

and deduce that

$$k=k(r)<k(\rho)+k(\rho)^{\frac{2}{3}}.$$

Writing $\tau=k-k_1$, in Lemma 7, we obtain

$$\tau<k_1^{\frac{2}{3}}.$$

Thus

$$\left(\frac{\rho}{r}\right)^{k-k_1}=e^{-\tau h}>\frac{1}{e}$$

and Lemma 7 yields

$$\text{(8.6)}\qquad \frac{u(\rho e^{i\vartheta_0})}{B(\rho)}<-A_2\frac{k_1+\tau}{\tau}(1-e^{-\tau h})<-A_2\frac{k_1}{\tau}\frac{\tau h}{e}=\frac{-A_2k_1h}{e}=\frac{-A_2}{e}k(\rho)^{\frac{1}{3}}.$$

The set E_1 for which (8.6) is false has finite logarithmic measure and so density zero. Thus (8.1) holds for some arbitrarily large ρ not in E_1 so that (8.1) and (8.6) hold simultaneously for such ρ. This contradiction completes the proof of Theorem 1.

9. The case $K=1$. Some preliminary results

We proceed to the proof of Theorems 2 and 3. Suppose then that (2.2) holds on a connected unbounded set G containing the origin. Let g be the set of all limiting directions of G, i.e. g is the set of all real ϑ, for which there exists a sequence $z_n=r_ne^{i\vartheta_0}\in G$ such that

$$r_n\to\infty,\quad\text{and}\quad \vartheta_n\to\vartheta.$$

We deduce from Lemma 1

Lemma 11. *If* $\vartheta\in g$ *then,*

$$u(re^{i\vartheta})\leqq 0,\quad 0<r<\infty.$$

In fact if z_n is defined as above we deduce from Lemma 1, that

$$u(re^{i\vartheta_n})\leqq 0,\quad 0<r<r_n.$$

Write $z_0 = re^{i\vartheta}$. Then we deduce that for any positive ε

$$\inf_{|z-z_0|=\varepsilon} u(z) \leqq 0 .$$

As we remarked after (5.12), this implies $u(z_0) \leqq 0$, and Lemma 11 is proved.

We deduce that g cannot contain any interval of length 2π, since otherwise $u(z)$ would be non-positive in the whole plane and so constant.

We shall be able to obtain an analogue of Lemma 6, but only with $\eta = 0$. In order to obtain a contradiction we need the following

Lemma 12. *Suppose that* $[\vartheta_1, \vartheta_2]$ *is a maximal interval such that*

$$u(re^{i\vartheta}) \leqq 0, \quad 0 < r < \infty, \quad \vartheta_1 \leqq \vartheta \leqq \vartheta_2 \tag{9.1}$$

and that $g \cap (\vartheta_1, \vartheta_2)$ *is not empty. Then*

$$A_0(r) = \inf_{\vartheta_1 \leqq \vartheta \leqq \vartheta_2} u(re^{i\vartheta}) < -\frac{1}{3} B(r), \quad r > r_0 . \tag{9.2}$$

The assumptions of Lemma 12 imply that $\vartheta_2 - \vartheta_1 = \delta > 0$. Also we can find ϑ_3, such that

$$\vartheta_1 - \delta < \vartheta_3 < \vartheta_1$$

and ϑ_3 is not in g. For if $(\vartheta_1 - \delta, \vartheta_1) \in g$ we deduce from Lemma 11 that

$$u(re^{i\vartheta}) \leqq 0, \quad 0 \leqq r < \infty, \quad \vartheta_1 - \delta \leqq \vartheta < \vartheta_1$$

and this contradicts the hypothesis that ϑ_1 is minimal subject to (9.1). Similarly, since ϑ_2 is maximal in (9.1) we can find ϑ_4 such that

$$\vartheta_2 < \vartheta_4 < \vartheta_2 + \delta$$

and ϑ_4 is not in g. Thus G meets the rays $\arg z = \vartheta_3, \vartheta_4$ only in bounded sets. We choose R_0 so that

$$re^{i\vartheta_3}, re^{i\vartheta_4} \text{ lie outside } G, r > R_0 . \tag{9.3}$$

We now suppose that $r > R_0$. Since g meets $(\vartheta_1, \vartheta_2)$ there exists $z_1 = re^{i\vartheta} \in G$ with $\vartheta_1 < \vartheta < \vartheta_2$ and $r_1 > r$. Let Γ_1 be a Jordan arc joining the origin to z_1 in G. If Γ_1 contains any arcs γ_1 outside the sector

$$S_1 : \vartheta_3 < \arg z < \vartheta_4$$

we replace γ_1 by segments γ on the boundary of S_1. In view of (9.3) γ must lie in $|z|<R_0$. Thus we may join the points $z=0$, z_1 by a Jordan arc Γ lying in $\bar{S}_1$ and such that every point of Γ either lies in G or satisfies

$$|z|<R_0 .$$

Writing $C=2B(R_0)$, we deduce that.

$$u(z)<-B(z)+2C, \quad z\in\Gamma .$$

Suppose now that Γ meets the arc

$$|z|=r, \quad \vartheta_1<\arg z<\vartheta_2 . \tag{9.4}$$

Then

$$A_0(r)\leqq -B(r)+2C<-\frac{1}{3}B(r)$$

if r is large enough. Suppose next that Γ does not meet the arc (9.4). Then Γ must contain an arc $\gamma: z_3z_4$ where $|z_3|<r<|z_4|$. z_3, z_4 are on the boundary of the sector

$$S_0: \vartheta_1\leqq \arg z\leqq \vartheta_2$$

but the interior points of γ lie outside S_0. We may, for instance, take for z_3 the last point in $S_0\cap\Gamma$ of modulus less than r, as Γ is described, starting from the origin.

Hence the arc γ lies either in $\vartheta_3\leqq\arg z\leqq\vartheta_1$ or in $\vartheta_2\leqq\arg z\leqq\vartheta_4$. Suppose e.g. the former. Then

$$z_3=r_3e^{i\vartheta_1}, \quad z_4=r_4e^{i\vartheta_1}, \quad \text{where} \quad r_3<r<r_4 .$$

In this case we reflect γ in the line $\arg z=\vartheta_1$ and obtain an arc γ^* which lies in S_0, since

$$\vartheta_1-\vartheta_3<\delta=\vartheta_2-\vartheta_1 .$$

Let D be the Jordan domain bounded by γ and γ^* and consider in D the s.h. function

$$v(z)=u(z)+u(z^*)$$

where z^* denotes the reflection of z in $\arg z=\vartheta_1$. Then if z is a boundary point of D either z lies on Γ and z^* lies in $\bar{S}_0$ or vice versa. Thus

$$v(z)\leqq -B(z)+2C$$

on the boundary of D and so in the whole of D. In particular

$$v(re^{i\vartheta_1})=2u(re^{i\vartheta_1})\leqq -B(r)+2C ,$$

so that

$$A_0(r) \leqq -\frac{1}{2}B(r)+C<-\frac{1}{3}B(r), \quad r>r_0 .$$

If γ lies in $\vartheta_2 \leqq \arg z \leqq \vartheta_4$ the conclusion is similar. This proves Lemma 12.

We also need

Lemma 13. *If* $u(z)$ *is s.h. and satisfies* (9.1) *then if* $A_0(r)$ *is defined as in* (9.2) *we have*

$$\lim \frac{A_0(r)}{r^k} = \alpha > -\infty$$

as $r \to \infty$ *outside a set* e *of finite logarithmic measure, where* $k = \pi/(\vartheta_2 - \vartheta_1)$.

Suppose first that $\vartheta_1 = -\vartheta_2 = \frac{\pi}{2}$. Then the first author proved [4] that

(9.5) $$\frac{u(re^{i\vartheta})}{r} \to \alpha \cos \vartheta$$

uniformly for $|\vartheta| < \frac{\pi}{2}$, as $r \to \infty$ outside e, where $\alpha > -\infty$. Thus

$$\lim \frac{A(r)}{r} = \alpha$$

as $r \to \infty$ outside e. In the general case we obtain the required conclusion by considering $u(z^k e^{i\lambda})$ for a suitable real λ.

We deduce

Lemma 14. *With the hypothesis of Lemma 12 we have*

(9.6) $$\overline{\lim_{r\to\infty}} \frac{B(r)}{r^k} < \infty ,$$

where $k = \pi/(\vartheta_2 - \vartheta_1)$. *Hence if* g *contains an interval of length* δ, u *has at most order* π/δ *with mean or minimal type.*

Suppose contrary to this that there is a sequence r_n such that

$$r_{n+1} > 2r_n$$

and

$$\frac{B(r_n)}{r_n^k} \to +\infty .$$

Let e be the union of the intervals $[r_n, 2r_n]$. Then e has infinite logarithmic measure. Also for $r_n \leqq r \leqq 2r_n$ and large n we deduce from Lemma 12 that

$$A_0(r) < -\frac{1}{3} B(r) < -\frac{1}{3} B(r_n).$$

Thus

$$\frac{A_0(r)}{r^k} \to -\infty, \quad \text{as} \quad r \to \infty \quad \text{in } e$$

and this contradicts Lemma 13.

We deduce at once that if g contains an interval of length δ, then $u(z)$ satisfies the hypothesis of Lemma 12 with $\vartheta_2 - \vartheta_1 \geqq \delta$, and hence (9.6) holds. Thus u has at most order k mean type, where $k = \pi/\delta$.

In particular if u has infinite order then g contains no intervals. This proves the conclusion (2.5) of Theorem 3, when $u(z)$ has infinite order, in a somewhat strengthened form. For if ϑ_1, ϑ_2 are the lower and upper limits of arg z on the path Γ as $z \to \infty$, the interval $[\vartheta_1, \vartheta_2]$ belongs to g, and so we must have $\vartheta_1 = \vartheta_2$.

10. Proof of Theorem 2

We now return to the reflection techniques of Section 3 in order to complete our proofs. Suppose that u has lower order μ. If $\mu = +\infty$, then u has infinite order and regular growth so that Theorem 2 is true in this case. Also, as we saw above, (2.5) holds in this case, so that Theorem 3 is also true.

Suppose then that $\mu < +\infty$. Then we choose a sequence R_n such that

$$R_n \to +\infty, \quad \text{as} \quad n \to \infty,$$

and

$$\log B(R_n) < (\mu + o(1)) \log R_n, \quad \text{as} \quad n \to \infty. \tag{10.1}$$

Let f be the set of all real ϑ (mod 2π), such that

$$u(re^{i\vartheta}) \leqq 0, \quad 0 < r < \infty. \tag{10.2}$$

It follows from Lemma 11 that $g \in f$, so that f is not empty. An argument similar to that after (5.12) shows that f is closed. Thus the complement of f consists of a union of disjoint intervals. Again, if (10.2) holds for $\vartheta = \vartheta_1, \vartheta_2$, where $\vartheta_2 - \vartheta_1 < \pi/\mu$ then it follows from (10.1) and the Phragmén–Lindelöf principle that (10.2) remains valid for $\vartheta_1 \leqq \vartheta \leqq \vartheta_2$. Thus the complementary intervals to f all have length at least π/μ and so are finite in number. Thus f itself consists of a finite number of closed intervals possibly reducing to points. At least one such interval $[\vartheta_1, \vartheta_2]$, say, contains a point of g, possibly as an endpoint.

We now choose Φ_1, Φ_2 in the complement of f and such that

$$\Phi_1 < \vartheta_1 \leqq \vartheta_2 < \Phi_2 .$$

Then the intersection of G with $\arg z = \Phi_j$ is bounded for $j = 1, 2$ in view of Lemma 11. We choose r_1, r_2 minimal positive numbers such that $re^{i\Phi_j}$ lies outside $\bar{G}$ for $r > r_j$. Thus $r_j e^{i\Phi_j} \in \bar{G}$.

We note that $\bar{G}$ is a closed connected set containing ∞, and so the complement of $\bar{G}$ in the closed plane consists of simply connected domains. Each ray

$$T_j : \arg z = \Phi_j, \quad r_j < |z| < \infty$$

forms a cross cut in one such domain and hence divides this domain into two simply connected domains, one of which, Δ_j say, contains points in the sector $S : \Phi_1 < < \arg z < \Phi_2$ near T_j. Since G is a connected set whose intersection with S has $r_1 e^{i\Phi_1}$ and ∞ as limit points, Δ_1 and Δ_2 are disjoint.

We define $D_j = \Delta_j \cup T_j \cup \Delta_j^*$, where the star denotes reflection in T_j as in section 3 and consider in D_j

$$v_j(z) = u(z) + u(z^*) .$$

We shall show that if $\Phi_2 - \Phi_1$ is small enough then

$$v_j(z) \leqq 0 , \quad z \in D_j \tag{10.3}$$

and this will lead to a contradiction.

For $R > r_j$ let $\gamma_j(R)$ be that arc of $D_j \cap (|z| = R)$, which contains the point $Re^{i\Phi_j}$, and let $2R\vartheta_j(R)$ be the length of $\gamma_j(R)$. Clearly $\gamma_j(R)$ divides D_j into two domains, one of which, $D_j(R)$ say, contains the segment

$$\arg z = \Phi_j , \quad r_j < |z| < R$$

and is bounded. We denote by $\omega(R, j, z)$ the harmonic measure of $\gamma_j(R)$ in $D_j(R)$. We now consider in $D_j(R)$

$$h_j(z) = v_j(z) - 2B(R)\omega(R, j, z)$$

and note that

$$h_j(z) \leqq 0 , \quad z \in D_j(R) . \tag{10.4}$$

In fact suppose that z approaches a boundary point ζ of $D_j(R)$. If ζ is an interior point of the arc $\gamma_j(R)$, then

$$\omega(R, j, z) \to 1$$

while

$$\lim u(z) \leqq B(R) , \quad \lim u(z^*) \leqq B(R) .$$

Thus

$$\overline{\lim}\ h_j(z) \leqq 0\,. \tag{10.5}$$

Otherwise ζ or ζ^* is a point of $\bar{G}$. In the former case every small circle $|z-\zeta|=\varepsilon$ meets G and so we deduce as at the end of Section 5, that

$$u(\zeta)+B(\zeta) \leqq 0\,,$$

while

$$u(\zeta^*) \leqq B(\zeta)\,.$$

Thus since $B(z)$ is continuous and $u(z)$ is upper semicontinuous, we deduce that

$$\overline{\lim}\ v_j(z) \leqq 0$$

as $z \to \zeta$ and so (10.5) holds in this case. If $\zeta^* \in \bar{G}$ the conclusion is similar. Thus (10.5) holds in all cases and now the maximum principle shows that (10.4) holds. In order to deduce (10.3) from (10.4) it is enough to show that, for $z \in D_j$, $j=1, 2$,

$$\lim_{n\to\infty} B(R_n)\omega(R_n, j, z)=0\,. \tag{10.6}$$

Since (10.3) yields $u(z) \leqq 0$ for $z \in T_j$, and since $r_j e^{i\Phi_j} \in \bar{G}$ we deduce from this and Lemma 1, that (10.2) holds for $\Phi=\Phi_j$, so that $\Phi_j \in f$ contrary to hypothesis. Thus (10.3) and so (10.6) must be false. Thus we have for all sufficiently large n, some point z in T_j and $j=1, 2$

$$\omega(R_n, j, z) > \delta/B(R_n) > R_n^{-\mu-o(1)} \tag{10.7}$$

in view of (10.1).

We now use Lemma 5. We set $|z|=\rho_j$, where z is a point in T_j satisfying (10.7) and deduce from (4.2) and (10.7) that for $j=1, 2$

$$\frac{\pi}{2}\int_{\rho_j}^{R_n} \frac{dt}{t\vartheta_j(t)} < (\mu+o(1)) \log R_n, \quad \text{as} \quad n\to\infty\,.$$

Suppose that $r_0=\max(\rho_1, \rho_2)$. Then we deduce by addition that

$$\int_{r_0}^{R_n} \frac{dt}{t}\left\{\frac{1}{\vartheta_1(t)}+\frac{1}{\vartheta_2(t)}\right\} < \left(\frac{4\mu}{\pi}+o(1)\right)\log\frac{R_n}{r_0}, \quad \text{as} \quad n\to\infty\,. \tag{10.8}$$

We note first that $\gamma_1(t)$, $\gamma_2(t)$ contain disjoint arcs of length $t\vartheta_1(t)$, $t\vartheta_2(t)$ lying on the arc $|z|=t$, $\Phi_1 \leqq \arg z \leqq \Phi_2$. Thus

$$\vartheta_1(t)+\vartheta_2(t) \leqq \Phi_2-\Phi_1$$

and hence

$$\frac{1}{\vartheta_1}+\frac{1}{\vartheta_2} \geqq \frac{4}{\Phi_2-\Phi_1}.$$

Thus (10.8) yields

$$\frac{4}{(\Phi_2-\Phi_1)}\log\frac{R_n}{r_0} < \left(\frac{4\mu}{\pi}+o(1)\right)\log\frac{R_n}{r_0}.$$

Thus $(\Phi_2-\Phi_1) \geqq \pi/\mu$. Since Φ_1, Φ_2 may be chosen as near as we please to ϑ_1, ϑ_2 we deduce that

$$\vartheta_2-\vartheta_1 \geqq \pi/\mu. \tag{10.9}$$

We also verify that G must have a limiting direction ϑ such that $\vartheta_1<\vartheta<\vartheta_2$. For suppose that g has no such direction. Then given $\varepsilon>0$ the arc

$$|z|=R, \quad \vartheta_1+\varepsilon<\arg z<\vartheta_2-\varepsilon \tag{10.10}$$

lies in the complement of G for large R and so lies entirely inside or entirely outside $\gamma_j(R)$. Since $\gamma_1(R)$, $\gamma_2(R)$ are disjoint, at least one of these two arcs does not meet the arc (10.10). We may suppose that $\Phi_2-\vartheta_2<\varepsilon$, $\Phi_1-\vartheta_1<\varepsilon$, and deduce that one of $\gamma_1(R)$, $\gamma_2(R)$ has length less than 2ε. Thus for all large t

$$\frac{1}{\vartheta_1(t)}+\frac{1}{\vartheta_2(t)} \geqq \frac{1}{2\varepsilon}$$

Now (10.8) yields

$$\frac{1}{2\varepsilon}\log\frac{R_n}{r_0} < \left(\frac{4\mu}{\pi}+o(1)\right)\log\frac{R_n}{r_0},$$

i.e. $\varepsilon \geqq \pi/(8\mu)$. This gives a contradiction and shows that g contains a point in $(\vartheta_1, \vartheta_2)$ and more precisely in $[\vartheta_1+\pi/(8\mu), \vartheta_2-\pi/(8\mu)]$.

We can now apply Lemmas 12 and 14 and deduce that $u(z)$ has at most mean type of order $\pi/(\vartheta_2-\vartheta_1)$. Thus (10.9) shows that $\mu \geqq \pi/(\vartheta_2-\vartheta_1) \geqq \lambda$, i.e.

$$\lambda=\mu=\pi/(\vartheta_2-\vartheta_1), \tag{10.11}$$

since $\lambda \geqq \mu$ always. Thus u has regular growth of order λ and mean or minimal type as stated in Theorem 2.

To complete the proof of Theorem 2 it remains to show that $\lambda > 1$. We note that the hypotheses of Theorem 2 imply that

$$A(r) < -B(r) + O(1).$$

This contradicts Theorem C, if $\lambda < 1$, and Theorem D if u has mean or minimal type of order one, unless u is linear. This completes the proof of Theorem 2.

11. Proof of Theorem 3

We proceed to prove Theorem 3. Having established (10.11) we may choose for R_n an arbitrary sequence tending to ∞ with R in (10.1) and so in (10.7). We may also choose $\Phi_2 - \Phi_1$ as near as we please to $\vartheta_2 - \vartheta_1$. We now take a fixed positive ε, write

$$\vartheta_2 - \vartheta_1 = 2h,$$

and claim that, with a suitable choice of Φ_1, Φ_2, we have

$$\vartheta_1(t) > h - \varepsilon$$

outside a set of logarithmic density zero.

Suppose that this is false. Then we have

$$\vartheta_1(t) \leqq h - \varepsilon \tag{11.1}$$

on a set E, such that if $E(r_0, R) = E \cap (r_0, R)$, we have

$$\overline{\lim_{R \to \infty}} \frac{1}{\log R} \int_{E(r_0, R)} \frac{dt}{t} > 0.$$

Hence there exists a sequence R_n tending to ∞ with n, such that

$$\int_{E(r_0, R_n)} \frac{dt}{t} > \eta \log \frac{R_n}{r_0}, \tag{11.2}$$

where η is a positive constant. We set $\delta = \min\left\{h, \frac{1}{8}\eta h^{-1}\varepsilon^2\right\}$, and choose Φ_1 Φ_2 so near ϑ_1, ϑ_2 respectively that

$$\Phi_2 - \Phi_1 < \vartheta_2 - \vartheta_1 + \delta = 2h + \delta \leqq 3h.$$

We write $S=2h+\delta$ and note that for every r

$$\frac{1}{\vartheta_1(r)}+\frac{1}{\vartheta_2(r)}\geqq\frac{1}{\vartheta_1(r)}+\frac{1}{S-\vartheta_1(r)}=\frac{4}{S}+\frac{(S-2\vartheta_1(r))^2}{S\vartheta_1(r)(S-\vartheta_1(r))}.$$

Thus for $r_0\leqq r\leqq R_n$, we have

$$\frac{1}{\vartheta_1(r)}+\frac{1}{\vartheta_2(r)}\geqq\frac{4}{S}=\frac{4}{2h+\delta}\geqq\frac{2}{h}-\frac{\delta}{h^2},$$

while if $r\in E$, we deduce from (11.1) that

$$\frac{1}{\vartheta_1(r)}+\frac{1}{\vartheta_2(r)}\geqq\frac{4}{S}+\frac{(2\varepsilon)^2}{\frac{1}{4}S^3}\geqq\frac{2}{h}-\frac{\delta}{h^2}+\frac{\frac{1}{2}\varepsilon^2}{h^3},$$

since $\delta\leqq h$, so that $S\leqq 3h$, and $S^3<27h^3$. Since $\frac{1}{2}\varepsilon^2>2\delta h$, this gives

$$\frac{1}{\vartheta_1(r)}+\frac{1}{\vartheta_2(r)}\geqq\frac{2}{h}+\frac{\frac{1}{4}\varepsilon^2}{h^3},\quad r\in E.$$

Hence if E' is the complement of E we have

$$\int_{r_0}^{R_n}\frac{dt}{t}\left\{\frac{1}{\vartheta_1(t)}+\frac{1}{\vartheta_2(t)}\right\}\geqq\int_{E(r_0,R_n)}+\int_{E'(r_0,R_n)}\geqq$$

$$\geqq\frac{2}{h}\log\frac{R_n}{r_0}+\int_{E(r_0,R_n)}\frac{\frac{1}{4}\varepsilon^2}{h^3}\frac{dt}{t}-\int_{E'(r_0,R_n)}\frac{\delta}{h^2}\frac{dt}{t}.$$

Using (11.2) we deduce that

$$\int_{r_0}^{R_n}\frac{dt}{t}\left\{\frac{1}{\vartheta_1(t)}+\frac{1}{\vartheta_2(t)}\right\}\frac{dt}{t}\geqq\log\frac{R_n}{r_0}\left\{\frac{2}{h}+\frac{\frac{1}{4}\eta\varepsilon^2}{h^3}-\frac{\delta}{h^2}\right\}.$$

Since by (10.11) we have $2/h=4\mu/\pi$ and $\delta<\frac{1}{4}\eta\varepsilon^2/h$, we obtain a contradiction from (10.8).

Thus for all r outside a set of zero logarithmic density (11.1) is false, so that G has no points $re^{i\vartheta}$, for which

$$\Phi_1\leqq\vartheta\leqq\Phi_1+h-\varepsilon$$

and hence no points for which

$$\vartheta_1\leqq\vartheta\leqq\vartheta_1+h-\varepsilon-\delta=\frac{1}{2}(\vartheta_2+\vartheta_1)-\varepsilon-\delta\,.$$

Since δ, ε may be chosen as small as we please, and since a similar inequality applies to $\vartheta_2(r)$, we deduce that if ε' is fixed and positive then all points $re^{i\vartheta}$ in G, for which $\vartheta_1-\delta\leqq\vartheta\leqq\vartheta_2+\delta$ and r lies outside a set of zero logarithmic density, satisfy $\left|\vartheta-\frac{1}{2}(\vartheta_1+\vartheta_2)\right|<\varepsilon'$.

We now choose $\varepsilon'=\varepsilon_n=\varepsilon 2^{-n}$, and choose R_n so large that if $R>R_n$, then we have for $z=re^{i\vartheta}\in G$, and $\vartheta_1\leqq\vartheta\leqq\vartheta_2$

$$|\vartheta-\vartheta_0|<\varepsilon_n$$

provided that r lies outside E_n where, for $R>R_n$,

$$\int\limits_{E_n(r_0,\,R)}\frac{dt}{t}<\varepsilon_n\log\frac{R}{r_0}\,. \tag{11.3}$$

We may suppose without loss of generality that

$$\frac{\log R_{n+1}}{\log R_n}\to\infty\quad\text{as}\quad n\to\infty\,,$$

and define $E=\bigcup\limits_{n=1}^{\infty}E_n(R_n,R_{n+1})$. Then if r lies outside E and $R_n<r<R_{n+1}$ we have, for $z=re^{i\vartheta}\in G$

$$|\vartheta-\vartheta_0|<\varepsilon_n,$$

so that for $z\in G$

$$\arg z\to\vartheta\quad\text{as}\ |z|\to\infty\quad\text{outside}\ E.$$

Also if $R_n < r < R_{n+1}$, we have

$$\int_{E(r_0,R)} \frac{dt}{t} \leqq \int_{r_0}^{R_{n-1}} \frac{dt}{t} + \int_{E_{n-1}(R_{n-1},R_n)} \frac{dt}{t} + \int_{E_n(R_n,R)} \frac{dt}{t} \leqq \log\frac{R_{n-1}}{r_0} +$$

$$+\varepsilon_{n-1}\log\frac{R_n}{r_0} + \varepsilon_n \log\frac{R}{r_0} \leqq (\varepsilon_n + \varepsilon_{n-1})\log R + o(\log R).$$

Thus E has zero logarithmic density and Theorem 3 is proved.

12. Conclusion

We have actually proved a little more than is stated in Theorem 3. Suppose that G is an unbounded connected set on which (2.2) holds and that u has finite lower order μ. Then G has a finite number of preferred directions $\arg z = \psi_j$, where $\psi_0 < \psi_1 < \ldots < \psi_N = \psi_0 + 2\pi$, and $\psi_{j+1} - \psi_j \geqq 2\pi/\mu$, so that $N \leqq \mu$.

There exists a set E of r having logarithmic density zero, such that for r outside E, $G \cap (|z| = r)$ lies in the union of small arcs

(12.1) $$|\arg z - \psi_j| < o(1), \quad j = 1 \text{ to } N$$

and G actually meets every one of these arcs. Further for $re^{i\vartheta} \in G$, where $r \in E$ we still have

(12.2) $$|\arg z - \psi_j| < \frac{\pi}{2\mu} + o(1).$$

For we may take $\psi_j = \frac{1}{2}(\vartheta_1 + \vartheta_2)$ with the notation of the previous section, so that $\vartheta_1 = \psi_j - \pi/(2\mu)$, $\vartheta_2 = \psi_j + \pi/(2\mu)$. Thus

$$u(z) \leqq 0, \quad \text{for} \quad |\arg z - \psi_j| \leqq \pi/(2\mu)$$

and $u(z) > 0$ is somewhere in each sector.

$$\psi_j + \pi/(2\mu) < \arg z < \psi_{j+1} - \pi/(2\mu).$$

Thus by the Phragmén–Lindelöf principle we must have

$$\psi_{j+1} - \pi/(2\mu) \geqq \psi_j + \pi/(2\mu) + \pi/\mu,$$

i.e. $\psi_{j+1}-\psi_j \geqq 2\pi/\mu$. Also from our construction G has no limiting direction ϑ in the complementary sectors

$$\psi_j+\pi/(2\mu)<\vartheta<\psi_{j+1}-\pi/(2\mu).$$

Thus G is confined to the regions (12.2). Further G meets each circle $|z|=r$ at some point in (12.2) and when z lies outside E, such a point satisfies (12.1).

References

[1] A. BEURLING, Some theorems on boundedness of analytic functions, *Duke Math. J.*, **16** (1949), 355–359.

[2] W. K. HAYMAN, Remarks on Ahlfors' distortion theorem, *Quart. J. Math., Oxford Ser.*, **19** (1948), 33–53.

[3] W. K. HAYMAN, The minimum modulus of large integral functions, *Proc. London Math. Soc.*, (3) **2** (1952), 469–512.

[4] W. K. HAYMAN, Questions of regularity connected with the Phragmén–Lindelöf principle, *J. Math. Pures Appl.*, (9) **35** (1956), 115–126.

[5] W. K. HAYMAN, The minimum modulus of integral functions of order one, *J. Analyse Math.*, **28** (1975), 171–212.

[6] M. H. HEINS, Entire functions with bounded minimum modulus; subharmonic function analogues, *Ann. of Math.*, **49** (1948), 200–213.

[7] M. H. HEINS, *Selected topics in the classical theory of functions of a complex variable*, Holt, Rinehart and Winston, New York 1962.

[8] B. KJELLBERG, A theorem on the minimum modulus of entire functions, *Math. Scand.*, **12** (1963), 5–11.

[9] J. E. LITTLEWOOD, A general theorem on integral functions of finite order, *Proc. London Math. Soc.*, (2) **6** (1908), 189–204.

[10] G. VALIRON, Sur les fonctions entières d'ordre nul et d'ordre fini et en particulier les fonctions à correspondance régulière, *Ann. Fac. Sci. Univ. Toulouse*, (3) **5** (1913), 117–257.

[11] A. WIMAN, Über eine Eigenschaft der ganzen Funktionen von der Höhe Null, *Math. Ann.*, **76** (1915), 197–211.

[12] A. WIMAN, Über den Zusammenhang zwischen dem Maximalbetrage einer analytischen Funktion und dem grössten Betrage bei gegebenem Argumente der Funktion, *Acta Math.*, **41** (1918), 1–28.

IMPERIAL COLLEGE
LONDON SW7,
ENGLAND

ROYAL INSTITUTE OF TECHNOLOGY
STOCKHOLM
SWEDEN

Studies in Pure Matematics
Dem Andenken Paul Turáns gewidmet

Benachbarte multiplikative Funktionen

von

E. HEPPNER und W. SCHWARZ (Frankfurt am Main)

1. Einleitung

Eine zahlentheoretische Funktion $f:\mathbf{N}\to\mathbf{C}$ heißt *vollständig multiplikativ* [bzw. *multiplikativ*], wenn für alle Paare m, n natürlicher Zahlen [bzw. für alle teilerfremden Paare m, n] die Gleichung $f(m\cdot n)=f(m)\cdot f(n)$ gilt. Die Menge $\mathcal{M}$ aller multiplikativen Funktionen, die nicht identisch Null sind, bildet mit der durch

$$(f*g)(n)=\sum_{d\mid n} f(d)\cdot g\left(\frac{n}{d}\right)$$

definierten *Faltung* eine kommutative Gruppe $(\mathcal{M},*)$ mit Einselement e; hierbei ist $e(1)=1$, $e(n)=0$ für $n\neq 1$. Die zu $f\in\mathcal{M}$ bezüglich der Faltung *inverse Funktion* werde mit $\check{f}$ bezeichnet; diese kann aus $f*\check{f}=e$ rekursiv bestimmt werden.

Multiplikative Funktionen sind durch ihre Werte an den Primzahlpotenzen festgelegt; wegen der Seltenheit der höheren Primzahlpotenzen p^k, $k\geqq 2$, kann erwartet werden, daß Funktionen $f, g\in\mathcal{M}$, die (im Mittel) an den Primzahlen p nur wenig voneinander abweichen, ein ähnliches Verhalten auf $\mathbf{N}$ (im Mittel) aufweisen. Wir definieren zunächst:

Die Funktionen $f, g\in\mathcal{M}$ heißen *benachbart*, wenn die Reihe

$$\sum_p \frac{1}{p}\cdot|f(p)-g(p)| \tag{1.1}$$

(absolut) konvergiert.

Man kann nach hinreichenden Bedingungen dafür fragen, daß für benachbarte multiplikative Funktionen f, g die Gültigkeit einer der folgenden Aussagen für f die Gültigkeit der entsprechenden Aussage für g impliziert[1]:

1) f besitzt einen *Mittelwert*

$$M(f)=\lim_{N\to\infty}\frac{1}{N}\cdot\sum_{n\leqq N} f(n).$$

[1] Entsprechende Sätze sind für manche dieser Aussagen bekannt (man vgl. [1], [9], [11], [12], [13]), für andere [wie etwa 6] unbekannt.

2) f besitzt *Fourierkoeffizienten*

$$\hat{f}(\gamma)=\lim_{N\to\infty}\frac{1}{N}\sum_{n\leq N} f(n)\cdot e^{-2\pi i\gamma n}, \quad (\gamma\in\mathbf{R}),$$

oder Ramanujan-Entwicklungskoeffizienten

$$a_q(f)=M(f\cdot c_q),$$

wobei $c_q: n\to \sum_{(a,q)=1}\exp\left(2\pi i\frac{a}{q}n\right)$ die q-te Ramanujan-Summe bezeichnet.

3) f besitzt eine *konvergente* Ramanujan-Entwicklung

$$f(n)=\sum_{q=1}^{\infty} a_q\cdot c_q(n).$$

4) f gehört zur Klasse B^1 der durch Linearkombinationen von Ramanujan-Summen (bzw. von Exponentialfunktionen $e^{2\pi i\frac{a}{q}\cdot n}$ in der Halbnorm

$$\|f\|_1=\limsup_{N\to\infty}\frac{1}{N}\cdot\sum_{n\leq N}|f(n)|$$

beliebig genau approximierbaren Funktionen.

5) Die Reihe $\sum n^{-1}f(n)$ *konvergiert.*

6) Die Reihe $\sum n^{-1}f(n)$ ist (nach einem vorgegebenen Verfahren) *summierbar.*

Sätze dieser Art sind beweistechnisch wichtig, denn sie erlauben, Beweise für Existenz eines Mittelwertes etc. für eine multiplikative Funktion g auf den Fall einer möglichst „einfachen" Funktion f zu reduzieren; demgemäß traten solche Sätze in der Literatur — wenigstens in impliziter Gestalt — häufiger auf (zum Beispiel in [1], [3], [4], [5], [9], [12], [13], [14]).

Die Beweise für solche Sätze beruhen darauf, daß für die in

$$g=f*h$$

auftretende multiplikative Funktion $h=g*\check{f}$ gezeigt werden kann, daß die Reihe

$$\sum_{n=1}^{\infty}\frac{1}{n}\cdot|h(n)|$$

absolut konvergiert. Für multiplikative, benarchbarte Funktionen vom Betrage ≤ 1 wurde dies 1961 von DELANGE [1] gezeigt, der zum Beweise mit Potenzreihen rechnete. In [12] wurde das Ergebnis ausgedehnt, wobei beweismethodisch ein Satz vom

WIENERschen Typ über die Inversion absolutkonvergenter Potenzreihen benutzt wurde. Eine durch ELLIOTTS Arbeit [3] motivierte, elegante Abrundung des Ergebnisses wurde in der Arbeit [9] von L. LUCHT gegeben.[2] Es bezeichnet $\mathscr{V}_q$ den $\mathbf{C}$-Vektorraum der Funktionen $f:\mathbf{N}\to\mathbf{C}$ mit endlicher Halbnorm

$$\|f\|_q := \left\{\limsup_{N\to\infty} \frac{1}{N}\cdot \sum_{n\leq N} |f(n)|^q\right\}^{\frac{1}{q}}. \tag{1.2}$$

Dann zeigte LUCHT:

Für ein gegebenes $q>1$ seien die Funktionen $f,g\in\mathscr{M}_q:=\mathscr{M}\bigcap\mathscr{V}_q$ benachbart. Für alle Primzahlen p seien die Faktoren

$$\varphi_f(p,s) := 1+\frac{f(p)}{p^s}+\frac{f(p^2)}{p^{2s}}+\ldots \tag{1.3}$$

der erzeugenden Dirichletreihe

$$\mathscr{D}(f,s) := \sum_{n=1}^{\infty}\frac{f(n)}{n^s} = \prod_p \varphi_f(p,s) \tag{1.4}$$

in der Halbebene $\operatorname{Re} s\geqq 1$ *von Null verschieden. Dann konvergiert die Reihe*

$$\sum_{n=1}^{\infty}\frac{1}{n}\cdot|h(n)| \tag{1.5}$$

mit der durch $h=g*\check{f}$ bestimmten Funktion h, und es gilt die Produktdarstellung

$$\sum\frac{1}{n}\cdot h(n) = \prod_p \varphi_g(p,1)\cdot\{\varphi_f(p,1)\}^{-1}. \tag{1.6}$$

Dieses Ergebnis läßt sich mit einer abgewandelten Beweismethode auf eine noch größere Funktionenklasse ausdehnen, die besonders günstige Eigenschaften in Bezug auf die Faltung besitzt. Wir stützen uns auf einen Satz vom WIENERschen Typus über die absolute Konvergenz der Inversen von Dirichletreihen[3], der von HEWITT und WILLIAMSON [6] gezeigt wurde. Wir führen die folgenden Teilmengen von $\mathscr{M}$ ein:

$$\mathscr{D} := \{h\in\mathscr{M};\ \sum n^{-1}\cdot|h(n)|<\infty\}, \tag{1.7}$$

$$\mathscr{G} := \{f\in\mathscr{M};\ \sum_p p^{-2}\cdot|f(p)|^2<\infty \quad \text{und} \quad \sum_p\sum_{k\geqq 2} p^{-k}\cdot|f(p^k)|<\infty\} \tag{1.8}$$

[2] Herrn LUCHT danken wir sehr für die Überlassung einer Kopie seines Manuskriptes [9].

[3] Abgesehen von der Anwendung dieses Satzes beruht der Beweis auf der Abschätzung gewisser unendlicher Reihen über Primzahlen.

und (wobei $\varphi_f(p, s)$ in (1.3) definiert wurde)

(1.9) $$\mathscr{G}^* := \{f \in \mathscr{G};\ \textit{für alle } p \textit{ ist } \varphi_f(p, s) \neq 0 \textit{ in } \operatorname{Re} s \geqq 1\}.$$

Schließlich sei

(1.10) $$\mathscr{B} := \{f \in \mathscr{G};\ f \textit{ benachbart zu } e\}.$$

Mit diesen Bezeichnungen gibt der folgende Satz unser Hauptergebnis.

Satz 1. (1) *$\mathscr{G}$ ist gegenüber der Faltung abgeschlossen, d. h. sind $f, g \in \mathscr{G}$, so ist auch $f * g$ aus $\mathscr{G}$.*
(2) *Sind $f, g \in \mathscr{G}^*$, so ist auch $f * g$ aus $\mathscr{G}^*$.*
(3) *Ist $f \in \mathscr{G}^*$, so ist die bezüglich der Faltung inverse Funktion $\check{f}$ aus $\mathscr{G}^*$.*
(4) *Die Mengen $\mathscr{D}$ und $\mathscr{B}$ stimmen überein.*

Wir bemerken, daß die in [9] verwendete Klasse $\mathscr{M}_q$ gegenüber der Faltung nicht abgeschlossen ist; denn die konstante Funktion $1: n \to 1$ liegt in $\mathscr{M}_q$, aber für jedes $q > 1$ liegt $\tau = 1 * 1$ nicht in $\mathscr{M}_q$. Hingegen ist $(\mathscr{G}^*)$ eine Halbgruppe mit Einselement e, und $\mathscr{G}^*$ ist bezüglich der Faltung eine Gruppe.
Aus Satz 1 folgt unmittelbar

Korollar 1. *Ist $f \in \mathscr{G}^*$, $g \in \mathscr{G}$ und sind f und g benachbart, so existiert ein $h \in \mathscr{D}$ mit $g = f * h$.*

Korollar 1 läßt sich auf Funktionen f, die nur in $\mathscr{G}$ liegen, folgendermaßen ausdehnen:
Sind $f \in \mathscr{G}$ und $g \in \mathscr{G}$ benachbart und ist $\varphi_f(p, s) \neq 0$ in $\operatorname{Re} s \geqq 1$ für alle p außerhalb einer endlichen Menge $\mathscr{E}$, so existiert ein $h \in \mathscr{D}$ mit $g = f * h$, falls für alle $p \in \mathscr{E}$ und alle k die Beziehung $f(p^k) = g(p^k)$ gilt.

Korollar 2. *Die in Korollar 1 gegebene Funktion h erfüllt* (1.6).

Die LUCHTschen Klassen $\mathscr{M}_q$ sind in $\mathscr{G}$ enthalten gemäß

Satz 2. *Für jedes $q > 1$ ist $\mathscr{M}_q \subset \mathscr{G}$.*

Satz 1, Satz 2 und Korollar 1 lassen sich sehr leicht auf *β-benachbarte* Funktionen ausdehnen; das sind solche Funktionen $f, g \in \mathscr{M}$, *die für ein festes β*, $0 < \beta \leqq 1$, die Bedingung

(1.11) $$\sum_p p^{-\beta} \cdot |f(p) - g(p)| < \infty$$

erfüllen; dies wird in §4 angedeutet.

Anwendungen werden in §5 skizziert.

2. Beweis von Satz 2 und Beginn des Beweises von Satz 1

Wegen $q>1$ kann ε so klein gewählt werden, daß $\frac{1+2\varepsilon}{q}<1$ ist. Mit $q'=\frac{q}{q-1}$ gibt die Höldersche Ungleichung

$$\sum_p \sum_{k\geqq 2} \frac{1}{p^k}\cdot|f(p^k)| \leqq \left\{\sum_p \sum_{k\geqq 2} \frac{1}{p^{(1+\varepsilon)k}}\cdot|f(p^k)|^q\right\}^{\frac{1}{q}} \cdot \tag{2.1}$$

$$\cdot\left\{\sum_p \sum_{k\geqq 2} p^{-k\left(1-\frac{1+\varepsilon}{q}\right)\cdot q'}\right\}^{\frac{1}{q'}}$$

Wegen $f\in\mathscr{V}_q$ (und partieller Summation) bzw. wegen $\left(1-\frac{1+\varepsilon}{q}\right)\cdot q'>\frac{1}{2}$ konvergieren die beiden Doppelreihen auf der rechten Seite von (2.1). Weiter hat $f\in\mathscr{V}_q$ die Beziehung $|f(n)|\leqq C'\cdot n^{1/q}$ zur Folge; also wird

$$\sum_p \frac{|f(p)|^2}{p^2} \leqq \left\{\sum_p \frac{|f(p)|^q}{p^{1+\varepsilon}}\right\}^{\frac{1}{q}} \cdot \left\{\sum_p p^{-\left(2-\frac{2+\varepsilon}{q}\right)q'}\right\}^{\frac{1}{q'}};$$

wegen $f\in\mathscr{V}_q$ und wegen $\left(2-\frac{2+\varepsilon}{q}\right)\cdot q'>1$ ist dieser Ausdruck endlich.

Zum Beweis von (1) aus Satz 1 definieren wir die multiplikative Funktion w durch $w=f*g$ und zeigen, daß w in $\mathscr{G}$ liegt, wenn f und g aus $\mathscr{G}$ sind.

Zunächst ist $w(p)=f(p)+g(p)$, also ist

$$\sum p^{-2}|w(p)|^2 \leqq 2\sum p^{-2}\cdot\{|f(p)|^2+|g(p)|^2\}<\infty.$$

Weiter ist nach Definition der Faltung

$$w(p^k)=\sum_{r+r'=k} f(p^r)\cdot g(p^{r'}). \tag{2.2}$$

Somit wird

$$\sum_p \sum_{k\geqq 2} p^{-k}\cdot|w(p^k)| \leqq \sum_{\substack{r \\ r+r'\geqq 2}} \sum_{r'} \sum_p \frac{|f(p^r)|}{p^r}\cdot\frac{|g(p^{r'})|}{p^{r'}} \leqq \sum\nolimits_1+\ldots+\sum\nolimits_4$$

mit den Einschränkungen

$r\geqq 2,\ r'\geqq 2$ in $\sum_1$,

$r=0$ oder $r=1,\ r'\geqq 2$ in $\sum_2$,

$r'=0$ oder $1,\ r\geqq 2$ in $\sum_3$,

und $r'=1=r$ in $\sum_4$.

Da f und g die zweite Eigenschaft aus Definition (1.8) von $\mathscr{G}$ erfüllen, ist $\sum_1$ beschränkt. Aus $\sum p^{-2}|f(p)|^2<\infty$ folgt $f(p)=O(p)$, also ist $\sum_2$ beschränkt wegen $\sum\limits_{p,r\geqq 2} p^{-r}|g(p^r)|<\infty$; entsprechend folgt $\sum_3<\infty$.

Die Endlichkeit von $\sum_4$ folgt aus der Cauchy'schen Ungleichung.

Damit ist Aussage (1) von Satz 1 bewiesen; wegen

$$\sum_{k=0}^{\infty}\frac{w(p^k)}{p^{ks}}=\sum_{r=0}^{\infty}\frac{f(p^r)}{p^{rs}}\cdot\sum_{r'=0}^{\infty}\frac{g(p^{r'})}{p^{r's}}$$

[vgl. (2.2)] ist Aussage (2) offensichtlich.

Zu (4). Ist $h\in\mathscr{D}$, so ist

$$\sum_p p^{-1}|h(p)|\leqq\sum_{n=1}^{\infty}n^{-1}|h(n)|<\infty,$$

also

$$|h(p)|=O(p)\text{ und}$$

$$\sum p^{-2}|h(p)|^2\ll\sum p^{-1}|h(p)|<\infty.$$

Weiter ist

$$\sum_p\sum_{k\geqq 2}p^{-k}|h(p^k)|\leqq\sum n^{-1}|h(n)|<\infty,$$

und damit ist $h\in\mathscr{G}$. Wegen

$$\sum p^{-1}|h(p)-e(p)|=\sum p^{-1}|h(p)|<\infty$$

ist h zu e benachbart, und damit $\mathscr{D}\subset\mathscr{B}$.

Ist $h\in\mathscr{B}$, so ist $\sum p^{-1}|h(p)|<\infty$ und $\sum\limits_p\sum\limits_{k\geqq 2}p^{-k}\cdot|h(p^k)|<\infty$. Hieraus folgt

$$\sum_{n\leqq x}n^{-1}|h(n)|\leqq\prod_p\left\{1+\sum_{k=1}^{\infty}p^{-k}\cdot|h(p^k)|\right\}$$

und damit die Inklusion $\mathscr{B}\subset\mathscr{D}$.

3. Hilfssätze und Beweisschluß für Satz 1

Lemma 1. *Ist $\mathscr{A}$ die Banachalgebra der Potenzreihen $P(z)=\sum\limits_0^{\infty}a_nz^n$ mit endlicher Norm*

$$||P||:=\sum|a_n|,$$

so gilt: Ist $P\in\mathscr{A}$ und $P(z)\neq 0$ in $|z|\leqq 1$, so liegt auch die Potenzreihe für die Funktion $z\to 1/P(z)$ in $\mathscr{A}$. (Man vgl. etwa [8], 23C).

Der entsprechende Satz für (gewöhnliche) Dirichletreihen lautet folgendermaßen.

Lemma 2. *Die Dirichletreihe* $\sum_1^\infty a_n n^{-s}$ *mit* $\sum_1^\infty |a_n| < \infty$ *hat dann und nur dann eine Inverse* $\sum_1^\infty b_n \cdot n^{-s}$ *mit* $\sum_1^\infty |b_n| < \infty$, *wenn eine Konstante* $\delta > 0$ *existiert, so daß*

$$\left|\sum a_n n^{-s}\right| \geqq \delta$$

für alle s mit Re $s \geqq 0$ *gilt.*

Ein Beweis dieses Hilfssatzes über Ideen aus der GELFANDschen Theorie der Banachalgebren wurde von E. HEWITT und J. H. WILLIAMSON [6] ausgeführt; nach HEWITT und WILLIAMSON kann dieser Hilfssatz auch aus Ergebnissen von R. S. PHILLIPS [10] gefolgert werden. Eine Ausdehnung auf allgemeine Dirichletreihen gab D. A. EDWARDS [2], wiederum mit Methoden der Funktionalanalysis; A. E. INGHAM [7] zeigte ein entsprechendes Ergebnis mit klassischen Methoden.

Wir kommen nun zum Beweis der Aussage (3) von Satz 1. Ist $f \in \mathscr{G}$ gegeben, so bestimmen wir multiplikative Funktionen f_0, f_1 und f_2 durch ihre Werte an den Primzahlpotenzen auf folgende Weise. Sei

$$f_0(p^k) = \begin{cases} \{f(p)\}^k & \text{für } p > P_0, \\ 0 & \text{für } p \leqq P_0; \end{cases} \tag{3.1}$$

weiter sei

$$f_1 = f_1' * f_1'', \tag{3.2}$$

wobei

$$f_1'(p^k) = \begin{cases} -f(p) & \text{für } k=1, p > P_0, \\ 0 & \text{sonst}, \end{cases} \tag{3.2'}$$

$$f_1''(p^k) = \begin{cases} f(p^k) & \text{für } p > P_0, \\ 0 & \text{für } p \leqq P_0, \end{cases} \tag{3.2''}$$

und schließlich sei

$$f_2(p^k) = \begin{cases} 0 & \text{für } p > P_0, \\ f(p^k) & \text{für } p \leqq P_0. \end{cases} \tag{3.3}$$

Dabei ist die Konstante P_0 so gewählt, daß

$$|f(p)| < \frac{1}{6} p \quad \text{für} \quad p > P_0 \tag{3.4'}$$

und

$$\sum_{p>P_0}\sum_{k\geqq 2} p^{-k}\cdot|f(p^k)|<\frac{1}{3} \tag{3.4''}$$

gilt; wegen $f\in\mathscr{G}$ ist dies möglich.

Wir zeigen nun

Lemma 3. *Sei $f\in\mathscr{G}$. Dann gelten die folgenden Aussagen:*
(a) $f=f_0*f_1*f_2$.
(b) f_0 *ist vollständig multiplikativ.*
(c) $f_0\in\mathscr{G}^*$ *und* $\check{f}_0\in\mathscr{G}^*$.
(d) $f_1\in\mathscr{D}\cap\mathscr{G}^*$.
(e) $\check{f}_1\in\mathscr{D}$.
(f) $f_2\in\mathscr{D}$.
(g) *Ist* $\varphi_f(p,s)\neq 0$ *für* Re $s\geqq 0$ *und für alle* $p\leqq P_0$, *so ist* $\check{f}_2\in\mathscr{D}$.

Bemerkung. Von diesen vielen Aussagen ist (e) die entscheidende, sie beruht auf Lemma 2.

Beweis. Die Betrachtung der zugeordneten Dirichletreihen zeigt, daß (a) richtig ist; dabei ist $f_0=f'_1$. (b) ist offensichtlich, (f) ist leicht zu zeigen, da die zugeordnete Dirichletreihe ein endliches Produkt von in Re $s\geqq 1$ absolut-konvergenten Dirichletreihen ist.

Zu (d). Wegen $f'_1\in\mathscr{G}$, $f''_1\in\mathscr{G}$ und dem schon bewiesenen Teil (1) von Satz 1 ist $f_1=f'_1*f''_1\in\mathscr{G}$. Sodann ist

$$f_1(p^k)=\begin{cases} f(p^k)-f(p^{k-1})\cdot f(p) & \text{für}\quad p>P_0\quad\text{und}\quad k\geqq 2,\\ 0 & \text{sonst}.\end{cases}$$

Demnach wird

$$\sum_{n=1}^{\infty}\left|\frac{f_1(n)}{n}\right|\leqq\prod_{p>P_0}\left\{1+\sum_{k\geqq 2}\frac{|f(p^k)|+|f(p^{k-1})(f(p))|}{p^k}\right\}.$$

Man prüft leicht nach, daß $f\in\mathscr{G}$ die Konvergenz dieses Produktes zur Folge hat. Somit ist $f_1\in\mathscr{D}$.

Schließlich ist für $p>P_0$

$$\begin{aligned} S_p:=\sum_{k=2}^{\infty}\frac{|f(p^k)|+|f(p^{k-1})f(p)|}{p^k}\leqq\\ \leqq\frac{|f(p)|^2}{p^2}+\left(1+\frac{|f(p)|}{p}\right)\cdot\sum_{k=2}^{\infty}\frac{|f(p^k)|}{p^k}\leqq\frac{1}{2},\end{aligned}\tag{3.5}$$

also ist für Re $s \geqq 1$

$$|\varphi_{f_1}(p, s)| \geqq 1 - S_p \geqq \frac{1}{2},$$

d. h. es ist $f_1 \in \mathscr{G}^*$.

Zu (e). Es ist wegen $S_p \leqq \frac{1}{2}$ für Re $s \geqq 1$

$$\left|\sum_{n=1}^{\infty} \frac{f_1(n)}{n^s}\right| \geqq \prod_{p>P_0} \left(1 - \sum_{k=2}^{\infty} \frac{|f(p^k)| + |f(p^{k-1}) f(p)|}{p^k}\right) \geqq$$

$$\geqq \exp(-2 \cdot \sum_{p \geqq P_0} S_p),$$

and ähnlich wie vorher [man vgl. (3.5)] wird wegen $f \in \mathscr{G}$

$$\sum_{p>P_0}' S_p \leqq \sum_{p>P_0} \frac{|f(p)|^2}{p^2} + \frac{7}{6} \cdot \sum_{p>P_0} \sum_{k \geqq 2} \frac{|f(p^k)|}{p^k} \leqq \gamma_1 < \infty,$$

somit ist

$$\left|\sum n^{-s} \cdot f_1(n)\right| \geqq \delta := e^{-2\gamma_1} \quad \text{in} \quad \operatorname{Re} s \geqq 1,$$

und nach Lemma 2 wird $\check{f}_1 \in \mathscr{D}$.

Schließlich gibt Lemma 1, daß die $\check{f}_2$ zugeordnete Dirichletreihe ein Produkt von endlich vielen in Re $s \geqq 1$ absolut konvergenten Dirichletreihen [nämlich der Inversen der Reihen $\varphi_{f_2}(p, s)$] ist, also wiederum absolut konvergiert. Somit ist $\check{f}_2 \in \mathscr{G}$, und (g) ist gezeigt.

Beweisschluß von Satz 1. Es steht nur der Beweis von (3) aus.

Wegen (a) von Lemma 3 wird

$$\check{f} = \check{f}_0 * \check{f}_1 * \check{f}_2 .$$

Zunächst ist $\check{f}_1 \in \mathscr{D}$ und $\check{f}_2 \in \mathscr{D}$ nach Lemma 3 (e) bzw. (g). Nach (4) von Satz 1 ist $\mathscr{D} = \mathscr{B} \subset \mathscr{G}$. Wegen (c) aus Lemma 3 ist $f_0 \in \mathscr{G}^* \subset \mathscr{G}$, also gibt (1) von Satz (1), daß $\check{f}$ aus $\mathscr{G}$ ist. Da die Dirichletreihen $\mathscr{D}(f_1, s)$ bzw. $\mathscr{D}(f_2, s)$ gemäß (d) und (f) aus Lemma 3 in Re $s \geqq 1$ absolut konvergieren, können die inversen Dirichletreihen in Re $s \geqq 1$ keine Nullstellen besitzen, also sind sogar $\check{f}_1 \in \mathscr{G}^*$ und $\check{f}_2 \in \mathscr{G}^*$, und (2) von Satz (1) gibt, daß $\check{f}$ in $\mathscr{G}^*$ liegt.

Beweis von Korollar 1 und 2. Wegen $f \in \mathscr{G}^*$ ist $\check{f} \in \mathscr{G}$, somit

$$h := \check{f} * g \in \mathscr{G}.$$

Da f zu g benachbart ist, wird

$$\sum p^{-1} \cdot |h(p)| = \sum p^{-1} |g(p) - f(p)| < \infty,$$

d. h. h ist zu e benachbart, also ist $h \in \mathscr{B}$. Wegen $\mathscr{B} = \mathscr{D}$ ist $\sum n^{-1} |h(n)| < \infty$.

4. Eine naheliegende Verallgemeinerung

Sei $0 < \beta \leqq 1$. Die (multiplikativen) Funktionen f und g heißen β-benachbart, wenn die Reihe

(4.1) $$\sum_p p^{-\beta} |f(p) - g(p)| < \infty$$

konvergiert. Die in §1 bis §3 genannten Ergebnisse lassen sich mühelos auf β-benachbarte Funktionen übertragen. Führt man analog zu den früheren Bezeichnungen die Mengen

(4.2) $$\mathscr{D}_\beta = \{h \in \mathscr{M}; \sum_n n^{-\beta} |h(n)| < \infty\},$$

(4.3) $$\mathscr{G}_\beta = \{f \in \mathscr{M}; \sum_p p^{-2\beta} \cdot |f(p)|^2 < \infty, \sum_p \sum_{k \geqq 2} p^{-k\beta} |f(p^k)| < \infty\}$$

und

(4.4) $$\mathscr{G}_\beta^* = \{f \in \mathscr{G}_\beta; \varphi_f(p, s) \neq 0 \quad \text{für} \quad \operatorname{Re} s \geqq \beta\}$$

ein, so erhält man

Satz 1'. (1) *Für* $f, g \in \mathscr{G}_\beta$ *ist* $f * g \in \mathscr{G}_\beta$.
(2) *Für* $f, g \in \mathscr{G}_\beta^*$ *ist* $f * g \in \mathscr{G}_\beta^*$.
(3) *Ist* $f \in \mathscr{G}_\beta^*$, *so ist* $\check{f} \in \mathscr{G}_\beta^*$.
(4) $\mathscr{D}_\beta = \{f \in \mathscr{G}_\beta;\ f\ \beta\text{-benachbart zu } e\}$.

Korollar 1'. *Ist* $f \in \mathscr{G}_\beta^*$, $g \in \mathscr{G}_\beta$ *und sind* f *und* g β*-benachbart, so existiert ein* $h \in \mathscr{D}_\beta$, *so daß*

$$g = f * h$$

gilt.

Satz 2'. *Ist* $q > 1$ *und* $\beta > \frac{1}{2} + \frac{1}{2q}$, *so ist*

$$\mathscr{M}_q \subset \mathscr{G}_\beta.$$

Die Beweise lassen sich entweder (nahezu) wörtlich übertragen — oder aber man führt die Ergebnisse mit $\tilde{f}(n) = f(n) \cdot n^{-(1-\beta)}$ für $f \in \mathscr{G}_\beta$ und mit analog erklärten Funktionen $\tilde{g}$ und $\tilde{h}$ auf den früheren Satz 1 zurück.

5. Anwendungen

Zur Erläuterung der Anwendbarkeit von Satz 1 (bzw. 1′) skizzieren wir mit wohlbekannten Beweismethoden einen Beweis für den folgenden

Satz 3. *Sei* $0<\beta\leqq 1$, $f\in\mathcal{G}_\beta^*$, $g\in\mathcal{G}_\beta$, *und seien* f *und* g β*-benachbart. Gilt für* $x\to\infty$

$$\sum_{n\leqq x} f(n)=A\cdot x+R(x) \tag{5.1}$$

mit dem Restglied

$$R(x)=O(x^\beta)\ [bzw.\ R(x)=o(x^\beta)]\,,$$

so gilt für $x\to\infty$

$$\sum_{n\leqq x} g(n)=A'\cdot x+R'(x)\,, \tag{5.2}$$

wobei $R'(x)=O(x^\beta)$ [*bzw.* $R'(x)=o(x^\beta)$] *und*

$$A'=A\cdot\prod_p\frac{\varphi_g(p,1)}{\varphi_f(p,1)} \tag{5.3}$$

ist.

Bemerkung. Die Voraussetzung $f\in\mathcal{G}_\beta^*$ läßt sich wie in der Bemerkung nach Korollar 1 abschwächen.

Als unmittelbare Folgerung ergibt sich ein Satz von Delange [1].

Sind f, g *multiplikativ, vom Betrag* $\leqq 1$ *und benachbart, so hat die Existenz von* $M(f)$ *die Existenz von* $M(g)$ *zur Folge, wenn noch für den Fall, daß* $f(2^r)=(-1)^r\{f(2)\}^r$ *für alle* $r\geqq 2$ *und* $|f(2)|=1$ *ist, vorausgesetzt wird, daß* $g(2^r)=f(2^r)$ *für alle* $r\geqq 1$ *ist.*

Beweis von Satz 3. Nach Satz 1′ gibt es ein $h\in\mathcal{D}_\beta$, so daß $g=f*h$ ist. Damit wird

$$\sum_{n\leqq x} g(n)=\sum_{d\leqq x} h(d)\cdot\sum_{m\leqq\frac{x}{d}} f(m)\,.$$

Setzt man die asymptotische Formel (5.1) ein und dehnt man die Summation über d bis ∞ aus, so folgt

$$\sum_{n\leqq x} g(n)=A\cdot x\cdot\sum_{d=1}^{\infty}\frac{h(d)}{d}+O\left(x\cdot\sum_{d>x}\frac{|h(d)|}{d}\right)+O\left(x^\beta\cdot\sum_{d\leqq x}\frac{|h(d)|}{d^\beta}\right).$$

Vergrößert man das erste Fehlerglied durch Anfügen des Faktors $\left(\frac{d}{x}\right)^{1-\beta}$ in der Summe, so folgt (5.2) unmittelbar. Eine ähnliche Rechnung führt für das Restglied $o(x^\beta)$ zum Ziel.

Korollar 3. *Sei $r \geqq 1$ eine natürliche Zahl; sei f eine multiplikative Funktion, die an allen Primzahlpotenzen gleichmäßig beschränkt ist, d. h. es gilt* $\sup_{p,k} |f(p^k)| < \infty$. *Sei $g \in \mathcal{M}$ derart, daß die Reihe*

$$\sum_p \sum_{k \geqq 2} \frac{|g(p^k)|^r}{p^k} < \infty \tag{5.4}$$

konvergiert, sei schließlich

$$\sum_p \frac{|f(p)-g(p)|}{p} < \infty \quad \text{und} \quad \sum_p \frac{|f(p)-g(p)|^r}{p} < \infty. \tag{5.5}$$

Ist dann $\varphi_{f^r}(p, s) \neq 0$ in $\operatorname{Re} s \geqq 1$, so folgt aus der Existenz des Mittelwertes $M(f^r)$ die Existenz von $M(g^r)$.

Beweis. Die Beschränktheit von $f(p^k)$ und die Bedingung über das Nichtverschwinden von $\varphi_{f^r}(p, s)$ zeigen, daß f^r in $\mathcal{G}^*$ liegt; mit (5.5) folgt die Konvergenz von $\sum p^{-2}|g(p)|^{2r}$, und zusammen mit (5.4) ist also $g^r \in \mathcal{G}$. Aus (5.5) folgt leicht, daß f^r und g^r benachbart sind, und die Behauptung ergibt sich aus Satz 3.

Bemerkung. Ist w eine multiplikative, beschränkte Funktion und sind $f \in \mathcal{G}$ und $g \in \mathcal{G}$ benachbart, so folgt aus der Existenz von $M(f \cdot w)$ die Existenz von $M(g \cdot w)$, wenn noch

$$\varphi_{f w}(p. s) \neq 0 \quad \text{in} \quad \operatorname{Re} s \geqq 1 \quad \text{für alle } p$$

vorausgesetzt wird. Man kann nämlich Satz 3 auf $\tilde{f} = f \cdot w \in \mathcal{G}^*$ und $\tilde{g} = g \cdot w \in \mathcal{G}$ anwenden.

Ist w vollständig multiplikativ und beschränkt, so folgt aus der Existenz von $M(f \cdot w)$ die Existenz von $M(g \cdot w)$, wenn $f \in \mathcal{G}^*$ und $g \in \mathcal{G}$ benachbart sind. Dies wird analog zu Satz 3 gezeigt.

B. SAFFARI[4] stellte folgendes Problem: Sind A, B *Teilmengen* von $\mathbf{N}$ derart, daß die multiplikative Halbgruppe $(\mathbf{N}, \cdot)$ direktes Produkt von A und B ist, so existieren die (natürlichen) Dichten δ_A bzw. δ_B von A bzw. B; er löste dieses Problem im „konvergenten" Falle $\mathcal{H}(B) := \sum_{b \in B} b^{-1} < \infty$. Die Lösung im „divergenten" Fall $\mathcal{H}(B) = \infty$ gaben P. ERDŐS, B. SAFFARI und R. C. VAUGHAN.[5] Im Spezialfall, daß die charakteristische Funktion χ_B der Menge B (und damit wegen $1 = \chi_A * \chi_B$ auch die charakteristische Funktion χ_A) multiplikativ ist, folgt im „konvergenten" Fall die Lösung des Problems aus Satz 3[6]. Die Bedingung $\mathcal{H}(B) < \infty$ impliziert nämlich, daß 1 und χ_A benachbart sind; da $M(1)$ existiert, zeigt Satz 3, daß $\delta(A) = M(\chi_A)$ existiert.

[4] On the asymptotic density of sets of integers, *J. London Math. Soc.*, (2) **13** (1976), 475–485.

[5] On the asymptotic density of sets of integers, II, to appear.

[6] Die Lösung folgt sogar schon aus dem nach Satz 3 zitierten Satz von DELANGE [1].

Den Beweis des folgenden Satzes, der demjenigen von Satz 3 ganz ähnlich ist, unterdrücken wir.

Satz 4. *Sind* $f \in \mathcal{G}^*$ *und* $g \in \mathcal{G}$ *benachbart, so folgt aus der Konvergenz der Reihe* $\sum n^{-1} f(n)$ *die Konvergenz der Reihe* $\sum n^{-1} g(n)$.

Wir bemerken noch, daß für benachbarte Funktionen f und g analytische Eigenschaften der Dirichletreihe $\mathcal{D}(f, s)$ für f entsprechende Eigenschaften von $\mathcal{D}(g, s)$ nach sich ziehen. Zum Beispiel gilt:

Sei $0 < \beta \leqq 1$. *Sind* $f \in \mathcal{G}_\beta^*$ *und* $g \in \mathcal{G}_\beta^*$ *β-benachbart und ist die (für* Re $s > 1$ *konvergente) Dirichletreihe* $\mathcal{D}(f, s)$ *bis auf eine Ausnahmemenge* $\mathcal{S}$ *von endlich vielen isolierten Singularitäten in die Halbebene* Re $s \geqq \beta$ *analytisch fortsetzbar, so ist* $\mathcal{D}(g, s)$ *nach* $\{s \in \mathbf{C};$ Re $s > \beta\} \setminus \mathcal{S}$ *analytisch und nach* $\{s;$ Re $s \geqq \beta\} \setminus \mathcal{S}$ *stetig fortsetzbar. Die Fortsetzungen von* $\mathcal{D}(f, s)$ *und* $\mathcal{D}(g, s)$ *haben in* Re $s > \beta$ *dieselben Singularitäten und in* Re $s \geqq \beta$ *dieselben Nullstellen.*

Denn auf Grund der Voraussetzungen gibt es Funktionen h, $h' \in \mathcal{D}_\beta$, $h' = \check{h}$, mit $g = h * f$ und $f = h' * g$. Wegen h, $h' \in \mathcal{D}_\beta$ sind $\mathcal{D}(h, s)$ und $\mathcal{D}(h', s) = \{\mathcal{D}(h, s)\}^{-1}$ in Re $s > \beta$ holomorph und in Re $s \geqq \beta$ stetig und nullstellenfrei; die Behauptung folgt aus $\mathcal{D}(g, s) = \mathcal{D}(h, s) \cdot \mathcal{D}(f, s)$.

Die Hauptergebnisse dieser Arbeit wurden inzwischen auf den Fall von Funktionen mehrerer Variabler verallgemeinert (vgl. E. Heppner, Über benachbarte multiplikative zahlentheoretische Funktionen mehrerer Variabler. Arch. Math. *35* (1980). 454–460 und Über Mittelwerte multiplikativer zahlentheoretischer Funktionen mehrerer Variabler. Monatsh. f. Math. *91* (1981), 1–9.

Literaturverzeichnis

[1] Delange, H., Sur les fonctions arithmétiques multiplicatives, *Ann. Sci. École Norm. Sup.*, **78** (1961), 273–304.

[2] Edwards, D. A., On absolutely convergent Dirichlet series, *Proc. Amer. Math. Soc.*, **8** (1957), 1067–1074.

[3] Elliott, P. D. T. A., A mean-value theorem for multiplicative functions, *Proc. London Math. Soc.*, (3) **31** (1975), 418–438.

[4] Galambos, J., On the asymptotic distribution of values of arithmetical functions, *Accad. Nazionale dei Lincei*, Ser. VIII., **52** (1972), 84–89.

[5] Halász, G., Über die Mittelwerte multiplikativer zahlentheoretischer Funktionen, *Acta Math. Sci. Hung.*, **19** (1968), 365–403.

[6] Hewitt, E. and J. H. Williamson, Note on absolutely convergent Dirichlet series, *Proc. Amer. Math. Soc.*, **8** (1957) 863–868.

[7] Ingham, A. E., On absolutely convergent Dirichlet series. *Studies in Mathematical Analysis and Related Topics. Essays in Honor of G. Pólya*, Stanford Calif., 1962, pp. 156–164.

[8] Loomis, L. H., *An introduction to abstract harmonic analysis*, Princeton N. J., 1953.

[9] Lucht, L. Über benachbarte multiplikative Funktionen, *Arch. Math.*, **30** (1978), 40–48.

[10] Phillips, R. S., Sprectral theory for semi-groups of linear operators, *Transactions Amer. Math. Soc.*, **71** (1951), 393–415.

[11] SCHWARZ, W., Eine weitere Bemerkung über multiplikative Funktionen, *Coll. Math.*, **28** (1973), 81–89.
[12] SCHWARZ, W., Ramanujan-Entwicklungen stark multiplikativer Funktionen, *J. Reine Angew. Math.*, **262/263** (1973), 66–73.
[13] SCHWARZ, W. and J. SPILKER, Mean values and Ramanujan expansions of almost even functions, *Coll. Math. Soc. J. Bolyai*, Debrecen 1974, 315–357 (1976).
[14] TUTTAS, F., Über die Entwicklung multiplikativer Funktionen und Ramanujan-Summen, *Acta Arithmetica*, **36** (1980), 257–270.
[15] WIRSING, E., Das asymptotische Verhalten von Summen über multiplikative Funktionen, *Math. Ann.*, **143** (1961), 75–102. — Teil II, *Acta Math. Acad. Sci. Hung.*, **18** (1967), 414–467.

FACHBEREICH MATHEMATIK
DER JOHANN-WOLFGANG-GOETHE-UNIVERSITÄT
6 FRANKFURT AM MAIN 1
ROBERT-MAYER-STRASSE 10, BRD

Studies in Pure Mathematics
Dem Andenken Paul Turáns gewidmet

Eine Bemerkung zur Theorie der Gleichverteilung

von

E. HLAWKA (Wien)

Es sei ω eine Dreiecksfolge;

(1) $$(x_{N1}, x_{N2}, \ldots, x_{NN})$$

für $N=1, 2, \ldots$ Die x_{Nk} sind reelle Zahlen in einem Intervall $I=<a, b<$. Es sei ω zur Dichte ρ gleichverteilt, wo ρ eine im Riemannschen Sinne integrierbare Funktion auf $I=<a, b>$ ist. Es sei ρ nicht negativ, wobei

$$\lambda(I)=\int_a^b \rho\, dx>0$$

ist. Dann gelte also für jede (im Riemannschen Sinne) integrierbare Funktion g auf I

(2) $$\lim_{N\to\infty}\frac{1}{N}\sum_{k=1}^{N} g(x_{Nk})=\frac{1}{\lambda(I)}\int_I g(x)\,\rho(x)\,dx\,.$$

Wir ordnen nun für jedes feste N die Zahlen in (1) der Größe nach

(3) $$z_{N1}, z_{N2}, \ldots, z_{NN}\,.$$

Wir wollen die so für $N=1, 2, \ldots$ entstehende Folge mit $\hat{\omega}$ bezeichnen.

Es sei nun weiter eine Folge (α_k) komplexer Zahlen gegeben. Sie sei beschränkt, d. h. es existiert ein M, so daß für alle k

(4) $$|\alpha_k|\leqq M\,.$$

(Wenn alle α_k reell und nicht negativ sind, so setzen wir (4) nicht voraus.) Weiters existiere

(5) $$\lim_{N\to\infty}\frac{1}{N}\sum_{k=1}^{N}\alpha_k=\alpha\,.$$

Dann behaupten wir folgenden

Satz: *Für jede im Riemannschen Sinne integrierbare Funktion existiert*

$$\lim_{N\to\infty} \frac{1}{N} \sum_{k=1}^{N} \alpha_k f(z_{Nk})$$

und es ist

$$\lim_{N\to\infty} \frac{1}{N} \sum_{k=1}^{N} \alpha_k f(z_{Nk}) = \frac{\alpha}{\lambda(I)} \int_a^b f(x)\,\rho(x)\,dx\,. \tag{6}$$

Wir wollen folgenden Spezialfall betrachten. Es sei ρ auf I stets gleich 1, weiter sei

$$\bar{x}_{Nk} = a + \frac{k}{N}(b-a) \quad \text{für} \quad k = 0, 1, \ldots, N\,.$$

Es sei (α_k) eine Folge von Zahlen der Gestalt 0 oder 1, welcher man die Zahl

$$t = 0, \alpha_1, \alpha_2, \ldots$$

zuordnen kann. Für diese Folge ist (4) erfüllt. Weiters gelte (5). Betrachten wir nun eine Folge $\omega = (x_{Nk})$ $(k = 1, \ldots, N)$, so daß stets x_{Nk} im Intervall

$$<\bar{x}_{Nk-1}, \bar{x}_{Nk}<$$

liegt, so ist $\omega^* = \omega$; nach Definition des Riemannschen Integrals gilt (2) mit $\rho = 1$, und es ist dann noch (6), mit $\lambda(I) = b - a$

$$\lim_{N\to\infty} \frac{1}{N} \sum_{k=1}^{N} \alpha_k f(x_{Nk}) = \frac{\alpha}{\lambda(I)} \int_a^b f(x)\,dx\,. \tag{6'}$$

Diese Formel (6′) wurde erstmals von Carr und Hill 1951 in *Am. Proc.*, **2** (242–245) gezeigt. Sie nennen die linke Seite von (6′) das *Pattern integral* von f. Das „Muster" wird dabei durch die Zahl t gegeben.

Wir wollen, bevor wir weitere Bemerkungen zu (6) geben, zunächst (6) beweisen. Wir werden dabei eine Methode benützen, wie sie in der Theorie der Gleichverteilung üblich ist. Sie dürfte sogar im Falle (6′) etwas einfacher sein, als die Methode von Carr und Hill. Wir können ohne Beschränkung der Allgemeinheit annehmen, daß I das Intervall $E = 0, 1<$ und $\lambda(I) = 1$ ist.

Wenn f auf E eine Konstante k ist, dann ist (6) richtig und folgt sofort aus (5). Wir setzen nun zunächst voraus, daß die α_k alle nicht negativ sind. Es sei nun f die Indikatorfunktion i des Teilintervalls $<0, c<$, wo $0 < c < 1$ ist. Es sei nun die natürliche Zahl $l = l(N)$, so gewählt, daß

$$z_{Nl} \leqq c < z_{N,l+1} \tag{7}$$

ist. Dann ist

$$\frac{1}{N}\sum_{k=1}^{N}\alpha_k i(z_{Nk})=\frac{1}{N}\sum_{k-1}^{l(N)}\alpha_k\,. \tag{8}$$

Nun ist

$$\frac{1}{N}\sum_{k=1}^{l(N)}\alpha_k=\frac{l(N)}{N}\,\frac{1}{l(N)}\sum_{k=1}^{l(N)}\alpha_k\,.$$

Es ist nun, nach Definition von 1 (vgl. (7))

$$l(N)=\sum_{k=1}^{N} i(z_{Nk})=\sum_{k=1}^{N} i(x_{Nk}) \tag{9}$$

denn es ist (3) nur eine Umordnung von (1) und die Summe in (9) ist eine symmetrische Funktion. Nach (2) gilt aber

$$\lim_{N\to\infty}\frac{l(N)}{N}=\lim_{N\to\infty}\frac{1}{N}\sum_{k=1}^{N} i(x_{Nk})=\int_0^1 i(x)\rho(x)dx\,. \tag{2'}$$

Weiters ist nach (5)

$$\lim_{N\to\infty}\frac{1}{l(N)}\sum_{k=1}^{l(N)}\alpha_k=\alpha$$

und damit ist (6) für f bewiesen, wenn $l(N)$ nicht beschränkt ist. Ist aber von einem N_0 an $l(N)=l_0$ fest, dann ist nach (2′)

$$0=\lim_{N\to\infty}\frac{l_0}{N}=\int_0^1 i(x)\rho(x)dx=\int_0^c \sigma(x)dx\,.$$

Dann ist aber (6) auch richtig.

Es gilt (6) auch dann, wenn i_1 die Indikatorfunktion des Intervalls $<c, 1<$ ist, denn es ist doch, wenn i die gleiche Bedeutung wie vorher hat.

$$l_1=1-i\,.$$

Es ist ja (6) linear und homogen in f. Liegt ein Intervall $<c_1, c_2<$ aus E vor und ist i_3 seine Indikatorfunktion so ist doch $i_3=i_2-i_1$, wo i_2 die Indikatorfunktion von $<0, c_2<$ und i_1 jene von $<0, c_1<$ ist. Daraus folgt nun, daß (6) für alle Treppenfunktionen bewiesen ist.

Um nun (6) für alle im Riemannschen Sinne integrierbare Funktionen f zu beweisen, benützen wir die Tatsache, daß es zu jedem solchen f und zu jedem $\varepsilon>0$

Treppenfunktionen f_1 und f_2 gibt, so daß in E

$$f_1 \leqq f \leqq f_2 \tag{10}$$

ist und

$$\int_0^1 (f_2 - f_1)\,dx < \varepsilon \tag{11}$$

ist. Ist M eine obere Schranke von ρ in E, so ist daher auch

$$\int_0^1 (f_2 - f)\,\rho(x)\,dx \leqq \int_0^1 (f_2 - f_1)\,\rho\,dx \leqq M\varepsilon \tag{11'}$$

und

$$\int_0^1 (f - f_1)\,\rho\,dx \leqq M\varepsilon \tag{11''}$$

Nun benützen wir *erstmals*, daß die α_k nicht negativ sind. Es ist dann nämlich, wenn wir

$$\lambda_N(f) = \frac{1}{N} \sum_{k=1}^{N} \alpha_k f(z_{Nk}) \quad \text{setzen}$$

$$\lambda_N(f_1) \leqq \lambda_N(f) \leqq \lambda_N(f_2)\,. \tag{12}$$

Weiter ist nach (6) angewendet auf f_1 und f_2 (für Treppenfunktionen haben wir ja schon (6) bewiesen) für großes N

$$|\lambda_N(f_k) - \alpha\lambda(f_k)| < \varepsilon \tag{13}$$

wo

$$\lambda(g) = \int_0^1 g\rho\,dx$$

ist. Es ist also nach (13) für großes N und nach (11')

$$\lambda_N(f_2) \leqq \alpha\lambda(f_2) + \varepsilon \leqq \alpha\lambda(f) + (M+1)\,\varepsilon$$

und nach (13) und (11'')

$$\lambda_N(f_1) \geqq \alpha\lambda(f_1) - \varepsilon \geqq \alpha\lambda(f) - (M+1)\,\varepsilon\,.$$

Es ist also und (12) für großes N

$$|\lambda_N(f)-\alpha\lambda(f)| \leqq (M+1)\,\varepsilon$$

und dies ist die Behauptung (6).

Es sei nun die Folge (α_k) eine beliebige reelle Folge mit (4) und (5), dann ist die Folge $(\alpha'_k)=(\alpha_k+M)$ eine nicht negative Folge mit

$$\lim_{N\to\infty}\frac{1}{N}\sum_{k=1}^{N}\alpha'_k=\alpha+M$$

und wir erhalten nach dem eben Bewiesenen

$$\lim_{N\to\infty}\frac{1}{N}\sum_{k=1}^{N}\alpha'_k f(z_{Nk})=(\alpha+M)\,\lambda(f)\,.$$

Da

$$\lim_{N\to\infty}\frac{1}{N}\sum f(z_{Nk})=\lambda(f)$$

wieder nach (6), mit $\alpha_k=1$ für alle k, so folgt durch Subtraktion jetzt die Behauptung für jede reelle Folge (α_k). Ist jetzt allgemein (α_k) eine beliebige Folge mit (4) und (5), so folgt daß die Folge (Re *al* α_k) und (Im α_k) die Behauptung (6) erfüllen und damit (α_k) selbst. Damit ist der Satz vollkommen bewiesen.

Wir wollen gleich noch auf eine Verallgemeinerung hinweisen.

Satz 2: *Es seien die Voraussetzung* (1), (2), (3) *erfüllt. Es sei weiter* (a_k) *eine Folge von Vektoren in* C^s, *so daß ein* M *existiert, so daß*

(14) $$|a_k| \leqq M$$

und

(15) $$\lim_{k\to\infty}\frac{1}{N}\sum_{k=1}^{N}a_k=a$$

dann gilt

(16) $$\lim_{N\to\infty}\frac{1}{N}\sum_{k=1}^{N}a_k f(z_{Nk})=a\int_I f\rho\,dx\,.$$

Der Beweis folgt aus (6) angewendet auf die Komponenten der Vektorenfolge.

Eine weitere Verallgemeinerung erhalten wir dadurch, daß wir statt dem eindimensionalen Intervall I ein l-dimensionales Intervall I^l nehmen.

Weiters seien jetzt l-Folgen $\omega^{(g)}$ $(g=1, \ldots, l)$ durch

$$\omega^{(g)}=(x_{N1}^{(g)}, \ldots, x_{NN}^{(g)}) \tag{17}$$

gegeben.

Es sei

$$\lambda_{N_1 \ldots N_l}(g)=\frac{1}{N_1, N_2, \ldots, N_l} \sum_{k_1=1, \ldots, k_l=1}^{N_1, \ldots, N_l} g(x_{N_1, k_1}, \ldots, x_{N_l, k_l}). \tag{18}$$

Es gelte, wo

$$\lambda(I)=\int_{I^l} \rho \, dx_1, \ldots, dx_l$$

$$\lim_{(N_1 \ldots N_l) \to \infty} \lambda_{N_1 \ldots N_l}(g)=\frac{1}{\lambda(I^l)} \int_{I^l} g(x_1 \ldots x_l)\, \rho(x_1 \ldots x_l)\, dx_1 \ldots dx_l \tag{19}$$

wo ρ eine Dichtefunktion auf I^l ist. Es gelte (18) und (19) für jede auf I^l (Hülle von I^l) im Riemannschen Sinn integrierbare Funktion. Wir bilden uns nach (3) zu den Folge $\omega^{(j)}$ die Folgen $\hat{\omega}^{(j)}$. Es sei weiter eine l-fache beschränkte Folge

$$(\alpha_{k_1, \ldots, k_l})$$

gegeben mit

$$\lim_{(N_1 \ldots N_l) \to \infty} \frac{1}{N_1 \ldots N_l} \sum_{k_1=1, \ldots, k_l=1}^{N_1, \ldots, N_l} \alpha_{k_1 \ldots k_l}=\alpha \tag{20}$$

dann gilt wieder

$$\lim_{(N_1, \ldots, N_l) \to \infty} \frac{1}{N_1 \ldots N_l} \sum_{k_1 \ldots k_l}^{N_1 \ldots N_l} \alpha_{k_1 \ldots k_l} f(z_{Nk_1}^{(1)}, \ldots, z_{Nk_l}^{(2)})=\alpha \int_{I^l} f\rho \, dx_1 \ldots dx_l \tag{21}$$

Der Beweis erfolgt wie vorher.

Wir wollen nun einige Folgerungen aus (6) besprechen. Aus (6) folgt zunächst einmal daß mit (x_{Nk}) auch (z_{Nk}) zur Dichte ρ gleichverteilt ist. Nehmen wir weiters eine Folge (y_k) welche zur Dichte σ gleichverteilt ist, d. h. für welche jetzt gilt (g komplexwertig)

$$\lim_{N \to \infty} \frac{1}{N} \sum_{k=1}^{N} g(y_k)=\int_I g(x)\, \sigma(x)\, dx$$

und setzen wir in (6)

$$\alpha_k=\bar{g}(y_k)$$

($\bar{g}$ komplex konjugiert zu g).

So erhalten wir

$$\lim_{N\to\infty}\frac{1}{N}\sum_{k=1}^{N}\bar{g}(x_k)f(z_{Nk})=\int\bar{g}(x)\,\sigma(x)\,dx\int f\rho\,dx\,. \tag{21}$$

Interessant erscheint der Fall, daß die Folge (x_{Nk}) gerade eine Folge (x_k) ist, dann entsteht die Folge (z_{Nk}) dadurch daß für jedes N die N Zahlen $x_1,\ldots,x_N$ nach der *Größe geordnet* werden. Wir haben dann

$$\lim_{N\to\infty}\frac{1}{N}\sum_{k=1}^{N}\bar{g}(x_k)f(z_{Nk})=\int\bar{g}\,\rho\,dx\int f\rho\,dx \tag{22}$$

und insbesondere

$$\lim_{N\to\infty}\frac{1}{N}\sum_{k=1}^{N}\bar{f}(x_n)f(z_{Nk})=\left|\int f\rho\,dx\right|^2. \tag{23}$$

Interessant ist auch der Fall in (20) daß $\sigma=1$ ist und wir

$$g(x)=e^{2\pi ihx}$$

nehmen ($h\neq 0$, $h\in\mathbf{Z}$). Dann ist

$$\int_0^1 g\,dx=0$$

und wir haben für jede gleichverteilte Folge (x_{Nk})

$$\lim_{N\to\infty}\frac{1}{N}\sum_{k=1}^{N}e^{2\pi ihx_k}f(z_{Nk})=0\,. \tag{24}$$

Nehmen wir z. B. $x_k=\beta k \bmod 1$, wo β irrational ist, so haben wir für die Folge (1)

$$\lim_{N\to\infty}\frac{1}{N}\sum_{k=1}^{N}e^{2\pi ih\beta k}f(z_{Nk})=0\,. \tag{25}$$

Es ist also z. B.

$$\lim_{N\to\infty}\frac{1}{N}\sum_{k=1}^{N}e^{2\pi i\beta k}f\left(\frac{k}{N}\right)=0\,.$$

Wir bemerken noch folgendes: Es kann (5) nicht durch

$$\lim_{N\to\infty}\sum_{k=1}^{N}\alpha_{Nk}=\alpha$$

ersetzt werden, so daß (6) richtig bleibt. Wäre dies der Fall, so könnte man $\alpha_{Nk}=\frac{1}{N}f(z_{Nk})$ nehmen und wir hätten

$$\lim_{N\to\infty}\frac{1}{N}\sum_{k=1}^{N}f^2(z_{Nk})=\left(\int_0^1 f\rho\right)^2 dx\,.$$

Andererseits wäre nach (6) ebenfalls mit f^2 statt f

$$\lim\frac{1}{N}\sum_{k=1}^{N}f^2(z_n)=\int_0^1 f^2\,\rho\,dx\,.$$

Für $\rho=1$ und $f(x)=x$ für alle x in E hätten wir sofort $3=4$. Aus (20) folgt, wenn

$$\alpha_{k_1\ldots k_l}=e^{2\pi i(\beta_1 k_1+\ldots+\beta_1 k_1)}$$

(*ein* β irrational), daß analog zu (24)

$$\lim_{(N_1\ldots N_l)\to\infty}\frac{1}{N_1\ldots N_l}\sum_{k_1\ldots k_l}^{N_1\ldots N_1}e^{2\pi i(\beta_1 k_1+\ldots+\beta_1 k_1)}f(z_{Nk_1}^{(1)},\ldots,z_{Nk_l}^{(l)})=0\,,$$

also insbesondere

$$\lim_{(N_1\ldots N_l)\to\infty}\frac{1}{N_1\ldots N_l}\sum_{k_1\ldots k_l}^{N_1\ldots N_l}e^{2\pi i(\beta_1 k_1+\ldots+\beta_l k_l)}f\left(\frac{k_1}{N_1},\ldots,\frac{k_l}{N_l}\right)=0\,.$$

Bemerkung: Wir können statt l-fachen Folgen auch den Fall betrachten, daß in (18) $N_1=N_2=\ldots=N_l$ ist, dann gilt wenn (20) beibehalten wird, daß

$$\lim_{N\to\infty}\frac{1}{N}\sum_{k_1\ldots k_l}^{N\ldots N}\alpha_{k_1\ldots k_l}f(z_{Nk_1}^{(1)},\ldots,z_{Nk_l}^{(2)})=\alpha\int_{I^l}f\rho\,dx_1\ldots dx_l\,.$$

Schlußbemerkung: Es sei (y_k) eine Folge eines kompakten, metrischen Raumes X, welcher zu einem Wahrscheinlichkeitsmaß auf X gleichverteilt ist. Es gilt also für jede stetige Funktion g auf X

$$\lim_{N\to\infty}\frac{1}{N}\sum_{k=1}^{N}g(y_k)=\int_X g(x)\,d\mu\,.$$

Aus (6) folgt mit $\alpha_k = \bar{g}(y_k)$

$$\lim_{N\to\infty} \frac{1}{N} \sum_{k=1}^{N} \bar{g}(y_k) f(z_{Nk}) = \frac{1}{\lambda(I)} \int_X g(x)\, d\mu \int_a^b f(x)\, \rho(x)\, dx$$

Ist $X = \{0, 1\}$, $\int_X g(x)\, d\mu = \frac{g(0)+g(1)}{2}$, dann erhält das Resultat von Carr und Hill.

INST. FÜR ANALYSIS
TECHN. UNIV. WIEN
GUSSHAUSSTRASSE 27–29
A-1040 WIEN
ÖSTERREICH

Studies in Pure Mathematics
To the Memory of Paul Turán

Laguerre entire functions and Turán inequalities

by

L. ILIEV (Sofia)

Definition 1. The entire function $f(z) \in L_1$, if it is a polynomial having only real nonpositive zeros, or, if in every finite domain it is a limit of such polynomials.

The entire function $f(z) \in L_2$, if it is a polynomial having only real zeros, or, if it is a limit of such polynomials in every finite domain.

Definition 2. The infinite sequence $\{\alpha_n\}_0^\infty \in \alpha$, if for any polynomial

$$b(z) = b_0 + b_1 z + \dots + b_n z^n \in L_2$$

the polynomial

$$b(z) * \{\alpha_n\} = b_0\alpha_0 + b_1\alpha_1 z + \dots + b_n\alpha_n z^n \in L_2 .$$

The infinite sequence $\{\beta_n\}_0^\infty \in \beta$, if for any polynomial

$$a(z) = a_0 + a_1 z + \dots + a_n z^n \in L_1$$

the polynomial

$$a(z) * \{\beta_n\} = a_0\beta_0 + a_1\beta_1 z + \dots + a_n\beta_n z^n \in L_2 .$$

The properties of the functions from L_1 and L_2 and of the sequences from α and β are studied in [1].

Let $J_\lambda(z)$ be the Bessel's function of the first type and

$$f_\lambda(z) = \Gamma(\lambda+1)\left(\frac{z}{2}\right)^{-\lambda} J_\lambda(z) = \sum_{\kappa=0}^{\infty} \frac{(-1)^\kappa}{\kappa!} \frac{\Gamma(\lambda+1)}{\Gamma(\lambda+\kappa+1)}\left(\frac{z}{2}\right)^{2\kappa},$$

(1)

$$f_\lambda^*(z) = f_\lambda(\sqrt{-2z}) = \sum_{\kappa=0}^{\infty} \frac{1}{\kappa!} \frac{\Gamma(\lambda+1)}{\Gamma(\lambda+\kappa+1)} z^\kappa .$$

For $\lambda > -1$ the function $1/\Gamma(\lambda+x+1) \in L_2$ has only negative zeros. According to [2], pp. 107—108, the sequence $\{\Gamma(\lambda+1)/\Gamma(\lambda+\kappa+1)\}_0^\infty \in \alpha$. Therefore, for $\lambda > -1$, $f_\lambda^*(z) \in L_1$, $f_\lambda(z) \in L_2$.

1. Let

$$f_1(z) = \alpha_0 + \frac{\alpha_1}{1!} z + \frac{\alpha_2}{2!} z^2 + \ldots \in L_2, \tag{1, α}$$

and

$$f_2(z) = \beta_0 + \frac{\beta_1}{1!} z + \frac{\beta_2}{2!} z^2 + \ldots \in L_2. \tag{1, β}$$

Then, for arbitrary real numbers x_1 and x_2:

$$f_1(x_1 z) f_2(x_2 z) = \sum_{n=0}^{\infty} Q_n(x_1, x_2) \frac{z^n}{n!} \in L_2, \tag{1.1}$$

where

$$Q_n(x_1, x_2) = Q_n(x_1, x_2, f_1, f_2) = \sum_{\kappa=0}^{n} \binom{n}{\kappa} \alpha_{n-\kappa} \beta_\kappa x_1^{n-\kappa} x_2^\kappa, \quad n = 0, 1, 2, \ldots. \tag{1.2}$$

The equality (1.1) defines classes of polynomial sequences (1.2) generated by functions from L_2.

1.1. Among the sequences of polynomials defined by (1.1), all classical systems of orthogonal polynomials can be found.

In view of (1), (1.1) and since $e^z \in L_1$, $e^{-z^2} \in L_2$ we obtain namely,

$$\begin{aligned}
&f_\lambda^*[-(1-x)z] f_\mu^*[(1+x)z] = \sum_{n=0}^{\infty} P_{n,\lambda,\mu}(x) \frac{z^n}{n!} \in L_2, \quad \lambda > -1, \mu > -1, -1 \leqq x \leqq 1, \\
&e^{xz} f_{\lambda-1/2}(z\sqrt{1-x^2}) = \sum_{n=0}^{\infty} P_{n,\lambda}(x) \frac{z^n}{n!} \in L_2, \quad \lambda > -1/2, -1 \leqq x \leqq 1; \\
&e^z f_\lambda^*(xz) = \sum_{n=0}^{\infty} L_{n,\lambda}(x) \frac{z^n}{n!} \in L_1, \quad \lambda > -1, 0 \leqq x < +\infty; \\
&e^{xz} e^{-z^2} = \sum_{n=0}^{\infty} H_n(x) \frac{z^n}{n!} \in L_2, \quad -\infty < x < +\infty;
\end{aligned} \tag{1.3}$$

where $\{P_{n,\lambda,\mu}(x)\}$, $\{P_{n,\lambda}(x)\}$, $\{L_{n,\lambda}(x)\}$, $\{H_n(x)\}$ are the Jacobi polynomials, ultraspheric polynomials, Laguerre polynomials and the Hermite polynomials, respectively, with a norm determined by (1.1) which is different from the one in [3], for example.

1.2. If for the functions from $(1, \alpha)$ and $(1, \beta)$ $f_1(z) \in L_1$ and $f_2(z) \in L_2$, respectively, then $\{\alpha_n\}_0^\infty \in \alpha$, $\{\beta_n\}_0^\infty \in \beta$. Whence

Theorem 1. *If $f_1(z) \in L_1$, $f_2(z) \in L_2$, the polynomials*

$$Q_n(1-x, 1+x, f_1, f_2) = \sum_{\kappa=0}^{n} \binom{n}{\kappa} \alpha_{n-\kappa}\beta_\kappa (1-x)^{n-\kappa}(1+x)^\kappa, \quad n = 1, 2, \ldots,$$

$$Q_n(x, \sqrt{1-x^2}, f_1, f_2(z) = f_2(-z)) = \sum_{\kappa=0}^{[n/2]} \binom{n}{2\kappa} \alpha_{n-2\kappa}\beta_{2\kappa} x^{n-2\kappa}(1-x^2)^\kappa,$$

$$n = 1, 2, \ldots, \tag{1.4}$$

$$Q_n(1, x, f_1, f_2) = \sum_{\kappa=0}^{n} \binom{n}{\kappa} \alpha_{n-\kappa}\beta_\kappa x^\kappa, \quad n = 1, 2, \ldots,$$

$$Q_n(x, 1, f_1, f_2) = \sum_{\kappa=0}^{n} \binom{n}{\kappa} \alpha_{n-\kappa}\beta_\kappa x^{n-\kappa}, \quad n = 1, 2, \ldots$$

have only real zeros.

1.3. The equalities (1.4) define four manifolds of polynomial sequences having only real zeros.

If in (1.4) we fix the function $f_1(z)$, setting for the first sequence $f_1(z) = f_\lambda^*(z)$, and for the other ones — $f_1(z) = e^z$, as it is in (1.3), then for arbitrary $f_2(z) \in L_2$ these manifolds are characterised by the following

Theorem 2. *If $f_2(z) \in L_2$, then*

(a) The unique orthogonal system among the sequences $\{Q_n(1-x, 1+x, f_\lambda^*, f_2)\}$ is the system $\{P_{n,\lambda,\mu}(x)\}$, $\lambda > -1$, $\mu > -1$ of Jacobi polynomials.

(b) The unique orthogonal system among the sequences

$$\{Q_n(x, \sqrt{1-x^2}, e^z, f_2(z) = f_2(-z))\}$$

is the system $\{P_{n,\lambda}(x)\}$, $\lambda > -1/2$ of ultraspheric polynomials.

(c) The unique orthogonal system among the sequences $\{Q_n(1, x, e^z, f_2)\}$ is the system $\{L_{n,\lambda}(x)\}$, $\lambda > -1$ of Laguerre polynomials.

(d) The unique orthogonal system among the sequences $\{Q_n(x, 1, e^z, f_2)\}$ is the system $\{H_n(x)\}$ of Hermite polynomials.

The proof of (b), (c) and (d) is given in [4].

According to (1.3) the Jacobi polynomials are among the polynomials $\{Q_n(1-x, 1+x, f_\lambda^*, f_2)\}$ in (a). The question whether they are the unique orthogonal system of this type remains open.

The question whether the theorem holds for arbitrary $f_1(z) \in L_1$, $f_2(z) \in L_2$ also remains open.

The mentioned characteristics give grounds to accept the following

Definition 3. If $f_1(z)\in L_1$, $f_2(z)\in L_2$, then

A. The sequences $\{Q_n(1-x,\ 1+x,\ f_1,\ f_2)\}$ are called sequences of Jacobi type.

B. The sequences $\{Q_n(x,\ \sqrt{1-x^2},\ f_1,\ f_2(z)=f_2(-z^2))\}$ are called sequences of ultraspheric type.

C. The sequences $\{Q_n(1,\ x,\ f_1,\ f_2)\}$ are called sequences of Laguerre type.

D. The sequences $\{Q_n(x,\ 1,\ f_1,\ f_2)\}$ are called sequences of Hermite type.

1.4. By $\bar{L}_2=\bar{L}_2(F)$ denote the set of functions $f(z)\in L_2$ represented in the form, as follows:

$$f(z) = \int_{-\infty}^{\infty} F(t)e^{itz}\,dt = \sum_{\kappa=0}^{\infty}\frac{i^\kappa z^\kappa}{\kappa!}\int_{-\infty}^{\infty} F(t)t^\kappa\,dt\,. \tag{1.5}$$

Since $f(z)$ has only real zeros, then $F(-t)=\overline{F(t)}$ and

$$f(z) = \int_{-\infty}^{\infty} F(t)e^{itz}\,dt = \sum_{\kappa=0}^{\infty}\frac{(-1)^\kappa z^{2\kappa}}{(2\kappa)!}\int_{-\infty}^{\infty} F(t)t^{2\kappa}dt\,. \tag{1.6}$$

If

$$J_n(f_1,z)=\alpha_0 z^n + \binom{n}{1}\alpha_1 z^{n-1}+\ldots+\alpha_n\,,\quad n=0,1,2,\ldots \tag{1.7}$$

are the Jensen polynomials of the function $f_1(z)$ from $(1,\alpha)$ let us set

$$J_n(f_1,x_1,x_2)=x_1^n J_n\left(f_1,\frac{x_2}{x_1}\right) = \sum_{\kappa=0}^{n}\binom{n}{\kappa}\alpha_\kappa x_1^\kappa x_2^{n-\kappa}\,,\quad n=0,1,2,\ldots. \tag{1.8}$$

In the partial case when $f_1(z)\in\bar{L}_2(F_1)$ we obtain

$$J_n(f_1,z) = \int_{-\infty}^{\infty} F_1(u)\,(z+iu)^n\,du\,,\quad n=0,1,2,\ldots, \tag{1.9}$$

$$J_n(f_1,x_1,x_2) = \int_{-\infty}^{\infty} F_1(u)\,(x_2+iux_1)^n\,du\,,\quad n=0,1,2,\ldots. \tag{1.10}$$

Note also that (1.5), for $f(z)\in\bar{L}_2$, yields

$$f(\sqrt{-z}) = f^*(z) = \sum_{\kappa=0}^{\infty}\frac{\kappa!}{(2\kappa)!}\frac{z^\kappa}{\kappa!}\int_{-\infty}^{\infty} F(t)t^{2\kappa}\,dt\in L_1$$

and, therefore, $\left\{\dfrac{\kappa!}{(2\kappa)!}\displaystyle\int_{-\infty}^{\infty} F(t)t^{2\kappa}\,dt\right\}_0^\infty \in\alpha\,.$

These results yield the following theorems:

Theorem 3. If $f_1(z) \in \bar{L}_2(F_1)$, $f_2(z) \in \bar{L}_2(F_2)$, then

$$Q_n(x_1, x_2) = i^n \int_{-\infty}^{\infty} F_2(v) dv \int_{-\infty}^{\infty} F_1(u)(vx_2 + ux_1)^n du, \quad n=0,1,2,\ldots$$

i.e.

$$Q_{2n+1}(x_1, x_2) \equiv 0, \quad n=0,1,2,\ldots$$

$$Q_{2n}(x_1, x_2) = (-1)^n \int_{-\infty}^{\infty} F_2(v) dv \int_{-\infty}^{\infty} F_1(u)(vx_2 + ux_1)^{2n} du, \quad n=0,1,2,\ldots.$$

Theorem 4. If $f_1(z) \in \bar{L}_2(F_1)$, $f_2(z) \in \bar{L}_2(F_2)$,

$$f_1(\sqrt{-z}) = f_1^*(z), \ f_2(\sqrt{-z}) = f_2^*(z), \quad x_1 > 0, \quad x_2 > 0$$

and

$$f_1^*(x_1 z) f_2^*(x_2 z) = \sum_{n=0}^{\infty} Q_n^*(x_1, x_2) \frac{z^n}{n!},$$

$$f_1^*(-x_1 z) f_2^*(x_2 z) = \sum_{n=0}^{\infty} \overline{Q_n^*(x_1, x_2)} \frac{z^n}{n!},$$

then

$$Q_n^*(x_1, x_2) = \frac{n!}{(2n)!} \int_{-\infty}^{\infty} F_2(v) dv \int_{-\infty}^{\infty} F_1(u)(v\sqrt{x_2} + u\sqrt{x_1})^{2n} du, \quad n=0,1,2,\ldots,$$

$$Q_n^*(x_1, x_2) = \frac{n!}{(2n)!} \int_{-\infty}^{\infty} F_2(v) dv \int_{-\infty}^{\infty} F_1(u)(v\sqrt{x_2} - u\sqrt{x_1})^{2n} du, \quad n=0,1,2,\ldots.$$

Theorem 5. If $f_1(z) \in \bar{L}_2$, $f_2(z) \in \bar{L}_2(F)$, then

$$Q_n(x_1, x_2) = \int_{-\infty}^{\infty} F(t) J_n(f_1, x_1, it x_2) dt, \quad n=0,1,2,\ldots.$$

These theorems yield the integral representations of all classical orthogonal systems.

So, since for $\lambda > -1/2$

$$f_\lambda(z) = \frac{\Gamma(\lambda+1)}{\sqrt{\pi}\Gamma(\lambda+1/2)} \int_{-1}^{1} (1-t^2)^{\lambda-1/2} e^{itz} dt,$$

we get the integral representation of Jacobi polynomials

$$P_{n,\lambda,\mu}(x)=\frac{n!}{(2n)!}\frac{\Gamma(\lambda+1)\Gamma(\mu+1)}{\pi\Gamma(\lambda+1/2)\Gamma(\mu+1/2)}\int_{-1}^{1}(1-v^2)^{\lambda-1/2}\,dv\times$$

$$\times\int_{-1}^{1}(1-u^2)^{\mu-1/2}(v\sqrt{1+x}-u\sqrt{1-x})^{2n}\,du$$

where $\lambda>-1/2$, $\mu>-1/2$, $n=0,1,2,\ldots$.

The already known integral representations of the other classical orthogonal systems are found analogically.

The integral representation

$$H_n(x)=\frac{2^n}{\sqrt{\pi}}\int_{-\infty}^{\infty}e^{-t^2}(x+it)^n\,dt\,,\quad n=0,1,2,\ldots$$

of the Hermite polynomials, for instance, is obtained immediately from Theorem 5 and the representation $e^{-z^2}=\int_{-\infty}^{\infty}e^{-t^2}e^{itz}\,dt$.

2. P. TURÁN proved for the polynomials $P_n(x)$ of Legendre the inequalities, as follows:

(2.1) $$P_n^2(x)-P_{n-1}(x)P_{n+1}(x)\geqq 0\,,\quad -1\leqq x\leqq 1\,,\quad n=1,2,\ldots.$$

2.1. If $\{\beta_n\}\in\beta$, $\{\alpha_n\}\in\alpha$, then (see [1], [6])

(2.2) $$\beta_n^2-\beta_{n-1}\beta_{n+1}\geqq 0\,,\quad n=1,2,\ldots$$

and

(2.3) $$\alpha_n^2-\alpha_{n-1}\alpha_{n+1}\geqq 0\,,\quad n=1,2,\ldots,$$
$$\alpha_n^2-\alpha_{n-2}\alpha_{n+2}\geqq 0\,,\quad n=2,3,\ldots,$$
$$\left(\frac{\alpha_{n-3}}{\alpha_n}\right)^2-\left(\frac{\alpha_{n-2}}{\alpha_n}\right)^3\leqq 0\,,\quad n=3,4,\ldots.$$

Let us repeat that if

(2.4) $$f(z)=\gamma_0+\frac{\gamma_1}{1!}z+\frac{\gamma_2}{2!}z^2+\ldots,$$

then, for $f(z)\in L_1$, $\{\gamma_n\}_0^\infty\in\alpha$, for $f(z)\in L_2$, $\{\gamma_n\}_0^\infty\in\beta$.

According to (1.1), (2.2) and (2.3) we get

Theorem 6. *If $f_1(z) \in L_2$, $f_2(z) \in L_2$ the polynomials* (1.2) *satisfy the Turán inequalities*

$$Q_n^2(x_1, x_2) - Q_{n-1}(x_1, x_2) Q_{n+1}(x_1, x_2) \geqq 0, \quad n = 1, 2, \ldots \tag{2.5}$$

for arbitrary real numbers x_1 and x_2.

If $f_1(z) \in L_1$, $f_2(z) \in L_2$, then for arbitrary positive numbers x_1 and x_2, the Turán inequalities

$$\begin{gathered} Q_n^2(x_1, x_2) - Q_{n-1}(x_1, x_2) Q_{n+1}(x_1, x_2) \geqq 0, \quad n = 1, 2, \ldots, \\ Q_n^2(x_1, x_2) - Q_{n-2}(x_1, x_2) Q_{n+2}(x_1, x_2) \geqq 0, \quad n = 2, 3, \ldots, \\ \left[\frac{Q_{n-3}(x_1, x_2)}{Q_n(x_1, x_2)}\right]^2 - \left[\frac{Q_{n-2}(x_1, x_2)}{Q_n(x_1, x_2)}\right]^3 \leqq 0, \quad n = 3, 4, \ldots \end{gathered} \tag{2.6}$$

hold true.

In a partial case, according to (1.3), we get

$$\begin{gathered} P^2_{n,\lambda,\mu}(x) - P_{n-1,\lambda,\mu}(x) P_{n+1,\lambda,\mu}(x) \geqq 0, \quad \lambda > -1, \quad \mu > -1, \quad -1 \leqq x \leqq 1, \quad n = 1, 2, \ldots, \\ P^2_{n,\lambda}(x) - P_{n-1,\lambda}(x) P_{n+1,\lambda}(x) \geqq 0, \quad \lambda > -1/2, \quad -1 \leqq x \leqq 1, \quad n = 1, 2, \ldots, \\ L^2_{n,\lambda}(x) - L_{n-1,\lambda}(x) L_{n+1,\lambda}(x) \geqq 0, \quad \lambda > -1, \quad 0 \leqq x < +\infty, \quad n = 1, 2, \ldots, \\ H_n^2(x) - H_{n-1}(x) H_{n+1}(x) \geqq 0, \quad -\infty < x < +\infty, \quad n = 1, 2, \ldots. \end{gathered} \tag{2.7}$$

Moreover,

$$\begin{gathered} L^2_{n,\lambda}(x) - L_{n-2,\lambda}(x) L_{n+2,\lambda}(x) \geqq 0, \quad \lambda > -1, \quad 0 \leqq x < +\infty, \quad n = 2, 3, \ldots, \\ \left[\frac{L_{n-3,\lambda}(x)}{L_{n,\lambda}(x)}\right]^2 - \left[\frac{L_{n-2,\lambda}(x)}{L_{n,\lambda}(x)}\right]^3 \leqq 0, \quad \lambda > -1, \quad 0 \leqq x < +\infty, \quad n = 3, 4, \ldots. \end{gathered} \tag{2.8}$$

2.2 Definition 4. The sequence $\{\lambda_n\}_0^\infty \in \lambda$, if for any polynomial with real coefficients

$$p(z) = a_0 + a_1 z + \ldots + a_n z^n \tag{2.9}$$

which has no real zeros, the polynomial

$$p(z) * \{\lambda_n\}_0^\infty = a_0 \lambda_0 + a_1 \lambda_1 z + \ldots + a_n \lambda_n z^n \tag{2.10}$$

has no real zeros.

Lemma. *If* $F(x)\in L_1$, *then* $\{1/F(n)\}_0^\infty \in \lambda$.

Let the polynomial (2.9) have no real zeros. By s denote the number of real zeros of

$$\frac{a_0}{F(0)}+\frac{a_1}{F(1)}z+\ldots+\frac{a_n}{F(n)}z^n=b_0+b_1z+\ldots+b_nz^n. \tag{2.11}$$

According to [2] (p. 9), the polynomial

$$b_0F(0)+b_1F(1)z+\ldots+b_nF(n)z^n=a_0+a_1z+\ldots+a_nz^n$$

has at least as many zeros as (2.11) does, i.e. $0\leqq s\leqq 0$ or $s=0$. Thus, the Lemma is established.

In particular, if $\Gamma(x)$ is the Euler function, in view of [2] (pp. 107–108), it follows that $\{1/\Gamma(x+n)\}_0^\infty\in\lambda$ for any $x\geqq 0$.

According to Hamburger's first and second criteria [7], if $\{\lambda_n\}_0^\infty\in\lambda$, then $\Delta_n(\lambda_{2\kappa})>0$, $n=0, 1, 2, \ldots$; $\kappa=0, 1, 2, \ldots$, where

$$\Delta_n(\lambda_{2\kappa}) = \begin{vmatrix} \lambda_{2\kappa} & \lambda_{2\kappa+1} & \ldots & \lambda_{2\kappa+n} \\ \lambda_{2\kappa+1} & \lambda_{2\kappa+2} & \ldots & \lambda_{2\kappa+n+1} \\ \ldots & \ldots & \ldots & \ldots \\ \lambda_{2\kappa+n} & \lambda_{2\kappa+n+1} & \ldots & \lambda_{2\kappa+2n} \end{vmatrix}, \quad \Delta_0(\lambda_{2\kappa})=\lambda_{2\kappa}.$$

The Lemma and the remark yield

Theorem 7. *If* $F(x)\in L_1$ *and* $x\geqq 0$, *then*

$$\Delta_n(1/F(x+\kappa))>0,\quad \Delta_n(1/F(\kappa x))>0,\quad n=0, 1, 2, \ldots;\quad \kappa=0, 1, 2, \ldots.$$

Theorem 8. *For* $x>0$

$$\Delta_n(\Gamma(x+\kappa))>0,\quad \Delta_n(\Gamma(x\kappa))>0,\qquad n=0, 1, 2, \ldots;\quad \kappa=0, 1, 2, \ldots,$$

where $\Gamma(x)$ *is the Euler function.*

In particular, from Theorem 7 and (1.3), for the Laguerre polynomials $L_{n,\lambda}(x)$, we find

$$\Delta_n(1/L_{n,\lambda}(x+\kappa))>0,\quad \Delta_n(1/L_{n,\lambda}(\kappa x))>0,\quad n=0, 1, 2, \ldots;\quad \kappa=0, 1, 2, \ldots.$$

2.3. Let $f_\kappa(z)\in L_2$, $\kappa=1, 2, \ldots, s$. If $x_1, x_2, \ldots, x_s$ are real numbers, then [8]

$$Q^{(s)}(z)=\prod_{\kappa=1}^{s} f_\kappa(x_\kappa z)=\sum_{n=0}^{\infty} Q_n(x_1, \ldots, x_s)\frac{z^n}{n!}=\sum_{n=0}^{\infty} Q_n^{(s)}\frac{z^n}{n!}\in L_2,$$

(2.12)

$$R^{(s)}(z) = \prod_{\kappa=1}^{p} f_\kappa(x_\kappa z) \prod_{\kappa=p+1}^{s} f_\kappa(x_\kappa + z) = \sum_{n=0}^{\infty} R_n(x_1, \ldots, x_s) \frac{z^n}{n!} = \sum_{n=0}^{\infty} R_n^{(s)} \frac{z^n}{n!} \in L_2,$$

$$S^{(s)}(z) = \prod_{\kappa=1}^{s} f_\kappa(x_\kappa + z) = \sum_{n=0}^{\infty} S_n(x_1, \ldots, x_s) \frac{z^n}{n!} = \sum_{n=0}^{\infty} S_n^{(s)} \frac{z^n}{n!} \in L_2.$$

For $f_\kappa \in L_1$, $\kappa = 1, 2, \ldots, s$ and $x_\kappa \geqq 0$, we obtain

$$Q^{(s)}(z) \in L_1, \quad R^{(s)}(z) \in L_1, \quad S^{(s)}(z) \in L_1. \tag{2.13}$$

(2.12) and (2.13) yield

Theorem 9. *If $f_\kappa(z) \in L_2$, $\kappa = 1, 2, \ldots, s$ and $x_1, x_2, \ldots, x_s$ are real numbers, then $\{Q_n(x_1, x_2, \ldots, x_s)\} \in \beta$; $\{R_n(x_1, \ldots, x_s)\} \in \beta$; $\{S_n(x_1, \ldots, x_s)\} \in \beta$.*

If $f_\kappa(z) \in L_1$, $x_\kappa \geqq 0$, $\kappa = 1, 2, \ldots, s$, then $\{Q_n(x_1, \ldots, x_s)\} \in \alpha$; $\{R_n(x_1, \ldots, x_s)\} \in \alpha$; $\{S_n(x_1, \ldots, x_s)\} \in \alpha$.

In accordance with (2.2) we get

Theorem 10. *If $f_\kappa(z) \in L_2$, $\kappa = 1, 2, \ldots, s$ and $x_1, x_2, \ldots, x_s$ are real numbers, then the functions $Q_n(x_1, \ldots, x_s)$, $R_n(x_1, \ldots, x_s)$, $S_n(x_1, \ldots, x_s)$ satisfy the Turán inequalities*

$$\begin{aligned} &Q_n^2(x_1, \ldots, x_s) - Q_{n-1}(x_1, \ldots, x_s) Q_{n+1}(x_1, \ldots, x_s) \geqq 0, \quad n = 1, 2, \ldots, \\ &R_n^2(x_1, \ldots, x_s) - R_{n-1}(x_1, \ldots, x_s) R_{n+1}(x_1, \ldots, x_s) \geqq 0, \quad n = 1, 2, \ldots, \\ &S_n^2(x_1, \ldots, x_s) - S_{n-1}(x_1, \ldots, x_s) S_{n+1}(x_1, \ldots, x_s) \geqq 0, \quad n = 1, 2, \ldots. \end{aligned} \tag{2.14}$$

References

[1] Pólya, G. und Schur, J., *Journal f. d. reine u. angewandte Mathematik*, **144** (1914), 89–113.
[2] Obrechkov, N., Zeros of Polynomials, Bulg. Acad. Sci., Sofia (1963).
[3] Szegő, G., Orthogonal Polynomials, New York (1959).
[4] Iliev, L., *C. R. Acad. Bulg. Sci.*, 18, No. *4* (1965), 295–298.
[5] Szegő, G., *Bull. Amer. Math. Soc.*, **54** (1948), 401–405.
[6] Iliev, L., *C. R. Acad. Bulg. Sci.*, *17*, No. *86* (1964), 693–696.
[7] Hamburger, H., *Math. Annalen*, **81** (1921), 120–164, 168–187.
[8] Iliev, L., *C. R. Acad. Bulg. Sci.*, **19**, No. 7 (1966), 575–577.

UNIVERSITY OF SOFIA
BULGARIA

Studies in Pure Mathematics
To the Memory of Paul Turán

On Turán's equivalent power series

by

K.-H. INDLEKOFER (Paderborn)

1. Introduction

Let $D=\{z\in\mathbb{C}: |z|<1\}$ be the open unit disk and $\bar{D}=\{z\in\mathbb{C}: |z|\leqq 1\}$ the closed unit disk of the complex plane and $H(D)$ the algebra of all holomorphic functions in D. If $\zeta_0\in D$, $\zeta_0\neq 0$, then

$$(1)\qquad \Phi_{\zeta_0}(z)=\frac{1-\bar{\zeta}_0}{1-\zeta_0}\cdot\frac{z-\zeta_0}{1-\bar{\zeta}_0 z}$$

defines a conformal and bijective mapping Φ_{ζ_0} of $\bar{D}$ onto itself. If $f\in H(D)$, then $f_1=f\circ\Phi_{\zeta_0}\in H(D)$ and the Taylor series representing f, respectively f_1, are called *conformally equivalent*.

P. TURÁN [17] was the first who investigated the periphery-convergence behaviour of equivalent power series, and he showed that the convergence is not conformally invariant. More explicitly this means the following: he proved the existence of functions $f\in H(D)$, the Taylor series $f(w)=\sum_{k=0}^{\infty} a_k w^k$ of which converges for $w=1$, whereas the power series $f_1(z)=f(\Phi_{\zeta_0}(z))=\sum_{n=0}^{\infty} b_n z^n$ diverges for $z=\Phi_{\zeta_0}^{-1}(1)=1$.[1] J. CLUNIE [5] showed that this phenomenon can occur even for functions f_1 in $H(D)$ which are continuous on $\bar{D}$. The author [10] succeeded in proving the same for functions $f\in H(D)$, satisfying the estimate

$$\omega(f;h)=\sup_{|\vartheta|\leqq\pi}\sup_{|t|\leqq h}|f(e^{i(\vartheta+t)})-f(e^{it})|=O\left(\left(\log\frac{1}{h/2\pi}\right)^{-1}\right)$$
$$\text{for } h\to 0+$$

for the modulus of continuity.

[1] Such a function is said to behave *konvergenz-schlecht* under the mapping Φ_{ζ_0}.

Many papers concerning various problems on the periphery-convergence behaviour followed that of TURÁN. For instance, L. ALPÁR [1], [2] dealt with Cesàro-summability and absolute convergence (cf. G. HALÁSZ [7] and K.-H. INDLEKOFER [9], [11]) and K.-H. INDLEKOFER [9] investigated absolute Cesàro-summability. For more details the reader is referred to the articles [8], [14], [18], [19].

Remarks. For now let l_1^+ be the algebra of all functions $f \in H(D)$ with absolutely convergent MacLaurin series with norm

$$\left\| \sum_{k=0}^{\infty} a_k z^k \right\|_1 = \sum_{k=0}^{\infty} |a_k| .$$

We wish to determine the automorphisms τ of l_1^+. In analytic terms this means to determine the functions Φ for which the mapping

$$\sum_{k=0}^{\infty} a_k z^k \mapsto \sum_{k=0}^{\infty} a_k \Phi^k(z)$$

takes l_1^+ onto l_1^+. Necessarily such Φ must be injective on $\bar{D}$ and must satisfy $\Phi(\bar{D}) \subset \bar{D}$. Moreover, $\Phi\colon \bar{D} \to \bar{D}$ is surjective (for the proof see [12]). Thus $\Phi\colon \bar{D} \to \bar{D}$ is a conformal and bijective mapping of $\bar{D}$ onto itself[2] and $(\tau f)(z) = f(\Phi(z))$, $z \in \bar{D}$, for alle $f \in l_1^+$. Moreover one can actually conclude that $\Phi(z) = e^{i\alpha} z$, $\alpha \in \mathbf{R}$ (cf. [12]). In [12] the author investigated certain subalgebras of l_1^+ and characterized their automorphisms.

The aim of this paper is (i) to give much simpler proofs of some results on equivalent power series, (ii) to restrict the above mentioned questions to functions $f \in H(D)$, which are holomorphic in[3] $\bar{D} \setminus \{1\}$, and (iii) to handle similar questions with functions $\Phi\colon \bar{D} \to \bar{D}$, $\Phi \in H(\bar{D})$, which are not necessarily bijective.

2. Euler and Sonnenschein type summability methods

In 1949 J. SONNENSCHEIN [15] defined a general class of sequence transformation matrices generated by a function $u(z) = \sum_{k=0}^{\infty} u_k z^k$ with positive radius of convergence R and satisfying $u(1) = 1$, the elements of the matrix $\{a_{nk}\}$ being given by

$$[u(z)]^n = \sum_{k=0}^{\infty} a_{nk} z^k \quad (n = 0, 1, 2, \ldots). \tag{2}$$

[2] $\Phi(z)$ is of the form $\Phi(z) = e^{i\alpha} \Phi_{\zeta_0}(z)$, $\alpha \in \mathbf{R}$, $\zeta_0 \in D$.

[3] That means: every point of $\partial D \setminus \{1\}$ is a regular point of f. We write $f \in H(\bar{D} \setminus \{1\})$.

Remark. By the classical theorem of Toeplitz–Schur, necessary and sufficient conditions for the permanence of the transformation matrix $\{a_{nk}\}$ are

$$\text{(a)} \qquad \lim_{n\to\infty} a_{nk}=0 \quad \text{for any} \quad k=0,1,\ldots,$$

$$\text{(b)} \qquad \lim_{n\to\infty} \sum_{k=0}^{\infty} a_{nk}=1,$$

$$\text{(c)} \qquad \sum_{k=0}^{\infty} |a_{nk}|=O(1) \quad \text{for} \quad n\to\infty.$$

It is easily seen that (a) and (b) holds, if $u(1)=1$ and $u(z)\in\bar{D}$ for $z\in\bar{D}$.

In 1956 B. Bajšanski [3] gave general sufficient conditions for the permanence of $\{a_{nk}\}$, namely:

(i) *u is holomorphic in $|z|<R$, where $R>1$;*
(ii) *$|u(z)|<1$ for $z\in\bar{D}$, except at a finite number of points ζ;*
(iii) *for each ζ the real part of $A_\zeta\neq 0$, A_ζ being defined by*

$$h_\zeta(z)-z^{\alpha(\zeta)}=A_\zeta i^p(z-1)^p+o(|z-1|^p), \quad z\to 1,$$

with

$$A_\zeta\neq 0, \quad p=p(\zeta), \text{ where}$$

$$h_\zeta(z)=u(\zeta z)/u(\zeta)$$

and

$$\alpha(\zeta)=h'_\zeta(1);$$

(iv) $u(1)=1$.

He then proved that if (i) holds then (iv) and (ii) are necessary, unless $u(z)=z^l$ for some positive integer l.

J. Clunie and P. Vermes [6] showed that if (i) holds then (iii) is *necessary* for permanence, and thus obtained a complete set of necessary and sufficient conditions when u is holomorphic on the unit circle.

Euler summability methods are transposed Sonnenschein-matrices, transforming series into series. If $w=u(z)$ fulfils the conditions (i), (ii) and (iv) and if $f(w)=\sum_{k=0}^{\infty} a_k w^k$ converges in D, then the same holds for $f(u(z))=\sum_{n=0}^{\infty} b_n z^n$. The (general) Euler transformation $\{a'_{nk}\}$ is defined by

$$\text{(3)} \qquad b_n=\sum_{k=0}^{\infty} a'_{nk}a_k \quad (n=0,1,\ldots),$$

and transforms the series $\sum_{k=0}^{\infty} a_k$ into the series $\sum_{n=0}^{\infty} b_n$. Clearly

$$a'_{nk} = a_{kn} \quad (n, k = 0, 1, \ldots).$$

We consider the partial sums $A_k = \sum_{l=0}^{k} a_l$ and $B_n = \sum_{m=0}^{n} b_m$, so that

$$\sum_{k=0}^{\infty} A_k w^k = \frac{f(w)}{1-w}, \quad \sum_{n=0}^{\infty} B_n z^n = \frac{f(u(z))}{1-z}.$$

Then corresponding to (3), we have the sequence to sequence transformation

$$B_n = \sum_{k=0}^{\infty} \alpha'_{nk} A_k \tag{4}$$

with

$$\alpha'_{nk} = \frac{1}{2\pi i} \int_{(\gamma)} \frac{u^k(z)}{z^{n+1}} \cdot \frac{1-u(z)}{1-z} \, dz,$$

where (γ) is a simple closed path in D surrounding the origin.

In 1958 B. BAJŠANSKI [4] proved that the conditions (i), (ii), (iii) and (iv) are sufficient for the permanence of (3) and (4). In a recent paper K.-H. INDLEKOFER and R. TRAUTNER [13] succeeded in proving the following: If the conditions (i), (ii) and (iv) hold, then (iii) is necessary for the permanence of the Euler transformation (3) and (4).

Remark. What happens, if (i) holds and if $|u(z)| = 1$ for infinitely many points on $|z| = 1$? Clearly $|u(z)| = 1$ for all points $|z| = 1$, and $u(z)$ is a finite Blaschke product, i.e. $u(z)$ is a product of a finite number of Möbius transformations Φ_ζ. B. BAJŠANSKI [3] has shown that in this case $u(z)$ does not define a permanent Sonnenschein transformation, if $u(z) \neq e^{i\alpha} z^k$ $(k = 0, 1, \ldots)$. We prove the same for the corresponding Euler transformation and observe that the case of a Blaschke product with one factor, i.e.

$$u(z) = \Phi_\zeta(z), \quad 0 \neq \zeta \in D,$$

can be subsumed under the problems of equivalent power series.

The principle of the proofs of BAJŠANSKI, CLUNIF–VERMES, INDLEKOFER–TRAUTNER and of most other results on equivalent power series is based on the investigation of one of

$$\sum_{k=0}^{\infty} |a_{nk}| \quad \text{for} \quad n \to \infty \tag{5}$$

(cf. the theorem of Toeplitz–Schur) or

$$\sum_{n=0}^{\infty} |a_{nk}| \quad \text{for} \quad k \to \infty. \tag{6}$$

(We remark that a theorem of K. Knopp and G. G. Lorentz states that $\{a_{nk}\}$ is absolutely permanent iff the sum (6) is $O(1)$ for $k \to \infty$.)

Bajšanski's proofs [3], [4] to ensure that the sums (5) and (6) be bounded if (iii) holds are rather subtle and difficult. The proofs of Clunie–Vermes and Indlekofer–Trautner do not give the rate of divergence of the sums (5) and (6). In the case of equivalent power series L. Alpár [1], III and K.-H. Indlekofer [9], II have shown that

$$\sum_{k=0}^{\infty} |a_{nk}| \gg n^{1/2}$$

and

$$\sum_{n=0}^{\infty} |a_{nk}| \gg k^{1/2}.$$

Their proofs are based on the saddle-point method and are very long and difficult.

In the present paper we intend to give

1) sharp estimates of the rates of growth of the sums (5) and (6),

2) independent and much shorter proofs of the above mentioned results of B. Bajšanski [3], L. Alpár [1], III and K.-H. Indlekofer [9], II,

3) a sharpening of the results of P. Turán [17] and the result of L. Alpár [2] on absolutely convergent power series.

Before formulating our main results we separate the finite set $\{\zeta\}$ occurring in (ii), (iii) into two subsets $\{\zeta_j\}$ and $\{\eta_j\}$ by the properties Re $A_{\zeta_j}=0$, Re $A_{\eta_j}\neq 0$. Using this notation we prove the following theorems.

Theorem 1. *Let the function u satisfy* (i), (ii), (iv) *and let us assume that the set* $\{\zeta_j\}$ *is not empty. Let* p' *be the maximum of the* $p(\zeta_j)$. *Then for the sums* (5) *and* (6) *the following holds: There exists an even positive integer* q, $q>p'\geqq 2$, *such that*

$$n^{(q-p')/2q} \ll \sum_{k=0}^{\infty} |a_{nk}| \ll n^{(q-p')/2q} \tag{7}$$

and

$$k^{(q-p')/2q} \ll \sum_{n=0}^{\infty} |a_{nk}| \ll k^{(q-p')/2q}. \tag{8}$$

Theorem 2. *Let u be a finite Blaschke product. Then for the sums* (5) *and* (6) *we have the estimates*

$$n^{1/2} \ll \sum_{k=0}^{\infty} |a_{nk}| \ll n^{1/2} \tag{9}$$

and for all $K \in \mathbf{N}$,

(10) $$K^{1/2} \ll \max_{k \leqq K} \sum_{n=0}^{\infty} |a_{nk}| \ll K^{1/2}.$$

The proof of CLUNIE and VERMES for the lower bound of (6) consisted of the following steps (also cf. [3], p. 143): With the notation $A_n = \sup_k |a_{nk}|$ they first proved that

$$A_n = o(n^{-1/q}) \quad \text{as} \quad n \to \infty$$

where q is an even positive integer associated with $u(z)$. They next showed that

$$\sum_k |a_{nk}|^2 > cn^{-1/q},$$

where c is a positive constant. Now

(11) $$A_n \sum_k |a_{nk}| \geqq \sum_k |a_{nk}|^2$$

and so

$$\sum_k |a_{nk}| > c/n^{1/q} A_n \to \infty.$$

The idea of our proof is to give a sharper bound for A_n and to use the Schwarz inequality instead of (11). But first of all we give four elementary estimates in the next section.

3. Elementary estimates

In the following we assume that $u(z)$ satisfies either (i), (ii) and (iv) with the restriction $|u(z)| < 1$ for $z \in \bar{D} \setminus \{1\}$, or $|u(z)| = 1$ for $|z| = 1$. Later we show how to handle the general case.

We write $A = (-1)^p bi$, so that near $z = 1$

$$u(z) - z^{\alpha} = (-1)^p bi^{p+1}(z-1)^p + O(|z-1|^{p+1}).$$

Hence, for small t,

(12) $$\begin{aligned} u(e^{it}) &= \exp(i\alpha t) + ibt^p + \ldots = \exp(i\alpha t)(1 + ibt^p + \ldots) = \\ &= \exp(i\alpha t + ibt^p + \ldots). \end{aligned}$$

If (iii) is satisfied, then p is even (because of (ii)) and $\operatorname{Im} b > 0$.

Otherwise b is real and non-zero and there is a smallest power t^q which does not have a purely imaginary coefficient, and this coefficient has negative real part $-\beta$; also q is even (and $q>p$). Hence

$$u(e^{it})=\exp\{i\alpha t+ip(t)-\beta t^q+\dots\},$$

where $\beta>0$, and where $p(t)$ is a real polynomial in t of degree at most q and having bt^p as its term of smallest degree. Clearly $p\geqq 2$. In the case $|u(z)|=1$ for $|z|=1$ we put $q=\infty$.

I. *There is a positive* ε, $\varepsilon<\pi$, *such that for* $|t|<\varepsilon$,

$$t^p \ll p(t) \ll t^p$$

$$t^{p-1} \ll p'(t) \ll t^{p-1}$$

$$t^{p-2} \ll p''(t) \ll t^{p-2},$$

and $p(t)$ *and* $p'(t)$ *are monotonic in each of the intervals* $(-\varepsilon, 0)$ *and* $(0, \varepsilon)$.

Putting $u^n(z)=\sum^{\infty} a_{nk}z^k$, we have

II. *There exist positive* λ_0 *and* $\delta_0<1$, *such that*

(13) $$\sum_{k>\lambda_0 n} |a_{nk}| \ll \delta_0^n .$$

Proof. Let $1<r<R$, and

$$a_{nk}=\frac{1}{2\pi i}\int_{|z|=r}\frac{u^n(z)}{z^{k+1}}\,dz .$$

Then we have for a suitable $\lambda^*=\dfrac{1}{\lambda_0}$

$$\sup_{|z|=r}\frac{|u(z)|^\lambda}{r}\leqq\delta^*<1 \quad \text{for} \quad \frac{n}{k}=\lambda\leqq\lambda^* .$$

Hence

$$|a_{nk}|\leqq\left(\sup_{|z|=r}\frac{|u(z)|^\lambda}{r}\right)^k\leqq\delta^{*k} .$$

Summing up we get the inequality (13).

In the same manner one can prove

III. *There exists a positive* λ_1, *such that*

$$\sum_{k \leqq \lambda_1 n} |a_{nk}| \ll 1 .$$

Also we have

$$\sum_{\lambda_1 n \leqq k \leqq \lambda_0 n} |a_{nk}| \leqq \left(\sum_{k=0}^{\infty} |a_{nk}|^2 \right)^{1/2} \left(\sum_{\lambda_1 n \leqq k \leqq \lambda_0 n} 1 \right)^{1/2} \ll$$

$$\ll n^{1/2} \left(\int_{-\pi}^{\pi} |u(e^{it})|^{2n} dt \right)^{1/2} \ll n^{1/2} .$$

The next inequality follows from II and III and the preceding observation.

IV.

$$\sum_{k=0}^{\infty} |a_{nk}| \ll n^{1/2}.$$

Writing $\|u^n\|_1 := \sum_{k=0}^{\infty} |a_{nk}|$ we have to give lower and upper bounds for $\|u^n\|_1$. We shall write, for a given $q \in \mathbf{N}$,

$$h_q(t) := \begin{cases} 1 - n^{1/q}|t| , & \text{if } \ |t| \leqq n^{-1/q} \\ 0, & \text{if } \ n^{-1/q} \leqq |t| \leqq \pi \end{cases}$$

and if $q = \infty$, i.e. $|u(e^{it})| = 1$ for $t \in [0, \pi]$,

$$h_\varepsilon(t) := \begin{cases} 1 - \dfrac{1}{\varepsilon}|t| , & \text{if } \ |t| \leqq \varepsilon \\ 0 , & \text{if } \ \varepsilon \leqq |t| \leqq \pi . \end{cases}$$

We observe that for all $\nu \in \mathbf{Z}$.

$$\text{(14)} \qquad \int_{-\pi}^{+\pi} h_q(t) e^{i\nu t} dt = n^{-1/q} \int_{-1}^{+1} (1 - |t|) e^{i\nu n^{-1/q} t} dt = n^{-1/q} \left[\frac{\sin \dfrac{\nu n^{-1/q}}{2}}{\dfrac{\nu n^{1/q}}{2}} \right]^2 \geqq 0 ,$$

so that

$$\|h_q\|_1 = h_q(0) = 1 .$$

Hence

$$\text{(15)} \qquad \|u^n\|_1 \geqq \|h_q u^n\|_1 .$$

Similarly $$\|h_\varepsilon\|_1 = 1 \text{ and}$$

$$\|u^n\|_1 \geqq \|h_\varepsilon u^n\|_1 . \tag{16}$$

For brevity we write h instead of h_q and h_ε, respectively.

4. Lower estimates

The main tool will be the following

Lemma 1 (Van der Corput). *If* $g\colon [a, b]\to\mathbf{C}$, $F\colon [a, b]\to\mathbf{R}$ *are continuously differentiable,* $F(t)$ *and* $F'(t)$ *are monotonic, then*

$$\left|\int_a^b e^{iF(t)}g(t)\,dt\right| \leqq \left\{\frac{1}{|F'(a)|}+\frac{1}{|F'(b)|}\right\}\times$$

$$\times\{2\max_{t\in[a,b]}|g(t)|+(b-a)\max_{t\in[a,b]}|g'(t)|\}.$$

Proof. We may suppose that F increases and $F'(t)>0$ (otherwise replace F by $-F$) and we integrate by parts. The integral becomes

$$\int_a^b e^{iF(t)}F'(t)\frac{g(t)}{F'(t)}\,dt = \left[e^{F(t)}\cdot\frac{g(t)}{F'(t)}\right]_a^b -$$

$$-\int_a^b e^{iF(t)}\cdot\frac{g'(t)}{F'(t)}\,dt - \int_a^b e^{iF(t)}g(t)\,d\frac{1}{F'(t)}.$$

Hence

$$\left|\int_a^b e^{iF(t)}g(t)\,dt\right| \leqq \max_{t\in[a,b]}|g(t)|\left(\frac{1}{F'(a)}+\frac{1}{F'(b)}\right)+$$

$$+\max_{t\in[a,b]} g'(t)\left(\frac{1}{F'(a)}+\frac{1}{F'(b)}\right)(b-a)+\max_{t\in[a,b]}|g(t)|\left(\frac{1}{F'(a)}+\frac{1}{F'(b)}\right),$$

and this completes the proof of the lemma.

We will apply this lemma to estimate the Fourier coefficients a^*_{nk} of hu^n. Observing that

$$a^*_{nk} = \frac{1}{2\pi} \int_{-\pi}^{\pi} h(t)u^n(e^{it})e^{ikt}\,dt\,,$$

$$u(e^{it}) = \exp(i\alpha t + ip(t) - \beta t^q + \ldots)$$

near $t=0$, we put

$$F(t) = (n\alpha - k)t + np(t)\,,$$

$$g(t) = h(t)\{u(e^{it})\exp(-i\alpha t - ip(t))\}^n\,,$$

so that

$$2\pi a^*_{nk} = \int_{-\pi}^{+\pi} g(t)e^{iF(t)}\,dt\,.$$

First we have

$$|g(t)| \leqq 1$$

and

$$|g'(t)| \leqq |h'(t)| + c\beta|t|^q \ll n^{1/q}\,.$$

Consider $\int_0^{\pi} g(t)e^{iF(t)}\,dt$. We do not apply Lemma 1 to the whole integral. First define an interval J by

$$|F'(t)| \leqq b(n)\,,$$

where $b(n)$ will be determined later. The interval J is defined to be the set of real t satisfying

$$|np'(t) + (n\alpha - k)| \leqq b(n)\,.$$

The left side of the last inequality is $\gg \big||np'(t)| - (1 + |n\alpha - k|)\big|$ if $n\alpha \neq k$. If $1 + |n\alpha - k| \leqq 2b(n)$, it follows that

$$|np'(t)| \leqq 4b(n)\,.$$

Therefore, by the estimate I

$$|t| \ll \left(\frac{b(n)}{n}\right)^{\frac{1}{p-1}}.$$

Now, let $A := 1 + |n\alpha - k| \geqq 2b(n)$. Define $t_0 > 0$ by $|np'(t_0)| = A$. Without loss of generality let $t_0 \in (0, \varepsilon)$. Then, for $t \in J$,

$$|np'(t)| \geqq \frac{|np'(t_0)|}{2}$$

so that

$$t^{p-1} \gg t_0^{p-1},$$

where

$$\left(\frac{A}{n}\right)^{\frac{1}{p-1}} \ll t_0 \ll \left(\frac{A}{n}\right)^{\frac{1}{p-1}}.$$

Using Taylor's formula we get

$$np'(t) = np'(t_0) + np''(t^*)(t - t_0),$$

where

$$np''(t^*) \gg nt^{*p-2} \gg nt_0^{p-2} \gg n\left(\frac{A}{n}\right)^{\frac{p-2}{p-1}}.$$

Hence

$$|t - t_0| \ll \frac{b(n)}{n}\left(\frac{A}{n}\right)^{-\frac{p-2}{p-1}}.$$

Gathering the estimates we have

$$(17) \qquad |J| \ll \begin{cases} \left(\frac{b(n)}{n}\right)^{\frac{1}{p-1}} & \text{if } A \leqq 2b(n) \\ \frac{b(n)}{n}\left(\frac{A}{n}\right)^{-1+\frac{1}{p-1}} & \text{if } A \geqq 2b(n). \end{cases}$$

We remove the interval J from $[0, \pi]$. On the remaining two intervals Lemma 1 applies ($(b-a) \leqq 2n^{-1/q}$) and gives the estimate

$$(18) \qquad \Big| \int_{[0,\pi]\setminus J} g(t)e^{iF(t)}\,dt \Big| \ll 1/b(n).$$

Comparing the orders of magnitude in (17) and (18) we choose

$$b(n) := n^{\frac{1}{2(p-1)}} \cdot A^{\frac{p-2}{2(p-1)}}.$$

Repeating this analysis for the integral $\int_{-\pi}^{0} g(t)e^{iF(t)}\,dt$ we have the following

Lemma 2. *Let $k \in \mathbf{Z}$. Then*

$$(19) \qquad |a_{nk}^*| \ll \{n(1 + |n\alpha - k|)^{p-2}\}^{-\frac{1}{2(p-1)}}.$$

Recalling from (12) that $|u(e^{it})| \geqq e^{-ct^q}$ for $t \in (-\varepsilon, \varepsilon)$, we conclude that

$$\sum_k |a_{nk}^*|^2 = \frac{1}{2\pi} \int_{-\pi}^{\pi} |u(e^{it})|^{2n} h^2(t)\, dt \geqq \frac{1}{2\pi} \int_{-\pi}^{\pi} e^{-2cnt^q} h^2(t)\, dt;$$

changing t into $n^{-1/q}\, t$ the right hand side becomes

$$\frac{n^{-1/q}}{2\pi} \int_{-1}^{+1} (1-|t|)^2 e^{-2ct^q} dt\,.$$

Hence we have

Lemma 3.

(20) $$\sum_k |a_{nk}^*|^2 \gg n^{-1/q}\,.$$

We split the sum $\sum_k |a_{nk}^*|^2$ into two parts

$$\sum_{1+|k-n\alpha| \leqq B} |a_{nk}^*|^2 + \sum_{1+|k-n\alpha| > B} |a_{nk}^*|^2 =: \sum_1 + \sum_2,$$

and use Lemma 2. Then

(21) $$\sum_1 \leqq n^{-\frac{2}{2(p-1)}} \sum_{1+|k-n\alpha| \leqq B} (1+|n\alpha-k|)^{-\frac{2(p-2)}{2(p-1)}} \ll n^{-\frac{1}{p-1}} B^{1-\frac{p-2}{p-1}}\,.$$

Next we have

(22) $$\sum_2 \leqq n^{-\frac{1}{2(p-2)}} B^{-\frac{p-2}{2(p-1)}} \sum_k |a_{nk}^*|\,.$$

Comparing the right hand sides of (21) and (22) we choose

$$B := n^{1/p} \Big(\sum_k |a_{nk}^*|\Big)^{\frac{2(p-1)}{p}}\,.$$

Adding the estimates of (21) and (22) we obtain

$$\sum_k |a_{nk}^*|^2 \ll n^{-1/p} \Big(\sum_k |a_{nk}^*|\Big)^{2/p}\,.$$

Inserting this in Lemma 3 yields the estimate

$$\sum_k |a^*_{nk}| \gg n^{-\frac{p}{2q}} \cdot n^{\frac{1}{2}} = n^{\frac{q-p}{2q}}.$$

An application of (15) and (16) completes the proof of the lower bound in (7) and (9).

5. Upper estimates

If $|u(e^{it})| < 1$ for $t \neq 0$, we immediately have

(23)
$$\sum_k |a_{nk}|^2 = \frac{1}{2\pi} \int_{-\pi}^{\pi} |u(e^{it})|^{2n}\,dt \ll$$
$$\ll \int_{-\varepsilon}^{\varepsilon} \exp(-cnt^q)\,dt + \sup_{|t| \geqq \varepsilon} |u(e^{it})|^{2n} \ll n^{-1/q}.$$

Recalling the estimates II and III we conclude that (instead of IV) we have

$$\sum_k |a_{nk}| \ll n^{1/2 - 1/2q}.$$

Now write

(24)
$$\sum |a_{nk}| = \sum_{|n\alpha - k| > B} |a_{nk}| + \sum_{|n\alpha - k| \leqq B} |a_{nk}| =: \sum_1 + \sum_2.$$

Then

$$\sum_1^2 \leqq \sum_k |k - n\alpha|^2 |a_{nk}|^2 \cdot \sum_{|k-n\alpha| > B} |k - n\alpha|^{-2} \ll B^{-1} \sum_k |k - n\alpha|^2 |a_{nk}|^2.$$

Next we have

$$\sum_2^2 \leqq \sum_k |a_{nk}|^2 \cdot \sum_{|k-n\alpha| \leqq B} 1 \ll B \sum_k |a_{nk}|^2.$$

Choosing

$$B := \Big(\sum_k |a_{nk}|^2 \Big/ \sum_k |k - n\alpha|^2 |a_{nk}|^2\Big)^{1/2},$$

(24) becomes

(25) $$\Bigl(\sum_k |a_{nk}|\Bigr)^4 \ll \sum_k |a_{nk}|^2 \cdot \sum_k |n\alpha - k|^2 |a_{nk}|^2 .$$

The last sum in (25) can be written in the form

$$\frac{1}{2\pi}\int_{-\pi}^{+\pi}\left|\frac{du^n(e^{it})}{dt} - in\alpha u^n(e^{it})\right|^2 dt .$$

Now, if $|t| \leqq \varepsilon$ we have

$$\frac{(u^n(e^{it}))'}{u^n(e^{it})} = i\alpha n + inp'(t) + \dots .$$

Hence by (12)

(26) $$\int_{-\varepsilon}^{\varepsilon}\left|\frac{du^n(e^{it})}{dt} - inu^n(e^{it})\right|^2 dt \ll \int_{-\varepsilon}^{\varepsilon} e^{-2nct^q}(nt^{p-1})^2 dt \ll$$
$$\ll n^{-1/q} \cdot n^{2-\frac{2(p-1)}{q}} \cdot \int_{-\infty}^{\infty} t^{2(p-1)} e^{-2ct^q} dt \ll n^{(2q-2p+1)/q} .$$

On the remaining two intervals where $|t| \geqq \varepsilon$, we have $|u(e^{it})| < \delta$ and $|u'(e^{it})| < \delta$, where $\delta < 1$. Hence

(27) $$\int_{|t| \geqq \varepsilon}\left|\frac{du^n(e^{it})}{du} - in\alpha u^n(e^{it})\right|^2 dt \ll n^2 \delta^{2n} \ll 1 .$$

Inserting (26), (27) and (23) into (25) yields the estimate

$$\sum_k |a_{nk}| \ll n^{-\frac{1}{4q}} \cdot n^{\frac{2q-2p+1}{4q}} = n^{\frac{q-p}{2q}} .$$

6. Remarks on the general case

Let there be a finite number of points, $\zeta_1, \dots, \zeta_m$, such that $|u(\zeta_i)| = 1, i = 1, 2, \dots, m$. We will use a suitable partition of unity. Therefore we choose functions $H_i(t)$ indicated in Fig. 1 which are equal to 1 on the interval from arg ζ_i one third of the way on both sides to arg ζ_j of neighbouring points $\zeta_j (j \neq i)$, 0 to past two thirds of the way, and linear between:

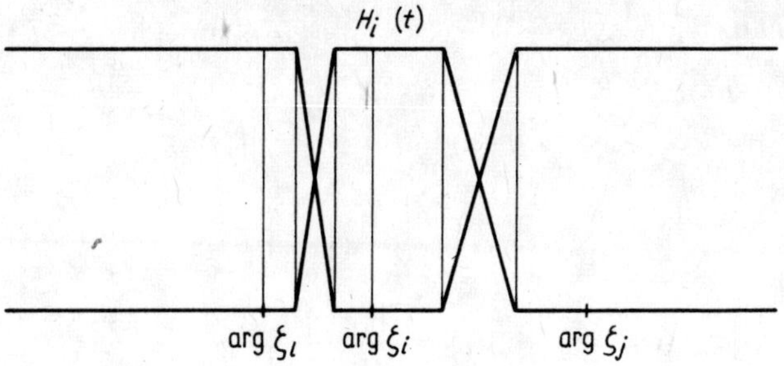

Fig. 1

Hence

$$\sum_{i=1}^{m} H_i(t) \equiv 1$$

and

$$\|u^n\|_1 \leqq \sum_{i=1}^{m} \|H_i u^n\|_1 \,.$$

Taking the corresponding numbers p_i, q_i in the local expansions about ζ_i and choosing the maximum

$$\frac{q_l - p_l}{2q_l} = \max_{i=1,\dots,m} \frac{q_i - p_i}{2q_i}$$

we get

$$\sum_k |a_{nk}| \ll n^{\frac{q_l - p_l}{2q_l}}$$

and in the same way as above

$$\sum_k |a_{nk}| \gg n^{\frac{q_l - p_l}{2q_l}}$$

Remark. In the case $q = \infty$ we proved

$$n^{1/2} \ll \sum_{k \leqq \lambda n} |a_{nk}| \ll n^{1/2}$$

and

(28) $$|a^*_{nk}| \ll n^{-1/2}$$

We cannot conclude that the same holds for a_{nk}, but it is not difficult to show that $\sum_{n=0}^{\infty} |a_{nk}|^2 = O(1)$ for all k.

Consider, namely,

$$a_{nk}=\frac{1}{2\pi i}\int\limits_{|z|=r<1}\frac{u^n(z)}{z^{k+1}}\,dz\,.$$

Then

$$v(w):=\sum_{n=0}^{\infty}a_{nk}w^n=\frac{1}{2\pi i}\int\limits_{|z|=r<1}\frac{1}{1-wu(z)}\,\frac{dz}{z^{k+1}}$$

for $w\in\bar{D}$. Observing that $u'(z)\neq 0$ for all z with $|z|=1$ we conclude by the residue theorem that $v(w)$ is uniformly bounded for $w\in\bar{D}$ and for all k. Therefore

$$\sum_{n=0}^{\infty}|a_{nk}|^2\ll 1\quad\text{for } k=0,\,1,\,2,\,\ldots\,. \tag{29}$$

Repeating the argument of §3, parts II and III with suitable positive constants λ_0', λ_1' and $\delta^*<1$, we get

$$|a_{nk}|\ll\delta^{*n}\quad\text{for } n<\lambda_1'k\,,\ \lambda_0'k<n\,. \tag{30}$$

7. Proof of (8) and (10)

The above proofs are not directly applicable here. Therefore, we handle the cases $q=\infty$ and $q<\infty$ separately.

The case $q=\infty$. Since (29) holds for all $k\in\mathbf{N}$, we have

$$\sum_{\lambda_1'k\leqq n\leqq\lambda_0'k}|a_{nk}|\leqq\Bigl(\sum_{n=0}^{\infty}|a_{nk}|^2\Bigr)^{1/2}\Bigl(\sum_{\lambda_1'k\leqq n\leqq\lambda_0'k}1\Bigr)^{1/2}\ll k^{1/2}\,.$$

On the other hand

$$K^{3/2}\ll\sum_{n\leqq K/\lambda}\ \sum_{k\leqq\lambda n\,.}|a_{nk}|\leqq\sum_{k\leqq K}\ \sum_{n=0}^{\infty}|a_{nk}|\leqq K\cdot\sup_{k\leqq K}\sum_{n=0}^{\infty}|a_{nk}|\,. \tag{31}$$

Inequality (10) now follows from the last inequalities and (30).

The case $q<\infty$. Let $|u(z)|<1$ for $z\in\bar{D}\backslash\{1\}$. Consider the integral

$$a_{nk}=\frac{1}{2\pi i}\int\limits_{(\gamma)}\frac{u^n(z)}{z^{k+1}}\,dz\,,$$

where (γ) is a simple closed path surrounding the origin and lying in the region of regularity of the function u. Choosing (γ) as in [4] (p. 105), we get

$$\sum_{n=0}^{\infty} |a_{nk}| = \sum_{n=0}^{\infty} p_{nk} + O(1)$$

where

$$p_{nk} = \frac{1}{2\pi i} \int_L \frac{u^n(z)}{z^{k+1}}\, dz$$

and L is defined by

$$|u(z)| = 1 \quad \text{for } -\varepsilon \leqq \arg u(z) \leqq \varepsilon\,.$$

On L the inverse function u^{-1} is regular for $w = e^{it}$, $-\varepsilon \leqq t \leqq \varepsilon$.[4] Let

$$z = u^{-1}(1/s) = \frac{1}{h(s)}\,.$$

Then

$$p_{nk} = \frac{1}{2\pi i} \int\limits_{\substack{|s|=1\\ |\arg s| \leqq \varepsilon}} \frac{h^k(s)}{s^{n+1}}\, h'(s)\, ds\,.$$

Writing

$$h(s) = s^{\alpha^*} + A^* i^d (s-1)^d + O(1)\,(s-1)^{d+1} \quad \text{for } s \to 1$$

with $\alpha^* = h'(1) = 1/\alpha$ and $A^* \neq 0$ and setting $s = e^{it}$ we see that $d = p$ and $\operatorname{Re} A^* = 0$. With the same arguments as above we get the assertions (8).

8. Examples

In the following we give some examples of regular and irregular Euler and Sonnenschein transformations.

Example 1. Let

$$u(z) = \frac{1 + iz + z^2}{2 + i}\,.$$

Clearly $u(1) = 1$ and $|u(-1)| = \left|\frac{2-i}{2+i}\right| = 1$. To prove that $u(z)$ satisfies (ii) except at $z = \pm 1$, we first consider $v(z) = 1 + z - z^2$, and observe that

$$|v(e^{it})|^2 = (1 + \cos t - \cos 2t)^2 + (\sin t - \sin 2t)^2 = 3 - 2\cos 2t\,.$$

[4] If u is a Möbius transformation (1) then the inverse function u^{-1} exists and with the same arguments as above we get the sharper estimate $k^{1/2} \ll \sum_{n=0}^{\infty} |a_{nk}|$ (cf. the case $q < \infty$).

This has maxima at $t = \pm\frac{\pi}{2}$. Now, $u(z) = \frac{v(iz)}{v(i)}$ and $|u(e^{it})|<1$ for $0<|t|<\pi$.

Also

$$\alpha = u'(1) = 1 .$$

Hence

$$u(z) - z = \frac{1}{2+i}(z-1)^2$$

and so

$$A_1 = -\frac{1}{2+i},$$

i.e. $\operatorname{Re} A_1 \neq 0$, $p = p(1) = 2$. At the other maximum we have $A_{-1} = \bar{A}_1$, $p(-1) = 2$. Therefore $u(z)$ generates a regular Euler and a regular Sonnenschein transformation.

Example 2. Another regular matrix $\{a_{nk}\}$ is generated by

$$u(z) = z^2 - \left(\frac{z-1}{2}\right)^4 .$$

Obviously we have $u(1)=1$, $|u(e^{it})|<1$ for $0<|t|\leqq\pi$, $u'(1)=2$, and therefore $p=4$, $A_1 = -1/16$.

Example 3. Contrary to Example 2 the function

$$u(z) = z - \left(\frac{z-1}{2}\right)^3$$

does not satisfy (iii). To prove this we first consider $|u(e^{it})|$.

Now

$$|u(e^{it})|^2 = 1 - \sin^4\frac{t}{2}\left(1+\cos^2\frac{t}{2}\right), \tag{32}$$

showing that $u(e^{it})$ has its only maximum at $t=0$. Since $u'(t)=1$, we have $p=3$, $A_1 = -i/8$. From (32) we conclude that $q=4$, and hence by (7) and (8)

$$n^{1/8} \ll \sum_{k=0}^{\infty} |a_{nk}| \ll n^{1/8} ,$$

$$k^{1/8} \ll \sum_{n=0}^{\infty} |a_{nk}| \ll k^{1/8} .$$

Example 4. Let

$$u(z) = \frac{15+10z-3(z-1)^2}{25}.$$

Then we have the identity

$$|u(e^{it})|^2 = 1 - \frac{36}{625}|e^{it}-1|^4. \tag{33}$$

Hence $u(1)=1$ and $|u(e^{it})|<1$ for $0<|t|\leqq\pi$. Furthermore $u'(1)=2/5$ and

$$u(z)-z^{2/5} = -\frac{8}{125}(z-1)^3 + O(|z-1|^4), \quad z\to 1.$$

Thus $A_1=-8i/125$ and $\{a_{nk}\}$ is not regular.

Equation (33) shows that $q=4$ and we get by our Theorem 1

$$n^{1/8} \ll \sum_{k=0}^{\infty} |a_{nk}| \ll n^{1/8},$$

$$k^{1/8} \ll \sum_{n=0}^{\infty} |a_{nk}| \ll k^{1/8}.$$

Example 5. Let $u(z)$ be as in Example 2 and let Φ_{ζ_0} be a Möbius transformation of the form (1), $\zeta_0\neq 0$. Then we define u^* by

$$u^*(z) = u(\Phi_{\zeta_0}(z)) = (\Phi_{\zeta_0}(z))^2 - \left(\frac{\Phi_{\zeta_0}(z)-1}{2}\right)^4.$$

We first consider the Taylor series of Φ_{ζ_0} about $z=1$. We have

$$\Phi_{\zeta_0}(z) = \sum_{m=0}^{3} d_m(z-1)^m + O(|z-1|^4)$$

where $d_0=1$ and

$$d_1 = \frac{1-\zeta_0\bar{\zeta}_0}{(1-\bar{\zeta}_0)(1-\zeta_0)} > 0,$$

$$d_2 = d_1\frac{\bar{\zeta}_0}{1-\zeta_0},$$

$$d_3 = d_1\left(\frac{\bar{\zeta}_0}{1-\zeta_0}\right)^2.$$

Hence

$$u^*(z)=1+2d_1(z-1)+(2d_2+d_1^2)(z-1)^2+$$

$$+(2d_3+2d_1d_2)(z-1)^3+O(|z-1|^4),$$

so that $\alpha=2d_1$. Next we observe that

$$z\alpha = \sum_{m=0}^{3}\binom{\alpha}{m}(z-1)^m+O(|z-1|^4).$$

Subtracting gives

$$u^*(z)-z^\alpha=c_2(z-1)^2+c_3(z-1)^3+O(|z-1|^4),$$

where

$$c_2 = 2d_2+d_1^2-\binom{\alpha}{2}=\frac{d_1(\bar{\zeta}_0-\zeta_0)}{(1-\bar{\zeta}_0)(1-\zeta_0)}.$$

In the case Im $\zeta_0\neq 0$ we get $p=2$, $A_1=-c_2\neq 0$, and Re $A_1=0$. If Im $\zeta_0=0$ we look at

$$c_3 = \frac{2}{3}d_1\frac{\zeta_0}{(1-\zeta_0)^2}.$$

Now $\zeta_0\neq 0$ and so $p=3$, $A_1=-ic_3\neq 0$, and A_1 is pure imaginary.

Next we determine q. Observing that

$$|u(z)|^2=1-z^2\left(\frac{\bar{z}-1}{2}\right)^4-z^{-2}\left(\frac{z-1}{2}\right)^4+\left|\frac{z-1}{2}\right|^8$$

on $|z|=1$ and putting, for $t\to 0$,

$$z:=\Phi_{\zeta_0}(e^{it})=1+itd_1+O(t^2),$$

so that

$$z^2=1+2itd_1+O(t^2)=1+O(|t|),$$

we conclude that

$$|u^*(e^{it})| = 1-\{1+O(|t|)\}\left\{\frac{d_1^4}{16}t^4+O(|t|^5)\right\}-$$

$$-\{1+O(|t|)\}\left\{\frac{d_1^4}{16}t^4+O(|t|^5)\right\}+O(t^8)=1-\frac{d_1^4}{8}t^4+O(|t|^5).$$

Thus in both cases $q=4$ and by Theorem 1 the following is proved:

(j) *If* $\operatorname{Im} \zeta_0 \neq 0$, *then*

$$n^{1/4} \ll \sum_{k=0}^{\infty} |a_{nk}| \ll n^{1/4},$$

$$k^{1/4} \ll \sum_{n=0}^{\infty} |a_{nk}| \ll k^{1/4}.$$

(jj) *If* $\operatorname{Im} \zeta_0 = 0$, *then*

$$n^{1/8} \ll \sum_{k=0}^{\infty} |a_{nk}| \ll n^{1/8},$$

$$k^{1/8} \ll \sum_{k=0}^{\infty} |a_{nk}| \ll k^{1/8}.$$

9. Continuable equivalent power series

If $f \in H(D)$, the structure of values of $f(w)$ in the neighbourhood of an arbitrary periphery point $w \in \partial D$ is "nearly the same" as that of $f_1(z) = f(\Phi_{\zeta_0}(z))$ for $z = \Phi_{\zeta_0}^{-1}(w)$ (cf. [17], p. 20). Therefore it was regarded as rather surprising that the convergence of $f(w) = \sum_{k=0}^{\infty} a_k w^k$ at $w=1$ does not imply the convergence of $f_1(z) = \sum_{n=0}^{\infty} b_n z^n$ at $z=1$. Moreover, all known examples of functions which behave konvergenz-schlecht under the mapping Φ_{ζ_0} (cf. for instance [5], [9] I) have ∂D as their natural boundary. Thus, one can discuss whether this phenomenon is characteristic. Generalizing the problem of TURÁN, we ask the following question.[5] *Let* $f \in H(\bar{D} \setminus \{e^{i\vartheta}\})$, $f(w) = \sum_{k=0}^{\infty} a_k w^k$. *If* $\sum_{k=0}^{\infty} a_k$ *has a property E* (for instance convergence, absolute convergence, (C, k)-summability), *does* $f_1(z) = f(\Phi_{\zeta_0}(z)) = \sum_{n=0}^{\infty} b_n z^n$ *have the same property E at* $z=1$?

The results of Theorem 1 allow us to give an answer in the case of convergence and absolute convergence, and even allow us to make certain restrictions on the growth of the coefficients a_k. Here we want only to give qualitative results and we show

Theorem 3. (See [13], Theorem 2.) *Let* $0 \neq \zeta_0 \in D$. *Then there exist functions* $f \in H(\bar{D} \setminus \{1\})$, *which behave konvergenz-schlecht under the mapping* Φ_{ζ_0}.

[5] The author formulated this question in a course of a lecture given at the University of Giessen on October 29, 1976.

Theorem 4. (See [13], Theorem 2.) *Let* $0 \neq \zeta_0 \in D$. *Then there exist functions* $f \in H(\bar{D} \setminus \{1\})$, $f(w) = \sum_{k=0}^{\infty} a_k w^k$, *such that* $\sum_{k=0}^{\infty} |a_k| < \infty$ *but the Taylor series* $f_1(z) = f(\Phi_{\zeta_0}(z)) = \sum_{n=0}^{\infty} b_n z^n$ *are absolutely divergent on* $|z| = 1$.

Proof of Theorem 3. Let $0 \neq \zeta_0 \in D$. We choose the functions u from Example 2 and u^* from Example 5. There exists a function $g \in H(D)$, $g(w) = \sum_{\nu=0}^{\infty} a'_\nu w^\nu$ converging at $w=1$, with the series $g(u^*(z)) = \sum_{n=0}^{\infty} b_n z^n$ divergent at $z=1$. Then $f(z) = g(u(z)) = \sum_{k=0}^{\infty} a_k z^k$ converges at $z=1$ and $f \in H(\bar{D} \setminus \{1\})$. Now f and $f \circ \Phi_{\zeta_0}$ are the required functions.

In the same manner we can show the assertions of Theorem 4.

Remark. If instead of one factor Φ_{ζ_0} one chooses a finite product of such Möbius transformations $\Phi = \Pi \Phi_{\zeta_0}$, then one can formulate

(a) the problems of TURÁN (and ALPÁR, CLUNIE, HALÁSZ, etc.) for functions $f \in H(D)$, resp. $f_1 = f \circ \Phi$,

(b) the same questions for continuable functions f, resp. $f \circ \Phi$.

By Theorem 2, in the case (a) the problem is solved for convergence and absolute convergence, but not much is known in the remaining cases.

References

[1] L. ALPÁR, Remarque sur la sommabilité des séries de Taylor sur leurs cercles de convergence I, II, III. *Magyar Tud. Akad. Mat. Kutató Int. Közl.*, **3** (1958), 1–12; **3** (1958), 141–158; **5** (1960), 97–152.

[2] L. ALPÁR, Sur certaines transformées des séries de puissances absolument convergentes sur la frontière de leur cercle de convergence. *Magyar Tud. Akad. Mat. Kutató int. Közl.*, **7** (1962), 287–316.

[3] B. M. BAJŠANSKI, Sur une classe générale de procédés de sommations du type d'Euler–Borel. *Acad. Serbe Sci. Publ. Inst. Math.*, **10** (1956), 131–152.

[4] B. M. BAJŠANSKI, Généralisation d'un théorème de Carlemann. *Acad. Serbe Sci. Publ. Inst. Math.*, **12** (1958), 101–108.

[5] J. CLUNIE, On equivalent power series. *Acta Math. Acad. Sci. Hung.*, **18** (1967), 165–169.

[6] J. CLUNIE and P. VERMES, Regular Sonnenschein type summability methods, *Acad. Roy. Belg. Cl. Sci.*, (5) **45** (1959), 930–945.

[7] G. HALÁSZ, On Taylor series absolutely convergent on the circumference of the circle of convergence I, II, III, *Publ. Math. Debrecen*, **14** (1967), 63–68; **15** (1968), 23–31; *Acta Math. Acad. Sci. Hung.*, **25** (1974), 81–87.

[8] G. HALÁSZ, On the behaviour of Taylor series under conformal mappings of the circle of convergence, *Studia Sci. Math. Hung.*, **1** (1966), 389–401.

[9] K.-H. INDLEKOFER, Summierbarkeitsverhalten äquivalenter Potenzreihen, I, II, III. *Arch. Math.*, **22** (1971), 385–393; *Math. Nachr.*, **50** (1971), 305–319; *Math. Nachr.*, **55** (1973), 265–286.

[10] K.-H. INDLEKOFER, Bemerkungen über äquivalente Potenzreihen von Funktionen mit einem gewissen Stetigkeitsmodul, *Monatsh. Math.*, **76** (1972), 124–129.

[11] K.-H. Indlekofer, Über die Invarianz der absoluten Konvergenz bei konformer Abbildung, *Math. Z.*, **134** (1973), 171–177.
[12] K.-H. Indlekofer, Automorphismen gewisser Funktionenalgebren, I, II. *Mitt. Math. Sem. Gießen*, **111** (1974), 68–79; *Acta Math. Acad. Sci. Hung.*, **28** (1976), 305–313.
[13] K.-H. Indlekofer and R. Trautner, Fortsetzbare äquivalente Potenzreihen, *Publ. Math. (Debrecen.)* **28** (1981), 25–30.
[14] W. Schwarz, Bemerkungen zu einem Satz der Herren Turán and Clunie über das Verhalten von Potenzreihen auf dem Rande des Konvergenzkreises, I, II. *Publ. Math. Debrecen.*, **16** (1969), 67–73; **18** (1971), 129–137.
[15] J. Sonnenschein, Sur les séries divergentes, *Bull. Acad. Royale de Belgique* **35** (1949), 594–601.
[16] J. Sonnenschein, *Sur les séries divergentes.* These, Bruxelles, 1946.
[17] P. Turán, A remark concerning the behaviour of a power series on the periphery of its convergence circle, *Publ. Inst. Math. Acad. Serbe Sci.*, **12** (1958), 19–26.
[18] P. Turán, Remarks on the preceding paper of J. Clunie entitled "On equivalent power series." *Acta Math. Acad. Sci. Hung.*, **18** (1967), 171–173.
[19] R. Warlimont, Euler-Summierbarkeit konform äquivalenter Reihen, *Monatsh. Math.*, **81** (1976), 63–68.

MATHEMATISCHES INSTITUT
DER UNIVERSITÄT PADERBORN
BRD

Studies in Pure Mathematics
To the Memory of Paul Turán

The avarage order of Gaussian sums

by

H. JAGER (Amsterdam)

1. Let G be a commutative semigroup with identity e on which a non-negative function $|.|: G \to \mathbf{R}$, called a *norm*, is defined such that $|ab| \leqq |a|\,|b|$ for all $a, b \in G$ and such that for every real x the number $N(x)$ of elements a of G with $|a| \leqq x$, is finite.

A function $G \to \mathbf{C}$ is called an *arithmetical function*. If f and g are two arithmetical functions defined on the same G we say that f and g have the same *average order*, notation $f \approx g$, when

$$\sum_{|a| \leqq x} f(a) \sim \sum_{|a| \leqq x} g(a), \quad x \to \infty.$$

The relation $\approx$ is an equivalence relation and an often occurring problem in number theory is to determine for a given function f a more smoothly behaving function g in the same equivalence class.

For $a, b \in G$ we denote by (a, b) the set of the common divisors of a and b. Let U denote the set of units of G, i.e. of all the divisors of e. If $(a, b) = U$ we say that a and b are *coprime*. An arithmetical function f is called *multiplicative* when

$$(a, b) = U \Rightarrow f(a\,b) = f(a) f(b).$$

In this note we consider the semigroup D, formed by the set of all Dirichlet characters χ mod m, on which a multiplication is defined by

$$(\chi_1 \bmod m_1)(\chi_2 \bmod m_2) := \chi_1 \chi_2 \bmod [m_1, m_2]$$

where $[m_1, m_2]$ stands for the least common multiple of m_1 and m_2. For the norm function we take

$$|\chi \bmod m| := m.$$

Clearly the above requirements on G are fulfilled, $N(x)$ being $\sum_{m \leqq x} \varphi(m)$. Note that $U = \{e\} = \{\chi \bmod 1\}$ and that $\chi_1 \bmod m_1$ and $\chi_2 \bmod m_2$ are coprime, if and only if $(m_1, m_2) = 1$.

The Gaussian sum of a Dirichlet character, defined by

$$\tau(\chi \bmod m) := \sum_{a=1}^{m} \chi(a) \exp\left(\frac{2\pi i a}{m}\right)$$

is an arithmetical function $\tau: D \to \mathbb{C}$. The purpose of this note is to determine a simple average order for $|\tau|$.

2. Let $\chi_i \bmod m_i$, $i=1, 2$ be two coprime Dirichlet characters with product $\chi \bmod m$. Then

$$\tau(\chi \bmod m) = \chi_1(m_2)\chi_2(m_1)\tau(\chi_1 \bmod m_1)\tau(\chi_2 \bmod m_2)\,. \tag{1}$$

This follows from the observation that if a_i runs through a complete set of reduced residues mod m_i, $i=1, 2$, then $a=a_2m_1+a_1m_2$ runs through such a set mod m. Hence

Lemma 1. *The arithmetical function* $|\tau|: D \to [0, \infty)$ *is multiplicative.*

Let $\chi \bmod m$ be induced by the, not necessarily primitive, character $\chi' \bmod m'$. Hence m'/m. Suppose that m' is a unitary divisor of m, i.e. let $\left(\frac{m}{m'}, m'\right)=1$; notation $m'//m$.
Then

$$\chi \bmod m = (\chi' \bmod m')\,(\chi_0 \bmod \frac{m}{m'})$$

where $\chi_0 \bmod \frac{m}{m'}$ denotes the principal character with modulus $\frac{m}{m'}$. Applying (1) and observing that $\tau\,(\chi_0 \bmod \frac{m}{m'}) = \mu\left(\frac{m}{m'}\right)$ we find that

$$\tau(\chi \bmod m) = \chi'\left(\frac{m}{m'}\right)\mu\left(\frac{m}{m'}\right)\tau(\chi' \bmod m')\,. \tag{2}$$

Now we show that (2) also holds when m' is not a unitary divisor of m. In that case $\chi'\left(\frac{m}{m'}\right)=0$ so we have to show that $\tau(\chi \bmod m)=0$. Put $v=\left[m', \frac{m}{m'}\right]$. Then $v<m$ and χ is also a character mod v. One has

$$\tau(\chi \bmod m) = \sum_{a=1}^{m} \chi(a+v) \exp\left(\frac{2\pi i(a+v)}{m}\right) = \exp\left(\frac{2\pi i v}{m}\right)\tau(\chi \bmod m)\,,$$

from which the desired $\tau(\chi \bmod m)=0$ follows. Hence we have proved

Lemma 2. *Let the character* $\chi \bmod m$ *be induced by the, not necessarily primitive, character* $\chi' \bmod m'$.

Then

$$\tau(\chi \bmod m) = \chi'\left(\frac{m}{m'}\right)\mu\left(\frac{m}{m'}\right)\tau(\chi' \bmod m').$$

For primitive χ' mod m' this formula can be found on p. 148 of [1] or in [5], formula 17. Since for a primitive character χ mod m one has $|\tau(\chi \bmod m)| = \sqrt{m}$ (see [1], p. 69), it follows from Lemma 2 that

$$0 \leqq |\tau(\chi \bmod m)| \leqq \sqrt{m}, \tag{3}$$

for every character χ mod m. Moreover, the right-hand equality in (3) occurs if and only if χ mod m is primitive. For a criterion for the occurrence of the left-hand equality see [4].

3. Theorem. *The absolute value of the Gaussian sum, $|\tau|: D \to [0, \infty)$, has the same average order as $g: D \to [0, \infty)$ where $g(\chi \bmod m) = c\sqrt{m}$, with*

$$c = \frac{\pi^2}{6}\prod_p\left(1 - \frac{2p^2 - p\sqrt{p} + \sqrt{p} - 1)}{p^4}\right), \quad c = .763\ldots.$$

Proof. Define the arithmetical function $T: \mathbf{N} \to \mathbf{R}$ by

$$T(m) = \sum_{\chi \bmod m} |\tau(\chi \bmod m)|,$$

where the sum is taken over the $\varphi(m)$ characters with modulus m. Denote by $\psi(m)$ the number of primitive characters with modulus m. In view of

$$\sum_{d|m} \psi(d) = \varphi(m),$$

the function ψ is multiplicative and from Möbius inversion formula we see that

$$\psi(p^k) = \varphi(p^k) - \varphi(p^{k-1}), \quad p \text{ prime}, k = 1, 2, \ldots. \tag{4}$$

From Lemma 2 it follows that

$$T(m) = \sum_{d|m} \left|\mu\left(\frac{m}{d}\right)\right| \psi(d)\sqrt{d} \tag{5}$$

and since the unitary convolution preserves multiplicativity (see [3]), T is multiplicative. Clearly

$$\sum_{|\chi \bmod m| \leqq x} |\tau(\chi \bmod m)| = \sum_{m \leqq x} T(m)$$

and thus the problem of determining an average order for a multiplicative function on D has been replaced by a similar problem for a function on $\mathbf{N}$. For the latter we have standard methods.

From (4) and (5) it follows that with p a prime number

$$T(p)=(p-2)\sqrt{p}+1,$$

$$T(p^k)=p^k\sqrt{p^k}\left(1-\frac{1}{p}\right)^2, \quad k>1.$$

For the function t, defined by $t(m)=m^{-3/2}\,T(m)$ we thus have, by a theorem of DELANGE, [2],

$$\sum_{m\leq x} t(m)=c'x+o(x), \quad x\to\infty$$

with

$$c'=\prod_p\left(1-\frac{2p^2-p\sqrt{p}+\sqrt{p}-1}{p^4}\right).$$

From this it is an easy step to

$$\sum_{m\leq x} T(m)=\frac{2}{5}c'x^{5/2}+o(x^{5/2}), \quad x\to\infty.$$

Finally,

$$\sum_{|\chi \bmod m|\leq x} g(\chi \bmod m)=\sum_{m\leq x} c\varphi(m)\sqrt{m}=\frac{2}{5}c'x^{5/2}+o(x^{5/2}), \quad x\to\infty,$$

from which the theorem follows.

References

[1] DAVENPORT, H., *Multiplicative Number Theory*, Lectures in advanced mathematics, vol. **1**, Chicago, 1967.
[2] DELANGE, H., Sur les fonctions arithmétiques multiplicatives, *Ann. Sci. Ecole Norm. Sup.*, (3) **78** (1961), 273–304.
[3] JAGER, H., The unitary analogues of some identities for certain arithmetical functions, *Ind. Math*, **23** (1961), 508–515.
[4] JAGER, H., Characters with non-zero Gauss sums, *Nieuw Archief voor Wiskunde (3)*, **24** (1976), 173–176.
[5] JORIS, HENRI, On the evaluation of Gaussian sums for non-primitive Dirichlet characters, *L'Enseignement Mathématique*, II Série, **23** (1977), 13–18.

MATHEMATICAL INSTITUTE
UNIVERSITY OF AMSTERDAM.
THE NETHERLANDS

Studies in Pure Mathematics
To the Memory of Paul Turán

Zeros of the zeta-function near the critical line

by

M. JUTILA (Turku)

1. Introduction

BOHR and LANDAU [2] were the first to prove that for any fixed $\varepsilon>0$ almost all complex zeros of the Riemann zeta-function $\zeta(s)$ lie in the strip $|\sigma-1/2|<\varepsilon$. Equivalently, there exists a positive decreasing function $f(t)$, tending to zero as t tends to infinity, such that

$$|\beta-1/2|<f(\gamma) \tag{1.1}$$

for almost all zeros $\rho=\beta+i\gamma$ of $\zeta(s)$ in the upper half plane. LITTLEWOOD [5] sharpened this result by showing that if $\Phi(t)$ is any positive increasing function, tending with t to infinity, then one may take in (1.1)

$$f(t)=\Phi(t)\log\log t/\log t\,. \tag{1.2}$$

The same conclusion also follows from the known zero-density estimate

$$N(\alpha,T)\ll T^{3(1-\alpha)/(2-\alpha)}\log^5 T \tag{1.3}$$

of INGHAM [4]; here $N(\alpha, T)$ denotes the number of zeros of $\zeta(s)$ in the rectangle $\alpha\leqq\sigma\leqq 1$, $|t|\leqq T$. SELBERG [8] made further progress by removing the factor $\log\log t$ in (1.2), and in [9] he proved the following quantitative result, superseding (1.3) for $\alpha\in[1/2,\ 1/2+(48/13)\log\log T/\log T]$:

$$N(\alpha,T)\ll T^{1-(\alpha-1/2)/4}\log T. \tag{1.4}$$

Our purpose is to give a fairly simple proof of a sharpened version of this estimate; actually SELBERG also pointed out that (1.4) is by no means the best possible result, obtainable by his method.

In the proofs of the above results the underlying idea is to introduce a "mollifier", i.e. a suitable Dirichlet polynomial

$$M(s)=\sum_{d\leqq z}\lambda_d d^{-s},$$

which behaves somewhat like $1/\zeta(s)$, so that the effect of multiplying $\zeta(s)$ by $M(s)$ is to damp the oscillations of the modulus of $\zeta(s)$. The most immediate choice is $\lambda_d = \mu(d)$, the Möbius function. This is suitable for a proof of (1.3), but no more for (1.4). In fact, the principal new idea of SELBERG was a construction of a more sophisticated mollifier, where the coefficients λ_d are suitably modified values of $\mu(d)$; in this problematics it can also be found the origin of Selberg's sieve method.

Since the zeta-function can be expressed in terms of partial sums of the zeta-series by the approximate functional equation, a problem naturally arising is to find a mollifier for a partial sum. However, it turns out that instead of the partial sum itself, it is more fruitful to consider a somewhat modified sum like

$$F(s) = F(s; v_1, v_2) = \sum_d \kappa_d(v_1, v_2) d^{-s}, \tag{1.5}$$

where $1 < v_1 < v_2$,

$$\kappa_d = \kappa_d(v_1, v_2) = \begin{cases} 1, & 1 \leqq d \leqq v_1, \\ \log(v_2/d)/\log(v_2/v_1), & v_1 < d < v_2, \\ 0, & d \geqq v_2. \end{cases} \tag{1.6}$$

A natural guess now is that a function like

$$M(s) = M(s; z_1, z_2) = \sum_d \lambda_d(z_1, z_2) d^{-s}, \tag{1.7}$$

where $1 < z_1 < z_2$ and

$$\lambda_d = \lambda_d(z_1, z_2) = \mu(d)\kappa_d(z_1, z_2), \tag{1.8}$$

might be a good mollifier for $F(s)$. This is, indeed, the case (see Lemma 2 below). It follows that a suitable function $M(s; z_1, z_2)$ can be taken as a mollifier for $\zeta(s)$, too; this is proved in Lemma 4. In passing, it should be noted that a mollifier with coefficients of the form $\lambda_d(z, z^2)$ was used by SELBERG [10] in proving a k-analogue of (1.4). Returning to the zeta-function, Lemma 4 and Littlewood's lemma easily lead to the following zero-density estimate. As is customary, we use notations like $\ll_\varepsilon$ to indicate the dependence of the implied constant on various parameters.

Theorem. *For* $1/2 \leqq \alpha \leqq 1$, $T \geqq 2$ *and any fixed* $\varepsilon > 0$, *we have*

$$N(\alpha, T) \ll_\varepsilon T^{1-(1-\varepsilon)(\alpha-1/2)} \log T. \tag{1.9}$$

Like (1.4), this estimate is of interest only for α near 1/2; more exactly, (1.9) supersedes (1.3) for $\alpha \in [1/2, 1/2 + (12-\varepsilon)\log\log T/\log T]$.

The usefulness of the mollifier (1.7)–(1.8) was anticipated by BARBAN and VEHOV [1], who sketched a proof of the following estimate:

$$\sum_{n \leqq x} \Big(\sum_{d|n} \lambda_d(z_1, z_2) \Big)^2 \ll x/\log(z_2/z_1). \tag{1.10}$$

Graham [3] sharpened this to an asymptotic formula with an estimate for the error. Let for $z>1$

(1.11) $$K_d(z)=\begin{cases}\log(z/d) & d\leqq z,\\ 0 & d>z,\end{cases}$$

(1.12) $$L_d(z)=\mu(d)K_d(z),$$

so that

(1.13) $$\kappa_d(v_1, v_2)=(K_d(v_2)-K_d(v_1))/\log(v_2/v_1),$$

(1.14) $$\lambda_d(z_1, z_2)=(L_d(z_2)-L_d(z_1))/\log(z_2/z_1).$$

An interesting result, related to (1.10), was recently obtained by Motohashi: for any positive integer k and any $z>1$, $\omega>1$, satisfying $1\ll(\omega-1)\log z\ll 1$

(1.15) $$\sum_{n=1}^{\infty}\tau_k(n)\left(\sum_{d|n}\mu(d)K_d^k(z)\right)^2 n^{-\omega}\ll_k(\log z)^{2k}$$

(see [7], proof of Lemma 5). Up to this estimate, our proof of (1.9) will be essentially self-contained. Actually, we do not by far need the full power of (1.15), rather the cases $k=1$, 2 only (moreover, $k=2$ without the factor $\tau(n)$).

The methods of this paper apply for the zeros of L-functions as well, but not in a completely straightforward manner, because the approximate functional equation of the L-functions is not as nice as that of the zeta-function. Hence, in order to keep the presentation as simple as possible, we leave aside possible analogues and generalizations to L-functions.

2. Preliminary lemmas

If the functions $F(s)$ and $M(s)$ are defined by (1.5)–(1.6) and (1.7)–(1.8), then we have

(2.1) $$M(s)F(s)=1+\sum_{u<n<v_2z_2}a_n n^{-s},$$

where $u=\min(v_1, z_1)$ and

(2.2) $$a_n=a_n(v_1, v_2, z_1, z_2)=\sum_{d|n}\lambda_d(z_1, z_2)\kappa_{n/d}(v_1, v_2).$$

By a mean-value estimate for Dirichlet polynomials (see [6], Theorem 6.1), we now have for $H>0$ and all σ and T

(2.3) $$\int_T^{T+H}|M(\sigma+it)F(\sigma+it)-1|^2\,dt\ll(H+v_2z_2)\sum_{u<n<v_2z_2}a_n^2 n^{-2\sigma}.$$

By (2.2), (1.13) and (1.14), the right-hand side can be estimated, for σ near 1/2, by the means of sums of the type

$$S(v, z) = \sum_{n < vz} \left(\sum_{d|n} L_d(z) K_{n/d}(v) \right)^2 n^{-1} .$$

Lemma 1. *Suppose that* $v > 1$, $z > 1$, $\log v \ll \log z \ll \log v$. *Then*

$$S(v, z) \ll \log^4 z . \tag{2.4}$$

Proof. For $n < vz$, we have

$$\sum_{d|n} L_d(z) K_{n/d}(v) = \sum_{\substack{d|n \\ n/v < d < z}} \mu(d) \log(z/d) \log(vd/n) =$$

$$= \sum_{\substack{d|n \\ d < z}} \mu(d) \log(z/d) \log(vd/n) - \sum_{d|n} \mu(d) \log(z/d) \log(vd/n) +$$

$$+ \sum_{\substack{d|n \\ d < v}} \mu(n/d) \log(zd/n) \log(v/d) = \sum_{\substack{d|n \\ d < z}} \mu(d) \log(z/d) \log(vz/n) - \sum_{\substack{d|n \\ d < z}} \mu(d) \log^2(z/d) -$$

$$- \sum_{d|n} \mu(d) \log(z/d) \log(vd/n) + \sum_{\substack{d|n \\ d < v}} \mu(n/d) \log(v/d) \log(vz/n) -$$

$$- \sum_{\substack{d|n \\ d < v}} \mu(n/d) \log^2(v/d) = \sum_{i=1}^{5} b_i(n) ,$$

say. Let

$$S_i(v, z) = \sum_{n < vz} b_i^2(n) n^{-1} .$$

For the proof of (2.4) it is enough to show that

$$S_i(v, z) \ll \log^4 z, \quad i = 1, \ldots, 5 . \tag{2.5}$$

For $i = 1, 2$ this follows immediately from (1.15). The case $i = 3$ may be reduced to known elementary estimates from prime number theory. Indeed,

$$b_3(n) = \Lambda(n) \log(zn/v) + \Lambda_2(n) ,$$

where $\Lambda(n)$ is von Mangoldt's function, and

$$\Lambda_2(n) = \sum_{d|n} \mu(d) \log^2 d .$$

The support of $\Lambda_2(n)$ consists of these positive integers which have at most two different prime factors. Now (2.5) for $i=3$ follows from the estimates

$$\sum_{n\leq x} \Lambda^2(n)n^{-1} \ll \log^2 x\,,$$

$$\sum_{n\leq x} \Lambda_2^2(n)n^{-1} \ll \log^4 x\,.$$

The desired estimates for S_4 and S_5 would also follow at once from (1.15) if n were restricted to square-free numbers. If $n=p_1^{a_1}\ldots p_r^{a_r}$, write $n=n_1n_2$, where

$$n_1=p_1\ldots p_r\,,\quad n_2=p_1^{a_1-1}\ldots p_r^{a_r-1}\,.$$

Then in the sums defining $b_4(n)$ and $b_5(n)$ only the divisors $d=n_2e$, where $e|n_1$, contribute something. Thus

$$|b_4(n)| \ll \Bigg|\sum_{\substack{e|n_1\\ e<v/n_2}} \mu(e)\log(v/n_2e)\Bigg| \log z\,, \tag{2.6}$$

$$|b_5(n)| = \Bigg|\sum_{\substack{e|n_1\\ e<v/n_2}} \mu(e)\log^2(v/n_2e)\Bigg|\,. \tag{2.7}$$

Consider, for a moment, numbers n with the same value for n_2. Let

$$n_2^* = \prod_{p|n_2} p\,.$$

Then $n_1=n_2^*m$, so that a divisor $e|n_1$ can be written uniquely as $e=fg$, where $f|n_2^*$, $g|m$. Thus by (2.6)

$$b_4^2(n) \ll \log^2 z\left\{\sum_{f|n_2^*}\mu(f)\sum_{\substack{g|m\\ g<v/n_2f}}\mu(g)\log(v/n_2fg)\right\}^2 \ll$$

$$\ll \log^2 z\tau(n_2^*)\sum_{f|n_2^*}\left\{\sum_{\substack{g|m\\ g<v/n_2f}}\mu(g)\log(v/n_2fg)\right\}^2\,.$$

Dividing this by $n=n_2n_2^*m$ and summing over all n under consideration, i.e. over $m<vz/n_2n_2^*$, we get

$$\ll \log^2 z(n_2n_2^*)^{-1}\tau(n_2^*)\sum_{f|n_2^*}\sum_{m<vz/n_2n_2^*}\mu^2(m)m^{-1}\left\{\sum_{\substack{g|m\\ g<v/n_2f}}\mu(g)\log(v/n_2fg)\right\}^2\,. \tag{2.8}$$

Here the m-sum is suitable for an application of (1.15). For $n_2 \leqq v^{1/3}$ the expression (2.8) is

$$\ll (n_2 n_2^*)^{-1} \tau^2(n_2^*) \log^4 z . \tag{2.9}$$

For $n_2 > v^{1/3}$ we estimate the m-sum in (2.8) roughly to be $\ll \log^6 z$, so that the whole expression (2.8) is in this case

$$\ll (n_2 n_2^*)^{-1} \tau^2(n_2^*) \log^8 z . \tag{2.10}$$

In order to carry out the summation over n_2 in (2.9) and (2.10), note that for a given square-free number n_2^* the numbers n_2 consist of the prime factors of n_2^*, so that

$$\sum_{n_2} n_2^{-1/2} \leqq \prod_{p \mid n_2^*} (1-p^{-1/2})^{-1} \ll \tau(n_2^*) .$$

Hence the amount of numbers $n_2 \leqq x$ for given n_2^* is $\ll \tau(n_2^*) x^{1/2}$, so that the sum over $n_2 \leqq v^{1/3}$ of (2.9) is

$$\ll \log^4 z \sum_{n_2^*} (n_2^*)^{-4/3} \ll \log^4 z ,$$

and the sum over $n_2 > v^{1/3}$ of (2.10) is

$$\ll v^{-1/7} \log^8 z \ll 1 .$$

This completes the proof of (2.5) for $i=4$. The case $i=5$ is analogous.

Having finished the proof of Lemma 1, we now get by the remarks made at the beginning of this section the following result.

Lemma 2. *Let* $1 < v_1 < v_2$, $1 < z_1 < z_2$, $u = \min(v_1, z_1)$, *and suppose that* $\log(v_2 z_2) \ll \log u$. *Then for all real* T *and all* $H > 0$, $1/2 \leqq \sigma \leqq 1$

$$\int_T^{T+H} |M(\sigma+it; z_1, z_2) F(\sigma+it; v_1, v_2) - 1|^2 dt \ll$$

$$\ll (H + v_2 z_2) u^{1-2\sigma} \log^4 z_2 \{\log(z_2/z_1) \log(v_2/v_1)\}^{-2} .$$

We shall also need a modified form of the approximate functional equation of $\zeta(s)$, which is usually stated as follows (see [11], Theorem 4.15): if $2\pi x y = t$, $x \geqq 1$, $y \geqq 1$, $0 \leqq \sigma \leqq 1$, then

$$\zeta(s) = \sum_{n \leqq x} n^{-s} + \chi(s) \sum_{n \leqq y} n^{s-1} + O(x^{-\sigma}) + O(t^{1/2-\sigma} y^{\sigma-1}) , \tag{2.11}$$

where

$$\chi(s) = 2^{s-1} \pi^s \sec\left(\frac{1}{2} s\pi\right) \Big/ \Gamma(s) = (2\pi/t)^{\sigma+it-1/2} e^{i(t+\pi/4)} (1 + O(t^{-1})) . \tag{2.12}$$

Lemma 3. *Let* $T \geqq 2$, $X=(T/2\pi)^{1/2}$, $0<H \leqq T$, $0<\eta \leqq 1/2$. *Then for* $1/2 \leqq \sigma \leqq 1$, $T \leqq t \leqq T+H$

$$\zeta(s)=F(s;X^{1-\eta},X^{1+\eta})+\chi(s)F(1-s;X^{1-\eta},X^{1+\eta})+R(s), \tag{2.13}$$

where

$$R(s) \ll T^{1/2-\sigma}(\eta \log X)^{-1} \int_{X^{1-\eta}}^{X^{1+\eta}} \Big| \sum_{y_1<n \leqq y} n^{\sigma-1+it} \Big| x^{-1}dx + T^{-1/8}, \tag{2.14}$$

$$y_1=y_1(x)=(2\pi x)^{-1}T, \quad y=y(x,t)=(2\pi x)^{-1}t.$$

Proof. Let in (2.11)

$$X^{1-\eta} \leqq x \leqq X^{1+\eta}, \tag{2.15}$$

and replace y by y_1, the error being by (2.12)

$$\ll T^{1/2-\sigma} \Big| \sum_{y_1<n \leqq y} n^{\sigma-1+it} \Big|.$$

The assertion now follows if we divide both sides of the equation by x, then integrate with respect to x over the interval (2.15), and finally divide by $2\,\eta \log X$.

3. The main lemma

We are now in a position to prove that $M(s)$ is a mollifier for $\zeta(s)$ near the critical line.

Lemma 4. *Let* $T \geqq 2$, $0<\eta \leqq 1/2$,

$$z_i=T^{\gamma_i}, \quad 1 \ll \gamma_1<\gamma_2<1/2, \tag{3.1}$$

$$T^{(1+\eta)/2} z_2 \leqq H \leqq T, \tag{3.2}$$

$$u=\min(T^{(1-\eta)/2}, z_1),$$

$$\Delta=\max\{\tau(n) \mid 1 \leqq n \leqq (T+H)\,z_2 X^{\eta-1}\}.$$

Then for $1/2 \leqq \sigma \leqq 1$

$$\int_T^{T+H} |M(\sigma+it;z_1,z_2)\zeta(\sigma+it)-1|^2\,dt \ll$$

$$\ll (\gamma_2-\gamma_1)^{-2}\eta^{-2}(u/\log^2 T)^{1-2\sigma}H+HT^{-1/5}+\Delta^3H^2T^{-1}\log^2 T. \tag{3.3}$$

Proof. Multiplying equation (2.13) by $M(s)$, we get

$$M(s)\zeta(s)-1=\{M(s)F(s)-1\}+M(s)\chi(s)F(1-s)+M(s)R(s)=\sum_{i=1}^{3} A_i(s), \tag{3.4}$$

say. By Lemma 2 and (3.1)–(3.2), we have

$$\int_T^{T+H} |A_1(\sigma+it)|^2 dt \ll (\gamma_2-\gamma_1)^{-2}\eta^{-2}u^{1-2\sigma}H. \tag{3.5}$$

Next, by the same lemma,

$$\int_T^{T+H} \left| A_2\left(\frac{1}{2}+it\right)\right|^2 dt \ll (\gamma_2-\gamma_1)^{-2}\eta^{-2}H,$$

and by standard estimates

$$\int_T^{T+H} |A_2(1+it)|^2 dt \ll HT^{-(1-\eta)/2}\log^2 T \ll Hu^{-1}\log^2 T,$$

so that by convexity, for $1/2 \leqq \sigma \leqq 1$,

$$\int_T^{T+H} |A_2(\sigma+it)|^2 dt \ll (\gamma_2-\gamma_1)^{-2}\eta^{-2}(u/\log^2 T)^{1-2\sigma}H. \tag{3.6}$$

By (2.14) and Schwarz's inequality (applied to the integral over x)

$$\int_T^{T+H} |A_3(\sigma+it)|^2 dt \ll$$

$$\ll T^{1-2\sigma}(\eta\log X)^{-1}\int_{X^{1-\eta}}^{X^{1+\eta}} x^{-1}\int_T^{T+H}\Big|\sum_{y_1(x)<n\leqq y(x,t)} n^{\sigma-1-it}M(\sigma+it)\Big|^2 dt\,dx + \tag{3.7}$$

$$+T^{-1/4}\int_T^{T+H} |M(\sigma+it)|^2\,dt.$$

The second term on the right-hand side is clearly

$$\ll HT^{-1/4}\log T \ll HT^{-1/5}.$$

Consider now the inner integral in the first term. Since y depends on t, one cannot immediately apply the mean value theorem for Dirichlet polynomials. The difficulty is, however, only technical. For orientation, let us make the following general estimations:

$$\int_T^{T+H}\Big|\Big(\sum_{m\leqq M} a_m m^{it}\Big)\Big(\sum_{n\leqq N} b_n n^{it}\Big)\Big|^2 dt = \int_T^{T+H}\Big|\sum_{q\leqq MN} c_q q^{it}\Big|^2 dt =$$

$$= H\sum_{q\leqq MN}|c_q|^2 + \sum_{\substack{q_1,q_2\leqq MN\\ q_1\neq q_2}} c_{q_1}\bar{c}_{q_2}\int_T^{T+H}(q_1/q_2)^{it}dt \ll (H+MN\log(MN))\sum_{q\leqq MN}|c_q|^2,$$

where

$$c_q = \sum_{mn=q} a_m b_n .$$

Let $\Delta = \max_{n \leqq MN} \tau(n)$. Then

$$\sum_{q \leqq MN} |c_q|^2 \leqq \sum_{q \leqq MN} \tau(q) \sum_{mn=q} |a_m b_n|^2 \leqq \Delta \sum_{m \leqq M} |a_m|^2 \sum_{n \leqq N} |b_n|^2 .$$

If, however, the coefficients a_m are piecewise constant functions $a_m(t)$ of t such that $a_m(t)$ is constant on two subintervals of $[T, T+H]$ which together make up the whole interval, then the coefficients c_q are also piecewise constant functions $c_q(t)$, taking at most Δ distinct values. If the above calculation is carried out in this case, the interval of integration must be split up into at most Δ^2 pieces, for each pair (q_1, q_2), in order that the function $c_{q_1}(t)c_{q_2}(t)$ be constant in each of these subintervals. Now, if $|a_m(t)| \leqq A_m$, we get

$$\int_T^{T+H} \left| \left(\sum_{m \leqq M} a_m(t) m^{it} \right) \left(\sum_{n \leqq N} b_n n^{it} \right) \right|^2 dt \ll \Delta (H + \Delta^2 MN \log (MN)) \sum_{m \leqq M} A_m^2 \sum_{n \leqq N} |b_n|^2 .$$

By this the inner integral in (3.7) is

$$\ll \Delta^3 H^2 T^{2\sigma - 2} x^{1 - 2\sigma} \log^2 T,$$

and hence

$$\int_T^{T+H} |A_3(\sigma + it)|^2 dt \ll \Delta^3 H^2 T^{-1} \log^2 T + HT^{-1/5} .$$

Together with (3.4)–(3.6), this gives (3.3).

4. Proof of the theorem

Proceeding in the familiar way, we consider zeros of the function

$$\varphi(s) = 1 - (M(s)\zeta(s) - 1)^2 ,$$

where $M(s)$ is as in Lemma 4. The zeros of $\zeta(s)$ occur among those of $\varphi(s)$, with at least the same multiplicities. Choose in Lemma 4

$$\eta = \varepsilon, \quad \gamma_1 = 1/2 - 2\varepsilon, \quad \gamma_2 = 1/2 - \varepsilon, \quad H = T^{1 - \varepsilon/2} ,$$

so that (3.1)–(3.2) hold, and $u = z_1$. Now (3.3) gives

$$\int_T^{T+H} |M(\sigma + it)\zeta(\sigma + it) - 1|^2 dt \ll_\varepsilon HT^{(1/2 - 3\varepsilon)(1 - 2\sigma)} + HT^{-\varepsilon/3} .$$

Using Littlewood's lemma (see [11], Theorem 9.16) and counting together the zeros in different strips of height H, we get for $\alpha \geqq 1/2$ (actually, in the first place for $\alpha \geqq 1/2 + 1/\log T$) the estimate

$$N(\alpha, 2T) - N(\alpha, T) \ll_\varepsilon T^{1-(1-6\varepsilon)(\sigma-1/2)} \log T + T^{1-\varepsilon/3} \log T.$$

This gives (1.9) for α near 1/2, and otherwise (1.9) follows from (1.3).

It can also be seen that the method of this paper, like that of Selberg, gives a non-trivial estimate for $N(\alpha, T+H) - N(\alpha, T)$ whenever $H \geqq T^{1/2+\varepsilon}$.

References

[1] BARBAN, M. B., VEHOV, P. P., Ob odnoi ekstremal'noi zadace, *Trudy Mosk. Mat. Obsc.*, **18** (1968), 83–90; English translation: *Trans. Moscow Math. Soc.*, **18** (1968), 91–99.

[2] BOHR, H. and LANDAU, E., Ein Satz über Dirichletsche Reihen mit Anwendung auf die ζ-Funktion und die *L*-Funktionen, *Rend. di Palermo*, **37** (1914), 269–272.

[3] GRAHAM, S., An Asymptotic Estimate Related to Selberg's Sieve, *J. Number Theory*, **10** (1978), 83–94.

[4] INGHAM, A. E., On the estimation of $N(\sigma, T)$, *Quart. J. Math.*, **11** (1940), 291–292.

[5] LITTLEWOOD, J. E., On the zeros of the Riemann zeta-function, *Proc. Cambridge Phil. Soc.*, **22** (1924), 295–318.

[6] MONTGOMERY, H. L., *Topics in Multiplicative Number Theory*. Lecture Notes in Mathematics 227, Springer, 1971.

[7] MOTOHASHI, Y., Primes in arithmetic progressions, *Inventiones Math.*, **44** (1978), 163–178.

[8] SELBERG, A., On the zeros of Riemann's zeta-function, *Skr. Norske Vid. Akad. Oslo* (1942) No. *10*.

[9] SELBERG, A., Contributions to the theory of the Riemann zeta-function, *Arch. for Math. og Naturv.*, **B 48** (1946), 89–155.

[10] SELBERG, A., Contributions to the theory of Dirichlet's L-functions, *Skr. Norske Vid. Akad. Oslo* (1946) No. *3*.

[11] TITCHMARSH, E. C., *The theory of the Riemann zeta-function*. Oxford 1951.

DEPARTMENT OF MATHEMATICS,
UNIVERSITY OF TURKU, FINLAND
AND
INSTITUT MITTAG-LEFFLER,
THE ROYAL SWEDISH ACADEMY OF SCIENCES,
DJURSHOLM, SWEDEN

Studies in Pure Mathematics
à la Mémoire de Paul Turán

Séries de Fourier des fonctions bornées

par
J.-P. KAHANE (Paris) et Y. KATZNELSON (Jerusalem)

Nous examinons ici trois questions. Les deux premières nous avaient été signalées, à tort, comme questions ouvertes. La troisième est inspirée par d'anciennes conversations avec P. TURÁN. On désigne par $f(t)$ une fonction mesurable bornée sur $\mathbf{T}=\mathbf{R}/2\pi\mathbf{Z}$, et par $S_n(t)$, ou $S_n(t, f)$, la n-ième somme partielle de sa série de Fourier:

$$S_n(t)=\sum_{-n}^{n}\hat{f}(m)e^{imt}.$$

Première question: existe-t-il $f\in L^\infty(\mathbf{T})$ telle que les normes $\|S_n\|=\sup_t |S_n(t)|$ tendent vers l'infini quand $n\to\infty$? (Question résolue par E. BUSKO [1] 1968.)

Deuxième question: existe-t-il $f\in L^\infty(\mathbf{T})$ telle que $|S_n(0)|$ tende vers l'infini quand $n\to\infty$? (Question essentiellement résolue par HARDY et LITTLEWOOD.)

Troisième question: existe-t-il $f\in C(\mathbf{T})$ (fonction continue sur $\mathbf{T}$) telle que non seulement les sommes partielles $S_n(f)$ divergent, mais aussi — dans un sens à préciser — les sommes partielles $S_n(\Phi\circ f)$ et $S_n(f\circ\varphi)$ des fonctions composées de f au moyen de fonctions qui opèrent sur f ou de changements de variable?

Avant d'indiquer les réponses, rappelons le contexte (cf. [3] [vol. I] chap. VIII).

L'existence d'une fonction continue dont la série de Fourier diverge en un point est connue depuis plus d'un siècle (PAUL DU BOIS-REYMOND). Il y a deux preuves classiques, l'une due à LEBESGUE, l'autre à FEJÉR. Celle de LEBESGUE consiste à ajouter, après régularisation et pondération, des fonctions

$$\operatorname{sign}\pi D_n(t),\quad \pi D_n(t)=\frac{1}{2}+\cos t+\cos 2+\ldots+\cos nt$$

($\pi D_n(t)$ s'appelle le noyau de Dirichlet, et sa convolution avec f donne $S_n(t, f)$). Celle de Fejér consiste à ajouter, après multiplication par des termes de haute fréquence, des polynômes trigonométriques

$$F_n(t) = \sum_1^n \frac{\sin mt}{m}.$$

On retrouvera dans notre étude ces deux outils fondamentaux.

Cependant, les sommes de Fourier ne peuvent pas être trop sauvages. D'abord, $S_{n+1} - S_n$ tend vers zéro. Ensuite, pour une fonction dont le module est borné par 1, S_n ne dépasse pas la norme-L^1 de D_n, qui est $O(\log n)$. Enfin, le théorème de sommabilité de Fejér dit que, pour f continue en 0,

$$\lim_{n\to\infty} \frac{1}{n} \sum_{m=1}^{n} (S_m(0) - f(0)) = 0$$

et le théorème de sommabilité forte de Hardy et Littlewood dit que

$$\lim_{n\to\infty} \frac{1}{n} \sum_{m=1}^{n} |S_m(0) - f(0)| = 0 .$$

(cf. ZII, p. 180). Un autre énoncé du théorème de sommabilité forte est que la suite $S_m(0)$ est "presque convergente" vers $f(0)$, c'est-à-dire que

$$\lim_{m\to\infty,\, m\notin\Lambda} S_m(0) = f(0),$$

où Λ est une suite d'entiers de densité nulle.

Un théorème de PÁL et BOHR, redémontré par SALEM (voir références dans [3], ZI, pp. 294–295), dit que pour toute $f \in C(\mathbf{T})$ à valeurs réelles il existe un homéomorphisme φ de $\mathbf{T}$ tel que la série de Fourier de $f \circ \varphi$ converge uniformément.

Nous bornerons là l'évocation du contexte. Dans les questions posées comme dans les résultats rappelés, on s'intéresse aux sommes partielles "symétriques", et non aux sommes

$$S_{n,n'}(t) = \sum_{-n'}^{n} \hat{f}(m) e^{imt}.$$

Une translation du spectre de f peut complètement modifier les S_n — c'est d'ailleurs l'intérêt des polynômes de FEJÉR $F_n(t)$ —.

La réponse à la première question est positive : c'est, comme nous l'avons dit, un théorème de BUSKO [1], amélioré depuis par K. I. OSKOLKOV [2]. Nous l'énonçons comme exemple 1.

La réponse à la seconde question est négative. C'est une conséquence très facile du théorème de sommabilité forte de Hardy et Littlewood. Nous donnerons (exemples 2 et 3) des exemples de suites n_j assez lacunaires pour que, quand f est convenablement choisi, $|S_{n_j}(0)|$ tende vers l'infini. Inversement (théorème 1), lorsque n_j se comporte comme une puissance de j, on a un analogue du théorème de HARDY et LITTLEWOOD qui entraîne $\underline{\lim}_{j \to 0} |S_{n_j}(0)| < \infty$ quel que soit $f \in L^\infty$. En passant, nous redémontrons le théorème de sommabilité forte de Hardy et Littlewood d'une manière très simple.

Nous éluciderons le comportement des suites $S_{n_j}(0)$ quand n_j croît comme une progression géométrique (exemple 2 et théorème 2).

Le théorème de PÁL et BOHR constitue une réponse partielle à la troisième question: la réponse est négative pour les $S_n(f \circ \varphi)$ si φ est un homéomorphisme arbitraire de $\mathbf{T}$. Nous donnons une nouvelle version de ce théorème, qui, au contraire de la version classique, permet de considérer le cas où f est complexe (théorème 3); nous répondons ainsi à une question posée oralement par A. ZYGMUND (1967).[1]

Cependant, la troisième question admet une réponse positive pour les $S_n(\Phi \circ f)$ dans des conditions très générales, et pour les $S_n(f \circ \varphi)$ à condition de se restreindre à des classes convenables de changements de variable φ (exemples 4 et 5).

Rappelons le théorème de BUSKO.

Exemple 1. *Il existe $f \in L^\infty(\mathbf{T})$ telle que $\|S_n\| > \log n$ pour tout n.*

Nous établirons les résultats suivants.

Exemple 2. *Il existe $f \in L^\infty(\mathbf{T})$ telle que $S_{10^j}(0)$ tende vers l'infini quand $j \to \infty$, et plus précisément telle que $S_{10^j}(0) > \sqrt{j}$.*

Exemple 3. *Soit $\{a_k\}$, $\{b_k\}$ deux suites d'entiers positifs telles que*

$$a_k < b_k < a_{k+1} \quad (k = 1, 2, \dots)$$

$$\lim_{k \to \infty} \frac{b_k}{a_k} = 1 , \quad \lim_{k \to \infty} \frac{a_{k+1}}{a_k} = \infty .$$

Posons $\Lambda = \bigcup_{k=1}^{\infty} [a_k, b_k]$; il existe une $f \in C(\mathbf{T})$ telle que $|S_n(0)|$ tende vers l'infini quand n tend vers l'infini dans Λ.

Exemple 4. *Il existe $f \in C(\mathbf{T})$ telle que, pour toute Φ continue telle que $\Phi \circ f$ soit définie et non constante, on ait*

$$\overline{\lim_{n \to \infty}} \, \| S_n(\Phi \circ f) \| = \infty . \tag{1}$$

[1] Le problème a été soulevé aussi par L. ALPÁR dans la note: Sur les transformées des séries de Fourier absolument convergentes (en hongrois), *Mat. Lapok*, **18** (1967), 97–104 (en particulier p. 98). — Il a proposé encore une fois ce problème en 1976 dans: Fourier analysis and approximation theory, *Colloquia Math. Soc. J. Bolyai*, **19** (1978), 918–919.

En d'autres termes, il existe une sous-algèbre fermée B de l'algèbre C(T) telle que, si g ∈ B et g n'est pas constante,

$$\overline{\lim_{n\to\infty}} \|S_n(g)\| = \infty. \text{ [2]}$$

Exemple 5. *Il existe $f \in C(\mathbf{T})$ telle que, pour toute fonction φ de classe C^1, nulle en 0, telle que $\varphi'(0) \neq 0$, on ait*

$$\overline{\lim_{n\to\infty}} \mid S_n(0, f\circ\varphi)| = \infty .$$

Même énoncé pour toute fonction φ analytique, nulle en 0, $\not\equiv 0$.

Théorème 1. *Soit $N \geqq 1$ et soit $\{n_j\}$ une suite d'entiers vérifiant $j^N \leqq n_j < (j+1)^N$ $(j=1, 2, \ldots)$. Alors, pour toute $f \in L^\infty(\mathbf{T})$ et tout entier $\nu \geqq 1$ on a*

$$\frac{1}{\nu}\sum_{j=1}^{\nu} |S_{n_j}(0)| \leqq C_N \|f\|_\infty . \tag{2}$$

Corollaire. *Supposons $f \in L^1(\mathbf{T})$ et f bornée au voisinage de 0 (resp. f continue en 0). Soit Λ une suite d'entiers telle que $|S_n(0)|$ tende vers l'infini (resp. $S_n(0)$ reste à distance $>\alpha>0$ de $f(0)$ quand $n\to\infty$, $n\in\Lambda$. Alors la suite des entiers j tels que $\Lambda \bigcap [j^N, (j+1)^N] \neq \emptyset$ est de densité nulle.*

Théorème 2. *Soit n_j une suite d'entiers positifs lacunaire à la Hadamard, c'est-à-dire $\dfrac{n_{j+1}}{n_j} \geqq q > 1$ $(j=1, 2, \ldots)$. Pour toute $f \in L^\infty(\mathbf{T})$ et tout entier $\nu \geqq 1$ on a*

$$\sum_{j=1}^{\nu} |S_{n_j}(0)| \leqq C_q \log n_\nu \cdot \sqrt{\nu}\, \|f\|_\infty . \tag{3}$$

Théorème 3. *Pour tout module de continuité ω, il existe un homéomorphisme croissant φ de* **T** *tel que pour toute $f \in C(\mathbf{T})$ dont le module de continuité est majoré par ω l'on ait $f\circ\varphi \in U(\mathbf{T})$.*

Corollaire. *Pour toute famille compacte $\mathscr{F} \subset C(\mathbf{T})$ il existe un homéomorphisme croissant φ de* **T** *tel que $\mathscr{F}\circ\varphi \subset U(\mathbf{T})$.*

On a noté $U(\mathbf{T})$ l'espace des fonctions continues sommes de séries de Fourier uniformément convergentes.

[2] **L'Exemple** 4 donne une réponse négative à la question suivante de N. K. BARY: "is it impossible for every continuous $\Phi(x)$ to choose a continuous monotonic $F(y)$ so that the Fourier series for $F[\Phi(x)]$ converges uniformly?" (A Treatise on Trigonometric Series I, p. 330. Pergamon Press, 1964.)

Remarques. L'exemple 1 a un caractère définitif puisque, pour toute $f \in L^\infty(\mathbf{T})$ on a $\|S_n\| = O(\log n)$. On ne peut pas y remplacer $L^\infty(\mathbf{T})$ par $C(\mathbf{T})$ puisque, pour toute $f \in C(\mathbf{T})$ on a $\|S_n\| = o(\log n)$.

L'exemple 2 et le théorème 2 montrent mutuellement que les majorations et minorations sont essentiellement inaméliorables. A la suite de l'exemple 2, nous indiquons quelques variantes.

L'exemple 3 montre qu'on peut imposer aux S_n d'être grands sur des blocs d'entiers consécutifs, à condition que ces blocs soient assez espacés.

Dans l'exemple 4, il est facile de se persuader qu'on ne peut pas remplacer $\|S_n(\Phi \circ f)\|$ par les valeurs au point 0, $S_n(0, \Phi \circ f)$.

L'exemple 5 impose à φ certaines restrictions. Le théorème 3 explique que de telles restrictions soient indispensables. Le cas $\varphi \in C^1$ est ouvert.

Construction de l'Exemple 2

Posons

$$f(t) = \sum_{n=1}^{\infty} \prod_{2^n < j \leqq 2^{n+1}} (1 + i2^{-\frac{n}{2}} \cos 10^j t) \sum_{10^{2^{n-1}} < m \leqq 10^{2^n}} \frac{\sin mt}{m}. \tag{4}$$

Le produit ("produit de Riesz imaginaire") comprend 2^n facteurs de module inférieur ou égal à $(1+2^{-n})^{1/2}$. Il est donc uniformément borné. On a d'autre part

$$\sum_{10^k < m \leqq 10^{k+1}} \frac{\sin mt}{m} \leqq \begin{cases} 10^{-k}|1-e^{it}|^{-1} \\ |t| \cdot 10^{k+1} \end{cases};$$

la première inégalité résulte de la transformation d'Abel, et la seconde de la majoration de chaque terme par $|t|$. Il en découle que

$$\sum_{k=1}^{\infty} \left| \sum_{10^k < m \leqq 10^{k+1}} \frac{\sin mt}{m} \right| \leqq C \quad \text{constante absolue} \tag{5}$$

et a fortiori

$$\sum_{n=1}^{\infty} \left| \sum_{10^{2^{n-1}} < m \leqq 10^{2^n}} \frac{\sin mt}{m} \right| \leqq C.$$

Donc $f \in L^\infty(\mathbf{T})$.

Les fréquences qui apparaissent dans le produit sont de la forme

$$\nu = \sum_{2^n < j \leqq 2^{n+1}} \varepsilon_j \cdot 10^j \qquad \varepsilon_j = 1, 0, -1. \tag{6}$$

Leurs distances mutuelles sont minorées par 10^{2^n+1}. Les bandes $[\nu - 10^{2^n}, \nu + 10^{2^n}]$ sont disjointes quand n varie et que ν parcourt les valeurs (6), et, dans une telle bande, le développement de f se réduit à

$$(i2^{-\frac{n}{2}})^{\sum|\varepsilon_j|}e^{i\nu t} \sum_{10^{2^{n-1}}<m\leqq 10^{2^n}} \frac{\sin mt}{m}.$$

Il s'ensuit que, pour chaque μ de la forme $\nu+10^{2^n}$ on a $S_\mu(0)=0$, et que pour $\nu=10^j$ $(2^n<j\leqq 2^{n+1})$

$$S_\nu(0)=\frac{1}{2}2^{-\frac{n}{2}} \sum_{10^{2^{n-1}}<m\leqq 10^{2^n}} \frac{1}{m}>c2^{n/2}>c'\sqrt{j}\,. \tag{7}$$

L'exemple 2 est donc achevé.

Remarques 1. Si on remplace dans (4) la somme $\sum_{n=1}^{\infty}\prod\sum$ par une somme $\sum_{n=1}^{\infty}\alpha_n\prod\sum$, où α_n est une suite tendant vers 0, on obtient une fonction continue. Etant donné n'importe quelle fonction $\omega(j)=o(\sqrt{j})$ $(j\to\infty)$, on obtient à la place de (7)

$$S_{10^j}(0)>\omega(j)$$

par un choix convenable des α_n.

2. Il existe des suites n_j croissant moins vite que 10^j pour lesquelles il existe une $f\in C(\mathbf{T})$ telle que $S_{n_j}(0)$ tende vers l'infini. Par exemple, on peut remplacer les puissances de 10, dans l'intervalle $\left[10^{2^n}, \frac{4^n}{n^4}\cdot 10^{2^n}\right]$, par une progression arithmétique de $\left[\frac{4^n}{n^4}\right]$ termes et de raison 10^{2^n}. Beaucoup plus facilement, on peut remplacer la suite 10^j par n'importe quelle suite n_j lacunaire à la Hadamard $\left(\frac{n_{j+1}}{n_j}>q>1\right)$.

Construction de l'Exemple 3

Posons $c_k=\max(a_{k-1}, b_k-a_k)$. L'hypothèse est $c_k=o(a_k)$. L'argument utilisé dans la construction précédente montre que pour toute suite $\{a_k\}$ telle que $\alpha_k\to 0$ l'on a

$$f(t)=\sum_k \alpha_k e^{i(a_k+c_k)t}\sum_{m=c_k}^{\frac{1}{2}a_k}\frac{\sin mt}{m}\in C(\mathbf{T})\,. \tag{8}$$

Il est clair que pour $a_k\leqq n\leqq a_k+2c_k$ l'on a

$$S_n(0)=\frac{i\alpha_k}{2}\sum_{m=c_k}^{\frac{1}{2}a_k}\frac{1}{m}\sim\alpha_k\log(a_k/c_k)\,. \tag{9}$$

Construction de l'Exemple 4

Nous allons construire f sur l'intervalle $I=[0,1]$, considéré comme plongé dans $\mathbf{T}$; le prolongement de f à $\mathbf{T}\backslash I$ sera arbitraire.

Soit E l'ensemble triadique de Cantor construit sur I, μ la mesure de probabilité naturelle sur E (donnant des masses égales à des parties égales), et $L(t)=\mu[0,t])$, $0\leqq t\leqq 1$. La fonction L prend la valeur $\dfrac{2p+1}{2^n}$ $(0\leqq p<2^{n-1};\ n=1,2,\ldots)$ sur un intervalle B_{np}, de longueur 3^{-n}, contigu à E.

Pour chaque couple (n,p), soit b'_{np} et b''_{np} les points qui divisent B_{np} en trois parties égales

$$(10)\qquad \varphi_{np}=\left[\begin{array}{lll} 1 \text{ si } & D_{\kappa_n}(t-b'_{np})\geqq 0 & \text{et } |t-b'_{np}|<3^{-n-2} \\ -1 \text{ si } & D_{\kappa_n}(t-b''_{np})\leqq 0 & \text{et } |t-b''_{np}||<3^{-n-2} \\ 0 \text{ sinon} & & \end{array}\right.$$

où D_κ est le noyau de Dirichlet et $\kappa_n\geqq 10^{4^n}$. Soit

$$\psi_{np}=2^{-n}\varphi_{np}*\delta_{\varepsilon_n}$$

où $\delta_\varepsilon(x)=\dfrac{1}{2\varepsilon}1_{[-\varepsilon,\varepsilon]}(x)$, et $\varepsilon_n=10^{-(\kappa_n)!}$. Nous posons

$$(11)\qquad f(t)=L(t)+\sum_{n=1}^{\infty}\sum_{p=0}^{2^{n-1}-1}\psi_{np}(t)\,.$$

Sur E, on a $f(t)=L(t)$, et l'oscillation de f sur chaque B_{np} est 2^{-n+1}. On a donc $f\in C(I)$, et $f(I)=I$, $f(0)=0$, $f(1)=1$.

Soit $g=\Phi\circ f$, non constante. Pour fixer les idées, supposons $g(I)=I$, $g(0)=0$, $g(1)=1$. On va montrer qu'il existe une suite b_n telle que $|S_{\kappa_n}(b_n,g)|$ tende vers l'infini.

Définissons par induction une suite d'intervalles dyadiques I_n, avec $I_0=I$, et les conditions que $|I_n|=2^{-n}$, $I_n\subset I_{n-1}$, I_n ait une extrémité commune avec I_{n-1}, et les valeurs prises par Φ aux extrémités de I_n soient distantes de plus de 2^{-n}.

I_n est de la forme $\left[\dfrac{2p}{2^n},\dfrac{2p+1}{2^n}\right]$ ou $\left[\dfrac{2p+1}{2^n},\dfrac{2p+2}{2^n}\right]$. Suivant le cas, on pose $b_n=b''_{np}$ ou $b_n=b'_{np}$. Soit $J_n=[b_n-3^{-n-2},\,b_n+3^{-n-2}]$.

On vérifie que

$$(12)\qquad S_{\kappa_n}(b_n,g)=S_{\kappa_n}(b_n,g\,1_{J_n})+O(1)>2^{-n}\log\kappa_n+O(1)$$

ce qui achève l'exemple 4.

Construction de l'Exemple 5

Nous pouvons supposer d'abord $|\varphi(t)-t|<\omega(|t|)$, où $\omega(t)$ est une fonction continue croissante pour $t \geqq 0$, $\omega(t)=o(t)$ quand $t \to 0$.

Choisissons par induction deux suites croissantes d'entiers a_k et κ_k, telles que

$$\log \kappa_k \gg k^2 a_{k-1} \tag{13}$$

$$\omega(\pi\kappa_k a_k^{-1}) \ll a_k^{-1} \tag{14}$$

et posons

$$\begin{aligned} &f_k(t)=k^{-2} \sin a_k t \quad \text{pour} \quad \frac{\pi}{a_k} \leqq t \leqq \frac{\kappa_k \pi}{a_k} \\ &f_k(t)=0 \quad \text{ailleurs} \end{aligned} \tag{15}$$

$$f(t)=\sum_1^\infty f_k(t)\,. \tag{16}$$

La condition (14) entraîne que

$$k^2 f_k(\varphi(t))=\sin a_k t+o(1) \quad \text{pour} \quad \frac{\pi}{a_k} \leqq t \leqq \frac{\kappa_k \pi}{a_k}$$

et par conséquent, en intégrant sur ce dernier intervalle,

$$k^2 S_{a_k}(0, f_k \circ \varphi)=\int \frac{\sin^2 a_k t}{\pi t}\, dt(1+o(1))=\log \kappa_k(1+o(1))\,.$$

La condition (13) entiraîne que

$$S_{a_k}\left(0, \sum_{j=1}^{k-1} f_j \circ \varphi\right)=O(a_{k-1})=o(k^{-2} \log \kappa_k)$$

(la première égalité tient à ce que le support des $f_j \circ \varphi$ est à droite de $\dfrac{\pi}{a_{k-1}}(1+o(1))$).

On a d'autre part

$$S_{a_k}\left(0, \sum_{j=k+1}^{\infty} f_j \circ \varphi\right)=O(1)\,.$$

La conclusion est

$$\lim S_{a_k}(0, f \circ \varphi)=\infty\,.$$

Cela s'applique, à un changement évident près, chaque fois que φ est de classe C^1, nulle en 0, avec $\varphi'(0) \neq 0$. La fonction f de (16) donne l'exemple 5, première partie.

Pour la seconde partie de l'exemple 5, une modification de la construction est nécessaire. Pour chaque entier positif j, posons

$$(17)\qquad \begin{cases} f_{k,j}(t^j) = f_k(t) & (t \geqq 0) \\ f_{k,j}(t^j) = 0 & (t \leqq 0) \end{cases}$$

où $f_k(t)$ est donné par (15). A chaque j attachons un ensemble infini Λ_j d'entiers positifs, de façon que 1) les Λ_j soient deux à deux disjoints, 2) les supports des $f_{k,j}$ ($j = 1, 2, \ldots$; $k \in \Lambda_j$) soient disjoints et se trouvent dans l'ordre des k, 3) pour $k \in \bigcup_j \Lambda_j$, $k^{-2} \log \kappa_k$ soit un infiniment grand d'ordre supérieur à l'inverse de la distance à 0 du support de la somme

$$\sum_{j,\, l \in \Lambda_j,\, l<k} f_{l,j}\,.$$

La condition 3) remplace (13) et est utilisée de la même façon. Pour construire les Λ_j, la plus simple est d'énumérer les entiers k et de décider pour chaque k s'il appartient ou non à $\bigcup_j \Lambda_j$, et dans le premier cas à quel Λ_j il appartient.

En posant

$$(18)\qquad f(t) = \sum_{j,\, k \in \Lambda_j} f_{k,j}(t)$$

on a alors

$$\overline{\lim_{n\to\infty}}\, S_n(0, f \circ \varphi^j) = \infty$$

pour tout entier positif j et toute φ de classe C^1, nulle en 0, vérifiant $\varphi'(0) \neq 0$. Donc

$$\overline{\lim_{n\to\infty}}\, S_n(0, \psi) = \infty$$

pour toute ψ analytique non nulle; il suffit d'écrire $\psi(x) = (\varphi(x))^j$.

Preuve du Théorème 1

Dans cette section nous supposerons f réelle. Le cas où f est complexe s'en déduit immédiatement.

Expliquons la méthode dans le cas où la suite $\{n_j\}$ est la suite de tous les entiers. La clé est l'inégalité

$$(19)\qquad \int_0^{\pi} \left| \sum_{n=1}^{\nu} \varepsilon_n \frac{\sin nt}{t} \right| dt \leqq 3\nu$$

quand les ε_n prennent les valeurs ± 1.

Pour démontrer (19), écrivons $\int_0^\pi = \int_0^\sigma + \int_\sigma^\pi$.

$$\int_0^\sigma \leqq \sigma \sum_{n=1}^{\nu} n = \frac{\sigma\nu(\nu+1)}{2}$$

$$\int_\sigma^\pi \leqq \left(\int_\sigma^\pi \left|\sum_{n=1}^{\nu} \varepsilon_n \sin nt\right|^2 dt \int_\sigma^\pi \frac{dt}{t^2}\right)^{1/2} \leqq \left(\frac{\pi\nu}{2\sigma}\right)$$

d'après l'inégalité de SCHWARZ et l'égalité de PARSEVAL. On obtient (19) pour $\sigma = \frac{1}{\nu}$.

Si $f \in L^\infty(\mathbf{T})$, (16) donne

$$\sum_{n=1}^{\nu} \varepsilon_n S_n^*(0, f) = \int_{-\pi}^{\pi} f(t) \sum_{n=1}^{\nu} \varepsilon_n \frac{\sin nt}{\pi t}\, dt \leqq 2\|f\|_\infty \nu$$

donc

$$\frac{1}{\nu} \sum_{n=1}^{\nu} |S_n^*(0, f)| \leqq 2\|f\|_\infty . \tag{20}$$

Comme conséquence de (20) on a le théorème de sommabilité forte de HARDY et LITTLEWOOD: si $f \in L^1(\mathbf{T})$ et si f est continue en 0, on a

$$\lim_{\nu\to\infty} \frac{1}{\nu} \sum_{n=1}^{\nu} |S_n(0, f) - f(0)| = 0 . \tag{21}$$

Il suffit pour le voir d'écrire $f = g + h$, avec $h = f$ dans un petit voisinage de 0 et $g = f$ hors de ce voisinage, puis d'appliquer (20) à la fonction h. C'est à notre connaissance la démonstration la plus simple de ce théorème de HARDY et LITTLEWOOD.

Dans le cas général, nous utiliserons le lemme suivant.

Lemme. *Soit Λ un ensemble fini d'entiers, contenu dans l'intervalle* $[0, A]$, *de pas δ (c'est-à-dire $\delta = \inf|\lambda - \lambda'|$, $\lambda, \lambda' \in \Lambda$, $\lambda \neq \lambda'$), et de cardinal μ. Soit $0 < \gamma < 1$. Alors*

$$\int_0^\pi \left|\sum_{n\in\Lambda} \varepsilon_n \frac{\sin nt}{t}\right| dt \leqq C_\gamma(\mu A^\gamma + \mu A \delta^{-1})^{1/2} + \mu \tag{22}$$

quand les ε_n prennent les valeurs ± 1, C_γ dépendant seulement de γ.

Preuve du lemme. Ecrivons encore $\int_0^\pi = \int_0^\sigma + \int_\sigma^\pi$. On a ici

(23) $$\int_0^\sigma \leqq \sigma\mu A$$

(24) $$\int_\sigma^\pi \leqq \left(\int_\sigma^\pi \left|\sum_{n\in\Lambda} \varepsilon_n \sin nt\right|^2 \varphi(t)\,dt\right)^{1/2} \left(\int_\sigma^\pi \frac{dt}{t^2\varphi(t)}\right)^{1/2},$$

$\varphi(t)$ étant une fonction positive à choisir. Prenons

$$\varphi(t) = 1 + 2\sum_1^\infty \frac{\cos nt}{n^\gamma}.$$

On sait que

$$\varphi(t) \geqq c_\gamma |t|^{\gamma-1} \quad (|t| \leqq \pi) \quad ([3], [ZI] \text{ p. } 186).$$

Donc

(25) $$\int_\sigma^\pi \frac{dt}{t^2\varphi(t)} \leqq C_\gamma \sigma^{-\gamma}.$$

On a

$$\frac{1}{\pi}\int_0^\pi \left|\sum_{n\in\Lambda} \varepsilon_n \sin nt\right|^2 \varphi(t)\,dt \leqq \frac{1}{2\pi}\int_{-\pi}^\pi \left|\sum_{n\in\Lambda} \varepsilon_n e^{int}\right|^2 \varphi(t)\,dt =$$

$$= \sum_{n,\, m\in\Lambda} \hat\varphi(n-m) = \mu\hat\varphi(0) + 2\sum_{n>m;\, n,\, m\in\Lambda} \hat\varphi(n-m).$$

Pour évaluer la dernière somme, faisons parcourir à j l'ensemble des entiers positifs tels que $2^j \leqq A$, posons

$$B_j = \sup_n \operatorname{card}(\{m\in\Lambda,\, 2^j \leqq n-m \leqq 2^{j+1}\})$$

et écrivons, en utilisant la décroissance de $\hat\varphi$,

$$\sum_{n>m;\, n,\, m\in\Lambda} \hat\varphi(n-m) = \sum_{n\in\Lambda}\sum_j \sum_{\substack{m\in\Lambda \\ 2^j\leqq n-m<2^{j+1}}} \hat\varphi(n-m) \leqq \mu\sum_j B_j\hat\varphi(2^j).$$

Comme $B_j \leqq 2^j/\delta$ et $\hat{\varphi}(2^j) = 2^{-j\gamma}$, et qu'on somme pour les j tels que $2^j \leqq A$, on obtient

$$\sum_{n>m;\, n,\, m \in \Lambda} \hat{\varphi}(n-m) \leqq C_\gamma \mu \delta^{-1} A^{1-\gamma}$$

d'où

$$(26) \qquad \int_0^\pi \left|\sum \varepsilon_n \sin nt\right|^2 \varphi(t)\, dt \leqq C_\gamma(\mu + \mu\delta^{-1} A^{1-\gamma}).$$

Choisissons $\sigma = A^{-1}$. Alors (23), (24), (25) et (26) donnent (22), ce qui achève la preuve du lemme.

Venons en à la preuve du théorème 1. Considérons séparément les suites $\{n_{2j}\}$ et $\{n_{2j+1}\}$, et, pour fixer les idées, considérons la première. On a $n_{2j} \sim (2j)^N$ et $n_{2j+2} - n_{2j} \geqq j^{N-1}$. Soit $\Lambda = \Lambda_k$ l'ensemble des n_{2j} contenus dans l'intervalle $[2^k, 2^{k+1}]$. Cet ensemble satisfait les hypothèses du lemme avec

$$A = A_k = 2^{k+1} \qquad \delta = \delta_k = 2^{k\frac{N-1}{N}} \qquad \mu = \mu_k \sim 2^{k/N}$$

et on a en application de (22)

$$\int_0^\pi \left|\sum_{n \in \Lambda_k} \varepsilon_n \frac{\sin nt}{t}\right| dt \leqq C_\gamma(\mu_k A_k^\gamma + \mu_k A_k \delta_k^{-1})^{1/2} + \mu_k$$

donc, en choisissant $\gamma < \dfrac{1}{N}$,

$$\int_0^\pi \left|\sum_{n \in \Lambda_k} \varepsilon_n \frac{\sin nt}{t}\right| dt \leqq C_\gamma \mu_k .$$

A fortiori, on a la même inégalité si on remplace Λ_k par une sous-suite. En ajoutant de telles inégalités, on obtient

$$\int_0^\pi \left|\sum_{j=1}^{l} \varepsilon_{n_{2j}} \frac{\sin n_{2j} t}{t}\right| dt \leqq Cl \quad (C = C_N).$$

Compte tenu de l'inégalité analogue concernant les n_{2j+1}, il vient

$$\int_0^\pi \left|\sum_{j=1}^{\nu} \varepsilon_j \frac{\sin n_j t}{t}\right| dt \leqq C\nu .$$

Si $f \in L^\infty(\mathbf{T})$, on a donc

$$\left|\sum_{j=1}^{\nu} \varepsilon_j S^*_{n_j}(0)\right| \leqq C\nu \|f\|_\infty ,$$

ce qui est l'inégalité désirée.

Cela achève la preuve du théorème. Le corollaire annoncé en dérive par des calculs classiques.

Preuve du Théorème 2

Elle est très voisine de celle du théorème 1. Il suffit de démontrer

$$\int_0^\pi \left|\sum_{j=1}^{\nu} \varepsilon_j \sin n_j t\right| \frac{dt}{t} \leqq C_q \nu^{1/2} \log n_\nu . \tag{27}$$

Ecrivons maintenant

$$\int_0^\pi = \sum_{k=0}^{\infty} \int_{\pi\cdot 10^{-k-1}}^{\pi\cdot 10^{-k}}$$

$$\int_{\pi\cdot 10^{-k-1}}^{\pi\cdot 10^{-k}} \left|\sum_{j=1}^{\nu} \varepsilon_j \sin n_j t\right| \frac{dt}{t} \leqq \int_{\pi\cdot 10^{-k-1}}^{\pi\cdot 10^{-k}} \left|\sum_{n_j \leqq 10^k}\right| + \left|\sum_{n_j > 10^k}\right| .$$

Dans la première somme nous majorons $|\sin n_j t|$ par $n_j t$; la somme est majorée par $C_q \inf(10^k, n_\nu)$ et son intégrale par $C_q \inf(1, n_\nu 10^{-k})$ (comme à l'accoutumé, C_q est un nombre ne dépendant que de q et de l'emplacement où il est écrit). Dans la seconde nous faisons le changement de variable $t = 10^{-k}\vartheta$ et nous posons $\lambda_j = n_j \cdot 10^{-k}$; on a

$$\int_{\pi\cdot 10^{-k-1}}^{\pi\cdot 10^{-k}} \left|\sum_{n_j > 10^k} \varepsilon_j \sin n_j t\right| \frac{dt}{t} = \int_{\pi/10}^{\pi} \left|\sum_j \varepsilon_j \sin \lambda_j \vartheta\right| \frac{d\vartheta}{\vartheta}$$

avec $\dfrac{\lambda j+1}{\lambda_j} \geqq q$, et le premier des λ_j supérieur à 1. On sait alors que la norme L^1 du polynôme trigonométrique lacunaire $\sum \varepsilon_j \sin \lambda_j t$ sur un intervalle fixé est équivalente à sa norme L^2, donc

$$\int_{\pi/10}^{\pi} \left|\sum_{j=1}^{\nu} \varepsilon_j \sin \lambda_j \vartheta\right| \frac{d\vartheta}{\vartheta} < C_q \sqrt{\nu} .$$

Finalement

$$\int_{\pi\cdot 10^{-k-1}}^{\pi\cdot 10^{-k}} \left| \sum_{j=1}^{\nu} \varepsilon_j \sin n_j t \right| \frac{dt}{t} \leqq \begin{cases} C_q n_\nu 10^{-k} & \text{si} \quad 10^k > n_\nu \\ C_q \nu^{1/2} & \text{si} \quad 10^k \leqq n_\nu . \end{cases}$$

En ajoutant, on obtient bien (27).

Preuve du Théorème 3

Au lieu de φ, construisons l'homéomorphisme réciproque, ψ.

La construction de ψ se fait en précisant deux suites $\{t_j\}$ et $\{x_j\}$ denses dans $\mathbf{T}$, y ayant le même ordre, de manière que si l'on écrit $\psi(t_j)=x_j$ on obtienne une fonction monotone qui se complète par continuité à un homéomorphisme. Les suites $\{t_j\}$ et $\{x_j\}$ sont définies par étapes, la première étant de prendre $\{t_j\}_{j=1}^{4}$ les racines de 1 d'ordre 4, et de poser $x_j=t_j$, $j=1, \ldots, 4$. Après n étapes nous aurons défini 4^n points t_j et les x_j correspondant. Ceci nous donne 4^n intervalles I_l (obtenus en divisant le cercle par les t_j, $j=1, \ldots, 4^n$) ainsi que $J_l=\psi(I_l)$ dont les extrémités sont les x_j correspondants (noter que ψ n'est pas encore définie à l'intérieur des I_l).

L'étape suivante consiste à diviser chaque I_l, ainsi que le J_l correspondant, en quatre par l'introduction de trois points t (resp. x) supplémentaires. On envoie le centre de I_l sur le centre de J_l et dans chaque moitié de I_l on prend le point dont la distance à l'extrémité gauche est ε_n, à préciser, et on lui fait correspondre le point dans la moitié correspondante de J_l dont la distance à l'extrémité droite est égale à η_n, à préciser (voir figure 1).

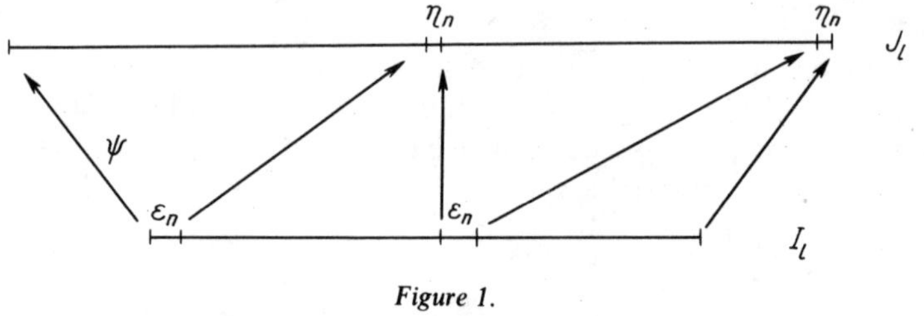

Figure 1.

On choisit ε_n et η_n suffisamment petits pour que $\varepsilon_n \leqq 4^{-2n}\varepsilon_{n-1}$, $\eta_n \leqq 4^{-2n}\eta_{n-1}$, et

$$\omega(\varepsilon_n) \leqq 4^{-2n}. \tag{28}$$

On précisera le choix de η_n plus tard. Une fois ce choix effectué, les homéomorphismes ψ et φ sont définis.

Soit f une fonction continue dont le module de continuité est borné par ω, et posons $F=f\circ\varphi$. Nous allons montrer que $F \in U(\mathbf{T})$. Notons par F_n l'interpolation linéaire de la restriction de F à l'ensemble $\{x_j\}_{j=1}^{4^n}$ obtenu après n étapes, et $G_n F_{n+1} - F_n G_n$ est nul aux extrémités de chaque J_l de la nième étape, et est linéaire par (quatre) morceaux sur J_l.

On écrit maintenant $G_n = G_n^* + \tilde{G}_n$ où G_n^* est égale à G_n sur les intervalles J_l de la nième étape telles que $|J_l| > \eta_{n-1}$ et nulle sur les J_l de longueur η_{n-1} (qui alternent avec les précédents). Si $|J_l| > \eta_{n-1}$ alors $J_l = \psi(I_l)$ avec $|I_l| = \varepsilon_{n-1}$ et l'on a par (28) $\max_{J_l} |G_n| < 4^{2-2n}$ d'où

$$\|G_n^*\|_\infty < 4^{2-2n}, \quad \text{Var}\,(G_n^*) < 4^{3-n}$$

et par conséquent $\sum_n G_n^*$ est continue à variation bornée, donc dans $U(\mathbf{T})$.

Passons à l'étude des $\tilde{G}_n$.

La fonction $\tilde{G}_n$ est la somme de $2 \cdot 4^{n-1}$ fonctions $\tilde{\gamma}_l$, portées par des intervalles J_l de longueur η_{n-1}, à distance mutuelle supérieure à $\frac{1}{2}\eta_{n-2} - \eta_{n-1}$. Chaque $\tilde{\gamma}_l$ a pour masse $\|\tilde{\gamma}_l\|_{L^1} \leqq \eta_{n-1}$ et pour variation $\|\tilde{\gamma}_l\|_V \leqq 6\omega(2^{-n})$. Pour chaque $t \in \mathbf{T}$, les $\tilde{\gamma}_l$ dont le support est à distance supérieure à $\frac{1}{4}\eta_{n-2}$ de t contribuent aux sommes $S_m(t, \tilde{G}_n)$ pour moins de $4^{n+1}\eta_{n-1}/\eta_{n-2}$, ce qui est $O(4^{-n})$ d'après la condition déjà imposée aux η_n. Il y a au plus un $\tilde{\gamma}_l$ restant, et sa contribution à $S_m(t, \tilde{G}_n)$ ne dépasse pas $2\|\tilde{\gamma}_l\|_V$. Donc

$$\|\tilde{G}_n\|_U \leqq 4^{n+1}\eta_{n-1}/\eta_{n-2} + 12\omega(2^{-n}) = o(1) \quad (n \to \infty).$$

On observe maintenant que $\tilde{G}_{n-2}$ ne dépend pas du choix de η_{n-1}, et que les coefficients de Fourier de $\tilde{G}_n$ ne dépassent pas $4^n\eta_{n-1}$. On peut choisir par induction η_{n-1} de façon que les sommes partielles de $\tilde{G}_n$ ne commencent à se faire sentir (disons, qu'elles ne dépassent 2^{-n}) qu'après que les sommes partielles de $\tilde{G}_{n-2}$ approchent cette fonction à moins de 2^{-n} près. De plus, on vérifie facilement que cette condition sur η_{n-1} ne dépend que des valeurs $\omega(2^{-n})$, η_{n-2} et η_{n-3}, qui permettent un bon contrôle des sommes partielles de $\tilde{G}_{n-2}$. Donc, bien qu'en général $\sum \|\tilde{G}_n\|_U = \infty$ on obtient $\sum \tilde{G}_n \in U$ et par conséquent $F = \sum G_n^* + \sum \tilde{G}_n \in U$.

Remarques. a) Les choix de $\{\varepsilon_n\}$ et de $\{\eta_n\}$ étant essentiellement indépendant on peut imposer $\omega(\varepsilon_n) = O(\eta_n)$. Il est facile de voir que dans ce cas on a $\sum G_n^* \in A(\mathbf{T})$. Si on enlève de $\mathbf{T}$ l'ensemble $\left\{t; \sum_{\kappa}^{\infty} \tilde{G}_n \neq 0\right\}$ on obtient un fermé E_κ de mesure arbitrairement voisine de 1 (pour $\kappa \to \infty$) tel que $F|_{E_\kappa}$ est une restriction d'une série de Fourier absolument convergente.

b) Malgré l'espoir que a) peut inspirer on ne peut pas remplacer, dans l'énoncé du théorème 3, $U(\mathbf{T})$ par $A(\mathbf{T})$. En effet, pour tout homéomorphisme φ, il existe des translatées de la fonction continue

$$\begin{cases} f(t)=\dfrac{t}{|t|}\left(\log\dfrac{t}{|t|}\right)^{-\frac{1}{2}} & \text{pour} \quad |t|<\dfrac{\pi}{4} \\ f(t) \text{ linéaire} & \text{pour} \quad \dfrac{\pi}{4}\leqq t\leqq\dfrac{7\pi}{4} \end{cases}$$

qui n'appartiennent pas à $A(\mathbf{T})$; il suffit de choisir la translation θ de façon que $0<\varphi'(\theta)\leqq\infty$.

References

[1] E. BUSKO, Sur le comportement dans $L^{\infty}(\pi)$ des sommes partielles de Fourier, *C. R. Acad. Sc., Paris*, **266** (1968), 17–20.

[2] К. И. ОСКОЛКОВ, Последовательности норм сумм Фурье ограничексых функций, *Труды МИАН СССР*, **143** (1977), 129–142.[3]

[3] A. ZYGMUND, *Trigonometric series*, Cambridge University Press, Vol. **I** (1959), Vol. **II** (1960).

Added in proof. Since this paper was written, the following papers appeared on the same or related topics:

А. А. СААКЯН Интегральные модули гладкости и коэффициенты Фурье у суперпозиции функций. Мат. Сборник 152 (1979), 597–608.

Long Jui Lin, Sommes partielles de Fourier des fonctions bornées. *C. R. Acad. Sc., Paris*, **288** (1979), 1009–1011.

— Sommes partielles de Fourier des fonctions bornées. *Prépubl. Math. Orsay*, 80T4 (1980), 25 p.

J.-P. KAHANE et Y. KATZNELSON, Homéomorphismes du cercle et séries de Fourier absolument convergentes. *C. R. Acad. Sc. Paris*, **292** (1981), 271–273.

Moreover, the paper by L. CARLESON in this volume was written between ours and the papers of LONG JUI LIN.

MATHÉMATIQUE (BÂT. 425)
UNIVERSITÉ DE PARIS SUD
91405 ORSAY (FRANCE)

DEPARTMENT OF MATHEMATICS
THE HEBREW UNIVERSITY
JERUSALEM (ISRAËL)

[3] Les auteurs doivent cette référence à P. L. ULIANOV (П. Л. Ульянов) qu'ils tiennent à remercier. L'article d'Oskolkov contient d'autres références intéressantes.

Studies in Pure Mathematics
To the Memory of Paul Turán

Appendix
to the Paper of J.-P. Kahane and Y. Katznelson

by

L. CARLESON (Djursholm)

The purpose of this note is to show that the two theorems 1 and 2 above can be combined into one statement which is actually sharp.

Theorem. *Let $\varphi(x)$ be a positive increasing convex function taking integer values for x integer. If $\psi(t)$ is the inverse function of φ we assume $\psi'(t)=O(\psi'(2t))$. Then*

$$Q_m(f)=\frac{1}{m}\sum_{j=1}^{m}|S_{\varphi(j)}(0)|\leqq \text{Const}\,\|f\|_\infty \tag{A1}$$

if and only it

$$\overline{\lim_{j\to\infty}}\frac{\log\varphi(j)}{\sqrt{j}}<\infty\,. \tag{A2}$$

Proof. Assume first that (A1) holds. Then

$$\sup_{\|f\|_\infty=1} Q_m(f)>\frac{1}{m}\int_{-\pi}^{\pi}\left|\sum_{j=1}^{m}D_{\varphi(j)}(x)\varepsilon_j\right|dx \tag{A3}$$

where D_ν is the Dirichlet kernel and $|\varepsilon_j|=1, j=1, 2, \ldots, m$. In (A3) we take the mean value over all choices of $\varepsilon_j=\pm 1$. By Chinchin's inequality we get

$$\int_{-\pi}^{\pi}\left(\sum_{1}^{m}D_{\varphi(j)}(x)^2\right)^{1/2}dx\leqq \text{Const}\cdot m\,.$$

From the explicit formula for $D_\nu(x)$ we get

$$\text{(A4)} \qquad \int\limits_{|t|>\varphi\left(\frac{m}{2}\right)^{-1}} \left(\sum_{j=\frac{m}{2}+1}^{m} \sin^2 \frac{\varphi(j)+1}{2} t \right)^{1/2} \frac{dt}{t} \leqq \text{Const} \cdot m \,.$$

Hence

$$\log \varphi\left(\frac{m}{2}\right) = \int\limits_{\varphi\left(\frac{m}{2}\right)^{-1}}^{1} \frac{dt}{t} \leqq \frac{\text{Const}}{\sqrt{m}} \frac{1}{\sqrt{m}} \int\limits_{\varphi\left(\frac{m}{2}\right)^{-1}}^{1} \left(\sum_{\frac{m}{2}+1}^{m} \sin^2 \frac{\varphi(j)+1}{2} t \right)^{1/2} \frac{dt}{t} \leqq \frac{\text{Const}}{\sqrt{m}} \cdot m$$

by (A4). This proves (A2).

For the converse we use the following lemma which is easy to prove.

Lemma. *Let* $1 \leqq \lambda_1 \leqq \lambda_2 \leqq \ldots \leqq \lambda_p$ *and*

$$g(x) = \sum_{1}^{p} a_j \sin \lambda_j x \,.$$

Then

$$\int_0^{2\pi} g(x)^2 dx \leqq \text{Const} \cdot \sum_{v=1}^{\infty} \left(\sum_{|\lambda_j - v| \leqq 1/2} |a_j| \right)^2 .$$

Let us assume that (A2) holds and take $\|f\|_\infty = 1$. For some choice of $\varepsilon_j = \pm 1$

$$Q_m(f) \leqq \text{Const} \int_0^{\pi} \frac{1}{m} \left| \sum_{j=1}^{m} \varepsilon_j \frac{\sin n_j x}{x} \right| dx \,.$$

For $|x| < n_m^{-1}$, the function under the integral sign is $\leqq n_m$ so this part gives a bounded contribution. For $x \in (2^{-k-1}, 2^{-k})$, $2^k \leqq n_m$, we have

$$\left| \sum_{1}^{m} \varepsilon_j \sin n_j x \right| \leqq 2^{-k} \sum_{n_j < 2^k} n_j + \left| \sum_{n_j > 2^k} \varepsilon_j \sin n_j x \right| .$$

The first term gives a bounded contribution:

$$\frac{\text{Const}}{m} \sum_{2^k \leqq n_m} 2^{-k} \sum_{n_j \leqq 2^k} n_j \leqq \frac{\text{Const}}{m} \sum_{j=1}^{m} n_j \sum_{2^k \geqq n_j} 2^{-k} \leqq \frac{\text{Const}}{m} \sum_{j=1}^{m} 1 \,.$$

For the second terms we use the lemma. If $A_\mu(x)$ denotes the number of n_j so that $1 \leqq \mu \leqq n_j x < \mu + 1$, then

$$\text{(A5)} \qquad Q_m(f) \leqq \frac{\text{Const}}{m} \sum_{2^k \leqq n_m} \left(\sum_\mu A_\mu(2^{-k})^2 \right)^{1/2} + \text{Const}\,.$$

Consider first those terms for which $A_\mu \geqq 2$. Then

$$A_\mu(2^{-k}) \leqq 2(\psi((\mu+1)2^k) - \psi(\mu 2^k))\,.$$

We set

$$a_k = \psi(2^k) - \psi(2^{k-1})\,, \quad 2^k \leqq n_m\,.$$

Then if

$$2^{p-1} \leqq \mu < 2^p$$

it follows from our assumption $\psi'(t) = O(\psi'(2t))$ that

$$A_\mu(2^{-k}) \leqq \text{Const}\; a_{k+p} 2^{-p}\,.$$

Hence

$$\sum_{\substack{\mu \\ A_\mu \geqq 2}} A_\mu(2^{-k})^2 \leqq \text{Const} \sum_{p \geqq 0} a_{k+p}^2 2^{-p}\,.$$

The trivial inequality $\left(\sum x_v^2\right)^{1/2} \leqq \sum x_v$ yields

$$\sum_k \left(\sum_\mu A_\mu(2^{-k})^2 \right)^{1/2} \leqq \text{Const} \sum a_{k+p} 2^{-p/2} \leqq \text{Const} \sum_{2^k \leqq n_m} a_k \leqq \text{Const}\; \psi(n_m) = m\,.$$

It remains to estimate the sum for $A_\mu(2^{-k}) = 1$. For every k, this can happen for at most m different μ so the total contribution is bounded by

$$\sum_{2^k \leqq n_m} m^{1/2} = m^{1/2} \log n_m \leqq \text{Const}\; m$$

by (A2). This completes the proof.

Studies in Pure Mathematics
To the Memory of Paul Turán

Characterization of $\log n$

by

I. KÁTAI (Budapest)

1. Introduction

A complex-valued function $f(n)$ of a positive integer is said to be *restrictedly additive* (or, simply, additive) if $(n_1, n_2)=1$ implies $f(n_1 n_2) = f(n_1)+f(n_2)$. If this equation is satisfied for any pair of integers n_1, n_2 then we say that $f(n)$ is *completely* (or totally) *additive.*

More than 30 years ago P. ERDŐS proved the following two assertions [1].

(A) *If $f(n)$ is restrictedly additive and monotonic then it is a constant multiple of* $\log n$.

(B) *If $f(n)$ is restrictedly additive and $f(n+1)-f(n)\to 0$ then it is a constant multiple of* $\log n$.

P. TURÁN [2] has discovered how to use these results for the characterization of the Dirichlet L-functions.

Later the author proved in [3] the following generalization of (A) and (B).

(C) *If $f(n)$ is real-valued, restrictedly additive and* $\liminf \Delta^k f(n)\geqq 0$ *for some integer $k\geqq 1$ where $\Delta^k f(n)$ denotes the k'th difference of $f(n)$, then $f(n)$ is a constant multiple of* $\log n$.

The following conjecture of P. ERDŐS was proved independently by E. WIRSING [4] and myself [5].

(D) *If $f(n)$ is restrictedly additive and*

$$\frac{1}{x}\sum_{n\leqq x}|\Delta f(n)| \to 0,$$

then $f(n)=c\log n$.

Later WIRSING deduced this assertion assuming only that

$$\liminf \frac{1}{x}\sum_{x\leqq n\leqq(1+\gamma)x}|\Delta f(n)|=0, \quad \gamma>\text{constant}.$$

I have proved [6] the following assertion.

(E) *If* $f(n)$ *is restrictedly additive and for some integer* $k \geqq 1$

$$\liminf \frac{1}{\log x} \sum_{n \leqq x} \frac{|\Delta^k f(n)|}{n} = 0,$$

then $f(n) = c \log n$.

A great progress has been achieved by E. WIRSING by proving the following theorem [7].

(F) *If* $f(n)$ *is complex valued, completely additive and*

$$\frac{\Delta f(n)}{\log n} \to 0 \quad (n \to \infty),$$

then $f(n)$ *is a constant multiple of* $\log n$.

Ten years ago I stated [8] the problem to determine all additive $f_0(n), \ldots, f_k(n)$ satisfying

$$\lim \sum_{i=0}^{k} f_i(a_i n + b_i) = C \quad (a_i > 0,\ b_i \text{ integers}).$$

In this paper we shall consider the special case $a_i = 1$, $f_i(n) = c_i f(n)$ $(i = 0, \ldots, k)$, $f(n)$ is completely additive.

Let $\varphi(z) = \alpha_0 + \alpha_1 z + \ldots + \alpha_k z^k$ be an arbitrary non-zero polynomial with complex coefficients. For a sequence y_n $(n = 1, 2, \ldots)$ let $E y_n = y_{n+1}$, $\Delta y_n = y_{n+1} - y_n$, $I y_n = y_n$, consequently

$$\varphi(E) y_n = \sum_{j=0}^{k} \alpha_j y_{n+j}.$$

Theorem 1. *Let* $f(n)$ *be a complex valued completely additive function. Suppose that there exists a non-zero polynomial* $\varphi(z)$ *with complex coefficients such that*

$$\frac{\varphi(E) f(n)}{\log n} \to 0. \tag{1.1}$$

Then, in the case $\varphi(1) = 0$, $f(n)$ *is a constant multiple of* $\log n$, *while in the case* $\varphi(1) \neq 0$, $f(n) = 0$ *identically.*

Theorem 2. *Let* $f(n)$ *be a complex valued completely additive function. Suppose that there exists a non-zero polynomial* $\varphi(z)$ *with complex coefficients and a constant* Γ *such that*

$$\liminf_{x \to \infty} \frac{1}{\log x} \sum_{n \leqq x} \frac{|\varphi(E) f(n) + \Gamma|}{n} = 0. \tag{1.2}$$

Then $\Gamma = 0$, *and in the case* $\varphi(1) = 0$, $f(n)$ *is a constant multiple of* $\log n$, *while in the case* $\varphi(1) \neq 0$, $f(n) = 0$ *identically.*

The basic idea is the following one. First we prove that the theorems hold if the conditions are satisfied by $\varphi(z)=(z-1)^k$.

Then we shall deduce the following statement. If the conditions hold with some $\varphi(z)$, then they hold with $\varphi(z)=(z-1)^k$ too.

2. The case $\varphi(z)=(z-1)^k$

Theorem 2 is an immediate consequence of (E). Indeed,

$$\sum_{n\leqq x}\frac{|\Delta^{k+1}f(n)|}{n}\leqq\sum_{n\leqq x}\frac{|\Delta^k f(n)+\Gamma|+|\Delta^k f(n+1)+\Gamma|}{n},$$

and so (1.2) implies

$$\liminf\frac{1}{\log x}\sum_{n\leqq x}\frac{|\Delta^{k+1}f(n)|}{n}=0.$$

To prove Theorem 1 we need to prove only the following

Lemma 1. *If $\Delta^k f(n)=o(\log n)$ for some $k\geqq 2$, then $\Delta^{k-1}f(n)=o(\log n)$; consequently $\Delta f(n)=o(\log n)$. Theorem* (F) *gives that $f(n)=c\log n$.*

Proof. Let $\Delta_2=E^2-I$. We have

$$\Delta_2^{k-1}f(2n)=\Delta_1^{k-1}f(n). \tag{2.1}$$

Furthermore

$$\Delta_2^{k-1}f(n)=\sum_{j=0}^{k-1}\binom{k-1}{j}\Delta^{k-1}f(n+j). \tag{2.2}$$

Consequently

$$\Delta_2^{k-1}f(2m)-2^{k-1}\Delta^{k-1}f(2m)=\sum_{h=0}^{k-1}\binom{k-1}{h}\{\Delta^{k-1}f(2m+h)-\Delta^{k-1}f(2m)\},$$

and so

$$\Delta^{k-1}f(m)-2^{k-1}\Delta^{k-1}f(2m)=\sum_{\nu=0}^{k-2}A(\nu,k\quad 2)\Delta^k f(2m+\nu), \tag{2.3}$$

$$A(\nu,k-2)=\sum_{j=\nu+1}^{k-1}\binom{k-1}{j}.$$

Suppose that

$$|\Delta^k f(n)| \leqq \delta(n) \log 2n\,, \quad \delta(n) \downarrow 0\,,$$

and let

$$\Delta^{k-1} f(n) = \psi(n) \log 2n\,. \tag{2.4}$$

From (2.3) we get

$$|\psi(n) \log 2n - 2^{k-1}\psi(2n) \log 4n| \leqq$$

$$\leqq \sum_{h=0}^{k-2} A(h, k-2)\delta(n) \log 4(n+h) \leqq \delta(n) 2^{2k-1} \log 4(n+k)\,.$$

Furthermore

$$\delta(n) \log 2n \geqq |\Delta^k f(n)| = |\Delta^{k-1} f(n+1) - \Delta^{k-1} f(n)| =$$

$$= |\psi(n+1) \log 2(n+1) - \psi(n) \log 2n|\,.$$

So we have

$$|\psi(2n)| \leqq \frac{|\psi(n)|}{2^{k-1}} \frac{\log 2n}{\log 4n} + \delta(n) \cdot 2^k \frac{\log 4(n+k)}{\log 2n}\,, \tag{2.5}$$

$$|\psi(2n+1)| \leqq |\psi(2n)| + \delta(2n)\,. \tag{2.6}$$

Let

$$\Gamma_t = \max_{2^t \leqq m < 2^{t+1}} |\psi(m)|\,.$$

From (2.5), (2.6) it follows that

$$\Gamma_{t+1} \leqq A\Gamma_t + \rho_t\,, \quad \rho_t \to 0\,, \quad A < 1\,,$$

if t is large. Consequently $\Gamma_t \to 0$ and Lemma 1 has been proved.

3. Completion of the proof of Theorem 1

Suppose that (1.1) holds with some $\varphi(z)$. If $\varphi(z)$ is a constant polynomial then the assertion is true. Let Φ denote the set of those polynomials $\psi(z)$ for which $\psi(E)f(n) = o(\log n)$. It is almost obvious that Φ is an ideal in the polynomial ring. Indeed, from ψ_1, $\psi_2 \in \Phi$ it follows immediately that $\psi_1 + \psi_2 \in \Phi$. Let $\psi \in \Phi$, and

$k(z)=\gamma_0+\gamma_1 z+\ldots+\gamma_h z^h$ be an arbitrary polynomial. Observing that

$$k(E)\psi(E)f(n) = \sum_{j=0}^{n} \gamma_1 \psi(E)f(n+j)=o(\log n),$$

we get $k(z)\psi(z)\in\Phi$.

Let $\psi(z)=\beta_0+\beta_1 z+\ldots+\beta_t z^t$ denote the generator element of Φ. We may suppose that $t\geqq 1$, $\beta_1=1$. Then $\psi(z)$ is uniquely determined, all elements of Φ are the multiple of it.

Let $\delta_1, \delta_2, \ldots, \delta_t$ denote the roots of $\psi(z)$,

$$\psi(z) = \prod_{j=1}^{t} (z-\delta_j). \tag{3.1}$$

For some integer $m\geqq 2$ let $1, \varepsilon_1, \varepsilon_2, \ldots, \varepsilon_{m-1}$ be the m-th roots of unity,

$$k(z) = \prod_{i=1}^{m-1} \prod_{j=1}^{t} (z-\varepsilon_i\delta_j). \tag{3.2}$$

Then

$$k(z)\psi(z) = \prod_{j=1}^{t} (z^m-\delta_j^m)=\rho(z^m),$$

$$\rho(z) = \prod_{j=1}^{t} (z-\delta_j^m)=\gamma_0+\gamma_1 z+\ldots+\gamma_{t-1}z^{t-1}+z^t. \tag{3.3}$$

We observe that

$$E^{mr} f(mn) = f(mn+rm)=E^r f(n)+f(m),$$

consequently

$$\rho(E^m)f(mn)=\rho(E)f(n)+f(m)\rho(1).$$

Otherwise

$$k(E)\psi(E)f(mn)=\rho(E^m)f(mn)=o(\log n) \quad (n\to\infty).$$

Hence it follows that

$$\rho(E)f(n)=o(\log n),$$

$\rho(z)\in\Phi$. Since it is monic, $\rho(z)\equiv\psi(z)$ and

$$\{\delta_1, \ldots, \delta_t\}=\{\delta_1^m, \ldots, \delta_t^m\} \tag{3.4}$$

counting the elements with multiplicity. We may suppose that $\delta_i \neq 0$ $(i=1, \ldots, t)$, since in the opposite case $\frac{\psi(z)}{z} \in \Phi$. By $m \to \infty$ from (3.4) we get $|\delta_i|=1$ $(i=1, \ldots, t)$. Let $\delta_j = e^{2\pi i \lambda_j}$ $(j=1, \ldots, t)$. The arguments λ_j must be rational numbers. Let N be a positive integer for which $N\lambda_j$ $(j=1, \ldots, t)$ are integers. Then by choosing $m=N$ we get $\{\delta_1^N, \ldots, \delta_t^N\} = \{1, \ldots, 1\} = \{\delta_1, \ldots, \delta_t\}$. So we deduced that

$$\psi(z) = (z-1)^t$$

but $\Delta^k f(n) = o(\log n)$ implies that $f(n) = c \log n$, as has been proved above.

Stating $f(n) = c \log n$, $c \neq 0$ in (1.1), we see that

$$\varphi(E)(c \log n) = c\varphi(1) \log(n) + o(1), \tag{3.5}$$

and it is a solution if and only if $\varphi(1)=0$.

4. Completion of the proof of Theorem 2

The proof is similar to that of Theorem 1. Let $\psi(z)$ be of the least degree polynomial satisfying

$$\liminf_{x \to \infty} \frac{1}{\log x} \sum_{n \leqq x} \frac{|\psi(E) f(n) + \Gamma_\psi|}{n} = 0. \tag{4.1}$$

Let $\delta_1, \ldots, \delta_t$, $k(z)$, $\rho(z)$ be defined as above. We get

$$\begin{aligned} \rho(1) f(m) + \rho(E) f(n) &= k(E)\psi(E) f(mn) = \\ &= k(E)[\psi(E) f(mn) + \Gamma_\psi] - k(1)\Gamma_\psi . \end{aligned} \tag{4.2}$$

Let $x_\nu \to \infty$ be a sequence such that

$$\sum_{n \leqq x_\nu} \frac{|\psi(E) f(n) + \Gamma_\psi|}{n} = o(\log x_\nu). \tag{4.3}$$

Then, for (4.3)

$$\sum_{n \leqq y_\nu} \frac{|\rho(E) f(n) + \Gamma_\rho|}{n} = o(\log y_\nu),$$

where

$$y_\nu = \frac{x_\nu - t(m-1)}{m}, \quad \Gamma_\rho = \rho(1) f(m) + k(1)\Gamma_\psi .$$

But (4.3) holds for y_ν, instead of x_ν, too. Consequently

$$\sum_{n\leqq y_\nu} \frac{|(\psi(E)-\rho(E))f(n)+(\Gamma_\psi-\Gamma_\rho)|}{n} = o(\log y_\nu).$$

So (4.1) holds for $\psi(z)-\rho(z)$ instead of $\psi(z)$, which contradicts the assumption that $\psi(z)$ has minimal degree, unless $\psi(z)-\rho(z)$ is the zero polynomial. Hence we deduce similarly as above that $\psi(z)=(z-1)^t$. Consequently

$$\liminf \frac{1}{\log x} \sum_{n\leqq x} \frac{|\Delta^t f(n)+\Gamma|}{n} = 0.$$

Hence it follows that

$$\frac{1}{\log x} \sum_{n\leqq x} \frac{|\Delta^{t+1} f(n)|}{n} = 0,$$

and by (E) that $f(n)=c\log n$.

To finish the proof it is enough to consider (3.5) $f(n)=c\log n$ $(c\neq 0)$ is a solution of (1.2) if and only if $\varphi(1)=0$, $\Gamma=0$.

References

[1] P. Erdős, On the distribution of additive functions, *Ann. of Math.*, **47** (1964), 1–20.

[2] P. Turán, On a characterization of Dirichlet's *L*-functions, *Annales Univ. Sci. Budapest. Eötvös Sect. Math.*, **8** (1965), 65–69.

[3] I. Kátai, A remark on additive arithmetical functions, *Annales Univ. Sci. Budapest. Eötvös Sect. Math.*, **10** (1967), 81–83.

[4] E. Wirsing, On a characterization of Log *n* as an additive function. *Proc. Rome Conference on Number Theory*, 1968.

[5] I. Kátai, On a problem of P. Erdős, *Journal of Number Theory*, **2** (1970), 1–6.

[6] I. Kátai, On additive functions, *Publ. Math.* (in print).

[7] E. Wirsing, Additive und vollständig additive Funktionen mit Wachstumsbeschränkungen. Seminarausarbeitung, Ulm, 1976.

[8] I. Kátai, On number-theoretical function, *Proc. Debrecen Conference of Number Theory*, 1968, 133–137.

EÖTVÖS LORÁND UNIVERSITY
H-1088 BUDAPEST, MÚZEUM KRT. 6–8.
HUNGARY

Studies in Pure Mathematics
To the Memory of Paul Turán

On a problem of Turán*

by

K. H. KIM and F. W. ROUSH (Montgomery)

Abstract

Let $T(n, k+1, k)$ denote the least number of k-subsets of an n-set such that every $k+1$-subset contains on of the chosen k-sebsets. We show

$$\lim_{n\to\infty} \frac{T(n, k+1, k)}{\binom{n}{k}}$$

is asymptotically less than or equal to

$$\frac{2 \log k}{k}$$

as a function of k.

TURÁN defined a function $T(n, k, m)$ as follows: $T(n, k, m)$ is the minimum size of a family F of m element subset of $N=\{1, 2, \ldots, n\}$ such that every k element subset of N contains some member of F. He determined $T(n, k, 2)$ exactly. Other authors [2], [3], [6] have studied $T(n, k, m)$ for $m>2$. Here we investigate the asymptotic behavior of $T(n, k+1, k)$. Namely we give an asymptotic upper bound on

$$g(k) = \lim_{n\to\infty} \frac{T(n, k+1, k)}{\binom{n}{k}}.$$

Our upper bound, $\frac{2 \log k}{k}$ differs considerably from the best known lower bound, $\frac{1}{k}$ [4]. It is an open problem to find which of the two is closer to the actual asymptotic value of $g(k)$.

* This work was supported by Alabama State University Faculty Research Grant R–78–6.

We will recast the problem in Boolean vector terms. By a *Boolean vector* we mean simply an n-tuple from the Boolean semiring $\{0, 1\}$. The *weight* of a Boolean vector is the number of ones in it. Problems of this nature have applications to information theory.

Question. *What is the least number of Boolean vectors of weight k such that every Boolean vector of weight $k+1$ is greater than at least one of weight k Boolean vectors?*

Proposition 1. (KATONA, NEMETZ and SIMONOVITS [4]).

$$\frac{T(n, k+1, k)}{\binom{n}{k}}$$

is nondecreasing in n for fixed k.

Theorem 2. *Asymptotically in k,*

$$g(k) \leqq \frac{2 \log k}{k}.$$

Proof. We divide the set of components into j classes $C_1, C_2, \ldots, C_j$, as nearly equal as possible. For a weight k vector v let n_i be the number of 1 components it has in C_i. Let S be the set of weight k vectors such that, either some $n_i = 0$ or $\sum in_i \equiv d \pmod{j}$. For any d this set will contain at least one vector less than any weight $k+1$ vector: if the weight $k+1$ vector has no 1 components in some C_i, remove any of its 1 components. If it has at least one 1 component in each C_i, by removing a 1 component from the proper C_i we can realize all values of $\sum in_i$, modulo j.

By choosing d we may assume that the number of vectors with $\sum in_i \equiv d \pmod{j}$ is less than or equal to $\frac{1}{j}\binom{n}{k}$. The number of vectors with some $n_i = 0$ is less than or equal to $j\binom{n-q}{k}$ where $q = \left[\frac{n}{j}\right]$.

This gives, asymptotically,

$$g(k) \leqq \frac{1}{j} + \left(1 - \frac{1}{j}\right)^k \leqq \frac{1}{j} + je^{-\frac{k}{j}}.$$

Choosing $j = \left[\frac{k}{2 \log k}\right]$ gives the theorem.

Remarks. Note that the theorem can be interpreted in terms of k-function hypergraphs [1], [5].

References

[1] C. Berge, *Graphes et Hypergraphes*, Dunod, Paris, 1970.
[2] V. Chvatal, Hypergraphs and Ramseyian theorems, *Proc. Amer. Math. Soc.*, **27** (1971), 434–440.
[3] P. Erdős and J. Spencer, *Probabilistic Methods in Combinatorics*, Akadémiai Kiadó, Budapest and Academic Press, New York, 1975.
[4] G. Katona, T. Nemetz and M. Simonovits, On a graph problem of Turán (in Hungarian), *Mat. Lapok*, **15** (1964), 228–238.
[5] M. Lorea, On Turán hypergraphs, *Discrete Mathematics*, **22** (1978), 281–286.
[6] J. Spencer, Turán's theorem for *k*-graphs, *Discrete Mathematics*, **2** (1972), 183–186.

MATHEMATICS RESEARCH GROUP
ALABAMA STATE UNIVERSITY
MONTGOMERY, ALABAMA 36101
U.S.A.

Studies in Pure Mathematics
To the Memory of Paul Turán

On the sum of powers of complex numbers

by

G. KOLESNIK (Austin) and E. G. STRAUS* (Los Angeles)

1. Introduction

In connection with the distribution of zeros of $\zeta(s)$, P. TURÁN [4] raised and gave a solution of the following problem.

Let $z_1, z_2, \ldots, z_n$ and $b_1, b_2, \ldots, b_n$ be complex numbers and let

$$S_k = b_1 z_1^k + b_2 z_2^k + \ldots + b_n z_n^k .$$

Find a lower bound for

$$M_{m,n} = \min_{z} \max_{m+1 \leqq k \leqq m+n} |S_k| ,$$

where the minimum is taken over all complex numbers z_j such that

$$1 = |z_1| \geqq |z_2| \geqq |z_3| \geqq \ldots \geqq |z_n| .$$

V. T. SÓS and P. TURÁN [3] proved that

$$M_{m,n} \geqq \left(\frac{n}{A(m+n)}\right)^n \min_{1 \leqq j \leqq n} |b_1 + \ldots + b_j| \tag{1}$$

holds with $A = 2e^{1+4/e}$.

It was noticed by S. UCHIYAMA [5], that the method of [3] gives (1) with $A = 8e$, and recently T. W. CUSICK and G. KOLESNIK improved [1] this constant to $A = 7.81e$.

E. MAKAI proved [2] that the best possible constant A in (1) is $\geqq 4e$.

In this paper we obtain (1) with the best possible constant $A = 4e$. Namely,

$$M_{m,n} \geqq 1.007 \left(\frac{n}{4e(m+n)}\right)^n \cdot \min_{1 \leqq j \leqq n} |b_1 + \ldots + b_j| . \tag{2}$$

* The research of the second author was supported in part by NSF Grant MPS71-2884.

In the case when $m \leqq 3n$ we get a larger lower bound:

$$M_{m,n} \geqq \frac{n!(2m+n)!}{2^n(2m+2n)!\sqrt{2m+2n+1}} \cdot \min_{1 \leqq j \leqq n} |b_1 + \ldots + b_j| . \tag{3}$$

Note that the constant 1.007 in (2) can be replaced by a larger number.

The proof of (2) and (3) is similar to the proof of Theorem 2 in [1] (or, in a more complicated way, to the method in[3]). The improvements are due to the following results (which replace Theorem 1 in [1]):

Theorem 1. *Let $n \geqq 1$ and $m \geqq 0$ be integers and let $P(x) = x^n + a_1 x^{n-1} + \ldots + a_n$ with real $a_1, a_2, \ldots, a_n$. Then*

$$\int_0^1 x^{2m}(P(x))^2\,dx \geqq \frac{(n!(2m+n)!)^2}{(2m+2n)! \cdot (2m+2n+1)!} \tag{4}$$

and

$$\max_{0 \leqq x \leqq 1} |x^m P(x)| \geqq \frac{n!(2m+n)!}{(2m+2n)!\sqrt{2m+2n+1}} . \tag{5}$$

Theorem 2. *Let $n \geqq 1$ and $m \geqq 0$ be integers and let $P(x) = x^n + a_1 x^{n-1} + \ldots + a_n$ with real $a_1, a_2, \ldots, a_n$. Then*

$$P_{m,n} \equiv \min_{a_1, \ldots, a_n} \max_{0 \leqq x \leqq 1} |x^m P(x)| \geqq 1.007 \left(\frac{n}{2e(m+n)} \right)^n . \tag{6}$$

We now obtain (2) with the help of the following theorem [1, Theorem 2].

Theorem 3. $M_{m,n} \geqq 2^{-n} P_{m,n} \min\limits_{1 \leqq j \leqq n} |b_1 + \ldots + b_j|$.

2. Proof of Theorem 1

Setting $a_0 = 1$ and $S_m(a_0, a_1, \ldots, a_n) = \int_0^1 x^{2m}(P(x))^2\,dx$, we obtain:

$$S_m(a_0, a_1, \ldots, a_n) = \int_0^1 x^{2m} \left(\sum_{j=0}^{n} a_j^2 x^{2n-2j} + 2 \sum_{j=1}^{n} \sum_{l=0}^{j-1} a_j a_l x^{2n-j-l} \right) dx =$$

$$= \sum_{j=0}^{n} \frac{a_j^2}{(2m+2n-2j+1)} + 2 \sum_{j=1}^{n} \sum_{l=0}^{j-1} \frac{a_j a_l}{(2m+2n-j-l+1)} .$$

Here $S_m(a_0, \ldots, a_n)$ is a positive definite quadratic form as a function of $a_0, \ldots, a_n$. We want to show by induction on n, that

$$S_m(a_0, a_1, \ldots, a_n) \geqq \frac{(n!(2m+n)!)^2}{(2m+2n)!(2m+2n+1)!}$$

for every $m \geqq 0$ and any set of real numbers $a_1, \ldots, a_n$ and $a_0 = 1$. If $n = 1$, then

$$S_m(a_0, a_1) = \frac{1}{2m+3} + \frac{a_1^2}{2m+1} + 2a_1 \cdot \frac{1}{2m+3} =$$

$$= \frac{1}{2m+1}\left(a_1 + \frac{2m+1}{2m+2}\right)^2 + \frac{1}{(2m+2)^2(2m+3)} \geqq \frac{(1!(2m+1)!)^2}{(2m+2)!(2m+3)!}.$$

Suppose, that $n > 1$, and let a_n be a real number. Then

$$S_m(a_0, a_1, \ldots, a_n) = \sum_{j=0}^{n-1} \frac{a_j^2}{(2m+2n-2j+1)} + 2\sum_{j=0}^{n-1}\sum_{l=0}^{j-1} \frac{a_j a_l}{(2m+2n-j-l+1)} +$$

$$+ \frac{a_n^2}{(2m+1)} + 2\sum_{l=0}^{n-1} \frac{a_n a_l}{(2m+n-l+1)} = \frac{1}{2m+1}\left(a_n + \sum_{l=0}^{n-1} a_l \cdot \frac{2m+1}{2m+n-l+1}\right)^2 +$$

$$+ \sum_{j=0}^{n-1} a_j^2 \left(\frac{1}{2m+2n-2j+1} - \frac{2m+1}{(2m+n-j+1)^2}\right) +$$

$$(7) \qquad +2\sum_{j=1}^{n-1}\sum_{l=0}^{j-1} a_j a_l \left(\frac{1}{2m+2n-j-l+1} - \frac{2m+1}{(2m+n-l+1)(2m+n-j+1)}\right) \geqq$$

$$\geqq \sum_{j=0}^{n-1} a_j^2 \cdot \frac{(n-j)^2}{(2m+2n-2j+1)(2m+n-j+1)^2} +$$

$$+2\sum_{j=0}^{n-1}\sum_{l=0}^{j-1} a_j a_l \frac{(n-l)(n-j)}{(2m+2n-j-l+1)(2m+n-l+1)(2m+n-j+1)} =$$

$$= \frac{n^2}{(2m+n+1)^2} \cdot S_{m+1}(b_0, b_1, \ldots, b_{n-1}),$$

where $b_j = a_j \cdot \dfrac{(n-j)(2m+n+1)}{n(2m+n-j+1)}$ for $j = 0, 1, \ldots, n-1$.

Using the induction hypothesis and (6), we obtain:

$$S_m(1, a_1, \ldots, a_n) \geqq \frac{n^2}{(2m+n+1)^2} \cdot S_{m+1}(1, b_1, \ldots, b_{n-1}) \geqq$$

$$\geqq \frac{n^2}{(2m+n+1)^2} \cdot \frac{((n-1)! \cdot (2m+2+n-1)!)^2}{(2m+2+2n-2)!(2m+2+2n-2+1)!} = \frac{(n!(2m+n)!)^2}{(2m+2n)!(2m+2n+1)!}.$$

Inequality (5) is an obvious corollary of (4). This proves Theorem 1 and, by Theorem 3, (5) implies (3). It is also clear from the proof that inequality (4) is sharp but (5) is not.

Note that performing a linear change of variables and using (5) with $m=0$, we obtain

$$\max_{-1 \leqq x \leqq 1} |P(x)| = \max_{0 \leqq x \leqq 1} |P(2x-1)| \geqq 2^n \cdot \frac{(n!)^2}{(2n)! \sqrt{2n+1}}.$$

The above inequality is almost as strong as Chebyshev's inequality, because, using Stirling's formula in the form

(8) $$n! \geqq n^n e^{-n} \sqrt{2\pi n}\, e^{1/12n - 1/360n^3}$$

and

(9) $$n! \leqq n^n e^{-n} \sqrt{2\pi n}\, e^{1/12n},$$

we obtain:

$$2^n \cdot \frac{(n!)^2}{(2n)! \sqrt{2n+1}} \geqq 2^n \cdot \frac{n^{2n} e^{-2n}\, 2\pi n \cdot e^{1/6n - 1/180n^3}}{(2n)^{2n} e^{-2n} \sqrt{4\pi n \cdot e^{1/24n}} \sqrt{2n+1}} \geqq 2^{-n} \sqrt{\frac{\pi n}{2n+1}} > 2^{-n}.$$

3. Proof of Theorem 2

We can suppose that the polynomial $P(x)$ is such that $\max_{0 \leqq x \leqq 1} |x^m P(x)| = P_{m,n}$. Let $x_1, x_2, \ldots, x_n$ be the roots of $P(x)$. It is clear that $0 \leqq x_j \leqq 1$, and we suppose

$$0 = x_0 \leqq x_1 \leqq x_2 \leqq \ldots \leqq x_n.$$

We can suppose $x_n > 0$, since otherwise $P_{m,n} = 1$. We can also suppose $x_1 > 0$. Indeed, if we know that (6) holds for all polynomials with $a_n \neq 0$, then $x^m \cdot P(x) = x^{m+l} \cdot P_1(x)$, where $P_1(x)$ is a polynomial of degree $n-l$ with $P(0) \neq 0$ and

$$\max_{0 \leqq x \leqq 1} |x^m P(x)| = \max_{0 \leqq x \leqq 1} |x^{m+l} P_1(x)| \geqq 1.007 \left(\frac{n-l}{4e(m+n)} \right)^{n-l}$$

But if $l \geqq 1$, then

$$\left(\frac{n-l}{4e(m+n)}\right)^{n-l} \Bigg/ \left(\frac{n}{4e(m+n)}\right)^{n} = \left(\frac{4e(m+n)}{n}\right)^{l} \cdot \left(1+\frac{l}{n-l}\right)^{-(n-l)} \geqq$$

$$\geqq \left(\frac{4e(m+n)}{n}\right)^{l} \cdot e^{-l} > 1$$

which proves the above statement.

Denoting

$$P_j = \max_{x_j \leqq x \leqq x_{j+1}} |x^m P(x)|, \quad j=0, 1, \ldots, n-1,$$

we can (similarly to the reasonings of P. L. CHEBYSHEV) show that $P_0 = P_1 = \ldots = P_{n-1} = P_{m,n}$; otherwise we could vary the x_j to construct another polynomial $Q(x)$ with smaller $\max\limits_{0<x<1} |x^m Q(x)|$.

If $n=1$, then $P(x) = x - x_1$, and

$$P_{m,n} = \max_{0 \leqq x \leqq 1} x^m |x - x_1| = \max \left\{1 - x_1; \left(\frac{m x_1}{m+1}\right)^m \cdot \frac{x_1}{m+1}\right\} \geqq \frac{1}{1.5e(m+1)}.$$

Also, if $m < 3n$, then Theorem 1 implies Theorem 2. For $n \geqq 4$, using (8) and (9), we get

$$\frac{n!(2m+n)!}{(2m+2n)!\sqrt{2m+2n+1}} \Bigg/ \left(\frac{n}{2e(m+n)}\right)^n \geqq$$

$$\geqq \frac{n^n \sqrt{2\pi n} \cdot (2m+n)^{2m+n} \sqrt{2\pi(2m+n)}}{(2m+2n)^{2m+2n} \sqrt{2\pi(2m+2n)} \cdot \sqrt{2m+2n+1}} \left(\frac{2e(m+n)}{n}\right)^n =$$

(10)

$$= \left(1+\frac{n}{2m+n}\right)^{-2m-n} e^n \cdot \sqrt{\frac{\pi n(2m+n)}{(m+n)(2m+2n+1)}} \geqq$$

$$\geqq \left(1+\frac{1}{7}\right)^{-7n} \cdot e^n \quad \frac{7\pi}{4\left(8+\frac{1}{n}\right)} \geqq 1.01,$$

because the functions $\left(1+\dfrac{n}{2x+n}\right)^{-2x-n}$ and $\dfrac{2x+n}{(x+n)(2x+2n+1)}$ decrease for $x \geqq 1$

and

$$\left(1+\frac{n}{2m+n}\right)^{-2m-n} \geqq \left(1+\frac{1}{7}\right)^{-7n},$$

$$\frac{(2m+n)n}{(m+n)(2m+n+1)} \geqq \frac{7n}{4(8n+1)} \geqq \frac{7}{4\left(8+\frac{1}{n}\right)} \geqq \frac{7}{33};$$

for $n=2$ and $n=3$ we also obtain

$$\frac{2!\cdot(2m+2)!}{(2m+4)!\sqrt{2m+5}} : \left(\frac{1}{e(m+2)}\right)^2 = e^2\cdot\frac{(m+2)}{(2m+3)\sqrt{2m+5}} \geqq \frac{e^2\cdot 7}{13\sqrt{15}} > 1.01$$

$$\left(\text{here } m \leqq 5 \text{ and } \frac{m+2}{2m+3} \geqq \frac{7}{13};\ \frac{1}{\sqrt{2m+5}} \geqq \frac{1}{\sqrt{15}}\right),$$

and

$$\frac{3!\cdot(2m+3)!}{(2m+6)!\sqrt{2m+7}} : \left(\frac{3}{2e(m+3)}\right)^3 = \frac{4e^3(m+3)^2}{9(m+2)(2m+5)\sqrt{2m+7}} \geqq$$

$$\geqq \frac{4e^3\cdot 11^2}{9\cdot 10\cdot 21\sqrt{23}} > 1.01\,.$$

(here $m \leqq 8$.)

So, we can suppose that $n \geqq 2$, $m \geqq 3n$ and $x_1 > 0$.

First we want to prove that

$$P_{m,n} \geqq 0.918\left(\frac{n}{2e(m+n)}\right)^n. \tag{11}$$

Let t be the smallest number in [0, 1] at which $|x^m\cdot P(x)|$ attains its maximum. Writing $y_0 = (n/4e(m+n))^{n/m}$ we can see, that $t \geqq y_0$, otherwise

$$P_{m,n} = \max_{0\leqq x\leqq 1} |x^m(x-x_1)\dots(x-x_n)| \leqq y_0^m = (n/4e(m+n))^n,$$

which contradicts the inequality

$$P_{m,n} \geqq (n/3.905e(m+n))^n > (n/4e(m+n))^n \tag{12}$$

of [1, Theorem 1].

Also $x_1 \geqq y_0$ because $t < x_1$. But

$$(n/4e(m+n))^n < P_{m,n} = t^m|t-x_1| \cdot |t-x_2| \ldots |t-x_n| \leqq t^m \cdot (1-y_0)^n$$

and therefore

$$t \geqq y_1 = (n/4e(m+n)(1-y_0))^{n/m}.$$

By induction we can prove, that $t \geqq y_j$ for $j=0, 1, 2, \ldots$, where $\{y_j\}$ is a monotone-increasing sequence of real numbers in $[0, 1)$, defined, by

$$y_{j+1} = (n/4e(m+n)(1-y_j))^{n/m}, \quad j=0, 1, 2, \ldots.$$

If $y = \lim_{j\to\infty} y_j$ then $x_1 > t \geqq y$, where y satisfies the equation

$$y^m(1-y)^n = (n/4e(m+n))^n.$$

Here $y \geqq 1 - \dfrac{3.7n}{(m+n)}$, because the function $f(x) = x^m(1-x)^n$ increases for $x \leqq \dfrac{m}{m+n} = 1 - \dfrac{n}{m+n}$, and

$$\begin{aligned} f\left(1-\frac{3.7n}{(m+n)}\right) &= \left(1-\frac{3.7n}{(m+n)}\right)^m \cdot \left(\frac{3.7n}{(m+n)}\right)^n \leqq e^{-3.7n} \cdot \left(\frac{3.7n}{m+n}\right)^n = \\ &= \left(\frac{3.7n}{e^{3.7}(m+n)}\right)^n < \left(\frac{n}{4e(m+n)}\right)^n, \end{aligned} \tag{13}$$

so, $x_1 \geqq t \geqq 1 - \dfrac{3.7n}{(m+n)} = t_0$, and

$$\int_0^{t_0} x^{2m}(P(x))^2\,dx = \int_0^{t_0} x^{2m}(x-x_1)^2 \ldots (x-x_n)^2\,dx \leqq$$

$$\leqq \int_0^{t_0} x^{2m}(1-x)^{2n}dx = I_{2m,2n}(t_0).$$

Estimating the integral, we obtain

$$I_{2m,2n}(t_0) = \int_0^{t_0} x^{2m}(1-x)^{2n}\,dx = \frac{x^{2m+1}(1-x)^{2n}}{2m+1}\Bigg|_0^{t_0} +$$

$$+ \frac{2n}{2m+1}\int_0^{t_0} x^{2m+1}(1-x)^{2n-1}\,dx = \frac{t_0^{2m+1}(1-t_0)^{2n}}{2m+1} + \frac{2n}{2m+1} I_{2m+1,2n-1}(t_0) \leqq$$

$$\leq \frac{t_0^{2m+1}(1-t_0)^{2n}}{2m+1} + \frac{n}{m}\cdot\frac{t_0^{2m+2}\cdot(1-t_0)^{2n-1}}{2m+2} + \frac{n\cdot(2n-1)}{m(2m+2)} I_{2m+2,2n-1}(t_0) \leq$$

$$\leq \frac{t_0^{2m+1}(1-t_0)^{2n}}{2m+1}\left(1+\frac{nt_0}{m(1-t_0)}+\ldots+\left(\frac{nt_0}{m(1-t_0)}\right)^n\right).$$

Here $\frac{nt_0}{m(1-t_0)} = \frac{m-2.7n}{3.7m} \leq \frac{10}{37}$, and we get (see (13))

$$\int_0^{t_0} x^{2m}(P(x))^2\,dx \leq I_{2m,2n}(t_0) \leq \frac{37}{27(2m+1)}\cdot\left(1-\frac{3.7n}{m+n}\right)^{2m+1}\cdot\left(\frac{3.7n}{m+n}\right)^{2n} \leq$$

$$\leq \frac{37}{27(2m+1)}\cdot\left(\frac{n}{4e(m+n)}\right)^{2n}.$$

We want to show that

$$\frac{37}{27(2m+1)}\cdot\left(\frac{n}{4e(m+n)}\right)^{2n} \leq \left(\frac{n!(2m+n)!}{(2m+2n)!}\right)^2\cdot\frac{1}{137(2m+2n+1)}. \tag{14}$$

If $n=2$, then $m \geq 6$ and

$$\left(\frac{2!(2m+2)!}{(2m+4)!}\right)^2\cdot\frac{1}{(2m+5)}\left[\frac{37}{27(2m+1)}\cdot\left(\frac{2}{4e(m+2)}\right)^4\right] =$$

$$= \frac{16\cdot 27\cdot e^4}{37}\cdot\frac{2m+1}{2m+5}\cdot\frac{(m+2)^q}{(2m+3)^2} \geq \frac{16\cdot 27\cdot e^4}{37}\cdot\frac{13}{17}\cdot\frac{8^2}{15^2} > 137,$$

because the function $f(x) = \frac{2x+1}{2x+5}\cdot\left(\frac{x+2}{2x+3}\right)^2$ increases for $x \geq 0$:

$$\frac{f'(x)}{f(x)} = \frac{2}{2x+1} - \frac{2}{2x+5} + \frac{2}{x+2} - \frac{4}{2x+3} = \frac{8}{(2x+1)(2x+5)} - \frac{2}{(x+2)(2x+3)} > 0.$$

If $n \geq 3$, then $m \geq 9$ and

$$\left(\frac{n!(2m+n)!}{(2m+2n)!}\right)^2\cdot\frac{2m+1}{2m+2n+1} \geq \left(\frac{n^n(2m+n)^{2m+n}\sqrt{2\pi n}\cdot\sqrt{2\pi(2m+n)}}{(2m+2n)^{2m+2n}\sqrt{2\pi(2m+2n)}}\right)^2\cdot\frac{2m+1}{2m+2n+1} =$$

$$= \left(\frac{n}{2(m+n)}\right)^{2n}\cdot\left(1+\frac{1}{2m+n}\right)^{-2(2m+n)}\cdot\frac{2\pi n(2m+n)(2m+1)}{(2m+2n)(2m+2n+1)} \geq$$

$$\geqq 6\pi\cdot\left(\frac{n}{2e(m+n)}\right)^{2n}\cdot\frac{(2m+n)(2m+1)}{(2m+2n)(2m+2n+1)}\geqq$$

$$\geqq 192\pi\cdot\left(\frac{n}{4e(m+n)}\right)^{2n}\cdot\frac{(2m+n)(2m+1)}{(m+n)(2m+2n+1)}\geqq$$

$$\geqq 137\cdot\frac{37}{27}\left(\frac{n}{4e(m+n)}\right)^{2n},$$

because the function $f(x)=\frac{(2x+n)(2x+1)}{(x+n)(2x+2n+1)}$ increases for $x\geqq 0$ as a function of x and $f(3n)=\frac{7}{4}\cdot\frac{6n+1}{8n+1}>\frac{21}{16}$. This proves (14) for all $n\geqq 2$, and

$$\int_0^{t_0} x^{2m}(P(x))^2\,dx\leqq\frac{1}{137}\cdot\left(\frac{n!(2m+n)!}{(2m+2n)!}\right)^2\cdot\frac{1}{2m+2n+1}.\tag{15}$$

Combining (4) with (15), we obtain:

$$\int_{t_0}^{1} x^{2m}(P(x))^2\,dx\geqq\frac{136}{137}\cdot\left(\frac{n!(2m+n)!}{(2m+2n)!}\right)^2\cdot\frac{1}{2m+2n+1},$$

and, like before, (8) and (9) lead to

$$P_{m,n}\geqq\max_{t_0\leqq x\leqq 1}|x^m P(x)|\geqq\frac{1}{1-t_0}\int_{t_0}^{1}x^{2m}(P(x))^2\,dx\geqq$$

$$\geqq\sqrt{\frac{m+n}{3.7n}\cdot\frac{136}{137}\cdot\left(\frac{n!(2m+n)!}{(2m+2n)!}\right)^2\cdot\frac{1}{2m+2n+1}}\geqq$$

$$\geqq\frac{n^n(2m+n)^{2m+n}}{(2m+2n)^{2m+2n}}\cdot\sqrt{\frac{(m+n)}{3.7n}\cdot\frac{136}{137}\cdot\frac{2\pi n\cdot 2\pi(2m+n)}{2\pi(2m+2n)}\cdot\frac{1}{2m+2n+1}}\geqq$$

$$\geqq\left(\frac{n}{2(m+n)}\right)^n\cdot\sqrt{\frac{136\pi(2m+n)}{3.7\cdot 137(2m+2n+1)}}\cdot\left(1+\frac{n}{2m+n}\right)^{-2m-n}$$

We can see that for $x=2m+n\geqq 7n$ the function $f(x)=\frac{x}{x+n+1}\cdot\left(1+\frac{n}{x}\right)^{-2x}$ decreases, because for $x\geqq 7n$, $n\geqq 2$ we get

$$\frac{f'(x)}{f(x)}=\frac{1}{x}-\frac{1}{x+n+1}-2\log\left(1+\frac{n}{x}\right)+\frac{2n}{n+x}<\frac{n+1}{x(x+n+1)}+\frac{2n}{n+x}-$$

$$-\frac{2n}{x}+\frac{n^2}{x^2}-\frac{n+1}{x(x+n)}-\frac{2n^2}{x(x+n)}+\frac{n^2}{x^2}=\frac{(n+1-n^2)x+n^3}{x^2(x+n)}\leqq \tag{16}$$

$$\leqq\frac{(n+1-n^2)7n+n^3}{x^2(x+n)}=\frac{n(-6n^2+7n+7)}{x^2(x+n)}<0.$$

So,

$$\sqrt{\frac{2m+n}{2m+2n+1}}\cdot\left(1+\frac{n}{2m+n}\right)^{-2m-n}<e^{-n}, \tag{17}$$

and, using (15) and (17), we complete the proof of (11):

$$P_{m,n}\geqq\left(\frac{n}{2(m+n)}\right)^n\cdot e^{-n}\cdot\sqrt{\frac{136\pi}{137\cdot 3.7}}\geqq 0.918\left(\frac{n}{2e(m+n)}\right)^n.$$

The proof of Theorem 2 is similar to the proof of (11). We start with inequality (11) instead of (12). As before, we can prove that $x_1>t\geqq y$, where y satisfies the equation

$$y^m(1-y)^n=0.918\cdot\left(\frac{n}{2e(m+n)}\right)^n.$$

Here

$$y\geqq 1-\frac{11n}{4(m+n)}=t_0,$$

because

$$\left(1-\frac{11n}{4(m+n)}\right)^m\cdot\left(\frac{11n}{4(m+n)}\right)^n\leqq(11/4e^{11/4})^n\cdot\left(\frac{n}{m+n}\right)^n=$$

$$=\left(\frac{11}{2e^{7/4}}\right)^2\cdot\left(\frac{n}{2e(m+n)}\right)^n<0.918\cdot\left(\frac{n}{2e(m+n)}\right)^n.$$

Using the inequality

$$\frac{nt_0}{m(1-t_0)}=\frac{4m-7n}{11m}<\frac{4}{11}$$

we obtain the following estimate:

$$\int_0^{t_0} x^{2m}(P(x))^2\,dx \leqq \frac{t_0^{2m+1}}{2m+1}\cdot(1-t_0)^{2n}\cdot\frac{11}{7} =$$

$$= \frac{11}{7(2m+1)}\cdot\left(1-\frac{11n}{4(m+n)}\right)^{2m+1}\cdot\left(\frac{11n}{4(m+n)}\right)^{2n} < \frac{11}{7(2m+1)}\cdot\left(\frac{11n}{4e^{11/4}(m+n)}\right)^{2n}.$$

Similarly to the proof of (14) we can show that

$$\frac{11}{7(2m+1)}\cdot\left(\frac{11n}{4e^{11/4}(m+n)}\right)^{2n} \leqq \left(\frac{n!(2m+n)!}{(2m+2n)!}\right)^2\cdot\frac{1}{9(2m+2n+1)}.$$

So,

$$\int_0^{t_0} x^{2m}(P(x))^2\,dx \leqq \frac{1}{9(2m+2n+1)}\cdot\left(\frac{n!(2m+n)!}{(2m+2n)!}\right)^2,$$

and

$$\int_{t_0}^{1} x^{2m}(P(x))^2\,dx \geqq \frac{8}{9(2m+2n+1)}\cdot\left(\frac{n!(2m+n)!}{(2m+2n)!}\right)^2;$$

$$P_{m,n} \geqq \frac{1}{1-t_0}\int_{t_0}^{1} x^{2m}(P(x))^2\,dx \geqq \frac{n!(2m+n)!}{(2m+2n)!}\sqrt{\frac{32(m+n)}{99n(2m+2n+1)}} \geqq$$

$$\geqq \frac{n^n(2m+n)^{2m+n}}{(2m+2n)^{2m+2n}}\cdot\sqrt{\frac{32\pi(2m+n)}{99(2m+2n+1)}} =$$

$$= \left(\frac{n}{2(m+n)}\right)^n\cdot\sqrt{\frac{32\pi}{99}}\cdot\sqrt{\frac{2m+n}{2m+2n+1}\cdot\left(1+\frac{n}{2m+n}\right)^{-4m-2n}} \geqq$$

$$\geqq \left(\frac{n}{2e(m+n)}\right)^n\sqrt{\frac{32\pi}{99}} \geqq 1.007\cdot\left(\frac{n}{2e(m+n)}\right)^n.$$

This completes the proof of Theorem 2. In view of Theorem 3 we have thus established (2).

Added in Proof

The inequality (2) can be replaced by a slightly stronger result.

(17) $$M_{m,n} \gg \sqrt{n} \cdot (n/4e(m+n))^{n-1} \min_{1 \leqq j \leqq n} |b_1 + \ldots + b_j| .$$

Note that E. MAKAI showed that

$$M_{m,n} \ll n \cdot \left(\frac{n}{4e(m+n)} \right)^{n-1} \min_{1 \leqq j \leqq n} |b_1 + \ldots + b_j|$$

so that (17) gives the correct exponent in m but the exponent in n differs by 1/2.

To prove (17), we can obviously suppose that $n \geqq 2$. Also, is $m \leqq 9n$, then we apply (3) and, using Stirling's formula, we obtain:

$$M_{m,n} \geqq \frac{n!(2m+n)!}{2^n \cdot (2m+2n)! \sqrt{2m+2n+1}} \gg \frac{n^n(2m+n)^{2m+n}}{(2m+2n)^{2m+2n} \cdot 2^n} =$$

$$= \left(\frac{n}{4(m+n)} \right)^n \cdot \left(\frac{2m+n}{2m+n} \right)^{2m+n} \gg n \cdot \left(\frac{n}{4e(m+n)} \right)^{n-1} .$$

So, we suppose $m > 9n$. By examining the proof of Theorem 2 in [1] one can see that (taking $N \to \infty$ in the last inequality on p. 211, [1])

$$M_{m,n} \gg \min_{1 \leqq j \leqq n} |b_1 + \ldots + b_j| \cdot \left\{ \min_{0 \leqq x \leqq 1} \sum_{k=1}^{n} 2^{n-k} I_{m,k}(x) \right\}^{-1} ,$$

where for some fixed x, $a_1, a_2, \ldots, a_n$ such that $0 \leqq x \leqq 1$ and $1 \geqq a_1 \geqq a_2 \geqq a_n \geqq 0$

$$I_{m,k}(x) = \max_{\mathbf{z}} \int_{-\pi}^{\pi} x^{-m} \prod_{j=k}^{n} |xe^{it} - z_j|^{-1} \, dt .$$

The maximum is taken over $\mathbf{z} = (z_1, \ldots, z_n)$ such that $|z_j| = a_j$, $j = 1, 2, \ldots, n$. So, we need an upper bound for $I_{m,k}(x)$. To find it, we use the following result of R. M. REDHEFFER and E. G. STRAUS:

(18) $$I_{m,k}(x) = \int_{-\pi}^{\pi} x^{-m} \prod_{j=k}^{n} |xe^{it} - a_j|^{-1} \, dt .$$

We take $r = [n/2]$ and consider two cases:

1) $$a_{r+1} \leqq 1 - \frac{2n}{(m+n)} .$$

Using Chebyshev's inequality, we can take x to satisfy $x\in\left[\frac{m}{m+n},\,1\right]$. Thus,

$$x^m\cdot|x-a_1|\dots|x-a_r|=\max_{\frac{m}{m+n}\leqq y\leqq 1} y^m\cdot|y-a_1|\dots|y-a_r|\geqq$$

$$\geqq\left(\frac{m}{m+n}\right)^m\cdot\left(\frac{n}{4(m+n)}\right)^r\geqq\left(\frac{n}{m+n}\right)^r\cdot(2e)^{-n}.$$

Then for $k\geqq r+1$ we have

$$I_{m,k}(x)\ll x^{-m}\prod_{j=k}^{n}|x-a_j|^{-1}\ll$$

$$\ll\left(\frac{m}{m+n}\right)^{-m}\cdot\left(\frac{n}{(m+n)}\right)^{-r}\ll\left(\frac{m+n}{n}\right)^r\cdot(2e)^n.$$

For $k\leqq r$ we use (18) and obtain:

$$I_{m,k}(x)=x^{-m}\int_{-\pi}^{\pi}\prod_{j=k}^{n}|xe^{it}-a_j|^{-1}\,dt\ll$$

$$\ll x^{-m}\prod_{j=1}^{r}|x-a_j|^{-1}\int_{-\pi}^{\pi}\prod_{j=r+1}^{n}|xe^{it}-a_j|^{-1}\,dt\ll$$

$$\ll(2e)^n\cdot\left(\frac{m+n}{n}\right)^r\cdot\int_{-\pi}^{\pi}\prod_{j=r+1}^{n}|xe^{it}-a_j|^{-1}\,dt.$$

Here

$$I\equiv\int_{-\pi}^{\pi}\prod_{j=r+1}^{n}|xe^{it}-a_j|^{-1}\,dt=4\int_{0}^{\pi/2}\prod_{j=r+1}^{n}\{(x-a_j)^2+4xa_j\sin^2 t\}^{-1/2}\,dt\ll$$

(19)

$$\ll\int_{0}^{\pi/4}\prod_{j=r+1}^{n}\left\{(x-a_j)^2+\frac{32}{\pi^2}xa_jt^2\right\}^{-1/2}+x^{r-n},$$

because for $t\leqq\frac{\pi}{4}$ we have $\sin t\geqq\frac{\sqrt{8}}{\pi}t$ and for $t\geqq\frac{\pi}{4}$ we have $(x-a_j)^2+4xa_j\sin^2 t\geqq x^2$.

Here $x\geqq\frac{m}{m+n}\geqq\frac{9}{10}$ and if $a_j\leqq\frac{2}{5}$, then $|x-a_j|\geqq 1/2$; if $a_j>2/5$ then $\frac{32}{2}xa_j\geqq 1$. So, if there are l values of a_j with $a_j\leqq 2/5$ then (19) yields

$$I\ll x^{r-n}+2^l\int_0^{\pi/4}\left(t^2+\frac{n^2}{(m+n)^2}\right)^{(r+l-n)/2}dt. \tag{20}$$

If $l \geqq n-r-3$ we get

$$I \ll x^{r-n} + 2^{n-r} \cdot \left(\frac{m+n}{n}\right)^3 \ll 2^n \cdot \left(\frac{m+n}{n}\right)^3.$$

If $l < n-r-3$ we set $s = t \cdot (m+n)/n$ and (20) yields

$$I \ll x^{r-n} + \max_{0 \leqq l \leqq n-r-4} 2^l \left(\frac{m+n}{n}\right)^{n-l-r-1} \int_0^\infty (s^2+1)^{(r+l-n)/2}\, ds. \tag{21}$$

For $q = [(n-l-r)/2] \geqq 2$ we have

$$\int_0^\infty (s^2+1)^{-q}\, ds = \pi i \operatorname{Res}((s^2+1)^{-q}, s=i) = \frac{\pi i}{(q-1)!} \frac{d^{q-1}}{ds^{q-1}} (s+i)^{-q} \Big|_{s=i} =$$

$$= \frac{\pi i}{(q-1)!} (-1)^{q-1} \frac{(2q-2)!}{(q-1)!} (2i)^{-2q+1} = 2\pi \binom{2q-2}{q-1} 4^{-q} \ll \frac{1}{\sqrt{q}}. \tag{22}$$

Thus substituting in (21) we get the maximum attained for $l=0$,

$$I \ll x^{r-n} + \frac{1}{\sqrt{n}} \left(\frac{(m+n)}{n}\right)^{n-r-1} \ll \frac{1}{\sqrt{n}} \left(\frac{m+n}{n}\right)^{n-r-1} \tag{23}$$

and

$$I_{m,k}(x) \ll (2e)^n \cdot \left(\frac{m+n}{n}\right)^r \cdot I \ll$$

$$\ll (2e)^n \cdot \frac{1}{\sqrt{n}} \cdot \left(\frac{m+n}{n}\right)^{n-1} \ll \frac{1}{\sqrt{n}} \cdot \left(\frac{2e(m+n)}{n}\right)^{n-1}.$$

So, in this case we obtain

$$M_{m,n} \Big/ \min_{1 \leqq j \leqq n} |b_1 + \ldots + b_j| \gg \sqrt{n} \cdot \left(\frac{n}{2e(m+n)}\right)^{n-1} \left(\sum_{k=1}^{n} 2^{n-k}\right)^{-1} \gg$$

$$\gg \sqrt{n} \cdot \left(\frac{n}{4e(m+n)}\right)^{n-1}.$$

2) $$a_{r+1} \geqq 1 - \frac{2n}{m+n}.$$

First, in a manner similar to the proof of (11), we can show that for $\delta=3.7n/(m+n)$

$$\max_{1-\delta\leqq y\leqq 1} y^m \prod_{j=1}^{n} |y-a_j| \gg \left(\frac{n}{2e(m+n)}\right)^n .$$

We take a number $x\in[1-\delta,\ 1]$, and obtain

$$(24)\qquad \begin{aligned} I_{m,k}(x) &\ll x^{-m}\prod_{j=k}^{n}|x-a_j|^{-1}\int_{-\pi}^{\pi}\prod_{j=k}^{n}|(x-a_j)/(xe^{it}-a_j)|\,dt \ll \\ &\ll (2e(m+n)/n)^n\cdot(3n/(m+n))^l\cdot I_1 , \end{aligned}$$

where $l=\min\{k-1;\ r+1\}$ and

$$I_1=\int_{-\pi}^{\pi}\prod_{j=k}^{n}|(x-a_j)/(xe^{it}-a_j)|\,dt .$$

Here $x\geqq 1-\delta\geqq 0.63$ and for $j\geqq r+1$

$$|x-a_j|\leqq\max\{1-x;\ 1-a_j\}\leqq\delta .$$

Set $a=a_{r+1}\geqq\frac{4}{5}$, and assume $k\leqq\log n+1$. Then, using (22), we get

$$\begin{aligned} I_1 &\ll \int_0^{\pi/2}\prod_{j=k}^{r+1}\{|x-a_j|^2/[(x-a_j)^2+4xa_j\sin^2 t]\}\,dt\ll \\ &\ll \int_0^{\pi/4}(\delta^2/(\delta^2+2xat^2))^{(r+2-k)/2}\,dt+\int_{\pi/4}^{\pi/2}(\delta^2/(\delta^2+a^2))^{(r+2-k)/2}\,dt\ll \\ &\ll \int_0^{\infty}(\delta^2/(t^2+\delta^2))^{(r+2-k)/2}\,dt+\frac{1}{m+n}\ll\frac{\delta}{\sqrt{r+2-k}}+\frac{1}{m+n}\ll\frac{\sqrt{n}}{m+n}. \end{aligned}$$

For $k>\log n+1$ we have

$$\left(\frac{3n}{m+n}\right)^l\ll\frac{\sqrt{n}}{m+n}\quad\text{and}\quad I_1\ll 1 .$$

Substituting in (24), we get

$$I_{m,k}(x)\ll\frac{\sqrt{n}}{m+n}\cdot\left(\frac{2e(m+n)}{n}\right)^n\ll\frac{1}{\sqrt{n}}\cdot\left(\frac{2e(m+n)}{n}\right)^{n-1},$$

which proves (17).

References

[1] T. W. CUSICK and G. KOLESNIK, "Turán's second theorem on the sums of powers of complex numbers", *Mich. Math. J.*, **26** (1979), 205–211.

[2] E. MAKAI, "On a minimum problem, II", *Acta Math. Acad. Sci. Hung.*, **15** (1964), 63–66.

[3] V. T. SÓS and P. TURÁN, "On some new theorems in the theory of Diophantine approximations", *Acta Math. Acad. Sci. Hung.*, **6** (1955), 241–255.

[4] P. TURÁN, *Eine neue Methode in der Analysis und deren Anwendungen*, Akadémiai Kiadó, Budapest, 1953.

[5] S. UCHIYAMA, "A note on the second main theorem of P. Turán", *Acta Math. Acad. Sci. Hung.*, **9** (1958), 379–380.

DEPARTMENT OF MATHEMATICS
UNIVERSITY OF TEXAS AT AUSTIN
U.S.A.

DEPARTMENT OF MATHEMATICS
UNIVERSITY OF CALIFORNIA, LOS ANGELES
U.S.A.

Studies in Pure Mathematics
To the Memory of Paul Turán

On a monotonicity property of some Hausdorff transforms of certain Fourier series[1]

by

L. LORCH (Downsview) and D. J. NEWMAN (Philadelphia)

1. Introduction

This paper, dedicated to PAUL TURÁN in admiration and affection, and with a lasting personal and scientific sense of loss, arises directly from his own work [5]. With him, we consider functions $f(\vartheta)$ which are positive and concave in $0<\vartheta<\pi$, with $f(0)=f(\pi)=0$. The class of such functions is denoted by $\mathscr{F}$.

For $f\in\mathscr{F}$,

$$f(\vartheta)=0+b_1\sin\vartheta+\ldots+b_n\sin n\vartheta+\ldots;\quad 0\leqq\vartheta\leqq\pi \tag{1}$$

$S_n^{(C,k)}(\vartheta)$ denotes the n-th Cesàro mean of order k of this series. TURÁN proved that these means form a monotonic sequence, i.e.,

$$S_n^{(C,1)}(\vartheta)>S_n^{(C,2)}(\vartheta)>\ldots>0,\quad 0<\vartheta<\pi,\quad n=1,2,\ldots, \tag{2}$$

and remarked that the same property holds also for the Hölder (H,k) means, $k=1,2,\ldots$, for which the corresponding quantities can be designated as $S_n^{(H,k)}(\vartheta)$.

Earlier, FEJÉR [1] had shown that, for $f\in\mathscr{F}$,

$$f(\vartheta)\geqq S_n^{(C,k)}(\vartheta)>0,\quad n,k=1,2,\ldots,\quad 0<\vartheta<\pi, \tag{3}$$

and had stated that this remains true when (C,k) is replaced by (H,k).

The positivity part of (3) holds for all $k\geqq 0$, non-integer as well as integer, for both (C,k) and (H,k) means, indeed for any totally regular [2, p. 10] Hausdorff method. This follows from a result due to L. KOSCHMIEDER [3] establishing this for $k=0$, since the matrix defining a totally regular Hausdorff method has exclusively non-negative elements [2, Theorem 199, p. 250, p. 257].

A result implying positivity is given as Theorem 3, with an example showing that it implies positivity in some cases not covered by KOSCHMIEDER's result. But the (C,k),

[1] This work was supported by the National Research Council of Canada.

(H, k) and $\{t^k\}$ methods considered in §§ 4, 5, 6, are all totally regular, and Theorem 3 yields less information in these cases than does Koschmieder's result.

Turán's monotonicity theorem leads one to wonder if (2) can be extended from (C, k) or (H, k), for $k = 1, 2, \ldots$, to all $k \geqq 1$, fractional as well as integral, or even to a broader class of Hausdorff summation methods, of which (C, k) and (H, k) are special cases. We shall consider this question here.

It will be shown, i.e., that $S_n^{(C,k)}(\vartheta)$ decreases for each $n = 1, 2, \ldots, 0 < \vartheta < \pi$, as $k\left(\geqq \frac{3}{2}\right)$ increases continuously, that $S_n^{(H,k)}(\vartheta)$ behaves similarly for $k \geqq 2$. Simple counter-examples (for $n = 2$) show that the $\frac{3}{2}$ in the Cesàro case cannot be reduced below $2^{1/2}$; in the Hölder case, 2 cannot go below $(\log\log 3 - \log\log 2)/(\log 3 - \log 2) = 1.13\ldots < 2^{1/2}$. But we do not know, in either case, the least value of k at which monotonicity starts uniformly in n. In both cases, this least value can be shown to approach 1 as $n \to \infty$.

On the other hand, it turns out that no result analogous to (2) holds for the Euler (E, k) means, another important subclass of the Hausdorff methods.

Our study of the (C, k) and (H, k) methods in this context is, nonetheless, based on their respective characterizations as Hausdorff methods. Criteria for the extension of (2) and the positivity part of (3) to a class of regular Hausdorff methods are established in §3, applied to (C, k) in §4, to (H, k) in §5, and to another special class of Hausdorff methods (considered by J. Mann [4]) in §6. Two elementary lemmas which are used in §§4 and 6 constitute §2.

The various definitions and properties of the summation methods examined here are the standard ones, as found, say, in [2].

Following Fejér [1], Turán [5] noted that the monotonicity properties at issue in his work follow for the entire class of functions under consideration once they are established for the "roof function" $R(\vartheta)$ whose sine series is

$$R(\vartheta) \sim \frac{2b}{a(\pi - a)}\left[\frac{\sin a \sin \vartheta}{1^2} + \ldots + \frac{\sin na \sin n\vartheta}{n^2} + \ldots\right],$$

where $0 < a < \pi$ and $b > 0$, and that, it is sufficient to consider the transformations of

$$\frac{\sin \vartheta}{1} + \ldots + \frac{\sin n\vartheta}{n} + \ldots,$$

obtained from the series for $R(\vartheta)$ by letting $a \downarrow 0$, and putting $b = \frac{1}{2}\pi$.

The same is true for the extensions discussed here and for the same reasons. Our calculations, therefore, will be confined to this test function.

2. Elementary lemmas

Two companion lemmas are applicable to the transition from the general criteria concerning general Hausdorff methods, the first to the Cesàro means (§4), the second to certain special Hausdorff means (§6) considered by J. MANN [4].

Lemma 1. *For* $0 \leqq a < b$, $a+b \geqq 1$, *the positive function*

$$F_1(t) = \frac{t^a - t^b}{1-t}$$

increases in $0<t<1$, *except for* $a=0$, $b=1$ *when* $F_1(t) \equiv 1$.

Proof. We may assume $a \leqq 1$, for, if $a>1$, then the increasing function t^{a-1} can be factored out, reducing the problem to the case $a=1$ (so that again $a+b \geqq 1$).

The positivity of the derivative of $F_1(t)$ can now be established as follows:

$$g(t) \equiv (1-t)^2 F_1'(t) = at^{a-1} - bt^{b-1} - at^a + bt^b + t^a - t^b .$$

Clearly, $g(1)=0$ and so $F_1'(t)$ will be seen to be positive once it is shown that $g'(t)<0$, $0<t<1$.

Now,

$$-g'(t) = a(1-a)t^{a-2}(1-t) - b(1-b)t^{b-2}(1-t),$$

so that it suffices to show that

$$a(1-a)t^a > b(1-b)t^b, \quad 0<t<1 .$$

But $a(1-a)-b(1-b)=(a+b-1)(b-a) \geqq 0$, while $t^a > t^b$, $0<t<1$, and the proof is complete.

Remark. The conclusion does not hold if $a+b<1$.

Lemma 2. *The positive function*

$$F_2(t) = \frac{t^a - t^b}{1-t}, \quad a \leqq 0 \leqq b, \quad a<b,$$

decreases in $0<t<1$, *provided* $a+b \leqq 1$, *in particular when* $b \leqq 1$, *except for* $a=0$, $b=1$, *when* $F_2(t) \equiv 1$.

Proof. Let $g(t)=(1-t)^2 F_2'(t)$ and $h(t)=t^{2-a}(1-t)^{-1}g'(t)$. Then

$$h(t) = a(a-1) - b(b-1)t^{b-a} .$$

When $b \leqq 1$, then clearly $h(t) > 0$ (except when $a=0$, $b=1$). When $b>1$, it suffices to show that $a(a-1)-b(b-1) \geqq 0$. But $a(a-1)-b(b-1)=(a-b)(a+b-1)$. Thus, $g'(t)>0$, $0<t<1$, and so $g(t)$ increases to $g(1)=0$. Hence, $F_2'(t)<0$, $0<t<1$, as required.

Remark. When $a=0$, $b>1$, or when $a>0$, the result is false.

3. Criteria for regular Hausdorff methods

Here are established general results which, with the aid of §2, will be applied to special cases in subsequent sections. These criteria are found in Theorems 2 and 3, which are essentially the applicable forms of Theorem 1.

Theorem 1. *If $\varphi(t)$ is a non-negative, non-increasing function (not identically zero) in $0<t<1$, then*

$$\operatorname{Im} \int_0^1 (1-t+te^{i\vartheta})^n (1-t)\varphi(t)dt > 0, \quad 0<\vartheta<\pi,$$

$n=1, 2, \ldots$.

Proof. The desired assertion would, from BONNET's form of the second mean-value theorem of integral calculus, follow from the inequalities

$$\operatorname{Im} \int_0^x (1-t+te^{i\vartheta})^n (1-t)\, dt > 0, \quad 0<x\leqq 1,$$

$0<\vartheta<\pi$, $n=1, 2, \ldots$. The integral becomes, on putting $s=1-(1-e^{i\vartheta})t$, $\alpha=1-(1-e^{i\vartheta})x$,

$$I_n(x) \equiv \int_0^x (1-t+te^{i\vartheta})^n(1-t)\, dt = (1-e^{i\vartheta})^{-2} \int_\alpha^1 s^n(s-e^{i\vartheta})\, ds =$$

$$= (1-e^{i\vartheta})^{-2}\left\{\left[\frac{1}{n+2}-\frac{e^{i\vartheta}}{n+1}\right]-\left[\frac{(1-(1-e^{i\vartheta})x)^{n+2}}{n+2}-\right.\right.$$

$$\left.\left.-\frac{e^{i\vartheta}(1-(1-e^{i\vartheta})x)^{n+1}}{n+1}\right]\right\}.$$

Now, $(1-e^{i\vartheta})^2=-2(1-\cos\vartheta)e^{i\vartheta}$, i.e., the left side is a negative constant times $e^{i\vartheta}$, and so

$$I_n(x) = \frac{-c}{e^{i\vartheta}(n+1)(n+2)}[(n+1)-(n+2)e^{i\vartheta}+$$

$$+\{e^{i\vartheta}-(n+1)(1-e^{i\vartheta})(1-x)\}(1-x+xe^{i\vartheta})^{n+1}],$$

where c is a positive constant.

Clearly, $I_n(0)=0$, while

$$I_n(1)=-c_1 e^{-i\vartheta}[e^{i(n+2)\vartheta}-(n+2)e^{i\vartheta}+n+1],$$

where c_1 is a positive constant. Hence

$$\operatorname{Im} I_n(1)=c_2[(n+1)\sin\vartheta-\sin(n+1)\vartheta],$$

where c_2 is a positive constant. Therefore,

$$\operatorname{Im} I_n(1)>0, \quad 0<\vartheta<\pi, \quad n=1, 2, \ldots .$$

For $0<x<1$, the definition of $I_n(x)$ as an integral shows that

$$\frac{d}{dx}\{\operatorname{Im} I_n(x)\}=(1-x)\operatorname{Im}\{(1-x+xe^{i\vartheta})^n\},$$

so that the extreme values of $\operatorname{Im} I_n(x)$, $0\leqq x\leqq 1$, occur either at the endpoints $x=0$, $x=1$, or where $(1-x+xe^{i\vartheta})^n$ is real.

Thus, from the integrated form of $I_n(x)$, we see that, at any extreme value of $I_n(x)$, $0<x<1$,

$$\operatorname{Im}\{c^{-1}(n+1)(n+2)I_n(x)\} =$$

$$=(n+1)\sin\vartheta+(n+1)(1-x+xe^{i\vartheta})^n(1-x)\operatorname{Im}\{(e^{-i\vartheta}-1)(1-x+xe^{i\vartheta})\},$$

since $(1-x+xe^{i\vartheta})^n$ is real at the extreme values, $0<x<1$.

But, $\operatorname{Im}\{(e^{-i\vartheta}-1)(1-x+xe^{i\vartheta})\}=-\sin\vartheta$, and so at the interior extreme values,

$$\operatorname{Im}\{c^{-1}(n+1)(n+2)I_n(x)\}=(n+1)\sin\vartheta[1-(1-x)(1-x+xe^{i\vartheta})^n].$$

The real number $(1-x+xe^{i\vartheta})^n\leqq 1$, while $1-x<1$, $0<x<1$, so that

$$\operatorname{Im} I_n(x)>0, \quad 0<\vartheta<\pi,$$

at any extreme value in $0<x<1$.

Clearly, therefore, $\operatorname{Im}\{I_n(x)\}>0$, $0<x\leqq 1$, $0<\vartheta<\pi$, since this quantity is positive at all extreme values in $0<x\leqq 1$ and $I_n(0)=0$.

This proves the theorem.

From this theorem there follows immediately a criterion for a result for Hausdorff means extending the TURÁN monotonicity theorem for (C, k) means of sine series of the functions in class $\mathscr{F}$.

But first we require a formula expressing the transform of $\sum \nu^{-1}\sin \nu\vartheta$ appropriately. This is provided by the next lemma.

Lemma 3. *Let* $S_n^{\{\mu\}}(\vartheta)$ *denote the transform of* $\sum_{\nu=1}^{n} \nu^{-1} \sin \nu\vartheta$ *under the regular Hausdorff method generated by* $\mu(t)$. *Then, for* $n=1, 2, \ldots,$

$$S_n^{\{\mu\}}(\vartheta) = \operatorname{Im} \int_0^1 (1-t+te^{i\vartheta})^n t^{-1}[1-\mu(t)]\, dt\,.$$

Proof. The result is clear for $\vartheta=0$, both sides vanishing there, so we need verify only that the derivatives are equal, i.e., that the sum

$$\cos \vartheta + \cos 2\vartheta + \ldots + \cos n\vartheta$$

is transformed, under $\mu(t)$, into

$$\operatorname{Im} \int_0^1 n(1-t+te^{i\vartheta})^{n-1} ie^{i\vartheta}[1-\mu(t)]\, dt\,,$$

But,

$$\cos \vartheta + \ldots + \cos n\vartheta = \operatorname{Im} \frac{e^{in\vartheta}-1}{1-e^{-i\vartheta}}\, i$$

and so, by definition, the transform by $\mu(t)$ is

$$\int_0^1 \operatorname{Im} \left\{ \frac{(te^{i\vartheta}+1-t)^n - 1}{1-e^{-i\vartheta}}\, i \right\} d\mu(t)\,.$$

Under integration by parts this becomes

$$\int_0^1 [1-\mu(t)] \operatorname{Im} \left\{ \frac{(e^{i\vartheta}-1)n(te^{i\vartheta}+1-t)^{n-1}}{1-e^{-i\vartheta}}\, i \right\} dt =$$

$$= \int_0^1 [1-\mu(t)] \operatorname{Im} \left\{ ine^{i\vartheta}(te^{i\vartheta}+1-t)^{n-1} \right\} dt\,,$$

as required, and the lemma is proved.

Theorem 2. *Let* $S_n^{\{\mu_j\}}(\vartheta)$ *denote the transform of the sine series of* $f(\vartheta) \in \mathcal{F}$ *by the regular Hausdorff mean with weight function* $\mu_j(t)$, $j=1, 2$. *Suppose that* $\mu_2(t) \geqq \mu_1(t)$, *with* $\mu_2(t) \not\equiv \mu_1(t)$, *and that*

$$\frac{\mu_2(t)-\mu_1(t)}{t(1-t)}$$

is non-increasing, $0<t<1$. *Then*

$$S_n^{\{\mu_1\}}(\vartheta) > S_n^{\{\mu_2\}}(\vartheta)\,, \quad 0<\vartheta<\pi\,, \quad n=1, 2, \ldots\,.$$

Proof. This is an immediate consequence of Theorem 1 and Lemma 3, since (as explained in [5]) we may restrict ourselves to the series $\sum_1^n \nu^{-1} \sin \nu\vartheta$. For this series we have, from Lemma 3,

$$S_n^{\{\mu_1\}}(\vartheta) - S_n^{\{\mu_2\}}(\vartheta) = \operatorname{Im} \int_0^1 (1-t+te^{i\vartheta})^n (1-t) \frac{\mu_2(t)-\mu_1(t)}{t(1-t)}\, dt,$$

to which Theorem 1 applies directly.

Another application of Theorem 1 is also immediate, one which permits further positivity results.

Theorem 3. *With the notation of Theorem 2, still applied to functions in* $\mathscr{F}$, *let*

$$\nu(t) = \frac{1-\mu(t)}{t(1-t)}$$

be non-negative and non-increasing. $0<t<1$. *Then* $S_n^{\{\mu\}}(\vartheta)>0$, $0<\vartheta<\pi$, $n=1, 2, \ldots$.

Proof. Again it suffices to use the test series $\sum_1^n \nu^{-1} \sin \nu\vartheta$, so that Theorem 1 applies, now with $\varphi(t)=t^{-1}(1-t)^{-1}[1-\mu(t)]$.

Remark. For the regular Hausdorff method generated by the weight function

$$\mu(t) = \begin{cases} 1-2\pi t(1-t)\csc 2\pi t, & 0 \leqq t \leqq 1/4, \\ 1, & 1/4<t\leqq 1, \end{cases}$$

we have $S_n^{\{\mu\}}(\vartheta)>0$, $0<\vartheta<\pi$, $n=1, 2, \ldots$, from Theorem 3, since here

$$\nu(t) = \begin{cases} 2\pi \csc 2\pi t, & 0<t\leqq 1/4, \\ 0, & 1/4<t<1, \end{cases}$$

a non-increasing function. However, this method, while regular, is not totally regular, since $\mu(1/4)=1-3\pi/8<0$; a Hausdorff method is totally regular only if $\mu(t)\geqq 0$, $0\leqq t\leqq 1$. Thus, this method is one for which KOSCHMIEDER's result does not imply that $S_n^{\{\mu\}}(\vartheta)>0$, $0<\vartheta<\pi$, $n=1, 2, \ldots$, while Theorem 3 does.

4. Cesàro means

The TURÁN monotonicity results (2) can now be extended to certain fractional orders of Cesàro summation.

Theorem 4. *For* $0<\vartheta<\pi$, $n=1, 2, \ldots$,

(i) $$S_n^{(C,k)}(\vartheta) > S_n^{(C,j)}(\vartheta), \quad \textit{when} \quad j>k\geqq 1 \quad \textit{and} \quad k+j\geqq 3,$$

so that, in particular,

(ii) $$S_n^{(C,k)}(\vartheta) > S_n^{(C,j)}(\vartheta), \quad \text{when} \quad j > k \geqq \frac{3}{2},$$

and

(iii) $$S_n^{(C,k)}(\vartheta) > S_n^{(C,k+1)}(\vartheta), \quad \text{when} \quad k \geqq 1.$$

Proof. The weight function for the (C, k) means is $\mu(t) = 1 - (1-t)^k$, so that (with $s = 1 - t$)

$$\varphi(t) = \frac{(1-t^k)-(1-t^j)}{t(1-t)} = \frac{s^k - s^j}{s(1-s)} = \frac{s^{k-1} - s^{j-1}}{1-s},$$

which, from Lemma 1, increases with s, $0 < s < 1$ (and hence decreases as t increases), when $0 \leqq k-1 < j-1$ and $(k-1)+(j-1) \geqq 1$, with the obvious exception of the case where $k=1$, $j=2$. Theorem 2 now yields the desired result, including the case $k=1$, $j=2$.

Remarks. It would be reasonable to ask if Theorem 4 (ii) holds for all $k \geqq 1$, not only for $k \geqq \frac{3}{2}$, $n = 1, 2, \ldots$. However, the answer is negative. It can be shown that the (C, k) mean of the second partial sum of $\sum_1^\infty \nu^{-1} \sin \nu\vartheta$, i.e., of $\sin \vartheta + \frac{1}{2} \sin 2\vartheta$, does not decrease for some ϑ, $0 < \vartheta < \pi$, when k passes through $2^{\frac{1}{2}}$. The details can be checked by considering $\frac{d}{dk} S_2^{(C,k)}(\vartheta)$ at $k = 2^{\frac{1}{2}}$.

5. Hölder means

Similar, but not identical, results can be established for the Hölder means (H, k). The weight function for these means is

$$\mu_k(t) = \frac{1}{\Gamma(k)} \int_0^t \log^{k-1}(1/x)\, dx, \quad 0 \leqq t \leqq 1,$$

rather more complicated than the (C, k) weights. However, TURÁN's assertion that (2) holds for Hölder means can be justified readily (by Theorem 2), even in the more general form of Theorem 4 (iii), where $k \geqq 1$ need not be an integer.

To see this, we note that

$$\varphi(t) = \frac{\mu_{k+1}(t) - \mu_k(t)}{t(1-t)} = \frac{1}{\Gamma(k+1)} \frac{\log^k(1/t)}{1-t}.$$

This formula can be proved by differentiation. We are required to prove that

$$f_1(t) \equiv \Gamma(k+1)[\mu_{k+1}(t) - \mu_k(t)] = t \log^k(1/t) \equiv f_2(t) .$$

From the definition of $\mu_k(t)$, and the familiar functional equation $\Gamma(k+1) = k\Gamma(k)$, it follows that

$$f'_1(t) = \log^k(1/t) - k \log^{k-1}(1/t) ;$$

$f'_2(t)$ clearly has the same value. Moreover, $f_1(0) = f_2(0+) = 0$ and so the formula for $\varphi(t)$ is verified.

Thus, Theorem 2 yields our assertion, once it is shown that $\varphi'(t) < 0$, $0 < t < 1$, for $k \geqq 1$.

Now,

$$\Gamma(k+1)(1-t)^2 t\varphi'(t) = [\log^{k-1}(1/t)]\,[t \log(1/t) - k(1-t)] .$$

The second factor on the right will be negative for all $k > 1$, if its value for $k = 1$, denoted by $\varphi_1(t)$, is negative, $0 < t < 1$. But this is clearly the case, since $\varphi_1(1) = 0$ and $\varphi'_1(t) = \log(1/t) > 0$, $0 < t < 1$.

A more comprehensive result can be established, but this requires more calculation. The next theorem incorporates both results.

Theorem 5. *For* $0 < \vartheta < \pi$, $n = 1, 2, \ldots,$ *we have*

(i) $$S_n^{(H,k)}(\vartheta) > S_n^{(H,j)}(\vartheta), \quad \textit{for} \quad j > k \geqq 2 ,$$

and

(ii) $$S_n^{(H,k)}(\vartheta) > S_n^{(H,k+1)}(\vartheta), \quad \textit{for} \quad k \geqq 1 .$$

Proof. The argument for (ii) has been given already.

To establish (i), it suffices (in view of Theorem 2) to show that the positive function

$$\frac{\mu_j(t) - \mu_k(t)}{t(1-t)}, \quad 0 < t < 1, \quad j > k ,$$

decreases in t for each fixed $j > k$ when $k \geqq 2$.

It simplifies matters considerably to note that it is sufficient to prove (i) for $k = 2$; its validity for $k > 2$ then follows from the group structure of the family (H, k) of Hölder methods. The point here is that the (H, α) transform of the (H, β) mean of a sequence s_n is the $(H, \alpha + \beta)$ mean of s and that (H, k) is a linear operator [2]. Moreover, when $\alpha > 0$, as in the present application, the coefficients in the transform are all non-negative so that if the (H, β) mean of s_n is positive, then the $(H, \alpha + \beta)$ mean of s_n is also positive for each $\alpha > 0$.

In the present instance, we take $\beta = 0$, $j > 2$, $s_n = S_n^{(H,2)}(\vartheta) - S_n^{(H,j)}(\vartheta)$, and we shall prove that $s_n > 0$, $0 < \vartheta < \pi$.

Once it is established that

$$\frac{\partial\mu_k(t)/\partial k}{t(1-t)}$$

is decreasing in t for $k=2$, then the monotonicity we require follows on integrating this last expression (with respect to k) from 2 to j.

Now,

$$\Gamma(k)\frac{\partial\mu_k(t)}{\partial k} = \int_0^t [\log(1/x)]^{k-1}\left[\log\log(1/x) - \frac{\Gamma'(k)}{\Gamma(k)}\right]dx\,.$$

Thus,

$$\left.\frac{\partial\mu_k(t)}{\partial k}\right|_{k=2} = \int_0^t [\log(1/x)]\,[\log\log(1/x) - \Gamma'(2)]\,dx\,.$$

To apply Theorem 2, we need to show that

$$\frac{\partial\mu_k(t)/\partial k}{t(1-t)}, \quad k=2\,,$$

decreases in $0<t<1$. Since $[\log(1/t)]/(1-t)$ decreases in $0<t<1$, it suffices to prove that

$$f(t)=[t\log(1/t)]^{-1}\int_0^t \log(1/x)\,[\log\log(1/x)-\Gamma'(2)]\,dx$$

decreases, $0<t<1$.

Changing variables, by putting $x=e^{-\tau}$ and writing $t=e^{-u}$, $f(t)$ becomes (with $s=\tau-u$)

$$\varphi(u)=u^{-1}e^{u}\int_u^\infty e^{-\tau}\tau(\log\tau-\Gamma'(2))\,d\tau=u^{-1}\int_0^\infty e^{-s}F(s+u)\,ds\,,$$

where

$$F(\tau)=\tau(\log\tau-\Gamma'(2))\,.$$

We wish to show that $\varphi(u)$ increases with u. To do so, we consider

$$\Phi(u)\equiv u^2\varphi'(u)=u\int_0^\infty e^{-s}F'(s+u)\,ds - \int_0^\infty e^{-s}F(s+u)\,ds\,.$$

Now,

$$\Phi(0) = -\int_0^\infty e^{-s}F(s)\,ds\,.$$

Differentiating the integral representation of $\Gamma(x)$ gives

$$\Gamma'(x) = \int_0^\infty e^{-s} s^{x-1} \log s \, ds$$

so that

$$\Gamma'(2) = \int_0^\infty e^{-s} s \log s \, ds\,;$$

hence $\Phi(0)=0$.

Moreover,

$$\Phi'(u) = u \int_0^\infty e^{-s} F''(s+u)\, ds\,.$$

But $F''(\tau)=1/\tau>0$ and so $\varphi'(u)>0$ and the theorem is proved.

6. Another family of special Hausdorff methods

Here we consider the regular Hausdorff means studied by J. MANN [4] chiefly for their associated Gibbs phenomenon. The weight function is $\mu_k(t)=t^k$, $k>0$. These methods are all equivalent to one another and consequently to $(C, 1)$, but they exhibit the Gibbs phenomenon when and only when $k \geqq n_0$ where n_0 is a certain constant such that $1<n_0<2$. Their behaviour in this context reflects a similar pattern. The notation is an obvious adaptation of that of §3.

Theorem 6. *If $j \geqq 1 \geqq k>0$, $j>k$, and $k+j \leqq 3$, then*

$$S_n^{\{t^j\}}(\vartheta) > S_n^{\{t^k\}}(\vartheta), \quad 0<\vartheta<\pi\,,$$

$n=1, 2, 3, \ldots.$

Proof. Here

$$0 < \frac{\mu_k(t)-\mu_j(t)}{t(1-t)} = \frac{t^{k-1}-t^{j-1}}{1-t}\,.$$

This decreases, under our hypotheses, according to Lemma 2 (with $a=k-1$, $b=j-1$), so that this theorem follows from Theorem 2.

Corollary. *If $1<j \leqq 2$, and $0<k<1$, then*

$$S_n^{\{t^j\}}(\vartheta) > S_n^{(C,1)}(\vartheta) > S_n^{\{t^k\}}(\vartheta) > 0,$$

$0<\vartheta<\pi$, $n=1, 2, \ldots.$

Remark. The left inequality displays a totally regular Hausdorff method which transforms the sine series of a function in $\mathscr{F}$ into a larger value than does $(C, 1)$.

References

[1] L. FEJÉR, Gestaltliches über die Partialsummen und ihre Mittelwerte bei der Fourierreihe und der Potenzreihe, *Zeits. f. angew. Math. und Mech.*, **13** (1933), 80–88.
[2] G. H. HARDY, *Divergent Series*, Oxford Univ. Press, 1949.
[3] L. KOSCHMIEDER, Vorzeicheneigenschaften der Abschnitte einiger physikalisch bedeutsamer Reihen, *Monatshefte f. Math. und Phys.*, **39** (1932), 321–344.
[4] J. MANN, Hausdorff means and the Gibbs phenomenon, *Trans. Amer. Math. Soc.*, **121** (1966), 277–295.
[5] P. TURÁN, Über die arithmetischen Mittel der Fourierreihe, *J. London Math. Soc.*, **10** (1935), 277–280.

YORK UNIVERSITY,
DOWNSVIEW, ONTARIO, CANADA.

TEMPLE UNIVERSITY,
PHILADELPHIA, PENNSYLVANIA, U.S.A.

Studies in Pure Mathematics
To the Memory of Paul Turán

Theorem of Budan–Fourier and Birkhoff interpolation

by

G. G. LORENTZ[1] (Austin)

In this note we would like to point out the close relation which exists between the theorem of BUDAN–FOURIER and lacunary or BIRKHOFF interpolation — a subject to which P. TURÁN himself made important contributions. In this way we obtain a generalization of this theorem, which in its simplest form asserts that the number Z_0 of zeros of a polynomial P of degree n in (a, b) satisfies

$$Z_0 \leqq S^- \{P^{(k)}(a)\} - S^+ \leqq P^{(k)}(b)\} . \tag{1}$$

As usual, we denote by $S^-\{c_k\}_0^n$ or $S^+\{c_k\}_0^n$ the number of changes of sign in the sequence c_k, when zero terms are disregarded, or respectively assigned signs $\pm$ so as to maximize this number. One has the identity $S^+\{(-1)^k c_k\} + S^-\{c_k\} = n$.

Let $\mathbf{E} = (e_{ik})$ be an $m \times (n+1)$ matrix of zeros and ones, which is conservative: contains no odd supported sequences (see [1], [2], [3]). It satisfies the PÓLYA *condition* if the number $M(k)$ of ones in the columns $0 \leqq l \leqq k$ of $\mathbf{E}$ is at least $k+1$, for $k = 0, \ldots, n$; it satisfies the BIRKHOFF *condition*, if $M(k) \geqq k+2$, $k = 0, \ldots, n-1$.

Let f be an n times continuously differentiable functions on $[a, b]$. We need the notion of zeros of f in *wide sense* in this interval. For $a < \alpha < b$, α is a zero of f if and only if $f(\alpha) = 0$, with usual multiplicity. On the other hand, $\alpha = a$ is a zero of f under the new definition, if either $f(a) = 0$ or else $f(a) f^{(k)}(a) > 0$, where k is the smallest integer $k = 1, \ldots, n$ with $f^{(k)}(a) \neq 0$. Similarly, b is a zero if $f(b) = 0$ or if $f(b)(-1)^k f^{(k)}(b) > 0$, with the similarly defined k. We shall say that a matrix $\mathbf{E}$ and the set of knots X: $a = x_0 < \ldots < x_m = b$ *annihilate* f, if for each pair i, k with $e_{ik} = 1$, x_i is a zero of $f^{(k)}$ in the wide sense.

Theorem 1. *If a conservative matrix* $\mathbf{E}$ *and a set of knots* X: $a = x_1 < \ldots < x_m = b$ *annihilate a polynomial* P *of (exact) degree* n, *and if* $\mathbf{E}$ *lists all zeros of* P *in wide sense at a*

[1] Supported, in part, by Grant MCS77-0946 of the National Science Foundation.

and b, then

$$S^+\{(-1)^k P^{(k)}(a)\} + Z + S^+\{P^{(k)}(b)\} \leqq n\,, \tag{2}$$

where Z is the number of zeros in (a, b) of various derivatives of P, listed by **E**.

Proof. It is essential that we have the following ROLLE's lemma for an n times continuously differentiable function f on $[a, b]$:

Lemma 1. *Between any two adjacent zeros $\alpha<\beta$ in wide sense of f on $[a, b]$, there is an odd number of zeros of f' (with multiplicities counted).*

Let, for example, $f(x)>0$ on (α, β). It is sufficient to show that $f'(x)>0$ for $x>\alpha$, x close to α, and that $f'(x)<0$ for $x<\beta$, x close to β. This is obvious for ordinary zeros α, β, but is also true if one or both of α, β are generalized zeros. Let, for example, $\beta=b$, $f(b)\neq 0$. Then $f(b)>0$, hence $(-1)^k f^{(k)}(b)>0$, and from Taylor's expansion,

$$f'(x)=\frac{(x-b)^{k-1}}{(k-1)!}f^{(k)}(b)+\ldots<0 \quad \text{for} \quad x<b\,,$$

if x is close to b. ∎

Lemma 2. *Let f be an n-times continuously differentiable function, annihilated in the wide sense by* **E**, *X, where* **E** *is a conservative matrix, having at least $n+1$ ones. Then for some α, $a\leqq\alpha\leqq b$, $f^{(n)}(\alpha)=0$.*

Proof. Let $\mathbf{E}_k$, $k=0, \ldots, n$, be the $m\times(n-k+1)$ matrix consisting of columns l of **E**, $k\leqq l\leqq n$. Since **E** has at least $n+1$ ones, for some k, $\mathbf{E}_k$ has at least $n-k+1$ ones. Let k_0 be the *largest* such k. One sees that E_{k_0} satistifes the PÓLYA condition, in fact even the BIRKHOFF condition. We apply to the function $f^{(k_0)}$ repeatedly ROLLE's Lemma 1 and by a standard argument ([1], [3]) arrive at the desired conclusion. ∎

To prove Theorem 1, we count the number of ones in the matrix **E**. Rows $1<i<m$ contain at least Z ones, corresponding to the listed zeros of derivatives of P in (a, b). For $i=1$, there are $s_a=C+N$ ones from zeros of $P^{(k)}$ for $x=a$ in the wide sense, where N is the number of ordinary zeros, and C is the number of constancies of sign in the sequence $P(a), \ldots, P^{(n)}(a)$ (disregarding zero terms). Thus, s_a is equal to the maximal number of constancies of sign in this sequence, when zero terms are assigned signs arbitrarily. In other words, $s_a=S^+\{(-1)^k P^{(k)}(a)\}_0^n$. Similarly, $s_b=S^+\{P^{(k)}(b)\}_0^n$.

It is now sufficient to remark that the number s_a+Z+s_b must be less than $n+1$, for otherwise $P^{(n)}(x)$ would vanish, and P would not be a polynomial of (exact) degree n. ∎

Remarks. 1) Theorem 1 remains valid even if only $\mathbf{E}_{k_0}$ (see proof) is conservative and has at least $n-k_0+1$ ones.

2) Inequality (2) can also be written in the form

$$Z \leqq S^{-}\{P^{(k)}(a)\} - S^{+}\{P^{(k)}(b)\}. \tag{3}$$

The example of $P_2 = 1 + x^2$ on $[-1, +1]$ shows that the difference of two sides in (3) need not be even, also that one can have strict inequality in (3) for all possible choices of $\mathbf{E}$.

3) Inequality (1) follows from Theorem 1, since one can always select $\mathbf{E}$ so that $Z_0 \leqq Z$. There are, in general, many possible choices of $\mathbf{E}$ in Theorem 1. The advantage of this theorem is that it counts different zeros than (1) and perhaps more of them. Only positions of zeros of $P^{(k)}(x)$ inside of (a, b) must be known, not the distribution of the signs of these derivatives.

4) It is instructive to compare Theorem 1 with the form of Budan–Fourier theorem proposed by Melkman [4, p. 257]. It is easy to see that it counts even sequences of zeros $P^{(k)}(x) = \ldots = P^{(k+2l-1)}(x) = 0$ in the same way as we do, but odd sequences are counted differently.

References

[1] G. G. Lorentz, Monotone approximation, pp. 201–215, in: *Inequalities III* (editor O. Shisha), Academic Press, New York, 1972.

[2] G. G. Lorentz and S. D. Riemenschneider, Recent progress in Birkhoff interpolation, pp. 187–236, in: *Approximation Theory and Functional Analysis* (editor J. B. Prolla), Nort-Holland, Inc., Amsterdam, 1979.

[3] G. G. Lorentz and K. L. Zeller, Birkhoff interpolation, SIAM *J. Numer. Anal.*, **8** (1971), 43–48.

[4] A. A. Melkman, The BUDAN–FOURIER theorem for splines, *Israel J. Math.*, **19** (1974), 256–263.

UNIVERSITY OF TEXAS
AUSTIN, U.S.A.

Studies in Pure Mathematics
To the Memory of Paul Turán

On the number of complete subgraphs of a graph II

by

L. LOVÁSZ and M. SIMONOVITS (Budapest)

Abstract

Generalizing some results of P. ERDŐS and some of L. MOSER and J. W. MOON we give lower bounds on the number of complete p-graphs K_p of graphs in terms of the numbers of vertices and edges. Further, for some values of n and E we give a complete characterization of the extremal graphs, i.e. the graphs S of n vertices and E edges having minimum number of K_p's. Our results contain the proof of the longstanding conjecture of P. ERDŐS that a graph G^n with $[n^2/4]+k$ edges contains at least $k\left[\frac{n}{2}\right]$ triangles if $k<n/2$.

0. Notation

The graphs in this paper will be denoted by capital letters. We shall exclude loops and multiple edges, and all graphs will be non-oriented.

Let G be a graph: $e(G)$ will denote the number of edges of G, $v(G)=n$ the number of vertices. If x is a vertex, $st(x)$ will denote the set of neighbors of x, that is the set of vertices joined to x. $\sigma(x)$ will denote the cardinality of $st(x)$, that is, the degree of x and if we consider more graphs on the same set of vertices, $st_G(x)$, $\sigma_G(x)$ will denote the star and the degree in G. If G is a graph and A is a set of vertices of G, then $G(A)$ will denote the subgraph spanned by A. For given $n_1, \ldots, n_d$ $K_d(n_1, \ldots, n_d)$ is the complete d-partite graph with n_i vertices in its ith class. $K_d := K_d(1, \ldots, 1)$ is the complete d-graph and $k_d(G)$ denotes the number of complete K_d's of G. If A is a set of vertices and edges of G, $G-A$ denotes the graph obtained by deleting the vertices and edges of A from G and deleting all the edges incident to a vertex in A. If (x, y) does not belong to G, $G+(x, y)$ is the graph obtained by adding the edge (x, y) to G.

1. Introduction

Let $f_p(n, E)=\min\{k_p(G): e(G)=E,\ v(G)=n\}$.

Problem 1. *Determine the function* $f_p(n, E)$.

Problem 2. *Characterize the extremal graphs for given* n *and* E, *i.e. those graphs* S *for which* $v(S)=n$, $e(S)=E$ *and* $k_p(S)=f_p(n, E)$.

The history of Problem 1 is the following.

In 1941 TURÁN [7] proved that if $n \equiv r \pmod{p-1}$ and $0 \leqq r \leqq p-2$ and if

$$m(n, p) = \frac{p-2}{2(p-1)}(n^2 - r^2) + \binom{r}{2},$$

then every G on n vertices having at least $m(n, p)+1$ edges contains at least one K_p. For $E = m(n, p)$ there exists exactly one graph $T^{n,p-1}$ having n vertices and E edges and containing no K_p. This $T^{n,p-1}$ is a $K_{p-1}(n_1, \ldots, n_{p-1})$ where $\sum n_i = n$ and $|n_i - n/d| < 1$. RADEMACHER proved (unpublished) that any G with n vertices and $\geqq m(n, 3)+1$ edges contains not only one but at least $\left[\frac{n}{2}\right]$ K_3's. ERDŐS [2, 3], (first only for $p=3$, then for any $p \geqq 3$) proved the following.

Theorem A. *Let U_k^n denote a graph obtained from $T^{n,p-1}$ by adding k edges to it so that the new edges belong to the same class having maximum number of vertices (i.e. $[n/d]+1$ if n/d is not an integer, n/d otherwise) and the new edges do not form triangles, if this is possible. Then there exists a constant $c_p > 0$ such that for $k < c_p n$, U_k^n is an extremal graph of Problem 1; i.e. if*

$$v(G) = n \quad e(G) = e(U_k^n) = m(n, p-1) + k\,,$$

then

$$k_p(G) \geqq k_p(U_k^n) = k \prod_{0 \leqq i \leqq p-3} \left[\frac{n+i}{p-1}\right].$$

Problem 3. (ERDŐS). *How large can c_p be in the theorem above?*

Remark 1. If we add $k+1$ or more edges to the first class of $G = K_{p-1}(k+1, k, k, \ldots, k, k-1)$, then each new edge will be contained only in $(k-1)k^{p-3}$ K_p's and it is easy to see that this construction is better than $U_k^{k(p-1)}$. Thus Theorem A does not hold for $c_p > \dfrac{1}{p-1}$.

This paper contains an improvement of Theorem A (see Theorem 4 below) which yields that in Problem 3 the answer is $c = 1/(p-1)$. For $p=3$ the proof of this was given in [5]. The result will follow from a much more general theorem characterizing the extremal graphs of Problem 1 for many values of n and E. Before stating our results we introduce some notation.

Let p, n and E be integers such that $p \geqq 3$ and $m(n, p) \leqq E \leqq \binom{n}{2}$. We write E in the form

$$E = \left(1 - \frac{1}{t}\right)\frac{n^2}{2}$$

and set $d = \lfloor t \rfloor$. Thus

$$m(n, d+1) \leqq E < m(n, d+2)\,.$$

We set $k=E-m(n,d+1)$. The numbers p and d will be considered fixed and n large relative to them.

The first theorem we state was proved for $p=3$ by GOODMAN [4] and it readily follows from results of MOON and MOSER [6]. We shall give a self-contained proof because some steps in the proof will be used later.

Theorem 1. *Let $v(G)=n$, $e(G)=E$, then*

$$k_p(G) \geqq \binom{t}{p}\left(\frac{n}{t}\right)^p. \tag{1}$$

Theorem 2. Let C be an arbitrary constant. There exist positive constants δ and C' such that if $0<k<\delta n^2$ and G is a graph on n vertices for which

$$k_p(G) \leqq \binom{t}{p}\left(\frac{n}{t}\right)^p + Ckn^{p-2} \tag{2}$$

then there exists a $K_d(n_1, \ldots, n_d)$ such that $\sum n_i = n$, $\left|n_i - \frac{n}{d}\right| < C'\sqrt{k}$, and G can be obtained from this $K_d(n_1, \ldots, n_d)$ by adding less than $C'k$ edges to it and then deleting less than $C'k$ edges from it.

Remark 2. *Theorem 2 is a "stability theorem" in the following sense: Let U_k^n be the graph obtained from $T^{n,d}$ by adding k edges to it (see Theorem A), then the k "extra edges" are contained in (approximately) $k\binom{d-1}{p-2}\left(\frac{n}{d}\right)^{p-2}$ K_p's and the graph $T^{n,d}$ has $\approx \binom{t}{p}\left(\frac{n}{t}\right)^p$ K_p's. Thus (2) means that G does not have much more K_p's than an extremal graph. Theorem 2 asserts that in this case G^n is very similar to $T^{n,d}$. This theorem is interesting only if k/n^2 is sufficiently small.*

Remark 3. Theorem 2 is sharp: $C'\sqrt{k}$ cannot be replaced by $o(\sqrt{k})$, $C'k$ cannot be replaced by $o(k)$. Indeed, if we add $3k$ edges to and delete k edges from $K_d\left(\frac{n}{d}+\sqrt{k}, \frac{n}{d}-\sqrt{k}, \frac{n}{d}, \ldots, \frac{n}{d}\right)$, then for the resulting graph G

$$k_p(G) \leqq \left(\frac{n}{d}\right)^p \binom{d}{p} + k\binom{d-1}{p-2}\left(\frac{n}{d}\right)^{p-2} < \left(\frac{n}{t}\right)^p \binom{t}{p} + k\binom{d-1}{p-2}\left(\frac{n}{d}\right)^{p-2}$$

while

$$e(G) = m(n, d+1) + k.$$

To formulate our main result we need to describe some classes of graphs.

Definition 1. Let $U_0(n, E)$ denote the class of those graphs with n points and E edges which arise from a complete d-partite graph S_0 by adding edges so that these new edges form no triangles. Let $U_1(n, E)$ denote the subclass where all new edges are contained in the same colorclass of S_0.

Definition 2. Let $U_2(n, E)$ denote the class of those graphs S with n points and E edges which have a set W of independent points such that $S-W$ is complete d-partite, and every point in W is connected to all points of all but one color-classes of $S-W$.

Theorem 3. *There exists a positive constant $\delta=\delta(p, d)$ such that if $0\leqq k<\delta n^2$ then every extremal graph for Problem 1 is in the class $U_1(n, E)$ if $p\geqq 4$ and is in the class $U_0(n, E)\cup U_2(n, E)$ if $p=3$. In this latter case there exists at least one extremal graph in $U_1(n, E)$.*

We regard this theorem as a complete solution of Problem 1 for the values of n and E under consideration. However, this interpretation requires some explanation, since not all graphs in the classes U_0, U_1 or U_2 have the same number of K_p's and hence, not all of them are extremal. But once we know that our graph is in U_0, U_1 or U_2, its structure is simple enough to determine the best choice by simple arithmetic. Some remarks are in order here:

Proposition 1. *Let $S\in U_1(n, E)$ be extremal. Let $S_0=K_d(n_1, \dots, n_d)$, $n_1\geqq\dots\geqq n_d$. Then all edges in $E(S)-E(S_0)$ are spanned by the largest class. Furthermore, $|n_i-n_j|\leqq 1$ for $i,j\geqq 2$.*

Given a sequence $n_1\geqq\dots\geqq n_d$, all graphs with the above structure have the same number of K_p's. Hence their structure is completely determined if we know the value of n_1. This can be done by simple arithmetic which is not discussed here. We remark that it turns out that

$$n_1=\frac{n}{d}+\frac{d-1}{d}\frac{k}{n}+o\left(\frac{k}{n}\right),\quad n_i=\frac{n}{d}-\frac{1}{d}\frac{k}{n}+o\left(\frac{k}{n}\right). \tag{3}$$

Proposition 2. *If $S\in U_0(n, E)$ is an extremal graph, then (for $k\leqq\delta n^2$) by moving all edges of $E(S)-E(S_0)$ to the largest color-class we can construct an $\ddot{S}\in U_1(n, E)$ for which $k_p(\ddot{S})\leqq k_p(S)$. If we moved edges from a smaller class to a larger one, or if $p\geqq 4$, then $k_p(S)>k_p(\ddot{S})$, which contradicts that S is extremal. Thus if $S\notin U_1(n, E)$, then $p=3$ and all the edges of $E(S)-E(S_0)$ belong to color-classes of maximum size in S.*

Proposition 3. *Let $S\in U_2(n, E)$ be an extremal graph. Then every $x\in W$ is connected to all points of all but a possibly smallest color-class of $S-W$. Let B_0 be a smallest color-class of $S-W$. Then, if we change the graph S by connecting every $x\in W$ to all points of $S-W-B_0$ and an appropriate number of points in B_0, we get another extremal graph S'. This graph S' is in $U_1(n, E)$.*

These remarks make the following conjecture plausible:

Conjecture: *For every n and E ($n \geqq n_0(p)$) there is an extremal graph in $U_1(n, E)$.*

Let us consider the case when $p = d+1$ and $k < \left[\frac{n}{d}\right]$. Let S be an extremal graph in $U_1(n, E)$. Let $S_0 = K_d(n_1, \ldots, n_d)$ and $n_1 \geqq \ldots \geqq n_d$. If the choice of S is not unique, choose one with n_1 minimal. We claim that $n_1 \leqq n_d + 1$, i.e. $S_0 = T^{n,d}$. Suppose that $n_1 \geqq n_d + 2$. Let r denote the number of edges in $E(S) - E(S_0)$. Then simple computation and (3) yield that

(4) $$r \leqq k + \sum_{i=1}^{d} \left(\frac{n}{d} - n_i\right)^2 \leqq \frac{n}{d} + O(1).$$

We have

$$k_p(S) = r \cdot n_2 \ldots n_d,$$

but if we add $r + n_d - n_1 + 1$ edges to $K_d(n_1 - 1, n_2, \ldots, n_{d-1}, n_d + 1)$, then we get a graph S' with the same number of edges but, by the extremality of S and n_1, with $k_p(S') \geqq k_p(S)$. Hence

$$r \cdot n_2 \ldots n_d \leqq (r + n_d - n_1 + 1) n_2 \ldots (n_d + 1),$$

or

(5) $$r \geqq (n_1 - n_d - 1)(n_d + 1).$$

Now, either $n_1 \leqq n_d + 1$ and hence $S_0 = T^{n,d}$, which we wish to prove, or by (3), $n_d = \frac{n}{d} + O(1)$, by (4) and (5)

$$(n_1 - n_d - 1)(n_d + 1) \leqq \frac{n}{d} + O(1),$$

and therefore $n_1 = n_d + 2$, if n is sufficiently large. By Proposition 1 $n_i \leqq n_d + 1 = n_1 - 1$ for $i \geqq 2$. Thus, if S'_0 is the complete d-partite graph of S', then $S'_0 = T^{n,d}$ and so $k = r + n_d - n_1 + 1 = r - 1$. By (5),

$$k \geqq n_d + 1 \geqq \left[\frac{n}{d}\right]$$

a contradiction.

Thus, assuming Theorem 3, we have proved

Theorem 4. *If $E = m(n, p-1) + k$, where $k < \left[\frac{n}{p-1}\right]$, then for $p > 3$ the only, for $p = 3$ one possible graph with n points and E edges, containing the least number of K_p's is obtained by adding k edges to a largest class of $T^{n,d}$.*

Theorem 4 is clearly a sharpening of ERDŐS's Theorem 1.

We investigate one more special case. Let $0<x<1$ and $E\approx x\cdot\binom{n}{2}$, $n\to\infty$. Let S be a graph in $U_1(n, E)$ with minimum number of K_p's. Then

$$k_p(S)\approx f(x)\binom{n}{p},$$

where $f(x)$ can be determined as follows. If $1-\frac{1}{d}\leqq x\leqq 1-\frac{1}{d+1}$ and S is obtained from $S_0=K_d(n_1, n_2, \dots, n_d)$, then we put $n_1=(1-\alpha)n$ and for $i=2, \dots, d$, by $|n_i-n_j|<1 n_i\approx\frac{\alpha}{d-1}n$. Clearly,

$$(*)\qquad \begin{aligned} k_p(S)\approx \left\{x\binom{n}{2}-\alpha(1-\alpha)n^2-\binom{d-1}{2}\left(\frac{\alpha}{d-1}\right)^2 n^2\right\}\left(\frac{\alpha n}{d-1}\right)^{p-2}\binom{d-1}{p-2}+\\ +(1-\alpha)n\binom{d-1}{p-1}\left(\frac{\alpha n}{d-1}\right)^{p-1}+\binom{d-1}{p}\left(\frac{\alpha n}{d-1}\right)^{p}.\end{aligned}$$

(Here $\{\dots\}$ is the number of edges in the first class of $K_d(n_1, \dots, n_d)$, $\{\dots\}\cdot\left(\frac{\alpha n}{d-1}\right)^{p-2}\binom{d-1}{p-2}$ is the number of K_p's containing such an edge. The next two terms are the numbers of K_p's containing 1 or 0 vertices from the first class.) Thus

$$\frac{k_p(S)}{\binom{n}{p}}\approx\{A\alpha^2+B\alpha+C\}\cdot\alpha^{p-2}=F(\alpha, x)$$

where $A=A(x, p, d)$, $B=B(x, p, d)$, $C=C(x, p, d)$ are constants easily calculated. $\frac{d}{d\alpha}F(\alpha, x)=0$ yields a quadratic equation, from which the optimal α can easily be determined. Substituting this α in (*) we obtain $f(x)$.

Define

$$g(x)=\liminf\left\{\frac{k_3(G^n)}{\binom{n}{3}}: e(G)\geqq x\binom{n}{2}\right\}.$$

Figure 1 shows what we know about the function $g(x)$. The dotted line shows the Goodman bound. This is equal to $g(x)$ when $x=1-\frac{1}{d}$, d integer. The broken line shows

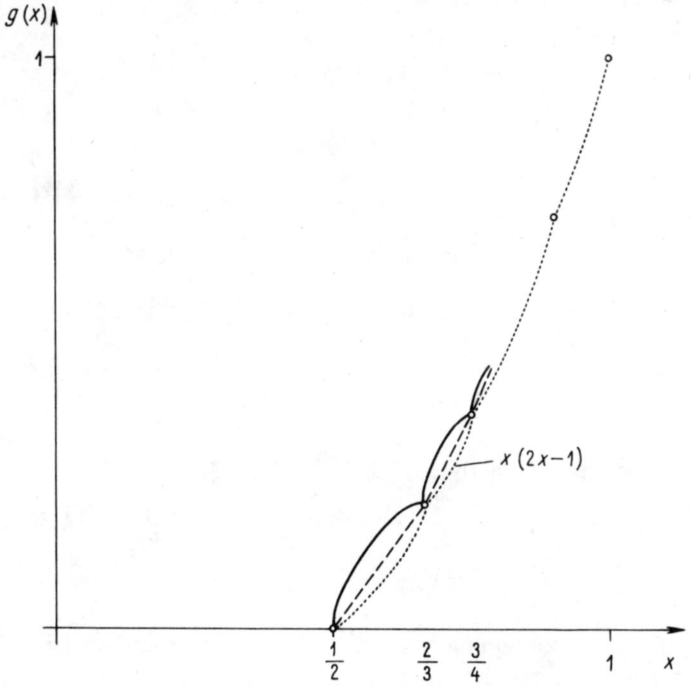

Fig. 1

the improvement given by Bollobás [1]. This proves that between these points $g(x)$ is above the chords. Finally, the continuous line shows the function $f(x)$. This is concave between the points $x=1-\frac{1}{d}$. If the conjecture formulated above is true, it follows that $g(x)=f(x)$. Clearly $g(x)\leqq f(x)$ and Theorem 3 implies that for each d there exists an $\varepsilon_d>0$ such that if $1-\frac{1}{d}\leqq x\leqq 1-\frac{1}{d}+\varepsilon_d$ then $f(x)=g(x)$. Unfortunately, ε_d is so small in our proof that we did not even dare to estimate ε_2.

2. Preliminaries: an inequality for the number of complete subgraphs

Let G be a graph with n points and E edges. Set $k_i=k_i(G)$. For each complete $(p-1)$-subgraph U, let $t_{i,U}$ denote the number of points connected to exactly $p-i-1$ points of U. Let t_i denote the number of induced subgraphs which consist of a K_{p-1} and a point joined to exactly $p-i-1$ points of this K_{p-1}. Clearly, for every U

$$\sum_{i=0}^{p-1} t_{i,U}=n-p+1$$

and

$$\sum_U t_{0,U} = p \cdot t_0 = pk_p, \quad \sum_U t_{1,U} = 2t_1,$$

$$\sum_U t_{i,U} = t_i \quad \text{for} \quad i \geqq 2.$$

So

$$k_{p-1} \cdot (n-p+1) = pt_0 + 2t_1 + t_2 + \ldots + t_{p-1}. \tag{6}$$

Denote, for each complete $(p-2)$-graph V, by r_V the number of complete $(p-1)$-graphs containing V. Then

$$\sum_V r_V = (p-1)k_{p-1}, \tag{7}$$

since each K_{p-1} contains exactly $p-1$ K_{p-2}'s.

Moreover

$$\sum_V \binom{r_V}{2} = t_1 + \binom{p}{2} k_p, \tag{8}$$

since any two K_{p-1}'s containing a given V yield a graph counted in $t_0 = k_p$ or t_1 depending on whether or not they are joined or not. Those subgraphs counted in t arise this way uniquely, and those counted in t_0 arise this way $\binom{p}{2}$ times.

Introducing the "deviation from average"

$$q_V = \frac{k_{p-1}}{k_{p-2}}(p-1) - r_V,$$

we have by (7)

$$\sum_V q_V = k_{p-1} \cdot (p-1) - \sum r_V = 0,$$

and hence

$$2\sum_V \binom{r_V}{2} = \sum_V 2 \binom{\frac{k_{p-1}}{k_{p-2}}(p-1) - q_V}{2} = \frac{k_{p-1}^2}{k_{p-2}}(p-1)^2 + \sum q_V^2 - (p-1)k_{p-1}.$$

This, $t_0 = k_p$, (6), and (8) yield that

$$nk_{p-1} = pk_p + 2\left(\sum \binom{r_V}{2} - \binom{p}{2} t_0\right) + t_2 + \ldots + t_{p-1} + (p-1)k_{p-1} =$$

$$= pk_p + \frac{k_{p-1}^2}{k_{p-2}}(p-1)^2 + \sum q_V^2 - p(p-1)k_p + (t_2 + \ldots + t_{p-1})$$

whence

$$p(p-2)k_p = \frac{k_{p-1}^2(p-1)^2}{k_{p-2}} - nk_{p-1} + \sum q_V^2 + (t_2 + \ldots + t_{p-1}).$$

Thus

(9) $$\frac{k_p}{k_{p-1}} = \frac{1}{p(p-2)} \left\{ \frac{k_{p-1}}{k_{p-2}} (p-1)^2 - n \right\} + R$$

where

(9*) $$R = \frac{1}{p(p-2)k_{p-1}} \{\sum q_V^2 + (t_2 + \ldots + t_{p-1})\}.$$

In particular,

(10) $$\frac{k_p}{k_{p-1}} \geqq \frac{1}{p(p-2)} \left\{ \frac{k_{p-1}}{k_{p-2}} (p-1)^2 - n \right\}.$$

This formula was remarked by MOON and MOSER [6].

3. Proof of Theorem 1

First we give a lower bound on k_j/k_{j-1}. We shall prove that

(11) $$k_j/k_{j-1} \geqq \frac{t-j+1}{j} \frac{n}{t}.$$

For $j=2$

$$k_2/k_1 = E/n = \left(1 - \frac{1}{t}\right).$$

By induction on j we obtain that

$$k_{j+1}/k_j \geqq \frac{1}{(j+1)(j-1)} \left\{ \frac{t-j+1}{j} \frac{n}{t} j^2 - n \right\} = \frac{t-j+2}{j+1} \frac{n}{t};$$

(we have used (10) for $p=j$ here). This proves (11). Since

$$k_p = k_1(k_2/k_1)(k_3/k_2)\ldots(k_p/k_{p-1}), \quad (k_1 = n),$$

we have, by (11),

$$k_p \geqq \left(\frac{n}{t}\right)^{p-1} \frac{(t-p+1)(t-p+2)\ldots(t-1)}{p(p-1)(p-2)\ldots 2.1} n = \left(\frac{n}{t}\right)^p \binom{t}{p}.$$

Thus Theorem 1 is proved.

4. Proof of Theorem 2

The basic inequality we shall use to prove Theorem 2 is (under the conditions of the theorem and with the notation of the previous proof

$$\sum q_V^2+(t_2+\dots+t_{p-1})=O(kn^{p-2}). \tag{12}$$

To establish (12) we shall carry out the proof of Theorem 1 a little more carefully. By Theorem 1 we know that

$$k_{p-1}\geqq\binom{t}{p-1}\left(\frac{n}{t}\right)^{p-1} \tag{13}$$

By (9), (9*), (11) (applied with $j=p-1$) and (13) we obtain that

$$(14)\quad k_p\geqq\frac{1}{p(p-2)}\{k_{p-1}\cdot((k_{p-1}/k_{p-2})(p-1)^2-n)+\sum q_V^2+(t_2+\dots+t_{p-1})\}\geqq$$

$$\geqq\frac{1}{p(p-2)}\left\{\binom{t}{p-1}\left(\frac{n}{t}\right)^{p-1}\left(\frac{t-(p-1)+1}{p-1}\frac{n}{t}(p-1)^2-n\right)+\right.$$

$$\left.+\sum q_V^2+(t_2+\dots+t_{p-1})\right\}=\binom{t}{p}\left(\frac{n}{t}\right)^p+\frac{1}{p(p-2)}\{\sum q_V^2+(t_2+\dots+t_{p-1})\}.$$

This proves (12).

The method we shall use is the following. By an averaging process we show that there must be a complete d-graph K_d in G such that

(i) almost all the vertices of $G-K_d$ are joined to exactly $d-1$ vertices of K_d;

(ii) dividing the vertices of $G-K_d$ into the classes $C_0,\dots,C_d$, where C_i contains the vertices joined to each vertex of K_d except the ith one ($i=1,\dots,d$) and C_0 contains the remaining ones almost all the pairs (x,y) ($x\in C_i$, $y\in C_j$, $i\neq j$) belong to G.

It is convenient to reduce the proof first to the case $p=3$. If $p'<p$ and we know that (2) holds for p, then by (11)

$$k_p/k_{p'}=(k_p/k_{p-1})(k_{p-1}/k_{p-2})\dots(k_{p'+1}/k_{p'})\geqq$$

$$\geqq\frac{(t-p+1)(t-p+2)\dots(t-p')}{p(p-1)\dots(p'+1)}\left(\frac{n}{t}\right)^{p-p'},$$

and hence (by (2))

$$k_{p'}\leqq\left(\frac{n}{t}\right)^{p'}\binom{t}{p'}+C''kn^{p'-2}.$$

In particular,

$$k_3(G)\leqq\binom{t}{3}\left(\frac{n}{3}\right)^3+C''kn. \tag{15}$$

On the other hand, by (14),

(16) $$k_3 \geqq \binom{t}{3}\binom{n}{3}^3 + \frac{1}{3}\{\sum q_V^2 + t_2\},$$

where (14) is applied with $p=3$, V is a vertex of G, r_V (of (7)) reduces to the degree of V, and t_2 is the number of (3,1)-graphs: of subgraphs of 3 vertices with 1 edges. Finally, $q_V = (p-1)\frac{k_2}{k_1} - r_V = \frac{2E}{n} - \sigma(V)$ measures how near is the valence of the vertex V is to the average valence. By (15) and (16)

$$\sum q_V^2 = O(kn), \quad t_2 = O(kn).$$

Let W be a complete d-graph of G and let A_W denote the number of vertices joined to at most $d-2$ vertices of W. If z is a vertex joined to at most $d-2$ vertices of A_W, then there is an edge (x, y) in W forming a (3,1)-graph with z. A given (3,1)-graph is counted only $O(n^{d-2})$ times in $\sum A_W$, hence

(17) $$\sum_W A_W = O(kn) \cdot O(n^{d-2}) = O(kn^{d-1}).$$

Let B_W be the number of pairs $(x, y) \notin E(G)$ such that either both x and y are joined to exactly $d-1$ vertices of W but these $d-1$ vertices are different for x and y, or x is joined to all vertices of W and y is joined to exactly $d-1$ ones. We can find a $z \in W$ joined to x but not joined to y and this triple (x, y, z) is a (3,1)-graph. For a given (3,1) graph we can find only $O(n^{d-1})$ W from which it can be obtained in the way given above. Hence

(18) $$\sum_W B_W = O(kn)O(n^{d-1}) = O(kn^d).$$

Let $Q_W =: \sum_{V \in W} q_V^2$. (Here V is a vertex!) Trivially,

(19) $$\sum_W \cdot Q_W = O(kn) \cdot O(n^{d-1}) = O(kn^d).$$

By (17), (18) and (19)

$$\sum_W (nA_W + B_W + Q_W) = O(kn^d).$$

By Theorem 1 applied with $p = d = \lfloor t \rfloor$ we know that the number of summands on the left, $k_d(G) \geqq c_1 n^d$ for some positive constant c_1. Therefore the average of $(nA_W + B_W + Q_W)$ is $O(k)$. Thus there exists a W in G for which

(20) $$A_W = O(k/n), \quad B_W = O(k), \quad \text{and} \quad q_V = O(\sqrt{k}) \quad \text{if} \quad V \in W.$$

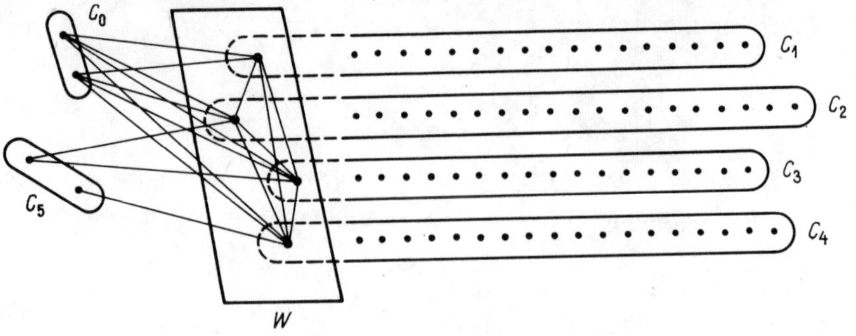

Fig. 2

Let C_i $(i=1, \ldots, d)$ be the set of vertices of G joined to all the vertices of W but to the ith one denoted by V_i. Let C_0 be the set of vertices joined to W completely and C_{d+1} be the set of vertices joined to at most $d-2$ vertices of W. By (20), $|C_{d+1}|=A_W=$ $=O\left(\frac{k}{n}\right)=O(\sqrt{k})$, and for every $V_j\in W$ $\sigma(V_j)=r_{V_j}=\frac{2E}{n}-q_{V_i}=\left(1-\frac{1}{t}\right)n+O(\sqrt{k})$. Thus, for $j=1, 2, \ldots, d$,

$$|C_i|=|\bigcap_{j\neq i} st(V_j)| \geqq \frac{n}{d}+O(\sqrt{k})$$

and therefore (by $\sum|C_i|\leqq n$)

$$|C_i|=\frac{n}{d}+O(\sqrt{k}), \quad \text{and} \quad |C_0|=O(\sqrt{k}).$$

A short computation gives that if $n_i=n/d+O(\sqrt{k})$, then $e(K_d(n_1, \ldots, n_d))=$ $=m(n, d+1)+O(k)$. Let us consider the following classification of the vertices of G: C_i is the ith class for $i=2, 3, \ldots, d$ and $C_0\cup C_1\cup C_{d+1}$ is the first one, n_i is the number of vertices in the ith class, $i=1, 2, \ldots, d$.

By (20), more precisely, by $B_W=O(k)$ and $|C_{d+1}|=O(k/n)$, the number of pairs (x, y) not belonging to G where x and y belong to different classes is only $O(k)+$ $+O(k/n)O(n)=O(k)$. Since

$$e(K_d(n_1, \ldots, n_d))=m(n, d+1)+O(k),$$

(i.e. it is not too small!), by (3) the number of edges of G the end vertices of which belong to the same class is at most

$$E-(e(K_d(n_1, \ldots, n_d))-B_W-n|C_{d+1}|)=O(k).$$

This completes the proof.

5. Proof of Theorem 3

The proof is rather long and subdivided into steps (A)–(U). Occasionally we shall insert some remarks telling our plans for the next few steps. In steps (A) and (B) we approximate the extremal graphs with complete d-partite graphs and introduce some notation. In (C) we show that if $K_d(n_1, \ldots, n_d)$ is the graph approximating our extremal graph S, then $n_i - n_j$ is small.

All the inequalities below are stated only for the sufficiently large values of n.

(A) Let S be an extremal graph for Problem 1 for some n, E, and let

$$d = \max\{t : m(n, t+1) \leqq E\},$$

while $k = E - m(n, d+1)$.

It is clear that we may assume that $k = o(n^2)$. Indeed, if the theorem is true for all possible functions $k = k(n)$ such that $k = o(n)$ then there exists an $\varepsilon > 0$ such that the theorem is true for $k < \varepsilon n^2$ (p and d are fixed throughout).

(B) We can apply Theorem 2 to S. Let Z be a graph obtained from Turán's graph $T^{n,d}$ by adding k edges to it. Then $e(Z) = E$ and so by the extremality of S we have

$$k_p(S) \leqq k_p(Z) = \binom{d}{p}\left(\frac{n}{d}\right)^p + O(kn^{p-2}).$$

Thus Theorem 2 applies and we conclude that there is a constant c_1 such that S can be obtained from a $K_d(n_1, \ldots, n_d)$ by deleting and adding at most $c_0 k$ edges. The construction of S this way is not unique. Let us choose the graph $K_d(n_1, \ldots, n_d)$ in such a way that the number of edges to add is minimal. Let $A_1, \ldots, A_d$ denote the classes of $K_d(n_1, \ldots, n_d)$, $|A_i| = n_i$. Call the edges to be added to $K_d(n_1, \ldots, n_d)$ *horizontal* edges; the edges to be deleted from $K_d(n_1, \ldots, n_d)$ *missing* edges; the edges which occur in both S and $K_d(n_1, \ldots, n_d)$ *vertical edges.*

Let h and m denote the number of horizontal and missing edges, respectively. Clearly, $h \leqq c_0 k$ and $m \leqq h \leqq c_0 k$. Moreover, $m \leqq h - k$:

$$k = E - m(n, d+1) = \{e(K_d(n_1, \ldots, n_d)) + h - m\} - m(n, d+1) \leqq h - m.$$

Set

$$\sigma_i^+(x) = |A_i \cap st\ x|$$

$$\sigma_i^-(x) = |A_i - st\ x|$$

If $x \in A_j$ then let

$$\sigma^+(x) = \sigma_j^+(x)$$

and

$$\sigma^-(x) = \sum_{i \neq j} \sigma_i^-(x).$$

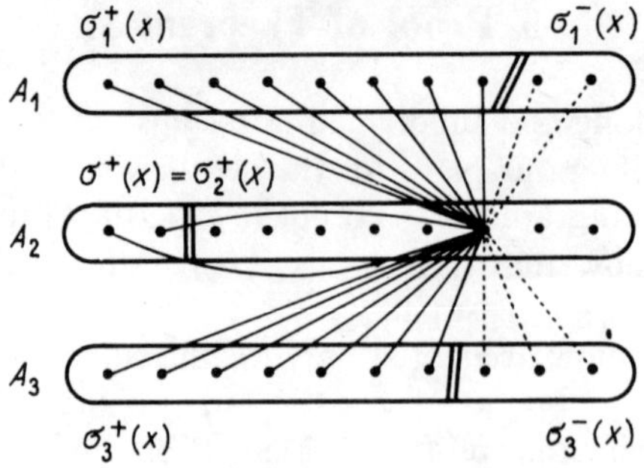

Fig. 3

Thus $\sigma^+(x)$ and $\sigma^-(x)$ denote the numbers of horizontal and missing edges adjacent to x, respectively.

Finally, set

$$\sigma^+ = \max_x \sigma^+(x)\,,$$

$$\sigma^- = \max_x \sigma^-(x)\,.$$

Note that the choice of the partition $\{A_1, \ldots, A_d\}$ implies that

(21) $$\sigma_i^+(x) \geqq \sigma^+(x) \quad (i=1, \ldots, d)\,.$$

Hence

$$\sigma^+(x) < \frac{n}{d}$$

for all x, so

(22) $$\sigma^+ < \frac{n}{d}\,.$$

Introduce the numbers

$$R_1 = \binom{d-1}{p-2}\left(\frac{n}{d}\right)^{p-2}, \quad R_i = \binom{d-2}{p-i}\left(\frac{n}{d}\right)^{p-1} \quad (i \geqq 2)\,.$$

These will occur frequently in various approximations.

Let

$$S_d^p(n_1, \ldots, n_d) = \sum_{i_1 \leqq \ldots \leqq i_p} \prod_{j=1}^{p} n_{i_j}\,.$$

If $n_1, \ldots, n_d$ are integers, clearly,

$$S_d^p(n_1, \ldots, n_d) = k_p(K_d(n_1, \ldots, n_d))\,.$$

(C) We show that $n_i = \frac{n}{d} + O(\sqrt{k})$. For let e.g. $n_1 = \max(n_1, \ldots, n_d)$, $n_2 = \min(n_1, \ldots, n_d)$. Then

$$e(S) \leq e(K_d(n_1, \ldots, n_d)) + c_1 k = S_d^2(n_1, \ldots, n_d) + c_1 k =$$

$$= S_d^2\left(\frac{n_1+n_2}{2}, \frac{n_1+n_2}{2}, n_3, \ldots, n_d\right) + c_1 k - \frac{1}{4}(n_1-n_2)^2 \leq$$

$$\leq S_d^2\left(\frac{n}{d}, \ldots, \frac{n}{d}\right) + c_1 k - \frac{1}{4}(n_1-n_2)^2 .$$

On the other hand,

$$e(S) = S_d^2\left(\frac{n}{d}, \ldots, \frac{n}{d}\right) + k + O(1),$$

which yields that $n_1 - n_2 = O(\sqrt{k})$.

(D) Let $u, v \in V(G)$. We denote by $a_S(u, v) = a(u, v)$ the number of K_p's in $S + (u, v)$ containing the edge (u, v). We can obtain quite accurate estimations on these numbers.

. . . The first part of the proof consists of steps (A)–(M). In steps (D)–(M) we obtain step by step more and more information, sharper and sharper inequalities for quantities like

(i) $a(x, y)$, when (x, y) is an edge, in particular, a horizontal one
(ii) $a(u, v)$, where (u, v) is a missing edge
(iii) $\sigma^+ = \max \sigma^+(x)$
(iv) $t = t(x) =: \min(\sigma^+(x), \sigma^-(x))$
(v) $\sigma^+(x) + \sigma^+(y)$ for the edges (x, y) and for the missing edges (x, y). . .

Let first (u, v) be a horizontal edge. Then

$$(23) \qquad a(u, v) \geq R_1 - [\sigma^-(u) + \sigma^-(v)] R_3 + O(\sqrt{k} \cdot n^{p-3}).$$

Indeed, let us count the K_p's containing (u, v), as follows. Let e.g. $u, v \in A_1$ and $\ddot{S}$ denote the graph obtained from S by filling in all the missing edges. The number of K_p's in $\ddot{S}$ containing (u, v) but no other horizontal edge is

$$S_{d-1}^{p-2}(n_2, \ldots, n_d) = S_{d-1}^{p-2}\left(\frac{n}{d}, \ldots, \frac{n}{d}\right) + O(\sqrt{k}\, n^{p-3}) = R_1 + O(\sqrt{k}\, n^{p-3}).$$

Let us delete now the missing edges which we have filled in. A missing edge disjoint from (u, v) destroys at most $O(n^{p-4})$ K_p's and since there are only $O(k)$ missing edges, this way we destroy only $O(k) \cdot O(n^{p-4}) < O(\sqrt{k}\, n^{p-3})$ K_p's. If we delete now a missing edge incident with u or v, say one connecting u to a point $w \in A_2$, then we destroy at most

$$S_{d-2}^{p-3}(n_3, \ldots, n_d) = R_3 + O(\sqrt{k}\, n^{p-4})$$

K_p's counted above. So deleting all such missing edges we destroy at most

$$(\sigma^-(u)+\sigma^-(v)) \cdot R_3 + (\sigma^-(u)+\sigma^-(v)) O(\sqrt{k}\, n^{p-4}) =$$

$$= (\sigma^-(u)+\sigma^-(v)) \cdot R_3 + O(\sqrt{k}\, n^{p-3})$$

K_p's counted above. This proves (23).

Similar computation yields that if (u, v) is a missing edge then

(24) $$a(u, v) \leqq R_2 + [\sigma^+(u)+\sigma^+(v)] R_3 + \sigma^+(u)\sigma^+(v) R_4 + O(\sqrt{k}\, n^{p-3}).$$

(E) The extremality of S implies that if $(x, y) \in E(S)$ but $(u, v) \notin E(S)$ then

(25) $$a(x, y) \leqq a(u, v).$$

Indeed filling in (u, v) creates $a(u, v)$ K_p's, and then deleting (x, y) destroys *at least* $a(x, y)$ of them: filling in (u, v) may create K_p's containing (x, y), this is why the deletion of (x, y) may destroy more than $a(x, y)$ K_p's. By the extremality of S

$$k_p(S) \leqq k_p(S + (u, v) - (x, y)) \leqq k_p(S) + a(u, v) - a(x, y),$$

proving (25).

Now (25) will be applied in the following way: knowing more and more about the structure of the graph we shall be able to obtain always better and better bounds on $a(x, y)$ and $a(u, v)$; then (25) in turn gives more information on the graph. Another inequality, similar to (24) and (25) is that

(26) $$a(x, y) \leqq R_1$$

if $(x, y) \in E(S)$. For using induction on k, we know that

$$k_p(S) = k_p(S - (x, y)) + a(x, y) \geqq k_p(G) + a(x, y)$$

for some $G \in U_1(n, E-1)$. Let $G' \in U_1(n, E)$ be obtained from the same $K_d(n_1, \ldots, n_d)$ as G. Let $n_1 \geqq n_i$. Then

$$k_p(G') = k_p(G) + S_{d-1}^{p-2}(n_2, \ldots, n_d) \leqq k_p(G) + R_1$$

and hence

$$k_p(S) \geqq k_p(G) + a(x, y) \geqq k_p(G') + a(x, y) - R_1.$$

Thus the extremality of S implies (26).

(F) Let (x, y) be a horizontal edge and (u, v) a missing edge. Then (23), (24) and (25) imply that

$$R_1 - R_2 \leqq [\sigma^-(x)+\sigma^-(y)+\sigma^+(u)+\sigma^+(v)] \cdot R_3 + \\ + \sigma^+(u)\sigma^+(v) \cdot R_4 + O(\sqrt{k}\, n^{p-3})$$

or, dividing by R_3,

$$\frac{n}{d} \leqq \sigma^-(x)+\sigma^-(y)+\sigma^+(u)+\sigma^+(v)+ \\ + \frac{d}{n}\frac{p-3}{d-p+2}\sigma^+(u)\cdot\sigma^+(v)+O(\sqrt{k})\,. \tag{27}$$

(G) The previous important inequality is used first to bound the number σ^+ from below. Using that

$$\sigma^+(u), \sigma^+(v) \leqq \sigma^+ < \frac{n}{d},$$

we obtain for each horizontal edge (x, y) that

$$\frac{n}{d} \leqq \sigma^-(x)+\sigma^-(y)+2\sigma^+ + \frac{p-3}{d-p+2}\sigma^+ + O(\sqrt{k})\,.$$

Summing for all horizontal edges (x, y), we get

$$h\cdot\frac{n}{d} \leqq \sum_x \sigma^+(x)\sigma^-(x) + h\sigma^+ \cdot \frac{2d-p+1}{d-p+2} + O(\sqrt{k}\,h) \leqq \\ \leqq \sigma^+ \sum_x \sigma^-(x) + h\sigma^+ \frac{2d-p+1}{d-p+1} + O(\sqrt{k}\,h) \leqq \\ \leqq \sigma^+ h\left(2+\frac{2d-p+1}{d-p+2}\right) + O(\sqrt{k}\,h)\,,$$

since $\sum_x \sigma^-(x) = 2m \leqq 2h$. Thus

$$\sigma^+ \geqq \frac{d-p+2}{4d-3p+5}\frac{n}{d} + O(\sqrt{k}) \geqq \frac{n}{4d^2} + O(\sqrt{k})\,. \tag{28}$$

(H) Our next aim is to show that for every x, one of $\sigma^+(x)$, $\sigma^-(x)$ must be small. More precisely, let

$$t = t_x = \min\,(\sigma^+(x), \sigma^-(x))\,.$$

We want to show that

(29) $$t=o(n).$$

Set $\sigma_j^+(x)=\sigma_j$. By the choice of the partition, more precisely, by (21),

$$\sigma_j \geqq \sigma^+(x) \geqq t \quad (j=1, \ldots, d).$$

The number of K_p's containing x is

$$k_{p-1}(K_d(\sigma_1, \ldots, \sigma_d))+O(kn^{p-3})=S_d^{p-1}(\sigma_1, \ldots, \sigma_d)+O(kn^{p-3})$$

where the second term accounts for the K_p's containing a horizontal edge not adjacent to x and also for those p-tuples consisting of x and $p-1$ neighbors of it which span a missing edge (since $h, m \leqq c_1 k$, see (B)).

Suppose that e.g. $x \in A_1$. One of the numbers $\sigma_2^-(x), \ldots, \sigma_d^-(x)$, say $\sigma_2^-(x)$, is at least t/d.

Replace $s=\lfloor t/d \rfloor$ edges connecting x to A_1 by $\lfloor t/d \rfloor$ edges connecting x to A_2. Then the K_p's not containing x remain the same while the number of K_p's containing x becomes

$$k_{p-1}(K_d(\sigma_1-s, \sigma_2+s, \sigma_3, \ldots, \sigma_d)+O(k\, n^{p-3})=$$
$$=S_d^{p-1}(\sigma_1-s, \sigma_2+s, \sigma_3, \ldots, \sigma_d)+O(k\, n^{p-3}).$$

The number of K_p's cannot decrease by this operation, hence

$$S_d^{p-1}(\sigma_1, \ldots, \sigma_d)-S_d^{p-1}(\sigma_1-s, \sigma_2+s, \sigma_3, \ldots, \sigma_d) \leqq O(k\, n^{p-3}).$$

But the left hand side is

(30) $$s(\sigma_2-\sigma_1+s)S_{d-2}^{p-3}(\sigma_3, \ldots, \sigma_d)>s^2 t^{p-3}>\frac{1}{2d^2}t^{p-1}$$

whence

$$t=O(k^{\frac{1}{p-1}} \cdot n^{\frac{p-3}{p-1}})=o(n).$$

(I) Let $x_0 \in A_i$ be a point with

$$\sigma^+(x_0)=\sigma^+.$$

Then by (28) and (29),

$$\sigma^-(x_0)=o(n).$$

Clearly x_0 has a neighbor $y_0 \in A_i$ with

$$\sigma^-(y_0) \leqq m/\sigma^+=O(k/n)=o(n).$$

Hence, by (23),

$$a(x_0, y_0) \geqq R_1 + o(n^{p-2}).$$

So, by (25), for every pair $(u, v) \notin E(G)$ we have

$$a(u, v) \geqq R_1 + o(n^{p-2}). \tag{31}$$

Applying (27) to the horizontal edge (x_0, y_0) and any missing edge (u, v) we obtain that

$$\sigma^+(u) + \sigma^+(v) + \frac{d}{n}\frac{p-3}{d-p+2}\sigma^+(u)\cdot\sigma^+(v) \geqq \frac{n}{d} + o(n). \tag{32}$$

(J) Now we can easily show that $\sigma^- = O(\sqrt{k})$. First we prove the weaker

$$\sigma^- = o(n). \tag{33}$$

Indeed, let v be a point with

$$\sigma^-(v) = \sigma^-.$$

For $c = \dfrac{1}{4d(p-3)}$ either $\sigma^+(v) \geqq cn$, and therefore (33) follows from (29), or $\sigma^+(v) \leqq cn$. In the second case for every missing edge (u, v) $\left(\text{by } \sigma^+(u) \leqq \dfrac{n}{d}\right)$

$$\frac{d}{n}\frac{p-3}{d-p+2}\cdot\sigma^+(u)\cdot\sigma^+(v) \geqq \frac{n}{4d}.$$

By (32)

$$\sigma^+(u) \geqq \frac{n}{d} + o(n) - \frac{n}{4d} - cn \geqq \frac{n}{6d}.$$

Therefore the number of such points u (i.e. $\sigma^-(v)$) is at most

$$h\Big/\frac{n}{6d} = O\left(\frac{k}{n}\right) = o(\sqrt{k}).$$

Now we improve (33). It implies that in (30) (in (H)) $\sigma_j = \sigma_j^+(x) = \dfrac{n}{d} + o(n)$, hence s^2t^{p-3} can be replaced by $s^2 \cdot \left(\dfrac{n}{2d}\right)^{p-3}$. Hence in (H) we can improve $t = o(n)$ to $t = O(\sqrt{k})$, in (29), thus $\sigma^-(x_0) = O(\sqrt{k})$, which, in turn, yields that

$$\sigma^- = O(\sqrt{k}). \tag{34}$$

An important consequence of (34) is that for any vertex $x\in V(S)$

$$\sigma(x)=\left(1-\frac{1}{d}\right)n+\sigma^+(x)+O(\sqrt{k}). \tag{35}$$

$\left(\text{Here we use } n_i=\frac{n}{d}+O(\sqrt{k}), \text{ too.}\right)$ Another consequence is that if $u\in A_i$ $v\in A_j$ and $i\neq j$, then

$$a(u,v)=R_2+[\sigma^+(u)+\sigma^+(v)]R_3+\sigma^+(u)\cdot\sigma^+(v)\cdot R_4+O(\sqrt{k}\,n^{p-3}). \tag{36}$$

Indeed, if we fill in all the missing edges adjacent to u or v, by (34), we create only $O(\sqrt{k}\,n^{p-3})$ K_p's containing (u, v). In the resulting graph an argument, similar to the proof of (23) works.

(K) Let $(x, y)\in E(S)$ (where (x, y) may be a horizontal or a vertical edge). We claim that

$$\sigma^+(x)+\sigma^+(y)\leqq\frac{n}{d}+O(\sqrt{k}). \tag{37}$$

By (35), an equivalent form of (37), independent of the partition is

$$\sigma(x)+\sigma(y)\leqq\left(2-\frac{1}{d}\right)\cdot n+O(\sqrt{k}). \tag{37*}$$

For let us assume first that x, y are in different classes. Then, by (26) and (36)

$$R_1\geqq a(x,y)\geqq R_2+[\sigma^+(x)+\sigma^+(y)]R_3+O(\sqrt{k}\,n^{p-3}),$$

proving (37). (Here we use that $R_1-R_2=R_3\cdot\frac{n}{d}$.) If $x, y\in A_1$, (say) then they have at least $\sigma^+(x)+\sigma^+(y)-|A_1|$ neighbors in A_1 in common and this yields

$$R_1\geqq a(x,y)\geqq R_1+O(\sqrt{k}\cdot n^{p-3})+(\sigma^+(x)+\sigma^+(y)-|A_1|)\cdot$$

$$\cdot\left(\binom{d-1}{p-3}\left(\frac{n}{d}\right)^{p-3}+O(\sqrt{kf}\,n^{p-4})\right).$$

This proves (37), for horizontal edges, too.

(L) An important consequence of (35), (36) and (37) *is that there exists a* $c_1>0$ *such that if* $\sigma(x)\geqq\left(1-\frac{1}{2d}\right)n+c_1\sqrt{k}$, *then the neighbors of* x *span no missing edge*. For suppose that (u, v) is a missing edge whose endpoints are adjacent to x. Let

$$\sigma(x)=\left(1-\frac{1}{2d}\right)n+r, \quad r>0.$$

Let $x\in A_i$ and $u\notin A_i$. By (25) and (36)

$$0\leqq a(u,v)-a(u,x)=[\sigma^+(v)-\sigma^+(x)]R_3+$$

$$+\sigma^+(u)[\sigma^+(v)-\sigma^+(x)]R_4+O(\sqrt{k}\cdot n^{p-3})=$$

$$=[\sigma^+(v)-\sigma^+(x)+O(\sqrt{k})]\,[R_3+\sigma^+(u)R_4].$$

Therefore

$$\sigma^+(v)\geqq\sigma^+(x)+O(\sqrt{k}).$$

This and (35) yield that

$$\sigma^+(v)+\sigma^+(x)\geqq\frac{n}{d}+2r+O(\sqrt{k}).$$

Since $(u, v)\in E(S)$, by (37), applied with $y=v$,

$$r=O(\sqrt{k}).$$

(M) Let us fix a $c_2>c_1$. Set

$$V=\left\{x\in V(G):\sigma^+(x)>\frac{n}{2d}+c_2\sqrt{k}\right\},$$

$$B_i=A_i-V,$$

$$b_i=|B_i|.$$

Let, further, h_i denote the number of horizontal edges spanned by B_i and m_{ij} the number of missing edges between B_i and B_j.

Note that if (u, v) is a missing edge, $u\in B_i$, $v\in B_j$ then, by $u\notin V$,

$$\sigma^+(u)\leqq\frac{n}{2d}+c_2\sqrt{k}$$

and hence (32) implies that there is a constant $c_3>0$ such that

$$\sigma^+(v)>c_3 n.$$

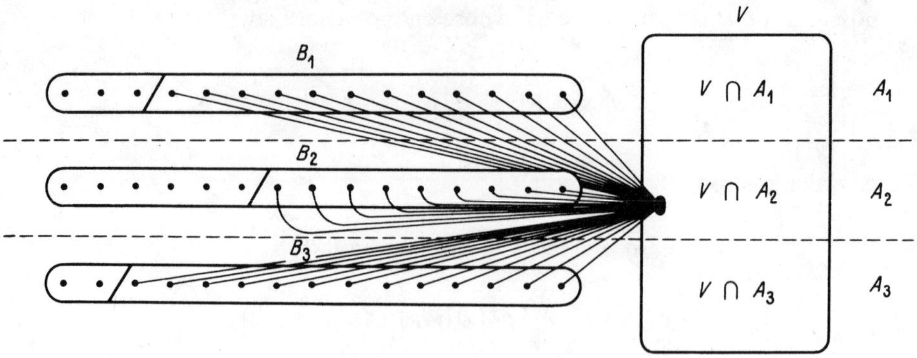

Fig. 4

Hence there are at most $h_j/c_3n = O(h_j/n)$ vertices in B_j incident with missing edges of $S-V$. This in particular implies that

$$m_{ij} = O\left(\frac{h_i h_j}{n^2}\right). \tag{38}$$

(N) *We shall carry out now a number of transformations which finally lead to a graph Q with $v(Q)=v(S)$, $e(Q)=e(S)$ and $k_p(Q)<k_p(S)$ unless S is of a very simple structure. (By the extremality of S the second one must be the case.)*

(i) First construct $S-V=S'$.

(ii) Second, fill in the missing edges in S', to get S''.

(iii) Third, rearrange the horizontal edges in S'' as follows. Let B_i span h_i horizontal edges. Find the least number t_i such that $t_i(|B_i|-t_i) \geqq h_i$. Clearly, $t_i = O\left(\frac{h_i}{n}+1\right) = o(n)$. Further, $h_i \leqq t_i n$. Let $F_i \subseteq B_i$, $|F_i| = t_i$ and $D_i = B_i - F_i$. Connect $t_i - 1$ points of F_i to all points of D_i, and the remaining point u_i of F_i to $h_i - (t_i-1)(|B_i|-t_i)$ points of D_i. This yields the graph S'''. (See Fig. 5.)

(iv) Delete m_{ij} edges spanned by $B_i \cup B_j$. The precise way of selecting these edges depends on the values of m_{ij}, t_i, t_j, h_i and h_j and will be given below, when these cases will be distinguished. To be able to start the general discussion, first we assume only the following.

Condition (*).
If $v \in B_i$ and $t_i > 1$, then we delete at most

$$\left[\frac{m_{ij}}{t_i - 1}\right]$$

edges (v, w), $w \in B_j$.

The resulting graph is S^{IV}. (See Fig. 5.)

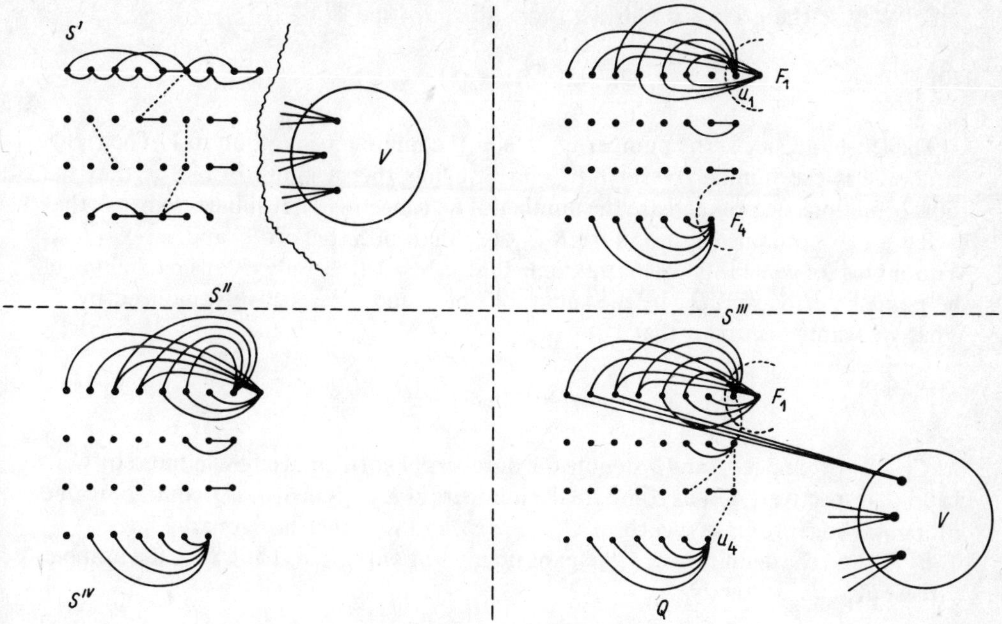

Fig. 5

(v) Connect each $x \in V$ to $\sigma_i^+(x)$ points of B_i which span the fewest edges in S^{IV}. The resulting graph is Q. Clearly $v(Q)=v(S)$ and $e(Q)=e(S)$.

(O) We first analyse the effect of (iii). Call a K_p *regular*, if it contains at most two points of each B_i. Clearly, every K_p in S''' is regular. On the other hand, it is easily seen that *S'' and S''' have the same number of regular K_p's*. Thus $k_p(S'') \geqq k_p(S''')$.

Another property of S''' we need is that *for every r ($0 \leqq r \leqq b_i$) the minimum number of edges spanned by a set X of r points of B_i is for S''' less than or equal to that of S''*. This is clear for $r \leqq b_i - t_i$, since then $X \subseteq B_i$ yielding the minimum is an independent set in S'''. If $r \geqq b_i - t_i + 1$, then X spans

$$h_i - (b_i - r)(b_i - t_i) \tag{39}$$

edges of S''': we take all points of B_i but $b_i - r$ ones from $F_i - u_i$. If $|X| = r$, $X \subseteq B_i$, then X spans at least

$$h_i - (b_i - r)\left(\frac{n}{2d} + c_2\sqrt{k}\right)$$

edges of S'', since $B_i - X$ represents at most $|B_i - X|\left(\frac{n}{2d} + c_2\sqrt{k}\right)$ edges. By $b_i - t_i = \frac{n}{d} + o(n)$ the minimum is smaller for S'''.

(P) We use the previous considerations to show that

$$k_p(Q)-k_p(S^{\mathrm{IV}})\leqq k_p(S)-k_p(S'). \tag{40}$$

The left-hand side is the number of K_p's in Q containing any point in V. The right-hand side is the number of such K_p's in S. (Thus the meaning of (40) is that the transformations do not increase the number of K_p's meeting V.) It suffices to prove that each $x\in V$ is contained in no more K_p's of Q than of S. Let $x\in V$ and set $X=st_S x$. Without loss of generality we may assume that $st_Q x=X$ (this only means relabelling of the points). Let S_X and Q_X be the subgraphs of Q and S respectively, induced by X. What we want to show is that

$$k_{p-1}(S_X)\geqq k_{p-1}(Q_X). \tag{41}$$

Set $C_i=B_i\cap X$, and let γ_i and δ_i denote the numbers of horizontal edges induced by C_i in S and Q, respectively. Let us compare the numbers of K_{p-1}'s in S and Q, containing one horizontal edge from, say, each of $C_1, \dots, C_v$ and no other horizontal edge.

By (L) and the definition of V, X spans no missing edges in S. Thus, in S, the number of these K_{p-1}'s is exactly

$$\gamma_1, \dots, \gamma_v\, S_{d-v}^{p-2v-1}(|C_{v+1}|, \dots, |C_d|). \tag{42}$$

The corrresponding number in Q is at most

$$\delta_1 \dots \delta_v\, S_{d-v}^{p-2v-1}(|C_{v+1}|, \dots, |C_d|). \tag{43}$$

Since $\delta_i\leqq\gamma_i$ by (O) and the construction, and furthermore, every K_{p-1} in Q_X, being regular, is taken into consideration in the terms (43), the inequality (41) follows. (S may contain K_{p-1}'s not counted in the terms (42), namely those containing three or more points of a C_i.)

(Q) The previous section and the extremality of S imply that

$$k_p(S^{\mathrm{IV}})\geqq k_p(S'). \tag{44}$$

Since every K_p in S^{IV} is regular, the number of regular K_p's in S^{IV} is at least as large as the number of regular K_p's in S'. Since step (iii) did not change the number of regular K_p's, it follows that the number of regular K_p's created in step (ii) is at least as large as the number of regular K_p's destroyed in step (iv).

Let Φ^{ij} denote the number of regular K_p's created when the missing edges between B_i and B_j are filled in; let Ψ^{ij} denote the number of regular K_p's destroyed when the m_{ij} edges corresponding to the missing edges between B_i and B_j are deleted in step (iv). Note that Φ^{ij} and Ψ^{ij} depend on the order in which the edges are filled in and deleted, so such an order must be fixed. However, this order will have no importance.

The following (unfortunately, rather tedious) analysis will show that *there is a* $c^*>0$ *such that*

$$\Psi^{ij} \geqq \Phi^{ij} - c^* \cdot \sqrt{k}\, n^{p-3} \tag{45}$$

and the stronger inequality

$$\Psi^{ij} \geqq \Phi^{ij} + d^2 \cdot c^* \sqrt{k}\, n^{p-3}. \tag{46}$$

holds, unless either $m_{ij}=0$ *or* $t_i=t_j=m_{ij}=1$.

The assertion above that "the number of regular K_p's created in step (ii) is at least as large as "the number of K_p's destroyed in step (iv)" means that

$$\sum_{i,j} \Psi^{ij} \leqq \sum_{i,j} \Phi^{ij}.$$

Therefore, by (45) and (46),

$$m_{ij}=0 \quad \text{or} \quad t_i=t_j=m_{ij}=1$$

for every i and j.

So let $i \neq j$ be given such that $m_{ij} \neq 0$ (if $m_{ij}=0$ we have nothing to do). Let us call a regular K_p to be of type ($\mu=0, 1, 2$) if it meets both B_i and B_j and contains μ horizontal edges in $B_i \cup B_j$. Let Φ_μ denote the type μ K_p's created in step (ii) and let Ψ_μ denote the type μ K_p's destroyed in step (iv).

Below *we shall first establish some upper bounds on* Φ_μ *and* (*lower*) *bounds on* Ψ_μ. Then, using some case distinction, we shall specify, how to delete the m_{ij} edges in step (iv) of (N) and show that in each case

$$\Psi^{ij} - \Phi^{ij} = (\Psi_0 + \Psi_1 + \Psi_2) - (\Phi_0 + \Phi_1 + \Phi_2)$$

is "too large", proving (46) or (45). What is an annoying but natural feature of our case distinction that *we shall have the most trouble with the cases, when* t_i *and* t_j *are very small* (1 *or* 2!).

When an edge between B_i and B_j is filled in, the number of type 0 K_p's created is at most

$$R_2 + O(\sqrt{k} \cdot n^{p-3}).$$

The corresponding numbers of type 1 and type 2 K_p's are

$$[\sigma_S^+(u) + \sigma_S^+(v)] R_3 + O(\sqrt{k} \cdot n^{p-3}) \leqq \frac{n}{d} R_3 + O(\sqrt{k} \cdot n^{p-3})$$

and

$$\sigma^+(u)\sigma^+(v) R_4 + O(\sqrt{k} \cdot n^{p-3}) \leqq \frac{n^2}{4d^2} R_4 + O(\sqrt{k} \cdot n^{p-3}),$$

(we have used the definition of V). So

(47) $$\Phi_0 \leqq m_{ij} R_2 + O(\sqrt{k} \cdot n^{p-3} m_{ij})$$

(48) $$\Phi_1 \leqq m_{ij} \frac{n}{d} R_3 + O(\sqrt{k} \cdot n^{p-3} m_{ij})$$

(49) $$\Phi_2 \leqq m_{ij} \frac{n^2}{4d} R_4 + O(\sqrt{k} \cdot n^{p-3} m_{ij}) .$$

On the other hand, the numbers of K_p's of types 0, 1 and 2 destroyed by deleting an edge (u, v) in step (iv) are

(50) $$R_2 + O(\sqrt{k} \cdot n^{p-3})$$

(51) $$[\sigma^+_{S'''}(u) + \sigma^+_{S'''}(v)] R_3 + O(\sqrt{k} \cdot n^{p-3})$$

and

(52) $$\sigma^+_{S'''}(u) \cdot \sigma^+_{S'''}(v) R_4 + O(\sqrt{k} \cdot n^{p-3}) ,$$

respectively. This would be trivial if we counted the K_p's in S''' containing (u, v). However, we fixed an order of deleting the edges between the classes B_i and B_j. More precisely, we fixed an order on the pairs (i, j), and if (i^*, j^*) preceeds (i, j), then we should not count here the K_p's containing (u, v) but at the same time containing a (u^*, v^*), $u^* \in B_{i^*}$, $u^* \in B_{j^*}$, already deleted. The number of such K_p's is $O(m \cdot n^{p-4}) = O(k \cdot n^{p-4})$, for the edges (u^*, v^*) disjoint from (u, v). Let us estimate the number of those destroyed by the removal of an edge (u, w). If $t_i = 1$, i.e. $F_i = \{u\}$ then $h_i < b_i$ and so, by (38),

$$m_{il} = O\left(\frac{h_i h_l}{n^2}\right) = O\left(\frac{n \cdot k}{n^2}\right) = O\left(\frac{k}{n}\right)$$

for every l. Thus only $O\left(\frac{k}{n}\right)$ edges adjacent to u are removed at most and so the number of K_p's containing (u, v) and an edge adjacent to u and removed previously is at most $O\left(\frac{k}{n} \cdot n^{p-3}\right) = O(k \cdot n^{p-4})$. If $t_i \geqq 2$ then, by Condition (*) of (N)/(iv), the number of edges adjacent to u and removed previously (by (38) and $h_l \leqq t_l \cdot n$) is at most

$$\sum_l O\left(\frac{m_{ij}}{t_l}\right) \leq \sum_l \left(\frac{h_i h_l}{t_l n^2}\right) = O\left(\frac{h_i}{n}\right) = O\left(\frac{k}{n}\right),$$

and we conclude as before. Thus (50), (51) and (52) are proved.

Now we need some case distinction. In the cases below we can always satisfy Condition (*) of step (iv) in (N).

Case (Q1). $m_{ij} \leqq (t_i - 1)(t_j - 1)$. Then we can remove m_{ij} edges connecting $F_i - u_i$ to $F_j - u_j$. For such an edge (u, v)

$$\sigma^+(u), \sigma^+(v) = \frac{n}{d} + O(\sqrt{k}),$$

whence by (50), (51) and (52),

$$\Psi_0 \geqq m_{ij} R_2 + O(m_{ij}\sqrt{k} \cdot n^{p-3})$$

$$\Psi_1 \geqq m_{ij} \frac{2n}{d} R_3 + O(m_{ij}\sqrt{k} \cdot n^{p-3})$$

$$\Psi_2 \geqq m_{ij} \frac{n^2}{d^2} R_4 + O(m_{ij}\sqrt{k} \cdot n^{p-3}).$$

Comparing with (47), (48) and (49) it follows that

$$\Psi^{ij} - \Phi^{ij} \geqq c_4 n^{p-2},$$

proving (46) and therefore (45), too.

Case (Q2). $(t_i - 1)(t_j - 1) < m_{ij} \leqq 4(t_i - 1)(t_j - 1)$. Then we can remove all edges between $F_i - u_i$ and $F_j - u_j$ and $m_{ij} - (t_i - 1)(t_j - 1)$ edges between $F_i - u_i$ and $B_j - F_j$. For the first $(t_i - 1)(t_j - 1)$ edges

$$\sigma^+(u), \sigma^+(v) \geqq \frac{n}{d} + O(\sqrt{k}),$$

for the rest still

$$\sigma^+(u) \geqq \frac{n}{d} + O(\sqrt{k}).$$

Hence, as before,

$$\Psi_0 - \Phi_0 \geqq O(\sqrt{k} \cdot n^{p-3} m_{ij}),$$

$$\Psi_1 - \Phi_1 \geqq (t_i - 1)(t_j - 1)\frac{n}{d} R_3 + O(\sqrt{k} \cdot n^{p-3} m_{ij}),$$

and

$$\Psi_2 - \Phi_2 \geqq \frac{4(t_i - 1)(t_j - 1) - m_{ij}}{4} \frac{n^2}{d^2} R_4 + O(\sqrt{k} \cdot n^{p-3} m_{ij}) \geqq O(\sqrt{k} \cdot n^{p-3} m_{ij}).$$

By $m_{ij} \leqq 4(t_i-1)(t_j-1)$ we have

$$\Psi^{ij} - \Phi^{ij} \geqq (t_i-1)(t_j-1)\frac{n}{d}R_3 + O(\sqrt{k}\cdot n^{p-3}m_{ij}) =$$
$$= (t_i-1)(t_j-1)\left[\frac{n}{d}R_3 + O(\sqrt{k}\cdot n^{p-3})\right] \geqq c_5 n^{p-2},$$

proving (46) (and also (45)).

Case (Q3). $m_{ij} \geqq t_i t_j$, $t_i \geqq 2$, $t_j \geqq 3$. In this case remove the m_{ij} edges so that all edges between F_i and F_j are removed. Then no type 2 K_p's remain and hence

$$\Psi_2 - \Phi_2 \geqq 0.$$

We have, similarly as before,

$$\Psi_0 - \Phi_0 \geqq O(\sqrt{k}\cdot n^{p-3}m_{ij}),$$

and since $(t_i-1)(t_j-1)$ of the removed edges satisfy $\sigma^+_{S''}(u), \sigma^+_{S''}(v) \geqq n/d + O(\sqrt{k})$, and all but at most one of the rest has at least one endpoint u with $\sigma^+_{S''}(u) \geqq \frac{n}{d} + O(\sqrt{k})$, we have

$$\Psi_1 - \Phi_1 \geqq ((t_i-1)(t_j-1)-1)\frac{n}{d}R_3 + O(\sqrt{k}\cdot n^{p-3}m_{ij}).$$

By (38),

$$m_{ij} = O\left(\frac{h_i h_j}{n^2}\right) = O(t_i t_j) = O((t_i-1)(t_j-1)-1).$$

We conclude as before.

Case (Q4). $t_i = t_j = 2$, $m_{ij} \geqq 4$. By (38), $m_{ij} = O(1)$. First we try the same construction as in case (Q3). As before we have

$$\Psi_2 - \Phi_2 \geqq 0,$$
$$\Psi_0 - \Phi_0 \geqq O(\sqrt{k}\cdot n^{p-3})$$

and looking also at the edges connecting u_i to $F_j - u_j$ and u_j to $F_i - u_i$ we get, similarly as above,

$$\Psi_1 - \Phi_1 \geqq [\sigma^+_{S''}(u_i) + \sigma^+_{S''}(u_j)]\cdot R_3 + O(\sqrt{k}\cdot n^{p-3}).$$

Now we are home, unless

$$\sigma^+_{S''}(u_i) + \sigma^+_{S''}(u_j) \leqq \sqrt[4]{k}\cdot n^{p-3+\frac{1}{2}}.$$

(Here and below we shall use $\sqrt[4]{kn^2}$ as a quantity which is $o(n)$ and for which $\sqrt{k}=o(\sqrt[4]{kn^2})$.) In the latter case we modify the rule used to delete the edges in step (iv). We do not delete (u_i, u_j), but delete an edge between F_i-u_i and B_j-F_j, instead. Putting (u_i, u_j) back creates at most

$$[\sigma^+_{S''}(u_i)+\sigma^+_{S''}(u_j)]R_3+\sigma^+_{S''}(u_i)\sigma^+_{S''}(u_j)R_4+O(\sqrt{k}\cdot n^{p-3})=o(n^{p-2})$$

K_p's, while deleting the edge between F_i-u_i and B_j-F_j destroys at least

$$\frac{n}{d}R_3+O(\sqrt{k}\cdot n^{p-3})$$

K_p's. Thus

$$\Psi^{ij}\geqq\Phi^{ij}+c_6n^{p-2}$$

proving (46). So we are finished again. The cases treated so far cover all cases with $t_i>1$ and $t_j>1$.

Case (Q5). $t_i=1$, $t_j\geqq 2$, $m_{ij}\leqq t_j-1$. The argument is basically the same as in case (Q1). However, we have to improve (48) and (49). Now $\sigma^+_S(u)\leqq\min\left(\frac{n}{2d}+c_2\sqrt{k}, h_i\right)$ for any $u\in B_i$. Thus for any missing edge (u, v) $(u\in B_i, v\in B_j)$

$$\sigma^+_S(u)+\sigma^+_S(v)\leqq\frac{n}{2d}+\min\left(\frac{n}{2d}, h_i\right)+O(\sqrt{k}).$$

Hence

$$\Phi_1\leqq m_{ij}\left(\frac{n}{2d}+\min\left(\frac{n}{2d}, h_i\right)\right)R_3+O(\sqrt{k}\cdot n^{p-3}m_{ij}), \tag{53}$$

and

$$\Phi_2\leqq m_{ij}\cdot\frac{n}{2d}\cdot\min\left(\frac{n}{2d}, h_i\right)R_4+O(\sqrt{k}\cdot n^{p-3}m_{ij}). \tag{54}$$

On the other hand, deleting m_{ij} edges connecting u_i to F_j-u_j we obtain that

$$\Psi_1\geqq m_{ij}\left(\frac{n}{d}+h_i\right)R_3+O(\sqrt{k}\cdot n^{p-3})$$

and

$$\Psi_2\geqq m_{ij}\cdot\frac{n}{d}\cdot h_iR_4+O(\sqrt{k}\cdot n^{p-3}).$$

By (47), (50), (53) and (54),

$$\Psi^{ij}\geqq\Phi^{ij}+c_7n^{p-2}.$$

We are home.

Case (Q6). $t_i=1, m_{ij}\geqq t_j\geqq 2$. By (38) $m_{ij}=O(1)$, again. Then we delete all lines between u_i and F_j and $m_{ij}-t_j$ other lines between F_j-u_j and B_i-u_i. Then, as above, we have

$$\Psi_1\geqq\left[(t_j-1)\left(\frac{n}{d}+h_i\right)+(\sigma^+_{S''}(u_j)+h_i)+(m_{ij}-t_j)\frac{n}{d}\right]R_3+O(\sqrt{k}\cdot n^{p-3})$$

and by the same argument as in case (Q3), $\Psi_2\geqq\Phi_2$. Hence we get in the case $h_i\geqq\frac{n}{2d}$, using (53),

$$\Psi^{ij}-\Phi^{ij}\geqq\left[t_jh_i+\sigma^+_{S''}(u_j)-\frac{n}{d}\right]R_3+O(\sqrt{k}\cdot n^{p-3})\geqq$$

$$\geqq\left[\left(\frac{t_j}{2}-1\right)\frac{n}{d}+\sigma^+_{S''}(u_j)+t_j\left(h_i-\frac{n}{2d}\right)\right]R_3+O(\sqrt{k}\cdot n^{p-3}),$$

and in case $h_i\leqq\frac{n}{2d}$,

$$\Psi^{ij}-\Phi^{ij}\geqq\left[m_{ij}\frac{n}{2d}-(m_{ij}-t_j)h_i+\sigma^+_{S''}(u_j)-\frac{n}{d}\right]R_3+O(\sqrt{k}\cdot n^{p-3})\geqq$$

$$\geqq\left[\left(\frac{t_j}{2}-1\right)\frac{n}{d}+\sigma^+_{S''}(u_j)\right]R_3+O(\sqrt{k}\cdot n^{p-3}).$$

Hence (46) is proved, unless $t_j=2$, $\sigma^+_{S''}(u_j)\leqq\sqrt[4]{kn^2}$, $h_i\leqq\frac{n}{2d}+\sqrt[4]{kn^2}$. Even in this latter case

$$\Psi^{ij}-\Phi^{ij}\geqq O(\sqrt{k}\cdot n^{p-3}).$$

Put the edge (u_i, u_j) back and delete a line between F_j-u_j and B_i-u_i instead. This way we destroy at least

$$\frac{n}{2d}R_3+o(n^{p-2}).$$

more K_p's than before. This settles this case.

Case (Q7). $t_i=t_j=1$, $m_{ij}\geqq 2$, and e.g. $h_i\geqq h_j$. Again, $m_{ij}=O(1)$. Now we delete (u_i, u_j) and $m_{ij}-1$ horizontal lines. As before,

$$\Psi_2\geqq\Phi_2.$$

Note that in this case we deleted only one vertical edge. Thus

$$\Psi_0=R_2+O(\sqrt{k}\cdot n^{p-3}).$$

For Φ_0 we of course still have (47). Moreover,

$$\Psi_1 \geqq (h_i+h_j)R_3+(m_{ij}-1)R_1+O(\sqrt{k}\cdot n^{p-3})=$$
$$=\left[h_i+h_j+(m_{ij}-1)\frac{n}{d}\right]R_3+(m_{ij}-1)R_2+O(\sqrt{k}\cdot n^{p-3}).$$

We have to estimate Φ_1 a little more carefully than before. Consider two missing lines (u, v) and (w, t) in S', $u,w \in B_i$, $v,t \in B_j$, where, say, $u \neq w$ (we allow $v=t$). Then

$$[\sigma_S^+(u)+\sigma_S^+(v)]+[\sigma_S^+(w)+\sigma_S^+(t)] \leqq$$
$$\leqq (h_i+1)+\sigma_S^+(v)+\sigma_S^+(t) \leqq h_i+h_j+\frac{n}{2d}+O(\sqrt{k}).$$

Hence

$$\Phi_1 \leqq \left(h_i+h_j+\frac{n}{2d}+(m_{ij}-2)\frac{n}{d}\right)R_3+O(\sqrt{k}\cdot n^{p-3}).$$

Thus

$$\Psi^{ij}-\Phi^{ij} \geqq \frac{n}{2d}R_3+O(\sqrt{k}\cdot n^{p-3}),$$

proving (46) again.

Observe that the cases (Q1)–(Q7) prove (46) unless either $m_{ij}=0$ or $m_{ij}=t_i=t_j=1$. Thus we have proved that for every (i, j) $m_{ij}=0$ or $m_{ij}=t_i=t_j=1$. Let us consider the latter case.

Case (Q8). $m_{ij}=t_i=t_j=1$. Of course, we remove (u_i, u_j). Denoting the missing edge of S' between B_i and B_j by (v_i, v_j) we have, by the same type calculations as above,

$$\Psi^{ij}-\Phi^{ij} \geqq [(h_i-\sigma_S^+(v_i))+(h_j-\sigma_S^+(v_j))]R_3+O(\sqrt{k}\cdot n^{p-3}).$$

Hence indeed $\Psi-\Phi \geqq (\sqrt{k}\cdot n^{p-3})$ and it also follows that

$$\sigma_S^+(v_i) \geqq h_i-\sqrt[4]{kn^2} \qquad \sigma_S^+(v_j) \geqq h_j-\sqrt[4]{kn^2}$$

As we have seen at the end of (M), $\sigma^+(v_i) \geqq c_3 n$. Thus $h_i \approx \sigma^+(v_i)$, which implies that v_i is the unique point in B_i with the largest horizontal degree. Hence we may assume that $v_i=u_i$ and $v_j=u_j$. Hence S' and S^{IV} have the same missing edges. Therefore step (ii) and (iv) can be ignored: Q is obtained from S by steps (i), (iii) and (v).

Let us consider step (iii) again. If step (iii) is applied to S' (instead of S''), then the number of regular K_p's remains the same, if B_i meets no missing edge (v_i, v_j), then the number of regular K_p's decreases when a horizontal edge in B_i non-adjacent to v_i is replaced by a horizontal edge adjacent to v_i. (40) is not influenced by omitting steps (ii) and (iv). Thus we get that $k_p(Q) \geqq k_p(S)$. By the extremality of S $k_p(Q) = k_p(S)$ and if (v_i, v_j) is a missing edge ($v_i \in B_i$, $v_j \in B_j$), then all the horizontal edges of B_i are adjacent to v_i. It also follows that no B_i contains a triangle in S. Hence, if $x \in V$, we must have equality in (41), which implies that then *either x is joined to all points of B_i or the neighbors of x in B_i are independent in S.*

(R) We study now Q. Since Q is another extremal graph, it follows that there is at most one i such that $t_i \geqq 2$. Indeed, if $t_i, t_j \geqq 2$ $(i \neq j)$ then, by (Q), $m_{ij} = 0$. Considering an edge connecting $F_i - u_i$ to $F_j - u_j$ we would get a contradiction with (37). So suppose that $t_2, \ldots, t_d \leqq 1$ and thus $F_i = \{u_i\}$ or $F_i = \emptyset$ for $i \geqq 2$.

Consider now a pair of points $x \in B_i$, $y \in B_j$. By $x, y \notin V$

(55) $$\sigma_i^+(x) < b_i - t_i$$

and

(56) $$\sigma_i^+(y) < b_j - t_j .$$

If $\sigma_i^+(x)$, $\sigma_i^+(y) > 0$, we define the *shifting* of edges from x to y as follows. Replace t horizontal edges of form (x, u) by t horizontal edges of form (y, v). Clearly, the number of K_p's of the resulting graph $Q(t)$ is a quadratic function of $t: At^2 + Bt + C$, where $A \leqq 0$. Therefore either $Q(1)$ or $Q(-1)$ has less K_p's than Q, unless $A = 0$, which means that

(57) either $p = 3$ or (x, y) is a missing edge.

In both cases no K_p is containing horizontal edges of type (x, u) and (y, v) at the same time. Now $k_p(Q(t))$ is linear:

$$k_p(Q(t)) = k_p(Q) - (a(x, u) - a(y, v))t ,$$

(where $a(x, u)$ and $a(y, v)$ are independent of the choices of u and v).

Since $k_p(Q) \leqq \min(k_p(Q(-1)), k_p(Q(1)))$, thus

(58) $$a(x, u) = a(y, v)$$

and taking t as large as possible we obtain a $Q' = Q(t)$ for which either

(59) $$st_{Q'}(x) \cap B_i = \emptyset$$

or

(60) $$st_{Q'}(y) \cap B_j - F_j .$$

This operation is called shifting of edges from x to y. We shall use it to prove that *there is at most one missing edge in $Q - V$ (i.e. in $S - V$).*

First we prove that

(61) $$\sigma_Q^+(x)=O(\sqrt{k}),$$

(62) $$\sigma_Q^+(y)=\frac{n}{d}+O(\sqrt{k}),$$

and

(63) $$\sigma_S^+(x)=\sigma_Q^+(x)=\frac{n}{2d}+O(\sqrt{k}).$$

Finally,

(64) x, y are not adjacent to any point in V.

Indeed, if (x, y) is a missing edge, then (Q8) describes the situation: $x=u_i$, $y=u_j$ and all the horizontal edges of B_i are adjacent to x in Q, and in S. Hence

(65) $$\sigma_Q^+(x)=\sigma_S^+(x)\leqq\frac{n}{2d}+O(\sqrt{k})\quad\text{and}\quad\sigma_Q^+(y)=\sigma_S^+(y)\leqq\frac{n}{2d}+O(\sqrt{k}).$$

Thus (60) implies

(66) $$\sigma_Q^+(x)=\sigma_Q^+(x)+\sigma_Q^+(y)-\sigma_Q^+(y)\leqq\frac{n}{d}-\sigma_Q^+(y)+O(\sqrt{k})\leqq O(\sqrt{k}).$$

This proves (61) in the second case and it is trivial, when (59) holds. (62) is trivial, when (60) holds. If we know only (59), then we apply (32) more precisely (to have $O(\sqrt{k})$), (34) *and* (27), *yielding* $\sigma^+(x)+\sigma^+(y)+\frac{d}{n}\cdot\frac{p-3}{d-p+2}\sigma^+(x), \sigma^+(y)<\frac{n}{d}+O(\sqrt{k})$, obtaining (62) again. (63) follows from (65) and (66), where we have equality.

Finally, if $w\in V$, then, by (62), $\sigma_Q^+(w)+\sigma_Q^+(y)\geqq\frac{3n}{2d}+O(\sqrt{k})$, therefore, applying (37) to (w, y) in Q' we obtain that w and y are not adjacent in Q, proving (64).

Let now (x, y) and (x', y') be two missing edges and assume that y and y' are in B_j and $B_{j'}$, where $j\neq j'$. By shifting the edges into y and y' we can achieve that $\sigma^+(y)+$ $+\sigma^+(y')=\frac{2n}{d}+o(n)$ in the obtained Q''.

By (35) and (37*), $(y, y')\notin E(Q'')$, hence (y, y') is a missing edge in Q and S as well. (Since the optimal partition may change during shifting the edges, we used (37*).) Now we shift the edges from y to x in Q but leaving $c_8\sqrt{k}$ edges at y, where c_8 is a sufficiently large constant. This will ensure that the arguments used to establish (32) in S work in Q as well. However, the missing edge (y, y') contradicts (32): $\sigma^+(y)=O(\sqrt{k})$ and

$\sigma^+(y') = \dfrac{n}{2d} + O(\sqrt{k})$. Thus we have proved that $Q-V$ and $S-V$ contain at most one missing edge.

(S) ... Below, in (S), (T) and (U) we complete the proof. In (S) we investigate the case, when $Q-V$ has no missing edges and at least two B_i's contain (horizontal) edges. In (U) we observe, that the remaining case, when $Q-V$ has (exactly) one missing edge, can be reduced to the cases (S), (T). Case (S) will be subdivided into (S1)–(S4) according to the distribution of the horizontal edges in B_i's. The basic method is to shift the edges so that the resulting graph contains an edge contradicting (37) of (K). Most of the difficulties occur when $p=3$.

First we prove the

Saturation principle. Every $x \in V$ is joined to all vertices of all but one sets $B_i - F_i$, where for $h_i=0$ $F_i=:\emptyset$.

Indeed, if there are a $B_i - F_i$ and a $B_j - F_j$ not all the vertices of which are joined to x, then delete an edge (x, u), $u \in B_j - F_j$ and add an edge (x, v), $v \in B_i - F_i$. One can easily check that the number of K_p's of the resulting graph Q' decreased if $\sigma_i^+(x) < \sigma_j^+(x)$:

All $B_i - F_i$ and $B_j - F_j$ are independent sets, and therefore the number of K_p's either not containing x or containing x and only one vertex from $B_i \cup B_j$ remains the same, while the number of K_p's containing x, a $u \in B_i - F_i$ and a $v \in B_j - F_j$ is proportional to $\sigma_i^+(x) \cdot \sigma_j^+(x)$, that is, decreases. This contradiction proves the saturation principle.

Now we describe the structure of S in the case when $Q-V$ (or $S-V$) has no missing edges and at least two sets B_i contain horizontal lines. Assume that the indices are chosen so that $h_1 \geqq h_2 \geqq \ldots \geqq h_f > 0$, $h_{f+1} = \ldots = h_d = 0$. So we deal with the case when $f \geqq 2$.

Case (S1). Suppose that $|F_1| \geqq 2$ and $\sigma_Q^+(u_1) < b_1 - t_1$. It follows by (Q) that $|F_2| = \ldots = |F_f| = 1$. Also note that $p=3$ by (57). Shift as many horizontal edges of Q incident with $u_1, \ldots, u_{f-1}$ to u_f as possible. Since u_f is adjacent to $F_1 - u_1$ whose points have degree $b_1 - t_1 = \dfrac{n}{d} + O(\sqrt{k})$, by (37) its horizontal degree cannot grow too big during this shift, i.e.

$$\sigma_Q^+(u_1) + \ldots + \sigma_Q^+(u_f) = O(\sqrt{k})\,.$$

We shall prove that each $x \in V$ is joined to each $v \in B_2 \cup \ldots \cup B_d$. Here we need the

Strong saturation principle. If $f \geqq 2$, then each $x \in V$ is joined to all the vertices of all but one sets B_1 $B_1 - F_1 + u_1$, $B_2, \ldots, B_d$. Indeed, fix a $u_i \in B_i - st(x)$ when $h_i = 0$. If e.g. $x \in V$ is not joined to a $v \in B_i$ and a $w \in B_j$, then it is neither joined to $u_i \in B_i$ and $u_j \in B_j$. Assume that $\sigma_i^+(x) \geqq \sigma_j^+(x)$. First shift all the h_i edges incident with u_i to some u_l (where $l=j$ is also allowed if $h_j > 0$). This does not change the number of K_3's. Thên replace an edge $(x, z) \in E(Q)$ by (x, u_i): now the number of K_3's decreases. This is a contradiction *proving that x is joined completely to each but one of* $B_1, B_2, \ldots, B_d$. A similar argument works if B_2 is replaced by $B_1 - F + u_1$.

We show that $x \in V$ cannot be joined to all points of $B_1 - F_1 + u_1$. As we have seen at the end of (Q8), any $x \in V$ is joined either to all the vertices of B_i or the neighbors of x are independent in S. If x is joined to all the vertices of $B_1 - F_1 + u_1$, then $st(x) \cap B_1$ contains edges in Q, thus in S as well. Therefore $st(x)$ contains a $u \in F_1 - u_1$, too. But $\sigma_Q^+(u) + \sigma_Q^+(x) \geqq \frac{3n}{2d} + o(n)$, contradicting (35) and (37*). Hence x must be adjacent to all points of $B_2 \cup \ldots \cup B_d$ in Q and in S as well. So considering the partition $D_1 = B_1 \cup V$, $D_2 = B_2$, $\ldots$, $D_d = B_d$, every edge between different classes will be in S. Thus $S \in U_0(n, E)$.

Case (S2). $\sigma_Q^+(u_1) \geqq \frac{3n}{4d}$. (We may have $|F_1| = 1$ or > 1.) By the saturation principle each $x \in V$ is connected to all points of all but one sets $B_1 - F_1, B_2, \ldots, B_d$. Suppose that x misses a point in B_2. Consider S. Since x is joined to all the vertices of $B_1 - F_1$ and by (37*) to none of F_1, it is joined to exactly $b_1 - t_1$ vertices of B_1 and these vertices are independent by the results of (Q8). Hence every horizontal edge of S in B_1 contains one of the t_1 points of B_1 non-adjacent to x in S. Thus for at least one of these vertices, say, for u, $\sigma_S^+(u) \geqq \frac{3n}{4d} + O(\sqrt{k})$, contradicting the definition of V. This proves that every $x \in V$ is connected to every y in $B_2 \cup \ldots \cup B_d$. We conclude as above.

Case (S3). $|F_1| = 1$ and $h_1 + \ldots + h_d \leqq \frac{3n}{4d}$. We know by the saturation principle that every $x \in V$ is adjacent to all points of all but at most one sets B_i. If x is not adjacent to all points of B_i, then it is not adjacent to u_i either. Also we have $p = 3$ again.

First let us assume that there exists an $x \in V$ not joined to u_1. Shift all but one horizontal edges of B_1 to B_2. (We know that B_1, B_2 contain horizontal edges!) This shifting results in another extremal graph Q'. Replace this last horizontal edge in B_1 (incident with u_1) by (u_1, x). This does not increase the number of triangles, moreover, it decreases, whenever at least one $y \in V$ is joined to u_1. This proves that no vertex of V is joined to u_1. Thus each $x \in V$ is joined to each $w \in B_2 \cup \ldots \cup B_d$. We conclude as in (S1).

So we may suppose that every $x \in V$ is adjacent to all points of B_1, and similarly to all points of $B_2, \ldots, B_f$. If every $x \in V$ is adjacent to all points in $B_1 \cup \ldots \cup B_d$ then we can again conclude as before. So suppose some $x \in V$ is non-adjacent to some point in B_{f+1} (say). Then $V = \{x\}$; in fact, if there exists another vertex $y \in V$, then we can shift edges connecting x to B_{f+1} to B_1 until the degree of u_1 becomes greater than $n - \frac{n}{3d}$. But then, being connected to y, it contradicts (37*). The case $V = \{x\}$ can be handled again in the same way as case (S1).

Case (S4). $|F_1| = 1$ and $h_1 + \ldots + h_d > \frac{3n}{4d}$, but $\sigma_Q^+(u_i) < b_i - 1$ $(i = 1, \ldots, f)$. Again, we have $p = 3$. It follows then (as before) that every $x \in V$ is joined to all points of all but at most one of $B_1-u_1, \ldots, B_f-u_f, B_{f+1}, \ldots, B_d$. Furthermore, since by shift we can increase the degree of any u_i $(i=1, \ldots, f)$ to more than $\frac{3n}{4d}$, no one of $u_1, \ldots, u_f$ is adjacent to any point in V.

Since the horizontal edges incident with $u_1, \ldots, u_f$ must be contained in the same number of triangles (by (58) in the definition of shift), it follows that

$$|B_1| = \ldots = |B_f|.$$

Shift now as many horizontal edges to B_i's with the smaller indices as possible. Even after this shifting each B_i $(2 \leqq i \leqq f)$ must contain horizontal edges, otherwise replacing an edge (x, u), $u \in B_1$ by (x, u_i) we could diminish $\sigma_1^+(x) \cdot \sigma_i^+(x)$, hence decreasing the number of K_3's of the resulting graph Q'. This is a contradiction, since Q' is extremal. Thus

$$h_1 + \ldots + h_f \geqq (f-1)(|B_1|-1)+1 \geqq |B_1|.$$

Hence

$$\sigma_Q^+(u_1) = |B_1| - 1$$

and

$$\sigma_Q^+(u_2) \geqq 1.$$

Since u_1 and u_2 are adjacent, by (37) $\sigma_Q^+(u_2) = o(n)$. Thus we can replace (u_1, u_2) by an edge connecting u_2 to $B_2 - u_2$. This decreases the number of K_3's, a contradiction.

(T) Suppose still that $Q-V$ has no missing edges but let now $h_2 = \ldots = h_d = 0$. The argument in (S2) works unless $|F_1| = 2$ and $h_1 \leqq \frac{n}{d} + O(\sqrt{k})$ or $|F_1| = 1$ and $h_1 \leqq \frac{n}{2d} + O(\sqrt{k})$. Thus $\sigma_Q^+(u_1) < b_1 - t_1$. Assume first $h_1 > 0$.

As above, each $x \in V$ is joined to all points of all but at most one sets $B_1 - F_1$, $B_2, \ldots, B_d$. *Our aim is to show that no $x \in V$ is joined to u_1.* This implies (by (Q8)) that no $x \in V$ is joined to F_1 at all. Thus each $x \in V$ is joined to each $v \in B_2 \cup \ldots \cup B_d$. Hence S satisfies Definition 2 with $W = V \cup F_1$: $S \in U_2(n, E)$.

Let us assume (indirectly) that an $x \in V$ is joined to u_1. By (Q8) x must be connected to all points of B_1. Hence, by (37*), $F_1 - u_1 = \emptyset$, that is, $F_1 = \{u_1\}$.

We show that each $y \in V - x$ is joined to each $v \in Q - V - u_1$. Suppose $y \in V - x$ is not connected to some $v \in B_i$ $(i \geqq 2)$, or some $v \in B_1 - u_1$. Then we can shift edges from y to u_1 and achieve $\sigma^+(u_1) \geqq \frac{n}{2d} + \sqrt[4]{kn^2}$. This contradicts (37*) since u_1 is adjacent to x.

There are two cases: x is joined to all vertices of $B_2 \cup \ldots \cup B_d$ or not. In the first case the vertices of Q can be partitioned into the classes $V \cup B_1, B_2, \ldots, B_d$ so that vertices belonging to different classes are always adjacent. Unless $h_1 = 0$, the first class contains a K_3, therefore we can rearrange the edges in $V \cup B_1$ ruining all the K_3's and (consequently) diminishing the number of K_3's. This is a contradiction.

In the other case there is a $v \in B_i$ ($i \geqq 2$) not joined to x. We can shift edges from x to u_1 until $\sigma^+(u_1) \geqq \frac{n}{2d} + \sqrt[4]{kn^2}$ is achieved. This proves (by (37*)) that no $y \in V-x$ is adjacent to u_1.

Also we can shift edges from u_1 to x. If this fills up x, i.e., in the resulting extremal graph Q' x is adjacent to all points of $Q-V$ and there is still a horizontal edge in Q' incident with u_1, then replacing (u_1, x) by a horizontal edge (u_1, w) we decrease the number of K_p's. This is a contradiction. Thus $Q'-V$ contains no horizontal edges. Carry out the same shifting of edges from u_1 to x but stop, when only one horizontal edge (u_1, w) is left. If $V-x \neq \emptyset$, we can replace (u_1, w) by (u_1, y), decreasing the number of K_p's, a contradiction. If $V=\{x\}$, then put x into the class B_i containing the v. Since x is joined to all the vertices of all the other classes, we are home: $Q \in U_0(n, E)$, which implies for $p \geqq 4$ that $Q \in U_1(n, E)$. The same holds for S, too.

The case $h_1=0$ is fairly simple, and left to the reader.

(U) We are left with the case when $Q-V$ has a missing edge (u_1, u_2) with, say, $u_i \in B_i$. Then we know that u_1, u_2 are not adjacent to any point in V. Then replacing V by $V+u_1$ and B_1 by B_1-u_1, the arguments in (S4) and (T) can be applied.

The proof of Theorem 3 is complete.

References

[1] Bollobás, B., Relations between sets of complete subgraphs, *Proc. of the Fifth British Combinatorial Conference (Aberdeen)*, 1975, 79–84.

[2] Erdős, P., On a theorem of Rademacher-Turán, *Illinois Journal of Math.*, **6** (1962), 122–127.

[3] Erdős, P., On the number of complete subgraphs contained in certain graphs, *Magy. Tud. Akad. Mat. Kut. Int. Közl.*, **7** (1962), 459–474.

[4] Goodman, A. W., On sets of acquaintances and strangers at any party, *Amer. Math. Monthly*, **66** (1959) 778–783.

[5] Lovász, L. and Simonovits, M., On the number of complete subgraphs of a graph, *Proc. of Fifth British Combinatorial Conference (Aberdeen)*, 1975, 431–442.

[6] Moon, J. W. and Moser, L., On a problem of Turán, *MTA Mat. Kut. Int. Közl.*, **7** (1962), 283–286.

[7] Turán, P., An extremal problem in graph theory (In Hungarian), *Mat. és Fiz. Lapok*, **48** (1941), 436–452.

EÖTVÖS LORÁND UNIVERSITY
H-1088 BUDAPEST, MÚZEUM KRT. 6—8.
HUNGARY

Studies in Pure Mathematics
To the Memory of Paul Turán

Zeros of approximations to the zeta function

by

H. L. MONTGOMERY* (Ann Arbor)

1. Statement of results

Let N be real, $N \geqq 5$, write $s=\sigma+it$, and put

$$U_N(s)=\sum_{n\leqq N} n^{-s}.$$

P. TURÁN [7, Theorem III] has shown that if $U_N(s)\neq 0$ for

(1) $$\sigma \geqq 1+N^{-\frac{1}{2}+\varepsilon} \quad (N>N_0(\varepsilon))$$

then the Riemann Hypothesis is true. We show that this implication is vacuous by demonstrating that $U_N(s)$ has zeros with much larger real part.

Theorem. *Let* $0<c<\frac{4}{\pi}-1$. *Then for all* $N>N_0(c)$, $U_N(s)$ *has zeros in the half-plane*

(2) $$\sigma>1+c(\log\log N)/\log N\,.$$

TURÁN [7, Theorem IV] has given a very simple proof that $U_N(s)\neq 0$ for

$$\sigma \geqq 1+2(\log\log N)/\log N \quad (N>N_0);$$

thus our Theorem is best possible, apart from the value of c. In fact, by using (6), (7) below and ideas of HALÁSZ [3] one may show that if $c>\frac{4}{\pi}-1$, $N>N_0(c)$, then $|U_N(s)-\zeta(s)|\leqq \frac{1}{2}|\zeta(s)|$ for s in the half-plane (2). Hence the constant $\frac{4}{\pi}-1$ in the Theorem is best possible.

* Work supported in part by National Science Foundation Grant MCS76-10346.

Let

$$C_N(s) = \sum_{n \leq N} (1 - n/N) n^{-s},$$

$$V_N(s) = \sum_{n \leq N} (-1)^n n^{-s},$$

$$A_N(s) = \sum_{n=1}^{\infty} e^{-n/N} n^{-s}.$$

TURÁN [7], Theorems VII, VIII] demonstrated that either of $C_N(s)$, $V_N(s)$ can take the place of $U_N(s)$ in deducing RH from the zerofree region (1), while N. WIENER and A. WINTNER [12] did the same for $A_N(s)$. However, our proof of the Theorem, mutatis mutandis, applies to these functions as well. TURÁN [8, 9, 10] has also considered zeros of $U_N(s)$ for restricted values of t. More precisely, TURÁN [9] has deduced RH from the supposition that for all $N > N_0$ there is a γ_N such that $U_N(s) \neq 0$ in the half-strip

$$\sigma \geqq 1 + N^{-\frac{1}{2}} (\log N)^3,$$

$$\gamma_N \leqq t \leqq \gamma_N + e^{N^{3/2}}.$$

We can make this redundant, for by the Lemma of TURÁN [9] we may show that for $N > N_0$ any interval

$$\gamma \leqq t \leqq \gamma + e^{N(\log N)^3}$$

contains the imaginary part of a zero of the sort asserted to exist in the Theorem.

We mention briefly other results concerning zeros of $U_N(s)$. C. B. HASELGROVE [4] demonstrated that $U_N(s)$ has zeros in $\sigma > 1$ for some N. R. SPIRA [6] proved the same for certain special values of N, such as $N = 19$, and J. VAN DE LUNE (unpublished) has located zeros in some such cases. N. LEVINSON [5] determined the asymptotic distribution of the zeros of $U_N(s)$ near $s = 1$. He found that all such zeros lie in $\sigma < 1$, although some are very close to $\sigma = 1$. Finally, S. M. VORONIN [11] has demonstrated that $U_N(s)$ has zeros in $\sigma > 1$ for infinitely many N.

2. Preliminary discussion

For $\sigma > 1$ let $f(s) = \sum_{n=1}^{\infty} a(n) n^{-s}$, where $|a(n)| = 1$ for all n, and $a(n)$ is totally multiplicative. Write

(3) $$F_N(s) = \sum_{n \leq N} a(n) n^{-s} = \frac{1}{2\pi i} \int_{2-i\infty}^{2+i\infty} f(s+w) \frac{N^w}{w} dw.$$

By the classical work of H. Bohr [2] (see also T. Apostol [1]), the values of $F_N(s)$ in a half-plane $\sigma > \sigma_0$ coincide with those of $U_N(s)$ in the same half-plane. Thus it suffices to choose the $a(n)$ so that the resulting $F_N(s)$ can be seen to have zeros which satisfy (2). Suppose that

$$\sigma \geqq 1 + 2/\log N, \quad |t| \leqq \frac{1}{2}. \tag{4}$$

If we move the contour in (3) to the abcissa $\alpha = 1 - \sigma + \dfrac{1}{\log N}$ then we have

$$F_N(s) = f(s) + \frac{1}{2\pi i} \int_{\alpha - i\infty}^{\alpha + i\infty} f(s+w) \frac{N^w}{w} \, dw. \tag{5}$$

We are thus concerned with the relative sizes of the two terms on the right. The following estimates are useful in estimating the integral. If $1 < \sigma_1 \leqq \sigma_2$ then

$$\frac{f(\sigma_1 + it)}{f(\sigma_2 + it)} \ll \frac{\sigma_2 - 1}{\sigma_1 - 1}. \tag{6}$$

If $\sigma > 1$, $0 \leqq |u| \leqq 1$, then

$$\frac{f(\sigma + i(t+u))}{f(\sigma + it)} \ll 1 + \left(\frac{|u|}{\sigma - 1} \right)^{4/\pi}. \tag{7}$$

We omit the proofs of these bounds, since all we require is the observation that (7) is best possible. It is not difficult to see that

$$\frac{f(\sigma + i)}{f(\sigma)} \approx (\sigma - 1)^{-4/\pi} \tag{8}$$

when the $a(p)$ are determined by the relation

$$\operatorname{Re} (p^{-i} - 1) a(p) = |p^{-i} - 1|.$$

That is, $a(p) = b_0(\log p/(2\pi))$, where $b_0(\vartheta)$ has period 1 and

$$b_0(\vartheta) = ie^{i\pi\vartheta} \quad (0 \leqq \vartheta \leqq 1). \tag{9}$$

This choice of the $a(p)$ is good in the sense that it yields (8), but the jump discontinuity of $b_0(\vartheta)$ at $\vartheta = 0$ gives rise to acute technical difficulties in estimating $f(s)$. Thus we let

$0<\delta\leqq\frac{1}{2}$ and put

$$a(p)=b_\delta\left(\frac{1}{2\pi}\log p\right) \tag{10}$$

where $b_\delta(\vartheta)$ has period 1 and

$$b_\delta(\vartheta)=\begin{cases} ie^{i\pi\vartheta} & (\delta\leqq\vartheta\leqq 1-\delta),\\ -e^{(1-(2\delta)^{-1})i\pi\vartheta} & (-\delta<\vartheta\leqq\delta).\end{cases} \tag{11}$$

When δ is small these $a(p)$ are almost as good as those provided by our first choice (9), but now it is of great advantage that the Fourier series of $b_\delta(\vartheta)$ is absolutely convergent. We write

$$b_\delta(\vartheta)=\sum_{-\infty}^{+\infty}\hat{b}_\delta(k)e(k\vartheta), \tag{12}$$

and find easily that

$$\hat{b}_\delta(k)=\frac{\sin 2\pi\left(k\delta-\frac{1}{2}\delta+\frac{1}{4}\right)}{(2k-1)\,2\pi\left(k\delta-\frac{1}{2}\delta+\frac{1}{4}\right)}. \tag{13}$$

We conclude this section by noting important properties of the Fourier coefficients $\hat{b}_\delta(k)$.

Lemma 1. *Suppose that* $0\leqq\delta\leqq\frac{1}{2}$. *Then*

(i) *for each* k, $\hat{b}_\delta(k)\in\mathbf{R}$;

(ii) $\hat{b}_\delta(k)\ll_\delta(k^2+1)^{-1}$;

(iii) *for each* k, $\lim\limits_{\delta\to 0^+}\hat{b}_\delta(k)=\dfrac{2}{\pi(2k-1)}=\hat{b}_0(k)$;

(iv) $\hat{b}_\delta(1)-\hat{b}_\delta(0)$ *is strictly decreasing in* δ;

(v) *for all* k, $\hat{b}_0(k)\leqq\frac{2}{\pi}$.

Proof. The first four assertions are clear from (13). From (13) we also see that $|\hat{b}_\delta(k)|\leqq\frac{1}{|2k-1|}$, so that in proving (v) we need consider only $k=0$, $k=1$. But $\hat{b}_\delta(0)\leqq 0$ for $0<\delta\leqq\frac{1}{2}$, and $\hat{b}_\delta(1)$ is a decreasing function of δ with $\hat{b}_0(1)=\frac{2}{\pi}$.

3. Estimates of $f(s)$

Let $b(\vartheta)=b_\delta(\vartheta)$, as given in (11), and put $a^*(n)=b\left(\frac{\log n}{2\pi}\right)$. We set

$$f^*(s)=\exp\left(\sum_n \frac{\Lambda(n)}{\log n}\, a^*(n)n^{-s}\right);$$

and by (12) this is

$$=\exp\left(\sum_n \frac{\Lambda(n)}{\log n}\, n^{-s}\sum_k \hat{b}(k)n^{ik}\right)=\prod_k \zeta(s-ik)^{\hat{b}(k)},$$

for $\sigma>1$. We write this product as

$$= \prod_{|k|\leqq K}\cdot \prod_{|k|>K} = f_1(s)\cdot f_2(s), \tag{14}$$

and hence we have

$$f(s)=f_1(s)f_2(s)f_3(s), \tag{15}$$

where

$$f_3(s)=f(s)/f^*(s)=\exp\left(\sum_n \frac{\Lambda(n)}{\log n}(a(n)-a^*(n))n^{-s}\right). \tag{16}$$

We now show that the interesting behaviour of f is due to that of f_1, and we describe this behaviour more precisely.

Lemma 2. *Let f_3 be defined by* (16). *Then* $\log f_3(s)$ *is regular in $\sigma>\frac{1}{2}$, and is uniformly bounded in the half-plane $\sigma\geqq\frac{3}{4}$.*

Proof. By definition $a(p)=a^*(p)$, $|a(n)|=|a^*(n)|=1$ for all n, and by (16) we see that

$$\log f_3(s)\ll \sum_{\substack{p^k\\ k\geqq 2}} p^{-k\sigma}\ll \sum_p p^{-2\sigma}.$$

Thus $\log f_3(s)$ is regular in $\sigma>\frac{1}{2}$, and is uniformly bounded for $\sigma\geqq\frac{3}{4}$.

Lemma 3. *If* $K \geqq \log\log N$ *then*

$$f_2(s) = 1 + O_\delta(K^{-1}\log\log N)$$

uniformly for $\sigma \geqq 1 + (\log N)^{-1}$.

Proof. For $\sigma > 1$,

$$\log f_2(s) = \sum_{|k|>K} \hat{b}(k)\log\zeta(s-ik).$$

By Lemma 1 (ii) this is

$$\ll_\delta (\max_t |\log\zeta(\sigma+it)|) \sum_{|k|>K} (k^2+1)^{-1} \ll_\delta K^{-1}\log\log N$$

for $\sigma \geqq 1 + (\log N)^{-1}$.

Let $c_1 > 0$ be a constant so that

$$\frac{\zeta'}{\zeta}(s) \ll \log t, \quad \log\zeta(s) \ll \log\log t \tag{17}$$

whenever $\sigma \geqq 1 - c_1(\log t)^{-1}$, $t \geqq 2$. Then we have

Lemma 4. *Suppose that* $K \geqq 2$, $\sigma \geqq 1 - c_1(\log 3K)^{-1}$, *and that* $|t-k| \leqq \frac{1}{2}$, *where* $|k| \leqq K$. *Put*

$$g_k(s) = f_1(s)(s-1-ik)^{\hat{b}(k)}.$$

Then

$$\log g_k(s) \ll_\delta \log\log(k^2+4), \tag{18}$$

and

$$\frac{g_k'}{g_k}(s) \ll_\delta \log(k^2+4). \tag{19}$$

Proof. By Lemma 1 (ii) and (17) we see that

$$\sum_{\substack{|m|\leqq K\\ m\neq k}} \hat{b}(m)\log\zeta(s-im) \ll_\delta \sum_m (m^2+1)^{-1}\log\log((k-m)^2+4) \ll_\delta$$

$$\ll_\delta \log\log(k^2+4),$$

which gives (18). The estimate (19) is derived similarly.

4. Completion of the proof of the Theorem

Put $\Delta=\frac{4}{\pi}-1-c$, and set $\delta=\frac{1}{4}\Delta$; from now on we regard δ as fixed. Suppose that (4) holds, and take $K=[\exp((\log\log N)^2)]$. Then by (5),

$$(20)\quad F_N(s)=f(s)+\frac{1}{2\pi i}\int_{\alpha-iK}^{\alpha+iK} f(s+w)\frac{N^w}{w}\,dw+O\left(N^{1-\sigma}\exp\left(-\frac{1}{2}(\log\log N)^2\right)\right),$$

where $\alpha=1-\sigma+(\log N)^{-1}$. On this contour we see by Lemma 3 that

$$f(s+w)=f_1(s+w)f_3(s+w)\left(1+O\left(\exp\left(-\frac{1}{2}(\log\log N)^2\right)\right)\right),$$

and by Lemmas 1 (ii), 2, 4 the above is

$$=f_1(s+w)f_3(s+w)+O\left(\exp\left(-\frac{1}{3}(\log\log N)^2\right)\right).$$

We use this in the integral in (20), and then move the contour to the abcissa $\gamma=1-\sigma-c_1(3\log K)^{-1}$, except for small loop contours Γ_k which start at $\gamma+i(k-t-\varepsilon)$, pass in the positive sense around the singularity at $1-s+ik$, and return to $\gamma+i(k-t+\varepsilon)$. We may let $\varepsilon\to 0$, in view of Lemma 1 (v). Thus

$$\frac{1}{2\pi i}\int_{\alpha-iK}^{\alpha+iK} f(s+w)\frac{N^w}{w}\,dw=\frac{1}{2\pi i}\left(\int_{\gamma-iK}^{\gamma+iK}+\sum_{|k|\le K}\int_{\Gamma_k}\right)f_1(s+w)f_3(s+w)\frac{N^w}{w}\,dw+$$

$$+O\left(N^{1-\sigma}\exp\left(-\frac{1}{4}(\log\log N)^2\right)\right).$$

By Lemmas 1 (iv), 2, 4 we see that

$$(21)\quad \int_{\Gamma_k}\ll N^{1-\sigma}(\log N)^{\delta(k)-1}(\log(k^2+4))^{c_2}|1-s+ik|^{-1},$$

and similarly

$$(22)\quad \int_{\gamma-iK}^{\gamma+iK}\ll\exp(-(\log\log N)^2).$$

For $k=1$ we argue more precisely than in (21). By Lemmas 2, 4 we find that

$$\frac{1}{2\pi i}\int_{\Gamma_1} = \frac{g_1(1+i)f_3(1+i)}{2\pi i(1+i-s)}\int_{\Gamma_1}(s+w-1-i)^{-\hat{b}(1)}N^w dw +$$

$$+O(N^{1-\sigma}(\log N)^{\hat{b}(1)-2}).$$

Put $D_1=-ig_1(1+i)f_3(1+i)$. Then $1\ll|D_1|\ll 1$ by these same Lemmas. Subsequent constants D_j will also have the property that $1\ll|D_j|\ll 1$. If

$$\sigma\geqq 1+2(\log N)^{-1},\quad |s-1|\leqq(\log N)^{-2/3}, \tag{23}$$

then the above is

$$=\frac{D_1N^{1+i-s}}{2\pi i}\int_C z^{-\hat{b}(1)}N^z dz+O(N^{1-\sigma}(\log N)^{\hat{b}(1)-\frac{5}{3}}),$$

where C is a contour starting at $-\infty-i\varepsilon$, passing in the positive sense around $z=0$, and continuing to $-\infty+i\varepsilon$. This latter integral is

$$=2i\Gamma(1-\hat{b}(1))\,(\sin\pi\hat{b}(1))\,(\log N)^{\hat{b}(1)-1},$$

so that

$$\frac{1}{2\pi i}\int_{\Gamma_1}=D_2N^{1+i-s}(\log N)^{\hat{b}(1)-1}(1+O((\log N)^{-2/3})).$$

But $\delta<\frac{1}{10}$, so that $\hat{b}(1)\geqq\frac{1}{2}$ and hence by (13), $\hat{b}(k)\leqq\hat{b}(1)-\frac{1}{6}$ for all $k\neq 1$. Thus by (21)

$$\sum_{|k|\leqq K}\int_{\Gamma_k}=D_2N^{1+i-s}(\log N)^{\hat{b}(1)-1}(1+O((\log N)^{-1/6}(\log K)^{c_2+1})).$$

Now $\log K\ll(\log\log N)^2$, so altogether we have

$$F_N(s)=f(s)+D_2N^{1+i-s}(\log N)^{\hat{b}(1)-1}(1+O((\log N)^{-1/7})). \tag{24}$$

But by Lemmas 2, 3, 4 we have

$$f(s)=D_3(s-1)^{-\mathfrak{b}(0)}(1+O((\log N)^{-2/3}))$$

provided that (23) holds; here $D_3=g_0(1)f_3(1)$.

We now complete our argument by Rouché's theorem. Write $F_N(s)=M(s)+R(s)$, where

$$M(s)=D_2N^{1+i-s}(\log N)^{\mathfrak{b}(1)-1}+D_3(s-1)^{-\mathfrak{b}(0)}. \tag{25}$$

Consider the two abcissae

$$\sigma_1=1+c(\log N)^{-1}\log\log N,$$

$$\sigma_2=1+\left(\frac{4}{\pi}-1+\Delta\right)(\log N)^{-1}\log\log N,$$

in the region (23). By Lemma 1 (iii, iv) we see that

$$\frac{4}{\pi}-1>\mathfrak{b}(1)-\mathfrak{b}(0)-1\geqq\frac{4}{\pi}-1-2\pi\delta^2>\frac{4}{\pi}-1-2\delta=\frac{4}{\pi}-1-\frac{1}{2}\Delta.$$

Thus of the two terms on the right in (25), the first is larger on σ_1, and the second is larger on σ_2. Choose t_1, $|t_1|\leqq 2\pi/\log N$, so that $D_2N^{1+i-it}D_3^{-1}>0$, and put $t_2=t_1+2\pi/\log N$. We consider the change of argument of $M(s)$ as s moves around a rectangle with vertices σ_j+it_k, $j, k=1, 2$. The change in argument on the horizontal sizes and on σ_2 is very small, while on σ_1 the change in argument is approximately 2π. Thus $M(s)$ has a zero in this rectangle. On this path, we have $R(s)\ll|M(s)|(\log N)^{-1/7}$, so that $|R(s)|<|M(s)|$, and by Rouché's theorem $F_N(s)$ also has a zero in this rectangle. This completes the proof of the theorem.

References

[1] T. Apostol, Sets of values taken by Dirichlet's L-series. *Proc. Sympos. Pure Math.*, vol. **8**, Amer. Math. Soc. (Providence, R. I., 1965), pp. 133–137.

[2] H. Bohr, Zur Theorie der allgemeinen Dirichletschen Reihen, *Math. Ann.*, **79** (1919), 136–156.

[3] G. Halász, On the distribution of additive and the mean values of multiplicative arithmetic functions, *Studia Sci. Math. Hungar.*, **6** (1971), 211–233.

[4] C. B. Haselgrove, A disproof of a conjecture of Pólya, *Mathematika* **5** (1958), 141–145.

[5] N. Levinson, Asymptotic formula for the coordinates of the zeros of sections of the zeta function, $\zeta_N(s)$, near $s=1$, *Proc. Nat. Acad. Sci. USA*, **70** (1973), 985–987.

[6] R. Spira, Zeros of sections of the zeta function, I, II, *Math. Comp.*, **20** (1966), 542–550; **22** (1968), 168–73.

[7] P. TURÁN, On some approximative Dirichlet-polynomials in the theory of the zeta-function of Riemann, *Danske Vid. Selsk. Mat.-Fys. Medd.*, **24** (1948), no. *17*, 36 pp.

[8] P. TURÁN, Nachtrag zu meiner Abhandlung "On approximative Dirichlet polynomials in the theory of zeta-function of Riemann", *Acta Math. Acad. Sci. Hungar.*, **10** (1959), 277–298.

[9] P. TURÁN, A theorem on diophantine approximation with application to Riemann zeta-function, *Acta Sci. Math. Szeged*, **21** (1960), 311–318.

[10] P. TURÁN, Untersuchungen über Dirichlet-Polynome, *Bericht von der Dirichlet-Tagung*, Akademie-Verlag (Berlin, 1963), pp. 71–80.

[11] S. M. VORONIN, On the zeros of partial sums of the Dirichlet series for the Riemann zeta-function, *Dokl. Akad. Nauk SSSR*, **216** (1974), 964–967; trans. *Soviet Math. Doklady*, **15** (1974), 900–903.

[12] N. WIENER and A. WINTNER, Notes on Pólya's and Turán's hypotheses concerning Liouville's factor, *Rend. Circ. Mat. Palermo*, (2) **6** (1957), 240–248.

DEPARTMENT OF MATHEMATICS
UNIVERSITY OF MICHIGAN,
ANN ARBOR, MICHIGAN
U.S.A.

Studies in Pure Mathematics
To the Memory of Paul Turán

Large sieve extensions of the Brun–Titchmarsh theorem

by

Y. MOTOHASHI (Tokyo)

1. Introduction and Statement of Results

In the present paper we are concerned with large sieve inequalities whose specializations imply results of the Brun–Titchmarsh type, i.e. good upper bounds for $\pi(x;k,l)$ the number of primes congruent to $l \pmod k$ and less than x. Such a result was obtained first by BOMBIERI and DAVENPORT in their important paper [2]. Being modified into a form convenient for our present discussion, their main result runs as follows: Let $\{a_n\}$ be a sequence of complex numbers such that $a_n = 0$ whenever n has a prime divisor less than Q. Then it holds that, uniformly for any positive M, N, Q, k, l.

(1.1)
$$\sum_{\substack{q \leqq Q \\ (q,k)=1}} \log(Q/q) \sum_{\chi \pmod q}^{*} \Big| \sum_{\substack{M<n\leqq M+N \\ n\equiv l \pmod k}} \chi(n) a_n \Big|^2 \leqq \frac{k}{\varphi(k)} \{N/k + O(Q^2)\} \sum_{\substack{M<n\leqq M+N \\ n\equiv l \pmod k}} |a_n|^2 ,$$

where φ is the Euler function, and $\sum^*$ denotes as usual a sum over primitive Dirichlet characters χ. From this it follows readily that, denoting prime numbers by p,

(1.2)
$$\sum_{\substack{q \leqq Q \\ (q,k)=1}} \sum_{\chi \pmod q}^{*} \Big| \sum_{\substack{M<p\leqq M+N \\ p\equiv l \pmod k}} \chi(p) \Big|^2 \leqq (2+\varepsilon) \frac{N}{\varphi(k)\log(N/kQ^2)} (\pi(M+N;k,l) - \pi(M;k,l)) .$$

provided

$$M < N, \quad (Nk^{-1}Q^2)^{1/2} \leqq M, \quad (kQ^2)^{1+\varepsilon} \leqq N .$$

Here and in what follows ε is a sufficiently small positive parameter whose value may differ at each occurrence, and other parameters are supposed to be sufficiently large, if necessary.

The special case $Q=1$ in (1.2) gives the classical form of the Brun–Titchmarsh theorem:

$$\pi(x;k,l)\leqq(2+\varepsilon)\frac{x}{\varphi(k)\log(x/k)},\quad k\leqq x^{1-\varepsilon}. \tag{1.3}$$

But recently this inequality has been improved under various conditions on the size of k. The present author [6], [7] obtained

$$\pi(x;k,l)\leqq(2+\varepsilon)\frac{x}{\varphi(k)\log(x/k^{\frac{3}{8}})},\quad k\leqq x^{\frac{1}{3}-\varepsilon}, \tag{1.4}$$

$$\pi(x;k,l)\leqq(2+\varepsilon)\frac{x}{\varphi(k)\log(x/k^{\frac{1}{2}})},\quad k\leqq x^{\frac{2}{5}-\varepsilon}, \tag{1.5}$$

$$\pi(x;k,l)\leqq(1+\varepsilon)\frac{x}{\varphi(k)\log(x/k^{\frac{3}{2}})},\quad x^{\frac{2}{5}}\leqq k\leqq x^{\frac{1}{2}}. \tag{1.6}$$

Later GOLDFELT [4] improved on these by proving (1.4) in the range $k\leqq x^{\frac{24}{71}-\varepsilon}$ and by refining (1.6). Further, but very modest, improvements were supplied by WOLKE [10]. And more recently substantial improvements on (1.4)–(1.6) have been announced by IWANIEC [5]; In his argument a remarkably improved version of the Rosser sieve, due to himself, plays a vital role, instead of the Selberg sieve which has been used by his predecessors. He has proved (1.4) for $k\leqq x^{\frac{8}{19}-\varepsilon}$, (1.5) for $k\leqq x^{\frac{1}{2}-\varepsilon}$ as well as

$$\pi(x;k,l)\leqq(2+\varepsilon)\frac{x}{\varphi(k)\log(x^{\frac{4}{3}}k^{-\frac{3}{2}})},\quad x^{\frac{4}{9}}\leqq k\leqq x^{\frac{2}{3}-\varepsilon},$$

which is certainly striking.

IWANIEC's investigations have revealed that the Rosser sieve has some advantages over the Selberg sieve, particularly in the case of linear sieve problems. However, the fact that the Selberg sieve can be considered, in a sense, to be dual to the large sieve suggests the possibility that the large sieve may better be crossed with the Selberg sieve than the Rosser sieve. More precisely speaking, we may expect that the argument developed in [6] can be adapted so as to produce some improvements on (1.1) or (1.2) which in turn imply improvements on (1.3) similar to (1.4)–(1.6). The main purpose of the present paper is to show that this is indeed possible. But, unfortunately, it does not seem to be an easy task to get a hybrid of the large sieve and the Rosser sieve, much less IWANIEC's version of it.* Also certain deficiencies inherent in our argument obstruct us to produce the improvement on (1.1) which implies (1.4) with the condition on k prescibed there or the corresponding result of GOLDFELT.

***Note added in proof: In the mean time we have obtained such a hybrid of the large sieve and the Rosser —Iwaniec combinatorial sieve. See Proc. Japan Acad. 56 (1980), 288–290, and also authors lecture notes „*Sieve Methods and Prime Number Theory*" which will be published by Tata Inst. Res. (Bombay).**

Neverthless we can proceed a little further by proving an improvement on the following large sieve inequality, due to SELBERG [9]: Let $c_r(n)$ be the Ramanujan sum, and let $\{a_n\}$ be arbitrary complex numbers. Then we have, uniformly for any positive M, N, Q, k, l.

$$\begin{aligned}(1.7)\qquad &\sum_{\substack{qr\leqq Q\\(q,r)=(qr,k)=1}}\frac{q}{\varphi(qr)}\sum_{\chi(\mathrm{mod}\,q)}^{*}\Big|\sum_{\substack{M<n\leqq M+N\\ n\equiv l(\mathrm{mod}\,k)}}\chi(n)c_r(n)a_n\Big|^2\\ &\leqq (N/k+O(Q^2))\sum_{\substack{M<n\leqq M+N\\ n\equiv l(\mathrm{mod}\,k)}}|a_n|^2.\end{aligned}$$

The proof of this can be found in [1; Theoreme 7A], but the above is a slightly modified form of the original result. If we observe that $c_r(n)=\mu(r)$ the Möbius function when $(r,n)=1$, and that for $x>1$ we have

$$(1.8)\qquad \sum_{\substack{r\leqq x\\(r,q)=1}}\frac{\mu^2(r)}{\varphi(r)}\geqq\frac{\varphi(q)}{q}\log x,$$

then we see that (1.1) is an immediate consequence of (1.7).

Now our main result, an improvement on (1.7), is as follows:

Theorem. *We have, for any positive* N, Q, R, k, l *with* $(k,l)=1$ *and* $\log(QRk)\ll\log N$, *and for any complex numbers* $\{a_n\}$,

$$\begin{aligned}&\sum_{\substack{q\leqq Q\\ r\leqq R\\(q,r)=(qr,k)=1}}\frac{q}{\varphi(qr)}\sum_{\chi(\mathrm{mod}\,q)}^{*}\Big|\sum_{\substack{n\leqq N\\ n\equiv l(\mathrm{mod}\,k)}}\chi(n)c_r(n)a_n\Big|^2\\ &\leqq\left\{\frac{N}{k}\left(1+O\left(\frac{1}{\log N}\right)\right)+O_\varepsilon(N^\varepsilon\Phi)\right\}\sum_{\substack{n\leqq N\\ n\equiv l(\mathrm{mod}\,k)}}|a_n|^2,\end{aligned}$$

where

$$\Phi=\mathrm{Min}\,\{QRk^{-\frac{1}{2}}(R+kQ^2),\,N^{\frac{1}{2}}Q^{\frac{3}{8}}k^{-\frac{13}{16}}(R+R^{\frac{1}{2}}Q^2k)\}.$$

Compared with (1.7) our result contains certain deficiencies: For instance (1.7) works for any intervals whereas ours is not capable to give any informations about short intervals. Also for larger values of Q (1.7) is better than ours, and moreover the ranges of r and q are now separated. But still the above inequality has an advantage over (1.7) in that here we can take R relatively large which controls the sieving-effect of our result, though only for restricted ranges of parameters.

Setting in our theorem $a_n=1$ if $n=p$, $M<p\leqq N$, and $a_n=0$ otherwise, and noticing (1.8), we obtain immediately the following improvement on (1.2):

Corollary.* *We have, for any positive N, Q, k, l with $(k, l)=1$,*

$$\sum_{\substack{q\leqq Q\\(q,k)=1}}\ \sum_{\chi(\mathrm{mod}\,q)}^{*}\Big|\sum_{\substack{M<p\leqq N\\p\equiv l(\mathrm{mod}\,k)}}\chi(p)\Big|^2$$

$$\leqq(1+\varepsilon)\frac{N}{\varphi(k)S(N;k,Q)}(\pi(N;k)-\pi(M;k,l)),$$

where $M<N$ and

$$S(N;k,Q)=\begin{cases}\frac{1}{2}\log(N/(Q^2k)^{\frac{3}{8}}) & \text{if}\quad (kQ^2)^2\leqq M,\ (kQ^2)^{\frac{35}{8}+\varepsilon}\leqq N,\\[2mm] \frac{1}{2}\log(N/Qk^{\frac{1}{2}}) & \text{if}\quad kQ^2\leqq M,\ (kQ^2)^{\frac{5}{2}+\varepsilon}\leqq N,\\[2mm] \log(N/Q^3k^{\frac{3}{2}}) & \text{if}\quad \frac{N}{M}\leqq(kQ^2)^{\frac{3}{2}}<N\leqq(kQ^2)^{\frac{5}{2}}.\end{cases}$$

From the case $Q=1$ the results (1.5) and (1.6) follow, but as has been remarked above, (1.4) comes out with an inferior condition on k. However, it may be worth remarking that already the case $k=1$ gives a new result, and because of its independent interest we single out the following: For $N\geqq Q^{5+\varepsilon}$ we have

$$\sum_{q\leqq Q}\ \sum_{\chi(\mathrm{mod}\,q)}^{*}\Big|\sum_{p<N}\chi(p)\Big|^2\leqq(2+\varepsilon)\frac{N^2}{\log N\log N/Q}.$$

We are inclined to believe that this holds even under the condition $N\geqq Q^{2+\varepsilon}$.

2. Proof of the Theorem

It is sufficient to consider the dual form

$$I(N)=\sum_{\substack{n\leqq N\\n\equiv l(\mathrm{mod}\,k)}}\Big|\sum_{\substack{q\leqq Q\\r\leqq R\\(q,r)=(qr,k)=1}}\ \sum_{\chi(\mathrm{mod}\,q)}^{*}\left(\frac{q}{\varphi(qr)}\right)^{\frac{1}{2}}\chi(n)c_r(n)b(r,\chi)\Big|^2$$

$$=\sum_{\substack{n\leqq N\\n\equiv l(\mathrm{mod}\,k)}}|B(n)|^2,$$

* A result related to this has been announced in [8], but there the insertion of the parameter M is erroneously overlooked.

say, where $b(r,\chi)$ are arbitrary complex numbers. Our aim is to prove

$$I(N)=\left\{\frac{N}{k}\left(1+O\left(\frac{1}{\log N}\right)\right)+O_\varepsilon(N^\varepsilon\Phi)\right\}\|b(r,\chi)\|^2 \tag{2.1}$$

with Φ defined in the theorem, and with

$$\|b(r,\chi)\|^2=\sum_{\substack{q\leqq Q,\,r\leqq R\\(q,r)=(qr,k)=1}}\ \sideset{}{^*}\sum_{\chi(\mathrm{mod}\,q)}|b(r,\chi)|^2 . \tag{2.2}$$

For this sake it is expedient to consider the Riesz mean

$$I(N)=\frac{1}{2}\sum_{\substack{n\leqq N\\ n\equiv l(\mathrm{mod}\,k)}}|B(n)|^2(\log N/n)^2 ,$$

which admits the analytic representation

$$I(N)=\frac{1}{2\pi i\varphi(k)}\sum_{\xi(\mathrm{mod}\,k)}\bar\xi(l)\int_{2-i\infty}^{2+i\infty}F(s,\xi)\frac{N^s}{s^3}\,ds , \tag{2.3}$$

where ξ is a Dirichlet character (mod k), and

$$F(s,\xi)=\sum_{n=1}^{\infty}\xi(n)|B(n)|^2n^{-s}.$$

As it is well known, we have

$$c_r(n)=\sum_{\substack{d|r\\d|n}}\mu(r/d)\,d .$$

So

$$B(n)=\sum_{\substack{q\leqq Q\\(q,k)=1}}\left(\frac{q}{\varphi(q)}\right)^{\frac{1}{2}}\sideset{}{^*}\sum_{\chi(\mathrm{mod}\,q)}\chi(n)\sum_{\substack{d|n\\d\leqq R\\(d,qk)=1}}d\sum_{\substack{u\leqq R/d\\(u,qk)=1}}\mu(u)(\varphi(du))^{-\frac{1}{2}}b(du,\chi) \tag{2.4}$$

$$=\sum_{\substack{q\leqq Q\\(q,k)=1}}\left(\frac{q}{\varphi(q)}\right)^{\frac{1}{2}}\sideset{}{^*}\sum_{\chi(\mathrm{mod}\,q)}\chi(n)\sum_{\substack{d|n\\d\leqq R\\(d,k)=1}}\lambda(d,\chi) ,$$

say. This gives, for any s,

$$F(s,\xi)=\sum_{\substack{q_1,q_2\leqq Q\\(q_1q_2,k)=1}}\left(\frac{q_1q_2}{\varphi(q_1)\varphi(q_2)}\right)^{\frac{1}{2}}\sideset{}{^*}\sum_{\substack{\chi_1(\mathrm{mod}\,q_1)\\ \chi_2(\mathrm{mod}\,q_2)}}L(s,\xi\chi_1\bar\chi_2)H(s;\xi,\chi_1,\chi_2) . \tag{2.5}$$

Here $L(s, \chi)$ is a Dirichlet L-function, and

$$H(s; \xi, \chi_1, \chi_2) = \sum_{d_1, d_2 \leqq R} \frac{\xi\chi_1\bar{\chi}_2([d_1, d_2])}{[d_1, d_2]^s} \lambda(d_1, \chi_1)\overline{\lambda(d_2, \chi_2)}$$

in which $[d_1, d_2]$ is the least common multiple of d_1 and d_2. Then, as in [6], we transform $H(s; \xi, \chi_1, \chi_2)$ into a form suitable for the application of the large sieve: A familiar device in the theory of the Selberg sieve gives

$$H(s; \xi, \chi_1, \chi_2) = \sum_{d \leqq R} \xi\chi_1\bar{\chi}_2(d) d^{-s} \prod_{p|d} (1 - \xi\chi_1\bar{\chi}_2(p) p^{-s}) \tag{2.6}$$
$$\times \Lambda_d^{(1)}(s; \xi, \chi_1, \chi_2) \Lambda_d^{(2)}(s; \xi, \chi_1, \chi_2),$$

where

$$\Lambda_d^{(1)}(s; \xi, \chi_1, \chi_2) = \sum_{u \leqq R/d} \xi\chi_1\bar{\chi}_2(u) \lambda(du, \chi_1) u^{-s},$$
$$\Lambda_d^{(2)}(s; \xi, \chi_1, \chi_2) = \sum_{u \leqq R/d} \xi\chi_1\bar{\chi}_2(u) \overline{\lambda(du, \chi_2)}\, u^{-s}. \tag{2.7}$$

Now we note that in (2.5) $L(s, \xi\chi_1\bar{\chi}_2)$ is entire except for the cases $\chi_1 = \chi_2$, $\xi = \xi_0$ the principal character (mod k). Hence, from (2.3) and (2.5), we get

$$I(N) = \frac{N}{k} \sum_{\substack{q \leqq Q \\ (q, k) = 1}} \sum_{\chi (\mathrm{mod}\, q)}^{*} H(1; \xi_0, \chi, \chi) + O(N^{\sigma + \varepsilon} k^{-1} J(\sigma)), \tag{2.8}$$

where $(\log N)^{-1} \leqq \sigma < 1$ and

$$J(\sigma) = \sum_{\xi (\mathrm{mod}\, k)} \sum_{\substack{q_1, q_2 \leqq Q \\ (q_1 q_2, k) = 1}} \sum_{\substack{\chi_1 (\mathrm{mod}\, q_1) \\ \chi_2 (\mathrm{mod}\, q_2)}}^{*} \int_{-\infty}^{\infty} |L(\sigma + it, \xi\chi_1\bar{\chi}_2) H(\sigma + it; \xi, \chi_1, \chi_2)| \frac{dt}{(|t| + 1)^3}. \tag{2.9}$$

First we have to calculate $H(1; \xi_0, \chi, \chi)$. From (2.4) and (2.7) we have, for χ (mod q),

$$\Lambda_d^{(1)}(1; \xi_0, \chi, \chi) = d \sum_{\substack{u \leqq R/d \\ (u, qk) = 1}} \sum_{\substack{v \leqq R/du \\ (v, qk) = 1}} \mu(v) \varphi(duv)^{-\frac{1}{2}} b(duv, \chi) =$$

$$= d \sum_{\substack{h \leqq R/d \\ (h, qk) = 1}} \varphi(dh)^{-\frac{1}{2}} b(dh, \chi) \sum_{v|h} \mu(v) = d\varphi(d)^{-\frac{1}{2}} b(d, \chi).$$

Also

$$\Lambda_d^{(2)}(1;\xi_0,\chi,\chi)=d\varphi(d)^{-\frac{1}{2}}\overline{b(d,\chi)}.$$

Thus, from these and (2.6), we get, for χ (mod q),

$$H(1;\xi_0,\chi,\chi)=\sum_{\substack{d\leqq R\\(d,qk)=1}}|b(d,\chi)|^2. \tag{2.10}$$

We now turn to the estimation of $J(\sigma)$ at $\sigma=1/2$ and $\sigma=(\log N)^{-1}$. Since they are similar, we treat in detail only the first case. According to Burgess [3] we have

$$L\left(\frac{1}{2}+it,\xi\chi_1\bar{\chi}_2\right)\ll(Q^2k)^{\frac{3}{16}+\varepsilon}(|t|+1),$$

and so, from (2.9),

$$J\left(\frac{1}{2}\right)\ll(Q^2k)^{\frac{3}{16}+\varepsilon}$$

(2.11)

$$\times\int_{-\infty}^{\infty}\sum_{\xi(\mathrm{mod}\,k)}\sum_{\substack{q_1,q_2\leqq Q\\(q_1q_2,k)=1}}\sideset{}{^*}\sum_{\substack{\chi_1(\mathrm{mod}\,q_1)\\\chi_2(\mathrm{mod}\,q_2)}}\left|H\left(\frac{1}{2}+it;\xi,\chi_1,\chi_2\right)\right|\frac{dt}{(|t|+1)^2}=(Q^2k)^{\frac{3}{16}+\varepsilon}\int_{-\infty}^{\infty}Y(t)\frac{dt}{(|t|+1)^2},$$

say. Then, from (2.6), we have

$$Y(t)\ll R^{\varepsilon}\sum_{d\leqq R}d^{-\frac{1}{2}}$$

$$\times\left\{\sum_{\substack{q_1\leqq Q\\(q_1,k)=1}}\sideset{}{^*}\sum_{\chi_1(\mathrm{mod}\,q_1)}\sum_{\xi(\mathrm{mod}\,k)}\sum_{\substack{q_2\leqq Q\\(q_2,k)=1}}\sideset{}{^*}\sum_{\chi_2(\mathrm{mod}\,q_2)}\left|\Lambda_d^{(1)}\left(\frac{1}{2}+it;\xi,\chi_1,\chi_2\right)\right|^2\right\}^{\frac{1}{2}} \tag{2.12}$$

$$\times\left\{\sum_{\substack{q_2\leqq Q\\(q_2,k)=1}}\sideset{}{^*}\sum_{\chi_2(\mathrm{mod}\,q_2)}\sum_{\xi(\mathrm{mod}\,k)}\sum_{\substack{q_1\leqq Q\\(q_1,k)=1}}\sideset{}{^*}\sum_{\chi_1(\mathrm{mod}\,q_1)}\left|\Lambda_d^{(2)}\left(\frac{1}{2}+it;\xi,\chi_1,\chi_2\right)\right|^2\right\}^{\frac{1}{2}}.$$

Here we appeal to the following inequality: For any complex numbers $\{a_n\}$ and for any positive M, N,

$$\sum_{\xi(\mathrm{mod}\,k)}\sum_{\substack{q\leqq Q\\(q,k)=1}}\sideset{}{^*}\sum_{\chi(\mathrm{mod}\,q)}\Big|\sum_{M<n\leqq M+N}\chi\xi(n)a_n\Big|^2\ll(N+kQ^2)\sum_{\substack{M<n\leqq M+N\\(n,k)=1}}|a_n|^2.$$

This is a slightly generalized form of the conventional multiplicative large sieve, and the proof is quite similar. Thus we get, from this and (2.7),

$$\sum_{\xi(\bmod k)} \sum_{\substack{q_2 \leqq Q \\ (q_2, k)=1}} \sideset{}{^*}\sum_{\chi_2(\bmod q_2)} \left| \Lambda_d^{(1)}\left(\frac{1}{2}+it; \xi, \chi_1, \chi_2\right)\right|^2$$

$$\ll (R/d + kQ^2) \sum_{\substack{r \leqq R/d \\ (r, kq_1)=1}} |\lambda(dr, \chi_1)|^2 r^{-1},$$

and also a similar result for the corresponding sum in the second brackets of (2.12).

Hence from (2.12) we have

$$Y(t) \ll N^{\varepsilon} \sum_{d \leqq R} d^{-\frac{1}{2}} (R/d + kQ^2) \sum_{\substack{q \leqq Q \\ (q, k)=1}} \sideset{}{^*}\sum_{\chi(\bmod q)} \sum_{\substack{r \leqq R/d \\ (r, qk)=1}} |\lambda(dr, \chi)|^2 r^{-1}.$$

On the other hand, by the definition of $\lambda(d, \chi)$ given in (2.4), we have

$$\sum_{\substack{r \leqq R/d \\ (r, qk)=1}} |\lambda(dr, \chi)|^2 r^{-1} \leqq d^2 \sum_{\substack{r \leqq R/d \\ (r, qk)=1}} r \sum_{\substack{u \leqq R/rd \\ (u, qk)=1}} \varphi(dru)^{-1} \sum_{\substack{u \leqq R/rd \\ (u, qk)=1}} |b(dru, \chi)|^2$$

$$\ll dN^{\varepsilon} \sum_{\substack{r \leqq R/d \\ (r, qk)=1}} |b(dr, \chi)|^2.$$

This implies

$$Y(t) \ll N^{\varepsilon} \sum_{\substack{q \leqq Q \\ (q, k)=1}} \sideset{}{^*}\sum_{\chi(\bmod q)} \sum_{\substack{d \leqq R \\ (d, qk)=1}} \sum_{\substack{r \leqq R/d \\ (r, qk)=1}} d^{\frac{1}{2}} (R/d + kQ^2) |b(dr, \chi)|^2$$

$$\ll N^{\varepsilon}(R + R^{\frac{1}{2}} Q^2 k) \|b(r, \chi)\|^2,$$

where the last factor has been defined by (2.2).

Inserting this into (2.11) and noticing (2.10) we obtain, by (2.8),

$$I(N) = \{N/k + O(N^{\frac{1}{2}+\varepsilon} Q^{\frac{3}{8}} k^{-\frac{13}{16}} (R + R^{\frac{1}{2}} kQ^2))\} \|b(r, \chi)\|^2.$$

Also, if we set $\sigma = (\log N)^{-1}$ in (2.8) and note

$$L((\log N)^{-1} + it, \xi\chi_1\bar{\chi}_2) \ll Qk^{\frac{1}{2}} (|t|+1)^{\frac{1}{2}} (\log N(|t|+1))^2,$$

we can deduce, just in the same manner as above,

$$I(N) = \{N/k + O(N^{\varepsilon} Qk^{-\frac{1}{2}} R(R + kQ^2))\} \|b(r, \chi)\|^2.$$

Combining these, we find

$$I(N) = \{N/k + O(N^{\varepsilon}\Phi)\} \, \|b(r, \chi)\|^2 \, .$$

Finally, appealing to the well-known smoothing device, we infer that the last result yields (2.1), and we end the proof of the theorem.

References

[1] Bombieri, E., Le grand crible dans la théorie analytique des nombres, *Soc. Math. France, Astérisque*, No. **18**, 1974.

[2] Bombieri, E. and Davenport, H., On the large sieve method, *Abhandlungen aus Zahlentheorie und Analysis zur Errinerung an Edmund Landau*, VEB Deutscher Verlag der Wiss., Berlin 1968, pp. 11–12.

[3] Burgess, D. A., On character sums and *L*-series, II, *Proc. London Math. Soc.*, (3) **13** (1963), 524–536.

[4] Goldfelt, D. A., A further improvement of the Brun–Titchmarsh theorem, *J. London Math. Soc.*, (2) **11** (1975), 434–444.

[5] Iwaniec, H., A new form of the error term in the linear sieve, To appear in *Acta Arith.*

[6] Motohashi, Y., On some improvements of the Brun–Titchmarsh theorem, *J. Math. Soc. Japan*, **26** (1974), 306–323.

[7] Motohashi, Y., On some improvements of the Brun–Titchmarsh theorem II. (Japanese) *Res. Inst. Math. Sci. Kyoto Univ. Kōkyūroku*, **193** (1973), 97–109.

[8] Motohashi, Y., A note on the large sieve, *Proc. Japan Acad.*, **53** (1977), 17–19.

[9] Selberg, A., Remarks on sieves, *Proc. 1972 Number Theory Conf.*, Boulder 1972, pp. 205–216.

[10] Wolke, D., Eine weitere möglichkeit zur Verbesserung des Satzes von Brun–Titchmarsh, *Manuscript.*

DEPARTMENT OF MATHEMATICS
COLLEGE OF SCIENCE AND TECHNOLOGY
NIHON UNIVERSITY
SURUGADAI, TOKYO 101, JAPAN

Studies in Pure Mathematics
To the Memory of Paul Turán

On a question of Alladi and Erdős on sums of squares

by

W. NARKIEWICZ (Wroclaw)

1. Let $1=a_0<a_1<\dots$ be an infinite sequence of integers. We shall consider the following algorithm giving a decomposition of any positive integer into a sum of elements of our sequence: choose $i_1 \leqq i_2 \leqq \dots$ with

$$a_{i_1} \leqq N < a_{i_1+1}$$
$$a_{i_2} \leqq N - a_{i_1} < a_{i_2+1}$$
$$\dots\dots\dots$$

and write $N=a_{i_1}+a_{i_2}+\dots+a_{i_r}$. Put $P(N)=\prod_{j=1}^{r} a_j$, $r(N)=r$ and $L(x)=\max_{N\leqq x} r(N)$. P. ERDŐS and K. ALLADI [1] recently asked for the behaviour of $P(N)$ in the case of the sequence of all squares. This algorithm was also considered by G. LORD [2], who dealt with the existence of integers N with prescribed value of $r(N)$. In this paper we consider sequences with differences growing not too fast and obtain an upper bound for $L(x)$ and $P(N)$. Then we return to the case of squares in which case we find the true order of growth for $P(N)$, incidentally disproving a conjecture stated in [1] and find a normal order for $r(N)$.

2. We start with a simple observation which shows that $P(N)$ can be small only for rather particular sequences:

(i) The evaluation $P(N)=O(N)$ holds if and only if the sequence $a_{i+1}-a_i$ is bounded.

Proof. Write $M(x)=\max_{N\leqq x} P(N)$ and assume that with a certain constant B we have $M(x)\leqq Bx$. Clearly for any N with $a_i \leqq N < a_{i+1}$ we have $P(N)=a_iP(N-a_i)$. If now $a_i \leqq x < a_{i+1}$ and $b \leqq x-a_i$ satisfies $P(b)=M(x-a_i)$ then $a_i<b+a_i\leqq x<a_{i+1}$ thus

$$M(x)\geqq P(b+a_i)=a_iP(b)=a_iM(x-a_i) \tag{1}$$

Now let a_j be an arbitrary element of our sequence. If $a_{j+1} \leqq 2a_j + 1$ then we apply (1) with $M(x) = a_{j+1} - 1 \leqq 2a_j$ to get

$$\frac{x}{2} M(x-a_j) \leqq a_j M(x-a_j) \leqq M(x) \leqq Bx$$

and $M(x-a_j) \leqq 2B$. This implies $x - a_j \leqq C_1$ hence $a_{j+1} - a_j \leqq 1 + C_1$ with a suitable positive constant C_1.

If $a_{j+1} > 2a_j + 1$ then we apply (1) with $x = 2a_j < a_{j+1}$ to get

$$a_j M(a_j) = a_j M(x-a_j) \leqq M(x) \leqq Bx = 2Ba_j$$

and $M(a_j) \leqq 2B$ giving $a_j \leqq C$. This shows that for all except finitely many j's we have $a_{j+1} - a_j \leqq 1 + C$. Adjusting the constant we get $a_{j+1} - a_j = O(1)$.

The converse implication is trivial.

Now we prove evaluations for $P(N)$ and $L(N)$ in the case when the differences of our sequence do not increase too rapidly:

Theorem 1. *Assume that there exist constants B and $d<1$ such that $a_{i+1} - a_i \leqq$ $\leqq Ba_i^d + 1$ holds for $i = 0, 1, \ldots$. Then*

(a) $$r(N) \leqq L(N) \leqq \frac{\log\log N}{\log d^{-1}} + O(1)$$

and

(b) $$P(N) \leqq C_2 N^a \log^b N$$

where C_2 is a constant, $a = (1-d)^{-1}$ and $b = \dfrac{\log B}{(1-d)\log d^{-1}}$

Proof. Observe first that if $a_i \leqq N < a_{i+1}$, then $r(N) = 1 + r(N - a_i)$, hence $L(N) \leqq$ $\leqq 1 + L\left(Ba_i^d\right) \leqq 1 + L(BN^d)$ and by recurrence

$$L(N) \leqq k + L(B^{1+d+\ldots+d^{k-1}} N^{d^k}) \leqq k + B^{(1-d)^{-1}} (NB^{-a})^{d^k}$$

holds for every k, due to $L(x) \leqq x$. Choosing now $k = \left[\dfrac{\log\log N}{\log d^{-1}}\right]$ we obtain

$$L(N) \leqq \frac{\log\log N}{\log d^{-1}} + O(1)$$

as asserted in (a).

The inequality (b) follows now by noting that if $N=a_{i_1}+\ldots+a_{i_r}$ is the decomposition obtained by our algorithm, then $a_{i_2}\leqq Ba_{i_1}^d, \ldots, a_{i_r}\leqq Ba_{i_{r-1}}^d$, hence

$$a_{i_2}a_{i_3}\ldots a_{i_r}\leqq B^{r-1}a_1^d\ldots a_{r-1}^d$$

and we get

$$P(N)\leqq NB^{r-1}P(N)^d$$

which inequality easily implies (b).

3. For the sequence of squares theorem 1 gives $P(N)=O(N^2\log^2 N)$. Erdős and Alladi asked whether in this case the bound $P(N)=O(N^2)$ holds. We shall show now that this is not true and in fact the bound obtained in theorem 1 cannot be improved in that case.

(ii) For the sequence of all squares we have $\limsup P(N)/N^2\log^2 N>0$.

Proof. Let $t_0=3$ and put $t_{i+1}=\frac{1}{2}(1+t_i^2)$ for $i=0, 1, 2, \ldots$ In view of $t_i^2-1=t_{i-1}^2-1+(t_i-1)^2$ we obtain that our algorithm leads to the decomposition

$$N_k=\sum_{i=0}^{k}(t_i-1)^2+2^2$$

for the number $N_k=t_k^2-1$, thus $P(N_k)=2^2\prod_{j=1}^{k}(t_j-1)^2$ holds for $k=1, 2, 3, \ldots$. Put $a_k=P(N_k)/N_k^2$. Then

$$\frac{a_{k+1}}{a_k}=4\cdot\left(1-\frac{2}{1+t_{k+1}}\right)^2$$

thus

$$a_m=a_0 4^m\prod_{k=1}^{m}\left(1-\frac{2}{1+t_k}\right)^2.$$

The infinite product

$$\prod_{k=1}^{\infty}\left(1-\frac{2}{1+t_k}\right)$$

being convergent we obtain $P(N_k)\geqq C_3N_k^2 4^k$ with a certain positive constant C_3. As obviously t_k does not exceed 3^{2^k} we obtain $\log N_k=O(2^k)$ and the inequality

$$P(N_k)\geqq DN_k^2\log^2 N_k$$

with $D>0$ follows.

Theorem 2. *For the sequence of all squares the function* $r(N)$ *has* $\frac{\log\log N}{\log 2}$ *for normal order, i.e. for all positive* ε *and almost all* N *one has* $(1-\varepsilon)\frac{\log\log N}{\log 2}\leqq r(N)\leqq$ $\leqq(1+\varepsilon)\frac{\log\log N}{\log 2}$.

Proof. For a given r denote by $A_r(x)$ the number of integer $N\leqq x$ with $r(N)\leqq r$. Observe that the equality $r(N)=r$ holds if and only if $r(N-[N^{1/2}]^2)=r-1$ and for a given x write $k_0=[x^{1/2}]$. If $k\leqq k_0-1$ then the numbers k^2+j with $j\leqq 2k$ satisfy $r(k^2+j)=1+r(j)$ and cover the interval $[1, k_0^2]$. This shows that

$$A_{r+1}(k_0^2)=\sum_{k\leqq k_0-1} A_r(2k)$$

and as obviously

$$A_{r+1}(x)=A_{r+1}(k_0^2)+A_r(x-k_0^2)$$

we arrive at

$$A_{r+1}(x)=\sum_{k<k_0} A_r(2k)+A_r(x-k_0^2),$$

hence for $r=1, 2, \ldots$ we have

(2) $$A_{r+1}(x)\leqq\sum_{k\leqq x^{1/2}} A_r(2k).$$

Assume that for a certain r we have the inequality

(3) $$A_r(x)\leqq B_r x^{a_r}$$

holding for all $x\geqq 1$ with fixed B_r and $1/2\leqq a_r\leqq 1$. This is certainly true for $r=1$, in which case we may take $a_1=1/2$ and $B_1=1$. By (2) we may write

$$A_{r+1}(x)\leqq B_r 2^{a_r}\sum_{k\leqq x^{1/2}} k^{a_r}$$

and an easy computation leads to

$$A_{r+1}(x)\leqq 3\cdot 2^{a_r}B_r x^{a_{r+1}}$$

with $a_{r+1}=\frac{1+a_r}{2}$. Putting $B_{r+1}=3\cdot 2^{a_r}\cdot B_r$ we obtain (3) for all r. Now observe that the obtained values for a_r, B_r satisfy $a_r=1-2^{-r}$ and $B_r\leqq 6^r$ thus

$$A_r(x)\leqq 6^r x^{1-2^{-r}}$$

holds for all r and $x \geqq 1$. Choosing now a positive ε and putting $r = \frac{1-\varepsilon}{\log 2} \log\log x$ we arrive at

$$A_r(x) \leqq x \exp\{\varepsilon \log\log x \log 6/\log 2 - \log^\varepsilon x\} = o(x).$$

This clearly implies that for every positive ε and almost all N we have

$$r(N) \geqq \frac{1-\varepsilon}{\log 2} \log\log N$$

As the inequality

$$r(N) \leqq \frac{1+\varepsilon}{\log 2} \log\log N$$

holds for all N by Theorem 1 (a) we are ready.

References

[1] ALLADI, K., On an additive arithmetic function, *Pacific Journal Math.*, **71** (1977), 275–294.
[2] LORD, G., Minimal elements in an integer representing algorithm, *Amer. Math. Monthly*, **83** (1976), 193–195.

INSTITUTE OF MATHEMATICS, WROCLAW UNIVERSITY
PL-50-384, WROCLAW, POLAND
PLAC GRUNWALDZKI 2–4.

Studies in Pure Mathematics
To the Memory of Paul Turán

A quasi-Monte Carlo method for the approximate computation of the extreme values of a function

by

H. NIEDERREITER* (Wien)

The applicability of Monte Carlo methods to a wide range of problems in numerical analysis is well known. If one replaces the random sampling procedure, on which a Monte Carlo method is based, by a deterministic selection scheme appropriate to the problem at hand, one arrives at techniques that are collectively called "quasi-Monte Carlo methods". These methods have the advantage that one can usually establish effective *a priori* error bounds for them which are often better than the probabilistic Monte Carlo bounds. Very successful implementations of such methods have been developed for the purposes of numerical integration and approximate solution of integral equations. We refer to [5] for a survey of quasi-Monte Carlo methods.

In this paper, we discuss a quasi-Monte Carlo method for approximating the extreme values of a function. Earlier investigations in this direction were carried out by Artobolevskii et al. [1] and Sobol' and Statnikov [9], who employed a search algorithm based on a special class of sequences, namely LP_τ-sequences in the sense of Sobol' [8]. The idea of approximating the supremum norm of a function by L^p norms and using quasi-Monte Carlo integration techniques for the integrals defining the L^p norms was considered by Hlawka [3]. However, the resulting method converges very slowly, since it involves an error bound of the order of magnitude $(\log\log N)^2/\log N$, where N is the number of nodes used in the numerical integration.

A Monte Carlo method for the approximate evaluation of the extreme values of a function was proposed by Zieliński [10]. Our method may be viewed as a deterministic version of Zieliński's algorithm. Let f be a bounded real-valued function defined on the bounded subset E of $\mathbf{R}^s$, $s \geqq 1$. We discuss the method only for the case where the supremum of f on E is desired. Obvious modifications lead to a method for approximating the infimum of f on E.

* Supported by NSF Grant MCS 77-01699.

With the above notation, let now $x_1, x_2, \ldots$ be a sequence of points in E. Then we compute numbers $m_1, m_2, \ldots$ by the following algorithm:

$$m_1 = f(x_1)$$

$$m_{n+1} = \begin{cases} m_n & \text{if} \quad f(x_{n+1}) \leqq m_n \\ f(x_{n+1}) & \text{if} \quad f(x_{n+1}) > m_n \end{cases} \qquad n = 1, 2, \ldots .$$

After a reasonably large number N of steps, we may expect m_N to be close to $M = \sup_{x \in E} f(x)$ in case f satisfies some regularity condition and the points $x_1, \ldots, x_N$ are scattered over E in some uniform manner. We introduce the following quantity to measure the uniformity of distribution of these points.

Definition. The *dispersion* $d_N(E)$ of the points $x_1, \ldots, x_N$ in E is defined by

$$d_N(E) = \sup_{x \in E} \min_{1 \leqq n \leqq N} d(x, x_n),$$

where $d(\cdot, \cdot)$ denotes the standard euclidean distance in $\mathbf{R}^s$.

If E is compact, we may replace "sup" by "max" in the above definition. The error between the approximate value m_N and the correct value M of the supremum of f on E can now be estimated in terms of $d_N(E)$ and the modulus of continuity of f. We recall that the modulus of continuity ω_E of f on E is given by

$$\omega_E(t) = \sup_{\substack{x, y \in E \\ d(x, y) \leqq t}} |f(x) - f(y)| \quad \text{for} \quad t \geqq 0 .$$

Theorem 1. *For any N points $x_1, \ldots, x_N$ in E with dispersion $d_N(E)$ and any bounded real-valued function f on E with modulus of continuity ω_E we have*

$$m_N \leqq M \leqq m_N + \omega_E(d_N(E)) .$$

Proof. The first inequality is trivial. For the proof of the second inequality, we choose $\varepsilon > 0$ and take a point $y \in E$ with $f(y) > M - \varepsilon$. Then for some i, $1 \leqq i \leqq N$, we have

$$d(y, x_i) = \min_{1 \leqq n \leqq N} d(y, x_n) .$$

It follows that $d(y, x_i) \leqq d_N(E)$. Furthermore, we have

$$f(y) - f(x_i) \leqq \omega_E(d_N(E)) ,$$

and so

$$M - \varepsilon < f(y) \leqq f(x_i) + \omega_E(d_N(E)) \leqq m_N + \omega_E(d_N(E)) ,$$

which implies the desired result.

If f is uniformly continuous on E, we have $\lim_{t\to 0+} \omega_E(t)=0$. In this case, Theorem 1 shows that if $x_1, x_2, \ldots$ is a sequence of points in E for which the dispersion $d_N(E)$ of the first N terms tends to 0 as $N\to\infty$ (or, equivalently, if $x_1, x_2, \ldots$ is dense in E), then $\lim_{N\to\infty} m_N = M$. By a direct argument, one sees easily that this holds also if f is only continuous on E.

Theorem 1 suggests that an efficient algorithm for the approximate computation of M is obtained by working with points $x_1, \ldots, x_N$ with small dispersion $d_N(E)$. The question of finding such points is closely related to covering problems. We say that the subsets F_j of $\mathbf{R}^s$, with j running through a nonempty index set J, form a *covering* of $F\subseteq\mathbf{R}^s$ if $\bigcup_{j\in J} F_j \supseteq F$. We denote by $B(x, r)$ the closed ball with center $x\in\mathbf{R}^s$ and radius r. Then it is easily seen that the following is an equivalent definition of the dispersion $d_N(E)$ of N points $x_1, \ldots, x_N$ in E:

(1) $$d_N(E)=\min\{r\geqq 0: B(x_1, r), \ldots, B(x_N, r) \text{ form a covering of } E\}.$$

We write $V(E)$ for the volume (= Lebesgue measure) of E and γ_s for the volume of the s-dimensional unit ball, i.e.,

(2) $$\gamma_s=\frac{\pi^{s/2}}{\Gamma((s/2)+1)}.$$

We denote by ϑ_s the covering density of the s-dimensional unit ball (cf. [7], p. 24). A bounded subset E of $\mathbf{R}^s$ of positive volume is called a tiling domain if there is a tiling of $\mathbf{R}^s$ by congruent copies of E (compare with [2], p. 65).

Theorem 2. *The dispersion $d_N(E)$ of any N points in the bounded subset E of $\mathbf{R}^s$ of outer Lebesgue measure $\bar{V}(E)$ satisfies*

(3) $$d_N(E)\geqq\left(\frac{\bar{V}(E)}{\gamma_s}\right)^{1/s} N^{-1/s}.$$

If E is a tiling domain, then

(4) $$d_N(E)\geqq\left(\frac{\vartheta_s V(E)}{\gamma_s}\right)^{1/s} N^{-1/s}.$$

Proof. Let $x_1, \ldots, x_N$ be N given points in E. For $r=d_N(E)$, the balls $B(x_1, r), \ldots, B(x_N, r)$ form a covering of E because of (1). By comparing measures, we get

$$N\gamma_s r^s\geqq\bar{V}(E),$$

which leads to (3). To prove (4), we set again $r=d_N(E)$ and suppose that

$$N\gamma_s r^s < \vartheta_s V(E). \tag{5}$$

Let $\mathcal{T}$ be a fixed tiling of $\mathbf{R}^s$ by congruent copies of E. Then the covering $B(x_1, r), \ldots, B(x_N, r)$ of E leads to a covering $\mathcal{K}$ of $\mathbf{R}^s$ by applying to these balls the various isometries that carry E onto the other elements of $\mathcal{T}$. Let C be a cube in $\mathbf{R}^s$ with edge-length $a(C)$, let U be the union of the elements of $\mathcal{T}$ that have a nonempty intersection with C, and let h be the number of elements of $\mathcal{T}$ making up U. If b is the diameter of E, then U is contained in a cube with edge-length $a(C)+2b$, and so

$$h=\frac{V(U)}{V(E)} \leqq \frac{(a(C)+2b)^s}{V(E)}. \tag{6}$$

Since there are at most hN balls from the covering $\mathcal{K}$ that are completely contained in C, we get

$$\frac{1}{V(C)} \sum_{\substack{B\in\mathcal{K}\\ B\subseteq C}} V(B) \leqq \frac{1}{V(C)} hN\gamma_s r^s \leqq \frac{(a(C)+2b)^s}{a(C)^s} \cdot \frac{N\gamma_s r^s}{V(E)}$$

by using (6), and so (5) yields

$$\limsup_{a(C)\to\infty} \frac{1}{V(C)} \sum_{\substack{B\in\mathcal{K}\\ B\subseteq C}} V(B) \leqq \frac{N\gamma_s r^s}{V(E)} < \vartheta_s,$$

which is a contradiction to the definition of ϑ_s. Therefore (4) is established.

The only known values of ϑ_s are $\vartheta_1=1$, which is trivial, and $\vartheta_2=2\pi/\sqrt{27}=1.209\ldots$ (cf. [7], p. 16). We also have $1.431\ldots \leqq \vartheta_3 \leqq 1.464\ldots$ and $1.658\ldots \leqq \vartheta_4 \leqq 1.765\ldots$ (cf. [7], p. 18). From the upper bounds for ϑ_s in [7] (p. 19), it follows that

$$\lim_{s\to\infty} \vartheta_s^{1/s}=1.$$

Because of (2) and Stirling's formula, the constants $\gamma_s^{-1/s}$ and $(\vartheta_s/\gamma_s)^{1/s}$ in (3) resp. (4) are then asymptotically equal to $(s/2\pi e)^{1/2}$ as $s\to\infty$. The lower bounds in (3) and (4) can be achieved up to a constant independent of s, as the following examples show.

Example 1. Let $E=I^s$, the s-dimensional unit cube. For a positive integer k, consider the $N=k^s$ points

$$\left(\frac{2n_1-1}{2k}, \frac{2n_2-1}{2k}, \ldots, \frac{2n_s-1}{2k}\right),$$

where the n_j, $1 \leqq j \leqq s$, run independently through the integers $1, 2, \ldots, k$. It is then clear that the dispersion $d^N(I^s)$ of these points is equal to the length of the diagonal in an s-dimensional cube with edge-length $(2k)^{-1}$, and so

$$d_N(I^s) = \frac{\sqrt{s}}{2} N^{-1/s}.$$

Somewhat better constants can be obtained by choosing points which are centers of balls forming an economical covering of I^s. See [2], pp. 58–59, for the case $s=2$.

Example 2. Let E be a bounded subset of $\mathbf{R}^s$ for which we assume, without loss of generality, that it is contained in I^s. For a positive integer k, we partition $[0, 1]$ into the intervals $I_h = [h/k, (h+1)/k)$ for $0 \leqq h \leqq k-2$ and $I_{k-1} = [(k-1)/k, 1]$. Then the cubes $I_{h_1} \times \ldots \times I_{h_s}$, with the h_j, $1 \leqq j \leqq s$, running independently through the integers $0, 1, \ldots, k-1$, form a partition of I^s. For each of those cubes C having a nonempty intersection with E, we select one point from $C \cap E$. In this way, we arrive at the points $x_1, \ldots, x_N$. Now let $x \in E$ be arbitrary. Then x lies in some cube C_0 from above having a nonempty intersection with E, and also $x_n \in C_0$ for some n, $1 \leqq n \leqq N$. Since the diameter of C_0 is $\sqrt{s}/k$, we get $d(x, x_n) \leqq \sqrt{s}/k$, and so the dispersion $d_N(E)$ of the points $x_1, \ldots, x_N$ satisfies $d_N(E) \leqq \sqrt{s}/k$. Now $N \leqq k^s$, and therefore $d_N(E) \leqq \sqrt{s} N^{-1/s}$.

Example 3. Let E be a bounded convex subset of $\mathbf{R}^s$ with $V(E) > 0$ for which we assume, without loss of generality, that it is contained in I^s. We choose a positive integer $k \geqq 2s/V(E)$ and construct the points $x_1, \ldots, x_N$ as in Example 2. Then we get $d_N(E) \leqq \sqrt{s}/k$ as before. Since N is the number of cubes C from Example 2 having a nonempty intersection with E, it follows from a lemma in [6] (p. 126), that

$$\frac{N}{k^s} - V(E) \leqq \frac{2s}{k}.$$

We conclude that $Nk^{-s} \leqq 2V(E)$, or $k^{-1} \leqq (2V(E)/N)^{1/s}$. Therefore,

$$d_N(E) \leqq \sqrt{s}(2V(E))^{1/s} N^{-1/s}.$$

There is a relationship between the dispersion and another measure for uniformity of distribution, the so-called discrepancy (cf. [4], Ch. 2). The *discrepancy* D_N of the points $x_1, \ldots, x_N$ in I^s is defined to be

$$D_N = \sup_K \left| \frac{A(K; N)}{N} - V(K) \right|, \tag{7}$$

where K runs through all subintervals of I^s and $A(K; N)$ is the number of n, $1 \leqq n \leqq N$, such that $x_n \in K$.

Theorem 3. *For $E \subseteq I^s$ and any points $x_1, \ldots, x_N$ in E we have*

$$d_N(E) \leqq \sqrt{s}\, D_N^{1/s}. \tag{8}$$

Proof. We can assume $d_N(E) > 0$. For given ε, $0 < \varepsilon < d_N(E)$, there exists an $x \in E$ such that $\min_{1 \leqq n \leqq N} d(x, x_n) > d_N(E) - \varepsilon$. Then the ball $B(x, d_N(E) - \varepsilon)$ contains none of the points x_n, $1 \leqq n \leqq N$. If we can show that we can inscribe a cube C into $B(x, d_N(E) - \varepsilon) \cap I^s$ with edge-length $(d_N(E) - \varepsilon)/\sqrt{s}$, then it follows that

$$D_N^{1/s} \geqq \left| \frac{A(C; N)}{N} - V(C) \right|^{1/s} = V(C)^{1/s} = \frac{d_N(E) - \varepsilon}{\sqrt{s}},$$

which implies (8). Therefore, it remains to prove that for a ball $B(y, r)$ with $y \in I^s$ and $r \leqq \sqrt{s}$ we can inscribe a cube C into $B(y, r) \cap I^s$ with edge-length $r/\sqrt{s}$. We note first that we can inscribe a cube C_0 into $B(y, r)$ which has center y and edge-length $2r/\sqrt{s}$. Now consider the interval $C_0 \cap I^s$. Each edge of this interval is a one-dimensional interval of the form $H = [t - (r/\sqrt{s}), t + (r/\sqrt{s})] \cap [0, 1]$ for some $t \in [0, 1]$. If $t + (r/\sqrt{s}) \leqq 1$, then H contains the interval $[t, t + (r/\sqrt{s})]$ of length $r/\sqrt{s}$. If $t + (r/\sqrt{s}) > 1$, then H contains the interval $[1 - (r/\sqrt{s}), 1]$ of length $r/\sqrt{s}$. Altogether, $C_0 \cap I^s$ contains a cube C with edge-length $r/\sqrt{s}$, and so $B(y, r) \cap I^s$ contains C.

The exponent $1/s$ in (8) is best possible. This follows from the lower bound in (3) and from the fact that for every $N \geqq 2$ there are points $x_1, \ldots, x_N$ in I^s such that D_N is of the order of magnitude $N^{-1} (\log N)^{s-1}$ (cf. [4], p. 130). The constant $\sqrt{s}$ in (8) is also best possible, as can be seen from the case where $E = I^s$ and the points $x_1, \ldots, x_N$ are all equal to the origin. The proof of Theorem 3 shows that the discrepancy D_N in (8) may be replaced by the "cube discrepancy", i.e., the discrepancy obtained by extending the supremum in (7) only over the cubes K contained in I^s.

It is obvious that some of the arguments in this paper can also be carried out in the framework of general metric spaces.

Added in proof. For numerical experiments using this method see NIEDERREITER, H., McCURLEY, K., Optimization of functions by quasi-random search methods, *Computing* **22** (1979), 119–123.

References

[1] ARTOBOLEVSKII, I. I., GENKIN, M. D., GRINKEVIČ, V. K., SOBOL', I. M., STATNIKOV, R. B., Optimization in the theory of machines by an LP-search (Russian). *Dokl. Akad. Nauk SSSR* **200** (1971), 1287–1290.

[2] FEJES TÓTH, L., *Lagerungen in der Ebene, auf der Kugel und im Raum*, 2. Aufl. Berlin–Heidelberg–New York: Springer-Verlag 1972.

[3] Hlawka, E., Anwendung zahlentheoretischer Methoden auf Probleme der numerischen Mathematik I. *Sitzgsber. Österreich. Akad. Wiss., math.-naturwiss. Kl. Abt. II*, **184** (1975), 217–225.

[4] Kuipers, L., Niederreiter, H., *Uniform Distribution of Sequences.* New York: Wiley–Interscience 1974.

[5] Niederreiter, H., Quasi-Monte Carlo methods and pseudo-random numbers, *Bull. Amer. Math. Soc.* **84** (1978), 957–1041.

[6] Niederreiter, H., Wills, J. M., Diskrepanz und Distanz von Massen bezüglich konvexer und Jordanscher Mengen, *Math. Z.*, **144** (1975), 125–134; Berichtigung, ibid. **148** (1976), 99.

[7] Rogers, C. A., *Packing and Covering.* London: Cambridge University Press 1964.

[8] Sobol', I. M., *Multidimensional Quadrature Formulas and Haar Functions.* (in Russian), Moscow: Izdat. „Nauka" 1969.

[9] Sobol', I. M., Statnikov, R. B., LP-search and problems of optimal design. (in Russian) In: *Problems of Random Search*, Vol. **1**, pp. 117–135. Riga: Izdat. "Zinatne" 1972.

[10] Zieliński, R., On the Monte Carlo evaluation of the extremal value of a function, *Algorytmy* **2, 4,** (1965), 7–13.

AUSTRIAN ACADEMY OF SCIENCES
VIENNA, AUSTRIA

Studies in Pure Mathematics
To the memory of Paul Turán

On a problem of P. Turán concerning Sylow subgroups

by

P. P. PÁLFY and M. SZALAY (Budapest)

1. In a sequence of papers (see [3]–[9]) P. Erdős and P. Turán developed a statistical theory of the symmetric group S_n on n letters. They proved in [3] that, for *almost all* elements σ of S_n (i.e., with the exception of $o(n!)$ σ's at most), the (group theoretical) order $\mathbf{O}(\sigma)$ of σ satisfies the inequality

$$\left|\log \mathbf{O}(\sigma) - \frac{1}{2}\log^2 n\right| < \omega(n) \log^{3/2} n \tag{1.1}$$

if $\omega(n) \nearrow \infty$ arbitrarily slowly. A generalization of (1.1) gives that $\mathbf{O}(\sigma)$ shows a "logarithmic Gaussian distribution" (see [5]). The analogue of this distribution theorem was proved for the symmetric semigroup S_n^* on n letters by B. Harris (see [10]).

The sequence [3]–[9] of P. Erdős and P. Turán contains a number of statistical results on the arithmetical structure of $\mathbf{O}(\sigma)$ for $\sigma \in S_n$, on the possible *different* values of $\mathbf{O}(\sigma)$ for $\sigma \in S_n$, on the cardinalities of the conjugacy classes of S_n, and on the common orders of the elements in a random conjugacy class of S_n. Some of these results imply the corresponding ones for the alternating group A_n on n letters.

The analogue of the above mentioned distribution theorem is proved for A_n in the paper [1] of J. Dénes, P. Erdős and P. Turán.

Concerning Abelian groups, K. Bognár, P. Erdős, R. R. Hall, R. J. Miech, A. Rényi, A. Sudbery, P. Turán and K. Wild proved statistical theorems of various type (see [6], [2] and their references).

Concerning the value distribution of the characters of the complex irreducible representations of S_n, see P. Turán [13], M. Szalay and P. Turán [12], A. M. Veršik and S. V. Kerov [14] and their references.

2. The analogue of (1.1) holds for A_n. P. Turán posed the problem of the analogue of (1.1) for other subgroups of S_n, especially for *Sylow subgroups*. In this paper we prove partial results in this direction.

For fixed prime p, let P_n be a Sylow p-subgroup of the symmetric group S_{p^n} on p^n letters. We have obviously

$$|P_n| = p^{1+p+\dots+p^{n-1}} \tag{2.1}$$

Owing to $|P_n| = o(|S_{p^n}|)$ (for $n \to \infty$), the result (1.1) cannot be used. Nevertheless, Corollary of our Theorem I asserts that if $\omega(n) \nearrow \infty$ arbitrarily slowly then the inequalities

$$p^{\mathbf{M}(\xi_n) - \omega(n)} \leqq \mathbf{O}(x) \leqq p^{\mathbf{M}(\xi_n) + \omega(n)} \tag{2.2}$$

hold for almost all elements x of P_n (i.e., with the exception of $o(|P_n|)$ x' es at most for $n \to \infty$) where $\mathbf{M}(\xi_n)$ is the mean value of a suitable random variable ξ_n. Concerning $\mathbf{M}(\xi_n)$, we are able to prove only the estimations

$$c_1(p) \cdot n \leqq \mathbf{M}(\xi_n) \leqq c_2(p) \cdot n \tag{2.3}$$

for sufficiently large n. Here, $c_1(p)$ and $c_2(p)$ are positive and independent of n (see Theorem II and Theorem III). Comparing (2.2)–(2.3) with (1.1), we can observe that $p^{c_2(p) \cdot n}$ is notably less than $\exp\left(\frac{1}{2} \log^2 (p^n)\right)$.

3. For the proof of our theorems, we need a recurrence formula. As it is well known (see, e.g., D. S. PASSMAN [11], p. 10), P_n is an iterated wreath product of n copies of the cyclic group Z_p of order p. Therefore, we have

$$P_{n+1} = P_n \operatorname{wr} Z_p \tag{3.1}$$

for non-negative integer n (with $P_0 = Z_1$).

Let us consider the random field consisting of all possible choices of elements from P_n with equal probabilities. The orders of the elements of P_n are powers of the prime p. Let ξ_n denote a random variable which assigns the non-negative integer $\log_p \mathbf{O}(x)$ to an $x \in P_n$. Our purpose is the investigation of ξ_n. Obviously, $0 \leqq \xi_n \leqq n$. For arbitrary integer k and non-negative integer n, let

$$b_n(k) = \operatorname{Prob}(\xi_n \leqq k)\,. \tag{3.2}$$

If $k < 0$ then $b_n(k) = 0$. For $k \geqq n$, we have $b_n(k) = 1$. From definition (3.2), we get

$$\operatorname{Prob}(\xi_n = k) = b_n(k) - b_n(k-1)\,. \tag{3.3}$$

Now we assert a recurrence relation as

Lemma 1. *For $n \geqq 1$, we have*

$$b_n(k) = \left(1 - \frac{1}{p}\right) b_{n-1}(k-1) + \frac{1}{p} b_{n-1}^p(k)\,. \tag{3.4}$$

Proof. According to the definition of the wreath product, the elements of P_n are expressed in the form $x=(f_x, x')$ where $f_x: Z_p \to P_{n-1}$ and $x' \in Z_p$. The elements x for which $x'=e$, the unit element of Z_p, form a normal subgroup D of index p in P_n. Now we have

$$\text{Prob}(\xi_n \leqq k) = \text{Prob}(x \notin D) \cdot \text{Prob}(\xi_n \leqq k | x \notin D) + \tag{3.5}$$
$$+ \text{Prob}(x \in D) \cdot \text{Prob}(\xi_n \leqq k | x \in D).$$

Obviously,

$$\text{Prob}(x \notin D) = 1 - \frac{1}{p} \quad \text{and} \quad \text{Prob}(x \in D) = \frac{1}{p}. \tag{3.6}$$

If $x \notin D$ (i.e., $x' \neq e$) then $x^p \in D$ and $x^p = (f_{x^p}, e)$ where

$$f_{x^p}(z) = f_x(z) f_x(zx') \cdot \ldots \cdot f_x(zx'^{p-1})$$

for arbitrary $z \in Z_p$. Further, for $z, y \in Z_p$, the relation $y = zx'^m$ holds for an appropriate m with $0 \leqq m \leqq p-1$ since x' generates Z_p owing to $x' \neq e$. Consequently, for $z \neq y$, we have

$$f_{x^p}(y) = (f_x(z) \cdot \ldots \cdot f_x(zx'^{m-1}))^{-1} f_{x^p}(z) (f_x(z) \cdot \ldots \cdot f_x(zx'^{m-1})).$$

Thus the values of f_{x^p} are conjugate in P_{n-1} and $\mathbf{O}(f_{x^p}(z)) = \frac{1}{p}\mathbf{O}(x)$ holds for arbitrary $z \in Z_p$. Let us fix $x'(\neq e)$, $f_x(x')$, $f_x(x'^2), \ldots, f_x(x'^{p-1})$ (the number of the possible choices is $(p-1) \cdot |P_{n-1}|^{p-1}$). Then, $f_{x^p}(e) = f_x(e) f_x(x') \cdot \ldots \cdot f_x(x'^{p-1})$ implies that $f_{x^p}(e)$ runs through P_{n-1} if $f_x(e)$ does. Hence, taking the relations

$$\mathbf{O}(f_{x^p}(e)) = \frac{1}{p}\mathbf{O}(x) \quad \text{and} \quad (p-1) \cdot |P_{n-1}|^{p-1} = \frac{|P_n - D|}{|P_{n-1}|}$$

into account, we get

$$\text{Prob}(\xi_n \leqq k | x \notin D) = \text{Prob}(\xi_{n-1} \leqq k-1) = b_{n-1}(k-1). \tag{3.7}$$

On the other hand, if $x = (f_x, e) \in D$ then we have

$$\mathbf{O}(x) = \max_{z \in Z_p} \mathbf{O}(f_x(z)).$$

Therefore, using the relation $|D| = |P_{n-1}|^p$, we get

$$\text{Prob}(\xi_n \leqq k | x \in D) = (\text{Prob}(\xi_{n-1} \leqq k))^p = b_{n-1}^p(k). \tag{3.8}$$

(3.5), (3.6), (3.7) and (3.8) prove Lemma 1.

Applying Lemma 1 repeatedly, we get

Lemma 2. *For $n \geqq 1$, $0 \leqq k \leqq n-1$. we have*

$$b_n(k) = \frac{1}{p} \sum_{j=0}^{k} \left(1 - \frac{1}{p}\right)^j b_{n-1-j}^p(k-j). \tag{3.9}$$

Next we shall prove three basic inequalities. We assert the first one as

Lemma 3. *The inequality*

$$b_n(k) \leqq b_{n+1}(k+1) \tag{3.10}$$

holds for $n \geqq 1$, $0 \leqq k \leqq n$.

Proof. We proceed by induction on $n-k$. If $n=k$ then $b_n(k) = 1 = b_{n+1}(k+1)$. Otherwise, Lemma 2 and the induction hypothesis yield that

$$b_{n+1}(k+1) = \frac{1}{p} \sum_{j=0}^{k+1} \left(1 - \frac{1}{p}\right)^j b_{n-j}^p(k+1-j) \geqq$$

$$\geqq \frac{1}{p} \sum_{j=0}^{k} \left(1 - \frac{1}{p}\right)^j b_{n-1-j}^p(k-j) = b_n(k)$$

owing to $b_{n-k-1}(0) \geqq 0$ and $b_1(1) = 1 = b_0(0)$. Q.e.d.

Lemma 4. *For $n \geqq 1$, $0 \leqq k \leqq n-1$, we have*

$$b_n(k) \leqq \left(1 - \left(1 - \frac{1}{p}\right)^{k+1}\right) b_{n-1}^p(k) < b_{n-1}^p(k). \tag{3.11}$$

Proof. Using Lemma 2 and Lemma 3, we obtain that

$$b_n(k) = \frac{1}{p} \sum_{j=0}^{k} \left(1 - \frac{1}{p}\right)^j b_{n-1-j}^p(k-j) \leqq$$

$$\leqq \frac{1}{p} \sum_{j=0}^{k} \left(1 - \frac{1}{p}\right)^j b_{n-1}^p(k) = \left(1 - \left(1 - \frac{1}{p}\right)^{k+1}\right) b_{n-1}^p(k) < b_{n-1}^p(k)$$

owing to $b_0(0) = 1 = b_{n-1}(n-1)$ and $b_{n-1}(k) > 0$. Q.e.d.

Lemma 5. *For $n \geqq 1$, $1 \leqq k \leqq n$, the inequality*

$$b_n(k-1) < b_n^p(k) \tag{3.12}$$

holds.

Proof. According to Lemma 1, $b_{n+1}(k)$ is a weighted average of $b_n(k-1)$ and $b_n^p(k)$ with positive weights. Therefore, our assertion follows from the consequence $b_{n+1}(k) < b_n^p(k)$ of Lemma 4.

4. In this section we investigate the variance $\mathbf{D}^2(\xi_n)$ and the mean value $\mathbf{M}(\xi_n)$ of ξ_n. The distribution of the orders of elements of P_n is highly concentrated, as the following theorem shows.

Theorem I. *For $n \geqq 1$, the inequalities*

$$\mathbf{D}^2(\xi_n) \leqq \frac{1}{4} + 48\frac{\log p}{p} < 18 \tag{4.1}$$

hold. (N. B., the estimation is independent of n.)

Proof. For the variance of ξ_n, we have

$$\mathbf{D}^2(\xi_n) = \sum_{j=0}^{n} (b_n(j) - b_n(j-1))(j - \mathbf{M}(\xi_n))^2 .$$

Owing to $b_n(0) \leqq \frac{1}{p} \leqq 1 - \frac{\log p}{p}$, we can choose a *maximal* k such that

$$b_n(k) \leqq 1 - \frac{\log p}{p}. \tag{4.2}$$

Clearly, $0 \leqq k < n$. Now,

$$\mathbf{D}^2(\xi_n) \leqq \mathbf{D}^2(\xi_n) + \left(k + \frac{1}{2} - \mathbf{M}(\xi_n)\right)^2 =$$

$$= \sum_{j=0}^{n} (b_n(j) - b_n(j-1))\left(j - k - \frac{1}{2}\right)^2 .$$

Decomposing this sum into two parts, set

$$D_1 = \sum_{j=0}^{k} (b_n(j) - b_n(j-1))\left(j - k - \frac{1}{2}\right)^2 =$$

$$= \frac{1}{4} b_n(k) + \sum_{j=0}^{k-1} b_n(j)\left(\left(j - k - \frac{1}{2}\right)^2 - \left(j + 1 - k - \frac{1}{2}\right)^2\right) = \tag{4.3}$$

$$= \frac{1}{4} b_n(k) + \sum_{j=0}^{k-1} 2(k-j) b_n(j),$$

$$D_2 = \sum_{j=k+1}^{n} (b_n(j) - b_n(j-1)) \left(j-k-\frac{1}{2}\right)^2 =$$

$$(4.4) \qquad = \frac{1}{4}(1-b_n(k)) + \sum_{j=k+1}^{n} (1-b_n(j)) \left(\left(j+1-k-\frac{1}{2}\right)^2 - \left(j-k-\frac{1}{2}\right)^2\right) =$$

$$= \frac{1}{4}(1-b_n(k)) + \sum_{j=k+1}^{n} 2(j-k)(1-b_n(j)).$$

Using (4.2), we get

$$b_n^p(k) \leqq \left(1 - \frac{\log p}{p}\right)^p < \frac{1}{p}.$$

Consequently, for $0 \leqq j < k$,

$$b_n(j) < b_n^{p^{k-j}}(k) \leqq (b_n(k))^{(k-j)p} < \frac{1}{p^{k-j}}$$

owing to Lemma 5. Hence, from (4.3), we obtain that

$$(4.5) \qquad D_1 \leqq \frac{1}{4} b_n(k) + \sum_{j=0}^{k-1} \frac{2(k-j)}{p^{k-j}} < \frac{1}{4} b_n(k) + \frac{2}{p\left(1 - \frac{1}{p}\right)^2}.$$

If $1 \geqq x > 1 - \frac{\log p}{p}$ then

$$(4.6) \qquad 1 - x^{1/p} = \frac{1-x}{1+x^{1/p}+\ldots+x^{(p-1)/p}} \leqq \frac{1-x}{p-\log p}.$$

Again by Lemma 5, for $k+1 \leqq j \leqq n$, we get

$$(4.7) \qquad b_n(j) \geqq (b_n(k+1))^{p^{-(j-k-1)}}.$$

For $k+1 \leqq j \leqq n$, (4.2), (4.6) and (4.7) give that

$$1 - b_n(j) \leqq 1 - (b_n(k+1))^{p^{-(j-k-1)}} \leqq$$

$$\leqq \frac{1-b_n(k+1)}{(p-\log p)^{j-k-1}} < \frac{\log p}{p \cdot (p-\log p)^{j-k-1}}.$$

Hence, from (4.4),

$$D_2 < \frac{1}{4}(1-b_n(k)) + \sum_{j=k+1}^{n} \frac{2(j-k)\log p}{p(p-\log p)^{j-k-1}} <$$

(4.8)

$$< \frac{1}{4}(1-b_n(k)) + \frac{2\log p}{p\left(1-\dfrac{1}{p-\log p}\right)^2}.$$

Adding (4.5) and (4.8), we obtain

$$\mathbf{D}^2(\xi_n) \leqq D_1 + D_2 < \frac{1}{4} + \frac{2\log p}{p}\left[\frac{1}{\left(1-\dfrac{1}{p}\right)^2\log p} + \frac{1}{\left(1-\dfrac{1}{p-\log p}\right)^2}\right] \leqq$$

$$\leqq \frac{1}{4} + \frac{2\log p}{p}\left[\frac{1}{\left(1-\dfrac{1}{2}\right)^2\log 2} + \frac{1}{\left(1-\dfrac{1}{2-\log 2}\right)^2}\right] < \frac{1}{4} + 48\frac{\log p}{p} < 18.$$

Q.e.d.

Corollary of Theorem I. *If $\omega(n) \nearrow \infty$ arbitrarily slowly then the inequalities*

(4.9) $$p^{\mathbf{M}(\xi_n)-\omega(n)} \leqq \mathbf{O}(x) \leqq p^{\mathbf{M}(\xi_n)+\omega(n)}$$

hold for almost all elements x of P_n (i.e., *with the exception of $o(|P_n|)$ x's at most for $n \to \infty$*).

Proof. Applying Chebyshev's inequality, we have

$$\text{Prob}\,(|\xi_n - \mathbf{M}(\xi_n)| > \omega(n)) < \frac{\mathbf{D}^2(\xi_n)}{\omega^2(n)} < \frac{18}{\omega^2(n)} \to 0$$

for $n \to \infty$. Q.e.d.

Unfortunately, we do not know the value of $\mathbf{M}(\xi_n)$. Using a computer for the calculations, we determined $\mathbf{M}(\xi_n)$ for $n \leqq 100$ and $p = 2, 3, 5, 7$. On the basis of these experiments, we set up the following conjecture.

Conjecture. $\mathbf{M}(\xi_n)/n$ is an increasing sequence and, for

$$c = \lim_{n\to\infty} \frac{\mathbf{M}(\xi_n)}{n},$$

the relations

(4.10) $$0 < c < 1$$

and

$$\frac{1-c}{c}\log(1-c)+\log c=\log\left(1-\frac{1}{p}\right) \tag{4.11}$$

hold.

The left-hand side of (4.11) is an increasing function of c in the interval (0, 1). The c-values corresponding to the smallest primes can be found in the table below.

p	c
2	0.772 907 80
3	0.884 183 66
5	0.945 686 99
7	0.965 849 43
11	0.981 153 84

5. We are able to prove only two estimates for $\mathbf{M}(\xi_n)/n$. We assert the first one as

Theorem II. *If* $c=c(p)$ *satisfies* (4.10) *and* (4.11) *then the inequality*

$$\mathbf{M}(\xi_n)<cn \tag{5.1}$$

holds for sufficiently large n.

For the proof of Theorem II we need

Lemma 6. *For* $n\geqq 1$, $k\geqq -1$, *the inequality*

$$b_n(k)\geqq 1-\binom{n}{k+1}\left(1-\frac{1}{p}\right)^{k+1} \tag{5.2}$$

holds and, for $n\geqq 1$, *we have*

$$b_n(n-1)=1-\left(1-\frac{1}{p}\right)^n. \tag{5.3}$$

Proof. For $n\geqq 1$, Lemma 1 yields that

$$1-b_n(k)=\left(1-\frac{1}{p}\right)(1-b_{n-1}(k-1))+\frac{1}{p}(1-b_{n-1}^p(k)) \tag{5.4}$$

and

$$1-b_n(n-1)=\left(1-\frac{1}{p}\right)(1-b_{n-1}(n-2)). \tag{5.5}$$

$b_1(0)=1/p$ and (5.5) prove (5.3).

Since, for $0 \leqq x \leqq 1$,

$$1 - x^p = (1-x)(1+x+\ldots+x^{p-1}) \leqq p(1-x),$$

it follows from (5.4) that

$$1 - b_n(k) \leqq \left(1 - \frac{1}{p}\right)(1 - b_{n-1}(k-1)) + (1 - b_{n-1}(k)) \tag{5.6}$$

for $n \geqq 1$.

For $n \geqq 1$, $k = -1$, (5.2) holds trivially. Now we can prove (5.2) by induction on n. If $n = 1$ then

$$b_1(0) = \frac{1}{p} = 1 - \binom{1}{1}\left(1 - \frac{1}{p}\right)^1$$

and

$$b_1(k) = 1 = 1 - \binom{1}{k+1}\left(1 - \frac{1}{p}\right)^{k+1} \quad \text{for} \quad k \geqq 1.$$

For $n \geqq 2$, $k \geqq 0$, the induction hypothesis and (5.6) yield that

$$1 - b_n(k) \leqq \left(1 - \frac{1}{p}\right)\binom{n-1}{k}\left(1 - \frac{1}{p}\right)^k + \binom{n-1}{k+1}\left(1 - \frac{1}{p}\right)^{k+1} =$$

$$= \binom{n}{k+1}\left(1 - \frac{1}{p}\right)^{k+1}.$$

Q.e.d.

Proof of Theorem II. Let $c = c(p)$ satisfy (4.10) and (4.11). Let $k = [cn] - 5$ and let us suppose that $\mathbf{M}(\xi_n) \geqq cn$. Now, Theorem I and Chebyshev's inequality yield that

$$b_n(k) \leqq \operatorname{Prob}(|\xi_n - \mathbf{M}(\xi_n)| \geqq 5) \leqq \frac{18}{5^2} = 0.72. \tag{5.7}$$

Since $1 > c > 0.77$, we have

$$\frac{1}{2} < \frac{k}{n} < \frac{[cn]+1}{n} < 1$$

for sufficiently large n. Using Lemma 6 we get

$$1 - b_n(k) \leqq \binom{n}{k+1}\left(1 - \frac{1}{p}\right)^{k+1} \leqq$$

$$\leqq \frac{(cn)^5}{((1-c)n)^5}\binom{n}{[cn]+1}\left(1 - \frac{1}{p}\right)^{k+1}.$$

Stirling's formula yields that

$$\log(1-b_n(k)) \leqq \left(-c\log c-(1-c)\log(1-c)+c\log\left(1-\frac{1}{p}\right)\right)n+$$

$$(5.8) \qquad +\frac{1}{12n}+\frac{9}{2}\log c-\frac{11}{2}\log(1-c)-\frac{1}{2}\log n-$$

$$-\frac{1}{2}\log 2\pi+1-5\log\left(1-\frac{1}{p}\right).$$

Since c satisfies (4.11), the coefficient of n in (5.8) is 0. Hence,

$$(5.9) \qquad 1-b_n(k) \leqq \frac{e^{13/12}c^{9/2}}{(1-c)^{11/2}\left(1-\frac{1}{p}\right)^5\sqrt{2\pi}}\cdot\frac{1}{\sqrt{n}}.$$

Consequently, for sufficiently large n, $b_n(k)>0.72$ in contradiction with (5.7). This proves Theorem II.

6. For the lower estimate we need

Lemma 7. *For* $n \geqq 1$, $0 \leqq k < n$, *the inequality*

$$(6.1) \qquad \mathbf{M}(\xi_n) \geqq k+2-\frac{1}{1-b_n(k)}$$

holds.

Proof. Using Lemma 5, we get

$$\mathbf{M}(\xi_n)=\sum_{j=0}^{n}(b_n(j)-b_n(j-1))j=$$

$$=n-\sum_{j=0}^{n-1}b_n(j) \geqq n-\sum_{j=0}^{k}b_n(j)-\sum_{j=k+1}^{n-1}1=$$

$$=k+1-\sum_{j=0}^{k}b_n(j) \geqq k+1-\sum_{j=0}^{k}b_n^{p^{k-j}}(k) \geqq$$

$$\geqq k+2-\sum_{i=0}^{\infty}b_n^i(k)=k+2-\frac{1}{1-b_n(k)}.$$

Q.e.d.

Finally, we assert

Theorem III. *For sufficiently large n, we have*

$$\mathbf{M}(\xi_n) > \frac{\log p}{\log p - \log\left(1-\frac{1}{p}\right)} n - 1.6. \tag{6.2}$$

Proof. For $n \geqq 1$, $0 \leqq k \leqq n-1$, Lemma 4 and (5.3) from Lemma 6 yield that

$$b_n(k) \leqq b_{k+1}^{p^{n-k-1}}(k) = \left(1-\left(1-\frac{1}{p}\right)^{k+1}\right)^{p^{n-k-1}}.$$

Thus,

$$\log b_n(k) \leqq p^{n-k-1} \log\left(1-\left(1-\frac{1}{p}\right)^{k+1}\right) < -p^{n-k-1}\left(1-\frac{1}{p}\right)^{k+1}. \tag{6.3}$$

Let

$$k_0 = \left[\frac{\log p}{\log p - \log\left(1-\frac{1}{p}\right)} n\right] - 1. \tag{6.4}$$

For sufficiently large n, we have

$$0 \leqq k_0 \leqq n-1 \quad \text{and} \quad \frac{k_0+1}{n} \leqq \frac{\log p}{\log p - \log\left(1-\frac{1}{p}\right)}.$$

Using (6.3), we get

$$\log b_n(k_0) < -\left(p^{1-(k_0+1)/n}\left(1-\frac{1}{p}\right)^{(k_0+1)/n}\right)^n \leqq -1.$$

Therefore, $b_n(k_0) \leqq e^{-1}$. Lemma 7 gives that

$$\mathbf{M}(\xi_n) \geqq k_0 + 2 - \frac{1}{1-b_n(k_0)} > \frac{\log p}{\log p - \log\left(1-\frac{1}{p}\right)} n - 1.6.$$

Q.e.d.

Acknowledgement

The authors wish to thank Dr. L. Babai for suggesting the important Lemma 1 and Lemma 6.

References

[1] J. DÉNES, P. ERDŐS and P. TURÁN, On some statistical properties of the alternating group of degree *n*, *L'Enseignement mathématique*, **XV** (1969), 89–99.

[2] P. ERDŐS and R. R. HALL, Probabilistic methods in group theory, II, *Houston Journal of Mathematics*, **2** (1976), 173–180.

[3] P. ERDŐS and P. TURÁN, On some problems of a statistical group theory, I, *Z. Wahrscheinlichkeitstheorie und verw. Gebiete*, **4** (1965), 175–186.

[4] P. ERDŐS and P. TURÁN, On some problems of a statistical group theory, II, *Acta Math. Acad. Sci. Hungar.*, **18** (1967), 151–163.

[5] P. ERDŐS and P. TURÁN, On some problems of a statistical group theory, III, *Acta Math. Acad. Sci. Hungar.*, **18** (1967), 309–320.

[6] P. ERDŐS and P. TURÁN, On some problems of a statistical group theory, IV, *Acta Math. Acad. Sci. Hungar.*, **19** (1968), 413–435.

[7] P. ERDŐS and P. TURÁN, On some problems of a statistical group theory, V, *Periodica Math. Hung.*, **1** (1971), 5–13.

[8] P. ERDŐS and P. TURÁN, On some problems of a statistical group theory, VI, *J. Indian Math. Soc.*, **34** (1970), 175–192.

[9] P. ERDŐS and P. TURÁN, On some problems of a statistical group theory, VII, *Periodica Math. Hung.*, **2** (1972), 149–163.

[10] B. HARRIS, The asymptotic distribution of the order of elements in symmetric semigroups, *J. Combinatorial Theory*, **15A** (1973), 66–74.

[11] D. S. PASSMAN, *Permutation Groups*, Benjamin, 1968.

[12] M. SZALAY and P. TURÁN, On some problems of the statistical theory of partitions with application to characters of the symmetric group, III, *Acta Math. Acad. Sci. Hungar.*, **32** (1978), 129–155.

[13] P. TURÁN, Combinatorics, partitions, group theory. In: *Colloquio Int. s. Teorie Combinatorie* (Roma, 3–15 settembre 1973), Roma, Accademia Nazionale dei Lincei, 1976, Tomo II, 181–200.

[14] A. M. VERŠIK and S. V. KEROV, Asymptotics of the Plancherel measure of the symmetric group and limiting form of Young tables, *Dokl. Akad. Nauk SSSR*, **233** (1977), 1024–1027 = *Soviet Math. Dokl.* **18** (1977), 527–531.

MATHEMATICAL INSTITUTE OF THE
HUNGARIAN ACADEMY OF SCIENCES
H-1053 BUDAPEST, REÁLTANODA U. 13–15.
HUNGARY

DEPARTMENT OF ALGEBRA AND NUMBER THEORY
EÖTVÖS LORÁND UNIVERSITY
H-1088 BUDAPEST
MÚZEUM KRT. 6–8.
HUNGARY

Studies in Pure Mathematics
To the Memory of Paul Turán

On polynomials with curved majorants

by

R. PIERRE (Sherbrooke) and Q. I. RAHMAN (Montréal)

At a conference held in Varna, Bulgaria in the year 1970 the late Professor P. TURÁN proposed the following problem:

Problem. *Let* $\varphi(x) \geqq 0$ *for* $-1 \leqq x \leqq 1$. *For fixed* x_0 *in* $[-1, 1]$ *what can be said for* $\sup |p_n'(x_0)|$ *if* $p_n(x)$ *belongs to the class* $\mathscr{P}_n$ *of all polynomials of degree n satisfying the inequality* $|p_n(x)| \leqq \varphi(x)$ *for* $-1 \leqq x \leqq 1$?

Besides, he singled out the case $\varphi(x) = \sqrt{1-x^2}$ as one of special interest since for real-valued polynomials the hypothesis means that the graph of $p_n(x)$ on the interval $-1 < x < 1$ is contained in the closed unit disk.

It has been shown [4] that if $p_n(x)$ is a polynomial of degree n such that $|p_n(x)| \leqq \sqrt{1-x^2}$ for $-1 < x < 1$, then

$$\max_{-1 \leqq x \leqq 1} |p_n'(x)| \leqq 2(n-1). \tag{1}$$

The case $\varphi(x) \equiv 1$ is classical and according to a well-known result of W. A. MARKOV

$$\max_{-1 \leqq x \leqq 1} |p_n'(x)| \leqq n^2 \tag{2}$$

in that case.

The majorants $\varphi(x) \equiv 1$ and $\varphi(x) = \sqrt{1-x^2}$ are both concave and one might wish to find out the role played by "the concavity of the majorant" in the above problem.

For a given non-negative function $\varphi(x)$ let $\mathscr{P}_{n,\varphi}$ denote the class of all polynomials of degree n such that $|p_n(x)| \leqq \varphi(x)$ for $-1 \leqq x \leqq 1$. It is easily seen that if $\varphi(x)$ is concave on $[-1, 1]$ and

$$\max \{\varphi(-1), \varphi(1)\} = c > 0$$

then

$$N_\varphi := \sup_{p_n \in \mathscr{P}_{n,\varphi}} \max_{-1 \leqq x \leqq 1} |p_n'(x)| \geqq \frac{c}{2} \{2(n-1)^2 + 1\}. \tag{3}$$

In fact, if $\max\{\varphi(-1), \varphi(1)\}=\varphi(1)$ say, then $\varphi(x)\geqq \frac{c}{2}(1+x)$ for $-1\leqq x\leqq 1$. Hence if $T_{n-1}(x)$ is the Chebyshev polynomial of the first kind of degree $n-1$ then $P_n(x)= = \frac{c}{2}(1+x)T_{n-1}(x)\in \mathscr{P}_{n,\varphi}$ and

$$\max_{-1\leqq x\leqq 1} |P_n'(x)|=|P_n'(1)|=\frac{c}{2}\{2(n-1)^2+1\}.$$

If $\varphi(-1)=\varphi(1)=0$, then

$$N_\varphi \geqq \frac{n-3}{4}M, \tag{4}$$

where $M=\max_{-1\leqq x\leqq 1} \varphi(x)$. To see this note that

$$D_1:=\left\{(x, y)\in \mathbf{R}^2: -1\leqq x\leqq 1, |y|\leqq \frac{M}{4}(1-x^2)\right\}\subset D_2:=$$

$$:=\left\{(x, y)\in \mathbf{R}^2: -1\leqq x\leqq 1, |y|\leqq \frac{M}{2}(1-|x|)\right\}$$

$$\subseteq D_3:=\{(x, y)\in \mathbf{R}^2: -1\leqq x\leqq 1, |y|\leqq \varphi(x)\}.$$

Thus the graph of $P(x):=\frac{M}{4}(1-x^2)T_{n-2}(x)$ lies in D_3 and for odd n,

$$\max_{-1\leqq x\leqq 1} |P'(x)|\geqq |P'(0)|=\frac{n-2}{4}M.$$

For even n we may consider $Q(x):=\frac{M}{4}(1-x^2)T_{n-3}(x)$.

On the other hand, the example $p_n(x)=M\cos\left\{n \arccos\left(x\cos\frac{\pi}{2n}\right)\right\}$ shows that N_φ can be as large as $Mn\cot\frac{\pi}{2n}\sim\frac{2M}{\pi}n^2$ even if $\varphi(-1)=\varphi(1)=0$ and all we know is that $\varphi(x)$ is concave on $[-1, 1]$. Without further information about the function $\varphi(x)$ we cannot be more precise. What appears to be important is the behaviour of $\varphi(x)$ near the end points -1 and 1.

In view of the above mentioned facts it is interesting to consider majorants of the form $(1-x^2)^\rho$ where ρ is an arbitrary non-negative number. As ρ varies from 0 to $\frac{1}{2}$ we would obtain a deformation of the square $\{(x, y)\in \mathbf{R}^2: -1\leqq x\leqq 1, -1\leqq y\leqq 1\}$ into the disk $\{(x, y)\in \mathbf{R}^2: x^2+y^2\leqq 1\}$ and see how the upper bound for the derivative varies from n^2 to $2(n-1)$ as this happens. The following result of Dzyadyk [2] provides us with an answer.

Theorem A. *If a polynomial of degree not exceeding n satisfies on the interval $(-1, 1)$ the inequality*

$$|p_n(x)| \leqq L \cdot (1-x^2)^{\rho/2} \quad \textit{when} \quad \rho \leqq 0, \tag{5}$$

and the inequality

$$|p_n(x)| \leqq L \cdot \{(1-x^2)^{\rho/2} + n^{-\rho}\} \quad \textit{when} \quad \rho \geqq 0, \tag{5'}$$

where L and ρ are constants, then the derivative $p_n'(x)$ satisfies for every x in $(-1, 1)$ the inequality

$$|p_n'(x)| \leqq CnL \min \{(1-x^2)^{(\rho-1)/2}, n^{1-\rho}\} \quad \textit{if} \quad \rho \leqq 1, \tag{6}$$

and the inequality

$$|p_n'(x)| \leqq CnL \left\{(1-x^2)^{(\rho-1)/2} + \frac{1}{n^{\rho-1}}\right\} \quad \textit{if} \quad \rho \geqq 1, \tag{6'}$$

where C is a constant depending only on ρ.

The question as to what extent these estimates of Dzyadyk are sharp has not been discussed before. From (4) it follows that (6) is best possible as far as the exponent of the factor n is concerned. For $\rho < 1$ the global bound $O(n^{2-\rho})$ implied by the estimate (6) is sharp too in as much as $n^{2-\rho}$ cannot be replaced by any function of n tending to infinity (with n) more slowly. Indeed, we have the following

Theorem 1. *For $\lambda < 1$, $\mu < 1$ let*

$$N(\lambda, \mu) := \sup \{ \max_{-1 \leqq x \leqq 1} |p_n'(x)| : \deg(p_n) \leqq n, |p_n(x)| \leqq (1-x)^{\lambda}(1+x)^{\mu}\}.$$

Then there exists a constant K independent of n such that

$$N(\lambda, \mu) \geqq Kn^{2(1-m)} \tag{7}$$

where $m = \min(\lambda, \mu)$.

Proof. Set $\alpha = \frac{3}{2} - 2\lambda$, $\beta = \frac{3}{2} - 2\mu$, so that $\alpha > -\frac{1}{2}$, $\beta > -\frac{1}{2}$, and consider the polynomial

$$f(x) = \sqrt{\pi}(n-2)^{1/2} 2^{(\lambda+\mu)}(1-x^2) P_{n-2}^{(\alpha,\beta)}(x)$$

where $P_n^{(\alpha,\beta)}(x)$ denotes the Jacobi polynomial of degree n with the normalization

$$P_n^{(\alpha,\beta)}(-1)=\binom{n+\alpha}{n}. \tag{8}$$

Using the following two properties of Jacobi polynomials, namely [6, p. 168]

$$\max|P_n^{(\alpha,\beta)}(x)|=\begin{cases}\binom{n+\alpha}{n} & \text{if } (\beta-\alpha)/(\alpha+\beta+1)\leqq x\leqq 1,\\[2mm] \binom{n+\beta}{n} & \text{if } -1\leqq x\leqq(\beta-\alpha)/(\alpha+\beta+1),\end{cases}$$

and for a fixed positive number c [6, Theorem 8.21.13]

$$P_n^{(\alpha,\beta)}(\cos\vartheta)=n^{-1/2}\pi^{-1/2}\left(\sin\frac{\vartheta}{2}\right)^{-\alpha-\frac{1}{2}}\left(\cos\frac{\vartheta}{2}\right)^{-\beta-\frac{1}{2}}\{\cos(N\vartheta+\gamma)+$$

$$+(n\sin\vartheta)^{-1}O(1)\},\ cn^{-1}\leqq\vartheta\leqq\pi-cn^{-1}$$

where $N=n+(\alpha+\beta+1)/2$, $\gamma=-\left(\alpha+\frac{1}{2}\right)\pi/2$ it can be shown that

$$f(x)=O(1)(1-x)^{\lambda}(1+x)^{\mu}.$$

On the other hand, from (8) in conjunction with [6, p. 59]

$$P_n^{(\alpha,\beta)}(-1)=(-1)^n\binom{n+\beta}{n} \tag{9}$$

it follows that

$$\max_{-1\leqq x\leqq 1}|f'(x)|\geqq\max\{|f'(-1)|,|f'(1)|\}=$$

$$=2\sqrt{\pi}(n-2)^{1/2}2^{(\lambda+\mu)}\cdot\max\left\{\binom{n-2+\alpha}{n-2},\binom{n-2+\beta}{n-2}\right\}$$

and hence (7) holds.

The constants C in DZYADYK's estimates are not precise. Apart from (1) and the classical inequality (2) there is one further interesting case where a certain pointwise estimate like (6) leads to the precise global bound for the derivative.

Theorem 2. *If $p_n(x)$ is a polynomial of degree n such that $|p_n(x)| \leqq (1-x^2)^{-1/2}$ for $-1<x<1$, then*

$$(10) \qquad \max_{-1 \leqq x \leqq 1} |p_n'(x)| \leqq \max_{-1 \leqq x \leqq 1} \left| \frac{T_{n+1}'(x)}{n+1} \right| = \frac{n(n+1)(n+2)}{3}$$

where $T_{n+1}(x)$ is the $(n+1)$-st Chebyshev polynomial of the first kind.

As an immediate consequence of Theorem 2 we obtain

Corollary 1. *If $p_n(x)$ is a polynomial of degree n such that $|p_n'(x)| \leqq \frac{n}{(1-x^2)^{1/2}}$ for $-1<x<1$, then*

$$(11) \qquad \max_{-1 \leqq x \leqq 1} |p_n''(x)| \leqq \frac{n^2(n^2-1^2)}{1 \cdot 3}.$$

Inequality (11) was first proved by W. A. Markov [3] under the hypotheses "$|p_n(x)| \leqq 1$ for $-1 \leqq x \leqq 1$" which is stronger since according to a famous result of S. N. Bernstein it implies "$|p_n'(x)| \leqq \frac{n}{(1-x^2)^{1/2}}$ for $-1<x<1$".

It is surprising that inequality (11) was never proved before since polynomials of degree n satisfying $|p_n(x)| \leqq (1-x^2)^{-1/2}$ for $-1<x<1$ have been considered in the past and it is well known (see for example [5, p. 90], [1, pp. 89–90], [7, pp. 36–37], etc.) that for such polynomials

$$(12) \qquad \max_{-1 \leqq x \leqq 1} |p_n(x)| \leqq n+1.$$

Proof of Theorem 2. Clearly $g(\vartheta) = \sin\vartheta\, p_n(\cos\vartheta)$ is a trigonometric polynomial of degree $n+1$ such that $|g(\vartheta)| \leqq 1$ for all real ϑ. Hence by Bernstein's inequality

$$|g'(\vartheta)| = |\cos\vartheta \cdot p_n(\cos\vartheta) - \sin^2\vartheta \cdot p_n'(\cos\vartheta)| \leqq n+1,$$

i.e.

$$|x\, p_n(x) - (1-x^2) p_n'(x)| \leqq n+1$$

for $-1 \leqq x \leqq 1$. Using (12) we get

$$|(1-x^2) p_n'(x)| \leqq (n+1) + |x|\, |p_n(x)| \leqq 2(n+1).$$

From this it can be easily deduced that

$$(13) \qquad |p_n'(x)| \leqq \frac{n(n+1)(n+2)}{3}$$

for $|x| \leqq \cos \frac{\pi}{n+1}$.

In order to prove (13) for $\cos\dfrac{\pi}{n+1}<|x|\leqq 1$, set

$$l(x)=T_{n+1}(x),$$

$$x_\nu=\cos\left\{\left(\nu+\frac{1}{2}\right)\frac{\pi}{n+1}\right\},\quad \nu=0,1,2,\ldots,n,$$

$$l_\nu(x)=\frac{l(x)}{x-x_\nu},\quad \nu=0,1,2,\ldots,n.$$

Then by Lagrange's interpolation formula

$$p_n(x)=\sum_{\nu=0}^{n} l_\nu(x)\frac{p_n(x_\nu)}{l'(x_\nu)}=\frac{1}{n+1}\sum_{\nu=0}^{n}\{l_\nu(x)(-1)^\nu(1-x_\nu^2)^{1/2}p_n(x_\nu)\}.$$

Differentiating with respect to x we obtain

$$p_n'(x)=\frac{1}{n+1}\sum_{\nu=0}^{n}\{l_\nu'(x)(-1)^\nu(1-x_\nu^2)^{1/2}p_n(x_\nu)\}. \tag{14}$$

Using the hypothesis we are led to the inequality

$$p_n'(x)=\frac{1}{n+1}\sum_{\nu=0}^{n}|l_\nu'(x)|. \tag{15}$$

Now we observe that

$$l_\nu'(x)>0,\quad \nu=0,1,2,\ldots,n \tag{16}$$

for $\cos\dfrac{\pi}{n+1}\leqq x\leqq 1$. In fact,

$$l_\nu'\left(\cos\frac{\pi}{n+1}\right)=\frac{1}{\left(\cos\dfrac{\pi}{n+1}-x_\nu\right)^2}>0$$

as well as

$$l_\nu'(1)=\frac{(n+1)^2(1-x_\nu)-1}{(1-x_\nu)^2}>0$$

for $\nu=0,1,2,\ldots,n$. Hence in $\left(\cos\dfrac{\pi}{n+1},1\right)$, $l_\nu'(x)$ must have an even number of zeros. But in $\left(\cos\dfrac{\pi}{2(n+1)},\infty\right)$ it can have at most one zero. So it has no zero in

$\left(\cos\frac{\pi}{n+1}, 1\right)$, i.e. (16) holds. Thus for $\cos\frac{\pi}{n+1} < x \leqq 1$, (15) may be written as

$$|p_n'(x)| \leqq \frac{1}{n+1} \sum_{\nu=0}^{n} l_\nu'(x). \tag{17}$$

But setting $p_n(x) = \frac{l'(x)}{n+1}$ in (14) we see that the right-hand side of (17) is equal to $\frac{l''(x)}{n+1}$, so that

$$|p_n'(x)| \leqq \frac{l''(x)}{n+1} = \frac{T_{n+1}''(x)}{n+1} \leqq \frac{T_{n+1}''(1)}{n+1} = \frac{n(n+1)(n+2)}{3},$$

i.e. (13) holds for $\cos\frac{\pi}{n+1} < x \leqq 1$. The same must obviously hold for $-1 \leqq x < -\cos\frac{\pi}{n+1}$ as well, and so the theorem is proved.

References

[1] E. W. Cheney, *Introduction to Approximation Theory*, McGraw-Hill, New York, 1966.

[2] V. K. Dzyadyk, Constructive characterization of functions satisfying a condition Lip $\alpha(0<\alpha<1)$ on a finite interval of the real axis, *Izvestiya Akad. Nauk SSSR, Ser. Mat.*, **20** (1956), 623–642.

[3] W. A. Markov, Über Polynome, die in einem gegebenen Intervalle möglichst wenig von Null abweichen, *Math. Ann.*, **77** (1916), 218–258.

[4] Q. I. Rahman, On a problem of Turán about polynomials with curved majorants, *Trans. Amer. Math. Soc.*, **163** (1972), 447–455.

[5] G. Pólya und G. Szegő, *Aufgaben und Lehrsätze aus der Analysis* II, Springer, Berlin, 1925.

[6] G. Szegő, *Orthogonal Polynomials*, Amer. Math. Soc. Colloq. Publ., vol. XXIII, Third Edition, Amer. Math. Soc., Providence, R. I., 1967.

[7] J. Todd, *Introduction to the Constructive Theory of Functions*, Academic Press, New York, 1963.

DÉPARTMENT DE MATHÉMATIQUES
UNIVERSITÉ DE SHERBROOKE, SHERBROOKE, QUÉBEC, CANADA

DÉPARTEMENT DE MATHÉMATIQUES ET DE STATISTIQUE
UNIVERSITÉ DE MONTRÉAL, MONTRÉAL, QUÉBEC, CANADA

Studies in Pure Mathematics
To the Memory of Paul Turán

Oscillatory properties of the remainder term of the prime number formula

by

J. PINTZ (Budapest)

1. The first oscillatory result for the remainder term

$$\Delta(x) \overset{\text{def}}{=} \Psi(x) - x \overset{\text{def}}{=} \sum_{n \leq x} \Lambda(n) - x \overset{\text{def}}{=} \sum_{p^m \leq x} \log p - x \tag{1.1}$$

of the prime number formula was proved in the last century by PHRAGMÉN [3]. He showed that if Θ denotes the least upper bound of the real parts of the ζ-zeros, then

$$\Delta(x) = \Omega(x^{\Theta-\varepsilon})^{1} \tag{1.2}$$

for any $\varepsilon > 0$. At the same time the proof could not substitute (1.2) with any explicit inequality.

LITTLEWOOD [2] wrote from this problem in 1937 the following lines.[2]

"Those familiar with the theory of the Riemann zeta-function in connection with the distribution of primes may remember that the interference difficulty arises with the function

$$f(x) = \sum_{\rho} \frac{x^\rho}{\rho} = \sum \frac{x^{\beta+i\gamma}}{\beta+i\gamma}$$

(where the ρ's are complex zeros of $\zeta(s)$).

There exist proofs that if Θ is the upper bound of the β's (so that $\Theta = \frac{1}{2}$ if Riemann hypothesis is true) then $f(x)$ is of order at least $x^{\Theta-\varepsilon}$ in x. But these proofs are curiously indirect: if $\left(\Theta > \frac{1}{2} \text{ and}\right)$ we are given a particular $\rho = \rho_0$ for which $\beta = \beta_0 > \frac{1}{2}$ they

[1] The notation $f(x) = \Omega(g(x))$ means $\limsup_{x\to\infty} \frac{|f(x)|}{g(x)} > 0$.

[2] His $f(x)$ is essentially $-\Delta(x)$.

provide no explicit X depending only upon β_0, γ_0 and ε such that $|f(x)|>X^{\beta_0-\varepsilon}$ for some x in $(0, X)$. There are no known ways of showing (for any explicit X) that the single term $\frac{x^{\beta_0+i\gamma_0}}{\beta_0+i\gamma_0}$ of f is not interfered with by other therms of the series over the range $(0, X)$."

So LITTLEWOOD asked for an explicit Ω-type estimation of $\Delta(x)$ depending on a single zero only. This important theoretical problem was solved by TURÁN [7] in 1950 who proved the following

Theorem A (TURÁN). *If $\rho_0=\beta_0+i\gamma_0$ is a zero of $\zeta(s)$ with $\beta_0 \geqq \frac{1}{2}$, further*

(1.3) $$T \geqq \max(c_1, \exp(|\rho_0|^{60}))$$

then

(1.4) $$\max_{1\leqq x\leqq T} |\Delta(x)| > \frac{T^{\beta_0}}{|\rho_0|^{10\log T/\log_2 T}} \exp\left(-c_2 \frac{\log T \log_3 T}{\log_2 T}\right)$$

where c_1, c_2 are explicitly calculable absolute constants.

2. The second problem is the connection between zero-free regions of $\zeta(s)$ and the remainder term of the prime number formula. The usual way is that assuming a zero-free domain we prove an upper estimate for the remainder term. Such a general theorem is due to INGHAM [1] (Theorem 22):

Theorem (INGHAM). *Suppose that $\zeta(s)$ has no zeros in the domain*

(2.1) $$\sigma > 1-\eta(|t|)$$

where $\eta(t)$ is, for $t \geqq 0$ a decreasing function having a continuous derivative $\eta'(t)$ and satisfying the following conditions

(2.2) $$0<\eta(t)\leqq\frac{1}{2}$$

(2.3) $$\eta'(t)\to 0 \quad as\ t\to\infty$$

(2.4) $$\frac{1}{\eta(t)} = O(\log t) \quad as\ t\to\infty.$$

Let ε be a fixed number satisfying $0<\varepsilon<1$ and let

(2.5) $$\omega(x) \stackrel{\text{def}}{=} \min_{t\geqq 1} (\eta(t)\log x+\log t).$$

[3] $\log_\nu(x)$ denotes the ν-times iterated logarithm function.

Then we have

$$\Delta(x) = O\left(\frac{x}{e^{1/2(1-\varepsilon)\omega(x)}}\right). \tag{2.6}$$

If we choose here

$$\eta(t) = \frac{c_3}{\log^\beta (t+2)} \tag{2.7}$$

we get the following

Corollary. *If* $\zeta(s) \neq 0$ *in the domain*

$$\sigma > 1 - \frac{c_3}{\log^\beta (t+2)} \tag{2.8}$$

then

$$\Delta(x) = O(x \exp(-c_4 (\log x)^{\frac{1}{1+\beta}})). \tag{2.9}$$

Again a very important theoretical problem is (restricting ourselves for the special case (2.7)) whether it is possible (perhaps with finer analytic methods) to deduce from the zero-free region (2.8) a better estimate for the remainder term than given by (2.9). An equivalent formulation of the problem is whether assuming the upper estimate (2.9) for the remainder term we get a domain of type (2.8) to be zero-free. With other words: assuming there are perhaps infinitely many zeros in the domain (2.8) — is it possible to prove (2.9) with Ω instead of O. These problems (in the special case (2.7)) were affirmatively answered in 1950 by the following theorem of P. Turán [8].

Theorem B (Turán). *If for a* β *with* $0 < \beta < 1$ *we have*

$$\Delta(x) = O(x \exp(-c_5 (\log x)^{\frac{1}{1+\beta}})) \tag{2.10}$$

then $\zeta(s) \neq 0$ *in the domain*

$$\sigma > 1 - \frac{c_6}{\log^\beta (|t|+2)}, \quad |t| \geqq c_7(\beta). \tag{2.11}$$

An equivalent formulation of this is:

Theorem B′ (Turán). *If for a* β *with* $0 < \beta < 1$ *there are infinitely many* ζ*-zeros in the domain*

$$\sigma > 1 - \frac{c_8}{\log^\beta (|t|+2)} \tag{2.12}$$

then

$$\Delta(x) = \Omega(x \exp(-c_9 (\log x)^{\frac{1}{1+\beta}})). \tag{2.13}$$

Both Theorems A and B of TURÁN were proved by his powersum method, the main tool being the so-called second main theorem of the powersum theory (this will be formulated explicitly later). The treatment of both theorems were separate but similar. As he mentioned in his book [9] (after Satz XXX) from Theorem A it is possible to deduce a theorem of type Theorem B′, namely under the suppositions of Theorem B′ one gets

$$\Delta(x)=\Omega\left(x \exp\left(-c_{10}\frac{\log x}{(\log_3 x)^{\beta}}\right)\right) \tag{2.14}$$

which is however much weaker than (2.13). This is the reason why a separate treatment of Theorem B is needed.

3. As an improvement of Theorem A we shall prove

Theorem 1. *If $\rho_1=\beta_1+i\gamma_1$ is a ζ-zero with $\beta_1 \geqq \frac{1}{2}$, $\gamma_1>0$, then for*

$$T \geqq \max(\gamma_1^{400}, c_{11}) \tag{3.1}$$

there exists an $x \in [T^{1/4}, T]$ for which

$$|\Delta(x)| > \frac{c_{12}x^{\beta_1}}{\gamma_1^{50}}. \tag{3.2}$$

A comparison with Theorem A shows that assuming a much weaker condition we get a much better lower bound for $|\Delta(x)|$, and even the proof is more simple. A further advantage of Theorem 1 is that applying this instead of Theorem A for the conversion of INGHAM's theorem we get Theorem B to be valid even for very general domains and the deduction from Theorem 1 will be very simple. So Theorem 1 makes possible the unique and simple treatment of the two phenomenons dealt in Theorems A and B of TURÁN.

Theorem 2. *Suppose $\zeta(s)$ has an infinity of zeros in*

$$\sigma \geqq 1-\eta(t) \tag{3.3}$$

where $\eta(t)$ is, for $t \geqq 0$ a continuous decreasing function and let

$$\omega(x) \overset{\text{def}}{=} \min_{t\geqq 0}(\eta(t)\log x+\log t). \tag{3.4}$$

Then we have

$$\Delta(x)=\Omega\left(\frac{x}{e^{54\omega(x)}}\right) \tag{3.5}$$

where the constant implied by the Ω-symbol is explicitly calculable (in fact it is equal to the constant c_{12} appearing in Theorem 1).

Theorem 2 shows that the conversion of INGHAM's theorem is true in an explicit form for more general domains than dealt in INGHAM's theorem. However, we may note that supposing for $\eta(t)$ only that it is a continuous decreasing function, (2.6) is true even with the sharper estimate

$$\Delta(x)=O\left(\frac{x}{e^{(1-\varepsilon)\omega(x)}}\right) \tag{3.6}$$

and thus the suppositions (2.2)–(2.4) and that $\eta(t)$ has a continuous derivative can be omitted in the formulation of INGHAM's theorem (see [5], Theorem 1).

The proof of Theorem 1 is based on TURÁN's method, more precisely on the second main theorem of the powersum theory which we state here as

Theorem C (T. Sós–TURÁN). *For arbitrary complex numbers z_j and $m>0$ the inequality*

$$\max_{m<\nu\leqq m+n}\frac{\left|\sum_{j=1}^{n} z_j^{\nu}\right|}{|z_1|^{\nu}}\geqq\left[\frac{1}{8e\left(\frac{m}{n}+1\right)}\right]^n \tag{3.8}$$

holds.

The proof is contained in [6]. If we choose here $m=a\frac{n}{d}$; $z_j=e^{\alpha_j\frac{u}{m}}=e^{\alpha_j\frac{d}{n}}$ we get

$$\max_{\frac{n}{d}a<\nu\leqq(a+d)\frac{n}{d}}\frac{\left|\sum_{j=1}^{n} e^{\alpha_j\frac{d}{n}\nu}\right|}{|z_1|^{\nu}}\geqq\left[\frac{1}{8e\left(\frac{a}{d}+1\right)}\right]^n. \tag{3.9}$$

From this we get immediately the continuous form of the second main theorem, which we formulate as

Theorem C′ (T. Sós–TURÁN). *For arbitrary complex numbers α_j, and for a, $d>0$ the inequality*

$$\max_{a<t\leqq a+d}\frac{\left|\sum_{j=1}^{n} e^{\alpha_j t}\right|}{|e^{\alpha_1 t}|}\geqq\left[\frac{1}{8e\left(\frac{a}{d}+1\right)}\right]^n \tag{3.10}$$

holds.

Finally we note that with far more complicated arguments but based also on TURÁN's method one can show the following sharper results:

Theorem I. *If $\rho_0=\beta_0+i\gamma_0$ is a non-trivial zero of $\zeta(s)$, $\varepsilon>0$ and $T>c(\rho_0,\varepsilon)$ (effective lower bound depending on ρ_0 and ε), then there exist*

$$x_1, x_2 \in [T, T^{50\log\gamma_0}] \tag{3.11}$$

such that the inequalities

$$\Delta(x_1)>(1-\varepsilon)\frac{x_1^{\beta_0}}{|\rho_0|} \tag{3.12}$$

and

$$\Delta(x_2)<-(1-\varepsilon)\frac{x_2^{\beta_0}}{|\rho_0|} \tag{3.13}$$

hold.

Theorem II. *If $\zeta(s)$ has infinitely many zeros in the domain*

$$\sigma>1-g(\log t) \tag{3.14}$$

where $g(u)$ is a continuous decreasing function and $g'(u)\nearrow 0$, $0<\varepsilon<1$, then

$$\Delta(x)=\Omega_{\pm}\left(\frac{x}{e^{(1+\varepsilon)\omega(x)}}\right) \tag{3.15}$$

with the $\omega(x)$ function defined by (3.4).

Theorem I is essentially optimal concerning the lower estimate, only the localisation in (3.11) is weaker than in Theorem 1. In Theorem II one has to require stronger conditions for the domain, i.e. for the $\eta(t)=g(\log t)$ function, but the Ω-type estimate is again essentially optimal in view of (3.6). A further advantage is that it gives $\Omega_{\pm}$ results, i.e. Theorems I and II assure "big positive" and "big negative" values too for the remainder term. The more elaborated proofs of Theorems I and II will appear in [4] and [5] resp.

4. For the indirect proof of Theorem 1 let μ be a real number, to be chosen later for which

$$\frac{\log T}{2}\leqq\mu\leqq\frac{2\log T}{3} \tag{4.1}$$

and let

$$k\overset{\text{def}}{=}\frac{\mu}{20}. \tag{4.2}$$

We shall start with the formula

$$\int_1^\infty \Delta(x)\frac{d}{dx}(x^{-s})\,dx=\frac{\zeta'}{\zeta}(s)+\frac{s}{s-1}\overset{\text{def}}{=}H(s), \tag{4.3}$$

which can be proved easily by partial integration. Using the well-known formula

$$\frac{1}{2\pi i}\int_{(2)} e^{As^2+Bs}\,ds = \frac{1}{2\sqrt{\pi A}}\exp\left(-\frac{B^2}{4A}\right), \tag{4.4}$$

which is valid for real $A>0$ and arbitrary complex **B** we get from (4.3)

$$\begin{aligned} U &\overset{\text{def}}{=} \frac{1}{2\pi i}\int_{(2)} H(s+i\gamma_1)e^{ks^2+\mu s}\,ds = \frac{1}{2\pi i}\int_{(2)}\int_1^\infty \Delta(x)\frac{d}{dx}(x^{-s-i\gamma_1}e^{ks^2+\mu s})\,dx\,ds = \\ &= \int_1^\infty \Delta(x)\frac{d}{dx}\left\{x^{-i\gamma_1}\frac{1}{2\pi i}\int_{(2)} e^{ks^2+(\mu-\log x)s}\,ds\right\}dx = \\ &= \int_1^\infty \Delta(x)\frac{d}{dx}\left\{x^{-i\gamma_i}\frac{1}{2\sqrt{\pi k}}\exp\left(-\frac{(\mu-\log x)^2}{4k}\right)\right\}dx = \\ &= \frac{1}{2\sqrt{\pi k}}\int_1^\infty \frac{\Delta(x)}{x}x^{-i\gamma_1}\exp\left(-\frac{(\mu-\log x)^2}{4k}\right)\left\{-i\gamma_1+\frac{\mu-\log x}{2k}\right\}dx. \end{aligned} \tag{4.5}$$

We split the integral U in (4.5) into three parts:

$$U_1 = \int_1^{e^{\mu/2}}, \quad U_2 = \int_{e^{\mu/2}}^{e^{3\mu/2}}, \quad U_3 = \int_{e^{3\mu/2}}^{\infty} \tag{4.6}$$

Using $|\Delta(x)|<x$ (if $x>x_0$) for $T>T_0$ we get

$$\begin{aligned} |U_3| &< \gamma_1 \int_{e^{\mu+10k}}^\infty \exp\left(-\frac{(\mu-\log x)^2}{4k}\right)\left(\frac{\log x-\mu}{2k}-1\right)dx = \\ &= \gamma_1\int_{10k}^\infty \exp\left(-\frac{r^2}{4k}\right)\left(\frac{r}{2k}-1\right)e^{r+\mu}\,dr = \gamma_1 e^{\mu+10k-\frac{100k^2}{4k}} = \gamma_1 e^{\frac{\mu}{4}} \end{aligned} \tag{4.7}$$

and analogously for $T>T_0$ we get

$$|U_1|<\gamma_1 e^{\frac{\mu}{4}}. \tag{4.8}$$

Now assuming Theorem 1 to be false we have

$$|U_2| < \frac{(\gamma_1+5)c_{12}}{2\sqrt{\pi k}\gamma_1^{50}} \int\limits_{e^{\mu-10k}}^{e^{\mu+10k}} x^{\beta_1} \exp\left(-\frac{(\mu-\log x)^2}{4k}\right)\frac{dx}{x} <$$

(4.9) $$< \frac{c_{12}}{\sqrt{\pi k}\,\gamma_1^{49}} \int\limits_{-10k}^{10k} \exp\left((\mu+r)\beta_1 - \frac{r^2}{4k}\right) dr <$$

$$< \frac{e^{\mu\beta_1+k\beta_1^2}c_{12}}{\sqrt{\pi k}\,\gamma_1^{49}} \int\limits_{-\infty}^{\infty} \exp\left\{-\left(\frac{r}{2\sqrt{k}} - \beta_1\sqrt{k}\right)^2\right\} dr = \frac{2c_{12}}{\gamma_1^{49}} e^{\mu\beta_1+k\beta_1^2}$$

Taking in account (3.1), (4.6)–(4.9) imply

(4.10) $$|U| < \frac{3c_{12}}{\gamma_1^{49}} e^{k\beta_1^2+\mu\beta_1}.$$

5. Shifting the line of integration in (4.5) to $\sigma = -\frac{1}{2}$ we get

(5.1) $$U = \sum_{\rho} e^{k(\rho-i\gamma_1)^2+\mu(\rho-i\gamma_1)} + \frac{1}{2\pi i} \int\limits_{(-\frac{1}{2})} H(s+i\gamma_1)e^{ks^2+\mu s}\, ds.$$

Estimating here the integral I trivially we have

(5.2) $$|I| = O(\log \gamma_1 e^{\frac{k}{4}-\frac{\mu}{2}}) = O(1)$$

since $|H(s+i\gamma_1)| = O(\log(|t+\gamma_1|+2))$.

Further the contribution of zeros with $|\gamma-\gamma_1| \geqq 4$ to the infinite powersum is

(5.3) $$O\left(\sum_{n=4}^{\infty} \log(\gamma_1+n)e^{k(1-n^2)+\mu}\right) = O(\log \gamma_1 e^{\mu-15k}).$$

Applying Jensen's inequality for the circle $|s-(3+i\gamma_1)| \leqq 10$ we get for the number n of zeros with $|\gamma-\gamma_1| < 4$

(5.4) $$1 \leqq n \leqq \frac{7.5\log \gamma_1 + c_{13}}{\log 2} < 10.83 \log \gamma_1 + c_{14}.$$

Thus we get from Theorem C′ the existence of a μ, satisfying (4.1) for which

$$\left|\sum_{|\gamma-\gamma_1|<4} \{e^{\frac{1}{20}(\rho-i\gamma_1)^2+(\rho-i\gamma_1)}\}^{\mu}\right| \geqq \frac{e^{k\beta_1^2+\mu\beta_1}}{(32e)^{10.83\log\gamma_1+c_{14}}} > c_{15}\frac{e^{k\beta_1^2+\mu\beta_1}}{\gamma_1^{48.4}}. \tag{5.5}$$

Owing to (3.1) the formulae (5.2), (5.3), (5.5) imply

$$|U| > c_{15}\frac{e^{k\beta_1^2+\mu\beta_1}}{\gamma_1^{49}} \tag{5.6}$$

which contradicts to (4.10) if we choose $c_{12} = \frac{c_{15}}{3}$.

6. We note that Theorem 2 trivially follows from Theorem 1 (applied with the zero ρ_0 of minimal imaginary part, $\rho_0 = \frac{1}{2} + i\gamma_0 \approx \frac{1}{2} + 14.13i$) if $\lim_{t\to\infty} \eta(t) \geqq 0.01$ since in this case $\omega(x) \geqq 0.01 \log x$ and thus $xe^{-54\omega(x)} \leqq x^{0.46}$.

If $\lim_{t\to\infty} \eta(t) < 0.01$, let $\rho_n = \beta_n + i\gamma_n$ $(0<\gamma_1<\gamma_2<\dots)$ be an infinite sequence of zeros with

$$\beta_n > 1-\eta(\gamma_n) \tag{6.1}$$

and let T_n be the unique real number defined by

$$\eta(\gamma_n)\log\sqrt[4]{T_n} = \log\gamma_n. \tag{6.2}$$

Then for $n > n_0(\eta)$ (3.1) is satisfied for ρ_n and T_n and therefore we have an $x_n \in [\sqrt[4]{T_n}, T_n]$ for which by Theorem 1

$$\begin{aligned}\frac{|\Delta(x_n)|}{x_n} &> \frac{c_{12}}{x_n^{1-\beta_n}\cdot\gamma_n^{50}} \geqq \frac{c_{12}}{e^{\eta(\gamma_n)\log x_n + 50\log\gamma_n}} \geqq \\ &\geqq \frac{c_{12}}{e^{4\eta(\gamma_n)\log\sqrt[4]{T_n}+50\log T_n}} \geqq \frac{c_{12}}{e^{\omega(\sqrt[4]{T_n})\cdot 54}} \geqq \frac{c_{12}}{e^{\omega(x_n)\cdot 54}},\end{aligned} \tag{6.3}$$

since $\omega(x)$ is trivially monotonically increasing, further by (6.2)

$$\begin{aligned}\omega(\sqrt[4]{T_n}) &\geq \min_{t\geqq 0}\{\max(\eta(t)\log\sqrt[4]{T_n}, \log t)\} \geqq \\ &\geqq \eta(\gamma_n)\log\sqrt[4]{T_n} = \log\gamma_n.\end{aligned} \tag{6.4}$$

(6.3) obviously proves Theorem 2.

References

[1] A. E. INGHAM, *The distribution of prime numbers*, University Press, Cambridge, 1932.
[2] J. E. LITTLEWOOD, Mathematical notes (12). An inequality for a sum of cosines, *Journ. Lond. Math. Soc.*, **12** (1937), 217–222.
[3] E. PHRAGMÉN, Sur le logarithme intégral et la fonction $\zeta(x)$ de Riemann, *Öfversigt of Kongl. Vetenskaps Akademiens Förhandlingar*, **48** (1891), 599–616.
[4] J. PINTZ, On the remainder term of the prime number formula I, On a problem of Littlewood, *Acta Arith.*, **36** (1979), 27–51.
[5] J. PINTZ, On the remainder term of the prime number formula II, On a theorem of Ingham, *Acta Arith.*, **37** (1980), 209–220.
[6] VERA T. SÓS and P. TURÁN, On some new theorems in the theory of diophantine approximations, *Acta Math. Acad. Sci. Hung.*, **6** (1955), 241–255.
[7] P. TURÁN, On the remainder-term of the prime-number formula, I., *Acta Math. Acad. Sci. Hung.*, **1** (1950), 48–63.
[8] P. TURÁN, On the remainder term of the prime-number formula II, *Acta Math. Acad. Sci. Hung.*, **1** (1950), 155–166.
[9] P. TURÁN, *Eine neue Methode in der Analysis und deren Anwendungen*, Akadémiai Kiadó, Budapest, 1953.

MATHEMATICAL INSTITUTE OF THE
HUNGARIAN ACADEMY OF SCIENCES
H-1053, BUDAPEST, REÁLTANODA U. 13–15.
HUNGARY

Studies in Pure Mathematics
To the Memory of Paul Turán

On some universal bounds for Fuchsian groups

by

CH. POMMERENKE (Berlin–Minneapolis) and N. PURZITSKY* (Toronto–Berlin)

1. Introduction

Let Γ be a group of Möbius transformations of the unit disk **D** or of the upper halfplane onto itself. The results of C. L. Siegel [15] and of A. Marden [10] show that, leaving aside the elementary groups, there is a sharp dividing line between discrete (Fuchsian) and non-discrete groups. The aim of this paper is to give a sharp quantitative form of Marden's theorem (see Section 4).

The paper is based on research by A. F. Beardon, J. Lehner and the authors; compare also [1], [8]. The approach will be algebraic-computational, and following Siegel [15] and the second author [12], [13], [14] it starts from the matrix representation of the elements in Γ. The results are essentially results about the subgroup generated by two given elements β and γ in Γ. We shall distinguish the cases that β is hyperbolic or elliptic; the parabolic case will be treated as a limit case of the hyperbolic.

The elementary groups (that is, groups with at most two limit points) play an exceptional role. The elementary Fuchsian groups [2, Chap. VI] are finite cyclic, infinite cyclic, or dihedral. If we consider the upper halfplane with 0, ∞ as limit points, then the dihedral group is generated by

$$\beta(z)=\rho^2 z,\quad \gamma(z)=-b^2/z\quad (1<\rho<\infty, 0<b<\infty).$$

The fixed points of the elliptic elements lie on the axis of the hyperbolic generator β.

We write $[\beta,\gamma]=\beta\circ\gamma\circ\beta^{-1}\circ\gamma^{-1}$ for the commutator while $\langle\beta,\gamma\rangle$ denotes the group generated by β and γ. The exceptional case in several results below will be that $\langle\beta,\gamma\rangle$ is elementary, thus cyclic or dihedral.

We want to thank M. Mittelhaus and F. Urbanski for pointing out several errors.

* The research of the second author was supported by the Alexander von Humboldt-Foundation.

2. The hyperbolic case

Let Γ be a Fuchsian group in the upper halfplane. We use the standard notation

$$(2.1)\qquad \gamma(z)=\frac{az+b}{cz+d},\quad a, b, c, d\in\mathbf{R},\ ad-bc=1.$$

The sign of the trace $\operatorname{tr}\gamma=a+d$ depends on the choice of sign in the matrix representation. If γ is hyperbolic then the *axis* $A(\gamma)$ is the non-euclidean line between the fixed points of γ.

The hyperbolic element $\beta\in\Gamma$ is called *simple* if, for all $\gamma\in\Gamma$,

$$(2.2)\qquad \gamma(A(\beta))\cap A(\beta)=\emptyset \quad\text{or}\quad A(\beta).$$

If Γ has no elliptic elements this means that the closed geodesic $A(\beta)/\Gamma$ on the corresponding Riemann surface does not cross itself properly. If $\beta(z)=\rho^2 z$ $(\rho>1)$ then [13, Th. 1]

$$(2.3)\qquad \beta\text{ simple}\Leftrightarrow ad\notin(0, 1)\quad\text{for all}\quad \gamma\in\Gamma;$$

the present definition differs slightly from that introduced in [13] (where β was called canonical) because the case $ad=1$ is now permitted.

We consider first the case that γ is simple.

Theorem 1. *Let $\beta(z)=\rho^2 z$ $(\rho>1)$ be a simple hyperbolic element of the Fuchsian group Γ in $\{\operatorname{Im} z>0\}$. Set $\kappa=(\rho-\rho^{-1})^2$. If $\gamma\in\Gamma$ and $ad\neq 0, 1$ then*

$$(2.4)\qquad ad\leqq-\frac{1}{\kappa}\quad\text{or}\quad ad\geqq 1+\frac{1}{\kappa},$$

and if Γ contains no elliptic elements then

$$(2.5)\qquad ad\leqq-\frac{4\rho}{(\rho-1)^2}\quad\text{or}\quad ad\geqq 1+\frac{4}{\kappa}.$$

All four bounds are sharp for each $1<\rho<\infty$.

These inequalities generalize results of C. L. SIEGEL [15]. They are stronger than JØRGENSEN's inequality [5, Lemma 1], [6] in the present case of a hyperbolic element in a Fuchsian group. The proof is essentially that of SIEGEL, except for the proof of the second inequality of (2.5) which is essentially contained in [12, Th. 8].

Proof. (a) We define $\gamma=\gamma_1$ and, recursively,

$$\gamma_{n+1}=[\gamma_n,\beta]\equiv\gamma_n\circ\beta\circ\gamma_n^{-1}\circ\beta^{-1}\in\Gamma\quad(n=1,2,\ldots). \tag{2.6}$$

Writing $\gamma_n(z)=(a_nz+b_n)/(c_nz+d_n)$ we see that

$$\begin{aligned}a_{n+1}&=a_nd_n-b_nc_n\rho^{-2},\quad b_{n+1}=-a_nb_n(\rho^2-1),\\ c_{n+1}&=c_nd_n(1-\rho^{-2}),\quad d_{n+1}=a_nd_n-b_nc_n\rho^2.\end{aligned} \tag{2.7}$$

Suppose now that $a_{n+1}=0$. Then $\gamma_{n+1}(\infty)=0$. Since Γ is discrete and since $0,\infty$ are the fixed points of β, it follows that $\gamma_{n+1}(0)=\infty$ hence that $d_{n+1}=0$. Therefore we conclude from (2.7) that $a_nd_n=0$. The same conclusion holds if $d_{n+1}=0$. Since $ad\neq 0$ we thus obtain by induction that $a_nd_n\neq 0$ for all n.

We set $y_n=a_nd_n$. Since $b_nc_n=y_n-1$ it follows from (2.7) that

$$y_{n+1}=(a_nd_n-b_nc_n\rho^{-2})(a_nd_n-b_nc_n\rho^2)=1-\kappa y_n(y_n-1). \tag{2.8}$$

Since $y_n\neq 0$ and $y_1=ad\neq 1$ we see by induction that $y_n\neq 1$.

Suppose that $-1/\kappa<y_1<1$. Since β is simple it follows from (2.3) that $y_1\leqq 0$, hence $-1/\kappa<y_1<0$. Therefore we easily deduce from (2.8) that $y_1<y_2<1$. Repeating this argument we see that $-1/\kappa<y_1<y_n<0$. Hence (2.8) shows that

$$\left|\frac{y_{n+1}-1}{y_n-1}\right|=\kappa|y_n|<\kappa|y_1|<1\quad(n=1,2,\ldots)$$

and therefore that $y_n\to 1$, which contradicts $y_n<0$. Hence we have shown that if $ad<1$ then $ad\leqq -1/\kappa$.

Suppose finally that $1<y_1<1+1/\kappa$. Then (2.8) implies that $-1/\kappa<y_2<0$. Since $y_2=a_2d_2$ this is impossible by our last result.

(b) We assume now that Γ has no elliptic elements. It follows from (2.8) that

$$\operatorname{tr}\gamma_{n+1}=2-\kappa(y_n-1). \tag{2.9}$$

If $y_1=ad>1$ then $\operatorname{tr}\gamma_2<2$ and thus $\operatorname{tr}\gamma_2\leqq -2$ because γ_2 is not elliptic. It follows from (2.9) that $y_1\geqq 1+4/\kappa$.

Let now $ad\leqq 1$. Then $ad<0$ by the previous remarks, say $a>0$, $d<0$. Since

$$t_n=\operatorname{tr}(\beta^n\circ\gamma)=a\rho^n+d\rho^{-n}\to\pm\infty\quad\text{as}\quad n\to\pm\infty$$

there exists $n\in\mathbf{Z}$ such that $t_n<0$, $t_{n+1}\geqq 0$. Since $\beta^n\circ\gamma$ and $\beta^{n+1}\circ\gamma$ are not elliptic we conclude that

$$a\rho^n+d\rho^{-n}=t_n\leqq -2,\quad a\rho^{n+1}+d\rho^{-n-1}=t_{n+1}\geqq 2.$$

It follows that

$$-a\rho^n(\rho^2-1)\cdot d\rho^{-n-2}(\rho^2-1)=(\rho t_{n+1}-t_n)(\rho^{-1}t_{n+1}-t_n)\geqq 4\rho^{-1}(\rho+1)^2$$

and therefore that $ad\leqq -4\rho(\rho-1)^{-2}$.

(c) We show now that the bounds are best possible for given $\rho\in(1,+\infty)$. We first choose γ such that $a+d>2$ and $ad=1+1/\kappa$. Then $\operatorname{tr}[\gamma,\beta]=\operatorname{tr}\gamma_2=1$ by (2.9). Hence [14, Th. 2] the group Γ generated by γ and β is a Fuchsian group with signature (0; 2, 2, 2, 3; 0). The element β is simple in this group by the following argument: From [14, p. 90] we see that γ and β are related to a suitably labelled standard set of generators of Γ, E_1, E_2, E_3 with $E_1^2=E_2^2=E_3^2=(E_1\circ E_2\circ E_3)^3=id$, by $\beta=E_3\circ E_2$ and $\gamma=E_1\circ E_2$ with $[\gamma,\beta]=(E_1\circ E_2\circ E_3)^2$. From $(E_1\circ E_2\circ E_3)^3=id$ we see that the triangle T on p. 91 of [14] is a hyperbolically convex fundamental domain for Γ. Now cutting along the geodesic joining the fixed points of E_2 and E_3, dividing T into a triangle Δ and a quadrilateral, and pasting the triangle onto the quadrilateral by taking $E_3(\Delta)$, we have a hyperbolically convex fundamental domain for Γ for which β identifies a pair of sides. Hence β is simple [13]. Thus the second bound in (2.4) is sharp, and the argument of part (a) shows that therefore the first bound is also sharp.

We now choose γ such that $a+d>2$, $ad=1+4/\kappa$. Then $\operatorname{tr}[\gamma,\beta]=-2$ by (2.9). Hence [12, Th. 8] the group Γ generated by β and γ is a free Fuchsian group, and β is simple because in the proof of Theorem 8 of [12] a convex fundamental domain is constructed in which β identifies a pair of sides. Thus the second bound in (2.5) is sharp.

Finally we choose γ such that $a+d=2$ and $\operatorname{tr}(\beta^{-1}\circ\gamma)=a/\rho+d\rho=-2$. By [12, Th. 1], $\langle\beta,\gamma\rangle$ is a free discrete group. By direct calculations we have $ad=\dfrac{-4\rho}{(\rho-1)^2}$.

We consider now the case that β is non-simple.

Theorem 2. *Let Γ be a Fuchsian group and let β be a non-simple hyperbolic element in Γ. Then*

$$|\operatorname{tr}\beta|\geqq\sqrt{6}=2.449\ldots \tag{2.10}$$

except in the following four cases of triangle groups:

$$\Gamma=T(2,3,7),\quad |\operatorname{tr}\beta|=2\cos\frac{2\pi}{7}+1=2.246\ldots$$

$$\Gamma=T(2,4,5),\quad |\operatorname{tr}\beta|=\sqrt{8}\cos\frac{\pi}{5}=2.288\ldots$$

$$\Gamma=T(3,3,4)\text{ or }T(2,4,8),\quad |\operatorname{tr}\beta|=\sqrt{2}+1=2.414\ldots.$$

If Γ does not have a compact fundamental domain or if Γ has no elliptic elements, then $|\operatorname{tr}\beta|\geqq\sqrt{8}$.

This theorem shows that

$$2<|\mathrm{tr}\ \beta|<2\cos\frac{2\pi}{7}+1\Rightarrow\beta \text{ is simple hyperbolic.} \tag{2.11}$$

The best previous bound was $\sqrt{5}$, due to SIEGEL. The situation becomes more complicated for elements with traces $\in(\sqrt{6}, \sqrt{8})$.

Proof. (a) By (2.3) there exists $\gamma\in\Gamma$ such that $0<y_1=ad<1$, using the notation of the proof of Theorem 1. It follows from (2.8) that

$$0<y_2-1=\kappa y_1(1-y_1)\leqq\frac{\kappa}{4}. \tag{2.12}$$

Hence we obtain from (2.9) that $\mathrm{tr}\ \gamma_3=2-\kappa(y_2-1)<2$. If we exclude the case that $1<\mathrm{tr}\ \gamma_3<2$, it follows that $y_2-1\geqq 1/\kappa$ and hence from (2.12) that $1/\kappa\leqq\kappa/4$, $\kappa\geqq 2$. This implies $|\mathrm{tr}\ \beta|\geqq\sqrt{6}$ because

$$\kappa=(\rho+\rho^{-1})^2-4=(\mathrm{tr}\ \beta)^2-4. \tag{2.13}$$

(b) We assume now that $1<\mathrm{tr}\ \gamma_3<2$. Let Γ_0 be the subgroup of Γ generated by β and γ_2. Since $\gamma_3=[\gamma_2, \beta]$ there are only three possible cases [14, Th. 4]:

$$\Gamma_0=T(2,3,q),\quad \mathrm{tr}\ \gamma_3=-2\cos\frac{6\pi}{q}\ (q \text{ prime to } 6),$$

$$\Gamma_0=T(2,4,q),\quad \mathrm{tr}\ \gamma_3=-2\cos\frac{4\pi}{q}\ (q \text{ odd}),$$

$$\Gamma_0=T(3,3,q),\quad \mathrm{tr}\ \gamma_3=-2\cos\frac{3\pi}{q}\ (q \text{ prime to } 3).$$

Only the choices $q=7, 5, 4$ respectively satisfy $\mathrm{tr}\ \gamma_3>1$.

We shall only consider the first case. By [14, Th. 4] there exists ψ with

$$t\equiv\mathrm{tr}\ \beta=\mathrm{tr}\ \psi=\mathrm{tr}(\beta\circ\psi),\quad \mathrm{tr}\ [\beta,\psi]=2\cos\frac{\pi}{7}.$$

This leads to the equation $t^2(3-t)=2+2\cos(\pi/7)$ which has $t=2\cos(2\pi/7)+1$ as its only solution with $|t|>2$. Since $T(2, 3, 7)$ is a maximal Fuchsian group by a result of L. GREENBERG [3], it follows from $\Gamma_0\subset\Gamma$ that $\Gamma_0=\Gamma$.

(c) Finally we assume that Γ has no compact fundamental domain or no elliptic elements. In the first case, HOARE and MACBEATH [4] have shown that Γ is the free product of cyclic groups. Since every elliptic element in Γ is conjugate to an elliptic element in one of the free factors [9, p. 187], it is easy to see that the commutator subgroup $[\Gamma, \Gamma]$ has no elliptic elements; this is trivially true if Γ itself has no elliptic elements.

We conclude now the argument as in part (a). Since γ_3 is non-elliptic we see that $\operatorname{tr} \gamma_3 = 2 - \kappa(y_2 - 1) \leqq -2$. Hence $y_2 - 1 \geqq 4/\kappa$, and (2.12) shows that $\kappa \geqq 4$ and thus $|\operatorname{tr} \beta| \geqq \sqrt{8}$.

Corollary 1. *Let Γ be a Fuchsian group in $\{\operatorname{Im} z > 0\}$. Let $\beta(z) = \rho^2 z$ and $\gamma(z)$ be elements in Γ such that the subgroup $\langle \beta, \gamma \rangle$ is non-elementary. If*

$$\kappa = (\rho - \rho^{-1})^2 < \left(2 \cos \frac{2\pi}{7} + 1\right)^2 - 4 = 1.048\ldots \tag{2.14}$$

then (2.4) holds. If Γ has no elliptic elements and if $\kappa < 4$ then (2.5) holds.

Proof. It follows from the description of elementary groups made at the end of the introduction that $ad \neq 0, 1$. Furthermore we see from (2.14), (2.13) and (2.11) that β is simple. Hence the assertions follow from Theorem 1.

3. The elliptic case

Let Γ be a Fuchsian group in $\mathbf{D}$. We use as standard notation

$$\gamma(z) = \frac{pz + q}{\bar{q}z + \bar{p}}, \quad p, q \in \mathbb{C}, \quad |p|^2 - |q|^2 = 1. \tag{3.1}$$

Theorem 3. *Let $k = 3, 4, \ldots$. Let $\beta(z) = e^{2\pi i/k} z$ and $\gamma(z)$ with $q \neq 0$ be elements in Γ. If Γ is not a triangle group then*

$$|p| \sin \frac{\pi}{k} \geqq 1. \tag{3.2}$$

If Γ is a triangle group then

$$|p| \sin \frac{\pi}{k} \geqq c_k, \tag{3.3}$$

where $c_3 = \cos \frac{\pi}{7}$, $c_4 = \cos \frac{\pi}{5}$, $c_5 = c_6 = \cos \frac{\pi}{4}$ and $c_k = \frac{1}{2}$ for $k \geqq 7$. All bounds are best possible.

This result (without the exact determination of the bounds) was proved by BEARDON [1]. We remark that there is no non-trivial lower bound in the case $k = 2$ as the dihedral group shows.

Proof. (a) Since Γ is discrete there exists $\gamma \in \Gamma$ such that $|q|$ is minimal for $q \neq 0$. We consider the NIELSEN transforms

$$\varphi = \gamma \circ \beta^n, \quad \psi = \gamma \circ \beta^{n+1} \quad (n = 0, \ldots, k-1) \tag{3.4}$$

and choose n such that

$$a \equiv \frac{1}{2} \operatorname{tr} \varphi = \operatorname{Re}\,[e^{\pi i n/k} p] \geqq 0, \quad -b \equiv \frac{1}{2} \operatorname{tr} \psi \leqq 0\,. \tag{3.5}$$

Hence $-b = a \cos(\pi/k) - \operatorname{Im}\,[e^{\pi i n/k} p] \sin(\pi/k)$, and we deduce that

$$|p|^2 = a^2 + (\operatorname{Im}[e^{\frac{\pi i n}{k}} p])^2 = \frac{a^2 + b^2 + 2ab\cos(\pi/k)}{\sin^2(\pi/k)}\,. \tag{3.6}$$

If φ and ψ are not both elliptic then $a \geqq 1, b \geqq 0$ or $a \geqq 0, b \geqq 1$, and (3.2) follows at once from (3.6).

(b) Let now φ be elliptic of order $m \geqq 2$ with fixed point ζ and let ψ be elliptic of order $l \geqq 2$. Then

$$a = \frac{1}{2} \operatorname{tr} \varphi = \cos \frac{\pi \mu}{m} \quad \left(1 \leqq \mu \leqq \frac{m}{2},\ \mu \text{ prime to } m\right) \tag{3.7}$$

by (3.5). Computation shows that

$$\varphi^\nu(z) = \frac{p_\nu z + q_\nu}{\bar{q}_\nu z + \bar{p}_\nu} \quad \text{with} \quad q_\nu = \frac{2i\zeta}{1 - |\zeta|^2} \sin \frac{\pi \nu \mu}{m}\,.$$

We determine ν so that $\mu\nu \equiv 1 \bmod m$. Since $|q_1| = |q|$ by (3.4) and since $|q|$ was chosen minimal, we conclude that

$$\left|\sin \frac{\pi \mu}{m}\right| \leqq \left|\sin \frac{\pi \nu \mu}{m}\right| = \sin \frac{\pi}{m}$$

and hence $\mu = 1$ by (3.7). Dealing the same way with ψ we obtain that

$$a = \cos(\pi/m), \quad b = \cos(\pi/l)\,. \tag{3.8}$$

Let Γ_0 be the subgroup of Γ generated by β and γ. We consider the lines $L = (-\zeta/|\zeta|, \zeta/|\zeta|)$ and $L' = e^{-\pi i/k} L$ through 0. Let B be the non-euclidean line from ζ to the fixed point ζ' of ψ. Since

$$\psi(e^{-2\pi i/k}\zeta) = \varphi \circ \beta(e^{-2\pi i/k}\zeta) = \varphi(\zeta) = \zeta$$

it follows that $e^{-2\pi i/k}\zeta$ and ζ have the same non-euclidean distance from ζ'. Hence $\zeta' \in L'$, and it follows from (3.8) that B and L' from the angle π/l at ζ'. We obtain from

$$\varphi(e^{-2\pi i/k}\zeta') = \psi \circ \beta^{-1}(e^{2\pi i/k}\zeta') = \psi(\zeta') = \zeta'$$

that B on L from the angle π/m at ζ. Hence we see that the non-euclidean triangle with vertices 0, ζ, ζ' has the angles π/k, π/m, π/l and that $\Gamma_0 = T(k, m, l)$. It follows from results of GREENBERG [3] that no triangle group is contained in a Fuchsian group that is not a triangle group. Hence we conclude that Γ itself is a triangle group.

We obtain from (3.6) and (3.8) that

$$|p|^2 \sin^2 \frac{\pi}{k} = \cos^2 \frac{\pi}{m} + \cos^2 \frac{\pi}{l} + 2 \cos \frac{\pi}{m} \cos \frac{\pi}{l} \cos \frac{\pi}{k}, \quad \frac{1}{k} + \frac{1}{m} + \frac{1}{l} < 1.$$

Numerical calculation shows that this expression becomes minimal for $m=2$, and $l=7$, 5, 4, 4 or 3 if $k=3$, 4, 5, 6 or $k>6$ respectively. This gives the estimates (3.3).

4. Quantitative form of Marden's theorem

The previous results will be used to prove

Theorem 4. *Let Γ be a Fuchsian group in* **D**. *Let β, γ be elements of Γ such that the subgroup $\langle \beta, \gamma \rangle$ is not elementary.*

(i) *If β is hyperbolic or parabolic and $|\beta(0)| < 1/\sqrt{5}$ then*

$$|\gamma(0)| \geqq \frac{1 - 5|\beta(0)|^2}{1 + 3|\beta(0)|^2}, \tag{4.1}$$

and equality is possible for every $|\beta(0)| < 1/\sqrt{5}$.

(ii) *If β is elliptic of order $k \geqq 3$ and if*

$$|\beta(0)| < \left[\left(c_k^2 - \sin^2 \frac{\pi}{k}\right) \Big/ \left(c_k^2 + \cos^2 \frac{\pi}{k}\right)\right]^{\frac{1}{2}} \tag{4.2}$$

where c_k are the constants defined in Theorem 3, then

$$|\gamma(0)|^2 \geqq 1 - \frac{(1 - |\beta(0)|^2) \sin^4 (\pi/k)}{\left[c_k \sqrt{\sin^2 \frac{\pi}{k} + |\beta(0)|^2 \cos^2 \frac{\pi}{k}} - |\beta(0)| \sqrt{c_k^2 - \sin^2 \frac{\pi}{k}}\right]^2} \tag{4.3}$$

and equality is possible for every $|\beta(0)|$ satisfying (4.2).

The bound (4.3) is minimal for $k=3$ and condition (4.3) is also most restrictive for $k=3$. If Γ is not a triangle group then we can use (3.2) instead of (3.3), and (ii) holds with c_k replaced by 1. This new inequality is sharp for $\Gamma=T(k, 2, \infty)$.

We now apply this theorem to give a new proof of a result of A. Marden [10, Th. 1]. We state Marden's theorem in its sharp quantitative form; a weaker result is contained in the paper of Lehner and Purzitsky [8].

Corollary 2. *Let Γ be a Fuchsian group in* **D** *and let $\beta, \gamma \in \Gamma$. If either*

$$\text{(4.4)} \qquad \max(|\beta(0)|, |\gamma(0)|) < \frac{\sqrt{4\cos^2(\pi/7)-3}}{2(1+\cos(\pi/7))} = 0.1307\ldots,$$

or if β is hyperbolic or parabolic and

$$\text{(4.5)} \qquad |\beta(0)| \leqq r, \quad |\gamma(0)| < \frac{1-5r^2}{1+3r^2} \quad \left(0 \leqq r < \frac{1}{\sqrt{5}}\right),$$

then the subgroup $\langle \beta, \gamma \rangle$ is elementary.

Proof. Suppose that $\langle \beta, \gamma \rangle$ is not elementary. Then not both β and γ can be elliptic of order 2 because otherwise $\langle \beta, \gamma \rangle$ would be dihedral. Hence we may assume that β is not elliptic of order 2.

First let β be elliptic of order $k \geqq 3$. We write $c=\cos(\pi/7)$ and $\rho=\max(|\beta(0)|, |\gamma(0)|)$. It follows from (4.4) that condition (4.2) of Theorem 4 (ii) is satisfied. Hence we obtain from (4.3) (for the worst case $k=3$) that

$$1-\rho^2 \leqq \frac{9(1-\rho^2)}{4[c\sqrt{3+\rho^2}-\rho\sqrt{4c^2-3}]^2}.$$

Hence $c\sqrt{3+\rho^2}-\rho\sqrt{4c^2-3} \leqq \frac{3}{2}$ and therefore

$$(2(1-c^2)\rho - \sqrt{4c^2-3})^2 \leqq c^2(4c^2-3).$$

This implies $\rho \geqq \sqrt{4c^2-3}/[2(1+c)]$ which contradicts (4.4).

Let now β be non-elliptic. If (4.4) holds then (4.5) holds with $r=1/5$, and (4.5) (for any $r<1/\sqrt{5}$) contradicts (4.1) in Theorem 4 (i).

In the theory of Riemann surfaces, the most important case is that Γ has no elliptic elements. In this case the above estimates can be considerably strengthened.

Theorem 5. *Let Γ be a Fuchsian group in* **D** *without elliptic elements. If the subgroup $\langle\beta, \gamma\rangle$ is not cyclic then*

(4.6) $$|\beta(0)|^2 + |\gamma(0)|^2 \geqq 1$$

and equality is possible for every value of $|\beta(0)|$.

We shall need the following elementary result.

Lemma. *If $\xi \geqq 0$, $u \geqq 0$ and*

(4.7) $$v \geqq \max\,[(1+\xi^2)(u-1), \xi^2(1-u)]$$

then $v-u+1 \geqq 0$, and the function

(4.8) $$h(u, v, \xi) = u + [\sqrt{(1+\xi^2)(v-u+1)} - \xi\sqrt{v}]^2$$

is increasing in u and in v; the value in the square bracket is non-negative.

Proof. We obtain from (4.7) that

$$\frac{\partial h}{\partial u} = \frac{\xi}{\sqrt{v-u+1}}(\sqrt{1+\xi^2)v} - \xi\sqrt{v-u+1}) \geqq 0,$$

$$\frac{\partial h}{\partial v} = \frac{\sqrt{(1+\xi^2)(v-u+1)} - \xi\sqrt{v}}{\sqrt{v(v-u+1)}}(\sqrt{(1+\xi^2)v} - \xi\sqrt{v-u+1}) \geqq 0.$$

Proof of Theorem 4 (i). (a) We consider first the case that β is hyperbolic. We may assume that 1 is a fixed point of β and map $\{|z|<1\}$ onto $\{\operatorname{Im} z^* > 0\}$ by

(4.9) $$z^* = i\frac{1+z}{1-z} + t$$

where we choose $t \in \mathbf{R}$ such that the other fixed point of β is mapped to 0. Then β and γ are transformed into elements of the form

(4.10) $$\beta^*(z^*) = \rho^2 z^*, \quad \gamma^*(z^*) = \frac{az^*+b}{cz^*+d}\,(ad-bc=1).$$

It follows from (4.9) and (4.10) by calculation that

(4.11) $$\frac{1}{1-|\gamma(0)|^2} = \left(\frac{a+d}{2}\right)^2 + \frac{1}{4}[-b+(d-a)t+c(t^2+1)]^2.$$

In particular for $a=\rho$, $b=c=0$, $d=\rho^{-1}$ we obtain that

$$\kappa=(\rho-\rho^{-1})^2=\frac{4}{1+t^2}\frac{|\beta(0)|^2}{1-|\beta(0)|^2}. \tag{4.12}$$

Hence it follows from $|\beta(0)|<1/\sqrt{5}$ that

$$\kappa\leqq\frac{4|\beta(0)|^2}{1-|\beta(0)|^2}<1. \tag{4.13}$$

Thus we conclude from Corollary 1 that $ad\leqq -1/\kappa$ or $ad\geqq 1+1/\kappa$.

(b) We consider first the case that $ad\geqq 1+1/\kappa$. Then it follows from (4.11) that

$$\frac{1}{1-|\gamma(0)|^2}\geqq\left(\frac{a+d}{2}\right)^2\geqq ad\geqq 1+\frac{1}{\kappa}$$

and therefore from (4.13) that

$$|\gamma(0)|^2\geqq\frac{1-|\beta(0)|^2}{1+3|\beta(0)|^2} \tag{4.14}$$

which is actually stronger than (4.1) because $|\beta(0)|<1/\sqrt{5}$.

(c) We consider now the case $ad\leqq -1/\kappa$. We set $s=(a+d)/2$ and $y=-ad$. Then $y\geqq 1/\kappa$ and $bc=-y-1<0$; we may assume that $b<0$, $c>0$. It follows from (4.11) that

$$\frac{1}{1-|\gamma(0)|^2}=s^2+\left[\frac{y+1}{2c}\pm t\sqrt{s^2+y}+\frac{c}{2}(t^2+1)\right]^2. \tag{4.15}$$

If $s^2\geqq 1+yt^{-2}$ then we obtain from $y\geqq 1/\kappa$ that

$$\frac{1}{1-|\gamma(0)|^2}\geqq 1+\frac{y}{t^2}\geqq 1+\frac{1}{t^2\kappa}$$

and we conclude from (4.12) that (4.14) and thus (4.1) holds.

Thus we may assume that

$$s^2<1+yt^{-2},\quad y\geqq(1+t^2)\frac{1-|\beta(0)|^2}{4|\beta(0)|^2}>1+t^2 \tag{4.16}$$

because of $y\geqq 1/\kappa$, (4.13) and $|\beta(0)|^2<1/5$. Thus the expression in the square bracket in (4.15) is positive and attains its minimum (as a function of c) for $c=[(1+y)/(1+t^2)]^{1/2}$.

It follows that, using definition (4.8),

$$\frac{1}{1-|\gamma(0)|^2} \geqq s^2 + [\sqrt{(1+y)(1+t^2)} - |t|\sqrt{s^2+y}]^2 = h(s^2, y+s^2, |t|). \tag{4.17}$$

Since condition (4.7) is satisfied because of (4.16), we obtain from the lemma and from (4.16) that, with $\lambda = (1-|\beta(0)|^2)/(4|\beta(0)|^2)$,

$$1-|\gamma(0)|^2 \leqq 1/h(0, (1+t^2)\lambda, |t|) = \frac{[\sqrt{1+(1+t^2)\lambda} + t\sqrt{\lambda}]^2}{(1+\lambda)^2(1+t^2)}.$$

Differentiation shows that the last expression is strictly increasing in $|t|$ (because $\lambda > 1$). By considering the limit as $|t| \to \infty$, we deduce that it is $< 4\lambda/(1+\lambda)^2$. It follows that

$$|\gamma(0)| > \frac{\lambda-1}{\lambda+1} = \frac{1-5|\beta(0)|^2}{1+3|\beta(0)|^2}. \tag{4.18}$$

(d) Finally let β be parabolic. Then Γ does not have a compact fundamental domain, so that we can approximate Γ by groups Γ_n without parabolic elements, for instance using the method developed in [11, Lemma 1]. Here β is approximated by a hyperbolic element in Γ_n and γ by some $\gamma_n \in \Gamma_n$. The groups $\langle \beta_n, \gamma_n \rangle$ are non-elementary for large n. Hence (4.18) shows that

$$|\gamma_n(0)| > (1-5|\beta_n(0)|^2)/(1+3|\beta_n(0)|^2)$$

and we obtain (4.1) by letting $n \to \infty$.

(e) To show that (4.1) is best possible, we transform the modular group by $z^* = iv(1+z)/(1-z)$ in $\{|z|<1\}$. The elements $\beta^*(z^*) = z^*+1$ and $\gamma^*(z^*) = -1/z^*$ are transformed into elements β and γ satisfying

$$|\beta(0)| = \frac{1}{\sqrt{1+4v^2}}, \quad |\gamma(0)| = \frac{v^2-1}{v^2+1} \quad (1 \leqq v < \infty).$$

Now equality holds in (4.1), and $|\beta(0)|$ assumes all values in $(0, 1/\sqrt{5}]$.

Proof of Theorem 4 (ii). (a) Let now β be elliptic of order $k \geqq 3$; we may assume that the fixed point x of β satisfies $0 \leqq x < 1$. If we map **D** onto **D** by

$$z^* = (x-z)/(1-xz) \tag{4.19}$$

then β and γ are transformed into

$$\beta^*(z^*) = e^{2\pi i v/k} z^*, \quad \gamma^*(z^*) = \frac{pz+q}{\bar{q}z+\bar{p}} \quad (|p|^2 - |q|^2 = 1). \tag{4.20}$$

We find that, with $s=\frac{1}{2}\operatorname{tr}\gamma=\operatorname{Re}p$,

$$\frac{1}{1-|\gamma(0)|^2}=s^2+\left(\frac{1+x^2}{1-x^2}\sqrt{|q|^2+1-s^2}\pm\frac{2x}{1-x^2}\operatorname{Im}q\right)^2. \tag{4.21}$$

Let $b_k=\sin(\pi/k)$ and let c_k be defined as in Theorem 3. Then we obtain from (4.21) (specializing to $p=e^{2\pi iv/k}$, $q=0$) that

$$\xi\equiv\frac{2x}{1-x^2}=\frac{|\beta(0)|}{\sin(\pi v/k)\sqrt{1-|\beta(0)|^2}}\leqq\frac{|\beta(0)|}{b_k\sqrt{1-|\beta(0)|^2}} \tag{4.22}$$

and from (3.3) that

$$|q|^2=|p|^2-1\geqq(c_k/b_k)^2-1\,. \tag{4.23}$$

If $s^2\geqq 1+|q|^2/(1+\xi^2)$ then, by (4.21), (4.23) and (4.22)

$$\frac{1}{1-|\gamma(0)|^2}\geqq s^2\geqq\frac{c_k^2+(1-c_k^2)|\beta(0)|^2}{b_k^2+(1-b_k^2)|\beta(0)|^2},$$

and this inequality is stronger than (4.3) under the condition (4.2).

(b) Thus we may assume that $s^2<1+(1+\xi^2)|q|^2$. It follows from (4.23), (4.2) and (4.22) that

$$|q|^2\geqq\left(\frac{c_k}{b_k}\right)^2-1\geqq\frac{|\beta(0)|^2}{b_k^2(1-|\beta(0)|^2)}\geqq\xi^2\geqq\xi^2(1-s^2)\,.$$

Thus the condition (4.7) of the lemma is satisfied with $u=s^2$, $v=|q|^2$. Since $1+\xi^2=$ $=[(1+x^2)/(1-x^2)]^2$ it follows therefore from (4.21) and (4.23) that

$$\frac{1}{1-|\gamma(0)|^2}\geqq h(s^2,|q|^2,\xi)\geqq h(0,c_k^2/b_k^2-1,\xi)=$$

$$=\left[\sqrt{1+\xi^2}\,\frac{c_k}{b_k}-\frac{\xi}{b_k}\sqrt{c_k^2-b_k^2}\right]^2. \tag{4.24}$$

Differentiation shows that the last expression is decreasing in $\xi\in[0,b_k^{-1}\sqrt{c_k^2-b_k^2}]$. Hence it follows by (4.22) and by (4.2) that it becomes minimal for $\xi=$ $=|\beta(0)|/(b_k\sqrt{1-|\beta(0)|^2})$, and this gives our estimate (4.3).

(c) To show that (4.4) is sharp we consider the triangle group $T(2,k,l)$ where $l=l(k)$ is determined as in the proof of Theorem 3. Then the transformation (4.19) leads to

$$s=\operatorname{Re}p=0,\quad q=i[(b_k/c_k)^2-1]^{1/2}\,.$$

Hence equality holds in (4.24), and if we choose x such that equality holds in (4.22), then equality holds in (4.3).

Proof of Theorem 5. (a) This proof is quite similar to that of Theorem 4 (i). We may assume that $|\beta(0)|<1/\sqrt{2}$. Then (4.13) shows that $\kappa<4$. Hence it follows from Corollary 1 that (2.5) holds.

If $ad \geqq 1+4/\kappa$ then $s^2 \geqq (a+d)^2/4 \geqq 1+4/\kappa \geqq |\beta(0)|^{-2}$ by (4.13), and (4.6) follows at once from (4.11). We may thus assume that (compare (4.16))

$$s^2<1+yt^{-2}, \quad y \geqq \frac{4\rho}{(\rho-1)^2} \quad (>4/\kappa)$$

because the case $s^2 \geqq 1+yt^{-2}$ is dealt with as above. Since $|s|=|\mathrm{tr}\,\gamma|/2 \geqq 1$ we obtain that (compare (4.17))

$$\frac{1}{1-|\gamma(0)|^2} \geqq h\left(1, \frac{4\rho}{(\rho-1)^2}+1, |t|\right)=1+\left(\frac{\rho+1}{\rho-1}\right)^2(\sqrt{1+t^2}-|t|)^2 .$$

If $\lambda=(1-|\beta(0)|^2)/(4|\beta(0)|^2)$ then $1+t^2=\rho^2(\rho^2-1)^{-2}\lambda^{-1}$ by (4.12). Hence we deduce that

$$\frac{\sqrt{1-|\gamma(0)|^2}}{|\gamma(0)|} \leqq \frac{\rho-1}{\rho+1}(\sqrt{1+t^2}+|t|)=\frac{\rho+\sqrt{\rho^2-\lambda(\rho^2-1)^2}}{\sqrt{\lambda}(\rho+1)^2} \leqq \frac{1}{2\sqrt{\lambda}}=\frac{|\beta(0)|}{\sqrt{1-|\beta(0)|^2}}$$

which implies (4.6) if β is hyperbolic. The parabolic case is again considered as a limit case of the hyperbolic case.

(b) To show that (4.6) is best possible we consider the free subgroup of the modular group generated by the parabolic elements $\beta^*(z^*)=z^*+2$ and $\gamma^*(z^*)=z^*/(2z^*+1)$. The transformation $z^*=iv(1+z)/(1-z)$ into **D** leads to elements β and γ with $|\beta(0)|^2= =1/(1+v^2)$ and $|\gamma(0)|^2=v^2/(1+v^2)$ so that equality holds in (4.6).

Remark. There is (at least) one other extremal case namely the free Fuchsian group in **D** generated by

$$\beta(z)=\frac{z+b}{1+bz}, \quad \gamma(z)=\frac{z+i\sqrt{1-b^2}}{1-i\sqrt{1-b^2}\,z}$$

where $0<b<1$; this corresponds to the fundamental group of a once punctured torus. This example (with $b=|\beta(0)|=|\gamma(0)|=1/\sqrt{2}$) seems to contradict the assertion of L. KEEN [7] that

$$\max(|\beta(0)|, |\gamma(0)|) \geqq \tan h(2^{1/2}/5^{1/4})>0.737 .$$

References

[1] BEARDON, A. F., On the isometric circles of elements in a Fuchsian group, *J. London Math. Soc.*, **10** (1975), 329–337.

[2] FORD, L. R., *Automorphic functions*, Chelsea Publ. Comp., New York 1951.

[3] GREENBERG, L., Maximal Fuchsian groups, *Bull. Amer. Math. Soc.*, **69** (1963), 569–573.

[4] HOARE, A. H. M. and MACBEATH, A. M., Groups of hyperbolic crystallography, *Math. Proc. Cambridge Philos. Soc.*, **79** (1976), 235–249.

[5] JØRGENSEN, T., On discrete groups of Möbius transformations, *Amer. J. Math.*, **98** (1976), 739–749.

[6] JØRGENSEN, T. and KIIKKA, M., Some extreme discrete groups, *Ann. Acad. Sci. Fenn., Ser. A I Math.*, **1** (1975), 245–248.

[7] KEEN, L. *Collars on Riemann surfaces*, Discont. Groups Riemann Surf., Proc. Conf. Univ. Maryland 1973, 263–268.

[8] LEHNER, J. and PURZITSKY, N., On the intersector subgroup and the diameter of a Fuchsian group. Preprint.

[9] MAGNUS, W., KARRASS, A. and SOLITAR, D., *Combinatorial group theory*, Interscience Publ., New York 1966.

[10] MARDEN, A., Universal properties of Fuchsian groups in the Poincaré metric. Discontinuous groups and Riemann surfaces, *Annals of Mathematics Studies*, **79** (1974), 315–339.

[11] POMMERENKE, CH., On the theta-operator for automorphic forms of weight 1, *Indiana Univ. Math. J.*, **25** (1976), 595–607.

[12] PURZITSKY, N., Two-generator discrete free products, *Math. Z.*, **126** (1972), 209–223.

[13] PURZITSKY, N., Canonical generators of Fuchsian groups, *Illinois J. Math.*, **18** (1974), 484–490.

[14] PURZITSKY, N., All two-generator Fuchsian groups, *Math. Z.*, *147* (1976), 87–92.

[15] SIEGEL, C. L., Über einige Ungleichungen bei Bewegungsgruppen in der nichteuklidischen Ebene, Math. Ann. *133* (1957), 127–138.

TECHNISCHE UNIVERSITÄT BERLIN
UNIVERSITY OF MINNESOTA, MINNEAPOLIS

YORK UNIVERSITY, TORONTO
TECHNISCHE UNIVERSITÄT BERLIN

Studies in Pure Mathematics
To the Memory of Paul Turán

On the variance of additive functions

by

I. Z. RUZSA (Budapest)

1. Introduction

Let f be a real-valued additive arithmetical function. The quantity

$$D^2(f, t) = x^{-1} \sum_{n \leq x} (f(n) - t)^2 \tag{1.1}$$

assumes its minimum at

$$t = M(f) \overset{\text{def}}{=} x^{-1} \sum_{n \leq x} f(n) = x^{-1} \sum_{p^k \leq x} \left[\frac{x}{p^k}\right] (f(p^k) - f(p^{k-1}));\tag{1.2}$$

we call its value

$$D^2(f) = D^2(f, M(f)) \tag{1.3}$$

the variance of f on the interval $[1, x]$. (If it does not lead to any ambiguity, we shall omit the argument "f" and write simply D^2 instead of $D^2(f)$ etc.) An upper bound for the variance is given by the celebrated Turán–Kubilius inequality; it states

$$D^2 \leq D^2(A) \ll B^2(f) \overset{\text{def}}{=} \sum_{p^k \leq x} p^{-k} f^2(p^k), \tag{1.4}$$

where the implied constant is absolute and

$$A = A(f) = \sum_{p \leq x} f(p)/p. \tag{1.5}$$

This was proved first for the special functions ν and κ (the number of prime divisors, counted with or without multiplicity) and next for a class of functions by TURÁN [4, 5]; the above-mentioned general form is due to KUBILIUS [2].

In many cases this gives the right order of the variance. However, applying it for the logarithmic function

$$f(n) = \log n$$

we get

$$B^2 = \sum_{p^k \leqq x} p^{-k} \log^2 p^k \sim \frac{1}{2} \log^2 x ,$$

while a simple computation yields

(1.6) $$D^2 \asymp D^2(A) \asymp 1 \qquad (f = \log) .$$

(The symbol $x \asymp y$ means that both $x \ll y$ and $y \ll x$.)[1] Our aim is to find a similar formula which gives the right order of variance for every additive function.

2. The results

Start with an arbitrary additive function f and regard the decomposition

$$f = g + \lambda \log , \qquad g = f - \lambda \log ,$$

where λ is a real parameter. (If we write "log" without any argument, it refers to the logarithm regarded as an arithmetical function.) Using the elementary inequality

(2.1) $$(x+y)^2 \leqq 2(x^2+y^2)$$

we get

(2.2) $$D^2(f, A(f)) \leqq 2(D^2(g, A(g)) + D^2(\lambda \log, A(\lambda \log))) .$$

Estimating the first member of (2.2) by the Turán–Kubilius inequality and the second by (1.6) we obtain[2]

(2.3) $$D^2(f) \leqq D^2(f, A(f)) \ll B^2(f, \lambda) \stackrel{\text{def}}{=} \lambda^2 + \sum_{p^k \leqq x} p^{-k} (f(p^k) - \lambda \log p^k)^2 .$$

We shall prove that (2.3) gives the right order of D^2 for a suitably chosen λ. $B^2(\lambda)$ is a quadratic polynomial in λ, so it is not hard to determine its minimum; it is attained at

(2.4) $$\lambda_1(f) = \frac{\sum_{p^k \leqq x} p^{-k} f(p^k) \log p^k}{1 + \sum_{p^k \leqq x} p^{-k} \log^2 p^k} .$$

[1] The symbol $x \ll y$ is equivalent to $x = O(y)$.

[2] Professor J. KUBILIUS informed me that this upper estimate was known to him and his students.

Moreover we shall show that the simpler expression

$$\lambda_2(f) = \frac{2}{\log^2 x} \sum_{p \leqq x} \frac{f(p) \log p}{p} \tag{2.5}$$

is also good. We sum up our statements in the following form.

Theorem. *For an arbitrary additive function we have*

$$D^2 \asymp D^2(A) \asymp B^2(\lambda_1) \asymp B^2(\lambda_2)\,;$$

the implied constants are absolute.

We note that this result remains valid for complex-valued functions or even for functions with values in a Hilbert space. To obtain this generalization we have only to apply the original form to the real functions

$$f_i(n) = \langle f(n), e_i \rangle ,$$

where $\{e_i\}$ runs over an orthonormal basis.

We also give a new proof for the Turán–Kubilius inequality, which seems to be somewhat simpler than the original one given in Kubilius's book [2].

3. Proof of the Turán–Kubilius inequality

With the notations (1.1—1.5) we have

$$D^2(t) = D^2 + (t-M)^2 , \tag{3.1}$$

thus in order to prove $D^2(A) \ll B^2$ it is sufficient to show that

$$D^2 \ll B^2 \tag{3.2}$$

and

$$A - M \ll B . \tag{3.3}$$

Instead of A we may use also the means

$$A_1 = \sum_{p^k \leqq x} p^{-k} f(p^k), \qquad A_2 = \sum_{p^k \leqq x} p^{-k}(f(p^k) - f(p^{k-1})) .$$

The inequalities

$$M - A_2 \ll B, \qquad A_1 - A_2 \ll B, \qquad A - A_1 \ll B,$$

which together imply (3.3), can be proved in the usual way, with the Cauchy-inequality. The essential point is the proof of (3.2).

Let g be the Möbius transform of f:

$$g(n)=\sum_{d|n}\mu(d)f(n/d),\qquad f(n)=\sum_{d|n}g(d);\tag{3.4}$$

for an additive f, g is given by

$$g(n)=\begin{cases}0, \text{ if } n \text{ is not a prime-power;}\\ f(p^k)-f(p^{k-1}), \text{ if } n=p^k.\end{cases}\tag{3.5}$$

We shall prove

$$D^2(f)\ll B_1^2(f)\overset{\text{def}}{=}\sum_{n\leqq x}\frac{g^2(n)}{n}\leqq 3\sum_{p^k\leqq x}\frac{f^2(p^k)}{p^k}.\tag{3.6}$$

The second inequality of (6) evidently follows from (3.5) and (2.1).

It is enough to prove the first part of (3.6) for nonnegative functions g. Namely let

$$g=g_+-g_-,\qquad g_+(n)=\max(0, g(n));$$

we have

$$f=f_1-f_2,\ f_1(n)=\sum_{d|n}g_+(d),\ f_2(n)=\sum_{d|n}g_-(d)$$

and thus

$$D^2(f)\leqq 2(D^2(f_1)+D^2(f_2))\ll\sum_{n\leqq x}\frac{g_+^2(n)+g_-^2(n)}{n}=\sum_{n\leqq x}\frac{g^2(n)}{n},$$

supposed we know the wanted inequality for the nonnegative functions g_+ and g_-.

Obviously

$$x^2D^2=x\sum_{n\leqq x}f^2(n)-\Big(\sum_{n\leqq x}f(n)\Big)^2.\tag{3.7}$$

We express these sums by g. For the first we have

$$\sum_{n\leqq x}f(n)=\sum_{d\leqq x}g(d)[x/d];\tag{3.8}$$

to get the second we square (3.4):

$$f^2(n)=\sum_{a,b|n}g(a)g(b),$$

and hence

$$\sum_{n\leqq x}f^2(n)=\sum_{a\leqq x}\sum_{b\leqq x}g(a)g(b)\left[\frac{x}{[a,b]}\right].\tag{3.9}$$

Combining (3.7), (3.8) and (3.9) we get

$$x^2D^2 = \sum_{a,b\leqq x} g(a)g(b)\left(x\left[\frac{x}{[a,b]}\right]-\left[\frac{x}{a}\right]\left[\frac{x}{b}\right]\right). \tag{3.10}$$

By virtue of (3.5) here only those summands differ from zero in which both a and b are prime-powers. Regard first the case when they are powers of the same prime:

$$a=p^i, \qquad b=p^j.$$

The corresponding part of (3.10) is

$$x^2 \sum_{p,i,j} g(p^i)g(p^j)p^{-\max(i,j)}. \tag{3.11}$$

Introducing the variables

$$u_i=g(p^i)p^{-i/2}$$

the part of (3.11) belonging to a fixed prime p can be estimated in the following way:

$$\leqq \sum_{i,j} u_iu_jp^{-|i-j|/2} \leqq \sum_{i,j}(u_i^2+u_j^2)p^{-|i-j|/2} \leqq c\sum_i u_i^2,$$

where

$$c = 2\sum_{i=-\infty}^{\infty} 2^{-|i|/2};$$

thus for this part of (3.10) we got the estimate

$$c\sum_{p^i\leqq x} g^2(p^i)p^{-i},$$

as wanted.

In the other case a and b are powers of different primes, so they are coprime. Therefore

$$x\left[\frac{x}{[a,b]}\right]-\left[\frac{x}{a}\right]\left[\frac{x}{b}\right]=x\left[\frac{x}{ab}\right]-\left[\frac{x}{a}\right]\left[\frac{x}{b}\right]\leqq x\min(a^{-1},b^{-1}).$$

(This is not true in absolute value; that is why we assumed g to be nonnegative.) Hence this part of (3.10) is

$$\leqq x\sum_{a,b\leqq x} g(a)g(b)\min(a^{-1},b^{-1}) \leqq 2x\sum_{a\leqq x} g(a)/a\sum_{b\leqq a} g(b). \tag{3.12}$$

By the Cauchy-inequality we have

(3.13) $$\sum_{n\leqq y} g(n) \leqq \left(\sum_{n\leqq y} \frac{g^2(n)}{n} \sum_{n\leqq y} n \right)^{1/2} \leqq B_1 y$$

(B_1 was defined in (3.6)), thus (3.12) can be continued as

$$\leqq x \sum_{a\leqq x} \frac{g(a)}{a} B_1 a = B_1 x \sum_{a\leqq x} g(a) \leqq B_1^2 x ,$$

again by (3.13). This completes the proof of (3.2).

4. Proof of the theorem

As we have

$$D^2 \leqq D^2(A) \ll B^2(\lambda_1) \leqq B^2(\lambda_2) ,$$

it is sufficient to prove

(4.1) $$B^2(\lambda_2) \ll D^2 .$$

First we show that λ_2 is an "almost minimum" for $B(\lambda)$, that is

(4.2) $$B(\lambda_2) \leqq c_1 B(\lambda)$$

for all λ with an absolute constant c_1.

Write $g = f - \log$. Then

$$\lambda_2 - \lambda = \frac{2}{\log^2 x} \sum_{p\leqq x} \frac{f(p)\log p}{p} - \lambda =$$

$$= \lambda \left(\frac{2}{\log^2 x} \sum_{p\leqq x} \frac{\log^2 p}{p} - 1 \right) + \frac{2}{\log^2 x} \sum_{p\leqq x} \frac{g(p)\log p}{p} .$$

Here the first term is

$$\ll |\lambda|/\log x \leqq B(\lambda)/\log x ;$$

the second can be estimated by the Cauchy-inequality:

$$\left| \sum_{p\leqq x} \frac{g(p)\log p}{p} \right| \leqq \left(\sum_{p\leqq x} \frac{g^2(p)}{p} \sum_{p\leqq x} \frac{\log^2 p}{p} \right)^{1/2} \ll B(\lambda) \log x ,$$

thus we got

$$\lambda_2 - \lambda \ll B(\lambda)/\log x .$$

According to (2.1) this implies

$$B^2(\lambda_2) \leqq 2(B^2(\lambda) + (\lambda_2 - \lambda)^2 + (\lambda_2 - \lambda)^2 \sum_{p^k \leqq x} p^{-k} \log^2 p^k) \lll B^2(\lambda) .$$

Now we have to show that

$$B(\lambda) \ll D \tag{4.3}$$

for a suitably chosen λ. This is based on the following two lemmas.

(4.4) **Lemma.** *Let f be a real-valued additive function. Suppose that for some number a*

$$f(n) \in [a, a+1]$$

holds for αx numbers $n \leqq x$. Then there is a λ such that

$$\lambda^2 + \sum_{p \leqq x} \frac{\min(1, (f(p) - \lambda \log p)^2)}{p} \ll \alpha^{-2}, \tag{4.5}$$

the implied constant is absolute.

See Ruzsa [3].

(4.6) **Lemma.** *Let P be a set of primes satisfying*

$$\sum_{p \in P} 1/p \leqq K .$$

For every $x \geqq 1$ the number of square-free natural numbers not exceeding x which are divisible by no element of P is

$$\geqq c(K)x , \qquad c(K) > 0 .$$

See Erdős–Ruzsa [1].

Now we start proving (3). After a normalization this takes the form if

$$\sum_{n \leqq x} (f(n) - M)^2 \leqq x , \tag{4.7}$$

then there is a λ such that

(4.8 $$|\lambda| \leqq c_2 , \qquad \sum_{p^k \leqq x} p^{-k} (f(p^k) - \lambda \log p^k)^2 \leqq c_3 ,$$

c_2, c_3 are absolute constants.

(7) obviously implies that $x/6$ of the numbers $f(n)$, $n \leqq x$ lie in an interval of unit length (via the Chebyshev-inequality). Applying Lemma (4.4) we conclude that there is a λ such that

$$(4.9) \qquad |\lambda| \leqq c_2; \qquad \sum_{p^k \leqq x} \frac{\min(1, (f(p) - \lambda \log p)^2}{p} \leqq c_2,$$

with an absolute constant c_2. We shall prove (4.8) with the same λ and c_2; the first inequality is already contained in (4.9).

Let $g = f - \lambda \log$ and define an additive function g_1 by

$$g_1(p^k) = \begin{cases} g(p^k), & \text{if } |g(p^k)| \leqq 1, \\ 0 & \text{otherwise} \end{cases};$$

finally let $g_2 = g - g_1$. We know:

$$(4.10) \qquad f = \lambda \log + g_1 + g_2,$$

$$(4.11) \qquad |\lambda| \leqq c_2,$$

$$(4.12) \qquad \sum_{p^k \leqq x} p^{-k} g_1^2(p^k) \leqq c_4$$

(the series over primes is estimated by (4.9), the higher powers obviously);

$$(4.13) \qquad g_2(p^k) = 0 \quad \text{or} \quad |g_2(p^k)| \geqq 1.$$

Now we show

$$(4.14) \qquad D^2(g_2) \leqq c_5.$$

As $g_2 = f - \lambda \log - g_1$, we have by (2.1)

$$D^2(g_2) \ll D^2(f) + D^2(\lambda \log) + D^2(g_1).$$

Here the first term is $\leqq 1$ by (4.7), the second is $O(1)$ by (4.11) and the third is also $O(1)$ by (4.12) and the Turán–Kubilius inequality.

Denoting

$$P = \{p : p \leqq x, \quad g_2(p) \neq 0\}$$

we have

$$(4.15) \qquad \sum_{p \in P} 1/p \leqq c_2$$

by (4.9).

Let T be the set of squarefree integers divisible by no element of P, and for a prime p let

$$T_p = \{n : n \in T,\ p \nmid n\} .$$

We shall use the same symbols to denote the counting functions of these sets, that is

$$T(y) = |T \cap [1, y]|$$

and similarly for T_p.

Applying Lemma (6) for the set $P \cup \{p\}$ we get

$$T(y) \geqq T_p(y) \geqq c_6 y \tag{4.16}$$

for all y, where $c_6 = c(K)$, $K = c_2 + 1/2$.

(4.14) means that

$$\sum_{n \leqq x} (g_2(n) - M_2)^2 \leqq c_5 x \tag{4.17}$$

for a number M_2. Summing over only T we get

$$\sum_{\substack{n \leqq x \\ n \in T}} (g_2(n) - M_2)^2 = M_2^2 T(x) \leqq c_5 x$$

(evidently $g_2(n) = 0$ if $n \in T$), and hence

$$M_2^2 \leqq c_7, \qquad c_7 = c_5/c_6 . \tag{4.18}$$

Now we note that the sets

$$p^k T_p, \qquad g_2(p^k) \neq 0 \tag{4.19}$$

are disjoint. Namely suppose

$$p_1^{k_1} t_1 = p_2^{k_2} t_2, \quad t_1 \in T_{p_1}, t_2 \in T_{p_2} .$$

If $p_1 \neq p_2$, then $p_2^{k_2} | t_1$, in contradiction with the definition of the sets T_p. If $p_1 = p_2 = p$, then $k_1 \neq k_2$, thus either $p | t_1 \in T_p$ or $p | t_2 \in T_p$, again a contradiction.

(4.17) yields, by the disjointness of the sets (4.19)

$$Q = \sum_{p^k}{}^* \sum_{\substack{n \in p^k T_p \\ n \leqq x}} (g_2(n) - M_2)^2 \leqq c_5 x ; \tag{4.20}$$

the asterisk indicates that the summation is over the prime-powers p^k such that $g_2(p^k) \neq 0$.

On the other hand, if $n \in p^k T_p$ and $g_2(p^k) \neq 0$, then

$$g_2(n) = g_2(p^k) = g(p^k),$$

so we get

$$Q = \sum_{p^k}^{*} (g(p^k) - M_2)^2 T_p(xp^{-k}) \geqq c_6 \times \sum_{p^k \leqq x}^{*} p^{-k}(g(p^k) - M_2)^2 . \tag{4.21}$$

Comparing (4.20) and (4.21) we conclude

$$\sum_{p^k \leqq x}^{*} p^{-k}(g(p^k) - M_2)^2 \leqq c_8 ;$$

together with (4.18), (4.15) and (2.1) this implies

$$\sum_{p^k \leqq x}^{*} p^{-k} g^2(p^k) \leqq c_9 .$$

Combined with (4.11) and (4.12) this gives us the desired inequality (4.8).

Acknowledgement

I am thankful to D. G. J. BABU for correcting an inaccuracy in this paper.

Added in proof. After submitting the paper I learned that this method of proving the Turán–Kubilius inequality (Sec. 3) had been published by P. D. T. A. Elliott. Proc. *Amer. Math. Soc. 65* (1977), 8–10.

References

[1] P. ERDŐS and I. Z. RUZSA, On the small sieve, to be published in *J. Number Theory*, **12** (1980), 385–394.

[2] J. KUBILIUS, *Probabilistic methods in the theory of numbers* (in Russian), Vilnius 1959, 1962; English translation New York, 1964.

[3] I. Z. RUZSA, On the concentration of additive functions, to be published in the *Acta Math. Acad. Sci. Hung.* **36** (1980), 215—232.

[4] P. TURÁN, On a theorem of Hardy and Ramanujan, *J. London Math. Soc.*, **9** (1934), 274–6.

[5] P. TURÁN, Über einige Verallgemeinerungen eines Satzes van Hardy and Ramanujan, *J. London Math. Soc.*, **11** (1936), 125–33.

MATHEMATICAL INSTITUTE OF THE
HUNGARIAN ACADEMY OF SCIENCES
H 1053 BUDAPEST
REÁLTANODA U. 13–15.
HUNGARY

Studies in Pure Mathematics
To the Memory of Paul Turán

Automorphism group and spectrum of a graph

by

H. SACHS and M. STIEBITZ* (Ilmenau)

Abstract

It is well known that there are close relations between the automorphism group **aut G** and the spectrum of a (finite, directed or undirected) graph **G** which can be investigated by the general methods of representation theory, or by more direct methods.

aut G can be represented as the group $\mathscr{G}$ (**A**) of all permutation matrices **P** which commute with the adjacency matrix **A** of **G**. Therefore, if **x** is any eigenvector of **A** belonging to the eigenvalue λ, then so is **Px** for each $\mathbf{P} \in \mathscr{G}(\mathbf{A})$. If, for some $P \in \mathscr{G}(A)$, **x** and **Px** prove linearly independent then λ must have a multiplicity $m > 1$. So, if **aut G** is rich enough, the occurrence of a simple (non-trivial) eigenvalue is an "exception". In this paper it is assumed that **aut G** is transitive, and it is investigated under what conditions simple eigenvalues can occur. In particular, a sharp upper bound for the number of simple eigenvalues (in terms of **aut G**) is given, and from the intermediate results some conclusions are drawn.

1. Introduction

In what follows $\mathbf{G} = (\mathbf{V}, \mathbf{E})$ will always denote a connected finite directed or undirected graph with vertex set $\mathbf{V} = \{1, 2, \ldots, n\}$ and edge set E, loops and multiple edges being admitted.

The *adjacency matrix* $\mathbf{A} = (a_{ij})$ *of* **G** is a square matrix of order n with a_{ij} being the number of (directed) edges issuing from vertex i and terminating in vertex j, where, conventionally, in the case of an undirected graph a_{ii} is twice the number of loops attached to the vertex i.

G is called *regular of degree r* if, for each row and each column of **A**, the sum of the a_{ij} is equal to r. The eigenvalues (eigenvectors) of **A** are also called *eigenvalues* (*eigenvectors*) *of* **G**.

The *automorphism group* of **G**, denoted by **aut G**, is the group of all adjacency preserving (1, 1)-mappings of **V** onto itself: $\gamma \in$ **aut G** if and only if γ is a permutation acting on the set $\{1, 2, \ldots, n\}$ and having the property $a_{\gamma(i)\gamma(j)} = a_{ij}$ for all $i, j = 1, 2, \ldots, n$. Let $\mathbf{P}_\gamma$ denote the permutation matrix which corresponds to the permutation γ. Clearly,

* The authors' thanks are due to Professor GERHARD PAZDERSKI (Wilhelm-Pieck-Universität Rostock) for valuable discussions and comments.

$\gamma \in \mathbf{aut}\,\mathbf{G}$ if and only if $\mathbf{P}_\gamma^{-1}\mathbf{A}\mathbf{P}_\gamma = \mathbf{A}$, i.e., if and only if $\mathbf{P}_\gamma$ commutes with the adjacency matrix $\mathbf{A}$ of $\mathbf{G}$.

A graph $\mathbf{G}$ will be called *transitive* if $\mathbf{aut}\,\mathbf{G}$ is transitive. If $\mathbf{x} = (x_1, x_2, \ldots, x_n)^\mathsf{T}$ and $y = (y_1, y_2, \ldots, y_n)^\mathsf{T}$ are any two vectors over the complex number field then, as usual, the hermitian scalar product $x_1\bar{y}_1 + x_2\bar{y}_2 + \ldots + x_n\bar{y}_n$ is denoted by $\langle \mathbf{x}, \mathbf{y} \rangle$, and $\mathbf{x}, \mathbf{y}$ are called *orthogonal* if $\langle \mathbf{x}, \mathbf{y} \rangle = 0$. The vector $\mathbf{u} = (1, 1, \ldots, 1)^\mathsf{T}$ is called the *identity vector*.

Let $\mathbf{U}_n(l) = \{\mathbf{x} = (x_1, x_2, \ldots, x_n)^\mathsf{T} | x_i^l = 1$ for $i = 1, 2, \ldots, n\}$. With respect to the composition $\otimes$ defined by

$$\mathbf{x} \otimes \mathbf{y} = (x_1y_1, x_2y_2, \ldots, x_ny_n)^\mathsf{T},$$

$\mathbf{U}_n(l)$ is an abelian group, namely (trivially) the direct product of n cyclic groups each of order l.

The cardinality of a set $\mathbf{S}$ will be denoted by $|\mathbf{S}|$.

Now let $\mathbf{x}$ be any eigenvector of $\mathbf{G}$ belonging to the eigenvalue λ, i.e., satisfying $\mathbf{A}\mathbf{x} = \lambda\mathbf{x}$. Then, for all $\gamma \in \mathbf{aut}\,\mathbf{G}$,

$$\mathbf{A} \cdot \mathbf{P}_\gamma\mathbf{x} = \mathbf{P}_\gamma\mathbf{A}\mathbf{x} = \mathbf{P}_\gamma\lambda\mathbf{x} = \lambda \cdot \mathbf{P}_\gamma\mathbf{x}\,.$$

That means that, together with $\mathbf{x}$, also $\mathbf{P}_\gamma\mathbf{x}$ is an eigenvector belonging to λ. Suppose that λ is a simple eigenvalue: then $\mathbf{x}$ and $\mathbf{P}_\gamma\mathbf{x}$ are linearly dependent. Therefore, for each $\gamma \in \mathbf{aut}\,\mathbf{G}$, there is a (complex) number $a_\gamma = a_\gamma(\mathbf{x})$ satisfying $\mathbf{P}_\gamma\mathbf{x} = a_\gamma\mathbf{x}$. Thus $\mathbf{x}$ is a common eigenvector of all permutation matrices $\mathbf{P}_\gamma$, $\gamma \in \mathbf{aut}\,\mathbf{G}$.

Let σ $(\mathbf{G})$ denote the number of simple eigenvalues of $\mathbf{G}$. From the preceding it follows that, in a sense, the "richer" $\mathbf{aut}\,\mathbf{G}$, the smaller $\sigma(\mathbf{G})$. In this paper we assume that $\mathbf{G}$ is a transitive graph, and we search for upper bounds for $\sigma(\mathbf{G})$.

Let Γ be a transitive permutation group of order g acting on the set $\{1, 2, \ldots, n\}$, and assume that $\mathbf{x} = (x_1, x_2, \ldots, x_n)^\mathsf{T} \neq 0$ satisfies $\mathbf{P}_\gamma\mathbf{x} = a_\gamma\mathbf{x}$ for all $\gamma \in \Gamma$: then $\{(a_\gamma)\}$ is a representation of Γ of degree 1, the numbers a_γ are g^{th} roots of unity and, by virtue of the transitivity of Γ, $|x_1| = |x_2| = \ldots = |x_n| \neq 0$.

Let $\mathbf{Z}(\Gamma) = \{\mathbf{x} |$ for each $\gamma \in \Gamma$ there is a number $a_\gamma(\mathbf{x})$ such that $\mathbf{P}_\gamma\mathbf{x} = a_\gamma(\mathbf{x}) \cdot \mathbf{x}$, and $x_1 = 1\}$; then according to the above considerations, $\sigma(\mathbf{G}) \leqq |\mathbf{Z}(\mathbf{aut}\,\mathbf{G})|$. $\mathbf{Z}(\Gamma)$ has the following properties:

(a) For some l, $\mathbf{Z}(\Gamma)$ is a subgroup of $\mathbf{U}_n(l)$.
(b) $\langle \mathbf{x}, \mathbf{y} \rangle = 0$ for any pair of distinct elements of $\mathbf{Z}(\Gamma)$.

Therefore, in Section 2 we shall be concerned with the problem of determining the maximum order a subgroup of $\mathbf{U}_n(l)$ with pairwise orthogonal elements can have. Using simple methods of representation theory, in Section 3 we shall determine the order of $\mathbf{Z}(\Gamma)$.

In Section 4 we shall prove that a transitive undirected graph with $n = 2^q k$ vertices (k being an odd integer) cannot have more than 2^q simple eigenvalues, and in Section 5 we shall construct sequences of undirected graphs which show that this bound is sharp for each n.

In Section 6 it will be shown that each $\mathbf{x} \in \mathbf{Z}(\mathbf{aut\ G})$ is an eigenvector of $\mathbf{G}$ (not necessarily belonging to a simple eigenvalue) and some conclusions concerning the form of the simple eigenvalues will be drawn. As a special result, for transitive undirected graphs also lower bounds for the number of rational eigenvalues (counted with their multiplicities) will be obtained.

The question how the bounds improve if only graphs without loops and multiple edges are taken into consideration, remains, however, an essentially unsolved problem (Section 7).

2. Feasible vector sets

Definition 1. A subgroup E of $\mathbf{U}_n(l)$ is called a *feasible vector set of degree l and dimension n* if any two distinct elements of E are orthogonal.

Let $\mathscr{E}_n(l)$ denote the set of all feasible vector sets of degree l and dimension n, and let $s_n(l) = \max_{E \in \mathscr{E}_n(l)} |E|$. For calculating $s_n(l)$ we shall frequently use a well-known lemma:

Lemma 1 (see, e.g., ZURMÜHL [7]). *Let* $\mathbf{M}_l(\varepsilon) = (\varepsilon^{ij})_{i,j=0,1,\dots,l-1}$ *where* ε *is a primitive* l^{th} *root of unity. Then*

(*i*) *the columns* (*rows*) *of* $\mathbf{M}_l(\varepsilon)$ *are pairwise orthogonal.*

(*ii*) det $\mathbf{M}_l(\varepsilon) \neq 0$.

The following Propositions (A), (B), (C) can easily be established:

(A) $d \mid l$ *implies* $\mathscr{E}_n(d) \subseteq \mathscr{E}_n(l)$ *and* $s_n(d) \leqq s_n(l)$.

(B) $s_n(l) \geqq 1$.

(C) $n \mid n'$ *implies* $s_n(l) \leqq s_{n'}(l)$.

(D) *If* $\mathbf{x} \in E \in \mathscr{E}_n(l)$ *and* $\mathbf{x}$ *has order d, then* $d \mid l$ *and* $d \mid n$.

Proof of (D). (*i*) d is the smallest positive integer satisfying $\mathbf{x}^d = \mathbf{u}$. Since $E \in \mathbf{U}_n(l)$, also $\mathbf{x}^l = \mathbf{u}$. Therefore, $d \mid l$.

(*ii*) For $k = 1, 2, \dots, d-1$ we have $\mathbf{x}^k = (x_1^k, x_2^k, \dots, x_n^k)^{\mathsf{T}} \neq \mathbf{u}$, therefore $\langle \mathbf{x}^k, \mathbf{u} \rangle = 0$. Now, $\langle \mathbf{x}, \mathbf{u} \rangle = x_1 + x_2 + \dots + x_n = m_0 + m_1\varepsilon + \dots + m_{d-1}\varepsilon^{d-1}$, where ε is a primitve d^{th} root of unity and where $m_0, m_1, \dots, m_{d-1}$ are non-negative integers with

$$(1) \qquad m_0 + m_1 + \dots + m_{d-1} = n\,.$$

With these numbers,

$$\langle \mathbf{x}^k, \mathbf{u} \rangle = m_0 + m_1\varepsilon^k + \dots + m_{d-1}\varepsilon^{k(d-1)},$$

and if $\mathbf{m} = (m_0, m_1, \dots, m_{d-1})^{\mathsf{T}}$ then $\mathbf{M}_d(\varepsilon)\mathbf{m} = (n, 0, 0, \dots, 0)^{\mathsf{T}}$. It follows from Lemma 1 that $m_0 = m_1 = \dots = m_{d-1}$, and because of (1), $n = d \cdot m_0$, i.e. $d \mid n$.

From the proof of (**D**) immediately follow (**E**) and (**F**):

(**E**) *$(l, n)=1$ implies $s_n(l)=1$*[1].
(**F**) *If $\mathbf{x}\in E\in\mathscr{E}_n(l)$ and $\mathbf{x}$ has order d, then, if ε is any primitive d^{th} root of unity,*

$$dm_k=n, \quad \text{where} \quad m_k=|\{i\,|\,x_i=\varepsilon^k\}| \quad (k=0, 1, \ldots, d-1).$$

(**G**) *For any prime p and any positive integer l, $p\,|\,l$ implies $ps_n(l)\leqq s_{np}(l)$.*

Proof of (G). Let $E\in\mathscr{E}_n(l)$ with $|E|=s_n(l)$ and let ε denote a primitive p^{th} root of unity. We shall show that the set

$$E'=\{\mathbf{x}'=(\mathbf{x}^{\mathsf{T}}, \varepsilon^k\mathbf{x}^{\mathsf{T}}, \ldots, \varepsilon^{(p-1)k}\mathbf{x}^{\mathsf{T}})^T\,|\,\mathbf{x}\in E \text{ and } k=0, 1, \ldots, p-1\}$$

is a member of $\mathscr{E}_{np}(l)$.

(*i*) If $\mathbf{x}'=(\mathbf{x}^{\mathsf{T}}, \rho\mathbf{x}^{\mathsf{T}}, \ldots, \rho^{p-1}\mathbf{x}^{\mathsf{T}})^T\in E'$ and $\mathbf{y}'=(\mathbf{y}^{\mathsf{T}}, \sigma\mathbf{y}^{\mathsf{T}}, \ldots, \sigma^{p-1}\mathbf{y}^{\mathsf{T}})^T\in E'$ with $\rho=\varepsilon^{k'}$ and $\sigma=\varepsilon^{k''}$ then also $\mathbf{x}'\otimes\mathbf{y}'=((\mathbf{x}\otimes\mathbf{y})^{\mathsf{T}}, \rho\sigma(\mathbf{x}\otimes\mathbf{y})^{\mathsf{T}}, \ldots, \rho^{p-1}\sigma^{p-1}(\mathbf{x}\otimes\mathbf{y})^{\mathsf{T}})^T\in E'$: thus E' is a subgroup of $\mathbf{U}_{np}(l)$.

(*ii*) To prove the orthogonality, note that $\langle\mathbf{x}', \mathbf{y}'\rangle=(1+\rho\bar{\sigma}+\ldots+\rho^{p-1}\bar{\sigma}^{p-1})\langle\mathbf{x}, \mathbf{y}\rangle$. Suppose that $x'\neq y'$: then either $\mathbf{x}\neq\mathbf{y}$ or $\rho\neq\sigma$ (or both). If $\mathbf{x}\neq\mathbf{y}$ then $\langle\mathbf{x}, \mathbf{y}\rangle=0$, and if $\rho\neq\sigma$ then, by virtue of Lemma 1, $1+\rho\bar{\sigma}+\ldots+\rho^{p-1}\bar{\sigma}^{p-1}=0$: thus, in every case, $\langle\mathbf{x}', \mathbf{y}'\rangle=0$.

(*i*) and (*ii*) imply $E'\in\mathscr{E}_{np}(l)$; consequently, $ps_n(l)=p\,|E|=|E'|\leqq s_{np}(l)$.

Lemma 2. *If p is a prime then*

$$s_{np}(p)=p\cdot s_n(p).$$

Proof. Because of (**G**), all that has to be shown is that $s_{np}(p)\leqq p\cdot s_n(p)$. Let $E^*\in\mathscr{E}_{np}(p)$ with $|E^*|=s_{np}(p)$, and let ε denote a primitive p^{th} root of unity.

There is an $\mathbf{x}\in E^*$ with $\mathbf{x}\neq\mathbf{u}$ and $\mathbf{x}^p=\mathbf{u}$. We conclude that

$$\langle\mathbf{x}, \mathbf{u}\rangle=x_1+x_2+\ldots+x_{np}=m_0+m_1\varepsilon+\ldots+m_{p-1}\varepsilon^{p-1}=0$$

with non-negative integers $m_0, \ldots, m_{p-1}$ having the sum np: this implies that $m_0=m_1=\ldots=m_{p-1}=n$. Therefore, we may assume that the vector components are labelled so that

$$\mathbf{x}=(\mathbf{u}^{\mathsf{T}}, \varepsilon\,\mathbf{u}^{\mathsf{T}}, \ldots, \varepsilon^{p-1}\mathbf{u}^{\mathsf{T}})^{\mathsf{T}}.$$

For $\mathbf{y}=(y_1, y_2, \ldots, y_{np})^{\mathsf{T}}\in E^*$, let $\pi_i(\mathbf{y})$ denote the partial vector $(y_{in+1}, y_{in+2}, \ldots, y_{(i+1)n})^{\mathsf{T}}$ $(i=0, 1, \ldots, p-1)$; then $\mathbf{y}=(\pi_0^{\mathsf{T}}(\mathbf{y}), \pi_1^{\mathsf{T}}(\mathbf{y}), \ldots, \pi_{p-1}^{\mathsf{T}}(\mathbf{y}))^T$.

[1] As usual, (a, b) denotes the greatest common divisor of the integers a, b.

Now consider the set

$$E=\{\pi_0(\mathbf{y}) \mid \mathbf{y}\in E^*\}.$$

We shall show: (*i*) $|E^*|\leqq p|E|$, (*ii*) $E\in\mathscr{E}_n(p)$.

(*i*) It suffices to show that in E^* there cannot be more than p vectors having the same projection π_0. Let $\mathbf{y}\in E^*$ and $\mathbf{y}_k=\mathbf{y}\otimes\mathbf{x}^k$ $(k=0, 1, \ldots, p-1)$: then $\mathbf{y}_k\in E^*$ and $\pi_0(\mathbf{y}_k)=\pi_0(\mathbf{y})$. Suppose that there is a vector $\mathbf{y}'\in E^*$, $\mathbf{y}'\neq\mathbf{y}_k$ for $k=0, 1, \ldots, p-1$ and satisfying $\pi_0(\mathbf{y}')=\pi_0(\mathbf{y})$. Then

$$\langle\mathbf{y}_k, \mathbf{y}'\rangle=\sum_{i=0}^{p-1}\langle\pi_i(\mathbf{y}_k), \pi_i(\mathbf{y}')\rangle=$$
$$=\sum_{i=0}^{p-1}\varepsilon^{ik}\langle\pi_i(\mathbf{y}), \pi_i(\mathbf{y}')\rangle=0$$

for $k=0, 1, \ldots, p-1$, or, equivalently,

$$M_p(\varepsilon)\cdot\mathbf{v}=0,$$

where

$$\mathbf{v}=(\langle\pi_0(\mathbf{y}), \pi_0(\mathbf{y}')\rangle, \ldots, \langle\pi_{p-1}(\mathbf{y}), \pi_{p-1}(\mathbf{y}')\rangle)^{\mathsf{T}}.$$

Because of Lemma 1, $\mathbf{v}=0$, contradicting

$$\langle\pi_0(\mathbf{y}), \pi_0(\mathbf{y}')\rangle=\langle\pi_0(\mathbf{y}), \pi_0(\mathbf{y})\rangle=n.$$

(*ii*) Clearly, $\pi_0(\mathbf{x}')\otimes\pi_0(\mathbf{x}'')=\pi_0(\mathbf{x}'\otimes\mathbf{x}'')$ for all $\mathbf{x}', \mathbf{x}''\in E^*$, hence E is a subgroup of $\mathbf{U}_n(p)$. Let $\mathbf{y}, \mathbf{y}'\in E^*$ with $\pi_0(\mathbf{y})\neq\pi_0(\mathbf{y}')$ and let $\mathbf{y}_k=\mathbf{y}\otimes\mathbf{x}^k$ $(k=0, 1, \ldots, p-1)$. Then $\mathbf{y}_k\neq\mathbf{y}'$ for $k=0, 1, \ldots, p-1$, and in the same way as under (*i*) we deduce from $\langle\mathbf{y}_k, \mathbf{y}'\rangle=0$ for $k=0, 1, \ldots, p-1$ that also

$$\langle\pi_i(\mathbf{y}), \pi_i(\mathbf{y}')\rangle=0 \quad \text{for} \quad i=0, 1, \ldots, p-1,$$

especially, $\langle\pi_0(\mathbf{y}), \pi_0(\mathbf{y}')\rangle=0$. Thus $E\in\mathscr{E}_n(p)$.

(*i*) and (*ii*) imply $s_{np}(p)=|E^*|\leqq p\cdot|E|\leqq p\cdot s_n(p)$. Lemma 2 is now proved.

From Lemma 2 and (*E*) we obtain

(H) If $n=p^k m$ *and* $(p, m)=1$ *then* $s_n(p)=p^k$.

Lemma 3. *If l is a positive integer and p is a prime with $(p, l)=1$ then, for $\alpha=0, 1, 2, \ldots,$*

$$s_n(l\cdot p^{\alpha})\leqq s_n(p)\cdot s_n(l).$$

Proof. Let $n=p^k\cdot m$ where $k\in\{0,1, \ldots\}$ and $(p, m)=1$. We proceed by induction over k.

(*i*) $k=0$ means $(p, n)=1$. According to (**H**), $s_n(p)=1$. Let $E \in \mathscr{E}_n(lp^\alpha)$ with $|E|=s_n(lp^\alpha)$: then, by (**D**), $E \in \mathscr{E}_n(l)$. Therefore,

$$s_n(lp^\alpha)=|E| \leqq s_n(l)=s_n(p) \cdot s_n(l) .$$

(*ii*) Let $n^*=p^{k+1}m=p(p^k m)=pn$ and $E^* \in \mathscr{E}_{n^*}(lp^\alpha)$ with $|E^*|=s_{n^*}(lp^\alpha)$. If E^* does not contain an element of order p then $\mathbf{x}^l=\mathbf{u}$ for each $\mathbf{x} \in E^*$, thus $E^* \in \mathscr{E}_{np}(l)$ implying

$$s_{np}(lp^\alpha)=|E^*| \leqq s_{np}(l) \leqq s_{np}(p) \cdot s_{np}(l) .$$

If, however, E^* contains an element of order p we proceed in the same way as in the proof of Lemma 2: we construct a set $E \in \mathscr{E}_n(lp^\alpha)$ with $|E^*| \leqq p|E|$ and conclude

$$s_{np}(lp^\alpha)=|E^*| \leqq p|E| \leqq ps_n(lp^\alpha) .$$

In connection with Lemma 2 and Proposition (**C**), the induction hypothesis now yields

$$\begin{aligned} s_{np}(lp^\alpha) &\leqq ps_n(lp^\alpha) \leqq ps_n(p) \cdot s_n(l) = \\ &= s_{np}(p) \cdot s_n(l) \leqq s_{np}(p) \cdot s_{np}(l) \end{aligned}$$

which proves Lemma 3.

Theorem 1. *Let* $p_1, p_2, \ldots, p_r$ *be distinct primes, let* $l=p_1^{\alpha_1} p_2^{\alpha_2} \ldots p_r^{\alpha_r}$, $n=p_1^{k_1} p_2^{k_2} \ldots p_r^{k_r} \cdot m$, *where the* α_ρ *and* m *are positive integers, the* k_ρ *are non-negative integers, and* $(l, m)=1$. *Then*

$$s_n(l)=p_1^{k_1} p_2^{k_2} \ldots p_r^{k_r}.$$

Proof. By Lemma 3 and Proposition (**H**),

$$s_n(l) \leqq s_n(p_1) s_n(p_2) \ldots s_n(p_r)=p_1^{k_1} p_2^{k_2} \ldots p_r^{k_r};$$

by Propositions (**G**) and (**E**),

$$s_n(l) \geqq p_1^{k_1} p_2^{k_2} \ldots p_r^{k_r} \cdot s_m(l)=p_1^{k_1} p_2^{k_2} \ldots p_r^{k_r} .$$

3. Sets of partition vectors

In this section Γ denotes a transitive permutation group acting on the set $\{1, 2, \ldots, n\}$ and $\mathbf{Z}(\Gamma)$ denotes the vector set defined in Section 1. By reasons soon to become evident, each element $\mathbf{x} \in \mathbf{Z}(\Gamma)$ is called a *partition vector* of Γ. The *exponent* l of Γ is defined to be the least positive integer α such that $\gamma^\alpha = id$ for all $\gamma \in \Gamma$.

We shall show that $\mathbf{Z}(\Gamma)$ is a group and, by simple means of group theory (in particular, representation theory), we shall determine its order $z(\Gamma)=|\mathbf{Z}(\Gamma)|$.

Lemma 4. $\mathbf{Z}(\Gamma) \in \mathscr{E}_n(l)$.

Proof. (*i*) To each pair $\gamma \in \Gamma$, $\mathbf{x} \in \mathbf{Z}(\Gamma)$ there exists a complex number $a = a_\gamma(\mathbf{x})$ such that $\mathbf{P}_\gamma \mathbf{x} = a\mathbf{x}$. Thus

$$\mathbf{x} = \mathbf{P}_{\gamma^l}\mathbf{x} = \mathbf{P}_\gamma^l \mathbf{x} = a^l \mathbf{x}$$

from which we conclude that all numbers $a_\gamma(\mathbf{x})$ are l^{th} roots of unity. By the transitivity of Γ, there is, for each $i \in \{1, 2, \ldots, n\}$, some permutation $\gamma_i \in \Gamma$ with $\gamma_i(1) = i$. From $\mathbf{P}_{\gamma_i}\mathbf{x} = a_{\gamma_i}(\mathbf{x})\mathbf{x}$ now follows $x_i = a_{\gamma_i}(\mathbf{x})x_1 = a_{\gamma_i}(\mathbf{x})$, therefore $x_i^l = 1$, i.e. $\mathbf{x} \in \mathbf{U}_n(l)$.

(*ii*) For any two elements $\mathbf{x}, \mathbf{y} \in \mathbf{Z}(\Gamma)$ and any $\gamma \in \Gamma$, $\mathbf{P}_\gamma \mathbf{x} = a\mathbf{x}$ and $\mathbf{P}_\gamma \mathbf{y} = b\mathbf{y}$ where $a = a_\gamma(\mathbf{x})$, $b = a_\gamma(\mathbf{y})$. Thus

$$\mathbf{P}_\gamma(\mathbf{x} \otimes \mathbf{y}) = (\mathbf{P}_\gamma \mathbf{x}) \otimes (\mathbf{P}_\gamma \mathbf{y}) = (a\mathbf{x}) \otimes (b\mathbf{y}) = ab \cdot (\mathbf{x} \otimes \mathbf{y}),$$

i.e., $\mathbf{x} \otimes \mathbf{y} \in \mathbf{Z}(\Gamma)$.

(*iii*) Let $\mathbf{x}, \mathbf{y} \in \mathbf{Z}(\Gamma)$ where $\mathbf{x} \neq \mathbf{y}$; then there is an $i \neq 1$ with $x_i \neq y_i$. There exists a $\gamma \in \Gamma$ with $\gamma(1) = i$. If $\mathbf{P}_\gamma \mathbf{x} = a\mathbf{x}$, $\mathbf{P}_\gamma \mathbf{y} = b\mathbf{y}$ (where a, b are l^{th} roots of unity) then, because of $x_i \neq y_i$, also $a \neq b$, thus $a\bar{b} \neq 1$. Now,

$$\langle \mathbf{x}, \mathbf{y} \rangle = \langle \mathbf{P}_\gamma \mathbf{x}, \mathbf{P}_\gamma \mathbf{y} \rangle = \langle a\mathbf{x}, b\mathbf{y} \rangle = a\bar{b} \langle \mathbf{x}, \mathbf{y} \rangle$$

implies $\langle \mathbf{x}, \mathbf{y} \rangle = 0$.

Lemma 4 is now proved.

Note that, for an arbitrary $\mathbf{x} \in \mathbf{Z}(\Gamma)$ ($\mathbf{x}$ fixed), $\{(a_\gamma(\mathbf{x}))\}_{\gamma \in \Gamma}$ is an irreducible representation of Γ of degree 1, and for an arbitrary $\gamma \in \Gamma$ (γ fixed), $\{(a_\gamma(\mathbf{x}))\}_{\mathbf{x} \in \mathbf{Z}(\Gamma)}$ is an irreducible representation of $\mathbf{Z}(\Gamma)$ of degree 1.

We shall use the following notation:

$$\mathbf{Z}_d(\Gamma) = \mathbf{Z}(\Gamma) \cap \mathbf{U}_n(d) \quad \text{and} \quad z_d(\Gamma) = |\mathbf{Z}_d(\Gamma)|.$$

The elements of $\mathbf{Z}(\Gamma)$ are called the *partition vectors* of Γ: suppose that $\mathbf{x} \in \mathbf{Z}(\Gamma)$ has the order d and let ε denote a primitive d^{th} root of unity, then the sets $\mathbf{X}_k = \{i \mid x_i = \varepsilon^k\}$ ($k = 0, 1, \ldots, d-1$) from a partition of $\{1, 2, \ldots, n\}$ where, by Proposition (**F**), $d \cdot |\mathbf{X}_k| = n$ for $k = 0, 1, \ldots, d-1$. If $\gamma \in \Gamma$ has the property that, for some $i \in \mathbf{X}_k$, the image $\gamma(i) \in \mathbf{X}_{k'+h}$, then $\mathbf{P}_\gamma \mathbf{x} = \varepsilon^h \mathbf{x}$ and, consequently, $\gamma(\mathbf{X}_k) = \mathbf{X}_{k+h}$ ($k = 0, 1, \ldots, d-1$; $k+h$ to be reduced mod d). Thus the sets $\mathbf{X}_0, \mathbf{X}_1, \ldots, \mathbf{X}_{d-1}$ present a partition of $\{1, 2, \ldots, n\}$ into systems of imprimitivity of Γ which are cyclically permuted by the permutations of Γ. With $d = 1$ or $d = n$ we obtain the trivial partitions. It is clear that, conversely, corresponding to each partition into systems of imprimitivity which are cyclically permuted by Γ, there is a partition vector generating this particular partition.

As a simple consequence, we have

Lemma 5. *If the transitive group Γ is primitive and n not a prime then* $z(\Gamma) = 1$.

If $n > 2$ then there are exactly $z_2(\Gamma) - 1$ distinct ways of partitioning the set $\{1, 2, \ldots, n\}$ into two systems of imprimitivity. Furthermore, since, for an arbitrary transitive group Γ and an arbitrary prime p dividing the order of Γ, any partitioning into p systems of imprimitivity with the property that these systems are cyclically permuted under Γ is generated by an intransitive normal subgroup of Γ of index p (and conversely), we have

Lemma 6. *Let Γ be a transitive permutation group, let p be a prime and let $v_p(\Gamma)$ denote the number of intransitive normal subgroups of Γ which have the index p. Then $v_p(\Gamma)$ and $z_p(\Gamma)$ are connected by the relation*

$$z_p(\Gamma)-1=(p-1)\,v_p(\Gamma)\,.$$

Proof. (*i*) For $\mathbf{x}\in\mathbf{Z}_p(\Gamma)$, $\mathbf{x}\neq\mathbf{u}$ (if there is such an $\mathbf{x}$), let $\Gamma(\mathbf{x})=\{\gamma\in\Gamma\mid\mathbf{P}_\gamma\mathbf{x}=\mathbf{x}\}$; since Γ is transitive, $\Gamma(\mathbf{x})\neq\Gamma$. Let ε denote an arbitrary primitive p^{th} root of unity and put $h(\gamma)=\varepsilon^k$ if $\mathbf{P}_\gamma\mathbf{x}=\varepsilon^k\mathbf{x}$. Then h is a homomorphism of Γ onto the cyclic group of order p, the kernel of h being $\Gamma(\mathbf{x})$. It follows that $\Gamma(\mathbf{x})$ is a normal subgroup of Γ of index p. Clearly, $\Gamma(\mathbf{x})$ is intransitive.

Let $\mathbf{X}_k=\{i\mid x_i=\varepsilon^k\}$ $(k=0,1,\ldots,p-1)$. By Proposition (**F**) (see also the remark preceding Lemma 5. $|\mathbf{X}_0|=|\mathbf{X}_1|=\ldots=|\mathbf{X}_{p-1}|=n/p$. Clearly, for $\gamma\in\Gamma(\mathbf{x})$ and $k=0,1,\ldots p-1$, $\gamma(\mathbf{X}_k)=\mathbf{X}_k$. In fact, the sets $\mathbf{X}_k$ are the orbits of $\Gamma(\mathbf{x})$: to prove this, let $i,j\in X_k$; since Γ is transitive there is a $\gamma\in\Gamma$ with $\gamma(i)=j$ implying $P_\gamma\mathbf{x}=\mathbf{x}$, thus $\gamma\in\Gamma(\mathbf{x})$.

Next we show that

(*) $\Gamma(\mathbf{y})=\Gamma(\mathbf{x})$ *if and only if* $\mathbf{y}=\mathbf{x}^l$, $l\in\{1,2,\ldots,p-1\}$.

(*a*) Clearly, $\mathbf{x}^l\in Z_p(\Gamma)$, $\mathbf{x}^l\neq\mathbf{u}$, $\Gamma(\mathbf{x}^l)=\Gamma(\mathbf{x})$.

(*b*) Suppose that $\Gamma(\mathbf{y})=\Gamma(\mathbf{x})$ where $\mathbf{x},\mathbf{y}\in\mathbf{Z}_p(\Gamma)$, $\mathbf{x}\neq\mathbf{u}$, $\mathbf{y}\neq\mathbf{u}$, $\mathbf{y}\neq\mathbf{x}^l$ for $l=1,2,\ldots,p-1$. Then $\mathbf{x}^l\otimes\mathbf{y}\neq\mathbf{u}$ for $l=0,1,\ldots,p-1$, therefore

$$\text{(2)}\qquad \langle\mathbf{x}^l\otimes\mathbf{y},\mathbf{u}\rangle=\sum_{i=1}^{n}x_i^l y_i=0,\quad l=0,1,\ldots,p-1.$$

Since the sets X_k are orbits of $\Gamma(\mathbf{y})=\Gamma(\mathbf{x})$, if $i,j\in\mathbf{X}_k$ then $y_i=y_j=\varepsilon^{\alpha_k}$ with some integer $\alpha_k\in\{0,1,\ldots,p-1\}$ $((\alpha_0,\alpha_1,\ldots,\alpha_{p-1})$ is a permutation of $(0,1,\ldots,p-1))$, and we obtain from 2

$$\sum_{i=1}^{n}x_i^l y_i=\sum_{k=0}^{p-1}\sum_{j\in\mathbf{X}_k}\varepsilon^{kl}\cdot\varepsilon^{\alpha_k}=(n/p)\sum_{k=0}^{p-1}\varepsilon^{kl}\varepsilon^{\alpha_k}=0\,.$$

$$l=0,1,\ldots,p-1\,,$$

i.e., $\mathbf{M}_p(\varepsilon)\cdot\mathbf{w}=\mathbf{0}$ where $\mathbf{w}=(\varepsilon^{\alpha_0},\varepsilon^{\alpha_1},\ldots,\varepsilon^{\alpha_{p-1}})^{\mathrm{T}}$, contradicting Lemma 1.

(*) is now proved.

From (*) it follows that the above construction of groups $\Gamma(\mathbf{x})$, $\mathbf{x}\in\mathbf{Z}_p(\Gamma)$, yields $(z_p(\Gamma)-1)/(p-1)$ distinct intransitive normal subgroups of Γ of index p, i.e.:

$$v_p(\Gamma)\geqq(z_p(\Gamma)-1)/(p-1)\,.$$

(*ii*) Let Γ' be an intransitive normal subgroup of Γ of index p. Then the quotient group Γ/Γ' is cyclic of order p, the group Γ' has p orbits $\mathbf{T}_0, \mathbf{T}_1, \ldots, \mathbf{T}_{p-1}$ partitioning the set $\{1, 2, \ldots, n\}$ into p systems of imprimitivity of Γ which are cyclically permuted by Γ. We may assume that the orbits are labelled so that $1 \in \mathbf{T}_0$ and that $\gamma(\mathbf{T}_0) = \mathbf{T}_i$ implies $\gamma(\mathbf{T}_k) = \mathbf{T}_{k+i}$ ($\gamma \in \Gamma$; $k = 0, 1, \ldots, p-1$; $k+i$ to be reduced mod p). Let ε be an arbitrary primitive p^{th} root of unity and define the vector $\mathbf{x} = (x_1, x_2, \ldots, x_n)^{\mathsf{T}}$ in the following way: $x_i = \varepsilon^k$ if $i \in \mathbf{T}_k$. Then $\mathbf{x} \in \mathbf{Z}_p(\Gamma)$, $\mathbf{x} \neq \mathbf{u}$, and $\Gamma' = \Gamma(\mathbf{x})$.

As there are exactly $p-1$ possible choices for ε, we obtain at least $(p-1)\, v_p(\Gamma)$ distinct vectors $\mathbf{x} \in \mathbf{Z}_p(\Gamma)$, $\mathbf{x} \neq \mathbf{u}$, i.e.:

$$z_p(\Gamma) - 1 \geqq (p-1)\, v_p(\Gamma)\,.$$

Lemma 6 is now proved.

Let $\mathbf{x} \in \mathbf{Z}(\Gamma)$. As we have seen above, $\{(a_\gamma(\mathbf{x}))\}_{\gamma \in \Gamma}$ is a representation of Γ of degree 1 which is contained in the matrix representation $\mathscr{R}^P := \{\mathbf{P}_\gamma\}_{\gamma \in \Gamma}$ of Γ as an irreducible component.

Let $\mathbf{x}, \mathbf{y} \in \mathbf{Z}(\Gamma)$, then, for all $\gamma \in \Gamma$, $\mathbf{P}_\gamma \mathbf{x} = a_\gamma(\mathbf{x}) \cdot \mathbf{x}$ and $\mathbf{P}_\gamma \mathbf{y} = a_\gamma(\mathbf{y}) \cdot \mathbf{y}$. Suppose that, for all $\gamma \in \Gamma$, $a_\gamma(\mathbf{x}) = a_\gamma(\mathbf{y})$; put $a_\gamma(\mathbf{x}) = a_\gamma$. Then, for each $i \in \{1, 2, \ldots, n\}$, there is a $\gamma_i \in \Gamma$ with $\gamma_i(1) = i$, and $\mathbf{P}_{\gamma_i} \mathbf{x} = a_{\gamma_i}\, \mathbf{x}$, $\mathbf{P}_{\gamma_i} \mathbf{y} = a_\gamma\, \mathbf{y}$ ($i = 1, 2, \ldots, n$) imply

$$x_i = a_{\gamma_i} x_1 = a_{\gamma_i} = a_{\gamma_i} y_1 = y_i\,,$$

i.e. $\mathbf{x} = \mathbf{y}$. This means that the representations of Γ (of degree 1) generated by the partition vectors are pairwise non-equivalent.

Conversely, let $\mathscr{R} = \{(R(\gamma))\}_{\gamma \in \Gamma}$ be any representation of Γ of degree 1 which is contained in the matrix representation $\mathscr{R}^P = \{\mathbf{P}_\gamma\}_{\gamma \in \Gamma}$ as an irreducible component: then there is a vector $\mathbf{x} = (x_1, x_2, \ldots, x_n)^{\mathsf{T}} \neq \mathbf{0}$ such that $\mathbf{P}_\gamma \mathbf{x} = R(\gamma) \cdot \mathbf{x}$, and with $\gamma_i \in \Gamma$ satisfying $\gamma_i(1) = i$ ($i = 1, 2, \ldots, n$) we obtain $x_i = R(\gamma_i) \cdot x_1$ which (having in view the fact that the $R(\gamma)$ are roots of unity) implies $|x_1| = |x_2| = \ldots = |x_n| \neq 0$: assuming $x_1 = 1$ we obtain $\mathbf{x} \in \mathbf{Z}(\Gamma)$.

This means that the representation of Γ by permutation matrices $\mathbf{P}_\gamma$ contains exactly $z(\Gamma)$ representations of degree 1 *as irreducible components* (*which are pairwise non-equivalent*).

Before proceeding, we need some more notations. Let $\Gamma_i = \{\gamma \in \Gamma \mid \gamma(i) = i\}$ denote the ith stabilizer subgroup of Γ and let $\Gamma^* = \langle \Gamma_1, \Gamma_2, \ldots, \Gamma_n \rangle$ be the subgroup of Γ generated by the stabilizer subgroups. Let Γ' denote the commutator subgroup of Γ. It is well known that Γ^* and Γ' are normal subgroups of Γ, and so is $\Gamma^* \cdot \Gamma'$.

By standard techniques of representation theory we shall now prove

Theorem 2. $z(\Gamma) = |\Gamma : (\Gamma^* \cdot \Gamma')|$.

Remark 1. If only d^{th} roots of unity are taken into consideration, then we obtain

$$z_d(\Gamma) = |\Gamma : (\Gamma^* \cdot \Gamma' \cdot \Gamma_d)|$$

where $\Gamma_d = \langle \{\gamma^d \mid \gamma \in \Gamma\} \rangle$.

Proof of Theorem 2. Note that the quotient group $\Gamma/(\Gamma^* \cdot \Gamma')$ is abelian, thus the number of its irreducible representations equals its order $|\Gamma:(\Gamma^* \cdot \Gamma')|$. We shall prove the theorem by establishing a (1,1)-correspondence between the $z(\Gamma)$ irreducible representations of Γ of degree 1 which are components of the representation $\mathscr{R}^P$ of Γ by permutation matrices and the irreducible components of $\Gamma/(\Gamma^* \cdot \Gamma')$.

(*i*) Let $\mathscr{R}_\mu = \{R_\mu(\gamma)\}_{\gamma \in \Gamma}$ $(\mu = 1, 2, \ldots, m)$ denote the irreducible components of $\mathscr{R}^P$, where $\mathscr{R}_\mu$ has degree 1 for $\mu = 1, 2, \ldots, t$ and degree >1 for $\mu = t+1, t+2, \ldots, m$; as we have seen above, $\mathscr{R}_1, \mathscr{R}_2, \ldots, \mathscr{R}_t$ are pairwise non-equivalent. We have

$$\mathbf{P}_\gamma \sim \mathbf{R}_1(\gamma) \dotplus \mathbf{R}_2(\gamma) \dotplus \ldots \dotplus \mathbf{R}_t(\gamma) \dotplus \mathbf{R}_{t+1}(\gamma) \dotplus \ldots \dotplus \mathbf{R}_m(\gamma).$$

Clearly, if $\mathbf{x} \in \mathbf{Z}(\Gamma)$ then $\mathbf{P}_\gamma \mathbf{x} = \mathbf{x}$ for all $\gamma \in \Gamma_i$; this, in particular, implies that, for $\tau = 1, 2, \ldots, t$, each stabilizer subgroup Γ_i is contained in the kernel N_τ of the homomorphism $\mathscr{R}_\tau$, and so is $\Gamma^* = \langle \Gamma_1, \Gamma_2, \ldots, \Gamma_n \rangle$. Since, by a well-known theorem, the quotient group Γ/N_τ is abelian, also Γ', and therefore also $\Gamma^* \cdot \Gamma'$, are contained in $N_\tau (\tau = 1, 2, \ldots, t)$. Now define, for $\tau = 1, 2, \ldots, t$, representations $\tilde{\mathscr{R}}_\tau$ of $\Gamma/(\Gamma^* \cdot \Gamma')$ by putting

$$\tilde{\mathbf{R}}_\tau(\gamma \cdot (\Gamma^* \cdot \Gamma')) = \mathbf{R}_\tau(\gamma).$$

Clearly, $\tilde{\mathscr{R}}_\tau$ has degree 1.

(*ii*) Let $\tilde{\mathscr{R}}$ be an irreducible representation of $\Gamma/(\Gamma^* \cdot \Gamma')$. Since $\Gamma/(\Gamma^* \cdot \Gamma')$ is abelian, $\tilde{\mathscr{R}}$ has degree 1, and the mapping $\mathscr{R}$ of Γ defined by

$$R(\gamma) = \tilde{R}(\gamma \cdot (\Gamma^* \cdot \Gamma'))$$

is a representation of Γ of degree 1.

The character χ of $\mathscr{R}$ satisfies $\chi(\gamma) = 1$ if $\gamma \in \Gamma^* \cdot \Gamma'$; for the character χ^P of the representation $\mathscr{R}^P = \{\mathbf{P}_\gamma\}_{\gamma \in \Gamma}$, clearly, $\chi^P(\gamma) = 0$ if $\gamma \notin \Gamma^* \cdot \Gamma'$; consequently,

$$\langle \chi, \chi^P \rangle := \frac{1}{|\Gamma|} \sum_{\gamma \in \Gamma} \chi(\gamma)\, \overline{\chi}^P(\gamma) = \frac{1}{|\Gamma|} \sum_{\gamma \in \Gamma^* \cdot \Gamma'} \overline{\chi^P}(\gamma) =$$

$$= \text{number of orbits of } \Gamma = 1;$$

$\langle \chi, \chi^P \rangle = 1$ means that $\mathscr{R}$ is contained in the representation of Γ by permutation matrices as an irreducible component with multiplicity 1.

Theorem 2 is now proved.

Remark 2. In fact, we have proved a bit more, namely, *$Z(\Gamma)$ is isomorphic to $\Gamma/(\Gamma^* \Gamma')$.*

Theorem 2′. $Z(\Gamma) \cong \Gamma/(\Gamma^* \cdot \Gamma')$.

4. Simple eigenvalues of transitive graphs

Let **G** be a transitive graph and let **x** be an eigenvector of **G** belonging to a simple eigenvalue. As we have seen above, **x** is a common eigenvector of all permutation matrices $\mathbf{P}_\gamma$, $\gamma \in$ **aut G**, i.e.: there is, for each $\gamma \in$ **aut G,** a (complex) number (namely, a root of unity) $a_\gamma(\mathbf{x})$ such that $\mathbf{P}_\gamma \mathbf{x} = a_\gamma(\mathbf{x}) \cdot \mathbf{x}$. Since $|x_1| = |x_2| = \ldots = |x_n| \neq 0$, we may and shall always suppose $x_1 = 1$. With this convention, $\mathbf{x} \in \mathbf{Z}(\textbf{aut G})$; therefore, the number $\sigma(\mathbf{G})$ of simple eigenvalues of **G** cannot exceed the number $z(\textbf{aut G})$ of partition vectors of **aut G.**

Thus we have proved

Theorem 3. $\sigma(\mathbf{G}) \leqq z(\textbf{aut G})$.

Theorem 3 is a simple consequence of the fact that $z(\textbf{aut G})$ equals the number of representations of aut **G** which are contained in $\mathscr{R}^P$ as irreducible components of degree 1.

If, in particular, **G** is undirected then **A** is symmetric, the eigen values are real, and the eigenvectors **x** can also be taken to be real. Then, for an eigenvector **x** belonging to a simple eigenvalue, the $a_\gamma(\mathbf{x})$ are real roots of unity, i.e., $a_\gamma(\mathbf{x}) = \pm 1$, and we conclude $\mathbf{x} \in Z_2(\textbf{aut G})$. Since $Z_2(\textbf{aut G}) \in \mathscr{E}_n(2)$, $z_2(\textbf{aut G}) \leqq s_n(2)$, and making use of Theorem 1 we obtain

Theorem 4. *Let* **G** *be an undirected transitive graph with n vertices where $n = 2^q k$, k being an odd integer. Then*

$$\sigma(\mathbf{G}) \leqq z_2(\textbf{aut G}) \leqq 2^q,$$

i.e.: **G** *cannot have more than 2^q simple eigenvalues.*

5. The bound of Theorem 4 is sharp

Theorem 5. *Let n be a given positive integer and put $n = 2^q \cdot k$ where k is an odd integer. There is a transitive undirected graph without loops which has n vertices and $s_n(2) = 2^q$ simple eigenvalues.*

First we prove

Lemma 7. *Let* **A** *be the adjacency matrix of a transitive undirected graph with n vertices and exactly s simple eigenvalues. Then there is a positive integer t such that the graph* **G′** *with adjacency matrix*

$$\mathbf{A}' = \begin{bmatrix} t\mathbf{A} & \mathbf{I} \\ \mathbf{I} & t\mathbf{A} \end{bmatrix}$$

has exactly 2s simple eigenvalues. **G′** *is undirected, transitive, and has 2n vertices.*

Proof. (*i*) Let $\lambda_1, \lambda_2, \ldots, \lambda_m$ be the distinct eigenvalues of $\mathbf{G}$, where $\lambda_1, \lambda_2, \ldots, \lambda_s$ are the s simple eigenvalues. Let t be any positive integer such that $t(\lambda_i - \lambda_j) \neq 2$ for $i, j \in \{1, 2, \ldots, m\}$. If $\mathbf{x}$ is an eigenvector of $\mathbf{G}$ belonging to the eigenvalue λ_i having multiplicity m_i then $\mathbf{x}' = (\mathbf{x}^T, \mathbf{x}^T)^T$ and $\mathbf{y}' = (\mathbf{x}^T, -\mathbf{x}^T)^T$ are eigenvectors of $\mathbf{G}'$ belonging to the eigenvalues $t\lambda_i + 1, t\lambda_i - 1$, respectively, both of which have multiplicity m_i. Thus $\mathbf{G}'$ has exactly $2s$ simple eigenvalues, namely $t\lambda_1 \pm 1, t\lambda_2 \pm 1, \ldots, t\lambda_s \pm 1$.

(*ii*) Clearly, $\mathbf{G}'$ is undirected and has $2n$ vertices. Since $\mathbf{G}$ is transitive and $\mathbf{G}'$ admits the permutation $(1, n+1)\,(2, n+2), \ldots, (n, 2n)$, the graph $\mathbf{G}'$ is transitive, too.

Theorem 5 can now easily be proved. Let $\mathbf{G}_1^0$ denote the graph with exactly one vertex and no edge, and let, for any odd integer $k \geq 3$, $\mathbf{G}_k^0$ be an odd circuit of length k; clearly, the graphs $\mathbf{G}_k^0$ $(k = 1, 3, 5, \ldots)$ have no loops, they are transitive, have exactly $k = 2^0 \cdot k$ vertices and exactly one simple eigenvalue. Starting from $\mathbf{G}_k^0$, Lemma 7 now enables a sequence of undirected transitive graphs $\mathbf{G}_k^q$ $(q = 0, 1, 2, \ldots)$ without loops, with exactly $2^q \cdot k$ vertices and exactly 2^q simple eigenvalues, to be constructed.

This proves Theorem 5.

Remark 3. For $k=1$ we may choose $t=2$ in each step of the construction; the resulting graphs $\mathbf{G}_1^q$ (see Fig. 1) have the following properties:

(*i*) $\mathbf{G}_1^q$ has 2^q vertices;
(*ii*) $\mathbf{G}_1^q$ is regular of degree $r_q = 2^q - 1$;
(*iii*) $\mathbf{G}_1^q$ is bipartite;
(*iv*) by replacing multiple edges by simple ones, $\mathbf{G}_1^q$ is transformed into the q-dimensional cube graph;
(*v*) all non-trivial automorphisms are involutions, i.e., **aut** $\mathbf{G}_1^q$ has the exponent 2;
(*vi*) all eigenvalues of $\mathbf{G}_1^q$ are simple;
(*vii*) the eigenvalues form the equidistant spectrum

$$[-r_q, -r_q+2, -r_q+4, \ldots, r_q-2, r_q].$$

From Theorem 2 and Remark 1 we deduce

Lemma 8. *Let* $\mathbf{G}$ *be an undirected transitive graph with* n *vertices. Then* $z_2(\mathbf{aut}\ \mathbf{G}) = n$ *if and only if all nontrivial automorphisms are involutions, i.e., if and only if* $\exp \mathbf{aut}\ \mathbf{G} = 2$.

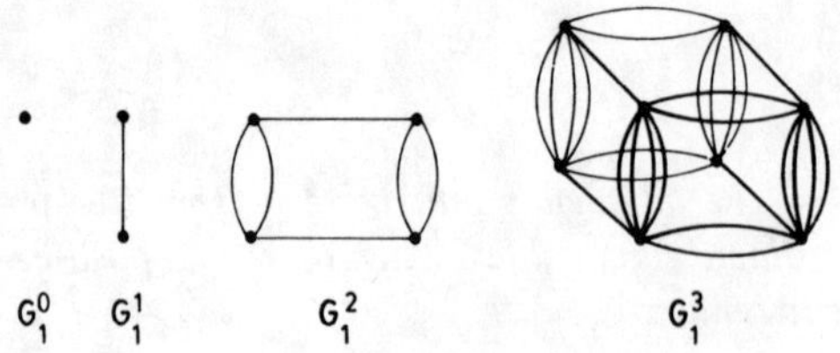

Fig. 1

6. Partition vectors, eigenvectors, and totally transitive graphs

Theorem 6. *Let* **G** *be a transitive (directed or undirected) graph with n vertices which is regular of degree r, and let Γ be a transitive subgroup of* **aut G**. *Then each vector* $\mathbf{x} \in \mathbf{Z}(\Gamma)$ *is an eigenvector of* **G**, *and if* **x** *has the order d then the corresponding eigenvalue has the form*

$$\lambda = r_0 + r_1 \varepsilon + r_2 \varepsilon^2 + \ldots + r_{d-1} \varepsilon^{d-1},$$

where $r_0, r_1, \ldots, r_{d-1}$ are non-negative integers with $r_0 + r_1 + \ldots + r_{d-1} = r$ and ε is a primitive d^{th} root of unity.

Proof. (*i*) Let $\mathbf{x} \in \mathbf{Z}(\Gamma)$ have order d and let ε be a primitive d^{th} root of unity. **x** induces a partitioning of the vertex set $\{1, 2, \ldots, n\}$ of **G** into sets $\mathbf{X}_k = \{i \mid x_i = \varepsilon^k\}$ $(k = 0, 1, \ldots, d-1)$ of equal cardinality $|\mathbf{X}_k| = n/d$.

Let $\mathbf{G}_{ik}$ denote the subgraph of **G** which consists of the vertex set $\mathbf{X}_i \cup \mathbf{X}_k$ and of the set of all those directed edges which issue from a vertex of $\mathbf{X}_i$ and terminate in a vertex of $\mathbf{X}_k$.[2]

(*ii*) Let $\gamma \in \Gamma$ and $\mathbf{P}_\gamma \mathbf{x} = \varepsilon^m \mathbf{x}$: then $\gamma(\mathbf{X}_k) = \mathbf{X}_{k+m}$ and γ is an isomorphism from $\mathbf{G}_{ik}$ to $\mathbf{G}_{i+m,k+m}$ (subscripts to be reduced mod d). Since Γ is transitive we conclude that all graphs $\mathbf{G}_{i+m,k+m}$ $(m = 0, 1, \ldots, d-1)$ are isomorphic to $\mathbf{G}_{ik}$.

(*iii*) Let $a, b \in \mathbf{X}_i$ and let $r(a)$, $r(b)$ be the numbers of directed edges issuing from a or b, respectively, and terminating in vertices of $\mathbf{X}_k$. There is a permutation $\gamma \in \Gamma$ with $\gamma(a) = b$; this permutation has the properties $\gamma(\mathbf{X}_j) = \mathbf{X}_j$ for $j = 0, 1, 2, \ldots, d-1$, and γ restricted to the set $\mathbf{X}_i \cup \mathbf{X}_k$ is an element of **aut** $\mathbf{G}_{ik}$, thus $r(a) = r(b)$; let r_{ik} denote the common value of $r(a)$ and $r(b)$: then r_{ik} is the number of directed edges issuing from any vertex of $\mathbf{X}_i$ and terminating in vertices of $\mathbf{X}_k$.

It follows from (*ii*) that the matrix (r_{ij}) is a circulant matrix.

(*iv*) Put $r_i = r_{0i}$ and $\lambda = r_0 + r_1 \varepsilon + \ldots + r_{d-1} \varepsilon^{d-1}$. We shall show that **x** is an eigenvector of **G** belonging to the eigenvalue λ.

For an arbitrary $k \in \{0, 1, \ldots, d-1\}$ and an arbitrary $i \in \mathbf{X}_k$,

$$\sum_{j=1}^{n} a_{ij} x_j = \sum_{m=0}^{d-1} \sum_{j \in \mathbf{X}_m} a_{ij} x_j = \sum_{m=0}^{d-1} r_{km} \varepsilon^m = \sum_{m=0}^{d-1} r_{0,m-k} \varepsilon^m =$$

$$= \varepsilon^k \cdot \sum_{m=0}^{d-1} r_{m-k} \varepsilon^{m-k} = \varepsilon^k \cdot \sum_{m=0}^{d-1} r_m \varepsilon^m = x_i \cdot \lambda .$$

Theorem 6 is now proved.

Remark 4. If **G** is an undirected transitive graph then **Z(aut G)** $=$ $\mathbf{Z}_2$**(aut G)**; thus z(**aut G**) $= z_2$(**aut G**). Clearly, for any transitive subgroup Γ of **aut G**, z(**aut G**) $\leq z(\Gamma)$; it

[2] If **G** is undirected then, as usual, each undirected edge is considered as a pair of antiparallel directed edges: the resulting directed graph **G**′ has the same adjacency matrix and also the same automorphism group as **G**, so no distinction will be made between **G** and **G**′.

does happen that $z(\mathbf{aut\ G})<z(\Gamma)$. If, e.g., **G** is an undirected circuit of length 4 then **aut G** is the dihedron group of order 8, thus $z(\mathbf{aut\ G})=z_2(\mathbf{aut\ G})=2$. If we choose for Γ the cyclic group of order 4 we obtain $z(\Gamma)=z_4(\Gamma)=4$, and if we choose Klein's group $\{(1), (12)(34), (13)(24), (14)(23)\}$ we have $z(\Gamma)=z_2(\Gamma)=4$.

Remark 5. The eigenvalues λ to which the vectors of $\mathbf{Z}_2(\Gamma)$ belong all have the form $\lambda=\rho-(r-\rho)=2\rho-r$ ($\rho\in\{0, 1, \ldots, r\}$), i.e., they are rational. Thus we have proved.

Theorem 7. *Let* **G** *be a transitive graph and let* Γ *be a transitive subgroup of* **aut G**. *Then* $z_2(\Gamma)$ *is a lower bound for the number of rational eigenvalues of* **G**, *counting their multiplicities.*

We now proceed to the investigation of totally transitive graphs:

A graph **G** is called *totally transitive* if **G** is transitive and if, for any two (directed) edges e going from a to b and e' going from a' to b' there is an automorphism γ which simultaneously maps a onto a' and b onto b' (and, therefore, e onto e').

A well-known theorem in N. BIGGS [1] (see also J. H. SMITH [6]) states that *if* **G** *is a connected undirected totally transitive graph, then* **G** *is regular of some degree r, and if* **G** *is non-bipartite then r is the only simple eigenvalue of* **G**, *and if* **G** *is bipartite then r and* $-r$ *are the only simple eigenvalues of* **G**. We shall now generalize this result for the case of an arbitrary connected totally transitive graph.

We need one more definition.

Definition 2. A (directed) graph **G** is called *cyclically d-partite* ($d\in\{1, 2, \ldots\}$) if it is strongly connected and if the vertex set **V** of **G** can be partitioned into d sets $\mathbf{X}_0, \mathbf{X}_1, \ldots, \mathbf{X}_{d-1}$ such that, for $i=0, 1, \ldots, d-1$, each edge issuing from a vertex of $\mathbf{X}_i$ terminates in a vertex of $\mathbf{X}_{i+1}$ (subscripts to be reduced mod d).

Remark 6. Trivially, each strongly connected graph is cyclically 1-partite.

Remark 7. Clearly, if **G** is cyclically k-partite and $d\,|\,k$, then **G** is also cyclically d-partite.

Lemma 9. *Let* $g, h\in\{1, 2, \ldots\}$, $(g, h)=1$, *and let* **G** *be a graph which is simultaneously cyclically g-partite and h-partite. Then* **G** *is also cyclically gh-partite.*

Proof. By hypothesis, there exist cyclic partitions $\{\mathbf{X}_0, \mathbf{X}_1, \ldots, \mathbf{X}_{g-1}\}$ and $\{\mathbf{Y}_0, \mathbf{Y}_1, \ldots, \mathbf{Y}_{h-1}\}$ of the vertex set **V** of **G**; consider the system of sets $\{\mathbf{Z}_i^j\,|\,i=0, 1, \ldots, g-1; j=0, 1, \ldots, h-1\}$ where $\mathbf{Z}_i^j=\mathbf{X}_i\cap\mathbf{Y}_j$. Obviously, all directed edges issuing from $\mathbf{Z}_i^j$ terminate in $\mathbf{Z}_{i+1}^{j+1}$ where the subscript or superscript is to be reduced mod g or mod h, respectively. Because of $(g, h)=1$, the $\mathbf{Z}_i^j$ form a single cycle of length $g\cdot h$ if arranged in the following way; $\mathbf{Z}_0^0, \mathbf{Z}_1^1, \ldots, \mathbf{Z}_i^j, \mathbf{Z}_{i+1}^{j+1}, \ldots, \mathbf{Z}_{q-1}^{h-1}$ (subscript mod g, superscript mod h). Since **G** is strongly connected, $\mathbf{Z}_i^j\neq\emptyset$ for $i=0, 1, \ldots, g-1; j=0, 1, \ldots, h-1$: thus the system $\{Z_i^j\}$ is a partition of **V** and, therefore, **G** is cyclically gh-partite.

Lemma 10. *Let the graph* **G** *be cyclically h-partite* ($h \in \{1, 2, \ldots\}$) *and let k be the greatest among all integers d for which* **G** *is cyclically d-partite.*[3] *Then* $h \mid k$.

Proof. Suppose the contrary. Then there are a prime p and non-negative integers α, β such that $h = p^\alpha h'$, $k = p^\beta k'$, $(h', p) = (k', p) = 1$, and $\alpha > \beta$. According to Remark 7, **G** is simultaneously cyclically p^α-partite and cyclically k'-partite, where $(p^\alpha, k') = 1$. Then, by Lemma 9, **G** is also cyclically $p^\alpha k'$-partite where $p^\alpha k' > k$ — contradicting the hypothesis that k has been chosen greatest possible.

The following lemma is a specialization of a well-known general theorem on non-negative square matrices (see, e.g., [7], p. 212 or [8], vol. II).

Lemma 11. *Each cyclically d-partite graph which is regular of degree r has* $r, r\varepsilon, r\varepsilon^2, \ldots, r\varepsilon^{d-1}$ (ε *being a primitive* d^{th} *root of unity) as simple eigenvalues.*

Remark 8. A. L. Dulmage and N. S. Mendelsohn [2] showed that the characteristic polynomial $\det(\lambda \mathbf{I} - \mathbf{A})$ of a cyclically d-partite graph **G** with adjacency matrix **A** has the form $\lambda^m \cdot Q(\lambda^d)$ where Q is a polynomial.

Theorem 8. *Let* **G** *be a connected totally transitive graph which is regular of degree r, let k be the greatest among all numbers d for which* **G** *is cyclically d-partite (possibly* $k = 1$), *and let* ε *denote a primitive* k^{th} *root of unity. Then*

$$\sigma(\mathbf{G}) = z(\mathbf{aut\ G}) = k,$$

and the simple eigenvalues of **G** *are precisely the numbers*

$$r, r\varepsilon, r\varepsilon^2, \ldots, r\varepsilon^{k-1}. \tag{3}$$

Proof. Note that a regular connected graph is also strongly connected.

(*i*) By Lemma 11, all of the numbers (3) are simple eigenvalues of **G**. Therefore, $k \leqq \sigma(\mathbf{G})$.

(*ii*) Let λ be a simple eigenvalue of **G** and let $\mathbf{x}$ (with $x_1 = 1$) be the eigenvector belonging to λ: then $\mathbf{x} \in \mathbf{Z}(\mathbf{aut\ G})$ (see Section 4). If $\mathbf{x}$ has order 1 then $\mathbf{x} = \mathbf{u}$ and $\lambda = r$. Suppose that $\mathbf{x}$ has order $d > 1$ and put, for $h = 0, 1, \ldots, d-1$, $\mathbf{X}_h = \{i \mid x_i = \delta^h\}$ where δ is a primitive d^{th} root of unity. Since **G** is connected there is a directed edge e issuing from a vertex $a \in \mathbf{X}_0$ and terminating in a vertex $b \in \mathbf{X}_j$ where $j \neq 0$. If $a' \in X_h$ and e' is any directed edge issuing from a' and terminating in a vertex b', then there is a permutation $\gamma \in \mathbf{aut\ G}$ mapping e onto e', i.e. γ satisfies $\gamma(a) = a'$, $\gamma(b) = b'$. Since $x_a = 1$, $x_{a'} = \delta^h$, $x_b = \delta^j$, we have $\mathbf{P}_\gamma \mathbf{x} = \delta^h \mathbf{x}$ and, therefore, $x_{b'} = \delta^h x_b = \delta^{h+j}$ implying $b' \in \mathbf{X}_{h+j}$ (subscripts to be reduced mod d). This means that, for $h = 0, 1, \ldots, d-1$, all directed edges issuing from a vertex of $\mathbf{X}_h$ terminate in vertices of $\mathbf{X}_{h+j}$. Necessarily, $(j, d) = 1$ for otherwise **G** would

[3] There is such a k because **G** is strongly connected.

not be connected. It follows that the sets $\mathbf{X}_h$ arranged in the order $\mathbf{X}_0, \mathbf{X}_j, \mathbf{X}_{2j}, \ldots, \mathbf{X}_{d-j}$ form a cyclic d-partition of $\mathbf{V}$. For λ we obtain

$$\lambda = \lambda x_a = \sum_{i \in \mathbf{X}_j} a_{ai} x_i = r \cdot \delta^j;$$

by virtue of Lemma 10, $d \mid k$, thus δ is a kth root of unity: this proves that in every case λ is one of the numbers (3).

(*iii*) Combining the results of (*i*) and (*ii*) we see that λ is a simple eigenvalue if and only if it is one of the numbers (3).

If we repeat the considerations of (*ii*) starting with any vector $\mathbf{x} \in \mathbf{Z}(\mathbf{aut\ G})$ we find that $\mathbf{x}$ is an eigenvector of $\mathbf{G}$ (see Theorem 6) which belongs to an eigenvalue of the form $r \cdot \varepsilon^h$, i.e., to a simple eigenvalue, and we conclude that $z(\mathbf{aut\ G}) \leqq k$. By Theorem 3, $\sigma(\mathbf{G}) \leqq z(\mathbf{aut\ G})$, and as a result of (*i*), $k \leqq \sigma(\mathbf{G})$. Combining these inequalities we find

$$\sigma(\mathbf{G}) = z(\mathbf{aut\ G}) = k\,.$$

Theorem 8 is now proved.

7. Concluding remarks

Let $\mathbf{G}$ be a transitive undirected connected graph which is regular of degree r and let $\mathbf{x}$ be an eigenvector belonging to the simple eigenvalue λ of $\mathbf{G}$. As we have seen in Section 4 we may assume $x_1 = 1$: then $\mathbf{x} \in \mathbf{Z}(\mathbf{aut\ G})$ and, according to Remarks 4 and 5 following Theorem 6, $\mathbf{x} \in \mathbf{Z}_2(\mathbf{aut\ G})$ and $\lambda = 2\rho - r$ for some $\rho \in \{0, 1, \ldots, r\}$ (see also [4]).

If $n = 2k$ where k is an odd integer we can say a bit more. Assume that $\lambda \neq r$, then $\mathbf{x} \neq \mathbf{u}$. By $\mathbf{x}$ the vertex set $\mathbf{V}$ of $\mathbf{G}$ is partitioned into two classes $\mathbf{X}_0 = \{i \mid x_i = 1\}$ and $\mathbf{X}_1 = \{i \mid x_i = -1\}$, where $|\mathbf{X}_0| = |\mathbf{X}_1| = k$. By virtue of the transitivity of **aut G**, the subgraph $\mathbf{G}_0$ spanned by $\mathbf{X}_0$ is regular of some degree ρ, and since $\mathbf{G}_0$ has $\frac{1}{2}\rho k$ edges ρ must be even: $\rho = 2\tau$, say. Then

$$\lambda = \rho - (r - \rho) = 4\tau - r, \quad \tau \in \left\{0, 1, \ldots, \left[\frac{1}{2}(r-1)\right]\right\}.$$

Combining this result with Theorems 4 and 5 we obtain

Theorem 9. *Let* $\mathbf{G}$ *be a transitive connected undirected graph with* $n = 2^q \cdot k$ *vertices,* k *being an odd integer.*

(*i*) *If* n *is odd* (*i.e.,* $q = 0$) *then* $\lambda = r$ *is the only simple eigenvalue of* $\mathbf{G}$.

(*ii*) *If* $n \equiv 2 \pmod 4$ (*i.e.,* $q = 1$) *then* $\mathbf{G}$ *has at most two simple eigenvalues, namely* $\lambda = r$

and possibly one more which is of the form

$$\lambda = 4\tau - r, \tau \in \left\{0, 1, \ldots, \left[\frac{1}{2}(r-1)\right]\right\}.$$

(iii) If $n \equiv 0 \pmod 4$ *(i.e.,* $q \geqq 2$*) then* **G** *has at most* 2^q *simple eigenvalues including* $\lambda = r$ *all of which have the form*

$$\lambda = 2\rho - r, \quad \rho \in \{0, 1, \ldots, r\}.$$

The bound is sharp for each value of n.

Corollary. *A transitive connected undirected graph which is regular of degree r cannot have more than* $r+1$ *simple eigenvalues.*

Consequently, a schlicht[4] *connected undirected graph with* $n \geqq 3$ *vertices which has all simple eigenvalues cannot be transitive.*

It remains an open question whether the bounds of Theorem 9 remain sharp if the considerations are restricted to the class of schlicht graphs. In this connection we just quote a general theorem on the eigenvalues of a regular schlicht graph:

Theorem 10 (E. Nosal [3]). *If* **G** *is a connected undirected graph which is schlicht and regular of degree r then all of its eigenvalues* $\lambda \neq r$ *satisfy*

$$\max(r-n, -r) \leqq \lambda \leqq \min(n-r, r) - 2.$$

Note that the last inequality is more restrictive than the inequality $-r \leqq \lambda \leqq r-2$ which ensues from Theorem 9 if and only if $2r > n$.

Remark 9. Only after the completion of the manuscript the authors proved:

For an arbitrary non-negative integer q and for each odd integer m containing q or more prime factors (which need not be distinct) a transitive undirected schlicht graph with $n = 2^q m$ *vertices and* $s_n(2) = 2^q$ *simple eigenvalues can be constructed.* (See [5].)

References

[1] Biggs, N., *Algebraic Graph Theory*, Cambridge University Press 1974 (see *Proposition* 16.7, p. 110).

[2] Dulmage, A. L. and N. S. Mendelsohn, *Graphs and matrices*. In: Graph Theory and Theoretical Physics (ed. F. Harary), Academic Press London–New York 1967; pp. 167–227.

[3] Nosal, E., *Eigenvalues of Graphs*. Master thesis, University of Calgary, 1970.

[4] Petersdorf, M. and Sachs, H., *Spektrum und Automorphismengruppe eines Graphen*. In: Combinatorial Theory and Its Applications, III. (eds. P. Erdős, A. Rényi and Vera T. Sós). North-Holland Publishing Company, Amsterdam–London 1970. pp. 891–907.

[4] A graph is called *schlicht* if it has neither loops nor multiple edges.

[5] SACHS, H. and STIEBITZ, M., Konstruktion schlichter transitiver Gruppen mit maximaler Anzahl einfacher Eigenwerte, *Math. Nachr.*, **100** (1981), 145–150.

[6] SMITH, J. H., *Some properties of the spectrum of a graph.* In: Combinatorial Structures and Their Applications. (eds. R. Guy, H. Hanani, N. Sauer, J. Schönheim). Gordon and Breach, New York–London–Paris 1970, pp. 403–406.

[7] ZURMÜHL, R., *Matrizen.* Springer-Verlag, Berlin–Göttingen–Heidelberg 1950; 2. Aufl. 1958.

[8] ГАНТМАХЕР, Р. Ф., *Теория Матриц.* Москва 1966.

English translation: GANTMACHER, F. R., *Theory of Matrices* I, II, New York 1959.

German translation: GANTMACHER, F. R., *Matrizenrechnung*, Teil 1 und Teil 2. Berlin 1959.

TECHNISCHE HOCHSCHULE ILMENAU
SEKTION MATHEMATIK, RECHENTECHNIK
UND ÖKONOMISCHE KYBERNETIK
DDR–63 ILMENAU
PSF 327

Studies in Pure Mathematics
To the Memory of Paul Turán

The joint distribution of the digits of certain integer s-tuples

by

W. M. SCHMIDT (Boulder, Tokyo)

1. Introduction

Let $B(n)$ denote the number of digits 1 in the representation of a natural number n in the binary scale. For example, since 5 in the binary scale is 101, we have $B(5)=2$. It is well known that for most integers n, the number $B(n)$ is about half the total number of digits in the binary representation of n, so that $B(n)$ is roughly equal to $\frac{1}{2}\nu$, where

$$\nu=\nu(n)={}_2\log n\,, \tag{1.1}$$

and where ${}_2\log$ is the logarithm to the base 2. In fact it follows from the Central Limit Theorem of probability theory that the numbers n with

$$\frac{B(n)-\frac{1}{2}\nu}{\sqrt{\nu}}\leqq\xi \tag{1.2}$$

have density

$$\varphi(\xi)=\sqrt{\frac{2}{\pi}}\int_{-\infty}^{\xi}e^{-2t^2}dt: \tag{1.3}$$

Here and always we say that a set S of natural numbers *has density* ψ if the number $N(S,x)$ of numbers $n\in S$, $n\leqq x$ satisfies the asymptotic relation $N(S,x)\sim\psi x$ as $x\to\infty$.

STOLARSKY was the first to compare $B(n)$ and $B(kn)$ where $k>1$ is a fixed odd integer. According to him a number n is k-*sturdy* if $B(n)\leqq B(kn)$, and it is simply *sturdy* if it is k-sturdy for every k. STOLARSKY proved [3] that the 3-sturdy numbers have density $\frac{1}{2}$. Here we shall prove that for any odd $k>1$, the k-sturdy numbers have density $\frac{1}{2}$, and in fact we shall prove rather more. Our main result is as follows.

Theorem 1. *Let $k_1, \ldots, k_s$ be distinct odd integers. The matrix $\mathbf{M}=(\mu_{ij})$ $(1 \leqq i, j \leqq s)$ with entries*

$$\mu_{ij}=k_i^{-1}k_j^{-1} \quad (\gcd(k_i, k_j))^2$$

has positive determinant. Let $\mathbf{Q}=(q_{ij})$ be its inverse; then the quadratic form

$$Q(\mathbf{t}) = \sum_{i,j=1}^{s} q_{ij}t_i t_j$$

is positive definite, and hence

$$\varphi(k_1, \ldots, k_s; \xi_1, \ldots, \xi_s) = \left(\frac{2}{\pi}\right)^{s/2} \frac{1}{(\det \mathbf{M})^{1/2}} \int_{-\infty}^{\xi_1} \cdots \int_{-\infty}^{\xi_s} e^{-2Q(\mathbf{t})}\, dt_1 \ldots dt_s \tag{1.4}$$

is well defined for $(\xi_1, \ldots, \xi_s) \in \mathbf{R}^s$.

The natural numbers n having simultaneously

$$\frac{B(k_i n) - \frac{1}{2}\nu}{\sqrt{\nu}} \leqq \xi_i \quad (i=1, \ldots, s) \tag{1.5}$$

have density $\varphi(k_1, \ldots, k_s; \xi_1, \ldots, \xi_s)$.

For $s=1$, $k_1=1$, we have $\mathbf{M}=(1)$, $Q(\mathbf{t})=t^2$, and (1.4) reduces to (1.3). In §2 we will deduce

Corollary 1A. *Let k_1, k_2 be distinct odd integers, and put $\mu=k_1^{-1}k_2^{-1}(\gcd(k_1, k_2))^2$. Write*

$$\psi(k_1, k_2; \eta)=(\pi(1-\mu))^{-1/2} \int_{-\infty}^{\eta} e^{-t^2/(1-\mu)}\, dt. \tag{1.6}$$

Then the numbers n with

$$\frac{B(k_1 n) - B(k_2 n)}{\sqrt{\nu}} \leqq \eta \tag{1.7}$$

have density $\psi(k_1, k_2; \eta)$.

An immediate consequence is

Corollary 1B. *Suppose that* $f(n)=o(\sqrt{v})=o((\log n)^{1/2})$. *Then the numbers n with*

$$|B(k_1 n)-B(k_2 n)| \leqq f(n)$$

have density zero.

A result of this type in the case when one of k_1, k_2 is 1 was given by MUSKAT and STOLARSKY [4, Corollary]. It may be seen that our conclusion still holds with $B(k_1 n)-B(k_2 n)$ replaced by

$$A(n)=c_1 B(k_1 n)+\ldots+c_s B(k_s n), \tag{1.8}$$

where $k_1, \ldots, k_s$ are distinct odd integers, where $c_1+\ldots+c_s=0$ and not all the c_i are zero.

Since the density (the integrand) in (1.6) is an even function of t, or directly from the case $s=2$ of Theorem 1, one gets

Corollary 1C. *Let* k_1, k_2 *be distinct odd integers. The numbers n with*

$$B(k_1 n) \leqq B(k_2 n) \tag{1.9}$$

have density $\frac{1}{2}$.

The inequality (1.9) here could be replaced by $A(n) \leqq 0$, with $A(n)$ defined in (1.8).

It is an easy consequence of Theorem 1 that for given odd $k_1, \ldots, k_r$, the integers n with

$$B(n) \leqq B(k_i n) \quad (i=1, \ldots, r)$$

have a certain density $\chi(k_1, \ldots, k_r)$.

Theorem 2. *There is a function* $g(r)$ *tending to zero as* $r \to \infty$ *such that* $\chi(k_1, \ldots, k_r) \leqq g(r)$, *for any r distinct odd numbers* $k_1, \ldots, k_r$.

Corollary 2A. *The sturdy numbers have density* 0.

The assertion concerning numbers n with (1.2) follows from the Central Limit Theorem for independent random variables. For a proof of Theorem 1, independent random variables no longer apply. In the present manuscript we will use Markov Chains, but probably the theory of "Mixing Sequences of Random Variables" (PHILIPP [2]) could be used instead. (On the other hand, Markov Chains with a single class of positive states could be considered as a special case of Mixing Sequences.)

The method of the present paper does not give a good upper estimate for the number of sturdy numbers $\leqq x$. The following question is left open: Given $K>0$, is it true that the numbers n with

$$B(n)\leqq KB(kn) \quad \text{for every } k$$

have density zero?

2. Deduction of Corollary 1A and of Theorem 2 from the Main Theorem

For $s=2$ we have $\mathbf{M}=\begin{pmatrix}1 & \mu\\ \mu & 1\end{pmatrix}$ and $\det\mathbf{M}=1-\mu^2$. It follows immediately from Theorem 1 that the numbers n with (1.7) have density

$$\rho(k_1,k_2;\eta)=\frac{2}{\pi(1-\mu^2)^{1/2}}\iint_{t_1-t_2\leqq\eta} e^{-2Q(\mathbf{t})}\,dt_1\,dt_2\,.$$

Now

$$2Q(t_1,t_2)=\frac{2}{1-\mu^2}(t_1^2-2\mu t_1t_2+t_2^2)=\frac{s_1^2}{1+\mu}+\frac{s_2^2}{1-\mu}$$

with $s_1=t_1+t_2$, $s_2=t_1-t_2$, so that

$$\rho(k_1,k_2;\eta)=\frac{1}{\pi(1-\mu^2)^{1/2}}\left(\int_{-\infty}^{\infty} e^{-\frac{s_1^2}{1+\mu}}ds_1\right)\left(\int_{-\infty}^{\eta} e^{-\frac{s_2^2}{1-\mu}}ds_2\right)=$$

$$=(\pi(1-\mu))^{-1/2}\int_{-\infty}^{\eta} e^{-t^2/(1-\mu)}\,dt\,.$$

But this is the quantity $\psi(k_1,k_2;\eta)$ of Corollary 1A.

As for Theorem 2, we may suppose that $k_1=1$. We note that for $2\leqq s\leqq r$ we have $\chi(k_1,\ldots,k_r)\leqq\chi(k_1,\ldots,k_s)$. Now if $\mathbf{M},Q(\mathbf{t})$ are defined as in Theorem 1, and if D_s is the set of points $\mathbf{t}=(t_1,\ldots,t_s)$ in $\mathbf{R}^s$ with $t_1\leqq t_2$, $t_1\leqq t_3$, $\ldots$, $t_1\leqq t_s$, then

$$\chi(k_1,\ldots,k_s)=\left(\frac{2}{\pi}\right)^{s/2}\frac{1}{(\det\mathbf{M})^{1/2}}\int\!\!\ldots\!\!\int_{D_s} e^{-2Q(\mathbf{t})}\,dt_1\ldots dt_s\,.$$

Now since

$$1=\left(\frac{2}{\pi}\right)^{s/2}\frac{1}{(\det\mathbf{M})^{1/2}}\int\!\!\ldots\!\!\int_{\mathbf{R}^s} e^{-2Q(\mathbf{t})}\,dt_1\ldots dt_s\,,$$

we obtain

$$\chi(k_1, \ldots, k_s) = \left(\int_{D_s} \ldots \int e^{-2Q(\mathbf{t})}\, d\mathbf{t} \right) \Big/ \left(\int_{\mathbf{R}^s} \ldots \int e^{-2Q(\mathbf{t})}\, d\mathbf{t} \right).$$

Write $A(x)$ for the volume of the ellipsoid $Q(\mathbf{t}) \leqq x$, and $B(x)$ for the volume of the intersection of this ellipsoid with the angular domain D_s. Then $A(x) = x^{s/2}A(1)$, $B(x) = x^{s/2}B(1)$. We have

$$\int_{\mathbf{R}^s} \ldots \int e^{-2Q(\mathbf{t})}\, d\mathbf{t} = \int_0^\infty e^{-2x} dA(x) = A(1) \int_0^\infty e^{-2x}(s/2)x^{(s/2)-1} dx,$$

and an analogous formula holds for the integral over D_s. We may conclude that

$$\chi(k_1, \ldots, k_s) = B(1)/A(1).$$

If the ellipsoid $Q(\mathbf{t}) \leqq 1$ is the unit ball, then $B(1)/A(1) = \frac{1}{s}$. Now if the matrix $\mathbf{Q}$ is close to the $(s \times s)$-identity matrix, then our ellipsoid is "almost" a ball, and $B(1)/A(1) \leqq 2/s$. Now $\mathbf{Q}$ will be close to the identity matrix if $\mathbf{M}$ is, and since $\mu_{ii} = 1$, this will be true if

(2.1) $$\mu_{ij} < \varepsilon \qquad (1 \leqq i < j \leqq s)$$

for a suitable small ε. Theorem 2 now follows from

Lemma 1. *Let s be natural, and $\varepsilon > 0$. If $r > r_0(s, \varepsilon)$ and if $1 = k_1, k_2, \ldots, k_r$ are distinct odd numbers, then there are s numbers $1 = h_1 < \ldots < h_s$ between 1 and r such that*

(2.2) $$\mu_{h_i h_j} < \varepsilon \qquad (1 \leqq i < j \leqq s).$$

Put differently, we can reorder $k_2, \ldots, k_r$ so that (2.1) holds.

Proof. For natural k, k', set $\mu(k, k') = k^{-1}k'^{-1}(\gcd(k, k'))^2$. For given k write

$$k' = k\frac{a}{b}$$

where $\gcd(a, b) = 1$. Then $\mu(k, k') = (ab)^{-1}$. Now $\mu(k, k') \geqq \varepsilon$ means that $ab \leqq \varepsilon^{-1}$, and hence for given k there are not more than ε^{-2} numbers k' with $\mu(k, k') \geqq \varepsilon$.

Set $h_1 = 1$. If $r > \varepsilon^{-2}$, then we may pick h_2 in $1 \leqq h_2 \leqq r$ with $\mu_{h_1 h_2} = \mu(k_{h_1}, k_{h_2}) < \varepsilon$. If $r > 2\varepsilon^{-2}$, then we can pick h_3 in $1 \leqq h_3 \leqq r$ with $\mu_{h_1 h_3} = \mu(k_{h_1}, k_{h_3}) < \varepsilon$ and $\mu_{h_2 h_3} = \mu(k_{h_2}, k_{h_3}) < \varepsilon$. And so forth. If $r > s\varepsilon^{-2}$, then we can pick $h_2, \ldots, h_s$ between 1 and r such that (2.2) holds. Since $\mu(h, h) = 1$, the numbers $h_1 = 1, h_2, \ldots, h_s$ will be distinct if, as we may suppose, $0 < \varepsilon < 1$.

3. A reduction

If $n=a_s a_{s-1} \dots a_1$ in the binary scale, write $B_h(n)$ for the number of digits among $a_1, a_2, \dots, a_h$ which equal 1. For example, since 6 is 110 in the binary scale, we have $B_2(6)=1$. Put $B_h(0)=0$. Given integers $k_1, \dots, k_s$ as in Theorem 1, write

$$N_h(k_1, \dots, k_s; \xi_1, \dots, \xi_s)$$

for the number of integers n in $0 \leqq n < 2^h$ with

$$\frac{B_h(k_i n) - \frac{1}{2}h}{\sqrt{h}} \leqq \xi_i \qquad (i=1, \dots, s). \tag{3.1}$$

Proposition 1. *As the integer h tends to infinity, we have*

$$\lim_{h \to \infty} 2^{-h} N_h(k_1, \dots, k_s; \xi_1, \dots, \xi_s) = \varphi(k_1, \dots, k_s; \xi_1, \dots, \xi_s).$$

Deduction of Theorem 1 from the Proposition. Fix a large integer g. For large x there is a natural integer h with

$$2^{h+g-1} \leqq x < 2^{h+g}.$$

There is a unique natural y_0 and a z_0 in $0 \leqq z_0 < 2^h$ with $x = 2^h y_0 + z_0$. In fact, there also is a natural y and a z with

$$x = 2^h y + z \quad \text{and} \quad 2^h \leqq z < 2^{h+1}.$$

There are $2^h y$ integers n in the interval

$$z < n \leqq x. \tag{3.2}$$

Each such n may uniquely be written as

$$n = 2^h q + n_0 \quad \text{with} \quad 0 \leqq n_0 < 2^h.$$

As n runs through (3.2), n_0 will run through $0 \leqq n_0 < 2^h$ exactly y times.

For n in (3.2) we have

$$B_h(k_i n_0) = B_h(k_i n) \leqq B(k_i n) \leqq B_h(k_i n) + g + k = B_h(k_i n_0) + g + k \quad (1 \leqq i \leqq s)$$

where $k = \max(k_1, \dots, k_s)$. Further

$$h < \nu(n) \leqq h + g,$$

whence

$$\frac{1}{\sqrt{h}} \leqq \frac{1}{\sqrt{v}}\left(1+\frac{g}{h}\right)^{1/2} < \frac{1}{\sqrt{v}}\left(1+\frac{g}{h}\right).$$

For such n, (3.1) implies that

$$\frac{B_h(k_i n_0) - \frac{1}{2}h}{\sqrt{h}} \leqq \frac{B(k_i n) - \frac{1}{2}v + \frac{1}{2}g}{\sqrt{v}}\left(1+\frac{g}{h}\right) \leqq \left(\xi_i + \frac{g}{\sqrt{h}}\right)\left(1+\frac{g}{h}\right),$$

so that

$$\frac{B(k_i n_0) - \frac{1}{2}h}{\sqrt{h}} \leqq \xi_i + \varepsilon \qquad (i=1, \ldots, s) \tag{3.3}$$

if x and hence h is large. By Proposition 1 the number of n_0 in $0 \leqq n_0 < 2^h$ with (3.3) is

$$\leqq (1+\varepsilon)2^h \varphi(k_1, \ldots, k_s; \xi_1+\varepsilon, \ldots, \xi_s+\varepsilon)$$

if h is large. Since n_0 runs y times through $0 \leqq n_0 < 2^h$ as n runs through (3.2), it follows that the number of natural $n \leqq x$ with (3.1) does not exceed

$$(1+\varepsilon)2^h y \varphi(k_1, \ldots, k_s; \xi_1+\varepsilon, \ldots, \xi_s+\varepsilon) + z\,.$$

Since $z/x \leqq 2^{2-g}$, we see that the numbers n with (3.1) have an upper density not exceeding

$$(1+\varepsilon)\varphi(k_1, \ldots, k_s; \xi_1+\varepsilon, \ldots, \xi_s+\varepsilon) + 2^{2-g}\,.$$

Since $\varepsilon > 0$ and g were arbitrary, and since φ is continuous in its last s arguments, the upper density is at most $\varphi(k_1, \ldots, k_s; \xi_1, \ldots, \xi_s)$. One proves in the same way that the lower density is at least $\varphi(k_1, \ldots, k_s; \xi_1, \ldots, \xi_s)$.

4. A probability space

If Ω_0 is the unit interval $0 \leqq \xi < 1$, $\mathfrak{J}_0$ the set of Borel subsets of Ω_0, and $\mathbf{P}_0$ the Borel measure, then $(\Omega_0, \mathfrak{J}_0, \mathbf{P}_0)$ is what is called a "probability triple".

We are not interested in Ω_0, but in the set Ω of 2-adic integers

$$\mathfrak{N} = a_1 + 2a_2 + 2^2 a_3 + \ldots, \tag{4.1}$$

where each "digit" a_i is either 0 or 1. The map

$$\sigma: \mathfrak{N} \to \cdot a_1 a_2 \ldots \text{ in the binary scale}$$

is from Ω onto Ω_0. For $\xi \in \Omega_0$ there is exactly one $\mathfrak{N}$ with $\sigma(\mathfrak{N})=\xi$, except for the countably many ξ of the form $.a_1a_2\ldots a_r100\ldots=.a_1a_2\ldots a_r011\ldots$, for which there are two 2-adic integers $\mathfrak{N}$ whose image is ξ. Writing $\mathfrak{J}$ for the collection of sets $S=\sigma^{-1}(S_0)$ with $S_0 \in \mathfrak{J}_0$ and $\mathbf{P}$ for the measure with $\mathbf{P}(S)=\mathbf{P}_0(S_0)$, we obtain a probability triple $(\Omega, \mathfrak{J}, \mathbf{P})$.

The 2-adic integers form a ring, and in particular products $k\mathfrak{N}$ are defined for natural integers k. For $\mathfrak{N}$ given by (4.1), put

$$\mathfrak{N}_t = a_1 + 2a_2 + \ldots + 2^{t-1}a_t .$$

For given k write $k\mathfrak{N}_t = b_{t1} + 2b_{t2} + \ldots + 2^{l-1}b_{tl}$ where each digit b_{ti} is 0 or 1, and where $l=l(k,t)$. Then $b_{tt}=b_{t+1,t}=b_{t+2,t}=\ldots=b_t$, say, and

$$k\mathfrak{N} = b_1 + 2b_2 + 2^2b_3 + \ldots .$$

In particular, if $k_1, \ldots, k_s$ are the integers of Theorem 1, put

$$k_i\mathfrak{N} = b_1^{(i)} + 2b_2^{(i)} + 2^2b_3^{(i)} + \ldots .$$

The first t digits of $k_i\mathfrak{N}_t$ are the same as the first digits of $k_i\mathfrak{N}$. Thus if [ ] denotes the integer part, then the first digit of $[2^{-t+1}k_i\mathfrak{N}_t]$ is $b_t^{(i)}$, or

$$[2^{-t+1}k_i\mathfrak{N}_t] \equiv b_t^{(i)} \pmod 2 . \tag{4.2}$$

Put

$$y_t^{(i)} = \begin{cases} \dfrac{1}{2} & \text{if } b_t^{(i)}=1 \\ -\dfrac{1}{2} & \text{if } b_t^{(i)}=0 \end{cases} \qquad (i=1, \ldots, s; t=1, 2, \ldots)$$

and $S_h^{(i)} = y_1^{(i)} + y_2^{(i)} + \ldots + y_h^{(i)}$. Then $S_h^{(i)}$ equals {the number of the first h digits of $k_i\mathfrak{N}$ which are 1} $-\frac{1}{2}h$, or $S_h^{(i)} = B_h(k_i\mathfrak{N}_h) - \frac{1}{2}h$. Now $\mathfrak{N}_t$, $b_t^{(i)}$, $y_t^{(i)}$, $S_h^{(i)}$ are random variables dependent on the "event" $\mathfrak{N} \in \Omega$. Write

$$\mathbf{R}_h(\xi_1, \ldots, \xi_s) = \mathbf{P}\{h^{-1/2}S_h^{(i)} \leqq \xi_i \qquad (i=1, \ldots, s)\} . \tag{4.3}$$

With N_h as in Proposition 1, it is clear that for given $k_1, \ldots, k_s$ we have

$$\mathbf{R}_h(\xi_1, \ldots, \xi_s) = 2^{-h}N_h(k_1, \ldots, k_s; \xi_1, \ldots, \xi_s) .$$

Thus it will suffice to prove that

$$\lim_{h\to\infty} \mathbf{R}_h(\xi_1, \ldots, \xi_s) = \varphi(k_1, \ldots, k_s; \xi_1, \ldots, \xi_s) . \tag{4.4}$$

5. A Markov chain

Given $\mathfrak{N} \in \Omega$, write $\mathbf{x}_0 = (0, \ldots, 0)$ (with s components) and

$$\mathbf{x}_t = \mathbf{x}_t(\mathfrak{N}) = ([2^{-t+1}k_1\mathfrak{N}_t], \ldots, [2^{-t+1}k_s\mathfrak{N}_t]) \quad (t = 1, 2, \ldots).$$

Then $\mathbf{x}_0, \mathbf{x}_1, \ldots$ are (vector valued) random variables.

A vector $\mathbf{x} = (x_1, \ldots, x_s)$ will be called *admissible* if there is an α in $0 \leqq \alpha < 2$ with

$$x_i = [k_i\alpha] \qquad (i = 1, \ldots, s). \tag{5.1}$$

It is clear that $\mathbf{x}_t(\mathfrak{N})$ is always admissible, and conversely if $\mathbf{x}$ is admissible, then there is a t and an $\mathfrak{N}$ with $\mathbf{x}_t(\mathfrak{N}) = \mathbf{x}$.

Given an admissible $\mathbf{x}$, the numbers α in $0 \leqq \alpha < 2$ with (5.1) constitute an interval $I(\mathbf{x})$ which is half open, of the type $\alpha_1 \leqq \alpha < \alpha_2$. The interval $0 \leqq \alpha < 2$ is the disjoint union of the intervals $I(\mathbf{x})$ with admissible $\mathbf{x}$. The end points of the intervals $I(\mathbf{x})$ are the rational numbers in $0 \leqq \alpha \leqq 2$ whose denominators are divisors of one of $k_1, \ldots, k_s$. In general, the number of admissible vectors is a complicated function of $k_1, \ldots, k_s$. It is usually easier to construct the intervals first.

For example, when $s = 2$, $k_1 = 1$, $k_2 = 3$, then the end points are $0, \frac{1}{3}, \frac{2}{3}, 1, \frac{4}{3}, \frac{5}{3}, 2$, and the intervals are

$$A = \left[0, \frac{1}{3}\right) = I(0, 0), \quad B = \left[\frac{1}{3}, \frac{2}{3}\right) = I(0, 1), \quad C = \left[\frac{2}{3}, 1\right) = I(0, 2),$$

$$D = \left[1, \frac{4}{3}\right) = I(1, 3), \quad E = \left[\frac{4}{3}, \frac{5}{3}\right) = I(1, 4), \quad F = \left[\frac{5}{3}, 2\right) = I(1, 5).$$

The admissible vectors are (0, 0), (0, 1), (0, 2), (1, 3), (1, 4), (1, 5).

It is clear that $\mathbf{0} = (0, \ldots, 0)$ is admissible. When (5.1) holds, then $[x_i/2] = [k_i\alpha/2]$ and $[x_i/2] + k_i = [k_i(\alpha + 2)/2]$ for $i = 1, \ldots, s$. Therefore if $\mathbf{x} = (x_1, \ldots, x_s)$ is admissible, then so are

$$\mathbf{x}^0 = ([x_1/2], \ldots, [x_s/2]) \quad \text{and} \quad \mathbf{x}^1 = ([x_1/2] + k_1, \ldots, [x_s/2] + k_s).$$

Lemma 2. *The random variables $\mathbf{x}_0, \mathbf{x}_1, \ldots$ form a Markov chain. The initial distribution is that always $\mathbf{x}_0 = \mathbf{0}$, and the transition probabilities are given by the rule that for given $\mathbf{x}_t$ we have*

$$\mathbf{x}_{t+1} = \begin{cases} \mathbf{x}_t^0 \text{ with probability } \frac{1}{2}, \\ \mathbf{x}_t^1 \text{ with probability } \frac{1}{2}. \end{cases}$$

Proof. We have $\mathfrak{N}_{t+1}=\mathfrak{N}_t+2^t a_{t+1}$, hence if $\mathbf{x}_t=(x_1,\ldots,x_s)$, then

$$\mathbf{x}_{t+1}=([2^{-t}k_1(\mathfrak{N}_t+2^t a_{t+1})],\ldots,[2^{-t}k_s(\mathfrak{N}_t+2^t a_{t+1})])=$$

$$=\left(\left[\frac{1}{2}2^{-t+1}k_1\mathfrak{N}_t\right]+k_1a_{t+1},\ldots,\left[\frac{1}{2}2^{-t+1}k_s\mathfrak{N}_t\right]+k_sa_{t+1}\right)=$$

$$=\left(\left[\frac{1}{2}x_1\right]+k_1a_{t+1},\ldots,\left[\frac{1}{2}x_s\right]+k_sa_{t+1}\right)=$$

$$=\begin{cases}\mathbf{x}_t^0 & \text{if } a_{t+1}=0,\\ \mathbf{x}_t^1 & \text{if } a_{t+1}=1.\end{cases}$$

Now $\mathbf{x}_0,\mathbf{x}_1,\ldots,\mathbf{x}_t$ depend only on the digits $a_1,\ldots,a_t$. Given these digits, we have

$$a_{t+1}=\begin{cases}0 \text{ with probability } \frac{1}{2},\\ 1 \text{ with probability } \frac{1}{2}.\end{cases}$$

The lemma follows.

When $s=2$, $k_1=1$, $k_2=3$, then we have 6 states, which may briefly be denoted by A, B, C, D, E, F. The transition probabilities are described by the following diagram:

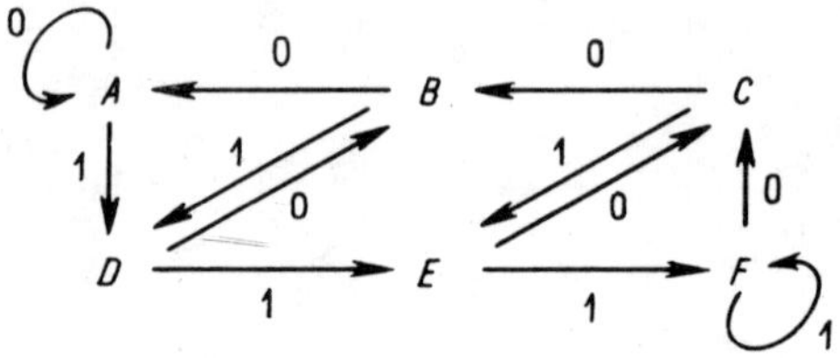

Fig. 1

Two arrows, denoted by 0 or 1, originate at each state. The arrow with 0 indicates a transition from $\mathbf{x}$ to $\mathbf{x}^0$, the arrow with 1 a transition from $\mathbf{x}$ to $\mathbf{x}^1$. Each arrow represents a probability of $\frac{1}{2}$. If $\mathbf{x}_t$ is in the state A, say, then $\mathbf{x}_{t+1}$ is in the state A or D, each with probability $\frac{1}{2}$. (In our diagram, two arrow lead to each state. In general this need not be.)

Lemma 3. *The states form one essential class. That is, if* $\mathbf{u}$, $\mathbf{v}$ *are admissible vectors, and if* $t \geqq 0$, *then there is an* $r > t$ *such that if* $\mathbf{x}_t = \mathbf{u}$, *then* $\mathbf{x}_r = \mathbf{v}$ *with positive probability. Put differently, the conditional probability*

$$\mathbf{P}\{\mathbf{x}_r = \mathbf{v} | \mathbf{x}_t = \mathbf{u}\}$$

is positive.

The lemma may be interpreted as saying that in the directed graph whose vertices are the states (the admissible vectors) and whose directed edges are the possible (one step) transitions, one can travel from any vertex to any other vertex by successively following directed edges.

Proof. Since $\mathbf{x}_t = \mathbf{x}_t(\mathfrak{N})$ depends only on $\mathfrak{N}_t$, it suffices to show that for a given integer n in $0 \leqq n < 2^t$, the conditional probability

$$\mathbf{P}\{\mathbf{x}_r = \mathbf{v} | \mathfrak{N}_t = n\} > 0 .$$

This is the same as

$$\mathbf{P}\{2^{-r+1}\mathfrak{N}_r \in I(\mathbf{v}) | \mathfrak{N}_t = n\} > 0 . \tag{5.2}$$

Now since $2^{-r+1}\mathfrak{N}_r = a_r \cdot a_{r-1} \ldots a_2 a_1$ (in the binary scale), it follows that for almost every $\mathfrak{N} \in \Omega$, the sequence $2^{-r+1}\mathfrak{N}_r$ $(r = 1, 2, \ldots)$ is uniformly distributed in the interval $0 \leqq \alpha < 2$. Given that $\mathfrak{N}_t = n$, we still have conditional probability 1 that the sequence is uniformly distributed, so that in particular $2^{-r+1}\mathfrak{N}_r$ will be in $I(\mathbf{v})$ infinitely often. So there is an $r > s$ with (5.2).

6. Some limits

The quantity $\pi_{\mathbf{x}}$ where $\mathbf{x}$ is a state is introduced in the theory of Markov Chains (Chung [1]), and could roughly be characterized as the "expected proportion of the time that $\mathbf{x}_t$ is in the state $\mathbf{x}$".

Lemma 4. $\pi_{\mathbf{x}} = \frac{1}{2}|I(\mathbf{x})|$, *where* $|\ldots|$ *denotes the measure of a set of real numbers.*

Proof. Let $l(\mathbf{x}, t) = l(\mathbf{x}, t, \mathfrak{N})$ be the number of r in $1 \leqq r \leqq t$ with $\mathbf{x}_r = \mathbf{x}$. The event $\mathbf{x}_r = \mathbf{x}$ is the same as $2^{-r+1}\mathfrak{N}_r \in I(\mathbf{x})$. Now since almost certainly $2^{-r+1}\mathfrak{N}_r$ is uniformly distributed in $0 \leqq \alpha < 2$, we have

$$\mathbf{P} \lim_{t \to \infty} t^{-1} l(\mathbf{x}, t) = \frac{1}{2}|I(\mathbf{x})| .$$

Our lemma now follows from [1, §I.14, Corollary 1].

Lemma 5. *For $1 \leqq i \leqq s$ we have*

$$\mathbf{P} \lim_{t \to \infty} \frac{1}{t} \sum_{r=1}^{t} y_t^{(i)} = 0 .$$

Proof. In view of (4.2) and the definition of $\mathbf{x}_t$, the random variable $y_t^{(i)}$ is a "functional" of $\mathbf{x}_t$: We have $y_t^{(i)} = f^{(i)}(\mathbf{x}_t)$, where

$$f^{(i)}(\mathbf{x}) = \begin{cases} \frac{1}{2} \text{ if the } i\text{-th component of } \mathbf{x} \text{ is odd}, \\ -\frac{1}{2} \text{ otherwise}. \end{cases} \tag{6.1}$$

In view of Theorem 2 in [1, §I.14] it will suffice for us to show that

$$\sum_{\mathbf{x}} \pi_{\mathbf{x}} f^{(i)}(\mathbf{x}) = 0 .$$

The states occur in pairs. To each state of the type $\mathbf{x} = ([k_1 \alpha], \ldots, [k_s \alpha])$ with $0 \leqq \alpha < 1$ there corresponds the dual state $\bar{\mathbf{x}} = ([k_1(\alpha+1)], \ldots, [k_s(\alpha+1)]) = \mathbf{x} + (k_1, \ldots, k_s)$. Since

$$\pi_{\mathbf{x}} = \pi_{\bar{\mathbf{x}}} \quad \text{and} \quad f^{(i)}(\mathbf{x}) = -f^{(i)}(\bar{\mathbf{x}}),$$

the lemma follows.

Lemma 6. *For $1 \leqq i, j \leqq s$ we have*

$$\mathbf{P} \lim_{t \to \infty} \frac{1}{t} \sum_{r=1}^{t} y_t^{(i)} y_t^{(j)} = \frac{1}{4} \mu_{ij},$$

where μ_{ij} is defined in Theorem 1.

Proof. $y_r^{(i)} y_r^{(j)} = f^{(i)}(\mathbf{x}_r) f^{(j)}(\mathbf{x}_r)$ is a functional of $\mathbf{x}_r$. Hence it will be enough to verify that

$$\sum_{\mathbf{x}} \pi_{\mathbf{x}} f^{(i)}(\mathbf{x}) f^{(j)}(\mathbf{x}) = \frac{1}{4} \mu_{ij} .$$

In view of Lemma 4 this is the same as

$$\frac{1}{2} |A| - \frac{1}{2} |B| = \mu_{ij} ,$$

where A, B are the subsets of $0 \leqq \alpha < 2$ where $[k_i\alpha]$ and $[k_j\alpha]$ have the same parity or the opposite parity, respectively. Since both k_i, k_j are odd, it is clear that the parity of $[k_i\alpha]-[k_j\alpha]$ depends only on α (modulo 1), and hence $|B|=2|C|$, where C consists of α in $0 \leqq \alpha < 1$ where $[k_i\alpha]$ and $[k_j\alpha]$ have opposite parity. Since $|A|+|B|=2$, it will therefore be enough to prove that

$$|C| = \frac{1}{2}(1-\mu_{ij}).$$

Write $k_i = k_i'd$ where $d = \gcd(k_i, k_j)$. Putting $\beta = d\alpha$ we see that C has d^{-1} times the measure of the set C' of β in $0 \leqq \beta < d$ where $[k_i'\beta]$, $[k_j'\beta]$ have opposite parity. Since the parity of $[k_i'\beta]-[k_j'\beta]$ depends only on β (modulo 1), we see that $|C|$ is the measure of the β in $0 \leqq \beta < 1$ where $[k_i'\beta]$, $[k_j'\beta]$ have the opposite parity. Since $\mu_{ij} = 1/(k_i'k_j')$, we may thus suppose without loss of generality that k_i, k_j are relatively prime, and we have to prove that

$$|C| = \frac{1}{2}\left(1 - \frac{1}{k_ik_j}\right). \tag{6.2}$$

Write $\alpha = (a/k_ik_j) + \varepsilon$ where $0 \leqq \varepsilon < 1/(k_ik_j)$ and a is an integer in $0 \leqq a < k_ik_j$. Then $|C| = Z/(k_ik_j)$ where Z is the number of integers a for which $[a/k_j]$ and $[a/k_i]$ are of opposite parity. The parity of the difference depends only on the residue class of a modulo k_ik_j. Since 2, k_i, k_j are prime in pairs, we may put $a = 2k_ib + 2k_jc$ with b, c, respectively, running through the residues mod k_j, k_i, and we have to compare the parities of $[2k_ib/k_j]$ and $[2k_jc/k_i]$. As b runs through a residue system modulo k_j, so does k_ib. The number of integers $b = 0, 1, \ldots, k_j - 1$ with

$$[2b/k_j] = \begin{cases} 0 \text{ equals } (k_j+1)/2\,, \\ 1 \text{ equals } (k_j-1)/2\,. \end{cases}$$

The number of integers $c = 0, 1, \ldots, k_i - 1$ with

$$[2c/k_i] = \begin{cases} 0 \text{ equals } (k_i+1)/2\,, \\ 1 \text{ equals } (k_i-1)/2\,. \end{cases}$$

Thus

$$Z = \frac{1}{4}((k_i+1)(k_j-1)+(k_i-1)(k_j+1)) = \frac{1}{2}(k_ik_j-1)\,.$$

(6.2) and hence the lemma follows.

7. Computation of variances

The random vectors $\mathbf{x}_t$, $\mathbf{x}_{t+1}$ are not independent. Similarly, the vectors $\mathbf{y}_t$, $\mathbf{y}_{t+1}$ where $\mathbf{y}_t=(y_t^{(1)}, \dots, y_t^{(s)})$, are not independent. However, given $a_1, \dots, a_t$, we have $a_{t+1}=0$ or 1, each with probability $\frac{1}{2}$. Hence for i in $1 \leqq i \leqq s$ and given $\mathbf{x}_t$, we have $y_{t+1}^{(i)} = -\frac{1}{2}$ or $\frac{1}{2}$, each with probability $\frac{1}{2}$, so that $\mathbf{x}_t$, $y_{t+1}^{(i)}$ are independent. Similarly, $\mathbf{y}_t$ and $y_{t+1}^{(i)}$ are independent. More generally, for $t<r$, the random variables $\mathbf{y}_t$ and $y_r^{(i)}$ are independent. Hence in *some* ways, $\mathbf{y}_1, \mathbf{y}_2, \dots$ behaves like a sequence of independent random variables.

For almost every $\mathfrak{R} \in \Omega$ and for every admissible $\mathbf{u}$, there are infinitely many t with $\mathbf{x}_t=\mathbf{u}$. So if Ω' is the subset of Ω where this is true, then the complement $\Omega \sim \Omega'$ is of measure zero. For $\mathfrak{R} \in \Omega'$, we write

$$\tau_1(\mathbf{u})<\tau_2(\mathbf{u})<\dots$$

for the increasing sequence of values of $t \geqq 1$ with $\mathbf{x}_t=\mathbf{u}$. We further put

$$Y_\nu^{(i)}(\mathbf{u}) = \sum_{t=\tau_\nu(\mathbf{u})+1}^{\tau_{\nu+1}(\mathbf{u})} y_t^{(i)} \qquad (1 \leqq i \leqq s;\ \nu=1, 2, \dots) \tag{7.1}$$

and $\mathbf{Y}_\nu(\mathbf{u})=(Y_\nu^{(1)}(\mathbf{u}), \dots, Y_\nu^{(s)}(\mathbf{u}))$. We note that this type of definition is standard, except that (in order to save a few lines below) our range of summation in (7.1) is different from the perhaps more common $\tau_\nu(\mathbf{u}) \leqq t < \tau_{\nu+1}(\mathbf{u})$ (CHUNG [1, §I. 14]). The essential fact on functionals on Markov Chains is that for every $\mathbf{u}$ *the random vectors* $\mathbf{Y}_\nu(\mathbf{u})$ ($\nu=1, 2, \dots$) *are independent and are identically distributed.* (See [1, §I. 14, Theorem 3], where a one dimensional distribution (the case $s=1$) is treated.)

Put

$$Y_\nu^{(i,j)}(\mathbf{u}) = \sum_{t=\tau_\nu(\mathbf{u})+1}^{\tau_{\nu+1}(\mathbf{u})} y_t^{(i)} y_t^{(j)} \qquad (1 \leqq i, j \leqq s;\ \nu=1, 2, \dots).$$

For fixed $i, j, \mathbf{u}$, the random variables $Y_\nu^{(i,j)}(\mathbf{u})$ ($\nu=1, 2, \dots$) are again independent and identically distributed. And also, for fixed $i, j, \mathbf{u}$, the random variables $Y_\nu^{(i)}(\mathbf{u})\, Y_\nu^{(j)}(\mathbf{u})$ ($\nu=1, 2, \dots$) are independent and identically distributed.

Write $\mathbf{E}(x)$ for the expectation value of a random variable x. In view of what we said above, $\mathbf{E}(Y_\nu^{(i)}(\mathbf{u}))$ does not depend on ν, hence may be denoted by $\mathbf{E}(Y^{(i)}(\mathbf{u}))$. We similarly define $\mathbf{E}(Y^{(i,j)}(\mathbf{u}))$ and $\mathbf{E}(Y^{(i)}(\mathbf{u})\,Y^{(j)}(\mathbf{u}))$.

Lemma 7. *For admissible* $\mathbf{u}$ *we have*

$$\mathbf{E}(Y^{(i)}(\mathbf{u}))=0 \qquad (1\leqq i\leqq s)$$

and

$$\pi_{\mathbf{u}}\mathbf{E}(Y^{(i,j)}(\mathbf{u})) = \frac{1}{4}\mu_{ij} \qquad (1\leqq i,j\leqq s).$$

Proof. Put $M^{(i)}(\mathbf{u})=\pi_{\mathbf{u}}\mathbf{E}(Y^{(i)}(\mathbf{u}))$ and $M^{(i,j)}(\mathbf{u})=\pi_{\mathbf{u}}\mathbf{E}(Y^{(i,j)}(\mathbf{u}))$. By combining Theorems 2, 4 of [1, §I. 15], we obtain

$$M^{(i)}(\mathbf{u}) = \mathbf{P}\lim_{t\to\infty}\frac{1}{t}\sum_{r=1}^{t} y_r^{(i)} \qquad (1\leqq i\leqq s),$$

and also

$$M^{(i,j)}(\mathbf{u})=\mathbf{P}\lim_{t\to\infty}\frac{1}{t}\sum_{r=1}^{t} y_r^{(i)}y_r^{(j)} \qquad (1\leqq i,j\leqq s).$$

Our assertions are now immediate consequences of Lemmas 5 and 6.

Lemma 8.

$$\mathbf{E}(Y^{(i)}(\mathbf{u})Y^{(j)}(\mathbf{u}))=\mathbf{E}(Y^{(i,j)}(\mathbf{u})) \qquad (1\leqq i,j\leqq s).$$

This lemma is a consequence of the quasi-independence mentioned at the beginning of this section.

Proof. We introduce a new state ∞, and given v and an admissible $\mathbf{u}$ we introduce the new sequence of random vectors

$${}_v\mathbf{x}_{\tau_v+1}=\mathbf{x}_{\tau_v+1}, \ldots, {}_v\mathbf{x}_{\tau_{v+1}}=\mathbf{x}_{\tau_{v+1}}, {}_v\mathbf{x}_{\tau_{v+1}+1}={}_v\mathbf{x}_{\tau_{v+1}+2}=\ldots=\infty.$$

For admissible $\mathbf{u}$ define $f^{(i)}(\mathbf{u})$ according to (6.1), and further put $f^{(i)}(\infty)=0$. Then

$$Y_v^{(i)}(\mathbf{u}) = \sum_{t=1}^{\infty} f^{(i)}({}_v\mathbf{x}_{\tau_v+t}).$$

This is formula (5) of [1, §I. 14], written in a different form. Similarly,

$$Y_v^{(i,j)}(\mathbf{u}) = \sum_{t=1}^{\infty} f^{(i)}({}_v\mathbf{x}_{\tau_v+t})f^{(j)}({}_v\mathbf{x}_{\tau_v+t}).$$

We obtain

$$\mathbf{E}(Y_v^{(i,j)}(\mathbf{u})) = \sum_{t=1}^{\infty}\sum_{\mathbf{v}} f^{(i)}(\mathbf{v})f^{(i)}(\mathbf{v})_{\mathbf{u}}\, Y_v p_{\mathbf{uv}}^{(t)},$$

where $\mathbf{v}$ runs through admissible vectors and ${}_{\mathbf{z}}p^{t}_{\mathbf{uv}}$ is the conditional probability

$$ {}_{\mathbf{z}}p^{(t)}_{\mathbf{uv}} = \mathbf{P}\{\mathbf{x}_{l+t} = \mathbf{v},\ \mathbf{x}_{l+r} \neq \mathbf{z} \quad \text{for} \quad 1 \leqq r < t \,|\, \mathbf{x}_l = \mathbf{u}\}, $$

which is independent of l. On the other hand,

$$ \mathbf{E}(Y^{(i)}_{v}(\mathbf{u})\,Y^{(j)}_{v}(\mathbf{u})) = \mathbf{E}\left(\left(\sum_{t_1=1}^{\infty} f^{(i)}({}_{v}\mathbf{x}_{\tau_v+t_1})\right)\left(\sum_{t_2=1}^{\infty} f^{(j)}({}_{v}\mathbf{x}_{\tau_v+t_2})\right)\right) = $$

(7.2)

$$ = \sum_{t_1=1}^{\infty}\sum_{t_2=1}^{\infty}\sum_{\mathbf{v}}\sum_{\mathbf{w}} f^{(i)}(\mathbf{v})\,f^{(j)}(\mathbf{w})\,{}_{\mathbf{u}}p^{(t_1,t_2)}_{\mathbf{uvw}}, $$

where $\mathbf{v}, \mathbf{w}$ are admissible vectors and ${}_{\mathbf{z}}p^{(t_1,t_2)}_{\mathbf{uvw}}$ is the conditional probability

$$ {}_{\mathbf{z}}p^{(t_1,t_2)}_{\mathbf{uvw}} = \mathbf{P}\{\mathbf{x}_{l+t_1} = \mathbf{v},\ \mathbf{x}_{l+t_2} = \mathbf{w},\ \mathbf{x}_{l+r} \neq \mathbf{z} \quad \text{for} \quad 1 \leqq r < \max(t_1, t_2) \,|\, \mathbf{x}_l = \mathbf{u}\}. $$

Now the admissible vectors $\mathbf{w}$ occur in pairs (see the proof of Lemma 5) and ${}_{\mathbf{u}}p^{(t)}_{\mathbf{v}\bar{\mathbf{w}}} = {}_{\mathbf{u}}p^{(t)}_{\mathbf{vw}}$, but $f^{(j)}(\mathbf{w}) = -f^{(j)}(\bar{\mathbf{w}})$. Moreover, if $t_1 < t_2$, then

$$ {}_{\mathbf{u}}p^{(t_1,t_2)}_{\mathbf{uvw}} = \begin{cases} {}_{\mathbf{u}}p^{(t_1)}_{\mathbf{uv}}\ {}_{\mathbf{u}}p^{(t_2-t_1)}_{\mathbf{vw}} & \text{if } \mathbf{v} \neq u, \\ 0 \quad \text{if } \mathbf{v} = \mathbf{u}. \end{cases} $$

So for $t_1 < t_2$,

$$ \sum_{\mathbf{w}} f^{(j)}(\mathbf{w})\,{}_{\mathbf{u}}p^{(t_1,t_2)}_{\mathbf{uvw}} = 0. $$

Hence in (7.2) it suffices to take summands with $t_1 = t_2$, and

$$ \mathbf{E}(Y^{(i)}_{v}(\mathbf{u})\,Y^{(j)}_{v}(\mathbf{u})) = \sum_{t=1}^{\infty}\sum_{\mathbf{v}} f^{(i)}(\mathbf{v})\,f^{(j)}(\mathbf{v})\,{}_{\mathbf{u}}p^{(t)}_{\mathbf{uv}} = \mathbf{E}(Y^{(i,j)}_{v}(\mathbf{u})). $$

8. The Central Limit Theorem

The results of the last section may be summarized by the equations

(8.1) $$ M^{(i)} = \pi_{\mathbf{u}}\mathbf{E}(Y^{(i)}(\mathbf{u})) = 0 \qquad (1 \leqq i \leqq s), $$

(8.2) $$ M^{(i,j)} = \pi_{\mathbf{u}}\mathbf{E}(Y^{(i)}(\mathbf{u})\,Y^{(j)}(\mathbf{u})) = \frac{1}{4}\mu_{ij} \qquad (1 \leqq i, j \leqq s). $$

Lemma 9. *The quadratic form*

$$F(\mathbf{z})=F(z_1, \ldots, z_s) = \sum_{i,j=1}^{s} \mu_{ij}z_iz_j$$

is positive definite.

Proof. That F is semidefinite is a direct consequence of (8.2). However, in order to prove the definiteness, we proceed directly as follows. Since $\mu_{ij}=h_{ij}^2k_i^{-1}k_j^{-1}$ where $h_{ij} = \gcd(k_i, k_j)$, we will have to prove that $\sum h_{ij}^2z_iz_j$ is definite. Let D be the least common multiple of $k_1, \ldots, k_s$. If d, e are divisors of D (in symbols: $d|D$, $e|D$), put $g_{de}=\gcd(d, e)$. Then in a new notation our form $\sum h_{ij}^2z_iz_j$ becomes $\sum_{d,e\in\sigma} g_{de}^2z_dz_e$, where $\sigma=\{k_1, \ldots, k_s\}$. So if $\mathbf{z}$ is the vector with components z_d with $d|D$, it will suffice to show that the form

$$G_D(\mathbf{z}) = \sum_{d|D}\sum_{e|D} g_{de}^2z_dz_e$$

is positive definite. This will be done by induction on the number of prime factors of D. Note that $G_D(\mathbf{z})=B_D(\mathbf{z}, \mathbf{z})$ where

$$B_D(\mathbf{z}, \mathbf{w}) = \sum_{d|D}\sum_{e|D} g_{de}^2z_dw_e$$

When $D=1$, then $G_D(\mathbf{z})=z_1^2$. If $D=p_1^{\gamma_1}\ldots p_l^{\gamma_l}q^{\gamma}=Eq^{\gamma}$ with distinct primes $p_1, \ldots, p_l, q$, then $d|D$, $e|D$ are of the form $d=aq^{\alpha}$, $e=bq^{\beta}$ with $a|E$, $b|E$ and $0\leqq\alpha, \beta\leqq\gamma$, and

$$g_{de}=g_{ab}\cdot q^{\min(\alpha,\beta)}.$$

Let $\mathbf{z}_0$ be the vector with components z_a (ordered in some fixed way) with $a|E$. More generally, let $\mathbf{z}_\alpha$ where $0\leqq\alpha\leqq\gamma$ be the vector with components z_d where $d=aq^{\alpha}$ and $a|E$. Then in some sense, $\mathbf{z}=\mathbf{z}_0+\ldots+\mathbf{z}_\gamma$, and

$$G_D(\mathbf{z})=B_D(\mathbf{z}, \mathbf{z})=B_D(\mathbf{z}_0+\ldots+\mathbf{z}_\gamma, \mathbf{z}_0+\ldots+\mathbf{z}_\gamma)=$$

$$=\sum_{\alpha=0}^{\gamma}\sum_{\beta=0}^{\gamma} q^{2\min(\alpha,\beta)}B_E(\mathbf{z}_\alpha, \mathbf{z}_\beta).$$

The coefficient of each term $B_E(\mathbf{z}_\alpha, \mathbf{z}_\beta)$ is at least 1. The terms with $\min(\alpha, \beta)\geqq 1$ have a coefficient at least $q^2=1+(q^2-1)$, etc. We obtain

$$G_D(\mathbf{z})=G_E(\mathbf{z}_0+\ldots+\mathbf{z}_\gamma)+(q^2-1)G_E(\mathbf{z}_1+\ldots+\mathbf{z}_\gamma)+$$

$$+(q^4-q^2)G_E(\mathbf{z}_2+\ldots+\mathbf{z}_\gamma)+\ldots+(q^{2\gamma}-q^{2\gamma-2})G_E(\mathbf{z}_\gamma).$$

Now G_E is positive definite by induction, and $G_D(\mathbf{z})=0$ only if $\mathbf{0}=\mathbf{z}_\gamma=\mathbf{z}_{\gamma-1}+\mathbf{z}_\gamma=$ $=\ldots=\mathbf{z}_0+\ldots+\mathbf{z}_\gamma$, i.e. if $\mathbf{z}=\mathbf{0}$.

Theorem 1 now follows rapidly. Since $F(\mathbf{z})$ is positive definite, the matrix (μ_{ij}) has positive determinant. Moreover, the quadratic form Q of Theorem 1 must also be positive definite. Define $S_h^{(i)}$ and $\mathbf{R}_h(\xi_1, \ldots, \xi_s)$ as in section 4. In view of (8.1), (8.2) and of Lemma 9, the Central Limit Theorem for Markov Chains implies the desired relation (4.4). This Central Limit Theorem is proved in [1, §I. 16, Theorem 1] for a one-dimensional distribution; the case of an s-dimensional distribution is an easy generalization.

References

[1] K. L. CHUNG, *Markov Chains with Stationary Transition Probabilities*, Springer Grundlehren, **104** (1967).

[2] W. PHILIPP, *Mixing Sequences of Random Variables and Probabilistic Number Theory*, Mem. A.M.S., **114** (1971).

[3] K. B. STOLARSKY, Integers whose multiples have anomalous digital frequencies, *Acta Arith.*, (to appear).

[4] K. B. STOLARSKY and J. B. MUSKAT, *The number of binary digits in multiples of n.* (to appear).

UNIVERSITY OF COLORADO, BOULDER
AND
OCHANOMIZU UNIVERSITY, TOKYO

Studies in Pure Mathematics
To the Memory of Paul Turán

On Jacobi–Bertrand's proof of a Theorem of Poncelet

by

I. J. SCHOENBERG (West Point)

1. Introduction

A result from the golden age of Geometry is the following:

Theorem 1 (Poncelet). *Let C and C' be two ellipses in the plane, C' being interior to C. From a point P on C we draw a tangent to C' intersecting C again in P_1. Again, from P_1 we draw the tangent to C', intersecting C at P_2, and we continue this construction n times until we obtain the tangent $P_{n-1}P_n$ to C', with $P_n \in C$. The result is the polygonal line $PP_1 \ldots P_n$ inscribed in C and circumscribed to C'. If after one revolution along C we have that $P_n = P$, so that the polygon $PP_1 \ldots P_n$ is closed, then this will happen no matter what point P on C we start from.*

We also state the following two special cases of Theorem 1.

Theorem 2. *Theorem 1 holds for the special case when C and C' are circles.*

Theorem 3. *Theorem 1 holds if C is an ellipse and C' is a circle having its center O in the center of C.*

Jacobi gave a beautiful proof of Theorem 2 which was improved by J. Bertrand in [1, pp. 575–577]. Bertrand liked it so much that he reproduced it also at the end of his note on elliptic functions in [2, pp. 534–536].

Here we want to show 1 (by means of suitable projective maps of the plane, a proof of Theorem 1 may be reduced to a proof of Theorem 3. 2) a simplified version of Jacobi's idea leads to a direct proof of Theorem 3.

2. Reducing Theorem 1 to Theorem 3

Let D and D' denote the closed elliptical domains bounded by C and C', respectively. Let $P \in D$, and let Δ denote the polar line of P with respect to the ellipse C. As Δ does not intersect the interior of D, it follows that $\Delta \cap D' = \emptyset$. Therefore the pole P' of Δ with respect to the ellipse C' is in the interior of D': $P' \in D'$. This construction produces a mapping

$$T:D \to D' \subset D.$$

By BROUWER's fixed-point theorem there is a point P_0 such that $P'_0 = TP_0 = P_0$. Let Δ_0 be the polar line of P_0 with respect to C, as well as with respect to C'. Now we perform a projective map changing Δ_0 into the line at infinity, while P_0 is mapped into the point O. If we denote by C_1 and C'_1 the images of C and C', it follows that O must be the common center of the ellipses C_1 and C'_1.

Finally, an obvious affine map that leaves the common center O in place, will change C'_1 into a circle C'_2, and C_1 into an ellipse C_2.

The final result is that the original ellipses C, C', have been projectively mapped into the ellipse C_2 and the circle C'_2, respectively, the last two curves having the common center 0. Now it is clear that Theorem 3 implies Theorem 1.

3. A proof of Theorem 3 using the Jacobi–Bertrand's idea

Let

$$C: \frac{x^2}{a^2} + \frac{y^2}{b^2} = 1 \quad (b < a) \tag{1}$$

and

$$C': x^2 + y^2 = r^2 \quad (r < b). \tag{2}$$

Furthermore let

$$P = (a \cos \varphi, b \sin \varphi), \quad P' = (a \cos \varphi, a \sin \varphi) \tag{3}$$

be a point of C and its corresponding point on the principal circle Γ of C.

We draw the tangent PP_1 touching C' at M, and let

$$\sphericalangle AOP' = \varphi, \quad \sphericalangle AOP'_1 = \varphi_1, \tag{4}$$

our objective being to find the value of the derivative

$$\frac{d\varphi_1}{d\varphi}. \tag{5}$$

To find it we consider the affine map

$$T: x = x', \quad y = \frac{b}{a} y', \tag{6}$$

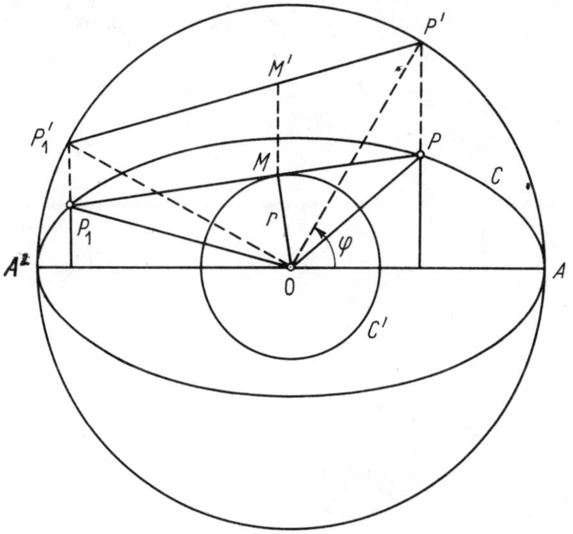

Fig. 1

which maps Γ into C. Let $M' = T^{-1}M$. If we let P move along C, the line PMP_1 being tangent to C at M, then the line $P'M'P_1'$ will envelope an ellipse $T^{-1}C'$, and will be tangent to it at M'. However, the line $P'M'P_1'$ intersects the circle Γ in equal angles, and it follows that

(7) $$\frac{d\varphi_1}{d\varphi} = \frac{M'P_1'}{M'P'} = \frac{MP_1}{MP}.$$

We also find that

$$(MP)^2 = (OP)^2 - (OM)^2 = a^2\cos^2\varphi + b^2\sin^2\varphi - r^2 =$$

$$= a^2(1-\sin^2\varphi) + b^2\sin^2\varphi - r^2 = a^2 - r^2 - (a^2 - b^2)\sin^2\varphi$$

and finally that

(8) $$MP = \sqrt{a^2 - r^2}\cdot\sqrt{1 - k^2\sin^2\varphi}$$

where

(9) $$k^2 = \frac{a^2 - b^2}{a^2 - r^2}.$$

Similarly

(10) $$MP_1 = \sqrt{a^2 - r^2}\cdot\sqrt{1 - k^2\sin^2\varphi_1}.$$

For the derivative (5) we now find, by (7), (8), and (10), the expression

$$\frac{d\varphi_1}{d\varphi}=\frac{\sqrt{1-k^2\sin^2\varphi_1}}{\sqrt{1-k^2\sin^2\varphi}},$$

whence the differential equation

$$\frac{d\varphi_1}{\sqrt{1-k^2\sin^2\varphi_1}}=\frac{d\varphi}{\sqrt{1-k^2\sin^2\varphi}}. \tag{11}$$

As in Jacobi's proof of Theorem 2, we consider the integral

$$J(\varphi,\varphi_1)=\int_{\varphi}^{\varphi_1}\frac{d\vartheta}{\sqrt{1-k^2\sin^2\vartheta}}, \tag{12}$$

whose differential

$$dJ(\varphi,\varphi_1)=\frac{d\varphi_1}{\sqrt{1-k^2\sin^2\varphi_1}}-\frac{d\varphi}{\sqrt{1-k^2\sin^2\varphi}}$$

vanishes, in view of (11). It follows that

(13) $J(\varphi,\varphi_1)=$ *a constant* ω, *independent of* φ.

If we now perform the successive constructions of the tangents n times, obtaining $P_1P_2,\ldots,P_{n-1}P_n$, all tangent to C', and the angles

$$\measuredangle AOP_2'=\varphi_2,\ \ldots\ \measuredangle AOP_n'=\varphi_n,$$

then, by (13), we find that

$$\int_{\varphi}^{\varphi_n}\frac{d\vartheta}{\sqrt{1-k^2\sin^2\vartheta}}=J(\varphi,\varphi_1)+J(\varphi_1,\varphi_2)+\ldots+J(\varphi_{n-1},\varphi_n)=n\omega. \tag{14}$$

In the case that the polygon $PP_1\ldots P_n$ closes after one revolution along C, hence $P_n=P$, then also $P_n'=P'$, and therefore $\varphi_n=\varphi+2\pi$. But then the equation (14) becomes

$$\int_{\varphi}^{\varphi+2\pi}\frac{d\vartheta}{\sqrt{1-k^2\sin^2\vartheta}}=n\omega. \tag{15}$$

This equation remains valid no matter how we choose φ, because 2π *is a period of the integrand of* (15). This establishes Theorem 3.

If the polygon $PP_1 \ldots P_n$ should close only after N revolutions along the ellipse C, then again (15) must hold, provided that we replace the upper limit of the integral by $\varphi + 2\pi N$. Since $2\pi N$ is again a period of the integrand, Theorem 3 holds also in this case.

References

[1] J. Bertrand, *Traité de Calcul Différentiel et de Calcul Intégral*, vol. **2**, Gauthier–Villars, Paris, 1870.
[2] J. Bertrand, *Note sur la Théorie des Fonctions Élliptiques*. An Appendix in J. M. C. Duhamel, *Éléments de Calcul Infinitésimal*, vol. **2**, pp. 526–536, Gauthier–Villars, Paris, 1876.

DEPARTMENT OF MATHEMATICS
UNITED STATES MILITARY ACADEMY
WEST POINT, NEW YORK 10996

Studies in Pure Mathematics
To the Memory of Paul Turán

Entire functions of bounded value distribution and gap power series

by

S. M. SHAH (Lexington)

Abstract

This paper discusses functions of bounded value distribution and bounded index. It is shown that there exist functions in these two classes for which the known inequality giving exponential type can be improved.

1. Introduction

In this paper we give a brief survey of known results on entire functions of bounded value distribution (b.v.d.) considered by the late Professor Paul Turán (see [6], [7]). We also give some new results on this class of functions with brief proofs.

Let $n(a, R, 1/(f-w))$ denote the number of zeros of an entire function $f(z)-w$ ($w \in \mathbf{C}$) in the disc $|z-a|<R$ ($a \in \mathbf{C}, R>0$). We define now functions of bounded index (b.i.) and b.v.d.

Definition 1.1. An entire function f is said to be of b.v.d. if for every $R>0$, there exists a fixed integer $P(R)>0$ such that

$$n\left(a, R, \frac{1}{f-w}\right) \leqq P(R)$$

for all $a \in \mathbf{C}$ and all $w \in \mathbf{C}$.

Definition 1.2. An entire function is said to be of bounded index if there exists an integer $N \geqq 0$ such that for all $z \in \mathbf{C}$ and for all positive integers k,

$$\max_{0 \leqq j \leqq N} \left\{ \frac{|f^{(j)}(z)|}{j!} \right\} \geqq \frac{|f^{(k)}(z)|}{k!}.$$

The least such integer N is called the index of f ([8], [12]).

The two concepts are related. In fact we have:

Theorem 1.3. [7]. *An entire function f has b.v.d. if and only if f' has b.i.*

Theorem 1.4. ([7], [11]). (i) *If f is any entire function such that f' is of b.i. $N(f')$ then f is also of b.i. $N(f)$ and $N(f) \leqq N(f')+1$.*

(ii) *There exists an entire function F of b.i. such that F' is of unbounded index.*

Note that the inequality in (i) is sharp. Consider for instance $f(z)=e^z+1$. Here $N(f)=1$, $N(f')=0$.

2. Growth problem

If f is an entire function of b.i. then f is necessarily of exponential type. More precisely we have:

Theorem 2.1. ([7], [10]). *Let f be an entire function of b.i. $N(f)$. Write $N(f)=N$. Then*

$$|f(z)| \leqq \left\{ \max_{0 \leqq k \leqq N} \left(\frac{|f^{(k)}(0)|}{(N+1)^k} \right) \exp (N+1)|z| \right\} \tag{2.1}$$

$$\limsup_{r \to \infty} \frac{\nu(r, f)}{r} \leqq N+1 \tag{2.2}$$

where $\nu(r, f)$ denotes the central index of f.

Let

$$\lim_{r \to \infty} \begin{Bmatrix} \sup \\ \inf \end{Bmatrix} \frac{\log M(r, f)}{r} = \begin{Bmatrix} T(f) \\ t(f) \end{Bmatrix}. \tag{2.3}$$

Then either of these inequalities (2.1), (2.2) imply that $T(f) \leqq N+1$. This result is sharp, for $f(z)=\exp((N+1)z)$ is of index N and type $T=N+1$. We now show that there exist functions for which (2.2) gives

$$T(f) \leqq \{N(f)+1\}/e.$$

Theorem 2.2. *Let $\{\lambda_n\}_1^\infty$ be a strictly increasing sequence of positive integers such that*

$$\lim_{n \to \infty} \lambda_n/\lambda_{n+1}=0, \quad \liminf_{n \to \infty} (\log \lambda_n)/(\log \lambda_{n+1})>0.$$

Let $\{a_n\}_1^\infty \in \mathbf{C}$ be such that

$$0< \lim_{n \to \infty} \begin{Bmatrix} \sup \\ \inf \end{Bmatrix} \frac{1}{\lambda_n} \left| \frac{a_{n-1}}{a_n} \right|^{1/(\lambda_n-\lambda_{n-1})} < \infty.$$

Then $g(z)=\sum_{n=1}^{\infty} a_n z^{\lambda_n}$ *is an entire function of exponential type and there exist two entire functions* f *of b.i. and* Φ *of b.v.d. such that*

(i) $\log M(r,g) \sim \log M(r,f) \sim \log M(r,\Phi), \quad r\to\infty;$

(ii) $T(f)=T(\Phi)\leqq \frac{1}{e}\min(N(f)+1, N(\Phi)+1, N(\Phi')+1).$

Proof. The hypothesis implies that, for $n>n_0$, $a_n\neq 0$. Let, for $n>n_0$,

$$x_n=\left|\frac{a_{n-1}}{a_n}\right|^{1/(\lambda_n-\lambda_{n-1})}; \quad \lim_{n\to\infty}\begin{Bmatrix}\sup\\ \inf\end{Bmatrix}\frac{x_n}{\lambda_n}=\begin{Bmatrix}B\\ A\end{Bmatrix}.$$

Then for $n>n_1(\varepsilon)$, $x_n<(B+\varepsilon)\lambda_n$, $x_{n+1}>(A-\varepsilon)\lambda_{n+1}$, $(B+\varepsilon)\lambda_n<(A-\varepsilon)\lambda_{n+1}$. Hence $x_n<x_{n+1}$. Now $\log 1/|a_n|=(\lambda_n\log\lambda_n)(1+o(1))$. Hence g is an entire function of order $\rho=1$. Further for $n>n_2$, and $x_n\leqq r<x_{n+1}$, $\mu(r)=|a_n|r^{\lambda_n}$, $\nu(r)=\lambda_n$ and it follows that the lower order λ of g is given by $\lambda=\liminf_{n\to\infty}(\log\lambda_n)/(\log\lambda_{n+1})>0$. Let

$$\begin{Bmatrix}\gamma(g)\\ \delta(g)\end{Bmatrix}=\lim_{r\to\infty}\begin{Bmatrix}\sup\\ \inf\end{Bmatrix}\frac{\nu(r,g)}{r}.$$

Then $\gamma(g)=1/A$, $\delta(g)=0$ and since $\rho=1$, $\delta\leqq t\leqq T\leqq\gamma\leqq Te$ [9], we have $T(g)\leqq 1/A$. Hence [4] there exists an entire function f of b.i. such that

$$\log M(r,g)\sim\log M(r,f), \quad r\to\infty.$$

Write

$$I(r,g)=\int_1^r\frac{\nu(t,g)}{t}\,dt.$$

Then $\log M(r,g)\sim I(r,g)$; and $I(r,g)=o(x_n)$ when $r=x_n$,

$$T(g)=\frac{1}{e}\limsup_{n\to\infty}\frac{\lambda_n}{x_n}=\frac{1}{eA}, \quad t(g)=0, \quad \gamma(f)=\frac{1}{A}=eT(f).$$

By (2.2) $\gamma(f)\leqq N(f)+1$.

By considering $g'(z)=\Sigma a_n\lambda_n z^{\lambda_n-1}$, we obtain similarly another entire function Φ of b.v.d. such that $\log M(r,g)\sim\log M(r,\Phi)$ and

$$T(g)=T(\Phi)=T(f)\leqq\frac{1}{e}\min(N(\Phi)+1, N(\Phi')+1).$$

The proof is complete.

Remarks. (i) See [5] for a similar theorem and an example.

(ii) These functions g, f, Φ are not bounded on the real axis. This follows from Theorem 6.6.6 of [1].

3. Functions of b.v.d.

(i) All solutions of linear differential equations with constant coefficients are of b.v.d. [10]. More generally entire solutions of the linear differential equation

$$P_0(z)w^{(n)}+P_1(z)w^{(n-1)}+\ldots+P_n(z)w=q(z) \tag{3.1}$$

where P_j and q are polynomials and $\deg P_0 \geqq \deg P_j$ $(j=1, 2, \ldots, n)$ are of b.v.d. For further extensions see [5], [12].

Consider the equation

$$w^{(n)}+\sum_{j=1}^{n} f_j(z)w^{(n-j)}=0\,, \tag{3.2}$$

where f_j are all entire functions. (i) If every solution of this equation has b.v.d., then the f_j are all constants [15]. (ii) TIJDEMAN ([2, p. 147], [13]) has shown that the coefficients f_j are polynomials if and only if there exist fixed numbers p and q such that each solution of (3.2) is p-valent in any disk

$$\{z:|z-z_0|<1/(1+|z_0|^q)\}\,. \tag{3.3}$$

Thus the equation $w^{(2)}+(z-1)w^{(1)}-zw=0$ has one solution of b.v.d., and another an entire function of order 2 and so not of b.v.d. Case (ii) gives p-valence of each solution in discs (3.3).

(ii) Functions of b.v.d. are not closed under addition [12].

(iii) Functions of b.v.d. are not closed under multiplication (unpublished result due to G. FRICKE).

(iv) A function of b.v.d. is of exponential type but the converse is not true [10].

(v) Every entire function of exponential type can be expressed as the difference of two entire functions of b.v.d. [12].

(vi) When f is of b.v.d. we write

$$p(R)=\sup_a \sup_w n\left(a, R, \frac{1}{f-w}\right)$$

where $R>0$ is fixed. Then $p(R)\leqq P(R)<\infty$ and we see that f does not take any value more than $p(R)$ times in every disc $|z-a|<R$. Further [7] $P(1)\leqq 3e(N(f')+1)$. Similarly, if f is of b.i.

$$\sup_a n(a, 1, 1/f)\leqq K(f)<\infty.$$

We show here that the converse is not true.

Theorem 3.1. *There exists an entire function f such that*

$$(3.4) \qquad T(f)=0, \quad \sup_a n(a, 1, 1/f)=1$$

and f is not of b.i.

Proof. Our construction of the required function f is similar to that in [3]. Let $\{N_k\}_{k=1}^{\infty}$ be a strictly increasing sequence of positive integers such that $N_k \geqq [\exp(k^2+k)+1]$, $k \geqq 1$. Define sequences $\{n_k\}_{k=1}^{\infty}$ and $\{d_i\}_{i=1}^{\infty}$ as follows:

$$n_1 = N_1,\ n_k = n_{k-1} + kN_k,\ k>1$$

$$d_i = \begin{cases} 4, & i \leqq n_4 \\ (kn_{k+1})^2, & i = n_k,\ k>4 \\ k, & n_k < i \leqq n_k + N_k,\ k>3 \\ i^2, & n_k + N_k < i < n_{k+1},\ k>3. \end{cases}$$

Then $\lim_{n\to\infty} d_n = \infty$. Let $a_n = \sum_{i=1}^{n} d_i$. Then $\sum_{n=1}^{\infty} 1/a_n < \infty$, $\sum_{j=1}^{\infty} 1/jd_j < \infty$. Let $f(z) = \prod_{n=1}^{\infty} (1 - z/a_n)$. Then $T(f)=0$ and (3.4) is satisfied. For $z_k = a(n_k)+2$, $k>4$, we have

$$\left| \sum_{i=1}^{\infty} \frac{1}{z_k - a_i} \right| > k.$$

Hence f is not of b.i. and consequently not of b.v.d.

(vii) Let B denote the class of all functions of b.i., B^{T} the class of all functions of b.v.d.; and B^* the class of all entire functions f which satisfy some differential equation of the form (3.1), where P_j and q are always polynomials such that $\deg P_j \leqq \deg P_0$ for each such equation with varying n, P_j and q.

Then it is easily seen that $B^* \subset B^{\mathrm{T}} \subset B$ and the inclusion is proper. The function Φ in Theorem 2.2 is in class B^{T} but not in class B^* since for every entire solution f of (3.1) we must have $T(f)=t(f)$ [14]. Further if [11]

$$f(z) = \prod_{j=1}^{\infty} \left(1 - \frac{z}{a_j}\right)^{k_j}$$

where $\{a_j\}$ and $\{k_j\}$ are certain strictly increasing sequences, then $f(z)+c$ ($c \in C, c \neq 0$) is in class B but not in B^{T}.

References

[1] R. P. BOAS, *Entire Functions*, Academic Press, New York, 1954.

[2] J. C. CLUNIE and W. K. HAYMAN, *Symposium on Complex Analysis*, Canterbury, Lond. Math. Soc. Lecture Notes, 1974.

[3] GERD H. FRICKE, Entire functions having positive zeros, *Indian J. Pure and Appl. Math.*, **5** (1974), 478–485.

[4] GERD H. FRICKE, Entire functions with prescribed asymptotic behavior, *Rocky Mountain J. Math.*, **6** (1976), 237–246.

[5] G. H. FRICKE and S. M. SHAH, On bounded value distribution and bounded index, *Nonlinear Analysis Theory Methods and Applications*, Vol. **2**, (1978), 423–435.

[6] W. K. HAYMAN, *Research problems in Function Theory*, Athlone Press, London, 1967.

[7] W. K. HAYMAN, Differential inequalities and local valency, *Pacific J. Math.*, **44** (1973), 117–137.

[8] B. LEPSON, Differential equations of infinite order, hyperdirichlet series and entire functions of bounded index, *Proc. Sympos. Pure Math.* vol. **XI**, Amer. Math. Soc. Providence, R. I., (1968), 298–307.

[9] S. M. SHAH, The maximum term of an entire series (III), *Quart. J. Math.* (Oxford), **19** (1948), 220–223.

[10] S. M. SHAH, Entire functions of bounded index, *Proc. Amer. Math. Soc.*, **19** (1968), 1017–1022.

[11] S. M. SHAH, On entire functions of bounded index whose derivatives are of unbounded index, *J. Lond. Math. Soc.*, (2) **4** (1971), 127–139.

[12] S. M. SHAH, *Entire functions of bounded index*, Springer Lecture Notes in Math. 599 (1977), 117–145.

[13] R. TIJDEMAN, *On the distribution of values of certain functions*, Doctoral dissertation, Univ. of Amsterdam, 1969.

[14] G. VALIRON, *Lectures on the General Theory of Integral Functions*, Chelsea, New York, 1949.

[15] H. WITTICH, *Zur Kennzeichung linearer Differentialgleichungen mit konstanten Koeffizienten*, Festband zum, 70 Geburstag von R. Nevanlinna, Springer–Berlin, 128–134, 1966.

DEPARTMENT OF MATHEMATICS
UNIVERSITY OF KENTUCKY
LEXINGTON, KENTUCKY 40506
U.S.A.

Studies in Pure Mathematics
To the Memory of Paul Turán

Estimates for the moduli of polynomials with algebraic coefficients at the values of E-functions

by

A. B. SHIDLOVSKY (Moscow)

§ 1. Definitions and notations

The paper establishes general theorems concerning lower estimates for moduli of polynomials with algebraic integer coefficients at the values at algebraic points of a set of E-functions, satisfying a system of linear differential equations with coefficients from $\mathbf{C}(z)$. In some cases such estimates are also obtained for polynomials depending on a subset of E-functions, for which the considered basic set consists of E-functions, algebraically dependent over $\mathbf{C}(z)$.

In the following let $\mathbf{A}$ denote the field of all algebraic numbers over $\mathbf{Q}$, $\mathbf{K}$ an algebraic field over $\mathbf{Q}$, $h=[\mathbf{K}:\mathbf{Q}]$ and $\mathbf{I}$ an imaginary quadratic field.

If $\xi \in \mathbf{K}$, then let $\overline{|\xi|} = \max\limits_{1\leq i\leq h} |\xi_i|$, where $\xi_1, \ldots, \xi_h$ are the conjugates to ξ in $\mathbf{K}$.

The algebraical independence measure of the numbers $\alpha_1, \ldots, \alpha_m$ is defined by the function

$$\Phi(\alpha_1, \ldots, \alpha_m; s; H) = \min |\mathscr{P}(\alpha_1, \ldots, \alpha_m)|, \tag{1}$$

where $\mathscr{P} = \mathscr{P}(z_1, \ldots, z_m) \in \mathbf{Z}[z_1, \ldots, z_m]$,

$$\mathscr{P} \neq 0, \qquad H_{\mathscr{P}} \leqq H,$$

$H_{\mathscr{P}}$ is the height of $\mathscr{P}$ (the maximum of the moduli of all coefficients of $\mathscr{P}$), $s = \deg \mathscr{P}$ in $z_1, \ldots, z_m$ and the minimum is taken over all the polynomials, satifying these conditions.

For $m=1$ the function

$$\Phi(\alpha; s; H) = \min |\mathscr{P}(\alpha)| \tag{2}$$

is called the transcendence measure of the number α.

With the help of Dirichlet's principle it is easy to obtain upper estimates for the measure (1) for any set of numbers α (cf. [1, 2].). In the transcendental number theory and its applications it is of interest to get lower estimates for the measures of various classes of numbers α.

If for example a lower estimate for $\Phi(\alpha; s; H)$ is known, then we know that the same estimate holds for $|\mathscr{P}(\alpha)|$ for each

$$\mathscr{P}(z) \in \mathbf{Z}[z], \quad \mathscr{P}(z) \not\equiv 0, \quad \deg \mathscr{P} \leqq s, \quad H_{\mathscr{P}} \leqq H,$$

as $\Phi(\alpha; s; H)$ is the least value of the modulus in the finite set of all such polynomials.

The modern analytical methods of the transcendental number theory enable us to obtain estimates of this type for the values of some classes of functions which are fairly close to their natural bounds.

The method, due to C. SIEGEL [3], which is a natural generalization of the classical Hermite-Lindemann method, enables us to prove some fairly general theorems on such estimates for the values of a class of entire functions, called E-functions by SIEGEL, which have algebraical coefficients in their Taylor expansions satisfying some arithmetical conditions and which satisfy linear differential equations with the coefficients from $\mathbf{C}(z)$. C. SIEGEL (cf. [3, 4]) calls an entire function

$$f(z) = \sum_{n=0}^{\infty} c_n \frac{z^n}{n!}$$

an E-function, if: 1) $c_n \in \mathbf{K}$, $n=0, 1, \ldots$, 2) for any $\varepsilon > 0$, $c_n = O(n^{\varepsilon n})$ as $n \to \infty$, 3) there exists a sequence of numbers $\{q_n\}$, $q_n \in \mathbf{N}$, such that the numbers $q_n c_k \in \mathbf{Z}_K$, $k=0, 1, \ldots, n$, for all $n=1, 2, \ldots$ and for any $\varepsilon > 0$, $q_n = O(n^{\varepsilon n})$ as $n \to \infty$.

The E-functions form a ring of functions, closed with respect to differentiating and integrating from 0 to z and substituting the argument λz for z, where $\lambda \in \mathbf{A}$.

E-functions with the coefficients of their power series from an algebraic field $\mathbf{K}$ will be called KE-functions.

In 1929 in his paper [3] C. SIEGEL published a method of proving the transcendence and the algebraical independence of the values of E-functions at algebraic points. With the help of this method he proved the algebraical independence of the numbers $J_0(z)$ and $J_0'(z)$, where $J_0(z)$ is the Bessel function.

He also obtained the estimate

$$\Phi(J_0(\xi), J_0'(\xi); s; H) > \sigma(\xi, s) H^{-123h^3 s^2},$$

$$\sigma(\xi, s) > 0,$$

where $\xi \neq 0$, $\xi \in \mathbf{A}$, and h is the degree of ξ over $\mathbf{Q}$.

In the same paper C. SIEGEL also obtained a series of results on the arithmetical properties of the values of E-functions at algebraic ponts, satisfying linear differential equations of the first or the second order.

In his monograph [4] SIEGEL summarized his method in the form of a general theorem about the algebraical independence of the values of E-functions.

In the midst of the fifties Siegel's method developed further (cf. the reviews [1, 5] and the papers [6, 7, 8]) which made it possible to obtain many new results about the arithmetical properties of the values of E-functions, satisfying linear differential equations of arbitrary orders.

We shall consider a set of KE-functions

$$f_1(z), \ldots, f_m(z) \tag{3}$$

which forms a solution of the system of linear differential equations

$$y'_k = Q_{k,i} + \sum_{i=1}^{m} Q_{k,i} y_i, \quad k=1, \ldots, m, \qquad Q_{k,i} \in \mathbf{C}(z), \tag{4}$$

or the system of homogeneous equations

$$y'_k = \sum_{i=1}^{m} Q_{k,i} y_i, \quad k=1, \ldots, m \qquad Q_{k,i} \in \mathbf{C}(z). \tag{5}$$

In this case (see [6]) the numerical coefficients of the polynomials (the numerators and the denomiators of the functions $Q_{k,i}$ in (4) or (5)) may be chosen from $\mathbf{Z}_{\mathbf{K}}[z]$, so $Q_{k,i} \in \mathbf{K}(z)$.

Let $T = T(z) \in \mathbf{Z}_{\mathbf{K}}[z]$ and $T_0 = T_0(z) \in \mathbf{Z}_{\mathbf{K}}[z]$ denote the polynomials, which are the least common multiples of the denominators of all the functions $Q_{k,i}$ in system (4) or (5) respectively. Then all the $TQ_{k,i} \in \mathbf{Z}_{\mathbf{K}}[z]$ and all the $T_0 Q_{k,i} \in \mathbf{Z}_{\mathbf{K}}[z]$, respectively.

It was proved (see [6]) that if the set of the KE-functions (3) forms a solution of system (4) (in particular of system (5)) and they are algebraically independent over $\mathbf{C}(z)$ and $\xi \in \mathbf{A}$, $\xi T(\xi) \neq 0$, then the numbers

$$f_1(\xi), \ldots, f_m(\xi) \tag{6}$$

are algebraically independent.

With the help of the generalization of Siegel's method given in paper [6] and SIEGEL's work [4] it is quite easy to get a general theorem concerning the estimate of the algebraical independence measure of the numbers (6). Such a theorem for the case of a homogenous system (5) was published by S. LANG in 1962 [9]. It states that under the conditions, formulated in the preceeding paragraph

$$\Phi(f_1(\xi), \ldots, f_m(\xi); s; H) > \sigma H^{-\gamma s^m}, \tag{7}$$

where $\sigma > 0$ is a constant depending only on the functions (3), system (5), the numbers ξ, m and s, and $\gamma > 0$ is a constant, depending only on the number m and the degree κ of the algebraic field got by adjoining the number ξ to the field $\mathbf{K}$ over $\mathbf{Q}$.

By the use of the refinements of the main lemmas of the method, established in a paper [8] in 1968, A. I. GALOCHKIN [10] replaced in the inequality (7) the constant γ by a concrete function of κ and m and established an analogous estimate in a more general situation.

In the papers [2, 11] some theorems are proved on the estimates of the algebraical independence measure of the values of IE-functions, for the case $\mathbf{K}=\mathbf{I}$ and $\xi \in \mathbf{I}$, fairly close to their natural bounds. A similar theorem has been published in the paper of V. G. CHIRSKY [12].

In the paper of JU. V. NESTERENKO [13] an estimate of the form (7), is proved in which $\gamma=4^m\kappa^m(m\kappa^2+\kappa+1)$, the constant σ effectively depends on s, and s may grow together with H up to some limit, depending on H. The formulation of a theorem of this type in the case $\mathbf{K}=\mathbf{I}$ and $\xi \in \mathbf{I}$ was published already in 1967 in the work [14].

In order to obtain the lower bounds for the moduli of the polynomials with algebraic integer coefficients in the considered numbers let us generalize the above defined measure concepts and consider the algebraical independence and the transcendence measures with respect to the field $\mathbf{K}$. The definitions of these measures are quite analogous to the definitions of the measures (1) and (2) with the only difference that the coefficients of the polynomial $\mathscr{P}$ belong to $\mathbf{Z_K}$ and its height with respect to the field $\mathbf{K}$ (the maximum of the moduli of the coefficients of the polynomial $\mathscr{P}$ and of all their conjugates) do not exceed H.

The corresponding measures will be denoted analogously to (1) and (2) but instead of Φ we shall write $\Phi_{\mathbf{K}}$.

In order to estimate homogeneous polynomials of the given numbers let us consider the homogeneous algebraical independence measures $\Phi^0(\alpha_1, \ldots, \alpha_m; s; H)$ and $\Phi^0_{\mathbf{K}}(\alpha_1, \ldots, \alpha_m; s; H)$, which are defined analogously to the measure (1) with the only difference that in their definitions $\mathscr{P}(z_1, \ldots, z_m)$ is a homogeneous polynomial from $\mathbf{Z}[z_1, \ldots, z_m]$ or $\mathbf{Z_K}[z_1, \ldots, z_m]$, resp.

In the subsequent we shall write "homogeneously algebraically independent" instead of "are not connected by a homogeneous algebraical equation".

One can deduce the estimates of Φ^0 and $\Phi^0_{\mathbf{K}}$ from the estimates of Φ and $\Phi_{\mathbf{K}}$ considering the number $\alpha_{m+1}=1$ and also the estimates of Φ and $\Phi_{\mathbf{K}}$ for the numbers $\alpha_1/\alpha_m, \ldots, \alpha_{m-1}/\alpha_m$.

As $\mathbf{Z}\subset\mathbf{Z_K}$, the established lower estimates imply the same estimates for Φ and Φ^0.

In the paper [11] estimates are obtained for the measures $\Phi^0_{\mathbf{I}}$and Φ^0 for the values of IE-functions.

In the paper [7] some theorems are proved on the algebraic independence of a subset of numbers (6) in the case, when the initial set of KE-functions is algebraically dependent over $\mathbf{C}(z)$. In the present paper in this situation estimates will be obtained for the algebraical independence measures of values of KE-functions in some cases.

Considering the measures of values of KE-functions (3) at the point ξ we can choose $\xi \in \mathbf{A}$ but $\xi \notin \mathbf{K}$ and also consider the coefficients of the polynomial $\mathscr{P}$ from $\mathbf{Z}_{\mathbf{K}^*}$ where $\mathbf{K}^*$ is different from $\mathbf{K}$. In the formulations of the theorems and in their proofs it is convenient to consider a field, containing the fields $\mathbf{K}$, $\mathbf{K}^*$ and the number ξ.

Therefore in the future we shall assume that the field $\mathbf{K}$ is such a field itself.

In what follows we shall use the following notations. The positive constants b (in § 2) and c (in §§ 2–6) with various indices and without indices will depend only on the given KE-functions (3), the system of the differential equations (4) or (5) for these functions, the number m of the functions (3) and the numbers s and ξ. The numbers b depend also on the numbers ε and N, introduced in § 2. The positive constants γ and γ_i with various indices will depend only on the function (3), on the numbers m (in § 2, 3, 4) and l (in § 5). Besides the letters c and γ in different cases denote different constants.

The proofs of the present work use the results of the papers [3, 6, 7, 8, 10]. The review of the results, connected with these subjects, is given in [1, 5].

§ 2. The main lemma

The above mentioned method of the transcendental number theory will be applied for estimating the measures of algebraical independence of the values of E-functions in various cases, depending on the number and structure of the algebraical equations that connect the considered E-functions over $\mathbf{C}(z)$. Therefore in order to avoid the repetition of similar arguments we shall sum up the situation in the form of a main lemma.

Consider the set (3) of KE-functions that satisfy system (5) of homogeneous differential equations.

Let L_N, $N \in \mathbf{N}$, denote the set of $\rho_{N,m} = \dfrac{(N+m-1)!}{N!(m-1)!}$ power products

$$\text{(8)} \qquad \begin{cases} f_1^{k_1}(z) \dots f_m^{k_m}(z), & k_1 + \dots + k_m = N, \\ k_i \geqq 0, \quad i = 1, \dots, m; & m \geqq 2, \end{cases}$$

for any $N = 1, 2, \dots$.

By Lemma 12 of the paper [6], setting in it $k_1 + k_2 + \dots + k_m = N$ we see, that the set of $\rho_{N,m}$ functions (8) forms a solution of a system of linear homogeneous differential equations of the form (5), in which the number m is replaced with $\rho_{N,m}$ and which has no poles except those of system (5).

Denote by B_N a set of the power products of functions, satisfying the conditions:

1) $B_N \subset L_N$,

2) the number of the elements of B_N is equal to $\mu = \varphi(N)$, where $\varphi(N)$ is some positive increasing function of N,

3) the elements of B_N are linearly independent over $\mathbf{C}(z)$,

(4) a set of μ functions of the set B_N forms a solution of a system consisting of μ linear homogeneous differential equations of the form (5), in which the number m is replaced by μ and the poles of the coefficients of this system belong to $\mathscr{D}$, where $\mathscr{D}$ is some finite set of numbers from $\mathbf{K}$.

Such a set B_N exists for every $N = 1, 2, \dots$ for the KE-functions (3), satisfying the system (5). For example, if the functions (3) are homogeneously algebraically independent over $\mathbf{C}(z)$, then we can set $B_N = L_N$ and $\varphi(N) = \rho_{N,m}$. If these functions are homogeneously algebraically dependent over $\mathbf{C}(z)$, then for B_N we can choose, for example, any subset of the functions (8), that forms a basis of the linear space, generated by the functions (8) over $\mathbf{C}(z)$. It is evident, that the four conditions hold for B_N.

Now denote by $L_{N,\xi}$ and $B_{N,\xi}$ the sets of numbers obtained from the sets L_N and B_N substituting in all their elements $z = \xi$, $\xi \in \mathbf{K}$, $\xi \neq 0$, $\xi \in \mathscr{D}$.

A homogenous polynomial

$$\mathscr{P}=\mathscr{P}(f_1(z), \ldots, f_m(z)), \quad \mathscr{P}(z_1, \ldots, z_m) \in \mathbf{Z}_{\mathbf{K}}[z_1, \ldots z_m],$$

(9)

$$\mathscr{P}(z_1, \ldots, z_m) \not\equiv 0, \quad \deg \mathscr{P}(z_1, \ldots, z_m)=s, \quad s \geqq 1,$$

for some N, $N \geqq s$, and $\xi \in \mathbf{K}$, $\xi \neq 0$, $\xi \notin \mathscr{D}$, will be called a $B_{N,\xi}$-polynomial, if for such N and ξ the polynomial of the numbers (6)

(10) $$f_1^{k_1}(\xi) \ldots f_m^{k_m}(\xi)\mathscr{P}(f_1(\xi), \ldots, f_m(\xi)), \quad k_1+\ldots+k_m=N-s$$

for every element $f_1^{k_1}(z) \ldots f_m^{k_m}(z) \in B_{N-s}$ after multiplying term by term in (10), happens to be a linear combination of the elements from $B_{N,\xi}$ or may be represented as a linear combination of elements from $B_{N,\xi}$ with coefficients from $\mathbf{K}$, by the help of the linear equations connecting the numbers of the set $L_{N,\xi}$ and in the latter case all the $\sigma_{N-s,m}$ linear forms of the elements of the set $B_{N,\xi}$ with coefficients from $\mathbf{K}$, obtained from different polynomials (10), will be linearly independent over $\mathbf{K}$ as linear forms in these elements (in the first case this is evident).

If the KE-functions (3) are algebraically independent over $\mathbf{C}(Z)$ and $B_N=L_N$, $N=1, 2, \ldots$, then any polynomial (9) will be a $B_{N,\xi}$-polynomial for every $N \geqq s$ and for any $\xi \in K$, $\xi T_0(\xi) \neq 0$.

Main lemma. *Let the polynomial $\mathscr{P}$ (9) of height H with respect to the field $\mathbf{K}$, for some N, $N \geqq s$, and $\xi \in \mathbf{K}$, $\xi \neq 0$, $\xi \notin \mathscr{D}$ be a $B_{N,\xi}$-polynomials, and further let $v=\varphi(N-s)$ and $w=\mu-v$. Then if N is such that*

(11) $$\mu-(2h-1)w>0,$$

then the inequality

(12) $$|\mathscr{P}(\xi)|=|\mathscr{P}(f_1(\xi), \ldots, f_m(\xi)|>CH^{-2h\mu}$$

holds.

Proof. Enumerate all the KE-functions belonging to B_N in an arbitrary order and denote them by

(13) $$\mathscr{F}_1(z), \ldots, \mathscr{F}_\mu(z), \quad \mu=\varphi(N).$$

Analogously denote the functions of the set B_{N-s} by

(14) $$\mathscr{G}_1(z), \ldots, \mathscr{G}_v(z), \quad v=\varphi(N-s).$$

Consider the set of v polynomials of the numbers (6)

(15)
$$\Psi_i(\xi)=r_i\mathcal{G}_i(\xi)\mathcal{P}(f_1(\xi),\ldots,f_m(\xi)),$$
$$r_i\in\mathbf{N},\quad i=1,\ldots,v.$$

Then, by the definition of a $B_{N,\xi}$-polynomial, for the corresponding numbers r_i the polynomials $\Psi_i(\xi)$ may be represented in the form

(16)
$$\Psi_i(\xi)=a_{i,1}\mathcal{F}_1(\xi)+\ldots+a_{i,\mu}\mathcal{F}_\mu(\xi),\quad i=1,\ldots,v,$$
$$a_{i,j}\in\mathbf{Z}_{\mathbf{K}},\quad \overline{|a_{i,j}|}\leqq b_1H,\quad i=1,\ldots,v,\quad j=1,\ldots,\mu.$$

This time $b_1=r_1=\ldots=r_v=1$ and the $a_{i,j}$'s are the coefficients of the polynomial $\mathcal{P}$ if all the polynomials (15) are the linear combinations of the numbers

(17)
$$\mathcal{F}_1(\xi),\ldots,\mathcal{F}_\mu(\xi)$$

and r_i are such that all the numbers $a_{i,j}\in\mathbf{Z}_{\mathbf{K}}$ in the case when the polynomials (15) may be represented in the form of linear combination of the numbers (17), by the help of the linear equations with coefficients from $\mathbf{K}$, connecting the numbers of the set $L_{N,\xi}$.

If in the lemma 1 of the work [6] we replace the number m by the number μ, the KE-functions (3) by the KE-functions (13) and use the refinement of the lemma, given in the paper [8], then for some $n\in\mathbf{N}$ we may construct an approximating linear functional form in the functions (13)

$$R_1(z)=\sum_{l=1}^{\mu}\mathcal{P}_{1,l}(z)\mathcal{F}_l(z),\quad R_1(z)\not\equiv 0,$$

$$\mathcal{P}_{1,l}(z)\in\mathbf{Z}_{\mathbf{K}}[z],\quad \deg\mathcal{P}_{1,l}(z)\leqq 2n-1,\quad l=1,\ldots\mu,$$

which has a "sufficiently large" order of zero at $z=0$ and "sufficiently sharp" estimates are valid for the coefficients of the polynomials $\mathcal{P}_{1,l}(z)$ and their conjugates in the field $\mathbf{K}$.

The derivative $R_1'(z)$ is a linear from in the functions (13) and their derivatives. In view of the 4th condition of the definition of the set B_N we may replace the derivatives $\mathcal{F}_l'(z)$ $=1$, $l=1,\ldots,\mu$ by the right-hand sides of the corresponding differential equations which are satified by the set of functions (13) and we may multiply the result by the polynomial $T_0(z)$, corresponding to the system.

Then $T_0(z)R_1'(z)$ is again a linear form in the functions (13) with coefficients from $\mathbf{C}[z]$. Therefore if we put

$$R_k(z)=T_0(z)R_{k-1}'(z),\quad k=2,3,\ldots,$$

we obtain a set of linear functional forms

$$R_k(z) = \sum_{l=1}^{\mu} \mathscr{P}_{k,l}(z)\mathscr{F}_l(z), \quad k=1, 2, \ldots, \mathscr{P}_{k,l}(z) \in \mathbf{Z_K}[z].$$

In the paper [6, 8] it is proved that there exists an $n_0 \in \mathbf{N}$ such that for $n \geqq n_0$ the linear forms $R_1(z), \ldots, R_\mu(z)$ are linearly independent and if $\xi \in \mathbf{K}$, $\xi T_0(\xi) \neq 0$ (i.e. $\xi \neq 0$ and $\xi \notin \mathscr{D}$), then for $n \geqq n_0$ among the numerical linear approximation forms in the numbers (17) with coefficients from $\mathbf{Z_K}$

$$R_k(\xi) = \sum_{l=1}^{\mu} \mathscr{P}_{k,l}(\xi)\mathscr{F}_l(\xi), \quad k=1, \ldots, \mu+t, \quad t=\varepsilon n+O(1),$$

(where $0<\varepsilon \leqq 1/2$) it is possible to select μ linearly independent forms; further

(19)
$$\overline{|\mathscr{P}_{k,l}(\xi)|}\, O(n^{(2+\varepsilon)n}), \qquad R_k(\xi)=O(n^{-(2\mu-2-\varepsilon)n}),$$
$$\max \deg \mathscr{P}_{k,l}(z)=O(n),$$
$$k=1, \ldots, \mu+t, \quad l=1, \ldots \mu.$$

Consider the numerical linear forms (16) in the numbers (17). By the definition of a $B_{N,\xi}$-polynomial they are linearly independent over $\mathbf{K}$.

Among the linearly independent forms (18) in the numbers (17) it is possible to select $w=\mu-v$ forms

(20)
$$R_{k_i}(\xi)=\mathscr{P}_{k_i,1}(\xi)\mathscr{F}_1(\xi)+\ldots+\mathscr{P}_{k_i,\mu}(\xi)\mathscr{F}_\mu(\xi),$$
$$k_i \leqq \mu+t, \quad i=v+1, \ldots, \mu,$$

which are linearly independent together with the v linear forms (16).

Denote by $\Delta(\xi)$ the determinant of the matrix of the coefficients of the μ linear forms (16) and (20). As they are linearly independent, $\Delta(\xi) \neq 0$.

As $\xi T_0(\xi) \neq 0$, at least one of the numbers (17) differs from zero. We may assume that $\mathscr{F}_1(\xi) \neq 0$ as the numbers of the functions (13) are arbitrary.

From (16) and (20) it follows that

(21)
$$\mathscr{F}_1(\xi)\Delta(\xi)=\Delta_1\Psi_1(\xi)+\ldots+\Delta_v\Psi_v(\xi)+$$
$$+\Delta_{v+1}R_{k_{v+1}}(\xi)+\ldots+\Delta_\mu R_{k_\mu}(\xi)$$

where Δ_i, $i=1, \ldots, \mu$, are the cofactors of the elements of the first column of $\Delta(\xi)$.

By the help of the estimates (16) and (19) we get

(22)
$$\Delta_i=O(H^{v-1}n^{(2+\varepsilon)wn}), \quad i=1, \ldots, v,$$
$$\Delta_i=O(H^v n^{(2+\varepsilon)(w-1)n}), \quad i=v+1, \ldots, \mu.$$

From equalities (15) and (21) by the help of (19) and (22) we obtain

$$\Delta(\xi)=O\left\{H^{v}n^{(2+\varepsilon)wn}\left(\frac{|\mathscr{P}(\xi)|}{H}+n^{-2\mu n}\right)\right\}. \tag{23}$$

Choose $a\in\mathbf{N}$ so that $a\xi\in\mathbf{Z}_{\mathbf{K}}$.

From the estimates (19) it follows that deg $\Delta(z)=O(n)$ and therefore $a^{O(n)}\Delta(\xi)\in\mathbf{Z}_{\mathbf{K}}$. If $N(\xi)$ is the norm of the algebraic number ξ in the field $\mathbf{K}$ then in view of $\Delta(\xi)\neq 0$, we have

$$|N(a^{O(n)}\Delta(\xi)|\geqq 1\,. \tag{24}$$

Using the estimates (16) and (19) we get

$$\overline{|\Delta(\xi)|}=O(H^{v}n^{(2+\varepsilon)wn})\,. \tag{25}$$

From the estimates (23)–(25) we obtain

$$b_2H^{hv}n^{(2+\varepsilon)hwn}\left(\frac{|\mathscr{P}(\xi)|}{H}+n^{-2\mu n}\right)\geqq 1\,. \tag{26}$$

Regard the least n which satisfy the conditions

$$n\geqq n_0,\quad n^n>(2b_2)^{1/v}H^h\,. \tag{27}$$

Under our assumptions for a sufficiently large H the inequality $(n-1)^{n-1}\leqq\leqq(2b_2)^{1/v}H^h$ holds and so

$$n^n<b_3H^h\ln H<b_3H^{h+\varepsilon}\,. \tag{28}$$

Choose N in such a way, that condition (11) hold. Then for a sufficiently small ε the inequality

$$2\mu-(2+\varepsilon)hw\geqq v \tag{29}$$

holds.

Inequalities (26), (27) and (29) imply

$$2b_2H^{hv-1}n^{(2+\varepsilon)hwn}|\mathscr{P}(\xi)|>1\,,$$

$$|\mathscr{P}(\xi)|>bH^{1-hv-(2+\varepsilon)h(h+\varepsilon)w}\,.$$

Hence with a sufficiently small ε in view of inequality (29) this implies inequality (12). The lemma is proved.

§3. The estimate of the algebraical independence measure of the values of E-functions, not connected by algebraical equations over $\mathbf{C}(z)$

Theorem 1. *Let the set of KE-functions (3) (with $m \geqq 2$) form a solution of a system of linear homogeneous differential equations (5) and be homogeneously algebraically independent over $\mathbf{C}(z)$. Let $\xi \in \mathbf{K}$, $\xi T_0(\xi) \neq 0$. Then the inequalities*

$$\Phi^0_{\mathbf{K}}(f_1(\xi), \ldots, f_m(\xi); s; H) > CH^{-2^m \frac{(m-1)^{m-1}}{(m-1)!} h^m s^{m-1}}, \tag{30}$$

$$\Phi_{\mathbf{K}}\left(\frac{f_1(\xi)}{f_m(\xi)}, \ldots, \frac{f_{m-1}(\xi)}{f_m(\xi)}; s; H\right) > CH^{-2^m \frac{(m-1)^{m-1}}{(m-1)!} h^m s^{m-1}} \tag{31}$$

hold.

Remark. As $m! > 2\left(\frac{m}{e}\right)^m$, the exponent of the right-hand sides of (30) and (31) may be replaced by $-(2e)^{m-1}h^m s^{m-1}$.

Proof. We use the main lemma setting $B_N = L_N$, $N = 1, 2, \ldots$. The set $\mathscr{D}$ coincides with the set of zeros of the polynomial $T_0(z)$. Let $\mathscr{P}$ be an arbitrary homogeneous polynomial (9) of height H with respect to the field $\mathbf{K}$. Then for any N, $N \geqq s$, and for any ξ under consideration, $\mathscr{P}$ is a $B_{N,\xi}$-polynomial. Therefore by the main lemma, if the number N is taken in such a way that condition (11) is satified, then inequality (12) holds.

We have

$$\mu = \varphi(N) = \frac{(N+m-1)!}{N!(m-1)!}, \quad v = \varphi(N-s), \quad w = \mu - v. \tag{32}$$

Therefore

$$\frac{w}{\mu} = 1 - \frac{v}{\mu} = 1 - \frac{(N-s+1)\ldots(N-s+m-1)}{(N+1)\ldots(N+m-1)} = 1 - \left(1 - \frac{s}{N+1}\right)\cdot\ldots \tag{33}$$

$$\ldots\left(1 - \frac{s}{N+m-1}\right) \leqq s\left(\frac{1}{N+1} + \ldots + \frac{1}{N+m-1}\right) \leqq \frac{(m-1)s}{N+1} < \frac{1}{2h-1},$$

if we set

$$N = (m-1)(2h-1)s. \tag{34}$$

This means that for such an N condition (11) is satisfied.

In view of equality (32) we have

(35)
$$\mu=\frac{1}{(m-1)!}(N+1)\ldots(N+m-1)\leqq\frac{1}{(m-1)!}(N+m-1)^{m-1}=$$
$$=\frac{1}{(m-1)!}[(m-1)(2h-1)s+m-1]^{m-1}<\frac{[2(m-1)hs]^{m-1}}{(m-1)!}.$$

which gives inequality (30) in view of (12).

Inequality (31) follows from inequality (30).

Theorem 2. *Let the set of KE-functions* (3), (*with* $m\geqq 1$) *form a solution of the system of linear differential equations* (4) *and be algebraically independent over* $\mathbf{C}(z)$. *Let* $\xi\in\mathbf{K}$ *and* $\xi T(\xi)\neq 0$. *Then the inequality*

(36)
$$\Phi_{\mathbf{K}}(f_1(\xi),\ldots,f_m(\xi);s;H)>CH^{-2^{m+1}\frac{m^m}{m!}h^{m+1}s^m}$$

holds.

Remark. As in case of Theorem 1 the exponent in the right-hand side of inequality (36) may be replaced by $-(2e)^m h^{m+1}s^m$.

Theorem 2 follows from Theorem 1 if in the latter we replace m by $m+1$ and set $f_{m+1}(z)=1$.

For $\mathbf{K}=\mathbf{Q}$ Theorem 2 follows from a more general theorem proved by A. I. Galochkin [10].

§ 4. The estimate of the algebraical independence measure of the values of E-functions, connected by a single algebraical equation over $\mathbf{C}(z)$

Considering the set L_N of the power products (3) of the KE-functions (3) and its subsets we suppose that the functions (8) are ordered in the lexicographical order of the power products of $f_m(z),\ldots,f_1(z)$.

Theorem 3. *Let the set of KE-functions* (3) (*with* $m\geqq 3$) *form a solution of the system of linear homogeneous differential equations* (5). *The functions* $f_1(z),\ldots,f_{m-1}(z)$ *are homogeneously algebraically independent over* $\mathbf{C}(z)$ *and are connected with the function* $f_m(z)$ *by an homogeneous algebraical equation*

(37)
$$A=A(f_1(z),\ldots,f_m(z))=0,$$

where A *is an irreducible and primitive homogeneous polynomial of degree* k *in the functions* (3) *and with coefficients from* $\mathbf{C}(z)$. *The major term of the polynomial* A *is of the form*

(38)
$$B(z)f_m^{\kappa_m}(z)\dots f_l^{\kappa_l}(z),\qquad \kappa_l+\dots+\kappa_m=k\,,$$
$$B(z)\in\mathbf{C}(z),\quad \kappa_m\geqq 1,\ \dots,\ \kappa_l\geqq 1\,,$$

where $3\leqq l\leqq m$. *Further,* $\xi\in\mathbf{K}$, $\xi T_0(\xi)B(\xi)\neq 0$. *Then the inequalities*

(39)
$$\Phi_{\mathbf{K}}^0(f_1(\xi),\dots,f_{l-1}(\xi);s;H)> >CH^{-\frac{k[2(m-1)h]^{m-1}}{(m-1)!}s^{m-2}},$$

(40)
$$\Phi_{\mathbf{K}}\left(\frac{f_1(\xi)}{f_{l-1}(\xi)},\dots,\frac{f_{l-2}(\xi)}{f_{l-1}(\xi)};s;H\right)> >CH^{\frac{-k[2(m-1)h]^{m-1}}{(m-1)!}s^{m-2}}$$

hold.

Remark. As in the case of theorem 1 the exponent in inequalities (39) and (40) may be replaced by $-k(2eh)^{m-1}s^{m-2}$.

Proof. First of all, according to Lemma 10 from [6] the numerical coefficients of the polynomial $B(z)$ may be chosen from $\mathbf{K}$.

We use the main lemma for the proof. Consider the set L_N (8) for any $N=1,2,\dots$. Denote by B_N the subset of L_N such that the element $f_1^{k_1}(z)\dots f_m^{k_m}(z)\in B_N$ if $k_i<\kappa_i$ at least for one i, $l\leqq i\leqq m$. The set $\mathscr{D}$ is the set of zeros of polynomials $T_0(z)$ and $B(z)$.

With the help of equation (37) we can easily verify that B_N satisfies all the conditions given in § 2 for any $N=1,2,\dots$, and

(41)
$$\mu=\varphi(N)=\begin{cases}\dfrac{(N+m-1)!}{N!(m-1)!} & \text{if } N<k\\[2ex] \dfrac{(N+m-1)!}{N!(m-1)!}-\dfrac{(N-k-m-1)!}{(N-k)!(-1)!} & \text{if } N\geqq k\end{cases}$$

Let us consider an arbitrary homogeneous polynomial

(42)
$$\mathscr{P}=\mathscr{P}(f_1(z),\dots,f_{l-1}(z)),\quad \mathscr{P}(z_1,\dots,z_{l-1})\in\mathbf{Z}_{\mathbf{K}}[z_1,\dots,z_{l-1}],$$
$$\mathscr{P}(z_1,\dots,z_{l-1})\not\equiv 0,\quad \deg\mathscr{P}(z_1,\dots,z_{l-1})=s,\quad s\geqq 1,$$

of height H with respect to $\mathbf{K}$.

Then for any $N\geqq 3$ and any considered ξ the polynomial $\mathscr{P}$ is evidently a $B_{N,\xi}$-polynomial. Therefore by the main lemma, if N is chosen so that the condition (11) holds, then (12) holds too.

We have $v=\varphi(N-s)$ and $w=\mu-v$. We set

$$N=(m-1)(2h-1)s. \tag{43}$$

Let us consider the three possible cases.

1) $k\leqq(m-1)(2h-1)s-s$. Then $N\geqq k+s$ and in view of equality (41) we obtain

$$\frac{w}{\mu}=1-\frac{v}{\mu}=1-\frac{(N-s+1)\dots(N-s+m-1)-(N-s-k+1)\dots(N-s-k+m-1)}{(N+1)\dots(N+m-1)-(N-k+1)\dots(N-k+m-1)}=$$

$$=1-\frac{(N-s+1)\dots(N-s+m-1)}{(N+1)\dots(N+m-1)}\,\frac{1-\dfrac{(N-s+k+1)\dots(N-s-k+m-1)}{(N-s+1)\dots(N-s+m-1)}}{1-\dfrac{(N-k+1)\dots(N-k+m-1)}{(N+1)\dots(N+m-1)}}=$$

$$=1-\left(1-\frac{s}{N+1}\right)\dots\left(1-\frac{s}{N+m-1}\right)\frac{1-\left(1-\dfrac{k}{N-s+1}\right)\dots\left(1-\dfrac{k}{N-s+m-1}\right)}{1-\left(1-\dfrac{k}{N+1}\right)\dots\left(1-\dfrac{k}{N+m-1}\right)}$$

As the fraction in the square brackets is greater than one and equality (43) holds, we have

$$\frac{w}{\mu}<1-\left(1-\frac{s}{N+1}\right)\left(1-\frac{s}{N+m-1}\right)\leqq s\left(\frac{1}{N+1}+\dots+\frac{1}{N+m-1}\right)<$$
$$<\frac{(m-1)}{N+1}<\frac{1}{2h-1}. \tag{44}$$

Thus for such an N in the considered case condition (11) is true.

In view of equation (43) we get

$$\mu=\frac{1}{(m-1)!}[(N+1)\dots(N+m-1)-(N-k+1)\dots(N-k+m-1)]=$$

$$=\frac{(N+1)\dots(N+m-1)}{(m-1)!}\left[1-\left(1-\frac{k}{N+1}\right)\dots\left(1-\frac{k}{N+m-1}\right)\right]<$$

$$<\frac{k}{(m-1)!}(N+1)\dots(N+m-1)\left(\frac{1}{N+1}+\dots+\frac{1}{N+m-1}\right)\leqq$$

$$\leqq\frac{k}{(m-2)!}(N+m-1)^{m-2}=\frac{k}{(m-2)!}[(m-1)(2h-1)s+m-1]^{m-2}$$

and this implies

$$\mu \leqq \frac{k}{(m-2)!}[2(m-1)hs]^{m-1}. \tag{45}$$

Inequalities (12) and (45) in the considered case imply inequality (39).

2) $$(m-1)(2h-1)s-s<k<(m-1)(2h-1)s.$$

In this case the inequality $k \leqq N < k+s$ holds, and this means that $N-s<k$. Then from equation (41) we deduce that

$$\mu = \frac{(N+m-1)!}{N!(m-1)!} - \frac{(N+k+m-1)!}{(N-k)!(m-1)!}, \quad v = \frac{(N-s+m-1)!}{(N-s)!(m-1)!}. \tag{46}$$

By the help of equalities (43), (47), arguing analogously to the first case we have

$$\begin{aligned} \frac{w}{\mu} = 1 - \frac{v}{\mu} = 1 - \left(1-\frac{s}{N+1}\right)\ldots\left(1-\frac{1}{N+m-1}\right) \times \\ \times \frac{1}{1-\left(1-\frac{k}{N+1}\right)\ldots\left(1-\frac{k}{N+m-1}\right)} < \\ < 1-\left(1-\frac{s}{N+1}\right)\ldots\left(1-\frac{s}{N+m-1}\right) < \frac{1}{2h-1}. \end{aligned} \tag{47}$$

As in view of the first of equations (46), inequality (45) also holds, the assertion of this theorem is also true in this case.

3) $k>(m-1)(2h-1)s$. Then the inequality $N<k$ holds. Therefore in the considered case the elements of the set L_N are linearly independent over $\mathbf{C}(z)$, $B_N = L_N$, $\varphi(N) = \frac{(N+m-1)!}{N!(m-1)!}$ and we deduce inequality (44) word for word so as it was done in the proof of Theorem 1. Further

$$\begin{aligned} \mu = \frac{1}{(m-1)!}(N+1)\ldots(N+m-1) < \frac{k(N+m-1)^{m-2}}{(m-1)!} = \\ = \frac{k[(m-1)(2h-1)s+m-1]^{m-2}}{(m-1)!} \leqq \frac{k[2(m-1)hs]^{m-2}}{(m-1)!} < \\ < \frac{k[2(m-1)h]^{m-2}s^{m-2}}{(m-2)!}, \end{aligned}$$

i.e. inequality (45) is true. This proves inequality (39) in the third case. Inequality (40) follows from inequality (39).

Theorem 3 implies

Theorem 4. *Let the set of KE-functions* (3), (*with* $m \geqq 2$) *form a solution of a system of linear differential equations* (4), *the functions* $f_1(z), \dots, f_{m-1}(z)$ *be algebraically independent over* $\mathbf{C}(z)$ *and be connected by an algebraical equation* (37) *with the function* $f_m(z)$, *where A is an irreducible and primitive polynomial of degree k in the functions* (3), *contaning* $f_m(z)$, *with coefficients from* $\mathbf{C}(z)$. *Let the major term of the polynomial A be of the form* (38) *where* $2 \leqq l \leqq m$. *Further let* $\xi \in \mathbf{K}$, $\xi T(\xi) B(\xi) \neq 0$. *Then the inequality*

$$\Phi_{\mathbf{K}}(f_1(\xi), \dots, f_{l-1}(\xi); s; H) > CH^{-\frac{k[2mh]^m}{m!} s^{m-1}}$$

is true.

The Remark to Theorem 4, analogous to Remark to Theorem 3 hold.

In Theorems 3 and 4 the case $l = m$, when the major term of A is of the form $B(z) f_m^k(z)$, is of special interest.

§ 5. The estimate of the algeraical measure of values of E-functions, connected by algebraic equations of a special form

Theorem 5. *Let a set of KE-functions form a solution of a system of linear homogeneous differential equations* (5). *Let the maximal quantity of homogeneously algebraically independent functions among them be equal to* l, $1 \leqq l \leqq m-1$, *either with respect to the field* $\mathbf{C}(z)$ *or with respect to the field* $\mathbf{C}$, *and let the functions* $f_1(z), \dots, f_l(z)$ *be homogeneously algebraically independent over* $\mathbf{C}(z)$. *Further let* $\xi \in \mathbf{K}$, $\xi \neq 0$, *and* $\mathscr{P} = \mathscr{P}(f_1(z), \dots, f_m(z))$ *be any homogeneous polynomial* (9) *of height H with respect to* $\mathbf{K}$ *such that* $\mathscr{P}(f_1(z), \dots, f_m(z)) \neq 0$. *Then the inequalities*

$$|\mathscr{P}(f_1(\xi), \dots, f_m(\xi))| > CH^{-\gamma h^l s^{l-1}}, \tag{48}$$

$$\Phi^0_{\mathbf{K}}(f_1(\xi), \dots, f_l(\xi); s; H) > CH^{-\gamma h^l s^{l-}}, \tag{49}$$

$$\Phi_{\mathbf{K}}\left(\frac{f_1(\xi)}{f_l(\xi)}, \dots, \frac{f_{l-1}(\xi)}{f_l(\xi)}; s; H\right) > CH^{-\gamma h^l s^{l-1}} \tag{50}$$

hold.

Proof. Again we use the main lemma. Let us consider the set L_N (8) for any $N = 1, 2, \dots$. Denote by r_N the number of elements of the basis of the linear space L_N, generated by the functions (8) over $\mathbf{C}$.

From the assumptions and the properties of the algebraical dependence easily follows, that the number of elements of the basis of the linear space L_N over $\mathbf{C}(z)$ also equals to r_N and that any basis of L_N over $\mathbf{C}$ is a basis of L_N over $\mathbf{C}(z)$.

There exists an N_0, depending only on the functions (3), such that for any N, $N \geqq N_0$, r_N is a polynomial of N precisely of degree $l-1$ (see, e.g. [15]).

For every $N=1, 2, \ldots$, we choose an arbitrary basis L_N and denote it by

$$v_{N,1}(z), \ldots, v_{N,r_N}(z). \tag{51}$$

If $r_N<\rho_{N,m}$, then we denote the elements of L_N, not contained in the basis (51) by

$$v_{N,r_N+1}(z), \ldots, v_{N,\rho_{N,m}}(z). \tag{52}$$

In the latter case any of the functions (52) may be represented in a unique way as a linear combination of the functions (51) with constant coefficients, which by Lemma 10 of the work [5] may be chosen from the field $\mathbf{K}$. In view of this the equations

$$v_{N,j}(z) - \sum_{i=1}^{r_N} \alpha_{N,j,i} v_{N,i}(z) = 0, \tag{53}$$

$$\alpha_{N,j,i} \in \mathbf{K}, \quad j=r_N+1, \ldots, \rho_{N,m}, \tag{53}$$

hold.

For every $N=1, 2, \ldots$ we take basis (51) for the set B_N. With the help of equations (53) one can easily verify that the set B_N satisfies all the four conditions formulated in § 2 and the set $\mathscr{P}$ coincides with the set of zeros of the polynomial $T_0(z)$.

We shall prove that for any N, $N \geqq 3$, and any considered ξ the polynomial $\mathscr{P}$ in (9) is a $B_{N,\xi}$-polynmial.

Consider the formulae

$$v_{N-s,j}(z)\mathscr{P}(f_1(z), \ldots, f_m(z)) = \sum_{i=1}^{\rho_{N,m}} \beta_{N,j,i} v_{N,i}(z), \quad \beta_{N,j,i} \in \mathbf{Z}_{\mathbf{K}}. \tag{54}$$

We shall prove that for $r_N<\rho_{N,m}$ the linear forms (53) and (54) of the variables (51) and (52) with coefficients from $\mathbf{K}$ are linearly independent over $\mathbf{K}$.

Suppose the contrary. Then identically in the variables (51) and (52) the equality

$$\begin{aligned} \sum_{j=1}^{r_{N-s}} a_j v_{N-s,j}(z)\mathscr{P}(f_1(z), \ldots, f_m(z)) &= \sum_{j=1}^{r_{N-s}} a_j \sum_{i=1}^{\rho_{N,m}} \beta_{N,j,i} v_{N,i}(z) = \\ &= \sum_{j=r_N+1}^{\rho_{N,m}} a_j\Big(v_{N,j}(z) - \sum_{i=1}^{r_N} \alpha_{N,j,i} v_{N,i}(z)\Big), \end{aligned} \tag{55}$$

holds, where at least one of the numbers a_j is different from zero. As the left-hand side of equations (53) are linearly independent over $\mathbf{K}$ regarded as linear forms in the variables (51) and (52), at least one of the numbers $a_1, \ldots, a_{r_{N-s}}$ is different from zero. This, in view of equations (53) and equality (55) implies

$$\sum_{j=1}^{r_{N-s}} a_j v_{N-s,j}(z)\mathscr{P}(f_1(z), \ldots, f_m(z)) = 0. \tag{56}$$

By the assumptions $\mathscr{P}(f_1(z), \ldots, f_m(z)) \neq 0$ and then equality (56) gives us

$$\sum_{j=1}^{r_{N-s}} a_j v_{N-s,j}(z) = 0. \tag{57}$$

But equation (57) is impossible because the functions (51) form a basis of L_{N-s} over $\mathbf{C}$.

So the linear forms (53) and (54) in the variables (5) and (52) are linearly independent over $\mathbf{C}$.

Replacing the functions (52) by the linear combinations of the functions (51) in the right-hand sides of the equalities (54) and using (53) we obtain:

$$\begin{cases} v_{N-s,j}(z)\mathscr{P}(f_1(z), \ldots, f_m(z)) = \sum_{i=1}^{r_N} \lambda_{N,j,i} v_{N,i}(z), \\ \lambda_{N,j,i} \in \mathbf{K}, \quad j = 1, \ldots, r_{N-s}. \end{cases} \tag{58}$$

As we have proved that the linear forms (53) and (54) in the variables (51) and (52) are linearly independent over $\mathbf{K}$, the linear forms (58) in the variables (51) are linearly independent over $\mathbf{K}$.

This implies that for any N, $N \geqq s$, for which $r_N < \rho_{N,m}$ and any considered ξ, the polynomial $\mathscr{P}$ in (9) is a $B_{N,\xi}$-polynomial. For those values of N, $N \geqq s$, for which $r_N = \rho_{N,m}$, the latter assertion is evident. Therefore by the main lemma, if we choose N, $N \geqq s$ so the condition (11) takes place, inequality (12) also holds.

We have $\mu = \varphi(N) = r_N$, $v = \varphi(N-s) = r_{N-s}$, $w = \mu - v$. Let $N \geqq N_0 + s$. As it is shown above for $N \geqq N_0$, the equality

$$\mu = r_N = \alpha_{l-1} N^{l-1} + \ldots + \alpha_1 N + \alpha_0, \quad \alpha_{l-1} > 0 \tag{59}$$

is valid and the inequalities

$$0 < \beta_1 N^{l-1} < r_N < \beta_2 N^{l-1} \tag{60}$$

hold too where the constants $\alpha_0, \alpha_1, \ldots, \alpha_{l-1}, \beta_1, \beta_2$ depend only on the functions (3).

In view of equality (59) and inequalities (60) for $N \geqq N_0 + s$ we have

$$\begin{aligned} \frac{w}{\mu} &= \frac{r_N - r_{N-s}}{r_N} < \frac{\sum_{k=1}^{l-1} \alpha_k [N^k - (N-s)]^k}{\beta_1 N^{l-1}} = \\ &= \frac{s}{\beta_1 N^{l-1}} \sum_{k=1}^{l-1} \alpha_k [N^{l-2} + N^{l-3}(N-s) + \ldots + (N-s)^{l-2}] \leqq \frac{(l-1)\alpha s}{\beta_1 N} < \frac{\gamma_0 s}{N} \end{aligned} \tag{61}$$

where

$$\alpha = \max_{l \leqq k \leqq l-1} \alpha_k, \quad \gamma_0 = \max\left(\left[\frac{\alpha(l-1)}{\beta_1}\right] + 1, 2N_0\right), \quad \gamma_0 \in \mathbf{N}. \tag{62}$$

We set

$$N = \gamma_0(2h-1)s. \tag{63}$$

Then by equalities (62) we have

$$N \geqq 2N_0 s \geqq 2\max(N_0, s) \geqq N_0 + s$$

and from equality (63) and inequality (61) we deduce the inequality

$$w < \frac{\mu}{2h-1}. \tag{64}$$

Therefore for such an N inequality (11) is true and thus inequality (12) holds.

From inequality (60) and equality (63) we get

$$\mu < B_2 N^{l-1} = \beta_0[\gamma_0(2h-1)s]^{l-1} < \gamma_1 h^{l-1} s^{l-1}. \tag{65}$$

Inequalities (12) and (65) imply inequality (48) which implies inequalities (49) and (50).

Theorem 6. *Let the set of KE-functions (3) (with $m \geqq 2$) form a solution of the system of linear differential equations (4). Let the maximal number of algebraically independent functions among them be equal to l, $1 \leqq l \leqq m-1$, either over $\mathbf{C}(z)$ or over $\mathbf{C}$, and let the functions $f_1(z), \ldots, f_l(z)$ be algebraically independent over $\mathbf{C}(z)$. Further, let $\xi \in \mathbf{K}$, $\xi \neq 0$, and $\mathscr{P} = \mathscr{P}(f_1(z), \ldots, f_m(z))$ be an arbitrary polynomial of the form (9) of the height H with respect to $\mathbf{K}$ such that $\mathscr{P}(f_1(z), \ldots, f_m(z)) \neq 0$.*

Then the inequalities

$$|\mathscr{P}(f_1(\xi), \ldots, f_m(\xi))| > CH^{-\gamma h^{l+1} s^l}$$

(66)

$$\Phi_{\mathbf{K}}(f_1(\xi), \ldots, f_l(\xi); s; H) > CH^{-\gamma h^{l+1} s^l}$$

hold.

Theorem 6 follows from Theorem 5.

Remark 1. In Theorems 2, 4 and 6 in the system of differential equations (4) $Q_{k,0}$ may be equal to zero, i.e. this system may be homogeneous.

Remark 2. The main lemma and Theorems 1–6 may be reformulated for the case, when instead of the KE-functions (3) we consider the functions $f(z)$, $f'(z)$, $\ldots$, $f^{(m-1)}(z)$, where $f(z)$ is a solution of a differential equation

$$\mathscr{P}_m y^{(m)} + \ldots + \mathscr{P}_1 y' + P_0 y = Q, \quad \mathscr{P}_0, \mathscr{P}_1, \ldots, \mathscr{P}_m \in \mathbf{C}[z],$$

or a solution of a homogeneous equation

$$\mathscr{P}_m y^{(m)} + \ldots + \mathscr{P}_1 y' + \mathscr{P}_0 y = 0$$

resp.

§ 6. Application of the proved theorems to concrete functions

Let us consider the E-functions

$$\omega_k(z) = 1 + \sum_{n=1}^{\infty} \frac{z^n}{n!n^k}, \qquad k = 0, 1, \ldots, m,$$

$$\Psi_k(z) = \sum_{n=0}^{\infty} \frac{1}{(n!)^k} \left(\frac{z}{k}\right)^{kn}, \quad k \geqq 1.$$

Using the results of the paper [6] and Theorems 1 and 2, we obtain the following inequalities

$$\Phi_{\mathbf{K}}(\omega_0(\xi), \omega_1(\xi), \ldots, \omega_m(\xi); s; H) > CH^{-2^{m+2}\frac{(m+1)^{m+1}}{(m+1)!}h^{m+2}s^{m+1}},$$

$$\Phi^0_{\mathbf{K}}(\Psi_k(\xi), \Psi'_k(\xi), \ldots, \Psi_k^{(k-1)}(\xi); s; H) > CH^{-2^k\frac{(k-1)^{k+1}}{(k-1)!}h^k s^{k-1}},$$

$$\Phi_{\mathbf{K}}\left(\frac{\Psi'_k(\xi)}{\Psi_k(\xi)}, \ldots, \frac{\Psi_k^{(k-1)}(\xi)}{\Psi_k(\xi)}; s; H\right) > CH^{-2^k\frac{(k-1)^{k-1}}{(k-1)!}h^k s^{k-1}},$$

$$\Phi_{\mathbf{K}}(\Psi_k(\xi), \Psi'_k(\xi), \ldots, \Psi_k^{(k-1)}(\xi); s; H) > CH^{-2^{k+1}\frac{k^k}{k!}h^{k+1}s^k},$$

$$\Phi_{\mathbf{K}}(\Psi_1(\xi), \Psi_2(\xi), \Psi'_2(\xi), \ldots, \Psi_k(\xi), \Psi'_k(\xi), \ldots, \Psi_k^{(k-1)}(\xi); s; H) >$$

$$> CH^{-\gamma s^{\frac{k(k+1)}{2}}},$$

$$\gamma = 2^{\frac{k^2+k+2}{2}} \frac{\left(\frac{k(k+1)}{2}\right)^{\frac{k(k+1)}{2}}}{\left(\frac{k(k+1)}{2}\right)!} h^{\frac{k^2+k+2}{2}}, \quad \xi \in \mathbf{A}, \quad \xi \neq 0.$$

Let us consider the E-function

$$K_\lambda(z) = \sum_{n=0}^{\infty} \frac{(-1)^n}{n!(\lambda+1)\ldots(\lambda+n)} \left(\frac{z}{2}\right)^{2n}, \quad \lambda \neq -1, -2, \ldots; \tag{67}$$

$$\lambda \in \mathbf{Q},$$

satisfying the equation $y'' + \frac{2\lambda+1}{z} y' + y = 0$. C. Siegel proved [3, 4] that if $\lambda \neq \frac{2k+1}{2}$, $k \in \mathbf{Z}$, then $K_\lambda(z)$ and $K'_\lambda(z)$ are algebraically independent. By Theorems 1 and 2 for such a λ the inequalities

$$\Phi^0_{\mathbf{K}}(K_\lambda(\xi), K'_\lambda(\xi); s; H) > CH^{-4h^2 s},$$
$$\Phi_{\mathbf{K}}\left(\frac{K'_\lambda(\xi)}{K_\lambda(\xi)}; s; H\right) > CH^{-4h^2 s},$$
$$\Phi_{\mathbf{K}}(K_\lambda(\xi)K'_\lambda(\xi); s; H) > CH^{-16h^3 s^2}$$
$$\xi \in \mathbf{A}, \quad \xi \neq 0$$

hold and in view of the equality

$$\frac{J'_\lambda(z)}{J_\lambda(z)} = \frac{K'_\lambda(z)}{K_\lambda(z)} + \frac{\lambda}{z}$$

where $J_\lambda(z)$ is the Bessel function, the inequality

$$\Phi_{\mathbf{K}}\left(\frac{J'_\lambda(\xi)}{J_\lambda(\xi)}; s; H\right) > CH^{-4h^2 s}, \quad \xi \in \mathbf{A}, \quad \xi \neq 0$$

holds too.

Consider the E-functions

$$\operatorname{si} z = \int_0^z \frac{\sin t}{t}\, dt, \quad \operatorname{ci} z = \int_0^z \frac{1-\cos t}{t}\, dt.$$

In the paper [16] it is proved that the functions si z and sin z, as well as the functions ci z and cos z are algebraically independent over $\mathbf{C}(z)$. Therefore, considering the triplets of functions si z, sin z, cos z and ci z, cos z, sin z each of them is connected by the equation $\sin^2 z + \cos^2 z = 1$ and satifies the corresponding system of differential equations

$$y'_1 = \frac{y_2}{z}, \quad y'_2 = y_3, \quad y'_3 = -y_2$$
$$y'_1 = \frac{1-y_2}{z}, \quad y'_2 = -y_3, \quad y'_3 = y_2.$$

By Theorem 4 we obtain the inequalities

$$\Phi_{\mathbf{K}}(\operatorname{si} \xi, \sin \xi; s; H) > CH^{-72h^3 s^2},$$
$$\Phi_{\mathbf{K}}(\operatorname{ci} \xi, \cos \xi; s; H) > CH^{-72h^3 s^2},$$
$$\xi \in \mathbf{A}, \quad \xi \neq 0.$$

Consider the E-functions

$$\varphi_k(z) = 1 + \sum_{n=1}^{\infty} \frac{(-1)^n z^{2n}}{(2n)!(2n)^k}, \quad k=0, 1, \dots m,$$

where $\varphi_0(z)=\cos z$. In the paper [16] it is proved that these functions are algebraically independent over $\mathbf{C}(z)$, connected with the function $\sin z$ by the equation $\sin^2 z + \cos^2 z = 1$ and satisfy a system of $m+2$ linear differential equations with coefficients from $\mathbf{C}(z)$ with a pole at $z=0$. Therefore by Theorem 4 we have

$$\Phi_{\mathbf{K}}(\varphi_0(\xi), \varphi_1(\xi), \dots, \varphi_m(\xi); s; H) > CH^{-\frac{2[2(m+2)h]^{m+2}}{(m+2)!}s^{m+1}},$$

$$\xi \in \mathbf{K}, \quad \xi \neq 0.$$

Let us return to the function $K_\lambda(z)$, see (67).

From SIEGEL's results [3] it follows, that if $\lambda_1, \lambda_2 \in \mathbf{Q}$; $\lambda, \lambda_1 \neq -1, \pm\frac{1}{2}, -2\pm\frac{3}{2}, \dots$ and $\lambda_1 \pm \lambda_2 \notin \mathbf{Z}$, then the four numbers $K_{\lambda_1}(\xi)$, $K'_{\lambda_1}(\xi)$ $K_{\lambda_2}(\xi)$, $K'_{\lambda_2}(\xi)$ are algebraically independent for any $\xi \in \mathbf{A}$, $\xi \neq 0$.

If we consider the functions $K_\lambda(z)$ and $K_{-\lambda}(z)$, $\lambda \in \mathbf{Q}$, $\lambda \neq 0$, $\pm\frac{1}{2}$, $-1\pm\frac{3}{2}, \dots$ then it turns out that the four functions $K_\lambda(z)$, $K'_\lambda(z)$, $K_{-\lambda}(z)$, $K'_{-\lambda}(z)$ are connected by the algebraical equation

$$K_\lambda(z)K'_\lambda(z) - K'_\lambda(z)K_{-\lambda}(z) - \frac{2\lambda}{z}K_\lambda(z)K_{-\lambda}(z) + \frac{2\lambda}{z} = 0$$

(see [7]). But from SIEGEL's work it follows that any three of these functions are algebraically independent over $\mathbf{C}(z)$.

We set $y_1 = K_\lambda(z)$, $y_2 = K'_\lambda(z)$, $y_3 = K_{-\lambda}(z)$, $y_4 = K'_{-\lambda}(z)$. These functions satisfy the system of equations

$$y'_1 = y_2, \quad y'_2 = -\frac{2\lambda+1}{z}y_2 - y_1,$$

$$y'_3 = y_4, \quad y'_4 = -\frac{2\lambda+1}{z}y_4 - y_3.$$

Let us denote by $\varphi_1(z)$ and $\varphi_2(z)$ any of the three pairs of functions $K'_\lambda(z)$ and $K_{-\lambda}(z)$, $K_\lambda(z)$ and $K'_{-\lambda}(z)$, K'_λ and $K'_{-\lambda}(z)$. Then by Theorems 3 and 4 (the indexing of the considered functions is arbitrary) under the assumptions given above the inequalities

$$\Phi^0_{\mathbf{K}}(K_\lambda(\xi), K'_\lambda(\xi), K_{-\lambda}(\xi), K'_{-\lambda}(\xi); s; H) > CH^{-72h^4s^3},$$

$$\Phi_{\mathbf{K}}(\varphi_1(\xi), \varphi_2(\xi); s; H) > CH^{-\frac{1024}{3}s^3},$$

$$\xi \in \mathbf{A}, \quad \xi \neq 0$$

hold.

Let the transcendental KE-function $f(z)$ be a solution of the differential equation with polynomial coefficients

(68) $$\mathscr{P}_2(z)y'' + \mathscr{P}_1(z)y' + \mathscr{P}_0(z)y = Q(z),$$

and let the functions $f(z)$ and $f'(z)$ be connected by the algebraic equation

(69) $$A = A(f(z), f'(z)) = 0,$$

where $A(z_1, z_2)$ is an irreducible and primitive polynomial with coefficients form $\mathbf{C}[z]$ of degree k.

If we take the derivative of the left-hand side of equation (69) and use the differential equation (68) we can easily prove, that among the homogeneous terms of the polynomial A of degree k there is a term

$$B(z)(f'(z))^k, \quad B(z) \in \mathbf{C}[z], \quad B(z) \neq 0.$$

Therefore by Theorem 4

$$\Phi_{\mathbf{K}}(f(\xi); s; H) > CH^{-8kh^2s}, \xi \in \mathbf{K}, \quad \xi B(\xi) \neq 0;$$

in particular

$$\Phi_{\mathbf{K}}(\sin \xi; s; H) > CH^{-16h^2s},$$

$$\Phi_{\mathbf{K}}(\cos \xi; s; H) > CH^{-16h^2s},$$

$$\xi \in \mathbf{A}, \quad \xi \neq 0.$$

By Theorem 1 we have:

$$\Phi_{\mathbf{K}}(\operatorname{tg} \xi; s; H) > CH^{-4h^2s}, \quad \xi \in \mathbf{A}, \quad \xi \neq 0.$$

If we use results of a number of published papers, where the algebraical independence of E-functions over $\mathbf{C}(z)$ is established, we are in a position to enlarge significantly the number of applications of Theorems 1–5 to concrete functions.

Finally we note that the idea of considering $B_{N,\xi}$-polynomials, which is fundamental for this work, is involved in the paper [17], published in 1960.

References

[1] Фельдман, Н. И., Шидловский, А. Б., Развитие и современное состояние теории трансцендентных чисел, *Успехи матем. наук*, **22**, (1967), 3–81.

[2] Шидловский, А. Б., Об оценке меры трансцендентности значений Е-функций, *Матем. заметки*, **2** (1967), 33–44.

[3] Siegel, C. L., Über einige Anwendungen Diophantischer Approximationen, *Abhand. preuss. Acad. Wiss.*, **1** (1929–1930), 1–70.

[4] Siegel, C. L., *Transcendental numbers*, Princeton, 1949.

[5] Шидловский, А. Б., Об арифметических свойствах значений аналитических функций, *Труды МИАН СССР им. В. А. Стеклова*, **132** (1973), 169–202.

[6] Шидловский, А. Б., О критерии алгебраической независимости значений одного класса целых функций, *Изв. АН СССР*, **23** (1959), 35–66.

[7] Шидловский, А. Б., О трансцендентности и алгебраической независимости значений *E*-функций, связанных любым числом алгебраических уравнений в поле рациональных функций, *Изв. АН СССР*, **26** (1962), 877–910.

[8] Шидловский, А. Б., К общей теореме об алгебраической независимости значений *E*-функций, *ДАН СССР*, **171** (1966), 810–813.

[9] Lang, S., A transcendence measure for E-functions, *Mathematika*, **9** (1962), 157–161.

[10] Галочкин, А. И., Оценка меры взаимной трансцендентности значений *E*-функций, *Матем. заметки*, **3** (1968), 377–386.

[11] Шидловский, А. Б., Об оценках меры трансцендентности значений *E*-функций, *Вестник МГУ*, **6** (1977), 3–10.

[12] Чирский, В. Г., Об арифметических свойствах значений аналитических функций, связанных алгебраическими уравнениями над полем рациональных функций, *Матем. заметки*, **14** (1973), 83–94.

[13] Нестеренко, Ю. В., Оценки порядков нулей функций одного класса и их приложения в теории трансцендентных чисел, *Изв. АН СССР*, **41** (1977), 83–84.

[14] Шидловский, А. Б., Об оценках меры трансцендентности значений *E*-функций, *Успехи матем. наук*, **22** (1967), 83–84.

[15] Олейников, В. А., О некоторых свойствах алгебраически зависимых величин, *Вестник МГУ*, **5** (1962), 11–17.

[16] Шидловский, А. Б., О трансцендентности и алгебраической независимости значений некоторых *E*-функций, *Вестник МГУ*, **5** (1961), 44–49.

[17] Шидловский, А. Б., О трансцендентности и алгебраической независимости значений *E*-функций, связанных алгебраическим уравнением в поле рациональных функций, *Вестник МГУ*, **5** (1960), 19–28.

Studies in Pure Mathematics
To the Memory of Paul Turán

Sieve methods and Siegel's zeros

by

H. SIEBERT (Mannheim)

0. Among number theorists it is a "well-known fact" that Siegel's theorem ([6], Satz 8.2, p. 144) could be proved with effective constants $c(\varepsilon)$ for every $\varepsilon \in \left(0, \frac{1}{2}\right]$ if the constant 2 in the so-called "Brun–Titchmarsh-inequality"

$$\pi(x, k, l) := \sum_{\substack{p \leqq x \\ p \equiv l (\mathrm{mod}\, k)}} 1 \leqq \frac{2}{\varphi(k)} \cdot \frac{x}{\log (x/k)}, \quad 1 \leqq k < x, (l, k) = 1$$

(stated here in a form proved by H. L. MONTGOMERY and R. C. VAUGHAN ([3], Theorem 2, p. 121)) could be improved to $2-\delta$, with an effectively computable $\delta > 0$. This observation seems to be due to K. A. RODOSSKII (see [2], Remark 1, p. 49). The purpose of this paper is to give a proof of this fact and to prove a general result of this kind (Theorem 7 below) showing that the linear Selberg sieve in the version of W. B. JURKAT and H.-E. RICHERT ([1], Theorem 5, p. 230) in the same sense just fails to give assertions on Siegel zeros for every value of the parameter $\alpha \in (0, 1)$. The proof also yields a direct arithmetic interpretation of the functions $f(u)$, $F(u)$ occurring in the Jurkat–Richert sieve.

Throughout the paper $c_1, c_2, \ldots$ denote effectively computable positive constants which may depend on α, δ and r where these parameters occur. As usual $L(s, \chi)$ is the Dirichlet function with character χ; χ_0 is the principal character and χ_1 the real exceptional character, β_1 the exceptional real zero; $\pi(x, k, l)$ and $\psi(x, k, l)$ are as usual defined by

$$\psi(x, k, l) = \sum_{\substack{n \leqq x \\ n \equiv l(k)}} \Lambda(n), \quad \pi(x, k, l) = \sum_{\substack{p \leqq x \\ p \equiv l(k)}} 1,$$

$\Lambda(n)$ being v. Mangoldt's function.

I wish to express my gratitude to Prof. Y. MOTOHASHI for making accessible his unpublished manuscript [5] to me, and to Prof. H.-E. RICHERT and Prof. E. WIRSING for their interest in this work.

1. The Brun–Titchmarsh inequality

Theorem 1. *If there exists a* $\delta>0$ *such that*

$$\pi(x,k,l)\leqq(2-\delta)\frac{x}{\log(x/k)},\quad 1\leqq k<x,\,(l,k)=1 \tag{1.1}$$

for all residue classes $l \bmod k$, *then there is an effective constant* $c(\delta)$ *such that*

$$L(s,\chi_1)\neq 0 \quad \text{in} \quad 1-\frac{c(\delta)}{\log^2 k}\leqq s\leqq 1\,. \tag{1.2}$$

The proof is very simple: From (1.1) we get

$$\begin{aligned}\psi(x,k,l)&\leqq\log x\cdot\pi(x,k,l)+O(\sqrt{x}\log x)\leqq\\ &\leqq(2-\delta)\frac{x\log x}{\varphi(k)\log(x/k)}+O(\sqrt{x}\log x)\,,\end{aligned} \tag{1.3}$$

while classical analytic methods (see for example [6], Satz 7.3, p. 136) give

$$\psi(x,k,l)=\frac{1}{\varphi(k)}\left(x-\chi_1(l)\frac{x^{\beta_1}}{\beta_1}\right)+O(xe^{-c_1\sqrt{\log x}}) \tag{1.4}$$

uniformly for $(l,k)=1$, $k\leqq\exp(c_2\sqrt{\log x})$. We choose a residue class l with $\chi_1(l)=-1$ and combine (1.3) and (1.4) to get

$$x+\frac{x^{\beta_1}}{\beta_1}=(2-\delta)x(1+o(1))+O(\varphi(k)xe^{-c_1\sqrt{\log x}})+O(\sqrt{x}\,\varphi(k)\log x)\,.$$

To make sure that there is such an l it is sufficient to have (1.1) for at least $\frac{1}{2}\varphi(k)+1$ residue classes. If we choose $c_3=\min\left(c_2,\frac{c_1}{2}\right)$ and x such that $k=\exp(c_3\sqrt{\log x})$, both O-terms are $o(x)$ and we have

$$x+\frac{x^{\beta_1}}{\beta_1}\leqq(2-\delta)x(1+o(1))\,.$$

Hence $\beta_1 \log x \leqq \log x - c_4 + o(1)$ from which

$$\beta_1 \leqq 1 - \frac{c_4 + o(1)}{\log x} \leqq 1 - \frac{c_5}{\log^2 k}.$$

for $k \geqq c_6$. This proves the theorem.

If one uses the theorem of Rodosskii–Tatuzawa ([6], Satz 2.1, p. 314) instead of (1.4), one gets $\beta_1 \leqq 1 - c_7(\log k \operatorname{loglog} k)^{-1}$ instead of $\beta_1 \leqq 1 - c \log^{-2} k$ for zero-free region in (1.2), as stated by Y. MOTOHASHI ([4], p. 306). Recently MOTOHASHI [5] gave a simple proof which gives $\beta_1 \leqq 1 - c_8\delta(\log k)^{-1}$. This seems to be best possible.

2. The linear sieve

We need some more notations:
For $\alpha \in (0, 1)$, $x \geqq 1$ let $A_\alpha(x, k, l)$ denote the number of integers $1 \leqq n \leqq x$, $n \equiv l (\operatorname{mod} k)$ with the property $p|n \Rightarrow p \geqq x^\alpha$, and $A_\alpha(x, k, l; r)$ the number of n counted in $A_\alpha(x, k, l)$ with the additional condition $\Omega(n) = r$, $\Omega(n)$ counting the number of prime divisors of n with multiplicity. Thus we have

$$A_\alpha(x, k, l) = \sum_{r=1}^{[\frac{1}{\alpha}]} A_\alpha(x, k, l; r). \tag{2.1}$$

Let further denote for $r \leqq \left[\frac{1}{\alpha}\right]$

$$D_1(\alpha) = 1,\ D_2(\alpha) = \frac{1}{2}\int_\alpha^{1-\alpha} \frac{dx}{x(1-x)} = \log\frac{1-\alpha}{\alpha}, \tag{2.2}$$

and in general $(r \geqq 2)$

$$D_r(\alpha) = \frac{1}{r!} \int\limits_{\substack{x_1 + \ldots + x_{r-1} \leqq 1 \\ x_i \geqq \alpha}} \cdots \int \frac{dx_1 \ldots dx_{r-1}}{x_1 \ldots x_{r-1}(1 - x_1 - \ldots - x_{r-1})}$$

and

$$J_r(x, \alpha) = \int\limits_{\substack{u_1 + \ldots + u_r \leqq 1 \\ u_i \geqq \alpha}} \cdots \int \frac{x^{u_1 + \ldots + u_r}}{u_1 \ldots u_r} du_1 \ldots du_r. \tag{2.3}$$

For example $J_1(x, \alpha) = \int_\alpha^1 \frac{x^u}{u} du = \operatorname{li} x - \operatorname{li}(x^\alpha)$. With these notations holds the following

Theorem 2. *For* $\alpha \in (0, 1)$, $r \leqq \left[\frac{1}{\alpha}\right]$, *and fixed* k *we have*

(2.4) $$A_\alpha(x, k, l; r) = \frac{1}{\varphi(k)}\left(J_r(x, \alpha) + O\left(\frac{x}{\log^2 x}\right)\right), \quad x \to \infty,$$

(2.5) $$A_\alpha(x, k, l; r) = \frac{1}{\varphi(k)}\left(D_r(\alpha)\frac{x}{\log x} + O\left(\frac{x}{\log^2 x}\right)\right), \quad x \to \infty.$$

For $r = 1$ the theorem follows from the prime number theorem for arithmetic progressions:

$$A_\alpha(x, k, l; 1) = \sum_{\substack{x^\alpha \leqq p \leqq x \\ p \equiv l(k)}} 1 = \pi(x, k, l) - \pi(x^\alpha, k, l) + O(1) =$$

$$= \frac{1}{\varphi(k)}\left(\operatorname{li} x - \operatorname{li} x^\alpha + O\left(\frac{x}{\log^2 x}\right)\right) = \frac{1}{\varphi(k)}\left(J_1(x, \alpha) + O\left(\frac{x}{\log^2 x}\right)\right).$$

For $r > 1$ the theorem can be proved by induction. To keep notations simple, we indicate only the case $r = 2$:

$$A_\alpha(x, k, l; 2) = \sum_{\substack{p_1 p_2 \leqq x \\ p_1 p_2 \equiv l(k) \\ p_i \geqq x^\alpha}} 1 = \sum_{\substack{a=1 \\ (a,k)=1}}^{k} \sum_{\substack{x^\alpha \leqq p_2 \leqq x^{1-\alpha} \\ p_2 \equiv la'(k)}} \sum_{\substack{x^\alpha \leqq p_1 \leqq \frac{x}{p_2} \\ p_1 \equiv a(k)}} 1,$$

where a and a' represent associated residue classes, i.e. $aa' \equiv 1 \bmod k$. Using the prime number theorem in the inner sum we get by partial summation

$$A_\alpha(x, k, l; 2) = \frac{1}{\varphi(k)} \sum_{\substack{a=1 \\ (a,k)=1}}^{k} \frac{1}{\varphi(k)}\left(\int_{x^\alpha}^{x^{1-\alpha}} \frac{x}{u^2 \log\frac{x}{u}} \int_{x^\alpha}^{u} \frac{dy}{\log y}\, du + \frac{1}{\varphi(k)} O\left(\frac{x}{\log^2 x}\right)\right) =$$

$$= \frac{1}{\varphi(k)}\left(J_2(x, \alpha) + O\left(\frac{x}{\log^2 x}\right)\right),$$

by an appropriate substitution in the integral. It is now obvious how to proceed in the induction step. The estimate (2.5) follows immediately from (2.4) if one applies

$$\operatorname{li} x = \frac{x}{\log x} + O\left(\frac{x}{\log^2 x}\right)$$

to the innermost integral in (2.3):

$$J_r(x,\alpha)=\iint\limits_{\substack{u_1+\ldots+u_{r-1}\leqq 1-\alpha\\ u_i\geqq\alpha}}\frac{x^{u_1+\ldots+u_{r-1}}}{u_1\ldots u_{r-1}}\left(\int\limits_{\alpha}^{1-(u_1+\ldots+u_{r-1})}\frac{x^{u_r}}{u_r}\,du_r\right)du_1\ldots du_{r-1}=$$

$$=\iint\limits_{\substack{u_1+\ldots+u_{r-1}\leqq 1-\alpha\\ u_i\geqq\alpha}}\frac{x^{u_1+\ldots+u_{r-1}}}{u_1\ldots u_{r-1}}(\operatorname{li}x^{1-(u_1+\ldots+u_{r-1})}-\operatorname{li}x^{\alpha})\,du_1\ldots du_{r-1}=$$

$$=\frac{x}{\log x}\iint\limits_{\substack{u_1+\ldots+u_{r-1}\leqq 1-\alpha\\ u_i\geqq\alpha}}\frac{du_1\ldots du_{r-1}}{u_1\ldots u_{r-1}(1-(u_1+\ldots+u_{r-1}))}+O\left(\frac{x}{\log^2 x}\right)+$$

$$+O\left(\frac{x^{\alpha}}{\log x}J_{r-1}\left(x^{1-\alpha},\frac{\alpha}{1-\alpha}\right)\right)=D_r(\alpha)\frac{x}{\log x}+O\left(\frac{x}{\log^2 x}\right).$$

This proves Theorem 2.

There is a very instructive heuristic argument which leads to Theorem 2 and which could be completed to a rigorous proof with a slightly weaker error term (P. Turán [9] did this in the case $r=3$): Let $W>0$ be a parameter. Then

$$A_\alpha(x,k,l;r)=\sum_{\substack{p_1\ldots p_r\leqq x\\ p_i\geqq x^{\alpha}\\ p_1\ldots p_r\equiv l(k)}}1\approx\frac{1}{r!}\sum_{\substack{p_1\ldots p_r\leqq x\\ x^{\alpha}\leqq p_1<\ldots<p_r\\ p_1\ldots p_r\equiv l(k)}}1=\sum_{\substack{\alpha W\leqq v_1<v_2<\ldots<v_r\\ v_1+\ldots+v_r\leqq W}}\sum_{\substack{p_i\in J_{v_i}\\ p_1\ldots p_r\equiv l(k)}}1,$$

where J_{v_i} denotes the interval $(x^{\frac{v_i-1}{W}}, x^{\frac{v_i}{W}}]$.

We replace the congruence condition $p_1\ldots p_r\equiv l(k)$ using the orthogonality of Dirichlet's characters:

$$A_\alpha(x,k,l;r)\approx\sum_{\substack{\alpha W\leqq v_1<\ldots<v_r\\ v_1+\ldots+v_r\leqq W}}\sum_{p_i\in J_{v_i}}\frac{1}{\varphi(k)}\sum_{\chi\bmod k}\bar\chi(l)\,\chi(p_1\ldots p_r)=$$

$$=\frac{1}{\varphi(k)}\sum_{\substack{\alpha W\leqq v_1<\ldots<v_r\\ v_1+\ldots+v_r\leqq W}}\sum_{\chi\bmod k}\bar\chi(l)\prod_{i=1}^{r}\sum_{p_i\in J_{v_i}}\chi(p_i).$$

In the inner sum we use

$$\sum_{p\leqq x}\chi(p)\log p=\begin{Bmatrix}x\\0\end{Bmatrix}+O(xe^{-c_9\sqrt{\log x}});\ \begin{cases}\chi=\chi_0\\ \chi\neq\chi_0\end{cases},\tag{2.6}$$

(this follows for fixed k from PRACHAR [6], Satz 7.2, p. 134), and get

$$A_\alpha(x,k,l;r)\approx\frac{1}{\varphi(k)}\sum_{\substack{\alpha W\leqq v_1<\ldots<v_r\\ v_1+\ldots+v_r\leqq W}}\prod_{i=1}^{r}\left[\frac{1}{\frac{v_i}{W}\log x}\left(x^{\frac{v_i}{W}}-x^{\frac{v_i-1}{W}}\right)\right]\approx$$

$$\approx\frac{1}{\varphi(k)}\sum_{\substack{\alpha W\leqq v_1<\ldots<v_r\\ v_1+\ldots+v_r\leqq W}}\frac{W}{v_1}\cdot\frac{W}{v_2}\cdot\ldots\frac{W}{v_r}\,x^{\frac{v_1}{W}+\ldots+\frac{v_r}{W}}\frac{1}{W^r}.$$

In the last step we used $x^{\frac{v_i}{W}}(1-x^{-\frac{1}{W}})\approx x^{\frac{v_i}{W}}\frac{\log x}{W}$ which follows from the mean value theorem.

This last r-fold sum can be interpreted as a Riemann sum for the r-fold integral $J_r(x,\alpha)$.

We now prove a uniform result for $A_\alpha(x,k,l;r)$ where the modulus k may increase with x:

Theorem 3. *For fixed* $\alpha\in(0,1)$ *and* $r\leqq\left[\frac{1}{\alpha}\right]$ *we have*

$$A_\alpha(x,k,l;r)=\frac{1}{\varphi(k)}\left(J_r(x,\alpha)+(-1)^r\chi_1(l)J_r(x^{\beta_1},\alpha)+O\left(\frac{x}{\log^2 x}\right)\right)=$$

$$=\frac{1}{\varphi(k)}D_r(\alpha)\left(\frac{x}{\log x}+(-1)^r\chi_1(l)\frac{x^{\beta_1}}{\beta_1\log x}\right)+O\left(\frac{x}{\varphi(k)\log^2 x}\right)$$

uniformly for $k\leqq\exp(c_{10}\sqrt{\log x})$, $(l,k)=1$.

The proof is again by induction with respect to r, starting with

$$\pi(x,k,l)=\frac{1}{\varphi(k)}(\operatorname{li}x-\chi_1(l)\operatorname{li}x^{\beta_1})+O(xe^{-c_{11}\sqrt{\log x}})$$

which follows from [6] (Satz 7.3, p. 136), by partial summation. Again the heuristic argument of Theorem 2 can be applied with (2.6) replaced by

$$(2.7)\qquad\sum_{p\leqq x}\chi(p)\log p=\begin{cases}x\\ -\dfrac{x^{\beta_1}}{\beta_1}\\ 0\end{cases}+O(xe^{-c_{12}\sqrt{\log x}})\quad\text{for}\quad\begin{cases}\chi=\chi_0\\ \chi=\chi_1\\ \chi\neq\chi_0,\chi_1\end{cases},$$

(see [6], Satz 7.2, p. 134). The heuristic argument makes it very transparent how the factor $(-1)^r$ in Theorem 3 arises. This factor is responsible for the form of the "Siegel-critical constants" in the following

Theorem 4. *If for a fixed* $\alpha \in (0,1)$ *there is an effectively computable* $\delta > 0$ *such that*

$$A_\alpha(x, k, l) \leqq \frac{1}{\varphi(k)} \Bigg(2 \sum_{\substack{r=1 \\ 2 \nmid r}}^{[\frac{1}{\alpha}]} D_r(\alpha) - \delta \Bigg) \frac{x}{\log x} (1 + o(1)) \tag{2.8}$$

or

$$A_\alpha(x, k, l) \geqq \frac{1}{\varphi(k)} \Bigg(2 \sum_{\substack{r=1 \\ 2 \mid r}}^{[\frac{1}{\alpha}]} D_r(\alpha) + \delta \Bigg) \frac{x}{\log x} (1 + o(1)) \tag{2.9}$$

uniformly for $k \leqq \exp(c_{13} \sqrt{\log x})$, *then there is an effectively computable* $c(\delta)$ *with*

$$L(s, \chi_1) \neq 0 \quad \textit{for} \quad 1 - \frac{c(\delta)}{\log^2 k} \leqq s \leqq 1 .$$

Proof. Theorem 3 and (2.1) give for a residue class l with $\chi_1(l) = -1$

$$A_\alpha(x, k, l) = \sum_{r=1}^{[\frac{1}{\alpha}]} A_\alpha(x, k, l; r) \geqq \sum_{\substack{r=1 \\ 2 \nmid r}}^{[\frac{1}{\alpha}]} A_\alpha(x, k, l; r) =$$

$$= \frac{1}{\varphi(k)} \sum_{\substack{r=1 \\ 2 \nmid r}}^{[\frac{1}{\alpha}]} D_r(\alpha) \left(\frac{x}{\log x} + \frac{x^{\beta_1}}{\beta_1 \log x} \right) + O\left(\frac{1}{\varphi(k)} \frac{x}{\log^2 x} \right).$$

This together with the assumption (2.8) gives

$$\frac{1}{\varphi(k)} \sum_{\substack{r=1 \\ 2 \nmid r}}^{[\frac{1}{\alpha}]} D_r(\alpha) \left(\frac{x}{\log x} + \frac{x^{\beta_1}}{\beta_1 \log x} \right) + O\left(\frac{1}{\varphi(k)} \frac{x}{\log^2 x} \right) \leqq$$

$$\leqq \frac{1}{\varphi(k)} \Bigg(2 \sum_{\substack{r=1 \\ 2 \nmid r}} D_r(\alpha) - \delta \Bigg) \frac{x}{\log x} (1 + o(1))$$

and the conclusion follows as in the proof of Theorem 1. In the case (2.9) the proof is somewhat more complicated since we cannot simply omit the contribution of the

$A_\alpha(x, k, l; r)$ with the "wrong" parity, but it is still essentially the same idea, and we can leave the proof for the reader.

For the quantity $A_\alpha(x, k, l)$ the linear sieve of W. B. JURKAT and H.-E. RICHERT [1] gives the following estimates:

Theorem 5. *For $\alpha \in (0, 1)$ we have*

$$A_\alpha(x, k, l) \leqq \frac{x}{\varphi(k) \log x} \cdot \frac{e^{-\gamma}}{\alpha} F\left(\frac{1}{\alpha}\right)(1+o(1)) \tag{2.10}$$

$$A_\alpha(x, k, l) \geqq \frac{x}{\varphi(k) \log x} \frac{e^{-\gamma}}{\alpha} f\left(\frac{1}{\alpha}\right)(1+o(1)) \tag{2.11}$$

uniformly for $k \leqq \exp(c_{14}\sqrt{\log x})$, $(l, k)=1$, where the functions $f(u)$, $F(u)$ are defined to be the continuous solutions of

$$\begin{cases} F(u)=\dfrac{2e^\gamma}{u}, \; f(u)=0 & \textit{for} \quad 0<u\leqq 2 \\ (uf(u))'=F(u-1), \; (uF(u))'=f(u-1) & \textit{for} \quad u \geqq 2 . \end{cases} \tag{2.12}$$

Proof. This is a very special and weak form of [1] (Theorem 5, p. 230).

The link between Siegel's zeros and the linear sieve is now given by

Theorem 6. *For $\alpha \in (0, 1)$ we have*

$$\frac{e^{-\gamma}}{\alpha} F\left(\frac{1}{\alpha}\right) = 2 \sum_{\substack{r=1 \\ 2 \nmid r}}^{[\frac{1}{\alpha}]} D_r(\alpha), \quad \frac{e^{-\gamma}}{\alpha} f\left(\frac{1}{\alpha}\right) = 2 \sum_{\substack{r=1 \\ 2 \mid r}}^{[\frac{1}{\alpha}]} D_r(\alpha) . \tag{2.13}$$

Proof. For $u>0$ define $G(u)$, $g(u)$ by

$$G(u) := \frac{2e^\gamma}{u} \sum_{\substack{r=1 \\ 2 \nmid r}}^{[u]} D_r\left(\frac{1}{u}\right), \quad g(u) := \frac{2e^\gamma}{u} \sum_{\substack{r=1 \\ 2 \mid r}}^{[u]} D_r\left(\frac{1}{u}\right).$$

We show that $G(u)=F(u)$, $g(u)=f(u)$ for $u \in (0, 2)$ and that $g(u)$, $G(u)$ satisfy the difference-differential equations (2.12) for $f(u)$ and $F(u)$. For $u<2$ we have

$$G(u)=\frac{2e^\gamma}{u} D_1\left(\frac{1}{u}\right) = \frac{2e^\gamma}{u} = F(u) ,$$

while $g(u)=0=f(u)$ since the sum is empty. The difference-differential equations reduce to

$$\frac{d}{du}\sum_{\substack{r=1\\2|r}}^{[u]} D_r\left(\frac{1}{u}\right)=\frac{1}{u-1}\sum_{\substack{r=1\\2\nmid r}}^{[u]} D_r\left(\frac{1}{u-1}\right),\quad u>2$$

and

$$\frac{d}{du}\sum_{\substack{r=1\\2\nmid r}} D_r\left(\frac{1}{u}\right)=\frac{1}{u-1}\sum_{\substack{r=1\\2|r}}=D_r\left(\frac{1}{u-1}\right),\quad u>2$$

and further to

$$\frac{d}{du}D_n\left(\frac{1}{u}\right)=\frac{1}{u-1}D_{n-1}\left(\frac{1}{u-1}\right),\qquad u\geqq n. \tag{2.14}$$

We substitute $\alpha=\frac{1}{u}$ and see that (2.14) is equivalent to

$$\frac{d}{d\alpha}D_n(\alpha)=\frac{1}{\alpha(\alpha-1)}D_{n-1}\left(\frac{\alpha}{1-\alpha}\right),\quad \alpha\leqq\frac{1}{n}. \tag{2.15}$$

This can be proved directly from the definition (2.2) by induction, if the integrals are written as repeated integrals.

From Theorems 4 and 6 now follows our main result.

Theorem 7. *If for some $\alpha\in(0,1)$ the main term constants $\frac{e^{-\gamma}}{\alpha}F\left(\frac{1}{\alpha}\right)$, $\frac{e^{-\gamma}}{\alpha}f\left(\frac{1}{\alpha}\right)$ in the linear Jurkat–Richert sieve could be replaced by $\frac{e^{-\gamma}}{\alpha}F\left(\frac{1}{\alpha}\right)-\delta$, $\frac{e^{-\gamma}}{\alpha}f\left(\frac{1}{\alpha}\right)+\delta$, resp., with an effectively computable $\delta>0$, Siegel's theorem could be proved with effectively computable constants $c(\varepsilon)$ for each $\varepsilon\in\left(0,\frac{1}{2}\right)$.*

For $\alpha=\frac{1}{2}$ Theorem 7 gives again Theorem 1. For $\alpha\in\left[\frac{1}{4},\frac{1}{3}\right]$ Theorem 4 is due to P. Turán ([9], p. 136); Theorem 6 was proved in this case by the author ([8], (2.2), p. 304).

The connection between the sieve constants and the contributions of odd and even numbers to the main term constants in the asymptotic estimate for $A_\alpha(x,k,l)$ does not surprise. It confirms Selberg's conclusion "that the weakness of the sieve-method lies in the fact that it is unable to distinguish between numbers with an odd or an even number of primefactors" ([7], p. 20).

References

[1] JURKAT, W. B. and RICHERT, H.-E., An improvement of Selberg's sieve method I, *Acta Arith.*, **11** (1965), 217–240.
[2] KLIMOV, N. I., Almost prime numbers, *Amer, Math. Soc. Translations* (2) **46**, 48–56.
[3] MONTGOMERY, H. L. and VAUGHAN, R. C., The large sieve. *Mathematika*, **20** (1973), 119–134.
[4] MOTOHASHI, Y., On some improvements of the Brun–Titchmarsh theorem. *Journal of the Math. Soc. of Japan*, **26** (1974), 306–323.
[5] MOTOHASHI, Y., A note on Siegel's zeros (to appear in *Proc. Japan Acad.*).
[6] PRACHAR, K., *Primzahlverteilung*, Springer, Berlin, Göttingen, Heidelberg, 1957.
[7] SELBERG, A., On elementary methods in prime-number-theory and their limitations, Den 11-te Skandinaviske Matematikerkongress, Trondheim (1952), 13–22.
[8] SIEBERT, H., On a question of P. Turán, *Acta Arith.*, **26** (1975), 303–305.
[9] TURÁN, P., Über die Siegel-Nullstelle der Dirichletschen Funktionen. *Acta Arith.*, **24** (1973), 135–141.

UNIVERSITÄT ULM
BRD

Studies in Pure Mathematics
To the Memory of Paul Turán

Extremal graph problems and graph products

by

M. SIMONOVITS (Budapest)

Abstract

In this paper we consider only graphs without loops and multiple edges. The product of two vertex disjoint graphs G_1 and G_2 is the graph obtained by joining each vertex of G_1 to each vertex of G_2. Given n and the sample graphs $L_1, \ldots, L_\lambda$, we shall consider those graphs on n vertices which contain no L_i as a subgraph and have maximum number of edges under this condition. These graphs will be called extremal graphs for the L_i's.

In many cases the extremal graphs are products of other extremal graphs (for some other families of sample graphs). The aim of this paper is to investigate, when are the extremal graphs products and when are not.

Notations

The graphs considered in this paper are undirected, have no loops and no multiple edges. They will be denoted by capitals, and the superscript will always denote the number of vertices. Thus G^n, H^n, S^n will all denote graphs of n vertices.

The number of vertices, edges, and the chromatic number of a graph G will be denoted by $v(G)$, $e(G)$ and $\chi(G)$, respectively. If x is a vertex of G, st(x) denotes the star of x, i.e. the set of vertices joined to it; $d(x)$ will denote the degree of x.

To simplify the definitions of graphs we shall use the following operations.

(a) $G=\sum G_i$, if the G_i's are spanned subgraphs of G the pairwise disjoint vertex sets of which cover G and no vertices belonging to different G_i's are joined. (SUM).

(b) $G=\times G_i$, if the G_i's are spanned subgraphs of G the pairwise disjoint vertex sets of which cover G and vertices belonging to different G_i's are *always* joined. (PRODUCT).

(c) If G_1 is a subgraph of G or a set of vertices and edges of it, then $G-G_1$ is the graph resulting by deleting all the vertices, edges, and also the vertices incident with some deleted edges of G_1 from G.

$K_d(r_1, \ldots, r_d)$ denotes the complete d-partite graph with r_i vertices in its ith class.

Introduction

A classical result of P. TURÁN [6, 7] asserts that if p and n are given integers and S^n is a graph not containing K_p as a subgraph and having maximum number of edges under this condition, then $S^n = K_{p-1}(n_1, \ldots, n_{p-1})$ where $n_1, \ldots, n_{p-1}$ is the most uniform partition of n into $p-1$ summands:

$$n_i = \left[\frac{n}{p-1}\right] \quad \text{or} \quad n_i = \left[\frac{n}{p-1}\right] + 1, \quad \text{and} \quad n_1 + \ldots + n_{p-1} = n .$$

To generalize the above theorem one can ask the following general problems.

Problem 1. Let $\mathscr{L}$ be a given finite or infinite family of graphs and let $\mathscr{A}(n, \mathscr{L})$ denote the class of graphs on n vertices not containing any $L \in \mathscr{L}$ as a subgraph. What is the maximum number of edges a graph $G^n \in \mathscr{A}(n, \mathscr{L})$ can have.

(The graphs of $\mathscr{L}$ will be called sample graphs, the graphs attaining the maximum will be called extremal graphs, the maximum will be denoted by $\operatorname{ex}(n, \mathscr{L})$ and the class of extremal graphs will be denoted by $\operatorname{EX}(n, \mathscr{L})$.)

Problem 2. Describe the structure of the extremal graphs.

Some general results obtained by P. ERDŐS [1, 2] and the author [4] independently, give a fairly good description of the extremal graphs. Thus e.g. we have proved that

Theorem A. *For a given* $\mathscr{L}$ *let*

$$d = \min\{\chi(L) : L \in \mathscr{L}\} - 1 . \tag{1}$$

There exists a $c > 0$ *such that if* S^n *is an extremal graph for* $\mathscr{L}$, *then* S^n *can be obtained from a* $K_d(n_1, \ldots, n_d)$ *by deleting from and adding to it* $O(n^{2-c})$ *edges. Further,* $n_i = \dfrac{n}{d} + O(n^{1-c})$, $i = 1, 2, \ldots, d$.

Corollary. *Under the conditions of Theorem A* S^n *can be obtained from some appropriate graphs* $G_1, \ldots, G_d$ *by deleting* $O(n^{2-c})$ *edges from* $\underset{i \leq d}{\times} G_i$.

Remark. 1. The basic content of Theorem A is that the extremal graphs depend only very loosely on $\mathscr{L}$, the minimum chromatic number determines their structure up to $O(n^{2-c})$ edges.

Problem 3. Under which condition is it true that $S^n = \underset{i \leq d}{\times} G^{n_i}$ where $n_i = \dfrac{n}{d} + o(n)$?

Originally ERDŐS and I thought that whenever $\mathscr{L}$ is finite and n is sufficiently large, all the extremal graphs for $\mathscr{L}$ are products of graphs of almost equal size. Later we found some counter examples. However, we think that the following conjecture holds.

Conjecture 1. Let L be a $d+1$-chromatic graph which *cannot* be coloured by $d+1$ colours "1", "2", ..., "$d+1$" so that the subgraph $L_{1,2}$ spanned by the vertices of colours "1" and "2" is a tree or a forest. Then there exists an n_0 such that for any $n>n_0$, if S^n is an extremal graph for L, then $S^n=\underset{i\leq d}{\times} G^{n_i}$ where $n_i=\frac{n}{d}+o(n)$.

One can generalize Conjecture 1 to finite families of sample graphs as follows.

Definition 1. Let $\mathscr{L}$ be a given family of sample graphs. Let d be defined by (1). We say that M belongs to the *decomposition* family $\mathscr{M}$ of $\mathscr{L}$ if there exists an $L\in\mathscr{L}$ and an integer r for which

$$L\subseteq M\times K_{d-1}(r,\ldots,r)\,. \tag{2}$$

Conjecture 2. Let $\mathscr{L}$ be a finite family of graphs and d be defined by (1). If the decomposition family $\mathscr{M}$ of $\mathscr{L}$ contains no trees or forests, then for any sufficiently large n each extremal graph S^n is a product: for some fixed integer t

$$S^n=S^{n_1}\times S^{n_2},\quad \text{where}\quad n_1=\frac{tn}{d}+o(n),\quad n_2=n-n_1\,.$$

Remark 2. One can ask, why to exclude the trees and forests in Conjectures 1 and 2. To motivate this we remark that

(a) as we shall see (Proposition 2 or Theorem 1 + Remark 3), Conjecture 2 does not hold if the decomposition is allowed to contain a path. This is, why we exclude the trees in Conjecture 2.

(b) It is known [2, 4], that the extremal graph S^n can be obtained from a $K_d(n_1,\ldots,n_d)\left(\text{where } n_i=\frac{n}{d}+o(n)\right)$, by changing *only* $O(n)$ edges in it if and only if the decomposition contains a tree or a forest: in all the other cases we must alter at least cn^{1+a} edges in $K_d(n_1,\ldots,n_d)$, where $a>0$ is a constant. There is a trivial, but very important difference between $f(n)=n$ and $f(n)=n^{1+a}$, namely, the latter one is *strictly* convex. Of course, this is only a heuristic motivation given in a very compact form.

It can be shown that if $\mathscr{L}$ contains more than one graph, the (stronger) assertion of Conjecture 1 does not necessarily hold.

Our assertions above are all trivial for $d=1$. Hence we shall assume that $d\geq 2$. (The case $d=1$ will be called *degenerate*.) The main idea of Conjectures 1 and 2 is to reduce the general case to the degenerate case as follows.

Proposition 1. *Let $\mathscr{L}$ be a finite family of sample graphs and $k=\max\{v(L):L\in\mathscr{L}\}$. Let d be defined by* (1) *and $\mathscr{M}$ be the decomposition family of $\mathscr{L}$. If S^n is an extremal graph for $\mathscr{L}$ and*

$$S^n=\underset{i\leq d}{\times} G^{n_i},\quad \textit{where}\quad n_i\geq k\,,$$

then there exist d families of sample graphs, $\mathscr{M}_1,\ldots,\mathscr{M}_d$ for which

(a) $\max\{v(M): M \in \mathscr{M}\} \leq k$.
(b) $\mathscr{M} \subseteq \mathscr{M}_i$ *and*

$$\min\{\chi(M): M \in \mathscr{M}_i\} = 2 .$$

(c) *If* H_i *contains no* $M \in \mathscr{M}_i$ $(i=1, \ldots, d)$, *then* $\underset{i \leq d}{\times} H_i$ *contains no* $L \in \mathscr{L}$.
(d) G^{n_i} *is an extremal graph for* $\mathscr{M}_i$ $(i=1, \ldots, d)$.

Proof. Let $\mathscr{M}_i$ be the family of graphs of at most k vertices not contained in G^{n_i}. Now (a) and (c)→(d) are trivial. If M is in the decomposition of $\mathscr{L}$ but $M \notin \mathscr{M}_i$, then there exists an $L \subseteq M \times K_{d-1}(k, \ldots, k)$ and by the definition of $\mathscr{M}_i$ $M \subseteq G^{n_i}$. Hence $M \times K_{d-1}(k, \ldots, k) \subseteq G^{n_i} \times \underset{j \neq i}{\times} G^{n_j} = S^n$, that is, $L \subseteq S^n$, which is a contradiction. This proves (b), since

$$\min\{\chi(M): M \in \mathscr{M}\} = 2$$

is obvious: we colour an appropriate $L \in \mathscr{L}$ by $d+1$ colours and denote by $L_{1,2}$ the subgraph spanned by the first two colours. Clearly, $L_{1,2}$ is bipartite and belongs to $\mathscr{M}$. To prove (c) observe that, since H_i contains no $M \in \mathscr{M}_i$, each subgraph of H_i of at most k vertices is also a subgraph of G^{n_i}. Thus each subgraph of $\underset{i \leq d}{\times} H_i$ of at most k vertices is also a subgraph of $S^n = \underset{i \leq d}{\times} G^{n_i}$. Thus it cannot belong to $\mathscr{L}$. This completes the proof.

Though the proof of Proposition 1 was fairly simple and straightforward, the proposition itself is worth some further explanation. Assume that Conjecture 1 holds. Then all the extremal problems satisfying the condition of Conjecture 1 can be reduced to degenerate extremal graph problems in the following sense:

Given a finite family $\mathscr{L}$ of sample graphs, the families $\mathscr{M}_1, \ldots, \mathscr{M}_d$ can be defined only in finitely many ways so that (a), (b) and (c) hold. Assume that we can solve the extremal problems corresponding to the degenerate families $\mathscr{M}_1, \ldots, \mathscr{M}_d$. If $H^{n_1}, \ldots, H^{n_d}$ are the corresponding extremal graphs, let $S^n = \times H^{n_i}$. Clearly,

$$e(S^n) = e(K_d(n_1, \ldots, n_d)) + \sum \mathrm{ex}(n_i, \mathscr{M}_i) = f(n_1, \ldots, n_d; \mathscr{M}_1, \ldots, \mathscr{M}_d). \tag{3}$$

At least in theory, we may find for each n and $\mathscr{M}_1, \ldots, \mathscr{M}_d$ the partition $n = n_1 + \ldots + n_d$ yielding the maximum in (3). Since there are only finitely many possible candidates for $\mathscr{M}_1, \ldots, \mathscr{M}_d$, we may find the one giving the highest maximum, and the corresponding S^n will be the extremal graph. In this sense we reduced the problem of $\mathscr{L}$ to the degenerate problems of $\mathscr{M}_1, \ldots, \mathscr{M}_d$.

This is, why Proposition 1 is important in theory. Another use of it is that in many cases we can guess the possible extremal graphs by assuming Conjecture 1, and finding the potentially possible sets $\mathscr{M}_1, \ldots, \mathscr{M}_d$, then the corresponding extremal graphs for $\mathscr{L}$. Knowing, which are the extremal graphs if Conjecture holds we can often prove that they are really extremal graphs, not using Conjecture 1 at all.

One can ask, whether Proposition 1 holds even if the decomposition family $\mathcal{M}$ contains a tree or a forest. The answer is that sometimes *yes* and sometimes *not*.

Proposition 2. *There exists a finite family $\mathcal{L}$ of sample graphs and an n_0 such that if $n > n_0$, then no extremal graph S^n (for $\mathcal{L}$) can be decomposed into the product of d nonempty graphs, where d is defined by* (1).

One way to prove Proposition 2 would be to show that for

$$\mathcal{L}^* = \{K_k(1, 3, 3), K_3 \times \bar{K}_3, (K_2 + K_2) \times \bar{K}_3, K_4)\}$$

Proposition 2 holds:

Let $\tilde{S}^n$ be obtained from $K_2(n_1, n_2)$, where $n_1 = \left[\frac{n}{2}\right]$ and $n_2 = n - n_1$, by adding two incident edges (x, y) and (y, z) and two further incident edges (x', y') and (y', z') to it and deleting (y', y), where x, y, z belong to the first class of $K_2(n_1, n_2)$ and x', y', z' to the other one. One can show that if n is sufficiently large, then this $\tilde{S}^n$ is the only extremal graph for $\mathcal{L}^*$ and $\tilde{S}^n$ cannot be decomposed into the product of two nonempty graphs. However, Proposition 2 will be derived as a consequence of a much deeper theorem, which could be called either an "inverse extremal graph theorem" or a compactness theorem.

An inverse extremal graph theorem

The aim of the next definition is to define a sequence of graphs which in some sense are very much alike and differ from each other only in size.

Definition 2. Let the graphs $A_1, \ldots, A_d$ and D be fixed and let also fix a subset B of the pairs $(x, y): x \in D, y \in \bigcup_{i \leq d} A_i$. Let us take an n for which $m_i = \frac{n - v(D)}{dv(A_i)}$ are all integers, take m_i vertex disjoint copies of A_i, denoted by $A_{i,j}$ and fix the isomorphisms $F_{i,j}: A_{i,j} \to A_i$. Let

$$Z^{n - v(D)} =: \mathop{\times}_{i=1}^{d} \sum_{j=1}^{m} A_{i,j}.$$

Let us join an $x \in D$ to a $y \in A_{i,j}$ iff $(x, F_{i,j}(y))$ belongs to B. Thus we obtain a graph S^n. A sequence

$$S^{n_1}, \ldots, S^{n_k}, \ldots$$

will be called a *q*-sequence if each S^{n_k} is obtained from the same $D, A_1, \ldots, A_d$ and B in the way described above. Sometimes we shall call D the head and $Z^{n-v(D)}$ the tail of the graph, respectively, though they are not uniquely defined by $\{S^{n_k}\}$.

Definition 3. Let $\{S^{n_k}\}$ be a q-sequence, obtained from $A_1, \ldots, A_d$, D and B. If for every q-sequence $\{T^{m_p}\}$ obtained from $A'_1 \subseteq A_1, \ldots, A'_d \subseteq A_d$, $D' \subseteq S^{n_h}$ (for some fixed h) and $B' \subseteq B$,

$$e(S^{n_k}) \geqq e(T^{m_p}) \quad \text{if} \quad n_k = m_p, \quad k > k_0, \tag{4}$$

then $\{S^{n_k}\}$ will be called *dense*. If we have strict inequality in (4), then $\{S^{n_k}\}$ will be called *strictly dense*.

Theorem 1. *The following two assertions are equivalent:*

(i) $\{S^{n_0+km}\}$ *is a (strictly) dense q-sequence.*

(ii) *There exists a* **finite** $\mathscr{L}$ *such that* $\{S^{n_0+km}\}$ *is (the only) extremal graph for* $\mathscr{L}$ *and* $n = n_0 + km$, $(n > n_1)$.

Remark 3. One can easily find strictly dense q-sequences which are not products. Such a strictly dense sequence is e.g. $\tilde{S}^n$ defined after Proposition 2. By Theorem 1 these are sequences of extremal graphs. Thus Proposition 2 follows from Theorem 1. (To be quite precise, S^n is a q-sequence if n is even and another q-sequence if n is odd. Thus Theorem 1 yields two families $\mathscr{L}_{\text{even}}$ and $\mathscr{L}_{\text{odd}}$ and if $\mathscr{L} = \mathscr{L}_{\text{even}} \cup \mathscr{L}_{\text{odd}}$, then obviously S^n is the only extremal graph for $\mathscr{L}$ if n is sufficiently large.)

Remark 4. In [5] we proved that if $\mathscr{L}$ is a finite family of sample graphs and the decomposition family of $\mathscr{L}$ contains a path or a subgraph of a path, then there exists an integer t such that for every h there is a strictly dense q-sequence $\{S^h : n \equiv h \pmod t\}$ of extremal graphs for $\mathscr{L}$ if n is large enough. In other words, in every residue class mod t there is a sequence of extremal graphs of similar structure. Theorem 1 shows that this (main) theorem of [5] is sharp: each strictly dense q-sequence is an extremal sequence for some finite $\mathscr{L}$. In this sense Theorem 1 is an *inverse extremal graph theorem*. It is also an *inverse extremal graph theorem* in the following sense: we first fix the extremal graphs and then find the corresponding $\mathscr{L}$.

Remark 5. One part of Theorem 1, namely (ii)→(i) is trivial: let us fix an $\mathscr{L}$ satisfying (ii). If $\{T^{m_p}\}$ is a q-sequence obtained from a family $A'_1 \subseteq A_1, \ldots, A'_d \subseteq A_d$, $D' \subseteq S^{n_h}$ and $B' \subseteq B$, then each T^{m_p} is a subgraph of an S^{n_k}. Thus T^{m_p} contains no $L \in \mathscr{L}$. Further, if $n_k = m_p$, then (4) holds (with strict inequality) since S^{n_k} is (the only) extremal graph for $\mathscr{L}$. Q.E.D.

Before turning to the proof of Theorem 1 we give some examples illustrating the notion of dense q-sequences.

Example 1. ERDŐS and RÉNYI called a graph A balanced if for every subgraph A'

$$\frac{e(A)}{v(A)} > \frac{e(A')}{v(A')}.$$

Let $A_1, \ldots, A_d$ be balanced and D arbitrary. If B is the whole direct product $\{(x, y): x \in D, y \in \bigcup_{i \leq d} A_i\}$, then the corresponding q-sequence is strictly dense. (A tree, a complete graph, a complete bipartite graph, a cycle are all balanced. A balanced graph is always connected.)

Example 2. Let $A_1, \ldots, A_d$ be given graphs and A_1 be strictly unbalanced in the sense that it has a subgraph A' for which

$$e(A_1):v(A_1)<e(A'):v(A').$$

Let D be arbitrary and B be again the whole direct product. Then the corresponding q-sequence is *not* dense.

Example 3. Let $d=2$, $A_1=A_2=C^4$ be a four-cycle and Z^{8k} be obtained by taking the corresponding graph $G^{4k}\times G^{4k}$, where G^{4k} is the union of k disjoint C^4. Let $D=\{x\}$. The corresponding q-sequence S^{8k+1} is not dense if x is joined to one vertex of each C^4: we obtain a better sequence T^{8k+1} by omitting x and 3 further points from S^{8k+5}. If x is joined to 3 vertices of each C^4, then the obtained S^{8k+1} is a strictly dense q-sequence.

Proof of Theorem 1

Let us fix the sequence S^{n_k}. A graph G will be called "small" if it is contained in an S^{n_k}. By Remark 5 it is enough to prove (i)→(ii). We shall prove that if r is sufficiently large and

$$\mathcal{L}_r=\{L: L \text{ is not "small"}, v(L)\leq r\},$$

then S^{n_k} is (the only) extremal graph for $\mathcal{L}_r$ (for $n=n_k$).

We need the following two lemmas.

Lemma 1. *Let $\{S^{n_k}\}$ be a dense q-sequence. There exists an N_0 such that if $n_k>N_0$ and G^{n_k} is "small", then*

$$e(G^{n_k})\leq e(S^{n_k}). \tag{5}$$

Further, if $\{S^{n_k}\}$ is strictly dense and the equality holds in (5), then $G^{n_k}=S^{n_k}$.

Lemma 2. *Given a dense q-sequence $\{S^{n_k}\}$, there exist two integers R and N_1 and a positive constant c such that if $n>N_1$, each vertex of G^n has valence $>\left(1-\frac{1}{d}-c\right)n$ and each subgraph G^R of G^n is "small", then G^n is also "small".*

The proofs of these lemmas will be given in the next paragraph. Here we show, how to complete the proof of Theorem 1 assuming the lemmas.

First we remark that if R is sufficiently large, then $\mathscr{L}_R$ contains an L with $\chi(L)=d+1$. Indeed, if e.g. $b=v(D)+v(A_1)+\ldots+v(A_d)$ then $K_{d+1}(2bd, \ldots, 2bd)\notin S^{n_k}$ is trivial, thus $K_{d+1}(2bd, \ldots, 2bd)\in\mathscr{L}_R$ for $R\geqq 4bd^2$. On the other hand, each $K_d(p, \ldots, p)\subseteq S^{n_k}$ if $k\geqq k_0(d, p)$. Hence $\mathscr{L}_R$ contains no $\leqq d$-chromatic graphs:

$$\min\{\chi(L): L\in\mathscr{L}_R\}=d+1 .$$

Hence, according to the main results of [1, 2] and [4], for $R\geqq 4bd^2$ if H^n is extremal for $\mathscr{L}_R$, then

$$e(H^n)=\mathrm{ex}\,(n, \mathscr{L}_R)=\frac{1}{2}\left(1-\frac{1}{d}+o(1)\right)n^2 ,$$

and each vertex of H^n is of valence $\geqq\left(1-\frac{1}{d}\right)n-o(n)$. Now we may apply Lemma 2 to H^n: there exist an $\tilde{R}$ and an N_1, further a $c>0$, such that if $N_1<n$ and the minimum degree of G^n exceeds $\left(1-\frac{1}{d}-c\right)n$ and each subgraph $G^{\tilde{R}}\subseteq G^n$ is "small", then G^n is also "small". Now we fix an $R=\max\{\tilde{R}, 4bd^2\}$ and get that if $n>N_2$, then the extremal graph H^n (for $\mathscr{L}_R$)

(a) contains no prohibited subgraphs $L\in\mathscr{L}_R$, hence each $G^{\tilde{R}}\subseteq H^n$ is "small", and therefore

(b) H^n itself is also "small".

Now, by Lemma 1, $e(H^{n_k})\leqq e(S^{n_k})$. On the other hand, S^{n_k} contains no prohibited subgraphs $L\in\mathscr{L}_R$, by the definition of $\mathscr{L}_R$, and H^{n_k} is extremal, thus $e(H^{n_k})\geqq e(S^{n_k})$, that is, S^{n_k} and H^{n_k} have the same number of edges and both are extremal for $\mathscr{L}_R$. If, in addition, $\{S^{n_k}\}$ is strictly dense, then, by Lemma 1, $S^{n_k}=H^{n_k}$. This completes the proof.

Proofs of the Lemmas

Proof of Lemma 1. Let $G^{n_k}\subseteq S^{n_l}$. To prove that $e(G^{n_k})\leqq e(S^{n_k})$ let us define $\tilde{G}^{n_k}$ as a "small" graph with the maximum number of edges on n_k vertices. It is enough to prove that

$$e(\tilde{G}^{n_k})\leqq e(S^{n_k}) \tag{6}$$

if $\tilde{G}^{n_k}$ is "small". Let S^∞ be defined as the infinite graph obtained from $Z^\infty =: \mathop{\times}\limits_{i=1}^{d}\sum\limits_{j=1}^{\infty}A_{i,j}$ and D in the way described in Definition 1. Since a graph is "small" iff it is a subgraph of S^∞, $\tilde{G}^{n_k}$ is the spanned subgraph of S^∞ of n_k vertices with the maximum number of edges. Let us abreviate n_k by n, and denote by v_i the number of vertices of $\tilde{G}^n$ in $\sum A_{i,j}=:\tilde{A}_i$.

Fixing these numbers v_i we also fix the number of edges joining different $\tilde{A}_i$'s. Let $\tilde{A}_{i,j}$ denote the subgraph of $\tilde{G}^n$ spanned by the vertices belonging to $A_{i,j}$, too. We may assume that $\tilde{G}^n$ is a spanned subgraph of S^α, therefore

$$(7)\qquad e(\tilde{G}^n)=e(K_d(v_1,\ldots,v_d))+\sum_i\sum_U c_i(U)\cdot(e(U)+e_U),$$

where $c_i(U)$ denotes the number of $\tilde{A}_{i,j}$'s isomorphic to U and in the same position as U, if U is a spanned subgraph of A_i. (Here the same position means that the mapping $F_{i,j}$ of Definition 1 maps $\tilde{A}_{i,j}$ onto U.) Further, e_U denotes the number of edges joining $\tilde{A}_{i,j}$ to D (or, in other words, the number of pairs (x, y) in B for which $y\in U\subseteq A_i$). The sum is taken for all the spanned subgraphs U of A_i.

Let $b=v(A_1)+v(A_2)+\ldots+v(A_d)+v(D)$. We assert that $e(U)+e_U$ is the same for all the graphs U such that $c_i(U)\geqq b!$ if i is fixed. Indeed, if $e(U)+e_U<e(U')+e_{U'}$ and $c_i(U)$, $c_i(U')\geqq b!$, then we may replace $b!/v(U)$ copies of U by $b!/v(U')$ copies of U', thus, by (7), increasing $e(\tilde{G}^n)$. This contradicts the maximality of $e(\tilde{G}^n)$. This very "replacement" argument also yields that we may assume that $c_i(U)\leqq b!$ for every U but one for each i: it may happen that this does not hold for the original $\tilde{G}^n$, but then it can be replaced by another one, $\tilde{\tilde{G}}^n$ for which this holds. After this replacement $\{\tilde{\tilde{G}}^n\}$ is already a q-sequence, and therefore (since S^{n_k} is a dense sequence) for $\tilde{G}^n=\tilde{G}^{n_k}$

$$(8)\qquad e(\tilde{G}^{n_k})\leqq e(\tilde{\tilde{G}}^{n_k})\leqq e(S^{n_k}),$$

what was to be proved. The second part of Theorem 1 concerning the strictly dense sequences can easily be proved: we have to show that if $e(G^{n_k})=e(S^{n_k})$, then $G^{n_k}=S^{n_k}$ for $k>k_0$. Indeed, in this case, by (8) $G^{n_k}=\tilde{G}^{n_k}$ can be assumed. If there exists a $U\neq A_i$ for which $c_i(U)\geqq b!$, then the above replacement technique yields a q-sequence $\{\tilde{\tilde{G}}^{n_k}\}$ different from $\{S^{n_k}\}$, since the sum of the block-sizes is smaller) and this contradicts $e(G^{n_k})=eS^{n_k})$ or that $\{S^{n_k}\}$ is strictly dense. This shows that $c_i(U)<b!$ if $U\neq A_i$, that is, $G^{n_k}=\tilde{G}^{n_k}$ itself is a q-sequence. Therefore, by the definition of strict density, $G^{n_k}=S^{n_k}$ if k is sufficiently large.

Proof of Lemma 2. The basic idea of the proof is to partition first the vertices of G^n into $d+1$ classes $\mathscr{A}_1,\ldots,\mathscr{A}_d$ and $\mathscr{A}_0$, then show that the subgraph of G^n spanned by $\mathscr{A}_i$ $(i=1,\ldots,d)$ is the sum of components of at most $b=v(A_1)+\ldots+v(A_i)+v(D)$ vertices. If we take all the occurring components as many times as they occur in case if they occur at most $2bd!$ times, otherwise we take only $2bd!$ copies and we take $\mathscr{A}_0$, for which $|\mathscr{A}_0|=O(1)$, the if the subgraph G^R spanned by these $O(1)$ vertices is "small", then the original graph G^n is "small" as well. In details:

First we fix the constants c, M and R as follows: $r=(3b)^{b^2}$,

$$(9)\qquad c=\frac{1}{100bd^2},\quad M=1000\frac{b}{c},\quad R=\max\{4bd^2g_b\cdot 2^{2br}, 30b^3d\}$$

where g_b denotes the number of graphs on $(3b)^{b^2}$ vertices. By the Erdős–Stone theorem [3] G^n contains a $K_d(M, \ldots, M)$, if n is large enough. Let the classes of this $K_d(M, \ldots, M)$ be $C_1, \ldots, C_d$. Now we partition the vertices of $G^n - K_d(M, \ldots, M) = G^{n-dM}$ into the following $d+2$ classes: P_i $(i=1, \ldots, d)$ contains those vertices which are joined to each C_j $(j \neq i)$ by at least $M\left(1-\frac{1}{6b}\right)$ edges and by at most $3b-1$ edges to C_i. E is the class of vertices joined to each C_j ($i=j$ included) by at least $3b$ edges. V contains the rest.

We assert that $|E| \leqq b$. Clearly, if $K_{d+1}(1, 3b, \ldots, 3b) \subseteq S^{n_k}$, then its single vertex of the first class belongs to the "head", of S^{n_k}. Therefore, if L can be covered with $b+1$ copies of $K_{d+1}(1, 3b, \ldots, 3b)$ with *different peaks*, then L is a prohibited subgraph. On the other hand, for each $x \in E$ we can find a $K_{d+1}(1, 3b, \ldots, 3b)$ with the first class $\{x\}$, thus $|E| \leqq v(D) \leqq b$. A similar argument shows that if $Q_i \subseteq P_i$ is the set of vertices joined to at least $3b$ vertices of $P_i \cup C_i$, then $|\bigcup Q_i| \leqq b$.

Next we show that

$$|V| \leqq 7bcd \cdot n. \tag{10}$$

Indeed, if T denotes the number of edges joining $K_d(M, \ldots, M)$ to G^{n-dM}, then on the one hand

$$T \geqq dM\left(1-\frac{1}{d}-c\right)n-(dM)^2 \tag{11}$$

since each $x \in K_d(M, \ldots, M)$ has valence $\geqq\left(1-\frac{1}{d}-c\right)n$. On the other hand,

$$T \leqq (n-dM)\cdot((d-1)M+3b)-|V|\frac{M}{6b}+bM \tag{12}$$

since the vertices of G^{n-dM} are generally joined by at most $(d-1)M+3b$ edges to $K_d(M, \ldots, M)$, however, in case, when $x \in E$, it may be joined to $K_d(M, \ldots, M)$ by dM edges and if $x \in V$, then it is joined to $K_d(M, \ldots, M)$ by less than $(d-1)M+3b-\frac{M}{6b}$ edges. (10) follows easily from (11), (12) and (9).

Now that (10) is established, one can easily show that the classes P_i are approximately of the same size:

(a) Let $x \in P_i - Q_i$. Since x is joined to $\leqq 3b$ vertices of its own class P_i and $d(x) \geqq \left(1-\frac{1}{d}-c\right)n$, thus

$$|P_i| \leqq n-d(x)+3b \leqq \left(\frac{1}{d}+c\right)n+3b. \tag{13}$$

This means that none of the classes P_i can be much larger than the average $\frac{n}{d}$. But this implies that none of them can be much smaller:

$$|P_i| \geqq n-(d-1)\left(\frac{1}{d}+c\right)n-3(d-1)b-|V| \geqq$$

(14)

$$\geqq \frac{n}{d}-((d-1)+8bd)cn \geqq \frac{n}{d}-10bcd\cdot n.$$

Let us subdivide the class V into $d+1$ subclasses now:

— V_0 contains the vertices of V joined to at least $3b$ vertices of each P_i-Q_i;
— V_i is the set of vertices of V joined to at most $3b-1$ vertices of P_i-Q_i, $i=1, 2, \ldots, d$.

By the valency condition each $x \in V_i$ is joined to P_j-Q_j $(j \neq i)$ by at least

(15) $$\frac{n}{d}-10bcd\cdot n-(10bcd\cdot n+cn+3b) \geqq \frac{n}{d}-22bcd\cdot n$$

edges, since it misses at least $\frac{n}{d}-10bcd\cdot n-3b$ vertices of P_i-Q_i and it misses altogether $n-d(x) \leqq \frac{n}{d}+cn$ vertices. Thus the classes V_i $(i=0, 1, \ldots, d)$ are well defined.
Let $\mathscr{A}_i =: P_i \cup V_i \cup C_i$ and W_i be the set of vertices of $\mathscr{A}_i$ joined to at least $3b$ vertices of the same $\mathscr{A}_i$. A slight modification of the above argument shows that $\sum_i |W_i| \leqq b$: we replace K_{d+1} 1, $3b, \ldots, 3b)$ by L defined as follows: for $j=1, 2, \ldots, 3b$, $p=1, 2, \ldots, d$; we fix the vertices $y_{p,j}$ joined to a vertex x (which will be called the "peak", and $y_{p,j}$ is joined to $3b$ vertices of the jth class of a fixed $K_d(10b, \ldots, 10b)$ for every $j \neq p$. If this L is a subgraph of an S^{n_k}, then we omit the head, D from S^{n_k} and obtain, that the "tail" $S^{n_k}-D$ contains $L-D$. Since $v(D) \leqq b$, one can easily see, that the "peak" x was also deleted: $x \in D$. Thus $\sum_i |W_i| \leqq v(D) \leqq b$, since each $x \in W_i$ is the "peak" of an $L \subseteq G^n$. Let now L^* be defined as follows: we take a K_d $(3b, \ldots, 3b)$ and the vertices $y_{p,j}$ $(p=1, 2, \ldots, d$, $j=1, 2, \ldots, 3b)$ are joined to all the vertices of $K_d(3b, \ldots, 3b)$ except to the vertices of the pth class. Further, we take b^2+1 vertices x_i forming a path $(x_1x_2 \ldots x_{b^2+1})$ and join each x_i to each $y_{p,j}$ but for a $p=p_0$. One can easily check that deleting b vertices of L^* we get an L^{**} not occurring in the "tail" $Z^{n-v(D)}=S^n-D$. If on the other hand $\mathscr{A}_{p_0}$ contained a path of length b^2+2b, then G^n contained an L^*. By $v(L^*) \leqq R$ this L^* would be "small", that is a subgraph of an S^{n_k} and therefore L^*-(at most b vertices)$=$ $=L^{**} \subseteq Z^{n-v(D)}$ would yield a contradiction, proving that $\mathscr{A}_p$ contains no path of b^2+1 vertices. Hence each connected component of the graph spanned by $\mathscr{A}_p-W_p$ has at

most $r=(3b)^{b^2}$ vertices. For a fixed p let us call two components equivalent iff they are isomorphic and connected to the vertices of $E\cup W_1\cup\ldots\cup W_d$ in the same way. The number of nonequivalent components is bounded by $g_b\cdot 2^{2br}$.

Let us take the subgraph of G^n defined as follows: we select all the vertices of $E\cup W_1\cup\ldots\cup W_d$ and for each $p=1,\ldots,d$ from each equivalence class of components (in $\bar{\mathscr{A}}_p-W_p$ we take $2bd$ copies of components if there exist that many members in the equivalence class, otherwise we take all of them, i.e. less than $2bd$ copies. These vertices define a graph $G^{\tilde{R}}\in G^n$ for some $\tilde{R}\leq R$, therefore $G^{\tilde{R}}$ is "small". We embed this $G^{\tilde{R}}$ in S^α. This embedding yields automatically an embedding of G^n into S^α: if U is a component of $\bar{\mathscr{A}}_p$ occurring in $G^n-G^{\tilde{R}}$, then it has multiplicity $\geq 2bd$, therefore it occurs at least $2bd$ times in $G^{\tilde{R}}\subseteq S^\alpha$. Hence it occurs at least b times in some class of the "tail" Z^α of S^α. Thus we may replace this b copies by an arbitrary number of copies from this class of the "tail". (If U and U' are two such components, joined to each other by at least an edge, then in the embedding of $G^{\tilde{R}}$ in S^α U and U' were put into different classes of the "tail", otherwise a class of the tail contained a K_b. Thus the increasing of the multiplicities of different connected components do not disturb each other!) Thus G^n is "small" as well. This proves Lemma 2.

References

[1] ERDÖS, P., Some recent results on extremal problems in graph theory (Results), *Theory of Graphs*, International Symposium, Rome (1966), 118–123.

[2] ERDÖS, P., New inequalities concerning extremal properties of graphs, *Theory of Graphs, Proc. Coll.*, held at Tihany, (Hungary, 1966), 77–81.

[3] ERDŐS P. and STONE, A. H., On the structure of linear graphs, *Bull. American Math. Soc.*, **52** (1946), 50–57.

[4] SIMONOVITS, M., A method for solving extremal problems in graph theory, stability problems, *Theory of Graphs, Proc. Coll.*, held at Tihany (Hungary, 1966), 279–319.

[5] SIMONOVITS, M., Extremal graph problems with symmetrical extremal graphs, *Discrete Math.*, **7** (1974), 349–376.

[6] TURÁN, P., Egy gráfelméleti szélsőértékfeladatról (In Hungarian, with German resume), *Mat. Phys. Lapok*, **48** (1941) 436–452.

[7] TURÁN, P., On the theory of graphs, *Colloq. Math.*, **3** (1954), 19–30.

EÖTVÖS LORÁND UNIVERSITY
H-1088 BUDAPEST
MÚZEUM KRT. 6–8.
HUNGARY

Studies in Pure Mathematics
To the Memory of Paul Turán

On the coefficients of rational functions

by

†G. SOMORJAI (Budapest)

Let $f(z)$ be a rational function of order $\leqq n$, i.e. the quotient of two polynomials of order $\leqq n$. Suppose that it has no poles on the unit circle $|z|=1$ and $\max_{|z|=1} |f(z)|=1$. Let

$$f(z) = \sum_{k=-\infty}^{\infty} a_k z^k$$

be its Laurent expansion valid on the unit circle. G. EHRLING raised the problem of estimating $\sum_{k=-\infty}^{\infty} |a_k|$ in terms of n and conjectured the upper bound const. n which, if true, would be best possible. H. S. SHAPIRO showed this (unpublished) if all the poles are inside the unit disc and in the general case for n replaced by n^2 (oral communication). Here we prove by a different method the

Theorem.

$$\sum_{k=-\infty}^{\infty} |a_k| \leqq 43n\sqrt{\log 3n}\,.$$

Proof. We have

$$a_k=(1/2\pi i)\int_{\Gamma} f(z)z^{-k-1}\,dz$$

implying, restricting ourselves first to negative indices,

$$(1)\qquad \sum_{k=-\infty}^{-1} |a_k| \leqq (\max_{z\in\Gamma} |f(z)|/2\pi)\int_{\Gamma} |dz|/(1-|z|)\,,$$

where Γ is any cycle (union of closed curves) lying inside the unit disk which surrounds every pole in $|z|<1$ of $f(z)$ exactly once.

Denoting these poles by z_i we have by the maximum principle

$$\log|f(z)| \leqq \sum_i g_i(z) \overset{\text{def}}{=} g(z) \quad (|z| \leqq 1),$$

where $g_i(z)$ is the Green function of the unit disc with pole at z_i:

$$g_i(z) = \log|(1 - z\bar{z}_i)/(z - z_i)|. \tag{2}$$

As Γ we shall choose an appropriate level set

$$\Gamma_\lambda = \{z : |z| \leqq 1, g(z) = \lambda\}, \tag{3}$$

where $1 \leqq \lambda \leqq 2$, implying

$$\max_{z \in \Gamma} |f(z)| \leqq e^2. \tag{4}$$

(Such a Γ surrounds in fact every pole of $f(z)$ lying inside the unit disc exactly once as follows easily by continuity since it holds for $\Gamma_0 = \{z : |z| = 1\}$.)

Let us consider the hyperbolic area of the set $\{z : |z| \leqq 1,\ 1 \leqq g(z) \leqq 2\}$:

$$I \overset{\text{def}}{=} \iint_{1 \leqq g(z) \leqq 2} (1 - |z|^2)^{-2}\, dx\, dy. \quad (z = x + iy) \tag{5}$$

Since we have at most n poles z_i, we see that

$$g(z) \leqq \sum_{g_i(z) \geqq 1/(2n)} g_i(z) + 1/2$$

implying

$$I \leqq \iint_{|z|<1} (1 - |z|^2)^{-2}\, 2 \sum_{g_i(z) \geqq 1/(2n)} g_i(z)\, dx\, dy =$$

$$= 2 \sum_i \iint_{g_i(z) \geqq 1/(2n)} (1 - |z|^2)^{-2} g_i(z)\, dx\, dy.$$

Recalling (2) and the fact that the hyperbolic area element is invariant under linear transformations of the unit disc onto itself, we see that the last integral has, independently of i, the value

$$\iint_{\log|1/z| \geqq 1/(2n)} (1 - |z|^2)^{-2} \log|1/z|\, dx\, dy =$$

$$= 2\pi \int_0^{\exp[-1/(2n)]} (1 - r^2)^{-2} \log(1/r) r\, dr \leqq 2\pi \int_0^{\exp[-1/(2n)]} (1 - r)^{-1}\, dr \leqq 2\pi \log 3n.$$

We thus obtain

$$I \leqq 4\pi n \log 3n . \tag{6}$$

On the other hand, rewriting integration in (5) with respect to λ and the level curves (3),

$$I = \int_1^2 \int_{\Gamma_\lambda} (1-|z|^2)^{-2} (\partial g/\partial n)^{-1} |dz| d\lambda ,$$

where $\partial g/\partial n$ denotes the derivative of $g(z)$ in the outer normal direction of Γ_λ. (6) then implies that there is a level curve $\Gamma = \Gamma_\lambda$ such that

$$\int_\Gamma (1-|z|^2)^{-2} (\partial g/\partial n)^{-1} |dz| \leqq 4\pi n \log 3n .$$

By Cauchy's inequality

$$\int_\Gamma (1-|z|^2)^{-1} |dz| \leqq \sqrt{\int_\Gamma (1-|z|^2)^{-2} (\partial g/\partial n)^{-1} |dz| \int_\Gamma (\partial g/\partial n) |dz|} \leqq$$

$$\leqq \sqrt{4\pi n \log 3n \cdot 2\pi n} = 2\sqrt{2}\pi n \sqrt{\log 3n} ,$$

using Green's formula for the last integral. This and (4) imply in (1)

$$\sum_{k=-\infty}^{-1} |a_k| \leqq 2\sqrt{2e^2}n\sqrt{\log 3n} .$$

Considering $f(z^{-1})$ in place of $f(z)$, the same estimation holds for the positive indices and since $|a_0| \leqq 1$ trivially, the result follows.

The author is grateful to Prof. H. S. Shapiro for communicating the problem.

MATHEMATICAL INSTITUTE OF THE
HUNGARIAN ACADEMY OF SCIENCES
H 1053 BUDAPEST, REÁLTANODA U. 13–15.
HUNGARY

Studies in Pure Mathematics
To the Memory of Paul Turán

On strong irregularities of the distribution of $\{n\alpha\}$ sequences

by

V. T. SÓS (Budapest)

Abstract

Let $U=\{u_n\}$ be a sequence in $[0, 1]^k$ and $\Delta_N^U = \sup_I |\Delta_N(I)| = \sup_I \left| \sum_{\substack{u_n \in I \\ 1 \leq n \leq N}} 1 - N|I| \right|$ (I a subinterval of $[0, 1]^k$). By Schmidt's theorem $\Delta_N > c_1 \log N$ for any N if $k=2$ while for $k=1$ only $\overline{\lim} \frac{\Delta_N}{\log N} > c_2 > 0$ holds and we have sequences (c.g. $\{n\alpha\}$ sequences) for which $\Delta_N \leqq 1$ for infinitely many N. Inspite of this fact we have the following Theorem: Let $u_n = \{n\alpha\}$. With a suitable $\delta \in (0, 1)$ and for every $N > N_0$

$$\Delta_n > c_3 \log N$$

holds for all but at most N^δ values of n, $1 \leqq n \leqq N$. (Here $c_3 > 0$ is an absolute constant.)

Introduction

Let $E^k = \{(x_1, \ldots, x_k) \in R^k, 0 \leqq x_i \leqq 1 \text{ for } 1 \leqq i \leqq k\}$ be the unit cube in R^k and for $\mathbf{x} \in E^k$.

$I(\mathbf{x}) = \{(t_1, \ldots, t_k): 0 \leqq t_i \leqq x_i \text{ for } 1 \leqq i \leqq k\}$; $|I| = \prod_{i=1}^{k} x_i$. For a sequence $\{\mathbf{u}_n\}$, $\mathbf{u}_n \in E^k$ put

(1) $$\Delta_N(I) = \sum_{\substack{\mathbf{u}_n \in I \\ 1 \leqq n \leqq N}} 1 - N|I|$$

and

(2) $$\|\Delta_N\|_p = \Big(\int_{E^k} |\Delta_N(I(\mathbf{x}))|^p \, dx \Big)^{\frac{1}{p}};$$

(3) $$\Delta_N = \|\Delta_N\|_\infty .$$

The infinite sequence $\{\mathbf{u}_n\}$ is uniformly distributed in E^k if $\lim_{N \to \infty} \frac{1}{N} \Delta_N = 0$. $D_N =: \frac{1}{N} \Delta_N$ is called the discrepancy function of the sequence $\{\mathbf{u}_n\}$. Δ_N resp. $\|\Delta_N\|_p$ measures in certain respect the irregularity of the finite sequence $\mathbf{u}_1, \ldots, \mathbf{u}_N$, their behaviour for $N \to \infty$ describes the irregularity of the infinite sequence $\{\mathbf{u}_n\}$.

It was conjectured by VAN DER COPRUT and proved first by VAN AARDENNE–EHRENFEST [22], [23] that for any infinite sequence $\{\mathbf{u}_n\}$ we have

$$\overline{\lim_{N\to\infty}}\ \Delta_N = \infty$$

i.e. there is no "too well" distributed sequence.

We recall some results which show how the situation changes with increasing dimension.

K. F. ROTH [13] proved, that for all $k \geqq 1$.

(A) for *any infinite* sequence $\{\mathbf{u}_n\}$ in E^k, for any $N > N_k$ there exists an n, $1 \leqq n \leqq N$ such that

$$\|\Delta_n\|_2 > c_k \log^{\frac{k}{2}} N$$

and consequently also

$$\Delta_n > c_k \log^{\frac{k}{2}} N\,.$$

(B) for *any* N *points* $\mathbf{u}_1, \ldots, \mathbf{u}_N$ in E^k with $N > N'_k$

$$\|\Delta_N\|_2 > c'_k \log^{\frac{k-1}{2}} N$$

and consequently also

$$\Delta_N > c'_k \log^{\frac{k-1}{2}} N\,.$$

Here N_k, N'_k, $c_k > 0$, $c'_k > 0$ depend only on k and are absolute constants.

ROTH also proved directly that the case (A) for k-dimension is equivalent to the case (B) for $k-1$ dimension.

Best possible results concerning the order of magnitudes of Δ_N are known only for $k=1$ and for finite sequences also for $k=2$. Namely, W. G. SCHMIDT [17] proved

(A^+) for any infinite sequence $(\mathbf{u}_n)$ in E^1 and for any $N > N_1$ there exists an n, $1 \leqq n \leqq N$ such that

$$\Delta_n > c \log N \tag{4}$$

and

(B^+) for any N points $\mathbf{u}_1, \ldots, \mathbf{u}_N$ in E^2 with $N > N_2$

$$\Delta_N > c' \log N\,. \tag{5}$$

(Here $c > 0$, $c' > 0$ are effective constants; the best possible constants are not known.)

As to the sharpness of these results, it is well known that there exist sequences in E^1 for which $\Delta_N = O(\log N)$. ROTH [13] constructed finite sequences in E^2 for which $\Delta_N = O(\log N)$. The best possible result concerning the order of magnitude of Δ_N is not known for $k > 2$. However for $\|\Delta_N\|_2$ DAVENPORT [3] constructed finite sequences in E^2 for which $\|\Delta_N\|_2 = O(\log^{\frac{1}{2}} N)$ and quite recently for any $k > 2$ ROTH [14], [15] constructed finite sequences in E^k for which

$$\|\Delta_N\|_2 = O(\log N^{\frac{k-1}{2}}).$$

The above results show, that the irregularities of a sequence increase with increasing dimension, which can be expressed in a quantitative form. Moreover, from $k=1$ to $k=2$ this phenomenon has also a qualitative feature.

Namely, for $k=1$ for *any* N we have sequences with $\Delta_N \leqq 1$, for example for the equipartition of E^1: $\frac{1}{N}, \frac{2}{N}, \ldots, \frac{N}{N}$ we have $\Delta_N \leqq 1$, while for $k \geqq 1$

$$\Delta_N \geqq c_k (\log N)^{\frac{k-1}{2}}$$

and consequently for infinite sequences for $k \geqq 2$

$$\lim_{N \to \infty} \Delta_N = \infty$$

while for $k=1$ we have only

$$\overline{\lim_{N \to \infty}}\, \Delta_N = \infty .$$

(For $k \geqq 2$ a "good equipartition" does not exist.) There are sequences in E^1 for which

$$\Delta_N \leqq 1$$

for infinitely many N. Now the question we are interested in is, the following: for a given sequence $\{\mathbf{u}_n\}$ in E^1 and for a fixed C how often may e.g.

$$\Delta_N \leqq C \tag{7}$$

hold, how often must

$$\Delta_N > c \log N \tag{8}$$

hold. The above theorem leaves open the possibility that for some sequences (8) holds with any $c > 0$ only for a sequence of integers of 0 density. The theorems we are going to prove show that at least for $(\{n\alpha\})$ sequences this is not possible.

As to ($\{n\alpha\}$) sequences it was proved already by HARDY–LITTLEWOOD [6] and OSTROWSKI [11] that for any ($\{n\alpha\}$) sequence

$$\Delta_N > c \log N \tag{9}$$

holds for infinitely many N, (where c is a positive absolute constant). This is a "best possible" result concerning the order of magnitude since for any α with bounded partial quotients

$$\Delta_N = O(\log N)\,. \tag{10}$$

(10) means that concerning the order of magnitude of Δ_N the ($\{n\alpha\}$) sequences for α with bounded partial quotients are among the "best" sequences.[1]

We also know that for any α

$$\Delta_n \leqq 1$$

holds for infinitely many n, e.g. for $n_i = q_i$ $(i=1, \dots)$ where q_i's are the denominators of the convergents of α.

The above results suggest that the behaviour of ($\{n\alpha\}$) sequences is quite characteristic for the general situation. Probably results analogous to the ones formulated below, hold for arbitrary sequences too.* See also Remark 2.

Here we are going to prove

Theorem. *Let α be irrational and Δ_n be defined by* (3) *belonging to the sequence* ($\{k\alpha\}$). *With a suitable $\vartheta \in (0, 1)$, for $N > N_0$*

$$\Delta_n > c \log N \tag{11}$$

holds for all but at most N^ϑ values of n; $1 \leqq n \leqq N$. Here $c > 0$ is an absolute constant.

Without proof we mention the following

Proposition 1. *Let α be irrational, $\alpha = [a_1, a_2, \dots]$ be the continued fraction expansion of α, q_i $(i=1, \dots)$ the denominators of the convergents of α. Then for every N*

$$\frac{1}{N} \sum_{n=1}^{N} \Delta_n > c\left(\sum_{k=1}^{\nu} (a_k + 1) + \frac{N}{q_{\nu+1}} \right) \tag{12}$$

where ν is determined by $q_{\nu+1} \leqq N < q_{\nu+2}$. Here $c > 0$ is an absolute constant.

[1] As to the best possible constant in (9) with Y. DUPAIN we proved in [2] that for

$$c(\alpha) = \overline{\lim_{N}} \frac{\Delta_N}{\log N}$$

we have

$$\inf_\alpha c(\alpha) = \min_\alpha c(\alpha) = c(\sqrt{2} - 1) = \frac{1}{4 \log(\sqrt{2} + 1)} \sim 0.2836\,.$$

* See "Added in proof".

Remark 1. Proposition 1 asserts more than our theorem in the case when α has "large" partial quotients; $\overline{\lim}\, \frac{\sum a_k}{\log N} = \infty$. The result in KUIPERS–NIEDERREITER [9], that for every n; $1 \leqq n \leqq N$

$$\Delta_n < c' \left(\sum_{k=1}^{\nu} (a_k + 1) + \frac{N}{q_{\nu+1}} \right)$$

holds with an absolute constant c', shows that in certain sense (12) is best possible.

Proposition 2. *Let α be irrational and $\Delta_n(\beta) = : \Delta_n([0, \beta])$ defined by* (1) *belonging to the sequence* $(\{k\alpha\})$. *Then for almost all $\beta \in (0, 1)$ we have*

$$\overline{\lim_{N \to \infty}} \frac{|\Delta_N(\beta)|}{\log N} > c. \tag{13}$$

Here $c > 0$ is an absolute constant.

Moreover, the exeptional set- the set of β's, for which (13) *does not hold — has Hausdorff-dimension* 0.

Remark 2. KESTEN [8] proved that for $\{n\alpha\}$ sequences $\Delta_n(I)$ is bounded only if $|I| = \{k\alpha\}$ for some integer k (and it is bounded for $|I| = \{k\alpha\}$ according to a theorem of HECKE [7])[2]

SCHMIDT [17] proved, that for any sequence the lengths of all intervals for which $\Delta_N(I)$ is bounded form a countable set. Moreover, a recent result of SCHMIDT [17] states that for any sequence

$$\lim_{N \to \infty} \frac{|\Delta_N(\beta)|}{\log \log N} > c$$

holds for almost every β, were $c > 0$ is an absolute constant. In [17] SCHMIDT asks whether the analogous result holds with $\log N$ instead of $\log \log N$. So Proposition 2 gives an affirmative answer in the case of $\{n\alpha\}$ sequences.

For the proofs of Proposition 1 and Proposition 2, see V. T. Sós [21].

[2] For ergodic-theoretical generalizations and proofs of KESTEN's theorem see e.g. FÜRSTENBERG–KEYNES–SHAPIRO [4], HALÁSZ [5], PETERSEN [12].

Notation

Let $\alpha=[a_1, \ldots, a_n, \ldots]$ be the continued fractions expansion of α. We shall use the notations and consequences

$$\frac{p_n}{q_n}=[a_1, \ldots, a_{n-1}]\,; \quad q_{n+1}=a_n q_n+q_{n-1}, \quad p_{n+1}=a_n p_n+p_{n-1},$$

$$\Theta_n=q_n\alpha-p_n\,; \quad \Theta_{n+1}=a_n\Theta_n+\Theta_{n-1},$$

$$\lambda_n=|\Theta_n|=(-1)^{n+1}\Theta_n\,;$$

$$\sum_{v=0}^{\infty} a_{k+2v}\Theta_{k+2v}=-\Theta_{k-1}\,; \quad k=1, \ldots \quad (\Theta_0=-1)$$

$$\sum_{v=0}^{n} a_{k+2v}q_{k+2v}=q_{k+2n+1}-q_{k-1}\,; \quad k=1, \ldots \quad (q_0=0)\,.$$

We shall say that the sequence of integers $(b_1, \ldots, b_v)$ is a "permitted" sequence if it satisfies

$$0\leqq b_1\leqq a_1-1, \quad 0\leqq b_k\leqq a_k \quad \text{if} \quad 2\leqq k\leqq v \tag{14}$$

and

$$b_k=0 \quad \text{if} \quad b_{k+1}=a_{k+1} \quad (1\leqq k\leqq v-1)\,. \tag{15}$$

It is well known that every positive integer $N<q_{v+1}$ can be uniquely represented in the form

$$N=\sum_{k=1}^{v} b_k q_k \tag{16}$$

where $(b_1, \ldots, b_v)$ is a "permitted" sequence (and conversely, for every "permitted" sequence $(b_1, \ldots, b_v)$

$$N=\sum_{v=1}^{v} b_i q_i<q_{v+1}).$$

It is also known (Descombes [1], Sós [20], Lesca [10]) that each β with $-\alpha\leqq\beta< <1-\alpha$ can be represented in the form

$$\beta=\sum_{k=1}^{\infty} d_k\Theta_k \tag{17}$$

where (d_k) is a "permitted" infinite sequence which satisfies

$$0\leqq d_1\leqq a_1-1, \quad 0\leqq d_k\leqq a_k \quad \text{if} \quad k\geqq 2, \tag{18}$$

(19) $$d_k=0 \quad \text{if} \quad d_{k+1}=a_{k+1},$$

(20) $$d_{2k+1}\neq a_{2k+1}$$

for infinitely many positive integer k.

Conversely, every sequence which satisfies (18)–(20) by (17) determines a $\beta\in(-\alpha, 1-\alpha)$.

The expansions above turned out to be useful for different types of investigations in diophantine approximation. Our proof will be based on the result that it is possible to handle Δ_N by these expansions.

Let

$$\Delta_N(\beta)=\Delta_N([0,\beta)) \quad \text{for} \quad 0<\beta<1$$

and

$$\Delta_N(\beta)=\Delta_N([0,1+\beta)) \quad \text{for} \quad -\alpha<\beta<0.$$

We shall use with the notation of (16) and (17) the "explicit" formula for $\Delta_N(\beta)$ (in this form see T. Sós [19]).

(21) $$\Delta_N(\beta) = \sum_{k=1}^{\infty} ((-1)^{k+1}\min(b_k, d_k)-d_k(q_k \sum_{i=k+1}^{\infty} b_i\Theta_i+\Theta_k \sum_{i=1}^{k} b_iq_i))+\sum_{k=1}^{\nu} \delta_k,$$

where

(22) $$\delta_k=\begin{cases} 1, \text{ if } k \text{ is odd}, \ d_k>b_k & \text{and } \sum_{i=1}^{k-1} b_iq_i>\sum_{i=1}^{k-1} d_iq_i \\ -1 \text{ if } k \text{ is even, } d_k<b_k & \text{and } \sum_{i=1}^{k-1} b_iq_i\leqq\sum_{i=1}^{k-1} d_iq_i \\ 0 \text{ otherwise.} \end{cases}$$

Proof of the Theorem

Let α be fixed. Without loss of generality we may assume that $N=c_{\nu+1}q_{\nu+1}$ for some ν with $0<c_{\nu+1}\leqq a_{\nu+1}$, $c_{\nu+1}$ integer.

For any n, $1\leqq n\leqq N$ we consider the expansion

$$n=\sum_{k=1}^{\nu+1} b_k(n)q_k$$

where b_i satisfies (14)–(15) if $1\leqq i\leqq \nu$ and $0\leqq b_{\nu+1}<c_{\nu+1}$. We shall write b_k instead of $b_k(n)$ when it is not misunderstandable. Instead of determining the number of values of n, $1\leqq n\leqq N$ with certain conditions on $b_k(n)$; $1\leqq k\leqq \nu+1$, we shall determine the permitted sequences with the given properties.

In order to obtain a good lower bound for Δ_n we shall define a β_n^+ resp. a β_n^- for which $\Delta_n(\beta_n^+)$ or $-\Delta_n(\beta_n^-)$ is large and we use

$$\Delta_n \geqq \frac{1}{2}(\Delta_n(\beta_n^+) - \Delta_n(\beta_n^-)).$$

Let $1 \leqq n \leqq N$, $n = \sum_{i=1}^{\nu+1} b_i q_i$. Let β_n^+, β_n^- be defined by

$$\beta_n^+ = \sum_{2k+1 \leqq \nu+1} b_{2k+1}\lambda_{2k+1}$$

$$\beta_n^- = -\sum_{2k \leqq \nu+1} b_{2k}\lambda_{2k}.$$

First for the values of δ_k in (22) we remark the following: For β_n^+ we have $\delta_{2k+1} = 0$ since $d_{2k+1} = b_{2k+1}$ $(k = 1, \ldots)$. Since $d_{2i} = 0$, $d_{2i+1} = b_{2i+1}$; we have $\sum_{i=1}^{k-1} b_i q_i \leqq \sum_{i=1}^{k-1} d_i q_i$ iff $b_{2i} = 0$ for $i < k$. This means that $\delta_{2k} = -1$ for at most one value of k. For β_n^- we have $\delta_{2k+1} = 0$, since $d_{2k+1} = 0$ and $\delta_{2k} = 0$, since $d_{2k} = b_{2k}$.

Hence using the discrepancy-formula (21) we get

$$\Delta_n \geqq \frac{1}{2}(\Delta_n(\beta_n^+) - \Delta_n(\beta_n^-)) =$$

(23)
$$= \frac{1}{2}\sum_{k=1}^{\nu+1} b_k\Big(1 - b_k q_k \lambda_k - \lambda_k \sum_{i<k} b_i q_i + q_k \sum_{i>k} (-1)^{i+1-k} b_i \lambda_i\Big) - 1.$$

Now we consider the k'th term:

$$s_k =: b_k\Big(1 - b_k q_k \lambda_k - \lambda_k \sum_{i<k} b_i q_i + q_i \sum_{i>k} (-1)^{i+1-k} b_i \lambda_i\Big).$$

Using

$$1 = q_{k+1}\lambda_k + q_k\lambda_{k+1} = a_k q_k \lambda_k + \lambda_k q_{k-1} + q_k \lambda_{k+1},$$

$$\sum_{i>k} (-1)^{i+1-k} b_i \lambda_i > -\lambda_{k+1},$$

$$\sum_{i<k} b_i q_i < q_k,$$

and in case $b_k = a_k$ $(b_{k-1} = 0)$

$$\sum_{i<k} b_i q_i = \sum_{i<k-1} b_i q_i < q_{k-1},$$

we get

$$s_k \geqq 0 \quad k=1, \ldots, v+1 . \tag{24}$$

We also have

$$s_k \geqq b_k\left((a_k - b_k)\lambda_k q_k + \lambda_k q_{k-1} - \lambda_k \sum_{i=1}^{k-1} b_i q_i\right).$$

By this we have the following positive lower bounds:

$$s_k > b_k(a_k - b_k - 1)\lambda_k q_k > \frac{b_k(a_k - b_k - 1)}{a_k + 2} \quad \text{if} \quad 0 < b_k < a_k - 1 \tag{25}$$

$$s_k > b_k \lambda_k q_{k-1} > \frac{1}{(a_k+2)(a_{k-1}+1)} \quad \text{if} \quad 0 < b_k = a_k - 1 \tag{26}$$

$$s_k > \lambda_k(q_{k-1} - q_{k-2}) > \left(\prod_{i=0}^{3} a_{k-i} + 2\right)^{-1} \quad \text{if} \quad b_k = a_k,\ b_{k-1} = b_{k-2} = 0 . \tag{27}$$

In order to prove the Theorem we shall show that for all but at most N^9 values of n, $1 \leqq n \leqq N$ at least one of the three cases holds for many values of k, and moreover in such cases these terms give an essential contribution to Δ_n. To prove this we need the following lemmas

Lemma 1. *Let* $N = c_{v+1} q_{v+1}$ *for an integer* $c_{v+1} \in [1, a_{v+1}]$, $1 < k_1 < \ldots < k_l \leqq \leqq v+1$, $\frac{3}{a_{k_i}+3} < t_{k_i} < 1$ *for* $i = 1, \ldots, l$ *and* $S(t_1, \ldots, t_l)$ *be the number of "permitted" sequences* $(b_1, \ldots, b_{v+1})$ *which satisfy also* $b_{v+1} < c_{v+1}$ *and*

$$\min(b_{k_i}, a_{k_i} - b_{k_i} - 1) < t_{k_i} a_{k_i}, \quad i = 1, \quad \ldots, \quad l,$$

$$\min(b_{v+1}, c_{v+1} - b_{v+1}) < t_{v+1} c_{v+1} \quad \textit{if} \quad k_l = v+1 .$$

Then

$$S(t_1, \ldots, t_l) < \prod_{i=1}^{l} (4 t_{k_i})\, c_{v+1} q_{v+1} . \tag{28}$$

Proof. Note that the total number of "permitted" sequences $(b_1, \ldots, b_{v+1})$ for which $b_{v+1} < c_{v+1}$ holds is just $c_{v+1} q_{v+1}$.

Now first let $l = 1$, $k_1 = k \leqq v$, $t_1 = t$. Assumption (18) means, that b_k can take only the values

$$0, \ldots, [t a_k], a_k - [t a_k] - 1, \ldots, a_k . \tag{29}$$

Put $a'_k = 2[t a_k] + 2$ and $q'_k = q_k$. Now the number of "permitted" sequences under the restriction that b_k can take only the $a'_k + 1$ different values in (29) is $c_{v+1} q'_{v+1}$ where q'_{v+1}

is determined by the recursive formulae

$$q'_{k+1}=a'_k q_k+q_{k-1},\ q'_k=q_k$$

$$q'_{k+j+1}=a_{k+j}q'_{k+j}+q'_{k+j-1} \quad \text{if} \quad 1\leqq j\leqq \nu-k\,.$$

Since

$$q'_{k+1}=\frac{a'_k q_k+q_{k-1}}{a_k q_k+q_{k-1}}\,q_{k+1}<\frac{a'_k+1}{a_k+1}\,q_{k+1}<3tq_{k+1}$$

and

$$q'_{k+2}=\frac{a_{k+1}q'_{k+1}+q_k}{a_{k+1}q_{k+1}+q_k}\,q_{k+2}<\frac{3ta_{k+1}+1}{a_{k+1}+1}\,q_{k+2}<4tq_{k+2}$$

we get (28) for $l=1$ by induction on j.

A similar argument holds in case $k=\nu+1$. Now by induction on l we get (28) for the general cases.

Lemma 2. *Let* $\delta>0$, $M>M_0(\delta)$

$$K_1=\{k\colon a_k\geqq M;\, 1\leqq k\leqq \nu+1\}$$

$$a'_k=\begin{cases} a_k\,, & \text{if} \quad k\leqq r \\ c_{r+1}\,, & \text{if} \quad k=r+1 \end{cases}$$

and

$$B_1(n)=\{k\colon \min\,(b_k(n),\, a'_k-b_k(n)-1)<\frac{1}{4}\log a'_k,\ k\in K_1\}\,,$$

$$N_1=\{n\colon \sum_{k\in B_1(n)}\log a'_k>\delta\log N,\quad 1\leqq n\leqq N\}\,.$$

Then with a suitable $\vartheta\in(0,1)$

$$|N_1|<N^{1-\vartheta}\,.$$

Proof. By the definition of N_1 we have $\prod_{k\in B_1(n)} a'_k>N^\delta$ if $n\in N_1$.

Let $A\subseteq K_1$ and

$$N_1(A)=\{n\colon B_1(n)=A,\, n\in N_1\}\,.$$

Let us fix a $\Theta\in(0,1)$. Then for $M>M_0$

$$\prod_{k\in A}(a'^{-1}_k\log a'_k)<\prod_{k\in A}a'^{-1+\Theta}_k<N^{-\delta(1-\Theta)}\,.$$

By Lemma 1

$$|N_1(A)| < N \cdot N^{-\delta(1-\Theta)}$$

and consequently by summation on A we obtain

$$|N_1| = \sum_A |N_1(A)| < N \cdot 2^{v_1} N^{-\delta(1-\Theta)}.$$

Now taking into consideration, that

$$N > \prod_{a'_k \geqq M} a'_k \geqq M^{v_1} \quad \text{and} \quad 2 < M^{\frac{\delta(1-\Theta)}{2}}, \quad \text{if} \quad M > M_0,$$

we obtain

$$|N_1| < N \cdot N^{\frac{\delta(1-\Theta)}{2}} \cdot N^{-\delta(1-\Theta)} = N^{1-\frac{1}{2}\delta(1-\Theta)}$$

Lemma 3. *Let* $K_2 = \{k : 2 \leqq a_k < M,\ 1 \leqq k \leqq v\}$ *and* $K'_2 \subset K_2$, $v'_2 = |K'_2|$,

$$B_2(n) = \{k : b_k \in \{0, a_k\}, k \in K'_2\},$$

$$N_2 = \{n : |B_2(n)| > (1-\delta)v'_2;\ 1 \leqq n \leqq N\}.$$

If $v'_2 > v_0$, $\delta > \delta_0$, *then* $|N_2| < \Theta^{v'_2} N$ *with a suitable* $\Theta = \Theta(\delta) \in (0, 1)$.

Proof. First let $1 \leqq k_1 < \ldots < k_l \leqq v$, $k_i \in K'_2$ $(i = 1, \ldots, l)$ and $S_l(k_1, \ldots, k_l)$ be the number of "permitted" sequences $b_1, \ldots, b_{v+1}$ satisfying

$$b_{k_i} \in \{0, a_{k_i}\} \quad i = 1, \ldots,$$

We shall prove

(30)
$$S_l \leqq \left(\frac{5}{6}\right)^l N.$$

First let $l = 1$, $k = k_1 \leqq v$. Similarly to the proof of Lemma 1 put

$$a'_k = 1, q'_k = q_k \quad \text{and} \quad q'_{k+1} = q_k + q_{k-1}$$

$$q'_{k+j+1} = a_{k+1} q'_{k+j} + q'_{k+j-1} \quad \text{for} \quad 1 \leqq j \leqq v - k.$$

Now we have

$$q'_{k+1} = \frac{q_k + q_{k-1}}{a_k q_k + q_{k-1}} q_{k+1} < \frac{2}{3} q_{k+1}$$

$$q'_{k+2} = \frac{a_{k+1} q'_{k+1} + q_k}{a_{k+1} q_{k+1} + q_k} q_{k+2} < \frac{\frac{2}{3} a_{k+1} + 1}{a_{k+1}} q_{k+2} < \frac{5}{6} q_{k+2}.$$

By induction on j we get

$$S_1(k)=q'_{v+1}<\left(\frac{5}{6}\right)q_{v+1}.$$

Hence by induction on l we obtain (30).

By (30) we have

$$|N_2|<\sum_{t>(1-\delta)v'_2}\binom{v'_2}{t}\left(\frac{5}{6}\right)^t N<\Theta^{v'_2}N$$

if $v'_2>v_0(\delta)$.

Lemma 4. *Let*

$$K_3=\{k:a_k=1,\ 1\leqq k\leqq v\},\ v_3=|K_3|>\frac{97}{100}v,$$

$$B_3(n)=\{k:b_{k-2}=b_{k-1}=0,\ b_k=1,\ a_{k-i}=1\quad \text{for}\quad 0\leqq i\leqq 3,\quad 1\leqq k\leqq v\}$$

$$N_3=\{n:|B_3(n)|<\delta v_3,\ 1\leqq n\leqq N\}.$$

Then, with a suitable $\Theta\in(0,1)$. $|N_3|<\vartheta^v N$, *if* $\delta>\delta_0$, $r>r_0$.

Proof. Consider the blocks of indices $I_j=\{10j+i,\ 1\leqq i\leqq 10\}$ for $0\leqq j\leqq\left[\frac{v}{10}\right]$ and let

$$J=\{I_j:a_k=1\quad\text{if}\quad k\in I_j\}.$$

By the assumption $v_3>\frac{97}{100}v$ we have $|J|>\frac{v}{20}$. Now we consider only the blocks in J and we shall show that for all but at most N values of n, $1\leqq n\leqq N$

$$B_3(n)\cap I_j\neq\emptyset$$

for at least $10^{-2}v_3$ values of j, $I_j\in J$.

Let $1\leqq j_1<\ldots<j_l\leqq v$, $I_{j_i}\in J$ and $S_l(j_1,\ldots,j_l)=\{n:B_3(n)\cap I_{j_i}=\emptyset,\ i=1,\ldots,l\}$. Then

(31) $$|S_l|<2^{-l}N.$$

To see this we have to remark only that

(a) the number of permitted 0,1 — sequences $d_1,\ldots,d_{10}$ for which

(32) $$(d_i,d_{i+1},d_{i+2})\neq(0,0,1)\quad\text{if}\quad 1\leqq i\leqq 8$$

is 11.

(b) the number of "permitted" 0,1 — sequences $d_1, \ldots, d_{10}$ for which

(33) $$d_1=0, \quad d_i=d_{i+1}=0, \quad d_{i+2}=1, \quad d_{10}=0$$

with some $1 \leqq i \leqq 6$ is >22.

Consequently to any $n \in S_l(j_1, \ldots, j_l)$ by replacing the blocks $(b_{10_j+i}, 1 \leqq i \leqq 10)$ of type (32) for blocks of type (33) we can order 2 different $n \notin S_l$ on such a way that to $n_1 \neq n_2$ we order different ones. ($d_1=d_{10}=0$ in (33) gives the possibility to choose sequences of type (33) for different blocks I_{j_1}, I_{j_2} independently.)

By (31), with the notation $v' = \frac{v_3}{20}$

$$|N_3| < \sum_{l>(1-\delta)v} \binom{v'}{t} 2^{-t} N < \Theta^{v'} N$$

if $v_3 > v_0$.

To finish the proof we distinguish three cases:

Case 1. Suppose, with the notation of Lemma 2,

(33) $$\sum_{k \in K_1} \log (a_k+1) > \frac{1}{200} \log N .$$

Let $n \notin N_1$. Then by Lemma 2, (23), (24) and (25) we have

$$\Delta_n \geqq \sum_{k=1}^{v+1} s_k \geqq \sum_{k \in K_1} s_k \geqq \sum_{k \in K_1 \setminus B_1(n)} \log (a_k+1) =$$

$$= \sum_{k \in K_1} \log (a_k+1) - \sum_{k \in B_1(n)} \log (a_k+1) > \frac{1}{5 \cdot 10^3} \log N .$$

Case 2. Let $K_2' = \{k: 2 \leqq a_k < M, a_{k-1} \leqq M, 1 \leqq k \leqq v\}$. Suppose, with the notation of Lemma 2 and Lemma 3,

$$\sum_{k \in K_1} \log (a_k+1) < \frac{1}{200} \log N$$

and

(34) $$\sum_{k \in K_2} \log (a_k+1) > \frac{1}{100} \log N .$$

By these we have

$$v_1 = |K_1| < \frac{1}{200 \log (M+1)} \log N$$

$$v_2 = |K_2| > \frac{1}{100 \log (M+1)} \log N$$

and consequently

$$\nu_2' = |K_2'| > \frac{1}{200 \log (M+1)} \log N .$$

Now we apply Lemma 3. Let $n \notin N_2$. Then by (23), (24) and (26) we have

$$\Delta_n > \sum_{k=1}^{\nu+1} s_k \geqq \sum_{k \in K_2' \setminus B_2(n)} b_k \lambda_k q_{k-1} \geqq \frac{1}{(M+1)^2} |K_2' \setminus B_2(n)| \geqq$$

$$\geqq \frac{1}{(M+1)^2} \cdot \frac{1}{10^3} \cdot \frac{1}{200} \cdot \frac{1}{\log (M+1)} \cdot \log N .$$

By (34) $\nu_2' > c_M \log N$. By this and by Lemma 2 we get with a suitable $\Theta \in (0, 1)$ and $\vartheta = \vartheta(\Theta, c_M) \in (0, 1)$ that $|N_2| < \Theta^{\nu_2'} N < \Theta^{c_M \log N} < N^{\vartheta}$.

Case 3. Suppose neither (33) nor (34) holds. In this case

$$\nu_1 < \frac{1}{200 \log (M+1)} \log N , \tag{35}$$

$$\nu_2 < \frac{1}{100 \log 3} \log N \tag{36}$$

and consequently

$$\nu_1 + \nu_2 < \frac{3}{200} \log N .$$

Since

$$N = c_{\nu+1} \prod_{k \in K_1}{}_1 \frac{q_{k+1}}{q_k} \prod_{k \in K_2}{}_2 \frac{q_{k+1}}{q_k} \prod_{\substack{k \notin K_1 \cup K_2 \\ k \leqq \nu}}{}_3 \frac{q_{k+1}}{q_k}$$

$$\log N = \log c_{\nu+1} + \Sigma_1 \log (a_k+1) + \Sigma_2 \log (a_k+1) + \log \Pi_3 ,$$

we obtain

$$\left(1 - \frac{3}{200}\right) \log N < \log \Pi_3 < \nu \log 2 < \nu .$$

By (35) and (36) we get

$$\nu_3 > \frac{98}{100} \nu .$$

Now using Lemma 4, by (27) we obtain for $n \notin N_3$

$$\Delta_3 \geqq \sum_{k=1}^{\nu+1} s_k > \sum_{k \notin B_3(n)} \lambda_k q_{k-3} > \frac{1}{10} |B_3(n)| > \frac{1}{10^3} \log N .$$

Now by the assumptions (35)–(36) we have

$$\log N < 2\nu_3, \qquad N < 10^{\nu_3}.$$

Therefore, using Lemma 4, with a suitable $\vartheta = \vartheta(\Theta) \in (0, 1)$ we have

$$|N_3| < \Theta^{\nu_3} N < N^{\vartheta}.$$

This completes the proof.

References

[1] I. R. Descombes, Sur la répartition des sommets d'une ligne polygonale réguliere nonfermée. *Ann. Sci. de l'École Normale Sup.*, **75** (1956), 284–355.

[2] Y. Dupain and V. T. Sós, On the discrepancy of $\{n\alpha\}$ sequences (to appear).

[3] H. Davenport, Note on irregularities of distribution, *Mathematika*, **3** (1956), 131–135.

[4] A. Fürstenberg, H. Keynes and L. Shapiro, Prime flows in topological dynamics, *Israel J. Math.*, **14** 26 –38.

[5] G. Halász, Remark on the remainder in Birkhoff's ergodic theorem. *Acta Math. Acad. Sci. Hung.*, **27** (1976), 389–396.

[6] G. H. Hardy and J. E. Littlewood, The lattice points of a right angled triangle I. *Proc. Lond. Math. Soc.*, (3) **20** (1922), 15–36.

[7] E. Hecke, Über analytische Funktionen und die Verteilung von Zahlan mod Eins. *Abh. Math. Sem. Hamburg*, **1** (1922), 54–76.

[8] N. Kesten, On a conjecture of Erdős and Szüsz related to uniform distribution mod 1. *Acta Arith.* **12** (1966), 193–212.

[9] L. Kuipers and H. Niederreiter, *Uniform distribution of sequences.* Wiley, New York, 1974.

[10] J. Lesca, Sur la repartition modulo 1 de la suite $\{n\alpha\}$. *Acta Arith.*, **20** (1972), 345–352.

[11] A. Ostrowski, Bemerkungen zur Theorie der diophantischen Approximationen, I. Qbh. Hamburt Sem. **1** (1922), 77–98.

[12] K. Petersen, On a series of cosecants related to a problem in ergodic theory. *Comp. Math.*, **26** (1973), 313 –317.

[13] K. F. Roth, On irregularities of distribution. *Mathematika*, **7** (1954), 73–79.

[14] K. F. Roth, On irregularities of distribution. *Mathematika*, **7** (1954), 73–79.

[14a] K. F. Roth, On irregularities of distribution III. *Acta Arith.*, (to appear)

[15] K. F. Roth, On irregularities of distribution IV. (to appear)

[16] W. G. Schmidt, Irregularities of distribution, VII. *Acta Arith.*, **21** (1972), 45–50.

[17] W. G. Schmidt, Lectures on irregularities of distribution, Tata Inst. of Fund. Res. Bombay, 1977, p. 40.

[18] W. G. Schmidt, Irregularities of distribution VIII. *Trans. Amer. Math. Soc.*, **198** (1974), 1–22.

[19] Vera T. Sós, On the discrepancy of the sequence $\{n\alpha\}$ *Coll. Math. Soc. J. Bolyai*, **13** (1974), 359–367.

[20] Vera T. Sós, On the theory of diophantine approximation II. *Acta Math. Acad. Sci. Hung.*, **9** (1958), 229–241.

[21] Vera T. Sós, On irregularities of $\{n\alpha\}$ sequences (to appear).

[22] Van Aardenne—Ehrenfest, Proof of the impossibility of a just distribution of an infinite sequence of points over an interval, *Indag. Math.*, **7** (1945), 71–76.

[23] Van Aardenne—Ehrenfest, On the impossibility of a just distribution, *Indag. Math.*, **11** (1949), 264–269.

Added in proof. This paper was submitted in 1978. I lectured on this topic and formulated the conjecture concerning arbitrary sequences in 1979 in Oberwolfach. On strong irregularities of the distribution of $(\{n\alpha\})$ sequences, *Tagungsbericht Oberwolfach* 23 (1979), 17–18. Since that G. HALÁSZ (On Roth's Method in the Theory of Irregularities of Point distributions, *Recent Progress in Analytic Number Theory*. Acad. Press, 1981, (79–94)) and R. TIJDEMAN, and G. WAGNER (A sequence has almost nowhere small discrepancy. *Monatshefte für Math.* **90** (1980), 315–329) proved the conjecture and more general results.

EÖTVÖS LORÁND UNIVERSITY
H-1088 BUDAPEST
MÚZEUM KRT. 6–8.
HUNGARY

Studies in Pure Mathematics
To the Memory of Paul Turán

On density-difference sets of sets of integers

by

C. L. STEWART (Waterloo) and R. TIJDEMAN (Leiden)

Abstract

This note is a continuation of our paper [4]. We prove that density-difference sets do not have the superset property, but that both the union and the intersection of any two density-difference sets is a density-difference set. Finally we show that by repeating the operation of forming the ordinary-difference set we obtain an arithmetical progression after a finite number of steps.

1. Introduction

Let $\mathbf{N}_0$ denote the non-negative integers and let A be any subset of $\mathbf{N}_0$. We denote the number of elements of A by $|A|$ and the number of elements of A which are less than x by $|A|_x$. As usual we define the upper density of A by $\bar{d}(A)=\limsup_{x\to\infty} |A|_x/x$ and the lower density of A by $\underline{d}(A)=\liminf_{x\to\infty} |A|_x/x$. If $\bar{d}(A)=\underline{d}(A)$, then we define this limit value to be the density $d(A)$ of A.

Let $d\in\mathbf{Z}$. By $A-d$ we denote the set of integers $b\in\mathbf{N}_0$ with $b+d\in A$. For the sake of brevity we write $A[d]$ instead of $A\cap(A-d)$. We define the ordinary-difference set $\mathscr{D}(A)$ of A by

$$\mathscr{D}(A)=\{d\in\mathbf{N}_0 \mid A[d]\neq\emptyset\}\,,$$

the infinite-difference set $\mathscr{D}_\infty(A)$ of A by

$$\mathscr{D}_\infty(A)=\{d\in\mathbf{N}_0 \mid |A[d]|=\infty\}$$

and the density-difference set $\mathscr{D}_0(A)$ of A by

$$\mathscr{D}_0(A)=\{d\in\mathbf{N}_0 \mid \bar{d}(A[d])>0\}\,.$$

In the last few years difference sets have been investigated by several people. See [5], or for recent results not mentioned in this survey paper [1], [2], [3]. Most authors have considered only ordinary-difference sets. Their results, however, can often be extended to the other types of difference sets. Our first theorem, which is an extension of Theorem 5 of [4], is sometimes useful in this connection.

Theorem 1. *Given a set* $A \subseteq \mathbf{N}_0$ *there exists a set* $B \subseteq \mathbf{N}_0$ *with* $\underline{d}(B) \geq \bar{d}(A)$ *such that* $\mathscr{D}(B) \subseteq \mathscr{D}_0(A)$.

In [4] we proved that the collection of infinite-difference sets associated with sets of positive upper density is a filter of the set of all subsets of $\mathbf{N}_0$. In particular this implies that if A has positive upper density and $\mathscr{D}_\infty(A) \subseteq K \subseteq \mathbf{N}_0$, then there exists a set B with positive upper density such that $\mathscr{D}_\infty(B) = K$. The analogous property does not hold for the other two types of difference sets. Let E be the set of non-negative even integers. We have $\mathscr{D}(E) = E$, but it is easy to see that $E \cup \{1\}$ is not the ordinary-difference set of any set. Similarly we have $\mathscr{D}_0(E) = E$.

Theorem 2. *There is no set A such that* $\mathscr{D}_0(A) = E \cup \{1\}$.

Another consequence of the filter property is that the union of two infinite-difference sets of sets of positive upper density is also an infinite-difference set of a set of positive upper density. The analogous assertion does not hold for ordinary-difference sets. Take $A = \{0, 1, 11, 21, 31, \ldots\}$ and $B = \{0, 3, 13, 23, 33, \ldots\}$. Then $\mathscr{D}(A) \cup \mathscr{D}(B) = \{c \mid c \equiv 0, 1 \text{ or } 3 \pmod{10}\}$ but this is not an ordinary-difference set. However, it is true that the union of any two density-difference sets is a difference set.

Theorem 3. *If A and B are subsets of* $\mathbf{N}_0$, *then there exists a set* $C \subseteq \mathbf{N}_0$ *such that* $\mathscr{D}_0(C) = \mathscr{D}_0(A) \cup \mathscr{D}_0(B)$.

A further consequence of the filter property is that the intersection of two infinite-difference sets associated with sets of positive upper density is also an infinite-difference set of a set of positive upper density. While the corresponding assertion does not hold for ordinary-difference sets (see [4]), it does hold for density-difference sets.

Theorem 4. *If A and B are subsets of* $\mathbf{N}_0$, *then there exists a set* $C \subseteq \mathbf{N}_0$ *such that* $\mathscr{D}_0(C) = \mathscr{D}_0(A) \cap \mathscr{D}_0(B)$. *Moreover,* $\bar{d}(C[d]) \geq \bar{d}(A[d]) \cdot \bar{d}(B[d])$ *for every* $d \in \mathbf{N}_0$.

On taking $d = 0$ we obtain $\bar{d}(C) \geq \bar{d}(A) \cdot \bar{d}(B)$. Hence, by Theorem 1 with $C = A$ and some simple arguments, there exists a set C' such that

$$\underline{d}(\mathscr{D}_0(A) \cap \mathscr{D}_0(B)) = \underline{d}(\mathscr{D}_0(C)) \geq \underline{d}(\mathscr{D}(C')) \geq \underline{d}(C') \geq \bar{d}(C) = \bar{d}(A) \cdot \bar{d}(B) .$$

So, by repeated application of Theorem 4, we find that for any sets $A_1, A_2, \ldots, A_h \subseteq \mathbf{N}_0$,

$$\underline{d}\left(\bigcap_{j=1}^{h} \mathscr{D}_0(A_j) \right) \geq \prod_{j=1}^{h} \bar{d}(A_j) . \tag{1}$$

In [4] we showed that this inequality cannot be improved. Inequality (1) is an improvement of [4] Theorem 1 and it was proved recently by Y. Katznelson and by I. Z. Ruzsa [3]. It follows from Theorem 4 that there even exists a set C with $\bar{d}(C) \geqq \prod_{j=1}^{h} \bar{d}(A_j)$ such that $\mathscr{D}_0(C) = \bigcap_{j=1}^{h} \mathscr{D}_0(A_j)$.

Up to now no simple characterization of any of the three sets of difference sets associated with sets of positive upper density has been found. Our last result, by contrast, demonstrates that if we iterate the operation of taking the ordinary-difference set, a simple stable set occurs after relatively few steps. Put $\mathscr{D}^1(A) = \mathscr{D}(A)$ and $\mathscr{D}^k(A) = \mathscr{D}(\mathscr{D}^{k-1}(A))$ for $k = 2, 3, \dots$.

Theorem 5. *Let A have positive upper density ε. Then there exists an integer k with $1 \leqq k \leqq \varepsilon^{-1}$ such that $\mathscr{D}^r(A) = \{jk\}_{j=0}^{\infty}$ for all integers r with $r > 2[(\log \varepsilon^{-1})/\log 2]$.*

The example of the set of integers A_l with $A_l = \{a \equiv 0 \text{ or } 1 \pmod{l}\}$ shows that the lower bound for r cannot be replaced by $[(\log \varepsilon^{-1})/\log 2]$. We wonder whether the assertion of Theorem 5 remains valid if we replace the last inequality by $r > [(\log \varepsilon^{-1})/\log 2] + 1$.

2. Proof of Theorem 1

Put $\varepsilon = \bar{d}(A)$ and let $n \in \mathbf{N}$. Note that we may assume that ε is positive, since otherwise the theorem plainly holds. We prove first that there exists a set

$$R = \{r_j\}_{j=1}^{\infty} \subseteq \mathbf{N}_0$$

with positive upper density such that

$$|A - r_j|_k \geqq \varepsilon k \quad \text{for } k = 1, \dots, n \quad \text{and} \quad j = 1, 2, \dots.$$

Suppose this statement is false. Put

$$\varepsilon' = \left\{ \max \frac{i}{k} \,\middle|\, i, k \in \mathbf{N}_0,\ 1 \leqq k \leqq n,\ \frac{i}{k} < \varepsilon \right\}.$$

Note that $\varepsilon' < \varepsilon$ and that for every m except for a set $M^* \subseteq \mathbf{N}_0$ of density zero we have $|A - m|_{k_m} \leqq \varepsilon' k_m$ for some k_m with $1 \leqq k_m \leqq n$. Put $k_m = 1$ if $m \in M^*$. Define the set M inductively by $m_1 = 1$, $m_{j+1} = m_j + k_{m_j}$ for $j = 1, 2, \dots$. Let $x \in \mathbf{N}$ and define J by the inequalities $m_J \leqq x < m_{J+1}$. It follows that

$$|A|_x \leqq \varepsilon' m_J + x - m_J + |M^*|_x \leqq \varepsilon' x + n + |M^*|_x.$$

Since $\bar{d}(M^*) = 0$, it follows that $\bar{d}(A) \leqq \varepsilon'$, which is a contradiction.

Let $\{r_j^{(n)}\}_{j=1}^{\infty}$ be a set of positive upper density such that $|A - r_j^{(n)}|_k \geqq \varepsilon k$ for $k = 1, 2, \dots, n$ and $j = 1, 2, \dots$. Denote $\{0, 1, \dots, n-1\}$ by $\hat{n}$. We consider the sets $(A - r_j^{(n)}) \cap \hat{n}$. By the pigeon hole principle there exists a subset $\{s_j^{(n)}\}_{j=1}^{\infty}$ of $\{r_j^{(n)}\}_{j=1}^{\infty}$ of positive upper density such that $(A-s_j^{(n)})\cap\hat{n}$ is the same set $S^{(n)}$ for every j. We obtain in this way a set $S^{(n)}$, for every positive integer n, such that for $k=1, 2, \dots, n$ the number of elements less than k is at least εk. We now construct the set B by induction. Suppose $B\cap\hat{n}$ has been constructed in such a way that there are infinitely many integers v with $S^{(v)}\cap\hat{n}=B\cap\hat{n}$. We put $n\in B$ if and only if there are infinitely many integers v' among these integers v with $n\in S^{(v')}$. It follows that there are infinitely many integers v with $S^{(v)}\cap\widehat{n+1}=$ $=B\cap\widehat{n+1}$. By construction, for some $v>n$,

$$|B|_n=|S^{(v)}|_n\geqq\varepsilon n\,.$$

Thus $\underline{\underline{d}}(B)\geqq\varepsilon=\bar{d}(A)$.

Let $d\in\mathscr{D}(B)$. Then $n\in B[d]$ for some n and hence $n\in S^{(v)}[d]$ for some integer v. Therefore $n+s_j^{(v)}\in A$ and $n+d+s_j^{(v)}\in A$ for a set $\{s_j^{(v)}\}$ of positive upper density. Thus $d\in\mathscr{D}_0(A)$. This completes the proof.

Note that we have even proved that the Schnirelmann density of $B+1$ is at least ε, since $|B|_n\geqq\varepsilon n$ for every positive integer n.

3. Proof of Theorem 2

Suppose that A is a set for which 1 is an element of $\mathscr{D}_0(A)$. Thus $\bar{d}(A[1])=\varepsilon>0$. We shall show that $\mathscr{D}_0(A)$ contains an odd integer less than $8\varepsilon^{-1}+1$ and larger than 1. This will establish the result. Let $a_1, a_2, \dots$ be the elements of $A[1]$ in increasing order. We have $\liminf_{j\to\infty} a_j/j=\varepsilon^{-1}$. Hence there exist infinitely many integers a_N for which $a_{N+2}/N<2\varepsilon^{-1}$. Now since

$$\frac{1}{N}\sum_{j=1}^{N}(a_{j+2}-a_j)\leqq\frac{2a_{N+2}}{N}<\frac{4}{\varepsilon},$$

at least one half of the integers a_j with $j\leqq N$ satisfy $a_{j+2}-a_j<8\varepsilon^{-1}$. Thus $a_{j+2}-a_j=d$ for some integer d with $1<d<8\varepsilon^{-1}$ for a set of integers a_j of positive upper density. Since $a_{j+2}+1\in A$ for every j, both d and $d+1$ are in $\mathscr{D}_0(A)$ and thus there is an odd integer different from 1 in $\mathscr{D}_0(A)$ as required.

4. Proof of Theorem 3

We may assume that the upper density of both A and B is positive. Define C by $j\in C$ if and only if

$$\begin{cases} j-2^{2i}\in A & \text{for } 2^{2i}\leqq j<2^{2i+1}, \\ j-2^{2i+1}\in B & \text{for } 2^{2i+1}\leqq j<2^{2i+2}, \end{cases} \qquad i=0, 1, 2, \dots .$$

Suppose that n is a positive integer such that $|A|_n > n\bar{d}(A)/2$. Take i such that $2^{2i-2} \leqq n < 2^{2i}$. Then

$$|C|_{2^{2i+1}} \geqq |A|_{2^{2i}} \geqq \frac{n\bar{d}(A)}{2} \geqq \frac{2^{2i+1}\bar{d}(A)}{16}.$$

Thus $\bar{d}(C) \geqq \bar{d}(A)/16 > 0$.

Let $d \in \mathscr{D}_0(A)$. Let $\varepsilon > 0$ be such that $|A[d]|_{n-d} > \varepsilon n$ for infinitely many n. For such an n define the integer i by $2^{2i-2} \leqq n < 2^{2i}$. Then

$$|C[d]|_{2^{2i+1}} \geqq |A[d]|_{2^{2i}-d} \geqq \varepsilon n \geqq \frac{\varepsilon \cdot 2^{2i+1}}{8}.$$

Hence, $d \in \mathscr{D}_0(C)$. Thus $\mathscr{D}_0(A) \subseteq \mathscr{D}_0(C)$. Similarly, $\mathscr{D}_0(B) \subseteq \mathscr{D}_0(C)$.

Finally, suppose $d \notin \mathscr{D}_0(A) \cup \mathscr{D}_0(B)$. Let $0 < \varepsilon < 1$. Take n_C so large that both $|A[d]|_n < \varepsilon n$ and $|B[d]|_n < \varepsilon n$ for $n \geqq n_0$. Let n and i be integers with $2^{2i} > n \geqq 2^{2i-2} \geqq n_0$. Then

$$|C[d]|_n \leqq \sum_{j=0}^{i-1} |A[d]|_{2^{2j}} + \sum_{j=0}^{i-1} |B[d]|_{2^{2j+1}} + 2id \leqq$$

$$\leqq \varepsilon \sum_{j=0}^{i-1} 2^{2j} + \varepsilon \sum_{j=0}^{i-1} 2^{2j+1} + c + 2id,$$

where c is some constant. Hence,

$$|C[d]|_n \leqq \varepsilon \cdot 2^{2i} + c + 2id \leqq 4\varepsilon n + c + d\frac{\log 4n}{\log 2}.$$

Thus $\bar{d}(C[d]) \leqq 4\varepsilon$. Since ε was arbitrary, $d \notin \mathscr{D}_0(C)$. This completes the proof of the theorem.

5. Proof of Theorem 4

For any positive integer n we denote the set $\{0, 1, \ldots, n-1\}$ by $\hat{n}$. Let $\kappa, \lambda \in \mathbf{N}_0$ with $\kappa > \lambda > 0$. Put $\tau = [\log \lambda]$ and $\sigma = (\kappa + \lambda)(\lambda + \tau)$. We define a subset $S = S_{\kappa,\lambda}$ of $\hat{\sigma}$ such that

$$(2) \qquad |S[d]| = |A[d]|_{\kappa - d} \cdot |B[d]|_{\lambda - d}$$

for every $d \in \hat{\tau}$. Namely, if $x = n(\lambda + \tau) + j$ with $n \in \widehat{\kappa + \lambda}, j \in \widehat{\lambda + \tau}$, then $x \in S$ if and only if $j \in ((A \cap \hat{\kappa}) - n + \lambda - 1) \cap B \cap \hat{\lambda}$. In the next paragraph we show that (2) holds.

Assume $d \in \hat{\tau}$, $a \in A[d] \cap \widehat{\kappa - d}$, $b \in B[d] \cap \widehat{\lambda - d}$. Then $a, a+d \in A \cap \hat{\kappa}$ and b, $b + d \in B \cap \hat{\lambda}$. Put $n = a - b + \lambda - 1$. It follows that $n(\lambda + \tau) + b \in S$ and $n(\lambda + \tau) + b + d \in S$.

Hence $n(\lambda+\tau)+b\in S[d]$. Since different pairs a, b lead to different numbers $n(\lambda+\tau)+b$, this proves that

$$|A[d]|_{\kappa-d}\cdot|B[d]|_{\lambda-d}\leqq|S[d]|\,.$$

On the other hand, assume $n(\lambda+\tau)+j\in S[d]$ with $n\in\widehat{\kappa+\lambda}$, $j\in\widehat{\lambda+\tau}$, $d\in\hat{\tau}$. Then both $n(\lambda+\tau)+j$ and $n(\lambda+\tau)+j+d$ belong to S. Hence $j<\lambda$, $j+d<\lambda+\tau$ and it follows that $j+d<\lambda$. Further we have $j, j+d\in(A\cap\hat{\kappa})-n+\lambda-1$ and $j, j+d\in B$. Put $a=j+n-\lambda+1$. We now also have $a, a+d\in A\cap\hat{\kappa}$. Thus $a\in A[d]\cap\widehat{\kappa-d}$ and $j\in B[d]\cap\widehat{\lambda-d}$. Since different numbers $n(\lambda+\tau)+j\in S[d]$ lead to different pairs a, j, we have proved that

$$|S[d]|\leqq|A[d]|_{\kappa-d}\cdot|B[d]|_{\lambda-d}\,.$$

This completes the proof of (2).

Put $\alpha_d=\bar{d}(A[d])$ and $\beta_d=\bar{d}(B[d])$ for $d\in\mathbf{N}_0$. In particular $\alpha_0=\bar{d}(A)$, $\beta_0=\bar{d}(B)$. Let $\{k_j^{(d)}\}_{j=1}^{\infty}$ and $\{l_j^{(d)}\}_{j=1}^{\infty}$ be strictly increasing sequences of positive integers such that

$$(3)\qquad |A[d]|_{k_j^{(d)}-d}\geqq\left(1-\frac{1}{j}\right)k_j^{(d)}\alpha_d \quad\text{and}\quad |B[d]|_{l_j^{(d)}-d}\geqq\left(1-\frac{1}{j}\right)l_j^{(d)}\beta_d$$

for $j=1, 2, 3, \ldots$. Next we define two sequences $\{\kappa(h)\}_{h=0}^{\infty}$ and $\{\lambda(h)\}_{h=0}^{\infty}$ by induction. Put $\kappa(0)=k_1^{(0)}$, $\lambda(0)=l_1^{(0)}$. If $h=m^2+d$ with $m\in\mathbf{N}$, $0\leqq d\leqq 2m$, then $\lambda(h)$ is a term of $\{l_j^{(d)}\}_{j=m}^{\infty}$ and $\kappa(h)$ is a term of $\{k_j^{(d)}\}_{j=m}^{\infty}$ chosen in such a way that for $h=1, 2, \ldots$

$$(4)\qquad \lambda(h)>\lambda(h-1) \quad\text{and}\quad \kappa(h)>h\{\lambda(h)+\sum_{j=0}^{h-1}(\kappa(j)+\lambda(j))(\lambda(j)+\log\lambda(j)\}\,.$$

Hence $\{\kappa(h)\}_{h=0}^{\infty}$ and $\{\lambda(h)\}_{h=0}^{\infty}$ are strictly increasing sequences of positive integers. Put $\tau(j)=[\log\lambda(j)]$ and $\sigma(j)=(\kappa(j)+\lambda(j))(\lambda(j)+\tau(j))$ for $j=0, 1, 2, \ldots$ and $M(-1)=0$ and $M(h)=\sum_{j=0}^{h}\sigma_j$ for $h=0, 1, 2, \ldots$. We define C by

$$(5)\qquad (C-M(h-1))\cap\widehat{\sigma(h)}=S_{\kappa(h),\,\lambda(h)}$$

for $h=0, 1, 2, \ldots$.

We prove first that

$$\bar{d}(C[d])\geqq\bar{d}(A[d])\cdot\bar{d}(B[d])$$

for $d\in\mathbf{N}_0$. We observe that, by (5), (2) and (3), for $0\leqq d\leqq\tau(m^2)$,

$$|C[d]|_{M(m^2+d)}\geqq|S_{\kappa(m^2+d),\,\lambda(m^2+d)}[d]|=$$
$$=|A[d]|_{\kappa(m^2+d)-d}\cdot|B[d]|_{\lambda(m^2+d)-d}\geqq$$
$$\geqq\left(1-\frac{1}{m}\right)\kappa(m^2+d)\alpha_d\cdot\left(1-\frac{1}{m}\right)\lambda(m^2+d)\beta_d\,.$$

On the other hand, by (4)

$$M(m^2+d)=\sum_{j=0}^{m^2+d}\sigma(j)\leqq\sigma(m^2+d)+\frac{1}{m}\kappa(m^2+d)\leqq$$

$$\leqq\left\{\left(1+\frac{1}{m^2+d}\right)\left(1+\frac{\log\lambda(m^2+d)}{\lambda(m^2+d)}\right)+\frac{1}{m}\right\}\kappa(m^2+d)\,\lambda(m^2+d).$$

Thus

$$\bar{d}(C[d])\geqq\left(1-\frac{1}{m}\right)^2\left\{\left(1+\frac{1}{m}\right)\left(1+\frac{\log\lambda(m^2+d)}{\lambda(m^2+d)}\right)+\frac{1}{m}\right\}^{-1}\alpha_d\beta_d.$$

If $m\to\infty$, then $\lambda(m^2+d)\to\infty$. Hence, for any $d\in\mathbf{N}_0$,

$$\bar{d}(C[d])\geqq\alpha_d\beta_d=\bar{d}(A[d])\cdot\bar{d}(B[d]).$$

Consequently, $\mathscr{D}_0(A)\cap\mathscr{D}_0(B)\subseteq\mathscr{D}_0(C)$.

The proof of the theorem will be complete after we show that $\mathscr{D}_0(C)\subseteq\mathscr{D}_0(A)\cap\mathscr{D}_0(B)$. Fix some positive integer d with $d\notin\mathscr{D}_0(A)\cap\mathscr{D}_0(B)$. Let $n\in\mathbf{N}$. Take m and y such that

(6) $$n=M(m-1)+y\quad\text{and}\quad y\in\sigma(m).$$

It follows that

(7) $$|C[d]|_n\leqq\sum_{j=0}^{m-1}|S_{\kappa(j),\lambda(j)}[d]|+|S_{\kappa(m),\lambda(m)}[d]|_y.$$

Choose j_0 such that $\tau(j)\geqq d$ for $j\geqq j_0$. We have, by (2), for $j\geqq j_0$,

(8) $$|S_{\kappa(j),\lambda(j)}[d]|\leqq|A[d]|_{\kappa(j)-d}\cdot|B[d]|_{\lambda(j)-d}.$$

Let ε be any positive number. Let c be a constant such that

(9) $$|A[d]|_n<\varepsilon n+c\quad\text{for every}\quad n\in\mathbf{N}$$

if $d\notin\mathscr{D}_0(A)$, and such that

(10) $$|B[d]|_n<\varepsilon n+c\quad\text{for every}\quad n\in\mathbf{N}$$

if $d\notin\mathscr{D}_0(B)$. Then

(11) $$|A[d]|_{\kappa(j)}|B[d]|_{\lambda(j)}<\max\{\varepsilon\kappa(j)+c)\lambda(j),\ \kappa(j)\,(\varepsilon\lambda(j)+c)\}\leqq$$
$$\leqq\varepsilon\kappa(j)\lambda(j)+c(\kappa(j)+\lambda(j)).$$

On combining (8) and (11) we obtain

$$\sum_{j=0}^{m-1} |S_{\kappa(j),\lambda(j)}[d]| \leqq \varepsilon \sum_{j=0}^{m-1} \kappa(j)\lambda(j) + c \sum_{j=0}^{m-1} (\kappa(j)+\lambda(j)) + c_1, \tag{12}$$

where c_1 is some constant larger than $\sum_{j=0}^{j_0} |S_{\kappa(j),\lambda(j)}[d]|$.

From now on we assume that $m \geqq j_0$. Put $y = (t-1)(\lambda(m)+\tau(m)) + u$ with $0 \leqq u < \lambda(m)+\tau(m)$. If (10) holds, then, by the construction of $S_{\kappa,\lambda}$,

$$\begin{aligned} |S_{\kappa(m),\lambda(m)}[d]|_y &\leqq (t-1)|B[d]|_{\lambda(m)} + |B[d]|_u \leqq \\ &\leqq (t-1)(\varepsilon\lambda(m)+c) + \varepsilon u + c \leqq \varepsilon y + tc \leqq \varepsilon y + (c+\varepsilon)\left(\frac{y}{\lambda(m)} + 1\right). \end{aligned} \tag{13}$$

If (9) holds, then, by the construction of $S_{\kappa,\lambda}$,

$$|S_{\kappa(m),\lambda(m)}[d]|_y \leqq \sum_{j=1}^{t} |(A+\lambda(m)-j)[d]|_{\lambda(m)}. \tag{14}$$

The elements of $(A+\lambda(m)-j)[d]$ correspond to elements of $A[d]$. If an element $a \in A[d]$ induces an element of $(A+\lambda(m)-j)[d] \cap \widehat{\lambda(m)}$, then $-\lambda(m)+j \leqq a < j \leqq t$. A fixed number a is counted therefore at most $\min(t, \lambda(m))$ times in the sum. Hence, by (9),

$$\sum_{j=1}^{t} |(A+\lambda(m)-j)[d]|_{\lambda(m)} \leqq \min(t, \lambda(m))|A[d]|_t \leqq \min(t, \lambda(m))(\varepsilon t + c). \tag{15}$$

On combining (14) and (15) we obtain

$$\begin{aligned} |S_{\kappa(m),\lambda(m)}[d]|_y &\leqq \min(t, \lambda(m))(\varepsilon(t-1)+\varepsilon+c) \leqq \\ &\leqq \varepsilon y + (c+\varepsilon)t \leqq \varepsilon y + (c+\varepsilon)\left(\frac{y}{\lambda(m)} + 1\right). \end{aligned} \tag{16}$$

From the inequalities (7), (12), (13) and (16), we find for $m \geqq j_0$,

$$|C[d]|_n \leqq \varepsilon\left(y + \sum_{j=0}^{m-1} \kappa(j)\lambda(j)\right) + c \sum_{j=0}^{m-1} (\kappa(j)+\lambda(j)) + c_1 + (c+\varepsilon)\left(\frac{y}{\lambda(m)} + 1\right).$$

Hence, by (6) and (4),

$$|C[d]|_n \leqq \varepsilon n + 3c\kappa(m-1) + c_1 + (c+\varepsilon)\left(\frac{n}{\lambda(m)} + 1\right).$$

If $n\to\infty$, then $m\to\infty$ and $\lambda(m)\to\infty$. Therefore, since $n\geqq\kappa(m-1)\lambda(m-1)$,

$$\bar{d}(C[d])\leqq \lim_{\substack{n\to\infty\\ m\to\infty}}\left\{\varepsilon+\frac{3c}{\lambda(m-1)}+\frac{c_1}{n}+(c+\varepsilon)\left(\frac{1}{\lambda(m)}+\frac{1}{n}\right)\right\}=\varepsilon .$$

Since ε was arbitrary, $\bar{d}(C[d])=0$ for every number $d\notin\mathscr{D}_0(A)\cap\mathscr{D}_0(B)$. Thus $\mathscr{D}_0(C)\subseteq\mathscr{D}_0(A)\cap\mathscr{D}_0(B)$. This completes the proof of the theorem.

6. Proof of Theorem 5

We remark that if $\mathscr{D}^r(A)=\mathscr{D}^{r+1}(A)$ then in fact $\mathscr{D}^r(A)=\mathscr{D}^s(A)$ for all $s\geqq r$. We also note that if $0\in A$ then $A\subseteq\mathscr{D}(A)$ and thus $\mathscr{D}(A)\subseteq\mathscr{D}^2(A)\subseteq\dots$. We shall prove first that if $\mathscr{D}(A)\neq\mathscr{D}^2(A)\neq\dots\neq\mathscr{D}^r(A)$, then $r\leqq 2[(\log\varepsilon^{-1})/\log 2]+1$.

Accordingly, let l be an integer which is in $\mathscr{D}^2(A)$ but not in $\mathscr{D}(A)$. We may then write

(17) $$l=(a_1-a_2)-(a_3-a_4),$$

where a_1, a_2, a_3, a_4 are integers from A with $a_1>a_2$ and $a_3\geqq a_4$. On replacing a_1 in the expression of (17) by any x from A which is larger than a_1 we again find a number which is in $\mathscr{D}^2(A)$. Thus $(A-a_1)+l\subseteq\mathscr{D}^2(A)$. Plainly $\mathscr{D}^2(A)$ also contains the set $A-a_1$. The sets $(A-a_1)+l$ and $A-a_1$ are disjoint, since l is not in $\mathscr{D}(A)$. Thus $\bar{d}(\mathscr{D}^2(A))\geqq 2\bar{d}(A)$. We may repeat the above argument with A replaced by $\mathscr{D}^{t-2}(A)$ and l replaced by an integer which is in $\mathscr{D}^t(A)$ but not in $\mathscr{D}^{t-1}(A)$, for any integer t with $2<t\leqq r$.

We then find that $\bar{d}(\mathscr{D}^t(A))\geqq 2\bar{d}(\mathscr{D}^{t-2}(A))$. In particular,

$$\bar{d}(\mathscr{D}^{2s}(A))\geqq 2^s\bar{d}(A)=2^s\varepsilon$$

for $s=[r/2]$. Since the upper density of $\mathscr{D}^{2s}(A)$ is at most 1, we have $s\leqq[(\log\varepsilon^{-1})/\log 2]$ and therefore $r\leqq 2[(\log\varepsilon^{-1})/\log 2]+1$ as was asserted previously.

Thus $\mathscr{D}^s(A)=\mathscr{D}^r(A)$ for all $s\geqq r$ whenever $r>2[(\log\varepsilon^{-1})/\log 2]$. Put $k\mathbf{N}_0=\{kt\}_{t=0}^{\infty}$. Plainly if $\mathscr{D}^r(A)=k\mathbf{N}_0$ then $1\leqq k\leqq\varepsilon^{-1}$, since $\bar{d}(\mathscr{D}^r(A))\geqq\varepsilon$ for $r\geqq 1$. Therefore to conclude the proof if suffices to show that if $A=\mathscr{D}(A)$ then $A=k\mathbf{N}_0$. Obviously $0\in A$, so we may write $A=\{0, a_1, a_2, \dots\}$ with $0<a_1<a_2<\dots$. Assume $A\neq a_1\mathbf{N}_0$ and let j be the first index for which $a_j\neq ja_1$. Then the difference a_j-a_1 is in $\mathscr{D}(A)$ but not in A contradicting the assumption that $A=\mathscr{D}(A)$. Therefore $A=a_1\mathbf{N}_0$ as required. This completes the proof.

References

[1] P. ERDŐS and A. SÁRKÖZY, On differences and sums of integers, I. *J. Number Theory*, **10** (1978), 430–450.
[2] P. ERDŐS and A. SÁRKÖZY, On differences and sums of integers, II. *Bull. Greek Math. Soc.* **18** (1977), 204 223.
[3] I. Z. RUZSA, On difference sets. *Studia Sci. Math. Hungar.*, **13** (1978), 319–326.
[4] C. L. STEWART and R. TIJDEMAN, On infinite-difference sets of sequences of positive integers, *Canad. J. Math.*, **31** (1979), 897–910.
[5] R. TIJDEMAN, Distance sets of sequences of integers, *Proc. Bicentennial Conf. Wiskundig Genootschap, MC Tract* 101, *Math. Centre, Amsterdam*, 1979. pp. 405–415.

DEPARTMENT OF PURE MATHEMATICS
THE UNIVERSITY OF WATERLOO
WATERLOO, ONT. N2L 3G1
CANADA

MATHEMATICAL INSTITUTE
P.O. BOX 9512
2300 RA LEIDEN
THE NETHERLANDS

Studies in Pure Mathematics
To the Memory of Paul Turán

Some notes on the power sums of complex numbers whose sum is 0[1]

by

J. SURÁNYI (Budapest)

1. Let $z_1, \ldots, z_n$ be complex numbers. The important method of P. TURÁN, based on estimating from below the maximum of the modulus of the power sums

(1) $$s_\nu = \sum_{j=1}^{n} z_j^\nu \quad 1 \leqq \nu \leqq n,$$

and of generalized power sums

$$\sum_{j=1}^{n} b_j z_j^\nu \quad m+1 \leqq \nu \leqq m+n$$

under different normations for the numbers z_j, provided unexpected new results on quite different fields of mathematics and many new problems emerge in the further development of the theory. One of them, raised by TURÁN in his lectures on the topic and in his posthumous book [4], is the estimation of the sums (1) under the following conditions:

(2) $$s_1 = 0$$

and either

(3) $$|z_j| = 1 \quad \text{for some } j, \quad 1 \leqq j \leqq n$$

or

(4) $$|z_j| \geqq 1 \quad (j = 1, \ldots, n).$$

Let us denote by m_n and M_n the minimal value[2] of $\max(|s_2|, \ldots, |s_n|)$ for all systems $(z_1, \ldots, z_n) = Z_n$ satisfying — besides (2) — (3) and (4) respectively.

[1] With a remark of M. SZALAY (Budapest).

[2] Weierstrass' theorem yields the existence of the *minimum* m_n (>0). For M_n — as an infimum in question — besides the adequate conditions, we can suppose that $\max\limits_{\nu=2,\ldots,n} |z_1^\nu + \ldots + z_n^\nu| \leqq M_n + 1$ which implies the inequality $\max\limits_{j=1,\ldots,n} |z_j| \leqq \dfrac{M_n+1}{m_n}$. It follows that M_n is a minimal value.

I will give some estimations for these quantities. §2 contains a rough lower bound for M_n and some upper estimations. In §3 I show a way of improving the lower estimation with some numerical results. Finally §4 contains upper bounds for m_n.

Clearly, a rotation of the system Z_n around the origin does not change the modulus of the s_ν and a contraction diminishes it (if $s_\nu \neq 0$). Thus we can suppose that 1 belongs to z_n and it has maximal or minimal modulus according to conditions (3) and (4), respectively.

We will make use of the polynomial

$$f(z)=\prod_{j=1}^{n}(z-z_j)=\sum_{\nu=0}^{n} a_\nu z^{n-\nu} \quad (a_0=1, \quad a_1=0).$$

2. In the case of M_n (4) gives then $|a_n| \geqq 1$. Let us denote by a_k, for an extremal system Z_n one of the coefficients with maximal modulus (and $k \geqq 2$). When $k>2$, we get, using the Newton–Waring–Girard formulae

$$k \leqq k|a_k| = |-s_k - \sum_{\nu=2}^{k-2} a_\nu s_{k-\nu}| \leqq |a_k|(k-2)M_n$$

which gives

$$M_n \geqq \frac{k}{k-2} \geqq \frac{n}{n-2}. \tag{5}$$

As (2) implies $s_2=-2a_2$, the case $k=2$ would lead to $M_n \geqq 2$. Thus, for $n>4$ we can only conclude the smaller lower bound $n/(n-2)$.

For $n \leqq 4$ M_n can be easily calculated. We have

$$M_2(=m_2)=2, \quad M_3=3, \quad M_4=2.$$

In fact, $Z_2=\{-1, 1\}$ is essentially unique and $Z_3=\{e^{j\frac{2\pi i}{3}} \mid j=0, 1, 2\}$, $Z_4=\{e^{j\frac{\pi i}{3}} \mid j=1, 2, 4, 5\}$ furnishes us $M_3 \leqq 3$, $M_4 \leqq 2$. On the other hand, for $n=3$, $s_1=a_1=0$, $|a_3| \geqq 1$ and $s_3=-3a_3$ yield that $M_3 \geqq 3$; for $n=4$, (5) or $s_2=-2a_2$ yields that $M_4 \geqq 2$; so that $n/(n-2)$ is best possible for $n=3, 4$.

The systems

$$Z_{2m}=\{e^{j\frac{\pi i}{m+1}} \mid 1 \leqq j \leqq 2m+1, \quad j \neq m+1\},$$

$$Z_{3m-1}=\{-1, \quad e^{j\frac{2\pi i}{3m}} \mid 0 \leqq j \leqq 3m-1, \quad j \neq m, 2m\},$$

$$Z_{6m-3}=\{e^{j\frac{\pi i}{3m}} \mid 0 \leqq j \leqq 6m-1, \quad j \neq m, 3m, 5m\}$$

provide the upper estimations

$$M_{2m} \leqq 2, \quad M_{3m-1} \leqq 3, \quad M_{6m-3} \leqq 3.$$

An absolute but rough upper estimation can be given for the outstanding case M_{6m+1} too.

Next we give a better upper bound for M_5 showing that

$$\min_{Z'_5} \max \{|s_2|, \ldots, |s_5|\} = \frac{\sqrt{981}-9}{10} = 2.232\,091\ldots,$$

where Z'_5 refers to the systems of the form

$$Z'_5 = \{1, u_j \pm iv_j \mid j=1,2;\quad u_1^2+v_1^2=u_2^2+v_2^2=1;\quad 1+2u_1+2u_2=0, \quad u_j, v_j \text{ real numbers}\}.$$

Calculating the power sums in terms of u_1 we obtain

$$s_1=0, \quad s_2=2(4u_1^2+2u_1-1),$$

$$s_3=-3(4u_1^2+2u_1-1)=-\frac{3}{2}s_2, \quad s_4=\frac{s_2^2}{2},$$

$$s_5=5\left(1-\frac{1}{4}s_2^2\right).$$

Clearly $|s_2| \leqq |s_3|$. According to $M_5 \leqq 3$, just shown, with a Z'_5, we may assume $|s_2| \leqq 3$. In this interval we also have $|s_4| \leqq |s_3|$. The minimal value of $\max(|s_2|, \ldots, |s_5|)$ is reached when $(3 \geqq)\, |s_3| = |s_5|$, (and is equal to this common value). The equality holds iff $|s_2| = \dfrac{\sqrt{109}-3}{5}$ which occurs e.g. for

$$u_1 = \frac{\sqrt{\sqrt{10\,900}+95}-5}{20} = 0.456\,050\,7\ldots.$$

In this case $|s_5| = |s_3| = \dfrac{3}{2}|s_2| = \dfrac{\sqrt{981}-9}{10}$ which proves our claim.

This furnishes the upper estimation

$$M_5 < 2.232\,092.$$

Similar calculations led me to three pairs of conjugate complex numbers on the unit circle (not necessarily the best ones) giving an upper bound for M_6 less than 2. The real parts are the roots of the equation

$$(10x)^3 - 51(10x) + 52 = 0.$$

This system gives the upper bound

$$M_6 \leqq 1.9968.$$

3. The lower bounds can also be improved. We can calculate from the Newton–Waring–Girard formulae the elementary symmetrical polynomials in terms of the power sums and obtain

$$a_k = \sum_{j_1+2j_2+\ldots+kj_k=k} \prod_{\nu=1}^{k} \frac{1}{j_\nu!}\left(-\frac{s_\nu}{\nu}\right)^{j_\nu}, \quad k=1,\ldots,n; \quad j_\nu \geqq 0.$$

For an extremal system this gives, according to (2) and (4), the inequality

$$1 \leqq |a_n| \leqq \sum_{2j_2+\ldots+nj_n=n} \prod_{\nu=2}^{n} \frac{M_n^{j_\nu}}{\nu^{j_\nu} j_\nu!}; \quad j_\nu \geqq 0.$$

This means that the (unique) positive root of the polynomial (of degree $[n/2]$)

$$f_n(x) = \sum_{2j_2+\ldots+nj_n=n} \prod_{\nu=2}^{n} \frac{x^{j_\nu}}{\nu^{j_\nu} j_\nu!} - 1$$

furnishes a lower bound for M_n. The first ones are as follows:

$$M_5 \geqq \frac{\sqrt{159}-3}{5} > 1.9219, \quad M_6 > 1.7936,$$

$$M_7 > 1.7199, \quad M_8 > 1.6625, \quad M_9 > 1.6185.$$

Though these values decrease slower than (5), I did not succeed in deducing some essentially better general estimates on this way.[3] The most interesting question is whether M_n tends to 1 or remains over a larger value.

4. For m_n too we can win upper estimations by finding appropriate systems Z_n. The choice

$$z_1 = \ldots = z_{n-1} = -\frac{1}{n-1}, \quad z_n = 1$$

e.g. gives

$$m_n \leqq 1 + \frac{1}{n-1},$$

but this can be improved essentially taking[4] (for $n \geqq 3$)

$$z_j = \frac{1}{2} e^{j\frac{2\pi i}{n-1}} \quad j=1,\ldots,n-2, \quad z_{n-1} = -\frac{1}{2}, \quad z_n =$$

[3] M. SZALAY improved (5) on this way. Cf. the remark at the end of the paper.

[4] This system was suggested by LÁSZLÓ SURÁNYI.

For this system the power sums do not exceed 1 except s_{n-1} which furnishes the estimation

$$m_n \leqq 1 + \frac{n-2+(-1)^{n-1}}{2^{n-1}}$$

For $n=3$ we infer from $3s_2+2s_3=6$ easily

$$m_3 = 1,2.$$

The corresponding extremal system is

$$-\frac{1}{2} \pm \frac{\sqrt{15}}{10} i, 1.$$

For $n=4$ I found a system Z_4 which is approximately

$$z_1 = -0.548\,801, \quad z_{2,3} = -0.225\,599\,5 \pm 0.419\,876 i, \quad z_4 = 1.$$

For this system we have

$$|s_2| = |s_3| = |s_4| = \frac{13-\sqrt{97}}{3} = 1.050\,380\,7\ldots.$$

This is the best one amongst the systems symmetrical to the real axis and containing 1, but there can be asymmetrical systems forcing m_4 perhaps even under 1, as without the restriction (2) the minimum is always under 1. (See J. LAWRYNOWICZ [1, 2, 3].) CASSELS has shown that this is possible only for asymmetrical systems. See in [4].

Remark by M. SZALAY
The arguments of §3 furnish also the estimation

$$M_n \geqq 1 + \frac{\log 2 - o(1)}{\log n}$$

by means of the formula

$$\sum_{\substack{j_1+2j_2+\ldots+nj_n=n \\ j_\nu \geqq 0}} \prod_{\nu=1}^{n} \frac{1}{j_\nu!} \left(\frac{x}{\nu}\right)^{j_\nu} = \binom{x+n-1}{n}$$

where the j_ν's are integers (see J. SURÁNYI, Problem 201, *Mat. Lapok*, **37** (1976–1979), 181–185). Indeed, this yields alternative representations of the polynomial

$$f_n(x) = \sum_{\substack{2j_2+\ldots+nj_n=n \\ j_\nu \geqq 0}} \prod_{\nu=2}^{n} \frac{1}{j_\nu!} \left(\frac{x}{\nu}\right)^{j_\nu} - 1,$$

namely, for $n \geqq 5$, we get

$$f_n(x) = -1 + \sum_{\substack{j_1+2j_2+\ldots+nj_n=n \\ j_\nu \geqq 0}} \prod_{\nu=1}^{n} \frac{1}{j_\nu!}\left(\frac{x}{\nu}\right)^{j_\nu} -$$

$$- \sum_{\substack{j_1+2j_2+\ldots+nj_n=n \\ j_\nu \geqq 0,\ j_1 \geqq 1}} \prod_{\nu=1}^{n} \frac{1}{j_\nu!}\left(\frac{x}{\nu}\right)^{j_\nu} = -1 + \binom{x+n-1}{n} -$$

$$- \sum_{\substack{(j_1-1)+2j_2+\ldots+(n-1)j_{n-1}=n-1 \\ j_\nu \geqq 0,\ j_1-1 \geqq 0}} \frac{x}{(j_1-1)+1} \cdot \frac{x^{j_1-1}}{(j_1-1)!} \prod_{\nu=2}^{n-1} \frac{1}{j_\nu!}\left(\frac{x}{\nu}\right)^{j_\nu} =$$

$$= -1 + \binom{x+n-1}{n} - x \sum_{\substack{j_1+2j_2+\ldots+(n-1)j_{n-1}=n-1 \\ j_\nu \geqq 0}} \frac{1}{j_1+1} \prod_{\nu=1}^{n-1} \frac{1}{j_\nu!}\left(\frac{x}{\nu}\right)^{j_\nu} =$$

$$= -1 + \binom{x+n-1}{n} - x\binom{x+n-2}{n-1} +$$

$$+ x \sum_{\substack{j_1+2j_2+\ldots+(n-1)j_{n-1}=n-1 \\ j_\nu \geqq 0,\ j_1 \geqq 1}} \frac{j_1}{j_1+1} \prod_{\nu=1}^{n-1} \frac{1}{j_\nu!}\left(\frac{x}{\nu}\right)^{j_\nu} =$$

$$= -1 + \binom{x+n-1}{n} - x\binom{x+n-2}{n-1} +$$

$$+ x \sum_{\substack{(j_1-1)+2j_2+\ldots+(n-2)j_{n-2}=n-2 \\ j_\nu \geqq 0,\ j_1-1 \geqq 0}} \frac{x}{(j_1-1)+2} \cdot \frac{x^{j_1-1}}{(j_1-1)!} \prod_{\nu=2}^{n-2} \frac{1}{j_\nu!}\left(\frac{x}{\nu}\right)^{j_\nu} =$$

$$= -1 + \binom{x+n-1}{n} - x\binom{x+n-2}{n-1} +$$

$$+ \frac{x^2}{2} \sum_{\substack{j_1+2j_2+\ldots+(n-2)j_{n-2}=n-2 \\ j_\nu \geqq 0}} \frac{2}{j_1+2} \prod_{\nu=1}^{n-2} \frac{1}{j_\nu!}\left(\frac{x}{\nu}\right)^{j_\nu}.$$

For $n \geqq 5$ and

$$x_n = 1 + \frac{\log 2 - \log\left\{1 + \left(1 - \frac{2}{n}\right)\frac{\log^2 2}{\log^2(en)} + \frac{2}{n}\frac{\log 2}{\log(en)}\right\}}{\log(en)},$$

this implies that

$$f_n(x_n) \leqq -1 + \binom{x_n+n-1}{n} - x_n \binom{x_n+n-2}{n-1} + \frac{x_n^2}{2}\binom{x_n+n-3}{n-2} =$$

$$= -1 + \frac{1}{2}\left(1 + \left(1 - \frac{2}{n}\right)(x_n-1)^2 + \frac{2}{n}(x_n-1)\right)\prod_{j=1}^{n-2}\left(1 + \frac{x_n-1}{j}\right) \leqq$$

$$\leqq -1 + \frac{1}{2}\left(1 + \left(1 - \frac{2}{n}\right)\frac{\log^2 2}{\log^2 (en)} + \frac{2}{n}\frac{\log 2}{\log (en)}\right)\exp\left(\sum_{j=1}^{n-2}\frac{x_n-1}{j}\right) <$$

$$< -1 + \frac{1}{2}\left(1 + \left(1 - \frac{2}{n}\right)\frac{\log^2 2}{\log^2 (en)} + \frac{2}{n}\frac{\log 2}{\log (en)}\right)\exp\left((x_n-1)\log (en)\right) = 0\,.$$

Consequently, for $n \geqq 5$,

$$M_n \geqq x_n \geqq 1 + \frac{\log 2 - \left(1 - \frac{2}{n}\right)\frac{\log^2 2}{\log^2 (en)} - \frac{2}{n}\frac{\log 2}{\log (en)}}{\log (en)} = 1 + \frac{\log 2 - o(1)}{\log n}\,.$$

References

[1] J. ŁAWRYNOWICZ, Remark on a Problem of P. Turán, *Bulletin de la Soc. Sci. et Lettres de Łódź*, **11,** 1 (1960), 1–4.

[2] J. ŁAWRYNOWICZ, Calculation of a Minimum Maximorum of Complex Numbers, *Ibid*, **11,** 2 (1960), 1–9.

[3] J. ŁAWRYNOWICZ, Remark on power-sums of complex numbers, *Acta Math. Acad. Sci. Hung.*, 18 (1967), 279–281.

[4] P. TURÁN, *On a new method in the analysis and its applications*, Wiley-Interscience Tracts Series (to appear).

EÖTVÖS LORÁND UNIVERSITY
H-1088 BUDAPEST
MÚZEUM KRT. 6–8.
HUNGARY

Studies in Pure Mathematics
To the Memory of Paul Turán

The field of definition of the Neron–Severi group

by

H. P. F. SWINNERTON-DYER (Cambridge)

1. Introduction

Let k be an algebraic number field, regarded as embedded in the field $\mathbf{C}$ of complex numbers, and let t be transcendental over $\mathbf{C}$. Let

$$\Gamma: Y^2 = X^3 + aX^2 + bX + c \tag{1}$$

be an elliptic curve defined over $k(t)$, which is not birationally equivalent over $\mathbf{C}(t)$ to a curve defined over $\mathbf{C}$. For any field $L \supset k(t)$ we denote by $\Gamma(L)$ the group of points on Γ defined over L. The main problem associated with such a curve Γ is to find the group $\Gamma(\mathbf{C}(t))$. It is known that this is finitely generated, and an upper bound can be given for its number of generators for any particular Γ and for its torsion part in general; but there is no reliable way of computing it. In particular, the standard method of descent may fail, for it is known that the Tate–Safarevic group of Γ over $\mathbf{C}(t)$ can have an infinitely divisible 2-component; see for example [1].

Since $\Gamma(\mathbf{C}(t))$ is finitely generated, there is a field $K_0 \subset \mathbf{C}$, finitely generated over k, such that $K_0(t)$ is the least field containing $k(t)$ over which $\Gamma(\mathbf{C}(t))$ is defined. Obviously K_0 is Galois over k, and hence is itself an algebraic number field. It would be useful to have a reliable method of finding K_0, or at least of finding an algebraic number field K_1 which contains K_0. For one reason, $\Gamma(\mathbf{C}(t)) = \Gamma(K_1(t))$ could then be calculated by means of a descent argument over $K_1(t)$, with the usual reservations; at least it is conjectured that the Tate–Safarevic group of Γ over $K_1(t)$ is always finite. The object of this paper is to obtain a slightly weaker result, but one which is just as useful for practical purposes — namely, that there is an explicitly computable integer $m > 0$ and an explicitly computable algebraic number field K_2, both depending on Γ, such that $m\Gamma(\mathbf{C}(t))$ is defined over $K_2(t)$. If

$$\Gamma(K_2(t)) \supset m\Gamma(\mathbf{C}(t))$$

can be computed, then it is easy to find $\Gamma(\mathbf{C}(t))$.

The importance of this result lies in its application to algebraic geometry. Equation (1) defines a surface V in the X, Y, t space; V is defined over k and has an obvious completion V^* in $\mathbf{P}^2 \times \mathbf{P}^1$, which will in general be singular. If P_0 denotes the base point of (1), and $P_1, \ldots, P_r$ span $\Gamma(\mathbf{C}(t))$ then the Neron-Severi group of V^* is spanned by

(i) the loci of $P_0, P_1, \ldots, P_r$ as t varies, and

(ii) a general fibre (1) and the components of the singular fibres.

More generally, let W be a surface over k containing a pencil of elliptic curves, and suppose that the generic curve is isomorphic to (1). Then in the notation above there is a birational map $V^* \to W$ and the Neron–Severi group of W is generated by the image of the Neron- Severi group of V^*, together with the exceptional curves of the map $V^* \to W$. A rather similar situation obtains if merely W contains a pencil of curves of genus 1 (that is, curves without basepoint) and the Jacobian of the generic such curve is isomorphic to (1). So the results in this paper can be applied to a large and important class of surfaces.

It may seem to the reader that the construction of K_2 in this paper is complicated and gives an unduly large K_2. But this seems to be in the nature of the problem. For let W be a non-singular cubic surface defined over k, and let l be a sufficiently general line defined over k in the ambient space. Assume that at least one of the points of $W \cap l$ is defined over k; then the planes through l cut out a pencil of elliptic curves on W. For this pencil, K_0 is the field of definition of the 27 lines on W, so that for suitable k, W we may have

$$[K_0:k] = 51\,840 = 2^7 \cdot 3^4 \cdot 5\,;$$

and $K_2 \supset K_0$ whatever value we take for m.

The main ideas of this paper are already to be found in CHRISTIE [2], though he did not push them to their logical conclusion. I am also indebted to Professor J. W. S. CASSELS for drawing my attention to the problem, and to A. BREMNER for helpful conversations.

2. The 2-coverings over C(t)

The argument of this paper depends on comparing the 2-coverings of Γ, and of the curves Γ^d defined in (16), over various fields $K(t)$ where $\mathbf{C} \supset K \supset k$. Without loss of generality we can take a, b, c in (1) to be in $k[t]$; we shall assume this for the rest of the paper. We start with the 2-coverings of Γ over $\mathbf{C}(t)$, writing (1) in the form

$$Y^2 = (X+\alpha_1)(X+\alpha_2)(X+\alpha_3) \tag{2}$$

where $\alpha_1, \alpha_2, \alpha_3$ are algebraic over $k(t)$ and their only poles lie above $t=\infty$. Let $(X(t), Y(t))$ be a point of Γ defined over $\mathbf{C}(t)$ other than the point at infinity; then apart possibly from $t=\infty$ the only poles of

$$X^3(t) + aX^2(t) + bX(t) + c \tag{3}$$

are poles of order $3n_i$ at the points $t=t_i$ at which $X(t)$ has a pole of order n_i. Since (3) is a square in $\mathbf{C}(t)$, every n_i is even and we can write

$$X(t) = U(t)/V^2(t)$$

where $U(t)$, $V(t)$ are in $C[t]$ and are coprime. This gives

(4) $$Y^2V^6=(U+\alpha_1V^2)(U+\alpha_2V^2)(U+\alpha_3V^2).$$

In the field $\mathbf{C}(t, \alpha_1, \alpha_2, \alpha_3)$ the only possible poles of any of the factors on the right are the points above $t=\infty$; and for example the only possible common zeros of the first two factors on the right are these points and the zeros of $(\alpha_1-\alpha_2)$. So the only points that can occur with odd multiplicity in the divisor of $(U+\alpha_1V^2)$ are the zeros of $(\alpha_1-\alpha_2)$ or $(\alpha_1-\alpha_3)$ and the points above $t=\infty$. Thus in the equation

(5) $$\text{Divisor of} \quad (U+\alpha_iV^2)=\mathfrak{a}_i\mathfrak{b}_i^2$$

the set of $\mathfrak{a}_i$ which need to be considered is finite and computable. Moreover, though this has been proved for the field $\mathbf{C}(t, \alpha_1, \alpha_2, \alpha_3)$ it clearly remains true in the field $\mathbf{C}(t, \alpha_i)$.

It follows from (5) that deg $(\mathfrak{a}_i)$ is even. Let $\mathfrak{c}_i$ run through a set of representatives of the finitely many divisor classes modulo linear equivalence whose square is the class of $\mathfrak{a}_i$; then

$$\text{Divisor of} \quad (U+\alpha_iV^2)\sim\mathfrak{c}_i^2\mathfrak{b}_i^2$$

so that the class of $\mathfrak{c}_i\mathfrak{b}_i$ has order at most 2. Thus for one of the choices of $\mathfrak{c}_i$ the divisor $\mathfrak{c}_i\mathfrak{b}_i$ is principal — say equal to the divisor of a function g_i in $C(t, \alpha_i)$. Let

$$\mathfrak{a}_i\mathfrak{c}_i^{-2}=(f_i)$$

so that f_i is in $\mathbf{C}(t, \alpha_i)$ and belongs to a finite computable list; then $(U+\alpha_iV^2)$ and $f_ig_i^2$ have the same divisor, and after absorbing a constant into g_i we can write

(6) $$U+\alpha_iV^2=f_ig_i^2.$$

This and (4) imply

$$f_1f_2f_3=(YV^3/g_1g_2g_3)^2.$$

Moreover, if say α_1 and α_2 are conjugate over $\mathbf{C}(t)$ then we can arrange for the possible f_2 to be conjugate to the possible f_1, so that the equations (6) for $i=1$ and $i=2$ are conjugate over $\mathbf{C}(t)$; hence $g_1g_2g_3$ is in $\mathbf{C}(t)$ and $f_1f_2f_3$ is a square in $\mathbf{C}(t)$. The modifications to the argument which are needed if $Y(t)=0$ are well known and can be left to the reader.

The triples (f_1, f_2, f_3) thus obtained correspond to 2-coverings of Γ over $\mathbf{C}(t)$, and all the soluble 2-coverings can be obtained in this way. They form a group under component-wise multiplication modulo squares, but we shall not need this fact. What is important is that the process above induces an embedding

(7) $$\Gamma(\mathbf{C}(t))/2\Gamma(\mathbf{C}(t))\to\text{Set of triples } (f_1, f_2, f_3).$$

To bring the three equations (6) into standard form, we divide cases as follows:

(i) $\alpha_1, \alpha_2, \alpha_3$ are conjugate over $\mathbf{C}(t)$;

(ii) α_1 is in $\mathbf{C}(t)$ and α_2, α_3 are conjugate over $\mathbf{C}(t)$;

(iii) $\alpha_1, \alpha_2, \alpha_3$ are all in $\mathbf{C}(t)$.

These correspond respectively to 0, 1 or 3 of the 2-division points of Γ being defined over $\mathbf{C}(t)$.

In case (i) we write

$$f_i = l + \alpha_i m + \alpha_i^2 n, \quad g_i = L + \alpha_i M + \alpha_i^2 N \tag{8}$$

where l, m, n are known and L, M, N unknown elements of $\mathbf{C}(t)$; that we can do this depends on the conjugacy arranged above. Equating coefficients of α_i and α_i^2 in (6) gives

$$V^2 = \Phi'(L, M, N), \quad 0 = \Phi''(L, M, N) \tag{9}$$

where Φ', Φ'' are quadratic polynomials with coefficients in $\mathbf{C}(t)$. Note first that the equation $\Phi''=0$ has a non-trivial solution in $\mathbf{C}(t)$. For without loss of generality we may assume that the coefficients of Φ'' are polynomials in t of degree at most r, where $r>0$. Writing L, M, N as general polynomials of degree $(r-1)$ and equating coefficients of powers of t, we obtain $(3r-1)$ homogeneous equations in the $3r$ undetermined coefficients; and these must have a non-zero solution. There are of course easier ways to find such a solution in practice. Since $\Phi''=0$ is soluble and quadratic, L, M, N can be written as quadratic polynomials in two new unknowns S and T, multiplied by an arbitrary common factor which is of no importance and which we shall ignore. Substituting this parametrization into $V^2=\Phi'$ we obtain

$$V^2 = \text{Homogeneous quartic in } S, T \tag{10}$$

which is a 2-covering of the original curve Γ.

Again in case (ii) we write

$$f_i = l + \alpha_i m, \quad g_i = L + \alpha_i M \quad (i = 2, 3) \tag{11}$$

where l, m are known and L, M unknown elements of $\mathbf{C}(t)$. Substituting into (6) and remembering that α_2, α_3 are now quadratic over $\mathbf{C}(t)$, we obtain

$$U = \Phi'(L, M), \quad V^2 = \Phi''(L, M) \tag{12}$$

with Φ', Φ'' homogeneous quadratic; and hence

$$f_1 g_1^2 = \Phi'(L, M) + \alpha_1 \Phi''(L, M). \tag{13}$$

Again, the second equation (12) leads us to write L, M as quadratic polynomials in two new unknowns S and T, multiplied by an arbitrary common factor; and so (13) reduces to the form

$$f_1 g_1^2 = \text{Homogeneous quartic in } S, T.$$

In case (iii) the three equations (6) are already defined over $\mathbf{C}(t)$. Eliminating U and using the relation

$$(\alpha_1-\alpha_2)f_3g_3^2+(\alpha_2-\alpha_3)f_1g_1^2+(\alpha_3-\alpha_1)f_2g_2^2=0$$

to write g_1, g_2, g_3 as quadratic polynomials in new unknowns S and T, we are once again led to an equation of the form (10). We omit the details, since in what follows we shall use a trick to avoid having to consider this case in this way.

3. Christie's Lemma and its consequences

There is considerable freedom in the choice of the triples (f_1, f_2, f_3), because the $\mathfrak{c}_i$ are only determined up to linear equivalence and the f_i can be multiplied by non-zero constants. But they can clearly all be chosen to lie in $K_3(t)$ for some computable algebraic number field $K_3 \supset k$; and by enlarging K_3 if necessary, we may also assume that each $f_1 f_2 f_3$ is a square in $K_3(t)$, that the parametrizations of the second equations (9) and (12) are defined over $K_3(t)$ and that

(14) $$k(\alpha_1, \alpha_2, \alpha_3, t)\cap\mathbf{C}\subset K_3.$$

In the course of the argument we shall impose further conditions on K_3, which may involve a further finite extension. Since $\Gamma(\mathbf{C}(t))$ is finitely generated, it is defined over $K_4(t)$ for some algebraic number field K_4; and by increasing K_4 if necessary we may assume that K_4 is a normal extension of K_3. Thus $G=\mathrm{Gal}\,(K_4/K_3)$ acts on $\Gamma(\mathbf{C}(t))$; and it acts trivially on $\Gamma(\mathbf{C}(t))/2\Gamma(\mathbf{C}(t))$ because its action commutes with the map (7) and its action on the right-hand side of (7) is trivial. Hence it acts trivially on $m\Gamma(\mathbf{C}(t))/2m\Gamma(\mathbf{C}(t))$ for any integer $m>0$.

The following result is Lemma 3 of Christie [2]:

Lemma 1. *Let G be a finite group and A a finitely generated torsion-free abelian group on which G acts. If G induces the trivial action on $A/2A$ then there is a basis $\{a_i\}$ for A such that $\sigma a_i=\pm a_i$ for each σ in G.*

In this we take $A=m\Gamma(\mathbf{C}(t))$, where m is large enough to kill the torsion part of $\Gamma(\mathbf{C}(t))$. Let $a_1, \ldots, a_r$ be the basis for A given by the lemma, and for each i let G_i be the subgroup of G which leaves a_i fixed. If $G_i=G$ then a_i is defined over $K_3(t)$; if not, then the fixed field of G_i is $K_3(d_i^{1/2})$ for some d_i in K_3 and $a_i=(x_i, y_i)$ with x_i and $d_i^{1/2}y_i$ in $K_3(t)$. Hence we can take

(15) $$K_2=K_3(d_1^{1/2}, \ldots, d_r^{1/2})$$

in the notation of §1. Unfortunately we do not know K_4 or the d_i; but we do know that the d_i are among those d in K_3 for which the curve

(16) $$\Gamma^d: d\,Y^2=X^3+aX^2+bX+c$$

has a point of infinite order defined over $K_3(t)$. The rest of this paper is concerned with investigating the set of such d and showing that, modulo squares, it is finite and computable. Specifically, we shall define a finite list of bad primes, depending on Γ and K_3, such that if d is divisible to an odd power by a prime not in this list then Γ^d does not have a point of infinite order defined over $K_3(t)$. We do this by considering the 2-coverings of Γ^d over a suitably chosen field, and showing that those among them which are soluble correspond to torsion points on Γ^d. The calculation of the 2-coverings mimics that in §2.

For completeness, we must show that m is computable. In fact we have

Lemma 2. *If m is the least positive integer which kills the torsion part of $\Gamma(\mathbf{C}(t))$ then $m \leqq 10$ or $m=12$.*

Proof. Suppose first that the invariant $j(\Gamma)$ is in $\mathbf{C}$. Without loss of generality we can assume $a=0$ in (1). Thus there exists s algebraic over $\mathbf{C}(t)$ such that the transformation $X=s^2x$, $Y=s^3y$ takes (1) into an equation in x, y defined over $\mathbf{C}$; call this new curve Γ^*. Let (X_0, Y_0) be a division point of Γ defined over $\mathbf{C}(t)$; then $(s^{-2}X_0, s^{-3}Y_0)$ is a division point of Γ^* and hence defined over $\mathbf{C}$. If X_0, Y_0 were both non-zero it would follow that s was in $\mathbf{C}(t)$, contrary to the hypothesis in the second sentence of §1. But there are only 5 points on Γ with $X_0=0$ or $Y_0=0$; and it follows that in this case $m \leqq 6$.

Now suppose that $j(\Gamma)$ is not in $\mathbf{C}$. The modular curve which parametrizes the structure

elliptic curve and an m-division point on it

is that conventionally called $X_1(m)$; for details see MAZUR [3]. If Γ has an m-division point defined over $\mathbf{C}(t)$, this induces a non-constant point on $X_1(m)$ defined over $\mathbf{C}(t)$. By Luroth's theorem, this can only happen if $X_1(m)$ has genus 0; and this happens precisely if $m \leqq 10$ or $m=12$. Conversely, it is easy to show that all these values of m are possible.

4. The case of no 2-division points

We now consider the 2-coverings of Γ^d over a field $K(t)$, where K will be chosen later but will satisfy $\mathbf{C} \supset K \supset K_3$. We can almost repeat the argument of §2, noting that

$$\mathfrak{c}_i^2 \mathfrak{b}_i^2 = \text{Divisor of } f_i^{-1}(U+\alpha_i V^2)$$

is defined over $K(\alpha_1, \alpha_2, \alpha_3, t)$ and hence so are $\mathfrak{c}_i \mathfrak{b}_i$ and g_i. The only difference is that we can no longer absorb the square root of a constant into g_i, so that instead of (6) we have

$$U+\alpha_i V^2 = \lambda_i f_i g_i^2 \tag{17}$$

for some constants λ_i; here λ_i is in $K(\alpha_i, t)$ and hence in K by (14). We have the same conjugacy statements as before, and (17) implies that

$$\lambda_1 \lambda_2 \lambda_3 / d \text{ is a square in } K. \tag{18}$$

We now split cases; in this section we assume that $\alpha_1, \alpha_2, \alpha_3$ are conjugate over $\mathbf{C}(t)$, so that $\Gamma(\mathbf{C}(t))$ has no 2-torsion. Now conjugacy implies $\lambda_1=\lambda_2=\lambda_3$; and since the λ_i are only determined modulo squares in K and satisfy (18), we may take

$$\lambda_1=\lambda_2=\lambda_3=d.$$

In (17) we make the substitution (8), which this time leads to

$$d^{-1}V^2=\Phi'(L, M, N), \quad 0=\Phi''(L, M, N)$$

with the same Φ', Φ'' as before; this time L, M and N are unknown elements of $K(t)$. Using the same parametric solution of $\Phi''=0$ as before, we obtain

(19) $$d^{-1}V^2=\text{Homogeneous quartic in } S, T=\psi(S, T),$$

say, where the right-hand side is the same as in (10) and does not depend on d. By multiplying V by an appropriate factor, we can assume that the coefficients of ψ are in $\mathfrak{o}_K[t]$.

For the rest of this section we take $K=K_3$. Let $\mathfrak{p}$ be a prime which divides d to an odd power; write $F=\mathfrak{o}_K/\mathfrak{p}$ and denote reduction mod $\mathfrak{p}$ by a tilde. If (19) is soluble, then it has a solution for which S and T are integral at $\mathfrak{p}$ and not both divisible by $\mathfrak{p}$; and then the left hand side of (19) is divisible by $\mathfrak{p}$. In other words, $\tilde{\psi}(S, T)$ must have a linear factor defined over $F(t)$. This motivates the following result.

Lemma 3. *In the notation above, suppose that $\tilde{\psi}$ has a linear factor defined over $F(t)$; then either ψ has a linear factor defined over $\mathbf{C}(t)$ or $\mathfrak{p}$ belongs to a finite computable set depending only on ψ.*

Proof. Assume that ψ does not have a linear factor defined over $\mathbf{C}(t)$, and denote by $\beta(t)$ the coefficient of S^4 in ψ. Since $\psi=0$ has no repeated root S/T and $\beta(t)\neq 0$, we can (after adding a constant to t if necessary) assume that both these still hold when $t=0$. Hence we can expand each root S/T as a formal power series in t, the coefficients being in the obvious quartic extensions of K. By writing down the iterative process explicitly, we see that the only primes which can occur in the denominators of the coefficients are those which lie above a factor either of $\beta(0)$ or of the discriminant of ψ at $t=0$. We may assume $\mathfrak{p}$ is not such a factor. The formal series for $\beta(t)S/T$ does not terminate, for if it did then S/T would be in $\mathbf{C}(t)$ contrary to hypothesis. But its reduction mod $\mathfrak{p}$ does terminate and has degree at most n_0, the sum of the degrees of $\beta(t)$ and the coefficient of T^4 in ψ; for the linear factor of $\tilde{\psi}$ defined over $F(t)$ must have the form

$$\tilde{\beta}(t)S-\tilde{\gamma}(t)T$$

where $\tilde{\gamma}$ is a polynomial. Write

$$\beta(t)S/T=\sum_0^{\infty}\eta_n t^n$$

and choose $n > n_0$ so that $\eta_n \neq 0$; then $\tilde{\eta}_n = 0$ and the list of $\mathfrak{p}$ for which this holds is finite and computable. This proves the lemma.

Now ψ has a linear factor defined over $\mathbf{C}(t)$ if and only if (19) has a solution in $\mathbf{C}(t)$ with $V = 0$. Such a solution corresponds to the point at infinity on Γ; hence there is just one such ψ. Leaving this aside, we see that there is a finite computable list of bad primes such that if any prime not in this list divides d to an odd power, none of the remaining equations (19) are soluble in $K(t)$. This means that Γ^d has only one soluble 2-covering and hence $\Gamma^d(K(t))$ is finite and of odd order.

Since we are only concerned with d in (16), or the d_i in (15), modulo squares, this means that we have only to consider a finite computable list of possible d_i; and this completes the construction of K_2 in this case.

5. The case of one 2-division point

In this and the next section we assume that α_1 is in $C(t)$ and α_2, α_3 are conjugate over $\mathbf{C}(t)$. The first part of §4 up to and including (18) remains valid; this time conjugacy implies $\lambda_2 = \lambda_3$ so that (18) gives

$$\lambda_1 = d, \quad \lambda_2 = \lambda_3 = \lambda$$

for some λ in K. By the substitution (11), where L, M are this time unknown elements of $K(t)$, we obtain

$$U = \lambda\Phi'(L, M), \quad V^2 = \lambda\Phi''(L, M), \tag{20}$$

$$\lambda^{-1} d f_1 g_1^2 = \Phi'(L, M) + \alpha_1 \Phi''(L, M) \tag{21}$$

with the same Φ', Φ'' as in (12), so that they do not depend on λ or d. Our aim is to show that if d is divisible to an odd power by a 'good' prime then only two of these 2-coverings can be soluble; these two will necessarily correspond to the base point and the 2-division point of Γ^d.

The base point and the 2-division point of Γ^d correspond to special triplets (f_1, f_2, f_3), which are the same if Γ has a 4-division point and distinct otherwise. We defer consideration of these triplets to §6, and discuss here the remaining ones.

Lemma 4. *Suppose that Φ'' is irreducible over $\mathbf{C}(t)$; then there is a finite computable set $\mathcal{S}_1$ of primes in K_3 with the following property. Let $K \supset K_3$ be an algebraic number field and $\mathfrak{p}$ a prime in K whose underlying prime in K_3 is not in $\mathcal{S}_1$; if λ in K is divisible to an odd power by $\mathfrak{p}$ then $V^2 = \lambda\Phi''$ has no non-trivial solutions in $K(t)$.*

Proof. Without loss of generality we can assume that the coefficients of Φ'', regarded as a polynomial in L, M, t, are algebraic integers. Denote reduction mod $\mathfrak{p}$ by a tilde; then as in the preamble to Lemma 3, if $V^2 = \lambda\Phi''$ is soluble in $K(t)$ then $\tilde{\Phi}''$ must have a linear factor defined over $F(t)$ where $F = \mathfrak{o}_K/\mathfrak{p}$. By an argument like that in the proof of Lemma 3, this happens only if $\mathfrak{p}$ divides a certain computable non-zero integer in K_3;

and the computation of this integer does not involve a knowledge of K. The lemma now follows at once.

Now suppose that Φ'' is irreducible over $\mathbf{C}(t)$ and that the only primes in K which divide λ to an odd power lie above primes in $\mathscr{S}_1$. There is a parametrization of $V^2=\Phi''(L, M)$ used in §2, in which V, L, M are quadratic polynomials in S and T with coefficients in $K_3(t)$; using the same formulae for L and M, we obtain a parametrization of the second equation (20) over $K(\lambda^{1/2}, t)$, and substituting this into (21) gives

$$\lambda^{-1} d f_1 g_1^2 = \psi(S, T) \tag{22}$$

where ψ is a quartic defined over $K_3(t)$ and independent of λ and d. We may assume that ψ does not have a linear factor defined over $\mathbf{C}(t)$; for if it did, we would have a solution of (20) and (21) over $\mathbf{C}(t)$ with $g_1=0$, and the triplet (f_1, f_2, f_3) would correspond to the 2-division point of Γ.

Lemma 5. *With the notation and hypotheses above, there is a finite computable set $\mathscr{S}_2$ of primes in K_3, depending only on f_1 and ψ, with the following property. If $\mathfrak{p}$ is a prime in K_3 which is not in $\mathscr{S}_2$ and is unramified for K/K_3, and if $\mathfrak{p}$ divides d to an odd power, then* (22) *is not soluble in $K(\lambda^{1/2}, t)$ for any λ in K.*

Proof. By the argument of Lemmas 3 and 4, we can find a finite computable set $\mathscr{S}_2$ such that if $\mathfrak{P}$ is a prime in $K(\lambda^{1/2})$ which divides $\lambda^{-1}d$ to an odd power, and whose underlying prime in K_3 is not in $\mathscr{S}_2$, then (22) is not soluble in $K(\lambda^{1/2}, t)$. We may further suppose that $\mathscr{S}_2$ contains the $\mathscr{S}_1$ of Lemma 4 and all the primes which divide 2. Now λ is a square in $K(\lambda^{1/2})$, so $\mathfrak{P}$ divides $\lambda^{-1}d$ to an odd power if and only if it divides d to an odd power. The only primes which can ramify in $K(\lambda^{1/2})/K$ are ones which divide λ to an odd power or which divide 2; so if $\mathfrak{p}$ satisfies the conditions of the lemma then every prime $\mathfrak{P}$ in $K(\lambda^{1/2})$ which divides $\mathfrak{p}$ divides $\lambda^{-1}d$ to an odd power. This proves the Lemma.

We now turn to the case when Φ'' factorizes over $\mathbf{C}(t)$. By increasing K_3 if necessary, we can assume it factorizes over $K_3(t)$; and by means of a linear transformation with coefficients in $K_3(t)$ we may assume that $\Phi''=LM$. Up to a common factor which is of no importance, the general solution of the second equation (20) is $L=\lambda S^2$, $M=T^2$; and now (21) takes the form

$$\lambda^{-1} d g_1^2 = \vartheta(\lambda S^2, T^2), \tag{23}$$

where ϑ is a quadratic polynomial with coefficients in $K_3(t)$ which is independent of λ and d.

Lemma 6. *Suppose that neither extreme coefficient of ϑ is a square in $\mathbf{C}(t)$, and that $\vartheta(S^2, T^2)$ has no linear factor defined over $\mathbf{C}(t)$. Then there is a finite computable set $\mathscr{S}_3$ of primes in K_3 with the following property. If $\mathfrak{p}$ is a prime which is not in $\mathscr{S}_3$ and is unramified for K/K_3, and if $\mathfrak{p}$ divides d to an odd power, then* (23) *is not soluble in $K(t)$ for any λ in K.*

Proof. Without loss of generality we can assume that $\vartheta(X, Y)$ is a polynomial in X, Y, t whose coefficients are algebraic integers. Let $\mathfrak{P}$ be a prime in K which divides λ to an odd power, and write $F = \mathfrak{o}_K/\mathfrak{P}$. If (23) has a solution, then λS^2 and T^2 cannot be divisible by the same power of $\mathfrak{P}$; assume say that T^2 is divisible by the lower power. The reduction mod $\mathfrak{P}$ of the last coefficient of ϑ must be a square in $F(t)$ multiplied by an element of F, by (23). Since this last coefficient is not a square in $C(t)$, this implies that the prime $\mathfrak{p}$ in K_3 which underlies $\mathfrak{P}$ belongs to a finite computable list $\mathscr{S}_4$ which depends on ϑ but not on K.

Suppose on the other hand that $\mathfrak{P}$ is a prime in K which divides λ to an even power but $\lambda^{-1}d$ to an odd power. If (23) has a solution, then the reduction mod $\mathfrak{P}$ of $\vartheta(S^2, T^2)$ must have a linear factor defined at worst over $F_2(t)$, where F_2 is the unique quadratic extension of $F = \mathfrak{o}_K/\mathfrak{P}$. As in Lemma 3, this implies that the prime $\mathfrak{p}$ in K_3 which underlies $\mathfrak{P}$ belongs to a finite computable set $\mathscr{S}_5$ which depends on ϑ but not on K. Now the lemma clearly holds with $\mathscr{S}_3 = \mathscr{S}_4 \cup \mathscr{S}_5$.

Note that if say the last coefficient of ϑ is a square in $C(t)$ then (23) has a solu ion in $\mathbf{C}(t)$ with $S=0$; this means that (20) and (21) have a solution in $\mathbf{C}(t)$ with $V=0$, so that the triple (f_1, f_2, f_3) is one corresponding to the base point of Γ. Similarly if $\vartheta(S^2, T^2)$ has a linear factor defined over $\mathbf{C}(t)$, then (23) has a solution in $C(t)$ with $g_1 = 0$; and the triple (f_1, f_2, f_3) is the one corresponding to the 2-division point of Γ.

We can sum up the results of this section as follows. Let $\mathscr{S}'$ be the union of all the sets $\mathscr{S}_1, \mathscr{S}_2, \mathscr{S}_3$ generated in Lemmas 4 to 6; note for future reference that $\mathscr{S}'$ contains all the primes in K_3 which divide 2. If d is divisible to an odd power by a prime which is not in $\mathscr{S}'$ and which does not ramify in K/K_3, then the only 2-coverings of Γ^d over $K(t)$ which are soluble are associated with either the base point or the 2-division point of Γ.

6. A subdivision of this case

Direct calculation shows that for the 2-covering which corresponds to the base points we have

$$f_1 = f_2 = f_3 = 1,$$

whereas for the 2-covering which corresponds to the 2-division point we have

$$f_2 = (\alpha_2 - \alpha_1), \quad f_3 = (\alpha_3 - \alpha_1), \quad f_1 = f_2 f_3.$$

We assume first that Γ has no 4-division point defined over $\mathbf{C}(t)$, so that these two coverings are inequivalent.

The equations (12) and (13) corresponding to the base point have a solution in $\mathbf{C}(t)$ with $V=0$, and by increasing K_3 we can assume this solution is in $K_3(t)$; so Φ'' factorizes over $K_3(t)$ and we can reduce to an equation of the form (23). This does not have a solution with $g_1 = 0$, because this covering does not correspond to the 2-division point; so $\vartheta(S^2, T^2)$ does not have a linear factor defined over $\mathbf{C}(t)$. By the relevant half of the proof of Lemma 6, there is a finite computable set $\mathscr{S}_4$ of primes in K_3 with the following property. If $\mathfrak{p}$ is a prime which is not in $\mathscr{S}_4$ and is unramified for K/K_3, and if a prime above $\mathfrak{p}$ divides $\lambda^{-1}d$ to an odd power, then (23) is not soluble in $K(t)$.

Similarly the equations (12) and (13) corresponding to the 2-division point have a solution in $\mathbf{C}(t)$ with $g_1=0$, and we can assume this solution is in $K_3(t)$. Thus the right-hand side of (13) splits over $K_3(t)$ and after a linear transformation on L, M with coefficients in $K_3(t)$ we can assume (21) has the form

$$\lambda^{-1}dg_1^2=LM.$$

Neglecting a common factor as usual, the general solution of this is

$$L=\lambda^{-1}dS^2, \quad M=T^2$$

which gives the equation

$$\lambda^{-1}V^2=\Phi''(\lambda^{-1}dS^2, T^2). \tag{24}$$

As in the previous paragraph, this cannot have a solution over $\mathbf{C}(t)$ with $V=0$; so $\Phi''(S^2, T^2)$ has no linear factor defined over $\mathbf{C}(t)$. Using once again the relevant half of the proof of Lemma 6, we find that there is a finite computable set $\mathscr{S}_5$ of primes in K_3 with the following property. If $\mathfrak{p}$ is a prime which is not in $\mathscr{S}_5$ and is unramified for K/K_3, and if a prime above $\mathfrak{p}$ divides λ^{-1} to an odd power, then (24) is not soluble in $K(t)$.

Write $\mathscr{S}=\mathscr{S}'\cup\mathscr{S}_4\cup\mathscr{S}_5$ and let K_5 be the maximal algebraic extension of K_3 unramified at any finite prime of K_3 outside $\mathscr{S}$. The group $\Gamma^d(K_5(t))$ is finitely generated, and is therefore defined over some $K_6(t)$, where K_6 is an algebraic number field depending on d, with $K_3\subset K_6\subset K_5$. We take $K=K_6$ and assume that d is divisible to an odd power by some prime not in $\mathscr{S}$. The only 2-coverings of Γ^d that can be soluble are those described in this paragraph. Suppose for example that (24) were soluble for $\lambda=\lambda'$ and for $\lambda=\lambda''$. By what we have just proved, any prime which divides λ'/λ'' to an odd power must be in $\mathscr{S}$, so $(\lambda'/\lambda'')^{1/2}$ is in K_5. Thus these 2-coverings correspond to the same coset in

$$\Gamma^d(K_5(t))/2\Gamma^d(K_5(t))=\Gamma^d(K_6(t))/2\Gamma^d(K_6(t))$$

and so they are already equivalent over $K_6(t)$. It follows that there are only two soluble 2-coverings of Γ^d over $K_6(t)$ and hence $\Gamma^d(K_6(t))$ is finite; a fortiori so is $\Gamma^d(K_3(t))$. Thus the only d_i which can appear in (15) are those which are not divisible to an odd power by any prime outside $\mathscr{S}$; and it follows that K_2 is computable.

We now turn to the case when Γ has 4-division points defined over $\mathbf{C}(t)$ — and indeed just two of them. We have only one triple (f_1, f_2, f_3) to consider, and in the associated equation (23) one extreme coefficient of ϑ is a square in $\mathbf{C}(t)$ and $\vartheta(S^2, T^2)$ has a linear factor defined over $\mathbf{C}(t)$. Without loss of generality, and after a further quadratic extension of K_3 if necessary, we can write the relevant equation (23) in the form

$$\lambda^{-1}dg_1^2=(\lambda S^2-\beta_1^2T^2)(\lambda S^2-\beta_2T^2) \tag{25}$$

where β_1, β_2 are in $K_3(t)$ and independent of λ and d. As usual, we can assume that β_1, β_2 are polynomials; and any common squared factor of β_1^2, β_2 can be absorbed into T. Moreover we may assume that $\beta_1^2-\beta_2$ is not constant — for if it is constant we write t^{-1} for t and absorb an appropriate power of t into T. After a possible further extension of K_3, we can assume that $\beta_1^2-\beta_2$ has at least one linear factor in $K_3[t]$, and after increasing t by a suitable constant we can take this factor to be t; thus $\beta_1^2-\beta_2$ is divisible by t and β_2 is not divisible by t^2.

Consider a solution of (25) in which S and T are coprime polynomials over K_3. If the two factors on the right have non-zero constant terms then these constants must be the same and so $\lambda^{-1}d$ is a square in K_3. If they both have zero constant term and β_1 is not divisible by t, then the shape of the first factor shows that λ is a square in K_3. Finally, suppose that both factors have zero constant term and β_1 is divisible by t; then the second factor is divisible by t but not t^2, because this is true of β_2. Hence the first factor is divisible by an odd power of t, and once again λ must be a square in K_3. Thus for given d, there are at most two values of λ modulo squares for which (25) is soluble in $K_3(t)$. Now take $K=K_3$ and choose $\mathscr{S}'$ as in the end of §5; we have proved that if d is divisible to an odd power by a prime not in $\mathscr{S}'$, then there are only two soluble 2-coverings of Γ^d over $K_3(t)$ and hence $\Gamma^d(K_3(t))$ is finite. So the only d_i which can appear in (15) are those which are not divisible to an odd power by any prime outside $\mathscr{S}'$; and once again it follows that K_2 is computable.

7. The case of three 2-division points

In principle, this case could be attacked in the same way as the previous ones, though the argument would be more complicated and the subdivision of cases more elaborate. For a specific example, this would be the right way to proceed; but to save trouble we shall use a trick to reduce to the previous case. As in the proof of Lemma 2, we divide cases according as the invariant $j(\Gamma)$ is or is not in $\mathbf{C}$.

Suppose first that $j(\Gamma)$ is in $\mathbf{C}$, so that

$$(\alpha_2-\alpha_1)/(\alpha_3-\alpha_1)$$

is constant in the notation of (2); we may assume K_3 so large that it is a square. If $(\alpha_2-\alpha_1)$ were a square in $\mathbf{C}(t)$ then Γ would be equivalent over $\mathbf{C}(t)$ to a curve defined over $\mathbf{C}$, contrary to hypothesis; so after extending K_3 and adding a constant to t if necessary, we can assume that it is divisible by an odd power of t. Now (17) gives

$$(26)\qquad dY^2V^6=\lambda_1 f_1 g_1^2\{\lambda_1 f_1 g_1^2+(\alpha_2-\alpha_1)V^2\}\{\lambda_1 f_1 g_1^2+(\alpha_3-\alpha_1)V^2\}.$$

If f_1 is not 1 or $(\alpha_2-\alpha_1)$, up to multiplication by a square in $\mathbf{C}(t)$, this is an equation to which we can apply Lemma 6 with $K=K_3$. If $f_1=1$ we consider a solution of (26) in which g_1 and V are coprime polynomials in $K_3[t]$; by considering the coefficient of the lowest power of t on the right-hand side, we find that λ_1/d is a square in K_3. Similarly if $f_1=(\alpha_2-\alpha_1)$, one of the two expressions in curly brackets must be divisible by an even power of t, and this means that $-\lambda_1$ is a square in K_3. Similar arguments apply to f_2 and f_3; moreover if each of f_1, f_2, f_3 is equal to 1 or $(\alpha_2-\alpha_1)$ then because $f_1 f_2 f_3$ is a square in $\mathbf{C}(t)$ we have only four choices instead of the apparent eight.

Summing up, we see that there is a finite computable set $\mathscr{S}''$ of primes in K_3 with the following property: if d is divisible to an odd power by a prime not in $\mathscr{S}''$ then Γ^d has at most four soluble 2-coverings. These must correspond to the base point and the three 2-division points; so $\Gamma^d(K_3(t))$ is finite. As usual we deduce that K_2 is computable.

We now suppose that $j(\Gamma)$ is not in $\mathbf{C}$. We can replace Γ by a curve isogenous to Γ without changing the probiem; so after the results of §§5 and 6 it is enough to show that there is a curve isogenous to Γ which has only one 2-division point. The modular curve which parametrizes the structure elliptic curve and a cyclic subgroup of order n on it is that conventionally called $X_0(n)$; and it is known that $X_0(32)$ has genus 1. Hence, by an argument like that in the last part of the proof of Lemma 2, there can be no cyclic subgroup of order 32 defined over $C(t)$ on Γ. Let H be a maximal cyclic subgroup of Γ whose order is a power of 2 and which is defined over $\mathbf{C}(t)$; by what has just been said, H exists. It is easy to see that Γ/H has only one 2-division point over $\mathbf{C}(t)$, so that we have reduced to the previous case.

References

[1] J. W. S. CASSELS, W. J. ELLISON and A. PFISTER, On sums of squares and on elliptic curves over function fields, *J. Number Theory*, **3** (1971), 125–149.

[2] M. R. CHRISTIE, Positive definite rational functions of two variables which are not the sum of three squares, *J. Number Theory*, **8** (1976), 224–232.

[3] B. MAZUR, Modular curves and the Eisenstein ideal, *Publ. IHES*, **47** (1978), 33–186.

ST. CATHARINE'S COLLEGE
CB2 1RL
CAMBRIDGE
ENGLAND

Studies in Pure Mathematics
To the Memory of Paul Turán

On Hadamard's gap theorem

by

P. SZÜSZ (Stony Brook)

Hadamard's classical gap theorem states the following:

Let $f(z)=\sum a_k z^k$ be a power-series with radius of convergence 1. Further, let $a_k=0$ if $k \neq k_l$, where $k_1, k_2, \ldots$ is a subsequence of the sequence of natural numbers satisfying

(1) $$k_{l+1}/k_l \geqq \vartheta > 1 .$$

Then the circle $|z|=1$ is the natural boundary of $f(z)$.

There are different improvements and generalizations of this theorem. I mention Fabry's gap theorem, replacing (1) by the weaker assumption

(2) $$k_l/l \to \infty$$

(see for instance LANDAU [1] p. 76, also TURÁN [2] p. 75) and Ostrowski's theorem on over-convergence (see TITCHMARSCH [3], p. 220).

Strangely, it seems to me to be unnoticed that the straightest approach to Hadamard's theorem gives the shortest and simplest proof and an improvement not contained even in Fabry's theorem.

In the present short note I prove the following

Theorem. *Suppose that* $f(z)=\sum a_k z^k$,

(4) $$\overline{\lim_{k\to\infty}} |a_k|^{1/k}=1 .$$

Further suppose that there is a subsequence $k_1, k_2, \ldots$ *of the sequence of natural numbers such that the relations*

(5) $$\overline{\lim_{l\to\infty}} |a_{k_l}|^{1/k_l}=1$$

and

$$a_k = 0 \quad \text{if} \quad |k - k_l| < \vartheta k_l, \quad k \neq k_l \tag{6}$$

hold, where ϑ *is a positive constant.*

Then $f(z)$ *cannot be continued beyond the circle* $|z| = 1$.

Remarks. 1) The result of the present paper is stronger than Hadamard's gap theorem, because (1) implies (6). On the other hand, (6) means that in $k_1, k_2, \ldots$ there is an infinity of Hadamard gaps, but (1) does not have to hold for all $l-s$.

2) The result of the present paper is not contained in Fabry's gap theorem; namely (6) and $k_l/l = O(1)$ are not incompatible. Of course, (2) does not imply (6) either.

Proof. We have to prove only that $z = 1$ is a singular point; to this end it suffices to show that, with some δ satisfying $0 < \delta < 1$ we have

$$\overline{\lim_{k \to \infty}} \left| \frac{f^{(k)}(\delta)}{k!} \right|^{1/k} = \frac{1}{1-\delta}$$

or expressed in terms of the $a_k - s$,

$$\overline{\lim_{k \to \infty}} \left| \sum_{l=k}^{\infty} \binom{l}{k}^{l-k} a_l \right|^{1/k} = \frac{1}{1-\delta}. \tag{8}$$

Now let k denote an integer belonging to the subsequence of integers satisfying (5) and (6).

Let δ denote any positive number for which

$$\delta < \vartheta/2 \tag{9}$$

holds, ϑ being defined by (6); further, let m be the greatest integer satisfying

$$\left[\frac{m}{1-\delta} \right] \leq k \tag{10}$$

($[y]$ is the greatest integer not exceeding y.)

Then we have

$$\begin{aligned} \frac{f^{(m)}(\delta)}{m!} &= \sum_{l=m}^{\infty} \binom{l}{m} \delta^{l-m} a_l = \binom{k}{m} \delta^{k-m} a_k + \\ &+ \sum_{l > (1+\delta)k} \binom{l}{m} \delta^{k-m} a_l; \end{aligned} \tag{11}$$

namely, because of (6) the only a_1 between m and $k(1+\delta)$ which is different from 0 is a_k.

Since k belongs to our subsequence with (5), we have

$$|a_k|^{1/k} = 1 + o(1) \quad \text{as} \quad k \to \infty. \tag{12}$$

Further we have, because of Stirling's formula

$$\binom{k}{m} \delta^{k-m} \sim \frac{1}{(1-\delta)^m} \frac{k}{\sqrt{m}} \tag{13}$$

as $m \to \infty$.

Finally we have to estimate the last sum in (11). Applying Stirling's formula again taking into account that for $l > (1+\delta)k$ we have

$$\frac{\binom{l+1}{m}}{\binom{l}{m}} \delta < 1/2$$

we obtain

$$\sum_{l > (1+\delta)k} \binom{l}{m} \delta^{l-m} a_l = O(1) \tag{14}$$

(5), (11), (13) and (14) yield

$$\frac{l^{(m)}(\delta)}{m!} \sim a_k (1-\delta)^{-m} k m^{-1/2},$$

which proves our theorem.

References

[1] Landau, L., *Darstellung und Begrundung einiger neuerer Ergebnisse der Funktionentheorie*, II. Aufl., Berlin, 1929.

[2] Turán, P., *Eine neue Methode in der Analysis und einige ihrer Anwendungen*. Akadémiai Kiadó, Budapest, 1952.

[3] Titchmarsh, E. C., *The theory of functions*, University Press, Oxford, 1952.

MATH. DEPARTMENT, SUNY AT STONY BROOK.
U.S.A.

Studies in Pure Mathematics
To the Memory of Paul Turán

A remark on Freud's tauberian theorem

by

R. C. VAUGHAN (London)

1. Introduction

FREUD [1] has shown that if the real sequence $\{a_n\}$ satisfies the tauberian condition

(1) $$na_n \leqq 1$$

and

(2) $$\sum_{n=0}^{\infty} a_n r^n = O((1-r)^{\Theta})$$

as $r \to 1-$, for some fixed Θ with $0 < \Theta < 1$, then

$$s_n = \sum_{m=0}^{n} a_m$$

satisfies

(3) $$s_n = O(1/\log n)$$

as $n \to \infty$. Here, as throughout for simplicity of exposition, we only state the most interesting special case in its most elementary form. GANELIUS [2] has given an alternative proof. An example of KOREVAAR [4] shows that the expression on the right of (3) cannot be replaced by $o(1/\log n)$.

It follows readily from this that if, in the hypothesis, (1) and (2) are replaced by $a_n \leqq 1$ and

$$\sum_{n=0}^{\infty} a_n r^n = O((1-r)^{-\Theta})$$

respectively, then

$$t_n = \sum_{m=0}^{n} \frac{a_m}{m+1}$$

satisfies

$$t_n = l + O(1/\log n)$$

as $n \to \infty$, for some fixed real number l. Consequently, by partial summation one has

$$s_n = O(n/\log n)\,. \tag{4}$$

Now consider instead the following. Suppose that

$$a_n \geqq 0 \tag{5}$$

and

$$\sum_{n=0}^{\infty} a_n r^n = (1-r)^{-1} + O((1-r)^{-\Theta}) \tag{6}$$

as $r \to 1+$, where again $0 < \Theta < 1$. Since $1 - a_n \leqq 1$ one has at once from the conclusion (4) (with a_n replaced by $1 - a_n$)

$$s_n = n + O(n/\log n) \tag{7}$$

Korevaar's example can be adapted to show that this is also essentially best possible. However, the a_n that arise therein are bounded. HAYMAN has recently enquired as to what can be said in general about the order of magnitude of the a_n on the hypothesis (5), (6). At once from (7) one has

$$a_n = O(n/\log n)\,. \tag{8}$$

Whilst not being able to completely answer this question we are able to give an example which shows that at any rate (8) cannot be radically improved.[1]

Theorem. *Suppose that $0 < \Theta < 1$. Then there is a sequence $\{a_n\}$ of positive real numbers such that*

$$\sum_{n=0}^{\infty} a_n r^n = (1-r)^{-1} + O((1-r)^{-\Theta}) \quad as \quad r \to 1- \tag{9}$$

and such that for infinitely many n

$$a_n \gg \Theta n (\log n)^{-1-1/\Theta},$$

in both expressions the implied constant being independent of Θ.

[1] Note added in proof. HALÁSZ has recently answered this question completely by giving an example in which (9) holds with $\vartheta = 0$ and $a_n = \Omega\,(n/\log n)$.

2. Proof of the theorem

It certainly suffices to prove the theorem for a suitable sequence $\{a_n\}$ of non-negative real numbers. For then we can write $a'_n = \frac{1}{2}(1+a_n)$. Let

$$\rho = \Theta/(1+2\Theta)$$

and choose k_0 so that whenever $k \geqq k_0$ we have

$$[\exp((k+1)^\rho)] > [\exp(k^\rho)].$$

For those n for which there is a $k \geqq k_0$ such that $n = [\exp(k^\rho)]$ let

$$a_n = \rho k^{\rho-1} \exp(k^\rho)$$

and otherwise let $a_n = 0$. This sequence will be seen to have the desired properties.

Let X be a large positive real number and write

(10) $$f(x) = \exp(-X^{-1}\exp(x^\rho)).$$

Then

$$\sum_{n=0}^{\infty} a_n e^{-n/x} = O(1) + \sum_{k=1}^{\infty} \rho k^{\rho-1} \exp(k^\rho)\exp(-X^{-1}[\exp(k^\rho)]) =$$

$$= O(1) - X(1+O(X^{-1})) \sum_{k=1}^{\infty} f'(k).$$

It suffices, therefore, to show that

(11) $$\sum_{k=1}^{\infty} f'(k) = -1 + O(X^{\Theta-1}).$$

By the Euler–Maclaurin sum formula (see, for instance, Hardy [3; Chapter XIII]),

$$\sum_{k=1}^{K} f'(k) = \int_1^K f'(x)dx + \frac{1}{2}f'(1) + \frac{1}{2}f'(K) +$$

$$+ \left[\sum_{r=1}^{R} \frac{(-1)^{r-1}B_r}{(2r)!} f^{(2r)}(x)\right]_1^K - \frac{1}{(2R+2)!}\int_1^K \Psi_{2R+2}(x) f^{(2R+3)}(x)\,dx$$

where

(12) $$B_r = \frac{2(2r)!}{(2\pi)^{2r}}\zeta(2r), \quad \Psi_{2r}(x) = \frac{(-1)^r 2(2r)!}{(2\pi)^{2r}} \sum_{m=1}^{\infty} \frac{1-\cos 2\pi m x}{m^{2r}}.$$

It is easily seen by induction on h that, for $h \geqq 1$,

$$f^{(h)}(x)=f(x)\sum_{i=1}^{h}(X^{-1}\exp(x^{\rho}))^{i}\sum_{j=i}^{h}c(h,i,j)\,x^{\rho j-h} \tag{13}$$

where

$$c(1,1,1)=-\rho, \quad c(1,i,j)=0 \quad \text{if} \quad i\neq 1 \quad \text{or} \quad j\neq 1, \tag{14}$$

and

$$\begin{aligned} c(h+1,i,j)&=-\rho c(h,i-1,j-1)+\\ &+\rho i c(h,i,j-1)+(\rho j-h)\,c(h,i,j). \end{aligned} \tag{15}$$

Thus $f^{(h)}(x)\to 0$ as $x\to\infty$ and $\sum_{k=1}^{\infty} f'(k)$ converges. Therefore

$$\begin{aligned} \sum_{k=1}^{\infty} f'(k)&=-f(1)+\frac{1}{2}f'(1)+\\ &+\sum_{r=1}^{R}\frac{(-1)^{r}B_r}{(2r)!}f^{(2r)}(1)-\frac{1}{(2R+2)!}\int_1^{\infty}\Psi_{2R+2}(x)f^{(2R+3)}(x)\,dx. \end{aligned} \tag{16}$$

Clearly $f(1)=\exp(-e/X)$ and $f'(1)=-\rho X^{-1}e\exp(-e/X)$, so that

$$f(1)=1+O(1/X), \quad f'(1)=O(1/X). \tag{17}$$

Let

$$C_h=\sum_{i=1}^{h}\sum_{j=1}^{h}|c(h,i,j)|. \tag{18}$$

Then, by (14) and (15),

$$\begin{aligned} C_{h+1}&\leqq\sum_{i=1}^{h+1}\sum_{j=i}^{h+1}\Big(\rho|c(h,i-1,j-1)|+\rho i|c(h,i,j-1)|+(h-\rho j)|c(h,i,j)|\Big)=\\ &=\sum_{i=1}^{h}\sum_{j=i}^{h}\Big(\rho|c(h,i,j)|+\rho i|c(h,i,j)|+(h-\rho j)|c(h,i,j)|\Big)\leqq(h+1)\,C_h. \end{aligned}$$

Hence $C_h\leqq h!$ and so, by (13) and (18),

$$|f^{(h)}(1)|\ll X^{-1}h!$$

and

$$\int_1^{\infty}|f^{(h)}(x)|dx\leqq h!\max_{\substack{i,j\\ 1\leqq i\leqq j\leqq h}}\int_1^{\infty}(X^{-1}\exp(x^{\rho}))^{i}x^{\rho j-h}f(x)\,dx. \tag{19}$$

Therefore, by (12) and Stirling's formula,

$$\sum_{r=1}^{R} \frac{(-1)^r B_r}{(2r)!} f^{(2r)}(1) \ll X^{-1} \exp(2R\log R). \tag{20}$$

Further, by (12) and (19),

$$\begin{aligned}\frac{1}{(2R+2)!}\int_1^\infty \Psi_{2R+2}(x) f^{(2R+3)}(x)\,dx &\ll \\ \ll (2\pi)^{-2R}(2R+3)! \max_{\substack{i,j\\ 1\leqq i\leqq j\leqq 2R+3}} X^{-i}\int_1^\infty \exp(ix^\rho)\, x^{\rho j-2R-3} f(x)\,dx\,.\end{aligned} \tag{21}$$

The number R will be chosen as a function of X which grows with X. Thus it can certainly be supposed to be large. For brevity write $H=2R+3$. Then it is necessary to examine the behaviour of

$$\int_1^\infty \exp(ix^\rho) x^{\rho j-H} f(x)\,dx$$

when $1\leqq i\leqq j\leqq H$. Now

$$\int_1^{(\log X)^{1/\rho}} \exp(ix^\rho)\, x^{\rho j-H} f(x)\,dx \ll \max_{x\in[1,(\log X)^{1/\rho}]} (\exp(ix^\rho)\, x^{\rho j-H+2}),$$

and the function $G(x)=\exp(ix^\rho)\, x^{\rho j-H+2}$ has only one local extremum, namely when $\rho i x^\rho = H-2-\rho j$. This is a minimum since $G(x)\to+\infty$ as $x\to 0+$. Thus

$$\int_1^{(\log X)^{1/\rho}} \exp(ix^\rho)\, x^{\rho j-H} f(x)\,dx \ll e^i + X^i(\log X)^{j-(H-2)/\rho}.$$

To estimate

$$\int_{(\log X)^{1/\rho}}^\infty \exp(ix^\rho)\, x^{\rho j-H} f(x)\,dx$$

we make the change of variables $y=X^{-1}\exp(x^\rho)$ and obtain

$$\rho^{-1}X^i \int_1^\infty y^{i-1}(\log Xy)^{j-1-(H-1)/\rho} e^{-y}\,dy$$

This is at most

$$\rho^{-1}X^i(\log X)^{j-1-(H-1)/\rho}\Gamma(i).$$

Therefore

$$\max_{\substack{i,j \\ 1\leq i\leq j\leq H}} X^{-i} \int_1^\infty \exp(ix^\rho)\, x^{\rho j-H} f(x)\, dx \ll$$

$$\ll X^{-1} + (\log X)^{H-(H-2)/\rho} + \Gamma(H)\,(\log X)^{(H-1)(1-1/\rho)}.$$

The choice

$$R = \left[\frac{1}{2}\,\Theta(\log X)/(\log\log X)\right] \tag{22}$$

gives

$$(\log X)^{1+1/\rho} \ll \Gamma(2R+3)$$

so that, by (21) and Stirling's formula,

$$\frac{1}{(2R+2)!}\int_1^\infty \Psi_{2R+2}(x) f^{(2R+3)}(x)\, dx \ll$$

$$\ll X^{-1}\exp(2R\log R) + \exp(4R(\log R) - (2R+2)(1/\rho - 1)\log\log X)\,. \tag{23}$$

By (22),

$$X^{-1}\exp(2R\log R) \leq X^{-1}\exp(\Theta\log X) = X^{\Theta-1}$$

and

$$\exp(4R(\log R) - (2R+2)(1/\rho-1)\log\log X) \leq$$

$$\leq \exp\left(2\Theta(\log X) - \Theta\left(\frac{1+2\Theta}{\Theta} - 1\right)\log X\right) = X^{\Theta-1}$$

Hence, by (16), (17), (20) and (23) we have (11) and thus the theorem.

References

[1] G. FREUD, Restglied eines Tauberschen Satzes I, *Acta Math. Acad. Sci. Hung.*, **2** (1951), 299–308.

[2] T. H. GANELIUS, *Tauberian Remainder Theorems*, Lecture Notes in Mathematics, Vol. **232**, Springer Verlag, Berlin, 1971.

[3] G. H. HARDY, *Divergent Series*, Clarendon Press, Oxford, 1949.

[4] J. KOREVAAR, An estimate of the error in tauberian theorems for power series, *Duke Math. J.*, **18** (1951), 723–734.

IMPERIAL COLLEGE,
LONDON, S. W. 7.
ENGLAND

Studies in Pure Mathematics
To the Memory of Paul Turán

Two problems of P. Turán

by

P. VÉRTESI (Budapest)

1. Summary

In this paper we deal, among others, with the convergence of the Lagrange interpolation supposing that the Hermite–Fejér interpolatory polynomials defined on the same nodes converge for any continuous functions; further we obtain estimations for the distribution of the nodes using the mentioned good property of the Hermite–Fejér interpolation (see P. TURÁN [1], Problems XVIII and XXIV).

2. Notations. Preliminary results. Some problems

2.1. Let us consider an arbitrary system of nodes

(2.1) $$-1 \leqq x_{n,n} < x_{n-1,n} < \ldots < x_{2,n} < x_{1,n} \leqq 1 \quad (n=1, 2, 3, \ldots)$$

in $[-1, 1]$, further denote

(2.2) $$\Omega_n(\mathbf{X}, x) \overset{\text{def}}{=} c(x-x_{1,n})(x-x_{2,n}) \ldots (x-x_{n,n}) \quad (c \neq 0),$$

(2.3) $$l_{k,n}(\mathbf{X}, x) \overset{\text{def}}{=} \frac{\Omega_n(\mathbf{X}, x)}{\Omega_n'(X, x_{k,n})(x-x_{k,n})} \quad (k=1, 2, \ldots, n),$$

(2.4) $$L_n(f; \mathbf{X}, x) \overset{\text{def}}{=} \sum_{k=1}^{n} f(x_{k,n}) l_{k,n}(X, x) \quad (n=1, 2, 3, \ldots).$$

(2.5) $$v_{k,n}(\mathbf{X}, x) \overset{\text{def}}{=} 1 - \frac{\Omega''(\mathbf{X}, x_{k,n})}{\Omega'(\mathbf{X}, x_{k,n})}(x-x_{k,n}) \quad (k=1, 2, \ldots, n),$$

(2.6) $$h_{k,n}(\mathbf{X}, x) \overset{\text{def}}{=} v_{k,n}(\mathbf{X}, x) l_{k,n}^2(\mathbf{X}, x) \quad (k=1, 2, \ldots, n),$$

(2.7) $$\mathfrak{H}_{k,n}(\mathbf{X}, x) \overset{\text{def}}{=} (x-x_{k,n}) l_{k,n}^2(\mathbf{X}, x) \quad (k=1, 2, \ldots, n),$$

(2.8) $$H_n(f;\mathbf{X},x) \overset{\text{def}}{=} \sum_{k=1}^{n} f(x_{k,n})\, h_{k,n}(\mathbf{X},x) \quad (n=1,2,3,\dots),$$

(2.9) $$H_n^*(f;\mathbf{X},x) \overset{\text{def}}{=} H_n(f;\mathbf{X},x)+\sum_{k=1}^{n} f'(x_{k,n})\, \mathfrak{H}_{k,n}(\mathbf{X},x) \quad (n=1,2,3,\dots),$$

where $\mathbf{X}$ is the matrix $\{x_{k,n}\}_{k=1}^{n}$ $(n=1, 2, 3, \dots)$, $f\in C$ $(=f(x)$ is continuous on $[-1,1])$, moreover in (2.9) we suppose that $f'\in C$, too.

2.2. As G. FABER [2] proved, for any fixed system of nodes $\mathbf{X}$, there exists a continuous function for which the Lagrange parabolas $L_n(f;\mathbf{X},x)$ do not converge uniformly to the function considered.

2.3. For the Hermite–Fejér step-parabolas $H_n(f;X,x)$, the situation is more favourable. Here, contrary the Faber's theorem, as L. FEJÉR [3] proved, for the Chebyshev matrix $\mathbf{T}=\left\{\cos\frac{2k-1}{2n}\pi\right\}$, $H_n(f;\mathbf{T},x)$ uniformly tends to $f(x)$ on $[-1,1]$, whenever $f\in C$. Generally, as G. GRÜNWALD [4], showed, if $\mathbf{X}$ is ρ-normal matrix, which means

(2.10) $$v_{k,n}(\mathbf{X},x)\geqq\rho>0 \quad (k=1,2,\dots,n;\, n=1,2,\dots;\, x\in[-1,1])$$

then for $f\in C$

(2.11) $$\lim_{n\to\infty}\|H_n(f;\mathbf{X},x)-f(x)\|=0.$$

(Here $\|g\|=\max_{-1\leqq x\leqq 1}|g(x)|$ if $g\in C$). As it is well known the roots of the Jacobi polynomials $P_n^{(\alpha,\beta)}(x)$ define a $\rho=\min(-\alpha,-\beta)$-normal system is $-1<\alpha,\ \beta<0$; further $\Omega_n(\mathbf{T};x)=P_n^{(-1/2,-1/2)}(x)$.

2.4. It is natural to ask whether there is any connection between the convergence-behaviours of the Lagrange- and Hermite–Fejér interpolations. More exactly:

a) If for a matrix $\mathbf{X}$ and a class of functions $A\subset C$

(2.12) $$\lim_{n\to\infty}\|L_n(f;\mathbf{X},x)-f(x)\|=0 \quad \text{if} \quad f\in A,$$

then determine the class $B\subset C$ such that for any $f\in B$, the relation (2.11) should hold (see P. TURÁN [1], Problem XXIII).

In my paper [9] I obtained a negative answer, which essentially says that generally B must be a trivial function-class (e.g., $f_1(x)\notin B$ where $f_1(x)=x$).

b) If for a matrix $\mathbf{X}$, (2.11) holds for each $f\in C$, determine the class $A\subset C$ such that (2.12) should hold (see P. TURÁN [1], Problem XXIV; actually at the mentioned place $A=\{f;\ f'\in C\}$ was the original hint).

To this problem, one can find two positive answers. In his paper [5] L. FEJÉR proved, that if $A = Lip\gamma$ with $\gamma > \frac{1}{2}$, then (2.12) holds whenever (2.10) is true for $\mathbf{X}$ (with a certain $\rho > 0$).

Later G. GRÜNWALD obtained that if $A = Lip\gamma$ with $\gamma > \frac{1-\rho}{2}$ then (2.12) holds for any closed subinterval of $(-1, 1)$ whenever (2.10) is true.

Now we intend to investigate the problem b) dropping the ρ-normality (Parts 3.1–3.4) then by these considerations we deal with another question raised by P. TURÁN (Part 3.5).

3. Results

3.1. Introducing the notations

$$\mu_n(\mathbf{X}) \overset{\text{def}}{=} \left\| \sum_{k=1}^{n} |h_{k,n}(\mathbf{X}, x)| \right\|, \tag{3.1}$$

$$\nu_n(\mathbf{X}) \overset{\text{def}}{=} \left\| \sum_{k=1}^{n} |\mathfrak{H}_{k,n}(\mathbf{X}, x)| \right\|, \tag{3.2}$$

we state, sometimes omitting the superfluous notations

Theorem 3.1. *For any matrix* $\mathbf{X}$ *we have*

$$\nu_n = O(n^3 \mu_n). \tag{3.3}$$

Here and later the sign "O" may depend on $\mathbf{X}$.

3.2. By Theorem 3.3. it is easy to obtain the following useful estimation. If

$$\lambda_n(\mathbf{X}) \overset{\text{def}}{=} \left\| \sum_{k=1}^{n} | l_{k,n}(\mathbf{X}, x)| \right\|, \tag{3.4}$$

we have

Theorem 3.2. *For arbitrary fixed matrix* $\mathbf{X}$

$$\lambda_n = O(n^{5/2} \sqrt{\ln n}\, \mu_n). \tag{3.5}$$

3.3. For certain matrix $\mathbf{X}$ we can prove better estimation. Namely one can get

Theorem 3.3. *If* $\mu_n = O(1)$, *the relation*

$$\lambda_n = O(n^{5/2}) \tag{3.6}$$

holds.

3.4. By Theorems 3.2 and 3.3 we can easily get

Corollary 3.4. *If* $A=\{f;\, E_n(f)=o(n^{-5/2}(\ln n)^{-1/2}\mu_n^{-1})$, *then* (2.12) *holds; supposing* $\mu_n=O(1)$, *A can be chosen as* $\{f;\, E_n(f)=o(n^{-5/2})\}$.

Here $E_n(f)$ is the best uniform approximation of $f(x)\in C$ in $[-1,1]$ by polynomials of degree $\leq n$. (The proof is simple: we use $f(x)-L_n(f;\,x)=f(x)-P_{n-1}(f;\,x)+ +L_n(P_{n-1};x)-L_n(f;x)$ where $P_n(f;x)$ is the best approximating polynomial of degree $\leq n$ to $f(x)$.)

Considering that if (2.11) holds whenever $f\in C$, then $\mu_n=O(1)$, by Corollary 3.4 we have got a possible answer to Problem b) (see 2.4.).

3.5. Let us denote by $N_n(\alpha_n,\beta_n)$ the number of $\vartheta_{k,n}$ in $[\alpha_n,\beta_n]$ where $x_{k,n}=\cos\vartheta_{kn}$ and $0\leq\alpha_n<\beta_n\leq\pi$.

c) One can ask how the differences

$$N_n(\alpha_n,\beta_n)-\frac{\beta_n-\alpha_n}{\pi}n\quad(n=1,2,\ldots)$$

are be estimated knowing only $\mu_n(\mathbf{X})$ (see P. TURÁN [1], Problem XVIIII).

Now, using Theorems 3.2 and 3.3 and the rather deep theorem of P. ERDŐS [8] which states that if

$$|l_{k,n}(X,x)|=O[f(n)]\quad(k=1,2,\ldots,n)\tag{3.7}$$

then for any sequence of intervals $[\alpha_n,\beta_n]$

$$N_n(\alpha_n,\beta_n)=\frac{\beta_n-\alpha_n}{\pi}n+O[\ln n\cdot\ln(nf(n))]\,,\tag{3.8}$$

we can conclude

Theorem 3.4. *We have for any fixed X*

$$N_n(\alpha_n,\beta_n)=\frac{\beta_n-\alpha_n}{\pi}n+O(\ln n\cdot\ln(n\mu_n))\,.\tag{3.9}$$

Indeed, by (3.5), $\lambda_n=O(n^3\mu_n)$, from where $|l_k(x)|=O(n^3\mu_n)$, i.e. by (3.8) we get (3.9).

It is worth to formulate the following special case

Corollary 3.5. *If* (2.11) *holds for each* $f\in C$ *then*

$$N_n(\alpha_n,\beta_n)=\frac{\beta_n-\alpha_n}{\pi}n+O(\ln^2 n)\,.\tag{3.10}$$

4. Proofs

4.1. Proof of Theorem 3.1. The proof is indirect. Supposing that (3.3) is not true one can choose a sequence $\varphi_n \nearrow \infty$ such that for suitable $z_n \in [-1, 1]$

$$v_n = \sum_{k=1}^{n} |z_n - x_k| l_k^2(z_n) \geqq 2n^3 \varphi_n \mu_n \quad (n = n_1, n_2, \ldots). \tag{4.1}$$

By (4.1), $\sum_{k=1}^{k} l_k^2(z_n) \geqq n^3 \varphi_n \mu_n$ $(n = n_1, n_2, \ldots)$, i.e. for certain $s = s(n)$ we obtain

$$l_s^2(z_n) \geqq n^2 \varphi_n \mu_n \quad (n = n_1, n_2, \ldots). \tag{4.2}$$

4.1.1. Now, applying a theorem of M. Riesz [6], which states that if $p_m(x)$ is a polynomial of degree m attaining its absolute maximum in $[-1, 1]$ at the point $u_0 = \cos \delta_0$, then $|\eta_k - \delta_0| \geqq \frac{\pi}{2m}$ $(k = 1, 2, \ldots, m)$, where $y_k = \cos \eta_k$ $(k = 1, 2, \ldots, m)$, denote the roots of $p_m(x)$, we obtain by (4.2) that using the $\tilde{w}_n$, for which $\|l_s^2\| = l_s^2(\tilde{w}_n)$, the relations

$$l_s^2(\tilde{w}_n) \geqq n^2 \varphi_n \mu_n \quad \text{and} \quad \min_{k \neq s} |\tilde{w}_n - x_k| \geqq \frac{\pi}{4n^2} \quad (n = n_1, n_2, \ldots) \tag{4.3}$$

hold.

4.1.2. If $|\tilde{w}_n - x_s| \geqq \frac{1}{8n^2}$, then let $w_n = \tilde{w}_n$. If not, consider $w_n = \tilde{w}_n + \frac{1}{8n^2}$ (if $w_n \notin [-1, 1]$ we use $w_n = \tilde{w}_n - \frac{1}{8n^2}$). Then by Markov's inequality

$$\begin{aligned} l_s^2(w_n) &= l_s^2(\tilde{w}_n + \int_{\tilde{w}_n}^{w_n} [l_s^2(t)]' \, dt \geqq \|l_s^2\| - \frac{4(n-1)^2 \|l_s^2\|}{8n^2} > \\ &> \frac{\|l_s^2\|}{2} \geqq \frac{n^2 \varphi_n \mu_n}{2} \quad (n = n_1, n_2, \ldots), \end{aligned} \tag{4.4}$$

further by construction

$$\min_{1 \leqq k \leqq n} |w_n - x_k| \geqq \frac{1}{8n^2} \quad (n = n_1, n_2, \ldots). \tag{4.5}$$

4.1.3. Using that $|v_s(w_n)l_s^2(w_n)| \leqq \mu_n$ we get by (4.4)

$$|v_s(w_n)| < \frac{2}{n^2 \varphi_n} \quad (n = n_1, n_2, \ldots). \tag{4.6}$$

Further $v_s(x)$ is linear with $v_s(x_s) = 1$. So if we consider the point t_n such that $|t_n - w_n| = \dfrac{1}{n^2 \sqrt{\varphi_n}}$ and $t_n \in [-1, 1]$, we get

$$|v_s(t_n)| \geqq \frac{1}{4n^2 \sqrt{\varphi_n}} \quad (n = n_1, n_2, \ldots; n \geqq n_0). \tag{4.7}$$

Using the argument of 4.1.2 it is easy to gain

$$l_s^2(t_n) > \frac{n^2 \varphi_n \mu_n}{4} \quad (n = n_1, n_2, \ldots; n \geqq n_0), \tag{4.8}$$

i.e.

$$|h_s(t_n)| = |v_s(t_n)| l_s^2(t_n) > \frac{\sqrt{\varphi_n}}{16} \mu_n \quad (n = n_1, n_2, \ldots; n \geqq n_0),$$

which is a contradiction.

4.2. Proof of Theorem 3.2. Let $\min\limits_{1 \leqq k \leqq n} |x - x_k| = |x - x_{j(n)}|$. Then we have

$$\sum_{k \neq j} |l_k(x)| \leqq \sqrt{\sum_{k \neq j} \frac{1}{|x - x_k|} \sum_{k \neq j} |x - x_k| \, l_k^2(x)}. \tag{4.9}$$

4.2.1. To estimate $\sum\limits_{k \neq j} |x - x_k|^{-1}$, we remark

$$\sum_{k \neq j} \frac{1}{|x - x_k|} = O(1) \sum_{k=1}^{n} \frac{1}{k d_n} = O(\ln n) \frac{1}{x_r - x_{r+1}} =$$

(4.10)

$$= O(\ln n) \frac{h_r(x_r) - h_r(x_{r+1})}{x_r - x_{r+1}} = O(\ln n) \|h_r'(\xi)\| = O(\ln n \cdot n^2 \mu_n), \text{[1]}$$

[1] (4.10) is due to A. KROÓ. I proved $O(n^3 \mu)$.

where $d_n = \min_{1 \leq t \leq n-1} (x_t - x_{t+1}) = x_r - x_{r+1}$. I.e., by (4.9), (4.10) and (3.3)

$$\sum_{k \neq j} |l_k(x)| = O(n^{5/2} \sqrt{\ln n}\, \mu_n)\,. \tag{4.11}$$

4.2.2. If $k=j$, first let

a) $$|x - x_j| > \frac{c}{\mu_n n^2 \ln n}\,.$$

By $|\eta_j(x)| = |x - x_j| l_j^2(x) = O(n^3 \mu_n)$ (see (3.3)), we get $l_j^2(x) = O(\mu_n^2 n^5 \ln n)$ from where

$$|l_j(x)| = O(n^{5/2} \sqrt{\ln n}\, \mu_n)\,. \tag{4.12}$$

On the other hand, if

b) $$|x - x_j| \leq \frac{c}{\mu_n n^2 \ln n}$$

we get by (4.10)

$$\left| \frac{\Omega''(x_j)}{\Omega'(x_j)} (x - x_j) \right| = \left| \left(\sum_{k \neq j} \frac{1}{x_j - x_k} \right) (x - x_j) \right| =$$

$$= O(\mu_n n^2 \ln n) \frac{c}{\mu_n n^2 \ln n} \leq \frac{1}{2}\,,$$

if $c>0$ is small enough. I.e., by (2.5) $v_j(x) \geq \frac{1}{2}$, which means

$$|l_j(x)| = O(\sqrt{\mu_n}) \tag{4.13}$$

because of $v_j(x)\, l_j^2(x) = O(\mu_n)$. These give (3.5).

4.3. Proof of Theorem 3.3. We use Part **4.2**, sharpening **4.2.1.** If $\mu_n = O(1)$ then by a theorem of P. Erdős and P. Turán

$$\vartheta_{k+1} - \vartheta_k \sim \frac{1}{n} \quad (k = 1, 2, \ldots, n-1) \tag{4.14}$$

where $x_k = \cos \vartheta_k$ (see [7], Part IV).

Now, using this theorem, we have, supposing $1<j<n$, as follows

$$\sum_{k\neq j}\frac{1}{|x-x_k|}\sim\sum_{k\neq j}\frac{1}{\sin\frac{\vartheta_j+\vartheta_k}{2}\sin\frac{|\vartheta_j-\vartheta_k|}{2}}\sim n^2\sum_{k\neq j}\frac{1}{(j+k)|j-k|}\sim$$

$$\sim n^2\left[\sum_{k<\frac{j}{2}}+\sum_{\frac{j}{2}\leq k\leq 2j}+\sum_{k\geq 2j}\right]\sim n^2.$$

Using similar arguments for $j=1$ (or $j=n$) we get (3.6) as at **4.2.**, if at **4.2.2.** a) we suppose $|x-x_j|>c\cdot n^{-2}$.

References

[1] P. TURÁN, On some open problems of approximation theory *J. Appr. Th.*, **29** (1980), 23–85.

[2] G. FABER, Über die interpolatorische Darstellung stetiger Funktionen, *Jahr. D. Math. Verein.*, **23** (1914), 194–210.

[3] L. FEJÉR, Die Abschätzungen eines Polynomes, *Math. Zeitschrift*, **32** (1930), 426–457.

[4] G. GRÜNWALD, On the theory of interpolation, *Acta Math.*, **75** (1942), 219–245.

[5] L. FEJÉR, Lagrangesche Interpolationen und die zugehörigen konjugierten Punkte, *Math. Ann.*, **106** (1932), 1–55.

[6] M. RIESZ, Eine trigonometrische Interpolationsform und einige Ungleichungen für Polynome, *Jahr. D. Math. Verein.*, **23** (1914), 354–368.

[7] P. ERDŐS–P. TURÁN, On interpolation. II, *Ann. of Math.*, **39** (1938), 703–724.

[8] P. ERDŐS, On the uniform distribution of the roots of certain polynomials, *Ann. of Math.*, **43** (1942), 59–64.

[9] P. VÉRTESI, Contribution to the theory of interpolation, *Acta Math. Acad. Sci. Hungar.*, **29** (1977), 165–176.

MATHEMATICAL INSTITUTE OF THE
HUNGARIAN ACADEMY OF SCIENCES
H-1053 BUDAPEST
REÁLTANODA U. 13–15.
HUNGARY

Studies in Pure Mathematics
à la mémoire de Paul Turán

Un lemme de Schwarz pour des intersections d'hyperplans

par

M. WALDSCHMIDT (Paris)

Résumé

Soit S un sous — ensemble fini de $\mathbf{C}^n$ qui est une intersection complète d'hyperplans. On donne, par une méthode élémentaire, une estimation du type "lemme de Schwarz" pour des fonctions analytiques s'annulant sur S.

1. Introduction

Soit S un sous-ensemble fini d'un polydisque D_r de $\mathbf{C}^n$:

$$D_r = \{(z_1, \ldots, z_n) \in \mathbf{C}^n; \quad |z_j| \leqq r, \quad 1 \leqq j \leqq n\}.$$

Soit $R > r$. L'algèbre $\mathscr{A}_R$ des fonctions f continues sur D_R et analytiques à l'intérieur de D_R est munie de la norme

$$|f|_R = \sup_{z \in D_R} |f(z)|.$$

On considère l'idéal $\mathscr{I}_R(S)$ des fonctions $f \in \mathscr{A}_R$ qui s'annulent sur S. Démontrer un "lemme de Schwarz" consiste à améliorer, pour les éléments de $\mathscr{I}_R(S)$, l'inégalité fournie par le principe du maximum:

$$|f|_r \leqq |f|_R.$$

Un exposé de ce problème se trouve dans [W] pour le cas complexe, et dans [R] pour le cas ultramétrique. On trouvera dans [W] des motivations arithmétiques pour cette étude.

Le cas $n = 1$ est facile: pour $f \in \mathscr{I}_R(S)$, on a

$$|f|_r \leqq |f|_R (3r/R)^{\mathrm{Card}\, S}. \tag{1}$$

Il y a trois manières de démontrer cette inégalité. La plus simple consiste à écrire

$$f(z) = f_1(z) \prod_{s \in S} (z - s),$$

où $f_1 \in \mathscr{A}_R$, et à utiliser le principe du maximum pour la fonction f_1:

$$|f_1|_r \leqq |f_1|_R,$$

avec les inégalités

$$|f|_r \leqq |f_1|_r (2r)^{\mathrm{Card}\, S}$$

et

$$|f_1|_R \leqq |f|_R (R-r)^{-\mathrm{Card}\, S}.$$

La deuxième démonstration repose sur la formule intégrale de Cauchy, et la troisième sur la formule de Jensen.

Les formules intégrales ont été itérées à $\mathbf{C}^n$ par TH. SCHNEIDER (1941), puis utilisées par S. LANG (1965) et A. BAKER (1967) pour traiter le cas de produits $S_1 \times \ldots \times S_n \subset \mathbf{C}^n$. Grâce à ces formules, on peut démontrer un lemme de Schwarz pour les produits cartésiens (cf. [W] lemme 1.2, et [R] théorème 3.1). D'autre part E. BOMBIERI et S. LANG (1970) ont montré comment la formule de Jensen pour les fonctions sous — harmoniques de plusieurs variables permet de donner un lemme de Schwarz dans lequel le rôle du nombre de zéros de f dans le disque $|z| \leqq r$ (quand $n=1$) est joué par la masse moyenne $\nu(f, r)$ des zéros de f dans la boule euclidienne de rayon r (mesure de Lelong). De plus, en utilisant les estimations L^2 de L. HÖRMANDER, E. BOMBIERI et H. SKODA, on peut montrer que l'exposant Card S dans (1) peut être remplacé essentiellement par $\frac{1}{n}\omega(S)$ quand $n \geqq 1$, où $\omega(S)$ est le plus petit degré des hypersurfaces algébriques contenant S. Il est facile de voir que cet exposant ne peut pas être supérieur à $\omega(S)$.

Notre but est de généraliser à plusieurs variables la première des démonstrations de (1) que nous venons de donner. Pour cela, on cherche une base $P_1, \ldots, P_h$ de l'idéal $\mathscr{I}_R(S)$, telle que toute $f \in \mathscr{I}_R(S)$ admette une décomposition

$$f = f_1 P_1 + \ldots + f_h P_h,$$

avec $f_1, \ldots, f_h \in \mathscr{A}_R$, et pour laquelle, c'est là le point essentiel, on ait de bonne majorations des $|f_j|_R$ en fonction de $|f|_R$.

Nous nous restreignons ici à un cas particulier pour lequel une méthode élémentaire suffit. Il s'agit du cas où il existe une base $P_1, \ldots, P_n$ de $\mathscr{I}_R(S)$, où chaque P_j est un produit de p_j polynômes de degré 1, et où Card $S = p_1 \ldots p_n$. Cette situation généralise celle d'un produit cartésien $S_1 \times \ldots \times S_n$, qui correspond à

$$(2) \qquad P_j(z_1, \ldots, z_n) = \prod_{s \in S_j} (z_j - s), \quad (1 \leqq j \leqq n).$$

Nous indiquerons ensuite comment traiter des cas plus généraux par la même méthode. De plus, on pourrait aussi introduire des multiplicités. Enfin, la démonstration vaut aussi bien dans le cas complexe que dans le cas ultramétrique; elle peut même être notablement simplifiée dans ce deuxième cas, aussi nous contenterons nous d'exposer la situation archimédienne.

2. Enoncés des résultats

Pour $z=(z_1, \ldots, z_n) \in \mathbf{C}^n$, on note $|z| = \max_{1 \leq j \leq n} |z_j|$.

Théorème 1. *Pour $1 \leqq j \leqq n$, soit $P_j \in \mathbf{C}[z_1, \ldots, z_n]$ un polynôme de degré total p_j, qui est produit de polynômes de degré 1. On suppose que l'ensemble*

$$S = \{s \in \mathbf{C}^n;\, P_1(s) = \ldots = P_n(s) = 0\}$$

a exactement $p_1 \ldots p_n$ éléments. Soit

$$r \geqq \max\{|s|;\, s \in S\}.$$

Il existe une constante $c_1 > 0$, ne dépendant que de $P_1, \ldots, P_n$, ayant la propriété suivante. Soit $R \geqq \max(2r, 1)$, et soit $f \in \mathscr{I}_R(S)$. Il existe des éléments $f_1, \ldots, f_n$ de $\mathscr{A}_R$ tels que

$$f = f_1 P_1 + \ldots + f_n P_n,$$

et

$$|f_j|_R \leqq c_1 R^{-p_j} |f|_R, \quad (1 \leqq j \leqq n).$$

Corollaire 2. *Sous les hypothèses du théorème* 1, *on a*

$$|f|_r \leqq c_2 (r/R)^{\omega(S)} |f|_R,$$

avec $\omega(S) = \min_{1 \leqq j \leqq n} p_j$, et c_2 ne dépend que de $P_1, \ldots, P_n$.

On peut multiplier chaque polynôme P_j par une constante non nulle sans modifier l'ensemble S. On peut donc choisir $P_1, \ldots, P_n$ de telle manière que $c_1 = 1$. Inversement, $P_1, \ldots, P_n$ étant donnés, la démonstration fournit une valeur explicite de c_1 et c_2. Par exemple, dans le cas d'un produit cartésien avec

$$P_j(z) = \prod_{s \in S_j} (z_j - s), \tag{2}$$

on trouve

(3) $$c_1 \leqq 12^{p_1+\cdots+p_n},$$

avec $p_j = \text{Card}\, S_j$, et

$$c_2 \leqq 24^{n\omega(S)},$$

avec $\omega(S) = \min_{1 \leqq j \leqq n} \text{Card}\, S_j$. Ces estimations ne sont pas optimales, mais elles sont suffisantes pour les applications de [W].

Bien qu'elle soit très simple, la méthode de démonstration du théorème 1 permet de considérer des situations plus générales que celle d'une intersection complète d'hyperplans. A titre d'exemple, nous démontrons le résultat suivant.

Théorème 3. *Soient P_1, $P_2 \in \mathbf{C}[z_1, z_2]$ deux polynômes de degré total p_1, p_2 respectivement, dont l'ensemble S des zéros communs a exactement $p_1 p_2$ éléments. On suppose que le polynôme P_2 est produit de polynômes de degré 1 ou 2. Il existe une constante $c_3 > 0$, ne dépendant que de P_1 et P_2, ayant la propriété suivante. Soit $R \geqq \max(2r, 1)$ et soit $f \in \mathscr{I}_R(S)$. Il existe des éléments $f_1, \ldots, f_n$ de $\mathscr{A}_R$ tels que*

$$f = f_1 P_1 + f_2 P_2$$

et

$$|f_j|_R \leqq c_3 R^{-p_j} |f|_R, \quad (j = 1, 2).$$

Nous verrons que si la fonction f du théorème 1 (resp. du théorème 3) est entière, alors les fonctions f_j sont entières, et les estimations de $|f_j|_R$ sont valables pour tout $R \geqq \max(2r, 1)$. En particulier si f est un polynôme, alors f_j est un polynôme de degré au plus $\deg f - p_j$, $(1 \leqq j \leqq n)$.

3. Démonstration du Théorème 1

Pour $1 \leqq j \leqq n$, notons

$$P_j = \prod_{h=1}^{p_j} P_{j,h}$$

où $P_{j,h}$ est un polynôme de degré 1 $(1 \leqq j \leqq n,\ 1 \leqq h \leqq p_j)$. Une telle décomposition n'est unique qu'à multiplication près par des constantes non nulles, et le nombre c_1 dépendra de notre choix. Soient $h_1, \ldots, h_n$ des entiers, $1 \leqq h_j \leqq p_j$, $(1 \leqq j \leqq n)$. Soit $s = (s_1, \ldots, s_n)$, dépendant de $h_1, \ldots, h_n$, le zéro commun à $P_{1,h_1}, \ldots, P_{n,h_n}$. On écrit

$$P_{j,h_j}(z_1, \ldots, z_n) = \sum_{\nu=1}^{n} a_{j,\nu,h_1,\ldots,h_n}(z_\nu - s_\nu).$$

Le déterminant

$$\Delta(h_1, \ldots, h_n) = \det [a_{j,\nu,h_1,\ldots,h_n}] \quad (1 \leqq j, \nu \leqq n)$$

n'est pas nul; soit $\Delta_{j,\nu}(h_1, \ldots, h_n)$ le cofacteur de $a_{j,\nu,h_1,\ldots,h_n}$, et soit c_4 tel que

$$c_4 \geqq \max_{j,h_1,\ldots,h_n} \sum_{\nu=1}^{n} \left| \frac{\Delta_{j,\nu}(h_1, \ldots, h_n)}{\Delta(h_1, \ldots, h_n)} \right| .$$

Il sera commode de choisir $c_4 \geqq 1/4$. Enfin, soit c_5 tel que

$$|P_{j,h}|_R \leqq c_5 R \quad \text{pour tout} \quad R \geqq r .$$

On va démontrer le théorème 1 avec

(4) $$c_1 \leqq (4c_4(1+c_5))^{p_1+\cdots+p_n-n} \cdot 4c_4 .$$

Lemme 4. *Supposons* $p_1 = \ldots = p_n = 1$. *Alors le théorème* 1 *est vrai avec*

$$c_1 \leqq 4c_4 .$$

Démonstration du lemme 4. Soit $s = (s_1, \ldots, s_n)$ l'élément de S. Soit $f \in \mathscr{A}_R$. On définit des éléments $\varphi_1, \ldots, \varphi_n$ de $\mathscr{A}_R$ par

$$f(s_1, \ldots, s_{\nu-1}, z_\nu, z_{\nu+1}, \ldots, z_n) - f(s_1, \ldots, s_{\nu-1}, s_\nu, z_{\nu+1}, \ldots, z_n) =$$
$$= (z_\nu - s_\nu)\varphi_\nu(z_\nu, z_{\nu+1}, \ldots, z_n), \quad (1 \leqq \nu \leqq n) .$$

On en déduit, en considérant le bord distingué du polydisque D_R,

$$(R-r)|\varphi_\nu|_R \leqq 2|f|_R, \quad (1 \leqq \nu \leqq n) ,$$

et

$$f(z_1, \ldots, z_n) - f(s_1, \ldots, s_n) = \sum_{\nu=1}^{n} (z_\nu - s_\nu)\varphi_\nu(z_\nu, \ldots, z_n) .$$

Supposons maintenant $f(s_1, \ldots, s_n) = 0$. Des relations

$$z_\nu - s_\nu = \sum_{j=1}^{n} \frac{\Delta_{j,\nu}}{\Delta} P_j(z), \quad (1 \leqq \nu \leqq n) ,$$

(où Δ et $\Delta_{j,\nu}$ correspondent à $(h_1, \ldots, h_n) = (1, \ldots, 1)$), on déduit

$$f(z) = \sum_{j=1}^{n} f_j(z) P_j(z) ,$$

avec

$$f_j(z)=\sum_{\nu=1}^{n}\frac{\Delta_{j,\nu}}{\Delta}\varphi_\nu(z_\nu,\ldots,z_n),\quad(1\leqq j\leqq n).$$

D'où

$$(R-r)|f_j|_R\leqq 2c_4|f|_R,$$

ce qui démontre le lemme 4.

Nous démontrons maintenant le théorème 1 *par récurrence sur* $p_1+\ldots+p_n$. Comme le résultat est vrai (par le lemme 4) pour $p_1+\ldots+p_n=n$, on peut supposer que l'un des p_j, disons p_1, est supérieur ou égal à 2. On note

$$P_1'=P_{1,1},\ P_1''=\prod_{2\leqq h\leqq p_1}P_{1,h},$$

et

$$S=S'\bigcup S'',$$

où S' est l'ensemble des zéros communs à $P_1', P_2, \ldots, P_n$, et S'' est l'ensemble des zéros communs à $P_1'', P_2, \ldots, P_n$.

Si $f\in\mathscr{I}_R(S')$, on a grâce à l'hypothèse de récurrence,

$$f=\varphi_1P_1'+\varphi_2P_2+\ldots+\varphi_nP_n,$$

avec

$$|\varphi_1|_RR\leqq c'|f|_R,$$

$$|\varphi_j|_RR^{p_j}\leqq c'|f|_R,\quad(2\leqq j\leqq n),$$

et

$$c'\leqq(4c_4(1+c_5))^{1+p_2+\ldots+p_n-n}\cdot 4c_4.$$

Si, de plus, $f\in\mathscr{I}_R(S'')$, alors comme S' et S'' sont disjoints, on a $\varphi_1\in\mathscr{I}_R(S'')$, et l'hypothèse de récurrence donne

$$\varphi_1=\psi_1P_1''+\psi_2P_2+\ldots+\psi_nP_n,$$

avec

$$|\psi_1|_RR^{p_1-1}\leqq c''|\varphi_1|_R,$$

$$|\psi_j|_RR^{p_j}\leqq c''|\varphi_1|_R,\quad(2\leqq j\leqq n),$$

et

$$c'' \leqq (4c_4(1+c_5))^{p_1-1+p_2+\dots+p_n-n} \cdot 4c_4 .$$

On en déduit

$$f = f_1 P_1 + \dots + f_n P_n ,$$

avec $f_1 = \psi_1$ et

$$f_j = \varphi_j + P'_1 \psi_j , \quad (2 \leqq j \leqq n) .$$

Par conséquent

$$|f_1|_R R^{p_1} \leqq c'c''|f|_R ,$$

et

$$|f_j|_R R^{p_j} \leqq (c' + c_5 c'c'')|f|_R .$$

On en déduit le résultat annoncé, avec la majoration (4).

Dans le cas d'un produit cartésien avec les polynômes (2), on peut choisir

$$P_{j,h}(z) = z_j - s_{j,h} , \quad (1 \leqq j \leqq n, 1 \leqq h \leqq p_j) ,$$

où

$$S_j = \{s_{j,1}, \dots, s_{j,p_j}\}, \quad (1 \leqq j \leqq n) ,$$

on a alors $c_4 = 1$, $c_5 = 2$, donc

(3) $$c_1 \leqq 12^{p_1 + \dots + p_n} .$$

Cette estimation peut évidemment être améliorée, par exemple en utilisant les formules intégrales de Baker [W].

4. Démonstration du corollaire 2

Soit $p = \min_{1 \leqq j \leqq n} p_j$. Quitte à remplacer chaque P_j par $\prod_{h=1}^{p} P_{j,h}$, on peut supposer $p_1 = \dots = p_n = p$. Du théorème 1 on déduit

$$|f|_r \leqq \sum_{j=1}^{n} |P_j|_r |f_j|_r \leqq \sum_{j=1}^{n} |P_j|_r |f_j|_R \leqq n c_1 c_5^p (r/R)^p |f|_R .$$

d'où

$$c_2 \leqq n c_1 c_5^p .$$

En choisissant pour f un polynôme et en faisant tendre R vers l'infini, on en déduit $p \leqq \deg f$, d'où $\omega(S) = p$.

5. Démonstration du Théorème 3

Nous démontrons le théorème 3 par récurrence sur p_2. Commençons par le cas $p_2=1$. On écrit

$$P_2(z)=az_1+bz_2+c\,.$$

Pour $s\in S$, on note

$$Q_s(z_1, z_2)=\bar{b}(z_1-s_1)-\bar{a}(z_2-s_2)\,,$$

où $\bar{a}$ et $\bar{b}$ sont les conjugués complexes de a et b. Alors S est l'ensemble des zéros communs à P_2 et au polynôme $Q=\prod_{s\in S} Q_s$. D'après le théorème 1, on a

$$f=\varphi_1 Q+\varphi_2 P_2\,,$$

avec

$$|\varphi_j|_R R^{p_j}\leqq c_5|f|_R\,,\quad (j=1,2)\,,$$

où c_5 ne dépend que de P_2 et S. D'autre part il existe $\lambda\in\mathbf{C}$ et $\psi\in\mathbf{C}[z_1, z_2]$ tels que

$$P_1=\lambda Q+\psi P_2\,,$$

avec $\deg\psi\leqq p_1-1$. On le voit soit en effectuant le changement de variables $w_1=$ $=az_1+bz_2$, $w_2=\bar{b}z_1-\bar{a}z_2$, soit en utilisant le théorème 1 et la remarque à la fin du §2.

Comme S est fini, on a $\lambda\neq 0$, d'où

$$f=f_1P_1+f_2P_2\,,$$

avec

$$f_1=-\frac{1}{\lambda}\varphi_1$$

et

$$f_2=\varphi_2-\frac{1}{\lambda}\varphi_1\psi\,,$$

ce qui démontre le théorème 3 pour $p_2=1$.

Par récurrence sur p_2, on en déduit facilement le théorème 3 quand P_2 est un produit de polynômes de degré 1.

Démontrons le théorème 3 quand P_2 est un polynôme quelconque de degré 2. On numérote les éléments de S:

$$S=\{s_1, \ldots, s_{2p_1}\}\,,$$

et on note

$$s_h=(\sigma_h, \sigma_h')\,,\quad (1\leqq h\leqq 2p_1)\,.$$

Pour $1 \leqq h \leqq p_1$ on considère la droite passant par s_h et s_{p_1+h}:

$$Q_h(z_1, z_2) = (z_1 - \sigma_h)(\sigma'_{p_1+h} - \sigma'_h) - (z_2 - \sigma'_h)(\sigma_{p_1+h} - \sigma_h).$$

Alors S est l'ensemble des zéros communs à P_2 et à $Q = \prod_{h=1}^{p_1} Q_h$. On peut donc reprendre les arguments précédents: si $f \in \mathscr{I}_R(S)$, on a

$$f = \varphi_1 Q + \varphi_2 P_2,$$

et il existe $\lambda \in \mathbf{C}$, $\lambda \neq 0$, et $\psi \in \mathbf{C}[z_1, z_2]$, tels que

$$P_1 = \lambda Q + \psi P_2.$$

On en déduit facilement le résultat pour $p_2 = 2$, et le cas général s'obtient aisément par récurrence sur p_2.

Références

[R] Robba, Ph., Lemmes de Schwarz et lemmes d'approximations p-adiques en plusieurs variables. *Invent. Math.*, **48** (1978), 245–277.

[W] Waldschmidt, M., Propriétés arithmétiques de fonctions de plusieurs variables; Sém. P. Lelong (Analyse), 15e année (1974/75) et 16e année (1975/76); *Lecture Notes in Math.*, **524** (1976), 106–129, et **578** (1977), 108–135.

UNIVERSITÉ P. ET M. CURIE (PARIS VI)
MATHÉMATIQUES, TOUR 45–46
4, PLACE JUSSIEU
75230 PARIS CEDEX 05
FRANCE

Studies in Pure Mathematics
To the Memory of Paul Turán

On the density of some sets of primes III

by

K. WIERTELAK (Poznań)

1. Introduction

Let q be a fixed prime. For primes $p \equiv 1 (\mathrm{mod}\ q)$ we denote by $m_q(p)$ the least positive integer belonging mod p to an exponent divisible by q. For primes $p \not\equiv 1$ (mod q) we put $m_q(p) = 0$. Let l be an integer, $l \geqq 1$. For primes $p \equiv 1$ (mod q) we denote by $n_{q^l}(p)$ the least q-th power non-residue (mod p). For primes $p \not\equiv 1$ (mod q) we put $n_{q^l}(p) = 0$ see [2], [3]). It is easily to notice that $q^l \| p - 1$ results $m_q(p) = n_{q^l}(p)$.

The purpose of this paper is to prove some asymptotic formulae for

$$\sum_{p \leqq x} m_q(p)$$

in the case q be an odd prime (Theorem 1) and in the remaining case $q = 2$ (Theorem 2). We prove also some asymptotic formulae for

$$\sum_{\substack{p \leqq x \\ q_r = m_q(p)}} 1$$

where q_r denotes the fixed r-th prime in the sequence of consecutive primes (Theorems 3 and 4). In the last part of the paper (Theorems 5 and 6) we refine some estimates obtained in [9].

In the following we denote by Q the field of rational numbers, by K an algebraic extension of Q, n and Δ denote the degree and the discriminant of K resp., $\overline{K}$ denotes the ring of algebraic integers of K, by $[a]$ we denote the principal ideal generated by $a \in \overline{K}$, $\mathfrak{p}$ denotes prime ideals, $c_0, c_1, \ldots$ are positive constants.

Let k be a positive rational integer, $\alpha \in \overline{Q(\sqrt[k]{1})}$, and let $\mathfrak{p}$ denote a prime ideal of the ring $\overline{Q(\sqrt[k]{1})}$, $\mathfrak{p} \nmid [k\alpha]$. We define as usually the power residue symbol of k-th degree for α

as follows

$$\left(\frac{\alpha}{\mathfrak{p}}\right)_k = \alpha^{\frac{1}{k}(N\mathfrak{p}-1)} (\operatorname{mod} \mathfrak{p}), \quad \left(\frac{\alpha}{\mathfrak{p}}\right)_k^k = 1 .$$

For each ideal $\mathfrak{a}$ of the ring $Q(\sqrt[k]{1})$, which is relatively prime with $[k\alpha]$, we put

$$\left(\frac{\alpha}{\mathfrak{a}}\right)_k = \prod_{\mathfrak{p}^\omega \| \mathfrak{a}} \left(\frac{\alpha}{\mathfrak{p}}\right)_k^\omega .$$

2. The main results

Theorem 1. *If* $q \neq 2$ *and* $c(q,r) = \frac{1}{q^r - 1} - \frac{1}{q^{r+1} - 1}$ *then for* $x \geqq \exp q^2$ *we have*

$$(1) \qquad \frac{1}{\pi(x)} \sum_{p \leqq x} m_q(p) = \sum_{r=1}^{x} q_r c(q,r) + O\left(q \frac{\log_2^{\frac{9}{2}} x}{\log x}\right)$$

and the constant implied by the O-notation is numerical.

Theorem 2. *If*

$$c(2,r) = \frac{1}{2^{r+1}}\left(1 + \frac{4}{2^r(2^r - 1)} - \frac{2}{2^{r+1}(2^{r+1} - 1)}\right)$$

then for $x \geqq \exp\exp 4$ *we have*

$$(2) \qquad \frac{1}{\pi(x)} \sum_{p \leqq x} m_2(p) = \sum_{r=1}^{x} q_r c(2,r) + O\left(\frac{\log_3^3 x}{\log_2 x}\right)$$

and the constant in O is numerical.

Theorem 3. *Suppose* $t \geqq 1$, $\frac{1}{2} \leqq \alpha \leqq 1$, $q \neq 2$, q_r *the r-th prime number. Then for*

$$x \geqq \exp\left((qq_r)^{\frac{2}{\alpha}} \left(\frac{t^2+2}{\alpha} \log(qq_r)\right)^{\frac{t+2}{\alpha}}\right)$$

and arbitrary positive constant c_1 *we have the estimate*

$$(3) \quad \frac{1}{\pi(x)} \sum_{\substack{p \leqq x \\ m_q(p) = q_r}} 1 = c(q,r) + O\left(qq_r \frac{\log_2^{t+2} x}{\log^\alpha x}\right)^r + O\left(\exp(-c_1 \log^{\frac{1-\alpha}{2}} x \log_2^{\frac{1+t}{2}} x)\right)$$

where the constant in O depends only on α, t *and* c_1.

Theorem 4. *If q_r is the r-th prime number, then for $x \geqq \exp\exp q_r^2$ we have*

$$(4) \qquad \frac{1}{\pi(x)} \sum_{\substack{p \leqq x \\ m_2(p) = q_r}} 1 = c(2, r) + O\left(\frac{q_r \log_3 x}{\log_2 x}\right)^r$$

and the constant in O is numerical.

For rational integers $a \neq 0, \pm 1$ and for $r = 0, 1, 2, \ldots$, we denote

$$B(a, q, r) = \{p : q^r \| \delta,\ \delta\text{-the exponent to which } a \text{ belongs mod } p\}$$

and

$$(5) \qquad N(x, a, q, r) = \sum_{\substack{p \leqq x \\ p \in B(a, q, r)}} 1 .$$

Let k be the maximal integer for which $|a|$ can be written in the form $|a| = b^{q^k}$, b being a positive integer (see [9]). With the above notations we have

Theorem 5. *If $|a| = b^{q^k}$, $q \neq 2$ and*

$$\frac{\log x}{\log_2^3 x} \geqq q^{k+r+1}, \quad x \geqq \exp b$$

then we have the estimate

$$(6) \qquad \frac{N(x, a, q, r)}{\pi(x)} = \alpha(a, q, r) + O\left(q^{k+r+2} \frac{\log_2^5 x}{\log^2 x}\right)$$

where the constant in O is numerical and $\alpha(a, q, r)$ are the constants depending on a, q and r (see [9], Theorem 2).

Theorem 6. *If $|a| = b^{2^k}$ and*

$$\frac{\log_2 x}{\log_3^{\frac{3}{2}} x} \geqq 2^{k+r}, \quad x \geqq \exp\exp b$$

then

$$(7) \qquad \frac{N(x, a, 2, r)}{\pi(x)} = \alpha(a, r) + O\left(2^{k+r} \left(\frac{\log_3 x}{\log_2 x}\right)^2\right)$$

where the constant in O is numerical and $\alpha(a, r)$ are constants depending on a and r (see [9], Theorem 1).

3. Lemmas used in the proofs of the theorems

Denote by K, $\mathfrak{f}$ and $\zeta(s, \chi)$ an algebraic number field of the degree n, an ideal of K and the Hecke zeta-function for $\chi \pmod{\mathfrak{f}}$, resp. Denote further

$$D = |\Delta| N\mathfrak{f}$$

where Δ is the discriminant of K and $N\mathfrak{f}$ is the norm of the ideal $\mathfrak{f}$.

Lemma 1. *There exists a numerical constant $c_0 > 0$, such that $\zeta(s, \chi) \neq 0$ in the region*

$$\sigma \geqq 1 - \frac{c_0}{n \log (D^{\frac{1}{n}}(2+|t|))}, \quad -\infty < t < \infty \tag{8}$$

for all $\chi \pmod{\mathfrak{f}}$ except the hypothetical real simple zero β_1 of $\zeta(s, \chi_1)$, $\chi_1 \bmod \mathfrak{f}$, χ_1-real.

The proof is similar to the proof of [10], Lemma 7.

Lemma 2. *Suppose that K is a normal extension of the field Q of rational numbers. Then for any $\varepsilon > 0$ and any ideal $\mathfrak{f}$ of $\bar{K}$ and any real $\chi \pmod{\mathfrak{f}}$,*

$$\zeta(s, \chi) \neq 0 \quad \text{for} \quad s > 1 - (c(\varepsilon))^n / D^{\varepsilon} \tag{9}$$

where $c(\varepsilon)$ denotes a constant depending only on ε.

This Lemma follows from Lemma 8 [10] applied to Dedekind zeta-function defined over a field, being an extension of degree two of the field K.

We introduce further the following notations:

$$E_0 = E_0(\chi) = \begin{cases} 1 \text{ for } \chi = \chi_0 \\ 0 \text{ for } \chi \neq \chi_0 \end{cases}$$

$$E_1 = E_1(\chi) = \begin{cases} 1, \text{ if there exists a real zero in the region (8)} \\ 0, \text{ otherwise} \end{cases}$$

$$\psi(x, \chi) = \sum_{n \leqq x} G(n, \chi) = \sum_{N\mathfrak{a} \leqq x} \chi(\mathfrak{a}) \Lambda(\mathfrak{a}) \quad (x \geqq 1)$$

where $G(n, \chi)$ *are the coefficients of the representation of the function* $-\frac{\zeta'}{\zeta}(s, \chi)$ by Dirichlet series and $\Lambda(\mathfrak{a})$ is the generalized Mangoldt function.

Lemma 3. *There exists a numerical constant c_2 such that*

$$\psi(x, \chi) = E_0 x - E_1 \frac{x^{\beta_1}}{\beta_1} + O(x \log 2D \log x \cdot \exp(\div c_2 \omega(x, D, n)) \tag{10}$$

where

(11) $$\omega(x, D, n) = \frac{\log x}{\max((n \log x)^{\frac{1}{2}}, \log D)}.$$

The proof of Lemma 3 follows from Lemma 1 similarly to the proof of Lemma 9 in[10].

Lemma 4. *If K is a normal extension of Q and χ is not a real character then*

(12) $$\sum_{N\mathfrak{p} \leqq x} \chi(\mathfrak{p}) = O\left(x \log 2D \cdot \exp\left(-c_2 \frac{\log x}{\max((n \log x)^{\frac{1}{2}}, \log D)}\right)\right)$$

and the constants in O is numerical.

Proof. From the definition of $\psi(x, \chi)$, we have

$$\psi(x, \chi) = \sum_{\substack{N\mathfrak{p}^\lambda \leqq x \\ \lambda \geqq 1}} \chi(\mathfrak{p}^\lambda) \log N\mathfrak{p} = \sum_{N\mathfrak{p} \leqq x} \chi(\mathfrak{p}) \log N\mathfrak{p} + O(x^{\frac{1}{2}} \log D).$$

Hence, owing to Lemma 3 we obtain

(13) $$\sum_{N\mathfrak{p} \leqq x} \chi(\mathfrak{p}) \log N\mathfrak{p} = E_0 x - E_1 \frac{x^{\beta_1}}{\beta_1} + O(x \log 2D \log x \exp(-c_2 \omega(x, D, n)))$$

and by partial summation we get (12).

Lemma 5. *If K is a normal extension of Q and χ is a real character, $\chi \neq \chi_0$ then with arbitrary numerical constants A and B we have the estimate*

(14) $$\sum_{N\mathfrak{p} \leqq x} \chi(\mathfrak{p}) = O\left(x \exp\left(-c_2 \left(\frac{\log x}{n}\right)^{1/2}\right)\right)$$

for

(15) $$1 \leqq D \leqq \log^A x, \quad 1 \leqq n \leqq B \frac{\log_2 x}{\log_3 x}$$

and the constant implied by the O-notation depends only on A and B.

This Lemma follows from (13) by the use of Lemmas 1 and 2.

Let k and r be positive integers, $k \geqq 2$ and denote by $a_1, a_2, \ldots, a_r$ any integers and by M the product of all different prime divisors of the product $a_1, a_2 \ldots a_r$. For the roots of unity of degree k: $\varepsilon_1, \ldots, \varepsilon_r$, we define

$$N(k, a_1, \ldots, a_r) = \sum_{\substack{\nu_1 = 1 \\ a_1^{\nu_1} \ldots a_r^{\nu_r} = \beta^k}}^{k} \ldots \sum_{\nu_r = 1}^{k} (\varepsilon_1^{\nu_1} \ldots \varepsilon_r^{\nu_r})^{-1}$$

where β is an algebraic integer belonging to the field $Q(\sqrt[k]{1})$. Denote further for real x

$$S(x, k, a_1, \ldots, a_r, \varepsilon_1, \ldots, \varepsilon_r) = \sum_{\substack{\mathfrak{p} \text{ of } Q(\sqrt[k]{1}) \\ N\mathfrak{p} \leqq x;\ \mathfrak{p} \nmid [ka_1 \ldots a_r] \\ \left(\frac{a_j}{\mathfrak{p}}\right)_k = \varepsilon_j}} 1 .$$

Lemma 6. *For k odd and $t \geqq 1$, $\frac{1}{2} \leqq \alpha \leqq 1$ and for any positive constant c_3 we have the estimate*

$$S(x, k, a_1, \ldots, a_r, \varepsilon_1, \ldots, \varepsilon_r) - k^{-r} N(k, a_1, \ldots, a_r)\pi(x) = \tag{16}$$
$$O\left(x \exp\left(-c_3 \log^{\frac{1-\alpha}{2}} x \log_2^{\frac{1+t}{2}} x\right)\right)$$

with the condition

$$(k^3 M)^{\varphi(k)} \leqq \exp\left(\left(\frac{c_2}{c_3+1}\right)^2 \frac{\log^\alpha x}{\log_2^t x}\right) \tag{17}$$

where the constant in O depends only on c_2, c_3, α and t.

Lemma 7. *For k-even, there exists a positive constant c_4 such that*

$$S(x, k, a_1, \ldots, a_r, \varepsilon_1, \ldots, \varepsilon_r) - k^{-r} N(k, a_1, \ldots, a_r)\pi(x) = \tag{18}$$
$$O\left(x \exp\left(-c_4 \left(\frac{\log x}{\log_2 x}\right)^{\frac{1}{2}}\right)\right)$$

with the condition

$$(k^3 M)^{\varphi(k)} \leqq \log^A x \tag{19}$$

where A is an arbitrary positive constant and the constant in O depends only on A.

The proof of Lemmas 6 and 7 is similar to the proof of [3] (Theorem 1). We have only to use the estimates (12) and (14).

Lemma 8. If $1 \leqq a_1 < a_2 < \ldots < a_z \leqq N$ *are different integers, r denote natural number, p is a prime and $Z(r, p)$ denotes the number of a_i which satisfy the congruence*

$a_i \equiv r \pmod p$, *then*

(20) $$\sum_{p \leqq N^{1/2}} p \sum_{r=0}^{p-1} \left(Z(r, p) - \frac{Z}{p}\right)^2 \leqq 2{,}2\, NZ\,.$$

The inequality (20) is very well known (see [1]).

Lemma 9. *Denote by $\psi(x, y)$ the number of integers $\leqq x$, which are divisible only by primes $p \leqq y$. If $h > 1$, $\varepsilon > 0$ then*

(21) $$\psi(x, (\log x)^h) > c(\varepsilon, h) x^{1 - \frac{1}{h} - \varepsilon}$$

where the constant $c(\varepsilon, h)$ depends only on ε and h.

For the proof of this lemma see [2].

Lemma 10. *If p is a prime and $k|(p-1)$, $k \neq \neq 1$ then we have*

(22) $$n_k(p) < c_5\, p^{\xi_k} (\log p)^2$$

where $\xi_k = \dfrac{1}{2} \exp\left(\dfrac{1}{k} - 1\right)$ and c_5 is a numerical constant.

For the proof of this lemma see [11].

4. The proof of Theorem 1

Denote

(23)

$$M(x, q^l, q_1^{\alpha_1}, \ldots, q_r^{\alpha_r}) = \sum_{\substack{p \leqq x,\ p \equiv 1 \pmod{q^l} \\ q_1^{\alpha_1}, \ldots, q_r^{\alpha_r} \text{ are } q^l\text{-th power residue} \pmod p}} 1 \qquad \text{where } \alpha_i \geqq 1 \text{ for } i = 1, 2, \ldots, r\,.$$

Hence

$$S = \sum_{p \leqq x} m_q(p) = \sum_{l \geqq 1} \sum_{\substack{p_l \leqq x \\ q^l \| p-1}} n_q(p) = \sum_{l \geqq 1} \sum_{q_r} q_r \{ M(x, q^l, q_1, \ldots, q_{r-1}) -$$

$$- M(x, q^l, q_1, \ldots, q_r) - M(x, q^{l+1}, q_1^q, \ldots, q_{r-1}^q) + M(x, q^{l+1}, q_1^q, \ldots, q_r^q) \} \stackrel{\text{def}}{=}$$

$$\stackrel{\text{def}}{=} \sum_{l \geqq 1} \sum_{q_r} q_r M_1(x, q, l, q_1, \ldots, q_r) = \sum_{l \geqq 1} \sum_{q_r} q_r M_1\,.$$

We split the sum S into four sums:

$$S=\sum_{q^{l+1}\leqq\xi}\sum_{q_r\leqq\eta_1}q_rM_1+\sum_{q^{l+1}>\xi}\sum_{q_r\leqq\eta_1}q_rM_1+\sum_{q^l\leqq x-1}\sum_{\eta_1<q_r\leqq\eta_2}q_rM_1+$$

(24)

$$+\sum_{q^l\leqq x-1}\sum_{q_r>\eta_2}q_rM_1=S_1+S_2+S_3+S_4$$

where

$$\xi=\frac{\log x}{\log_2^3 x},\quad \eta_1=\log_2^{3/2}x,\quad \eta_2=\log^4 x,\quad x\geqq\exp q^2.$$

From the definition of

$$S(x,q^l,q_1^{\alpha_1},\ldots,q_r^{\alpha_r},1,\ldots,1)=S(x,q^l,q_1^{\alpha_1},\ldots,q_r^{\alpha_r})$$

we get

$$M(x,q^l,q_1^{\alpha_1},\ldots,q_r^{\alpha_r})=\frac{1}{q^{l-1}(q-1)}S(x,q^l,q_1^{\alpha_1},\ldots,q_r^{\alpha_r})+O(x^{\frac{1}{2}}).\tag{25}$$

Hence

$$S_1=\sum_{q^{l+1}\leqq\xi}\sum_{q_r\leqq\eta_1}q_r\left\{\frac{1}{q^{(l+1)}(q-1)}(S(x,q^l,q_1,\ldots,q_{r-1})-S(x,q^l,q_1,\ldots,q_r))-\right.$$

$$\left.-\frac{1}{q^l(q-1)}(S(x,q^{l+1},q_1^q,\ldots,q_{r-1}^q)-S(x,q^{l+1},q_1^q,\ldots,q_r^q))\right\}+O(x^{\frac{1}{2}}\log_2^4 x).$$

We estimate $S(x,q^{l+1},q_1^q,\ldots,q_r^q)$ by the use of Lemma 6 for $t=1$, $\alpha=1$, $c_3=2$, $M=q_1,\ldots,q_r$, $k=q^{l+1}$. Condition (17) is satisfied since

$$\log(k^3M)^{\varphi(k)}<\xi(3\log\xi+3\eta_1)=O\left(\frac{\log x}{\log_2^{\frac{3}{2}}x}\right).$$

Therefore owing to (16) we have

$$S(x,q^{l+1},q_1^q,\ldots,q_r^q)=\left(\frac{1}{q^{l+1}}\right)^r N(q^{l+1},q_1^q,\ldots,q_r^q)\pi(x)+O\left(x\frac{1}{\log^2 x}\right).$$

For the remaining terms of the sum S_1 we get similar estimates. Hence

$$S_1 = \sum_{q^{l+1}\leqq\xi}\sum_{q_r\leqq\eta_1} q_r\left\{\frac{1}{q^{l-1}(q-1)}\left(\frac{N(q^l, q_1, \ldots, q_{r-1})}{q^{(r-1)l}} - \frac{N(q^l, q_1, \ldots; q_r)}{q^{rl}}\right) - \right.$$

$$\left. - \frac{1}{q^l(q-1)}\left(\frac{N(q^{l+1}, q_1^q, \ldots, q_{r-1}^q)}{q^{(r-1)(l+1)}} - \frac{N(q^{l+1}, q_1^q, \ldots, q_r^q)}{q^{r(l+1)}}\right)\right\}\pi(x) +$$

$$+ \sum_{q^{l+1}\leqq\xi}\sum_{q_r\leqq\eta_1} q_r(q^{-l}x(\log x)^{-2}) + O(x^{\frac{1}{2}}\log_2^4 x) =$$

$$= \sum_{q^{l+1}\leqq\xi}\sum_{q_r\leqq\eta_1} q_r\left(\frac{1}{q^{rl}} - \frac{1}{q^{(r+1)l}}\right)\pi(x) + O\left(x\left(\frac{\log_2 x}{\log x}\right)^2\right)$$

and

$$\frac{S_1}{\pi(x)} = \sum_{q_r\leqq\eta_1} q_r\left(\frac{1}{q^r-1} - \frac{1}{q^{r+1}-1}\right) + O\left(q\frac{\eta_1}{\xi}\right) + O\left(\frac{\log_2^2 x}{\log x}\right) =$$

(26)

$$= \sum_{q_r} q_r\left(\frac{1}{q^r-1} - \frac{1}{q^{r+1}-1}\right) + O\left(q\frac{\log_2^{\frac{9}{2}} x}{\log x}\right)$$

for $x \geqq \exp q^2$.

Next we estimate the sum S_2. From definition (23) we get

$$S_2 = O(\eta_1 \sum_{q^{l+1}>\xi}\sum_{\substack{p\leqq x\\ q^l\|p-1}} 1) = O\left(\frac{qx\log_2^{\frac{9}{2}} x}{\log^2 x}\right).$$

Hence

$$\frac{S_2}{\pi(x)} = O\left(q\frac{\log_2^{\frac{9}{2}} x}{\log x}\right) \quad \text{for} \quad x \geqq \exp q^2. \tag{27}$$

For the sum S_3 we have

$$S_3 \leqq \eta_2 \sum_{q^l\leqq x-1}\sum_{\eta_1<q_r\leqq\eta_2}\{M(x, q^l, q_1, \ldots, q_{r-1}) - M(x, q^l, q_1, \ldots, q_r) -$$

$$- M(x, q^{l+1}, q_1^q, \ldots, q_{r-1}^q) + M(x, q^{l+1}, q_1^q, \ldots, q_r^q)\}.$$

Let r_0 be the smallest natural number, such that $q_{r_0} > \eta_1$. Then

$$(28)\qquad \begin{aligned} S_3 &\leqq \eta_2 \sum_{q^l \leqq x-1} \{M(x, q^l, q_1, \ldots, q_{r_0-1}) - M(x, q^{l+1}, q_1^q, \ldots, q_{r_0-1}^q)\} \leqq \\ &\leqq \eta_2 M(x, q, q_1, \ldots, q_{r_0-1}) = O\left(\frac{\log^4 x}{q} S(x, q, q_1, \ldots, q_{r_0-1})\right) + O(x^{\frac{1}{2}} \log x)\,. \end{aligned}$$

We estimate the sum $S(x, q, q_1, \ldots, q_{r_0-1})$ using Lemma 6 with $t=1$, $\alpha=1$, $c_3=6$, $M = q_1 \cdot \ldots \cdot q_{r_0-1}$, $k=q$. Hence owing to (28) we get

$$(29)\qquad \frac{S_3}{\pi(x)} = O\left(\frac{1}{\log x}\right) \quad \text{for} \quad x \geqq \exp q^2\,.$$

For the last sum S_4, owing to Lemma 10 we have

$$(30)\qquad S_4 = \sum_{l \geqq 1} \sum_{\substack{p \leqq x \\ q^l \| p-1 \\ m_q(p) > \log^4 x}} n_{q^l}(p) \leqq c_6 x^{\frac{1}{3}} \sum_l \sum_{\substack{p \leqq x \\ q^l \| p-1 \\ m_q(p) > \log^4 x}} 1\,.$$

Suppose $q^l \| p-1$, $m_q(p) > \log^4 x = y$. Therefore each prime $\leqq y$ is a power residue of degree $q^l \pmod p$. Hence each integer formed of primes $\leqq y$ is a power residue of degree $q^l \pmod p$. For each $x \geqq 2$ we consider the set of integers $\leqq x^2$ formed of primes $\leqq y$. Denote these integers by a_i, $i = 1, 2, \ldots z$ where $z = \psi(x^2, y)$. These integers belong to at most $t \leqq \frac{p-1}{q^l}$ residue classes (mod p). Denote by $Z(r, p)$ the number of such a_i which satisfy the congruence $a_i \equiv r \pmod p$. Hence

$$p \sum_{r=0}^{p-1} \left(Z(r, p) - \frac{z}{p}\right)^2 \geqq p \frac{\left(z - t\frac{z}{p}\right)^2}{t} + p(p-t)\frac{z^2}{p^2} \geqq z^2(q^l - 1)$$

and further

$$(31)\qquad \sum_{\substack{p \leqq x \\ q^l \| p-1 \\ m_q(p) > y}} p \sum_{r=0}^{p-1} \left(Z(r, p) - \frac{z}{p}\right)^2 \geqq \sum_{\substack{p \leqq x \\ q^l \| p-1 \\ m_q(p) > y}} z^2(q^l - 1)\,.$$

From Lemma 8 and estimate (31) we get

$$\sum_{\substack{p \leqq x \\ q^l \| p-1 \\ m_q(p) > y}} 1 \leqq \frac{2{,}2}{q^l - 1} \frac{x^2}{\psi(x^2, y)}\,.$$

Hence owing to Lemma 9, for $\varepsilon>0$ it follows

(32) $$\sum_{\substack{p\leqq x\\ q^l\| p-1\\ m_q(p)>y}} 1 \leqq c_7 \frac{x^{\frac{1}{2}+\varepsilon}}{q^l}.$$

From (30) and (32) we get for sufficiently small ε

(33) $$\frac{S_4}{\pi(x)} = O\left(\frac{1}{q} x^{-\frac{1}{7}}\right) \quad \text{with} \quad x \geqq \exp q^2 .$$

From the inequality (24) and owing to (26), (27), (29) and (33) we get (1).

5. The proof of Theorem 2

Using the notations from the proof of Theorem 1, we can write the sum $S=\sum_{p\leqq x} m_q(p)$ as follows

(34) $$S = \sum_{2^l\leqq \xi}\sum_{q_r\leqq\eta_1} q_r M_1 + \sum_{2^l>\xi}\sum_{q_r\leqq\eta_1} q_r M_1 + \sum_{2^l\leqq x-1}\sum_{\eta_1<q\leqq\eta_2} q_r M_1 +$$
$$+ \sum_{2^l\leqq x-1}\sum_{\eta_2<q_r\leqq\eta_3} q_r M_1 + \sum_{2^l\leqq x-1}\sum_{q_r>\eta_3} q_r M_1 = S_1+S_2+S_3+S_4+S_5,$$

where

$$\xi = \frac{\log_2 x}{\log_3^{\frac{3}{2}}}, \quad \eta_1=\log_3^{\frac{3}{2}} x, \quad \eta_2=\log_2^{\frac{2}{3}} x, \quad \eta_3=\log^4 x, \quad x\geqq \exp\exp 4 .$$

Applying Lemma 7 we have

(35) $$\frac{S_1}{\pi(x)} = \sum_{q_r} q_r c(2,r) + O\left(\frac{\log_3^{\frac{3}{2}} x}{\log_2 x}\right),$$
$$\frac{S_2}{\pi(x)} = O\left(\frac{\log_3^3 x}{\log_2 x}\right),$$
$$\frac{S_3}{\pi(x)} = O\left(\frac{1}{\log_2 x}\right),$$
$$\frac{S_4}{\pi(x)} = O\left(\frac{1}{\log x}\right).$$

Estimating as in the proof of Theorem 1 we also get

$$\frac{S_5}{\pi(x)} = O(x^{-\frac{1}{7}}). \tag{36}$$

From (34)–(36) we get (2).

6. The proof of Theorem 3

Under the notation from the proof of Theorem 1 we get

$$\sum_{\substack{p \leqq x \\ m_q(p) = q_r}} 1 = \sum_{l=1}^{x} M_1 = \sum_{q^l \leqq \xi} M_1 + \sum_{q^l > \xi} M_1 = S_1 + S_2 \tag{37}$$

where

$$\xi = \frac{1}{qq_r} \frac{\log^\alpha x}{\log_2^{t+2} x}, \quad x \geqq \exp\left\{(qq_r)^{\frac{2}{\alpha}}\left(\frac{t^2+2}{\alpha}\log qq_r\right)^{\frac{t+2}{\alpha}}\right\}.$$

From (25) and Lemma 6 we have

(38)

$$\frac{S_1}{\pi(x)} = \frac{1}{q^r-1} - \frac{1}{q^{r+1}-1} + O\left(qq^r \frac{\log_2^{t+2} x}{\log^\alpha x}\right)^r + O\left(\frac{1}{q}\exp\left(-\frac{c_3}{2}\log^{\frac{1-\alpha}{2}} x \log_2^{\frac{1+t}{2}} x\right)\right).$$

Next we get

$$S_2 = O\left(\frac{1}{q^{l_0}} S(x, q^{l_0}, q_1, \ldots, q_{r-1})\right) + O(x^{\frac{1}{2}} \log_2 x)$$

where l_0 is the smallest natural number l for which $q^l > \eta$. Owing to Lemma 6 it follows

$$S_2 = O\left(qq_r \frac{\log_2^{t+2} x}{\log^\alpha x}\right)^r + O\left(\frac{1}{q}\exp\left(-\frac{c_3}{2}\log_x^{\frac{1-\alpha}{2}} x(\log_2 x)^{\frac{1+t}{2}}\right)\right). \tag{39}$$

Finally from (37) and the estimates (38) and (39) we get (3).

The proof of Theorem 4 follows analogously to the proof of Theorem 3, we have only to use Lemma 7 instead of Lemma 6.

The proofs of Theorems 5 and 6 can be performed analogously to the proof of Theorem 1, by splitting the sums under consideration into two sums (see [9]) and by applying Lemma 6 or Lemma 7, resp. and using the relations obtained in [9].

References

[1] H. Davenport and H. Halberstam, The values of a trigonometrical polynomial at well spaced points, *Mathematika*, **13** (1966), 91–96.
[2] P. D. T. A. Elliott, A problem of Erdös concerning power residue sums, *Acta Arith.*, **13** (1967), 131–149.
[3] P. D. T. A. Elliott, The distribution of power residues and certain related results, *Acta Arith.*, **17** (1970), 141–159.
[4] P. D. T. A. Elliott, On the mean value of $f(p)$, London Math. Soc., *Davenport Memorial Volume*.
[5] H. Hasse, Über die Dichte der Primzahlen p, für die eine vorgegebene ganzrationale Zahl $a \neq 0$ von gerader bzw. ungerader Ordnung mod p ist, *Math. Ann.*, **166** (1966), 19–23.
[6] H. Hasse, Über die Dichte der Primzahlen p, für die eine vorgegebenen granzrationale Zahl $a \neq 0$ von durch eine vorgegebenen Primzahl $1 \neq 2$ teilbarer bzw. unteilbarer Ordnung mod p ist, ibid., **162** (1965), 74–76.
[7] E. Landau, Über Ideale und Primideale in Idealklassen, *Math. Zeit.*, **2** (1918), 52–154.
[8] K. Prachar, *Primzahlverteilung*, Berlin 1957.
[9] K. Wiertelak, On the density of some sets of primes, I, *Acta Arithm.*, **34** (1978), 183–196.
[10] K. Wiertelak, On the density of some sets of primes, II, *Acta Arithm.* **34** (1978), 197–210.
[11] I. M. Vinogradov, On the bounds of the least non-residue of k-th powers, *Trans. Amer. Math. Soc.*, **29** (1927), 218–226.

INSTITUTE OF MATHEMATICS
OF THE ADAM MICKIEWICZ UNIWERSITY,
POZNAŃ, POLAND